TREASURY OF WORLD MASTERPIECES

ROGET'S THESAURUS

THE EVERYMAN EDITION

TREASURY OF WORLD MASTERPIECES

ROGET'S THESAURUS

OF ENGLISH WORDS AND PHRASES

THE EVERYMAN EDITION

REVISED FROM PETER ROGET BY

D. C. BROWNING

MA (GLASGOW), BA, B LITT (OXON)

OCTOPUS BOOKS LIMITED

Everyman's Thesaurus of English Words and Phrases was
first published in Great Britain in 1952, revised 1971

This edition first published in Great Britain in 1982 by

Octopus Books Limited
59 Grosvenor Street
London W1

under license from

J.M. Dent & Sons Limited
Aldine House
33 Welbeck Street
London W1

This edition © 1982 by J.M. Dent & Sons Limited

ISBN 0 7064 1651 1

Printed in the United States of America
by R.R. Donnelley and Sons Company

CONTENTS

'Proper words in proper places, make the true
definition of a style.'

JONATHAN SWIFT
Letter to a young clergyman
9th January, 1720

Note

PETER ROGET'S UNIQUE *Thesaurus of English Words and Phrases* was first published in 1852. When J.M. Dent & Sons Ltd. decided to produce a single-volume edition for the Everyman Library, D.C. Browning was asked to undertake a complete revision of the work, bearing in mind the changes and developments of the English language which had inevitably taken place during the intervening period.

Every paragraph was carefully reviewed and over 10,000 words and phrases were added, following the logical order which agrees with the original plan. Since the first publication in 1952, several reprints and substantial revisions in 1962 and 1971 have taken account of recent developments in English vocabulary.

This edition includes the complete plan of classification as laid down by Peter Roget himself and explained in his original introduction to the 1852 edition.

Every effort has been made to ensure that the index is as complete as possible and cross-references have been included in many cases where one paragraph is closely associated in meaning with another.

Original Introduction
By Peter Roget

THE PRESENT WORK is intended to supply, with respect to the English language, a desideratum hitherto unsupplied in any language; namely, a collection of the words it contains and of the idiomatic combinations peculiar to it, arranged, not in alphabetical order, as they are in a dictionary, but according to the *ideas* which they express. The purpose of an ordinary dictionary is simply to explain the meaning of words; and the problem of which it professes to furnish the solution may be stated thus: The word being given, to find its signification, or the idea it is intended to convey. The object aimed at in the present undertaking is exactly the converse of this; namely, the idea being given, to find the word, or words, by which that idea may be most fitly and aptly expressed. For this purpose, the words and phrases of the language are here classed, not according to their sound or their orthography, but strictly according to their *signification*.

The communication of our thoughts by means of language, whether spoken or written, like every other object of mental exertion, constitutes a peculiar art, which, like other parts, cannot be acquired in any perfection but by long and continued practice. Some, indeed, there are, more highly gifted than others with a facility of expression, and naturally endowed with the power of eloquence; but to none is it at all times an easy process to embody in exact and appropriate language the various trains of ideas that are passing through the mind, or to depict in their true colours and proportions the diversified and nicer shades of feeling which accompany them. To those who are unpractised in the art of composition, or unused to extempore speaking, these difficulties present themselves in their most formidable aspect. However distinct may be our views, however vivid our conceptions, or however fervent our emotions, we cannot but be often conscious that the phraseology we have at our command is inadequate to do them justice. We seek in vain the words we need, and strive ineffectually to devise forms of expression which shall faithfully portray out thoughts and sentiments. The appropriate terms, notwithstanding out utmost efforts, cannot be conjured up at will, Like 'spirits from the vasty deep,' they come not when we call; and we are driven to the employment of a set of words and phrases either too general or too limited, too strong or too feeble, which suit not the occasion, which hit not the mark we aim at; and the result of our prolonged exertion is a style at once laboured and obscure, vapid and redundant, or vitiated by the still graver faults of affectation or ambiguity.

It is to those who are thus painfully groping their way and struggling with the difficulties of composition, that this work professes to hold out a helping hand. The assistance it gives is that of furnishing on every topic a copious store of words and phrases, adapted to express all the recognizable shades and modifications of the general idea under which those words and phrases are arranged. The inquirer can readily select, out of the ample collection spread out before his eyes in the following pages, those expressions which are best suited to his purpose, and which might not have occurred to him without such assistance. In order to make this selection, he scarcely ever need engage in any elaborate or critical study of the subtle distinctions existing between synonymous terms; for if the materials set before him be sufficiently abundant, an instinctive tact will rarely fail to lead him to the proper choice. Even while glancing over the columns of this work, his eye may chance to light upon a particular term, which may save the cost of a clumsy paraphrase, or spare the labour of a tortuous circumlocution. Some felicitous turn of expression thus introduced will frequently open to the mind of the reader a whole vista of collateral ideas, which could not, without an extended and obtrusive episode, have been unfolded to his view; and often will the judicious insertion of a happy epithet, like a beam of sunshine in a landscape, illumine and adorn the subject which touches it, imparting new grace, and giving life and spirit to the picture.

Every workman in the exercise of his art should be provided with proper implements. For the fabrication of complicated and curious pieces of mechanism the artisan requires a corresponding assortment of various tools and instruments. For giving proper effect to the fictions of the drama, the actor should have at his disposal a well-furnished wardrobe, supplying the costumes best suited to the personage he is to represent. For the perfect delineation of the beauties of nature, the painter should have within reach of his pencil every variety and combination of hues and tints. Now the writer, as well as the orator, employs for the accomplishment of his purposes the instrumentality of words; it is in words that he clothes his thoughts; it is by means of words that he depicts his feelings. It is therefore essential to his success that he be provided with a copious vocabulary, and that he possess an entire command of all the resources and appliances of his language. To the acquisition of this power no procedure appears more directly conducive than the study of a methodized system such as that now offered to his use.

The utility of the present work will be appreciated more especially by those who are engaged in the arduous process of translating into English a work written in another language. Simple as the operation may appear, on a superficial view, of rendering into English each of its sentences, the task of transfusing, with perfect exactness, the sense of the original, preserving at the same time the style and character of its composition, and reflecting with fidelity the mind and the spirit of the author, is a task of extreme difficulty. The cultivation of this useful department of literature was in ancient times strongly recommended both by Cicero and by Quintilian as essential to the formation of a good writer and accomplished orator. Regarded simply as a mental exercise, the practice of translation is the best training for the attainment of that mastery of language and felicity of diction which are the sources of the highest oratory and are requisite for the possession of a graceful and persuasive eloquence. By rendering ourselves the faithful interpreters of the thoughts and feelings of others, we are rewarded with the acquisition of greater readiness and facility in correctly expressing our own; as he who has best learned to execute the orders of a commander becomes himself best qualified to command.

In the earliest periods of civilization, translations have been the agents for propagating knowledge from nation to nation, and the value of their labours has been inestimable; but, in the present age, when so many different languages have become the depositories of the vast treasures of literature and of science which have been accumulating for centuries, the utility of accurate translations has greatly increased, and it has become a more important object to attain perfection in the art.

The use of language is not confined to its being the medium through which we communicate our ideas to one another; it fulfils a no less important function as an *instrument of thought,* not being merely its vehicle, but giving it wings for flight. Metaphysicians are agreed that scarcely any of our intellectual operations could be carried on to any considerable extent without the agency of words. None but those who are conversant with the philosophy of mental phenomena can be aware of the immense influence that is exercised by language in promoting the development of our ideas, in fixing them in the mind, and detaining them for steady contemplation. In every process of reasoning, language enters as an essential element. Words are the instruments by which we form all our abstractions, by which we fashion and embody our ideas, and by which we are enabled to glide along a series of premises and conclusions with a rapidity so great as to leave in the memory no trace of the successive steps of the process; and we remain unconscious how much we owe to this potent auxiliary of the reasoning faculty. It is on this ground, also, that the present work founds a claim to utility. The review of a catalogue of words of analogous signification will often suggest by association other trains of thought, which, presenting the subject under new and varied aspects, will vastly expand the sphere of our mental vision. Amidst the many objects thus brought within the range of our contemplation, some striking similitude or appropriate image, some excursive flight or brilliant conception, may flash on the mind, giving point and force to our arguments, awakening a responsive chord in the imagination or sensibility of the reader, and procuring for our reasonings a more ready access both to his understanding and to his heart.

It is of the utmost consequence that strict accuracy should regulate our use of language, and that every one should acquire the power and the habit of expressing his thoughts with perspicuity and correctness. Few, indeed, can appreciate the real extent and importance of that influence which language has always exercised on human affairs, or can be aware how often these are determined by causes much slighter than are apparent to a superficial observer. False logic, disguised under specious phraseology, too often gains the assent of the unthinking multitude, disseminating far and wide the seeds of prejudice and error. Truisms pass current, and wear the semblance of profound wisdom, when dressed up in the tinsel garb of antithetical phrases, or set off by an imposing pomp of paradox. By a confused jargon of involved and mystical sentences, the imagination is easily inveigled into a transcendental region of clouds, and the understanding beguiled into the belief that it is acquiring knowledge and approaching truth. A misapplied or misapprehended term is sufficient to give rise to fierce and interminable disputes: a misnomer has turned the tide of popular opinion; a verbal sophism has decided a party question; an artful watchword, thrown among combustible materials, has kindled the flames of deadly warfare, and changed the destiny of an empire.

In constructing the following system of classification of the ideas which are expressible by language, my chief aim has been to obtain the greatest amount of practical utility. I have accordingly adopted such principles of arrangement as appeared to me to be the simplest and most natural, and which would not require, either for their comprehension or application, any disciplined acumen, or depth of metaphysical or antiquarian lore. Eschewing all needless refinements and subtleties, I have taken as my guide the more obvious characters of the ideas for

15

which expressions were to be tabulated, arranging them under such classes and categories as reflection and experience had taught me would conduct the inquirer most readily and quickly to the object of his search. Commencing with the ideas expressing mere abstract relations, I proceed to those which relate to the phenomena of the material world, and lastly to those in which the mind is concerned, and which comprehend intellect, volition, and feeling; thus establishing six primary Classes of Categories.

1. The first of these classes comprehends ideas derived from the more general and ABSTRACT RELATIONS among things, such as *Existence, Resemblance, Quantity, Order, Number, Time, Power.*

2. The second class refers to SPACE and its various relations, including *Motion,* or change of place.

3. The third class includes all ideas that relate to the MATERIAL WORLD; namely, the *Properties of Matter,* such as *Solidity, Fluidity, Heat, Sound, Light,* and the *Phemomena* they present, as well as the simple *Perceptions* to which they give rise.

4. The fourth class embraces all ideas of phenomena relating to the INTELLECT and its operations, comprising the *Acquisition,* the *Retention,* and the *Communication of Ideas.*

5. The fifth class includes the ideas derived from the exercise of VOLITION, embracing the phenomena and results of our *Voluntary and Active Powers,* such as *Choice, Intention, Utility, Action, Antagonism, Authority, Compact, Property,* etc.

6. The sixth and last class comprehends all ideas derived from the operation of our SENTIENT AND MORAL POWERS, including our *Feelings, Emotions, Passions,* and *Moral and Religious Sentiments.*

It must necessarily happen in every system of classification framed with this view, that ideas and expressions arranged under one class must include also ideas relating to another class; for the operations of the *Intellect* generally involve also those of the *Will,* and vice versa; and our *Affections* and *Emotions,* in like manner, generally imply the agency both of the *Intellect* and the *Will.* All that can be effected, therefore, is to arrange the words according to the principal or dominant idea they convey. *Teaching,* for example, although a Voluntary act, relates primarily to the Communication of Ideas, and is accordingly placed at No. 537, under Class IV, Division II. On the other hand, *Choice, Conduct, Skill,* etc., although implying the co-operation of Voluntary with Intellectual acts, relate principally to the former, and are therefore arranged under Class V.

It often happens that the same word admits of various applications, or may be used in different senses. In consulting the Index the reader will be guided to the number of the heading under which that word, in each particular acceptation, will be found, by means of *supplementary words,* printed in italics; which words, however, are not to be understood as explaining the meaning of the word to which they are annexed, but only assisting in the required reference. I have also, for shortness' sake, generally omitted words immediately derived from the primary one inserted, which sufficiently represents the whole group of correlative words referable to the same heading. Thus the number affixed to *Beauty* applies to all its derivatives, such as *Beautiful, Beauteous, Beautify, Beautifulness, Beautifully,* etc., the insertion of which was therefore needless.

The object I have proposed to myself in this work would have been but imperfectly attained if I had confined myself to a mere catalogue of words, and had omitted the numerous phrases and forms of expression, composed of several words, which are of such frequent use as to entitle them to rank among the constituent parts of the language. For example: To take time by the forelock; to turn over a new leaf; to show the white feather; to have a finger in the pie; to let the cat out of the bag; to take care of number one; to kill two birds with one stone, etc. Very few of these verbal combinations, so essential to the knowledge of our native tongue, and so profusely abounding in its daily use, are to be met with in ordinary dictionaries. These phrases and forms of expression I have endeavoured diligently to collect and to insert in their proper places, under the general ideas they are designed to convey. Some of these conventional forms, indeed, partake of the nature of proverbial expressions; but actual proverbs, as such, being wholly of a didactic character, do not come within the scope of the present work, and the reader must therefore not expect to find them here inserted.

The study of correlative terms existing in a particular language may often throw valuable light on the manners and customs of the nations using it. Thus Hume has drawn important inferences with regard to the state of society among the ancient Romans, from certain deficiencies which he remarked in the Latin language. 'It is an universal observation,' he remarks in his Essay on the Populousness of Ancient Nations, 'which we may form upon language, that where two related parts of a whole bear any proportion to each other, in numbers, rank, or consideration, there are always correlative terms invented which answer to both the parts and express their mutual relation. If they bear no proportion to each other, the term is only invented for the less, and marks its distinction from the whole. Thus *man* and *woman, master* and *servant, father* and *son, prince* and *subject, stranger* and *citizen,* are correlative terms. But the words *seaman, carpenter, smith, tailor,* etc., have no correspondent terms which express those who are no seamen, no carpenters, etc. Languages differ very much with regard to the particular words where this distinction obtains; and may thence afford very strong inferences concerning the manners and customs of different nations. The military government of the Roman emperors had exalted the soldiery so high, that they balanced all the other orders of the state: hence *miles* and *paganus* became relative terms; a thing, till then, unknown to ancient, and still so to modern, languages.' 'The term for a slave, born and bred in the family, was *verna.* As *servus* was the name of the genus, and *verna* of the species without any correlative, this forms a strong presumption that the latter were by far the least numerous: and from the same principles I infer that if the number of slaves brought by the Romans from foreign countries had not extremely exceeded those which were bred at home, *verna* would have had a correlative, which would have expressed the former species of slaves. But these, it would seem, composed the main body of the ancient slaves, and the latter were but a few exceptions. The warlike propensity of the same nation may in a like manner be inferred from the use of the word *hostis* to denote both a *foreigner* and an *enemy.*

In many cases, two ideas, which are completely opposed to each other, admit of an intermediate or neutral idea, equidistant from both: all these being expressible by corresponding definite terms. Thus, in the following examples, the words in the first and third columns; which express opposite ideas, admit of

17

the intermediate terms contained in the middle column having a neutral sense with reference to the former:

Identity	*Difference*	*Contrariety*
Beginning	*Middle*	*End*
Past	*Present*	*Future*

In other cases, the intermediate word is simply the negative to each of two opposite positions; as, for example:

Convexity	*Flatness*	*Concavity*
Desire	*Indifference*	*Aversion*

Sometimes the intermediate word is properly the standard with which each of the extremes is compared; as in the case of

Insufficiency	*Sufficiency*	*Redundance*

For here the middle term, *Sufficiency,* is equally opposed on the one hand to *Insufficiency* and on the other to *Redundance*.

It often happens that the same word has several correlative terms, according to the different relations in which it is considered. Thus to the word *Giving* are opposed both *Receiving* and *Taking*; the former correlation having reference to the *persons* concerned in the transfer, while the latter relates to the *mode* of transfer. *Old* has for opposite both *New* and *Young,* according as it is applied to *things* or to *living beings. Attack* and *Defence* are correlative terms, as are also *Attack* and *Resistance. Resistance,* again, has for its other correlative *Submission. Truth in the abstract* is opposed to *Error,* but the opposite of *Truth communicated* is *Falsehood. Acquisition* is contrasted both with *Deprivation* and with *Loss. Refusal* is the counterpart both of *Offer* and of *Consent. Disuse* and *Misuse* may either of them be considered as the correlative of *Use. Teaching,* with reference to what is taught, is opposed to *Misteaching,* but with reference to the act itself, its proper reciprocal is *Learning*.

Words contrasted in form do not always bear the same contrast in their meaning. The word *Malefactor,* for example, would, from its derivation, appear to be exactly the opposite of *Benefactor,* but the ideas attached to these two words are far from being directly opposed; for while the latter expresses one who confers a benefit, the former denotes one who has violated the laws.

Many considerations, interesting in a philosophical point of view, are presented by the study of correlative expressions. It will be found, on strict examination, that there seldom exists an exact opposition between two words which may at first sight appear to be the counterparts of one another; for, in general, the one will be found to possess in reality more force or extent of meaning than the other, with which it is contrasted. The correlative term sometimes assumes the form of a mere negative, although it is really endowed with a considerable positive force. Thus *Disrespect* is not merely the absence of *Respect*; its signification trenches on the opposite idea, namely, *Contempt*. In like manner, *Untruth* is not merely the negative of *Truth*; it involves a degree of *Falsehood. Irreligion,* which is properly *the want of Religion,* is understood as being nearly synonymous with *Impiety*.

There exist comparatively few words of a general character to which no correlative term, either of negation or of opposition, can be assigned. The correlative idea, especially that which constitutes a sense negative to the primary one, may, indeed, be formed or conceived; but, from its occurring rarely, no word has been framed to represent it; for in language, as in other matters, the supply fails when there is no probability of a demand. Occasionally we find this deficiency provided for by the contrivance of prefixing the syllable *non*; as, for instance, the negatives of *existence, performance, payment,* etc., are expressed by the compound words, *non-existence, non-performance, non-payment,* etc. Functions of a similar kind are performed by the prefixes *dis-* (the word *disannul*, however, had the same meaning as *annul*), *anti-, contra-, mis-, in-,* and *un-.* In the case of adjectives, the addition to a substantive of the terminal syllable *less*, gives it a negative meaning: as *taste, tasteless; care, careless; hope, hopeless; friend, friendless; fault, faultless,* etc. With respect to all these great latitude is allowed according to the necessities of the case, a latitude which is limited only by the taste and discretion of the author.

On the other hand, it is hardly possible to find two words having in all respects the same meaning, and being therefore interchangeable; that is, admitted of being employed indiscriminately, the one or the other, in all their applications. The investigation of the distinctions to be drawn between words apparently synonymous forms a separate branch of inquiry which I have not presumed here to enter upon; for the subject has already occupied the attention of much abler critics than myself, and its complete exhaustion would require the devotion of a whole life. The purpose of this work, it must be borne in mind, is not to explain the signification of words, but simply to classify and arrange them according to the sense in which they are now used, and which I presume to be already known to the reader. I enter into no inquiry into the changes of meaning they may have undergone in the course of time.

Such changes are innumerable; for instance, the words *tyrant, parasite, sophist, churl, knave, villain,* anciently conveyed no opprobrious meaning. *Impertinent* merely expressed *irrelative,* and implied neither *rudeness* nor *intrusion,* as it does at present. *Indifferent* originally meant *impartial; extravagant* was simply *digressive*; and to *prevent* was properly to *precede* and *assist.* The old translations of the Scriptures furnish many striking examples of the alterations which time has brought in the signification of words. Much curious information on this subject is contained in Trench's *Lectures on the Study of Words.*

I am content to accept word meanings at the value of their present currency, and have no concern with their etymologies, or with the history of their transformations; far less do I venture to thrid the mazes of the vast labyrinth into which I should be led by any attempt at a general discrimination of synonyms. The difficulties I have had to contend with have already been sufficiently great without this addition to my labours.

The most cursory glance over the pages of a dictionary will show that a great number of words are used in various senses, sometimes distinguished by slight shades of difference, but often diverging widely from their primary signification, and even, in some cases, bearing to it no perceptible relation. It may even happen that the very same word has two significations quite opposite to one another. This is the case with the verb *to cleave,* which means *to adhere tenaciously,* and also *to separate by a blow. To propugn* sometimes expresses *to attack*; at other times, *to defend. To ravel* means both *to entangle* and *to disentangle.* The alphabetical index at could I have presumed to erect any absolute standard of purity. My object, be it remembered, is not to regulate the use of words, but simply to supply and to suggest such as may be wanted on occasion, leaving the proper selection entirely to the discretion and taste of the employer. If a novelist or a dramatist, for example, proposed to delineate some vulgar personage, he would wish to have the power of putting into the mouth of the speaker expressions that would accord with his character, just as the actor, to revert to a former comparison, who had to personate a peasant, would choose for his attire the most homely garb, and would have just reason to complain if the theatrical wardrobe furnished him with no suitable costume.

Words which have, in process of time, become obsolete, are, of course, rejected from this collection. On the other hand, I have admitted a considerable number of words and phrases borrowed from other languages, chiefly the French and Latin, some of which may be considered as already naturalized; while others, though avowedly foreign, are frequently introduced in English composition, particularly in familiar style, on account of their being peculiarly expressive, and because we have no corresponding words of equal force in our own language. All these words and phrases are printed in italics. The rapid advances which are being made in scientific knowledge, and consequent improvement in all the arts of life, and the extension of those arts and sciences to so many new purposes and objects, create a continual demand for the formation of new terms to express new agencies, new wants, and new combinations. Such terms, from being at first merely technical, are rendered, by more general use, familiar to the multitude, and having a well-defined acceptation, are eventually incorporated into the language, which they contribute to enlarge and to enrich. *Neologies* of this kind are perfectly legitimate, and highly advantageous; and they necessarily introduce those gradual and progressive changes which every language is destined to undergo. Thus in framing the present classification I have frequently felt the want of substantive terms corresponding to abstract qualities or ideas denoted by certain adjectives, and have been tempted to invent words that might express these abstractions; but I have yielded to this temptation only in the four following instances: having framed from the adjectives *irrelative, amorphous, sinistral,* and *gaseous* the abstract nouns *irrelation, amorphism, sinistrality,* and *gaseity.* I have ventured also to introduce the adjective *intersocial* to express the active voluntary relations between man and man. Some modern writers, however, have indulged in a habit of arbitrarily fabricating new words and a new-fangled phraseology without any necessity, and with manifest injury to the purity of the language. This vicious practice, the offspring of indolence or conceit, implies an ignorance or neglect of the riches in which the English language already abounds, and which would have supplied them with words of recognized legitimacy, conveying precisely the same meaning as those they so recklessly coin in the illegal mint of their own fancy.

A work constructed on the plan of classification I have proposed might, if ably executed, be of great value in tending to limit the fluctuations to which language has always been subject, by establishing an authoritative standard for its regulation. Future historians, philologists, and lexicographers, when investigating the period when new words were introduced, or discussing the import given at the present time to the old, might find their labours lightened by being enabled to appeal to such a standard, instead of having to search for data among the scattered writings of the age. Nor would its utility be confined to a single language, for the principles of its construction are universally applicable to all languages, whether living or dead. On the same plan of classification there might be formed a French, a German, a Latin, or a Greek Thesaurus, possessing, in their respective spheres, the same advantages as those of the English model. Still more useful would be a conjunction of these methodized compilations in two languages, the French and the English, for instance; the columns of each being placed in parallel juxtaposition. No means yet devised would so greatly facilitate the acquisition of the one language by those who are acquainted with the other: none would afford such ample assistance to the translator in either language; and none would supply such ready and effectual means of instituting an accurate comparison between them, and of fairly appreciating their respective merits and defects. In a still higher degree would all those advantages be combined and multiplied in a *Polyglot Lexicon* constructed on this system.

Metaphysicians engaged in the more profound investigation of the Philosophy of Language will be materially assisted by having the ground thus prepared for them in a previous analysis and classification of our ideas, for such classification of ideas is the true basis on which words, which are their symbols. should be classified. It is by such analysis alone that we can arrive at a clear perception of the relation which these symbols bear to their corresponding ideas, or can obtain a correct knowledge of the elements which enter into the formation of compound ideas, and of the exclusions by which we arrive at the abstractions so perpetually resorted to in the process of reasoning and in the communication of our thoughts.

The principle by which I have been guided in framing my verbal classification is the same as that which is employed in the various departments of natural history. Thus the sectional divisions I have formed correspond to natural families in botany and zoology, and the filiation of words presents a network analogous to the natural filiation of plants or animals.

The following are the only publications that have come to my knowledge in which any attempt has been made to construct a systematic arrangement of Ideas with a view to their expression. The earliest of these, supposed to be at least nine hundred years old, is the AMERA CÓSHA, or *Vocabulary of the Sanscrit Language,* by Amera Sinha, of which an English translation, by the late Henry T. Colebrooke, was printed at Serampoor in the year 1808. The classification of words is there, as might be expected, exceedingly imperfect and confused, especially in all that relates to abstract Ideas or mental operations. This will be apparent from the very title of the first section, which comprehends '*Heaven, Gods, Demons, Fire, Air, Velocity, Eternity, Much*'; while *Sin, Virtue, Happiness, Destiny, Cause, Nature, Intellect, Reasoning, Knowledge, Senses, Tastes, Odours, Colours,* are all included and jumbled together in the fourth section. A more logical order, however, pervades the sections relating to natural objects, such as *Seas, Earth, Towns, Plants,* and *Animals,* which form separate classes, exhibiting a remarkable effort at analysis at so remote a period of Indian literature.

The well-known work of Bishop Wilkins, entitled *An Essay towards a Real Character and a Philosophical Language,* published in 1668, had for its object the formation of a system of symbols which might serve as a universal language. It professed to be founded on a 'scheme of analysis of the things or notions to which names were to be assigned'; but notwithstanding the immense labour and ingenuity expended in the construction of this system, it was soon found to be far the end of this work sufficiently shows the multiplicity of uses to which, by the elasticity of language, the meaning of words has been stretched so as to adapt them to a great variety of modified significations in subservience to the nicer shades of thought which, under peculiarity of circumstances, require corresponding expression. Words thus admitting of different meanings have therefore to be arranged under each of the respective heads corresponding to these various acceptations. There are many words, again, which express ideas compounded of two elementary ideas belonging to different classes. It is therefore necessary to place these words respectively under each of the generic heads to which they relate. The necessity of these repetitions is increased by the circumstance that ideas included under one class are often connected by relations of the same kind as the ideas which belong to another class. Thus we find the same relations of *order* and of *quantity* existing among the ideas of *Time* as well as those of *Space*. Sequence in the one is denoted by the same terms as sequence in the other, and the measures of time also express the measures of space. The cause and the effect are often designated by the same word. The word *Sound,* for instance, denotes both the impression made upon the ear by sonorous vibrations, and also the vibrations themselves, which are the cause or source of that impression. *Mixture* is used for the act of mixing, as well as for the product of that operation. *Taste* and *Smell* express both the sensations and the qualities of material bodies giving rise to them. *Thought* is the act of thinking, but the same word denotes also the idea resulting from that act. *Judgment* is the act of deciding, and also the decision come to. *Purchase* is the acquisition of a thing by payment, as well as the thing itself so acquired. *Speech* is both the act of speaking and the words spoken; and so on with regard to an endless multiplicity of words. Mind is essentially distinct from Matter, and yet, in all languages, the attributes of the one are metaphorically transferred to those of the other. Matter, in all its forms, is endowed by the figurative genius of every language with the functions which pertain to intellect; and we perpetually talk of its phenomena and of its powers as if they resulted from the voluntary influence of one body on another, acting and reacting, impelling and being impelled, controlling and being controlled, as if animated by spontaneous energies and guided by specific intentions. On the other hand, expressions of which the primary signification refers exclusively to the properties and actions of matter are metaphorically applied to the phenomena of thought and volition, and even to the feelings and passions of the soul; and in speaking of a *ray of hope,* a *shade of doubt,* a *flight of fancy,* a *flash of wit,* the *warmth of emotion,* or the *ebullitions of anger,* we are scarcely conscious that we are employing metaphors which have this material origin.

As a general rule, I have deemed it incumbent on me to place words and phrases which appertain more especially to one head also under the other heads to which they have a relation, whenever it appeared to me that this repetition would suit the convenience of the inquirer, and spare him the trouble of turning to other parts of the work; for I have always preferred to subject myself to the imputation of redundance, rather than incur the reproach of insufficiency. Frequent repetitions of the same series of expressions, accordingly, will be met with under various headings. For example, the word *Relinquishment,* with its synonyms, occurs as a heading at No. 624, where it applies to *intention,* and also at No. 782, where it refers to *property.* The word *Chance* has two significations, distinct from one another: the one implying the *absence of an assignable* cause, in which case it comes under the category of the relation of Causation, and occupies the No. 156; the other, the *absence of design,* in which latter sense it ranks under the operations of the Will, and has assigned to it the place No. 621. I have, in like manner, distinguished *Sensibility, Pleasure, Pain, Taste,* etc., according as they relate to *Physical* or to *Moral Affections*; the former being found at Nos. 375, 377, 378, 390, etc., and the latter at Nos. 822, 827, 828, 850, etc.

When, however, the divergence of the associated from the primary idea is suføiently marked, I have contented myself with making a reference to the place where the modified signification will be found. But in order to prevent needless extension, I have, in general, omitted *conjugate words* (different parts of speech from the same root exactly corresponding in point of meaning) which are so obviously derivable from those that are given in the same place, that the reader may safely be left to form them for himself. This is the case with adverbs derived from adjectives by the simple addition of the terminal syllable *-ly,* such as *closely, carefully, safely,* etc., from *close, careful, safe,* etc., and also with adjectives or participles immediately derived from the verbs which are already given. In all such cases, an 'etc.' indicates that reference is understood to be made to these roots. I have observed the same rule in compiling the index, retaining only the primary or more simple word, and omitting the conjugate words obviously derived from them. Thus I assume the word *short* as the representative of its immediate derivatives *shortness, shorten, shortening, shortened, shorter, shortly,* which would have had the same references, and which the reader can readily supply.

The same verb is frequently used indiscriminately either in the active or transitive, or in the neuter or intransitive sense. In these cases I have generally not thought it worth while to increase the bulk of the work by the needless repetition of that word, for the reader, whom I suppose to understand the use of the words, must also be presumed to be competent to apply them correctly.

There are a multitude of words of a specific character, which although they properly occupy places in the columns of a dictionary, yet, having no relation to general ideas, do not come within the scope of this compilation, and are consequently omitted. The names of objects in Natural History, and technical terms belonging exclusively to Science or to Art, or relating to particular operations, and of which the signification is restricted to those specific objects, come under this category. Exceptions must, however, be made in favour of such words as admit of metaphorical application to general subjects with which custom has associated them, and of which they may be cited as being typical or illustrative. Thus the word *Lion* will find a place under the head of *Courage,* of which it is regarded as the type. *Anchor,* being emblematic of *Hope,* is introduced among the words expressing that emotion; and, in like manner, *butterfly* and *weathercock,* which are suggestive of fickleness, are included in the category of *Irresolution.*

With regard to the admission of many words and expressions which the classical reader might be disposed to condemn as vulgarisms, or which he, perhaps, might stigmatize as pertaining rather to the slang than to the legitimate language of the day, I would beg to observe that, having due regard to the uses to which this work was to be adapted, I did not feel myself justified in excluding them solely on that ground, if they possessed an acknowledged currency in general intercourse. It is obvious that, with respect to degrees of conventionality, I could not have attempted to draw any strict lines of demarcation, and far less too abstruse and recondite for practical application.

In the year 1797 there appeared in Paris an anonymous work, entitled *Pasigraphie, ou Premiers Éléments du nouvel Art-Science d'écrire et d'imprimer une langue de manière à être lu et entendu dans toute autre langue sans traduction,* of which an edition in German was also published. It contains a great number of tabular schemes of categories, all of which appear to be excessively arbitrary and artificial, and extremely difficult of application, as well as of apprehension.

Lastly, such analyses alone can determine the principles on which a strictly *Philosophical Language* might be constructed. The probable result of the construction of such a language would be its eventual adoption by every civilized nation, thus realizing that splendid aspiration of philanthropists—the establishment of a Universal Language. 'The languages,' observes Horne Tooke in his Επεα Πτεροσενπα, 'which are commonly used throughout the world, are much more simple and easy, convenient and philosophical, than Wilkins's scheme for a *real character*; or than any other scheme that has been at any other time imagined or proposed for the purpose.' However Utopian such a project may appear to the present generation, and however abortive may have been the former endeavours of Bishop Wilkins and others to realize it, its accomplishment is surely not beset with greater difficulties than have impeded the progress to many other beneficial objects which in former times appeared to be no less visionary, and which yet were successfully achieved, in later ages, by the continued and persevering exertions of the human intellect. Is there at the present day, then, any ground for despair that, at some future stage of that higher civilization to which we trust the world is gradually tending, some new and bolder effort of genius towards the solution of this great problem may be crowned with success, and compass an object of such vast and paramount utility? Nothing, indeed, would conduce more directly to bring about a golden age of union and harmony among the several nations and races of mankind than the removal of that barrier to the interchange of thought and mutual good understanding between man and man which is now interposed by the diversity of their respective languages.

PLAN OF CLASSIFICATION

PLAN OF CLASSIFICATION

CLASS ONE
Abstract relations

Section 1
Existence

Abstract	1 EXISTENCE	2 INEXISTENCE
Concrete	3 SUBSTANTIALITY	4 UNSUBSTANTIALITY
	Internal	*External*
Formal	5 INTRINSICALITY	6 EXTRINSICALITY
	Absolute	*Relative*
Modal	7 STATE	8 CIRCUMSTANCE

Section 2
Relation

Absolute	9 RELATION	10 IRRELATION
	11 CONSANGUINITY	
	12 CORRELATION	
	13 IDENTITY	14 CONTRARIETY
		15 DIFFERENCE
Continuous	16 UNIFORMITY	16a NON-UNIFORMITY
	17 SIMILARITY	18 DISSIMILARITY
	19 IMITATION	20 NON-IMITATION
		20a VARIATION
	21 COPY	22 PROTOTYPE
General	23 AGREEMENT	24 DISAGREEMENT

Section 3
Quantity

Simple	*Absolute*	*Relative*
	25 QUANTITY	26 DEGREE
	27 EQUALITY	28 INEQUALITY
		29 MEAN
		30 COMPENSATION
	By Comparison with a Standard	
Comparative	31 GREATNESS	32 SMALLNESS
	By Comparison with a Similar Object	
	33 SUPERIORITY	34 INFERIORITY
	Changes in Quantity	
	35 INCREASE	36 NON-INCREASE
		DECREASE
	37 ADDITION	38 NON-ADDITION
		SUBDUCTION
	39 ADJUNCT	40 REMAINDER
		40a DECREMENT
Conjunctive	41 MIXTURE	42 SIMPLENESS
	43 JUNCTION	44 DISJUNCTION
	45 VINCULUM	
	46 COHERENCE	47 INCOHERENCE
	48 COMBINATION	49 DECOMPOSITION

30

CLASS TWO
Space

Section 1
Space in General

Abstract Space	*Indefinite*	*Definite*
	180 SPACE	181 REGION
		Limited
		182 PLACE
Relative Space	183 SITUATION	
	184 LOCATION	185 DISPLACEMENT
Existence in Space	186 PRESENCE	187 ABSENCE
	188 INHABITANT	189 ABODE
	190 CONTENTS	191 RECEPTACLE

Section 2
Dimensions

Dimensions	*General*	192 SIZE	193 LITTLENESS
		194 EXPANSION	195 CONTRACTION
		196 DISTANCE	197 NEARNESS
		198 INTERVAL	199 CONTIGUITY
	Linear	200 LENGTH	201 SHORTNESS
		202 BREADTH	203 NARROWNESS
		THICKNESS	THINNESS
		204 LAYER	205 FILAMENT
		206 HEIGHT	207 LOWNESS
		208 DEPTH	209 SHALLOWNESS
Linear – continued		210 SUMMIT	211 BASE
		212 VERTICALITY	213 HORIZONTALITY
		214 PENDENCY	215 SUPPORT
		216 PARALLELISM	217 OBLIQUITY
		218 INVERSION	
		219 CROSSING	
	Centrical	220 EXTERIORITY	221 INTERIORITY
	(General)	222 COVERING	
		223 CENTRALITY	224 LINING
		225 INVESTMENT	226 DIVESTMENT
		227 CIRCUMJACENCE	228 INTERJACENCE
		229 OUTLINE	
		230 EDGE	
		231 CIRCUMSCRIPTION	
		232 ENCLOSURE	
		233 LIMIT	
	(Special)	234 FRONT	235 REAR
		236 LATERALITY	237 ANTIPOSITION
		238 DEXTRALITY	239 SINISTRALITY

Section 3
Form

Form	*General*	240 FORM	241 AMORPHISM
		242 SYMMETRY	243 DISTORTION
	Special	244 ANGULARITY	
		245 CURVATURE	246 STRAIGHTNESS
		247 CIRCULARITY	248 CONVOLUTION
		249 ROTUNDITY	

CLASS THREE
Matter

CLASS FOUR
Intellect
Division I Formation of Ideas

CLASS FIVE
Volition
Division I Individual Volition

Division II Intersocial Volition

CLASS SIX
Affections

Section 1
General

820 AFFECTIONS
821 FEELING
822 SENSIBILITY
824 EXCITATION
825 EXCITABILITY

823 INSENSIBILITY

826 INEXCITABILITY

Section 2
Personal

Passive

827 PLEASURE
829 PLEASUREABLENESS
831 CONTENT

828 PAIN
830 PAINFULNESS
832 DISCONTENT
833 REGRET

834 RELIEF
836 CHEERFULNESS
838 REJOICING
840 AMUSEMENT
842 WIT
844 HUMORIST

835 AGGRAVATION
837 DEJECTION
839 LAMENTATION
841 WEARINESS
843 DULLNESS

Discriminative

845 BEAUTY
847 ORNAMENT

846 UGLINESS
848 BLEMISH
849 SIMPLICITY

850 TASTE
852 FASHION

851 VULGARITY
853 RIDICULOUSNESS
854 FOP
855 AFFECTION
856 RIDICULE
857 LAUGHING-STOCK

Prospective

858 HOPE

861 COURAGE
863 RASHNESS
865 DESIRE

859 HOPELESSNESS
860 FEAR
862 COWARDICE
864 CAUTION
867 DISLIKE

866 INDIFFERENCE

868 FASTIDIOUSNESS
869 SATIETY

Contemplative

870 WONDER
872 PRODIGY

871 EXPECTANCE

Extrinsic

873 REPUTE
875 NOBILITY
877 TITLE
878 PRIDE
880 VANITY
882 OSTENTATION
883 CELEBRATION
884 BOASTING
885 INSOLENCE
887 BLUSTERER

874 DISREPUTE
876 COMMONALTY

879 HUMILITY
881 MODESTY

886 SERVILITY

Section 3
Sympathetic

Social	888 FRIENDSHIP	889 ENMITY
	890 FRIEND	891 ENEMY
	892 SOCIALITY	893 SECLUSION
	894 COURTESY	895 DISCOURTESY
	896 CONGRATULATION	
	897 LOVE	898 HATE
	899 FAVOURITE	900 RESENTMENT
		901 IRASCIBILITY
	902 ENDEARMENT	
	903 MARRIAGE	904 CELIBACY
		905 DIVORCE
Diffusive	906 BENEVOLENCE	907 MALEVOLENCE
		908 MALEDICTION
		909 THREAT
	910 PHILANTHROPY	911 MISANTHROPY
	912 BENEFACTOR	913 EVILDOER
Special	914 PITY	
	915 CONDOLENCE	
Retrospective	916 GRATITUDE	917 INGRATITUDE
	918 FORGIVENESS	919 REVENGE
		920 JEALOUSY
		921 ENVY

Section 4
Moral

Obligations	922 RIGHT	923 WRONG
	924 DUENESS	925 UNDUENESS
	926 DUTY	927 DERELICTION
		927a EXEMPTION
Sentiments	928 RESPECT	929 DISRESPECT
		930 CONTEMPT
	931 APPROBATION	932 DISAPPROBATION
	933 FLATTERY	934 DETRACTION
	935 FLATTERER	936 DETRACTOR
	937 VINDICATION	938 ACCUSATION
Conditions	939 PROBITY	940 IMPROBITY
		941 KNAVE
	942 UNSELFISHNESS	943 SELFISHNESS
	944 VIRTUE	945 VICE
	946 INNOCENCE	947 GUILT
	948 GOOD MAN	949 BAD MAN
	950 PENITENCE	951 IMPENITENCE
	952 ATONEMENT	
Practice	953 TEMPERANCE	954 INTEMPERANCE
	955 ASCETICISM	
	956 FASTING	957 GLUTTONY
	958 SOBRIETY	959 DRUNKENNESS
	960 PURITY	961 IMPURITY
		962 LIBERTINE

THESAURUS

CLASS ONE

Words relating to abstract relations

Section I – Existence

1 EXISTENCE

Substantives: being, life, vital principle, entity, ens, essence, quiddity, subsistence; coexistence (120).

Reality, actuality, positiveness, absoluteness, fact, truth (494); actualization.

Presence; existence in space (186).

Science of existence, ontology; existentialism.

Phrases: The sober reality; hard fact; matter of fact; the whole truth; no joke.

Verbs: To be, to exist, have being, subsist, live, breathe, stand, abide, remain, stay, obtain, occur, prevail, be so, find itself, take place, eventuate, consist in, lie in; to vegetate, pass the time.

To come into existence, arise, come out, emerge, come forth, appear (448).

To bring into existence, produce, bring forth, discover (161), objectify.

Adjectives: Existing, being, subsisting, subsistent, in being, in existence, extant, living, breathing, obtaining, prevailing, prevalent, current, afoot.

Real, actual, positive, absolute, essential, substantial, substantive, self-existing, self-existent; undestroyed, tangible, not ideal, not imagined, not supposititious, not potential, virtual, effective, unideal, true, authentic, genuine, mere, objective.

Adverbs: Actually, really, absolutely, positively, etc., in fact, *de facto, ipso facto.*

Phrase: *In esse; cogito ergo sum.*

2 INEXISTENCE

Substantives: non-existence, not-being, nonentity, *nihil,* nil, non-subsistence, nulity, vacuity, blank (4), negativeness, absence (187), removal (185).

Annihilation, abeyance, extinction (162); nirvana.

Philosophy of non-existence, nihilism.

Phrases: No such thing; Mrs. Harris; 'men in buckram.'

Verbs: Not to be, not to exist, etc.

To cease to be, pass away, perish, vanish, fade away, dissolve, melt away, disappear (449), to be annihilated, extinct, etc., to die (360), to die out.

Phrases: To have no being; to have no existence; to be null and void; *non est*; to be no more; 'to leave not a rack behind'; to disappear into thin air; to be brought out of existence.

Adjectives: Inexistent, non-existent, non-existing, etc., negative, blank, absent.

Unreal, potential, virtual, baseless, unsubstantial (4), imaginary, ideal, vain, fanciful, unpractical, shadowy, fabulous (515), supposititious (514).

Unborn, uncreated, unbegotten, unproduced, unmade.

Annihilated, destroyed, extinct, gone, lost, perished, melted, dissolved, faded, exhausted, vanished, missing, disappeared, departed, extinct, defunct (360).

Adverbs: Negatively, virtually, etc.

Phrase: *In nubibus.*

3 SUBSTANTIALITY

Substantives: hypostasis, person, thing, being, something, existence, entity, reification, corporeity, body, physique, substance, object, article, creature, matter, material, stuff (316), substratum, protoplasm.

Totality of existences, world (318), continuum, plenum.

Phrase: Something or other.

Adjectives: Substantive, substantial, personal, bodily, tangible, true, real, concrete, corporal, corporeal, material, objective, hypostatic.

Verbs: Substantialize, actualize, materialize, reify, embody.

Adverbs: Substantially, etc., essentially.

4 UNSUBSTANTIALITY

Substantives: insubstantiality, nothingness, nihility, nothing, naught, damn-all, *nihil*, nil, nix, love, zero, cipher, a duck, duck's-egg, pair of spectacles; nonentity, nobody, no one (187).

A shadow, phantom, phantasm, phantasmagoria, dream, mockery, air, thin air, idle dream, pipe dream, castle in Spain (515), idle talks, ignis fatuus, *fata morgana,* mirage.

Void, vacuum, vacuity, vacancy, voidness, vacuousness, inanity, emptiness, hollowness, blank, chasm, gap, hiatus (198); empty space, ether.

Phrases: Nothing at all; nothing whatever; nothing on earth; nothing under the sun; not a particle.

A man of straw; *vox et praetera nihil;* 'such stuff as dreams are made on.'

Verbs: To vanish, fade, dissolve, evaporate.

Adjectives: Unsubstantial, immaterial, void, vacant, vacuous, blank, null, inane, idle, hollow, airy, visionary (515).

5 INTRINSICALITY

Substantives: inbeing, immanence, inherence, inhesion, essence; essentiality, essentialness, subjectiveness, subjectivity, essential part, soul, quintessence, quiddity, gist, pith, core, backbone, marrow, sap, lifeblood; incarnation.

Nature, constitution, character, type, quality (157), temperament, temper, manner, spirit, ethos, habit, humour, grain, endowment, capacity, capability, moods, declensions, features, aspects, specialities, peculiarities (79), particularities, idiosyncrasy, idiocrasy, diagnostics.

Verbs: To be innate, inborn, etc.

Phrases: To be in the blood; to be born like that.

Adjectives: Derived from within, subjective, intrinsic, intrinsical, inherent, essential, natural, internal, implanted, inborn, innate, inbred, engrained, inherited, immanent, indwelling, radical, constitutional, congenital, connate, hereditary, instinctive, indigenous.

Phrases: In the grain; in the blood; bred in the bone.

Characteristic, peculiar, qualitative, special, diagnostic (79), invariable.

Adverbs: Intrinsically, subjectively, substantially, at bottom, *au fond,* at the core.

6 EXTRINSICALITY

Substantives: extraneousness, objectiveness, objectivity, accident, superficiality, incident.

Adjectives: Derived from without, objective, extrinsic, extrinsical, extraneous, modal, adventitious, adscititious, incidental, accidental, non-essential, outward (220).

Implanted, engrafted.

Adverbs: Extrinsically, etc.

7 STATE

Substantives: condition, category, class, kind, estate, lot, case, constitution, habitude, diathesis, mood, temper, morale.

Frame, fabric, structure, texture, contexture (329), conformation, organism.

Mode, modality, schesis, form, shape (240), figure, cut, cast, mould, stamp, set, fit, tone, tenor, trim, turn, guise, fashion, aspect, complexion, style, manner, character, kind, get-up, set-up, format, *genre.*
Verbs: To be in a state, to be in condition, to be on a footing, etc.

To do, fare; to have, possess, enjoy, etc., a state, condition, etc.

To bring into a state, etc. (144).
Adjectives: Conditional, modal, formal, structural, organic, textual.
Phrases: As the matter stands; as things are; such being the case.
Adverbs: Conditionally, etc.

8 CIRCUMSTANCE
Substantives: situation, phase, position, posture, attitude, place, point, bearings, terms, fare, regime, footing, standing, status, predicament, contingency, occasion, juncture, conjuncture, emergency, exigence, exigency, crisis, pinch, impasse, pass, push, plight, fix.
Phrases: How the land lies; how the wind blows; how the cat jumps.
Adjectives: Circumstantial; given, conditional, provisional, modal, critical, contingent, incidental (6, 151), circumstanced, placed.
Verb Phrases: To bow before the storm; to take things as they come; to cut one's coat according to the cloth.
Adverbs: In or under the circumstances, conditions, etc.; thus, so; in such a case, contingency, etc.; accordingly, such being the case; since, sith, seeing that, as matters stand, as things go.

Conditionally, provided, if, and if, if so, if so be, if it be so, if it so prove, or turn out, or happen; in the event of, provisionally, unless, without.
Phrases: According to circumstances; as it may happen, or turn out; as the case may be; *pro re nata;* wind and weather permitting; D.V.; rain or shine; sink or swim; at all events; other things being equal; *ceteris paribus.*

Section II – Relation

9 RELATION
Substantives: relationship, bearing, reference, standing, concern, cognation, correlation (12), analogy, affinity, homology, alliance, homogeneity, connection, association, approximation, similarity (17), filiation, affiliation, etc. (11, 166), interest, habitude; relativity.

Relevancy, pertinency, fitness, etc. (646, 23).

Aspect, point of view, comparison (464); ratio, proportion.

Link, tie (45), homologue.
Verbs: To be related, have a relation, etc., to relate to, refer to, have reference to, bear upon, regard, concern, touch, affect, have to do with, pertain to, belong to, appertain to, answer to, interest.

To bring into relation with, correlate, associate, connect, affiliate, link (43), bring near (197), homologize; to bring to bear upon.
Phrase: To draw a parallel with.
Adjectives: Relative, correlative, cognate, relating to, relative to, relevant, in relation with, referable to, pertinent (23), germane, belonging to, pat, to the point, apposite, to the purpose, apropos, *ad rem,* just the thing, quite the thing; pertaining to, appertaining to, appurtenant, affiliated, allied, related, implicated, connected, associated, *en rapport,* in touch with, bound up with, homological, homologous.

Approximate, approximative, approximating, proportional, proportionate, proportionable, allusive, comparable, like, similar (17).
Adverbs: Relatively, thereof, as to, about, connecting, concerning, anent,

touching, as relates to, with relation to, relating to, as respects, with respect to, in respect of, respecting, as regards, with regard to, regarding, in the matter of, with reference to, according to, while speaking of, apropos of, in connection with, inasmuch as, whereas, in consideration of, in point of, as far as, on the part of, on the score of, under the head of, *in re*; pertinently, etc. (23).

10 IRRELATION
Substantives: disconnection, dissociation, disassociation, misrelation, independence, isolation (44), multifariousness, disproportion; commensurability, irrelevancy; heterogeneity, irreconcilableness (24), impertinence.

Verbs: To have no relation with, or to, to have nothing to do with, to have no business there, not to concern, not to admit of comparison.

To isolate, separate, detach, disconnect, segregate (44).

Adjectives: Irrelative, irrespective, unrelated, without reference, etc., to, arbitrary, episodic, remote, far-fetched, forced, out of place, out of tune (414), inharmonious, malapropos, irrelevant, foreign to, alien, impertinent, inapposite, extraneous to, strange to, stranger to, independent, parenthetical, incidental, outlandish, exotic, unallied, unconnected, disconnected, unconcerned, adrift, detached, isolated, insular.

Not comparable, incommensurable, inapplicable (24), irreconcilable, heterogeneous (83), unconformable.

Phrases: Foreign to the purpose; nothing to the purpose; having nothing to do with; *nihil ad rem*; neither here nor there; beside the mark; *à propos des bottes*; dragged in by the scruff of the neck.

Adverbs: Parentetically, by the way, by the by, *obiter dicta, en passant*, incidentally, irrespectively, irrelevantly, etc.

11 CONSANGUINITY
Substantives: relationship, kindred, blood, parentage (166), filiation, affiliation, lineage, agnation, connection, alliance, family connection, family tie, nepotism.

A kinsman, kinswoman, kinsfolk, kith and kin, relation, relative, friend, sibling, one's people, clan, connection, one's own flesh and blood, brother, sister, father, mother, uncle, aunt, nephew, niece, stepfather, etc., brother-in-law, etc., guid-brother, etc., cousin, cousin-german; first, second cousin; cousin once, twice, etc., removed; grand- or great-grandfather, etc., great-uncle, etc., a near relation, a blood-relation, a distant relation or relative, congener, collateral.

Family, issue, fraternity, sisterhood, brotherhood, parentage, cousinhood, etc.; race, stock, generation, sept, clan, tribe, strain.

Verbs: To be related, to have or claim relationship with.

Adjectives: Related, akin, consanguineous, congeneric, family, kindred, affiliated, allied, collateral, sib, agnate, agnatic, fraternal, of the same blood, nearly or close related, remotely or distantly related.

Phrase: Blood is thicker than water.

12 RECIPROCALNESS
Substantives: reciprocity, mutuality, correlation, correlativeness, interdependence, interchange, interaction, reciprocation, etc. (148), alternation (149), barter (794).

Verbs: To reciprocate, alternate, interchange, interact, exchange, counterchange, interdepend.

Adjectives: Reciprocal, mutual, common, correlative, alternate, alternative; interchangeable, interdependent, international.

Adverbs: Reciprocally, mutually, etc.

Phrases: *Mutatis mutandis*; each other; vice versa; turn and turn about.

13 IDENTITY
Substantives: sameness, oneness, coincidence, coalescence, convertibility; selfness, self, ego, oneself, number one; identification, monotony; equality (27), tautology (104).

Synonym; facsimile (21), counterpart (17).

Verbs: To be identical, to be the same, etc., to coincide, to coalesce.

To render the same.

To recognize the identity of, to identify, recognize.

Adjectives: Identical, identic, same, self, selfsame, very same, no other, ilk, one and the same, ditto, unaltered, coincident, coinciding, coessential, coalescing, coalescent, indistinguishable, tantamount, equivalent, equipollent, convertible, much the same.

Adverbs: All one, all the same, *ibidem*, ibid, identically, likewise.

Phrases: *Semper idem; toujours la même chose; alter ago*; on all fours; much of a muchness.

14 CONTRARIETY
Substantives: contrast, foil, set-off, antithesis, contradiction, opposition, oppositeness, antagonism (179, 708), distinction (15).

Inversion, reversion (218).

The opposite, the reverse, inverse, converse, antonym, the antipodes (237).

Phrases: The reverse of the medal; the other side of the shield; the tables being turned.

Verbs: To be contrary, etc., to contrast with, contradict, contravene, oppose, negate, antagonize, invert, reverse, turn the tables, to militate against.

Adjectives: Contrary, opposite, counter, converse, reverse, antithetical, opposed, antipodean, antagonistic, opposing, conflicting, inconsistent, contradictory, contrarious, contrariant, negative.

Phrases: Differing *toto caelo*; diametrically opposite; as black to white; light to darkness; fire to water; worlds apart; poles asunder.

Adverbs: Contrarily, contrariously, contrariwise, *per contra,* oppositely, *vice versa,* on the contrary, *tout au contraire,* quite the contrary, no such thing.

15 DIFFERENCE
Substantives: variance, variation, variety, diversity, modification, allotropy, shade of difference, nuance; deviation, divergence, divarication (291), disagreement (24), dissimilarity (18), disparity (28).

Distinction, contradistinction, differentiation, discrimination (465); a nice or fine or subtle distinction.

Phrases: A very different thing; *a tertium quid*; a horse of a different colour; another pair of shoes.

Verbs: To be different, etc., to differ, vary, mismatch, contrast, differ *toto caelo.*

To render different, etc., to vary, change, modify, varify, diversify, etc. (140).

To distinguish, differentiate, severalize (465), split hairs, discriminate.

Adjectives: Different, differing, disparate, heterogeneous, heteromorphic, allotropic, varying, distinguishable, discriminative, varied, modified, diversified, deviating, diverging, devious, disagreeing (24), various, divers, all manner of, multifarious, multiform, variform (81), variegated (440), diacritical.

Other, another, other-guess, not the same.

Unmatched, widely apart, changed (140).

Phrase: As different as chalk is from cheese.

Adverbs: Differently, variously, otherwise.

16 UNIFORMITY
Substantives: homogeneity, homogeneousness, consistency, connaturality, conformity (82), homology, accordance, agreement (23), regularity (58), routine, monotony, constancy.
Verbs: To be uniform, etc., to accord with, harmonize with, hang together, go together.

To become uniform, conform with, fall in with, follow suit.

To render uniform, to assimilate, level, smooth (255).
Adjectives: Uniform, homogeneous, homologous, of a piece, of a kind, consistent, connatural, monotonous, even, unvarying, flat, level, constant.
Adverbs: Uniformly, uniformly with, conformably (82), consistently with, in unison with, in harmony with, in conformity with, according to (23).

Regularly, at regular intervals, invariably, constantly, always, without exception.
Phrases: In a rut (or a groove); *ab uno disce omnes*; 'forty feeding like one.'

16A NON-UNIFORMITY
Substantives: variety, multiformity (81), diversity, unevenness, irregularity, unconformity (83).
Adjectives: Multiform, multifarious, various (81), diversified, inconsistent, of various kinds.

17 SIMILARITY
Substantives: resemblance, likeness, similitude, affinity, semblance, approximation, parallelism (216), analogy, brotherhood, family likeness; alliteration, head-rhyme, rhyme, pun, assonance, repetition (104), reproduction.

An analogue, copy (21), the like, facsimile, match, double, pendant, fellow, pair, mate, twin, *alter ego*, parallel, counterpart, brother, sister; simile, metaphor (521), resemblance, imitation (19).
Phrases: One's second self; *Arcades ambo*; birds of a feather; *et hoc genus omne*; a chip off the old block; the very spit (and image) of.
Verbs: To be similar, like, resembling, etc., to look like, resemble, bear resemblance, favour, approximate, parallel, match, imitate, take after (19), represent, simulate, personate, savour of, have a flavour of, favour, feature.

To render similar, assimilate, approximate, reproduce, bring near, copy, plagiarize.
Adjectives: Similar, like, alike, resembling, twin, analogous, analogical, parallel, allied to, of a piece, such as, connatural, congener, matching, conformable, on all fours with.

Near, something like, suchlike, mock, pseudo, simulating, representing, approximating, a show of, a kind of, a sort of.

Exact, accurate, true, faithful, close, speaking, lifelike, breathing.
Phrases: True to nature; to the life; for all the world like; like as two peas; *comme deux gouttes d'eau*; cast in the same mould; like father, like son.
Adverbs: As if, so to speak, as it were, quasi, as if it were, just as, after, in the fashion or manner of, *à la*.

18 DISSIMILARITY
Substantives: unlikeness, dissimilitude, diversity, divergence, difference (15), novelty (123), originality (515), disparity (28).
Verbs: To be unlike, etc., to vary (15, 20).

To render unlike, to diversify (140).
Phrase: To strike out something new.
Adjectives: Dissimilar, unlike, disparate, of a different kind, class, etc. (75); diversified, novel, new (123), unmatched, unique, unprecedented (83).
Phrases: Nothing of the kind; far from it; cast in a different mould; as different as chalk is from cheese.
Adverbs: Otherwise.

19 IMITATION
Substantives: assimilation, copying, transcription, transcribing, following, repetition (104), duplication, reduplication, quotation, reproduction.

Mockery, mocking, mimicry, mimicking, echoing, reflection, simulation, counterfeiting, plagiarism, forgery, fake, fakement, acting, personation, impersonation, representation (554), copy (21), parody, paraphrase, travesty, burlesque, semblance, mimesis.

An imitator, mimic, impersonator, echo, cuckoo, parrot, ape, monkey, mocking-bird.

Plagiary, plagiarist, forger, counterfeiter.

Phrase: *O imitatores, servum pecus.*

Verbs: To imitate, copy, plagiarize, forge, fake, reproduce, photograph, repeat (104), echo, re-echo, transcribe, match, parallel, emulate, do like, take off, hit off, reflect, mirror, model after (554).

To mock, mimic, ape, simulate, personate, impersonate (554), act, represent, adumbrate, counterfeit, parody, travesty, caricature, burlesque.

Phrases: To take or catch a likeness; to take after; to follow or tread in the steps of, or in the footsteps of; to take a leaf out of another's book; to follow suit; to go with the stream; to be in the fashion.

Adjectives: Imitated, copied, matched, repeated, paralleled, mock, mimic, parodied, etc., modelled after, moulded on, paraphrastic, imitative, mimetic, slavish, mechanical, synthetic, second-hand, imitable.

Adverbs: Literally, verbatim, to the letter, *literatim, sic, totidem verbis,* so to speak, in so many words, word for word, *mot à mot* (562).

20 NON-IMITATION
Substantives: originality, inventiveness, novelty.

Adjectives: Unimitated, uncopied, unmatched, unparalleled, inimitable, unique, original, novel.
Verb: To originate.

20A VARIATION
Substantives: alteration, modification, difference (15), change (140), deviation (279), divergence (291); moods and tenses.
Verbs: To vary, modify, change, alter, diversify (140).
Phrase: To steer clear of.
Adjectives: Varied, modified, diversified, etc.
Adverbs: Variously, in all manner of ways.

21 COPY
Substantives: facsimile, counterpart, effigies, effigy, form, likeness, similitude, semblance, reflex, portrait, photograph (556), photostat, microfilm, enlargement, miniature, study, cast, autotype, electrotype, imitation, replica, representation, adumbration.

Duplicate, transcript, transcription, repetition (104), réchauffé, reflection, shadow, record, recording.

Rough copy, fair copy, revise, carbon copy, tracing, rubbing, squeeze, draft or draught, proof, pull, reprint.

Counterfeit, parody, caricature, burlesque, travesty, paraphrase, forgery.
Phrases: A second edition; a twice-told tale.

22 PROTOTYPE
Substantives: original, model, pattern, standard, type, scale, scantling, archetype, protoplast, antitype, module, exemplar, example, ensample, protoplast, paradigm, fugleman, lay figure.

Text, copy, design, plan, blue-print, keynote.

Mould, matrix, last, plasm, proplasm, mint, die, seal, stamp, negative.
Verbs: To set a copy, to set an example.

23 AGREEMENT

Substantives: accord, accordance, unison, uniformity, harmony, union, concord, concert, concordance (714), cognation, conformity, conformance (82), consonance, consentaneousness, consensus, consistency, congruity, congruence, congeniality, correspondence keeping, parallelism.

Fitness, pertinence, suitableness, adaptation, meetness, patness, relevancy, aptness, aptitude, coaptation, propriety, apposition, appositeness, reconcilableness, applicability, applicableness, admissibility, commensurability, compatibility, adaptability.

Adaptation, adjustment, graduation, accommodation, reconciliation, reconcilement, concurrence (178), consent (488), co-operation (709).

Verbs: To be accordant, to agree, accord (714), correspond, tally, jibe, respond, harmonize, match, suit, fit, befit, hit, fall in with, chime in with, quadrate with, square with, cancel with, comport with, assimilate, unite with.

To render accordant, to adapt, accommodate, adjust, reconcile, fadge, dovetail, dress, square, regulate, comport, graduate, gradate, grade.

Phrases: To become one; to fit like a glove; to suit one to a T.

Adjectives: Agreeing, accordant, concordant, consonant, congruous, consentaneous, consentient, corresponding, correspondent, congenial, harmonizing, harmonious with, tallying with, conformable with, in accordance with, in harmony with, in unison with, in keeping with, squaring with, quadrating with, falling in with, of one mind, of a piece, consistent with, compatible, reconcilable with, commensurate.

Apt, apposite, pertinent, germane, relating to, pat, bearing upon (9), applicable, relevant, fit, fitting, suitable, happy, felicitous, proper, meet, appropriate, suiting, befitting, becoming, seasonable, deft, accommodating, topical.

Phrases: The cap fits; to the point; to the purpose; *rem acu tetigisti*; at home; in one's element.

24 DISAGREEMENT

Substantives: discord, discordance, dissonance, disharmony, dissidence, discrepancy, unconformity, disconformity, nonconformity, incongruity, incongruence, *mésalliance,* discongruity, jarring, clashing, jostling (713), inconsistency, inconsonance, disparity, disproportion, disproportionateness, variance, divergence, jar, misfit.

Unfitness, repugnance, unsuitableness, unsuitability, unaptness, ineptitude, inaptness, impropriety, inapplicability, inadmissibility, irreconcilableness, irreconcilability, incommensurability, inconcinnity, incompatability, inadaptability, interference, intrusion, irrelation (10).

Verbs: To disagree, belie, clash, jar, oppose (708), interfere, jostle (713), intrude.

Phrase: To have no business there.

Adjectives: Disagreeing, discordant, discrepant, jarring, clashing, repugnant, incompatible, irreconcilable, intransigent, inconsistent with, unconformable, incongruous, disproportionate, disproportioned, unproportioned, inharmonious, inconsonant, mismatched, misjoined, misjudged, unconsonant, incommensurable, incommensurate, divergent (291).

Unapt, inapt, inept, inappropriate, improper, unsuited, unsuitable, inapposite, inapplicable, irrelevant, not pertinent, impertinent, malapropos, ill-timed, intrusive, clumsy, unfit, unfitting, unbefitting, unbecoming, misplaced, forced, unseasonable, far fetched, inadmissible, uncongenial, ill-assorted, ill-sorted, repugnant to, unaccommodating, irreducible.

Phrases: Out of season; out of character; out of keeping; out of joint; out of tune; out of place; out of one's element; at odds; a fish out of water.

Adverbs: Discordantly, etc.; at variance with, in defiance of, in contempt of, in spite of, despite

Section III – Quantity

25 QUANTITY
Substantives: magnitude (192), amplitude, size, mass, amount, volume, area, quantum, measure, substance.

Science of quantity, mathematics.

Definite or finite quantity, handful, mouthful, spoonful, bucketful, pailful, etc.; stock, batch, lot.

Adjective: Quantitative.

Phrase: To the tune of.

26 DEGREE
Substantives: grade, gradation, extent, measure, ratio, stint, standard, height, pitch, reach, sweep, radius, amplitude, magnitude, water, calibre, range, scope, shade, tenor, compass, sphere, rank, station, standing, rate, way, sort.

Point, mark, stage, step, position, slot, peg; term (71).

Intensity, might, fullness, strength (31), conversion (144), limit (233).

Adjectives: Comparative, gradual, shading off.

Adverbs: By degrees, gradually, *gradatim*, inasmuch, *pro tanto*, however, howsoever, step by step, rung by rung, bit by bit, little by little, by inches, inch by inch, by slow degrees, by little and little, in some degree, to some extent.

27 EQUALITY
Substantives: parity, co-extension, evenness, equipoise, level, balance, equivalence, equipollence, equilib-

rium, poise, equiponderance, par, quits.

Equalization, equation, equilibration, co-ordination, adjustment, symmetry.

A drawn game or battle, a dead heat, a draw, a tie.

A match, peer, compeer, equal, mate, fellow, brother (17), equivalent, makeweight.

Phrases: A distinction without a difference; a photo finish.

Verbs: To be equal, etc., to equal, match, come up to, keep pace with; come to, amount to, balance, cope with.

To render equal, equalize, level, balance, equate, aequiparate, trim, dress, adjust, fit, accommodate, poise, square; to readjust, equipoise, equilibrate, set against.

Phrases: To be or lie on a level with; to come to the same thing.

To strike a balance; to establish or restore equality; to stretch on the bed of Procrustes; to cry quits.

Adjectives: Equal, even, quit, level, coequal, co-ordinate, equivalent, synonymous, tantamount, convertible, equipollent, equiponderant, equiponderous, square.

Rendered equal, equalized, equated, drawn, poised, levelled, balanced, symmetrical, trimmed, dressed.

Phrases: On a par with; on a level with; much of a muchness; as broad as it is long; as good as; all the same; all one; six to one and half a dozen of the other; not a pin to choose between them; tarred with the same brush; diamond cut diamond.

Adverbs: *Pari passu*, equally, symmetrically, *ad eundem*, practically, to all intents and purposes, neck and neck.

28 INEQUALITY
Substantives: disparity, imparity, imbalance, odds, handicap, bisque, difference (15), unevenness.

Preponderance, preponderation, inclination of the balance, advantage, prevalence, partiality.

Superiority (33), a casting vote; inferiority (34).

Verbs: To be unequal, etc., to preponderate, outweigh, outbalance, overbalance, prevail, countervail, predominate, overmatch, outmatch (33).

To fall short of, to want (304), not to come up to.

Phrases: To have or give the advantage; to turn the scale; to kick the beam; to topple over.

Adjectives: Unequal, uneven, disparate, partial, unbalanced, overbalanced, top-heavy, lopsided, preponderating, outweighing, prevailing.

Phrases: More than a match for, above par; below par; *haud passibus aequis.*

29 MEAN

Substantives: medium, intermedium, compromise, average, norm, balance, middle (68), *via media, juste milieu.*

Neutrality, mediocrity, middle course, shuffling.

Phrases: The golden mean; the average man; the man in the street.

Verbs: To compromise, pair off, cancel out.

Phrases: To sit on the fence; split the difference; strike a balance; take the average; reduce to a mean; to take a safe course.

Adjectives: Mean, intermediate, middle, median, normal, average, mediocre, middling, ordinary (82), neutral.

Adverb phrases: On an average; in the long run; half-way; taking the one with the other; taking all things together; in round numbers.

30 COMPENSATION

Substantives: equation, commutation, compromise (774), idemnification, neutralization, nullification,

counteraction (179), recoil (277), atonement (952).

A set-off, offset, makeweight, counterpoise, ballast, indemnity, hush-money, amends, equivalent.

Phrases: Measure for measure; give and take; *quid pro quo*; tit for tat.

Verbs: To compensate, make up for, indemnify, countervail, counterpoise, balance, compromise, outbalance, overbalance, counterbalance, counteract, set off, hedge, redeem, neutralize (27), cover.

Phrases: To make good; split the difference; fill up; make amends.

Adjectives: Compensating, compensatory, countervailing, etc., equivalent, equipollent (27).

Phrase: In the opposite scale.

Adverbs: However, yet, but, still, all the same, for all that, nevertheless, none the less, notwithstanding, be that as it may, on the other hand, although, though, albeit, *per contra.*

Phrases: As broad as it's long; taking one thing with another; it is an ill wind that blows nobody any good.

31 GREATNESS

Substantives: largeness, magnitude, size (192), multitude (102), fullness, vastness, immensity, enormity, infinity (105), intensity (26), importance (642), strength.

A large quantity, deal, power, world, macrocosm, mass, heap (72), pile, sight, pot, volume, peck, bushel, load, stack, cart-load, wagon-load, truck-load, ship-load, cargo, lot, flood, spring tide, mobs, bags, oodles, abundance (639), wholesale, store (636).

The greater part (50).

Verbs: To be great, etc., run high, soar, tower, transcend, rise, carry to a great height (305).

Phrases: To know no bounds; to break the record.

Adjectives: Great, gross, large, considerable, big, ample, above par, huge, full, saturated, plenary, deep, signal, extensive, sound, passing, goodly, famous, noteworthy, noble, heavy, precious, mighty (157), arch, sad, piteous, arrant, red-hot, downright, utter, uttermost, crass, lamentable, consummate, rank, thorough-paced, thorough-going, sovereign, unparalleled, matchless, unapproached, extraordinary, intense, extreme, pronounced, unsurpassed, unsurpassable.

Vast, immense, enormous, towering, inordinate, severe, excessive, monstrous, shocking, extravagant, exorbitant, outrageous, whacking, thumping, glaring, flagrant, preposterous, egregious, overgrown, stupendous, monumental, prodigious, marked, pointed, remarkable, astonishing, surprising (870), incredible, marvellous, transcendent, incomparable, tremendous, terrific, formidable, amazing, phenomenal, superhuman, titanic, immoderate.

Indefinite, boundless, unbounded, unlimited, incalculable, illimitable, immeasurable, infinite, unapproachable, unutterable, indescribable, unspeakable, inexpressible, beyond expression, swingeing, unconscionable, fabulous, uncommon, unusual (83).

Undiminished, unrestricted, unabated, unreduced, unmitigated, unredeemed, untempered.

Absolute, positive, decided staring, unequivocal, serious, grave, essential, perfect, finished, completed, abundant (639).

Adverbs: In a great degree, much, muckle, well, considerably, largely, grossly, greatly, very, very much, a deal, not a little, no end, pretty, pretty well, enough, richly, to a large extent, to a great extent, ever so, mainly, ever so much, on a large scale, insomuch, all lengths, wholesale, in a great measure.

In a positive degree, truly (494), positively, verily, really, indeed, actually, in fact, fairly, assuredly, decidedly, surely, clearly, obviously, unequivocally, purely, absolutely, seriously, essentially, fundamentally, radically, downright, in grain, altogether, entirely, completely.

In a comparative degree, comparatively, *pro tanto*, as good as, to say the least, above all, most, of all things, pre-eminently.

In a complete degree, completely (52), altogether, quite, entirely, wholly, totally, *in toto, toto coelo,* utterly, thoroughly, out and out, outright, out and away, fairly, clean, to the full, in every respect, *sous tous les rapports,* in all respects, on all accounts, nicely, perfectly, fully, amply, richly, wholesale, abundantly, consummately, widely, as . . . as . . . can be, every inch, *à fond, de fond,* far and wide, over head and ears, to the backbone, through and through, *ne plus ultra.*

In a greater degree, even, yea, *a fortiori,* still more.

In a high degree, highly, deeply, strongly, mighty, mightily, powerfully (157), profoundly, superlatively, ultra, in the extreme, extremely, exceedingly, excessively, consumedly, sorely, intensely, exquisitely, acutely, soundly, vastly, hugely, immensely, enormously, stupendously, passing, surpassing, supremely, beyond measure, immoderately, monstrously, inordinately, tremendously, over head and ears, extraordinarily, exorbitantly, indefinitely, immeasurably, unspeakably, inexpressibly, ineffably, unutterably, incalculably, infinitely, unsurpassably.

In a marked degree, particularly, remarkably, singularly, uncommonly, unusually, peculiarly, notably, *par excellence,* eminently, pre-eminently, superlatively, signally, famously, egregiously, prominently, glaringly, emphatically, strangely, wonderfully, amazingly, surprisingly, astonishingly, prodigiously, monstrously, incredibly, inconceivably, marvellously, awfully, stupendously.

In a violent degree, violently, severely, furiously, desperately, tremendously, outrageously, extravagantly, confoundedly, deucedly, devilishly, diabolically, with a vengeance, *à outrance,* like mad (173).

In a painful degree, sadly, grievously, woefully, wretchedly, piteously, sorely, lamentably, shockingly, frightfully, dreadfully, fearfully, terribly, horribly.

32 SMALLNESS
Substantives: littleness, minuteness (193), tenuity, scantness, scantiness, slenderness, meanness, mediocrity, insignificance (643), paucity, fewness (103).

A small quantity, modicum, atom, particle, molecule, corpuscle, microcosm, jot, iota, dot, speck, mote, gleam, scintilla, spark, ace, minutiae, thought, idea, suspicion, *soupçon,* whit, tittle, shade, shadow, touch, cast, taste, grain, scruple, spice, sprinkling, drop, droplet, driblet, globule, minim, dash, smack, nip, sip, scantling, dole, scrap, mite, slip, snippet, tag, bit, morsel, crumb, paring, shaving (51), trifle, thimbleful, toothful, spoonful, cupful, mouthful, handful, fistful.

Finiteness, a finite quantity.
Phrases: The shadow of a shade; a drop in a bucket or in the ocean.
Verbs: To be small, etc., to run low, diminish, shrink, decrease (36), contract (195).
Phrases: To lie in a nutshell; to pass muster.
Adjectives: Small, little, wee, scant, inconsiderable, diminutive, minute (193), tiny, minikin, puny, petty, sorry, miserable, shabby, wretched, paltry (643), weak (160), slender, feeble, faint, slight, scrappy, fiddling,

trivial, scanty, light, trifling, moderate, low, mean, mediocre, passable, passing, light, sparing.

Below par, below the mark, under the mark, at a low ebb, imperfect, unfinished, partial (651), inappreciable, evanescent, infinitesimal, atomic, homoeopathic.

Mere, simple, sheer, bare.
Adverbs: In a small degree, on a small scale, to a small extent, a wee bit, something, somewhat, next to nothing, little, inconsiderably, slightly, so-so, minutely, faintly, feebly, lightly, imperfectly, scantily, shabbily, miserably, wretchedly, sparingly, weakly, slenderly, modestly.

In a limited degree, in a certain degree, to a certain degree or extent, partially, in part, some, somewhat, rather, in some degree, in some measure, something, simply, only, purely, merely, in a manner, at least, at most, ever so little, thus far, *pro tanto,* next to nothing.

Almost, nearly, well-nigh, all but, short of, not quite, close upon, near the mark.

In an uncertain degree, about, thereabouts, scarcely, hardly, barely, somewhere about, say, more or less, *à peu près,* there or thereabouts.

In no degree, noways, nowise, nohow, in no wise, by no means, not in the least, not at all, not a bit, not a bit of it, not a whit, not a jot, in no respect, by no manner of means, on no account.
Phrases: As little as may be; after a fashion; in a way.

Within an ace of; on the brink of; next door to; a close shave (or call).

33 SUPERIORITY
Substantives: majority, supremacy, primacy, advantage, preponderance, excess (641), prevalence, pre-eminence, championship.

Maximum, acme, climax, zenith,

summit, utmost height, record, culminating point (210), the height of, lion's share, overweight.

Phrases: A Triton among the minnows; cock of the walk; *ne plus ultra; summum bonum.*

Verbs: To be superior, etc.; to exceed, surpass, excel, eclipse, transcend, top, overtop, o'ertop, cap, beat, cut out, outclass, override, outmatch, outbalance, overbalance, overweigh, overshadow, outdo; preponderate, predominate, prevail.

To render larger, magnify (194).

Phrases: To have the advantage of; to have the upper hand; to bear the palm; to have one cold; to beat hollow; to take the shine out of; to throw into the shade; to be a cut above.

Adjectives: Superior, greater, major, higher, surpassing, exceeding, excelling, passing, ultra, vaulting, transcending, transcendent, unequalled, unsurpassed, peerless, matchless, unparalleled, without parallel.

Supreme, greatest, utmost, paramount, pre-eminent, foremost, crowning, sovereign, culminating, superlative, topmost, top-hole, highest, first-rate, champion, A1, the last word, the limit.

Phrases: *Facile princeps; nulli secundus; primus inter pares.*

Adverbs: Beyond, more, over and above the mark, above par, over and above, at the top of the scale, at its height.

In a superior degree, eminently, pre-eminently, egregiously, prominently, superlatively, supremely, above all, of all things, principally, especially, particularly, peculiarly, *par excellence, a fortiori.*

34 INFERIORITY

Substantives: minority, subordination, shortcoming (304); deficiency, minimum.

Verbs: To be less, inferior, etc., to fall or come short of, not to pass (304); to want, be wanting.

To become smaller, to render smaller (195); to subordinate.

Phrases: To be thrown into the shade; to hide one's diminished head; to give a person best; to play second fiddle.

Adjectives: Inferior, deficient, smaller, minor, less, lesser, lower, sub, subordinate, subaltern, secondary, second-rate, second-best.

Least, smallest, wee-est, minutest, etc., lowest.

Phrases: Weighed in the balance and found wanting; not fit to hold a candle to.

Adverbs: Less, under or below the mark, below par, at the bottom of the scale, at a low ebb, short of, at a disadvantage.

35 INCREASE

Substantives: augmentation, enlargement, extension, dilatation (194), increment, accretion, development, rise, growth, swell, swelling, expansion, aggrandizement, aggravation, exacerbation, spread, climax, exaggeration, diffusion (73), flood-tide; accession (37).

Verbs: To increase, augment, enlarge, amplify, extend, dilate, swell, wax, expand, grow, stretch, shoot up, mushroom, rise, run up, sprout, burgeon, advance, spread, gather head, aggrandize, add, superadd, raise, heighten, strengthen, greaten, exalt, enhance, magnify, redouble, aggravate, exaggerate, exasperate, exacerbate, escalate.

Phrases: To add fuel to the flame; to pour oil on the flames.

Adjectives: Increased, augmented, enlarged, etc., undiminished; cumulative; additional (37).

Adverb: Crescendo.

36 NON-INCREASE. DECREASE

Substantives: diminution, reduction,

depreciation, lessening, abatement, bating, declension, falling off, dwindling, contraction (195), shrinking, attentuation, extenuation, anticlimax, abridgment, curtailment (201), coarctation, narrowing; deduction (38). Subsidence, wane, ebb, decrement.

Verbs: To decrease, diminish, lessen, dwindle, decay, crumble, shrink, contract, shrivel, fall off, fall away, waste, wear, wane, ebb, subside, decline, languish, wear off, run low, grow downward.

To abridge, reduce, curtail, cut down, pare down, substract, shorten, cut short, dock (201), bate, abate, fritter away, attenuate, extenuate, lower, weaken, dwarf; to mitigate (174), to throw in the shade.

Phrase: To hide its diminished head.

Adjectives: Decreased, diminished, lessened, etc., shorn, short by, decreasing, on the wane.

Adverbs: *Diminuendo, decrescendo.*

37 ADDITION

Substantives: adjection, introduction, superinduction, annexation, superposition, superaddition, subjunction, supervention, increment, accession, superfetation, corollary, reinforcement, supplement, accompaniment (88), interposition (228), insertion (300).

Verbs: To add, annex, affix, superadd, supplement, reinforce, subjoin, superpose, throw in, clap on, tack to, append, tag, engraft, saddle on, saddle with, superinduce, introduce, work in, interleave, extra-illustrate, grangerize.

To become added, to accrue, advene, supervene.

Phrase: To swell the ranks of.

Adjectives: Added, annexed, etc., additional, supplementary, supplemental, suppletory, subjunctive, adscititious, additive, accessory, cumulative.

Adverbs: Additionally, in addition, more, *plus*, extra, and, also, likewise, too, furthermore, forby, item, and also, and eke, else, besides, to boot, etcetera, and so forth, into the bargain, over and above, moreover.

With, together with, withal, along with, including, inclusive, as well as, not to mention, to say nothing of; jointly, conjointly (43).

38 NON-ADDITION. SUBDUCTION

Substantives: subtraction, abstraction, deduction, deducement, retrenchment, removal, elimination, ablation (789), purgation, curtailment, etc. (36), garbling, mutilation, truncation, abscission, excision, amputation, detruncation, sublation, castration, apocope.

Subtrahend, minuend; decrement, discount.

Verbs: To subduct, exclude, deduct, subtract, abscind, retrench, remove, withdraw, eliminate, bate, detract, deduce, take away, deprive of, curtail (36), garble, truncate, mutilate, eviscerate, exenterate, detruncate, castrate, spay, geld, purge, amputate, cut off, excise, cut out, dock, lop, prune, pare, dress, clip, thin, shear, decimate, abrade (330).

Adjectives: Subtracted, deducted, etc., subtractive.

Adverbs: In deduction, etc., less, *minus*, without, except, excepting, with the exception of, but for, barring, save, exclusive of, save and except (83).

39 ADJUNCT

Substantives: additament, addition, affix, appendage, annex, suffix, postfix, inflexion, augment, increment, augmentation, accessory, item, garnish, sauce, supplement, extra, bonus (810), adjective, addendum, complement, corollary, continuation, increment, reinforcement, pendant, apanage.

Sequel (65), postscript, codicil, envoy, rider, corollary, heel-piece, tag, tab, skirt, flap, lappet, trappings, tail, tailpiece (67), queue, train, suite, cortège, accompaniment (88).
Phrase: More last words.

40 REMAINDER
Substantives: residue, remains, remnant, the rest, relics, leavings, heel-tap, odds and ends, cheese-parings, candle-ends, off-scourings, orts.

Residuum, *caput mortuum,* dregs, refuse (645), scum, recrement (653), ashes, dross, cinders, slag, sediment, silt, alluvium, stubble; slough, exuviae, result, educt.

Surplus, overplus, surplusage, superfluity, excess (641), balance, complement, fag-end, stump, butt, rump, wreck, wreckage, ruins, skeleton.
Verbs: To remain, be left, be left behind, exceed, survive.
Adjectives: Remaining, left, left behind, residual, exuvial, residuary, sedimentary, outstanding, net, cast off, odd, over, unconsumed, surviving, outlying.

Superfluous, over and above, exceeding, redundant (641), supernumerary.

41 MIXTURE
Substantives: admixture, commixture, commixtion, intermixture, alloyage, marriage, miscegenation.

Impregnation, infusion, infiltration, diffusion, suffusion, interspersion, transfusion, seasoning, sprinkling, interlarding, interpolation, interposition (228), intrusion; adulteration, sophistication.

Thing mixed, a touch, spice, tinge, tincture, dash, smack, sprinkling, seasoning, infusion, suspicion, *soupçon,* shade, bit, portion, dose.

Compound resulting from mixture, blend, alloy, amalgam, magma, *mélange,* half and half, hybrid, *tertium*

quid, miscellany, medley, pastiche, pasticcio, patchwork, odds and ends; farrago, jumble (59), mess, salad, sauce, hash, hodge-podge or hotchpotch or hotchpot, mash, mish-mash, job lot, omnium gatherum, gallimaufry, olla podrida, olio, salmagundi, pot-pourri, Noah's ark, cauldron, marquetry, mosaic (440), complex.

A cross, hybrid, mongrel, half-breed, Eurasian, mulatto, quadroon, octoroon, sambo.
Phrases: A mingled yarn; a scratch team.
Verbs: To mix, commix, immix, intermix, associate, join (43), mingle, commingle, intermingle, bemingle, interlard, intersperse, interpose, interpolate (228); shuffle together, hash up, huddle together, deal, pound together, stir up, knead, brew, jumble (59); impregnate with.

To be mixed, to get among, to be entangled with.

To instil, imbue, infuse, infiltrate, dash, tinge, tincture, season, sprinkle, besprinkle, suffuse, transfuse, attemper, medicate, blend, alloy, amalgamate, compound (48), adulterate, sophisticate, infect, cross, intercross, interbreed, interblend.
Adjectives: Mixed, mingled, intermixed, etc., motley, miscellaneous, promiscuous; complex, composite, mixed up with, half-and-half, linsey-woolsey, mongrel, heterogeneous; miscible.

42 SIMPLENESS
Substantives: singleness, purity, clearness, homogeneity.

Purification (652), elimination, sifting, winnowing.
Verbs: To render simple, simplify, sift, winnow, bolt, screen, sort, eliminate; to separate, disjoin (44).

To purify (652).
Adjectives: Simple, uniform, of a

piece, homogeneous, single, pure, clear, sheer, blank, neat, absolute, elemental, elementary; unmixed, unmingled, untinged, unblended, uncombined, uncompounded, undecomposed, unadulterated, unsophisticated, undiluted, straight.

Free from, exempt from.

Phrase: Pure and simple.

43 JUNCTION

Substantives: joining, joinder, union, connection, connecting, hook-up, conjunction, conjugation, annexion, annexation, annexment, attachment, compagination, astriction, ligation, alligation, colligation, fastening, linking, accouplement, coupling, matrimony (903), grafting; infibulation, inosculation, symphysis, anastomosis, association (72), concatenation, communication, approach (197).

Joint, join, juncture, pivot, hinge, suture, articulation, commissure, mitre, seam, stitch, meeting, reunion, mortise.

Closeness, firmness, tightness, compactness, attachment, communication.

Verbs: To join, conjoin, unite, connect, associate, put together, embody, re-embody, hold together, lump together, pack, fix together, attach, affix, saddle on, fasten, bind, secure, make fast, grapple, moor, clench (or clinch), catch, tie, pinion, strap, sew, lace, string, stitch, tack, knit, tat, crochet, knot, button, buckle, hitch, lash, truss, bandage, braid, splice, swathe, gird, tether, picket, harness, inspan, bridge over.

Chain, enchain, shackle, pinion, fetter, manacle, handcuff, lock, latch, belay, brace, hook, clap together, leash, couple, link, yoke, bracket, hang together, pin, nail, bolt, hasp, clasp, clamp, screw, rivet, solder, weld, impact, wedge, rabbet, mortise, mitre, jam, dovetail, enchase, engraft, interlink, inosculate, entwine, enlace, interlace, intertwine, intertwist, interweave, interlock.

To be joined, etc., to hang or hold together, cohere (46).

Adjectives: Joined, conjoined, coupled, etc., bound up together, conjunct, corporate, compact.

Firm, fast, close, tight, taut, secure, set, fixed, impacted, jammed, locked, etc., intervolved, intertwined, inseparable, indissoluble, inseverable, untearable.

Phrases: Hand in hand; rolled into one.

Adverbs: Conjointly, jointly, etc.

With, along with, together with, in conjunction with.

Fast, firmly, closely, etc.

44 DISJUNCTION

Substantives: disconnection, disunity, disunion, disassociation, disengagement, abstraction, abstractedness, isolation, insularity, oasis, separateness, severalness, severality.

Separation, parting, detachment, divorce, sejunction, seposition, segregation, insulation, diduction, discerption, elision, caesura, division, subdivision, break, fracture, rupture, dismemberment, disintegration, dislocation, luxation, severance, disseverance, severing, fission, scission, rescission, abscission, laceration, dilaceration, wrenching, abruption, disruption, avulsion, divulsion, tearing asunder, section, cutting, resection, cleavage, fissure, breach, rent, split, crack, slit, tear, rip, dispersion (73), incision, dissection, vivisection anatomy.

Anatomist, prosector.

Phrase: *Disjecta membra.*

Verbs: To be disjoined, separated, etc., to come off, fall off, get loose, fall to pieces.

To disjoin, disconnect, disunite, part, dispart, detach, separate, space, space out, cut off, rescind, segregate, insulate, dissociate, isolate, disengage, set apart, liberate, loose, set free (750), unloose, unfasten, untie, unbind, disband, unfix, unlace, unclasp, undo, unbutton, unbuckle, unchain, unfetter, untack, unharness, ungird, unpack, unbolt, unlatch, unlock, unlink, uncouple, unpin, unclinch, unscrew, unhook, unrivet, untwist, unshackle, unyoke, unknit, unsolder, ravel out, unravel, disentangle, unpick, unglue, switch off, shut off.

Sunder, divide, subdivide, divorce, sever, dissever, abscind, cut, scissor, incide, incise, snip, nib, cleave, rive, slit, split, split in twain, splinter, chip, crack, snap, burst, rend, break or tear asunder, shiver, crunch, chop, cut up, rip up, hack, hew, slash, whittle, haggle, hackle, discind, tear, lacerate, mangle, mince, gash, hash, knap.

Dissect, cut up, carve, slice, castrate, detruncate, anatomize; take, pull or pick to pieces; unseam, tear to tatters, tear piecemeal, divellicate, disintegrate; dismember, disembowel, eviscerate, disbranch, dislocate, joint, disjoint, behead, mince, break up, crunch, gride, comminute (330), vivisect.
Phrase: To tear limb from limb.
Adjectives: Disjoined, disconnected, etc., snippety, disjointed, multipartite, abstract, disjunctive, isolated, insular, separate, discrete, apart, asunder, loose, free, liberated, disengaged, unattached, unannexed, distinct, unassociated, unconnected, adrift, straggling, dispersed, disbanded, segregated.
Cut off, rescinded, etc., rift, reft.
Capable of being cut, scissile, fissile, discerptible.
Adverbs: Separately, etc., one by one, severally, apiece, apart, adrift, asunder; in the abstract, abstractedly.

45 VINCULUM
Substantives: link, connective, connection, junction (43), conjunction, copula, intermedium, hyphen, bridge, stepping-stone, isthmus, span, girder.

Bond, filament, fibre (205), hair, cordage, cord, thread, string, packthread, twine, twist, whipcord, tape, ferret, raffia, line, snood, ribbon, riband, rope, cable, hawser, painter, halyard, guy, guy-rope, wire, chain.

Fastening, tie, tendril, tendon, ligament, ligature, strap, tackle, rigging, traces, harness, yoke, band, withe, withy, brace, bandage, roller, fillet, thong, braid, inkle, girth, cinch, cestus, girdle, garter, halter, noose, lasso, lariat, surcingle, knot, running-knot, slip-knot, reef-knot, sailor's knot, granny-knot, etc.

Pin, corking-pin, safety-pin, nail, brad, tack, skewer, staple, clamp, vice, bracket, cramp, screw, button, buckle, brooch, clasp, slide, clip, hasp, hinge, hank, bolt, catch, latch, latchet, tag, hook, tooth, hook and eye, lock, locket, holdfast, padlock, rivet, anchor, grappling-iron, stake, post, gyve, shackle (752).

Cement, adhesive, mucilage, glue, gum, paste, size, goo, solder, lute, putty, bird-lime, mortar, stucco, plaster, grout.

46 COHERENCE
Substantives: cohesion, adherence, adhesion, accretion, concretion, agglutination, conglutination, aggregation, consolidation, set, cementation, soldering, welding, grouting.

Sticking, clinging, adhesiveness, stickiness, gumminess, gummosity, glutinosity (352), cohesiveness, density (321), inseparability, inseparableness, tenaciousness, tenacity.

Clot, concrete, cake, lump, conglomerate (321).
Verbs: To cohere, adhere, stick, cling, cleave, hold, take hold of, hold fast, hug, grow or hang together, twine round.

To concrete, curdle, cake.

To glue, agglutinate, conglutinate,

agglomerate, consolidate, solidify (321); cement, lute, paste, gum, grout, stick, solder, weld.

Phrases: To stick like a leech; to stick like wax; to cling like ivy, like a bur, like a limpet.

Adjectives: Cohesive, adhesive, cohering, tenacious, sticky, tacky, glutinous, gluey, gooey, gummy, viscous (352), agglutinatory.

United, unseparated, sessile, inseparable, inextricable, infrangible (321).

47   INCOHERENCE
Substantives: non-adhesion, immiscibility, looseness, laxity, slackness, relaxation, freedom, disjunction.

Phrases: A rope of sand; *disjecta membra*.

Verbs: To loosen, make loose, slacken, relax, unglue, unsolder, etc., detach, untwist, unravel, unroll (44, 313), to comminute (330).

Adjectives: Incoherent, immiscible, detached, non-adhesive, loose, slack, lax, relaxed, baggy.

Segregated, flapping, streaming, dishevelled, unincorporated, unconsolidated, uncombined.

Phrase: Like grains of sand.

48   COMBINATION
Substantives: union, unification, synthesis, incorporation, amalgamation, coalescence, crasis, fusion, embodiment, conflation, absorption, blending, centralization; mixture (41).

Compound, composition, amalgam, impregnation, decompound, decomposite, resultant.

Verbs: To combine, unite, unify, incorporate, amalgamate, synthesize, embody, unify, re-embody, blend, merge, fuse, absorb, melt into one, consolidate, coalesce, centralize; to impregnate, to put together, to lump together.

Adjectives: Combined, compound,

composite, coalescent, synthetic, synthetical, impregnated with, engrained.

49   DECOMPOSITION
Substantives: analysis, resolution, dissolution, disintegration, catalysis, electrolysis, corruption (653), dispersion (73), disjunction (44).

Verbs: To decompose, rot, disembody, analyse, electrolyse, decompound, resolve, take to pieces, separate into its elements, dissect, unravel (313), break up.

Adjectives: Decomposed, etc., catalytic, analytic, analytical, corrupted, dissolved.

50   WHOLE
Substantives: totality, integrity, integrality, allness, entireness, entirety, *ensemble,* collectiveness, individuality, unity (87), indivisibility, indiscerptibility, indissolubility; embodiment, integration.

All, the whole, total, aggregate, integer, gross amount, sum, sum total, *tout ensemble,* upshot, trunk, hull, skeleton, hulk, lump, heap (72).

The principal part, bulk, mass, tissue, staple, body, compages, the main, the greater part, major part.

Phrases: The whole caboodle; the whole boiling.

Verbs: To form or constitute a whole, to integrate, embody, aggregate, amass (72), to total, amount to, come to.

Adjectives: Whole, total, integral, entire, one, unbroken, uncut, undivided, seamless, individual, unsevered, unclipped, uncropped, unshorn, undiminished, undemolished, undissolved, unbruised, undestroyed, indivisible, indissoluble, indissolvable, indiscerptible.

Wholesale, sweeping.

Adverbs: Wholly, altogether, totally, entirely, all, all in all, as a whole, wholesale, in the aggregate, in the mass, *en masse,* in the lump, *en bloc,* on the whole, *in toto,* in the gross, *in extenso,* in the bulk, to the full, throughout, every inch.

Phrases: To long and short of it; nearly or almost all; root and branch; lock, stock, and barrel; hook, line and sinker; in the long run; in the main; neck and crop; from end to end; from beginning to end; from first to last; from head to foot; from top to toe; fore and aft; from alpha to omega.

51 PART
Substantives: portion, item, division, subdivision, section, chapter, verse, extract, passage, gobbet, sector, segment, fraction, fragment, frustum, detachment, piece, bit, lump, chunk, dollop, scrap, whit, swatch, morsel, mouthful, scantling, cantle, cantlet, slip, crumb (32), fritter, rag, tag, shred, tatter, splinter, snatch, cut, cutting, snip, snippet, snick, collop, slice, chip, chipping, shiver, sliver, matchwood, spillikin, smithereens, driblet, clipping, paring, shaving, debris, odds and ends, oddments, sundries, detritus, lamina, shadow, flotsam and jetsam, pickings.

Parcel, share, instalment, contingent, compartment, department, dividend, dose, particular, article, clause, paragraph.

Member, limb, lobe, lobule, arm, branch, scion, bough, joint, link, ramification (256), twig, bush, spray, sprig, offshoot, leaf, leaflet, stump, stub, butt, rump, torso.

Verbs: To part, divide, subdivide, break (44); to partition, parcel out, portion, apportion (786), to ramify, branch, branch out.

Adjectives: Part, fractional, fragmentary, scrappy, lobular, sectional, aliquot, divided, multifid, partitioned, isomeric.

Adverbs: Partly, in part, partially,

piecemeal, in detail, part by part, by driblets, bit by bit, little by little, by inches, inch by inch, foot by foot, drop by drop, in snatches, by fits and starts.

52 COMPLETENESS
Substantives: entirety, fullness, impletion, completion (729), perfection (650), solidity, stop-gap, makeweight, padding, filling up, integration, absoluteness, sufficiency; complement, supplement (39).

Fill, load, bumper, brimmer, bellyful, skinful.

Verbs: To be complete, etc., suffice (639).

To render complete or whole, to complete, exhaust, perfect, finish, make up, fill up, charge, load, replenish, make good, piece out, eke out.

Phrases: To give the finishing touch; to supply deficiencies; to go to all lengths; to go the whole hog; to thrash out.

Adjectives: Complete, entire, whole (50), absolute, perfect, full, plenary, solid, undivided, with all its parts, supplementary, adscititious, thorough, exhaustive, radical, sweeping, searching; consummate, thorough-paced, regular, sheer, unmitigated, unqualified.

Crammed, saturated, brimful, chock-full.

Adverbs: Completely, entirely, to the full, outright, wholly, totally, thoroughly (31), *in toto, toto caelo,* in all respects.

Phrases: To the top of one's bent; up to the ears; *à fond;* from first to last; from beginning to end; *ab ovo usque ad mala.*

53 INCOMPLETENESS
Substantives: deficiency, defectiveness, shortcoming (304), unreadiness, defalcation, failure, imperfection (651), hollowness, patchiness.

Part wanting, omission, defect,

69

break, deficit, ullage, caret, lacuna, hiatus (198).
Verbs: To be incomplete, etc., to fail, fall short (304).
To dock, lop, mutilate, garble, truncate, castrate (38).
Adjectives: Incomplete, unfinished, imperfect, defective, deficient, wanting, failing, short by, hollow, meagre, insufficient, half-baked, perfunctory, sketchy, scrappy, patchy.
Mutilated, garbled, docked, lopped, truncated; proceeding, in progress.
Phrase: *Cetera desunt.*

54 COMPOSITION
Substantives: make-up, constitution, constituency, crasis.
Inclusion, admission, comprehension, reception.
Verbs: To be composed of, to consist of, be made of, formed of, made up of, be resolved into.
To contain, include, hold, comprehend, take in, admit, embrace, involve, implicate.
To compose, constitute, form, make, make up, fill up, build up, put together, embody.
To enter into the composition of, to be or form part of (51), to merge in, be merged in.
Adjectives: Comprehending, containing, including, comprising, etc.
Component, constituent, formative, forming, constituting, composing, etc., belonging to, appertaining to, inclusive.

55 EXCLUSION
Substantives: non-admission, omission, exception, rejection, proscription, repudiation, exile, banishment, excommunication.
Separation, segregation, elimination, seposition.
Verbs: To be excluded from, etc., to be out of it.
To exclude, shut out, bar, leave out,

omit, reject, repudiate, neglect, blackball; lay, put, or set apart or aside; segregate, pass over, throw overboard, slur over, neglect (460), excommunicate, banish, expatriate, extradite, deport, ostracize, relegate, rusticate, send down (297), rule out.
To eliminate, weed, winnow, screen, bar, separate (44), strike off.
Phrase: 'Include me out.'
Adjectives: Excluding, omitting, etc., exclusive.
Excluded, omitted, etc., unrecounted, inadmissible.
Adverbs: Except, save, bar, barring, excepting.

56 COMPONENT
Substantives: component part, integral part, element, constituent, ingredient, member, limb (51), part and parcel, contents (190), appurtenance, feature, personnel.

57 EXTRANEOUSNESS
Substantives: extrinsicality (5), exteriority (220).
A foreign body, alien, stranger, intruder, outsider, incomer, interloper, foreigner, dago, wop, *novus homo*, parvenu, immigrant, newcomer, new chum, pommy, greenhorn, tenderfoot.
Adjectives: Extraneous, foreign, alien, tramontane, ultramontane, interloping.
Adverbs: Abroad, in foreign parts, overseas.

Section IV – Order

58 ORDER
Substantives: regularity, orderliness, tidiness, uniformity, even tenor, symmetry.
Gradation, progression, pedigree, line, descent, subordination, course, series (69), array, routine.

Method, disposition, arrangement, system, economy, discipline, pattern, plan.

Rank, station, hierarchy, place, status, stand, scale, step, stage, period, term (71), footing; rank and file, pecking order.

Verbs: To be or become in order, to form, fall in, arrange itself, place itself, range itself, fall into its place, fall into rank.

Adjectives: Orderly, regular, in order, arranged, etc. (60), in its proper place, correct, tidy, shipshape, trim, *en règle,* well regulated, methodical, business-like, uniform, symmetrical, systematic, unconfused, undisturbed, untangled, unruffled, unravelled, still, etc. (265).

Phrases: In apple-pie order; Bristol fashion.

Adverbs: Systematically, methodically, etc., in turn, in its turn.

Step by step, by regular steps, gradations, stages, periods, or intervals, periodically (138).

At stated periods (138), *gradatim, seriatim.*

Phrase: Like clockwork.

59 DISORDER
Substantives: irregularity, asymmetry, anomaly, confusion, confusedness, disarray, untidiness, jumble, huddle, litter, lumber, farrago, mess, hash, clutter, pie, muddle, mix-up, upset, hotchpotch, hugger-mugger, anarchy, anarchism, imbroglio, chaos, tohubohu, omnium gatherum (41), derangement (61).

Complexness, complexity, complication, intricacy, intricateness, implication, perplexity, involution, ravelling, tangle, entanglement, snarl, knot, coil, skein, sleave, network, labyrinth, Gordian knot, jungle.

Turmoil, *mêlée,* tumult, ferment, stew, fermentation, pudder, pother riot, uproar, bobbery, rough-house,

rumpus, scramble, fracas, vortex, whirlpool, maelstrom, hurly-burly, bear-garden, Babel, Saturnalia, Donnybrook, pandemonium.

Tumultuousness, riotousness, inquietude (173), derangement (61), topsyturvydom (218).

Phrases: Wheels within wheels; confusion worse confounded; most admired disorder; *concordia discors;* hell broke loose.

A pretty kettle of fish; a fine state of things; a how-d'ye-do; the fat in the fire; a bull in a china shop; the devil to pay.

The cart before the horse; hysteron proteron.

Verbs: To be out of order, irregular, disorderly, etc., to ferment.

To derange, put out of order (61).

Phrases: To be at cross-purposes; to make hay of.

Adjectives: Disorderly, orderless, out of order, disordered, misplaced, out of place, deranged, disarranged (61), irregular, desultory, anomalous, untidy, sloppy, slovenly, tousled, straggling, unarranged, immethodical, unsymmetrical, unsystematic, unmethodical, undigested, unsorted, unclassified, unclassed, asymmetrical.

Disjointed, out of joint, out of gear, out of kilter, confused, tangled, involved, intricate, complicated, inextricable, irreducible.

Mixed, scattered, promiscuous, indiscriminate, casual.

Tumultuous, turbulent, riotous, troublous, tumultuary (173), rough-and-tumble.

Adverbs: Irregularly, etc., by fits and snatches, pell-mell; higgledy-piggledy, hugger-mugger; at sixes and sevens; helter-skelter, harum-scarum, anyhow.

60 ARRANGEMENT
Substantives: disposal, disposition, collocation, allocation, distribution,

sorting, assortment, allotment, apportionment, marshalling, alignment, taxis, taxonomy, gradation, organization, ordination; plan (626).

Analysis, sifting, screening, classification.

Result of arrangement, digest, synopsis, analysis, table, register (551).

Instrument for sorting, sieve, riddle, screen (260).

Verbs: To order, reduce to order, bring into order, introduce order into.

To arrange, dispose, place, form; to put, set, place, etc., in order; to set out, collocate, pack, marshal, range, align (or aline), rank, group, parcel out, allot, distribute, assort, sort, sift, riddle.

To class, classify, categorize, file, string, thread, tabulate, pigeon-hole, catalogue, index, register, take stock.

To methodize, digest, regulate, size, grade, gradate, graduate, alphabetize, co-ordinate, systematize, organize, settle, fix, rearrange.

To unravel (246), disentangle, ravel, card, disembroil.

Phrases: To put or set to rights; to assign places to.

Adjectives: Arranged, methodical (58), embattled, in battle array.

Phrase: A place for everything, and everything in its place.

61 DERANGEMENT

Substantives: disarrangement, misarrangement, displacement, misplacement, dislocation, discomposure, disturbance, bedevilment, disorganization, perturbation, shuffling, rumpling, embroilment, corrugation (258), inversion (218), jumble, muddle, disorder (59).

Verbs: To derange, disarrange, misarrange, misplace, mislay, discompose, disorder, embroil, unsettle, disturb, confuse, perturb, jumble, tumble, huddle, shuffle, muddle, toss, hustle, fumble; to bring, put, or throw into

disorder, trouble, confusion, etc., break the ranks, upset.

To unhinge, put out of joint, dislocate, turn over, invert; turn topsy-turvy; turn inside out (218), bedevil, throw out of gear.

To complicate, involve, perplex, tangle, entangle, embrangle (or imbrangle), ravel, ruffle, tousle, rumple, dishevel, muss, litter, scatter, make a mess of, monkey with, make hay of.

Adjectives: Deranged, etc., disordered (59).

62 PRECEDENCE

Substantives: coming before, antecedence, antecedency, anteposition, priority (116), anteriority, the *pas,* the lead.

Superiority (33), precession (280).

Verbs: To precede, come before, lead, introduce, usher in.

To place before; to prefix, affix, premise, prelude, preface, prologize.

Phrases: To have the *pas*; to take the lead; to have the start; set the fashion; to open the ball.

Adjectives: Preceding, precedent, antecedent, anterior, prior, previous, before, ahead of, leading.

Former, foregoing; coming or going before; precursory, precursive, prevenient, inaugural, prodromal, prodromic, preliminary, aforesaid, said, aforementioned, prefatory, introductory, prelusive, prelusory, proemial, preparatory, preambulatory.

Adverbs: In advance, ahead, in front of, before, in the van (234).

63 SEQUENCE

Substantives: coming after, consecution, succession, posteriority (117), secondariness; following (281).

Continuation, order of succession, successiveness; alternation (138).

Subordination, inferiority (34).

Phrase: *Proxime accessit.*

Verbs: To succeed, come after, follow, come next, ensue, come on, tread close upon; to alternate.

To place after, to suffix, append.

Phrases: To be in the wake or trail of; to tread on the heels of; to step into the shoes of; to assume the mantle of.

Adjectives: Succeeding, coming after, following, subsequent, ensuing, sequent, sequacious, consequent, next; consecutive, amoebean, alternate (138).

Latter, posterior.

Adverbs: After, subsequently, since, behind, in the wake of, in the train of, at the tail of, in the rear of (234).

64 PRECURSOR

Substantives: antecedent, precedent, predecessor, forerunner, pioneer, outrider, avant-courier, leader, bellwether, herald, harbinger.

Prelude, preamble, preface, foreword, prologue, prodrome, protasis, prolusion, overture, premise, proem, prolepsis, prolegomena, prefix, introduction, heading, advertisement, frontispiece, groundwork (673).

Adjectives: Precursory, prefatory (62).

65 SEQUEL

Substantives: afterpart, aftermath, suffix, successor, tail, runner-up, queue, train, wake, trail, rear, retinue, suite, appendix (39), postscript, epilogue, peroration, excursus, afterpiece, tailpiece, tag, colophon, afterthought, second thoughts, *arrière pensée*, codicil, continuation, sequela, apodosis.

Phrases: More last words; to be continued.

Adjectives: Subsequent, ensuing (63).

66 BEGINNING

Substantives: commencement, opening, outset, incipience, inception, inchoation, initiative, overture, exordium, introduction (64), inauguration, début, onset, brunt, alpha.

Origin, source, rise, conception, birth, infancy, bud, embryo, germ, egg, rudiment, *incunabula*, start, cradle, starting-point, starting-post (293); dawn, morning (125).

Van, vanguard, title-page, heading, front (234), fore-part, head (210).

Opening, entrance, entry, inlet, orifice, porch, portal, portico, gateway, door, gate, postern, wicket, threshold, vestibule, mouth, *fauces,* lips.

Alphabet, A B C, rudiments, elements.

Phrase: The rising of the curtain; the thin end of the wedge.

Verbs: To begin, commence, inchoate, rise, arise, originate, initiate, open, dawn, set in, take its rise, enter upon, embark on, set out (293), recommence, undertake (676).

To usher in, lead off, lead the way, take the lead or the initiative; head, stand at the head, stand first; broach, set on foot, set a-going, set abroach, set up, handsel, institute, launch, strike up.

Phrases: To make a beginning; to cross the Rubicon; to break ground; set the ball in motion; take the initiative; break the ice; fire away; open the ball; kick off; tee up; pipe up.

Adjectives: Beginning, commencing, arising, initial, initiatory, initiative, inceptive, incipient, proemial, inaugural, inchoate, inchoative, embryonic, primigenial, aboriginal, rudimental, nascent, natal, opening, dawning, entering.

First, foremost, leading, heading, maiden.

Begun, commenced, etc.

Adverbs: At, or in the beginning, at first blush, first, in the first place, *imprimis,* first and foremost, *in limine,* in the bud, in embryo.

From the beginning, *ab initio, ab ovo.*

67 END

Substantives: close, termination, desinence, conclusion, finish, finis, finale, period, term, terminus, limit, last, omega, extreme, extremity, butt-end, fag-end, stub, tail, nib, tip, after-part, rear (235), colophon, coda, tail-piece, tag, *cul-de-lampe,* peroration, swan-song.

Completion (729), winding-up, *dénouement,* catastrophe, consummation, expiration, expiry, finishing stroke, knock-out, K.O., death-blow, *coup de grâce,* upshot, issue, fate, doom, Day of Judgment, doomsday.

Phrases: The *ne plus ultra*; the fall of the curtain; *'le commencement de la fin.'*

Verbs: To end, close, finish, expire, terminate, conclude; come or draw to an end, close or stop, be all over, pass away, give out, peter out, run its course; to say one's say, perorate, be through with.

To come last, bring up the rear.

To bring to an end, close, etc., to put a period, etc., to; to make an end of; to close, finish, seal, wind up, complete, achieve (729), crown, determine.

Phrases: To cut the matter short; to shut up shop.

Adjectives: Ending, closing, etc., final, terminal, eschatological, desistive, definitive, crowning.

Last, ultimate, penultimate, antepenultimate, hindermost, rear, caudal, conterminal, conterminous.

Ended, closed, terminated, etc., through.

Unbegun, fresh, uncommenced.

Adverbs: Once for all, in fine, finally, at the end of the day, for good, for good and all.

68 MIDDLE

Substantives: midst, mean, medium, happy medium, *via media,* middle term, centre (223), *mezzo termine, juste milieu,* half-way house, hub, nave, navel, omphalos, bull's-eye, nucleus.

Equidistance, equator, diaphragm, midriff; bisection (91).

Intervenience, interjacence, intervention (228), mid-course (628).

Adjectives: Middle, medial, median, mesial, mean, mid, middlemost, midmost, mediate, intermediate (29), intervenient, interjacent (228), central (222), equidistant, embosomed, merged.

Mediterranean, equatorial.

Adverbs: In the middle, amid, amidst, midway, amidships, half-way.

Phrases: In the thick of; *in medias res.*

69 CONTINUITY

Substantives: consecution, consecutiveness, succession, suite, progression, series, train, chain, catenation, concatenation, scale, gradation, course, procession, column, retinue, cortège, cavalcade, rank and file, line of battle, array, pedigree, genealogy, lineage, race.

File, queue, echelon, line, row, rank, range, tier, string, thread, team, tandem, randem, suit, flush, colonnade.

Verbs: To follow in, form a series, etc.; to fall in.

To arrange in a series, to marshal (60); to string together, file, thread, graduate, tabulate.

Adjectives: Continuous, sequent, consecutive, progressive, serial, successive, continued, uninterrupted, unbroken, entire, linear, in a line, in a row, etc., gradual, constant, unremitting, unintermitting, evergreen (110).

Adverbs: Continuously, consecutively, etc., *seriatum*; in a line, row, series, etc., in succession, etc., running, gradually, step by step; uninterruptedly, at a stretch, at one go.

Phrase: In Indian file.

70 DISCONTINUITY

Substantives: interruption, pause, period, interregnum, break, interval, interlude, episode, lacuna, cut, gap, fracture, fault, chasm, hiatus (198), caesura, parenthesis, rhapsody, anacoluthon.

Intermission, alternation (138); a broken thread, broken melody.

Verbs: To be discontinuous, etc.; to alternate, intermit.

To discontinue, pause, interrupt, break, interposte (228); to break in upon, disconnect (44); to break or snap the thread.

Adjectives: Discontinuous, inconsecutive, broken, interrupted, unsuccessive, desultory, disconnected, unconnected, fitful, spasmodic, sporadic, scattered.

Alternate, every other, intermitting, alternating (138).

Phrase: Few and far between.

Adverbs: At intervals, by snatches, *per saltum,* by fits and starts, *longo intervallo.*

71 TERM

Substantives: rank, station, stage, step, rung, round, degree (26), remove, grade, link, place, peg, mark, point, *pas,* period, pitch, stand, standing, status, footing, range.

Verbs: To hold, occupy, find, fall into a place, station.

72 ASSEMBLAGE

Substantives: collection, dozen, collocation, compilation, levy, gathering, ingathering, muster, round-up, colligation, contesseration, *attroupement,* association, concourse, conflux, convergence, meeting, assembly, congregation, at home (892), levee, club, reunion, gaudy, soirée, conversazione, accumulation, cumulation, array, mobilization.

Congress, convocation, convention, *comitium,* committee, quorum, conclave, synod, caucus, conventicle, eisteddfod, mass-meeting.

Miscellany, olla podrida, museum, *collectanea,* menagerie (636), Noah's ark, anthology, encyclopaedia, portfolio, file.

A multitude (102), crowd, throng, rabble, mob, press, crush, horde, posse, body, tribe, crew, gang, knot, band, party, swarm, school, shoal, bevy, galaxy, covey, flock, herd, drove, corps, troop, troupe, squad, squadron, phalanx, platoon, company, regiment, battalion, legion, host, army, division.

A sounder (of swine), skulk (of foxes), pride (of lions), charm (of finches), flush (of mallards), gaggle (of geese), wedge (of swans).

Clan, brotherhood, fraternity, sisterhood, party (712).

Volley, shower, storm, cloud, flood, deluge.

Group, cluster, clump, set, batch, battery, pencil, lot, pack, budget, assortment, bunch, parcel, packet, package, bundle, fascicle, fascicule, *fasciculus,* faggot, wisp, truss, tuft, rosette, shock, rick, fardel, stack, sheaf, stook, haycock.

Accumulation, congeries, heap, hoard, lump, pile, rouleau, tissue, mass, pyramid, bale, drift, snowball, acervation, cumulation, glomeration, agglomeration, conglobation, conglomeration, conglomerate, coacervation, coagmentation, aggregation, concentration (290), congestion, omnium gatherum.

Collector, tax-gatherer, whip, whipper-in.

Verbs: To assemble, collect, muster, meet, unite, cluster, swarm, flock, herd, crowd, throng, associate, congregate, conglomerate, concentrate, congest, rendezvous, resort, flock together, get together, reassemble.

To bring, get or gather together, collect, draw together, group, convene, convoke, convocate, collocate, colligate, round-up, scrape together, rake up, dredge, bring into a focus, amass, accumulate, heap up, pile, pack, do up, stack, truss, cram, pack together, congest, acervate, coagment, agglomerate, garner up, lump together, make a parcel of; to centralize; to mobilize.

Phrases: To heap Pelion upon Ossa; to collect in a drag-net.

Adjectives: Assembled, collected, etc., undispersed, met together, closely packed, dense, crowded, serried, huddled together, teeming, swarming, populous.

Phrases: Packed like sardines; crowded to suffocation.

73 NON-ASSEMBLAGE. DISPERSION

Substantives: scattering, dissemination, diffusion, dissipation, spreading, casting, distribution, apportionment, sprinkling, respersion, circumfusion, interspersion, divergence (291), demobilization.

Odds and ends, waifs and strays, flotsam and jetsam.

Verbs: To disperse, scatter, sow, disseminate, diffuse, shed, spread, overspread, dispense, disband, disembody, distribute, dispel, cast forth; strew, bestrew, sprinkle, sparge, issue, deal out, utter, resperse, intersperse, set abroach, circumfuse; to decentralize, demobilize; to hive-off.

Phrases: To turn adrift; to scatter to the four winds; to sow broadcast; to spread like wildfire.

Adjectives: Unassembled, uncollected, dispersed, scattered, diffused, sparse, spread, dispread, widespread, sporadic, cast, broadcast, epidemic, adrift.

Adverbs: *Sparsim,* here and there, *passim.*

74 FOCUS

Substantives: point of convergence, corradiation, rendezvous, home, headquarters, club, centre (222), gathering-place, meeting-place, trysting-place, rallying-ground, haunt, howff, resort, museum, repository, depot (636).

75 CLASS

Substantives: division, category, predicament, head, order, section, department, domain, province.

Kind, sort, variety, type, genus, species, family, phylum, race, tribe, caste, sept, clan, *gens,* phratry, breed, kith, sect, set, assortment, feather, stripe, suit, range, run.

Gender, sex, kin, kidney, manner, nature, description, denomination, designation, character, stamp, stuff, *genre.*

Adjectives: Generic, racial, tribal, etc.

Verbs: To classify, catalogue (60).

76 INCLUSION

Substantives: comprehension under a class, reference to a class, admission, comprehension, reception, subsumption.

Inclusion in a compound, composition (54).

Verbs: To be included in, to come under, to fall under, to range under; to belong, or pertain to, appertain; to range with, to merge in, to be of.

To include, comprise, comprehend, contain, admit, embrace, receive; to enumerate among, reckon among, reckon with, number among, refer to, place under, class with or among, arrange under or with, take into account, subsume.

Adjectives: Including, inclusive, all-embracing, congener, congeneric, congenerous, *et hoc genus omne,* etcetera.

Included, merged, etc.

Phrase: Birds of a feather.

77 EXCLUSION from a class

Substantives: Rejection, proscription.

Exclusion from a compound (55).

Verbs: To be excluded from, etc.; to exclude, proscribe, debar, rule out, set apart (55).

Phrase: To shut the door upon.
Adjectives: Exclusive, excluding, etc.

78 GENERALITY
Substantives: university, catholicism, catholicity.

Every man, every one, everybody, all, all hands.

Miscellaneousness, miscellany, encyclopaedia, generalization, prevalence, drag-net.
Phrases: The world and his wife; N or M.
Verbs: To be general, common, or prevalent, to prevail.

To render general, to generalize.
Adjectives: General, generic, collective, comprehensive, encyclopaedic, panoramic, bird's-eye, sweeping, radical, universal, world-wide, cosmopolitan, catholic, common, oecumenical, transcendental, prevalent, prevailing, all-pervading, epidemic, all-inclusive.

Unspecified, impersonal; every, all.
Adverbs: Whatever, whatsoever, to a man; generally, universally, on the whole, for the most part.

79 SPECIALITY
Substantives: particularity, peculiarity, individuality, haecceity, thisness, personality, characteristic, mannerism, idiosyncrasy, trick, gimmick, specificness, specificity, eccentricity, singularity (83).

Version, reading (522).

Particulars, details, items, counts.

I, myself, self, I myself, *moi qui vous parle.*
Phrases: *Argumentum ad hominem;* local colour.
Verbs: To specify, particularize, individualize, realize, specialize, designate, determine.
Phrases: To descend to particulars; to enter into detail.
Adjectives: Special, particular, individual, specific, proper, appropriate, personal, private, respective, several, definite, determinate, especial, certain, esoteric, endemic, partial, party, peculiar, characteristic, distinctive, typical, unique, diagnostic, exclusive, *sui generis,* singular, exceptional (83).

This, that, yonder, yon, such and such.
Adverbs: Specially, specifically, etc., in particular, respectively, personally, individually, *in propria persona.*

Each, apiece, one by one, severally, seriatim, namely, *videlicet,* viz., to wit.

80 RULE
Substantives: regularity, uniformity, constancy, standard, model, nature, principle, the order of things, routine, prevalence, practice, usage, custom, use, habit (613), regulation, precept (697), convention, *convenances*

Form, formula, law, canon, principle, keynote, catchword.

Type, archetype, pattern, precedent, paradigm, the normal, natural, ordinary or model state or condition; norm, control.
Phrases: A standing order; the bed of Procrustes; law of the Medes and Persians.
Adjectives: Regular, uniform, constant (82).

81 MULTIFORMITY
Substantives: variety, diversity, multifariousness, allotropy, allotropism.
Adjectives: Multiform, variform, polymorphic, multifold, manifold, multifarious, multigenerous, omnifarious, omnigenous, heterogeneous, motley, epicene, indiscriminate, desultory, irregular, diversified, allotropic; different (15).
Phrase: Of all sorts and kinds.

82 CONFORMITY
Substantives: conformance, observance, naturalization, harmony, convention (613).

Example, instance, specimen, sample, ensample, exemplar, exemplification, illustration, pattern (22), object lesson, case in point, quotation, the rule.

Phrases: The order of the day; the common or ordinary run of things (23); a matter of course.

Verbs: To conform to rule, be regular, orthodox, etc., to follow, observe, go by, bend to, obey rules; to be guided or regulated by, be wont, etc. (613), to comply or chime in with, to be in harmony with, follow suit; to standardize, naturalize.

To exemplify, illustrate, cite, quote, put a case, produce an instance, set an example.

Phrases: To go with the crowd; to do in Rome as the Romans do; to follow the fashion; to swim with the stream; to keep one in countenance.

Adjectives: Conformable to rule, regular, uniform, constant, steady, according to rule, *en règle, de rigueur,* normal, well regulated, formal, canonical, orthodox, conventional, strict, rigid, positive, uncompromising (23).

Ordinary, natural, usual, common, wonted, accustomed, habitual (613), household, average, everyday, current, rife, prevailing, prevalent, established, received, stereotyped, acknowledged, typical, accepted, recognized, representative, hackneyed, well-known, familiar, vernacular, commonplace, trite, banal, cut and dried, naturalized, orderly, shipshape, run of the mill.

Exemplary, illustrative, in point, of daily or everyday occurrence, in the order of things.

Phrases: Regular as clockwork; according to Cocker (or Hoyle).

Adverbs: Conformably, by rule, regularly, etc., agreeably to; in accordance, conformity, or keeping with.

Usually, generally, ordinarily, commonly, for the most part, as usual, *more solito, more suo, pro more;* of course, as a matter of course, *pro forma.*

Always, uniformly (16), invariably, without exception, never otherwise.

For example, for instance, *exempli gratia, inter alia.*

Phrases: *Ab uno disce omnes; ex pede Herculem; ex ungue leonem;* birds of a feather.

83   UNCONFORMITY

Substantives: nonconformity, unconventionality, informality, arbitrariness, abnormity, abnormality, anomaly, anomalousness, lawlessness, peculiarity, exclusiveness; infraction, breach, violation, of law or rule; individuality, idiosyncrasy, mannerism, eccentricity, aberration, irregularity, unevenness, variety, singularity, rarity, oddity, oddness, exemption, salvo.

Exception, nondescript, a character, original, nonesuch, monster, monstrosity, prodigy (872), *lusus naturae, rara avis,* freak, curiosity, crank, queer fish; half-caste, half-breed, crossbreed, mongrel, hybrid, mule, mulatto (41), *tertium quid,* hermaphrodite, sport.

Phoenix, chimera, hydra, sphinx, minotaur, griffin, centaur, hippocentaur, hippogriff, basilisk, cockatrice, tragelaph, kraken, dragon, wyvern, roc, sea-serpent, mermaid, merman, cyclops, unicorn.

Phrases: Out of one's element; a fish out of water; neither one thing nor another; neither fish, flesh, nor fowl, nor good red herring; a law to oneself.

Verbs: To be unconformable to rule, to be exceptional, etc.; to violate a law or custom, to stretch a point.

Phrases: To have no business there; to beggar description.

Adjectives: Unconformable, exceptional, abnormal, anomalous, anomalistic, out of order, out of place, misplaced, irregular, unorthodox, uneven, arbitrary, informal, aberrant, stray, peculiar, funny, exclusive, unnatural, eccentric, unconventional, Bohemian, beatnick, hippy, yippy.

Unusual, unaccustomed, unwonted, uncommon, rare, singular, unique, curious, odd, extraordinary, strange, *outré*, out of the way, egregious, out of the ordinary, unheard of, queer, quaint, old-fashioned, unfashionable, nondescript, undescribed, unexampled, *sui generis,* unprecedented, unparalleled, unfamiliar, fantastic, newfangled, grotesque, bizarre, weird, eerie, outlandish, exotic, preternatural, unrepresentative, uncanny, denaturalized.

Heterogeneous, epicine, heteroclite, amorphous, out of the pale of, mongrel, amphibious, half-blood, hybrid (41), androgynous, betwixt and between.

Phrases: 'None but himself could be his parallel'; caviare to the general.

Adverbs: Unconformably, etc.; except, unless, save, barring, beside, without, but for, save and except, let alone, to say nothing of; however, yet, but.

Section V – Number

84 NUMBER

Substantives: symbol, numeral, figure, cipher, digit, integer, counter, a round number, notation, a formula; series.

Sum, difference, subtrahend, complement, product, factorial, multiplicand, multiplier, multiplicator, coefficient, multiple, least common multiple, dividend, divisor, factor, highest common factor, greatest common measure, quotient, sub-multiple, fraction, vulgar fraction, mixed number, numerator, denominator, decimal, circulating decimal, recurring decimal, repetend, common measure, aliquot part, reciprocal, prime number; permutation, combination, election.

Ratio, proportion, progression (arithmetical, geometrical, harmonical), percentage.

Power, root, exponent, index, function, logarithm, antilogarithm; differential, integral, fluxion, fluent; incommensurable, surd.

Adjectives: Numeral, complementary, divisible, aliquot, reciprocal, prime, fractional, decimal, factorial, fractional, mixed, incommensurable.

Proportional, exponential, logarithmic, logometric, differential, fluxional, integral.

Positive, negative, rational, irrational, surd, radical, real, imaginary, impossible.

85 NUMERATION

Substantives: numbering, counting, tale, telling, tally, calling over, recension, enumeration, summation, reckoning, computation, ciphering, calculation, calculus, algorism, dactylonomy, rhabdology.

Arithmetic, analysis, algebra, differential and integral calculus.

Statistics, dead reckoning, muster, poll, census, capitation, roll-call, muster-roll, account, score, recapitulation, demography.

Addition, subtraction, multiplication, division, proportion, rule of three, reduction, involution, evolution, practice, equations, extraction of roots, approximation, interpolation, differentiation, integration.

Abacus, logometer, ready-reckoner, slide-rule, sliding-rule, tallies, Napier's bones, calculating machine, tabulator, totalizator, totalizer, tote, cash-register.

Verbs: To number, count, tell, tally, call over, take an account of, enumerate, muster, poll, run over, recite, recapitulate; sum, sum up, cast up, tell off, score, cipher, compute, calculate, reckon, estimate, figure up, tot up; add, subtract, multiply, divide; amount to.

Check, prove, demonstrate, balance, audit, overhaul, take stock.

Adjectives: Numerical, arithmetical, logarithmic, numeral, analytic, algebraic, statistical, computable, calculable, commensurable, incommensurable, incommensurate.

86 LIST

Substantives: catalogue, inventory, schedule, register, census, return, statistics, record (551), account, registry, syllabus, roll, terrier, cadastre, cartulary, tally, file, muster-roll, roster, rota, bead-roll, panel, calendar, index, table, book, ledger, day-book, synopsis, bibliography, contents, invoice, bill of lading, bill of fare, menu, red book, peerage, baronetage, Almanach de Gotha, Debrett, Domesday Book, prospectus, programme, directory, gazetteer, who's who.

Registration, etc. (551).

87 UNITY

Substantives: unification, oneness, individuality, singleness, solitariness, solitude, isolation (893), abstraction; monism.

One, unit, ace, monad.

Someone, somebody, no other, none else, an individualist; monist.

Verbs: To be alone, etc.; to isolate (44), insulate, set apart.

To render one, unify.

Phrase: To dine with Duke Humphrey.

Adjectives: One, sole, single, individual, apart, alone, lone, isolated, solitary, lonely, lonesome, desolate, dreary, insular, insulated, disparate, discrete, detached; monistic.

Unaccompanied, unattended, *solus,* single-handed, singular, odd, unique, unrepeated, azygous.

Inseverable, irresolvable, indiscerptible, compact.

Adverbs: Singly, etc., alone, by itself, *per se,* only, apart, in the singular

number, in the abstract, one by one; one at a time.

One and a half, sesqui-.

88 ACCOMPANIMENT

Substantives: coexistence, concomitance, company, association, companionship, partnership, collaboration, copartnership, coefficiency.

Concomitant, adjunct, context, accessory (39), coefficient, companion, attendant, fellow, associate, consort, spouse, colleague, collaborator, partner, copartner, side-kick, buddy, satellite, escort, hanger-on, parasite, shadow; travelling tutor, chaperon, duenna.

Verbs: To accompany, chaperon, coexist, attend, associate or be associated with, keep company with, collaborate with, hang on, shadow, wait on, to join, tie together.

Phrases: To go hand in hand with; to be in the same boat.

Adjectives: Accompanying, coexisting, attending, attendant, concomitant, fellow, twin, joint, associated with, accessory.

Adverbs: With, withal, together with, along with, in company with, collectively, hand in hand, together, in a body, cheek by jowl, side by side; therewith, herewith, moreover, besides, also, and (37), not to mention.

89 DUALITY

Substantives: dualism, duplicity, twofoldness, doubleness, biformity; polarity.

Two, deuce, couple, brace, pair, dyad (or duad), twins, Siamese twins, Castor and Pollux, Damon and Pythias, fellows, gemini, yoke, span, file, conjugation, twosome; dualist.

Verbs: To unite in pairs, to pair, pair off, couple, match, mate, bracket, yoke.

Adjectives: Two, twain, dual, binary, dualistic, duplex (90), duplicate, dyadic, binomial, twin, tête-à-tête, Janus-headed, bilateral, bicentric, bifocal.

Coupled, bracketed, paired, etc., conjugate.

Both, both the one and the other.

90 DUPLICATION
Substantives: doubling, gemination, reduplication, ingemination, repetition, iteration (104), renewal.
Verbs: To double, redouble, geminate, reduplicate, repeat, iterate, re-echo, renew (660).
Adjectives: Double, doubled, redoubled, second.

Biform, bifarious, bifold, bilateral, bifacial, twofold, two-sided, two-faced, duplex, duplicate, ingeminate.
Adverbs: Twice, once more, over again, *da capo, bis, encore,* anew, as much again, twofold (104, 136).

Secondly, in the second place, again.

91 BISECTION
Substantives: bipartition, dichotomy, halving, dimidiation, bifurcation, forking, branching, ramification, divarication, splitting, cleaving.

Fork, prong, fold, branch, Y.

Half, moiety, semi-, demi-, hemi-.
Verbs: To bisect, halve, divide, split, cut in two, cleave, dimidiate, dichotomize.

To separate, fork, bifurcate, branch out, ramify.
Verbs: To go halves; to go fifty-fifty; to split the difference.
Adjectives: Bisected, halved, divided, etc., bipartite, bicuspid, bind, bifurcated, bifurcate, cloven, cleft, split, etc.

92 TRIALITY
Substantives: trinity.

Three, triad, triangle, triplet, trey, trio, tern, trinomial, leash, threesome, trefoil, triquetra, *terza rima,* trilogy.

Third power, cube.

Adjectives: Three, triform, trine, trinal, trinary, ternary, ternal, ternate (93), trinomial, tertiary, tri-.

93 TRIPLICATION
Substantives: triplicity, trebleness, trine.
Verbs: To treble, triple, triplicate, cube.
Adjectives: Treble, triple, tern, ternary, ternate, triplicate, trigeminal, threefold, third.
Adverbs: Three times, thrice, threefold, in the third place, thirdly.

94 TRISECTION
Substantives: tripartition, trichotomy; third part, third.
Verbs: To trisect, divide into three parts.
Adjectives: Trifid, trisected, tripartite, trichotomous, trisulcate, triform.

95 QUATERNITY
Substantives: four, tetrad, quadruplet, quad, quarter, quaternion, foursome, square, tetragon, tetrahedron, tessara, quadrature; tetralogy.
Verbs: To reduce to a square, to square.
Adjectives: Four, quaternary, quaternal, quadratic, quartile, tetractic, tetra-, quadri-.

96 QUADRUPLICATION
Verbs: To multiply by four, quadruplicate, biquadrate.
Adjectives: Fourfold, quadruple, quadruplicate, fourth.
Adverbs: Four times, in the fourth place, fourthly, to the fourth degree.

97 QUADRISECTION
Substantives: quadripartition, quartering, a fourth, a quarter.
Verbs: To quarter, to divide into four parts.
Adjectives: Quartered, etc., quadrifid, quadripartite.

98 FIVE, etc.
Substantives: cinque, cinqfoil, quint, quincunx, pentad, pentagon, pentahedron, quintuplet, quin, quintet.
Adjectives: Five, quinary, quintuple, fivefold, fifth.

Six, half a dozen, hexad, hexagon, hexahedron, sextet.
Adjectives: Senary, sextuple, sixfold, sixth.

Seven, heptad, heptagon, heptahedron, septet.
Adjectives: Septenary, septuple, sevenfold, seventh.

Eight, octad, octagon, octahedron, octet, ogdoad.
Adjectives: Octonary, octonal, octuple, eightfold, eighth.

Nine, ennead, nonagon, enneagon, enneahedron, novena.
Adjectives: Enneatic, ninefold, ninth.

Ten, decad, decagon, decahedron, decade.
Adjectives: Decimal, denary, decuple, tenfold, tenth.

Twelve, a dozen.
Adjectives: Duodenary, duodecimal, twelfth.

Thirteen, a long dozen, a baker's dozen.

Twenty, a score, icosahedron.
Adjectives: Vigesimal, twentieth.

Forty, twoscore.
Adjectives: Quadragesimal.

Fifty, twoscore and ten.
Adjectives: Quinquagesimal.

Sixty, threescore.
Adjectives: Sexagesimal, sexagenary.

Seventy, threescore and ten.

Eighty, fourscore.

Ninety, fourscore and ten.

Hundred, centenary, hecatomb, century. One hundred and forty-four, a gross.
Verbs: To centuriate.
Adjectives: Centesimal, centennial, centenary, centurial, centuple, centuplicate, hundredfold, hundredth.

Thousand, chiliad, millennium.
Adjective: Millesimal.
Myriad, lac, crore.
Million, billion, trillion, etc.

99 QUINQUESECTION, etc.
Adjectives: Quinquefid, quin-quarticular, quinquepartite.
Sexpartite.
Septempartite.
Octopartite.
Decimation, tithe.
Verb: To decimate.

100 PLURALITY
Substantives: a number, a certain number, a few, a wheen, a round number.
Adjectives: Plural, more than one, upwards of, some, a few, one or two, two or three, umpteen, certain.
Adverb: Etcetera.

101 ZERO
Substantives: nothing (4), nought (or naught), cipher; nobody, *nemo*.
Adjectives: None, not one, not any, not a soul.

102 MULTITUDE
Substantives: numerousness, numerosity, numerality, multiplicity, majority, profusion, legion, host, a great or large number, numbers, array, power, lot, sight, army, sea, galaxy, populousness (72), a hundred, thousand, myriad, million, etc.

A shoal, swarm, draught, bevy, flock, herd, drove, flight, covey, hive, brood, litter, mob, nest, crows (72).

Increase of number, multiplication, multiple; greater number, majority.
Verbs: To be numerous, etc., to swarm, teem, crowd, come thick upon, outnumber, multiply, to people.
Phrase: To swarm like locusts or bees.
Adjectives: Many, several, a wheen, sundry, divers, various, a great many, very many, full many, ever so many,

no end of, numerous, profuse, manifold, multiplied, multitudinous, multiple, multinomial, endless (105), teeming, populous, peopled.

Frequent, repeated, reiterated, outnumbering, thick, crowding, crowded; galore.

Phrases: Thick as hail; thick as leaves in Vallombrosa; plentiful as blackberries; in profusion; numerous as the sands on the seashore; their name is Legion.

103 FEWNESS
Substantives: paucity, a small number, handful, scantiness, rareness, rarity, thinness.

Diminution of number, reduction, weeding, elimination, thinning; smaller number, minority.
Verbs: To be few, etc.

To render few, reduce, diminish in number, weed, weed out, prick off, eliminate, thin, thin out, decimate.
Adjectives: Few, scanty, scant, rare, infrequent, sparse, scattered, hardly or scarcely any, reduced, thinned, etc.
Phrases: Few and far between; you could count them on the fingers of one hand.

104 REPETITION
Substantives: iteration, reiteration, harping, recapitulation, run, recurrence (136), recrudescence, tautology, monotony; cuckoo-note, chimes, repetend, echo, burden of a song, refrain, jingle, renewal, rehearsal, réchauffé, rehash, reproduction (19).

Cuckoo, mocking-bird, mimic, imitator, parrot.

Periodicity (138), frequency (136).
Phrase: A twice-told tale.
Verbs: To repeat, iterate, reiterate, recapitulate, renew, reproduce, echo, re-echo, drum, hammer, harp on, plug, rehearse, redouble, recrudesce, reappear, recur, revert, recommence.
Phrases: Do or say over again; ring the

changes on; to harp on the same string; to din or drum in the ear; to go over the same ground; to begin again.
Adjectives: Repeated, repetitional, repetitionary, repetitive, recurrent, recurring, reiterated, renewed, ever-recurring, thick-coming, monotonous, harping, sing-song, mocking, chiming; above-mentioned, said, aforesaid.
Phrases: It's that man again; cut and come again; *crambe repetita*.
Adverbs: Repeatedly, often (136), again, anew, over again, afresh, ditto, *encore, de novo, da capo, bis* (90).
Phrases: *Toties quoties*; again and again; in quick succession, over and over again; ever and anon; time after time; year after year; times out of number; *ad nauseam*.

105 INFINITY
Substantives: infiniteness, infinitude.
Adjectives: Infinite, numberless, innumerable, countless, sumless, untold, unnumbered, unsummed, incalculable, unlimited, limitless, illimitable, immeasurable, unmeasured, measureless, unbounded, boundless, endless, interminable, unfathomable, exhaustless, termless, indefinite, without number, without limit, without end, unending.
Adverbs: Infinitely, etc., without measure, limit, etc., *ad infinitum,* world without end.

Section VI – Time

106 DURATION
Substantives: time, period, term, space, span, spell, season, era, epoch, decade, century, chiliad, age, cycle, aeon.

Intermediate time, while, interval, interim, pendency, intervention, intermission, interregnum, interlude, recess, break, intermittence, respite (265).

Long duration (110).
Phrases: The enemy; the whirligig of time.
Verbs: To continue, last, endure, remain, go on; to take, take up, fill or occupy time, to persist, to intervene.

To pass, pass away, spend, employ, while away or consume time, waste time.
Adjectives: Continuing, lasting, enduring, remaining, persistent, perpetual, permanent (150).
Adverbs: While, whilst, so long as, during, pending, till, until, up to, during the time or interval, the whole time or period, all the time or while, in the long rung, all along, throughout, from beginning to end (52).

Pending, meantime, meanwhile, in the meantime, in the interim, *ad interim, pendente lite,* from day to day, for a time, for a season, for good, yet, up to this time.

107   TIMELESSNESS
Substantives: neverness, absence of time, no time, *dies non.*

Short duration (111).
Adverbs: Never, ne'er, at no time, on no occasion, at no period, nevermore, *sine die.*
Phrases: On Tib's eve; at the Greek Calends; *jamais de ma vie;* 'jam every other day.'

108   PERIOD
Substantives: second, minute, hour, day, week, fortnight, month, lunation, quarter, year, leap-year, lustrum, quinquennium, decade, lifetime, generation, century, age, millennium, *annus magnus.*
Adjectives: Hourly, horary; daily, diurnal, quotidian; weekly, hebdomadal, menstrual, monthly, annual, secular, centennial, bicentennial, etc., bissextile, seasonal.
Adverbs: From day to day, from hour to hour.

Once upon a time; Anno Domini, A.D.; Before Christ, B.C.

108a   CONTINGENT DURATION.
During pleasure, during good behaviour, *quamdiu se bene gesserit.*

109   COURSE
Substantives: progress, process, succession, lapse, flow, flux, stream, tract, current, tide, march, step, flight, etc., of time.

Indefinite time, aorist.
Verbs: To elapse, lapse, flow, run, proceed, roll on, advance, pass, slide, press on, flit, fly, slip, glide, run its course.
Adjectives: Elapsing, passing, etc.; aoristic.
Adverbs: In course of time, in due time of season, in process of time, in the fullness of time.
Phrase: *Labuntur anni.*

110   DIUTURNITY
Substantives: a long time, an age, a century, an eternity, aeon.
Phrases: *Temporis longinquitas;* a month of Sundays.

Durableness, durability, persistence, lastingness, continuance, permanence (150), longevity, survival.

Distance of time, protraction, extension or prolongation of time, delay (133).
Verbs: To last, endure, stand, remain, continue, abide, tarry, protract, prolong, outlast, outlive, survive; spin out, draw out, eke out, temporize, linger, loiter, lounge (275), wait.
Phrase: To live to fight another day.
Adjectives: Durable, of long duration, permanent, enduring, chronic, intransient, intransitive, intransmutable, lasting, abiding, persistent; live-long, longeval, long-lived, macrobiotic, diuturnal, evergreen, perennial, unintermitting, unremitting, perpetual (112).

Protracted, prolonged, spun out, long-winded, surviving, lingering.
Adverbs: Long, a long time, permanently.
Phrases: As the day is long; all the day long; all the year round; the livelong day; hour after hour; morning, noon, and night; for good; for many a long day.

111 TRANSIENTNESS
Substantives: transitoriness, impermanence, evanescence, transitiveness, fugitiveness, fugacity, fugaciousness, caducity, mortality, span, shortness, brevity.
Quickness, promptness (132), suddenness, abruptness.
A *coup de main,* bubble, Mayfly, nine days' wonder.
Verbs: To be transient, etc., to flit, pass away, fly, gallop, vanish, fade, intromit.
Adjectives: Transitory, transient, transitive, passing, impermanent, evanescent, fleeting, momentary, fugacious, fugitive, flitting, vanishing, shifting, flying, temporary, temporal, makeshift, provisional, provisory, rough and ready, cursory, galloping, short-lived, ephemeral, deciduous, meteoric.
Brief, sudden, quick, prompt, brisk, abrupt, extemporaneous, summary, hasty, precipitate.
Adverbs: Temporarily, etc., *en passant, in transitu,* extempore.
In a short time, soon, at once, awhile, anon, by and by, briefly, presently, apace, eftsoons, straight, straightway, quickly, speedily, promptly, presto, slapdash, directly, immediately, incontinently, forthwith; suddenly, *per saltum,* at one bound.
Phrases: At short notice; the time being up; before the ink is dry; here to-day and gone to-morrow (149); *sic transit gloria mundi.*

112 PERPETUITY
Substantives: eternity, sempiternity, immortality, athanasy, everlastingness, perpetuation.
Verbs: To last or endure for ever, to have no end: to eternize, pertetuate.
Adjectives: Perpetual, eternal, everlasting, sempiternal, coeternal; endless, unending, ceaseless, incessant, unceasing, uninterrupted, interminable, having no end, unfading, evergreen, never-fading, amaranthine, ageless, deathless, immortal, undying, never-dying, imperishable, indestructible.
Adverbs: Always, ever, evermore, aye, for ever, for aye, for evermore, still, perpetually, eternally, etc., in all ages, from age to age.
Phrases: For ever and a day; *esto perpetua*; for ever and ever; world without end; time without end; *in secula seculorum*; to the end of time; till Doomsday; till hell freezes; to a cinder.

113 INSTANTANEITY
Substantives: instantaneousness, moment, instant, second, split second, minute, twinkling, trice, flash, breath, span, jiffy, flash of lightening, suddenness (111).
Verbs: To twinkle, flash, to be instantaneous.
Adjectives: Instantaneous, push-button, sudden, momentary, extempore.
Phrases: Quick as thought; quick as a flash; quick as lightening.
Adverbs: Instantly, momentarily, *subito,* presto, instanter, suddenly, plump, slap, slapdash, in a moment, in an instant, in a second, in no time, in a trice, in a twinkling, at one jump, in a breath, extempore, *per saltum,* in a crack, out of hand.
Phrases: Before one can say 'Jack Robinson'; in a brace of shakes; between the cup and the lip; on the spur of the moment; in the twinkling of an eye; in a jiffy; in two ticks; on the

instant; in less than no time; at one fell swoop; no sooner said than done.

114 CHRONOMETRY
Substantives: chronology, horology, horometry, registry, date, epoch, style, era.

Greenwich, standard, mean, local, solar, sidereal time; summer time, double summer time.

Almanac, calendar, ephemeris, chronicle, annals, register, journal, diary, chronogram, time-book.

Instruments for the measurement of time, clock, watch, stop-watch, repeater, chronograph, chronometer, sextant, timepiece, dial, sun-dial, horologe, pendulum, hour-glass, water-clock, clepsydra; time signal.

Chronographer, chronologer, chronologist, time-keeper, annalist.

Verbs: To chronicle, to fix or mark the time, date, register, etc., to bear date, to measure time, to beat time, to make time, to time.

Adjectives: Chronological, chronometrical, chronogrammatical.

Adverb: O'clock.

115 ANACHRONISM
Substantives: error in time, prolepsis, metachronism, prochronism, parachronism, anticipation.

Disregard or neglect of time.

Verbs: To anachronize, misdate, antedate, postdate, overdate, anticipate.

Adjectives: Anachronistic, anachronous, misdated, undated, overdue, postdated, antedated.

Phrases: To take no note of time; to prophesy after the event.

116 PRIORITY
Substantives: antecedence, anteriority, precedence, pre-existence.

Precursor, predecessor, prelude, forerunner (64), harbinger, antecedent; the past (122).

Verbs: To precede, come before, fore-run, pre-exist, prelude, usher in, dawn, announce (511), foretell, anticipate, forestall.

Phrases: To be beforehand; to steal a march upon.

Adjectives: Prior, previous, preceding, precedent, anterior, antecedent, pre-existent, pre-existing, former, foregoing, aforesaid, said, abovementioned, prehistoric, antediluvian, pre-Adamite.

Precursory, prelusive, prelusory, proemial, introductory, prefatory (62), prodromal, prodromic.

Adverbs: Before, prior to, previously, anteriorly, antecedently, aforetime, ere, ere now, erewhile, before now, heretofore, ultimo, yet, beforehand, above, *supra*.

Phrase: Before the flood.

117 POSTERIORITY
Substantives: succession, sequence, subsequence, supervention, sequel, successor (65), postlude.

Verbs: To follow, come or go after, succeed, supervene, ensue.

Phrases: To tread on the heels of; to follow in the footsteps of.

Adjectives: Subsequent, posterior, following, after, later, succeeding, post-glacial, post-diluvial, post-diluvian, puisne, posthumous, post-prandial, post-classical.

Adverbs: Subsequently, after, afterwards, since, later, later on, at a subsequent or later period, proximo, next, in the sequel, close upon, thereafter, thereupon, whereupon, upon which, eftsoons, below, *infra*.

118 THE PRESENT TIME
Substantives: the existing time, the time being, the present moment, juncture, crisis, epoch, day, hour; the twentieth century.

Age, time of life.

Verb: To strike while the iron is hot.

Adjectives: Present, actual, current, existing, that is.

Adverbs: At this time, moment, etc., now, at present, at this time of day, at the present time, day, etc., to-day, nowadays, instant, already, even now, but now, just now, upon which.

Phrases: For the time being; for the nonce; *pro hac vice*; on the nail; on the spot; on the spur of the moment; now or never.

119 DIFFERENT TIME
Substantives: other time.

Indefinite time, aorist.

Adjectives: Aoristic.

Adverbs: At that time, moment, etc., then, at which time, etc., on that occasion, upon, in those days.

When, whenever, whensoever, upon which, on which occasions, at another or a different time, etc., otherwhile, otherwhiles, at various times, ever and anon.

Phrases: Once upon a time; one day; some other time; one of these days.

120 SYNCHRONISM
Substantives: synchronization, coinstantaneity, coexistence, coincidence, simultaneousness, coevality, contemporaneousness, contemporaneity, concurrence, concomitance.

Having equal times, isochronism.

A contemporary, coeval, coetanean.

Verbs: To coexist, concur, accompany, synchronize.

Phrase: To keep pace with.

Verbs: Synchronous, synchronal, synchronistic, simultaneous, coexisting, coincident, concomitant, concurrent, coeval, coetaneous, contemporary, contemporaneous, coeternal, isochronous.

Adverbs: At the same time, simultaneously, etc., together, during the same time, etc., in the interim, in the same breath, in concert, *pari passu*; meantime, meanwhile (106), while, whilst.

121 FUTURITY
Substantives: the future, futurition, the approaching time, hereafter, the time to come, posteriority (117), after time, after age, the coming time, the morrow, after days, hours, years, ages; after life, millennium, doomsday, the day of judgment, the crack of doom.

The approach of time, the process of time, advent, time drawing on, the womb of time.

Prospection, anticipation, prospect, perspective, expectation (507), horizon, outlook, look-out.

Heritage, heirs, progeny, issue, posterity, descendants, heir apparent, heir presumptive.

Future existence, future state, post-existence, after-life, beyond.

Verbs: To look forward, anticipate, forestall (132), have in prospect, keep in view, expect (507).

To impend, hang over, lie over, approach, await, threaten, overhang, draw near, prepare.

Phrases: Lie in wait for; bide one's time; to wait impatiently; kick one's heels.

To be in the wind; to be cooking; to loom in the future.

Adjectives: Future, to come, coming, going to happen, approaching, impending, instant, at hand, about to be or happen, next, hanging, awaiting, forthcoming, near, near at hand, imminent, threatening, brewing, preparing, in store, eventual, ulterior, in view, in prospect, prospective, in perspective, in the offing, in the wind, on the cards, that will be, overhanging.

Unborn, in embryo, in the womb of time.

Adverbs: Prospectively, hereafter, by and by, some fine day, one of these days, anon, in future, to-morrow, in course of time, in process of time, sooner or later, *proximo*, in after time.

On the eve of, ere long, at hand,

near at hand, on the point of, beforehand, against the time.

After a time, from this time, henceforth, henceforwards, thence, thenceforth, thenceforward, whereupon, upon which.

Phrases: All in good time; in the fullness of time.

122 PRETERITION

Substantives: The past, past time, *status quo,* days of yore, time gone by, priority (116), former times, old times, the olden time, ancient times, antiquity, antiqueness, lang syne, time immemorial, prehistory.

Archaeology, palaeology, palaeontology, palaeography, archaism, retrospection, retrospect, looking back.

Archaeologist, antiquary, medievalist, palaeographer, palaeologist, Dr. Dryasdust.

Ancestry (166), pre-existence.

Phrases: The good old days; the golden age; the rust of antiquity.

Verbs: To pass, be past, lapse, go by, elapse, run out, expire, blow over; to look back, cast the eyes back, retrospect, trace back, dig up, exhume.

Phrases: To have run its course; to have had its day.

Adjectives: Past, gone, gone by, over, bygone, foregone, pristine, prehistoric, quondam, lapsed, elapsed, preterlapsed, expired, late, *ci-devant,* run out, blown over, that has been.

Former, foregoing, late, last, latter, recent, overnight, preterperfect, preterpluperfect, forgotten, irrecoverable, out of date.

Looking back, retrospective, retroactive, *ex post facto*; archaeological, etc.

Pre-existing, pre-existent.

Adverbs: Formerly, of old, erst, whilom, erewhile, before now, time was, ago, over, in the olden time, anciently, in days of yore, long since, retrospectively, ere now, before now,

till now, once, once upon a time, hitherto, heretofore, *ultimo.*

The other day, yesterday, last night, week, month, year, etc.; just now, recently, lately, of late, latterly.

Long ago, a long while or time ago, some time ago.

Phrases: Once upon a time; from time immemorial; in the memory of man; time out of mind.

Already, yet, at length, at last.

123 NEWNESS

Substantives: novelty, recentness, recency, modernity, freshness, greenness, immaturity, youth (127), rawness.

Innovation, renovation (660), renewal.

Nouveau riche, parvenu, upstart, mushroom; latest fashion, *dernier cri.*

Verbs: Renew, renovate, restore (660), modernize.

Adjectives: New, novel, recent, fresh, green, evergreen, raw, immature, untrodden, advanced, twentieth-century, modern, modernistic, avant-garde, neoteric, new-born, nascent, new-fashioned, up-to-date, new-fangled, vernal, renovated, brand-new, split-new, virgin.

Phrases: Fresh as a rose; fresh as a daisy; fresh as paint; just out; spick and span.

Adverbs: Newly, recently, lately, afresh, anew.

124 OLDNESS

Substantives: age (128), antiquity, eld, ancientry, primitiveness, maturity, decline, decay, obsolescence; seniority, eldership, primogeniture.

Archaism, relic, antique, fossil, eolith; elder, doyen.

Verbs: To be or become old, mature, mellow; to age, fade, decay.

Adjectives: Old, ancient, antique, antiquated, out-of-date, of long standing, time-honoured, venerable, hoary, primitive, diluvian, antediluvian, fossil, palaeozoic, preglacial, palaeolithic, neolithic, primeval, primordial, prime, pre-Adamite, prehistoric, antemundane, archaic, classic, medieval.

Immemorial, inveterate, rooted, traditional.

Senior, elder, eldest, oldest, firstborn (128).

Obsolete, obsolescent, out-of-date, stale, time-worn, faded, decayed, effete, declining, played-out, crumbling, decrepit (128), passé.

Phrases: Nothing new under the sun; old as the hills; old as Methuselah; old as Adam; before the Flood; time out of mind; since the year one.

125 MORNING

Substantives: morn, morrow, forenoon, a.m., prime, dawn, daybreak, dayspring, peep of day, break of day, matins, aurora, first blush of the morning, prime of the morning, twilight, crepuscule, sunrise, sun-up, cockcrow.

Noon, midday, noontide, meridian, noonday, prime; spring, summer, midsummer.

Adjectives: Matutinal, auroral, vernal, midsummer.

126 EVENING

Substantives: eve, e'en, decline of day, close of day, eventide, nightfall, curfew, vespers, evensong, dusk, twilight, gloaming, eleventh hour, sunset, sundown, afternoon, p.m., bedtime, midnight; autumn, Indian summer, St. Martin's summer, St. Luke's summer, winter the fall.

Phrases: The witching time of night; the dead of night; blind-man's holiday.

Adjectives: Nocturnal, vespertine, autumnal, heimal, brumal.

127 YOUTH

Substantives: infancy, babyhood, boyhood, juvenility, childhood, youthhood, juniority, juvenescence, adolescence (131), minority, nonage, teens, tender age, bloom, heyday, boyishness, girlishness.

Cradle, nursery, leading strings, pupilage, pupilship, puberty.

Phrases: Prime or flower of life; the rising generation; salad days; schooldays.

Adjectives: Young, youthful, juvenile, callow, sappy, beardless, under age, in one's teens, boyish, girlish, junior, younger.

Phrase: In statu pupillari.

128 AGE

Substantives: old age, senility, senescence, oldness, longevity, years, anility, grey hairs, climacteric, decrepitude, hoary age, caducity, crow's feet, superannuation, dotage, anecdotage, seniority, green old age, eldership.

Phrases: The vale of years; decline of life; the sere and yellow leaf; second childhood.

Adjectives: Aged, old, elderly, senile, matronly, anile, in years, ripe, mellow, grey, grey-headed, hoary, hoar, venerable, timeworn, declining, antiquated, passé, rusty, effete, decrepit, superannuated.

Patriarchal, ancestral, primitive, older, elder, senior; eldest, oldest, firstborn, bantling, firstling.

Phrases: With one foot in the grave; marked with crow's feet; advanced in life, or in years; stricken in years; no chicken; long in the tooth; old as the hills.

129 INFANT

Substantives: babe, baby, nursling, suckling.

Child, baird, wean, little one, brat, toddler, kid, chit, urchin, bantling, bratling, papoose, elf, piccaninny.

Youth, boy, lad, laddie, stripling, youngster, teenager, callant, younker, gossoon, nipper, whipster, whippersnapper, schoolboy, young hopeful, hobbledehoy, cadet, minor.

Girl, lass, lassie, wench, miss, colleen, flapper, bobbysoxer, damsel, maid, maiden, *jeune fille*.

Scion, sapling, seedling, tendril, mushroom, nestling, chicken, larva, chrysalis, tadpole, whelp, cub, pullet, fry, foetus, calf, lamb, lambkin, colt, filly, pup, puppy, foal, kitten.

Adjectives: Infantine, infantile, puerile, boyish, girlish (127), virginal, childish, baby, babyish, unfledged, new-fledged, kittenish, callow.

Phrases: In leading-strings; at the breast; in arms; in one's teens; tied to mother's apron-strings.

130   VETERAN

Substantives: old man, seer, patriarch, greybeard, gaffer, grandsire, grandam, dowager, matron, crone, beldam, hag, sexagenarian, old-timer, old stager, old buffer, fogy, geezer.

Methuselah, Nestor; elders, forefathers, forbears, fathers, ancestors, ancestry.

Adjectives: Veteran, aged, old, grey-headed (128).

131   ADOLESCENCE

Substantives: puberty, pubescence, majority, adultness, maturity, ripeness, manhood, virility.

A man, adult (373), a woman, matron (374), *parti*; ephebe.

Phrases: Prime of life; man's estate; flower of age; meridian of life; years of discretion; *toga virilis*.

Adjectives: Adolescent, pubescent, of age, out of one's teens, grown up, mature, middle-aged, manly, virile, adult.

Womanly, matronly, nubile, marriageable, out.

132   EARLINESS

Substantives: timeliness, punctuality, readiness, promptness (682), promp-

titude, expedition, quickness, haste, acceleration, hastening, hurry, bustle, precipitation, anticipation, precociousness, precocity.

Suddenness, abruptness (111).

Phrases: A stitch in time saves nine; the early bird catches the worm.

Verbs: To be early, to be in time, keep time, be beforehand.

To anticipate, forestall, book, engage, bespeak, reserve.

To expedite, hasten, haste, quicken (274), press, dispatch, accelerate, precipitate, hurry, bustle (684).

Phrases: To take time by the forelock; to steal a march upon; to be beforehand with; to be pressed for time.

Adjectives: Early, prime, rathe, timely, timeous, punctual, matutinal, forward, ready, quick, expeditious, precipitate, summary, prompt, premature, precocious, prevenient, anticipatory, pre-emptive.

Sudden, abrupt, unexpected (508), subitaneous, extempore.

Adverbs: Early, soon, anon, betimes, apace, eft, eftsoons, in time, ere long, presently, shortly, punctually, to the minute, on time, on the dot.

Beforehand, prematurely, before one's time, in anticipation.

Suddenly, abruptly, at once, extempore, instanter.

Phrases: In good time; at sunrise; with the lark; early days.

On the point of; at short notice; on the spur of the moment; all at once; before you can say 'knife'; no sooner said than done.

133   LATENESS

Substantives: tardiness, slowness (275), delay, cunctation, procrastination, deferring, lingering, lagging, etc., postponement, dilatoriness, adjournment, shelving, prorogation, remand, moratorium.

Protraction, prolongation, leeway.

Phrase: Fabian tactics.

Verbs: To be late, etc., tarry, wait, stay, bide, take time, dally, dawdle, linger, loiter, lag, bide one's time, shuffle (275, 683).

To stand over, lie over, hang fire.

To put off, defer, delay, leave over, suspend, stave off, postpone, adjourn, carry over, shelve, procrastinate, temporize, stall, filibuster, prolong, protract, draw out, spin out, hold up, prorogue.

Phrases: To tide it over; to bide one's time; to let the matter stand over; to sleep on it; to kick (or cool) one's heels.

Adjectives: Late, tardy, slow, dilatory (275), posthumous, backward, unpunctual, procrastinatory, behindhand, belated, overdue.

Delayed, etc., suspended, pending, in abeyance.

Adverbs: Late, after time, too late, behind time; at length, at last.

Slowly, leisurely, deliberately.

Phrases: Late in the day; a day after the fair; at the eleventh hour; after death, the doctor.

134 OCCASION

Substantives: opportunity, chance, opening, break, show, room, suitable or proper time or season, high time, opportuneness, tempestivity, seasonableness, crisis, turn, juncture, conjuncture.

Spare time, leisure, holiday (685), spare moments, hours, etc., time on one's hands.

Phrases: Golden (or favourable) opportunity; the nick of time;

Verbs: To use, make use of, employ, profit by, avail oneself of, lay hold of, embrace, catch, seize, snatch, clutch, pounce upon, grasp, etc., the opportunity.

To give, offer, present, afford, etc., the opportunity.

To time well; to spend or consume time.

Phrases: To turn the occasion to account; to seize the occasion; to strike the iron while it is hot; to make hay while the sun shines; *carpe diem*; to take the tide at the flood; to furnish a handle for.

Adjectives: Opportune, timely, well-timed, timeful, timeous, seasonable, happy, lucky, providential, fortunate, favourable, propitious, auspicious, critical.

Adverbs: Opportunely, etc., on the spot, in proper or due time or season, high time, for the nonce.

By the way, by the by, *en passant, à propos,* parenthetically.

Phrases: In the nick of time; on the spur of the moment (612); now or never; at the eleventh hour; time and tide wait for no man.

135 INTEMPESTIVITY

Substantives: untimeliness, unsuitable time, improper time, unseasonableness, inopportuneness, evil hour.

Hitch, impediment (706), check, *contretemps.*

Verbs: To be ill-timed, etc., to mistime, intrude, come amiss.

To lose, omit, let slip, let go, neglect, pretermit, allow, or suffer the opportunity or occasion to pass, slip, go by, escape, lapse; to lose time, to fritter away time (683).

Phrases: to let slip through the fingers; to lock the stable door when the steed is stolen.

Adjectives: Ill-timed, untimely, untimeous, mistimed, unseasonable, out of season, unpunctual, inopportune, untoward, intrusive, too late (133), too early (132), malapropos, unlucky, inauspicious, unpropitious, unfortunate, unfavourable, unsuited, unsuitable.

Adverbs: Inopportunely, etc.

Phrases: As ill luck would have it; in evil hour; after meat, mustard; a day before (or after) the fair.

136 FREQUENCY
Substantives: oftness, recurrence, repetition (104), recrudescence, reiteration, iteration, run, reappearance, renewal, *ritornello, ritournelle,* burden.
Frequenter, *habitué,* fan, client.
Verbs: To recur, revert, return, repeat, reiterate, reappear, renew, reword.
To frequent, resort to, visit, attend, haunt, infest.
Adjectives: Frequent, common, not rare, repeated, reiterated, thickcoming, recurring, recurrent, incessant, everlasting, perpetual, rife; habitual (613).
Adverbs: Often, oft, oft-times, not infrequently, frequently, often-times, many times, several times, repeatedly.
Again, anew, afresh, *de novo, ditto,* over again, *da capo,* again and again, over and over, ever and anon, many times over, time after time, time and again, repeatedly (104).
Perpetually, continually, constantly, incessantly, everlastingly, without ceasing.
Sometimes, occasionally, at times, now and then, now and again, from time to time, at intervals, between whiles, once in a while, there are times when.
Most ofte, for the most part, generally, usually, commonly, most frequently, as often as not.
Phrases: A number of times; many a time (and oft); times out of number.

137 INFREQUENCY
Substantives: rareness, rarity, uncommonness, scarcity, fewness (103), seldomness.
Verbs: To be rare etc.
Adjectives: Infrequent, rare, scarce, unfrequent, uncommon, unprecedented, unheard-of.
Phrase: In short supply.
Adverbs: Seldom, rarely, scarcely, hardly, scarcely ever, ever, hardly ever, not often, unfrequently.

Once, once for all, once in a way.
Phrases: Once in a blue moon; angels' visits.

138 PERIODICITY
Substantives: intermittence, beat, ictus, pulse, pulsation, rhythm, lilt, swing, alternation, alternateness, bout, round, revolution, rotation, turn.
Anniversary, jubilee; silver, golden, wedding; centenary, bicentenary, tercentenary, etc.; feast, festival, birthday.
Regularity of return, rota, cycle, period, stated time, routine.
Phrase: The swing of the pendulum.
Verbs: To recur in regular order or succession, to come round, return, revolve, alternate, come in its turn, beat, pulsate, intermit; to regularize.
Adjectives: Periodic, periodical, recurrent, cyclical, revolving, intermittent, remittent, alternate, every other, alternating, rhythmic, rhythmical, steady, punctual.
Hourly, daily, diurnal, tertian, quotidian, weekly, hebdomadal, fortnightly, bi-monthly, monthly, biannual, annual, yearly, biennial, triennial, centennial.
Phrase: Regular as clockwork.
Adverbs: Periodically, at regular intervals, at stated times, at fixed periods, punctually, from day to day.
By turns, in turn, in rotation, alternately, in shifts, off and on, ride and tie, hitch and hike.

139 IRREGULARITY
Substantives: of recurrence, uncertainty, unpunctuality, fitfulness.
Adjectives: Irregular, uncertain, unpunctual, capricious, desultory, unrhythmic, unrhythmical, fitful, spasmodic, flickering, casual.
Adverbs: Irregularly, etc., by snatches, by fits and starts, skippingly, now and then, occasionally.

Section VII – Change

140 CHANGE

Substantives: alteration, mutation, permutation, variation, modification, modulation, inflexion, mood, qualification, innovation, metastasis, metabolism, deviation, turn, diversion, inversion, reversion, reversal, eversion, subversion (162), *bouleversement*, upset, organic change, revolution (146), substitution (147), transposition (148), transit, transition.

Transformation, transmutation, transfiguration, metamorphosis, transmigration, transubstantiation, transmogrification, metempsychosis, avatar.

Vicissitude, flux, unrest (149); change of mind, tergiversation (607).

Phrase: The wheel of fortune.

Verbs: To change, alter, vary, modify, modulate, diversify, qualify, tamper with, edit, turn, shift, veer, tack, chop, shuffle, swerve, warp, deviate, turn aside, turn topsy-turvy, upset, invert, reverse, introvert, subvert, evert, turn inside out.

Form, fashion, mould, model, vamp, warp, work a change, superinduce, resume, disturb (61), innovate, reform, remodel, refound, new-model, modernize, revolutionize.

Transform, transume, transmute, transfigure, transmogrify, metamorphose, pass to, leap to, transfer.

Phrases: To ring the changes; to turn over a new leaf; to introduce new blood; to shuffle the cards; to turn the corner; to wax and wane; to ebb and flow; *tempora mutantur; nous avons changé tout cela.*

Adjectives: Changed, altered, new-fangled, warped, etc.; transitional, metamorphic, metabolic, metastatic.

Adverb: *Mutatis mutandis.*

141 PERMANENCE

Substantives: persistence, endurance, *status quo*; maintenance, preservation, conservation, conservatism, *laissez-faire*, rest, sleep, establishment, truce, suspension, settledness (265), perdurability, stability (150).

Phrase: The law of the Medes and Persians.

Verbs: To remain, stay, stop, persist, tarry, hold, last, endure, continue, dwell, bide, abide, maintain, keep, hold on, stand, subsist, live, stand still, outlive, survive.

To let alone, let be.

Phrases: To keep one's footing; to hold one's ground; to stick to one's guns; to stand fast.

Adjectives: Persisting, etc., permanent, established, unchanged, unmodified, unrenewed, unaltered, fixed, settled, unvaried, intact, inviolate, persistent, stagnant, rooted, monotonous, unreversed, conservative, unprogressive, undestroyed, unrepelled, unsuppressed, unfailing, stationary (265), stereotyped, perdurable.

Adverbs: *In statu quo,* for good, finally, at a stand, at a standstill, *uti possidetis.*

Phrases: *J'y suis, j'y reste; plus cela change, plus cela est la même chose; esto perpetua.*

142 CESSATION

Substantives: discontinuance, desistance, quiescence.

Intermission, remission, suspension, interruption, suspense, stand, halt, closure, stop, stoppage, pause, rest, lull, breathing-space, respite, truce, drop, interregnum, abeyance.

Comma, colon, semicolon, period, full stop.

Verbs: To discontinue, cease, desist, break off, leave off, hold, stop, pause, rest, drop, lay aside, give up, have done with, stick, hang fire, pull up, give over, shut down, knock off, relinquish (624), surcease.

To come to a stand, or standstill, suspend, cut short, cast off, go out, be at an end; intromit, interrupt, arrest, intermit, remit; put an end or stop to.

To pass away, go off, pass off, blow over, die away, wear away, wear off (122).

Phrases: To shut up shop; to stay one's hand; to rest on one's oars; to rest on one's laurels.

Interjections: Hold! hold on! stop! enough! avast! *basta!* have done! a truce to! stop it! drop it! cheese it! chuck it! stow it! cut it out!

143 CONTINUANCE in action
Substantives: continuation, perseverance, repetition (104), persistence, run.
Verbs: To continue, persist, go on, keep on, abide, keep, pursue, hold on, run on, follow on, carry on, keep up, uphold, sustain, perpetuate, persevere, keep it up, stick it, peg away, maintain, maintain one's ground, harp upon, repeat (104), take root.
Phrases: To keep the pot boiling; to keep the ball rolling.
Adjectives: Continual, continuous, continuing, etc., uninterrupted, inconvertible, unintermitting, unreversed, unstopped, unrevoked, unvaried, unshifting, perpetual (112).

144 CONVERSION
Substantives: reduction, transmutation, resolution, assimilation; chemistry, alchemy; growth, lapse, progress, becoming; naturalization.

Passage, transit, transition, transmigration, flux, shifting, sliding, running into, etc.; phase, conjugations; convertibility.

Laboratory, alembic, crucible (691).

Convert, pervert, vert, turncoat, renegade, apostate.
Verbs: To be converted into; to become, get, wax, come to turn to, turn into, assume the form of, pass into, slide into, glide into, lapse, shift, run into, fall into, merge into, melt, grow, grow into, open into, resolve itself into, settle into, mature, mellow; assume the form, shape, state, nature, character, etc., of; illapse.

To convert into; to make, render, form, mould, reduce, resolve into; transume (140), fashion, model, remodel, reorganize, shape, modify, transmogrify; assimilate to; reduce to; bring to; refound, re-form, reshape.
Adjectives: Converted into, become, etc., convertible, transitional.
Adverbs: Gradually, *gradatim,* by degrees, step by step, by inches, inch by inch, by little and little, by slow degrees, consecutively, seriatim, *in transitu.*

145 REVERSION
Substantives: return, reconversion, relapse (661), recidivism, atavism, throwback, reaction, recoil (277), backlash, rebound, ricochet, revulsion, alternation (138), inversion, regression (283).

Reinstatement, re-establishment (660).
Phrases: The turning-point; the turn of the tide; *status quo ante bellum.*
Verbs: To revert, turn back, return to, relapse, recoil, rebound, react; to restore (660), to undo, unmake.
Phrase: To turn the tables (719).
Adjectives: Reverting, etc., restored, etc., regressive, retrogressive, atavistic, revulsive, reactionary.
Interjection: As you were!

146 REVOLUTION
Substantives: counter-revolution, revolt, rebellion (742), transilience, jump, leap, plunge, jerk, start, spasm, convulsion, throe, storm, earthquake, catastrophe, cataclysm (173).

Legerdemain, conjuration, sleight of hand, hocus-pocus (545), harlequinade, witchcraft (992).

A revolutionary, revolutionist, counter-revolutionist, deviationist; the red flag.
Verbs: To revolutionize, remodel, recast, refashion, reconstruct.
Adjectives: Revolutionary, radical, extreme, intransigent, catastrophic, cataclysmic.
Adverbs: Root and branch.

147 SUBSTITUTION
Substantives: commutation, supplanting, replacement, supersession, enallage, metonymy, synecdoche, antonomasia.

Thing substituted, substitute (634), succedaneum, makeshift, shift, apology, stand-in, pinch-hitter, locumtenens, representative, proxy; understudy, deputy (759), vice, double, dummy, changeling, scapegoat, stooge; stop-gap, jury-mast, palimpsest, metaphor (521).
Phrase: Borrowing of or robbing Peter to pay Paul.
Verbs: To substitute, put in place of, commute, supplant, cut out, change for, supersede, take over from.

To give place to; to replace.
Phrases: To serve as a substitute, etc.; to do duty for; to stand in the shoes of; to take the place of.
Adjectives: Substituted, etc., vicarious, subdititious, makeshift, provisional.
Adverbs: Instead, in place of, in lieu of, in the room of, *faute de mieux*.

148 INTERCHANGE
Substantives: exchange, commutation, intermutation, reciprocation, transposition, permutation, shuffling, castling (at chess), hocus-pocus, interchangeableness, interchangeability.

Reciprocity (12), retaliation (718), barter (794).
Phrases: A Roland for an Oliver; tit for tat; *quid pro quo*.
Verbs: To interchange, exchange, bandy, transpose, shuffle, change hands, swap, dicker, permute, reciprocate, commute, counterchange.
Phrases: To play at puss in the corner; to play musical chairs; to return the compliment; to give and take; you scratch my back and I'll scratch yours.
Adjectives: Interchanged, etc., reciprocal, mutual, commutative, interchangeable, intercurrent.
Adverbs: In exchange, vice versa.

149 MUTABILITY
Substantives: changeableness, changeability, inconstancy, variableness, mobility, instability, unsteadiness, vacillation, unrest, restlessness, slipperiness, impermanence, fragility, fluctuation, vicissitude, alternation, vibration, oscillation (314), flux, ebbing and flowing, ebbs and flows, ups and downs, fidgets, fidgetiness, fugitiveness, disquiet, disquietude.

A Proteus, chameleon, quicksilver, weathercock, kaleidoscope, harlequin; the moon.
Phrases: April showers; shifting sands; the wheel of fortune; the Cynthia of the minute.
Verbs: To fluctuate, vary, waver, flounder, vibrate, flicker, flit, flitter, shift, shuffle, shake, totter, tremble, vacillate, ebb and flow, turn and turn about, change and change about.

To fade, pass away like a cloud, shadow, or dream.
Adjectives: Mutable, changeable, variable, ever-changing, inconstant, impermanent, unsteady, unstable, protean, proteiform, unfixed, fluctuating, vacillating, shifting, versatile, fickle, wavering, flickering, flitting, restless, erratic, unsettled, mobile, fluttering, oscillating, vibratory, vagrant, wayward, desultory, afloat, alternating, plastic, disquiet, alterable, casual, unballasted, volatile, capricious (608).

Frail, tottering, shaking, shaky, trembling, fugitive, ephemeral, transient (111), fading, fragile, deciduous, slippery, unsettled, irresolute (605), rocky, groggy.

Kaleidoscopic, prismatic, iridescent, opalescent, shot.

Phrases: Unstable as water; changeable as the moon, or as a weathercock; *sic transit gloria mundi*; here to-day and gone to-morrow.

150 IMMUTABILITY

Substantives: Stability, unchangeableness, unchangeability, constancy, permanence, persistence (106), invariableness, durability, steadiness (604), immobility, fixedness, stableness, settledness, stabiliment, firmness, stiffness, anchylosis, solidity, aplomb, ballast, incommutability, insusceptibility, irrevocableness.

Rock, pillar, tower, foundation, fixture.

Phrase: The law of the Medes and Persians.

Verbs: To be permanent, etc. (265), to stand, stand fast, stand pat, remain.

To settle, establish, stablish, perpetuate, fix, set, stabilitate, retain, keep, hold, make sure, nail, clinch, rivet, fasten (43), settle down, set on its legs.

Phrases: To build one's house on a rock; to weather the storm.

Adjectives: Immutable, incommutable, unchangeable, unaltered, unalterable, not to be changed, constant, permanent, invariable, undeviating, stable, durable (265), perennial (110), valid.

Fixed, steadfast, firm, fast, steady, confirmed, immovable, irremovable, rooted, riveted, stablished, established, incontrovertible, stereotyped, indeclinable, settled, stationary, stagnant.

Moored, anchored, at anchor, on a rock, firmly seated, deep-rooted, ineradicable.

Stranded, aground, stuck fast, high and dry.

Indefeasible, irretrievable, intransmutable, irresoluble, irrevocable, irreversible, inextinguishable, irreducible, indissoluble, indissolvable, indestructible, undying, imperishable, indelible, indeciduous, insusceptible of change.

Phrases: *J'y suis, j'y reste; stet*; can the Ethiopian change his skin, or the leopard his spots?

151 EVENTUALITY

Substantives: event, happening, occurrence, incident, affair, transaction, proceeding, fact, matter of fact, phenomenon, advent.

Business, concern, circumstance, particular, casualty, accident, adventure, passage, crisis, episode, pass, emergency, contingency, consequence (154).

The world, life, things, doings, course of things, the course, tide, stream, current, run, etc., of events.

Phrases: Stirring events; the ups and downs of life; a chapter of accidents; the cast of the dice (156).

Verbs: To happen, occur, take place, take effect, come, come of, become of, come about, come off, pass, come to pass, fall, fall out, run, be on foot, fall in, befall, betide, bechance, turn out, go off, prove, eventuate, draw on, turn up, crop up, supervene, survene, issue, arrive, ensue, arise, spring, start, come into existence, fall to one's lot.

To pass off, wear off, blow over.

To experience, meet with, go through, pass through, endure (821), suffer, fare.

Adjectives: Happening, occurring, etc., going on, current, incidental, eventful, stirring, bustling.

Phrase: The plot thickening.

Adverbs: Eventually, in the event of, on foot, on the *tapis*, as it may happen, happen what may, at all events, sink or swim, come what may.

Phrases: In the course of things; in the long run; as the world wags.

152 DESTINY
Substantives: fatality, fate, doom, destination, lot, fortune, star, planet, preordination, predestination, fatalism, inevitableness, kismet, karma, necessity (601), after life, futurity (121).
Phrases: The decrees of fate; the wheel of fortune.
Verbs: To impend, hang over, overhang, be in store, loom, threaten, await, come on, approach, stare one in the face, foreordain, preordain, predestine, doom, must be.
Phrase: To dree one's weird.
Adjectives: About to happen, impending, coming, destined, imminent, inevitable, ineluctable, inexorable, fated, doomed, devoted.
Phrases: On the cards; on the knees of the gods.
Adverbs: Necessarily, inevitably.
Phrases: What must be, must; *che sarà sarà*; 'It is written'; the die is cast.

Section VIII – Causation

153 CAUSE
Substantives: origin, source, principle, element, occasioner, prime mover, *primum mobile,* spring, mainspring, agent, seed, leaven, groundwork, basis (215), fountain, well, fount, fountain-head, spring-head, author (164), parent (166), *fons et origo, raison d'être.*

Pivot, hinge, turning-point, key, lever.

Final cause, proximate cause, immediate cause, ground, reason, the reason why, the why and the wherefore, rationale, occasion, derivation, provenance.

Rudiment, germ, embryo, bud, root, *radix,* radical, etymon, nucleus,

seed, ovum, stem, stock, trunk, taproot.

Nest, cradle, womb, *nidus,* birthplace, hot-bed, forcing-bed.

Causality, origination, causation, production (161), aetiology.

Theories of causation, creationism; evolution, Lamarckism, Darwinism, Spencerism, orthogenesis.
Verbs: To be the cause of, to originate, germinate, give origin to, cause, occasion, give rise to, kindle, suscitate, bring on, bring to pass, give occasion to, produce, bring about, institute, found, lay the foundation of, lie at the root of, procure, draw down, induce, realize, evoke, provoke, elicit, entail, develop, evolve, operate (161).

To conduce, contribute, tend to (176); to determine, decide.
Phrases: To have a hand in; to have a finger in the pie; to open the door to; to be at the bottom of; to sow the seeds of; to turn the scale.
Adjectives: Caused, occasioned, etc., causal, original, primary, primordial, having a common origin, connate, radical, embryonic, embryotic, in embryo.

Evolutionary, Darwinian; aetiological.
Phrase: Behind the scenes.

154 EFFECT
Substantives: consequence, product, result, resultant, resultance, upshot, issue, end (67), fruit, crop, aftermath, harvest, development, outgrowth, derivative, deriva-tion.

Production, produce, work, handiwork, performance, creature, creation, offshoot, fabric, offspring, first-fruits, firstlings, output, *dénouement,* derivation, heredity, evolution (161).
Verbs: To be the effect, work, fruit, result, etc., of; to be owing to, originate in or from, rise from, take its rise from, arise, spring, proceed, evolve, come of, emanate, come, grow, ger-

minate, bud, sprout, stem, issue, flow, result, follow, accrue, etc., from; come to; to come out of, be derived from, be caused by, depend upon, hinge upon, turn upon, result from, to be dependent upon, hang upon; to pan out.
Phrase: To take the consequences.
Adjectives: Owing to, due to, attributable to, ascribable to, resulting from, through, etc., all along of, hereditary, genetic, derivative.
Adverbs: Of course, consequently, necessarily, eventually.
Phrases: *Cela va sans dire*; thereby hangs a tale.

155 ATTRIBUTION
Substantives: theory, aetiology, ascription, reference to, rationale, accounting for, imputation to, derivation from, filiation, affiliation, genealogy, pedigree, paternity, maternity (166), explanation (522), cause (153).
Verbs: To attribute, ascribe, impute, refer to, derive from, lay to, point to, charge on, ground on, invest with, assign as cause, trace to, father upon, account for, theorize, ground, etc.
Phrases: To put the saddle on the right horse; to point out the reason of; to lay at the door of.
Adjectives: Attributable, imputable, assignable, traceable, ascribable, referable, owing to, derivable from.
Putative, attributed, imputed, etc.
Adverbs: Hence, thence, therefore, because, from that cause, for that reason, on that account, owing to, thanks to, forasmuch as, whence, *propter hoc,* wherefore, since, inasmuch as.
Why? wherefore? whence? how comes it? how is it? how happens it? how does it happen?
In some way, somehow, somehow or other, in some such way.
Phrase: *Hinc illae lacrimae.*

156 CHANCE
Substantives: indetermination, acci-

dent, fortune, hazard, hap, haphazard, chance-medley, luck, lot, fate (152), casualty, contingency, adventure, venture, pot-luck, lucky dip, treasure trove, hit.
A lottery, toss-up, game of chance, *sortes Virgiliance, rouge et noir,* heads or tails, gambling (621), sweepstake.
Possibility, probability, odds, long odds, a near shave, bare chance.
Phrases: The turn of the cards; a cast or throw of the dice; a pig in a poke, a blind date.
Verbs: To chance, hap, turn up; to fall to one's lot, to be one's fate (152); to light upon; stumble upon.
To game, gamble, cast lots, raffle, play for.
Phrases: To take one's chance; to toss up for; to chance one's arm; to take a flyer.
Adjectives: Casual, fortuitous, random, accidental, adventitious, causeless, incidental, contingent, uncaused, undertermined, indeterminate, suppositional, possible (470); aleatory.
Adverbs: By chance, by accident, perchance, peradventure, perhaps, maybe, mayhap, haply, possibly.
Casually, etc., at random, at a venture, as it may be, as it may chance, as it may turn up, as it may happen; as chance, luck, fortune, etc., would have it.

157 POWER
Substantives: potentiality, potency, prepotence, prepotency, propollence, puissance, strength (159), might, force, energy, metal, dint, right hand, ascendancy, sway, control, almightiness, ability, ableness, competency, efficiency, effectiveness, efficacy, efficaciousness, validity, cogency, enablement; agency (170), casualty (153), influence (175), authority (737).
Capability, capacity, faculty, quality, attribute, endowment, virtue, gift, property.

Pressure, high pressure, mechanical energy, applied force, motive power.
Verbs: To be powerful, etc., to gain power; to exercise power, sway, etc., to constrain.

To be the property, virtue, attribute, etc., of; to belong to, pertain to, appertain to, to lie or be in one's power.

To give or confer power, to empower, enable, invest, endue, endow, arm, render strong (159).
Adjectives: Powerful, high-powered, potent, puissant, potential, capable, able, equal to, cogent, valid, effective, effectual, efficient, efficacious, adequate, competent.

Forcible, energetic, vigorous, nervous, dynamic, sturdy, rousing, all-powerful, omnipotent, resistless, irresistible, vivid, inextinguishable, sovereign, invincible, unconquerable, indomitable.
Adverbs: Powerfully, etc., by virtue of, in full force.

158 IMPOTENCE
Substantives: inability, disability, disablement, impuissance, weakness (160), imbecility, paralysis, inaptitude, incapacity, incapability, invalidity, inefficacy, inefficiency, inefficaciousness, ineffectualness, disqualification, helplessness, incompetence.
Phrases: A dead letter; waste paper; *brutum fulmen*; blank cartridge.
Verbs: To be impotent, powerless, etc.; to collapse, fail, flunk, break down, fizzle out, fold up.

To render powerless, etc., to deprive of power, disable, disenable, incapacitate, disqualify, unfit, invalidate, nullify, deaden, cripple, cramp, paralyse, muzzle, hamstring, bowl over, render weak (160).
Phrases: To go by the board; to end in smoke.

To clip the wings of; spike the guns; to tie a person's hands; to put a spoke in one's wheel; to take the wind out of one's sails.
Adjectives: Powerless, impotent, unable, incapable, incompetent, inadequate, unequal to, inefficient, inefficacious, inept, ineffectual, ineffective, inoperative, nugatory, incapacitated, harmless, imbecile, disqualified, disabled, armless, disarmed, unarmed, weaponless, defenceless; unnerved, paralysed, palsied, disjointed, nerveless, adynamic, unendowed.
Phrases: Laid on the shelf; *hors de combat*; not having a leg to stand on.

159 STRENGTH
Substantives: energy (171), power (157), vigour, vitality, force, main force, physical force, brute force, spring, elasticity, tone, tension, tonicity.

Stoutness, sturdiness, lustiness, lustihood, stamina, physique, nerve, muscle, thews and sinews, backbone, pith, pithiness.

Feats of strength, athletics, gymnastics.

Strengthening, invigoration, bracing, recruital, recruitment, refreshment, refocillation (689).

Science of forces, dynamics, statics.

Adamant, steel, iron, oak, heart of oak.

An athlete, gymnast, acrobat; an Atlas, a Hercules, Sampson, Cyclops, Goliath.
Phrases: A giant refreshed; a tower of strength.
Verbs: To be strong, etc., to be stronger, to overmatch.

To render strong, etc., to give strength, tone, etc., to strengthen, invigorate, brace, buttress, sustain, fortify, harden, case-harden, steel, gird up, screw up, wind up, set up, tone up.

To reinforce, refit, recruit, vivify, restore (660), refect, refocillate (689).
Phrase: To set on one's legs.
Adjectives: Strong, mighty, vigor-

ous, stout, robust, sturdy, powerful, puissant, hard, adamantine, invincible, able-bodied, athletic, Herculean, muscular, brawny, sinewy, made of iron, strapping, well-set, well-knit, stalwart, doughty, husky, lusty, hardy, irresistible; strengthening, etc., invigorative, tonic.

Manly, manlike, masculine, male, virile, manful, full-blooded.

Unweakened, unallayed, unwithered, unshaken, unworn, unexhausted, unrelaxed, undiluted, unwatered, neat.
Phrases: Made of iron; as strong as a lion, as a horse; in great form; fit as a fiddle.
Adverbs: Strongly, forcibly, etc., by main force, *vi et armis*, by might and main, tooth and nail, hammer and tongs, for all one is worth.

160 WEAKNESS
Substantives: feebleness, impotence (158), debility, atony, relaxation, helplessness, languor, slackness, enervation, nervousness, faintness, languidness, infirmity, emasculation, effeminacy, feminality, femineity, flaccidity, softness, defencelessness.

Childhood, etc. (127, 129); orphan, chicken.

Declension, loss, failure, etc., of strength, invalidation, delicacy, delicateness, decrepitude, asthenia, neurasthenia, anaemia, bloodlessness, palsy, paralysis, exhaustion, collapse, prostration, faintness, cachexy (or cachexia).

A reed, thread, rope of sand, house of cards; a weakling, sissy, jellyfish.
Verbs: To be weak, etc., to droop, fade, faint, swoon, languish, decline, flag, fail, totter, drop, crock; to go by the board.

To render weak, etc., to weaken, enfeeble, debilitate, devitalize, deprive of strength, relax, enervate, unbrace, unman, emasculate, castrate, geld, hamstring, disable, unhinge, cripple,

cramp, paralyse, maim, sprain, exhaust, prostrate, blunt the edge of, deaden, dilute, water, water down.
Adjectives: Weak, feeble, debile, strengthless, nerveless, imbecile, unnerved, relaxed, unstrung, unbraced, enervated, nervous, sinewless, spineless, lustless, effeminate, feminine, womanly, unmanned, emasculated, castrated.

Crippled, maimed, lamed, shattered, broken, frail, fragile, flimsy, gimcrack, halting, shaken, crazy, shaky, paralysed, palsied, paralytic, decrepit, puny, shilpit, drooping, languid, faint, sickly, flagging, dull, slack, limp, spent, effete, weatherbeaten, worn, seedy, exhausted, deadbeat, all in, whacked, done up, languishing, wasted, washy, vincible, untenable, laid low, run down, asthenic, neurasthenic, neurotic, rickety, invertebrate, feckless.

Unstrengthened, unsustained, unsupported, unaided, unassisted, defenceless, indefensible, unfortified, unfriended, fatherless, etc.
Phrases: On one's last legs; the worse for wear; weak as a child, as a baby, as a kitten, as water; good or fit for nothing.

161 PRODUCTION
Substantives: creation, formation, construction, fabrication, manufacture, building, architecture, erection, edification, coinage, organization, putting together, establishment, setting up, performance (729), workmanship, output.

Development, breeding, evolution, flowering, genesis, generation, *epigenesis,* procreation, propagation, fecundation, impregnation, gestation, birth, bringing forth, parturition, growth, proliferation.

Theory of development, Mendelism, eugenics.
Verbs: To produce, effect, perform,

operate, do, make, form, construct, fabricate, frame, contrive, manufacture, weave, forge, coin, carve, sculp, chisel, build, raise, edify, rear, erect, run up, establish.

To constitute, compose, organize, institute, work out, realize, bring to bear, bring to pass, accomplish, bring off.

To create, generate, engender, beget, bring into being, breed, propagate, proliferate, conceive, bear, procreate, give birth to, bring forth, yield, flower, fructify, hatch, develop, bring up.

To induce, superinduce, suscitate (153).

Phrases: To be brought to bed of; to usher into the world.

Adjectives: Produced, etc., producing, productive of, etc., creative, formative, parturient, pregnant, *enceinte,* genetic; eugenic.

Phrase: In the family way.

162 DESTRUCTION

Substantives: waste, dissolution, breaking up, disruption, consumption, disorganization, falling to pieces, crumbling, etc.

Fall, downfall, ruin, perdition, crash, smash, havoc, desolation, *bouleversement, débacle,* upset, wreck, shipwreck, cataclysm, extinction, annihilation; doom, destruction of life (360), prang (716, 732).

Demolition, demolishment, overthrow, subversion, suppression, dismantling, cutting up, corrosion, erosion, crushing, upsetting, abolition, abolishment, sacrifice, immolation, holocaust, dilapidation, devastation, *razzia,* ravaging, extermination, eradication, extirpation, rooting out, averruncation, sweeping, etc., death-blow, *coup de grâce,* the crack of doom.

Verbs: To be destroyed, etc., to perish, waste, fall to pieces, break up, crumble, break down, crack.

To destroy, do or make away with, demolish, overturn, upset, throw down, overthrow, overwhelm, subvert, put an end to, uproot, eradicate, extirpate, root out, grub up, break up, pull down, do for, dish, ditch, crumble, smash, crash, crush, quell, quash, squash, squelch, cut up, shatter, shiver, batter, tear or shake to pieces, tear to tatters, pick to pieces, put down, suppress, strike out, throw or knock down, cut down, knock on the head, stifle, dispel, fell, sink, swamp, scuttle, engulf, submerge, wreck, corrode, erode, consume, sacrifice, immolate, burke, blow down, sweep away, erase, expunge, liquidate, wipe out, mow down, blast.

To waste, lay waste, ravage, dilapidate, dismantle, disorganize, devour, swallow up, desolate, devastate, sap, mine, blow up, stifle, dispatch, exterminate, extinguish, quench, annihilate, kill (361), unroot, root out, rout out, averruncate, deracinate.

Phrases: To go to the dogs, or to pot; to go to the devil, or to rack and ruin; to be all over with one.

To lay the axe at the root of; to make short work of; make a clean sweep of; to make mincemeat of; to scatter to the winds; cut up root and branch; knock on the head; to wipe the floor with; to knock into a cocked hat; to sap the foundations of; to nip in the bud; to strike at the root of; to pluck up by the root; to ravage with fire and sword.

Adjectives: Destroyed, done for, dished, etc.; destructive, subversive, pernicious, ruinous, deadly, indendiary, demolitionary.

163 REPRODUCTION

Substantives: renovation, restoration (660), reconstruction, revival, regeneration, revivication, resuscitation, reanimation, resurrection, resurgence, reappearance, palingenesis, reincarnation, multiplication; phoenix.

Verbs: To reproduce, revive, renew, renovate, rebuild, reconstruct, regenerate, revivify, resurrect, resuscitate, reanimate, reincarnate, quicken; come again into life, reappear.
Phrase: To spring up like a mushroom.
Adjectives: Reproduced, etc., renascent, reappearing; hydra-headed.

164 PRODUCER
Substantives: originator, author, artist, creator, prime mover, founder, workman, doer, performer, manufacturer, forger, agent (690), builder, architect, factor.

165 DESTROYER
Substantives: extinguisher, exterminator, assassin (361), executioner (975), ravager, annihilator, subverter, demolisher; iconoclast, vandal.

166 PATERNITY
Substantives: fatherhood, maternity, motherhood, parentage, parent, father, sire, paterfamilias, pater, dad, daddy, papa, pa; mother, mamma, ma, mummy, mum, dam, materfamilias, mater, procreator, progenitor, begetter, ancestor, ancestry, forefathers, forbears, grandsire; house, parent stem, trunk, stock, pedigree.
Adjectives: Paternal, maternal, parental, fatherly, motherly, family, ancestral, patriarchal.

167 POSTERITY
Substantives: progeny, breed, issue, offspring, brood, seed, litter, spawn, scion, offset, child, son, daughter, grandchild, grandson, granddaughter, etc., bantling, shoot, sprout, sprig, slip, branch, line, lineage, filiation, family, offshoot, ramification, descendant, heir, heiress, heir apparent, heir presumptive.

Straight, descent, sonship, primogeniture, ultimogeniture.

Adjectives: Filial, daughterly, dutiful, lineal, hereditary.
Phrase: A chip off the old block; the rising generation.

168 PRODUCTIVENESS
Substantives: fecundity, fruitfulness, fertility, prolificness; creativeness, inventiveness.

Pregnancy, gestation, pullulation, fructification, multiplication, propagation, procreation.

A milch cow, rabbit, warren, hydra.
Phrase: A land flowing with milk and honey.
Verbs: To procreate (161), multiply, teem, pullulate, fructify, proliferate, generate, fertilize, impregnate, conceive.
Adjectives: Productive, prolific, teeming, fertile, fruitful, luxuriant, fecund, pregnant, great, gravid, *enceinte,* with child, with young.

Procreant, procreative, generative, propagable, life-giving.

169 UNPRODUCTIVENESS
Substantives: infertility, barrenness, sterility, unfruitfulness, unprofitableness, infecundity, fruitlessness (645), non-agency.
Verbs: To be unproductive, etc., to come to nothing.

To render unproductive, sterilize, castrate, spay, pasteurize.
Adjectives: Unproductive, inoperative, barren, addle, infertile, unprolific, sterile, unfruitful, fallow, fruitless, infecund, issueless, unprofitable (645).

170 AGENCY
Substantives: operation, force, working, strain, function, office, hand, intervention, intercession, interposition, exercise, work, swing, play, causation (153), impelling force, mediation (631), action (680).
Modus operandi, quickening power, maintaining power.

Verbs: To be in action, to operate, function, work, act, perform, play, support, sustain, strain, maintain, take effect, quicken, strike, strike hard, strike home, bring to bear.

Phrases: To come into play; to make an impression.

Adjectives: Acting, operating, etc., operative, practical, efficient, efficacious, effectual, in force.

Acted upon, wrought upon.

171 PHYSICAL ENERGY

Substantives: force, power, activity, keenness, intensity, sharpness, pungency, vigour, strength, edge, point, raciness, metal, mettle, vim, dash, fire, punch, go, pep.

Seasoning, mordant, pepper, mustard, cayenne, caviare (392).

Mental energy (604), mental excitation (824), voluntary energy (682).

Exertion, activity, stir, bustle, hustle, agitation, effervescence, fermentation, ferment, ebullition, splutter, perturbation, briskness, voluntary activity (682), quicksilver.

Verbs: To give energy, energize, stimulate, invigorate, kindle, galvanize, electrify, intensify, excite, exert (173).

Adjectives: Strong, energetic, emphatic, forcible, forceful, active, keen, vivid, intense, severe, sharp, acute, pungent, poignant, racy, brisk, ebullient, mettlesome, enterprising, go-ahead, double-edged, double-barrelled, double-distilled, drastic, intensive, trenchant.

Phrases: *Fortiter in re*; with telling effect; with full steam; at high pressure; flat out.

172 PHYSICAL INERTNESS

Substantives: inertia, *vis inertiae,* inertion, passiveness, passivity, inactivity, torpor, latency, torpidity, dullness, stagnation, deadness, heaviness, flatness, slackness, tameness, slowness,

languor, lentor, quiescence (265), sleep (683), intermission (141).

Mental inertness, indecision (605), placidity (826).

Verbs: To be alert, inactive, passive, etc.; to hang fire, smoulder.

Phrase: To sit on the fence.

Adjectives: Inert, inactive, passive, torpid, flaccid, limp, lymphatic, sluggish, dull, heavy, flat, slack, tame, slow, supine, slothful, stagnant, blunt, lifeless, dead.

Latent, dormant, smouldering, unexerted, unstrained, uninfluential.

Adverbs: Inactively, in suspense, in abeyance.

173 VIOLENCE

Substantives: inclemency, vehemence, might, impetuosity, boisterousness, abruptness, ebullition, turbulence, horseplay, bluster, uproar, shindy, row, riot, rumpus, fierceness, rage, wildness, fury, hear, exacerbation, exasperation, malignity, fit, paroxysm, orgasm, force, brute force, *coup de main,* strain, shock, spasm, convulsion, throe.

Outbreak, burst, outburst, dissilience, discharge, volley, explosion, blow-up, blast, detonation, rush, eruption, displosion, torrent.

Turmoil, tumult, storm, tempest, squall, hurricane, tornado, typhoon, cyclone, earthquake, volcano, thunder-storm.

A rowdy (949), berserk (or berserker), spitfire, fireater, hellhound, fury, termagant, virago, vixen, hellcat, dragon, demon, tiger, beldam, Tisiphone, Megaera, Alecto, Maenad.

Verbs: To be violent, etc., to run high, ferment, effervesce, run wild, run riot, run amuck, rush, tear, rush headlong, bluster, rage, rampage, riot, storm, boil, fume, let off steam, foam, wreak, bear down.

To break out, fly out, bounce, go off, explode, displode, fly, fulminate, detonate, blow up, flash, flare, burst, burst out, shock, strain.

To render violent, sharpen, stir up, quicken, excite, incite, stimulate, kindle, lash, suscitate, urge, accelerate, foment, aggravate, exasperate, exacerbate, convulse, infuriate, madden, lash into fury, inflame, let off, discharge.

Phrases: To break the peace; to see red; to out-herod Herod; add fuel to the flame.

Adjectives: Violent, vehement, warm, acute, rough, rude, wild, boisterous, impetuous, ungentle, tough, brusque, abrupt, rampant, knockabout, rampageous, bluff, turbulent, blustering, riotous, rowdy, noisy, thundering, obstreperous, uproarious, outrageous, frantic, phrenetic, headstrong, rumbustious, disorderly (59).

Savage, fierce, ferocious, fiery, fuming, excited, unquelled, unquenched, unextinguished, unrepressed, unbridled, unruly, boiling, boiling over, furious, outrageous, raging, running riot, storming, hysteric, hysterical, wild, running wild, ungovernable, unappeasable, immitigable, uncontrollable, insuppressible, irrepressible, raging, desperate, mad, rabid, infuriate, exasperated.

Tempestuous, stormy, squally, spasmodic, spastic, paroxysmal, convulsive, galvanic, bursting, explosive, detonating, volcanic, meteoric, seismic.

Phrases: Fierce as a tiger; all the fat in the fire.

Adverbs: Violently, etc., by force, by main force, like mad.

Phrases: By might and main; tooth and nail; *vi et armis*; at the point of the sword, or bayonet.

174 MODERATION

Substantives: gentleness, temperateness, calmness, mildness, composure, sobriety, slowness, tameness, quiet (740), restfulness, reason.

Relaxation, remission, measure, golden mean, mitigation, tranquillization, assuagement, soothing, allaying, etc., contemperation, pacification (723), restraint, check (751), lullaby, sedative, lenitive, demulcent, palliative, opiate, anodyne, balm, opium.

Mental calmness (826).

Verbs: To be moderate, etc., to keep within bounds or within compass, to settle down, to keep the peace, to sober down, remit, relent.

To moderate, soften, soothe, mitigate, appease, temper, attemper, contemper, mollify, lenify, tame, dull, take off that edge, blunt, obtund, tone down, subdue.

To tranquillize, assuage, appease, lull, cool, compose, still, calm, quiet, hush, quell, sober, pacify, damp, lay, allay, rebate, slacken, smooth, soften, alleviate, rock to sleep, deaden (376), check, restrain, slake, curb, bridle, rein in, hold in, repress, smother, counteract (179).

Phrases: To pour oil on the waves; to pour balm into; to throw cold water on.

Adjectives: Moderate, gentle, mild, sober, temperate, measured, reasonable, tempered, calm, unruffled, tranquil, smooth, untroubled; unexciting, unirritating, soft, bland, oily, demulcent, lenitive, cool, quiet, anodyne, hypnotic, sedative, peaceful, peaceable, pacific, lenient, tame, halcyon, restful.

Phrases: Gentle as a lamb; mild as milk.

Adverbs: Moderately, gently, temperately, softly, etc.

Phrases: Softly, softly, catchee monkey; *suaviter in modo; est modus in rebus.*

175 INFLUENCE

Substantives: weight, pressure, prevalence, sway, ascendancy (or ascendency), preponderance, predominance, predominancy, dominance, prepotency, importance (642), reign, ableness, capability (157).

Footing, hold, foothold, purchase, fulcrum, stance, *point d'appui, pou sto, locus standi,* leverage, vantage-ground; aegis, protection, patronage, auspices.
Phrases: A tower of strength; a host in himself.
Verbs: To have influence, etc., to have a hold upon, to have a pull, to gain a footing, work upon, take root, take hold, permeate, penetrate, infiltrate, prevail, dominate, predominate, outweigh, overweigh, carry weight, weigh, tell, to bear upon.
Phrases: To be in the ascendant; to cut some ice; to pull wires; to pull the strings; to set the fashion; to have a voice.
Adjectives: Influential, valid, weighty, prevailing, prevalent, dominant, regnant, predominating, predominant, prepotent, ascendant, rife.
Adverbs: With telling effect.

175A Absence of INFLUENCE
Substantives: impotence (158), weakness (160), inertness (172).
Verbs: To have no influence.
Phrase: To cut no ice.
Adjectives: Uninfluential.

176 TENDENCY
Substantives: aptness, proneness, proclivity, conduciveness, bent, bias, quality, inclination, trend, propensity, predisposition, leaning, drift, conducement, temperament, idiosyncrasy, vein, humour, mood.
Verbs: To tend, contribute, conduce, lead, dispose, incline, trend, verge, bend to, affect, carry, promote, redound to, subserve to (644), bid fair to, make for, gravitate towards.
Adjectives: Tending, contributing, conducing, conducive, working towards, calculated to, disposing, inclining, bending, leading, carrying to, subservient, subsidiary (644, 707);

apt, liable, prone, disposed, predisposed.
Adverbs: For, whither, in a fair way to.

177 LIABILITY
Substantives: subjection to, dependence on, exposure to, contingency, possibility (156), susceptivity, susceptibility.
Verbs: To be liable, etc., incur, to lay oneself open to, lie under, expose oneself to, stand a chance, to open a door to.
Phrase: To stick one's neck out.
Adjectives: Liable, apt, prone, subject, open to, incident to, exposed to, dependent on; answerable, accountable, responsible.
Contingent, incidental, possible, casual.
Phrases: Within range of; at the mercy of.

178 CONCURRENCE
Substantives: co-operation, collaboration (709), union, agreement, consent (488), pulling together, alliance; complicity, connivance, collusion.
Voluntary concurrence (709).
Verbs: To concur, co-operate, conspire, agree, conduce, contribute, unite, to pull together, hang together, join forces.
Phrases: To have a hand in; to be in the same boat; to go hand in hand (709).
Adjectives: Concurring, concurrent, conjoined, concomitant, associate, co-operating, conspiring, agreeing, correspondent, conformable, pulling together, etc., of one mind, in alliance with, with one consent, of one mind, with one accord,

179 COUNTERACTION
Substantives: opposition, antagonism, polarity, clashing, etc., collision, contrariety (14), resistance, interference, friction.

Neutralization, nullification, compensation (30).

Reaction, retroaction (277), repercussion, rebound, recoil, ricochet, counterblast.

Check, obstacle, hindrance (706); antidote, counter-irritant, preventive, corrective, remedy (662).

Voluntary counteraction (708).

Verbs: To counteract, oppose, cross, contravene, antagonize, interfere or conflict with, collide with, clash, neutralize, undo, nullify, render null; to militate against, withstand, resist (719), hinder (706), repress, control, curb, check, rein in (174).

To react (277), countervail, counterpoise (30), overpoise.

Adjectives: Counteracting, opposing, etc., counteractive, antagonistic, conflicting, reactionary, recalcitrant, opposite, retroactive, cohibitive, counter, contrary (14).

Adverbs: Counter, notwithstanding, nevertheless, nathless, none the less, yet, still, although, though, albeit, howbeit, maugre, at all events.

But, even, however, in defiance of, in the teeth of, in the face of, in spite of, in despite of (708).

Phrases: For all that; all the same; be that as it may; even so.

CLASS TWO

Words relating to space

Section 1 –
Space in General

180 SPACE
Substantives: extension, extent, expanse, room, scope, range, purview, way, expansion, compass, sweep, play, amplitude, latitude, field, swing, spread, stretch; spare room, headway, elbow-room, freedom, house-room, stowage, roomage, margin.

Open space, void space, vacuity (4), opening, waste, wilderness, moor, moorland, campagna, tundra.

Abyss (198); unlimited space, infinity (105).
Adjectives: Spatial, two-dimensional, three-dimensional.

Spacious, roomy, commodious, extensive, expansive, capacious, ample.

Boundless, unlimited, unbounded, limitless, illimitable, infinite, uncircumscribed, shoreless, trackless, pathless.
Adverbs: Extensively, etc., wherever, everywhere.
Phrases: The length and the breadth of the land; far and near, far and wide; all over; all the world over; from China to Peru; from Land's End to John o' Groat's; in every quarter; in all quarters; in all lands; every hole and corner; here, there, and everywhere; from pole to pole; throughout the world; to the four winds; under the sun.

181 REGION
Substantives: sphere, ground, area, realm, quarter, district, orb, circuit, circle, compartment, domain, tract, department, territory, country, canton, county, shire, township, riding, hundred, parish, bailiwick, province, satrapy, *arrondissement,* commune, enclave, principality, duchy, kingdom, empire, dominion, colony, protectorate, mandate.

Arena, precincts, *enceinte,* walk, patch, plot, paddock, enclosure, field, compound.

Clime, climate, zone, meridian.
Adjectives: Regional, territorial, provincial, parochial, local, etc.

182 PLACE
Substantives: spot, point, nook, corner, recess, hole, niche, compartment, premises, precinct, station, pitch, venue, abode (189).

Indefinite place.
Adverbs: Somewhere, in some place, wherever it may be.

183 SITUATION
Substantives: position, locality, locale, status, latitude and longitude, footing, standing, post, stage, bearings, aspect, orientation, attitude, posture, lie, emplacement.

Place, site, station, pitch, seat, venue, whereabouts, direction, azimuth, etc. (278).

Topography, geography, chorography.

A map, chart, plan (554).
Verbs: To be situated, to lie, to have its seat in.
Adjectives: Local, topical; situate.
Adverbs: *In situ,* here and there, *passim,* whereabouts.

184 LOCATION
Substantives: localization, lodgment, deposition, reposition, stowage, establishment, settlement, fixation, grafting, insertion (300), lading, encampment, billet, installation.

A colony, settlement, cantonment.

A habitation, residence, dwelling (189).

Phrases: *Genius loci*; the spirit of the place.

Verbs: To place, situate, locate, localize, put, lay, set, seat, station, lodge, park, post, install, house, settle, stow, dump, establish, fix, root, plant, graft, stick in, tuck in, insert, wedge in, shelve, pitch, camp, posit, deposit, reposit, cradle, encamp, moor, pack, embed (or imbed), vest, stock, populate, people, colonize, domicile.

To billet on, quarter upon.

To pocket, pouch, put up, bag, load.

To inhabit, reside (186), domesticate, put up at, colonize.

Phrase: To pitch one's tent.

Adjectives: Placed, located, etc., situate, situated, ensconced, nestled, embosomed, housed, moored, rooted, unremoved.

185 DISPLACEMENT
Substantives: dislodgment, eviction, ejectment (297), deportation, extradition, expatriation, banishment, exile.

Removal, remotion, transposition, relegation (270).

Verbs: To displace, dislodge, unhouse, unkennel, break bulk, take off, eject, evict, chuck out, hoof out, expel, etc. (297), extradite, expatriate, banish, exile, relegate, oust, rusticate, ostracize, remove, transfer, transpose, transplant, transport (270), empty, clear, clear out, sweep off, sweep away, do away with, get rid of, root out, disestablish, unpeople, depopulate.

To vacate, leave (293), get out, heave out, bale out, lade out, pour out (297).

Phrase: To make a clean sweep of.
Adjectives: Displaced, etc., unhoused, houseless, homeless, stateless.
Phrase: Like a fish out of water.

186 PRESENCE
Substantives: occupancy, occupation, attendance, whereness.

Diffusion, permeation, pervasion, interpenetration, dissemination (73).

Ubiquity, ubiety, ubiquitousness, omnipresence.

Verbs: To exist in space, to be present, attend, remain.

To occur in a place, lie, stand, occupy, colonize.

To inhabit, dwell, reside, live, abide, sojourn, lodge, nestle, perch, roost, put up at, hang out at, stay at, stop at, squat, hive, burrow, camp, encamp, bivouac, anchor, settle, take up one's quarters, pitch one's tent, get a footing, frequent, haunt, tenant, take root, strike root, revisit.

To fill, pervade, permeate, penetrate, interpenetrate, infiltrate, be diffused through, be disseminated through, overspread, run through.

Adjectives: Present, occupying, inhabiting, etc., moored, at anchor, resident, residentiary, domiciled.

Ubiquitous, omnipresent.

Adverbs: Here, there, where? everywhere, in residence, aboard, on board, at home, afield, etc., on the spot.

Phrases: Here, there, and everywhere; at every turn.

187 ABSENCE
Substantives: non-existence (2), non-residence, non-attendance, alibi, absenteeism.

Emptiness, void, vacuum, voidness, vacuity, vacancy, vacuousness.

An absentee, truant, nobody, nobody on earth.

Verbs: To be absent, not present, etc., vacate, to keep away, to keep out of the way.

Phrases: Make oneself scarce; absent oneself; take oneself off; stay away; play truant; be conspicuous by one's absence.
Adjectives: Absent, not present, away, gone from home, missing, non-resident.

Empty, void, vacant, vacuous, blank, untenanted, tenantless, uninhabited, deserted, devoid, unoccupied, unpeopled.
Phrases: Nowhere to be found; AWOL (absent without leave); *non est inventus*; not a soul; nobody present; the bird being flown.
Adverbs: Without, minus, nowhere, elsewhere, sans.
Phrases: One's back being turned; behind one's back.

188 INHABITANT
Substantives: resident, residentiary, dweller, indweller, occupier, occupant, lodger, boarder, paying guest, inmate, tenant, sojourner, settler, squatter, backwoodsman, national, colonist, denizen, citizen, cit, cockney, townsman, burgess, countryman, villager, cottar, compatriot, garrison, crew, population, people.
Native, indigene, aborigines, autochthones, son of the soil.
A colony, settlement, household.
Newcomer (57).
Adjectives: Indigenous, native, aboriginal, autochthonous, domestic, domiciliated, domesticated, domiciliary.

189 ABODE
Substantives: dwelling, lodging, domicile, residence, address, habitation, berth, seat, lap, sojourn, housing, quarters, accommodation, headquarters, throne, ark, tabernacle.
Nest, nidus, lair, haunt, eyrie (or aerie), den, hole, earth, warren, rookery, hive, habitat, haunt, resort, retreat, nidification, perch, roost.

Bivouac, camp, encampment, cantonment, castrametation, tent, marquee, teepee, igloo.
Cave, cavern, cell, grove, grot, grotto, alcove, bower, arbour, cove, chamber (191).
Home, fatherland, motherland, native land, country, homestead, homestall, fireside, snuggery, hearth, Lares and Penates, household gods, roof, household, housing; 'dulce domum', Blighty.
Building, structure, edifice, fabric, erection, pile, tenement, messuage, farm, farmhouse, steading, grange.
Cot, cabin, hut, shack, chalet, croft, shed, hangar, penthouse, lean-to, booth, stall, hovel, outhouse, barn, kennel, sty, coop, hutch, cage, cote, stable, garage, offices.
House, mansion, villa, flat, flatlet, prefab, maisonnette, cottage, box, lodge, *pied-à-terre,* bungalow, hermitage, summer-house, gazebo, folly, rotunda, tower, temple (1000), château, castle, pavilion, court, hall, palace, kiosk, house-boat.
Inn, hostel, hotel, roadhouse, motel, tavern, caravansery, hospice, rest-house, dak-bungalow, barrack, lodging-house, guest-house, doss-house, lodgings, apartments, diggings, digs.
Hamlet, village, clachan, thorp, dorp, kraal, borough, burgh, municipality, town, city, garden city, metropolis, suburb (227), conurbation, province, country.
Street, place, terrace, parade, road, avenue, row, lane, alley, court, wynd, close, yard, passage, rents, slum; square, polygon, quadrant, circus, crescent, mall, place, piazza, arcade, gardens.
Anchorage, roadstead, dock, basin, wharf, quay, port, harbour, haven.
Adjectives: Urban, civic, metropolitan, municipal, provincial, rural, rustic, countrified; home-like, homy.

190 CONTENTS
Substantives: cargo, lading, filling, stuffing, freight, load, burden, ware (798).

191 RECEPTACLE
Substantives: recipient, receiver, reservatory, compartment (636).

Cell, cellule, loculus, follicle, hole, corner, niche, recess, nook, crypt, stall, pigeon-hole, lodging (189), bed, berth, bunk, doss, etc. (215), store-room, strong-room.

Capsule, vesicle, cyst, bladder, pod.

Stomach, belly, paunch, ventricle, crop, craw, maw, gizzard, bread-basket, kyte, ovary, womb (221).

Pocket, pouch, sporran, fob, sheath, scabbard, socket, bag, sac, sack, wallet, scrip, poke, kit, knapsack, rucksack, haversack, sabretache, satchel, cigar-case, cigarette-case, reticule, powder-box, flapjack, compact, vanity-case, vanity-bag, portfolio, budget.

Chest, box, hutch, coffer, case, casket, caddy, pyx (or pix), caisson, desk, davenport, escritoire, bureau, cabinet, reliquary; trunk, portmanteau, saratoga, grip-sack, grip, bandbox, valise, hold-all, attaché-case, dispatch-case, dispatch-box, writing-case, suit-case, dressing-case, kit-bag, brief-bag, brief-case, gladstone bag, boot, creel, crate, packing-case, snuff-box, mull.

Vessel, vase, bushel, barrel, canister, jar, can, pottle, basket, pannier, corbeille, punnet, hamper, tray, hod.

For liquids: cistern, reservoir, tank, vat, cauldron, barrel, cask, keg, runlet, firkin, kilderkin, demijohn, carboy, amphora, bottle, jar, decanter, carafe, tantalus, ewer, cruse, crock, kit, canteen, flagon, flask, flasket, thermos flask, vacuum flask, stoup, noggin, vial (or phial), cruet, caster, urn, samovar, billy.

Tub, bucket, pail, pot, tankard, beaker, jug, pitcher, mug, noggin, pipkin, gallipot, matrass, receiver, alembic, retort, test-tube, pipette, capsule, kettle, spittoon.

Bowl, basin, jorum, punch-bowl, cup, goblet, chalice, quaich, tumbler, glass, horn, can, pan, pannikin, plate, dish, trencher, tray, salver, patera, calabash, porringer, saucepan, skillet, casserole, tureen, saucer, platter, hod, scuttle, baikie, shovel, trowel, spoon, spatula, ladle.

Closet, cupboard, cellaret, chiffonier, wardrobe, bunker, locker, bin, buffet, press, safe, sideboard, whatnot, drawer, chest of drawers, tallboy, lowboy, till.

Chamber, flat, storey, apartment, room, cabin, bower, office, court, hall, saloon, *salon*, parlour, state-room, presence-chamber, reception-room, drawing-room, sitting-room, living-room, gallery, cabinet, nursery, boudoir, library, study, snuggery, adytum, sanctum, den, phrontistery, lumber-room (636), dormitory, bedroom, dressing-room, refectory, dining-room, breakfast-room, billiard-room, smoking-room, pew, harem, seraglio, zenana.

Attic, loft, garret, cockloft, belfry, cellar, vault, hold, cockpit, ground-floor, *rez-de-chaussée*, basement, kitchen, kitchenette, pantry, scullery, bathroom, lavatory, water-closet, w.c., urinal, latrine, rear, toilet, convenience, comfort station, heads, thunder-box, offices.

Portico, porch, veranda, piazza, stoop, lobby, court, hall, vestibule, foyer, lounge, corridor, loggia, passage, anteroom, antechamber.

Adjectives: Capsular, saccular, sacculate, recipient, ventricular, cystic, vascular, celled, cellular, cellulous, cellulose, camerated, chambered, locular, multilocular, roomed, two-roomed, etc., polygastric, pouched, marsupial.

Section II – Dimensions

192 SIZE

Substantives: magnitude, dimension, bulk, volume, largeness, bigness, greatness (31), expanse, amplitude, mass, massiveness.

Capacity, capaciousness, tonnage (or tunnage), calibre, scantling.

Average size, stock size.

Corpulence, adiposity, obesity, chubbiness, plumpness, *embonpoint*, stoutness, out-size; corporation, flesh and blood, brawn, brawniness.

Hugeness, vastness, enormousness, enormity, immensity, monstrousness, monstrosity; expansion (194), infinity (105).

A giant, Goliath, Brobdingnagian, Antaeus, Gargantua, monster, whale, leviathan, elephant, mammoth, colossus, tun, lump, chunk, bulk, block, boulder, mass, bushel, whacker, thumper, whopper, spanker, behemoth.

A mountain, mound, heap (72).

Phrases: A Triton among the minnows; the lion's share.

Verbs: To be large, etc., to become large (194).

Adjectives: Large, big, great, considerable, bulky, voluminous, ample, massive, massy, capacious, comprehensive, mighty, king-sized.

Corpulent, obese, stout, fat, plump, rotund, buxom, sonsy, lusty, strapping, bouncing, portly, burly, brawny, fleshy, beefy, goodly, in good case, chopping, jolly, chubby, full-grown, chub-faced, lubberly, hulking, unwieldy, lumpish, husky, stalwart.

Squab, dumpy (202), tubby, roly-poly, pursy, blowsy.

Huge, immense, enormous, mighty, unbounded, vast, vasty, amplitudinous, stupendous, inordinate, herculean, thumping, whacking, whopping, spanking, thundering, monstrous, monster; gigantic, giant-like, colossal, titanic, mountainous, elephantine, mammoth, cyclopean, Antaean, Gargantuan, Falstaffian, Brobdingnagian; infinite, unbounded.

Phrases: Large as life; plump as a partridge; fat as a pig; fat as butter; fat as bacon.

193 LITTLENESS

Substantives: smallness (32), minuteness, diminutiveness, exiguity, inextension, puniness, dwarfishness, epitome, duo-decimo, rudiment, microcosm.

Leanness, emaciation, thinness, macilency, flaccidity, meagreness.

A dwarf, runt, pygmy, midget, Lilliputian, chit, bantam, urchin, elf, doll, puppet, skeleton, ghost, spindleshanks, shadow, Tom Thumb, manikin, *homunculus*.

Animalcule, mite, insect, emmet, fly, gnat, midge, shrimp, minnow, worm, grub, tit, tomtit, mouse, small fry, smout, mushroom, pollard, millet-seed, mustard-seed, grain of sand, molehill.

Atom, point, speck, dot, mote, ace, jot, iota, tittle, whit, particle, corpuscle, electron, molecule, monad, granule, grain, crumb, globule, nutshell, minim, drop, droplet, mouthful, thimbleful, sprinkling, dash, suspicion, *soupçon*, minimum, powder (330), driblet, patch, scrap, chip, inch, mathematical point; minutiae.

Phrases: The shadow of a shade; a drop in the ocean; chicken feed; tip of the ice-berg.

Verbs: To be small, etc., to become small, contract (195).

Adjectives: Little, small, minute, diminutive, inconsiderable, exiguous, puny, tiny, wee, weeny, teeny-weeny, petty, mini, minikin, hop-o'-my-thumb, miniature, bijou, *petite*, pygmy, undersized, half-pint, dwarf, stunted, dwarfed, dwarfish, pollard,

Lilliputian; pocket, thumb-nail, portative, portable, duodecimo.

Microscopic, infra-microscopic, evanescent, impalpable, imperceptible, invisible, inappreciable, infinitesimal, homoeopathic, atomic, corpuscular, molecular, rudimentary, rudimental.

Lean, thin, gaunt, meagre, emaciated, lank, macilent, ghostly, starved, starveling, fallen away, scrubby, reduced, shrunk, shrunken, attenuated, extenuated, shrivelled, tabid, flaccid, starved, skinny, wizen wizened, scraggy, lanky, raw-boned, scrawny, spindle-shanked, lantern-jawed (203).

Phrases: In a small compass; in a nutshell; on a small scale.

Worn to a shadow; skin and bone.

194 EXPANSION

Substantives: enlargement, extension, augmentation, increase of size, amplification, ampliation, aggrandisement, spread, increment, growth, development, pullulation, swell, dilatation, rarefaction, turgescence, turgidity, thickening, tumefaction, intumescence, swelling, tumour, diastole, distension, puffing, inflation.

Overgrowth, hypertrophy, overdistension, tympany.

Bulb, knot, knob (249).

Superiority of size.

Verbs: To become larger, to expand, widen, enlarge, extend, grow, increase, swell (202), gather, fill out, deploy, dilate, stretch, largen, spread, mantle, bud, burgeon, shoot, spring up, sprout, germinate, vegetate, pullulate, open, burst forth, put on flesh, outgrow.

To render larger, to expand, aggrandize, etc., distend, develop, open out, broaden, thicken, largen, amplify, tumefy, magnify, rarefy, inflate, puff, blow up, stuff, cram, pad, fill out.

To be larger than, to surpass, exceed, be beyond, cap, overtop (206, 33).

Adjectives: Expanded, enlarged, increased, etc., swelled out, swollen, distended, bulbous; exaggerated, bloated, tumid, turgid, puffy, full-blown, full-grown, full-formed, over-grown, hypertrophied, pot-bellied, swag-bellied, dropsical, oedematous.

Phrase: 'A-swellin' wisibly.'

195 CONTRACTION

Substantives: reduction, diminution, decrease of size, defalcation, lessening, decrement, shrinking, shrivelling, systole, collapse, emaciation, attenuation, tabefaction, tabes, consumption, marasmus, atrophy; hour-glass, neck (203).

Condensation, compression, squeezing.

Inferiority of size.

Corrugation, contractility, astringency.

Verbs: To become smaller, to lessen, diminish, decrease, dwindle, shrink, contract, shrivel, collapse, wither, wilt, lose flesh, wizen, fall away, decay, purse up, waste, wane, ebb, to grow less.

To render smaller, to contract, lessen, etc., draw in, to condense, reduce, clip, compress, constrict, cramp, squeeze, attenuate, chip, drawf, bedwarf, stunt, cut short (201), corrugate, crumple, crush, purse up, pinch (203), deflate.

To be smaller than, to fall short of, not to come up to.

Phrases: To grow 'small by degrees, and beautifully less' (659); to be on the wane; to hide its diminished head.

Adjectives: Contracting, etc., astringent, styptic, tabid, contracted, lessened, etc., shrivelled, wasted, wizened, stunted, waning, ebbing, etc., neap, condensed.

Unexpanded, contractile, compressible.

Phrase: *Multum in parvo.*

196 DISTANCE

Substantives: remoteness, farness, longinquity, elongation, offing, removedness, parallax, reach, span.

Antipodes, outpost, outskirts, aphelion, apogee, horizon.

Separation (44), transference (270).

Diffusion, disperson (73).

Phrases: *Ultima Thule; ne plus ultra*; the uttermost parts of the earth; the back of beyond.

Verbs: To be distant, etc.; to extend to, stretch to, reach to, spread to, go to, get to, stretch away to; outgo, outstep (303); to go to great lengths.

To remain at a distance, keep away, stand off, keep off, keep clear, stand aloof, hold off.

Adjectives: Distant, far, far off, remote, removed, distal, wide of, clear of, yon, yonder, at arm's length, apart, aloof, asunder, ulterior, transalpine, transatlantic, ultramundane, hyperborean, antipodean, hull down.

Inaccessible, un-get-at-able, out of the way, unapproachable, unreachable; incontiguous.

Adverbs: Far, away, far away, afar, off, a long way off, afar off, wide away, aloof, wide of, clear of, out of the way, a great way off, out of reach, abroad.

Apart, asunder, few and far between.

Yonder, farther, beyond, *longo intervallo,* wide apart, poles apart.

Phrases: Far and near; far and wide; over the hills and far away; a far cry to; from end to end; from pole to pole; from Indus to the Pole; from China to Peru; from Dan to Beersheba; to the ends of the earth; out of the sphere of; wide of the mark.

197 NEARNESS

Substantives: nighness, proximity, propinquity, vicinity, vicinage, neighbourhood, adjacency, closeness; perihelion, perigee.

A short distance, a step, an earshot, close quarters, a stone's throw, a hair's breadth, a span, bowshot, gunshot, pistol-shot.

Purlieus, neighbourhood, environs (227), vicinity, *alentours,* suburbs, whereabouts, *banlieue,* borderland.

A bystander, neighbour.

Approach, approximation, appropinquation, appulse (286), junction (43), concentration, convergence (290).

Meeting, *rencontre* (292).

Verbs: To be near, etc., to adjoin, hang about, trench on, border upon, stand by, approximate, tread on the heels of, cling to, clasp, hug, crowd, get near, etc., to aproach (287), to meet (290).

To bring near, to crowd, pack, huddle together.

Adjectives: Near, nigh, close, close at hand, neighbouring, proximate, approximate, adjacent, adjoining, intimate, bordering upon, close upon, hard upon, trenching on, treading on the heels of, verging on, at hand, handy, near the mark, home, at the point of, near run, in touch with, nearish.

Adverbs: Near, nigh, hard by, fast by, close to, next door to, within reach, within call, within hearing, within an ace of, close upon, at hand, on the verge of, near the mark, in the environs, round the corner, at one's door, at one's feet, at one's elbow, at close quarters; within range, pistol-shot, a stone's throw, etc.; cheek by jowl, beside, alongside, at the heels of, at the threshold.

About, hereabouts, thereabouts, in the way, in presence of, in round numbers, approximately, roughly, as good as, *à peu près* (32).

198 INTERVAL

Substantives: interspace (70), break, gap, opening (260), chasm, hiatus, caesura, interstice, lacuna, cleft, fosse, mesh,

crevice, chink, creek, cranny, crack, slit, fissure, scissure, chap, rift, flaw, gash, cut, leak, dike (350), ha-ha, fracture, breach, rent, oscitation, gaping, yawning, pandiculation, insertion (300), pass, gorge, defile, ravine, canyon (or cañon), crevasse, chimney, couloir, *bergschrund,* gulf, gully, gulch, nullah, strait, sound, kyle, frith, furrow (*see* 259).

Thing interposed, go-between, interjacence (228).

Verbs: To separate (44), gape, yawn.

199 CONTIGUITY
Substantives: contact, proximity, apposition, juxtaposition, touching, tangency, tangent, osculation, meeting (292), syzygy, coincidence, register, co-existence, adhesion (46).

Confine, frontier, demarcation, border (233).

Verbs: To be contiguous, etc., to touch, meet, adhere (46), osculate, coincide, register, coexist, join, adjoin, abut on, graze, border, march with.

Adjectives: Contiguous, touching, bordering on, meeting, in contact, conterminous, osculating, osculatory, tangential, proximate.

Phrases: Hand to hand; end to end; tête-à-tête; next door to; with no interval; in juxtaposition, apposition, etc.; in register.

200 LENGTH
Substantives: longitude, span, stretch.

A line, bar, rule, stripe, spoke, radius.

Lengthening, elongation, prolongation, production, producing, protraction, extension, tension, stretching.

Verbs: To be long, etc., to extend to, reach, stretch to.

To render long, lengthen, extend, elongate, prolong, produce, stretch, draw out, protract, spin out, drawl.

Phrase: To drag its slow length along.

Adjectives: Long, longsome, lengthy, tedious, tiresome, wiredrawn, outstretched, lengthened, produced, etc., sesquipedalian, interminable, endless, unending, never-ending, there being no end of.

Linear, lineal, longitudinal, oblong.

Phrases: As long as my arm; as long as to-day and to-morrow.

Adverbs: Lengthwise, longitudinally, in a line, along, from end to end, endways, from stem to stern, fore and aft, from head to foot, from top to toe, cap-à-pie.

201 SHORTNESS
Substantives: brevity, briefness, a span, etc., *see* Smallness (193).

Shortening, abbreviation, abbreviature, abridgment, curtailment, reduction, contraction, compression (195), retrenchment, elision, ellipsis, compendium (596), conciseness (in style) (572).

Verbs: To be short, brief, etc.

To render short, to shorten, curtail, abridge, abbreviate, epitomize, reduce, contract, compress, scrimp, skimp, boil down.

To retrench, cut short, cut down, pare down, whittle down, clip, dock, lop, poll, prune, pollard, crop, bob, shingle, bingle, snub, truncate, cut, hack, hew, foreshorten.

Adjectives: Short, brief, curt, laconic, compendious, compact, stubby, squab, squabby, squat, chunky, stubby, stocky, dumpy, podgy, fubsy, skimpy, stumpy, pug, snub.

Oblate, elliptical.

Concise (572), summary.

202 BREADTH
Substantives: width, latitude, amplitude, diameter, bore, calibre, superficial, extent, expanse.

Thickness, crassitude (192), thickening, expansion, dilatation, etc. (194).
Verbs: To be broad, thick, etc.

To broaden, to swell, dilate, expand, outspread, etc. (194); to thicken, incrassate.

Adjectives: Broad, wide, ample, extended, fan-like, outstretched, etc.

Thick, corpulent, fat (192), squab, squabby, squat, chunky, stubby, stocky, dumpy, podgy, fulsy, thickset.

Phrases: Wide as a church door; thick as a rope.

203 NARROWNESS

Substantives: slenderness, closeness, scantiness, exility, lankness, lankiness, fibrousness.

A line (205), a hair's breadth, a finger's breadth, strip, streak, vein.

Thinness, tenuity, leanness, meagreness.

A shaving, a slip (205), a mere skeleton, a shadow, an anatomy.

A middle constriction, stricture, neck, waist, isthmus, wasp, hourglass, bottle-neck, ridge, ravine, defile, gorge, pass (198).

Narrowing, coarctation, tapering, compression, squeezing, etc. (195).

Phrases: A bag of bones; a living skeleton.

Verbs: To be narrow, etc., to taper, contract, shrink.

To render narrow, etc., to narrow, contract, coarctate, attenuate, constrict, constringe, cramp, pinch, squeeze, compress, tweak, corrugate, warp.

To shave, pare, shear, etc.

Adjectives: Narrow, strait, slender, thin, fine, tenuous, filiform, filamentary, filamentous, fibrous, funicular, capillary, stringy, wiredrawn, finespun anguine, taper, dapper, slim, slight, gracile, scanty, scant, spare, delicate.

Meagre, lean, emaciated, lank, lanky, weedy, rangy, gangling, starveling, attenuated, pinched, skinny, scraggy, gaunt, cadaverous, skin and bone, raw-boned, scrawny, spindle-shanked (193), hatchet-faced, wasp-waisted, herring-gutted, spidery, spindly, reedy.

Phrases: Thin as a lath; thin as a whipping-post; lean as a rake; thin as a thread-paper; thin as a wafer; thin as a shadow.

204 LAYER

Substantives: stratum, bed, zone, substratum, slab, escarpment, floor, flag, stage, course, storey, tier.

Plate, lamina, lamella, sheet, flake, scale, coat, pellicle, membrane, film, slice, shive, cut, shaving, rasher, board, plank, platter, trencher, spatula, leaf.

Stratification, scaliness, a nest of boxes, coats of an onion.

Verbs: To slice, shave, etc.

Adjectives: Lamellar, laminated, lamelliform, laminiferous, scaly, squamous, filmy, membranous, flaky, foliated, foliaceous, stratified, stratiform, tabular, nested.

205 FILAMENT

Substantives: line, fibre, fibril, tendril, hair, gossamer, wire, thread, cord, funicle, rope, yarn, string, twine (45), cilium, gimp.

Strip (51), shred, slip, spill, list, string, band, fillet, fascia, ribbon (or riband); roll, lath, slat, splinter, sliver, shiver, shaving; arborescence (256); strand.

A hair-stroke.

Adjectives: Filamentary, fibrous, hairy, capillary, thread-like, wiry, funicular, stringy.

206 HEIGHT

Substantives: altitude, elevation, eminence, pitch, loftiness, sublimity.

Stature, tallness, procerity, culmination (210).

A giant, grenadier, guardsman, colossus, giraffe.

Alp, mountain, mount, hill, butte, ben, brae, hillock, kopje, monticule, fell, moorland, hummock, knap, knoll, cape, headland, foreland, promontory, ridge, *arète,* peak, pike, uplands, highlands, rising ground, downs, dune, mound, mole, steep, bluff, cliff, crag, vantage-ground, tor, eagle's nest, aerie.

Orography, orology.

Tower, pillar, column, obelisk, monument, steeple, spire, *flèche,* campanile, belfry, minaret, turret, cupola, pilaster, skyscraper.

Pole, pikestaff, maypole, flagstaff, topmast, topgallant mast, crow's nest.

Ceiling, roof, awning, canopy (*see* 210), attic, loft, garret, housetop.

Growth, upgrowth (194).

Verbs: To be high, etc., to tower, soar, ride, beetle, hover, cap, overtop, culminate, overhang, hang over, impend, overlie, bestride, mount, surmount, to cover (222), perch.

To render high, to heighten, exalt (307).

To become high, grow, upgrow, soar, tower, rise (305).

Adjectives: High, elevated, eminent, exalted, lofty, supernal, tall, towering, beetling, soaring, colossal, gigantic (192), Patagonian, culminating, raised, elevated, etc., perched up, hanging (gardens), crowning, coronary.

Upland, moorland, hilly, mountainous, cloud-touching, heaven-kissing, cloud-topt, cloud-capt, Alpine, subalpine, aerial; orographical.

Upper, uppermost (210), topgallant.

Overhanging, impending, incumbent, overlying, superincumbent, supernatant, superimposed, hovering.

Phrases: Tall as a maypole; tall as a steeple; tall as a poplar.

Adverbs: On high, high up, aloft, above, upstairs, overhead, in the clouds, on tiptoe, on stilts, on the shoulders of, over head and ears.

Over, upwards, from top to bottom, from top to toe, from head to foot, cap-à-pie.

Interjection: Excelsior!

207 LOWNESS
Substantives: lowlands, depression, a molehill, recumbency, prostration.

Dwarf, pygmy, bantam, Lilliputian.

Lowlands; molehill.

A ground-floor, basement, cellar, *rez de chaussée* (191), hold.

Verbs: To be low, etc., lie low, grovel, wallow, crouch, slouch, lie flat.

To lower, depress (306), take down a peg, prostrate, subvert.

Adjectives: Low, low-lying, neap, nether, prostrate, flat, level with the ground, grovelling, crouched, crouching, subjacent, underground, underlying, squat.

Adverbs: Under, beneath, underneath, below, down, adown, downstairs, below stairs, over head and ears, downwards, underfoot, at the foot of, underground, at a low ebb.

208 DEPTH
Substantives: deepness, profundity, profoundness, depression, bathos, anti-climax, depth of water, draught.

A hollow, pit, shaft, well, crater, gulf, abyss, abysm, bottomless pit, hell.

Soundings, submersion, plunge, dive (310).

Plummet, lead, sounding-rod, probe; bathymetry.

Bathysphere, diving-bell, caisson, submarine; diver, frogman.

Verbs: To be deep, etc.

To render deep, etc., to deepen, sink, submerge, plunge, dip, dlive (310).

To dig, scoop out, hollow, sink, delve (252).

Adjectives: Deep, deep-seated, profound, sunk, buried, submerged, etc., subaqueous, submarine, subterranean, underground, subterrene, abysmal; bathymetrical, bathymetric.

Bottomless, soundless, fathomless, unfathomed, unsounded, unplumbed, unfathomable.

Phrases: Deep as a well; ankle-deep; breast-deep; chin-deep.

Adverbs: Beyond one's depth, out of one's depth, underground.

Phrases: Over head and ears; to Davy Jones's locker; in the bowels of the earth.

209 SHALLOWNESS

Substantives: shoaliness, shoals.

Adjectives: Shallow, skin-deep, superficial, shoaly.

210 SUMMIT

Substantives: top, vertex, apex, zenith, pinnacle, acme, climax, culminating, point, apogee, pitch, meridian, sky, pole, watershed.

Tip, tiptop, crest, crow's nest, mast-head, truck, peak, turning-point, pole.

Crown, brow, nib, head, nob, noddle, pate.

Capital, cornice, sconce, architrave, pediment, entablature, frieze.

Roof, ceiling, thatch, tiling, slating, awning, canopy (222).

Adjectives: Top, topmost, upper-most, tiptop, culminating, meridian, capital, head, polar, supreme, crowning, coronary.

Phrase: At the top of the tree.

211 BASE

Substantives: basement, plinth, foundation, substratum, ground, earth, pavement, floor, paving, flag, ground floor, deck, substructure, infrastructure, footing, groundwork.

The bottom, rock-bottom, nadir, foot, sole, toe, root, keel.

Dado, wainscot, skirting-board.

Adjectives: Bottom, undermost, nethermost, fundamental, basic.

212 VERTICALITY

Substantives: erectness, uprightness, perpendicularity, aplomb, right angle, normal, plummet, plumb-line, azimuth, circle.

Wall, precipice, cliff.

Erection, raising, rearing.

Verbs: To be vertical, etc., to stand up, to stand on end, to stand erect, to stand upright, to stick up.

To render vertical, to set up, stick up, erect, rear, raise up, cock up, prick up, raise on its legs.

Adjectives: Vertical, upright, erect, perpendicular, sheer, normal, straight, standing up, etc., up on end, bolt upright, rampant.

Adverbs: Up, vertically, etc., on end, up on end, endways, endwise.

Phrase: Straight up and down.

213 HORIZONTALITY

Substantives: a level, plane, dead level, flatness (251).

Recumbency, lying, lying down, reclination, decumbence, decumbency, supination, resupination, prostration; spirit-level.

A plain, floor, level, flat, platform, bowling-green, billiard-table, plateau, terrace, estrade, esplanande, parterre, table-land (204, 215).

Verbs: To be horizontal, recumbent, etc., to lie, recline, lie down, couch, sit down, squat, lie flat, lie prostrate, sprawl, loll.

To render horizontal, etc., to lay, lay down, lay out, level, flatten, prostrate, knock down, fell, floor.

Adjectives: Horizontal, level, plane, flat, even, discoid.

Recumbent, decumbent, lying, prone, supine, couchant, couching, jacent, prostrate, squat, squatting, sitting, reclining.

Adverbs: Horizontally, etc., on one's back, on all fours, on one's hunkers.

Phrase: Like a millpond.

117

214 PENDENCY

Substantives: dependency, suspension, hanging.

A pendant, pedicel, peduncle, tail, train, flap, skirt, plait, pigtail, queue, tassel, earring, pendulum.

A peg, knob, button, stud, hook, nail, ring, fastener, zipper, clip, staple, knot (45), tenterhook.

Verbs: To be pendant, etc., to hang, swing, dangle, swag, daggle, flap, trail.

To suspend, append, hang, sling, hook up, hitch, fasten to.

Adjectives: Pendant, pendulous, pensile, hanging, dependent, swinging, etc., suspended, etc., loose, flowing, caudal.

Having a peduncle, etc., pedunculate, tailed, caudate.

Adverbs: Dingle-dangle.

Phrase: In the air.

215 SUPPORT

Substantives: ground, foundation, base, basis, *terra firma*, fulcrum, foothold, toehold, *point d'appui, pou sto, locus standi*, landing, landing-place, resting-place, ground-work, substratum, floor, bed, stall, berth, lap, mount.

A supporter, prop, stand, strut, stray, shore, boom, yard, outrigger, truss, sleeper, staff, stick, walking-stick, crutch, stirrups, stilts alpenstock, baton, anvil.

Post pillar, shaft, column, buttress, pedicle, pedestal, plinth (211), baluster, banister.

A frame, framework, scaffold, scaffolding, skeleton, cadre, beam, rafter, lintel, joist, jamb, mullion, cornerstone, stanchion, summer, girder, cantilever, sponson, tie-beam (45), columella, backbone, keystone, axle, axle-tree, axis, fuselage, chassis.

A board, form, ledge, platform, floor, stage, shelf, hob, bracket, arbor, rack, mantel, mantelpiece, mantel-shelf, counter, slab, console, dresser, flange, corbel, table, trestle, shoulder, perch, truss, horse, easel, desk.

A seat, throne, dais, divan, musnud, chair, arm-chair, easy-chair, *chaise longue,* hammock-chair, deck-chair, bench, sofa, davenport, lounge, settee, chesterfield, couch, *fauteuil,* stool, tripod, footstool, *tabouret,* trivet, woolsack, ottoman, settle, squab, bench, saddle, pillion, dicky, hassock, pouffe, cushion, howdah.

Bed, bedstead, chair-bedstead, bedding, pillow, bolster, mattress, shakedown, tester, pallet, hammock, bunk, stretcher, crib, cradle, cot, palliasse, donkey's breakfast, sleeping-bag, flea-bag.

Atlas, Persides, Atlantes, Caryatides, Hercules, Yggdrasil.

Verbs: To be supported, etc., to lie, sit, recline, lean, loll, lounge, abut, bear, rest, stand, step, repose, etc., on, be based on, bestride, straddle, bestraddle.

To support, bear, carry, hold, sustain, shoulder, uphold, hold on, upbear, prop, underprop, shore up, underpin, bolster up, pillow.

To give, furnish, afford, supply, lend, etc., support on foundations; to bottom, found, ground, base, embed.

Adjectives: Supported, etc., astride, astraddle; fundamental, basic.

216 PARALLELISM

Substantives: coextension.

Verbs: To be parallel, etc.

Adjectives: Parallel, coextensive.

Adverbs: Alongside, abreast, beside.

Phrases: Side by side; cheek by jowl.

217 OBLIQUITY

Substantives: inclination, slope, leaning, slant, crookedness, bias, bend, bevel, tilt, list, dip, swag, cant, lurch, skew, skewness, bevelling, squint.

Acclivity, uphill, rise, ascent, gradient, rising ground, bank, ramp.

Declivity, downhill, fall, devexity.

A gentle or rapid slope, easy ascent or descent, chute, helter-skelter, switchback, *montagnes russes*.

Steepness, precipitousness, cliff, precipice, talus, scarp, escarp, escarpment; measure of inclination, clinometer.

Diagonal, zigzag, distortion, hypotenuse, angle (244).

Phrase: The leaning tower of Pisa.

Verbs: To be or render oblique, etc., to slope, slant, tilt, lean, incline, shelve, stoop, descend, bend, heel, careen, sag, swag, slouch, cant, sidle, skew, scarp, escarp, bevel, distort.

Adjectives: Oblique, inclined, leaning, recumbent, sloping, shelving, skew, askew, skew-whiff, slant, aslant, slanting, slantendicular, plagioclastic, indirect, distorted, wry, awry, ajee, drawn, crooked, canted, tilted, biased, saggy, bevel, slouched, slouching, etc., out of the perpendicular, backhanded.

Uphill, rising, ascending, acclivitous.

Downhill, falling, descending, declining, declivitous, anticlinal.

Steep, abrupt, precipitous, breakneck.

Diagonal, transverse, athwart, transversal, antiparallel.

Adverbs: Obliquely, etc., on one side, askew, edgewise, askant, askance, sideways, aslope, slopewise, all on one side, crinkum-crankum, asquint, at an angle.

Phrase: *Facilis descensus Averni.*

218 INVERSION

Substantives: contraposition, overturn, somersault (or somerset), *culbute,* subversion, retroversion, reversion, reversal, introversion, eversion, transposition, pronation and supination.

Anastrophe, metathesis, hysteron, proteron, spoonerism, palindrome.

Verbs: To be inverted, etc., to turn turtle, loop the loop, bunt.

To render inverted, etc., to invert, reverse, upset, overset, overturn, turn over, upturn, subvert, retrovert, transpose, turn topsy-turvy, tilt over, *culbuter,* keel over, topple over, capsize.

Adjectives: Inverted, inverse, upside down, topsy-turvy, top-heavy.

Adverbs: Inversely, topsy-turvy, etc., inside out.

Phrases: To turn the tables; to put the cart before the horse; to the right about; bottom upwards; head over heels; the wrong side up; base over apex.

219 CROSSING

Substantives: intersection, decussation, transversion, convolution.

Reticulation, network, inosculation, anastomosis, interweaving, twining, intertwining, matting, plaiting, interdigitation, mortise (or mortice).

Net, knot, plexus, web, mesh, twill, skein, hank, felt, lace, tulle, wattle, wicker, basket-work, basketry, mat, matting, plait, trellis, lattice, grille, *cancelli,* grid, griddle, grating, gridiron, tracery, fretwork, filigree, reticle, diaper.

Cross, chain, wreath, braid, cat's cradle, dovetail, Greek cross, Latin cross, Maltese cross, cross of St. Anthony, St. Andrew's cross, cross of Lorraine, swastika, fylfot.

Verbs: To cross, lace, intersect, decussate, interlace, intertwine, intertwist, pleach, plash, entwine, enlace, enmesh, weave, interweave, inweave, twine, twist, wreathe, interdigitate, interlock, anastomose, inosculate, dovetail, splice (43).

To mat, plait, plat, braid, felt, twill, tangle, entangle, ravel, net, knot (43), dishevel, raddle.

Adjectives: Crossing, intersecting, etc., crossed, intersected, matted, etc., crucial, cruciform.

Retiform, reticulate, areolar,

areolate, cancellated, grated, barred, streaked, traceried.
Adverbs: Across, thwart, athwart, transversely, crosswise.

220 EXTERIORITY
Substantives: externality, outness, outside, exterior, surface, superficies, superstratum, eccentricity, extremity, frontage.
Disk, face, facet, front (234), skin (222).
Verbs: To be exterior, etc.
To place exteriorly, or outwardly, to turn out.
Adjectives: Exterior, external, outer, outward, outlying, outdoor, outside, extramural, superficial, skin-deep, frontal, discoid, eccentric, extrinsic.
Adverbs: Externally, etc., out, without, outwards, outdoors, abroad.
Phrases: Out of doors; *extra muros; ab extra*; in the open air; *sub Jove; à la belle étoile*; al fresco.

221 INTERIORITY
Substantives: inside, interior, hinterland, backblocks, interspace, substratum, subsoil.
Vitals, viscera, pith, marrow, heart, bosom, breast, entrails, bowels, belly, intestines, guts, inwards, womb, lap, backbone, *penetralia,* inmost recesses, cave, cavern (191).
Verbs: To be interior, internal, within, etc.
To place or keep within, to enclose, circumscribe (*see* 231, 232).
Adjectives: Interior, internal, inner, inside, intramural, inward, inlying, inmost, innermost, deep-seated, intestine, intestinal, splanchnic, intercostal, inland, interstitial, subcutaneous, intrinsic.
Home, domestic, indoor.
Adverbs: Internally, inwards, inwardly, within, inly, therein, *ab intra,* withinside, indoors, within doors, ben, at home, *chez soi,* up country.

222 COVERING
Substantives: cover, roof, ceiling, slates, tiles, thatch, cowling, canopy, baldachin, awning, tarpaulin, tilt, tent (189), lid, hatch, operculum (263), shed.
Integument, skin, tegument, pellicle, fleece, cuticle, scarf-skin, epidermis, hide, pelt, peel, crust, bark, rind, cortex, husk, scale, shell, carapace, capsule, coat, tunic, tunicle, sheath, case, casing, calyx, theca, sheathing, scabbard, wrapping, wrapper, envelope, tarpaulin, cloth, table-cloth, blanket, rug, quilt, eiderdown, coverlet (or coverlid), counterpane, carpet, drugget, oilcloth, wax-cloth, linoleum.
Superposition, coating, facing, veneer, paint, enamel, varnish, anointing, inunction, incrustation, plaster, stucco, wash, parget, patina.
Verbs: To cover, superpose, superimpose, overspread, over-canopy, wrap, lap, overlap, face, case, encase, veneer, pave, upholster.
To coat, paint, enamel, varnish, pave, plaster, beplaster, daub, bedaub, encrust, stucco, dab, smear, besmear, anoint, spray, do over, gild, japan, lacquer (or lacker), plate, electroplate, parget.
Phrase: To lay it on thick.
Adjectives: Covering, etc., cutaneous, dermal, cortical, cuticular, tegumentary, skinny, scaly, squamous, imbricated, epidermal, loricated, armour-plated, iron-clad.

223 CENTRALITY
Substantives: centre (68), middle, focus, epicentre, hub, core, kernel, marrow, pith, nucleus, nucleolus, heart, pole, axis, bull's-eye, nave, navel, umbilicus, omphalos; concentration, centralization.
Verbs: To be central, etc.
To render central, centralize, concentrate.

To bring to a focus.
Adjectives: Central, centrical, middle, middlemost, midmost, median, azygous, axial, focal, umbilical, concentric.
Adverbs: Midway, centrally, etc.

224 LINING
Substantives: coating, facing, internal incrustation, puddle, stalactite, stalagmite, wainscot, dado, wall.
Filling, stuffing, wadding, padding.
Verbs: To line, encrust, stuff, pad, wad, face, puddle, bush.
Adjectives: Lined, encrusted, etc.

225 INVESTMENT
Substantives: dress, clothing, raiment, drapery, costume, attire, toilet, trim, rig, rig-out, fig, habiliment, vesture, apparel, underwear, full dress, evening dress, soup-and-fish, glad rags, dinner-jacket, tuxedo, fancy dress, accoutrement, outfit, wardrobe, trousseau, uniform, regimentals, battle-dress, kit, equipment, livery, gear, harness, turn-out, caparison, suit, dress suit, lounge suit, bathing suit, swim-suit, tweeds, flannels, rigging, trappings, slops, traps, duds, togs, clobber, frippery, bloomers, haberdashery, housing.
Dishabille, morning dress, dressing-gown, undress, mufti, civvies, rags, *négligé,* tea-gown.
Clothes, garment, garb, garniture, vestment, pontificals, robe, tunic, caftan, paletot, habit, gown, coat, dress-coat, claw-hammer, frock, stole, blouse, shirt-waist, toga, haik, smock-frock, kimono, bikini.
Cloak, opera-cloak, cape, mantle, mantlet, dolman, shawl, wrap, wrapper, veil, fichu, yashmak, tippet, kirtle, plaid, mantilla, tabard, burnous, overcoat, great-coat, British warm, duffle coat, surtout, spencer, rain-coat, ulster, mackintosh, water-proof, oil-skin, slicker, burberry, poncho, surplice, alb, cassock, pallium, etc., mask, domino, cardinal, pelerine.
Jacket, vest, under-vest, semmit, singlet, jerkin, lumberjacket, waist-coat, cardigan, sweater, jersey, pull-over, slipover, jumper, windbreaker, windcheater, doublet, gaberdine, camisole, combinations, stays, corset, bodice, under-bodice, brassière, bra, corsage, cestus, petticoat, kilt, filibeg (or philibeg), stomacher, skirt, kirtle, crinoline, farthingale, underskirt, slip, apron, pinafore.
Trousers, trews, breeches, galligaskins, knickerbockers, plus-fours, knickers, drawers, scanties, pantaloons, pants, overalls, dungarees, boiler suit, rompers, unmentionables, inexpressibles, smalls, tights, bags, breeks, slacks, shorts, jeans, briefs.
Cap, hat, top-hat, silk hat, tile, bowler, panama, slouch-hat, trilby, Stetson, titfer, deerstalker, billycock, wide-awake, sou'wester, beaver, castor, bonnet, forage-cap, tam-o'-shanter, tammy, balmoral, glengarry, toque, sun-bonnet, hood, head-gear, head-dress, kerchief, scarf, muffler, comforter, boa, snood, coiffure, coif, skull-cap, calotte, biretta, cowl, chaplet, capote, calash, pelt, wig, peruke, periwig, toupee, transformation, chignon, turban, puggaree, fez, helmet, topi, shako, busby, képi, casque, beret.
Shirt, smock, shift, chemise, chemisette, nightshirt, nightgown, nightdress, pyjamas, bed-jacket, bed-gown, collar, cravat, neck-cloth, neck-tie, stock, handkerchief.
Shoe, pump, high-low, Oxford shoe, sabot, brogue, sand-shoe, plimsoll, rubbers, sneakers, boot, jack-boot, top-boot, Wellington, gum-boot, slipper, mule, galosh, overshoe, legging, puttee, buskin, greaves, mocassin, gaiter, spatterdash, spat, stocking, sock, nylons, hose, sandal, clog, babouche.
Glove, gauntlet, mitten, sleeve, cuff, muff.

Outfitter, tailor, clothier, milliner, sempstress, costumier, hatter, hosier, shoemaker, cobbler.

Verbs: To invest, cover, envelop, lap, involve, drape, enwrap, wrap up, lap up, sheathe, vest, clothe, array, enrobe, dress, dight, attire, apparel, accoutre, trick out, rig, fit out, fig out, caparison, adonize, dandify, titivate, don, put on, wear, have on, huddle on, slip on, roll up in, muffle, perk up, mantle, swathe, swaddle, equip, harness.

Adjectives: Invested, clothed, arrayed, dight, etc., clad, shod, etc.; sartorial.

226 DIVESTMENT

Substantives: nudity, bareness, nakedness, baldness, undress, dishabille, threadbareness.

Denuding, denudation, stripping, uncovering, decortication, peeling, flaying, excoriation, desquamation, moulting, exfoliation.

Verbs: To divest, uncover, denude, bare, strip, unclothe, undress, unrobe, disrobe, disapparel, debag, disarray, take off, doff, cast off, peel, pare, decorticate, husk, uncoif, unbonnet, excoriate, skin, flay, expose, exfoliate, lay open, dismantle, unroof, uncase, unsheathe, moult, mew.

Adjectives: Bare, naked, nude, stripped, denuded, undressed, unclothed, unclad, undraped, uncovered, unshod, barefoot, bareheaded, unbonneted, exposed, in dishabille, in buff, bald, threadbare, ragged, callow, roofless.

Phrases: In a state of nature; stark-naked; *in puris naturalibus*; stripped to the buff; in one's birthday suit; bald as a coot; as bare as the back of one's hand; out at elbows.

227 CIRCUMJACENCE

Substantives: circumambiency, encompassment, surroundings, environment, atmosphere, medium, setting,

scene, outpost, skirt, outskirts, boulevards, suburbs, suburbia, rurbania, purlieus, precincts, faubourgs, environs, entourage, *banlieue*, green belt.

Verbs: To lie around, surround, beset, set about, compass, encompass, environ, enclose, encircle, embrace, lap, gird, begird, engirdle, orb, enlace, skirt, twine round, hem in (231).

Adjectives: Circumjacent, ambient, circumambient, surrounding, etc., circumfluent, circumferential, suburban, extramural, embosomed.

Adverbs: Around, about, without, on every side, on all sides, right and left, all around, round about.

228 INTERJACENCE

Substantives: interlocation, intervention, insertion, interposition, interspersion, interpenetration, interdigitation, interpolation, interlineation, intercurrence, intrusion, obtrusion, insinuation, intercalation, insertion, intertwinement, interference, permeation, infiltration.

An intermedium, intermediary, a go-between, bodkin, intruder, interloper; interlude, episode; parenthesis, gag, flyleaf, *entresol* (68).

A partition, septum, panel, diaphragm, midriff, party-wall.

A half-way house, no-man's-land.

Verbs: To lie, come, or get between, intervene, intrude, butt in, slide in, permeate, put between, put in, interpose, interject, chip in, throw in, wedge in, thrust in, foist in, insert, intercalate, interpolate, parenthesize, interline, interleave, interlard, interdigitate, dovetail, sandwich, worm in, insinuate, obtrude (300), intersperse, infiltrate; to gag.

Phrases: To put one's oar in; to stick one's nose into; to have a finger in the pie.

Adjectives: Interjacent, intervening, etc., intermediary, intermediate, intercalary, interstitial, parenthetical, mediterranean.

Adverbs: Between, betwixt, 'twixt, among, amongst, amid, amidst, midst, betwixt and between, sandwich-wise. parenthetically, between the lines, in the thick of.

229 OUTLINE

Substantives: circumference, perimeter, periphery, ambit, circuit, lines, tournure, contour, profile, silhouette, sky-line.

Zone, belt, girth, band, baldric, zodiac, cordon, girdle, cingulum, clasp (247).

230 EDGE

Substantives: verge, brink, brow, brim, margin, marge, border, skirt, rim, side, mouth, jaws, lip, muzzle, door, porch, portal (260), kerb; shore, coast.

Frame, flounce, frill, ruffle, jabot, list, fringe, valance, edging, trimming, hem, selvedge, welt, furbelow.

Verbs: To border, edge, skirt, coast, verge on.

Adjectives: Border, marginal, coastal, skirting.

231 CIRCUMSCRIPTION

Substantives: limitation, enclosure, confinement, shutting up, circumvallation, entombment.

Imprisonment, incarceration (751).

Verbs: To circumscribe, limit, delimit, localize, bound, confine, enclose, surround (227), compass about, impound, restrict, restrain (751), shut in , shut up, lock up, bottle up, dam, hem in, hedge in, wall in, rail in, fence, picket, pen, enfold, coop, corral, encage, cage, mew, entomb, bury, immure, encase, pack up, seal up, wrap up (225), etc.

Adjectives: Circumscribed, etc., imprisoned, pent up (754), landlocked.

Phrase: Not room to swing a cat.

232 ENCLOSURE

Substantives: envelope, case, box (191), pen, penfold, fold, sheep-fold, pound, paddock, enclave, *enceinte,* corral, ring fence, wall, hedge, hedgerow, espalier, exclosure, play-pen.

Barrier, bar, gate, gateway, door, barricade, cordon.

Dike (or dyke), ditch, fosse, moat.

Fence, pale, paling, balustrade, rail, railing, hurdle, palisade, battlement, rampart, embankment, breakwater, mole, groyne (717), circumvallation, contravallation.

233 LIMIT

Substantives: boundary, bounds, confine, term, bourne, line of demarcation, termination, stint, frontier, border, precinct, marches, line of circumvallation, pillars of Hercules, Rubicon, turning-point, last word, *ne plus ultra.*

Adjectives: Definite, conterminal, terminal, frontier.

Phrases: To cross the Rubicon; thus far and no farther.

234 FRONT

Substantives: face, anteriority, forepart, front rank, foreground, van, vanguard, advanced guard, outpost, proscenium, façade, frontage, foreword, preface, frontispiece (64).

Forehead, visage, physiognomy, phiz, countenance, mug, dial, puss, pan, beak, rostrum, bow, stem, prow.

Pioneer, avant-courier (64).

(In a medal) obverse; (in a coin) head.

Verbs: To be in front, etc., to front, face, envisage, confront, bend forward, etc.

Adjectives: Fore, anterior, front, frontal, facial.

Adverbs: Before, in front, ahead, right ahead, in the van, foremost, vis-à-vis, in the foreground, face to face, before one's eyes.

235 REAR
Substantives: back, posteriority, the rear rank, rearguard, the background, heels, tail, scut, rump, croup, crupper, breech, backside, posterior, fanny, catastrophe, buttocks, haunches, hunkers, hurdies, hind quarters, *dorsum*, dorsal region, stern, poop, after-part, tailpiece, wake.

(In a medal) reverse; (in a coin) tail.
Verbs: To be in the rear, behind, etc., to fall astern, to bend backwards, to back on.
Phrases: Turn the back upon; bring up the rear.
Adjectives: Back, rear, postern, hind, hinder, hindmost, sternmost, posterior, dorsal, after.
Adverbs: Behind, in the rear, aft, abaft, astern, aback, rearward.
Phrases: In the background; behind one's back; at the heels of; at the tail of; at the back of; back to back.

236 LATERALITY
Substantives: side, flank, quarter, hand, cheek, jowl, wing, profile, temple, loin, haunch, hip, broadside, lee-side, lee.

East, orient; West, occident.
Verbs: To be on one side, etc., to flank, outflank, to sidle, skirt.
Adjectives: Lateral, sidelong, collateral, sideling, bilateral, trilateral, quadrilateral, multilateral, many-sided, eastern, oriental, western, occidental, eastward, westward.
Adverbs: Sideways, side by side (216), sidelong, abreast, abeam, alongside, aside, by the side of, to windward, to leeward.
Phrases: Cheek by jowl; broadside on.

237 ANTIPOSITION
Substantives: opposite side, contraposition, reverse, inverse, antipodes, opposition, inversion (218).

Polarity, opposite poles, North and South.

Verbs: To be opposite, etc., subtend.
Adjectives: Opposite, reverse, inverse, antipodal, subcontrary.

Fronting, facing, diametrically opposite, vis-à-vis.

Northern, boreal, septentrional, arctic; southern, austral, antarctic.
Adverbs: Over, over the way, over against, facing, against, fronting (234), face to face, vis-à-vis.

238 DEXTRALITY
Substantives: right, right hand, dexter, offside, starboard, recto.
Adjectives: Dextral, right-handed; ambidextrous, ambidexter.

239 SINISTRALITY
Substantives: left, left hand, sinister, near side, port, larboard, verso.
Adjectives: Sinistral, left-handed.

Section III – Form

240 FORM
Substantives: figure, shape, configuration, make, formation, frame, construction, conformation, cut, set, trim, build, make, stamp, cast, mould, fashion, structure.

Feature, lineament, phase (448), turn, attitude, posture, pose.

Morphology, isomorphism.

Formation, figuration, efformation, sculpture.
Phrase: The cut of one's jib.
Verbs: To form, shape, figure, fashion, carve, cut, chisel, chase, emboss, hew, rough-hew, cast, rough-cast, hammer out, block out, trim, work, lick into shape, knock together, mould, sculpture, sculp, grave, stamp.
Adjectives: Formed, graven, etc., receiving form, plastic, fictile.

Giving form, formative, plastic, plasmatic, plasmic.

241 AMORPHISM

Substantives: amorphousness, formlessness, shapelessness, disfigurement, defacement, mutilation (846).

Vandalism, vandal, Goth.

Verbs: To destroy form, deform, deface, disfigure, disfeature (846), mutilate.

Adjectives: Shapeless, amorphous, formless, unhewn, rough, rude, Gothic, unfashioned, unshapen, misshapen, inchoate.

242 SYMMETRY

Substantives: shapeliness, eurhythmy, uniformity, finish, beauty (845), proportion, balance.

Adjectives: Symmetrical, regular, shapely, eurhythmic, well-set, uniform, finished, well-proportioned, balanced, chaste, classic.

Phrase: *Teres atque rotundus.*

243 DISTORTION

Substantives: twist, kink, wryness, asymmetry, gibbosity, contortion, malformation, ugliness, etc. (846), teratology.

Verbs: To distort, twist, wrest, writhe, wring, contort, kink, buckle.

Adjectives: Irregular, unsymmetrical, asymmetrical, distorted, twisted, wry, awry, askew, crooked, on one side, misshapen, deformed, ill-proprtioned, ill-made, round-shouldered, pigeon-chested, humpbacked, hunchbacked, gibbous, gibbose; knock-kneed, bandy-legged, bow-legged, club-footed, splay-footed.

Phrases: All manner of ways; all over the place.

244 ANGULARITY

Substantives: angulation, angle, cusp, bend, elbow, knee, knuckle, groin, crinkle-crankle, kink, crotch, crutch, crane, fluke, scythe, sickle, zigzag, anfractuosity, refraction; fold (258), corner (182).

Fork, bifurcation, dichotomy.

Right angle (212), salient angle, re-entrant angle, acute angle, obtuse angle.

A polygon, square, rectangle, triangle, pentagon, hexagon, heptagon, octagon, nonagon, decagon, lozenge, diamond, rhomb, rhombus, rhomboid, parallelogram, gore, gusset, wedge.

Cube, parallelepiped, pyramid, prism, rhombohedron, tetrahedron, pentahedron, hexahedron, octahedron, dodecahedron, icosahedron.

T-square, set-square, protractor, goniometer, theodolite, sextant, quadrant, clinometer.

Verbs: To bend, refract, diffract, fork, bifurcate, angulate, crinkle, crankle, splay.

Adjectives: Angular, triangular, quadrangular, rectangular, bent, crooked, hooked, aduncous, aquiline, jagged, serrated, falciform, falcated, furcated, forked, bifurcate, zigzag; dovetailed, knock-kneed, crinkled, akimbo, geniculated, polygonal, trigonal, pentagonal, etc., fusiform, sagittate, arrow-headed, wedge-shaped, cuneate, cuneiform, splayed, angulate, cubical, pyramidal, rhombohedral, tetrahedral, etc.

245 CURVATURE

Substantives: curvation, incurvity, incurvation, bend, flexure, flexion, hook, crook, camber, bending, deflexion, inflexion, arcuation, diffraction, turn, deviation, detour, sweep, sinuosity, curl, curling, winding, recurvature, recurvation, refraction, flexibility (324).

A curve, arc, circle, ellipse (247), parabola, hyperbola, catenary, festoon, arch, arcade, vault, bow, crescent, half-moon, lunette, horse-shoe, loop bight, crane-neck, conchoid, ogee.

Verbs: To be curved, etc., to bend, curve, etc., decline, turn, trend, deviate, re-enter, sweep.

To render curved; to bend, curve, incurvate, camber, deflect, inflect, crook, hook, turn, round, arch, arcuate, bow, curl, recurve, loop, frizzle.
Adjectives: Curved, vent, etc., curvilinear, curviform, recurved, recurvous, circular, oval (247), parabolic, hyperbolic, bowed, crooked, bandy, arched, vaulted, arcuated, camerated, hooked, falcated, falciform, crescent-shaped, semilunar, semicircular, conchoidal, lunular, lunulate, cordiform, heart-shaped, reniform, pear-shaped; bow-legged, bandy-legged, knock-kneed, devious.

246 STRAIGHTNESS
Substantives: rectilinearity, directness.

A straight line, a right line, a direct line; inflexibility (323).
Verbs: To be straight, etc.

To render straight, to straighten, rectify, set or put straight, take the curl out of, unbend, unfold, uncurl, uncoil, unroll, unwind, unravel, untwist, unwreathe, unwrap.
Adjectives: Straight, rectilinear (or rectilineal), direct, even, right, in a line; unbent; not inclining, not bending, not turning, not deviating to either side, undeviating, unturned, undistorted, unswerving.
Phrases: Straight as an arrow; as the crow flies; in a bee line.

247 CIRCULARITY
Substantives: roundness, rotundity (249).

A circle, circlet, ring, areola, hoop, roundlet, *annulus*, annulet, bracelet, bangle, armlet, anklet, ringlet, eye, loop, wheel, cycle, orb, orbit, rundle, zone, belt, cordon, band, sash, girdle, cestus, cincture, baldric, bandolier, fillet, cummerbund, fascia, wreath, garland, crown, corona, coronal, coronet, chaplet, necklace, rivière; noose, lasso.

An ellipse, oval, ovule, ellipsoid, cycloid, epicycloid, epicycle, semicircle, quadrant, sextant, sector, segment.
Verbs: To make round, round, circle, encircle, environ (227).
Adjectives: Round, rounded, circular, annular, orbicular.

Oval, elliptical, elliptic, ovate, egg-shaped; cycloidal, etc., moniliform.

248 CONVOLUTION
Substantives: winding, wave, undulation, circuit, tortuosity, anfractuosity, sinuosity, involution, sinuation, circumvolution, meander, circumbendibus, twist, twirl, squiggle, curl, curlicue, curlie-wurlie, tirliewhirlie, crimp, frizz, frizzle, permanent wave, perm, windings and turnings, *ambages*, inosculation, peristalsis.

A coil, reel, roll, spiral, helix, corkscrew, worm, volute, scroll, cartouche, rundle, scallop (or scollop), escallop.

Serpent, eel, maze, labyrinth.
Verbs: To be convoluted, etc.

To wind, twine, twist, coil, roll, turn and twist, weave, twirl, wave, undulate, meander, scallop, curl, crimp, frizz, frizzle, perm, inosculate, entwine (219), enlace, twist together, goffer.
Adjectives: Convoluted, winding, twisting, contorted, waving, waved, wavy, curly, undulating, undulant, undulatory, undated, serpentine, anguilline, mazy, labyrinthine, Daedalian, tortuous, sinuous, flexuous, snaky, involved, sigmate, sigmoid, sigmoidal, vermiform, vermicular, peristaltic, meandrine; scalloped (or scolloped), wreathed, wreathy, crisped, crimped, frizzed, frizzy, frizzled, frizzly, ravelled, twisted, dishevelled (61).

Spiral, coiled, helical, turbinate.
Adverb: In and out.

249 ROTUNDITY
Substantives: roundness, cylindricity; cylinder, barrel, drum, cylindroid, roll, roller, rouleau, column, rolling-pin, rundle.

Cone, conoid; pear-shape, bell-shape.

Sphericity, spheroidity, globosity; a sphere, globe, ball, spheroid, ellipsoid, drop, spherule, globule, vesicle, bulb, bullet, pellet, pill, clue, marble, pea, knob, pommel.

Verbs: To form into a sphere, render spherical, to sphere, ensphere, to roll into a ball, round off, give rotundity, etc.

Adjectives: Rotund, round, cylindric, cylindrical, cylindroid, columnar, lumbriciform; conic, conical, conoidal.

Spherical, spheral, spheroidal, globular, globated, globous, globose, ovoid, egg-shaped, gibbous, bulbiform, bulbous, bell-shaped, campaniliform, campaniform, campanulate, fungiform, bead-like, moniliform, pyriform, cigar-shaped.

Phrases: Round as an apple; round as a ball; *teres atque rotundus.*

250 CONVEXITY
Substantives: prominence, projection, swelling, gibbosity, bulge, protuberance, intumescence, tumour, cancer, tuberosity, tubercle, tooth, knob, excrescence, elbow, process, condyle, bulb, nub, nubble, node, nodule, nodosity, tongue, *dorsum*, hump, hunch, hunk, bunch, boss, embossment, bump, lump, clump, sugarloaf, point (253), bow, bagginess.

Pimple, wen, papula, pustule, carbuncle, corn, wart, polyp, boil, furuncle, fungus, fungosity, bleb, blister, blain, chilblain, bunion.

Papilla, nipple, teat, pap, breast, dug, udder, mamilla, proboscis, nose, neb, beak, snout, nozzle, belly, paunch, corporation, kyte, back, shoulder, elbow, lip, flange.

Peg, button, stud, ridge, rib, jetty, snag, eaves, mole, cupola, dome, balcony.

Cameo, high and low relief, bas-relief, *basso rilievo, alto rilievo*; repoussé work.

Mount, hill (206); cape, promontory, foreland, headland, ness, mull, salient, point of land, hummock, spur, hog's back, offset.

Verbs: To be prominent, etc., to project, bulge, belly, jut out, bristle up, to hang over, overhang, beetle, bend over, protrude, stand out, stick out, poke out, stick up, start up, cock up, shoot up, swell.

To render prominent; to raise (307), to emboss, chase, stud, bestud, ridge.

Adjectives: Convex, prominent, projecting, bulging, etc., bold, bossed, bossy, knobby, nubbly, lumpy, bumpy, nodose, embossed, chased, gibbous, salient, mamilliform, in relief, bowed, arched, bellied, baggy, cornute, odontoid, tuberous, tuberculous, ridged, ridgy.

251 FLATNESS
Substantives: plane; horizontality (213), layer (204), smoothness (255); plate, platter, slab, table, tablet; level.

Verbs: To render flat, flatten, smooth, level.

Adjectives: Flat, plane, even, level, etc. (213), flush, scutiform, scutellate.

Phrases: Flat as a pancake; flat as a flounder; flat as a board; flat as my hand; a dead flat; a dead level.

252 CONCAVITY
Substantives: depression, hollow, hollowness, indentation, intaglio, cavity, dent, dint, dimple, follicle, pit, sinus, alveolus, lacuna, honeycomb, excavation, trough (259).

Cup, basin, crater, etc. (191); socket, thimble.

Valley, vale, dale, dell, dingle, coombe, strath, bottom, corrie, glade,

127

glen, cave, cell, cavern, cove, grotto, grot, alcove, gully (198), cul-de-sac.
Verbs: To be depressed, etc., to cave in, subside, retire.

To depress, hollow, scoop, gouge, dig, delve, excavate, dent, dint, stave in, mine, undermine, burrow, tunnel.
Adjectives: Depressed, concave, hollow, stove in, retiring, retreating, cavernous, honeycombed, alveolar, cellular, funnel-shaped, infundibular, bell-shaped, campaniliform, porous (260).

253 SHARPNESS
Substantives: keenness, pointedness, acuteness, acuity, acumination, spinosity, prickliness.

A point, spike, spine, spicule, needle, bodkin (262), aiguille, pin, prickle, prick, prong, tine, caltrop, *chevaux de frise*, arrow, spear, bayonet, pike, sword, dagger (727), spur, rowel, barb, spit, cusp, horn, antler, snag, tag, jag, thorn, brier, bramble, thistle, nib, tooth, tusk, denticle, spoke, cog, ratchet, comb, bristle, beard, awn, *arête*, crest, cone, peak, spire, pyramid, steeple, porcupine, hedgehog.

Cutlery, blade, edge-tool, knife, jack-knife, penknife, clasp-knife, bowie, jocteleg, chisel, razor, scalpel, bistoury, lancet, axe, hatchet, pole-axe, pick-axe, pick, mattock, spade, adze, coulter, ploughshare, scythe, sickle, reaping-hook, bill, billhook, cleaver, scissors, shears, sécateurs.

Sharpener, knife-sharpener, strop, hone, grinder, grindstone, whet-stone, steel, emery, carborundum.
Verbs: To be sharp, etc., to taper to a point, to bristle with.

To render sharp, etc., to sharpen, point, aculeate, set, whet, strop, hone, grind, barb, bristle up.
Adjectives: Sharp, keen, pointed, conical, acute, acicular, aculeated, arrowy, needle-shaped, spiked, spiky,

spicular, spiculate, mucronate, mucronated, ensiform, peaked, acuminated, salient, cusped, cuspidate, cuspidated, cornute, prickly, spiny, spinous, thorny, jagged, bristling, muricate, pectinated, studded, thistly, briery, snaggy, digitated, barbed, spurred, two-edged, tapering, fusiform, dentiform, denticular, denticulated, toothed, odontoid, cutting, trenchant, sharp-edged.

Starlike, stellated, stelliform.
Phrases: Sharp as a needle, as a razor.

254 BLUNTNESS
Substantives: obtuseness, dullness.
Verbs: To be blunt, etc., to render blunt, etc., to obtund, dull, take off the point or edge, turn.
Adjectives: Blunt, obtuse, dull, bluff.

255 SMOOTHNESS
Substantives: evenness, level (213), polish, gloss, glossiness, sleekness, slipperiness, lubricity, lubrication (332), down, velvet, velveteen, velour, silk, satin, plush, glass, ice, enamel, macadam.

Burnisher, calender, mangle, iron, file, plane, sandpaper, emery-paper, roller.
Verbs: To smooth, smoothen, plane, polish, burnish, calender, mangle, enamel, glaze, iron, file, roll, lubricate, macadamize.
Adjectives: Smooth, even, level, plane, sleek, slick, polished, glazed, glossy, sleeky, silken, silky, satiny, velvety, glabrous, slippery, oily, soft, unwrinkled.
Phrases: Smooth as glass, as velvet, as satin, as soil; slippery as an eel.

256 ROUGHNESS
Substantives: unevenness, asperity, regosity, ruggedness, scabrousness, salebrosity, cragginess, craggedness, corrugation, nodosity, crispness, plumosity, villosity; grain, texture, nap, pile.

Arborescence, branching, ramification.

Brush, bur, beard, shag, whisker, dundreary, mutton-chop, sideboards, side-burns, down, goatee, imperial, moustache, feather, plume, crest, tuft, *panache,* byssus, hair, chevelure, toupee, wool, fur, mane, cilia, fringe, *fimbriae,* tress, moss, plush, velvet, velveteen, velour, stubble.
Verbs: To be rough, etc.

To render rough, to roughen, crisp, crumple, corrugate, rumple.
Adjectives: Rough, uneven, scabrous, gnarled, rugged, rugose, rugous, salebrous, unpolished, matt, frosted, rough-hewn, craggy, cragged, prickly, scrubby.

Arborescent, dendroid, dendriform, arboriform, branching, ramose, ramulose.

Feathery, plumose, plumous, plumigerous, tufted, fimbriated, hairy, ciliated, hirsute, flocculent, bushy, hispid, tomentous, downy, woolly, velvety, villous (or villose), bearded, pilous, shaggy, shagged, stubbly, fringed, befringed, setaceous, filamentous.
Phrases: Rough as a nutmeg-grater; like quills upon the fretful porcupine; against the grain.

257 NOTCH
Substantives: dent, dint, nick, cut, indent, indentation, dimple.

Embrasure, battlement, machicolation, machicoulis, saw, tooth, sprocket, crenelle, scallop (or scollop).
Verbs: To notch, nick, cut, dent, indent, dint, jag, scotch, slash, scallop (or scollop), crenelate.
Adjectives: Notched, etc., jagged, crenate, crenated, crenelated, dented, dentated, denticulated, toothed, palmated, indented, serrated.

258 FOLD
Substantives: plication, plait, ply,

crease, pleat, tuck, hem, flexion, flexure, joint, elbow, doubling, duplicature, gather, wrinkle, crow's-foot, rimple, crinkle, crankle, crumple, rumple, rivel, ruck, ruffle, ruche, dog's-ear, corrugation, flounce, frounce, lapel, pucker, crimp.
Verbs: To fold, double, plicate, plait, crease, wrinkle, crinkle, crankle, curl, cockle up, cocker, rimple, frizz, frizzle, rumple, flounce, frounce, rivel, twill, corrugate, ruffle, crimple, crumple, pucker, to turn down, turn under, tuck, ruck.
Adjectives: Folded, dog's-eared (or dog-eared), etc.

259 FURROW
Substantives: groove, rut, slit, scratch, streak, stria, crack, score, rib.

Channel, gutter, trench, ditch, dike, moat, fosse, trough, kennel, chamfer, ravine (198), fluting.
Verbs: To furrow, etc., flute, plough.
Adjectives: Furrowed, etc., ribbed, striated, striate, sulcated, fluted, canaliculate, bisulcate, trisulcate, etc., corduroy, corded, corrugated.

260 OPENING
Substantives: hole, foramen, perforation, eye, eyelet, keyhole, loophole, porthole, scuttle, mouse-hole, pigeonhole, eye of a needle, pinhole, peephole, puncture.

Aperture, hiatus, yawning, oscitancy, dehiscence, patefaction, slot, chink, crevice (198).

Window, light, fanlight, skylight, casement, lattice, embrasure.

Orifice, inlet, intake, outlet, mouth, throat, muzzle, gullet, weasand, nozzle, portal, porch, gate, lych-gate, wicket, postern, gateway, door, embouchure, doorway, exit, vomitory, hatch, hatchway, gangway, arcade.

Channel (350), passage, pass, tube, pipe, vessel, tubule, canal, thoroughfare, gut, fistula, ajutage, tap, faucet, chimney, flue, vent, funnel, gully, tunnel, main, adit, pit, shaft, gallery, alley, aisle, glade, vista, bore, mine, calibre, pore, follicle, porosity, porousness, lacuna.

Sieve, cullender, colander, strainer, tamis, riddle, screen, honeycomb.

Apertion, perforation, piercing, boring, mining, terebration, drilling, etc., impalement, pertusion, puncture, acupuncture, penetration (302).

Opener, tin-opener, key, master-key.

Verbs: To open, ope, gape, yawn.

To perforate, lay open, pierce, empierce, tap, bore, mine, drill, scoop out, canalize, tunnel, transpierce, transfix, enfilade, rake, impale, spike, spear, gore, stab, pink, stick, prick, lance, puncture, riddle, honeycomb, punch, jab; uncover, unrip, stave in.

Phrase: To cut a passage through.

Adjectives: Open, pierced, perforated, etc., perforate, wide open, ajar, unclosed, unstopped, patulous, gaping, yawning, patent.

Tubular, tubulous, tubulate, tubuliform, cannular, fistulous, fistular, fistulate, pervious, permeable, foraminous, porous, follicular, cribriform, honeycombed, infundibular, windowed, fenestrated.

Phrase: Open sesame!

261 CLOSURE

Substantives: occlusion, blockade, shutting up, filling up, plugging, sealing, obstruction, impassableness, blocking up, obstipation, constipation, blind alley, blind corner, cul-de-sac, impasse, caecum.

Imperforation, imperviousness, impermeability, imporosity.

Verbs: To close, occlude, steek, plug, block up, fill up, blockade, obstruct, bar, stop, bung up, seal, clinch, plumb, cork up, shut up, choke,

throttle, ram down, dam up, cram, stuff up.

Adjectives: Closed, shut, unopened, occluded, etc., impervious, imperforate, caecal, impassable, invious, pathless, untrodden, unpierced, unventilated, impermeable, imporous, operculated, tight, water-tight, air-tight, hermetic.

Phrase: Hermetically sealed.

262 PERFORATOR

Substantives: borer, auger, gimlet, stylet, drill, wimble, awl, bradawl, brog, scoop, corkscrew, dibble, trepan, probe, bodkin, needle, stiletto, lancet, punch, spike, bit, brace and bit, gouge, fleam.

Verbs: To spike, gouge, scoop, punch, lance.

263 STOPPER

Substantives: stopple, plug, cork, bung, spigot, spike, spile, vent-peg, stopcock, tap, stopgap, rammer, ramrod, piston, wad, dossil, wadding, tompion, stuffing, tourniquet.

Cover, lid, operculum, covering, covercle, door, etc. (222), valve.

A janitor, door-keeper, commissionaire, chucker-out, ostiary, concierge, porter, warder, beadle, Cerberus.

Section IV – Motion

264 MOTION

Substantives: movement, transit, transition, move, going, etc., passage, course, stir.

Step, gait, stride, tread, port, footfall, carriage, transference (270), locomotion, travel (266), voyage (267).

Mobility, restlessness, unrest, movability, movableness, inquietude, flux; kinematics.

Verbs: To be moving, etc., to move, go, stir, hie, gang, budge, pass, flit, shift, glide, roll, roll on, flow (347, 348), sweep along, wander (279), change or shift one's place or quarters, dodge, keep going.

To put in motion, impel, etc. (276); to propel, project (284); to mobilize, motorize.

Adjectives: Moving, in motion, on the move, going, transitional; kinematic.

Shifting, movable (270), mobile, restless, nomadic, wandering, vagrant, discursive, erratic (279), mercurial, unquiet.

Adverbs: *In transitu,* under way, on the move.

265 QUIESCENCE

Substantives: rest, stillness, stagnation, stagnancy, fixedness, immobility, catalepsy, paralysis.

Quiet, quietness, quietude, tranquillity, calm, calmness, sedentariness, peace; steadiness, balance, equilibrium.

Pause, suspension, suspense, lull, stop, stoppage, interruption, stopping, stand, standstill, standing still, lying to, repose (687), respite.

Lock, deadlock, dead stop, embargo.

Resting-place, anchorage, moorings, bivouac, port (189, 666), bed, pillow, etc. (215).

Verbs: To be quiescent, etc., to remain, stand, stand still, lie to, pull up, hold, halt, stop, anchor, stop short, stop dead, freeze, heave to, rest, pause, repose, keep quiet, take breath, stagnate, vegetate, settle; to mark time.

To stay, tarry, sojourn, dwell (186), pitch one's tent, cast anchor, settle, encamp, bivouac, moor, tether, picket, plant oneself, alight, land, etc. (292), ride at anchor.

Phrases: Not to stir a peg (or step or inch); *'j'y suis, j'y reste';* to come to a standstill; to come to a deadlock; to rest on one's oars or laurels.

To stop, suspend, arrest, lay to, hold one's hand, interrupt, intermit, discontinue (142), put a stop to, quell, becalm.

Phrases: To bring to a standstill; to lay an embargo on.

Adjectives: Quiescent, still, motionless, moveless, at rest, stationary, untravelled, stay-at-home, at a stand, at a standstill, stock-still, standing still, sedentary, undisturbed, unruffled, fast, stuck fast, fixed, transfixed, rooted, moored, aground, at anchor, tethered, becalmed, stagnant, quiet, calm, breathless, peaceful, unmoved, unstirred, immovable, immobile, restful, cataleptic, paralysed, frozen, irremovable, stable, steady, steadfast.

Phrases: Still as a statue; still as a post; quiet or still as a mouse.

Interjections: Soho! stop! stay! avast! belay! halt! as you were! hold hard! hold your horses! hold on! whoa!

266 JOURNEY

Substantives: travel, travelling, excursion, expedition, tour, trip, trek, circuit, peregrination, discursion, ramble, outing, pilgrimage, Odyssey, course, ambulation, march, route march, marching, walk, walking, promenade, stroll, saunter, dander, turn, trot, tramp, hike, stalk, noctambulation, perambulation, ride, equitation, drive, jog-trot, airing, constitutional, spin, jaunt, joy-ride, change of scene.

Roving, vagrancy, flit, flitting, migration, emigration, immigration, intermigration; *Wanderlust.*

Map, plan, itinerary, road-book, guide, Baedeker, Bradshaw, ABC.

Procession, caravan, cavalcade, column, cortège.

Organs and instruments of locomotion, legs, feet, pins, stilt, skate, ski, snow-shoe, locomotive, vehicle (272, 273), velocipede, penny-farthing, bone-shaker, bicycle, cycle, bike, push

131

cycle, tandem, tricycle, fairy-cycle, scooter.

Phrase: Shanks's mare.

Verbs: To travel, journey, trek, walk, ramble, roam, rove, course, wander, itinerate, perambulate, stroll, straggle, expatiate, range, gad about, gallivant, knock about, to go or take a walk, journey, tour, turn, trip, etc.; to prowl, stray, saunter, tour, make a tour, knock about, emigrate, flit, migrate.

To walk, march, counter-march, step, tread, pace, wend, wend one's way, promenade, permabulate, cir-cumambulate, take a walk, go for a walk, take the air, trudge, trapes, stalk, stride, straddle, strut, foot it, hoof it, stump, clump, plod, peg along, bundle, toddle, patter, shuffle on, tramp, hike, footslog, traverse, bend one's steps, thread one's way, make one's way, find one's way, tread a path, take a course, take wing, take flight, defile, file off.

Ride, jog on, trot, amble, canter, gallop, take horse, prance, frisk, tittup, caracole, have a run, ride and tie, hitch-hike, lorry-hop.

To drive, slide, glide, skim, skate, toboggan, ski.

To go to, repair to, resort to, hie to.

Phrases: To pad the hoof; to hump bluey.

Adjectives: Travelling, etc., ambulatory, itinerant, wayfaring, peripatetic, discursive, vagrant, migratory, nomadic, on the wing, etc., circum-foranean, overland.

Adverbs: By the way, *chemin faisant,* on the road, *en passant, en route,* on foot, afoot.

267 NAVIGATION

Substantives: voyage, sail, cruise, Odyssey, circumnavigation, periplus, seafaring, yachting, boating; drifting, headway, sternway, leeway.

Natation, swimming, surf-riding.

Flight, flying, flip, volitation, aero-station, aeronautics, aerostatics, ballooning, aviation, gliding.

Space travel, astronautics.

Wing, pinion, fin, flipper; oar, scull, canvas, sail, rotor, paddle, punt-pole, paddle-wheel, screw, turbine, jet.

Verbs: To sail, make sail, warp, put to sea, navigate, take ship, get under way, spread sail, spread canvas, carry sail, plough the waves, plough the deep, scud, boom, drift, course, cruise, coast, circumnavigate, aviate.

To row, pull, paddle, scull, punt, steam.

To swim, float, buffet the waves, skim, *effleurer,* dive, wade.

To fly, aviate, hedge-hop, be wafted, hover, soar, glide, wing; to flush.

Phrases: To take wing; to take flight.

Adjectives: Sailing, etc., seafaring, under way, under sail, on the wing, volant, nautical; airborne, aeronautic, aeronautical, aerostatic; astronautical.

Phrases: In sail; under canvas.

268 TRAVELLER

Substantives: wayfarer, voyager, itinerant, passenger, commuter, tourist, tripper, excursionist, wanderer, rover, straggler, rambler, hiker, bird of passage, gad-about, globe-trotter, vagrant, tramp, hobo, bum, swagman, sundowner, vagabond, rolling-stone, nomad, pilgrim, hadji, palmer, runner, courier, pedestrian, peripatetic, emigrant, fugitive.

Rider, horseman, equestrian, cavalier, jockey, postilion, rough-rider, scout, motorist.

Mercury, Iris, Ariel.

269 MARINER

Substantives: navigator, seaman, sailor, seafarer, shipman, tar, old salt, bluejacket, marine, jolly, boatman, *voyageur,* ferryman, waterman, lighter-man, bargee, gondolier, longshore-man, crew, oarsman.

An aerial navigator, aeronaut, balloonist, aviator, airman, flying man, pilot.

Astronaut, cosmonaut, spaceman.

270 TRANSFERENCE

Substantives: transfer, displacement, metathesis, transposition (148), remotion, removal (185), relegation, deportation, extradition, conveyance, draft, carriage, carrying, convection, conduction, export, import.

Transmission, passage, transit, transition, ferry, transport, gestation, portage, porterage, cartage, carting, shovelling, shipment, transhipment, air lift, air drop, freight, wafture, transportation, transumption, transplantation, transfusion, translation, shifting, dodging, dispersion (73), traction (285).

Verbs: To transfer, convey, transmit, transport, transplant, transfuse, carry, bear, carry over, hand over, pass forward, remove (185), transpose (148), shift, export, import, convey, conduct, convoy, send, relegate, extradite, turn over to, deliver, waft, ship, tranship, ferry over.

To bring, fetch, reach, draft.

To load, lade, charge, unload, shovel, ladle, decant, empty, break bulk.

Adjectives: Transferred, etc., movable portable, portative.

Adverbs: From hand to hand, on the way, *en route, en passant, in transitu,* from pillar to post.

271 CARRIER

Substantives: porter, bearer, coolie, *hammal*, conveyer, transport-worker, stevedore (690), conductor, locomotive (285).

Beast of burden, cattle, horse, blood-horse, arab, steed, nag, palfrey, galloway, charger, destrier, war-horse, courser, racer, racehorse, hunter, pony, filly, colt, foal, barb, jade, hack, *bidet,* pad, cob, tit, punch, roadster, goer, pack-horse, draught-horse, cart-horse, post-horse, shelty, jennet, bayard, mare, stallion, gelding, gee-gee, gee, stud.

Ass, donkey, moke, cuddy, jackass, mule, hinny, sumpter-mule.

Camel, dromedary, llama, zebra, reindeer, yak, elephant, carrier-pigeon.

272 VEHICLE

Substantives: conveyance.

Carriage, caravan, van, furniture van, pantechnicon, wagon, stage-wagon, wain, dray, cart, float, trolley, sledge, sleigh, bob-sleigh, *luge*, toboggan, truck, tumbril, pontoon, barrow, wheelbarrow, hand-barrow, lorry.

Train, railway train, goods train, freight train, rolling stock, Pullman car, parlour car, restaurant-car, dining-car, diner, buffet-car, sleeping-car, sleeper, horse-box, cattle-truck, rail-car, tender.

Equipage, turn-out, carriage coach, chariot, chaise, post-chaise, phaeton, curricle, tilbury, whisky, victoria, landau, brougham, clarence, gig, calash, dog-cart, governess-cart, trap, buggy, carriole, jingle, wagonette, jaunting-car, shandrydan, droshky, kibitka, berlin, stage, stage-coach, diligence, car, omnibus, bus, charabanc, brake, cabriolet, cab, hackney cab, four-wheeler, growler, fly, hansom.

Motor-car, motor, automobile, autocar, touring-car, tourer, sports car, torpedo, landaulette, limousine, saloon, sedan, two-seater, runabout, coupé, jalopy, tricar, motor-cycle, side-car, autocycle, moped, corgi, motor-bus, motor-coach, autobus, taxi-cab, taxi, motor-van, jeep; trolley-bus, tram-car, tram, street-car.

Tank, armoured car, half-track, amtrac, duck.

Bath-chair, wheel-chair, sedan chair, palanquin (or palankeen), litter, jinricksha (or rickshaw), brancard, stretcher, perambulator, pram, mail-cart, bassinette, baby-carriage.

Shovel, spoon, spatula, ladle, hod.

273 SHIP
Substantives: vessel, bottom, craft, shipping, marine, fleet, flotilla, squadron, three-master, barque (or bark), barquentine, brig, brigantine, schooner, sloop, cutter, skiff, yawl, ketch, smack, dogger, hoy, lugger, barge, wherry, lighter, hulk, buss, packet, clipper, rotor ship.

Navy, armada, warship, man-of-war, ironclad, capital ship, super-dreadnought, dreadnought, battle-ship, battle-cruiser, cruiser, frigate, corvette, gunboat, aircraft-carrier, monitor, torpedo boat destroyer, destroyer, torpedo boat, mine-sweeper, mine-layer, submarine, Q-boat, troop-ship, trooper, transport, hospital ship, flagship; ship of the line, first-rate, seventy-four, fireship.

Liner, merchantman, tramp, slaver, steamer, steamboat, steam-packet, paddle-steamer, stern-wheeler, screw-steamer, turbine, tender, tug, collier, whaler, coaster, tanker.

Argosy, bireme, trireme, quad-rireme, quinquereme, galley, galleon, carrack, caravel, galliot, polacca, tartan, junk, praam, saic, dhow, proa, sampan, xebec.

Boat, motor-boat, long-boat, pinnace, launch, cabin cruiser, yacht, shallop, jolly-boat, gig, funny, dinghy, bumboat, fly-boat, wherry, coble, cock-boat, punt, cog, kedge, outrigger, catamaran, fishing-boat, coracle, hooker, life-boat, gondola, felucca, dahabeeyah, caique, canoe, dug-out, raft, float.

Adverbs: Afloat, aboard.

273A AIRCRAFT
Substantives: flying machine, aero-plane, monoplane, biplane, seaplane, hydroplane, plane, flyingboat, amphi-bian, air-liner, flying wing, strato-cruiser, stratoliner, sky-master, jet aircraft, jet, turbo-jet, autogiro, heli-copter, hoverplane, whirlybird, plani-copter, glider; fighter, bomber, fighter-bomber, flying fortress, super-fortress.

Balloon, air-balloon, aerostat, Montgolfier, pilot balloon, blimp, kite, airship, dirigible, Zeppelin.

Space ship, rocket, sputnik, lunik, satellite.

Adjectives: Airborne; orbital.

274 VELOCITY
Substantives: speed, celerity, swift-ness, rapidity, fleetness, expedition, speediness, quickness, nimbleness, briskness, agility, promptness, promp-titude (682), dispatch, acceleration (684).

Gallop, full gallop, canter, trot, run, rush, scamper, scoot, scorch, hand-gallop, lope; flight, dart, bolt, dash, spurt, sprint.

Haste, hurry, scurry, bounce, bolt, precipitation, precipitancy (684), forced march, race, steeplechase, Marathon race.

Rate, pace, step, gait, course, prog-ress.

Lightning, light, cannon-ball, bullet, wind, rocket, arrow, dart, quicksilver, telegraph, express train, clipper.

An eagle, antelope, doe, courser, racehorse, racer, gazelle, greyhound, hare, squirrel, bandersnatch.

Mercury, Ariel, Camilla.

Speed indicator, speedometer, tachometer, log, log-line.

Verbs: To move quickly; to trip, speed, haste, hie, hasten, hurry, fly, press, press on, press forward, post, push on, whip, scamper, run, sprint, race, scud, scour, scurry, scuttle, spin, scoot, scorch, rip, clip, shoot, tear, whisk, sweep, skim, brush, glance, cut along, dash on, dash forward, trot, gallop, lope, rush, bound, bounce, flounce, frisk, tittup, bolt, flit, spring, boom, dart.

To hasten, accelerate, expedite, dispatch, urge, whip, forward, buck up, express, speed-up, hurry, precipitate, quicken pace, gather way, ride hard.

To keep up with, keep pace with, race, race with, outpace, outmarch, distance, outdistance, lap, leave behind, outrun, outstrip, gain ground.

Phrases: To cover the ground; to clap on sail; take to one's heels; clap spurs to one's horse; to run like mad; ride hard; outstrip the wind; to make rapid strides; wing one's way; be off like a shot; run a race; stir one's stumps; do a scoot; get a move on; get cracking; step on it; give her the gun; let it rip.

Adjectives: Fast, speedy, swift, rapid, full-drive, quick, double-quick, fleet, nimble, agile, expeditious, prompt, brisk, frisky, hasty, hurried, flying, etc., precipitate, furious, light-footed, nimble-footed, winged, eagle-winged, mercurial, electric, telegraphic, light-legged; accelerative.

Phrases: Swift as an arrow, as a doe, as a lamplighter; off like a shot; quick as lightning; quick as thought.

Adverbs: Swiftly, with speed, speedily, trippingly, etc., full-tilt, full speed, apace, post-haste, *presto*, tantivy, by express, by telegraph, slap, slap-dash, headlong, hurry-scurry, hand over hand, at a round trot.

Phrases: Under press of sail, or canvas; *velis et remis*; on eagle's wings; at the double, in double-quick time; with giant, or gigantic steps; *à pas de géant*; in seven-league boots; whip and spur; *ventre à terre*; as fast as one's legs or heels will carry one; *sauve qui peut*; the devil take the hindmost; *vires acquirit eundo*; with rapid strides; at top speed; in top gear; flat out; all out; like greased lightning; like the wind.

275 SLOWNESS
Substantives: tardiness, dilatoriness, slackness, lentor, languor (683), drawl.

Hobbling, creeping, lounging, etc., shambling, claudication, halting, walk, amble, jog-trot, dog-trot, mincing steps, foot-pace, crawl.

A slow-goer, dawdle, dawdler, lingered, slow-coach, lame duck, drone, tortoise, snail, slug, sluggard, slacker.

Retardation, slackening, slowing down, delay (133).

Verbs: To move slowly, to creep, crawl, lag, slug, drawl, dawdle, linger, loiter (683), plod, trudge, flag, saunter, lounge, lumber, trail, drag, grovel, glide, laze, amble, steal along, inch along, jog on, rub on, bundle on, toddle, waddle, shuffle, halt, hobble, limp, claudicate, shamble, mince, falter, totter, stagger.

To retard, slacken, relax, check, rein in, curb, strike sail, reef, slow up, slow down.

Phrases: To 'drag its slow length along'; to hang fire; to march in slow time, in funeral procession; to lose ground.

To put on the drag; apply the brake; clip the wings; take in sail; take one's time; ca'canny; *festina lente*.

Adjectives: Slow, slack, tardy, dilatory, easy, gentle, leisurely, deliberate, lazy, languid, drawsy, sleepy, heavy, drawling, leaden, sluggish, snail-like, creeping, crawling, etc., dawdling, lumbering, hobbling, tardi-grade.

Adverbs: Slowly, etc., gingerly, softly, leisurely, deliberately, gradually, etc. (144) *piano, adagio, largo*.

Phrases: In slow motion; just ticking over; under easy sail; at a snail's pace; with mincing steps; with clipped wings; by degrees; little by little; inch by inch.

276 IMPULSE
Substantives: momentum, impetus, push, impulsion, thrust, shove, fling, jog, jolt, brunt, throw, volley, explosion (173), propulsion (284).

Percussion, collision, concussion, impact, clash, encounter, cannon, carom, carambole, appulse, shock, crash, bump, charge, tackle (716), foul.

Blow, stroke, knock, tap, fillip, pat, rap, dab, dig, jab, smack, slap, hit, putt, cuff, bang, crack, whack, thwack, slog, belt, wipe, clout, swipe, clip, squash, dowse, punch, thump, pelt, kick, lunge, buffet, beating (972).

Hammer, mallet, mall, maul, beetle, flail, cudgel, bludgeon, life-preserver, cosh, baton, truncheon, knobkerrie, shillelagh, staff, lathi, cane, stick, club, racket, bat, driver, brassy, baffy, spoon, putter, cleek, iron, mashie, niblick, ram, battering-ram, monkey-engine, catapult, pile-driver, rammer, sledge-hammer, steam hammer.

Dynamics; seismometer.

Verbs: To impel, push, give impetus, etc., drive, urge, hurtle, boom, thrust, elbow, shoulder, charge, tackle, jostle, justle, hustle, jog, jolt, encounter, collide, clash, cannon, foul.

To strike,, knock, tap, slap, dab, pat, slam, hit, bat, putt, rap, prod, jerk, dig, cuff, smite, butt, impinge, thump, bethump, beat, bang, whang, biff, punch, thwack, whack, spank, skelp, swat, lay into, shin, slog, clout, wipe, swipe, batter, dowse, baste, pummel, pelt, patter, drub, buffet, belabour, cane, whip (972), poke at, hoof, jab, pink, lunge, kick, recalcitrate.

To throw, etc. (284), to set going, mobilize.

Adjectives: Impelling, etc., impulsive, impellent, impelled, etc., dynamic, dynamical.

Interjections: Bang! boom! wham!

277 RECOIL

Substantives: retroaction, revulsion, reaction, rebound, bounce, stot, repercussion, ricochet, rebuff, reverberation, reflux, reflex, kick, springing back, ducks and drakes.

A boomerang, spring (325).

Verbs: To recoil, react, spring back, fly back, bound back, rebound, stot, reverberate, repercuss.

Adjectives: Recoiling, etc., on the recoil, etc., refluent, repercussive, reactionary, retroactive.

Phrase: On the rebound.

278 DIRECTION

Substantives: bearing, course, route, bent, inclination, drift, tenor, tendency, incidence, set, leaning, bending, trend, dip, steerage, tack, steering, aim, alignment (or alinement), orientation, collimation.

A line, bee-line, path, road, aim, range, quarter, point of the compass, rhumb, great circle, azimuth, line of collimation.

Verbs: To tend towards, go to, point to, or at; trend, verge, align (or aline), incline, conduct to, determine.

To make for, or towards, aim at, take aim, level at, steer for, keep or hold a course, be bound for, bend one's steps towards, direct or shape one's course.

To ascertain one's direction, orient (or orientate) oneself, to see which way the wind blows.

Adjectives: Directed, etc., direct, straight, undeviating, unswerving, aligned (or alined) with, determinate, point-to-point.

Adverbs: Towards, to, *versus*, thither, directly, straight, point-blank, full tilt at, whither, in a line with, as the crow flies.

By way of, via, in all directions, *quaquaversum,* in all manner of ways, to the four winds.

279 DEVIATION

Substantives: swerving, aberration, obliquation, *ambages,* warp, bending, flexion, deflection, refraction, sidling, side-slip, skid, half-roll, barrel-roll, loop, straying, straggling, warping, etc., digression, circuit, detour, departure from, divergence (291), desultory motion; slice, pull, hook, leg-break, off-break, googly.

Motion sideways, side-step.

Verbs: To alter one's course, divert, deviate, depart from, turn, bend, swerve, break, switch, skid, side-slip, zoom, bank, loop, bunt, jib, shift, warp, stray, straggle, sidle, diverge (291), digress, wander, meander, veer, wear, tack, yaw, turn aside, turn a corner, turn away from, face about, wheel, wheel about, steer clear of, ramble, rove, go astray, step aside, shunt, side-track, jay walk.

Phrases: To fly off at a tangent; to face to the right-about; to go out of one's way; to lose one's way.

Adjectives: Deviating, etc., aberrant, discursive, devious, desultory, erratic, vagrant, stray, undirected, circuitous, roundabout, crab-like, zigzag.

Adverbs: Astray from, round about.

Phrases: To the right-about; all manner of ways; like the knight's move in chess.

280 PRECESSION

Substantives: leading, heading.

Precedence in order (62), priority (116), precursor (64), front (234).

Verbs: To precede, forerun, lead, head, herald, introduce, usher in (62), go ahead.

Phrases: Go in the van; take the lead; lead the way; open the ball; have the start; to get before; steal a march.

Adjectives: Preceding, leading, etc.

Adverbs: In advance, before (62), in the van, ahead.

281 SEQUENCE

Substantives: following, pursuit, chase, hunt (622).

A follower, pursuer, attendant, shadow, satellite, hanger-on, train.

Sequence in order (63), in time (117).

Verbs: To follow, pursue, chase, hunt, hound, shadow, dog, tail, trail, lag.

Phrases: Go in the rear, or in the wake of; tread in the steps of; tread on the heels of; go after; fly after; to follow as a shadow; to lag behind; to bring up the rear; to fall behind; to tail off.

Adjectives: Following, etc.

Adverbs: Behind, in the rear, etc.

282 PROGRESSION

Substantives: advance, advancement, progress (658), on-going, progressiveness, progressive motion, flood-tide, headway, advancing, etc., pursuit, steeplechase (622), journey, march (266).

Verbs: To advance, proceed, progress, go, move, bend or pass forward, go on, move on, pass on, get on, get along, jog on, push on, go one's way, go ahead, forge ahead, make head, make way, make headway, work one's way, press forward, edge forward, get over the ground, gain ground, make progress, keep or hold on one's course, keep up with, get forward, distance.

Phrases: To make up leeway; to go with the stream; to make rapid strides; to push or elbow or cleave one's way; to go full tilt at.

Adjectives: Advancing, etc., progressive, go-ahead, avant-garde, profluent, undeviating.

Adverbs: Forward, onward, forth, on, in advance, ahead, under way, straightforward.

Phrases: *Vestigia nulla retrorsum; en avant.*

283 REGRESSION

Substantives: regress, recess, retrogression, retrogradation, retreat, withdrawal, retirement, recession (287), refluence, reflux, retroaction, return, reflexion, reflex (277), ebb, countermovement, countermarch, veering, regurgitation, back-wash.

Verbs: To recede, retrograde, return,

rebound, back, fall back, fall or drop astern, lose ground, put about, go back, turn back, hark back, double, countermarch, turn tail, draw back, get back, retrace one's steps, wheel about, back water, regurgitate, yield, give.

Phrases: Dance the back step; beat a retreat.

Adjectives: Receding, etc., retrograde, retrogressive, regressive, refluent, reflex, recidivous, resilient.

Adverbs: Backwards, reflexively, to the right-about, about turn, *à reculons, à rebours.*

Phrase: *Revenons à nos moutons.*

284 PROPULSION

Substantives: push, pushing (276), projection, jaculation, ejaculation, throw, fling, fillip, toss, shot, discharge, shy.

Ballistics, gunnery; *vis a tergo.*

Missile, projectile, shot, shell, ball, bolt, dart, arrow, bullet, stone, shaft, brickbat, discus, quoit, caber.

Bow, sling, pea-shooter, catapult, etc. (727).

Verbs: To propel, project, throw, fling, cast, pitch, chuck, bung, toss, lob, loft, jerk, jaculate, ejaculate, hurl, boost, bolt, drive, sling, flirt, flip, flick, shy, dart, send, roll, send off, let off, discharge, fire off, shoot, launch, let fly, dash, punt, volley, heave, pitchfork.

To bowl, trundle, roll along (312).

To put in motion, start, give an impulse, impel (276), expel (297).

Phrases: To carry off one's feet; to put to flight.

Adjectives: Propelling, etc., propulsive, projectile, etc.

285 TRACTION

Substantives: drawing, draught, pull, pulling, towage, haulage.

Traction engine, locomotive; hauler, haulyer, tractor, tug; trailer.

Phrase: A long pull, a strong pull, and a pull all together.

Verbs: To draw, pull, haul, lug, drag, tug, tow, trail, train, wrench, jerk, twitch, yank.

Phrase: To take in tow.

Adjectives: Drawing, etc., tractile.

286 APPROACH

Substantives: approximation, appropinquation, access, appulse, afflux, affluxion, pursuit (622), collision (276), arrival (292).

Verbs: To approach, draw near, approximate, to near; to come, get, go, etc., near; to set in towards, make up to, snuggle up to, gain upon, gain ground upon.

Phrases: To tread on the heels of; to hug the shore.

Adjectives: Approaching, etc., approximative.

287 RECESSION

Substantives: retirement, withdrawal, retreat, retrocession (283), departure (293), recoil (277), decampment, flight, stampede, skedaddle.

A runaway, a fugitive.

Verbs: To recede, go, move or fly from, retire, retreat, withdraw, come away, go or get away, draw back, shrink, move away.

To move off, stand off, draw off, buzz off, fall back, turn tail, march off, decamp, absquatulate, skedaddle, vamoose, sheer off, bolt, scram, hop it, beat it, slip away, run away, pack off, fly, remove, abscond, sneak off, slink away.

Phrases: To take French leave; to cut and run; take to one's heels; to give leg-bail; take one's hook; *sauve qui peut;* the devil take the hindmost; beat a retreat; make oneself scarce; do a bolt; do a guy; make tracks; cut one's lucky.

Adjectives: Receding, etc., fugitive, runaway (671).

288 ATTRACTION

Substantives: drawing to, pulling towards, adduction, attractiveness, magnetism, gravity, gravitation.

A loadstone, magnet.

Verbs: To attract, draw, pull, drag, etc., towards, adduce.

Adjectives: Attracting, etc., adducent, attrahent, adductive, attractive, magnetic, gravitational.

Interjections: Come! come here! approach! come near!

289 REPULSION

Substantives: push (276), driving from, repulse, expulsion (297).

Verbs: To repel, repulse; push, drive, etc., from, drive away, cold-shoulder, send packing.

Phrases: To give the frozen mitt to; send away with a flea in one's ear; send to the right-about (678).

Adjectives: Repelling, etc., repellent, repulsive, forbidding.

Interjections: Get out! be off! scram! avaunt! (293, 297).

290 CONVERGENCE

Substantives: appulse, meeting, confluence, concourse, conflux, congress, concurrence, concentration.

Resort, assemblage, synod (72), focus (74), asymptote.

Verbs: To converge, come together, unite, meet, fall in with, close in upon, centre in, enter in, meet, come across, come up against.

To gather together, unite, concentrate, etc.

Adjectives: Converging, etc., convergent, confluent, concurring, concurrent, centripetal, asymptotical.

291 DIVERGENCE

Substantives: aberration, peregrination, wandering, divarication, radiation, ramification, separation (44), dispersion, diffusion, dissemination (73); deviation (279).

Verbs: To diverge, divaricate, deviate, wander, stray (279), radiate, branch off, ramify, file off, draw aside.

To spread, disperse, scatter, distribute, decentralize, diffuse, disseminate, shed, sow broadcast, broadcast, sprinkle.

To part, part company, turn away from, wander from, separate (44).

Phrase: To go or fly off at a tangent.

Adjectives: Diverging, etc., divergent, radiant, wandering, aberring, aberrant, centrifugal.

Adverb: Broadcast.

292 ARRIVAL

Substantives: advent, reception, welcome, return, disembarkation, debarkation, remigration.

Home, goal, resting-place, destination, journey's end, harbour, haven, port, dock, pier, landing-place, landing-stage, landing-ground, airfield, airstrip, airstop, airport, aerodrome, helidrome, terminus, station.

Meeting, rencontre, rencounter, encounter.

Caller, visitor, visitant, guest.

Verbs: To arrive, get to, come, come to, reach, attain, come up with, come up to, catch up, make, fetch, overtake, overhaul.

To light, alight, land, dismount, disembark, debark, detrain, outspan, debus, put in, put into, visit, cast, anchor.

To come upon, light upon, pitch upon, hit, drop in, pop upon, bounce upon, plump upon, bump against, run against, run across, close with.

To come back, return, get back, get home, sit down.

To meet, encounter, rencounter, contact, come in contact (199).

Phrase: To be in at the death.

Adjectives: Arriving, etc., homeward bound.

Adverbs: Here, hither.

Interjections: Welcome! hallo! hail! all hail! good day! good morrow! *ave!*

293 DEPARTURE

Substantives: outset, removal, exit, exodus, decampment, embarkation, flight, hegira.

Valediction, adieu, farewell, good-bye, leave-taking, send-off; stirrup-cup, doch-an-doris, one for the road.

A starting point or post, place of departure or embarkation, airfield, terminus, etc. (292).

Phrase: The foot being in the stirrup.

Verbs: To depart, go, set out, set off, start, start off, issue, go forth, sally, debouch, sally forth, set forward, be off, move off, pack off, buzz off, scram, begone, get off, sheer off, clear out, vamoose, skedaddle, absquatulate.

To leave a place, quit, retire, withdraw, go one's way, take wing, flit, embus, inspan, entrain, embark, go on board, set sail, put to sea, weigh anchor, slip cable, decamp (671).

Phrases: To take leave; bid or take adieu; bid farewell; to say good-bye; make one's exit; take a run-out powder.

Adjectives: Departing, etc., valedictory, outward bound.

Adverbs: Whence, hence, thence.

Interjections: Be off! get out! clear out! scram! buzz off! hop it! beat it! begone! get you gone! go along! off with you! avaunt! away with you! go about your business!

Good-bye! bye-bye! 'bye! ta ta! farewell! fare you well! adieu! *au revoir! auf wiedersehen! a rivederci! bon voyage! vale! hasta la vista! sayonara!* so long! cheerio! chin-chin! tinkety-tonk! pip-pip! tootle-oo! bung-ho!

294 INGRESS

Substantives: ingoing, entrance, entry, introgression, admission, admittance, intromission, introduction, insinuation, insertion (300), intrusion, inroad, incursion, influx, irruption, invasion, penetration, interpenetra-tion, infiltration, import, importation, illapse, immigration.

A mouth, door (260); an entrant.

Verbs: To enter, go into, come into, set foot in, intrude, invade, flow into, pop into, insinuate itself, penetrate, interpenetrate, infiltrate, soak into; to put into, etc., bring in, insert, drive in, run in, wedge in, ram in (300), intromit, introduce, import, smuggle.

Phrases: To find one's way into; creep into; worm oneself into; to darken one's door; have the *entrée*; to open the door to.

Adjectives: Ingoing, incoming, penetrative, penetrant.

Adverb: Inwards.

295 EGRESS

Substantives: exit, issue, emersion, emergence.

Exudation, extravasation, transudation (348), leakage, seepage, percolation, distillation, oozing, effluence, efflux, effusion, drain, dropping, dripping, dribbling, drip, dribble, drainage, filtering, defluxion, trickling, eruption, outbreak, outburst, outpouring, gush (348), emanation, aura.

Export, expatriation, emigration, remigration, repatriation, exodus (293).

An outlet, vent, spout, tap, faucet, sluice, flue, chimney, pore, drain, sewer (350).

Verbs: To emerge, emanate, issue, go, come, move, pass, pour, flow, etc., out of, find vent, pass off, evacuate.

To transude, exude, leak, seep, well out, percolate, transcolate, strain, distil, drain, ooze, filter, filtrate, dribble, trickle, drizzle, drip, gush, spout, run, flow out, effuse, extravasate, disembogue, debouch (348).

Adjectives: Dripping, outgoing, etc., oozy, leaky, trickly, dribbly.

296 RECEPTION

Substantives: admission, admittance,

importation, immission, introduction, ingestion, imbibition, absorption, resorption, ingurgitation, inhalation (300).

Eating, swallowing, deglutition, devouring, gulp, gulping, gorge, gorging,
carousal.

Drinking, potation, sipping, supping, suction, sucking, draught, libation; smoking, snuffing.

Mastication, manducation, rumination, chewing; hippophagy, ichthyophagy, anthropophagy.

Verbs: To admit, receive, intromit, import, ingest, absorb, resorb, imbibe, inhale, let in, take in, readmit, resorb, reabsorb, snuff up, sop up, suck, suck in, swallow, take down, ingurgitate, engulf.

To eat, fare, feed, devour, tuck in, gulp, bolt, snap, get down, pick, peck, gorge, engorge, fall to, stuff, cram, gobble, guttle, guzzle, wolf, raven, eat heartily, do justice to, overeat, gormandize (957), dispatch, discuss.

To feed upon, live on, feast upon, regale, carouse, batten upon, fatten upon, dine, etc., browse, graze, crop, chew, champ, munch, gnaw, nibble, crunch, ruminate, masticate, manducate, mumble.

To drink, quaff, swill, swig, booze, drench, sip, sup, lap, drink up, drain up, toss off, drain the cup, tipple (959).

Phrases: To give entrance or admittance to; open the door to; usher in.

To refresh the inner man; restore one's tissues; play a good knife and fork; get outside of; wrap oneself round.

To drink one's fill; wet one's whistle; empty one's glass; crook or lift one's elbow; crack a bottle.

Adjectives: Admitting, etc., admitted, etc., admissible; absorbent, absorptive.

Hippophagous, ichthyophagous, anthropophagous, herbivorous, graminivorous, granivorous, omnivorous.

297 EJECTION

Substantives: emission, effusion, rejection, expulsion, detrusion, extrusion, eviction.

Discharge, egestion, evacuation, vomition, eructation, belch; bloodletting, venesection, phlebotomy, tapping.

Deportation, exile, rustication, banishment, relegation, extradition.

Phrases: The rogue's march; the bum's rush.

Verbs: To emit, eject, expel, export, reject, discharge, give out, let out, cast out, clear out, sweep out, clean out, gut, fillet, wipe off, turn out, chuck out, elbow out, kick out, hoof out, sack, dismiss, bounce, drive out, root out, pour out, ooze, shed, void, evacuate, disgorge, extrude, empty, detrude, throw off, spit, spit out, expectorate, spirt, spill, slop, drain.

To vomit, spue, cat, puke, cast up, keck, retch, spatter, splutter, slobber, slaver, slabber, squirt, eructate, belch, burp, give vent to, tap, broach, open the sluices, heave out, bale out, shake off.

To throw, project (284); to push, thrust (276).

To unpack, unlade, unload (270).

To banish, exile, extradite, deport; ostracize, boycott, send to Coventry.

Phrases: To send packing; to send to the right about; to send about one's business; to give the sack to; to show the door to; to turn out neck and crop; to make a clean sweep of; to send away with a flea in one's ear.

Adjectives: Emitting, etc., emitted, etc.

Interjections: Be off! get out! scram! (293), scat! fade! chase yourself! *allez-vous-en!*

298 FOOD

Substantives: pabulum, aliment,

nourishment, nutriment, sustenance, sustentation, nurture, subsistence, provender, fodder, provision, prey, forage, pasture, pasturage, keep, fare, cheer, rations, diet, regimen.

Comestibles, eatables, victuals, prog, grub, chow, chuck, toke, eats, meat, bread, breadstuffs, cake, pastry, viands, cates, delicacy, delicatessen, dainty, creature comforts, belly-timber, staff of life, dish, flesh-pots, pottage, pudding, ragout, omelet, sundae, kickshaws.

Table, board, commons, good cheer, bill of fare, menu, commissariat, table d'hôte, ordinary, cuisine.

Canteen, Naffy, restaurant, chop-house, café, cafeteria, eating-house, tea-room, tea-shop, coffee-house, coffee-stall, bar, milk bar, snack bar, public-house, pot-house, ale-house, wineshop, brasserie, bodega, tavern (189).

Meal, repast, feed, mess, spread, course, regale, regalement, entertainment, feast, banquet, junket, refreshment, refection; breakfast, *chota hazri*, elevenses, *déjeuner*, lunch, bever, luncheon, tiffin, tea, afternoon tea, five-o'clock tea, high tea, dinner, supper, whet, appetizer, aperitif, bait, dessert, *entremet, hors d'œuvre*, picnic, bottle-party, wayz-goose, beanfeast, blow-out, tuck-in, snack, pot-luck, table d'hôte, *déjeuner à la fourchette*.

Mouthful, bolus, gobbet, sip, sup, sop, tot, snort, hoot, dram, peg, cock-tail (615), nip, *chasse, liqueur*.

Drink, hard drink, soft drink, tipple, beverage, liquor, broth, soup, etc., symposium.
Phrases: A good tuck-in; a modest quencher.
Adjectives: Eatable, edible, esculent, comestible, alimentary, cereal, culinary, nutritious, nutritive, nutrient, nutrimental, succulent, potable, drinkable.

298A TOBACCO
Substantives: the weed, bacca, baccy, honeydew, cavendish, bird's-eye, shag, virginia, latakia, perique, plug, twist.

Cigar, segar, cheroot, havana, manila, weed, whiff, cigarette, fag, gasper, stinker, coffin-nail.

Snuff, rappee.

A smoke, draw, puff, pinch, quid, chew, chaw.

Tobacco-pipe, pipe, briar, meerschaum, calabash, corncob, clay pipe, clay, churchwarden, dudeen (or dudheen), cutty, hookah, hubble-bubble, chibouque, narghile, calumet.
Verbs: To smoke, chew, take snuff.
Adjectives: Nicotian.

299 EXCRETION
Substantives: discharge, emanation, exhalation, exudation, secretion, extrusion, effusion, extravasation, evacuation, faeces, excrement (653), perspiration, sweat, saliva, salivation, spittle, diaphoresis; bleeding, haemorrhage, flux.
Verbs: To emanate, exhale, excern, excrete, exude, effuse, secrete, secern, extravasate, evacuate, urinate, discharge, etc. (297).

300 INSERTION
Substantives: putting in, implantation, introduction, interjection, insinuation, planting, intercalation, embolism, injection, inoculation, vaccination, importation, intervention (228), dovetailing, tenon, wedge.

Immersion, dip, plunge, bath (337), submergence, submersion, souse, duck, soak.

Interment, burying, etc. (363).
Verbs: To insert, introduce, intromit, put into, import, throw in, interlard, inject, interject, intercalate, infuse, instil, inoculate, vaccinate, pasteurize, impregnate, imbue, imbrue, graft,

engraft, bud, plant, implant, embed, obtrude, foist in, worm in, thrust in, stick in, ram in, stuff in, tuck in, plough in, let in, dovetail, mortise (or mortice), insinuate, wedge in, press in, impact, drive in, run in, empierce (260).

To immerse, dip, steep, immerge, merge, submerge, bathe, plunge, drop in, souse, douse, soak, duck, drown.

To inter, bury, etc. (363).

Adjectives: Inserting, inserted, implanted, embedded, etc., in-growing.

301 EXTRACTION
Substantives: taking out, removal, elimination, extrication, evulsion, avulsion, eradication, extirpation, wrench.

Expression, squeezing; ejection (297).

Extractor, corkscrew, pincers, pliers, forceps.

Verbs: To extract, take out, draw, draw out, pull out, tear out, pluck out, extort, wring from, prise, wrench, rake out, rake up, grub up, root up, uproot, eradicate, extirpate, dredge, remove, get out (185), elicit, extricate, eliminate.

To express, squeeze out, wring out, pick out, disembowel, eviscerate, exenterate.

Adjectives: Extracted, etc.

302 PASSAGE
Substantives: transmission, permeation, penetration, interpenetration (294), filtration, infiltration, percolation, transudation, osmosis (or osmose), capillary attraction, endosmosis (or endosmose), exosmosis (or exosmose), intercurrence; way, path (627); channel, pipe (350).

Terebration, impalement, etc. (260).

Verbs: To pass, pass through, traverse, terebrate, stick, pierce, impale, spear, spike, spit (260), pene-trate, percolate, permeate, thread, thrid, enfilade, go through, cross, go across, go over, pass over, get over, clear, negotiate, cut across, pass and repass; work, thread or worm one's way, force a passage; to transmit.

Adjectives: Passing, intercurrent, penetrative, transudatory, etc.

303 TRANSCURSION
Substantives: Transilience, transgression, trespass, encroachment, infringement, extravagation, transcendence, enjambement, overrunning.

Verbs: To transgress, overstep, surpass, overpass, overrun, overgo, beat, outstrip, outgo, outstep, outrun, outdo, overreach, overleap, outleap, pass, go by, strain, overshoot the mark, overjump, overskip, overlap, go beyond, outpace, outmarch, transcend, distance, outdistance, lap, encroach, exceed, trespass, infringe, trench upon.

Phrases: To stretch a point; to steal a march on; to pass the Rubicon; to shoot ahead of; to throw into the shade.

Adverbs: Beyond the mark, out of bounds.

304 SHORTCOMING
Substantives: failure, falling short (732), defalcation, default, backlog, leeway, incompleteness (53); imperfection (651); insufficiency (640).

Verbs: To come or fall short of, not to reach, keep within bounds, keep within compass, to stop short, be wanting, lose ground, miss the mark.

Adjectives: Unreached, deficient (53), short, minus.

Adverbs: Within the mark, within compass, within bounds, etc., behind-hand.

305 ASCENT
Substantives: rise, climb, ascension, upgrowth, leap (309).

A rocket, sky-rocket, lark, skylark; a climber, mountaineer, Alpinist, stegophilist.

Verbs: To ascend, rise, mount, arise, uprise, go up, get up, climb, clamber, swarm, shin, scale, scramble, escalade, surmount, aspire.

To tower, soar, zoom, hover, spire, plane, swim, float, surge.

Phrase: To make one's way up.

Adjectives: Rising, etc., scandent, buoyant, floating, supernatant, superfluitant.

Adverbs: Uphill, on the up grade.

Interjections: Excelsior!

306 DESCENT

Substantives: fall, descension, declension, declination, drop, cadence, subsidence, lapse, downfall, tumble, tilt, toppling, trip, lurch, *culbute,* spill, cropper, purler, crash.

Titubation, shamble, shambling, stumble.

An avalanche, landslip, landslide, debacle, slump.

Phrase: The fate of Icarus.

Verbs: To descend, come or go down, fall, sink, gravitate, drop, drop down, droop, decline, come down, dismount, alight, light, settle, subside, slide, slip, slither, glissade, toboggan, coast, volplane, dive (310).

To tumble, slip, trip, stumble, pitch, lurch, swag, topple, topple over, swoop, tilt, sprawl, plump down, measure one's length, bite the dust, heel over, careen (217), slump, crash.

To alight, dismount, get down.

Adjectives: Descending, etc., descendent, decurrent, decursive, deciduous.

Phrase: Nodding to its fall.

Adverbs: Downhill, on the down grade.

307 ELEVATION

Substantives: raising, lifting, erection, lift, uplift, upheaval, upcast.

Lift, elevator, hoist, escalator, crane, derrick, winch, windlass, jack, lever.

Verbs: To elevate, raise, lift, uplift, upraise, set up, erect, stick up, rear, uprear, upbear, upcast, hoist, uphoist, heave, upheave, weigh, exalt, promote, give a lift, help up, prick up, perk up.

To drag up, fish up, dredge.

To stand up, rise up, ramp.

Phrases: To set on a pedestal; to get up on one's hind legs.

Adjectives: Elevated, etc., rampant.

Adverbs: On stilts, on the shoulders of.

308 DEPRESSION

Substantives: lowering, abasement, abasing, detrusion, reduction.

Overthrow, upset, prostration, subversion, overset, overturn, precipitation.

Bow, curtsy (or curtsey), genuflexion, obeisance, kowtow, salaam.

Verbs: To depress, lower, let down, take down, sink, debase, abase, reduce, demote, detrude, let fall, cast down, to grass, send to grass.

To overthrow, overturn, upset, overset, subvert, prostrate, level, raze, fell; cast, take, throw, fling, dash, pull, cut, knock, hew, etc., down.

To stoop, bend, bow, curtsy (or curtsey), bob, duck, kneel, crouch, cower, lout, kowtow, salaam, bend the head or knee; to recline, sit, sit down, couch, squat.

Phrases: To take down a peg; to pull about one's ears; to trample in the dust.

Adjectives: Depressed, sunk, prostrate.

309 LEAP

Substantives: jump, hop, spring, bound, vault, saltation.

Dance, caper, curvet, caracole, *entrechat,* gambade, gambado, capriole, dido, demivolt.

Kangaroo, jerboa, chamois, goat, frog, grasshopper, flea, buck-jumper.

Phrases: Hop, skip, and jump; on the light fantastic toe.
Verbs: To leap, jump, bound, spring, take off, buck, buck-jump, hop, skip, vault, dance, bob, curvet, romp, caracole, caper, cut capers.
Adjectives: Leaping, etc., saltatory, Terpsichorean, frisky.

310 PLUNGE

Substantives: dip, dive, ducking, header.
Diver, frogman.
Verbs: To plunge, dip, souse, duck, dive, plump, plop, submerge, submerse, bathe, douse, sink, engulf, founder.

311 CIRCUITION

Substantives: turn, wind, circuit, curvet, detour, excursion, circumbendibus, circumvention, circumnavigation, north-west passage, circulation.
Turning, winding, twist, twisting, wrench, evolution, twining, coil, circumambulation, meandering.
Verbs: To turn, bend, wheel, put about, switch, circle, go round, or round about, circumnavigate, circumambulate, turn a corner, double a point, wind, meander, whisk, twirl, twist (248), twill; to turn on one's heel.
Phrases: To lead a pretty dance; to go the round; to turn on one's heel.
Adjectives: Turning, etc., circuitous, circumforaneous, circumfluent.
Adverb: Round about.

312 ROTATION

Substantives: revolution, gyration, roll, circumrotation, circumgyration, gurgitation, pirouette, circumvolution, convolution, turbination, whir, whirl, eddy, vortex, whirlpool, cyclone, anticyclone, tornado, typhoon, whirlwind, willy-willy, waterspout, surge, dizzy round, maelstrom, Charybdis.

A wheel, flywheel, screw, reel, whirligig, rolling stone, windmill, top, teetotum, merry-go-round, roundabout, gyroscope, gyrostat.
Axis, axle, spindle, pivot, pin, hinge, pole, swivel, gimbals, mandrel.
Verbs: To rotate, roll, revolve, spin, turn, turn round, circumvolve, circulate, gyre, gyrate, gimble, wheel, reel, whirl, twirl, birl, thrum, trundle, troll, twiddle, bowl, roll up, furl, wallow, welter.
Phrases: To box the compass; to spin like a top.
Adjectives: Rotating, etc., rotatory, rotary, circumrotatory, turbinate, trochoid, vortiginous, vortical, gyratory.
Phrase: Like a squirrel in a cage.
Adverbs: Clockwise, with the sun, deiseal (or deisil); counter-clock-wise, against the sun, withershins (or widdershins).

313 EVOLUTION

Substantives: unfolding, etc., development, introversion, reversion, eversion.
Verbs: To evolve, unfold, unroll, unwind, uncoil, untwist, unfurl, untwine, unravel, disentangle (44), develop, introvert, reverse.
Adjectives: Evolving, evolved, etc.
Adverbs: Against.

314 OSCILLATION

Substantives: vibration, undulation, pulsation, pulse, systole, diastole, libration, nutation, swing, beat, shake, seesaw, alternation, wag, evolution, vibratiuncle, coming and going, ebb and flow, flux and reflux; vibratility.
Fluctuation, vacillation, dance, lurch, dodge, rolling, pitching, tossing, etc.
A pendulum, seesaw, rocker, rocking-chair, rocking-horse, etc.
Verbs: To oscillate, vibrate, undulate, librate, wave, rock, swing, sway, pulsate, beat, wag, waggle, wiggle,

wobble, shoogle, nod, bob, tick, play, wamble, wabble, waddle, dangle, swag, curtsy.

To fluctuate, vacillate, alternate, dance, curvet, reel, quake, quiver, quaver, roll, top, pitch, flounder, stagger, totter, brandish, shake, flicker, flourish, seesaw, teeter, move up and down, to and fro, backwards and forwards, to pass and repass, to beat up and down.

Adjectives: Oscillating, etc., oscillatory, vibratory, vibratile, vibrant, vibrational, undulatory, pulsatory, pendulous, libratory, systaltic.

Adverbs: To and fro, up and down, backwards and forwards, seesaw, zigzag, wibble-wabble.

315 AGITATION

Substantives: stir, tremor, shake, ripple, jog, jolt, jar, succussion, trepidation, quiver, quaver, dance, jactitation, jactitancy, restlessness, shuffling, twitter, flicker, flutter, bobbing.

Disturbance, perturbation, commotion, turmoil, welter, bobbery; turbulence, tumult, tumultuation, bustle, fuss, flap, tirrivee, jerk, throw, convulsion, spasm (173), twitch, tic, staggers, St. Vitus's dance, epilepsy, writhing, ferment, fermentation, effervescence, ebullition, hurly-burly, hubbub, stramash, *tohu-bohu*; tempest, storm, whirlwind, cyclone (312), ground swell.

Verbs: To be agitated, to shake, tremble, quiver, quaver, shiver, dither, twitter, twire, writhe, toss about, tumble, stagger, bob, reel, sway, wag, waggle, wiggle, wobble, shoogle, dance, wriggle, squirm, stumble, flounder, shuffle, totter, dodder, shamble, flounce, flop, curvet, prance, cavort, throb, pulsate, beat, palpitate, go pit-a-pat, fidget, flutter, flitter, flicker, bicker, twitch, jounce, ferment, effervesce, boil.

To agitate, shake, convulse, toss, tumble, bandy, wield, brandish, flap, flourish, whisk, switch, jerk, hitch, jolt, jog, hoggle, jostle, hustle, disturb, shake up, churn.

Phrases: To jump like a parched pea; to be in a spin; to shake like an aspen leaf; to drive from pillar to post.

Adjectives: Shaking, etc., agitated, tremulous, shivery, tottery, jerky, shaky, shoogly, quivery, quavery, trembly, choppy, rocky, wriggly, desultory, subsultory, shambling, giddy-paced, saltatory.

Phrases: All of a tremble or twitter; like a pea on a drum; like a cat on hot bricks; like a hen on a hot griddle.

Adverbs: By fits and starts; subsultorily, *per saltum* (139).

Words relating to matter

Section 1 –
Matter in General

316 MATERIALITY
Substantives: corporeity, corporality, materialness, substantiality, physical, condition.

Matter, body, substance, brute matter, stuff, element, principle, parenchyma, material, substratum, frame, *corpus pabulum*, flesh and blood.

Thing, object, article, still life, stocks and stones.

Physics, somatology, somatics, natural philosophy, physiography, physical science, experimental philosophy, positivism, materialism.

Verbs: To materialize, embody, incarnate, objectify, externalize.

Adjectives: Material, bodily, corporeal, corporal, carnal, temporal, physical, somatic, somatological, materialistic, sensible, palpable, tangible, ponderable, concrete, impersonal, objective, bodied.

317 IMMATERIALITY
Substantives: incorporeity, spirituality, spirit, etc. (450), inextension.

Personality, I, me, myself, ego.

Spiritualism, spiritism, idealism, immaterialism.

Verbs: To disembody, spiritualize, immaterialize.

Adjectives: Immaterial, incorporeal, ideal, unextended, intangible, impalpable, imponderable, bodiless, unbodied, disembodied, extra-sensory, astral, psychical, psychic. extra-

mundane, unearthly, supernatural, supranatural, transcendent, transcendental, pneumatoscopic, spiritualistic, spiritual (450).

Personal, subjective.

318 WORLD
Substantives: nature, creation, universe; earth, globe, wide world, cosmos, sphere, macrocosm.

The heavens, sky, welkin, empyrean, starry heaven, firmament, ether; vault or canopy of heaven; celestial spaces, starry host, heavenly bodies, star, constellation, galaxy, Milky Way, *via lactea*, nebula, etc., sun, moon, planet, asteroid, planetoid, satellite, comet, meteor, meteorite, shooting star.

Zodiac, ecliptic, colure, orbit.

Astronomy, astrophysics, uranography, uranology, cosmology, cosmography, cosmogony; planetarium, orrery.

An astronomer, star-gazer, cosmographer; observatory.

Adjectives: Cosmic, cosmical, mundane, terrestrial, terraqueous, terrene, telluric, sublunary, under the sun, subastral, worldwide, global.

Celestial, heavenly, spheral, starry, stellar, nebular, etc., sidereal, sideral, astral, solar, lunar.

319 HEAVINESS
Substantives: weight, gravity, gravitation, ponderosity, ponderousness, avoirdupois, pressure, load, burden, ballast; a lump, mass, weight, counterweight, counterpoise; ponderability.

Lead, millstone, mountain.
Balance, spring balance, scales, steelyard, weighbridge.
Statics.
Phrase: Pelion on Ossa.
Verbs: To be heavy, to gravitate, weigh, press, cumber, load.
Adjectives: Weighty, heavy, ponderous, gravitating, weighing, etc., ponderable, lumpish, cumbersome, hefty, massive, unwieldy, cumbrous, incumbent, superincumbent; gravitational.
Phrase: Heavy as lead.

320 LIGHTNESS
Substantives: levity, imponderability, subtlety, buoyancy, airiness, portability, volatility.
A feather, dust, mote, down, thistledown, flue, ooss, fluff, cobweb, gossamer, straw, cork, bubble; float, buoy; featherweight.
Verbs: To be light, float, swim, be buoyed up.
Adjectives: Light, subtle, airy, vaporous, imponderous, astatic, weightless, imponderable, ethereal, sublimated, floating, swimming, buoyant, airborne, portable, uncompressed, volatile.
Phrases: Light as a feather; light as thistledown; 'trifles light as air'.

Section II –
Inorganic matter

321 DENSITY
Substantives: denseness, solidness, solidity, impenetrability, incompressibility, cohesion, coherence, cohesiveness (46), imporosity, impermeability, closeness, compactness, constipation, consistence, spissitude, thickness.
Specific gravity; hydrometer, araeometer.
Condensation, consolidation, solidi-

fication, concretion, coagulation, conglomeration, petrifaction, lapidification, vitrification, crystallization, precipitation, inspissation, thickening, grittiness, knottiness, induration (323).
Indivisibility, indiscerptibility, indissolubility.
A solid body, mass, block, knot, lump, concretion, concrete, cake, clot, stone, curd, coagulum, clinker, nugget; deposit, precipitate.
Verbs: To be dense, etc.
To become or render solid; solidify, solidate, concrete, set, consolidate, congeal, jelly, jell, coagulate, curdle, curd, fix, clot, cake, cohere, crystallize, petrify, vitrify, condense, incrassate, thicken, inspissate, compact, concentrate, compress, squeeze, ram down, constipate.
Adjectives: Dense, solid, solidified, consolidated, etc., coherent, cohesive, compact, close, thick-set, serried, substantial, massive, lumpish, impenetrable, incompressible, impermeable, imporous, constipated, concrete, knotted, gnarled, crystalline, crystallizable, vitreous, coagulated, thick, incrassated, inspissated, curdled, clotted, grumous.
Undissolved, unmelted, unliquefied, unthawed.
Indivisible, indiscerptible, infrangible, indissolvable, indissoluble, insoluble, infusible.

322 RARITY
Substantives: tenuity, absence of solidity, subtility, sponginess, compressibility; hollowness (252).
Rarefaction, expansion, dilatation, inflation, dilution, attenuation, subtilization.
Ether, vapour, air, gas (334).
Verbs: To rarefy, expand, dilate, dilute, attenuate, subtilize, thin out.
Adjectives: Rare, subtle, sparse, slight, thin, fine, tenuous, compressible.

Porous, cavernous, spongy, bibulous, spongious, spongeous.

Rarefied, expanded, dilated, subtilized, unsubstantial, hollow (252).

323 HARDNESS
Substantives: rigidity, rigescence, firmness, renitence, inflexibility, stiffness, starchiness, starchedness, temper, callosity, durity, induration, grittiness, petrifaction, etc. (321), ossification, sclerosis.

A stone, pebble, flint, marble, rock, granite, brick, iron, steel, corundum, diamond, adamant, bone, callus.

Verbs: To render hard, harden, stiffen, indurate, petrify, vitrify, temper, ossify.

Adjectives: Hard, horny, corneous, bony, osseous, rigid, rigescent, stiff, firm, starch, stark, unbending, unyielding, inflexible, tense, indurate, indurated, gritty, stony, proof, adamantean, adamantine.

Phrases: Hard as iron, etc.; hard as a brick; hard as a nail; hard as a deal board; 'as hard as a piece of the nether millstone'; stiff as buckram; stiff as a poker.

324 SOFTNESS
Substantives: tenderness, flexibility, pliancy, pliableness, pliantness, litheness, pliability, suppleness, sequacity, ductility, malleability, tractility, extensibility, plasticity, inelasticity, laxity, flaccidity, flabbiness, limpness.

Clay, wax, butter, dough; a cushion, pillow, featherbed, down, padding, wadding, cotton-wool.

Mollification, softening, etc.

Verbs: To render soft, soften, mollify, relax, temper, mash, pulp, knead, squash.

To bend, yield, give, relent, relax.

Adjectives: Soft, tender, supple, pliable, limp, limber, flexible, flexile, lithe, lissom, *svelte,* willowy, pliant, plastic, waxen, ductile, tractile, tract-able, malleable, extensile, sequacious.

Yielding, bending, flabby, flaccid, lymphatic, flocculent, downy, flimsy, spongy, oedematous, doughy, argillaceous, mellow; emollient, softening, etc.

Phrases: Soft as butter; soft as down; soft as silk; yielding as wax; tender as a chicken.

325 ELASTICITY
Substantives: springiness, spring, resilience, buoyancy, renitency, contractility (195), compressibility.

Indiarubber, rubber, caoutchouc, whalebone, elastic.

Verbs: To be elastic, etc., to spring back, fly back, rebound, recoil (277).

Adjectives: Elastic, tensile, springy, resilient, buoyant.

326 INELASTICITY
Substantives: want or absence of elasticity, softness, etc. (324).

Adjectives: Inelastic, ductile, limber, etc. (324).

327 TOUGHNESS
Substantives: tenacity, strength, cohesion (46), stubbornness (606).

Leather, gristle, cartilage.

Verbs: To be tenacious, etc., to resist fracture.

Adjectives: Tenacious, tough, wiry, sinewy, stringy, stubborn, cohesive, strong, resisting, resistant, leathery, coriaceous.

Phrase: Tough as leather.

328 BRITTLENESS
Substantives: fragility, crispness, friability, frangibility, fissility.

Verbs: To be brittle, break, crack, snap, split, shiver, splinter, fracture, crumble, break short, burst, fly.

Adjectives: Brittle, frangible, fragile, frail, jerry-built, gimcrack, shivery, fissile, splitting, splintery, lacerable, crisp, friable, short, crumbling.

Phrases: Brittle as glass; a house of cards.

329 TEXTURE
Substantives: structure, construction, organization, set-up, organism, anatomy, frame, mould, fabric, framework, carcass, architecture, *compages*; substance, stuff, parenchyma, constitution, intertexture, contexture, tissue, grain, web, warp, woof, nap (256).

Fineness or coarseness of grain.

Histology.

Adjectives: Textural, structural, organic, anatomic, anatomical; fine, delicate, subtle, fine-grained; coarse, homespun, rough-grained, coarse-grained; flimsy, unsubstantial, gossamery, filmy, gauzy.

330 PULVERULENCE
Substantives: state of powder, powderiness, efflorescence, sandiness, friability.

Dust, stour (or stoor), powder, sand, shingle, sawdust, grit, meal, bran, flour, limature, filings, debris, detritus, moraine, scobs, crumb, seed, grain, spore, atom, particle (32), flocculence.

Reduction to powder, pulverization, comminution, granulation, disintegration, weathering, subaction, contusion, trituration, levigation, abrasion, detrition, filing, etc. (331).

Mill, quern, grater, nutmeg grater, rasp, file, pestle and mortar.

Verbs: To reduce to powder, to pulverize, comminute, granulate, triturate, levigate, scrape, file, abrade, rub down, grind, grate, rasp, mill, pound, bray, bruise, contuse, contund, beat, crush, crunch, scrunch, crumble, disintegrate, weather.

Adjectives: Powdery, granular, mealy, floury, branny, farinaceous, furfuraceous, flocculent, dusty, sandy, sabulous, arenaceous, gritty, efflorescent, impalpable; pulverizable, pulverulent, friable, crumbly, shivery, pulverized, etc., attrite.

331 FRICTION
Substantives: attrition, rubbing, massage, abrasion, rub, scouring, limature, filing, rasping, frication, elbowgrease.

Grindstone, whetstone, buff, hone, strop (253).

Verbs: To rub, abrade, scratch, scrape, scrub, grate, fray, rasp, pare, scour, polish, massage, curry, shampoo, rub out.

332 LUBRICATION
Substantives: prevention of friction, oiling, etc., anointment.

Lubricant, oil, lard, grease, etc. (356); synovia, saliva.

Verbs: To lubricate, oil, grease, anoint, wax; smooth (255).

Adjectives: Lubricated, etc.

333 FLUIDITY
Substantives: fluid (including both inelastic and elastic fluids).

Liquidity, liquidness, aquosity, a liquid, liquor, lymph, humour, juice, sap, blood, serum, serosity, gravy, chyle, rheum, ichor, sanies; solubility.

Hydrology, hydrostatics, hydrodynamics.

Verbs: To be fluid or liquid, to flow, run (348).

Adjectives: Liquid, fluid, fluent, running, flowing, serous, juicy, succulent, sappy, lush.

Liquefied, uncongealed, melted, etc. (335).

334 GASEITY
Substantives: vaporousness, flatulence, flatulency; gas, air, vapour, ether, steam, fume, reek, effluvium.

Smoke, cloud (353).

Pneumatics, aerostatics, aerodynamics; gas-meter, gasometer.

Verbs: To emit vapour, evaporate, to steam, fume, reek, smoke, puff, smoulder.
Adjectives: Gaseous, aeriform, ethereal, aerial, airy, vaporous, vapoury, flatulent, volatile, evaporable.

335 LIQUEFACTION
Substantives: liquescence, fusion, melting, thaw, deliquation, deliquescence, lixiviation.
Solution, dissolution, decoction, infusion, apozem, flux.
Solvent, menstruum, alkahest.
Verbs: To render liquid, to liquefy, deliquesce, run, melt, thaw, fuse, solve, dissolve, resolve, to hold in solution.
Adjectives: Liquefied, melted, unfrozen, molten, liquescent, liquefiable, deliquescent, diffluent, soluble, dissoluble.

336 VAPORIZATION
Substantives: gasification, volatilization, evaporation, distillation, sublimation, exhalation, volatility.
Vaporizer, retort, still.
Verbs: To render gaseous, vaporize, volatilize, evaporate, exhale, distil, sublime, sublimate.
Adjectives: Volatilized, etc., volatile, evaporable, vaporizable.

337 WATER
Substantives: heavy water, serum, lymph, rheum, whey.
Dilution, immersion, maceration, humectation, infiltration, sprinkling, washing, spraying, aspersion, affusion, irrigation, douche, balneation, bath, shower-bath, inundation, deluge (348), a diluent.
Verbs: To be watery, etc., to reek.
To add water, to water, wet, moisten (339), dilute, dip, immerse, plunge, merge, immerge, steep, souse, duck, submerge, drown, soak, saturate, sop, macerate, pickle, blunge, wash, lave, sprinkle, asperge, asperse, dabble, bedabble, affuse, splash, splatter, spray, swash, douse, drench, slop, slobber, irrigate, inundate, deluge, flood.
To take a bath, to tub, bathe, bath, paddle.
To syringe, inject, gargle.
Adjectives: Watery (339), aqueous, aquatic, lymphatic, diluted, etc., reeking, dripping, sodden, drenched, soaking, sopping.
Wet, washy, sloppy, squashy, splashy, soppy, soggy, slobbery, diluent, balneal.
Phrases: Wet as a drowned rat; soaked to the skin; wet as a rag; wet through.

338 AIR
Substantives: common air, atmospheric air.
The atmosphere, troposphere, tropopause, stratosphere, ionosphere, Heaviside layer, Appleton layer; the sky, the ether, the open air, ozone, weather, climate.
Meteorology, climatology, isobar, barometer, aneroid barometer, weather-glass, weather-chart, weather station, weather ship
Exposure to the air or weather, airing, weathering (33o).
Verbs: To aerate, oxygenate, arterialize, ventilate, air-condition.
Adjectives: Containing air, windy, flatulent, aerated, effervescent.
Atmospheric, airy, open-air, *plein-air,* alfresco, aerial, aeriform; meteorological, barometric, weatherwise.
Adverbs: In the open air, *à la belle étoile, sub Jove.*

339 MOISTURE
Substantives: moistness, humidity, dampness, damp, wetness, wet, humectation, madefaction, dew, muddiness, march (345).
Hygrometer, hygrometry, hygrology.

Verbs: To be moist, etc.

To moisten, wet, humectate, sponge, damp, dampen, bedew, imbue, infiltrate, imbrue; soak, saturate (337).

Adjectives: Moist, damp, watery, humid, wet, dank, muggy, dewy, roral, rorid, roscid, juicy, swampy (345), humectant, sopping, dripping, sodden.

Phrase: Wringing wet.

340 DRYNESS

Substantives: siccity, aridity, drought.

Exsiccation, desiccation, arefaction, drainage.

Verbs: To be dry, etc.

To render dry, to dry, dry up, sop up, swab, wipe, blot, exsiccate, desiccate, dehydrate, drain, parch.

Adjectives: Dry, anhydrous, dehydrated, arid, dried, etc., unwatered, undamped, waterproof, husky, juiceless, sapless; siccative, desiccative.

Phrases: Dry as a bone; dry as dust; dry as a stick; dry as a mummy; dry as a biscuit; dry as a limekiln.

341 OCEAN

Substantives: sea, main, the deep, brine, salt water, blue water, high seas, offing, tide, wave, surge, ooze, etc. (348).

Hydrography, oceanography.

Neptune, Thetis, Triton, Oceanid, Nereid, sea-nymph, siren, mermaid, merman, dolphin; trident.

Phrases: The vasty deep; the briny; the ditch; the drink.

Adjectives: Oceanic, marine, maritime, thalassic, pelagic, pelagian, sea-going, hydrographic.

Adverbs: At sea, on sea, afloat.

342 LAND

Substantives: earth, ground, terra firma, continent, mainland, peninsula, delta, alluvium, polder, tongue of land, neck of land, isthmus, oasis.

Coast, shore, seaboard, seaside, seabank, strand, beach, bank, lea.

Cape, promontory, etc. (250), headland, point of land, highland (206).

Soil, glebe, clay, humus, loam, marl, clod, clot, rock, crag, chalk, gravel, mould, subsoil.

Adjectives: Terrene, continental, earthy, terraqueous, terrestrial.

Littoral, riparian, alluvial, midland.

Adverbs: Ashore, on shore, on land.

343 GULF

Substantives: bay, inlet, bight, estuary, roadstead, roads, arm of the sea, armlet, sound, frith, firth, fiord, lagoon, cove, creek, strait, belt, kyle, Euripus.

Adjectives: Estuarine.

343A LAKE

Substantives: loch, lough, mere, tarn, linn, plash, broad, pond, dew-pond, pool puddle, well, reservoir, standing water, dead water, a sheet of water, fish-pond, ditch, dike, backwater.

Adjectives: Lacustrine (or lacustrian), lacuscular.

344 PLAIN

Substantives: tableland, open country, the face of the country, champaign country, basin, downs, waste, wild, weald, steppe, pampas, savanna, llano, prairie, tundra, heath, common, wold, moor, moorland, the bush; plateau, flat (213).

Meadow, mead, haugh, pasturage, park, field, lawn, green, plot, plat, terrace, esplanade, sward, turf, sod, heather, lea, grounds, pleasure-grounds, playing-fields, campus.

Phrase: A weary waste.

Adjectives: Campestrian, champaign, lawny.

345 MARSH

Substantives: marish, swamp,

morass, moss, fen, bog, quag, quagmire, slough, sump, wash.

Adjectives: Marshy, marish, swampy, boggy, quaggy, fenny, soft, plashy, poachy, paludal.

346 ISLAND
Substantives: isle, islet, ait, eyot, inch, holm, reef, atoll; archipelago.
Adjectives: Insular, sea-girt.

347 STREAM
Substantives: flow, current, jet, undercurrent, course (348).
Verbs: To flow, stream, issue, run.

348 RIVER
Substantives: running water, jet, spurt, squirt, spout, splash, rush, gush, water-spout, sluice, linn, waterfall, cascade, force, catadupe, cataract, debacle, cataclysm, inundation, deluge, avalanche, spate.

Rain, shower, scud, driving rain, downpour, drencher, soaker, cloudburst, mizzle, drizzle, Scotch mist, smirr, dripping, stillicidium; flux, flow, profluence, effluence, efflux, effluxion, defluxion.

Irrigation (337).

Spring, fountain, fount, rill, rivulet, gill, gullet, rillet, streamlet, runnel, sike, burn, beck, brooklet, brook, stream, reach, torrent, rapids, race, flush, flood, swash.

Tide, spring tide, high tide, tidal wave, bore, eagre, freshet, current, indraught, reflux, eddy, whirlpool, vortex, maelstrom, regurgitation.

Tributary, confluent, effluent, billabong; corrivation, confluence, effluence.

Wave, billow, surge, swell, chop, ripple, ground swell, surf, breaker, roller, comber, white caps, white horses.

Irrigation (337); sprinkler, sprayer, spray, atomizer, aspergillum, aspersorium, water-cart, watering-pot, watering-can, pump, syringe, hydrant.

Hydraulics, hydrodynamics, hydrography; rain-gauge.

Verbs: To flow, run, meander, gush, spout, roll, billow, surge, jet, well, drop, drip, trickle, dribble, ooze (295), percolate, distil, transude, stream, sweat, perspire (299), overflow, flow over, splash, swash, guggle, murmur, babble, bubble, purl, gurgle, sputter, spurt, regurgitate, surge.

To rain, rain hard, pour with rain, drizzle, spit, mizzle, set in.

To flow into, fall into, open into, drain into, discharge itself, disembogue, disgorge, debouch.

Phrases: To rain cats and dogs; to rain in torrents.

To cause a flow, to pour, drop, distil, splash, squirt, spill, drain, empty, discharge, pour out, open the sluices or flood-gates; shower down, irrigate (337).

To stop a flow, to stanch, dam, dam up (261), intercept.

Adjectives: Fluent, profluent, affluent, confluent, diffluent, tidal, flowing, etc., babbling, bubbling, gurgling, meandering, meandrous.

Fluviatile, fluvial, riverine, streamy, showery, drizzly, rainy, pluvial, pouring.

349 WIND
Substantives: draught, current, breath, air, breath of air, puff, whiff, zephyr, blow, drift, aura.

Gust, blast, breeze, squall, gale, storm, tempest, hurricane, whirlwind, tornado, cyclone, typhoon, blizzard, simoom, samiel, harmattan, monsoon, trade wind, sirocco, mistral, *bise, tramontana, föhn,* pampero; windiness, ventosity.

Aeolus, Boreas, Auster, Euroclydon, the cave of Aeolus.

Bellow, blowpipe, fan, ventilator, punkah.

Anemometer, anemograph, wind-gauge, weathercock, vane.

Insufflation, sufflation, perflation, blowing, fanning, ventilation, blowing up, inflation, afflation; respiration, inspiration, expiration, sneezing, sternutation, cough, hiccup.

Phrase: A capful of wind.

Verbs: To blow, waft, blow hard, blow a hurricane, breathe, respire, inspire, expire, insufflate, puff, whiff, sough, whiffle, wheeze, gasp, snuffle, sniffle, sneeze, cough.

To fan, ventilate, inflate, perflate, blow up.

Phrase: To blow great guns.

Adjectives: Blowing, etc., rough, blowy, windy, breezy, gusty, squally, puffy, stormy, tempestuous, blustering.

350 CONDUIT

Substantives: channel, duct, watercourse, watershed, race, adit, aqueduct, canal, sluice, dike, main, gully, moat, ditch, lode, leat, rhine, trough, gutter, drain, sewer, culvert, cloaca, sough, kennel, siphon,, pipe (260), emunctory, gully-hole, artery, aorta, pore, spout, funnel, tap, faucet, scupper, adjutage (or ajutage), wastepipe, hose, rose, gargoyle, artesian well.

Floodgate, dam, weir, levee, watergate, lock, valve.

351 AIR-PIPE

Substantives: air-tube, shaft, flue, chimney, lum, funnel, smoke-stack, exhaust-pipe, exhaust, vent, blowhole, nostril, nozzle, throat, weasand, trachea, larynx, windpipe, thrapple, spiracle, ventiduct.

Ventilator, louvre, register.

Tobacco-pipe, pipe, etc. (298A).

352 SEMILIQUIDITY

Substantives: pulpiness, viscidity, viscosity, ropiness, sliminess, gumminess, glutinosity, gummosity, siziness, clamminess, mucosity, spissitude, lentor, thickness, crassitude.

Inspissation, thickening, incrassation.

Jelly, mucilage, gelatine, mucus, chyme, phlegm, gum, glue, gluten, goo, colloid, albumen, size, milk, cream, emulsion, soup, broth, starch, treacle, squash, mud, clart, glaur, slush, slime, ooze, dope, glycerine; lava.

Pitch, tar, bitumen, asphalt, resin, rosin, varnish, copal, mastic, wax, amber.

Verbs: To inspissate, thicken, incrassate, jelly, jellify, mash, squash, churn, beat up, pulp.

Adjectives: Semi-fluid, semi-liquid, milky, emulsive, creamy, lacteal, lacteous, curdy, curdled, soupy, muddy, slushy, clarty, thick, succulent, squashy.

Gelatinous, albuminous, gummy, colloid, amylaceous, mucilaginous, glairy, slimy, ropy, stringy, clammy, glutinous (46), viscid, viscous, sticky, gooey, slab, slabby,sizy, lentous, tacky.

Tarry, pitchy, resinous, bituminous.

353 BUBBLE

Substantives: soda-water, aerated water, foam, froth, head, spume, lather, bleb, spray, spindrift, surf, yeast, barm, suds.

Cloud, vapour, fog, mist, smog, haze, steam, nebulosity (422); scud, rack, cumulus, cirrus, stratus, nimbus, mare's tail, mackerel sky.

Nephelology; Fido.

Effervescence, foaming, mantling, fermentation, frothing, etc.

Verbs: To bubble, boil, foam, froth, mantle, sparkle, guggle, gurgle, effervesce, fizz, ferment.

Adjectives: Bubbling, etc., frothy, yeasty, barmy, nappy, effervescent, fizzy, up, boiling, fermenting, sparkling, mantling, *mousseux*.

Cloudy, foggy, misty, vaporous, nebulous.

354 PULPINESS
Substantives: pulp, paste, dough, curd, pap, pudding, poultice, soup, squash, mud, slush, grume, jam, preserve.
Adjectives: Pulpy, pulpous, pultaceous, doughy, grumous.

355 UNCTUOUSNESS
Substantives: unctuosity, oiliness, greasiness, slipperiness, lubricity.
Lubrication (332), anointment, unction; ointment (356).
Verbs: To oil, grease, anoint, wax, lubricate (332).
Adjectives: Unctuous, oil, oleaginous, adipose, sebaceous, fat, fatty, greasy, waxy, butyraceous, soapy, saponaceous, pinguid, stearic, lardaceous.

356 OIL
Substantives: fat, butter, margarine, cream, grease, tallow, suet, lard, dripping, blubber, pomatum, pomade, stearin, lanoline, soap, soft soap, wax, beeswax, sealing-wax, ambergris, spermaceti, adipocere, ointment, unguent, liniment, paraffin, kerosene, gasolene, petroleum, petrol, mineral oil, vegetable oil, olive oil, castor oil, linseed oil, train oil.

Section III –
Organic matter

357 ORGANIZATION
Substantives: the organized world, organized nature, living nature, animated nature, living beings; protoplasm, protein.
Biology, ecology (or oecology), natural history, organic chemistry, zoology (368), botany (369).
Adjectives: Organic, animate.

358 INORGANIZATION
Substantives: the mineral world or kingdom; unorganized, inorganic, brute or inanimate matter.
Mineralogy, geognosy, petrology, lithology, geology, metallurgy, inorganic chemistry.
Adjectives: Inorganic, azoic, mineral, inanimate.

359 LIFE
Substantives: vitality, animation, viability, the vital spark or flame or principle, the breath of life, life-blood; existence (1).
Vicification, revivification.
Physiology, biology; metabolism.
Phrase: The breath of one's nostrils.
Verbs: To be living, alive, etc., to live, subsist (1), breathe, fetch breath, respire, draw breath, to be born, be spared.
To come to life, to revive, come to.
To give birth to (161); to bring, restore, or recall to life, to vivify, revive, revivify, quicken, reanimate, vitalize.
Phrases: To see the light; to come into the world; to walk the earth; to draw breath.
To keep body and soul together; to support life.
Adjectives: Living, alive, in life, above ground, breathing, animated, quick, viable.
Vital, vivifying, vivified, Promethean, metabolic.
Phrases: Alive and kicking; in the land of the living; on this side of the grave.

360 DEATH
Substantives: decease, dissolution, demise, departure, obit, expiration; termination, close or extinction of life, existence, etc.; mortality, fall, doom, fate, release, rest, end, quietus, loss, bereavement, euthanasia, katabolism.
Last breath, last gasp, last agonies, the death-rattle, dying breath, agonies of death, dying agonies.

155

Necrology, death-roll, obituary.
Phrases: The ebb of life; the king of terrors; the jaws of death; the swan-song; the Stygian shore; the sleep that knows no waking; a watery grave.
Verbs: To die, perish, expire.
Phrases: Breathe one's last; cease to live; depart this life; end one's days; be no more; go off; drop off; pop off; peg out; lose one's life; drop down dead; resign, relinquish, lay down, or surrender one's life; drop or sink into the grave; close one's eyes; break one's neck.

To give up the ghost; to be all over with one; to pay the debt to nature; to make the great change; to take one's last sleep; to shuffle off this mortal coil; to go to one's last home; to go the way of all flesh; to kick the bucket; to hop the twig; to turn up one's toes; to slip one's cable; to cross the Stygian ferry.

To snuff out; to go off the hooks; to go to one's account; to go aloft; to join the majority; to go west; to have had it; to be numbered with the dead; to die a natural death; to hand in one's checks; to pass away or over.
Adjectives: Dead, lifeless, deceased, demised, gone, departed, defunct, exanimate, inanimate, *kaput,* out of the world, mortuary; still-born.

Dying, expiring, moribund, *in articulo mortis, in extremis,* in the agony of death, etc., going, life ebbing, going off, life failing, *aux abois,* booked, having received one's death warrant.
Phrases: Dead and gone; dead as a door-nail, as mutton, as a door-post, as a herring; stone-dead; launched into eternity; gone to one's last home; gathered to one's fathers; gone to Davy Jones's locker; gone west; gone for a Burton; pushing up the daisies.

At death's door; on one's death-bed; in the jaws of death; death staring one in the face; one's hour being come; one's days being numbered; one's race being run; one foot in the grave; on one's last legs; life hanging by a thread; at one's last gasp.
Adverbs: Post-mortem, post-obit.

361 KILLING
Substantives: homicide, parricide, matricide, fratricide, sororicide, infanticide, regicide, tyrannicide, vaticide, genocide, manslaughter, murder, assassination, blood, gore, bloodshed, slaughter, carnage, butchery, massacre, immolation, holocaust, fusillade, *noyade,* thuggee, thuggery, thuggism; casualty, fatality.

Death-blow, kiss of death, *coup de grâce,* grace-stroke, mercy killing, euthanasia.

Suicide, felo-de-se, hara-kiri, happy dispatch, suttee, martyrdom, execution.

Destruction of animals, slaughtering, battue, hecatomb.

Slaughter-house, shambles, abattoir.

A butcher, slayer, murderer, homicide, parricide, matricide, etc., assassin, cut-throat, bravo, thug, executioner (975).
Verbs: To kill, put to death, do to death, slay, murder, assassinate, slaughter, butcher, immolate, massacre, decimate, take away or deprive of life, make away with, dispatch, burke, lynch, settle, do for, do in, bump off, brain, spiflicate.

To strangle, throttle, bowstring, choke, garrotte, stifle, suffocate, smother, asphyxiate, drown, hang, turn off, string up.

To cut down, sabre, cut to pieces, cut off, cut the throat, stab, knife, bayonet, shoot, behead, decapitate, stone, lapidate, execute (972).

To commit suicide, to make away with oneself.
Phrases: To put to the sword; put to the edge of the sword; give no quarter to; run through the body; knock on the head; give one the works; put one on the spot; blow the brains out; give the

death blow, the *coup de grâce*; put out of one's misery; launch into eternity; give a quietus to.

Adjectives: Killing, etc., murderous, slaughterous, sanguinary, ensanguined, gory, bloody, blood-stained, blood-guilty, red-handed.

Mortal, fatal, deadly, lethal, internecine, suicidal, homicidal, fratricidal, etc.

362 CORPSE

Substantives: corse, carcass, bones, skeleton, carrion, defunct, relic, remains, ashes, earth, dust, clay, mummy.

Shade, ghost, *manes*; the dead, the majority, the great majority.

Phrases: All that was mortal; this tenement of clay; food for worms or fishes.

Adjectives: Cadaverous, corpse-like.

363 INTERMENT

Substantives: burial, sepulture, inhumation, obsequies, exequies, funeral, wake, lyke-wake, pyre, funeral pile, cremation.

Funeral rite or solemnity, knell, passing-bell, tolling, dirge, lament, coronach, keening (839), requiem, epicedium, obit, elegy, funeral oration, epitaph, death march, dead march, lying in state.

Grave-clothes, shroud, winding-sheet, cerecloth, cerement.

Coffin, casket, shell, sarcophagus, urn, pall, bier, hearse, catafalque.

Grave, pit, sepulchre, tomb, vault, catacomb, mausoleum, house of death, burial-place, cemetery, necropolis, churchyard, graveyard, God's acre, burial-ground, cromlech, dolmen, barrow, tumulus, cairn, ossuary, charnel-house, morgue, mortuary, crematorium, cinerator; Valhalla.

Monument, tombstone, gravestone, shrine, cenotaph.

Exhumation, disinterment; autopsy, necropsy, post-mortem.

Undertaker, mortician, mute, sexton, grave-digger.

Verbs: To inter, bury, lay in the grave, consign to the grave or tomb, entomb, inhume, cremate, lay out, embalm, mummify.

To exhume, disinter.

Adjectives: Buried, etc., burial, funereal, funebrial, funerary, mortuary, sepulchral, cinerary; elegiac.

Phrases: *Hic jacet*; RIP.

364 ANIMALITY

Substantives: animal life, animality, animation, breath, animalization.

Flesh, flesh and blood, physique.

Verbs: To animalize.

Adjectives: Fleshly, corporal, carnal.

365 VEGETABILITY

Substantives: vegetable life, vegetation.

Adjectives: Lush, rank, luxuriant.

366 ANIMAL

Substantives: the animal kingdom, brute creation, fauna, avifauna.

A beast, brute, creature, created being; creeping or living thing, dumb creature, flocks and herds, live-stock.

Cattle, kine, etc.

Game, *fera natura,* wild life.

Mammal, quadruped, bird, reptile, fish, mollusc, worm, insect, zoophyte, animalcule, etc.

Phrases: The beasts of the field; fowls of the air; denizens of the deep.

Adjectives: Animal, zoological, piscatory, fishy, molluscous, vermicular, etc., feral.

367 PLANT

Substantives: vegetable, the vegetable kingdom, flora.

Tree, fruit-tree, shrub, bush, creeper, herb, herbage, grass, fern, fungus, lichen, moss, weed, seaweed, alga; annual, biennial, perennial; exotic.

Forest, wood, hurst, holt, green-wood, woodland, brake, grove, copse, coppice, hedgerow, boscage, plantation, thicket, spinney, underwood, undergrowth, brushwood, clump of trees, park, chase, weald, scrub, jungle, prairie.

Foliage, florescence, flower, blossom, branch, bough, spray, twig, leaf.

Adjectives: Vegetable, vegetal, arboreal, herbaceous, herbal, botanic, sylvan, woodland, woody, wooded, well-wooded, shrubby, grassy, verdurous, verdant, floral, mossy.

368 ZOOLOGY
Substantives: zoography, anatomy, zootomy, comparative anatomy, physiology, morphology.

Ornithology, ichthyology, herpetology, ophiology, malacology, helminthology, entomology; palaeontology.

369 BOTANY
Substantives: phytography, phytology, vegetable physiology, herborization, dendrology, mycology, Pomona, Flora, Ceres.

Herbarium, herbal, *hortus siccus,* vasculum.

Verbs: To botanize, herborize.

370 TAMING
Substantives: domestication, domesticity; training, breaking-in, manège, breeding, pisciculture; veterinary art.

Menagerie, zoological garden, game reserve, aviary, apiary, vivarium, aquarium, fishery, fish-pond, duck-pond.

Verbs: To tame, domesticate, train, tend, break in.

Adjectives: Pastoral, bucolic.

371 AGRICULTURE
Substantives: cultivation, culture, intensive cultivation, husbandry, agronomy, geoponics, hydroponics, georgics, tillage, gardening, horticul-ture, forestry, vintage, etc., arboriculture, floriculture, the topiary art.

Vineyard, vinery, garden, kitchen garden, market garden, nursery, bed, plot, herbaceous border, parterre, hot-house, greenhouse, conservatory, espalier, shrubbery, orchard, rock garden, rockery, winter garden, pinery, arboretum, allotment.

A husbandman, horticulturist, gardener, florist, agriculturist, agriculturalist, woodcutter, backwoodsman, forester, land girl, farmer, yeoman, cultivator.

Verbs: To cultivate, till, garden, farm; delve, dibble, dig, sow, plant, graft; plough, harrow, rake, reap, mow, cut, weed.

Adjectives: Agricultural, agrarian, arable, rural, country, rustic, agrestic.

372 MANKIND
Substantives: the human race or species; man, human nature, humanity, mortality, flesh, generation; Everyman.

Anthropology, anthropography, ethnology, ethnography, demography, sociology, social economics; civics.

Anthropomorphism.

Human being, person, individual, type, creature, fellow creature, mortal, body, somebody, one, someone, a soul, living soul, earthling, party personage, inhabitant; *dramatis personae.*

People, persons, folk, population, public, world, race, society, community, the million, commonalty (876), nation, state, realm, community, commonwealth, republic, commonweal, polity, nationality; civilized society, civilization.

Anthropologist, ethnologist, sociologist, etc.

Phrases: The lords of creation; the body politic.

Adjectives: National, civic, public, human, mortal, personal, individual, social, cosmopolitan, ethnic, racial; sociological, anthropological, ethnological, anthropomorphic, anthropomorphous, anthropoid, manlike.

373 MAN

Substantives: manhood, manliness, virility, he, menfolk.

A human being, man, male, mortal, person, body, soul, individual, fellow creature, one, someone, somebody, so-and-so.

Personage, a gentleman, sir, master, yeoman, citizen, denizen, burgess, burgher, cosmopolite, wight, swain, fellow, blade, bloke, beau, chap, guy, bod, type, cove, gossoon, buffer, gaffer, goodman; husband (903).

Adjectives: Human, manly, male, masculine, manlike, mannish, virile, mannish, unwomanly, unfeminine.

Phrase: The spear side.

374 WOMAN

Substantives: female, feminality, femininity, womanhood, muliebrity, girlhood, she, womenfolk.

Womankind, the sex, the fair, the fair sex, the softer sex, the weaker vessel, a petticoat, skirt.

Dame, madam, madame, ma'am, mistress, lady, gentlewoman, donna, belle, matron, dowager, goody, gammer, good woman, goodwife; wife (903).

Damsel, girl, lass, lassie, maid (209), maiden, *demoiselle,* flapper, miss, missie, nymph, wench, bint, floosy, popsy, pusher, jade, dona, grisette, colleen.

Adjectives: Female, feminine, womanly, ladylike, matronly, maidenly, girlish; womanish, effeminate, unmanly, pansy.

Phrase: The distaff side.

375 PHYSICAL SENSIBILITY

Substantives: sensitiveness, sensitivity, feeling, perceptivity, acuteness; allergy, idiosyncrasy; moral sensibility (822).

Sensation, impression, consciousness (490).

The external senses.

Verbs: To be sensible of, to feel, perceive, be conscious of, respond to, react to.

To render sensible, to sharpen, cultivate, train, tutor, condition.

To cause sensation; to impress, excite, or produce an impression.

Adjectives: Sensible, conscious, sensitive, sensuous, aesthetic, perceptive.

Hypersensitive, thin-skinned, neurotic, hyperaesthetic, allergic.

Acute, sharp, keen, vivid, lively, impressive.

Adverb: To the quick.

376 PHYSICAL INSENSIBILITY

Substantives: obtuseness, dullness, paralysis, anaesthesia, analgesia, sleep, trance, stupor, coma, catalepsy; moral insensibility (823).

Anaesthetic, opium, ether, chloroform, chloral, cocaine, morphia, laudanum, nitrous oxide, laughing gas.

Anaesthetics.

Verbs: To be insensible, etc.

To render insensible, to blunt, dull, obtund, benumb, deaden, stupefy, stun, paralyse, anaesthetize, dope, hocus, gas.

Adjectives: Insensible, unfeeling, senseless, impercipient, impassable, thick-skinned, pachydermatous, hardened, proof, apathetic, obtuse, dull, anaesthetic, paralytic, palsied, numb, dead, unaffected, untouched.

Phrase: Having a rhinoceros hide.

377 PHYSICAL PLEASURE

Substantives: bodily enjoyment, gratification, titillation, comfort, luxury, voluptuousness, sensuousness, sensuality; mental pleasure (827).

Phrases: The flesh-pots of Egypt; creature comforts; a bed of roses; a bed of down; on velvet; in clover.

Verbs: To feel, experience, receive, etc., pleasure; to enjoy, relish, luxuriate, revel, riot, bask, wallow in, feast on, gloat over, have oneself a ball.

To cause or give physical pleasure, to gratify, tickle, regale, etc. (829).

Adjectives: Enjoying, etc., luxurious, sensual, voluptuous, comfortable, cosy, snug.

Pleasant, pleasing, agreeable, grateful, refreshing, comforting.

378 PHYSICAL PAIN
Substantives: bodily pain, suffering, sufferance, dolour, ache, aching, smart, smarting, shoot, shooting, twinge, twitch, gripe, headache, toothache, earache, sore, hurt, discomfort, malaise; mental pain (828).

Spasm, cramp, nightmare, crick, stitch, convulsion, throe.

Pang, anguish, agony, torment, torture, rack, cruciation, crucifixion, martyrdom.

Verbs: To feel, experience, suffer, etc., pain; to suffer, ache, smart, bleed, tingle, shoot, twinge, lancinate, wince, writhe, twitch.

Phrases: To sit on thorns; to sit on pins and needles.

To give or inflict pain; to pain, hurt, chafe, sting, bite, gnaw, pinch, tweak, grate, gall, fret, prick, pierce, gripe, etc., wring, torment, torture, rack, agonize, break on the wheel, put on the rack, convulse.

Adjectives: In pain, in a state of pain; uncomfortable, pained, etc.

Painful, aching, etc., sore, raw, agonizing, excruciating.

379 TOUCH
Substantives: taction, tactility, feeling, palpation, manipulation, tangibility, palpability.

Organ of touch: hand, finger, fore-finger, thumb, paw, feeler, antenna.

Verbs: To touch, feel, handle, finger, thumb, paw, fumble, grope, grabble, scrabble; pass, or run the fingers over, manipulate.

Phrase: To throw out a feeler.

Adjectives: Tactual, tangible, palpable, tactile.

380 SENSATIONS OF TOUCH
Substantives: itching, titillation, formication, etc., creeping, aura, tingling, thrilling.

Verbs: To itch, tingle, creep, thrill; sting, prick, prickle, tickle, kittle, titillate.

Adjectives: Itching, etc., ticklish, kittly.

381 NUMBNESS
Substantives: deadness, anaesthesia (376); pins and needles.

Verbs: To benumb, paralyse, anaesthetize; to chloroform, inject with cocaine, etc. (376).

Adjectives: Numb, bebumbed; intangible, impalpable.

382 HEAT
Substantives: caloric, temperature, warmth, fervour, calidity, incalescence, candescence, incandescence, glow, flush, hectic, fever, pyrexia, hyperpyrexia.

Fire, spark, scintillation, flash, flame, blaze, bonfire, firework, wildfire, pyrotechny, ignition (384).

Insolation, summer, dog-days, tropical heat, heat-wave, summer heat, blood heat, sirocco, simoom; isotherm.

Hot spring, thermal spring, geyser.

Pyrology, thermology, thermotics, calorimetry, thermodynamics; thermometer (389).

Phrase: The devouring element.

Verbs: To be hot, to glow, flush, sweat, swelter, bask, smoke, reek, stew, simmer, seethe, boil, burn, broil, bake, parch, fume, blaze, smoulder.

Phrases: To be in a heat, in a glow, in a fever, in a blaze, etc.

Adjectives: Hot, warm, mild, unfrozen, genial, tepid, lukewarm, blood-hot, thermal, thermotic, calorific, sunny, close, sweltering, stuffy, sultry, baking, boiling, broiling, torrid, tropical, aestival, canicular, glowing, piping, scalding, reeking, etc., on fire, afire, ablaze, alight, aglow, fervid, fervent, ardent, unquenched; isothermal, sotheral; feverish, pyretic, pyrexial, pyrexical.

Igneous, plutonic, fiery, candescent, incandescent, red-hot, white-hot, incalescent, smoking, blazing, unextinguished, smouldering.

Phrases: Hot as fire; warm as toast; warm as wool; piping hot; like an oven; hot enough to roast an ox.

383 COLD

Substantives: coldness, frigidity, coolness, coolth, gelidity, chill, chilliness, freshness, inclemency; cold storage.

Frost, ice, snow, snowflake, sleet, hail, hailstone, rime, hoar-frost, icicle, iceberg, ice-floe, glacier, winter.

Sensation of cold: chilliness, shivering, shuddering, goose-skin, goose-pimples, goose-flesh, rigor, horripilation, chattering of teeth.

Verbs: To be cold, etc., to shiver, quake, shake, tremble, shudder, dither, quiver, starve.

Adjectives: Cold, cool, chill, chilly, gelid, frigid, algid, bleak, raw, inclement, bitter, biting, cutting, nipping, piercing, pinching, clay-cold, fresh, keen; pinched, starved, perished, shivering, etc., aguish, frozen, frost-bitten, frost-nipped, frost-bound, unthawed, unwarmed; isocheimal, isochimenal.

Icy, glacial, frosty, freezing, wintry, brumal, hibernal, boreal, arctic, hiemal, hyperborean, icebound.

Phrases: Cold as a stone; cold as marble; cold as a frog; cold as charity; cold as Christmas; cool as a cucumber; cool as a custard.

384 CALEFACTION

Substantives: increase of temperature, heating, tepefaction.

Melting, fusion, liquefaction, thaw, liquescence (335), liquation, incandescence.

Burning, combustion, incension, accension, cremation, cautery, cauterization, roasting, broiling, frying, ustulation, torrefaction, scorification, branding, calcination, carbonization, incineration, cineration.

Boiling, coction, ebullition, simmering, scalding, decoction, smelting.

Ignition, inflammation, setting fire to, flagration, deflagration, conflagration, arson, incendiarism, fire-raising; *auto da fé, suttee.*

Inflammability, combustibility; incendiary, fire-bug, fire-ship, *pétroleur.*

Transmission of heat, diathermancy.

Verbs: To heat, warm, mull, chafe, fire, set fire to, set on fire, kindle, enkindle, light, ignite, relume, rekindle.

To melt, thaw, fuse, liquefy (335); defrost, de-ice.

To burn, inflame, roast, toast, broil, fry, grill, brander, singe, parch, sweal, scorch, brand, scorify, torrify, bake, cauterize, sear, char, carbonize, calcine, incinerate, smelt.

To boil, stew, cook, seethe, scald, parboil, simmer.

To take fire, catch fire, kindle, light, ignite.

Phrases: To stir the fire; blow the fire; fan the flame; apply a match to; make a bonfire of; to take the chill off.

To consign to the flames; to reduce to ashes; to burn to a cinder.

Adjectives: Combustible, inflammable, heating, etc., heated, warmed, melted, molten, unfrozen, boiled, stewed, sodden, adust.

385 REFRIGERATION
Substantives: infrigidation, reduction of temperature, cooling, freezing, congealing, congelation, glaciation.

Fire-brigade, fire-extinguisher, fire-engine, fireman; incombustibility.

Verbs: To cool, refrigerate, congeal, freeze, glaciate, ice, benumb, refresh, damp, slack, quench, put out, blow out, extinguish, starve, pinch, pierce, cut.

To go out.

Adjectives: Cooled, frozen, benumbed, etc., shivery, frigorific, refrigerant.

Incombustible, non-inflammable, fire-proof.

386 FURNACE
Substantives: Fire, gas fire, electric fire, stove, kiln, oven, bakehouse, hot-house, conservatory, fire-place, grate, hearth, radiator, register, reverberatory, range, hob, hypocaust, crematorium, incinerator, forge, blast-furnace, brasier, salamander, geyser, heater, hot-plate, hot-water bottle, electric blanket, warming-pan, stew-pan, boiler, cauldron, kettle, pot, urn, chafing-dish, gridiron, saucepan, frying-pan; sudatorium, sudatory, Turkish bath, *hammam,* vapour bath.

387 REFRIGERATORY
Substantives: refrigerator, frig, ice-pail, ice-bag, ice-house, freezing-mixture, cooler, freezer.

388 FUEL
Substantives: firing, coal, anthracite, coke, charcoal, briquette, peat, combustible, log, tinder, touchwood.

Lucifer, ingle, brand, match, vesuvian, vesta, safety-match, fusee, lighter, spill, embers, faggot, firebrand, incendiary, port-fire, fire-ball, fire-barrel.

389 THERMOMETER
Substantives: clinical thermometer, pyrometer, calorimeter, thermoscope, thermograph, thermostat, thermopile.

Fahrenheit, Centigrade, Celsius, Réaumur.

Thermometry, therm.

390 TASTE
Substantives: flavour, gust, gusto, zest, savour, sapor, tang, twang, smack, relish, aftertaste, smatch, sapidity.

Tasting, gustation, degustation.

Palate, tongue, tooth, sweet tooth, stomach.

Verbs: To taste, savour, smack, smatch, flavour, twang.

Phrases: To tickle the palate; to smack the lips.

Adjectives: Sapid, gustable, gustatory, saporific, strong, appetizing, palatable (394).

391 INSIPIDITY
Substantives: tastelessness, insipidness, vapidness, vapidity, mawkishness, wershness, mildness; wish-wash, milk and water, slops.

Verbs: To be void of taste, tasteless, etc.

Adjectives: Insipid, tasteless, savourless, mawkish, wersh, flat, vapid, *fade,* wishy-washy, watery, weak, mild; untasted.

392 PUNGENCY
Substantives: *haut-goût,* strong taste, twang, raciness, race, saltness, sharpness, roughness.

Ginger, caviare, cordial, condiment (393).

Verbs: To be pungent, etc.

To render pungent, to season, spice, salt, pepper, pickle, brine, devil.

Adjectives: Pungent, high-flavoured, high-tasted, high, sharp, strong, rough, stinging, piquant, racy, biting, mordant, spicy, seasoned, hot, peppery, gingery, high-seasoned, gamy, salt, saline, brackish.

Phrases: Salt as brine; salt as a herring; salt as Lot's wife; hot as pepper.

393 CONDIMENT

Substantives: salt, mustard, pepper, cayenne, vinegar, curry, chutney, seasoning, spice, ginger, sauce, dressing, *sauce piquante,* caviare, pot-herbs, pickles, onion, garlic, sybo.

394 SAVOURINESS

Substantives: palatableness, toothsomeness, daintiness, delicacy, relish, zest.

A titbit, dainty, delicacy, ambrosia, nectar, *bonne-bouche.*

Verbs: To be savoury, etc.

To render palatable, etc.

To relish, like, fancy, be partial to.

Adjectives: Savoury, well-tasted, palatable, nice, good, dainty, delectable, toothsome, tasty, appetizing, delicate, delicious, exquisite, rich, luscious, ambrosial, meaty, fruity.

395 UNSAVOURINESS

Substantives: unpalatableness, bitterness, acridness, acridity, acrimony, roughness, acerbity, austerity; gall and wormwood, rue; sickener, scunner.

Verbs: To be unpalatable, etc.

To sicken, disgust, nauseate, pall, turn the stomach.

Adjectives: Unsavoury, unpalatable, ill-flavoured, bitter, acrid, acrimonious, unsweetened, rough, austere, uneatable, inedible.

Offensive, repulsive, nasty, fulsome, sickening, nauseous, nauseating, disgusting, loathsome, palling.

Phrases: Bitter as gall; bitter as aloes.

396 SWEETNESS

Substantives: dulcitude, dulcification, sweetening.

Sugar, saccharine, glucose, syrup, treacle, molasses, honey, manna, confection, confectionery, candy, conserve, jam, jelly, marmalade, preserve, liquorice, julep, sugar-candy, toffee, caramel, butterscotch, plum, sugar-plum, lollipop, bonbon, jujube, lozenge, pastille, comfit, fudge, chocolate, sweet, sweetmeat, marzipan, marchpane, fondant, nougat; mead, nectar, hydromel, honeysuckle.

Verbs: To be sweet, etc.

To render sweet, to sweeten, sugar, mull, edulcorate, candy, dulcify, saccharify.

Adjectives: Sweet, saccharine, sacchariferous, sugary, dulcet, candied, honeyed, luscious, edulcorated, nectarous, nectareous, sweetish, sugary.

Phrases: Sweet as a nut; sweet as honey.

397 SOURNESS

Substantives: acid, acidity, tartness, crabbedness, hardness, roughness, acetous, fermentation.

Vinegar, verjuice, crab, alum.

Verbs: To be sour, etc.

To render or turn sour, to sour, acidify, acidulate.

Phrase: To set the teeth on edge.

Adjectives: Sour, acid, acidulous, acidulated, sourish, subacid, vinegary, tart, crabbed, acerb, acetic, acetous, acescent, acetose, styptic, hard, rough.

Phrases: Sour as vinegar; sour as a crab.

398 ODOUR

Substantives: smell, scent, effluvium, emanation, fume, exhalation, essence; trail, nidor, redolence.

The sense of smell, act of smelling.

Verbs: To have an odour, to smell of, to exhale, to give out a smell, etc.

To smell, scent, snuff, sniff, inhale, nose, snowk.

Adjectives: Odorous, odorant, odoriferous, smelling, strong-scented, graveolent, redolent, nidorous, pungent.

Relating to the sense of smell: olfactory, keen-scented.

399 INODOROUSNESS
Substantives: absence or want of smell; deodorization.
Verbs: To be inodorous, etc., deodorize (652).
Adjectives: Inodorous, odourless, scentless, smell-less, wanting smell.

400 FRAGRANCE
Substantives: aroma, redolence, perfume, savour, bouquet.

Incense, musk, myrrh, frankincense, ambrosia, attar (or otto), eau-de-Cologne, civet, castor, ambergris, bergamot, lavender, sandalwood, orris root, balm, pot-pourri, pulvil; scent-bag, scent-bottle, sachet, nosegay.
Phrase: 'All the perfumes of Arabia.'
Verbs: To perfume, scent, embalm.
Adjectives: Fragrant, aromatic, redolent, balmy, scented, sweet-smelling, sweet-scented, ambrosial, perfumed, musky.

401 FETOR
Substantives: bad smell, empyreuma, stench, stink, mustiness, fustiness, frowziness, frowst, fug, rancidity, foulness, putrescence, putridity, mephitis.

A pole-cat, skunk, badger, teledu, asafoetida, cacodyl, stinkard, stink-bomb, stinkpot.
Verbs: To smell, stink, hum, niff, pong.
Phrase: To stink in the nostrils.
Adjectives: Fetid, strong-smelling, smelly, whiffy, malodorous, noisome, offensive, rank, rancid, reasty, mouldy, fusty, musty, stuffy, frowsty, fuggy, foul, frowzy, olid, nidorous, stinking, rotten, putrescent, putrid, putrefying, tainted, high (653), mephitic, empyreumatic.

402 SOUND
Substantives: sonance, noise, strain, voice (580), accent, twang, intonation, tone, resonance (408); sonority, sonorousness, audibleness, audibility.

Acoustics, phonics, phonetics, phonology, diacoustics.
Verbs: To produce sound; to sound, make a noise, give out or emit sound, to resound.
Adjectives: Sonorous, sounding, soniferous, sonorific, sonoriferous, resonant, canorous, audible, distinct, phonic, phonetic.

403 SILENCE
Substantives: stillness, quiet, peace, calm, hush, lull; muteness (581).

A silencer, mute, damper, sordine.
Verbs: To be silent, etc.

To render silent, to silence, still, hush, stifle, muffle, stop, muzzle, mute, damp, gag.
Phrases: To keep silence; to hold one's tongue; to hold one's peace.
Adjectives: Silent, still, stilly, noiseless, soundless, inaudible, hushed, etc., mute, mum, mumchance (581), solemn, awful, deathlike.
Phrases: Still as a mouse; deathlike silence; silent as the grave; one might hear a pin drop.
Adverbs: Silently, softly, etc., *sub silentio*.
Interjections: Hush! silence! soft! mum! whist! chut! *tace!*

404 LOUDNESS
Substantives: clatter, din, clangour, clang, roar, uproar, racket, hubbub, flourish of trumpets, tucket, tantara, taratantara, fanfare, blare, alarum, peal, swell, blast, boom, echo, fracas, shindy, row, rumpus, bobbery, clamour, hullaballoo, chorus, hue and cry, shout, yell, whoop, charivari, shivaree, vociferation; Stentor, Boanerges.

Speaking-trumpet, megaphone, loud-speaker, microphone, mike, amplifier, resonator.

Artillery, cannon, thunder.
Verbs: To be loud, etc., to resound, echo, re-echo, peal, swell, clang, boom, blare, thunder, fulminate, roar, whoop, shout (411).
Phrases: To din in the ear; to pierce, split, or rend the ears, or head; to shout, or thunder at the pitch of one's breath, or at the top of one's voice; to make the welkin ring; to rend the air; *faire le diable à quatre*.
Adjectives: Loud, sonorous, resounding, etc., high-sounding, big-sounding, deep, full, swelling, clamorous, clangorous, multisonous, noisy, blatant, plangent, vocal, vociferous, stunning, piercing, splitting, rending, thundering, deafening, ear-deafening, ear-piercing, obstreperous, blaring, deep-mouthed, open-mouthed, trumpet-tongued, uproarious, rackety, stentorian.
Phrases: Enough to split the head or ears; enough to wake the dead; enough to wake the Seven Sleepers.
Adverbs: Loudly, aloud, etc., *forte, fortissimo*.
Phrases: At the top of one's voice; in full cry.

405 FAINTNESS
Substantives: lowness, faint sounds, whisper, undertone, breath, underbreath, murmur, mutter, hum, susurration, tinkle, rustle.
Hoarseness, huskiness, raucity.
Verbs: To whisper, breathe, murmur, mutter, mumble, purl, hum, croon, gurgle, ripple, babble, tinkle.
Phrases: Steal on the ear; melt, float on the air.
Adjectives: Inaudible, scarcely audible, low, dull, stifled, muffled, hoarse, husky, gentle faint, breathed, etc., soft, floating, purling, etc., liquid, mellifluous, dulcet, flowing, soothing.
Adverbs: In a whisper, with bated breath, under one's breath, *sotto voce*, between the teeth, from the side of one's mouth, aside, *piano, pianissimo, à la sourdine*.

406 SNAP
Substantives: knock, rap, tap, click, clash, slam, clack, crack, crackle, crackling, crepitation, decrepitation, report, pop, plop, bang, thud, thump, ping, zip, clap, burst, explosion, discharge, crash, detonation, firing, salvo, atmospherics.
Squib, cracker, gun, pop-gun.
Verbs: To snap, knock, etc.
Adjectives: Snapping, etc.

407 ROLL
Substantives: rumble, rumbling, hum, humming, shake, trill, whirr, chime, tick, beat, toll, ticking, ticktack, patter, tattoo, ding-dong, drumming, quaver, tremolo, ratatat, tantara, rataplan, rat-tat, clatter, clutter, rattle, racket, rub-a-dub; reverberation (408).
Phrases: The devil's tattoo; tuck of drum.
Verbs: To roll, beat, tick, toll, drum, etc., rattle, clatter, patter, shake, trill, whirr, chime, beat; to drum or din in the ear.
Adjectives: Rolling, rumbling, etc.

408 RESONANCE
Substantives: ring, ringing, jingle, chink, tinkle, ting, tink, tintinnabulation, gurgle, chime, toot, tootle, clang, etc. (404).
Reflection, reverberation, echo.
Verbs: To resound, reverberate, re-echo, ring, jingle, clink, chime, tinkle, etc.
Adjectives: Resounding, resonant, tintinnabular, ringing, etc.
Phrase: Clear as a bell.
BASS (*Substantives*), low, flat or grave note, chest-note, baritone, contralto.
Adjectives: Deep-toned, deep-sounding, deep-mouthed, hollow, sepulchral, *basso profondo*.

165

409 SIBILATION
Substantives: hiss, swish, buzz, whiz, rustle, fizz, fizzle, wheeze, whistle, snuffle, sneeze, sternutation.
Verbs: To hiss, buzz, etc.
Adjectives: Sibilant, hissing, buzzing, etc., wheezy.
SOPRANO (*Substantives*), high note (410).

410 STRIDOR
Substantives: jar, grating, creak, clank, twang, jangle, jarring, creaking, rustling, roughness, gruffness, sharpness, cacophony,
High note, shrillness, acureness, soprano, falsetto, treble, alto, counter-tenor, penny trumpet, head-note.
Verbs: To creak, grate, jar, burr, pipe, twang, jangle, rustle, clank; to shrill, shriek, screech, squeal, skirl (411), stridulate.
Phrases: To set the teeth on edge; to grate upon the ear.
Adjectives: Strident, stridulous, jarring, etc., harsh, hoarse, horrisonous, discordant, scrannel (414), cacophonous, rough, gruff, sepulchral, grating.
Sharp, high, acute, shrill, piping, screaming.

411 CRY
Substantives: voice (580), vociferation, outcry, roar, shout, bawl, bellow, brawl, halloo, hullaballoo, hoop, whoop, yell, cheer, hoot, howl, chorus, scream, screech, screak, shriek, squeak, squawk, squeal, skirl, yawp, squall, whine, pule, pipe, grumble, plaint, groan, moan, snore, snort.
Verbs: To vociferate, roar, shout, bawl, etc., sing out, thunder, raise or lift up the voice.
Adjectives: Vociferating, etc., clamant, clamorous, vociferous, stertorous.

412 ULULATION
Substantives: latration, cry, roar, bel-

low, reboation, bark, yelp, howl, bay, baying, yap, growl, grunt, gruntle, snort, neigh, nicker, whinny, bray, croak, snarl, howl, caterwauling, mew, mewl, miaow, miaul, purr, pule, bleat, baa, low, moo, boo, caw, coo, croodle, cackle, gobble, quack, gaggle, squeak, squawk, squeal, chuckle, chuck, cluck, clack, chirp, chirrup, crow, woodnote, twitter, peep.
Insect cry, drone, buzz, hum.
Cuckoo, screech-owl.
Verbs: To cry, bellow, rebellow, etc., bell, boom, trumpet, give tongue.
Phrases: To bay the moon; to roar like a bull or lion.
Adjectives: Crying, etc., blatant, latrant, remugient.

413 MELODY
Substantives: melodiousness, *melos*.
Pitch, note, interval, tone, intonation, timbre; high or low, acute or grave notes, treble, alto, tenor, bass, soprano, mezzo-soprano, contralto, counter-tenor, baritone, *basso profondo*.
Scale, gamut, diapason; diatonic, chromatic, enharmonic, whole-tone, etc., scales; key, clef; major, minor, Dorian, Phrygian, Lydian, etc., modes; tetrachord, hexachord, pentatonic scale; tuning, modulation, temperament; solmization, solfeggio, sol-fa.
Staff (or stave), lines, spaces, brace; bar, double bar, rest.
Notes of the scale: sharps, flats, naturals, accidentals; breve, semibreve, minim, crotchet, quaver, semiquaver, demisemiquaver, etc.
Tonic, keynote, supertonic, mediant, subdominant, dominant, submediant, leading note, octave; primes, seconds, triads, etc.
Harmonic, overtone, partial, fundamental, note, hum-note.
Harmony, harmoniousness, concord, concordance, unison,

homophony, chord, chime, consonance, concent, euphony; counterpoint, polyphony; tonality, atonality; thorough-bass, figured bass.

Rhythm, time, tempo; common, duple, triple, six-eight, etc., time; *tempo rubato,* syncopation, ragtime, jazz, swing, jive, boogie-woogie, bebop, skiffle, rock-and-roll.

Verbs: To harmonize, chime, be in unison; put in tune, tune, accord.

Adjectives: Harmonious, harmonic, harmonical, in harmony, in tune, etc., unisonant, unisonal, univocal, symphonic, homophonous; contrapuntal, chordal; diatonic, chromatic, enharmonic, tonal, atonal.

Measured, rhythmical, in time, on the beat, hot.

Melodious, musical, tuneful, tunable, sweet, dulcet, canorous, mellow, mellifluous, silver-toned, silvery, euphonious, euphonic, euphonical; enchanting, ravishing, etc., Orphean.

414 DISCORD

Substantives: discordance, dissonance, jar, jarring, caterwauling, cacophony.

Hoarseness, croaking, etc. (410).

Confused sounds, babel, Dutch concert, cat's concert, marrow-bones and cleavers, charivari (404).

Verbs: To be discordant, etc., to croak, jar (410).

Adjectives: Discordant, dissonant, out of tune, sharp, flat, tuneless, absonant, unmusical, inharmonious, unmelodious, untuneful, untunable, singsong.

Cacophonous, harsh, hoarse, croaking, jarring, stridulous, etc. (410).

415 MUSIC

Substantives: tune, air, lilt, melody, refrain, burden, cadence, theme, motive, motif, *leit-motiv,* subject, counter-subject, episode, modulation, introduction, finale, etc.

Solo, duet, trio, quartet, etc., concerted music, chorus, chamber music.

Instrumental music: Symphony, *sinfonietta,* symphonic poem, tone-poem, concerto, sonata, sonatina; *allegro, andante, largo,* scherzo, rondo, etc.; overture, prelude, intermezzo, postlude, voluntary; ballade, nocturne, serenade, aubade, barcarolle, *berceuse,* etc.; fugue, fugato, canon; variations, humoresque, rhapsody, caprice, *capriccio,* fantasia, impromptu; arrangement, pot-pourri; march, pibroch, minuet, gavotte, waltz, mazurka, etc. (840); accompaniment, *obbligato*; programme music.

Vocal music: Chant, plain-song, Gregorian music, neume, psalmody, psalm, hymn, anthem, motet, antiphon, canticle, introit, etc., service, song, ballad, *lied, chanson,* cavatina, canzonet, serenade, lullaby, ditty, chanty, folk-song, dithyramb; part-song, glee, catch, round, canon, madrigal, chorus, cantata, oratorio, etc.; opera (599).

Dirge, requiem, nenia, knell, lament, coronach, dead march.

Musical ornament; grace-note, appoggiatura, trill, shake, turn, beat, mordent, etc.; cadenza, roulade, bravura, colorature, *coloratura.*

Scale, run, arpeggio, chord; five-finger exercise, study, *étude,* toccata.

Performance, execution, technique, touch, expression, tone-colour, rendering, interpretation; voice-production, *bel canto; embouchure,* lipping, bowing.

Concert, recital, performance, ballad concert, etc., musicale, sing-song.

Minstrelsy, musicianship, musicality, musicalness, an ear for music; composition, composing, orchestration, scoring, filling in the parts.

Composer, harmonist, contrapuntist.

Apollo, the Muses, Erato, Euterpe, Terpsichore.

Verbs: To play, fiddle, bow, strike, strike up, thrum, strum, grind, touch, tweedle, scrape, blow, pipe, tootle, blare, etc.; to execute, perform, render, interpret, conduct, accompany, vamp, arrange, prelude, improvise (612).

To sing, chant, vocalize, warble, carol, troll, lilt, hum, croon, chirp, chirrup, twitter, quaver, trill, shake, whistle, yodel.

To compose, set to music, score, harmonize, orchestrate.

To put in tune, tune, attune, accord, string, pitch.

Adjectives: Musical, harmonious, etc. (413), instrumental, orchestral, pianistic, vocal, choral, operatic, etc.; musicianly, having a good ear.

Phrase: *Fanatico per la musica.*

Adverbs: *Adagio, largo, larghetto, andante, andantino, maestoso, moderato, allegretto, con moto, vivace, veloce, allegro, presto, prestissimo, strepitoso, etc.; scherzando, legato, staccato, crescendo, diminuendo, morendo, sostenuto, sforzando, accelerando, stringendo, più mosso, meno mosso, allargando, rallentando, ritenuto, a piacere, etc.; arpeggiando, pizzicato, glissando, martellato, da capo.*

416 MUSICIAN

Substantives: minstrel, performer, player, soloist, virtuoso, maestro.

Organist, pianist, violinist, fiddler, cellist, harper, harpist, flautist, fifer, clarinettist, trombonist, etc., trumpeter, bugler, piper, bagpiper, drummer, timpanist; campanologist; band, orchestra, brass band, military band, string band, pipe band, waits; conductor, bandmaster, drum-major, leader, *chef d'orchestre,* etc., accompanist.

Vocalist, singer, songster, songstress, chanter, chantress, *cantatrice, lieder*-singer, ballad-singer, etc.; troubadour, minnesinger, gleeman; nightingale, Philomel, thrush, throstle, Orpheus.

Choris, choir, chorister.
Phrase: The tuneful Nine.

417 MUSICAL INSTRUMENTS

1. Stringed instruments: Monochord, polychord, harp, lyre, lute, theorbo, mandolin, guitar, gittern, cithern, banjo, ukelele, balalaika.

Violin, fiddle, Cremona, Stradivarius (or Strad), kit, viola (or tenor), violoncello (or cello), double-bass (or bass-viol), viol, viola d'amore, viola da gamba, violone, rebeck, psaltery.

Pianoforte (or piano), harpsichord, clavier, clavichord, clavicembalo, spinet, cembalo, virginal, zither, dulcimer.

2. Wind instruments: Organ, siren, pipe, pitch-pipe, Pan-pipes; piccolo, flute, bass-flute, oboe (or hautboy), oboe d'amore, cor anglais, clarinet, basset-horn, bass-clarinet, bassoon, double-bassoon, saxophone, horn, French horn, tuba, trumpet, cornet, cornet-à-piston, fife, trombone, euphonium; flageolet, whistle, pennywhistle, ocarina, bugle, serpent, ophicleide, clarion, bagpipe, musette; harmonium, American organ, seraphina, concertina, accordion, melodeon, mouth-organ, etc.; great, swell, choir, solo and echo organs.

3. Vibrating surfaces: Cymbal, bell, carillon, gong, tabor, tambourine, timbrel, drum, side-drum, bass-drum, kettle-drum, timpano, military drum, tom-tom, castanet; musical glasses, harmonica, glockenspiel; sounding-board.

4. Vibrating bars: Tuning-fork, triangle, xylophone, Jew's harp.

5. Mechanical instruments: Musical box, hurdy-gurdy, barrel-organ, piano-organ, orchestrion, piano-player, pianola, etc.; gramophone, phonograph, tape recorder, juke box, nickelodeon.

Key, string, bow, drumstick, bellows, sound-box, pedal, stop; loud or sustaining pedal, soft pedal, mute, sordine, sourdine, damper, swell-box; keyboard, finger-board, console; organ-loft, concert platform, orchestra, choir, singing-gallery, belfry, campanile.

418 HEARING
Substantives: audition, auscultation, listening, eavesdropping; audibility.

Acuteness, nicety, delicacy, of ear.

Ear, auricle, acoustic organs, auditory apparatus, lug, ear-drum, tympanum.

Telephone, speaking-tube, ear-trumpet, audiphone, audiometer, earphone, phone, gramophone, phonograph, dictaphone, intercom, receiver.

Wireless telephony, broadcasting, wireless, radio, transmitter, walkie-talkie, radiogram, microphone, mike.

A hearer, auditor, listener, eavesdropper, auditory, audience.
Verbs: To hear, overhear, hark, listen, list, hearken, give or lend an ear, prick up one's ears, give a hearing or audience to, listen in.

To become audible, to catch the ear, to be heard.
Phrases: To hang upon the lips of; to be all ears.
Adjectives: Hearing, etc., auditory, auricular, acoustic.
Interjections: Hark! list! hear! listen! oyez! (or oyes!)
Adverbs: *Arrectis auribus*; with ears flapping.

419 DEAFNESS
Substantives: hardness of hearing, surdity; inaudibility.
Verbs: To be deaf, to shut, stop, or close one's ears.

To render deaf, to stun, deafen.
Phrase: To turn a deaf ear to.
Adjectives: Deaf, stone deaf, tone deaf, hard of hearing, earless, surd,

dull of hearing, deaf-mute, stunned, deafened, having no ear.

Inaudible, out of earshot.
Phrases: Deaf as a post; deaf as a beetle; deaf as an adder.

420 LIGHT
Substantives: ray, beam, stream, gleam, streak, pencil, sunbeam, moonbeam, starbeam.

Day, daylight, sunshine, sunlight, moonlight, starlight, the light of day, the light of heaven, noontide, noonday, noontide light, broad daylight.

Glimmer, glimmering, glow, afterglow, phosphorescence, lambent flame, play of light.

Flush, halo, aureole, nimbus, glory, corona.

Spark, sparkle, scintilla, sparkling, scintillation, flame, flash, blaze, coruscation, fulguration, lightning, flood of light, glint.

Lustre, shine, sheen, gloss, tinsel, spangle, brightness, brilliancy, refulgence, dazzlement, splendour, resplendence, luminousness, luminosity, luminescence, lucidity, lucidness, incandescence, radiance, illumination, irradiation, glare, flare, flush, effulgence, fulgency, fluorescence, lucency, lambency.

Optics, photology, photometry, dioptrics, catoptrics.

Radioactivity, radiography, radiograph, radiometer, radioscopy, radiotherapy.
Verbs: To shine, glow, glitter, glisten, glister, glint, twinkle, gleam, flicker, flare, glare, beam, radiate, shoot beams, shimmer, sparkle, scintillate, coruscate, flash, blaze, fizzle, daze, dazzle, bedazzle; to clear up, to brighten.

To illuminate, illume, illumine, lighten, enlighten, light, light up, irradiate, flush, shine upon, cast lustre upon; cast, throw, or shed a light upon, brighten, clear, relume.

Phrase: To strike a light.
Adjectives: Luminous, luminiferous, shining, glowing, etc., lambent, glossy, lucid, lucent, luculent, lustrous, lucific, glassy, clear, bright, scintillant, light, lightsome, unclouded, sunny, orient, noonday. noontide, beaming, beamy, vivid, alight, splendent, radiant, radiating, cloudless, unobscured; radioactive, fluorescent, phosphorescent.

Garish, resplendent, refulgent, fulgent, effulgent, in a blaze, ablaze, relucent, splendid, blazing, rutilant, meteoric, burnished.
Phrases: Bright as silver, as day, as noonday.

421 DARKNESS
Substantives: night, midnight, obscurity, dusk (422), duskiness, gloom, gloominess, murk, mirk, murkiness, shadow, shade, umbrage, shadiness, umbra, penumbra, Erebus.

Obscuration, adumbration, obumbration, obtenebration, obfuscation, black-out, extinction, eclipse, gathering of the clouds, dimness (422).
Phrases: Dead of night; darkness visible; darkness that can be felt; blind man's holiday.
Verbs: To be dark, etc.; to lour (or lower).

To darken, obscure, shade, shadow, dim, bedarken, overcast, overshadow, obfuscate, obumbrate, adumbrate, cast in the shade, becloud, overcloud, bedim, put out, snuff out, blow out, extinguish, dout, douse.

To cast, throw, spread a shade or gloom.
Phrase: To douse the glim.
Adjectives: Dark, obscure, darksome, darkling, tenebrous, tenebrific, rayless, beamless, sunless, moonless, starless, pitch-dark, pitchy; Stygian, Cimmerian.

Sombre, dusky, unilluminated, unillumined, unlit, unsunned, nocturnal, dingy, lurid, overcast, louring (or lowering), cloudy, murky, murksome, shady, shadowy, umbrageous.

Benighted, noctivagant, noctivagous.
Phrases: Dark as pitch; dark as a pit; dark as Erebus; dark as a wolf's mouth; the palpable obscure.

422 DIMNESS
Substantives: dim-out, brown-out, paleness, glimmer, glimmering, owl-light, nebulousness, nebulosity, nebula, cloud, film, mist, haze, fog, brume, smog, smoke, haziness, eclipse, dusk, cloudiness, dawn, aurora, twilight, crepuscule, cockshut time, gloaming, daybreak, dawn, half-light, moonlight; moonshine, moonbeam, starlight, starshine, starbeam, candle-light.
Verbs: To be dim, etc., to glimmer, loom, lour, twinkle.

To grow dim, to fade, to render dim, to dim, obscure, pale.
Adjectives: Dim, dull, lack-lustre, dingy, darkish, glassy, faint, confused.

Cloudy, misty, hazy, foggy, brumous, muggy, fuliginous, nebulous, lowering, overcast, crepuscular, muddy, lurid, looming.
Phrase: Shorn of its beams.

423 LUMINARY
Substantives: sun, Phoebus, star, orb, meteor, galaxy, constellation, blazing star, glow-worm, firefly.

Meteor, northern lights, aurora borealis, aurora australis, fire-drake, ignis fatuus, jack-o'-lantern, will-o'-the-wisp, friar's lantern.

Artificial light, flame, gas-light, incandescent gas-light, electric light, limelight, acetylene, torch, candle, flash-lamp, flashlight, flambeau, link, light, taper, lamp, arc-lamp, mercury vapour lamp, neon lighting, lantern (or lanthorn), rushlight, farthing rushlight, night-light, firework, rocket, Very light, blue lights, fizgig, flare.

Chandelier, gaselier, electrolier, candelabra, girandole, lustre, sconce, gas-bracket, gas-jet, gas-burner, batswing; gas-mantle, electric bulb, filament.

Lighthouse, lightship, pharos, beacon, watch-fire, cresset, brand.

Adjectives: Self-luminous, phosphoric, phosphorescent, radiant (420).

424 SHADE
Substantives: awning, parasol, sunshade, screen, curtain, veil, mantle, mask, gause, blind, shutter, cloud, mist.

A shadow, chiaroscuro, umbrage, penumbra (421).

Adjectives: Shady, umbrageous.

425 TRANSPARENCY
Substantives: clarity, transparence, diaphaneity, translucence, translucency, lucidity, pellucidity, limpidity.

Glass, crystal, mica, lymph, water.

Verbs: To be transparent, etc., to transmit light.

Adjectives: Transparent, pellucid, lucid, diaphanous, translucent, relucent, limpid, clear, crystalline, vitreous, transpicuous, glassy, hyaline.

Phrase: Clear as crystal.

426 OPACITY
Substantives: thickness, opaqueness, turbidity, turbidness, muddiness.

Cloud, film, haze.

Verbs: To be opaque, etc., to obfuscate, not to transmit, to obstruct the passage of light.

Adjectives: Opaque, turbid, roily, thick, muddy, opacous, obfuscated, fuliginous, cloudy, hazy, misty, foggy, impervious to light.

427 SEMITRANSPARENCY
Substantives: opalescence, pearliness, milkiness.

Film, gause, muslin.

Adjectives: Semitransparent, semidiaphanous, semi-opaque, opalescent, gauzy, pearly, milky.

428 COLOUR
Substantives: hue, tint, tinge, dye, complexion, shade, spectrum, tincture, blazonry, cast, livery, coloration, glow, flush, tone, key.

Pure or positive colour, primary colour.

Broken colour, secondary or tertiary colour.

Chromatics; prism, spectroscope.

A pigment, colouring matter, medium, paint, dye, wash, stain, distemper, mordant.

Verbs: To colour, dye, tinge, stain, tinct, tincture, paint, wash, illuminate, blazon, emblazon, bedizen, imbur, distemper.

Adjectives: Coloured, colorific, chromatic, prismatic, full-coloured, lush, dyed; tinctorial.

Bright, deep, vivid, florid, fresh, high-coloured, unfaded, gay, showy, gaudy, garish, flaunting, vivid, gorgeous, glaring, flaring, flashy, tawdry, meretricious, raw, intense, double-dyed, loud, noisy.

Mellow, harmonious, pearly, light, quiet, delicate, pastel.

429 ACHROMATISM
Substantives: decoloration, discoloration, paleness, pallidity, pallidness, pallor, etiolation, anaemia, chlorosis, albinism, neutral tint, colourlessness; monochrome, black and white.

Verbs: To lose colour, to fade, pale, blanch, become colourless.

To deprive of colour, discolour, bleach, tarnish, decolour, decolorate, decolorize, achromatize, tone down.

Adjectives: Colourless, uncoloured, untinged, untinctured, achromatic, aplanatic, hueless, undyed, pale, pallid, pale-faced, pasty, etiolated, anaemic,

chlorotic, faint, faded, dull, cold, muddy, wan, sallow, dead, dingy, ashy, ashen, cadaverous, glassy, lacklustre, tarnished, bleached, discoloured.
Phrases: Pale as death, as ashed, as a witch, as a ghost, as a corpse.

430 WHITENESS
Substantives: milkiness, hoariness.
Albification, etiolation.
Snow, paper, chalk, milk, lily, sheet, ivory, silver, alabaster.
Verbs: To be white, etc.
To render white, whiten, bleach, whitewash, blanch, etiolate.
Adjectives: White, milk-white, snow-white, snowy, niveous, chalky, hoary, hoar, silvery, argent.
Whitish, off-white, cream-coloured, creamy, pearly, fair, blonde, etiolated, albescent.
Phrases: White as the driven snow; white as a sheet.

431 BLACKNESS
Substantives: darkness (421), swarthiness, dinginess, lividity, inkiness, pitchiness, nigritude.
Nigrification.
Jet, ink, ebony, coal, pitch, charcoal, soot, sloe, smut, raven, crow; negro, nigger, darkie, coon, blackamoor.
Verbs: To be black, etc.
To render black, to blacken, nigrify, denigrate, blot, blotch, smirch, smutch.
Adjectives: Black, sable, swarthy, swart, sombre, inky, ebon, livid, coal-black, jet-black, pitch-black, fuliginous, dingy, dusky, Ethiopic, nigrescent.
Phrases: Black as my hat; black as ink; black as coal; black as a crow; black as thunder.

432 GREY
Substantives: neutral, tint, dun.
Adjectives: Grey, etc., drab, dingy, sombre, leaden, livid, ashen, mouse-coloured, slate-coloured, stone-coloured, cinereous, cineritious, grizzly, grizzled.

433 BROWN
Substantives: bistre, ochre, sepia.
Adjectives: Brown, etc., bay, dapple, auburn, chestnut, nut-brown, umber, cinnamon, fawn, russet, olive, hazel, tawny, fuscous, chocolate, liver-coloured, tan, brunette, maroon, khaki, foxy, bronzed, sunburnt, tanned.
Phrases: Brown as a berry, as mahogany, as a gipsy.
Verbs: To render brown, embrown, to tan, bronze, etc.

434 REDNESS
Substantives: red, scarlet, vermilion, crimson, carmine, pink, lake, maroon, carnation, damask, ruby, rose, blush colour, peach colour, flesh colour, gules, solferino.
Rust, cinnabar, cochineal, madder, red lead, ruddle; blook, lobster, cherry, pillar-box.
Erubescence, rubescence, rubefaction, rosiness, rufescence, ruddiness, rubicundity.
Verbs: To become red, to blush, flush, mantle, redden, colour.
To render red, redden, rouge, rubefy, rubricate, incarnadine.
Adjectives: Red, scarlet, vermilion, carmine, rose, ruby, crimson, pink, etc., ruddy, rufous, florid, rosy, roseate, auroral, rose-coloured, blushing, mantling, etc., erubescent, blowzy, rubicund, stammel, blood-red, ensanguined, rubiform, cardinal, cerise, *sang-de-bœuf,* murrey, carroty, sorrel, brick-coloured, brick-red, lateritic, cherry-coloured, salmon-coloured.
Phrases: Red as fire, as blood, as scarlet, as a turkey-cock, as a cherry.

435 GREENNESS
Substantives: verdure, viridescence, viridity.

Emerald, jasper, verd-antique, verdigris, beryl, aquamarine, malachite, grass.
Adjectives: Green, verdant, pea-green, grass-green, apple-green, sea-green, turquoise-green, olive-green, bottle-green, glaucous, virescent, aeruginous, vert.
Phrase: Green as grass.

436 YELLOWNESS
Substantives: buff colour, orpiment, yellow ochre, gamboge, crocus, saffron, xanthin, topaz.
Lemon, mustard, jaundice, gold.
Adjectives: Yellow, citron, gold, golden, aureate, citrine, fallow, tawny, flavous, fulvous, saffron, croceate, lemon, xanthic, xanthous, sulphur, amber, straw-coloured, sandy, lurid, Claude-tint, luteous, primrose-coloured, cream-coloured, buff, chrome.
Phrases: Yellow as a quince, as a guinea, as a crow's foot.

437 PURPLE
Substantives: violet, plum, prune, lavender, lilac, peach colour, puce, gridelin, lividness, lividity, bishop's purple, magenta, mauve.
Amethyst, murex.
Verb: To empurple.
Adjectives: Purple, violet, plum-coloured, lilac, mauve, livid, etc.

438 BLUENESS
Substantives: bluishness, azure, indigo, ultramarine, Prussian blue, mazarine, bloom, bice.
Sky, sea, lapis lazuli, cobalt, sapphire, turquoise.
Adjectives: Blue, cerulean, sky-blue, sky-coloured, sky-dyed, watchet, azure, bluish, sapphire, Garter-blue.

439 ORANGE
Substantives: gold, flame, copper, brass, apricot colour; aureolin, nacarat.

Ochre, cadmium.
Adjectives: Orange, golden, ochreous, etc., buff, flame-coloured.

440 VARIEGATION
Substantives: dichroism, trichroism, iridescence, play of colours, *reflet,* variegatedness, patchwork, check, plaid, chess-board, tartan, maculation, spottiness, pointillism, parquetry, marquetry, mosaic, inlay, buhl, striae, spectrum.
A rainbow, iris, tulip, peacock, chameleon, butterfly, tortoise-shell, leopard, zebra, harlequin, motley, mother-of-pearl, nacre, opal, marble.
Verbs: To be variegated, etc.
To variegate, speckle, stripe, streak, chequer, bespeckle, fleck, freckle, inlay, stipple, spot, dot, damascene, embroider, tattoo.
Adjectives: Variegated, varicoloured, many-coloured, versicolour, many-hued, divers-coloured, particoloured, polychromatic, bicolour, tricolour, dichromatic.
Iridescent, prismatic, opaline, nacreous, pearly, opalescent, shot, watered, *chatoyant, gorge de pigeon,* all manner of colours, pied, piebald, skewbald, daedal, motley, mottled, veined, marbled, paned, dappled, clouded, cymophanous.
Mosaic, inlaid, tessellated, chequered, tartan, tortoiseshell.
Dotted, spotted, bespotted, spotty, speckled, bespeckled, punctate, maculated, freckled, fleckered, flecked, flea-bitten, studded, tattooed.
Striped, striated, streaked, barred, veined, brinded, brindled, tabby, roan, grizzled, listed, stippled.
Phrase: All the colours of the rainbow.

441 VISION
Substantives: sight, optics, eyesight.
View, espial, glance, glimpse, peep, peek, look, squint, dekko, gander, the

once-over, gaze, stare, leer, perlustration, contemplation, sight-seeing, regard, survey, reconnaissance, introspection, inspection, speculation, watch, *coup d'œil,* œillade, glad eye, bo-peep, ocular demonstration, autopsy, visualization, envisagement.

A point of view, gazebo, vista, loop-hole, peep-hole, look-out, belvedere, field of view, watch-tower, observation post, crow's nest, theatre, amphitheatre, horizon, arena, commanding view, bird's-eye view, coign of vantage, observatory, periscope.

The organ of vision, eye, the naked or unassisted eye, retina, pupil, iris, cornea, white, optics, peepers.

Perspicacity, penetration, discernment.

Cat, hawk, lynx, eagle, Argus.

Evil eye; cockatrice, basilisk.

Verbs: To see, behold, discern, have in sight, descry, sight, catch a sight, glance, or glimpse of, spy, espy, to get a sight of.

To look, view, eye, open one's eyes, glance on, cast or set one's eyes on, clap eyes on, look on or upon, turn or bend one's looks upon, turn the eyes to, envisage, visualize, peep, peer, peek, pry, scan, survey, reconnoitre, contemplate, regard, inspect, recognize, mark, discover, distinguish, see through, speculate; to see sights, lionize.

To look intently, strain one's eyes, be all eyes, look full in the face, look hard at, stare, gaze, pore over, gloat on, leer, to see with half an eye, to blink, goggle, ogle, make eyes at; to play at bo-peep.

Phrases: To have an eye upon; keep in sight; look about one; glance round; run the eye over; lift up one's eyes; see at a glance, or with half an eye; keep a look-out for; to keep one's eyes skinned; to be a spectator of; to see with one's own eyes.

Adjectives: Visual, ocular, optic, optical, ophthalmic.

Seeing, etc., the eyes being directed to, fixed, riveted upon.

Clear-sighted, sharp-sighted, quick-sighted, eagle-eyed, hawk-eyed, lynx-eyed, keen-eyed, Argus-eyed, piercing, penetrating.

Phrase: The scales falling from one's eyes.

Adverbs: Visibly, etc., at sight, in sight of, to one's face, before one's face, with one's eyes open, at a glance, at first sight, at sight.

Interjections: Look! behold! see! lo! mark! observe! lo and behold!

442 BLINDNESS

Substantives: night-blindness, snow-blindness, cecity, amaurosis, cataract, ablepsy, nictitation, wink, blink.

A blinkard.

Verbs: To be blind, etc., not to see, to lose sight of.

Not to look, to close or shut the eyes, to look another way, to turn away or avert the eyes, to wink, blink, nictitate.

To render blind, etc., to put out the eyes, to blind, blindfold, hoodwink, daze, dazzle.

Phrase: To throw dust in the eyes.

Adjectives: Blind, eyeless, sightless, visionless, dark, stone-blind, sand-blind, stark-blind, mope-eyed, dazzled, hoodwinked, blindfolded, undiscerning.

Phrases: Blind as a bat, as a buzzard, as a beetle, as a mole, as an owl.

Adverbs: Blindly, etc., blindfold, darkly.

443 DIMSIGHTEDNESS

Substantives: purblindness, lippitude, confusion of vision, scotomy, failing sight, short-sightedness, near-sightedness, myopia, nictitation, long-sightedness, amblyopia, presbyopia, hypermetropia, nyctalopia (or nyctalopy), nystagmus, astigmatism, squint, strabismus, wall-eye, swivel-eye, cast of the eye, double sight; an albino, blinkard.

Fallacies of vision: *deceptio visus,* refraction, false light, phantasm, anamorphosis, distortion, looming, mirage, *fata morgana,* the spectre of the Brocken, ignis fatuus, phantasmagoria, dissolving views.

Colour-blindness, Daltonism.

Limitation of vision, blinker, screen.

Verbs: To be dim-sighted, etc., to see double, to have a mote in the eye, to squint, goggle, look askance (or askant), to see through a prism, wink, nictitate.

To glare, dazzle, loom.

Adjectives: Dim-sighted, half-sighted, short-sighted, near-sighted, purblind, myopic, long-sighted, hypermetropic, presbyopic, moon-eyed, mope-eyed, blear-eyed, goggle-eyed, wall-eyed, one-eyed, nictitating, winking, monoculous, amblyopic, astigmatic.

444 SPECTATOR

Substantives: looker-on, onlooker, watcher, sightseer, bystander, *voyeur,* inspector, snooper, rubberneck (455), spy, beholder, witness, eye-witness, observer, star-gazer, etc., scout.

Verbs: To witness, behold, look on at, spectate.

445 OPTICAL INSTRUMENTS

Substantives: lens, meniscus, magnifier, reading-glass, microscope, megascope, spectacles, specs, glasses, barnacles, goggles, pince-nez, lorgnette, folders, eye-glass, monocle, contact lens, periscope, telescope, spyglass, monocular, binoculars, fieldglass, night-glass, opera-glass, glass, view-finder, range-finder.

Mirror, reflector, speculum, looking-glass, pier-glass, cheval-glass, kaleidoscope.

Prism, camera, cine-camera, cinematograph (448), camera lucida, camera obscura, magic lantern, phantasmagoria, thaumatrope, chromatrope, stereoscope, pseudoscope, bioscope.

Photometer, polariscope, spectroscope, collimator, polemoscope, eriometer, actinometer, exposure meter, lucimeter.

446 VISIBILITY

Substantives: perceptibility, conspicuousness, distinctness, conspicuity, appearance, exposure.

Verbs: To be visible, etc., to appear, come in sight, come into view, heave in sight, open to the view, catch the eye, show its face, present itself, show itself, manifest itself, produce itself, discover itself, expose itself, come out, come to light, come forth, come forward, stand forth, stand out, arise, peep out, peer out, show up, turn up, crop up, start up, loom, burst forth, break through the clouds, glare, reveal itself, betray itself.

Phrases: To show its colours; to see the light of day; to show one's face; to tell its own tale; to leap to the eye; *cela saute aux yeux*; to stare one in the face.

Adjectives: Visible, perceptible, perceivable, discernible, in sight, apparent, plain, manifest, patent, obvious (525), clear, distinct, definite, well-defined, well-marked, recognizable, evident, unmistakable, palpable, naked, bare, barefaced, ostensible, conspicuous, prominent, staring, glaring, notable, notorious, overt; periscopic, panoramic, stereoscopic.

Phrases: Open as day; clear as day; plain as a pikestaff; there is no mistaking; plain as the nose on one's face; before one's eyes; above-board; exposed to view; under one's nose; in bold relief; in the limelight.

447 INVISIBILITY

Substantives: indistinctness, inconspicuousness, imperceptibility, non-appearance, delitescence, latency (526), concealment (528).

Verbs: To be invisible, escape notice, etc., to lie hidden, concealed, etc. (528), to be in or under a cloud, in a mist, in a haze, etc.; to lurk, lie in ambush, skulk.

Not to see, etc., to be blind to.

To render invisible, to hide, conceal (528).

Adjectives: Invisible, imperceptible, unseen, unbeheld, undiscerned, viewless, undiscernible, indiscernible, sightless, undescried, unespied, unapparent, non-apparent, inconspicuous, unconspicuous, hidden, concealed, etc. (528), covert, eclipsed.

Confused, dim, obscure, dark, misty, hazy, foggy, indistinct, ill-defined, indefinite, ill-marked, blurred, shadowy, nebulous, shaded, screened, veiled, masked.

Phrases: Out of sight; not in sight; out of focus.

448 APPEARANCE

Substantives: phenomenon, sight, spectacle, show, premonstration, scene, species, view, *coup d'Œil,* lookout, prospect, outlook, vista, perspective, bird's-eye view, scenery, landscape, seascape, streetscape, picture, tableau, *mise en scène,* display, exposure, exhibition, manifestation.

Pageant, pageantry, peep-show, raree-show, panorama, diorama, cosmorama, georama, *coup de théâtre, jeu de théâtre.*

Bioscope, biograph, magic lantern, epidiascope, cinematograph (or kinematograph).

Phantasm, phasma, phantom, spectrum, apparition, spectre, mirage, etc.

(4, 443).

Aspect, phase, *phasis,* seeming, guise, look, complexion, shape, mien, air, cast, carriage, manner, bearing, deportment, port, demeanour, presence, expression.

Lineament, feature, trait, lines, outline, contour, face, countenance, physiognomy, visage, phiz, mug, dial, puss, pan, profile, *tournure.*

Verbs: To seem, look, appear; to present, wear, carry, have, bear, exhibit, take, take on, or assume the appearance of; to play, to look like, to be visible, to reappear; to materialize.

To show, to manifest.

Adjectives: Apparent, seeming, etc., ostensible.

Adverbs: Apparently, to all appearance, etc., ostensibly, seemingly on the face of it, *prima facie,* at the first blush, at first sight.

449 DISAPPEARANCE

Substantives: evanescence, eclipse, occultation.

Dissolving views, fade-out.

Verbs: To disappear, vanish, dissolve, fade, melt away, pass, be gone, be lost, etc.

To efface, blot, blot out, erase, rub out, expunge (552).

Phrase: To go off the stage.

Adjectives: Disappearing, etc., lost, vanishing, evanescent, gone, missing.

Inconspicuous, unconspicuous (447).

Phrases: Lost in the clouds; leaving no trace; out of sight.

Interjections: Avaunt! vanish! disappear!
(297).

CLASS FOUR

Words relating to the intellectual faculties

I

*Section I –
Operations of Intellect
in General*

450 INTELLECT

Substantives: mind, understanding, reason, thinking principle, nous, noesis, faculties, sense, common sense, consciousness, capacity, intelligence, percipience, intellection, intuition, instinct, conception, judgment, talent, genius, parts, wit, wits, shrewdness, intellectuality; the five senses; rationalism; ability, skill (698); wisdom (498).

Subconsciousness, subconscious mind, unconscious, id.

Soul, spirit, psyche, ghost, inner man, heart, breast, bosom.

Organ or seat of thought: *sensorium,* sensory, brain, head, headpiece, pate, noddle, nut, loaf, skull, brain-pan, grey matter, pericranium, cerebrum, cerebellum, cranium, upper storey, belfry.

Science of mind, phrenology, mental philosophy, metaphysics, psychology, psychics, psycho-analysis; ideology, idealism, ideality, pneumatology, immaterialism, intuitionism, realism; transcendentalism, spiritualism.

Metaphysician, psychologist, psychiatrist, psychotherapist, psychoanalyst.

Verbs: Appreciate, realize, be aware of, be conscious of, take in, mark, note, notice.

Adjectives: Intellectual, noetic, rational, reasoning, gnostic, mental, spiritual, subjective, metaphysical, psychical, psychological, noumenal, ghostly, immaterial (317), cerebral; subconscious, subliminal, Freudian.

450A ABSENCE OR WANT OF INTELLECT

Substantives: imbecility (499), materialism.

Adjectives: Material, objective, unreasoning.

451 THOUGHT

Substantives: reflection, cogitation, cerebration, consideration, meditation, study, lucubration, speculation, deliberation, pondering, head-work, brain-work, application, attention (457).

Abstraction, contemplation, musing, brown study, reverie (458); depth of thought, workings of the mind, inmost thoughts, self-counsel, self-communing, self-examination, introspection; succession, flow, train, current, etc., of thought or of ideas, brain-wave.

Afterthought, second thoughts, hindsight, reconsideration, retrospection, retrospect (505), examination (461), imagination (515).

Thoughtfulness, pensiveness, intentness.

Telepathy, thought-transference,

mind-reading, extra-sensory perception, retrocognition, telekinesis.

Verbs: To think, reflect, cogitate, excogitate, consider, deliberate, speculate, contemplate, mediate, introspect, ponder, muse, ruminate, think over, brood over, reconsider, animadvert, con, con over, mull over, study, bend or apply the mind, digest, discuss, hammer at, puzzle out, weigh, perpend, fancy, trow, dream of.

To occur, present itself, pass in the mind, suggest itself, strike one.

To harbour, entertain, cherish, nurture, etc., an idea, a thought, a notion, a view, etc.

Phrases: Take into account; take into consideration; to take counsel; to commune with oneself; to collect one's thoughts; to advise with one's pillow; to sleep on or over it; to chew the cud upon; revolve in the mind; turn over in the mind; to rack or cudgel one's brains; to put on one's thinking-cap.

To flash on the mind; to flit across the view; to enter the mind; come into the head; come uppermost; run in one's head.

To make an impression; to sink or penetrate into the mind; fasten itself on the mind; to engross one's thoughts.

Adjectives: Thinking, etc., thoughtful, pensive, meditative, reflective, ruminant, introspective, wistful, contemplative, speculative, deliberative, studious, abstracted, introspective, sedate, philosophical, conceptual.

Close, active, diligent, mature, deliberate, laboured, steadfast, deep, profound, intense, etc., thought, study, reflection, etc.

Intent, engrossed, absorbed, deep-musing, rapt (or wrapt), abstracted; sedate.

Phrases: Having the mind on the stretch; lost in thought; the mind or head running upon.

452 INCOGITANCY

Substantives: vacancy, inanity, fatuity (499), thoughtlessness (458).

Verbs: Not to think, to take no thought of, not to trouble oneself about, to put away thought; to inhibit, dismiss, discard, or discharge from one's thoughts, or from the mind; to drop the subject, set aside, turn aside, turn away from, turn one's attention from, abstract oneself, dream.

To unbend, relax, divert the mind.

Adjectives: Vacant, unintellectual (499), unoccupied, unthinking, inconsiderate, thoughtless, idealess, unidea'd, absent, *distrait,* abstracted, inattentive (458), diverted, distracted, distraught, unbent, relaxed.

Unthought-of, unconsidered, incogitable, undreamed-of, off one's mind.

Phrase: *In nubibus.*

453 IDEA

Substantives: notion, conception, apprehension, concept, thought, fancy, conceit, impression, perception, apperception, percept, ideation, image, eidolon, sentiment (484), fantasy, flight of fancy.

Point of view, light, aspect (448), field of view, standpoint; theory (514); fixed idea (481).

454 TOPIC

Substantives: subject, matter, theme, motif, thesis, text, subject-matter, point, proposition, theorem, business, affair, case, matter in hand, question, argument, motion, resolution, moot point (461), head, chapter; nice or subtle point, quodlibet.

Phrases: Food for thought; mental pabulum.

Adverbs: In question under consideration, on the carpet, *sur le tapis,* relative to, *re, in re* (9), concerning, touching.

Section 2 –
Precursory Conditions
and Operations

455 CURIOSITY

Substantives: curiousness, inquisitiveness, an inquiring mind.

A quidnunc, busybody, eavesdropper, snooper, rubberneck, Peeping Tom, Nosy Parker, Paul Pry, newsmonger, gosspi.

Verbs: To be curious, etc., to take an interest in, to stare, gape, pry, snoop, rubber, lionize.

Adjectives: Curious, inquisitive, inquiring, inquisitorial, all agog, staring, prying, snoopy, gaping, agape, over-curious, nosy.

Adverbs: With open mouth, on tiptoe, with ears flapping, *arrectis auribus.*

456 INCURIOSITY

Substantives: incuriousness, insouciance, nonchalance, want of interest, indifference (866).

Verbs: To be incurious, etc., to have no curiosity, take no interest in, not to care, not to mind; to mind one's own business.

Phrases: Not to trouble oneself about; one couldn't care less; the devil may care; san fairy ann.

Adjectives: Incurious, uninquisitive, indifferent, *sans souci,* insouciant, nonchalant, aloof, detached, apathetic, uninterested.

457 ATTENTION

Substantives: advertence, advertency, observance, observation, interest, notice, heed, look, regard, view, remark, inspection, introspection, heedfulness, mindfulness, look-out, watch, vigilance, circumspection, surveillance, consideration, scrutiny, revision, revisal, recension, review, revise, particularity (459).

Close, intense, deep, profound, etc., attention, application, or study.

Verbs: To be attentive, etc.; to attend, advert to, mind, observe, look, look at, see, view, look to, see to, remark, heed, notice, spot, twig, pipe, take heed, take notice, mark; give or pay attention to; give heed to, have an eye to; turn, apply, or direct the mind, the eye, or the attention to; look after, give a thought to, animadvert on, occupy oneself to, give oneself up to, see about.

To examine cursorily; to glance at, upon, or over; cast or pass the eyes over, run over, turn over the leaves, dip into, skim, perstringe.

To examine closely or intently, scrutinize, consider, give one's mind to, overhaul, pore over, perpend, note, mark, inspect, review, size up, take stock of, fix the eye, mind, thoughts, or attention on, keep in view, contemplate, revert to, etc. (451).

To fall under one's notice, observation, etc., to catch the eye; to catch, awaken, wake, invite, solicit, attract, claim, excite, engage, occupy, strike, arrest, fix, engross, monopolize, preoccupy, obsess, absorb, rivet, etc., the attention, mind, or thoughts; to interest.

To call attention to, point out, indicate (550).

Phrases: To trouble one's head about; lend or incline an ear to; to take cognizance of; to prick up one's ears; to have one's eyes open; to keep one's eyes skinned.

To have one's wits about one; to bear in mind; to come to the point; to take into account; to read, mark, learn.

Adjectives: Attentive, mindful, heedful, regardful, alive to, awake to, bearing in mind, occupied with, engaged, taken up with, interested, engrossed, wrapped in, absorbed, rapt.

Awake, watchful, on the watch (459), broad awake, wide awake, agape, intent on, with eyes fixed on,

179

open-eyed, unwinking, undistracted, with bated breath, breathless, upon the stretch.

Interjections: See! look! say! attention! hey! oy! mark! lo! behold! *achtung! nota bene!* NB.

458 INATTENTION

Substantives: inconsideration, inconsiderateness, inadvertence, inadvertency, non-observance, inobservance, disregard, oversight, unmindfulness, giddiness, respectlessness, thoughtlessness (460), in-souciance; wandering, distracted, etc., attention.

Absence of mind, abstraction, preoccupation, distraction, reverie, brown study, day-dream, day-dreaming, wool-gathering.

Phrases: The wits going wool-gathering; the attention wandering; building castle in the air, or castles in Spain.

Verbs: To be inattentive, etc., to overlook, disregard, pass by, slur over, pass over, gloss over, blink, miss, skim the surface, *effleurer* (460).

To call off, draw off, call away, divert, etc., the attention; to distract; to disconcert, put out, rattle, discompose, confuse, perplex, bewilder, bemuse, moider, bemuddle, muddle, dazzle, obfuscate, faze, fluster, flurry, flummox, befog.

Phrases: To take no account of; to drop the subject; to turn a deaf ear to; to come in at one ear and go out of the other; to reckon without one's host.

Adjectives: Inattentive, mindless, unobservant, unmindful, uninterested, inadvertent, heedless, regardless, respectless, careless (460), insouciant, unwatchful, listless, cursory, blind, deaf, etc.

Absent, abstracted, *distrait,* absent-minded, lost, preoccupied, bemused, dreamy, moony, napping.

Disconcerted, put out, etc., dizzy, muzzy (460).

Phrase: Caught napping.

Adverbs: Cavalierly, inattentively, etc.

459 CARE

Substantives: caution, heed, heedfulness, attention (457), wariness, prudence, discretion, watch, watchfulness, alertness, vigil, vigilance, circumspection, watch and ward, deliberation, forethought (510), predeliberation, solicitude, precaution (673), scruple, scrupulousness, scrupulosity, particularity, surveillance.

Phrases: The eyes of Argus; *l'œil du maître.*

Verbs: To be careful, etc., to take care, have a care, beware, look to it, reck, heed, take heed, provide for, see to, see after, keep watch, keep watch and ward, look sharp, look about one, set watch, take precautions, take tent, see about.

Phrases: To have all one's wits about one; to mind one's P's and Q's; to speak by the card; to pick one's steps; keep a sharp look out; keep one's weather eye open; to keep an eye on.

Adjectives: Careful, cautious, heedful, wary, canny, guarded, on one's guard, alert, on the alert, on the watch, watchful, on the look out, *aux aguets,* awake, vigilant, circumspect, broad awake, having the eyes open, Argus-eyed.

Discreet, prudent, sure-footed, provident, scrupulous, particular, meticulous.

Phrase: On the *qui vive.*

Adverbs: Carefully, etc., with care, etc., gingerly, considerately.

Phrases: Let sleeping dogs lie; catching a weasel asleep.

Interjections: Look out! mind your eye! watch! beware! cave! fore! heads!

460 NEGLECT

Substantives: negligence, omission, trifling, laches, heedlessness, carelessness, perfunctoriness, remissness, imprudence, secureness, indiscretion, *étourderie,* incautiousness, indiscrimination, rashness (863), recklessness, nonchalance, inattention (458); slovenliness, sluttishness.

Trifler, flibbertigibbet, Micawber; slattern, slut, sloven.

Verbs: To be negligent, etc., to neglect, scamp, pass over, cut, omit, pretermit, set aside, cast or put aside.

To overlook, disregard, ignore, slight, pay no regard to, make light of, trifle with, blink, wink at, connive at; take or make no account of; gloss over, slur over, slip over, skip, skim, miss, shelve, sink, jump over, shirk (623), discount.

To waste time, trifle, frivol, fribble (683).

To render neglectful, etc., to put or throw off one's guard.

Phrases: To give to the winds; take no account of; turn a deaf ear to; shut one's eyes to; not to mind; think no more of; set at naught; give the go-by to.

Adjectives: Neglecting, etc., unmindful, heedless, careless, *sans souci,* negligent, neglectful, slovenly, sluttish, remiss, perfunctory, thoughtless, unthoughtful, unheedful, off one's guard, unwary, incautious, unguarded, indiscreet, inconsiderate, imprudent, improvident, rash, headlong, reckless, heels over head, witless, hare-brained, giddy-brained, offhand, slapdash, happy-go-lucky, cursory, brain-sick, scatterbrained.

Neglected, missed, abandoned, shunted, shelved, unheeded, unperceived, unseen, unobserved, unnoticed, unnoted, unmarked, unattended to, untended, unwatched, unthought-of, overlooked, unmissed, unexamined, unsearched, unscanned, unweighed, unsifted, untested, unweeded, undetermined.

Phrases: In an unguarded moment; buried in a napkin.

Adverbs: Negligently, etc., anyhow, any old way.

Interjections: Let is pass! never mind! no matter! I should worry! san fairy ann! *nichevo!*

461 INQUIRY

Substantives: search, research, quest, pursuit (622), examination, review, scrutiny, investigation, perquisition, perscrutation, referendum, straw vote, Gallup poll; discussion, symposium, inquest, inquisition, exploration, exploitation, sifting, screening, calculation, analysis, dissection, resolution, induction; the Baconian method.

Questioning, asking, interrogation, interpellation, interrogatory, the Socratic method, examination, cross-examination, cross-questioning, third degree, quiz, catechism.

Reconnoitring, reconnaissance, feeler, *ballon d'essai,* prying, spying, espionage, the lantern of Diogenes, searchlight.

QUESTION, query, difficulty, problem, proposition, desideratum, point to be solved; point or matter in dispute; moot point, question at issue, bone of contention, plain question, fair question, open question, knotty point, vexed question, crux.

Enigma, riddle, conundrum, crossword, bone to pick, quodlibet, Gordian knot.

An inquirer, querist, questioner, heckler, inquisitor, scrutator, scrutineer, examiner, inspector, analyst, quidnunc, newsmonger, gossip (527, 532); investigator, detective, bloodhound, sleuth-hound, sleuth, inquiry agent, private eye, Sherlock Holmes, busy, dick, rozzer, flattie, G-man; secret police, Cheka, Ogpu, Gestapo.

Verbs: To inquire, seek, search, look for, look about for, look out for, cast about for, beat up for, grope for, feel for, reconnoitre, explore, sound, rum-

181

mage, fossick, ransack, pry, snoop, look round, look over, look through, scan, peruse.

To pursue, hunt, track, trail, mouse, dodge, trace, shadow, tail, dog (622), nose out, ferret out, unearth, hunt up.

To investigate; to take up, follow up, institute, pursue, conduct, carry on, prosecute, etc., an inquiry, etc.; to overhaul, examine, study, consider, fathom, take into consideration, dip into, look into, calculate, pre-examine, dive into, to delve into, rake, rake over, discuss, canvass, thrash out, probe, fathom, sound, scritinize, analyse, anatomize, dissect, sift, screen, winnow, resolve, traverse, see into.

To ask, speer, question, query, demand; to put, propose, propound, moot, raise, stir, suggest, put forth, start, pop, etc., a question; to interrogate, catechize, pump, cross-question, cross-examine, grill, badger, heckle, dodge, require an answer.

Phrases: To look, peer, or pry into every hole and corner, to beat the bushes; to leave no stone unturned; to seek a needle in a bundle of hay; to scratch the head.

To subject to examination; to grapple with a question; to put to the proof; pass in review; take into consideration; to ventilate a question; seek a clue; throw out a feeler.

To undergo examination; to be in course of inquiry; to be under consideration.

Adjectives: Inquiring, etc., inquisitive, requisitive, requisitory, catechetical, inquisitorial, heuristic, analytic, in search of, in quest of, on the look out for, interrogative, zetetic.

Undetermined, untried, undecided, to be resolved, etc., in question, in dispute, under discussion, under consideration, *sub judice,* moot, proposed, doubtful.

Adverbs: Why? wherefore? whence? *quaere?* how comes it? how happens it?

how is it? what is the reason? what's in the wind? what's cooking?

462 ANSWER

Substantives: response, reply, replication, riposte, rejoinder, rebutter, surrejoinder, surrebutter, retort, comeback, repartee, rescript, antiphony, rescription, acknowledgment.

Explanation, solution, deduction, resolution, exposition, rationale, interpretation (522).

A key, master-key, open sesame, *passepartout,* clue.

Oedipus, oracle (513); solutionist.

Verbs: To answer, respond, reply, rebut, retort, rejoin, return for answer, acknowledge, echo.

To explain, solve, resolve, expound, decipher, spell, interpret (522), to unriddle, unlock, cut the knot, unravel, fathom, pick or open the lock, discover, fish up, to find a clue to, get to the bottom of.

Phrases: To turn the tables upon; QED

Adjectives: Answering, responding, etc., responsive, respondent.

Adverb: On the right scent.

Interjection: Eureka!

463 EXPERIMENT

Substantives: essay, trial, tryout, tentative method, *tâtonnement,* verification, probation, proof, criterion, test, acid test, reagent, check, control, touchstone, pyx, assay, ordeal; empiricism, rule of thumb method of trial and error.

A feeler, *ballon d'essai,* pilot-balloon, messenger-balloon: pilot-engine: straw to show the wind.

Verbs: To experiment, essay, try, explore, grope, angle, cast about, beat the bushes; feel or grope one's way; the thread one's way; to make an experiment, make trial of.

To subject to trial, etc., to experiment upon, try over, rehearse, give a

trial to, put, bring, or submit to the test or proof; to prove, verify, test, assay, touch, practise upon.
Phrases: To see how the land lies; to see how the wind blows; to feel the pulse; to throw out a feeler; to have a try; to have a go.
Adjectives: Experimental, crucial, tentative, probationary, empirical, *sub judice,* under probation, on trial, on approval.
Adverbs: *A tâtons.*

464 COMPARISON

Substantives: collation, contrast, antithesis, identification.

A comparison, simile, similitude, analogy, parallel, parable, metaphor, allegory (521).
Verbs: To compare to or with; to collate, confront, place side by side or in juxtaposition, to draw a parallel, institute a comparison, contrast, balance, identify.
Adjectives: Comparative, metaphorical, figurative, allegorical, comparable, compared with, pitted against, placed by the side of.

465 DISCRIMINATION

Substantives: distinction, differentiation, perception or appreciation of difference, nicety, refinement, taste (850), judgment, discernment, nice perception, tact, critique.
Verbs: To discriminate, distinguish, differentiate, draw the line, sift, screen.
Phrases: To split hairs; to cut blocks with a razor; to separate the chaff from the wheat or the sheep from the goats.
Adjectives: Discriminating, etc., discriminative, distinctive, diagnostic, nice, judicial.

465A INDISCRIMINATION

Substantives: indistinctness, indistinction (460).

Verbs: Not to distinguish or discriminate, to confound, confuse; to neglect, overlook, lose sight of a distinction.
Adjectives: Indiscriminate, undistinguished, undistinguishable, sweeping, unmeasured, wholesale.

466 MEASUREMENT

Substantives: admeasurement, mensuration, triangulation, survey, valuation, appraisement, assessment, assize, estimation, reckoning, evaluation, gauging; mileage, voltage, horse power.

Geometry, geodetics, geodesy, orthometry, altimetry, sounding, surveying, weighing, ponderation, trutination, dead reckoning, metrology.

A measure, standard, rule, yardstick, compass, callipers, dividers, gauge, meter, line, rod, plumb-line, plummet, log, log-line, sound, sounding-rod, sounding-line, lead-line, index, flood-mark, Plimsoll line (or mark), check.

Scale, graduation, graduated scale, vernier, quadrant, theodolite, slide-rule, balance, spring balance, scales, steelyard, beam, weather-glass, barometer, aneroid, barograph, araeometer, altimeter, clinometer, graphometer, goniometer, thermometer, speedometer, tachometer, pedometer, ammeter, voltmeter, micrometer, etc.

A surveyor, geometer, leadsman, etc.
Verbs: To measure, mete, value, assess, rate, appraise, estimate, form an estimate, set a value on, appreciate, span, pace, step; apply the compass, rule, scale, etc., gauge, plumb, probe, sound, fathom, heave the log, survey, weigh, poise, balance, hold the scales, take an average, graduate, evaluate, size up, to place in the beam, to take into account, price.
Adjectives: Measuring, etc., metrical, ponderable, measurable, mensurable.

Section 3 –
Materials for Reasoning

467 EVIDENCE, on one side
Substantives: premises, data, grounds, *praecognita,* indication (550).

Oral, hearsay, internal, external, documentary, presumptive evidence.

Testimony, testimonial, deposition, declaration, attestation, testification, authority, warrant, warranty, guarantee, surety, handwriting, autograph, signature, endorsement, seal, sigil, signet (550), superscription, entry, fingerprint.

Voucher, credential, certificate, deed, indenture, docket, dossier, probate, affidavit, diploma; admission, concession, allegation, deposition, citation, quotation, reference; admissibility.

Criterion, test, reagent, touchstone, check, control, prerogative, fact, argument, shibboleth.

A witness, eye-witness, indicator, ear-witness, deponent, telltale, informer, sponsor, special pleader.

Assumption, presumption, show of reason, postulation, postulate, lemma.

Reason, proof (478), circumstantial evidence.

Ex-parte evidence, one-sided view.

Secondary evidence, confimation, corroboration, ratification, authentication, support, approval, compurgation.

Phrases: A case in point; *ecce signum; ex pede Herculem.*

Verbs: To be evidence, etc., to evidence, evince, show, indicate (550), imply, involve, entail, necessitate, argue, bespeak, admit, allow, concede, homologate, certify, testify, attest, bear testimony, depose, depone, witness, vouch for, sign, seal, set one's hand and seal to, endorse, confirm, ratify, corroborate, support, establish, uphold, bear upon, bear out, warrant, guarantee.

To adduce, cite, quote, refer to, appeal to, call, bring forward, produce, bring into court, confront witnesses, collect, bring together, rake up evidence, to make a case, make good, authenticate, substantiate, go bail for.

To allege, plead, assume, postulate, posit, presume; to beg the question.

Phrases: To hold good, hold water; to speak volumes; to bring home to; to bring to book; to quote chapter and verse; to speak for itself; tell its own tale.

Adjectives: Showing, etc., indicating, indicative, indicatory, evidential, evidentiary, following, deducible, consequential, collateral, corroborative, confirmatory, postulatory, presumptive.

Sound, logical, strong, valid, cogent, decisive, persuasive, persuasory, demonstrative, irrefragable, irresistible, etc. (578).

Adverbs: According to, witness, admittedly, confessedly, *a fortiori,* still more, still less, all the more reason for.

468 COUNTER-EVIDENCE
Substantives: disproof, contradiction, rejoinder, rebutter, answer (462), weak point, conflicting evidence, refutation (479), negation (536).

Phrases: A *tu quoque* argument; the other side of the shield.

Verbs: To countervail, oppose, rebut, check, weaken, invalidate, contradict, contravene.

Phrases: To tell another story; to cut both ways.

Adjectives: Countervailing, etc., contradictory; unauthenticated, unattested, unvouched-for.

Adverbs: Although, though, albeit, but, *per contra.*

Phrase: *Audi alteram partem.*

469 QUALIFICATION

Substantives: limitation, modification, allowance, grains of allowance, consideration, extenuating circumstance, condition, proviso, saving clause, penalty clause, exception (83), assumption (514).

Verbs: To qualify, limit, modify, tone down, colour, discount, allow for, make allowance for, take into account, introduce new conditions, admit exceptions, take exception.

Adjectives: Qualifying, etc., conditional, exceptional (83), contingent, postulatory, hypothetical, suppositious (514).

Adverbs: Provided, if, unless, but, yet, according as, conditionally, admitting, supposing, granted that; on the supposition, assumption, presumption, allegation, hypothesis, etc., of; with the understanding, even, although, for all that, at all events, after all.

Phrases: With a grain of salt; *cum grano salis.*

470 POSSIBILITY

Substantives: potentiality, contingency (156), what may be, what is possible, etc.

Practicability, feasibility (705), compatibility (23).

Verbs: To be possible, etc., to admit of, to bear.

To render possible, etc., to put into the way of.

Adjectives: Possible, contingent (475), conceivable, credible.

Practicable, feasible, achievable, performable, viable, accessible, surmountable, attainable, obtainable, compatible.

Adverbs: Possibly, by possibility, maybe, perhaps, mayhap, haply, perchance, peradventure, *in posse* (156).

Phrases: Wind and weather permitting; within the bounds of possibility; on the cards; DV.

471 IMPOSSIBILITY

Substantives: what cannot be, what can never be, imposs, no go, hopelessness (859).

Impracticability, incompatibility (704), incredibility.

Verbs: To be impossible, etc., to have no chance whatever.

Phrases: To make a silk purse out of a sow's ear; to wash a blackamoor white; to make bricks without straw; to get blood from a stone; to take the breeks off a highlandman; to square the circle; to eat one's cake and have it too.

Adjectives: Impossible, contrary to reason, inconceivable, unreasonable, absurd, incredible, visionary, chimerical, prodigious (870), desperate, hopeless, unheard-of, unthinkable.

Impracticable, unattainable, unachievable, unfeasible, infeasible, beyond control, unobtainable, unprocurable, insuperable, unsurmountable, inaccessible, inextricable.

Phrases: Out of the question; sour grapes; *non possumus.*

472 PROBABILITY

Substantives: likelihood, *vraisemblance,* verisimilitude, plausibility, show of, colour of, credibility, reasonable chance, favourable chance, fair chance, hope, prospect, presumption, presumptive evidence, circumstantial evidence, the main chance, a *prima facie* case.

Probabilism, probabiliorism.

Verbs: To be probable, likely, etc.; to think likely, dare say, expect (507).

Phrases: To bid fair; to stand fair for; to stand a good chance; to stand to reason.

Adjectives: Probable, likely, hopeful, well-founded.

Plausible, specious, ostensible, colourable, standing to reason, reasonable, credible, tenable, easy of belief, presumable, presumptive, *ben trovato.*

Phrases: Likely to happen; in a fair

way; appearances favouring; according to every reasonable expectation; the odds being in favour.

Adverbs: Probably, etc., belike, in all probability, or likelihood, apparently, to all appearance, on the face of it, in the long run, *prima facie,* very likely, like enough, arguably, ten to one.

Phrase: All Lombard Street to a china orange.

473 IMPROBABILITY

Substantives: unlikelihood, unfavourable chances, small chance, off-chance, bare possibility, long odds, incredibility.

Verbs: To be improbable, etc., to have or stand a small, little, poor, remote, etc., chance; to whistle for.

Adjectives: Improbable, unheard-of, incredible, unbelievable, unlikely.

Phrases: Contrary to all reasonable expectation; having scarcely a chance; a chance in a thousand.

474 CERTAINTY

Substantives: certitude, positiveness, a dead certainty, dead cert, infallibleness, infallibility, gospel, scripture, surety, assurance, indisputableness, moral certainty.

Fact, matter of fact, *fait accompli.*

Bigotry, dogmatism, *ipse dixit.*

Bigot, dogmatist, Sir Oracle.

Verbs: To be certain, etc., to believe (484).

To render certain, etc., to ensure, to assure, clinch, determine, decide.

To dogmatize, lay down the law.

Phrases: To stand to reason; to make assurance doubly sure.

Adjectives: Certain, sure, assured, solid, absolute, positive, flat, determinate, categorical, unequivocal, inevitable, unavoidable, avoidless, unerring, infallible, indubitable, indubious, indisputable, undisputed, uncontested, undeniable, incontestable, irrefutable, unimpeachable, incontrovertible, undoubted, doubtless, without doubt, beyond a doubt, past dispute, unanswerable, decided, unquestionable, beyond all question, unquestioned, questionless, irrefragable, evident, self-evident, axiomatic, demonstrable (478), authoritative, authentic, official, unerring, infallible, trustworthy (939).

Phrases: Sure as fate; and no mistake; sure as a gun; clear as the sun at noonday; sure as death (and taxes); bet your life; you bet; *cela va sans dire;* it's in the bag; that's flat.

Adverbs: Certainly, assuredly, etc., for certain, *in esse,* sure, surely, sure enough, to be sure, of course, as a matter of course, yes (488), depend upon it, that's so, by all manner of means, beyond a peradventure.

475 UNCERTAINTY

Substantives: incertitude, doubt (485), doubtfulness, dubiety, dubiousness, suspense, precariousness, indefiniteness, indetermination, slipperiness, fallibility, perplexity, embarrassment, dilemma, ambiguity (520), hesitation, vacillation (605), equivoque, vagueness, peradventure, touch-and-go.

Phrases: A blind bargain; a pig in a poke; a leap in the dark; a moot point; an open question.

Verbs: To be uncertain, etc; to vacillate, hesitate, waver.

To render uncertain, etc., to perplex, embarrass, confuse, moider, confound, bewilder, disorientate.

Phrases: To be in a state of uncertainty; not to know which way to turn; to be at a loss; to be at fault; to lose the scent.

To tremble in the balance; to hang by a thread.

Adjectives: Uncertain, doubtful, dubious, precarious (665), chancy, casual, random, contingent, indecisive, dependent on circumstances, undecided, unsettled, undetermined, pending, pendent, vague, indeterminate, indefinite, ambiguous, undefined, equivocal, undefinable, puzzling, enigmatic, debatable, disputable, questionable, apocryphal, problematical, hypothetical, controvertible, fallible, fallacious, suspicious, fishy, slippery, ticklish.

Unauthentic, unconfirmed, undemonstrated, undemonstrable, unreliable, untrustworthy.

Section 4 –
Reasoning Processes

476 REASONING
Substantives: ratiocination, dialectics, induction, deduction, generalization; inquiry (461).

Argumentation, discussion, *pourparler,* controversy, polemics, debate, wrangling, logomachy, apology, apologetics, ergotism, disputation, disceptation.

The art of reasoning, logic, process, train or chain of reasoning, analysis, synthesis, argument, lemma, proposition, terms, premises, postulate, data, starting-point, principle, inference, result, conclusion.

Syllogism, prosyllogism, enthymeme, sorites, dilemma, *perilepsis,* pros and cons, a comprehensive argument.

Correctness, soundness, force, validity, cogency, conclusiveness.

A thinker, reasoner, disputant, controversialist, logician, dialectician, polemic, wrangler, arguer, debater.
Phrases: A paper war; a war of words; a battle of the books; a full-dress debate.

The horns of a dilemma; *reductio ad absurdum; argumentum ad hominem; onus probandi.*
Verbs: To reason, argue, discuss,

debate, dispute, wrangle; bandy words or arguments; hold or carry on an argument, controvert, contravene (536), consider (461), comment upon, moralize upon, spiritualize.
Phrases: To open a discussion or case; to moot; to join issue; to ventilate a question; to talk it over; to have it out; to take up a side or case.

To chop logic; to try conclusions; to impale on the horns of a dilemma; to cut the matter short; to hit the nail on the head; to take one's stand upon; to have the last word.
Adjectives: Reasoning, etc., rational, rationalistic, ratiocinative, argumentative, controversial, dialectic, polemical, discursory, discursive, debatable, controvertible, disputatious; correct, just, fair, sound, valid, cogent, logical, demonstrative (478), relevant, pertinent (9, 23).
Phrases: To the point; in point; to the purpose; *ad rem.*
Adverbs: For, because, for that reason, forasmuch as, inasmuch as, since, hence, whence, whereas, considering, therefore, consequently, *ergo,* then, thus, accordingly, wherefore, *a fortiori, a priori, ex concesso.*
Phrases: In consideration of; in conclusion; in fine; after all; *au bout du compte;* on the whole; taking one thing with another.

477 INTUITION
Substantives: instinct, association, presentiment, insight, second sight, sixth sense.

False or vicious reasoning, show of reason.

Misjudgment, miscalculation (481).
SOPHISTRY
Substantives: paralogy, fallacy, perversion, casuistry, jesuitry, quibble, equivocation, evasion, chicanery, special pleading, quiddity, mystification; nonsense (497).

Sophism, solecism, paralogism,

elenchus, fallacy, quodlibet, subterfuge, subtlety, quillet, inconsistency, antilogy.

Speciousness, plausibility, illusiveness, irrelevancy, invalidity; claptrap, hot air.

Quibbler, casuist, *advocatus diaboli*.

Phrases: Begging the question; *petitio principii*; *ignoratio elenchi*; reasoning in a circle; *post hoc, ergo propter hoc*; *ignotum per ignotius*.

The meshes or cobwebs of sophistry; a flaw in an argument; an argument falling to the ground.

Verbs: To envisage, to judge intuitively, etc.

To reason ill, falsely, etc.; to pervert, quibble, equivocate, mystify, evade, elude, gloss over, varnish, misjudge, miscalculate (481).

To refine, subtilize, cavil, sophisticate, mislead.

Phrases: To split hairs; to cut blocks with a razor; throw off the scent; to beg the question; reason in a circle; beat about the bush; prove that black is white; not have a leg to stand on; lose one's reckoning.

Adjectives: Intuitive, instinctive, impulsive, unreasoning, independent of or anterior to reason.

Sophistical, unreasonable, irrational, illogical, false, unsound, not following, not pertinent, inconsequent, inconsequential, unwarranted, untenable, inconclusive, incorrect, fallacious, inconsistent, groundless, fallible, unproved, indecisive, deceptive, illusive, illusory, specious, hollow, jesuitical, plausible, irrelevant.

Weak, feeble, poor, flimsy, trivial, trumpery, trashy, puerile, childish, irrational, silly, foolish, imbecile, absurd (499), extravagant, far-fetched, pettifogging, quibbling, fine-spun, hair-splitting.

Phrases: *Non constat*; *non sequitur*; not holding water; away from the point; foreign to the purpose or subject; hav-ing nothing to do with the matter; not of the essence; *nihil ad rem*; not bearing upon the point in question; not the point; beside the mark.

478 DEMONSTRATION

Substantives: proof, conclusiveness, probation, comprobation, clincher, *experimentum crucis,* test, etc. (463), argument (476).

Verbs: To demonstrate, prove, establish, show, evince, verify, substantiate; to follow.

Phrases: Make good; set at rest; settle the question; reduce to demonstration; to make out a case; to prove one's point; to clinch an argument; bring home to bear out.

Adjectives: Demonstrating, etc., demonstrative, probative, demonstrable, unanswerable, conclusive, final, apodictic (or apodeictic), irrefutable, irrefragable, unimpeachable, categorical, decisive, crucial.

Demonstrated, proved, proven, etc., unconfuted, unrefuted; evident, self-evident, axiomatic (474); deducible, consequential, inferential.

Phrases: *Probatum est*; it stands to reason; it holds good; there being nothing more to be said; QED.

Adverbs: Of course, in consequence, consequently, as a matter of course, no wonder.

479 CONFUTATION

Substantives: refutation, disproof, conviction, redargution, invalidation, exposure, exposition; demolition of an argument; answer, come-back, counter, retort.

Phrases: *Reductio ad absurdum*; a knock-down argument; a *tu quoque* argument.

Verbs: To confute, refute, disprove, redargue, expose, show the fallacy of, knock the bottom out of, rebut, parry, negative, defeat, overthrow, demolish, explode, riddle, overturn, invalidate, silence, reduce to silence, shut up, put down.

Phrases: To cut the ground from one's feet; to give one a set-down.
Adjectives: Confuting, etc., confuted, etc., capable of refutation, refutable, confutable, etc.; unproved, etc.
Phrases: The argument falls to the ground; it won't hold water; that cock won't fight.

Section 5 –
Results of Reasoning

480 JUDGMENT
Substantives: conclusion, determination, deduction, inference, result, illation, corollary, rider, porism, consectary.

Estimation, valuation, appreciation, judication, adjudication, arbitrament, arbitration, assessment, award, ponderation.

Decision, sentence, verdict, moral, ruling, finding; detection, discovery, estimate; *chose jugée.*

Criticism, critique, review, report, notice; plebiscite, casting vote.

A judge, umpire, arbiter, arbitrator, assessor, censor, referee, critic, connoisseur, reviewer. **Verbs:** To judge, deduce, conclude, draw a conclusion, infer, make a deduction, draw an inference, put two and two together; come to, arrive or jump at a conclusion; to derive, gather, collect.

To estimate, appreciate, value, count, assess, rate, account, rank, regard, review, settle, decide, pronounce, arbitrate, perpend, size up.
Phrases: To sit in judgment; to hold the scales; to pass an opinion; to pass judgment.
Adjectives: Judging, etc., deducible (467); impartial, unbiased, unprejudiced, unwarped, unbigoted, equitable, fair, sound, rational, judicious, shrewd.

480A DETECTION
Substantive: discovery.
Verbs: To ascertain, determine, find, find out, make out, detect, discover, elicit, recognize, trace, get at; get or arrive at the truth; meet with, fall upon, light upon, hit upon, fall in with, stumble upon, lay the finger on, spot, solve, resolve, unravel, fish out, worm out, ferret out, root out, nose out, disinter, unearth, grub up, fish up, investigate (461).

To be near the truth, to get warm, to burn.
Phrase: To smell a rat.
Interjection: Eureka!

481 MISJUDGMENT
Substantives: obliquity of judgment, misconception, error (495), miscalculation, miscomputation, presumption.

Prejudgment, prejudication, prejudice, prenotion, *parti pris,* prevention, preconception, predilection, prepossession, preapprehension, presentiment, *esprit de corps,* clannishness, party spirit, partisanship, partiality.

Bias, warp, twist, fad, whim, crotchet, fike; narrow-mindedness, bigotry, dogmatism, intolerance, tenacity, obstinacy (606); blind side; one-sided, partial, narrow or confined views, ideas, conceptions, or notions; *idée fixe,* fixed idea, obsession, monomania, infatuation.
Phrases: A bee in one's bonnet; a mote in the eye; a fool's paradise.
Verbs: To midjudge, misestimate, misconceive, misreckon, etc. (495).

To prejudge, forejudge, prejudicate, dogmatize, have a bias, etc., presuppose, presume.

To produce a bias, twist, etc.; to bias, warp, twist, prejudice, obsess, infatuate, prepossess.
Phrases: To have on the brain; to look only at one side of the shield; to view with jaundiced eye; to run away with the notion; to jump to a conclusion.

Adjectives: Prejudging, midjudging, etc., prejudiced, jaundiced, narrow-minded, dogmatic, intolerant, illiberal, blimpish, besotted, infatuated, fanatical, *entêté,* positive, obstinate (606), tenacious, pig-headed, having a bias, twist, etc., warped, partial, one-sided, biased, bigoted, hide-bound, tendentious, opinionated, opinionative, opinioned, self-opinioned, self-opinionated, crotchety, pernickety, faddy, fussy, fiky.
Phrases: Wedded to an opinion; the wish being father to the thought.

482 OVERESTIMATION
Substantive: exaggeration.
Phrases: Much ado about nothing; much cry and little wool; a storm in a tea-cup.
Verbs: To overestimate, estimate too highly, overrate, overvalue, overprize, overpraise, overweigh, outreckon; exaggerate, extol, puff, boost, make too much of, overstrain.
Phrases: To set too high a value upon; to make a mountain out of a molehill; *parturiunt montes, nascetur ridiculus mus;* to make two bites of a cherry; all his geese are swans.
Adjectives: Overestimated, etc.

483 UNDERESTIMATION
Substantives: depreciation, disparagement, detraction (934), underrating, undervaluing, etc.
Verbs: To depreciate, disparage, detract, underrate, underestimate, undervalue, underreckon, underprize, misprize, disprize, not to do justice to, make light of, slight, belittle, knock, slam, make little of, think nothing of, hold cheap, cheapen, disregard, to care nothing for, despise, set at naught, minimize, discount, deride, derogate, decry, cry down, crab, denigrate, smear, vilipend, run down (934).

To scout, deride, pooh-pooh, mock, scoff at, laugh at, whistle at, play with,

trifle with, fribble, niggle, ridicule (856).
Phrases: To snap one's fingers at; throw into the shade; not to care a pin, rush, hoot, tinker's cuss, etc., for; to damn with faint praise.
Adjectives: Depreciating, etc., derogatory, cynical.

Depreciated, etc., unvalued, unprized.

484 BELIEF
Substantives: credence, faith, trust, troth, confidence, credit, dependence on, reliance, assurance.

Opinion, notion, idea (453), conception, apprehension, impression, conceit, mind, view, persuasion, conviction, convincement, sentiment, voice, conclusion, judgment (480), estimation, self-conviction.

System of opinions, creed, credo, religion (983, 987), doctrine, tenet, dogma, principle, school, ideology, articles of belief, way of thinking, popular belief, *vox populi,* public opinion, *esprit de corps,* partisanship; ism, doxy.

Change of opinion (607), proselytism, propagandism (537).

A convert, pervert, vert, proselyte.
Verbs: To believe, credit, receive, give faith to, give credit to, rely upon, make no doubt, reckon, doubt not, confide in, count upon, depend upon, build upon, calculate upon, take upon trust, swallow, gulp down, take one's word for, take upon credit, swear by.

To be of opinion, to opine, presume; to have, hold, possess, entertain, adopt, imbibe, embrace, foster, nurture, cherish, etc., a notion, idea, opinion, etc.; to think, look upon, view, consider, take, take it, hold, trow, ween, conceive, fancy, apprehend, regard, esteem, deem, account; meseems, methinks.

To cause to be believed, thought, or esteemed; to satisfy, persuade, assure, convince, convert, bring over, win over, indoctrinate, proselytize (537), evangelize; to vert.

Phrases: To pin one's faith to; to take at one's word.

To take it into one's head; to run away with the notion; to come round to an opinion.

To cram down the throat; to bring home to; to find credence; to carry conviction; pass current; pass muster; to hold water; to go down.

Adjectives: Believing, etc., impressed with, imbued with, wedded to, unsuspecting, unsuspicious, void of suspicion, etc., credulous (486), convinced, positive, sure, assured, cocksure, certain, confident.

Believed, etc., credited, accredited, unsuspected, received, current, popular.

Worthy of deserving of belief, commanding belief, believable, persuasive, impressive, reliable, dependable, trustworthy (939), credible, probable (572), fiducial, fiduciary; relating to belief, doctrinal.

Adverbs: In the opinion of, in the eyes of, on the strength of, to the best of one's belief, *me judice.*

485 UNBELIEF

Substantives: disbelief, misbelief, discredit, agnosticism, atheism (988), heresy (984), dissent (489).

Doubt, dubitation, scepticism, *diaporesis,* misgiving, demur, cliffhanging, suspense; shade or shadow of doubt, distrust, mistrust, misdoubt, suspicion, shyness, embarrassment, hesitation, uncertainty (475), scruple, qualm, dilemma; casuistry, paradox; schism (489), incredulity (487).

Unbeliever, sceptic (487); Doubting Thomas.

Verbs: To disbelieve, discredit, not to believe; refuse to admit or believe; misbelieve, controvert; put or set aside; join issue, dispute, etc.

To doubt, be doubtful, etc., diffide, distrust, mistrust, suspect, scent, jalouse; have, harbour, entertain, etc., doubts; demur, stick at, pause, hesitate, scruple, question, query, call in question, look askance (or askant).

To cause, raise, suggest, or start a doubt; to pose, stagger, floor, startle, embarrass, puzzle (704); shake or stagger one's faith or belief.

Phrases: Not to know what to make of; to smell a rat; to hang in doubt; to have one's doubts; to float in a sea of doubts.

Adjectives: Unbelieving, doubting, etc., incredulous, scrupulous, suspicious, sceptical, shy of belief, at sea, at a loss (487).

Unworthy or undeserving of belief, hard to believe, doubtful (475), dubious, unreliable, fishy, questionable, suspect, staggering, puzzling, etc., paradoxical, incredible, inconceivable.

Phrases: With a grain of salt; *cum grano salis; timeo Danaos et dona ferentes;* all is not gold that glitters; the cowl does not make the monk.

486 CREDULITY

Substantives: credulousness, gullibility, infatuation, self-delusion, self-deception, superstition, gross credulity, bigotry, dogmatism.

A credulous person, gull, gobemouche; dupe (547).

Verbs: To be credulous, etc., to follow implicitly, swallow, take on trust, take for gospel.

To impose upon, practise upon, palm off upon, cajole, etc., deceive (545).

Phrases: *Credo quia absurdum;* the wish being father to the thought.

Adjectives: Credulous, gullible, confiding, trusting; easily deceived, cajoled, etc.; green, verdant, superstitious, simple, unsuspicious, etc. (484), soft, childish, silly, stupid, overcredulous, over-confident.

487 INCREDULITY

Substantives: incredulousness, scepticism, pyrrhonism, nihilism, suspicion (485), suspiciousness, scrupulousness, scrupulosity.

An unbeliever, sceptic, misbeliever, pyrrhonist; nihilist.

Verbs: To be incredulous, etc., to distrust (485).

Adjectives: Incredulous, hard of belief, sceptical, unbelieving, inconvincible, shy of belief, doubting, distrustful, suspicious (485).

Phrases: Oh yeah? says you! a likely story! rats! that be hanged for a tale; tell that to the marines; it won't wash; that cock won't fight; *credat Judaeus Apella.*

488 ASSENT

Substantives: acquiescence, admission, assentation, nod, consent, concession, accord, accordance, agreement (23), concord (714), concordance, concurrence, ratification, confirmation, corroboration, approval, recognition, acknowledgment, acceptance, granting, avowal, confession.

Unanimity, chorus; affirmation (535), common consent, acclamation, consensus.

Yes-man, sycophant, echo.

Verbs: To assent, acquiesce, agree, yield assent, accord, concur, consent, nod assent, accept, coincide, go with, go along with, be at one with, chime in with, strike in with, close with, vote for, conform with, defer to; say yes, ay, ditto, amen, etc.

To acknowledge, own, avow, confess, concede, subscribe to, abide by, admit, allow, recognize, grant, endorse, ratify, countersign, OK, okay, approve, carry.

Phrases: To go or be solid for; to come to an understanding; to come to terms; one could not agree more.

Adjectives: Assenting, etc., acquiescent, content, consentient, willing; approved, agreed, carried; uncon-

tradicted, unchallenged, unquestioned, uncontroverted; unanimous.

Phrase: Of one mind.

Adverbs: Affirmatively, in the affirmative (535).

Yes, yea, yeah, yep, ay, aye, uh-huh, sure, very well, even so, just so, quite so, to be sure, all right, right oh! right you are, you said it, definitely, absolutely, exactly, precisely, truly, certainly, assuredly, no doubt, doubtless, verily, very true (494), *ex concesso.*

Be it so, so be it, by all means, granted, OK, okay, oke, okeydoke, by all manner of means, *à la bonne heure,* amen, willingly, etc. (602).

With one voice, with one accord, *una voce,* unanimously, in chorus, as one man, to a man, *nem. con.* or *nemine contradicente, nemine dissentiente, en bloc,* without a dissentient voice, one and all, on all hands.

489 DISSENT

Substantives: dissidence, discordance, denial (536), dissonance, disagreement; difference or diversity of opinion, recusancy, contradiction, nonconformity, schism (984), secession; protest.

A dissentient, dissenter, protestant, nonconformist, recusant, heretic; deviationist, nonjuror, schismatic seceder.

Verbs: To dissent, demur, deny, disagree, refuse assent, say no, differ, cavil, ignore, protest, contradict, secede, repudiate, refuse to admit.

Phrases: To shake the head; to shrug the shoulders; to join issue; to give the lie; to differ *toto caelo.*

Adjectives: Dissenting, etc., dissentient, dissident, discordant, protestant, nonconforming, recusant, nonjuring, non-content, schismatic, deviationist; unconvinced, unconverted, unavowed, unacknowledged.

Unwilling, reluctant, extorted, etc.

Adverbs: Negatively, in the negative (536), at variance with.

No, nay, nope, nit, na, not, not so, not at all, nohow, nowise, not in the least, not a bit, not a whit, not a jot, by no means, by no manner of means, not for the world, on no account, in no respect.

Phrases: Many men, many minds; *quot homines, tot sententiae; tant s'en faut*; the answer is in the negative; *il s'en faut bien.*

Interjections: No sir! God forbid! I'll be hanged first! I'll see you far enough! not bloody likely! not on your nelly! not if I know it! over my dead body! pardon me! I beg your pardon!

490 KNOWLEDGE

Substantives: cognizance, cognition, cognoscence, awareness, gnosis, acquaintance, experience, ken, privity, insight, familiarity, apprehension, comprehension, understanding, recognition; discovery (480), appreciation; knowability.

Intuition, clairvoyance, consciousness, conscience, perception, precognition, light, enlightenment, glimpse, inkling, glimmer, dawn, scent, suspicion; conception, notion, idea (453).

Self-consciousness, self-knowledge, apperception.

System or body of knowledge, science, philosophy, pansophy, pandect, doctrine, ideology, theory, aetiology, literature, *belles-lettres, literae humaniores,* the humanities, humanism; ology.

Erudition, learning, lore, scholarship, letters, book-learning, bookishness, bibliomania, bibliolatry, education, instruction, information, acquisitions, acquirements, accomplishments, attainments, proficiency, cultivation, culture; a liberal education, encyclopaedic knowledge, omniscience.

Elements, rudiments, abecedary (542), cyclopaedia, encyclopaedia, school, academy, etc.

Depth, extent, profoundness, profundity, stores, etc., solidity, accuracy, etc., of knowledge.

Phrases: The march of intellect; the progress, advance, etc., of science; the schoolmaster being abroad.

Verbs: To know, be aware of, savvy, ken, wot, ween, trow, have, possess, perceive, conceive, apprehend, ideate, understand, comprehend, make out, recognize, be master of, know full well, possess the knowledge of, experience, discern, perceive, see, see through, have in one's head.

Phrases: To know what's what; to know how the wind blows; to know the ropes; to have at one's fingertips or finger-ends.

Adjectives: Knowing, aware of, etc., cognizant of, acquainted with, privy to, conscious of, no stranger to, *au fait, au courant,* versed in, hep, up in, up to, alive to, wise to, conversant with, proficient in, read in, familiar with.

Apprised of, made acquainted with, informed of; undeceived.

Erudite, instructed, learned, well-read, lettered, literate, educated, cultivated, cultured, knowledgeable, enlightened, well-informed, shrewd, bookish, scholarly, scholastic, deep-read; self-taught, well-grounded, well-conned.

Known, etc., well-known, recognized, received, notorious, noted, proverbial, familiar; hackneyed, trite, commonplace; cognoscible, knowable; experiential.

Phrases: Behind the scenes; in the know; at home in; the scales fallen from one's eyes.

Adverbs: To one's knowledge, to the best of one's knowledge.

Phrase: *Experto crede.*

491 IGNORANCE

Substantives: nescience, nescientness, unacquaintance, unconsciousness, darkness, blindness, incomprehension, incognizance, inexperience, emptiness.

Imperfect knowledge, smattering, sciolism, glimmering; bewilderment, perplexity (475); incapacity.

Affectation of knowledge, pedantry, charlatanry, quackery, dilettantism.

Phrases: Crass ignorance; monumental ignorance.

A sealed book; unexplored ground; an unknown quantity; *terra incognita*.

Verbs: To be ignorant, etc., not to know, to know nothing of, not to be aware of, to be at a loss, to be out of it, to be at fault, to ignore, to be blind to, etc., not to understand, etc.

Phrases: To be caught tripping; not to know what to make of; to have no idea or notion; not to be able to make head or tail of; not to know a hawk from a handsaw; to lose one's bearings.

Adjectives: Ignorant, unknowing, unconscious, unaware, unwitting, witless, a stranger to, unacquainted, unconversant, unenlightened, unilluminated, incognizant, unversed, uncultivated, clueless.

Uninformed, uninstructed, untaught, unapprised, untutored, unschooled, unguided.

Shallow, superficial, green, verdant, rude, half-learned, illiterate, unread, uneducated, unlearned, uncultured, Philistine, unlettered, empty-headed, having a smattering, etc., pedantic.

Confused, puzzled, bewildered, bemused, muddled, bemuddled, lost, benighted, belated, at sea, at fault, posed, blinded, abroad, distracted, in a maze, misinformed, hoodwinked, in the dark, at a loss, *désorienté*.

Unknown, novel, unapprehended, unexplained, unascertained, uninvestigated, unexplored, untravelled, uncharted, chartless, unheard-of, unperceived, unknowable.

Phrases: Having a film over the eyes; wide of the mark; at cross purposes.

Adverbs: Ignorantly, unwittingly, unawares; for anything one knows; for aught one knows.

Phrase: 'A little learning is a dangerous thing.'

492 SCHOLAR

Substantives: student (541), savant, scientist, humanist, grammarian, intellectual, pundit, schoolman, don, professor, lecturer, reader, demonstrator, graduate, doctor, master of arts, licentiate, wrangler, gownsman, philosopher, philomath, clerk, encyclopaedist.

Linguist; *littérateur, literati, illuminati,* intelligentsia.

Pedant, pedagogue, bookworm, *helluo librorum,* bibliomaniac, bibliophile, blue-stocking, *bas-bleu,* high-brow, bigwig, bookman; swot, grind.

Phrases: Man of letters; man of learning; at the feet of Gamaliel; a walking dictionary.

Adjectives: Erudite, learned, scholarly (490).

493 IGNORAMOUS

Substantives: sciolist, smatterer, novice, greenhorn, half-scholar, schoolboy, booby, dunce (501); bigot (481); quack, mountebank, charlatan, dilettante, low-brow, amateur, Philistine, obscurant, obscurantist.

Phrase: The wooden spoon.

Adjectives: Bookless, shallow (499), ignorant, etc. (491), prejudiced (481), obscurantist.

494 TRUTH

Substantives: verity, actual, existence (1), reality, fact, matter of fact, actuality, nature, principle, orthodoxy, gospel, holy writ, substantiality, genuineness, authenticity, realism.

Accuracy, exactness, exactitude, precision, preciseness, nicety, delicacy, fineness, strictness, rigour, punctuality.

Phrases: The plain truth; the honest truth; the naked truth; the sober truth; the very thing; a stubborn fact; not a dream, fancy, illusion, etc.; the exact truth; 'the truth, the whole truth, and nothing but the truth'; 'a round unvarnished tale'; *ipsissima verba*; the real Simon Pure.

Verbs: To be true, real, etc., to hold good, to be the case.

To render true, legitimatize, legitimize, substantiate, realize, actualize, to make good, establish.

To get at the truth (480).

Phrases: *Vitam impendere vero; magna est veritas et praevalebit.*

Adjectives: True, real, veritable, veracious, actual, certain, positive, absolute, existing (1), substantial, categorical, realistic, factual; unrefuted, unconfuted, unideal, unimagined.

Exact, accurate, definite, precise, well-defined, just, correct, right, strict, hard-and-fast, literal, rigid, rigorous, scrupulous, conscientious, religious, punctilious, nice, mathematical, axiomatic, demonstrable, scientific, unerring, constant, faithful, *bona fide,* curious, delicate, meticulous.

Genuine, authentic, legitimate, pukka, orthodox, official, *ex officio,* pure, sound, sterling, hall-marked, unsophisticated, unadulterated, unvarnished; solid, substantial, undistorted, undisguised, unaffected, unflattering, unexaggerated, unromantic.

Phrases: Just the thing; neither more nor less; to a hair.

Adverbs: Truly, verily, veritable, troth, certainly, certes, assuredly, in truth, in good truth, of a truth, really, indubitably, in sooth, forsooth, in reality, in fact, in point of fact, as a matter of fact, strictly speaking, *de facto,* indeed, in effect, actually, *ipso facto,* definitely, literally, positively, virtually, at bottom, *au fond.*

Precisely, accurately, *ad amussim,* etc., mathematically, to a nicety, to a hair, to a T, to an inch; to the letter, *au pied de la lettre.*

In every respect, in all respects, *sous tous les rapports,* at any rate, at all events, by all means.

Phrases: Joking apart; in good earnest; in sober earnest; sooth to say.

495 ERROR

Substantives: mistake, miss, fallacy, misconception, misapprehension, misunderstanding, inaccuracy, incorrectness, inexactness, misconstruction (523), miscomputation, miscalculation (481).

Fault, blunder, *faux pas,* bull, Irish bull, Irishism, bloomer, howler, floater, clanger, boner, lapse, slip of the tongue, *lapsus linguae,* Spoonerism, slip of the pen, malapropism, equivoque, cross purposes, oversight, flaw, misprint, erratum; heresy, misstatement, misreport, bad shot.

Illusion, delusion, self-deceit, self-deception, hallucination, monomania, aberration; fable, dream, shadow, fancy, bubble, false light (443), the mists of error, will-o'-the-wisp, jack-o'-lantern, ignis fatuus, chimera (515), *maya.*

Verbs: To be erroneous, false, etc., to cause error, to mislead, lead astray, lead into error, delude, give a false impression or idea, to falsify, misstate, misrelate, misinform, misrepresent (544), deceive (545), beguile.

To err, be in error, to mistake, to receive a false impression; to lie or labour under an error, mistake, etc., to blunder, be in the wrong, be at fault, to misapprehend, misconceive, misunderstand, misremember, misreckon, miscalculate, miscount, misestimate, misjudge, misthink, flounder, trip.

Phrases: To take the shadow for the substance; to go on a fool's errand; to have the wrong sow by the ear; to put one's foot in it; to pull a boner; to drop a brick.

Adjectives: Erroneous, untrue, false, fallacious, duff, unreal, unsubstantial, baseless, groundless, ungrounded,

195

unauthenticated, untrustworthy, heretical.

Inexact, incorrect, wrong, illogical, partial, one-sided. unreasonable, absonous, absonant, indefinite, unscientific, inaccurate, aberrant.

In error, mistaken, etc., tripping, floundering, etc.

Illusive, illusory, ideal, imaginary, fanciful, chimerical, visionary, shadowy, mock, futile.

Spurious, apocryphal, bogus, illegitimate, phoney, pseudo, bastard, meretricious, deceitful, sophisticated, adulterated.

Phrases: Wide of the mark; on the wrong scent; barking up the wrong tree; out of it; without a leg to stand upon.

496 MAXIM
Substantives: aphorism, apophthegm, dictum, saying, *mot*, adage, gnome, saw, proverb, wisecrack, sentence, precept, rule, formula, tag, code, motto, slogan, catchword, word, byword, moral, sentiment, phylactery, conclusion, reflection, thought, golden rule, axiom, theorem, scholium, lemma, truism.

Catechism, creed (484), profession of faith.
Adjectives: Aphoristic, gnomic, proverbial, phylacteric, axiomatic; hackneyed, trite.
Phrases: 'Wise saws and modern instances'; as the saying is or goes.

497 ABSURDITY
Substantives: absurdness, nonsense, folly, paradox, inconsistency, quibble, sophism (477), stultiloquy, stultiloquence, Irish bull, Irishism, Hibernicism, sciamachy, imbecility (499).

Jargon, gibberish, rigmarole, double-Dutch, fustian, rant, bombast, bathos, amphigouri, rhapsody, extravagance, rodomontade, romance; nonsense verse, limerick, clerihew.

Twaddle, claptrap, flapdoodle, bunkum, blah, fudge, rubbish, piffle, verbiage, trash, truism, stuff, balderdash, slipslop, *bavardage,* palaver, *baragouin,* moonshine, fiddlestick, wish-wash, platitude, cliché, flummery, inanity, fiddle-faddle, rot, tommy-rot, bosh, tosh, hot air, havers, blethers, tripe, bilge, bull, hooey, hokum, boloney.

Vagary, foolery, tomfoolery, mummery, monkey-trick, monkey-shine, dido, *boutade,* lark, escapade, ploy, rag.
Phrases: A cock-and-bull story; a mare's-nest; a wild-goose chase; talking through one's hat; 'a tale told by an idiot, full of sound and fury, signifying nothing'; clotted nonsense; arrant rot.
Adjectives: Absurd, nonsensical, foolish, senseless, preposterous (499), sophistical, inconsistent, extravagant, ridiculous, cock-and-bull, quibbling, trashy, washy, wishy-washy, twaddling, etc.; topsy-turvy, Gilbertian.

498 INTELLIGENCE
Substantives: capacity, nous, parts, talent, sagacity, sagaciousness, wit, mother-wit, *esprit,* gumption, comprehension, understanding, quick parts, grasp of intellect.

Acuteness, acumen, shrewdness, astuteness, arguteness, sharpness, aptness, aptitude, quickness, receptiveness, subtlety, archness, penetration, perspicacity, perspicaciousness, clearsightedness, discrimination, discernment, flair, refinement (850).

Head, brains, headpiece, a long head.

WISDOM
Substantives: sapience, sense, good sense, common sense, plain sense, horse-sense, reason, reasonableness, rationality, judgment, judiciousness, solidity, depth, profoundness, catholicity, breadth of view, enlarged views, reach or compass of thoughts.

Genius, inspiration, the fire of genius.

Wisdom in action, prudence, discretion, self-possession, aplomb (698), sobriety, tact, ballast.

Phrase: Discretion being the better part of valour.

Verbs: To be intelligent, wise, etc., to reason (476), to discern (441), discriminate (465), to penetrate, to see far into.

Phrases: To have all one's wits about one; to see as far through a brick wall as anybody.

Adjectives: Applied to persons: Intelligent, sagacious, receptive, quick, sharp, acute, fly, smart, shrewd, gumptious, canny, astute, sharp-sighted, quick-sighted, quick-eyed, keen, keen-eyed, keen-sighted, keen-witted, sharp-witted, quick-witted, needle-witted, penetrating, piercing, clear-sighted, perspicacious, discerning, discriminating, discriminative, clever (698), knowledgeable.

Wise, sage, sapient, sagacious, reasonable, rational, sound, common-sense, sane, sensible, judicious, judgmatic, enlightened, impartial, catholic, broad-minded, open-minded, unprejudiced, unbiased, unprepossessed, undazzled, unperplexed, judicial, impartial, fair, progressive.

Cool, cool-headed, long-headed, hard-headed, long-sighted, calculating, thoughtful, reflective, oracular, heaven-directed.

Prudent, discreet, sober, staid, deep, solid, considerate, provident, politic, diplomatic, tactful.

Applied to actions: Wise, sensible, reasonable, judicious, well-judged, well-advised, prudent, prudential, politic (646), expedient.

Phrases: Wise as a serpent; wise in one's generation; not born yesterday; up to snuff; no flies on him; wise as Solomon.

499 IMBECILITY
Substantives: incapacity, vacancy of mind, poverty of intellect, shallowness, dullness, stupidity, asininity, obtuseness, stolidity, hebetude, doltishness, muddleheadedness, vacuity, short-sightedness, incompetence.

Silliness, simplicity, childishness, puerility, babyhood; dotage, second childhood, anility, fatuity, idiocy, idiotism (503).

FOLLY
Substantives: unwisdom, absurdity, infatuation, irrationality, senselessness, foolishness, frivolity, inconsistency, lip-wisdom, conceit, vanity, irresponsibility, giddiness, extravagance, oddity, eccentricity (503), ridiculousness, desipience.

Act of folly (497), imprudence (699), rashness, fanaticism.

Phrases: A fool's paradise; apartments to let; one's wits going wool-gathering; the meanest capacity.

Verbs: To be imbecile, foolish, etc., to trifle, drivel, ramble, dote, *radoter,* blether, haver; to fool, to monkey, to footle.

Phrases: To play the fool; to play the giddy goat; to make an ass of oneself; to go on a fool's errand; to pursue a wild-goose chase; *battre la campagne;* Homer nods.

Adjectives: Applied to persons: Unintelligent, unintellectual, witless, reasonless, not bright, imbecile, shallow, *borné,* weak, soft, simple, sappy, spoony, weak-headed, weak-minded, feeble-minded, half-witted, short-witted, half-baked, not all there, deficient, wanting, shallow-pated, shallow-brained, dull, dumb, dense, crass, stupid, heavy, obtuse, stolid, doltish, asinine, addle-headed, dull-witted, blunt, dull-brained, dim-sighted, vacuous.

Childish, infantine, infantile, babyish, childlike, puerile, callow; anile.

Fatuous, idiotic, lack-brained, drivelling, blatant, brainless, blunt-witted, beef-witted, fat-witted, fat-headed, boneheaded, insulse, having

197

no head or brains, thick-skulled, ivory-skulled, blockish, Boeotian.

Foolish, silly, senseless, irrational, insensate, nonsensical, blunder-headed, chuckle-headed, puzzle-headed, muddle-headed, muddy-headed, undiscerning, unenlightened, unphilosophical; prejudiced, bigoted, purblind, narrow-minded, wrong-headed, tactless, crotchety, conceited, self-opinionated, pig-headed, mulish, unprogressive, one-ideaed, stick-in-the-mud, reactionary, blimpish, besotted, infatuated, unreasoning.

Wild, giddy, dizzy, thoughtless, eccentric, odd, extravagant, quixotic, light-headed, rantipole, high-flying, crack-brained, cracked, cranky, hare-brained, scatter-brained, scatter-pated, unballasted, ridiculous, frivolous, balmy (or barmy), daft (503).

Applied to actions: Foolish, unwise, injudicious, improper, imprudent, unreasonable, nonsensical, absurd, ridiculous, silly, stupid, asinine, ill-imagined, ill-advised, ill-judged, ill-devised, tactless, inconsistent, irrational, unphilosophical, extravagant, preposterous, egregious, footling, imprudent, indiscreet, improvident, impolitic, improper (645, 647).

Phrases: Dead from the neck up; concrete above the ears.

Without rhyme or reason; penny-wise and pound-foolish.

500 SAGE
Substantives: wise man, master-mind, thinker, *savant*, expert, luminary, adept, authority, egghead.

Oracle, a shining light, *esprit fort,* intellectual, high-brow, pundit, academist, academician, philomath, schoolman, magi, a Solomon, Nestor, Solon, Socrates, a second Daniel.
Adjectives: Venerable, reverend, authoritative.
Phrases: 'A Daniel come to judgment'; the wise men of the East.

Ironically: Wiseacre, bigwig, know-all.

501 FOOL
Substantives: blockhead, bonehead, idiot, tom-fool, low-brow, simpleton, simp, sap, softy, sawney, witling, ass, donkey, goat, goose, ninny, dolt, booby, boob, noodle, muff, mug, muggins, juggins, owl, cuckoo, gowk, numskull, noddy, dumb-bell, gomeril, half-wit, imbecile, ninnyhammer, mutt, driveller, cretin, moron, natural, lackbrain, child, infant, baby, innocent, green-horn, zany, zombie, gaby.

Dunce, lout, loon, oaf, dullard, duffer, calf, colt, buzzard, block, stick, stock, clod-poll, clot-poll, clod-hopper, clod, lubber, bull-calf, bull-head, fat-head, thick-skull, dunder-head, addle-head, dizzard, hoddy-doddy, looby, Joe Soap, nincompoop, poop, put, *un sot à triple étage,* logger-head, sot, shallow-brain, jobbernowl, changeling, dotard, driveller, moon-calf, giddy-head, gobemouche, ranti-pole, muddler, stick-in-the-mud, old woman, April fool.
Phrases: One who is not likely to set the Thames on fire; one who did not invent gunpowder; one who is no conjurer; *qui n'a pas inventé la poudre*; who could not say 'Bo' to a goose; one with his upper storey to let; no fool like an old fool.

Men of Gotham; men of Boeotia.

502 SANITY
Substantives: rationality; being in one's senses, in one's right mind, in one's sober senses; sobriety, lucidity, lucid interval, sound mind, *mens sana.*
Verbs: To be sane, etc., to retain one's senses, reason, etc.

To become sane, come to one's senses, sober down.

To render sane, bring to one's senses, to sober.
Adjectives: Sane, rational, reasonable,

compos, in one's sober senses, in one's right mind, sober-minded.
Phrase: In full possession of one's faculties.
Adverbs: Sanely, soberly, etc.

503   INSANITY
Substantives: lunacy, madness, unsoundness, derangement, psychosis, neurosis, alienation, aberration, schizophrenia, split personality, dementia, paranoia, mania, melancholia, hypochondria, calenture, frenzy, phrenitis, raving, monomania, megalomania, kleptomania, dipsomania, etc., disordered intellect, incoherence, wandering, delirium, hallucination, lycanthropy, eccentricity (499), dementation; Bedlam.
Phrases: The horrors; the jim-jams; pink spiders; snakes in the boots.
Verbs: To be or become insane, etc., to lose one's senses, wits, reason, faculties, etc., to run mad, run amuck, go off one's head, rave, dote, ramble, wander, drivel.

To render or drive mad; to madden, dementate, turn the brain, addle the wits, turn one's head, befool, infatuate, craze.
Phrases: *Battre la campagne; avoir le diable au corps.*
Adjectives: Insane, mad, lunatic, crazy, crazed, *non compos*, cracked, cranky, loco, touched, deficient, wanting, out of one's mind, off one's head or nut or onion, bereft of reason, unsettled in one's mind, unhinged, insensate, reasonless, beside oneself.

Demented, daft, dotty, potty, dippy, scatty, loopy, batty, bats, wacky, crackers, cuckoo, haywire, bughouse, bugs, nuts, possessed, maddened, moon-struck, mad-brained, maniac, maniacal, delirious, incoherent, rambling, doting, doited, gaga.

Wandering, frantic, phrenetic, paranoiac, schizophrenic, megalomaniacal, kleptomaniacal, etc., raving, corybantic, dithyrambic, rabid, pixillated, light-headed, giddy, vertiginous, wild, haggard, flighty, neurotic, distracted, distraught, hag-ridden, *écervelé, tête montée.*
Phrases: The head being turned; having a screw (or a tile) loose; far gone; stark staring mad; mad as a March hare; mad as a hatter; of unsound mind; up the pole; bats in the belfry; the devil being in one; dizzy as a goose; candidate for Bedlam; like one possessed.

The wits going wool-gathering or bird's-nesting.

504   MADMAN
Substantives: lunatic, maniac, bedlamite, energumen, raver, monomaniac, paranoiac, schizophrenic, nut, screwball, crack pot, madcap, megalomaniac, dipsomaniac, kleptomaniac, psychopath, hypochondriac, *malade imaginaire,* crank, maenad.

Section 6 –
Extension of Thought

505   MEMORY
Substantives: remembrance, reminiscence, recognition, anamnesis, retention, retentiveness, readiness, tenacity.

Recurrence, recollection, retrospection, retrospect, flash-back, afterthought, hindsight.

Token of remembrance, reminder, memorial, memento, souvenir, keepsake, relic, reliquary, memorandum, aide-mémoire, remembrancer, prompter.

Things to be remembered, *memorabilia.*

Art of memory, artificial memory, *memoria technica,* mnemonics; Mnemosyne.
Phrases: The tablets of the memory; *l'esprit de l'escalier.*

Verbs: To remember, retain, mind, bear or keep in mind, have or carry in the memory, know by heart or by rote; recognize.

To be deeply impressed, live, remain, or dwell in the memory; to be stored up, bottled up, to sink in the mind, to rankle, etc.

To recollect, call to mind, bethink oneself, recall, call up, retrace, carry one's thoughts back, review, look back, rake up, brush up, think upon, call to remembrance, tax the memory.

To suggest, prompt, hint, recall to mind, put in mind, remind, whisper, call up, summon up, renew, commend to.

To say by heart, repeat by rote, say one's lesson, repeat as a parrot.

To commit to memory, get or learn by heart or rote, memorize, con, con over, repeat; to fix, imprint, impress, stamp, grave, engrave, store, treasure up, bottle up, embalm, enshrine, etc., in the memory; to load, store, stuff, or burden the memory with; to commemorate (883).

Phrase: To have at one's fingers' ends.

To jog or refresh the memory; to pull by the sleeve; to bring back to the memory; to keep the memory alive; to keep the wound green; to reopen old sores; to put in remembrance.

Adjectives: Remembering, etc., mindful, remembered, etc., fresh, green, unforgotten, present to the mind; living in, being in, or within one's memory; indelible, ineffaceable, green in remembrance, reminiscential, commemorative.

Adverbs: By heart, by rote, *memoriter*, without book; in memory of, in memoriam.

506 OBLIVION

Substantives: forgetfulness, amnesia, obliteration (552), a short memory; a lapse of memory; the memory failing, being in fault, or deserting one; the waters of Lethe, Nepenthe, *tabula rasa*.

Verbs: To forget, lose, unlearn, efface, expunge, blot out, etc. (552); discharge from the memory.

To slip, escape, fade, die away from the memory, to sink into oblivion.

Phrases: To cast behind one's back; to have a short memory; to put out of one's head; to apply the sponge; to think no more of; to consign to oblivion; to let bygones be bygones.

Adjectives: Forgotten, etc., lost, effaced, blotted out, obliterated, discharged, sponged out, buried or sunk in oblivion, out of mind, clean out of one's head or recollection, past recollection, unremembered.

Forgetful, oblivious, unmindful, mindless; Lethean.

507 EXPECTATION

Substantives: expectance, expectancy, anticipation, forestalling, foreseeing (510); reckoning, calculation.

Contemplation, prospect, look-out, outlook (121), perspective, horizon, vista, hope, trust (858), abeyance, waiting, suspense.

Phrase: The torments of Tantalus.

Verbs: To expect, look for, look out for, look forward to, anticipate, contemplate, flatter oneself, to dare to say, foresee (510), forestall, reckon upon, count upon, lay one's account to, to calculate upon, rely upon, build upon, make sure of, prepare oneself for, keep in view, not to wonder at.

To wait, tarry, lie in wait, watch for, abide, to bide one's time.

To hold out, raise, or excite expectation, to bid fair, to promise, to augur, etc. (511).

Phrases: To count one's chickens before they are hatched.

To have in store for; to have a rod in pickle.

Adjectives: Expectant, expecting, etc., prepared for, gaping for, ready for, agog, anxious, ardent, eager, breathless, sanguine.

Expected, anticipated, foreseen, etc., long expected, impending, prospective, in prospect.

Adverbs: With breathless expectation, on tenterhooks.

Phrases: On the tiptoe of expectation; on edge; looming in the distance; the wish father to the thought; we shall see; *nous verrons.*

508 INEXPECTATION

Substantives: non-expectation; blow, shock, surprise (870).

False or vain expectation, miscalculation.

Phrase: A bolt from the blue.

Verbs: Not to expect, not to look for, etc., to be taken by surprise, to start, come upon, to fall upon, not to bargain for, to miscalculate.

To be unexpected, etc., to crop up, pop up, to come unawares, suddenly, abruptly, like a thunderbolt, creep upon, burst upon, bounce upon; surprise, take aback, stun, stagger, startle.

Phrases: To reckon without one's host; to trust to a broken reed.

To drop from the clouds; you could have knocked me down with a feather.

Adjectives: Non-expectant, surprised, taken by surprise, unwarned, unaware, startled, etc., taken aback.

Unexpected, abrupt, unanticipated, unlooked-for, unhoped-for, unforeseen, beyond expectation, sudden, contrary to or against expectation, unannounced, unheralded; back-handed.

Adverbs: Suddenly, abruptly, unexpectedly, plump, pop, *à l'improviste,* unawares, without notice or warning (113).

Phrases: Like a thief in the night; who would have thought it?

509 DISAPPOINTMENT

Substantives: vain expectation, bligh-

ted hope, surprise, astonishment (870); balk, after-clap, miscalculation.

Phrase: 'There's many a slip 'twixt cup and lip.'

Verbs: To be disappointed, etc., to miscalculate; to look blank, to look blue, to look or stand aghast.

To disappoint, balk, bilk, tantalize, let down, play false, stand up, dumbfound, dash one's hope (859), sell.

Adjectives: Disappointed, disconcerted, aghast, blue, out of one's reckoning.

Happening, contrary to or against expectation.

Phrase: Parturiunt montes, nascetur ridiculus mus.

510 FORESIGHT

Substantives: prospiscience, prescience, foreknowledge, forethought, forecast, prevision, prognosis, precognition, second sight, clairvoyance.

Anticipation, foretaste, prenotion, presentiment, foregone conclusion, providence, discretion, prudence, sagacity.

Announcement, prospectus, programme, policy (626).

Verbs: To foresee, foreknow, forejudge, forecast, predict (511), anticipate, look forwards or beyond; look, peep, or pry into the future.

Phrases: To keep a sharp look out for; to have an eye to the future; *respice finem.*

Adjectives: Foreseeing, etc., prescient, weather-wise, far-sighted, far-seeing; provident, prudent, rational, sagacious, perspicacious.

511 PREDICTION

Substantives: announcement, prognosis, forecast, weird, prophecy, vaticination, mantology, prognostication, astrology, horoscopy, haruspicy, auguration, auspices, bodement, omination, augury, foreboding, abodement, aboding, horoscope, nativity, genethliacs, fortune-telling, crystal-gazing, palmistry, chiromancy, oneiromancy, sortilege, *sortes Virgilianae,* soothsaying, ominousness, divination (992).

Place of prediction, adytum, tripod.

Verbs: To predict, prognosticate, prophesy, vaticinate, presage, augur, bode, forebode, divine, foretell, croak, soothsay, auspicate, to cast a horoscope or nativity, tell one's fortune, read one's hand.

To foretoken, betoken, prefigure, portend, foreshadow, foreshow, usher in, herald, signify, premise, announce, point to, admonish, warn, forewarn, advise.

Adjectives: Predicting, etc., predictive, prophetic, fatidical, vaticinal, oracular, Sibylline.

Ominous, portentous, augural, auspicious, monitory, premonitory, significant of, pregnant with, weather-wise, bodeful, big with fate.

Phrase: 'Coming events cast their shadows before.'

512 OMEN

Substantives: portent, presage, prognostic, augury, auspice, sign, forerunner, precursor (64), harbinger, herald, monition, warning, avant-courier, pilot-balloon, handwriting on the wall, rise and fall of the barometer, a bird of ill omen, a sign of the times, gathering clouds.

Phrases: Touch wood! *absit omen.*

513 ORACLE

Substantives: prophet, seer, soothsayer, haruspex, fortune-teller, spaewife, palmist, gipsy, wizard, witch, geomancer, Sibyl, Python, Pythoness, *Pythia,* Pythian oracle, Delphic oracle, Old Moore, Zadkiel, Mother Shipton, Witch of Endor, Sphinx, Tiresias, Cassandra, Oedipus, Sibylline leaves.

Section 7 –
Creative Thought

514 SUPPOSITION

Substantives: conjecture, surmise, presurmise, speculation, inkling, guess, guess-work, shot, divination, conceit; assumption, postulation, hypothesis, presupposition, postulate, *postulatum,* presumption, theory, thesis; suggestion, proposition, motion, proposal, allusion, insinuation, innuendo.

Phrases: A rough guess; a lucky shot.

Verbs: To suppose, conjecture, surmise, guess, divine, theorize, give a guess, make a shot, hazard a conjecture, throw out a conjecture, etc., presuppose, fancy, wis, take it, dare to say, take it into one's head, assume, believe, postulate, posit, presume, presurmise.

To suggest, hint, insinuate, put forth, propound, propose, start, allude to, prompt, put a case, move, make a motion.

To suggest, hint, insinuate, put forth, propound, propose, start, allude to, prompt, put a case, move, make a motion.

To suggest, itself, occur to one, come into one's head; to run in the head; to haunt (505).

Phrases: To put it into one's head; 'thereby hangs a tale.'

Adjectives: Supposing, etc., supposed, supposititious, suppositious, suppositive, reputed, putative, suggestive, allusive, conjectural, presumptive, hypothetical, theoretical, warranted, authorized, mooted, conjecturable, supposable.

Adverbs: If, if so be, an, gin, maybe, perhaps, on the supposition, in the event of, as if, *ex hypothesi, quasi.*

515 IMAGINATION

Substantives: fancy, conception, ideality, idealism, inspiration, afflatus, verve, dreaming, somnambulism, frenzy, ecstasy, excogitation, reverie, *Schwärmerei,* trance, imagery, vision; Pegasus.

Invention, inventiveness, originality, fertility, romanticism, utopianism, castle-building.

Conceit, maggot, figment, coinage, fiction, romance, novel (594), myth, Arabian Nights, fairyland, faerie, the man in the moon, dream, day-dream, pipe-dream, nightmare, vapour, chimera, phantom, phantasy, fantasia, whim, whimsy, vagary, rhapsody, extravaganza, air-drawn dagger, bugbear, men in buckram, castle in the air, air-built castle, castle in Spain, will-o'-the-wisp, *ignis fatuus,* jack-o'-lantern, Utopia, Atlantis, Shangri-la, land of Prester John, millennium, golden age, *fata morgana* (443).

A visionary, romancer, rhapsodist, high-flyer, enthusiast, idealist, energumen, dreamer, seer, fanatic, knight-errant, Don Quixote.

Phrases: Flight of fancy; fumes of fancy; fine frenzy; thick-coming fancies; coinage of the brain; the mind's eye; a stretch of imagination; 'such stuff as dreams are made on.'

Verbs: To imagine, fancy, conceive, ideate, idealize, realize, objectify; fancy or picture to oneself; create, originate, devise, invent, coin, fabricate, make up, mint, improvise, excogitate, conjure up.

Phrases: To take into one's head; to figure to oneself; to strain or crack one's invention; to strike out something new; to give a loose to the fancy; to give the reins to the imagination; to set one's wits to work; to rack or cudgel one's brains.

Adjectives: Imagining, imagined, etc.; ideal, unreal, unsubstantial, imaginary, *in nubibus,* fabulous, fictitious, legendary, mythological, chimerical, *ben trovato,* fanciful, faerie,

fairylike, air-drawn, air-built, original, fantastic, fantastical, whimsical, high-flown.

Imaginative, inventive, creative, fertile, romantic, flighty, extravagant, high-flown, fanatic, enthusiastic, Utopian, Quixotic.

II

Section 1 –
Nature of Ideas
Communicated

516 MEANING

Substantives: signification, sense, import, purport, significance, drift, gist, acceptation, acceptance, bearing, interpretation (522), reading, tenor, allusion, spirit, colouring, expression.

Literal meaning, literality, obvious meaning, grammatical sense, first blush, *prima facie* meaning; after-acceptation.

Equivalent meaning, synonym, synonymity.

Thing signified: Matter, subject, substance, pith, marrow, argument, text; sum and substance.

Verbs: To mean, signify, express, import, purport, convey, breathe, imply, bespeak, speak of, tell of, touch on, bear a sense, involve, declare (527), insinuate, allude to, point to, indicate, drive at; to come to the point, give vent to; to stand for.

To take, understand, receive, or accept in a particular sense.

Adjectives: Meaning, etc., significant, significative, significatory, literal, expressive, explicit, suggestive, allusive; pithy, pointed, epigrammatic, telling, striking, full of meaning, pregnant with meaning.

517 UNMEANINGNESS
Substantives: empty sound, a dead

letter, scrabble, scribble; inexpressiveness, vagueness (519).

Nonsense, stuff, balderdash (497), jabber, gibberish, palaver, rigmarole, twaddle, tosh, bosh, bull, rubbish, rot, empty babble, empty sound, verbiage, *nugae*, truism, moonshine, inanity.

Verbs: To mean nothing, to be unmeaning, etc.; to scribble, jabber, gibber, babble.

Adjectives: Unmeaning, meaningless, nonsensical, void of meaning, of sense, etc., senseless, not significant, undefined, tacit, not expressed.

Inexpressible, indefinable, undefinable, unmeant, unconceived.

Trashy, trumpery, twaddling, etc.

Phrases: *Vox et praeterea nihil*; 'a tale told by an idiot, full of sound and fury, signifying nothing'; 'sounding brass and tinkling cymbal.'

Adverb: Tacitly.

518 INTELLIGIBILITY

Substantives: clearness, lucidity, perspicuity, explicitness, distinctness, plain speaking, expressiveness, legibility, visibility (446); precision (494).

Intelligence, comprehension, understanding, learning (539).

Phrases: A word to the wise; *verbum sapienti*.

Verbs: To be intelligible, etc.

To render intelligible, etc., to simplify, clear up, throw light upon.

To understand, comprehend, follow, take, take in, catch, catch on to, twig, dig, get the hang of, get wise to, grasp, sense, make out, get, collect; master, tumble to, rumble.

Phrases: It tells its own tale; he who runs may read; to stand to reason; to speak for itself.

To come to an understanding; to see with half an eye.

Adjectives: Intelligible, clear, lucid, understandable, explicit, expressive, significant, express, distinct, precise, definite, well-defined, perspicuous,

transpicuous, striking, plain, obvious, manifest, palpable, glaring, transparent, above-board, unambiguous, ummistakable, legible, open, positive, expressive (516), unconfused, unequivocal, pronounced, graphic, readable.

Phrases: Clear as day; clear as crystal; clear as noonday; not to be mistaken; plain to the meanest capacity; plain as a pikestaff; in plain English.

519 UNINTELLIGIBILITY

Substantives: incomprehensibility, inconceivability, darkness (421), imperspicuity, obscurity, confusion, perplexity, imbroglio, indistinctness, mistiness, indefiniteness, vagueness, ambiguity, looseness, uncertainty, mysteriousness (526), paradox, inexplicability, incommunicability, spinosity.

Jargon, gibberish, rigmarole, rodomontade, etc. (497); paradox, riddle, enigma, puzzle (533).

Double or High Dutch, Greek, Hebrew, etc.

Verbs: To be unintelligible, etc., to pass comprehension.

To render unintelligible, etc., to perplex, confuse, confound, bewilder, darken, moither (475).

Not to understand, etc., to lose, miss, etc., to lose the clue.

Phrases: Not to know what to make of; not to be able to make either head or tail of; to be all at sea; to play at cross purposes; to beat about the bush.

Adjectives: Unintelligible, incognizable, inapprehensible, incomprehensible, inconceivable, unimaginable, unknowable, inexpressible, undefinable, incommunicable, above or past or beyond comprehension, inexplicable, illegible, undecipherable, inscrutable, unfathomable, beyond one's depth, paradoxical, insoluble, impenetrable.

Obscure, dark, confused, indistinct,

indefinite, misty, nebulous, intricate, undefined, ill-defined, indeterminate, perplexed, loose, vague, ambiguous, disconnected, incoherent, unaccountable, puzzling, enigmatical, hieroglyphic, mysterious, mystic, mystical, at cross purposes.

Hidden, recondite, abstruse, crabbed, transcendental, far-fetched, *in nubibus,* searchless, unconceived, unimagined.

Phrases: Greek to one; without rhyme or reason; *obscurum per obscurius; lucus a non lucendo.*

520 EQUIVOCALNESS

Substantives: double meaning, quibble, equivoque, equivocation, *doubleentendre,* paragram, anagram, amphibology, amphiboly, ambiloquy, prevarication, white lie, mental reservation, tergiversation, slip of the tongue,
lapsus linguae, a pun, play on words, homonym.

Having a doubtful meaning, ambiguity (475), homonymy.

Having a false meaning (544), *suggestio falsi.*

Verbs: To be equivocal, etc., to have two senses, etc., to equivocate, prevaricate, tergiversate, palter to the understanding, to pun.

Adjectives: Equivocal, ambiguous, amphibolous, amphibological, homonymous, double-tongued, double-edged, left-handed, equivocatory, paltering.

Adverb: Over the left.

521 METAPHOR

Substantives: figure, metonymy, trope, catachresis, synecdoche, figure of speech, figurativeness, image, imagery, metalepsis, type (22), symbol, symbolism (550), troplogy.

Personification, prosopopaeia, allegory, apologue, parable.

Implication, inference, allusion, application, adumbration, hidden meaning.

Allegorist, tropist, symbolist.

Verbs: To employ metaphore, etc., to personify, allegorize, adumbrate, shadow forth, imply, understand, apply, allude to.

Adjectives: Metaphorical, figurative, catachrestical, typical, tropical, parabolic, allegorical, allusive, symbolic (550), symbolistic, implied, inferential, implicit, understood.

Adverbs: So to speak, as it were.

Phrases: Where more is meant than meets the ear; in a manner of speaking; *façon de parler*; in a Pickwickian sense.

522 INTERPRETATION

Substantives: exegesis, explanation, meaning (516), explication, expounding, exposition, rendition, reddition.

Translation, version, rendering, construction, reading, spelling, restoration, metaphrase, literal translation, free translation, paraphrase.

Comment, commentary, inference, illustration, exemplification, definition, *éclaircissement,* elucidation, crib, cab, gloss, glossary, annotation, *scholium,* marginalia, note, clue, key, sidelight, master-key (631), rationale, denouement, solution, answer (462), object lesson.

Palaeography, dictionary, glossology, etc. (562), semantics, semasiology, oneirocritics, oneirocriticism, hermeneutics.

Verbs: To interpret, expound, explain, clear up, construe, translate, render, English, do into, turn into, transfuse the sense of.

To read, spell, make out, decipher, decode, unfold, disentangle, elicit the meaning of, make sense of, find the key of, unriddle, unravel, solve, resolve (480), restore.

To elucidate, throw light upon, illustrate, exemplify, expound, annotate,

comment upon, define, unfold.
Adjectives: Explanatory, expository, explicatory, explicative, exegetical, hermeneutic, constructive, inferential.

Paraphrastic, metaphrastic; literal, plain, simple, strict, synonymous; polyglot.
Adverbs: That is to say, *id est* (or i.e), *videlicet* (or viz.), in other words, in plain words, simply, in plain English.

Literally, word for word, verbatim, *au pied de la lettre,* strictly speaking (494).

523 MISINTERPRETATION
Substantives: misapprehension, misunderstanding, misacception, misconstruction, misspelling, misapplication, catachresis, mistake (495), cross-reading, cross-purpose.

Misrepresentation, perversion, falsification, misquotation, garbling, exaggeration (549), false colouring, abuse of terms, parody, travesty, misstatement, etc. (544).
Verbs: To misinterpret, misapprehend, misunderstand, misconceive, misdeem, misspell, mistranslate, misconstrue, misapply, mistake (495).

To misstate, etc. (544); to pervert, falsify, distort, misrepresent, torture, travesty; to stretch, strain, wring, or wrest the sense or meaning; to put a bad or false construction on; to misquote, garble, belie, explain away.
Phrases: To give a false colouring to; to be or play at cross-purposes; to put a false construction on.
Adjectives: Misinterpreted, etc., untranslated, untranslatable.
Phrase: *Traduttori traditori.*

524 INTERPRETER
Substantives: expositor, expounder, exponent, demonstrator, scholiast, commentator, annotator, metaphrast, paraphrast, palaeographer, spokesman, speaker, mouthpiece, guide, dragoman, cicerone, conductor, courier, showman, barker, oneirocritic; Oedipus (513).

Section 2 – Modes of Communication.

525 MANIFESTATION
Substantives: expression, showing, etc., disclosure (529), presentation, indication, exposition, demonstration, exhibition, production, display, showing off.

An exhibit, an exhibitor.

Openness, frankness, plain speaking (543), publication, publicity (531).
Verbs: To manifest, make manifest, etc., show, express, indicate, point out, bring forth, bring forward, trot out, set forth, exhibit, expose, produce, present, bring into view, set before one, hold up to view, set before one's eyes, show up, shadow forth, bring to light, display, demonstrate, unroll, unveil, unmask, disclose (529).

To elicit, educe, draw out, bring out, unearth, disinter.

To be manifested, etc., to appear, transpire, come to light (446), to come out, to crop up, get wind.
Phrases: Hold up the mirror; draw, lift up, raise, or remove the curtain; show one's true colours; throw off the mask.

To speak for itself; to stand to reason; to stare one in the face; to tell its own tale; to give vent to.
Adjectives: Manifest, clear, apparent, evident, visible (446), prominent, in the foreground, salient, signal, striking, notable, conspicuous, palpable, patent, overt, flagrant, stark, glaring, open.

Manifested, shown, expressed, etc., disclosed (529), frank, capable of being shown, producible.

Phrases: As plain as a pikestaff; as plain as the nose on one's face.

Adverbs: Openly, before one's eyes, face to face, above-board, in open court, in open daylight, in the light of day, in the open streets, on the stage, on show.

526 LATENCY

Substantives: secrecy, secretness, privacy, invisibility (447), mystery, occultness, darkness, reticence, silence (585), closeness, reserve, inexpression; a sealed book, a dark horse, an undercurrent.

Retirement, delitescence, seclusion (893).

Phrases: More is meant than meets the ear (or eye).

Verbs: To be latent, etc., to lurk, underlie, escape observation, smoulder; to keep back, reserve, suppress, keep close, etc. (528).

To render latent (528).

Phrases: Hold one's tongue; hold one's peace; leave in the dark; to keep one's own counsel; to keep mum; to seal the lips; not to breathe a syllable about.

Adjectives: Latent, lurking, secret, close, unapparent, unknown (491), dark, delitescent, in the background, occult, cryptic, snug, private, privy, *in petto*, anagogic, sequestered, dormant, smouldering.

Inconspicuous, unperceived, invisible (447), unseen, unwitnessed, impenetrable, unespied, unsuspected.

Untold, unsaid, unwritten, unpublished, unmentioned, unbreathed, untalked-of, unsung, unpronounced, unpromulgated, unreported, unexposed, unproclaimed, unexpressed, not expressed, tacit, implicit, implied, undeveloped, embryonic, unsolved, unexplained, undiscovered, untraced, untracked, unexplored.

Phrase: No news being good news.

Adverbs: Secretly, etc., *sub silentio*.

Phrases: In the background; behind one's back; under the table; behind the scenes; between the lines.

527 INFORMATION

Substantives: gen, pukka gen, low-down, enlightenment, communication, intimation, notice, notification, enunciation, announcement, annunciation, statement, specification, report, advice, monition, mention, acquaintance (490), acquainting, etc., outpouring, intercommunication, communicativeness.

An informant, teller, tipster, spy, nose, nark, stool-pigeon, intelligencer, correspondent, reporter, messenger, newsmonger, gossip (532).

Hint, suggestion (514), wrinkle, tip, pointer, insinuation, innuendo, wink, glance, leer, nod, shrug, gesture, whisper, implication, cue, office, by-play, eye-opener.

Phrases: A word to the wise; *verbum sapienti*; a broad hint; a straight tip; a stage whisper.

Verbs: To inform, acquaint, tell, mention, express, intimate, impart, communicate, apprise, post, make known, notify, signify to, let one know, advise, state, specify, give notice, announce, annunciate, publish, report, set forth, bring word, send word, leave word, write word, declare, certify, depose, pronounce, explain, undeceive, enlighten, put wise, set right, open the eyes of, convey the knowledge of, give an account of; instruct (537).

To hint, give an inkling of; give, throw out, or drop a hint, insinuate, allude to, glance at, touch on, make allusion to, to wink, to tip the wink, glance, leer, nod, shrug, give the cue, give the office, give the tip, wave, whisper, suggest, prompt, whisper in the ear, give one to understand.

To be informed, etc., of, made

acquainted with; to hear of, get a line on, understand.

To come to one's ear, to come to one's knowledge, to reach one's ears.

Adjectives: Informed, etc., of, made acquainted with, in the know, hep; undeceived.

Reported, made known (531), bruited.

Expressive, significant, pregnant with meaning, etc. (516), declaratory, enunciative, nuncupatory, expository, communicatory, communicative, insinuative.

Adverbs: Expressively, significantly, etc.

Phrases: A little bird told me; *on dit*; from information received.

528 CONCEALMENT

Substantives: hiding, occultation, etc., secrecy, stealth, stealthiness, slyness (702), disguise, incognito, privacy, masquerade, camouflage, smoke screen, mystery, mystification, freemasonry, reservation, suppression, secretiveness, reticence, reserve, uncommunicativeness; secret path.

A mask, visor, ambush, etc. (530), enigma, etc. (533).

Phrases: A needle in a bundle of hay; a nigger in the woodpile; a skeleton in the cupboard; a family skeleton.

Verbs: To conceal, hide, put out of sight, secrete, cover, envelop, screen, cloak, veil, shroud, enshroud, shade, muffle, mask, disguise, camouflage, ensconce, eclipse.

To keep from, lock up, bury, cache, sink, suppress, stifle, withhold, reserve, burke, hush up, keep snug or close or dark.

To keep in ignorance, blind, hoodwink, mystify, pose, puzzle, perplex, embarrass, flummox, bewilder, bamboozle, etc. (545).

To be concealed, etc., to lurk, skulk, smoulder, lie hid, lie in ambush, lie perdu, lie low, lie doggo, sneak, slink, prowl, gumshoe, retire, steal into, steal along.

To conceal oneself, put on a veil, etc. (530), masquerade.

Phrases: To draw or close the curtain; not breathe a word about; let it go no farther; keep it under your hat.

To play at bo-peep; to play at hide-and-seek; to hide under a bushel; to throw dust in the eyes.

Adjectives: Concealed, hid, hidden, etc., secret, clandestine, perdu, close, private, privy, furtive, surreptitious, stealthy, feline, underhand, sly, sneaking, skulking, hole-and-corner, undivulged, unrevealed, undisclosed, incognito, incommunicado.

Mysterious, mystic, mystical, dark, enigmatical, problematical, anagogical, paradoxical, occult, cryptic, gnostic, cabbalistic, esoteric, recondite, abstruse, unexplained, impenetrable, undiscoverable, inexplicable, unknowable, bewildering, baffling.

Covered, closed, shrouded, veiled, masked, screened, shaded, disguised, under cover, under a cloud, veil, etc., in a fog, haze, mist, etc., under an eclipse; inviolate, inviolable, confidential, under wraps.

Reserved, uncommunicative, secretive, buttoned up, taciturn (585).

Phrase: Close as wax.

Adverbs: Secretly, clandestinely, incognito, privily, in secret, *in camera,* with closed doors, *à huis clos, à la dérobée,* under the rose, *sub rosa,* privately, in private, aside, on the sly, *sub silentio,* behind one's back, under the counter, behind the curtain, behind the scenes.

Confidentially, between ourselves, between you and me, *entre nous, inter nos,* in strict confidence, on the strict q.t., off the record, it must go no farther.

Phrases: Like a thief in the night; under the seal of secrecy, of confession; between you and me and the gate-post;

'tell it not in Gath'; nobody any the wiser.

529 DISCLOSURE
Substantives: revealment, revelation, disinterment, exposition, show-down, exposure, effusion, outpouring.

Acknowledgment, avowal, confession; an *exposé,* denouement.

A telltale, talebearer, informer, stool-pigeon, nark, nose.

Verbs: To disclose, open, lay open, divulge, reveal, bewray, discover, unfold, let drop, let fall, let out, let on, spill, lay open, acknowledge, allow, concede, grant, admit, own, own up, confess, avow, unseal, unveil, unmask, uncover, unkennel, unearth (525).

To blab, peach, squeal, let out, let fall, let on, betray, give away, tell tales, speak out, blurt out, vent, give vent to, come out with, round on, split; publish (531).

To make no secret of, to disabuse, unbeguile, undeceive, set right, correct.

To be disclosed, revealed, etc., to come out, to transpire, to ooze out, to leak out, to creep out, to get wind, to come to light.

Phrases: To let into the secret; to let the cat out of the bag; to spill the beans; to unburden or disburden one's mind or conscience; to open one's mind; to unbosom oneself; to make a clean breast of it; to come clean; to give the show away; to own the soft impeachment; to tell tales out of school; to show one's hand; to turn Queen's (or King's or State's) evidence.

Murder will out.

Adjectives: Disclosed, revealed, divulged, laid open, etc., unriddled, etc.; outspoken, etc. (543).

Open, public, exoteric.

Interjection: Out with it!

530 AMBUSH
Substantives: hiding-place, hide, retreat, cover, lurking-hole, secret place, cubby-hole, recess, closet, priest's hole, crypt, cache, ambuscade, *guet-apens, adytum,* dungeon, oubliette.

A mask, veil, visor (or vizor), eye-shade, blinkers, cloak, screen, hoarding, curtain, shade, cover, disguise, masquerade dress, domino.

Verbs: To lie in ambush, lurk, couch, lie in wait for, lay or set a trap for (545).

531 PUBLICATION
Substantives: announcement, notification, enunciation, annunciation, advertisement, promulgation, circulation, propagation, edition, redaction, proclamation, hue and cry, the Press, journalism, wireless, radio, broadcasting, television.

Publicity, notoriety, currency, cry, bruit, rumour, fame, report (532), *on dit,* flagrancy, limelight, town-talk, small talk, table-talk, puffery, ballyhoo, *réclame,* the light of day, daylight.

Notice, notification, manifesto, propaganda, advertisement, blurb, circular, placard, bill, *affiche,* poster, newspaper, journal, daily, periodical, weekly, gazette; personal column, agony column.

Publisher (593), publicity agent, advertising agent: tout, barker, town crier.

Phrases: An open secret; *un secret de Polichinelle.*

Verbs: To publish, make known, announce, notify, annunciate, gazette, set forth, give forth, give out, broach, voice, ⸱utter, advertise, circularize, placard, *afficher,* circulate, propagate, spread, spread abroad, broadcast, edit, redact, rumour, diffuse, disseminate, celebrate, blaze about; blaze or noise abroad; bruit, buzz, bandy, hawk about, trumpet, proclaim, herald, puff, boost, splash, plug, boom, give tongue, raise a cry, raise a hue and cry, tell the world, popularize; bring, lay or drag before the public, give currency to, ventilate, bring out.

Phrases: To proclaim from the house-tops; to publish in the gazette; to send round the crier; with beat of drum.

To be published, etc., to become public, to go forth, get abroad, get about, get wind, take air, get afloat, acquire currency, get in the papers, spread, go the rounds, buzz about, blow about.

To pass from mouth to mouth; to spread like wildfire.

Adjectives: Published, etc., made public, in circulation, exoteric, rumoured, rife, current, afloat, notorious, flagrant, whispered, buzzed about, in every one's mouth, reported, trumpet-tongued; encyclical.

Phrases: As the story runs; to all whom it may concern.

Interjections: Oyez! O yes! notice is hereby given!

532 NEWS

Substantives: piece of information, intelligence, tidings, budget of news, word, advice, message, communication, errand, embassy, dispatch, bulletin.

Report, story, scoop, beat, rumour, canard, hearsay, *on dit,* fame, talk, gossip, tittle-tattle, *ouï-dire,* scandal, buzz, bruit, *chronique scandaleuse,* town talk.

Letter, postcard, airgraph, telegram, wire, cable, wireless message, radiogram.

Newsmonger, scandalmonger, scaremonger, alarmist, talebearer, tattler, gossip (527), local correspondent, special correspondent, reporter (590).

533 SECRET

Substantives: *arcanum, penetralia,* profound secret, mystery, crux, problem, enigma, teaser, poser, riddle, puzzle, conundrum, charade, rebus, logogriph, anagram, acrostic, cross-word, cipher, code, cryptogram, monogram,

paradox, maze, labyrinth, perplexity, chaos (528), the Hercynian wood; *terra incognita.*

Iron curtain, bamboo curtain, censorship, counter-intelligence.

Phrases: The secrets of the prison-house; a sealed book.

Adjectives: Secret, top secret, hush-hush, undercover, clandestine (528).

534 MESSENGER

Substantives: envoy, nuncio, internuncio, intermediary, go-between, herald, ambassador, legate, emissary, *corps diplomatique.*

Marshal, crier, trumpeter, pursuivant, *parlementaire,* courier, runner, postman, telegraph-boy, errand-boy, bell-boy, bell-hop, Mercury, Hermes, Iris, Ariel, carrier pigeon.

Narrator, etc., talebearer, spy, secretservice agent, scout.

Mail, post (592), post office, telegraph, telephone, wireless, radio; grapevine, bush telegraph.

535 AFFIRMATION

Substantives: statement, predication, assertion, declaration, word, averment, asseveration, protestation, swearing, adjuration, protest, profession, deposition, avouchment, affirmance, assurance, allegation, acknowledgment, avowal, confession, confession of faith, oath, affidavit; vote, voice.

Remark, observation, position, thesis, proposition, saying, dictum, theorem, sentence.

Positiveness (474), dogmatism, *ipse dixit.*

A dogmatist, doctrinaire.

Phrase: The big bow-wow style.

Verbs: To assert, make an assertion, etc., say, affirm, predicate, enunciate, state, declare, profess, aver, avouch, put forth, advance, express, allege, pose, propose, propound, broach, set forth, maintain, contend, pronounce, pretend, pass an opinion, etc.; to re-assert, reaffirm, reiterate; quoth, *dixit, dixi*.

To vouch, assure, vow, swear, take oath, depose, depone, recognize, avow, acknowledge, own, confess, announce, hazard or venture an opinion.

To dogmatize, lay down, lay down the law; to call heaven to witness, protest, certify, warrant, posit, go bail for.

Phrases: I doubt not; I warrant you; I'll engage; take my word for it; depend upon it; I'll be bound; I am sure; I have no doubt; sure enough; to be sure; what I have said, I have said; faith! that's flat.

To swear till one is black in the face; to swear by all the saints in the calendar; to call heaven to witness.

Adjectives: Asserting, etc., dogmatic, positive, emphatic, declaratory, affirmative, predicable, pronounced, unretracted.

Positive, broad, round, express, explicit, pointed, marked, definitive, distinct, decided, formal, solemn, categorical, peremptory, absolute, flat, pronounced.

Adverbs: *Ex cathedra,* positively, avowedly, confessedly, broadly, roundly, etc.; ay, yes, indeed; by Jove, by George, by James, by jingo.

536 NEGATION

Substantives: abnegation, denial, denegation, disavowal, disclaimer, abjuration, contradiction, *démenti,* contravention, recusation, retraction, retractation, recantation, renunciation, palinode, recusancy, protest.

Qualification, modification (469); rejection (610); refusal (764).

Verbs: To deny, disown, contradict, negative, gainsay, contravene, disclaim, withdraw, recant, disavow, retract, revoke, abjure, negate.

Phrases: To deny flatly; eat one's words; go back from, or upon one's word.

To dispute, impugn, controvert, confute (479), question, call in question, give the lie to, rebut, belie.

Adjectives: Denying, etc., denied, etc., negative, contradictory, recusant.

Adverbs: No, nay, not, nohow, not at all, by no means (489), far from it, anything but, on the contrary, quite the reverse.

537 TEACHING

Substantives: instruction, direction, guidance, tuition, culture, inculcation, inoculation, indoctrination.

Education, co-education, initiation, preparation, practice, training, up-bringing, schooling, discipline, exercise, drill, exercitation, breaking in, taming, drilling, etc., preachment, persuasion, edification, proselytism, propagandism.

A lesson, lecture, prolusion, prelection, exercise, 'task; curriculum, course.

Rudiments, ABC, elements, three Rs, grammar, text-book, vademecum, school-book (593).

Physical training, PT, gymnastics, callisthenics.

Verbs: To teach, instruct, enlighten, edify, inculcate, indoctrinate, instil, imbue, inoculate, infuse, impregnate, graft, infix, engraft, implant, sow the seeds of, infiltrate, give an idea of, cram, coach, put up to.

To explain, expound, lecture, hold forth, read a lecture or sermon, give a lesson, preach; sermonize, moralize, point a moral.

To educate, train, discipline, school, form, ground, tutor, prepare, qualify prime, drill, exercise, practise, bring up, rear, nurture, dry-nurse, breed, break in, tame, domesticate, condition.

To direct, guide, initiate, put in the way of, proselytize, bring round to an opinion, bring over, win over, brainwash, re-educate, persuade, convince, convict, set right, enlighten, give one new ideas, put one up to, bring home to.

Phrases: To teach the young idea how to shoot; to sharpen the wits; to enlarge the mind.

Adjectives: Teaching, etc., taught, etc., educational.

Didactic, academic, doctrinal, disciplinal, disciplinary, instructive, scholastic, persuasive.

538 MISTEACHING

Substantives: misdirection, misleading, misinformation, misguidance, perversion, false teaching, sophistry.

Indocility, incapacity, misintelligence, dullness, backwardness.

Verbs: To misinform, misteach, mislead, misdirect, misguide, miscorrect, pervert, lead into error, bewilder, mystify (528), throw off the scent; to unteach.

Phrases: To teach one's grandmother; *obscurum per obscurius*; the blind leading the blind.

Adjectives: Misteaching, etc., unedifying.

539 LEARNING

Substantives: acquisition of knowledge, acquirement, attainment, scholarship, erudition, instruction, study, etc. (490).

Docility (602), aptitude (698), aptness to be taught, teachableness, persuasibility, capacity.

Verbs: To learn; to acquire, gain, catch, receive, imbibe, pick up, gather, collect, glean, etc., knowledge or information.

To hear, overhear, catch hold of, take in, fish up, drink in, run away with an idea, to make oneself acquainted with, master, read, spell, turn over the leaves, pore over, run through, peruse, study, grind, cram, mug, swot, go to school; to get up a

subject; to serve one's time or apprenticeship.

To be taught, etc.

Adjectives: Docile, apt, teachable, persuasible, studious, industrious, scholastic, scholarly.

Phrase: To burn the midnight oil.

540 TEACHER

Substantives: instructor, apostle, master, director, tutor, preceptor, institutor, mentor, adviser, monitor, counsellor, expositor, dry-nurse, trainer, coach, crammer, grinder, governor, bear-leader, disciplinarian, martinet, guide, cicerone, pioneer, governess, duenna.

Orator, speaker, mouthpiece (582).

Professor, lecturer, reader, demonstrator, praelector, prolocutor, schoolmaster, schoolmistress, schoolmarm, usher, pedagogue, monitor, pupil-teacher, dominie, dame, moonshee; missionary, propagandist.

Adjectives: Tutorial, professorial.

541 LEARNER

Substantives: scholar, student, alumnus, disciple, pupil, *élève,* schoolboy, schoolgirl, beginner, tyro (or tiro), abecedarian, novice, neophyte, chela, inceptor, probationer, apprentice, tenderfoot, freshman, bejan (or bejant), undergraduate, undergraduette, sophomore.

Proselyte, concert, catechumen, sectator; class, form.

Pupilage, pupilarity, pupilship, tutelage, apprenticeship, novitiate, leading-strings, matriculation.

Phrases: Freshwater sailor; *in statu pupillari.*

542 SCHOOL

Substantives: day school, boarding school, public school, council school, national school, board school, private school, preparatory school, elementary school, primary school, secondary school, senior school, grammar school, high school, academy, university, Alma Mater, university extension, correspondence school, college, seminary, lyceum, polytechnic, nursery, institute, institution, palaestra, gymnasium, class, form, standard; nursery school, infant school, kindergarten, crèche; reformatory, Borstal, approved school.

Horn-book, rudiments, vademecum, abecedary, manual, primer, school-book, text-book.

Professorship, lectureship, readership, chair; pulpit, ambo, theatre, amphitheatre, forum, stage, rostrum, platform.

Adjectives: Scholastic, academic, collegiate.

543 VERACITY
Substantives: truthfulness, truth, sincerity, frankness, straightforwardness, ingenuousness, candour, honesty, fidelity, bona fides, openness, unreservedness, bluntness, plainness, plain speaking, plain dealing; simplicity, bonhomie, naïveté, artlessness (703), love of truth.

A plain-dealer, truth-teller, man of his word.

Verbs: To speak the truth, speak one's mind, open out, think aloud.

Phrases: Tell the truth and shame the devil; to deal faithfully with; to show oneself in one's true colours.

Adjectives: Truthful, true, veracious, uncompromising, veridical, veridicous, sincere, candid, frank, open, outspoken, unreserved, free-spoken, open-hearted, honest, simple, simple-hearted, ingenuous, blunt, plain-spoken, true-blue, straightforward, straight, fair, fair-minded, single-minded, artless, guileless, natural, unaffected, simple-minded, undisguised, unfeigned, unflattering, warts and all.

Adverbs: Truly, etc. (494), above-board, broadly.

Phrases: In plain English: without mincing the matter: honour bright: honest Injun; bona fide; *sans phrase.*

544 FALSENESS
Substantives: falsehood, untruthfulness, untruth (546), falsity, mendacity, falsification, perversion of truth, perjury, fabrication, romance, forgery, prevarication, equivocation, shuffling, evasion, fencing, duplicity, double-dealing, unfairness, dishonesty, fraud, misrepresentation, *suggestio falsi, suppressio veri,* Punic faith, giving the go-by, disguise, disguisement, irony, understatement.

Insincerity, dissimulation, dissembling, deceit (545), shiftiness, hypocrisy, cant, humbug, gammon, jesuitry, pharisaism, mental reservation, lip-service, simulation, acting, sham, malingering, pretending, pretence, crocodile tears, false colouring, art, artfulness (702).

Deceiver (548).

Verbs: To be false, etc., to play false, speak falsely, lie, fib, tell a lie or untruth, etc. (546), to mistake, misreport, misrepresent, misquote, belie, falsify, prevaricate, equivocate, quibble, palter, shuffle, fence, hedge, understate, mince the truth.

To forswear, swear false, perjure oneself, bear false witness.

To garble, gloss over, disguise, pervert, distort, twist, colour, varnish, cook, doctor, embroider, fiddle, wangle, gerrymander, put a false colouring or construction upon (523).

To invent, make up, fabricate, concoct, trump up, forge, fake, romance.

To dissemble, dissimulate, feign, pretend, assume, act or play a part, simulate, pass off for, counterfeit, sham, malinger, make believe, cant, put on.

Phrases: To play the hypocrite; to give the go-by; to play fast and loose; to

213

play a double game; to blow hot and cold; to lie like a conjurer; sham Abraham; to look as if butter would not melt in one's mouth; to sail under false colours; to ring false.

Adjectives: False, dishonest, faithless, deceitful, mendacious, unveracious, truthless, trothless, unfair, uncandid, disingenuous, shady, shifty, underhand, underhanded, hollow, insincere, canting, hypocritical, jesuitical, sanctimonious, pharisaical, tartuffian, double, double-tongued, double-faced, smooth-spoken, smooth-tongued, plausible, mealymouthed, snide.

Artful, insidious, sly, designing, diplomatic, Machiavellian.

Untrue, unfounded, fictitious, invented, made up, *ben trovato*, forged, falsified, counterfeit, spurious, factitious, self-styled, bastard, sham, bogus, phoney, mock, pseudo, disguised, simulated, artificial, colourable, catchpenny, meretricious, tinsel, Brummagem, postiche, pinchbeck, illusory, elusory, supposititious, surreptitious, ironical, apocryphal.

Phrase: All is not gold that glitters.

Adverbs: Falsely, etc., slyly, stealthily, underhand.

545 DECEPTION

Substantives: falseness (544), fraud, deceit, imposition, artifice, juggle, juggling, sleight of hand, legerdemain, conjuration, hocus-pocus, jockeyship, trickery, coggery, fraudulence, imposture, *supercherie,* chicane, chicanery, covin, cozenage, circumvention, ingannation, prestidigitation, subreption, collusion, complicity, guile, gullery, hanky-panky, jiggery-pokery, rannygazoo.

Quackery, charlatanism, charlatanry, empiricism, humbug, hokum, eye-wash, hypocrisy, gammon, flapdoodle, bunkum, *blague,* bluff, mummery, borrowed plumes.

Stratagem, trick, cheat, wile, artifice, cross, deception, take-in, camouflage, make-believe, ruse, manoeuvre, finesse, hoax, canard, hum, kid, chouse, bubble, fetch, catch, spoof, swindle, plant, sell, hocus, dodge, bite, forgery, counterfeit, sham, fake, fakement, rig, delusion, stalking-horse.

Snare, trap, pitfall, decoy, gin, spring, noose, hook, bait, net, meshes, mouse-trap, trap-door, false bottom, ambush, ambuscade (530), masked battery, mine, mystery-ship, Q-boat.

Phrases: A wolf in sheep's clothing; a whited (or painted) sepulchre; a pious fraud; a man of straw.

Verbs: To deceive, mislead, cheat, impose upon, practise upon, circumvent, play upon, put upon, bluff, dupe, mystify, blind, hoodwink, best, outreach, trick, hoax, kid, gammon, spoof, hocus, bamboozle, hornswoggle, juggle, trepan, nick, entrap, beguile, lure, inveigle, decoy, lime, ensnare, entangle, lay a snare for, trip up, stuff the go-by.

To defraud, fiddle, take in, jockey, do, do brown, cozen, diddle, have, have on, chouse, welsh, bilk, bite, pluck, swindle, victimize, outwit, over-reach, nobble, palm upon, work off upon, foist upon, fob off, balk, trump up.

Phrases: To throw dust in the eyes; to play a trick upon; to pull one's leg; to try it on; to cog the dice; to mark the cards; to live by one's wits; to play a part; to throw a tub to the whale.

Adjectives: Deceiving, cheating, etc.; hypocritical, Pecksniffian; deceived, duped, done, had, etc., led astray.

Deptive, deceitful, deceptious, illusive, illusory, delusory, prestigious, elusive, bogus, counterfeit, insidious, *ad captandum, ben trovato.*

Phrases: *Fronti nulla fides; timeo Danaos et dona ferentes.*

546 UNTRUTH

Substantives: falsehood, lie, falsity, fiction, fabrication, fib, whopper, bouncer, cracker, crammer, tarradiddle, story, fable, novel, romance, flam, bull, gammon, flim-flam, *guet-apens,* white lie, pious, fraud, canard, nursery tale, fairy-tale, tall story.

Falsification, perjury, forgery, false swearing, misstatement, misrepresentation, inexactitude.

Pretence, pretext, subterfuge, irony, evasion, blind, disguise, plea, claptrap, shuffle, make-believe, shift, mask, cloak, visor, veil, masquerade, gloss, cobweb.

Phrases: A pack of lies; a tissue of falsehoods; a cock-and-bull story; a trumped-up story; all my eye and Betty Martin; a mare's-nest.

547 DUPE

Substantives: gull (486), gudgeon, gobemouche, cully, victim, sucker, flat, greenhorn, puppet, cat's-paw, April fool, simple Simon, Joe Soap, pushover, soft mark.

Phrases: To be the goat; to hold the baby; to carry the can; *qui vult decipi, decipiatur.*

548 DECEIVER

Substantives: liar, hypocrite, taleteller, shuffler, shammer, dissembler, serpent, cockatrice; Janus, Tartuffe, Pecksniff, Joseph Surface, Cagliostro.

Pretender, impostor, knave, cheat, rogue, trickster, swindler, spiv, adventurer, humbug, sharper, jockey, welcher, leg, blackleg, rook, shark, confidence man, con man, confidence trickster, decoy, decoy-duck, stool-pigeon, gipsy.

Quack, charlatan, mountebank, empiric, quacksalver, *saltimbanco,* medicaster, *soi-disant.*

Actor, player, mummer, tumbler, posture-master, jack-pudding; illusionist, conjurer (994).

Phrases: A wolf in sheep's clothing; a snake in the grass; one who lives by his wits.

549 EXAGGERATION

Substantives: hyperbole, overstatement, stretch, strain, colouring, bounce, flourish, vagary, bombast (884), yarn, figure of speech, flight of fancy, *façon de parler,* extravagance, rhodomontade, heroics, sensationalism, highfalutin; tale of Baron Munchausen, traveller's tale.

Phrases: A storm in a teacup; much ado about nothing.

Verbs: To exaggerate, amplify, magnify, heighten, overcharge, overstate, overcolour, overlay, overdo, strain, stretch, bounce, flourish, embroider; to hyperbolize, aggravate, to make the most of.

Phrases: To make a song about; spin a long yarn; draw the long bow; deal in the marvellous; out-herod Herod; lay it on thick; pile it on; make a mountain of a molehill.

Adjectives: Exaggerated, etc., hyperbolical, turgid, tumid, fabulous, extravagant, magniloquent, bombastic, *outré,* highly coloured, high-flying, high-flown, high-falutin, sensational, blood-and-thunder, lurid.

Phrases: All his geese are swans; much cry and little wool.

Section 3 –
Means of Communicating Ideas

550 INDICATION

Substantives: symbolization, symbolism, typification, notation, connotation, prefigurement, representation (554), exposition, notice (527), trace (551), name (564).

A sign, symbol, index, placard,

exponent, indicator, pointer, mark, token, symptom, type, emblem, figure, cipher, code, device, epigraph, motto, posy.

Science of signs, sematology, semeiology, semeiotics.

Lineament, feature, line, stroke, dash, trait, characteristic, idiosyncracy, score, stripe, streak, scratch, tick, dot, point, notch, nick, asterisk, red letter, rubric, italics, print, stamp, impress, imprint, sublineation, underlining, display, jotting.

For identification: Badge, criterion, check, countercheck, countersign, stub, counterfoil, duplicate, tally, label, book-plate, *ex-libris,* ticket, billet, card, visiting-card, *carte de visite,* identity-card, passport, bill, bill-head, facia, sign-board, witness, voucher, coupon, trade mark, hall-mark, signature, hand-writing, sign manual, monogram, seal, sigil, signet, chop, autograph, autography, superscription, endorsement, *visé,* title, heading, caption, docket, watchword, password, shibboleth, *mot du guet,* catchword; fingerprint.

Insignia: Banner, banneret, flag, colours, bunting, streamer, standard, eagle, ensign, pennon, pennant, pendant, burgee, jack, ancient, labarum, oriflamme; gonfalon, banderole, Union Jack, Royal Standard, Stars and Stripes, Tricolour, etc.; crest, arms, coat of arms, armorial bearings, shield, scutcheon, escutcheon, uniform, livery, cockade, epaulet, chevron, cordon, totem.

Indication of locality: Beacon, cairn, post, staff, flagstaff, hand, pointer, vane, guide-post, finger-post, signpost, landmark, sea-mark, lighthouse, light-ship, pole-star, lodestar, cynosure, guide, address, direction, rocket, blue-light, watch-fire, blaze.

Indication of an event: Signal, nod, wink, glance, leer, shrug, beck, cue, gesture, gesticulation, deaf-and-dumb alphabet, by-play, dumb-show, pantomime, touch, nudge, freemasonry, telegraph, heliograph, semaphore.

Indication of time: Time-signal, clock (114), alarm-clock, hooter, blower, buzzer, siren; tattoo, reveille, last post, taps.

Indication of danger: Alarm, alarum, alarm-bell, alert, fog-signal, detonator, red light, tocsin, fire-hooter, maroon, S O S, beat of drum, fiery cross, sound of trumpet, war-cry, war-whoop, slogan.

Indication of safety: all-clear, green light.

Verbs: To indicate, point out, be the sign, etc., of, denote, betoken, connote, connotate, represent, stand for, typify, symbolize, shadow forth, argue, bear the impress of, witness, attest, testify.

To put an indication, mark, etc.; to note, mark, stamp, impress, earmark, brand, label, ticket, docket, endorse, sign, countersign; put, append, or affix a seal or signature; dot, jot down, book, score, dash, trace, chalk, underline, italicize, print, imprint, engrave, stereotype, rubricate, star, obelize, initial.

To make a sign, signal, etc., signalize; give or hang out a signal; give notice, gesticulate, beckon, beck, nod, wink, nudge, tip the wink; give the cue, tip, or office; wave, unfurl, hoist, or hang out a banner, flag, etc., show one's colours, give or sound an alarm, beat the drum, sound the trumpets, raise a cry, etc.

Adjectives: Indicating, etc., indicatory, indicative, sematic, semeiological, denotative, representative, typical, typic, symbolic, symbolical, diacritical, connotative, pathognomic, symptomatic, exponential, emblematic, pantomimic, attesting; armorial, totemistic.

Indicated, etc., typified, impressed, etc.

Capable of being denoted, denotable, indelible.
Phrases: *Ecce signum*; in token of.

551 RECORD
Substantives: trace, mark, tradition, vestige, footstep, footmark, footprint, footfall, wake, track, trail, slot, spoor, pug, scent.

Monument, relic, remains, trophy, hatchment, achievement, obelisk, monolith, pillar, stele, column, slab, tablet, medal, testimonial, memorial.

Note, minute, register, registry, index, inventory, catalogue, list (86), memorandum, jotting, document, account, score, tally, invoice, docket, voucher, protocol, inscription.

Paper, parchment, scroll, instrument, deed, indenture, debenture, roll, archive, schedule, file, dossier, cartulary, table, *procès verbal,* affidavit, certificate, attestation, entry, diploma, protest, round-robin, roster, rota, musterroll, muster-book, notebook, commonplace-book, *adversaria,* portfolio.

Chronicle, annals, gazette, Hansard, history (594), newspaper, magazine, gazetteer, blue-book, almanac, calendar, ephemeris, diary, log, journal, day-book, ledger.

Registration, tabulation, enrolment, booking.
Verbs: To record, note, register, chronicle, calendar, make an entry of, enter, book, take a note of, post, enrol, jot down, take down, mark, sign, etc. (550), tabulate, catalogue, file, index, commemorate (883).
Adjectives: Registered, etc.
Adverbs: Under one's hand and seal, on record.

552 OBLITERATION
Substantives: erasure, rasure, cancel, cancellation, circumduction, deletion.
Verbs: To efface, obliterate, erase, raze, expunge, cancel, delete, blot out, take out, rub out, scrach out, strike

out, elide, wipe out, wash out, black out, write off, render illegible.

To be effaced, etc., to leave no trace.
Phrases: To draw the pen through; to apply the sponge.
Adjectives: Obliterated, effaced, etc., printless, leaving no trace.

Unrecorded, unattested, unregistered, intestate.
Interjections: *Dele*; out with it!

553 RECORDER
Substantives: notary, clerk, registrar, registrary, register, prothonotary, secretary, stenographer, amanuensis, scribe, remembrancer, journalist, historian, historiographer, annalist, chronicler, biographer, book-keeper.

Recordership, secretaryship, secretariat, clerkship.

554 REPRESENTATION
Substantives: delineation, representment, reproduction, depictment, personification.

Art, the fine arts, the graphic arts, design, designing, illustration, imitation (19), copy (21), portraiture, iconography, photography.

A picture, drawing, tracing, photograph.

An image, likeness, icon, portrait, effigy, facsimile, autotype, imagery, figure, puppet, dummy, lay figure, figurehead, doll, manikin, *mannequin* mammet, marionette, *fantoccini* (599), statue (557), waxwork.

Hieroglyphic, hieroglyph, inscription, diagram, monogram, draught (or draft), outline, scheme, *schema,* schedule.

Map, plan, chart, ground-plan, projection, elevation, ichnography, atlas; cartography, chorography.
Verbs: To represent, present, depict, portray, photograph, delineate, design, figure, adumbrate, shadow forth, copy, draft, mould, diagrammatize, schematize, map.

217

To imitate, impersonate, personate, personify, act, take off, hit off, figure as; to paint (556); carve (557); engrave (558).

Adjectives: Representing, etc.; artistic, imitative, representative, illustrative, figurative, hieroglyphic, hieroglyphical, diagrammatic, schematic.

555 MISREPRESENTATION
Substantives: distortion (243), caricature, burlesque (856), a bad likeness, daub, scratch, sign-painting, anamorphosis; misprint, *erratum*.
Verbs: To misrepresent, distort, falsify, caricature, wrest the sense (or meaning).

556 PAINTING
Substantives: depicting, drawing; perspective, composition, treatment.

Drawing in pencil, crayon, pastel, chalk, water-colour, etc.

Painting in oils, in distemper, in gouache, in fresco; encaustic painting, enamel painting, scene-painting; wash (428), body-colour, impasto.

A picture, drawing, painting, sketch, illustration, scratch, *graffito*, outline, tableau, cartoon, fresco, illumination; pencil, pen-and-ink, etc., drawing; oil, etc., painting; photograph; silver print; POP, bromide, gaslight, bromoil, platinotype, carbon print; autochrome, Kodachrome; daguerreotype, calotype; mosaic, tapestry, etc., picture-gallery.

Portrait, portraiture, likeness, full-length, etc., miniature, kitcat, shade, profile, silhouette, still, snapshot.

Landscape, seascape, nocturne, view, still-life, *genre,* panorama, diorama.

Pre-Raphaelitism, impressionism, etc. (559).
Verbs: To paint, depict, portray, limn, draw, sketch, pencil, scratch, scrawl, block in, rough in, dash off, chalk out, shadow forth, adumbrate,

outline, illustrate, illuminate; to take a portrait, take a likeness, to photograph, snap, pan.
Phrases: *Fecit, pinxit, delineavit.*
Adjectives: Painted, etc.; pictorial, graphic, picturesque, Giottesque, Raphaelesque, Turneresque, etc.; like, similar (17).

557 SCULPTURE
Substantives: insculpture, carving, modelling.

A statue, statuary, statuette, figure, figurine, model, bust, image, high relief, low relief, alto-rivievo, mezzo-rilievo, basso-rilievo, bas-relief, cast, marble, bronze, intaglio, anaglyph; medallion, cameo.
Verbs: To sculpture, sculp, carve, cut, chisel, model, mould, cast.
Adjectives: Sculptured, etc., sculptural, sculpturesque, anaglyphic, ceroplastic, ceramic.

558 ENGRAVING
Substantives: etching, wood-engraving, process-engraving, xylography, chalcography, cerography, glyptography; poker-work.

A print, engraving, impression, plate, cut, wood-cut, steel-cut, linocut, vignette.

An etching, dry-point, stipple, roulette; copper-plate, mezzotint, aquatint, lithography, chromolithograph, chromo, photo-lithograph, photogravure, anastatic-printing, collotype, electrotype, stereotype.

Matrix, flong.
Verbs: To engrave, etch, lithograph, print, etc.

559 ARTIST
Substantives: painter, limner, draughtsman, black-and-white artist, cartoonist, caricaturist, drawer, sketcher, pavement artist, screever, designer, engraver, copyist, photographer.

Academician; historical, landscape, portrait, miniature, scene, sign, etc., painter; an Apelles.

Primitive, Pre-Raphaelite, old master, quattrocentist, cinquecentist, impressionist, post-impressionist, futurist, vorticist, cubist, surrealist, Dadaist, pointillist.

A sculptor, carver, modeller, goldsmith, silversmith, *figuriste*; a Phidias, Praxiteles, Royal Academician, RA.

Implements of art: pen, pencil, brush, charcoal, chalk, pastel, crayon; paint (428); stump, graver, style, burin; canvas, easel, palette, maulstick, palette-knife; studio, *atelier*.

560 LANGUAGE
Substantives: tongue, speech, lingo, vernacular, mother-tongue, native tongue, standard English, King's (or Queen's) English, the genius of a language.

Dialect, local dialect, class dialect, provincialism, vulgarism, colloquialism, Americanism, Scotticism, Cockney speech, brogue, patois, patter, slang, cant, argot, Anglic, Basic English, broken English, pidgin English, lingua franca.

Universal languages: Esperanto, Volapük, Ido, Interglossa.

Philology, etymology (562), linguistics, glossology, dialectology, phonetics.

Literature, letters, polite literature, belles-lettres, the muses, humanities, the republic of letters, dead languages, classics, *literae humaniores*.

Scholarship (490), linguist, scholar (492), writer (593), glossographer.
Verbs: To express by words, to couch in terms, to clothe in language.
Adjectives: Literary, belletristic, linguistic, dialectal, vernacular, colloquial, slang, current, polyglot, pantomimic.
Adverbs: In plain terms, in common parlance, in household words.

561 LETTER
Substantives: alphabet, ABC, abecedary, spelling-book, horn-book, criss-cross-row; character (591), writing (590), hieroglyph, hieroglyphic; consonant, vowel, diphthong, triphthong; mute, liquid, labial, palatal, dental, guttural; spelling, orthography, phonetic spelling, misspelling; spelling-bee.

Syllable, monosyllable, dissyllable, trisyllable, polysyllable; anagram.
Verbs: To speel, spell out.
Adjectives: Literal, alphabetical, abecedarian, orthographic; syllabic, disyllabic, etc.

562 WORD
Substantives: term, vocable, terminology, part of speech (567), root, etymon.

Word similarly pronounced, homonym, homophone, paronym.

A dictionary, vocabulary, lexicon, index, polyglot, glossary, thesaurus, concordance, onomasticon, gradus; lexicography, lexicographer.

Derivation, etymology, glossology.
Adjectives: Verbal, literal, titular, nominal, etymological, terminological.

Similarly derived, conjugate, paronymous.
Adverbs: Nominally, etc., *verbatim,* word for word, in so many words, literally, *sic, totidem verbis, ipsissimis verbis, literatim.*

563 NEOLOGY
Substantives: neologism, slang, cant, byword, hard word, jaw-breaker, dog Latin, monkish Latin, loan word, vogue word, nonce word, Gallicism.

A pun, play upon words, paronomasia, *jeu de mots, calembour,* palindrome, conundrum, acrostic, anagram (533).

Dialect (560).

Neologian, neologist.

Verbs: To neologize, archaize, pun.
Phrase: To coin or mint words.
Adjectives: Neological, neologistic, paronomastic.

564 NOMENCLATURE
Substantives: nomination, naming, nuncupation.

A name, appellation, designation, appellative, denomination, term, expression, noun, byword, moniker, epithet, style, title, prenomen, forename, Christian name, baptismal name, given name, cognomen, agnomen, patronymic, surname, family name.

Synonym, namesake; euphemism, antonomasia, onomatopoeia.

Quotation, citation, chapter and verse.

Verbs: To name, call, term, denominate, designate, style, clepe, entitle, dub, christen, baptize, characterize, specify, label (550).

To be called, etc., to take the name of, pass under the name of; to quote, cite.

Phrases: To call a spade a spade; to rejoice in the name of.

Adjectives: Named, called, etc., hight, yclept, known as; nuncupatory, nuncupative, cognominal, titular, nominal.

Literal, verbal, discriminative.

565 MISNOMER
Substantives: missaying, malaprop, malapropism, antiphrasis, nickname, sobriquet, byname, assumed name or title, alias, *nom de guerre, nom de plume,* pen-name, pseudonym, pet name, euphemism.

So-and-so, what's-his-name, thingummy, thingumbob, thingumajig, dingus, *je ne sais quoi.*

A Mrs Malaprop.

Phrase: *Lucus a non lucendo.*

Verbs: To misname, missay, miscall, misterm, nickname.

To assume a name.

Adjectives: Misnamed, etc., malapropian, pseudonymous, *soi-disant,* self-called, self-styled, so-called.

Nameless, anonymous, without a name, having no name, innominate, unnamed.

566 PHRASE
Substantives: expression, phraseology, paraphrase, periphrasis, circumlocution (573), set phrase, round terms; mode or turn of expression; idiom, wording, *façon de parler,* mannerism, plain terms, plain English.

Sentence, paragraph, motto.

Figure, trope, metaphore (521), wisecrack, proverb (496).

Verbs: To express, phrase, put; couch, clothe in words, give words to; to word.

Adjectives: Expressed, etc., couched in, phraseological, idiomatic, paraphrastic, periphrastic, circumlocutory (573), proverbial.

Phrases: As the saying is; in good set terms; *sans phrase.*

567 GRAMMAR
Substantives: accidence, syntax, parsing, analysis, praxis, punctuation, conjugation, declension, inflexion, case, voice, person, number; philology (560), parts of speech.

Phrase: *Jus et norma loquendi.*

Verbs: To parse, analyse, conjugate, decline, inflect, punctuate.

Adjectives: Grammatical, syntactic, inflexional.

568 SOLECISM
Substantives: bad or false grammar, slip of the pen or tongue, bull, howler, floater, clanger, *lapsus linguae,* barbarism, vulgarism; dog Latin.

Verbs: To use bad or faulty grammar, to solecize, commit a solecism.

Phrases: To murder the king's English; to break Priscian's head.

Adjectives: Ungrammatical, barbarous, slipshod, incorrect, faulty, inaccurate.

569 STYLE

Substantives: diction, phraseology, wording, turn of expression, idiom, manner, strain, composition, authorship; stylist.

Adjectives: Stylistic, idiomatic, mannered.

Phrases: Command of language; a ready pen; *le style, c'est l'homme même.*

570 PERSPICUITY

Substantives: lucidity, lucidness, clearness, clarity, perspicacity, plain speaking, intelligibility (518).

Adjectives: Perspicuous, clear (525), lucid, intelligible, plain, transparent, explicit.

571 OBSCURITY

Substantives: ambiguity (520), unintelligibility (519), involution, involvedness, vagueness.

Adjectives: Obscure, confused, crabbed, ambiguous, vague, unintelligible, etc., involved, wiredrawn, tortuous.

572 CONCISENESS

Substantives: brevity, terseness, compression (195), condensation, concision, closeness, laconism, portmanteau word, telegraphese, pithiness, succinctness, quaintness, stiffness, ellipsis, ellipse, syncope.

Abridgment, epitome (596).

Verbs: To be concise, etc., to condense, compress, abridge, abbreviate, cut short, curtail, abstract.

Phrase: To cut the cackle and come to the horses.

Adjectives: Concise, brief, crisp, curt, short, terse, laconic, sententious, gnomic, snappy, pithy, nervous, pregnant, succinct, *guindé,* stiff, compact, summary, compendious (596), close,

cramped, elliptical, telegraphic, epigrammatic, lapidary.

Adverbs: Concisely, briefly, etc., in a word, to the point, in short.

Phrases: The long and short of it; *multum in parvo;* it comes to this; for shortness' sake; to make a long story short; to put it in a nutshell.

573 DIFFUSENESS

Substantives: prolixity, verbosity, macrology, pleonasm, tautology, copiousness, exuberance, laxity, looseness, verbiage, flow, flow of words, fluency, *copia verborum,* loquacity (584), redundancy, redundance, digression, amplification, *longueur,* padding, circumlocution, ambages, periphrasis, officialese, commercialese, gobbledygook, episode, expletive.

Verbs: To be diffuse, etc., to expatiate, enlarge, launch out, dilate, expand, pad out, spin out, run on, amplify, swell out, inflate, dwell on, harp on, descant, digress, ramble, maunder, rant.

Phrases: To beat about the bush; to spin a long yarn; to make a long story of.

Adjectives: Diffuse, wordy, verbose, prolix, copious, exuberant, flowing, fluent, bombastic, lengthy, long-winded, talkative (584), prosy, spun out, long-spun, loose, lax, slovenly, washy, slipslop, sloppy, frothy, flatulent, windy, digressive, discursive, excursive, tripping, rambling, ambagious, pleonastic, redundant, periphrastic, episodic, circumlocutory, roundabout.

Minute, detailed, particular, circumstantial.

Adverbs: In detail, at great length, *in extenso,* about it and about, *currente calamo, usque ad nauseam.*

574 VIGOUR

Substantives: energy, power, force,

221

spirit, point, vim, snap, punch, ginger, *élan,* pep, go, raciness, liveliness, fire, glow, verve, piquancy, pungency, spice, boldness, gravity, warmth, sententiousness, elevation, loftiness, sublimity, eloquence, individuality, distinction, emphasis, virility.

Phrase: 'Thoughts that glow and words that burn.'

Adjectives: Vigorous, energetic, powerful, strong, forcible, nervous, spirited, vivid, virile, expressive, lively, glowing, sparkling, racy, bold, slashing, incisive, trenchant, snappy, mordant, poignant, piquant, pungent, spicy, meaty, pithy, juicy, pointed, antithetical, sententious, emphatic, athletic, distinguished, original, individual, lofty, elevated, sublime, Miltonic, eloquent.

575 FEEBLENESS

Substantives: baldness, tameness, meagreness, coldness, frigidity, poverty, puerility, childishness, dullness, dryness, jejuneness, monotony.

Adjectives: Feeble, bald, dry, flat, insipid, tame, meagre, invertebrate, weak, mealy-mouthed, wishy-washy, wersh, banal, uninteresting, jejune, vapid, cold, frigid, poor, dull (843), languid, anaemic, prosy, prosaic, pedestrian, platitudinous, conventional, mechanical, decadent, trashy, namby-pamby (866), puerile, childish, emasculate.

576 PLAINNESS

Substantives: simplicity, homeliness, chasteness, chastity, neatness, monotony, severity.

Adjectives: Simple, unornamented, unvarnished, straightforward, artless, unaffected, downright, plain, unadorned, unvaried, monotonous, severe, chaste, blunt, homespun.

577 ORNAMENT

Substantives: floridness, floridity,

flamboyance, richness, opulence, turgidity, tumidity, pomposity, inflation, altiloquence, spreadeagleism, pretension, fustian, affectation, euphuism, gongorism, mannerism, metaphor, preciosity, inversion, figurativeness, sesquipedalianism, *sesquipedalia verba,* rant, bombast, frothiness; flowers of speech, high-sounding words, well-rounded periods, purple patches.

A phrase-monger, euphuist.

Verbs: To ornament, overcharge, overlay with ornament, lard or garnish with metaphors, lay the colours on thick, round a period, mouth.

Adjectives: Ornamented, etc., ornate, florid, flamboyant, rich, opulent, golden-mouthed, figurative, metaphorical, pedantic, affected, pretentious, falsetto, euphuistic, Della Cruscan, pompous, fustian, high-sounding, mouthy, inflated, high-falutin (or high-faluting), bombastic, stilted, mannered, high-flowing, frothy, flowery, luscious, turgid, tumid, swelling, declamatory, rhapsodic, rhetorical, orotund, sententious, grandiose, grandiloquent, magniloquent, altiloquent, sesquipedalian, Johnsonian, ponderous.

Adverb: *Ore rotundo.*

578 ELEGANCE

Substantives: grace, ease, naturalness, purity, concinnity, readiness, euphony; a purist.

Phrases: A ready pen; flowing periods; *curiosa felicitas.*

Adjectives: Elegant, graceful, Attic, Ciceronian, classical, natural, easy, felicitous, unaffected, unlaboured, chaste, pure, correct, flowing, mellifluous, euphonious, rhythmical, puristic, well-expressed, neatly put.

Phrases: To round a period; 'to point a moral and adorn a tale.'

579 INELEGANCE

Substantives: stiffness, uncouthness,

barbarism, archaism, rudeness, crudeness, bluntness, brusquerie, ruggedness, abruptness, artificiality, cacophony.
Phrases: Words that dislocate the jaw, that break the teeth.
Verbs: To be inelegant, etc.
Phrase: To smell of the lamp.
Adjectives: Inelegant, ungraceful, stiff, forced, laboured, clumsy, contorted, tortuous, harsh, cramped, rude, rugged, dislocated, crude, crabbed, uncouth, barbarous, archaic, archaistic, affected (577), artificial, abrupt, blunt, brusque, incondite.

580 VOICE
Substantives: vocality, vocalization, utterance, cry, strain, articulate sound, prolation, articulation, enunciation, delivery, vocalism, pronunciation, orthoepy, euphony.
Cadence, accent, accentuation, emphasis, stress, tone, intonation, exclamation, ejaculation, vociferation, ventriloquism, polyphonism.
A ventriloquist, polyphonist.
Phonetics, phonology; voice-production.
Verbs: To utter, breathe, cry, exclaim, shout, ejaculate, vociferate; raise, lift, or strain the voice or lungs; to vocalize, prolate, articulate, enunciate, pronounce, accentuate, aspirate, deliver, mouth, rap out, speak out, speak up.
Phrase: To whisper in the ear.
Adjectives: Vocal, oral, phonetic, articulate.
Silvery, mellow, soft (413).

581 APHONY
Substantives: obmutescence, absence or want of voice, dumbness, muteness, mutism, speechlessness, aphasia, hoarseness, raucity; silence (585).
A dummy, a mute, deaf-mute.
Verbs: To render mute, to muzzle, muffle, suppress, smother, gag (585); to whisper (405).
Phrases: To stick in the throat; to close

one's lips; to shut up.
Adjectives: Aphonous, dumb, speechless, mute, tongueless, muzzled, tongue-tied, inarticulate, inaudible, unspoken, unsaid, mum, mumchance, lips close or sealed, wordless; raucous, hoase, husky, sepulchral.
Phrases: Mute as a fish; hoarse as a raven; with bated breath; *sotto voce*; with the finger on the lips; mum's the word.

582 SPEECH
Substantives: locution, talk, parlance, verbal intercourse, oral communication, word of mouth, palaver, prattle, effusion, narrative (594), tale, story, yarn, oration, recitation, delivery, say, harangue, formal speech, speechifying, sermon, homily, discourse (998), lecture, curtain lecture, pi-jaw, address, tirade, pep-talk, screed; preamble, peroration; soliloquy (589).
Oratory, elocution, rhetoric, declamation, eloquence, gift of the gab, *copia verborum,* grandiloquence, magniloquence.
A speaker, spokesman, prolocutor, mouthpiece, lecturer, orator, stumporator, speechifier; a Cicero, a Demosthenes.
Verbs: To speak, break silence, say, tell, utter, pronounce (580), open one's lips, give tongue, hold forth, make or deliver a speech, sheechify, harangue, talk, discourse, declaim, stump, flourish, spout, rant, recite, rattle off, intone, breathe, let fall, whisper in the ear, expatiate, run on; to lecture, preach, address, sermonize, preachify; to sililoquize (589); quoth he.
Phrases: To have a tongue in one's head; to have on the tip of one's tongue; to have on one's lips; to pass one's lips; to find one's tongue.
Adjectives: Speaking, etc., oral, spoken, unwritten, elocutionary, oratorical, rhetorical, declamatory, outspoken.

223

Adverbs: Viva voce; *ore rotundo*; by word of mouth.

583 STAMMERING

Substantives: inarticulateness, stuttering, impediment in one's speech, titubancy, faltering, hesitation, lisp, drawl, jabber, gibber, sputter, splutter, mumbling, mincing, muttering, mouthing, twang, a broken or cracked voice, broken accents or sentences, tardiloquence, falsetto, a whisper (405), mispronunciation.

Verbs: To stammer, stutter, hesitate, falter, hem, haw, hum and ha, mumble, lisp, jabber, gibber, mutter, sputter, splutter, drawl, mouth, mince, lisp, croak, speak through the nose, snuffle, clip one's words, mispronounce, missay.

Phrases: To clip the King's (or Queen's) English; *parler à tort et à travers*; not to be able to put two words together.

Adjectives: Stammering, etc., inarticulate, guttural, nasal, tremulous.

584 LOQUACITY

Substantives: loquaciousness, talkativeness, garrulity, flow of words, prate, gas, jaw, gab, gabble, jabber, chatter, prattle, cackle, clack, clash, blether (or blather), patter, rattle, twaddle, bibble-babble, gibble-gabble, talkee-talkee, gossip.

Fluency, flippancy, volubility, verbosity, *cacoethes loquendi*, anecdotage.

A chatterer, chatterbox, blatherskite, babbler, wind-bag, gas-bag, rattle, ranter, tub-thumper, sermonizer, proser, driveller, gossip.

Magpie, jay, parrot, poll; Babel.

Phrases: A twice (or thrice) told tale; a long yarn; the gift of the gab.

Verbs: To be loquacious, etc., to prate, palaver, chatter, prattle, jabber, jaw, rattle, twaddle, blether, babble, gabble, gas, out-talk, descant, dilate, dwell on, reel off, expatiate, prose, launch out, yarn, gossip, wag one's tongue, run on.

Phrases: To din in the ears; to drum into the ear; to spin a long yarn; to talk at random; to bum one's chat; to talk oneself out of breath; to talk nineteen to the dozen.

Adjectives: Loquacious, talkative, garrulous, gassy, gabby, open-mouthed, chatty, chattering, etc.

Fluent, voluble, glib, flippant, long-tongued, long-winded, verbose, the tongue running fast.

Adverb: Trippingly on the tongue.

585 TACITURNITY

Substantives: closeness, reverse, reticence (528), muteness, silence, curtness; aposiopesis; a clam, oyster.

Phrases: A Quaker meeting; a man of few words.

Verbs: To be silent, etc. (403), to hold one's tongue, keep silence, hold one's peace, say nothing, hold one's jaw, close one's mouth or lips, fall silent, dry up, shut up, stow it.

To render silent, silence, put to silence, seal one's lips, smother, suppress, stop one's mouth, gag, muffle, muzzle (581).

Adjectives: Taciturn, silent, close, reserved, mute, sparing of words, buttoned up, curt, short-spoken, close-tongued, tight-lipped, reticent, secretive, uncommunicative, inconversable.

Phrases: Not a word escaping one; not having a word to say.

Interjections: Hush! silence! mum! *chut!* hist! whist! wheesht!

586 ALLOCUTION

Substantives: address, apostrophe, interpellation, appeal, invocation, alloquialism, salutation, accost, greeting (894).

Feigned dialogue, imaginary conversation; inquiry (461).

Phrase: A word in the ear.

Verbs: To speak to, address, accost,

buttonhole, apostrophize, appeal to, invoke, hail, make up to, take aside, call to, halloo (or hallo), salute.
Phrases: To talk with one in private; to break the ice.
Adjectives: Accosting, etc., alloquial, invocatory, apostrophic.
Interjections: Hallo! hello! hullo! I say! hoy! oi! hey! what ho! psst!

587 RESPONSE
Substantives: answer, reply (462).
Verbs: To answer, respond, reply, etc.
Phrase: To take up one's cue.
Adjectives: Answering, responding, etc., responsive, respondent.

588 INTERLOCUTION
Substantives: collocution, colloquy, conversation, converse, confabulation, confab, talk, discourse, verbal intercourse, dialogue, duologue, logomachy, communication, intercommunication, commerce, debate.

Chat, chit-chat, crack, small talk, table-talk, tattle, gossip, tittle-tattle, babblement, clack, prittle-prattle, idle talk, town-talk, bazaar talk, *on dit,* causerie, *chronique scandaleuse.*

Conference, parley, interview, audience, tête-à-tête, reception, conversazione, palaver, pow-wow; council (686).

A talker, interlocutor, interviewer, gossip, tattler, chatterer, babbler (584), conversationalist, *causeur; dramatis personae.*
Phrases: 'The feast of reason and the flow of soul'; a heart-to-heart talk.
Verbs: To talk together, converse, collogue, commune, debate, discourse with, engage in conversation, interview; hold or carry on a conversation; chat, gossip, have a crack, put in a word, chip in, tattle, babble, prate, clack, prattle.

To confer with, hold conference, etc., to parley, palaver, commerce, hold intercourse with, be closeted with, commune with, have speech with, compare notes, intercommunicate.
Adjectives: Conversing, etc., interlocutory, verbal, colloquial, discursive, chatty, gossiping, etc., conversable, conversational.

589 SOLILOQUY
Substantives: monologue, apostrophe, aside.

Soliloquist, monologist, monologuist.
Verbs: To soliloquize, monologize; to say or talk to oneself, to say aside, to think aloud, to apostrophize.
Adjectives: Soliloquizing, etc.

590 WRITING
Substantives: chirography, pencraft, penmanship, long-hand, calligraphy, quill-driving, pen-pushing, typewriting, typing.

Scribble, scrawl, scratch, cacography, scribbling, etc., jotting, interlineation, palimpsest.

Uncial writing, court hand, cursive writing, picture writing, hieroglyphics, hieroglyph, cuneiform characters, demotic text, heiratic text, ogham, runes.

Pothooks and hangers.

Transcription, inscription, superscription, minute.

Shorthand, stenography, phonography, brachygraphy, tachygraphy, steganography.

Secret writing, writing in cipher, cryptography, polygraphy, stelography; cryptogram.

Automatic writing, planchette.

Composition, authorship, *cacoethes scribendi.*

Manuscript, MS, copy, transcript, rough copy, fair copy, carbon, black, duplicate, flimsy, handwriting, hand, fist, script, autograph, signature, signmanual, monograph, holograph, endorsement, paraph.

A scribe, amanuensis, scrivener, secretary, clerk, penman, calligraphist, copyist, transcriber, stenographer, typist.

Writer, author, scribbler, quill-driver, ink-slinger, pamphleteer, essayist, critic, reviewer, novelist (593), journalist, editor, subeditor, reporter, pressman, penny-a-liner, hack, free-lance; Grub Street, Fleet Street.

Pen, quill, fountain-pen, stylograph, stylo, ball-point, Biro, pencil, stationery, paper, parchment, vellum, tablet, slate, marble, pillar, table, etc.

Phrase: A dash or stroke of the pen.

Verbs: To write, pen, typewrite, type, write out, copy, engross, write out fair, transcribe, scribble, scrawl, scratch, interline; to sign, undersign, countersign, endorse (497), set one's hand to.

To compose, indite, draw up, draft, minute, jot down, dash off, make or take a minute of, put or set down in writing; to inscribe, to dictate.

Phrases: To take up the pen; to spill ink; to sling ink; set or put pen to paper; put on paper; commit to paper.

Adjectives: Writing, etc., written, in writing, penned, etc., scriptorial; uncial, cursive, cuneiform, runic, hieroglyphical; editorial, journalistic, reportorial.

Phrases: Under one's hand; in black and white; pen in hand; *currente calamo*.

591 PRINTING

Substantives: print, letterpress, text, context, note, page, proof, pull, revise; presswork.

Typography, stereotypography, type, character, black-letter, fount (or font), capitals, majuscules, lower-case letters, minuscules, etc.; roman, italic, type; braille.

Folio, quarto, octavo, etc.(593).

Printer, pressman, compositor, corrector of the press, proof-reader, copy-holder; printer's devil.

Printing-press, linotype, monotype, etc.

Verbs: To print, put to press, publish, edit, get out a work, etc.

Adjectives: Printed, etc.

592 CORRESPONDENCE

Substantives: letter, epistle, note, line, airgraph, postcard, chit, billet, missive, circular, favour, *billet-doux,* dispatch, bulletin, memorial, rescript, rescription.

Letter-bag, mail, post; postage.

Verbs: To correspond, write to, send a letter to.

Phrase: To keep up a correspondence.

Adjectives: Epistolary, postal.

593 BOOK

Substantives: writing, work, volume, tome, codex, opuscule, tract, manual, pamphlet, chap-book, booklet, brochure, enchiridion, circular, publication, part, issue, number, journal, album, periodical, magazine, digest, serial, ephemeris, annual, yearbook.

Writer, author, publicist, scribbler, pamphleteer, poet, essayist, novelist, fabulist, editor (590).

Book-lover, bibliophile, bibliomaniac, paperback.

Bibliography, *incunabula,* Aldine, Elzevir, etc.; library.

Publisher, bookseller, bibliopole, bibliopolist, librarian.

Folio, quarto, octavo, duodecimo, sextodecimo, octodecimo.

Paper, bill, sheet, leaf, fly-leaf, page, title-page.

Chapter, section, paragraph, passage, clause.

Adjectives: Auctorial, bookish, bibliographical, etc.

594 DESCRIPTION

Substantives: account, statement, report, return, delineation, specification, particulars, sketch, representation

(554), narration, narrative, yarn, relation, recital, rehearsal, annals, chronicle, saga, *adversaria,* journal (551), itinerary, log-book.

Historiography; historicity, historic muse, Clio.

Story, history, memoir, tale, tradition, legend, folk-tale, folk-lore, anecdote, ana, analects (596), fable, fiction, novel, novelette, thriller, whodunit, romance, short story, *conte, nouvelle,* apologue, parable; word-picture; local colour.

Biography, necrology, obituary, life, personal narrative, adventures, autobiography, confessions, reminiscences.

A historian, historiographer, narrator, *raconteur,* annalist, chronicler, biographer, fabulist, novelist, fictionist, story-teller.

Verbs: To describe, state (535), set forth, sketch, delineate, represent (554), portray, depict, paint, shadow forth, adumbrate.

To relate, recite, recount, sum up, run over, recapitulate, narrate, chronicle, rehearse, tell, give or render an account of, report, draw up a statement, spin a yarn, unfold a tale, novelize, actualize.

To take up or handle a subject; to enter into particulars, detail, etc., to characterize, particularize, detail, retail, elaborate, write up; to descend to particulars; to Boswellize.

Phrases: To plunge *in medias res*; to fight one's battles over again.

Adjectives: Descriptive, narrative, graphic, realistic, naturalistic, novelistic, historic, traditional, traditionary, legendary, storied, romantic, anecdotic, Boswellian, described, etc.

595 DISSERTATION

Substantives: treatise, tract, tractate, thesis, theme, monograph, essay, discourse, article, leading article, leader, leaderette, editorial, feuilleton, criticism, critique, review, memoir, prolusion, disquisition, exposition, exercitation, compilation, sermon, lecture, teach-in, homily, pandect, *causerie,* pamphlet (593).

Commentator, lecturer, critic, leader-writer, pamphleteer.

Verbs: To dissert, descant, treat of, discuss, write, compile, touch upon, ventilate, canvass; deal with, do justice to a subject.

Adjectives: Discursive, disquisitional, expository, compiled.

596 COMPENDIUM

Substantives: compend, summary, abstract, précis, epitome, *aperçu,* analysis, digest, sum and substance, *compte rendu, procès verbal,* draft, *exposé,* brief, recapitulation, résumé, conspectus, abridgment, abbreviation, minute, note, synopsis, argument, plot, syllabus, contents, heads, prospectus.

Scrap-book, album, note-book, commonplace-book, compilation, extracts, cuttings, clippings, text-book, analects, *analecta,* excerpts, flowers, anthology, *collectanea,* memorabilia.

Verbs: To abridge, abstract, excerpt, abbreviate, recapitulate, run over, make or prepare an abstract, etc. (201), epitomize, sum up, summarize, boil down, anthologize.

Adjectives: Compendious, etc., synoptic, abridged, etc., analectic.

Phrases: In a nutshell; in substance; in short.

597 POETRY

Substantives: poetics, poesy, the Muse, the Nine, Calliope, Parnassus, Helicon, the Pierian spring.

Verse, metre, measure, foot, numbers, strain, rhyme (or rime), head-rhyme, alliteration, rhythm, heroic verse, Alexandrine, octosyllables, *terza rima,* blank verse, free verse, *vers libre,* sprung rhythm, assonance, versification, macaronics, doggerel, jingle, prosody, orthometry, scansion.

Poem, epic, epopee, epic poem, ballad, ode, epode, idyll, lyric, eclogue, pastoral, bucolic, macaronic, dithyramb, anacreontic, sonnet, lay, roundelay, rondeau, rondel, ballade, villanelle, triolet, sestina, rhyme royal, madrigal, canzonet, libretto, posy, anthology; distich, stanza, stave, strophe, antistrophe, couplet, triplet, quatrain, cento, monody, elegy, *vers de société*.

Iambic (or iamb), trochee, spondee, dactyl, anapaest, amphibrach, amphimacer, tribrach, paeon, etc.

A poet, laureate, bard, scald, poetess, rhymer, rhymist, versifier, rhymester, sonneteer, poetaster, minor poet, minnesinger, meistersinger, troubadour, *trouvère*.

Phrase: *Genus irritabile vatum.*
Verbs: To rhyme, versify, sing, make verses, scan, poetize.
Adjectives: Poetical, poetic, Castalian, Parnassian, Heliconian, lyric, lyrical, metrical, epic, heroic; catalectic, dithyrambic, doggerel, macaronic, leonine; Pindaric, Homeric, Virgilian, Shakespearian, Miltonic, Tennysonian, etc.

598 PROSE

Substantives: prose-writer, proser, prosaist.
Verbs: To prose.
Adjectives: Prosaic, prosaical, prosing, prosy, rhymeless, unrhymed, unpoetical, commonplace, humdrum.

599 THE DRAMA

Substantives: stage, theatre, the histrionic art, dramatic art, histrionics, acting; stage effect, *mise en scène*, stage production, setting, scenery; buskin, sock, cothurnus; Melpomene, Thalia, Thespis; play-writing, dramaturgy.

Play, stage-play, piece, tragedy, comedy, tragi-comedy, morality, mystery, melodrama, farce, knockabout farce, comedietta, curtain-raiser, interlude, after-piece, vaudeville, extravaganza, *divertissement,* burletta, burlesque, variety show, revue; opera, grand opera, music-drama, comic opera, *opéra bouffe,* operetta, ballad opera, *singspiel,* musical comedy; ballet, pantomime, harlequinade, charade, wordless play, dumb-show, by-play; monodrama, monologue, duologue; masque, pageant, show; scenario, libretto, book of words, part, role; matinée, benefit; act, scene, prologue, epilogue.

Theatre, playhouse, music-hall, variety theatre; stage, the boards, the footlights, green-room, foyer, proscenium, flies, wings, stalls, box, pit, circle, dress-circle, balcony, amphitheatre, gallery.

An actor, player, stage-player, performer, artiste, comedian, comedienne, tragedian, tragedienne, Thespian, Roscius, clown, harlequin, pantaloon, *buffo*, buffoon, pierrot, pierrette, impersonator, entertainer, etc., strolling player; ballet dancer, *ballerina,* figurant, mime, star; prima donna, *primo tenore,* etc., leading lady, heavy lead, juvenile lead, *ingénue,* soubrette; supernumerary, super, walking, gentleman or lady, chorus girl; *dramatis personae*, cast, company, stock company, touring company, repertory company; a star turn.

Mummer, guiser, masquer; dancer, nautch-girl, bayadère, geisha.

Stage manager, impresario, producer, prompter, stage hands, call-boy, etc.

Dramatic writer, pantomimist, playwright, play-writer, dramatist, dramaturge, librettist.
Phrase: The profession.
Verbs: To act, enact, play, perform, personate (554), play or interpret a part, rehearse, spout, rant, gag, star, walk on.

To produce, present, stage, stage-manager.

Phrases: To strut and fret one's hour on the stage; to tread the boards.

Adjectives: Dramatic, theatre, theatrical, scenic, histrionic, comic, tragic, buskined, farcical, knock-about, slapstick, tragi-comic, melodramatic, transpontine, stagy, operatic.

599a   CINEMA

Substantives: picture theatre, picturedrome, film, motion picture, pictures, movies, flicks, pix, silver screen; silent film, sound film, talkie, flattie; three-dimensional film, 3-D, wide-screen film, deepie; documentary, trailer.

Close-up, flash-back, fade-out.

Scenario, star, vamp; cinema-goer, cinemaddict, film fan.

Verbs: To feature, screen; dub.

599b   RADIO

Substantives: wireless, receiving set, transistor, walkie-talkie; broadcast, radio play; teleprompter.

Announcer, listener.

Television, TV, video, telly; telecast, telefilm, newscast, script.

Looker-in, televiewer, viewer.

Verbs: To broadcast, televise, telecast.

To listen in, look in, view, teleview.

Phrase: On the air.

Adjective: Telegenic.

CLASS FIVE

Words relating to the voluntary powers

I

Section 1 –
Volition in General

600 WILL

Substantives: volition, voluntariness, velleity, conation, free-will, spontaneity, spontaneousness, freedom (748).

Pleasure, wish, mind, animus, breast, mood, bosom, *petto*, heart, discretion, accord.

Libertarianism.

Determination (604), predetermination (611), intention (620), choice (609).

Verbs: To will, list, think fit, see fit, think proper, determine, etc. (604), settle, choose (609), to take upon oneself, to have one's will, to do as one likes, wishes, or chooses; to use or exercise one's own discretion, to volunteer, lend oneself to.

Phrases: To have a will of one's own; *hoc volo, sic jubeo, stet pro ratione voluntas*; to take the will for the deed; to know one's own mind; to know what one is about; to see one's way; to have one's will; to take upon oneself; to take the law into one's own hands.

Adjectives: Voluntary, volitional, willing, content, minded, spontaneous, free, left to oneself, unconstrained, unfettered, autocratic, bossy, unbidden, unasked, unurged, uncompelled, of one's own accord, gratuitous, of one's own head, prepense, advised, express, designed, intended, calculated, premeditated, precon-

certed, predetermined, deliberate.

Adverbs: At will, at pleasure, *à volonté, à discrétion, ad libitum, ad arbitrium*, spontaneously, freely, of one's own accord, voluntarily, advisedly, designedly, intentionally, expressly, knowingly, determinately, deliberately, pointedly, in earnest, in good earnest, studiously, purposely, *proprio motu, suo motu, ex mero motu; quo animo.*

Phrases: With one's eyes open; in cold blood.

601 NECESSITY

Substantives: instinct, blind impulse, necessitation, ἀνάγκη, fate, fatality, destiny, doom, kismet, weird (152), foredoom, destination, election, predestination, preordination, fore-ordination, compulsion (744), subjection (749), inevitability, inevitableness.

Determinism, necessitarianism, fatalism, automatism.

A determinist, necessarian, necessitarian; robot, automaton.

The Fates, Parcae, the Three Sisters, fortune's wheel, the book of fate, the stars, astral influence, spell (152).

Phrases: Hobson's choice; what must be; a blind bargain; a *pis aller*.

Verbs: To lie under a necessity, to be fated, doomed, destined, etc. (152), to need be, have no alternative.

To necessitate, destine, doom, foredoom, predestine, preordain.

To compel, force, constrain, etc. (744), cast a spell, etc. (992).

Phrases: To make a virtue of necessity; to be pushed to the wall; to dree one's weird.

230

Adjectives: Necessitated, fated, destined, predestined, foreordained, doomed, elect, spellbound.

Compelled, forced, etc., unavoidable, inevitable, irresistible, irrevocable.

Compulsory, involuntary, unintentional, undesigned, unintended, instinctive, automatic, blind, mechanical, impulsive, unconscious, reflex, unwitting, unaware.

Deterministic, necessitarian, fatalistic.

Phrase: Unable to help it.

Adverbs: Necessarily, needs, of necessity, perforce, forcibly, compulsorily; on or by compulsion or force, willy-nilly, *nolens volens*; involuntarily, etc., impulsively (612), unwittingly (491).

Phrases: It must be; it needs must be; it is written; one's fate is sealed; *che sarà sarà*; there is no help for it; there is no alternative; nothing for it but; necessity knows no law; needs must when the devil drives.

602 WILLINGNESS

Substantives: voluntariness, disposition, inclination, leaning, *penchant,* humour, mood, vein, bent, bias, propensity, proclivity, aptitude, predisposition, predilection (865), proneness, docility, pliability (324), alacrity, earnestness, readiness, assent (448).

Phrases: A labour of love; *labor ipse voluptas.*

Verbs: To be willing, etc., to incline to, lean to, not mind (865), to propend; to volunteer.

Phrases: To find in one's heart; to set one's heart upon; to make no bones of; have a mind to; have a great mind to; 'Barkis is willin'.'

Adjectives: Willing, fain, disposed, inclined, minded, bent upon, set upon, forward, predisposed, content, favourable, hearty, ready, wholehearted, cordial, genial, keen, prepense, docile, persuadable, persuasible, facile, tract-able, easy-going, easily led.

Free, spontaneous, voluntary, gratuitous, unforced, unasked, unsummoned, unbiased, unsolicited, unbesought, undriven.

Adverbs: Willingly, freely, readily, lief, heartily, with a good grace, without reluctance, etc., as soon, of one's own accord (600), certainly, be it so (488).

Phrases: With all one's heart, *con amore*; with heart and soul; with a right good will; with a good grace; *de bon cœur*; by all means; by all manner of means; nothing loth; *ex animo*; to one's heart's content.

603 UNWILLINGNESS

Substantives: indisposition, indisposedness, backwardness, disinclination, averseness, aversion, reluctance, repugnance, demur, renitence, remissness, slackness, lukewarmness, indifference, nonchalance.

Hesitation, shrinking, recoil, suspense, dislike (867), scrupulousness, scrupulosity, delicacy, demur, scruple, qualm.

A recusant, pococurante.

Verbs: To be unwilling, etc., to demur, stick at, hesitate (605), waver, hang in suspense, scruple, stickle, boggle, falter, to hang back, hang fire, fight shy of, jib, grudge.

To decline, reject, refuse (764), refrain, keep from, abstain, recoil, shrink, reluct.

Phrases: To stick in the throat; to set one's face against; to draw the line at; I'd rather not.

Adjectives: Unwilling, unconsenting, disinclined, indisposed, averse, reluctant, not content, laggard, backward, shy, remiss, slack, indifferent, lukewarm, frigid, scrupulous, repugnant, disliking (867).

Demurring, wavering, etc., refusing (764), grudging.

Adverbs: Unwillingly, etc., perforce.

Phrases: Against the grain; *invita Minerva; malgré lui; bon gré, mal gré; nolens volens*; in spite of one's teeth; with a bad grace; not for the world; willy-nilly.

604 RESOLUTION

Substantives: determination, decision, resolve, resolvedness, fixedness, steadiness, constancy, indefatigability, unchangeableness, inflexibility, decision, finality, firmness, doggedness, tenacity of purpose, pertinacity, perseverance, constancy, solidity, stability.

Energy, manliness, vigour, spirit, spiritedness, pluck, bottom, backbone, stamina, gameness, guts, grit, sand, will, iron will; self-reliance; self-mastery; self-control.

A devotee, zealot, extremist, ultra, enthusiast, fanatic, fan; bulldog, British lion.

Verbs: To be resolved, etc., to have resolution, etc., to resolve, decide, will, persevere, determine, conclude, make up one's mind; to stand, keep, or remain firm, etc., to come to a determination, to form a resolution, to take one's stand, to stand by, hold by, hold fast, stick to, abide by, adhere to, keep one's ground, persevere, keep one's course, hold on, hang on, not to fail.

To insist upon, to make a point of.

Phrases: To determine once for all; to form a resolution; to steel oneself; to pass the Rubicon; take a decisive step; to burn one's boats; to nail one's colours to the mast; to screw one's courage to the sticking-place; to take the bull by the horns; to mean business; to set one's teeth; to keep a stiff upper lip; to keep one's chin up.

Adjectives: Resolved, resolute, game, firm, steady, steadfast, staunch, constant; solid, manly, stout.

Decided, strong-willed, determined, uncompromising, purposive, self-possessed, fixed, unmoved, unshaken, unbending, unyielding, unflagging, unflinching, inflexible, unwavering, unfaltering, unshrinking, undiverted, undeterred, immovable, not to be moved, unhesitating, unswerving.

Peremptory, inexorable, indomitable, persevering, pertinacious, persistent, irrevocable, irreversible, reverseless, decisive, final.

Strenuous, bent upon, set upon, intent upon, proof against, master of oneself, steeled, staid, serious, stiff, stiff-necked, obstinate (606).

Phrases: Firm as a rock; game to the last; true to oneself; master of oneself; *in utrumque paratus.*

Adverbs: Resolutely, etc., without fail.

Phrases: Through thick and thin; through fire and water; at all hazards; sink or swim; *coûte que coûte; fortiter in re*; like grim death.

605 IRRESOLUTION

Substantives: indecision, indetermination, demur, hesitation, suspense, uncertainty (475), hesitancy, vacillation, unsteadiness, inconstancy, wavering, fluctuation, flickering changeableness, mutability, fickleness, caprice (608), levity, *légèreté*, trimming, softness, weakness, instability.

A weathercock, trimmer, timeserver, turncoat, shuttlecock, butterfly, harlequin, chameleon.

Verbs: To be irresolute, etc., to hesitate, hang in suspense, demur, waver, vacillate, quaver, fluctuate, shuffle, boggle, flicker, falter, palter, debate, dilly-dally, shilly-shally, dally with, coquette with, swerve, etc.

Phrases: To hang fire; to hum and ha; to blow hot and cold; not to know one's own mind; to leave 'ad referendum'; letting 'I dare not' wait upon 'I would.'

Adjectives: Irresolute, undecided, unresolved, undetermined, vacillating, wavering, hesitating, faltering, shuffling, etc., half-hearted, double-minded, indicisive.

Unsteady, unsteadfast, fickle, flighty, changing, changeable, versatile, variable, inconstant, mutable, protean, fluctuating, unstable, unsettled, unhinged, unfixed, weak-kneed, spineless.

Weak, feeble-minded, frail, soft, pliant, giddy, capricious, coquettish, volatile, fitful, frothy, freakish, lightsome, light-minded, invertebrate.

Revocable, reversible.

Phrases: Infirm of purpose; without ballast; waiting to see which way the cat jumps, or the wind blows.

Adverbs: Irresolutely, etc.; off and on.

606 OBSTINACY

Substantives: obstinateness, wilfulness, self-will, pertinacity, pertinaciousness, pervicacity, pervicaciousness, tenacity, tenaciousness, inflexibility, immovability, doggedness, stubbornness, steadiness (604), restiveness, contumacy, cussedness, obduracy, obduration, unruliness.

Intolerance, dogmatism, bigotry, opinionatedness, opiniativeness, fanaticism, zealotry, infatuation, monomania, indocility, intractability, intractableness (481), pig-headedness.

An opinionist, *opiniâtre*, crank, diehard, blimp, stickler, enthusiast, monomaniac, zealot, dogmatist, fanatic, mule.

A fixed idea, rooted prejudice, blind side, obsession (481), King Charles's head.

Phrase: A bee in one's bonnet.

Verbs: To be obstinate, etc., to persist, stickle, opiniate.

Phrases: To stick at nothing; to dig in one's heels; not yield an inch.

Adjectives: Obstinate, opinionative, opinative, opinionated, opinioned, wedded to an opinion, self-opinioned, prejudiced (481), cranky, wilful, self-willed, positive, tenacious.

Stiff, stubborn, stark, rigid, stiff-necked, dogged, pertinacious, restive, pervicacious, dogmatic, arbitrary, bigoted, unpersuadable, mulish, unmoved, uninfluenced, hard-mouthed, unyielding, inflexible, immovable, pig-headed, wayward, intractable, hide-bound, headstrong, restive, refractory, unruly, infatuated, *entêté*, wrong-headed, cross-grained, obdurate, contumacious, fanatical, rabid, inexorable, impracticable.

Phrases: Obstinate as a mule; impervious to reason.

Adverbs: Obstinately, etc.

Phrases: *Non possumus; vestigia nulla retrorsum.*

607 TERGIVERSATION

Substantives: retractation, recantation, revocation, revokement, reversal, palinode, volteface, renunciation, disavowal (536), abjuration, abjurement, apostasy, relinquishment (624), repentance (950), vacillation, etc. (605).

A turncoat, rat, Janus, renegade, apostate, pervert, backslider, recidivist, trimmer, time-server, opportunist, Vicar of Bray, deserter, weathercock, etc. (605), Proteus.

Verbs: To change one's mind, etc., to retract, recant, revoke, forswear, unsay, take back, abjure, renounce, apostatize, relinquish, trim, straddle, veer round, change sides, rat, go over; pass, change, or skip from one side to another; back out, back down, swerve, flinch, balance.

Phrases: To eat one's words; turn over a new leaf; think better of it; play fast and loose; blow hot and cold; box the compass; swallow the leek; eat dirt.

Adjectives: Changeful, changeable, mobile, unsteady (605), trimming, double-faced, ambidexter, fast and loose, time-serving, facing both ways.

Fugacious, fleeting (111), revocatory.

608 CAPRICE
Substantives: fancy, fantasy, humour, whim, crotchet, fad, fike, craze, *capriccio*, quirk, freak, maggot, vagary, whimsy, whim-wham, kink, prank, shenanigans, fit, flim-flam, escapade, ploy, dido, contrariety, monkey-tricks, rag, monkey-shines, *boutade*, wild-goose chase, freakishness, skittishness, volatility, fancifulness, whimsicality, giddiness, inconsistency; a madcap.
Verbs: To be capricious, etc.
Phrases: To strain at a gnat and swallow a camel; to take it into one's head.
Adjectives: Capricious, inconsistent, fanciful, fantastic, whimsical, full of whims, etc., erratic, crotchety, faddy, maggoty, fiky, perverse, humoursome, wayward, captious, contrary, contrarious, skittish, fitful.
Phrases: The head being turned; the deuce being in him; by fits and starts.

609 CHOICE
Substantives: option, election, arbitrament, adoption, selection, excerption, co-optation, gleaning, eclecticism, lief, preference, predilection, preoption, discretion (600), fancy.

Decision, determination, adjudication, award, vote, suffrage, ballot, poll, plebiscite, referendum, verdict, voice, plumper.

Alternative, dilemma (704).

Excerpt, extract, cuttings, clippings; pick, *élite*, cream (650).

Chooser, elector, voter, constituent; electorate, constituency.
Verbs: To choose, decide, determine, elect, list, think fit, use one's discretion, fancy, shape one's course, prefer, have rather, have as lief, take one's choice, adopt, select, fix upon, pitch upon, pick out, single out, vote for, plump for, co-opt, pick up, take up, catch at, jump at, cull, glean, pick, winnow.

Phrases: To winnow the chaff from the wheat; to indulge one's fancy; to pick and choose; to take a decided step; to pass the Rubicon (604); to hold out; offer for choice; commend me to; to swallow the bait; to gorge the hook; to yield to temptation.
Adjectives: Optional, discretional, eclectic, choosing, etc., chosen, etc., decided, etc., choice, preferential; left to oneself.
Adverbs: Discretionally, at pleasure, *à plaisir, a piacere,* at discretion, at will, *ad libitum.*

Decidedly, etc., rather; once for all, either the one of the other, for one's money, for choice.

610 ABSENCE OF CHOICE
Substantives: Hobson's choice, necessity (601).

Indifference, indecision (605).
Phrase: First come, first served.
Adjectives: Neutral; indifferent, undecided.
Phrase: To sit on the fence.

REJECTION
Substantives: refusal (764); declining, repudiation, exclusion.
Verbs: To reject, refuse, etc., decline, give up, repudiate, exclude, lay aside, pigeon-hole, refrain, spare (678), abandon, turn down, blackball; to fail, plough, pluck, spin, cast.
Phrases: To lay on the shelf; to return to store; to throw overboard; to draw the line at.
Adjectives: Rejecting, etc., rejected, etc., not chosen, etc.
Phrases: Not to be thought of; out of the question.
Adverbs: Neither; neither the one nor the other, nothing to choose between them.

611 PREDETERMINATION
Substantives: premeditation, predeliberation, foregone conclusion, *parti pris.*

Verbs: To predetermine, premeditate, preconcert, resolve beforehand.

Adjectives: Prepense, premeditated, predetermined, advised, predesigned, aforethought, calculated, studied, designed (620).

Adverbs: Advisedly, deliberately, etc., with the eyes open, in cold blood.

612 IMPULSE

Substantives: sudden thought, improvisation, inspiration, flash, spurt.

Improvisator, improvisatore, improvisatrice, creature of impulse.

Verbs: To flash on the mind; to improvise, improvisate, make up, extemporize, vamp, ad-lib.

Adjectives: Extemporaneous, extemporary, impulsive, unrehearsed, unpremeditated (674), improvised, improvisatorial, improvisatory, unprompted, instinctive, spontaneous, natural, unguarded, unreflecting, precipitate.

Adverbs: Extempore, offhand, impromptu, *à l'improviste,* out of hand.

Phrases: On the spur of the moment, or of the occasion.

613 HABIT

Substantives: habitude, wont, rule, routine, jog-trot, groove, rut.

Custom, consuetude, use, usage, practice, trick, run, run of things, way, form prevalence, observance, fashion (852), etiquette, prescription, convention, *convenances,* red tape, red-tapery, red-tapism, routinism, conventionalism, vogue.

Seasoning, training, hardening, etc. (673), acclimatization, acclimation, acclimatation.

Second nature, *cocoethes,* taking root, diathesis.

A victim of habit, etc., an addict, junkie, *habitué.*

Verbs: To be habitual, etc., to be in the habit of, be wont, be accustomed to, etc.

To follow, observe, conform to, obey, bend to, comply with, accommodate oneself to, adapt oneself to; fall into a habit, convention, custom, or usage; to addict oneself to, take to, get the hang of.

To become a habit, to take root, to gain or grow upon one, to run in the blood.

To habituate, inure, harden, season, form, train, accustom, familiarize, naturalize, acclimatize, conventionalize, condition.

To acquire a habit, to get into the way of, to learn, etc.

Phrases: To follow the multitude; go with the current, stream, etc.; run on in a groove; do in Rome as the Romans do.

Adjectives: Habitual, accustomed, prescriptive, habituated, etc.; in the habit, etc., of; used to, addicted to, attuned to, wedded to, at home in; usual, wonted, customary, hackneyed, commonplace, trite, ordinary, set, stock, established, accepted, stereotyped, received, acknowledged, recognized; groovy, fixed, rooted, permanent, inveterate, ingrained, running in the blood, hereditary, congenital, innate, inborn, besetting, natural, instinctive, etc. (5).

Fashionable, in fashion, in vogue, according to use, routine, conventional, etc.

Phrases: Bred in the bone; in the blood.

Adverbs: Habitually; as usual, as the world goes, *more suo, pro more, pro forma,* according to custom, *de rigueur.*

614 DESUETUDE

Substantives: disuse, want of habit or of practice, inusitation, newness to.

Non-observance (773), infraction, violation, infringement.

Phrase: 'A custom more honoured in the breach than the observance.'

Verbs: To be unaccustomed, etc., to

be new to; to leave off, wean oneself of, break off, break through, infringe, violate, etc., a habit, usage, etc.; to disuse, to wear off.

Adjectives: Unaccustomed, unused, unusual, unwonted, unpractised, unprofessional, unfashionable, non-observant, lax, disused, weaned.

Unseasoned, uninured, untrained, green.

Unhackneyed, unconventional, Bohemian (83).

615 MOTIVE

Substantives: reason, ground, principle, mainspring, *primum mobile,* account, score, sake, consideration, calculation, *raison d'être.*

Inducement, recommendation, encouragement, attraction, allectation, temptation, enticement, bait, allurement, charm, witchery, bewitchment.

Persuasibility, softness, susceptibility, attractability, impressibility.

Influence, prompting, dictate, instance, impulse, impulsion, incitement, incitation, press, instigation, excitement, provocation, invitation, solicitation, advocacy, call, suasion, persuasion, hortation, exhortation, seduction, cajolery, tantalization, *agacerie,* seducement, fascination, blandishment, inspiration, honeyed words.

Incentive, stimulus, spur, fillip, urge, goad, rowel, provocative, whet, dram, cocktail, pick-me-up, appetizer.

Bribe, graft, sop, lure, decoy, charm, spell, magnetism, magnet, loadstone.

Prompter, tempter, seducer, seductor, siren, Circe, instigator, *agent provocateur.*

Phrases: The pros and cons; the why and wherefore.

The golden apple; a red herring; a sop for Cerberus; the voice of the tempter; the song of the sirens.

Verbs: To induce, move, lead, draw, draw over, carry, bring, to influence, to weigh with, bias, to operate, work upon, engage, incline, dispose, predispose, put up to, prompt, whisper, call, call upon, recommend, encourage, entice, invite, solicit, press, enjoin, entreat (765), court, plead, advocate, exhort, enforce, dictate, tantalize, bait the hook, tempt, allure, lure, seduce, decoy, draw on, captivate, fascinate, charm, bewitch, conciliate, wheedle, coax, speak fair, carny (or carney), cajole, pat on the back or shoulder, talk over, inveigle, persuade, prevail upon, get to do, bring over, procure, lead by the nose, sway, over-persuade, come over, get round, turn the head, enlist, retain, kidnap, bribe, suborn, tamper with.

To act upon, to impel, excite, suscitate, stimulate, key up, motivate, incite, animate, instigate, provoke, set on, urge, pique, spirit, inspirit, inspire, awaken, buck up, give a fillip, light up, kindle, enkindle, rekindle, quicken, goad, spur, prick, edge, egg on, hurry on, stir up, work up, fan, fire, inflame, set on fire, fan the flame, blow the coals, stir the embers, put on one's mettle, set on, force, rouse, arouse, lash into fury, get a rise out of.

Phrases: To grease the palm; to gild the pill; to work the oracle.

To follow the bent of; to follow the dictates of; to yield to temptation; to act on principle.

Adjectives: Impulsive, motive, persuasive, hortative, hortatory, seductive, carnying, suasory, suasive, honey-tongued, attractive, tempting, alluring, piquant, exciting, inviting, tantalizing, etc.

Persuadable, persuasible, suasible, soft, yielding, facile, easily persuaded, etc.

Induced, moved, disposed, led, persuaded, etc., spellbound, instinct with or by.

Adverbs: Because, for, since, on

account of, out of, from; by reason of, for the sake of, on the score of.

As, forasmuch as, therefore, hence, why, wherefore; for all the world.
Phrase: *Hinc illae lacrimae.*

616 ABSENCE OF MOTIVE
Substantives: caprice (608).
Adjectives: Aimless, motiveless, pointless, purposeless (621); uninduced, unmoved, unactuated, uninfluenced, unbiased, unimpelled, unswayed, impulsive, wanton, unprovoked, uninspired, untempted, unattracted.
Phrase: Without rhyme or reason.

DISSUASION
Substantives: dehortation, discouragement, remonstrance, expostulation, deprecation (766).

Inhibition, check, restraint, curb (752), bridle, rein, stay, damper, chill; deterrent, disincentive.

Scruple, qualm, demur (867), reluctance, delicacy (868); counterattraction.
Phrase: A wet blanket.
Verbs: To dissuade, dehort, discourage, disincline, indispose, dispirit, damp, choke off, dishearten, disenchant, disillusion, deter, keep back, put off, render averse, etc.

To withhold, restrain, hold, hold back, check, bridle, curb, rein in, keep in, inhibit, censor, repel (751).

To cool, blunt, calm, quiet, quench, slake, stagger, remonstrate, expostulate, warn, deprecate (766).

To scruple, refrain, abstain, etc. (603).
Phrases: To throw cold water on; to turn a deaf ear to.
Adjectives: Dissuading, etc., dissuasive, dehortatory, expostulatory, deprecatory.

Dissuaded, discouraged, etc.

Repugnant, averse, scrupulous, etc. (867), unpersuadable (606).

617 PLEA
Substantives: allegation, pretext, pretence, excuse, alibi, cue, colour, gloss, salvo, loophole, handle, shift, quirk, guise, stalking-horse, makeshift, white lie, evasion, get-out, special pleading (477), claptrap, advocation, soft sawder, blarney (933), moonshine; a lame excuse or apology.
Verbs: To make a pretext, etc., of; to use as a plea, etc.; to plead, allege, pretend, excuse, make a handle, etc., of, make capital of.
Adjectives: Ostensible, colourable, pretended, alleged, etc.
Phrases: *Ad captandum; qui s'excuse s'accuse*; playing to the gallery.

618 GOOD
Substantives: benefit, advantage, service, interest, weal, boot, gain, profit, velvet, good turn, blessing, boon; behoof, behalf.

Luck, piece of luck, windfall, strike, treasure trove, godsend, bonus, bunce, bonanza, prize; serendipity.

Goodness (648), utility (644), remedy (662).
Phrases: The main chance; *summum bonum; cui bono?*
Adjectives: Good, etc. (648), gainful (644).
Adverbs: Aright, well, favourably, satisfactorily, for the best.

In behalf of, in favour of.

619 EVIL
Substantives: harm, ill, injury, wrong, scathe, curse, detriment, hurt, damage, disservice, ill-turn, bale, grievance, prejudice, loss, mischief, devilry (or deviltry), gravamen.

Disadvantage, drawback, trouble, vexation (828), annoyance, nuisance, molestation, oppression, persecution, plague, corruption (659).

Blow, dunt, knock (276), bruise, scratch, wound, mutilation, outrage, spoliation, mayhem, plunder, pillage, rapine, destruction (791), dilapidation, havoc, ravage, devastation, inroad, sweep, sack, foray (716), desolation, *razzia,* dragonnade.

Misfortune, mishap, woe, disaster, calamity, affliction, catastrophe, downfall, ruin (735), prostration, curse, wrack, blight, blast; Pandora's box; a plague-spot.

Cause of evil, bane (663).

Phrases: Bad show; there's the devil to pay.

Adjectives: Bad, hurtful, etc. (649).

Adverbs: Amiss, wrong, evil, ill.

Section 2 – Prospective Volition

620 INTENTION

Substantives: intent, purpose, design, purport, mind, meaning, drift (516), animus, view, set purpose, point, bent, turn, proposal, study, scope, purview.

Final cause, object, aim, end, motive (615), *raison d'être*; destination, mark, point, butt, goal, target, prey, quarry, game, objective; the philosophers' stone.

Decision, determination, resolve, resolution (604), predetermination (611); set purpose.

A hobby, ambition, wish (865).

Study of final causes, teleology; study of final issues, eschatology.

Verbs: To intend, purpose, plan (626), design, destine, mean, aim at, propose to oneself.

To be at, drive at, be after, point at, level at, take aim, aspire at or after, endeavour after.

To meditate, think of, dream of, premeditate (611), contemplate, compass.

To propose, project, devise, take into one's head.

Phrases: To have in view; to have an eye to; to take upon oneself; to have to do; to see one's way; to find in one's heart.

Adjectives: Intended, etc., inten-tional, deliberate, advised, studied, minded, express, prepense (611), aforethought; set upon, bent upon, intent upon, in view, *in petto,* in prospect; teleological, eschatological.

Phrases: In the wind; *sur le tapis*; on the stocks; in contemplation.

Adverbs: Intentionally, etc., expressly, knowingly, wittingly, designedly, purposely, on purpose, with a view to, with an eye to, for the purpose of, with the view of, in order to, to the end that, on account of, in pursuance of, pursuant to, with the intent, etc.

Phrases: In good earnest; with one's eyes open; to all intents and purposes.

621 CHANCE

Substantives: fortune, accident, hazard, hap, haphazard (156), lot, fate (601), chance-medley, hit, fluke, casualty, contingency, exigency, fate, adventure, random shot, off chance, toss-up, gamble.

A godsend, luck, a run of luck, a turn of the dice or cards, a break, windfall, etc. (618).

Drawing lots, sortilege, *sortes Virgilianae.*

Wager, bet, flutter, betting, gambling; pitch-and-toss, *roulette, rouge-et-noir.*

Phrases: A blind bargain; a pig in a poke.

Verbs: To chance, hap, turn up; to stand a chance.

To risk, venture, hazard, speculate, stake; incur or run the risk; bet, wager, punt, gamble, plunge, raffle.

Phrases: To take one's chance; to chance it; to chance one's arm; try one's luck; shuffle the cards; put into a lottery; lay a wager; toss up; spin a coin; cast lots; draw lots; stand the hazard.

To buy a pig in a poke; *alea jacta est*; the die being cast; to go nap on; to put one's shirt on.

Adjectives: Casual, fortuitous, accidental, inadvertent, fluky, contingent, random, hit-or-miss, happy-go-lucky, adventitious, incidental.

Unintentional, involuntary, aimless, driftless, undesigned, undirected; purposeless, causeless, without purpose, etc., unmeditated, unpurposed, indiscriminate, promiscuous.

On the cards, possible (470), at stake.

Adverbs: Casually, etc., by chance, by accident, accidentally, etc., at haphazard, at a venture; heads or tails.

Phrase: As luck would have it.

622 PURSUIT

Substantives: pursuance, undertaking, enterprise (676), emprise, adventure, game, hobby, endeavour.

Prosecution, search, angling, chase, venery, quest, hunt, shikar, race, battue, drive, course, direction, wild-goose chase, steeplechase, point-to-point.

Pursuer, huntsman, hunter, Nimrod, shikari, hound, greyhound, foxhound, whippet, bloodhound, sleuth-hound, beagle, harrier.

Verbs: To pursue, undertake, engage in, take in hand, carry on, prosecute (461), endeavour.

To court, seek, angle, chase, give chase, course, dog, stalk, trail, hunt, drive, follow, run after, hound, bid for, aim at, take aim, make a leap at, rush upon, jump at, quest, shadow, tail, chivy.

Phrases: Take or hold a course; tread a path; shape one's course; direct or bend one's steps or course; run a race; rush headlong; rush head-foremost; make a plunge; snatch at, etc.; start game; follow the scent; to run or ride full tilt at.

Adjectives: Pursuing, etc., in hot pursuit; in full cry.

Adverbs: In order to, in order that, for the purpose of, with a view to, etc. (620); on the scent of.

Interjections: Yoicks! tally-ho!

623 AVOIDANCE

Substantives: forbearance, abstention, abstinence, sparing, refraining.

Flight, escape (671), evasion, elusion.

Motive for avoidance, counter-attraction.

Shirker, slacker, quitter, truant, fugitive, runaway.

Verbs: To avoid, refrain, abstain; to spare, hold, shun, fly, slope, flee, eschew, run away from, shrink, hold back, draw back (287), recoil from, flinch, blench, shy, elude, evade, shirk, blink, parry, dodge, let alone.

Phrases: To give the slip or go-by; to part company; to beat a retreat; get out of the way; to give one a wide berth; steer clear of; fight shy of; to take to one's heels.

Adjectives: Avoiding, etc., elusive, evasive, flying, fugitive, runaway, shy, retiring; unattempted, unsought.

Adverbs: Lest, with a view to prevent.

Phrases: *Sauve qui peut*; the devil take the hindmost.

624 RELINQUISHMENT

Substantives: dereliction, abandonment (782), renunciation, desertion (607), discontinuance (142).

Dispensation, riddance.

Verbs: To relinquish, give up (782); lay, set, or put aside; drop, yield, resign, abandon, renounce, discard, shelve, pigeon-hole, waive, desist from, desert, defect, leave, leave off, back out of, quit, throw up, chuck up, give over, forgo, give up, forsake, throw over, forswear, swerve from (279), put away, discontinue (681).

Phrases: To drop all idea of; to think better of it; to wash one's hands of; to turn over a new leaf; to throw up the sponge; to have other fish to fry; to draw in one's horns; to lay on the shelf; to move the previous question.

To give warning; to give notice; to ask for one's books.

Adjectives: Relinquishing, etc., relinquished, etc., unpursued.

Interjections: Hands off! keep off! give over! chuck it!

625 BUSINESS

Substantives: affair, concern, matter, task, work, job, job of work, assignment, darg, chore, stint, stunt, errand, agenda, commission, office, charge, part, duty, role; a press of business.

Province, department, beat, round, routine, mission, function, vocation, calling, avocation, profession, occupation, pursuit, cloth, faculty, trade, industry, commerce, art, craft, mystery, walk, race, career, walk of life, *métier*.

Place, post, orb, sphere, field, line, capacity, employment, engagement, exercise, occupation; situation, undertaking (676).

Verbs: To carry on or run a business, ply one's trade, keep a shop, etc.; to officiate, serve, act, traffic.

Phrases: To have to do with; have on one's hands; betake oneself to; occupy or concern oneself with; go in for; have on one's shoulders; make it one's business; go to do; act a part; perform the office of or functions of; to enter or take up a profession; spend time upon; busy oneself with, about, etc.

Adjectives: Business-like, official, functional, professional, workaday, commercial, in hand.

Adverbs: On hand, on foot, afoot, afloat, going.

Phrase: In the swim.

626 PLAN

Substantives: scheme, device, design, project, proposal, proposition, suggestion.

Line of conduct, game, card course,

tactics, strategy, policy, polity (692), craft, practice, campaign, platform, plank, ticket, agenda, orders of the day, gambit.

Intrigue, cabal, plot, conspiracy, complot, racket, machination, *coup d'état*.

Measure, step, precaution, proceeding, procedure, process, system, economy, set-up, organization, expedient, resource, contrivance; invention, artifice, shift, makeshift, gadget, stopgap, manœuvre, stratagem, fetch, trick, dodge, machination, intrigue, stroke, stroke of policy, masterstroke, great gun, trump card.

Alternative, loophole, counterplot, counter-project, side-wind, last resort, *dernier ressort, pis aller*.

Sketch, outline, blue-print, programme, draft (or draught), scenario, *ébauche*, rough draft, skeleton, forecast, prospectus, *carte du pays*, bill of fare, menu.

After-course, after-game, after-thought, *arrière-pensée*, under-plot.

A projector, designer, schemer, contriver, strategist, promoter, organizer, *entrepreneur*, artist, schematist, intriguant.

Verbs: To plan, scheme, devise, imagine, design, frame, contrive, project, plot, conspire, cabal, intrigue (702), think out, invent, forecast, strike out, work out, chalk out, rough out, sketch, lay out, lay down, cut out, cast, recast, map out, countermine, hit upon, fall upon, arrange, mature, organize, systematize, concert, concoct, digest, pack, prepare, hatch, elaborate, make shift, make do, wangle.

Phrases: To have many irons in the fire; to dig a mine; to lay a train; to spring a project; to take or adopt a course; to make the best of a bad job; to work the oracle.

Adjectives: Planned, etc., strategic; planning, scheming, etc.

Well-laid, deep-laid, cunning, well-devised, etc., maturely considered, well-weighed, prepared, organized, etc.

Adverbs: In course of preparation, under consideration, on the anvil, on the stocks, in the rough, *sur le tapis; faute de mieux.*

627 WAY
Substantives: method, manner, wise, form, mode, guise, fashion.

Path, road, gait, route, channel, walk, access, course, pass, ford, ferry, passage, line of way, trajectory, orbit, track, ride, avenue, approach, beaten track, pathway, highway, roadway, causeway, footway, pavement, sidewalk, subway, *trottoir*, footpath, bridle path, corduroy road, cinder-path, turnpike road, high road, arterial road, *autobahn*, clearway, boulevard, the King's (or Queen's) highway, thoroughfare, street, lane, alley, gang-way, hatchway, cross-road, crossway, flyover, cut, short cut, royal road, cross-cut, *carrefour*, promenade.

Railway, railroad, tramway, tube, underground, elevated; canal.

Bridge, viaduct, stepping-stone, stair, corridor, aisle, lobby, staircase, moving staircase, escalator, companion-way, flight of stairs, ladder, step-ladder, stile, scaffold, scaffolding, lift, hoist, elevator; speedwalk, travolator.

Indirect way: By-path, by-way, by-walk, by-road, back door, backstairs.

Inlet, gate, door, gateway (260), portal, porch, doorway, adit, conduit, tunnel.

Phrase: *Modus operandi.*

Adverbs: How, in what way, in what manner, by what mode.

By the way, *en passant*, by the by, via, *in transitu, chemin faisant.*

One way or another, somehow, anyhow, by hook or by crook.

Phrases: All roads lead to Rome; *hae*

tibi erunt artes; where there's a will there's a way.

628 MID-COURSE
Substantives: middle course, middle (68), mean (29), golden mean, *juste milieu, mezzo termine.*

Direct, straight, straightforward, course or path; great-circle sailing.

Neutrality, compromise.

Verbs: To keep in a middle course, etc.; to compromise, go half-way.

Adjectives: Undeviating, direct, straight, straightforward.

Phrases: *In medio tutissimus ibis*; to sit on the fence.

629 CIRCUIT
Substantives: roundabout way, zig-zag, circuition, detour, circumbendibus (311), wandering, deviation (279), divergence (291).

Verbs: To perform a circuit, etc., to deviate, wander, go round about, meander, etc. (279).

Phrases: To beat about the bush; to make two bites of a cherry; to lead one a pretty dance.

Adjectives: Circuitous, indirect, roundabout, tortuous, zigzag, etc.

Adverbs: By a roundabout way, by an indirect course, etc.

630 REQUIREMENT
Substantives: requisition, need, occasion, lack, wants, requisites, necessities, desideratum, exigency, pinch, *sine qua non,* the very thing, essential, must.

Needfulness, essentiality, necessity, indispensability, urgency, call for.

Phrases: Just what the doctor ordered; a crying need; a long-felt want.

Verbs: To require, need, want, have occasion for, stand in need of, lack, desire, be at a loss for, desiderate; not to be able to do without or dispense with; to want but little.

To render necessary, to necessitate,

to create a necessity for, demand, call for.

Adjectives: Requisite, required, etc., needful, necessary, imperative, exigent, essential, indispensable, irreplaceable, prerequisite, that cannot be spared or dispensed with, urgent.

631 INSTRUMENTALITY

Substantives: medium, intermedium, vehicle, channel, intervention, mediation, dint, aid (707), agency (170).

Minister, handmaid; obstetrician, midwife, *accoucheur.*

Key, master-key, passport, safe-conduct, passe-partout, 'open sesame'; a go-between, middleman (758), a cat's-paw, jackal, pander, tool, ghost, main-stay, trump card.

Phrase: Two strings to one's bow.

Verbs: To subserve, minister, intervene, mediate, devil, pander to.

Adjectives: Instrumental, intervening, intermediate, intermediary, subservient, auxiliary, ancillary.

Adverbs: Through, by, with, by means of, by dint of, *à force de,* along with, thereby, through the medium, etc., of, wherewith, wherewithal.

632 MEANS

Substantives: resources, wherewithal, appliances, ways and means, convenience, expedients, step, measure (626), aid (707), intermedium, medium.

Machinery, mechanism, mechanics, engineering, mechanical powers, automation, scaffolding, ladder, mainstay.

Phrases: Wheels within wheels; a shot in the locker.

Adjectives: Instrumental, accessory, subsidiary, mechanical.

Adverbs: How, by what means, by all means, by all manner of means, by the aid of, by dint of.

Phrases: By hook or by crook; somehow or other; for love or money; by fair means or foul; *quocumque modo.*

633 INSTRUMENT

Substantives: tool, implement, appliance, contraption, apparatus, utensil, device, gadget, craft, machine, engine, motor, dynamo, generator, mill, lathe.

Equipment, gear, tackle, tackling, rigging, harness, trappings, fittings, accoutrements, paraphernalia, equipage, outfit, appointments, furniture, material, plant, appurtenances.

A wheel, jack, clockwork, wheelwork, spring, screw, turbine, wedge, flywheel, lever, bascule, pinion, crank, winch, crane, capstan, windlass, pulley, hammer, mallet, mattock, mall, bat, racket, sledge-hammer, mace, club, truncheon, pole, staff, bill, crow, crowbar, poleaxe, handspike, crutch, boom, bar, pitchfork, etc.

Organ, limb, arm, hand, finger, claw, paw, talons, tentacle, wing, oar, paddle, pincer, plier, forceps, thimble.

Handle, hilt, haft, shaft, shank, heft, blade, trigger, tiller, helm, treadle, pummel, peg (214, 215), key.

Edge-tool, hatchet, axe, pickaxe, etc. (253), axis (312).

634 SUBSTITUTE

Substantives: shift, makeshift, succedaneum (147), stop-gap, expedient, *pis aller,* surrogate, understudy, pinch-hitter, stand-in, locum tenens, proxy, deputy (759).

635 MATERIALS

Substantives: material, matter, stuff, constituent, ingredient (56), pabulum, fuel, grist, provender, provisions, food (298).

Supplies, munition, ammunition, reinforcement, relay, contingents.

Baggage, luggage, bag and baggage, effects, goods, chattels, household stuff, equipage, paraphernalia, impedimenta, stock-in-trade, cargo, lading (780).

Metal, stone, ore, brick, clay, wood, timber, composition, compo, plastic.

636 STORE

Substantives: stock, fund, supply, reserve, relay, budget, quiver, *corps de réserve,* reserve fund, mine, quarry, vein, lode, fountain, well, spring, milch cow.

Collection, accumulation, heap (72), hoard, cache, stockpile, magazine, pile, rick, nest-egg, savings, bank (802), treasury, reservoir, repository, repertory, repertoire, album, depot, depository, treasure, thesaurus, museum, storehouse, promptuary, reservatory, conservatory, menagerie, aviary, aquarium, receptacle, ware-house, godown, *entrepôt,* dock, larder, cellar, garner, granary, store-room, box-room, lumber-room, silo, cistern, well, tank, gasometer, mill-pond, armoury, arsenal, coffer (191).

Verbs: To store, stock, stockpile, trea-sure up, lay in, lay by, lay up, file, garner, save, husband, hoard, deposit, amass, accumulate (72).

To reserve, keep back, hold back.

Phrase: To husband one's resources.

Adjectives: Stored, etc., in store, in reserve, spare, surplus, extra.

637 PROVISION

Substantives: supply, providing, sup-plying, sustentation (707), purveyance, purveying, reinforcement, husband-ing, commissariat, victualling.

Forage, pasture, food, provender (298).

A purveyor, caterer, contractor, commissary, quartermaster, sutler, victualler, *restaurateur,* feeder, batman; bum-boat.

Verbs: To provide, supply, furnish, purvey, suppeditate, replenish, fill up, feed, stock with, recruit, victual, cater, find, fend, keep, lay in, lay in store, store, stockpile, forage, husband (636), upholster.

Phrase: To bring grist to the mill.

638 WASTE

Substantives: consumption, expendi-ture, exhaustion, drain, leakage, wear and tear, dispersion (73), ebb, loss, misuse, prodigality (818), seepage, squandermania.

Verbs: To waste, spend, expend, use, consume, spill, leak, run out, run to waste, disperse (73), ebb, dry up, impoverish, drain, empty, exhaust; to fritter away, squander.

Phrases: To cast pearls before swine; to burn the candle at both ends; to employ a steam-hammer to crack nuts; to break a butterfly on a wheel; to pour water into a sieve.

Adjectives: Wasted, spent, profuse, lavish, etc., at a low ebb.

Phrase: Penny wise and pound foolish.

639 SUFFICIENCY

Substantives: adequacy, competence; enough, satiety.

Fullness, fill, plenitude, plenty, abundance, copiousness, amplitude, affluence, richness, fertility, lux-uriance, uberty, foison.

Heaps, lots, bags, piles, lashings, oceans, oodles, mobs.

Impletion, repletion, saturation.

Riches (803), mine, store, fund, (636); a bumper, a brimmer, a bellyful, a cart-load, truck-load, ship-load; a plumper; a charge.

A flood, draught, shower, rain (347), stream, tide, spring tide, flush.

Phrases: The horn of plenty; the horn of Amalthea; cornucopia; the fat of the land.

Verbs: To be sufficient, etc., to suffice, serve, pass muster, to do, satisfy, satiate, sate, saturate, make up.

To abound, teem, stream, flow, rain, shower down, pour, swarm, bristle with.

To render sufficient, etc., to make up, to fill, charge, replenish, pour in; swim in, wallow in, roll in.

Adjectives: Sufficient, enough,

adequate, commensurate, what will just do.

Moderate, measured.

Full, ample, plenty, copious, plentiful, plenteous, plenary, wantless, abundant, abounding, flush, replete, laden, charged, fraught; well stocked or provided, liberal, lavish, unstinted, to spare, unsparing, unmeasured; *ad libitum,* wholesale.

Brimful, to the brim, chock-full, saturated, crammed, up to the ears, fat, rich, affluent, full up, luxuriant, lush.

Unexhausted, unwasted, exhaustless, inexhaustible.

Phrases: Enough and to spare; cut and come again; full as an egg; ready to burst; plentiful as blackberries; flowing with milk and honey; enough in all conscience; enough to go round; *quantum sufficit.*

Adverbs: Amply, etc., galore.

640 INSUFFICIENCY

Substantives: inadequacy, inadequateness, incompetence.

Deficiency, stint, paucity, defect, defectiveness, default, defalcation, deficit, shortcoming, falling short (304), too little, what will not do, scantiness, slenderness, a mouthful, etc. (32).

Scarcity, dearth, shortage, want, need, lack, exigency, inanition, indigence, poverty, penury (804), destitution, dole, pittance, short allowance, short commons, a banian day, fast (956), a mouthful, starvation, malnutrition, famine, drought, depletion, emptiness, vacancy, flaccidity, ebbtide, low water.

Phrase: 'A beggarly account of empty boxes.'

Verbs: To be insufficient, etc., not to suffice, to come short of, to fall short of, fail, run out of, stop short, to want, lack, need, require (630); caret.

To render insufficient, etc., to stint, grudge, hold back, withhold, starve, pinch, skimp, scrimp, famish.

Phrase: To live from hand to mouth.

Adjectives: Insufficient, inadequate, incompetent, too little, not enough, etc., scant, scanty, skimpy, scrimpy, deficient, defective, in default, scarce, empty, empty-handed, devoid, short of, out of, wanting, etc., hard up for.

Destitute, dry, drained, unprovided, unsupplied, unfurnished, unreplenished, unfed, unsorted, untreasured, bare, meagre, poor, thin, spare, skimpy, stinted, starved, famished, pinched, fasting, starveling, jejune, without resources (735), short-handed, undermanned, understaffed, etc.

Phrases: In short supply; not to be had for love or money; at the end of one's tether; at one's last gasp.

641 REDUNDANCE

Substantives: superabundance, superfluity, superfluence, glut, exuberance, profuseness, profusion, plethora, engorgement, congestion, surfeit, gorge, load, turgidity, turgescence, dropsy.

Excess, nimiety, overdose, oversupply, overplus, surplus, surplusage, overflow, inundation, deluge, extravagance, prodigality (818), exorbitance, lavishness, immoderation.

An expletive (908), pleonasm.

Phrases: *Satis superque*; a drug in the market; the lion's share.

Verbs: To superabound, overabound, run over, overflow, flow over, roll in, wallow in.

To overstock, overdose, overlay, gorge, engorge, glut, sate, satiate, surfeit, cloy, load, overload, surcharge, overrun, choke, drown, drench, inundate, flood, whelm, deluge.

Phrases: To go begging; it never rains but it pours; to paint the lily; to carry coals to Newcastle.

Adjectives: Redundant, superfluous, exuberant, superabundant, immoderate, extravagant, excessive, in excess, *de trop*, needless, unnecessary, uncalled-for, over and above (40), more than enough, buckshee, running to waste, overflowing, running over.

Turgid, gorged, plethoric, dropsical, replete, profuse, lavish, prodigal, supervacaneous, extra, spare, duplicate, supernumerary, supererogatory, expletive, surcharged, overcharged, sodden, overloaded, overladen, overburdened, overrun, overfed, overfull.
Phrase: Enough and to spare.
Adverbs: Over, over and above, too much, overmuch, over and enough, too far, without measure, without stint.
Phrase: Over head and ears.

642 IMPORTANCE
Substantives: consequence, moment, weight, gravity, seriousness, consideration, concern, significance, import, influence (175), pressure, urgency, instancy, stress, emphasis, interest, preponderance, prominence (250), greatness (31).

The substance, essence, quintessence, core, kernel, nub, gist, pith, marrow, soul, point, gravamen.

The principal, prominent, or essential part.

A notability, somebody, personage (875), VIP, bigwig, toff, big pot, big gun, his nibs; great doings, *notabilia,* a red-letter day.
Phrases: *A sine qua non*; a matter of life and death; no laughing matter.
Verbs: To be important, or of importance, etc., to signify, import, matter, boot, weigh, count, to be prominent, etc., to take the lead.

To attach, or ascribe importance to; to value, care for, etc. (897); overestimate, etc. (482), exaggerate (549).

To mark, underline, italicize, score, accentuate, emphasize, stress, rub in.
Phrases: To be somebody; to fill the bill; to make much of; to make a stir, a

fuss, a piece of work, a song and dance; set store upon; to lay stress upon; to take *au grand sérieux*.
Adjectives: Important, of importance, etc., grave, serious, material, weighty, influential, significant, emphatic, momentous, earnest, pressing, critical, preponderating, pregnant, urgent, paramount, essential, vital.

Great, considerable, etc. (31), capital, leading, principal, superior, chief, main, prime, primary, cardinal, prominent, salient, egregious, outstanding.

Signal, notable, memorable, remarkable, etc., grand, solemn, eventful, stirring, impressive; not to be despised, or overlooked, etc., unforgettable, worth while.
Phrases: Being no joke; not to be sneezed at; no small beer.

643 UNIMPORTANCE
Substantives: indifference, insignificance, triflingness, triviality, triteness; paltriness, emptiness, nothingness, inanity, lightness, levity, frivolity, vanity, frivolousness, puerility, child's play.

Poverty, meagreness, meanness, shabbiness, etc. (804).

A trifle, small matter, minutiae, bagatelle, cipher, moonshine, molehill, joke, jest, snap of the fingers, flea-bite, pinch of snuff, old song, *nugae,* fiddlestick, fiddlestick end, bubble, bulrush, nonentity, lay figure, nobody.

A straw, pin, fig, button, rush, feather, farthing, brass farthing, red cent, dime, dam, doit, peppercorn, pebble, small fry.

Trumpery, trash, codswallop, stuff, *fatras,* frippery, chaff, drug, froth, smoke, cobweb.

Toy, plaything, knick-knack, gimcrack, gewgaw, thingumbob, bauble, kickshaw, bric-à-brac, fal-lal, whim-wham, whigmaleerie, curio, bibelot.

Refuse, lumber, junk, litter, orts,

tares, weeds, sweepings, scourings, off-scourings; rubble, debris, dross, scoriae, dregs, scum, flue, dust (653).

Phrases: 'Leather and prunella'; *peu de chose*; much ado about nothing; much cry and little wool; flotsam and jetsam; a man of straw; a stuffed shirt; a toom tabard.

Verbs: To be unimportant, to be of little or no importance, etc.; not to signify, not to deserve, merit, or be worthy of notice, regard, consideration, etc.

Phrases: To catch at straws; to make much ado about nothing; to cut no ice; *le jeu ne vaut pas la chandelle.*

Adjectives: Unimportant, secondary, inferior, immaterial, inconsiderable, inappreciable, insignificant, unessential, non-essential, beneath notice, indifferent; of little or no account, importance, consequence, moment, interest, etc.; unimpressive, subordinate.

Trifling, trivial, trite, banal, mere, common, so-so, slight, slender, flimsy, trumpery, foolish, idle, puerile, childish, infantile, frothy, trashy, catchpenny, fiddling, frivolous, commonplace, contemptible, cheap.

Vain, empty, inane, poor, sorry, mean, meagre, shabby, scrannel, vile, miserable, scrubby, weedy, niggling, beggarly, piddling, peddling, pitiful, pitiable, despicable, paltry, ridiculous, farcical, finical, finicking, finicky, finikin, fiddle-faddle, wishy-washy, namby-pamby, gimcrack, twopenny, twopenny-halfpenny, two-by-four, one-horse, piffling, jerry, jerry built.

Phrases: Not worth a straw; as light as air; not worth mentioning; not worth boasting about; no great shakes; nothing to write home about; small potatoes; neither here nor there.

Interjections: No matter! pshaw! pooh! pooh-pooh! shucks! I should worry! fudge! fiddle-de-dee! nonsense! boloney! hooey! nuts! rats! stuff! *n'importe!*

Adverbs: Meagrely, pitifully, vainly, etc.

644 UTILITY

Substantives: service, use, function, office, sphere, capacity, part, role, task, work.

Usefulness, worth, stead, avail, advantageousness, profitableness, serviceableness, merit, *cui bono,* applicability, adequacy, subservience, subserviency, efficacy, efficiency, help, money's worth.

Verbs: To be useful, etc., of use, of service.

To avail, serve, subserve, help (707), conduce, answer, profit, advantage, accrue, bedstead.

To render useful, to use (677), to turn to account, to utilize, to make the most of.

Phrases: To stand in good stead; to do yeoman service; to perform a function; to serve a purpose; to serve a turn.

Adjectives: Useful, beneficial, advantageous, serviceable, helpful, gainful, profitable, lucrative, worthwhile.

Subservient, conducive, applicable, adequate, efficient, efficacious, effective, effectual, seaworthy.

Applicable, available, handy, ready.

Adverbs: Usefully, etc.; *pro bono publico.*

645 INUTILITY

Substantives: uselessness, inefficacy, inefficiency, ineptness, ineptitude, inadequacy, inaptitude, unskilfulness, fecklessness, fruitlessness, inanity, worthlessness, unproductiveness, barrenness, sterility, vanity, futility, triviality, paltriness, unprofitableness, unfruitfulness, rustiness, obsoleteness, discommodity, supererogation, obsolescence.

Litter, rubbish, lumber, trash, junk, punk, job lot, orts, weeds (643), bilge, hog-wash. A waste, desert, Sahara, wild, wilderness.

Phrases: The labour of Sisyphus; the work of Penelope; a slaying of the slain; a dead loss; a work of supererogation.

Verbs: To be useless, etc., to be of no avail, use, etc. (644).

To render useless, etc.; to dismantle, disable, disqualify, cripple.

Phrases: To use vain efforts; to beat the air; to fish in the air; to lash the waves; to plough the sands.

Adjectives: Useless, inutile, inefficient, inefficacious, unavailing, inadequate, inoperative, bootless, supervacaneous, unprofitable, unremunerative, unproductive, sterile, barren, unsubservient, supererogatory.

Worthless, valueless, at a discount, gainless, fruitless, profitless, unserviceable, rusty, effete, vain, empty, inane, wasted, nugatory, futile, feckless, inept, withered, good for nothing, wasteful, ill-spent, obsolete, obsolescent, stale, dud, punk, dear-bought, rubbishy.

Unneeded, unnecessary, uncalled-for, unwanted, incommodious, discommodious.

Phrases: Not worth having; leading to no end; no good; not worthwhile; of no earthly use; a dead letter.

Adverbs: Uselessly, etc., to no purpose.

646 EXPEDIENCE

Substantives: expediency, fitness, suitableness, suitability, aptness, aptitude, appropriateness, propriety, pertinence, seasonableness (134), adaptation, congruity, consonance (23), convenience, eligibility, applicability, desirability, seemliness, rightness.

An opportunist, time-server.

Verbs: To be expedient, etc.

To suit, fit, square with, adapt itself to, agree with, consort with, accord with, tally with, conform to, go with, do for.

Adjectives: Expedient, fit, fitting, worth while, suitable, applicable, eligible, apt, appropriate, adapted, proper, advisable, politic, judicious, desirable, pertinent, congruous, seemly, consonant, becoming, meet, due, consentaneous, congenial, well-timed, pat, seasonable, opportune, apropos, befitting, happy, felicitous, auspicious, acceptable, etc., convenient, commodious, right.

Phrases: Being just the thing; just as well.

647 INEXPEDIENCE

Substantives: inexpediency, disadvantageousness, unserviceableness, disservice, unfitness, inaptitude, ineptitude, ineligibility, inappropriateness, impropriety, undesirability, unseemliness, incongruity, impertinence, inopportuneness, unseasonableness.

Inconvenience, incommodiousness, incommodity, discommodity, disadvantage.

Inefficacy, inefficiency, inadequacy.

Verbs: To be inexpedient, etc., to embarrass, cumber, lumber, handicap, be in the way, etc.

Adjectives: Inexpedient, disadvantageous, unprofitable, unfit, unfitting, unsuitable, undesirable, amiss, improper, unapt, inept, impolitic, injudicious, ill-advised, unadvisable, ineligible, objectionable, inadmissible, unseemly, inopportune, unseasonable, inefficient, inefficacious, inadequate.

Inconvenient, incommodious, cumbrous, cumbersome, lumbering, unwieldy, unmanageable, awkward, clumsy.

648 GOODNESS

Substantives: excellence, integrity (939), virtue (944), merit, value, worth, price, preciousness, estimation, rareness, exquisiteness.

Superexcellence, superiority, supereminence, transcendence, perfection (650).

Mediocrity (651), innocuousness, harmlessness, inoffensiveness.

Masterpiece, *chef d'œuvre,* flower, pick, cream, *crème de la crème, élite,* gem, jewel, treasure; a good man (948).

Phrases: One in a thousand (or in a million); the salt of the earth.

Verbs: To be good, beneficial, etc.; to be superior, etc., to excel, transcend, top, vie, emulate (708).

To be middling, etc. (651); to pass, to do.

To produce good, benefit, etc., to benefit, to be beneficial, etc., to confer a benefit, etc., to improve (658).

Phrases: To challenge comparison; to pass muster; to speak well for.

Adjectives: Good, beneficial, valuable, estimable, serviceable, advantageous, precious, favourable, palmary, felicitous, propitious.

Sound, sterling, standard, true, genuine, household, fresh, in good condition, unfaded, unspoiled, unimpaired, uninjured, undemolished, undamaged, unravaged, undecayed, natural, unsophisticated, unadulterated, unpolluted, unvitiated.

Choice, select, picked, nice, worthy, meritorious (944), fine, rare, unexceptionable, excellent, admirable, first-rate, splendid, swell, bully, wizard, priceless, smashing, super, topping, top-hole, clipping, ripping, nailing, prime, tiptop, crack, jake, cardinal, superlative, superfine, super-excellent, pukka, gradely, champion, exquisite, high-wrought, inestimable, invaluable, incomparable, transcendent, matchless, peerless, inimitable, unrivalled, *nulli secundus,* second to none, *facile princeps,* spotless, immaculate, perfect (650), *récherché,* first-class,

first chop.

Moderately good (651).

Harmless, innocuous, innoxious, unoffending, inoffensive, unobjectionable.

Phrases: The goods; the stuff to give them; a bit of all right; of the first water; precious as the apple of the eye; *ne plus ultra;* sound as a roach; worth its weight in gold; right as a trivet; up to the mark; an easy winner.

649 BADNESS

Substantives: hurtfulness, disserviceableness, injuriousness, banefulness, mischievousness, noxiousness, malignancy, malignity, malevolence, tender mercies, venomousness, virulence, destructiveness, scathe, curse, pest, plague, bane (663), plague-spot, evil star, ill wind; evildoer (913).

Vileness, foulness, rankness, depravation, depravity; injury, outrage, ill treatment, annoyance, molestation, oppression; sabotage; deterioration (659).

Phrases: A snake in the grass; a fly in the ointment; a nigger in the woodpile; a thorn in the side; a skeleton in the cupboard.

Verbs: To be bad, etc.

To cause, produce, or inflict evil; to harm, hurt, injure, mar, damage, damnify, endamage, scathe, prejudice, stand in the light of, worsen.

To wrong, molest (830), annoy, harass, infest, grieve, aggrieve, trouble, oppress, persecute, weigh down, run down, overlay.

To maltreat, abuse, ill use, ill treat, bedevil, bruise, scratch, maul, mishandle, man-handle, strafe, knock about, strike, smite, scourge (972), wound, lame, maim, scotch, cripple, mutilate, hamstring, hough, stab, pierce, etc., crush, crumble, pulverize.

To corrupt, corrode, pollute, etc. (659).

To spoil, despoil, sweep, ravage, lay

waste, devastate, dismantle, demolish, level, raze, consume, overrun, sack, plunder, destroy (162).

Phrases: To play the deuce with; to break the back of; crush to pieces; crumble to dust; to grind to powder; to ravage with fire and sword; to knock the stuffing out of; to queer one's pitch; to let daylight into.

Adjectives: Bad, evil, ill, wrong, prejudicial, disadvantageous, unprofitable, unlucky, sinister, left-handed, obnoxious, untoward, unadvisable, inauspicious, ill-omened.

Hurtful, harmful, injurious, grievous, detrimental noxious, pernicious, mischievous, baneful, baleful.

Morbific, rank, peccant, malignant, tabid, corroding, corrosive, virulent, cankering, mephitic, narcotic.

Deleterious, poisonous, venomous, envenomed, pestilent, pestilential, pestiferous, destructive, deadly, fatal, mortal, lethal, lethiferous, miasmal.

Vile, sad, wretched, sorry, shabby, scurvy, base, low, low-down (940), scrubby, lousy, stinking, horrid.

Hateful, abominable, loathsome, detestable, execrable, iniquitous, cursed, accursed, confounded, damnable, diabolic, devilish, demoniacal, infernal, hellish, Satanic, villainous, depraved, shocking (898).

Adverbs: Wrong, wrongly, badly, to one's cost.

Phrases: *Corruptio optimi pessima*; if the worst comes to the worst.

650 PERFECTION

Substantives: perfectness, indefectibility, impeccability, infallibility, unimpeachability, *beau idéal,* summit (210).

Masterpiece, *chef d'œuvre, magnum opus,* classic, model, pattern, mirror, phoenix, *rara avis,* paragon, cream, nonsuch (or nonesuch), nonpareil, *élite.*

Gem, bijou, jewel, pearl, diamond, ruby, brilliant.

A Bayard, a Galahad, an Admirable Crichton.

Phrases: The philosophers' stone; the flower of the flock; the cock of the roost; the pink or acme of perfection; the pick of the bunch; the *ne plus ultra.*

Verbs: To be perfect, etc., to excel, transcend, overtop, etc. (33).

To bring to perfection, to perfect, to ripen, mature, etc. (52, 729).

Phrases: To carry everything before it; to play first fiddle; bear away the bell; to sweep the board.

Adjectives: Perfect, best, faultless, finished, indeficient, indefectible, immaculate, spotless, impeccable, transcendent, matchless, peerless, unparagoned, etc. (648), inimitable, unimpeachable, superlative, superhuman, divine, classical.

Phrases: Right as a trivet; sound as a bell; *ad unguem factus; sans peur et sans reproche.*

651 IMPERFECTION

Substantives: imperfectness, unsoundness, faultiness, deficiency, disability, weak point, drawback, inadequacy, inadequateness (645), handicap.

Fault, defect, flaw, lacuna (198), crack, twist, taint, blemish, shortcoming (304), peccancy, vice.

Mediocrity, mean (29), indifference, inferiority.

Verbs: To be imperfect, middling, etc., to fail, fall short, lie under a disadvantage, be handicapped.

Phrases: To play second fiddle; barely to pass muster.

Adjectives: Imperfect, deficient, defective, faulty, dud, inferior, inartistic, inadequate, wanting, unsound, vicious, cracked, warped, lame, feeble, frail, flimsy, sketchy, botched, gimcrack, gingerbread, tottering, wonky, decrepit, rickety, ramshackle, rattletrap, battered, worn out, threadbare, seedy, wormeaten, moth-eaten, played out, used up, decayed, mutilated, unrectified, uncorrected.

Indifferent, middling, mediocre, below par, so-so, *couci-couci*, secondary, second-rate, third-rate, etc., second-best, second-hand.

Tolerable, passable, bearable, pretty well, well enough, rather good, decent, fair, admissible, not bad, not amiss, not so dusty, unobjectionable, respectable, betwixt and between.

Phrases: Having a screw loose; out of order; out of kilter; no great catch; milk and water; no great shakes; nothing to boast of; on its last legs; no class.

652 CLEANNESS
Substantives: cleanliness, asepsis, purity (960), neatness, tidiness, spotlessness, immaculateness.

Cleaning, purification, mundification, lustration, abstersion, depuration, expurgation, purgation, castration.

Washing, ablution, lavation, elutriation, lixiviation, clarification, defecation, edulcoration, filtration.

Fumigation, ventilation, antisepsis, decontamination, disinfection, soap; detergent, shampoo, antiseptic, disinfectant.

Washroom, wash-house, laundry; washerwoman, laundress, charwoman, cleaner, scavenger, dustman, sweep.

Brush, broom, besom, vacuum-cleaner, duster, handkerchief, napkin, face-cloth, towel, sponge, toothbrush, nail-brush; mop, sieve, riddle, screen, filter.

Verbs: To be clean, etc.

To render, clean, etc., to clean, to mundify, cleanse, wipe, mop, sponge, scour, swab, scrub, brush, sweep, vacuum, dust, brush up.

To wash, lave, sluice, buck, launder, steep, rinse, absterge, deterge, descale,

clear, purify, depurate, defecate, elutriate, lixiviate, edulcorate, clarify, drain, strain, filter, filtrate, fine, fine down.

To disinfect, deodorize, fumigate, delouse, ventilate, purge, expurgate, bowdlerize.

To sift, winnow, pick, screen, weed.

Phrase: To make a clean sweep of.

Adjectives: Clean, cleanly, pure, spotless, unspotted, immaculate, unstained, stainless, unsoiled, unsullied, taintless, untainted, sterile, aseptic, uninfected.

Cleansing, etc., detergent, detersive, abstersive, abstergent, purgatory, purificatory, etc., abluent, antiseptic.

Spruce, tidy, washed, swept, etc., cleaned, disinfected, purified, etc.

Phrases: Clean as a whistle; clean as a new penny; neat as ninepence.

653 UNCLEANNESS
Substantives: immundicity, uncleanliness, soilure, sordidness, foulness, impurity (961), pollution, nastiness, offensiveness, beastliness, muckiness, defilement, contamination, abomination, taint, tainture, corruption, decomposition (49).

Slovenliness, slovenly, untidiness, sluttishness, coarseness, grossness, dregginess, squalor.

Dirt, filth, soil, slop, dust, flue, ooss, cobweb, smoke, soot, smudge, smut, stour, clart, glaur, grime, *sordes,* mess, muck.

Slut, slattern, sloven, frump, mudlark, riff-raff.

Dregs, grounds, sediment, lees, settlement, dross, drossiness, precipitate, scoriae, slag, clinker, scum, sweepings, off-scourings, garbage, *caput mortuum,* residuum, draff, fur, scurf, scurfiness, furfur, dandruff, vermin.

Mud, mire, slush, quagmire, slough, sludge, alluvium, silt, slime, spawn, offal, faeces, excrement, ordure, dung, droppings, guano, manure, compost, dunghill, midden, bog, laystall, sink, cesspool, sump, sough, *cloaca,* latrine, lavatory, water-closet, w.c., toilet, urinal, rear, convenience, privy, jakes, comfort station, heads, thunder-box, drain, sewer; hog-wash, bilge-water.

Sty, pigsty, dusthole, lair, den, slum.

Rottenness, corruption, decomposition, decay, putrefaction, putrescence, putridity, purulence, pus, matter, suppuration, feculence, rankness, rancidity, mouldiness, mustiness, mucidness, mould, mother, must, mildew, dry-rot, fetor, (401).

Scatology, coprology.

Phrases: A sink of corruption; an Augean stable.

Verbs: To be unclean, dirty, etc., to rot, putrefy, corrupt, decompose, go bad, mould, moulder, fester, etc.

To render unclean, etc., to dirt, dirty, soil, tarnish, begrime, smear, besmear, mess, smirch, besmirch, smudge, besmudge, bemire, spatter, bespatter, splash, bedaggle, bedraggle, daub, bedaub, slobber, beslobber, beslime, to cover with dust.

To foul, befoul, sully, pollute, defile, debase, contaminate, taint, corrupt, deflower, rot.

Adjectives: Unclean, dirty, soiled, filthy, grimy, clarty, dusty, dirtied, etc., smutty, sooty, smoky, reechy, thick, turbid, dreggy, slimy, filthy, mucky.

Slovenly, untidy, sluttish, blowzy, draggle-tailed, dowdy, frumpish, slipshod, unkempt, unscoured, unswept, unwiped, unwashed, unstrained, unpurified, squalid.

Nasty, foul, impure, offensive, abominable, beastly, lousy.

Mouldy, musty, mildewed, fusty, rusty, mouldering, moth-eaten, reasty, rotten, rotting, tainted, rancid, high, fly-blown, maggoty, putrescent, putrid, putrefied, bad, festering, purulent,

feculent, fecal, stercoraceous, exrementitious.

Phrases: Wallowing in the mire; rotten to the core.

654 HEALTH

Substantives: sanity, soundness, heartiness, haleness, vigour, freshness, bloom, healthfulness, euphoria, incorruption, incorruptibility.

Phrases: *Mens sana in corpore sano*; a clean bill.

Verbs: To be in health, etc., to flourish, thrive, bloom.

To return to health, to recover, convalesce, recruit, pull through, to get the better of.

To restore to health, to cure, recall to life, bring to.

Phrases: To keep on one's legs; to take a new or fresh lease of life; to turn the corner.

Adjectives: Healthy, in health, well, sound, healthful, hearty, hale, fresh, whole, florid, staunch, flush, hardy, vigorous, chipper, spry, bobbish, blooming, weather-proof, fit.

Unscathed, uninjured, unmaimed, unmarred, untainted.

Phrases: Sitting up and taking nourishment; being on one's legs; sound as a bell, or roach; fresh as a daisy or rose; in fine or high feather; in good case; fit as a fiddle; in the pink of condition; in the pink; in good form.

655 DISEASE

Substantives: illness, sickness, ailment, ailing, indisposition, complaint, disorder, malady, distemper.

Attack, visitation, seizure, stroke, fit.

Sickliness, sickishness, infirmity, diseasedness, tabescence, invalidation, delicacy, weakness, cachexy, witheredness, atrophy, marasmus, incurableness, incurability, palsy, paralysis, decline, consumption, prostration.

251

Taint, pollution, infection, septicity, epidemic, endemic, murrain, plague, pestilence, virus, pox.

A sore, ulcer, abscess, fester, boil, gathering, issue, rot, canker, cancer, carcinoma, sarcoma, caries, gangrene, mortification, eruption, rash, congestion, inflammation, fever.

A valetudinarian, invalid, patient, case, cripple.

Pathology, aetiology, nosology.

Verbs: To be ill, etc., to ail, suffer, be affected with, etc., to complain of, to droop, flag, languish, halt, sicken, gasp; to malinger.

Phrases: To be laid up; to keep one's bed.

Adjectives: Diseased, ill, taken ill, seized, indisposed, unwell, sick, sickish, seedy, queer, crook, toutie, ailing, suffering, confined, bedridden, invalided.

Unsound, sickly, poorly, delicate, weakly, cranky, healthless, infirm, groggy, unbraced, drooping, flagging, withered, palsied, paralytic, paraplectic, decayed, decrepit, lame, crippled, battered, halting, worn out, used up, run down, off colour, moth-eaten, worm-eaten.

Morbid, tainted, vitiated, peccant, contaminated, tabid, tabescent, mangy, poisoned, immedicable, gasping, moribund (360).

Phrases: Out of sorts; good for nothing; on the sick-list; on the danger list; in a bad way; *hors de combat*; on one's last legs; at one's last gasp.

656 SALUBRITY

Substantives: healthiness, wholesomeness, innoxiousness.

Preservation of health, prophylaxis, hygiene, sanitation.

A health resort, spa, hydropathic, sanatorium (662).

Verbs: To be salubrious, etc., to agree with.

Adjectives: Salubrious, wholesome, healthy, sanitary, hygienic, salutary, salutiferous, healthful, tonic, prophylactic, bracing, benign.

Innoxious, innocuous, harmless, uninjurious, innocent.

Remedial, restorative, sanatory (662), nutritious, alterative (660).

657 INSALUBRITY

Substantives: unhealthiness, unwholesomeness, deadliness, fatality.

Microbe, germ, virus, etc. (663).

Adjectives: Insalubrious, insanitary, unsanitary, unhealthy, ungenial, uncongenial, unwholesome, morbific, mephitic, septic, deleterious, pestilent, pestiferous, pestilential, virulent, poisonous, toxic, contagious, infectious, catching, epidemic, epizotic, endemic, pandemic, zymotic, deadly, pathogenic, pathogenetic, lowering, relaxing; innutritious (645).

Phrase: 'There is death in the pot.'

658 IMPROVEMENT

Substantives: melioration, amelioration, betterment, mend, amendment, emendation, advance, advancement, progress, elevation, promotion, preferment, convalescence, recovery, recuperation, curability.

Repair, reparation, cicatrization, correction, reform, reformation, rectification, epuration, purification, etc. (652), refinement, relief, redress, second thoughts.

New edition; *réchauffé, refacimento,* revision, revise, recension, rehash, redaction.

Verbs: To be, become, or get better, etc., to improve, mend, advance, progress (282), to get on, make progress, gain ground, make way, go ahead, pick up, rally, recover, get the better of, get well, get over it, pull through, convalesce, recuperate.

To render better, improve, amend, better, meliorate, ameliorate, advance, push on, promote, prefer, forward, enhance.

To relieve, refresh, restore, renew, redintegrate, heal (660); to palliate, mitigate.

To repair, refit, cannibalize, retouch, revise, botch, vamp, tinker, cobble, clout, patch up, touch up, cicatrize, darn, fine-draw, rub up, do up, furbish, refurbish, polish, bolster up, caulk, careen; to stop a gap, to staunch.

To purify, depurate (652), defecate, strain, filter, rack, refine, disinfect, chasten.

To correct, rectify, redress, reform, review, remodel, prune, restore (660), mellow, set to rights, sort, fix, put straight, straighten out, revise.

Phrases: To turn over a new leaf; to take a new lease of life; to make the most of; to infuse new blood into.

Adjectives: Improving, etc., improved, etc., progressive, corrective, reparatory, emendatory, revisory, sanatory, advanced.

Curable, corrigible, capable of improvement.

659 DETERIORATION

Substantives: wane, ebb, debasement, degeneracy, degeneration, degradation, degenerateness, demotion, relegation.

Impairment, injury, outrage, havoc, devastation, inroad, vitiation, adulteration, sophistication, debasement, perversion, degradation, demoralization, corruption, prostitution, pollution, contamination, alloy, venenation.

Decline, declension, declination, going downhill, recession, retrogression, retrogradation (283), caducity, decrepitude, decadence, falling off, pejoration.

Decay, disorganization, damage, scathe, wear and tear, mouldiness, rottenness, corrosion, moth and rust, dry-rot, blight, marasmus, atrophy, emaciation, falling to pieces, *délâbrement*.

Verbs: To be, or become worse, to deteriorate, worsen, disimprove, wane, ebb, degenerate, fall off, decline, go downhill, sink, go down, lapse, droop, be the worse for, recede, retrograde, revert (283), fall into decay, fade, break, break up, break down, fall to pieces, wither, moulder, rot, rust, crumble, totter, shake, tumble, fall, topple, perish, die (360).

To render less good; to weaken, vitiate, debase, alloy, pervert.

To spoil, embase, defile, taint, infect, contaminate, sophisticate, poison, canker, corrupt, tamper with, pollute, deprave, demoralize, envenom, debauch, prostitute, defile, degrade, downgrade, demote, adulterate, stain, spatter, bespatter, soil, tarnish (653), addle.

To corrode, erode, blight, rot, wear away, wear out, gnaw, gnaw at the root of, sap, mine, undermine, shake, break up, disorganize, dismantle, dismast, lay waste, do for, ruin, confound.

To embitter, acerbate, aggravate.

To wound, stab, maim, lame, cripple, mutilate, disfigure, deface.

To injure, harm, hurt, impair, dilapidate, damage, endamage, damnify, etc. (649).

Phrases: To go to rack and ruin; to have seen better days; to go to the dogs; to go to pot; to go on from bad to worse; to go farther and fare worse; to run to seed; to play the deuce with; to sap the foundations of.

Adjectives: Deteriorated, worse, impaired, etc., degenerate, *passé*, on the decline, on the down-grade, deciduous, unimproved, unrecovered, unrestored.

Decayed, etc., moth-eaten, worm-eaten, mildewed, rusty, time-worn, moss-grown, effete, wasted, worn, crumbling, tumbledown, dilapidated, overblown.

Phrases: Out of the frying-pan into the fire; the worse for wear; worn to a thread; worn to a shadow; reduced to a skeleton; the ghost of oneself; a hopeless case.

660 RESTORATION

Substantives: restoral, reinstatement, replacement, rehabilitation, instauration, re-establishment, rectification, revendication, redintegration, refection, reconstitution, cure, sanation, refitting, reorganization, recruiting, redress, retrieval, refreshment.

Renovation, renewal, reanimation, recovery, resumption, reclamation, reconversion, recure, resuscitation, revivification, reviviscence, revival, renascence, renaissance, rejuvenation, rejuvenescence, regeneration, regeneracy, regenerateness, palingenesis, redemption; a Phoenix.

Réchauffé, *rifacimento* (658), recast.

Phrases: A new lease of life; second youth; new birth; 'Richard's himself again.'

Verbs: To return to the original state, to right itself, come to, come round, rally, revive, recover.

To restore, replace, re-establish, reinstate, reseat, replant, reconstitute, redintegrate, set right, set to rights, sort, fix, rectify, redress, reclaim, redeem, recover, recoup, recure, retrieve, cicatrize.

To refit, recruit, refresh, refocillate, rehabilitate, reconvert, renew, renovate, revitalize, revivify, reinvigorate, regenerate, rejuvenesce, rejuvenate, resuscitate, reanimate, recast, reconstruct, rebuild, reorganize.

To repair, retouch, revise (658).

To cure, heal, cicatrize, remedy, doctor, physic, medicate.

Phrases: Recall to life; set on one's legs.

Adjectives: Restoring, etc., restored, etc., restorative, recuperative, reparative, sanative, remedial, curative (662).

Restorable, sanable, remediable, retrievable, recoverable.

Adverbs: *In statu quo*; as you were; Phoenix-like.

661 RELAPSE

Substantives: lapse, falling back, back-sliding, retrogression, reaction, set-back, recidivism, retrogradation, etc. (659).

Return to or recurrence of a bad state.

A recidivist, backslider, throwback.

Verbs: To relapse, lapse, backslide, fall back, slide back, sink back, return, retrograde.

662 REMEDY

Substantives: help, redress, cure, antidote, counterpoison, vaccine, antitoxin, antibiotic, antiseptic, specific, prophylactic, corrective, restorative, pick-me-up, bracer, sedative, anodyne, opiate, hypnotic, nepenthe, tranquillizer.

Febrifuge, diaphoretic, diuretic, carminative, purgative, laxative, emetic, palliative.

Physic, medicine, drug, tonic, medicament, nostrum, placebo, recipe, prescription, catholicon.

Panacea, elixir, *elixir vitae,* balm, balsam, cordial, cardiac, theriac, ptisan.

Pill, pilule, pellet, tablet, tabloid, pastille, lozenge, powder, draught, lincture, suppository.

Salve, ointment, plaster, epithem, embrocation, liniment, lotion, cataplasm, styptic, poultice, compress, pledget.

Treatment, diet, dieting, regimen.

Pharmacy, pharmacology, materia medica, therapeutics, homoeopathy, allopathy, faith healing, radiotherapy, actinotherapy, heliotherapy, thallassotherapy, hydrotherapy, hydropathy, osteopathy, dietetics, dietary, chirurgery, surgery, gynaecology, midwifery, obstetrics, paediatrics, geriatrics; psycho-analysis, psychiatry, psychotherapy.

A hospital, infirmary, pest-house, lazaretto, madhouse, asylum, lunatic asylum, mental hospital, *maison de santé*, ambulance, clinic, dispensary, sanatorium, spa, hydropathic, nursing home.

A doctor, physician, general practitioner, GP, surgeon, anaesthetist, dentist, aurist, oculist, specialist, alienist, psycho-analyst, psychiatrist, psycho-therapist; apothecary, druggist; midwife, nurse.

Verbs: To dose, physic, attend, doctor, nurse.

Adjectives: Remedial, medical, medicinal, therapeutic, surgical, chirurgical, sanatory, sanative, curative, salutary, salutiferous, healing, paregoric, restorative, tonic, corroborant, analeptic, balsamic, anodyne, sedative, lenitive, demulcent, emollient, depuratory, detersive, detergent, abstersive, disinfectant, antiseptic, corrective, prophylactic, antitoxic, febrifuge, alterative, expectorant; veterinary.

Dietetic, alexipharmic, nutritious, nutritive, peptic, alimentary.

663 BANE

Substantives: scourge, curse, scathe, sting, fang, gall and wormwood.

Poison, virus, venom, toxin, microbe, germ, bacillus, miasma, mephitis, malaria, pest, rust, canker, cancer, canker-worm.

Hemlock, hellebore, nightshade, henbane, aconite, upas-tree.

Sirocco.

A viper, adder, serpent, cobra, rattlesnake, cockatrice, scorpion, wireworm, torpedo, hornet, vulture, vampire.

Science of poisons, toxicology.

Adjectives: Poisonous, venomous, virulent, toxic, mephitic, pestilent, pestilential, miasmatic, baneful (649).

664 SAFETY

Substantives: security, surety, impregnability, invulnerability, invulnerableness, escape (671).

Safeguard, guard, guardianship, chaperonage, protection, tutelage, wardship, wardenship, safe-conduct, escort, convoy, garrison.

Watch, watch and ward, sentinel, sentry, scout, watchman, patrol, vedette, picket, bivouac.

Policeman, policewoman, police officer, constable, cop, copper, bobby, peeler, slop, bull, dick, rozzer.

Watch-dog, bandog, Cerberus.

Protector, guardian, guard (717), defender, warden, warder, preserver, chaperon, tutelary saint, guardian angel, palladium.

Custody, safe-keeping (751).

Isolation, segregation, quarantine; insurance, assurance; cover.

Verbs: To be safe, etc.

To render safe, etc., to protect, guard, ward, shield, shelter, flank, cover, screen, shroud, ensconce, secure, fence, hedge in, entrench, house, nestle.

To defend, forfend, escort, convoy, garrison, mount guard, patrol, chaperon, picket.

Phrases: To save one's bacon; to light upon one's feet; to weather the storm; to bear a charmed life; to make assurance doubly sure; to take no chances.

To play gooseberry.

Adjectives: Safe, in safety, in security, secure, sure, protected, guarded, etc., snug, fireproof, waterproof, seaworthy, airworthy.

Defensible, tenable; insurable.

Invulnerable, unassailable, unattackable, impregnable, inexpugnable.

Protecting, etc., guardian, tutelary.

Unthreatened, unmolested, unharmed, scatheless, unhazarded.

Phrases: Out of harm's way; safe and sound; under lock and key; on sure ground; under cover; under the shadow of one's wing; the coast being

clear; the danger being past; out of the wood; proof against.
Interjections: All's well! *salva est res!* safety first!

665 DANGER
Substantives: peril, insecurity, jeopardy, risk, hazard, venture, precariousness, slipperiness.

Liability, exposure (177), vulnerability, vulnerable point, Achilles heel.

Hopelessness (859), forlorn hope, alarm (860), defencelessness.
Phrases: The ground sliding from under one; breakers ahead; a storm brewing; the sword of Damocles.
Verbs: To be in danger, etc., to be exposed to, to incur or encounter danger, run the danger of, run a risk.

To place or put in danger, etc., to endanger, expose to danger, imperil, jeopardize, compromise, adventure, risk, hazard, venture, stake.
Phrases: To sit on a barrel of gunpowder; stand on a volcano; to engage in a forlorn hope.
Adjectives: In danger, peril, jeopardy, etc., unsafe, insecure, unguarded, unscreened, unsheltered, unprotected, guardless, helpless, guideless, exposed, defenceless, vulnerable, at bay.

Unwarned, unadmonished, unadvised.

Dangerous, perilous, hazardous, parlous, risky, chancy, untrustworthy, fraught with danger, adventurous, precarious, critical, touch-and-go, breakneck, slippery, unsteady, shaky, tottering, top-heavy, harbourless, ticklish, dicky.

Threatening, ominous, alarming, minacious (909).
Phrases: Not out of the wood; hanging by a thread; neck or nothing; in a tight place; between two fires; out of the frying-pan into the fire; between the devil and the deep sea; between Scylla and Charybdis; on the rocks; hard bested.

666 REFUGE
Substantives: asylum, sanctuary, fastness, retreat, ark, hiding-place, dug-out, funk-hole, fox-hole, loophole, shelter, lee, cover.

Roadstead, anchorage, breakwater, mole, groyne, port, haven, harbour, harbour of refuge, pier.

Fort, citadel, fortification, stronghold, strong point, keep, shield, etc. (717).

Screen, covert, wing, fence, rail, railing, wall, dike, ditch, etc. (232).

Anchor, kedge, grapnel, grappling-iron, sheet-anchor, prop, stay, mainstay, jury-mast, lifeboat, lifebuoy, lifebelt, plank, stepping-stone, umbrella, parachute, lightning-conductor, safety-valve, safety curtain, safety-lamp.

667 PITFALL
Substantives: rocks, reefs, sunken rocks, snags, sands, quicksands, breakers, shoals, shallows, bank, shelf, flat, whirlpool, rapids, current, undertow, precipice, lee shore, air-pocket.

Trap, snare, gin, springe, deadfall, toils, noose, net, spring-net, spring-gun, masked battery, mine.
Phrases: The sword of Damocles; a snake in the grass; trusting to a broken reed; a lion's den; a hornet's nest; an ugly customer.

668 WARNING
Substantives: caution, *caveat,* notice, premonition, premonishment, lesson, dehortation, monition, admonition (864); alarm (669).

Beacon, lighthouse, lightship, pharos, watch-tower, signal-post, guide-post (550).

Sentinel, sentry, watch, watchman, patrol, vedette (664); monitor, Cassandra.
Phrases: The writing on the wall; the yellow flag; a red light; a stormy petrel; gathering clouds.

Verbs: To warn, caution, forewarn, premonish, give notice, give warning, admonish, dehort, threaten, menace (909).

To take warning; to beware; to be on one's guard (864).

Phrases: To put on one's guard; to sound the alarm.

Adjectives: Warning, etc., monitory, premonitory, dehortatory, cautionary, admonitory.

Warned, etc., careful, one one's guard (459).

Interjections: Beware! look out! mind what you are about! watch your step! let sleeping dogs lie! *foenum habet in cornu!* fore! heads! mind your back! cave!

669 ALARM

Substantives: alert, alarum, alarm-bell, horn, siren, maroon, fog-signal, tocsin, tattoo, signal of distress, SOS, hue and cry.

False alarm, cry of wolf, bugbear, bugaboo, bogy.

Verbs: To give, raise, or sound an alarm, to alarm, warn, ring the tocsin, dial 999; to cry wolf.

Adjectives: Alarming, etc., threatening.

Phrases: Each for himself; *sauve qui peut.*

670 PRESERVATION

Substantives: conservation, maintenance (141), support, upkeep, sustentation, deliverance, salvation, rescue, redemption, self-preservation, continuance (143).

Means of preservation, prophylaxis, preservative, preserver.

Verbs: To preserve, maintain, support, keep, sustain, nurse, save, rescue, file (papers).

To embalm, mummify, dry, dehydrate, cure, kipper, smoke, salt, pickle, marinade, season, kyanize, bottle, pot, can, tin.

Adjectives: Preserving, conservative, prophylactic, preservatory, hygienic.

Preserved, intact, unimpaired, uninjured, unhurt, unsinged, unmarred.

671 ESCAPE

Substantives: getaway, flight, elopement, evasion, retreat, reprieve, reprieval, deliverance, redemption, resuce.

Narrow escape, hair's-breadth, escape, close shave, close call, narrow squeak.

Means of escape: Bridge, drawbridge, loophole, ladder, plank, stepping-stone, trap-door, fireescape, emergency exit.

A fugitive, runaway, refugee, evacuee.

Verbs: To escape, elude, evade, wriggle out of, make or effect one's escape, make off, march off, pack off, skip, skip off, slip away, steal away, slink away, flit, decamp, run away, abscond, levant, skedaddle, scoot, fly, flee, bolt, bunk, scarper, scram, hop it, beat it, vamoose, elope, whip off, break loose, break away, get clear.

Phrases: To take oneself off; play truant; to beat a retreat; to give one the slip; to slip the collar; to slip through the fingers; to make oneself scarce; to fly the coop; to take to one's heels; to show a clean pair of heels; to take French leave; to do a bunk; to do a guy; to cut one's lucky; to cut and run; to live to fight another day; to run for one's life; to 'make tracks.

Interjections: *Sauve qui peut!* the devil take the hindmost!

Adjectives: Escaping, etc., escaped, etc., runaway.

Phrase: The bird having flown.

672 DELIVERANCE

Substantives: extrication, rescue, reprieve, respite, redemption, salvation, riddance, release, liberation (750); redeemableness, redeemability.

Verbs: To deliver, extricate, rescue, save, salvage, redeem, ransom, help out, bring off, *tirer d'affaire,* to get rid, to work off, to rid.

Phrases: To save one's bacon; to find a hole to creep out of.

Adjectives: Delivered, saved, etc., scot-free, scatheless.

Extricable, redeemable, rescuable.

673 PREPARATION

Substantives: making ready, providing, provision, providence, anticipation, preconcertation, rehearsal, precaution; laying foundations, ploughing, sowing, semination, cooking, brewing, digestion, gestation, hatching, incubation, concoction, maturation, elaboration, predisposition, premeditation (611), acclimatization (613).

Physical preparation, training, drill, drilling, discipline, exercise, exercitation, gymnastics, callisthenics, eurhythmics, athletics, gymnasium, *palaestra,* prenticeship, apprenticeship, qualification, inurement, education, novitiate (537).

Putting or setting in order, putting to rights, clearance, arrangement, disposal, organization, adjustment, adaptation, disposition, accommodation, putting in tune, tuning, putting in trim, dressing, putting in harness, outfit, equipment, accoutrement, armament.

Groundwork, basis, foundation, pedestal, etc. (215), stepping-stone, first stone, scaffold, scaffolding, cradle, sketch (626).

State of being prepared, preparedness, ripeness, maturity, readiness, mellowness.

Preparer, pioneer, avant-courier, sappers and miners.

Phrases: A stitch in time; clearing decks; a note of preparation; a breather; a trial bout; a practice swing.

Verbs: To prepare, get ready, make ready, get up, anticipate, forecast, pre-establish, preconcert, settle preliminaries, to found.

To arrange, set or put in order, set or put to rights, organize, dispose, cast the parts, mount, adjust, adapt, accommodate, trim, tidy, fit, predispose, inure, elaborate, mature, mellow, season, ripen, nurture, hatch, cook, concoct, brew, tune, put in tune, attune, set, temper, anneal, smelt, undermine, brush up, get up.

To provide, provide against, discount, make provision, keep on foot, take precautions, make sure, lie in wait for (507).

To equip, arm, man, fit out, fit up, furnish, rig, dress, dress up, furbish up, accoutre, array, fettle, vamp up, wind up.

To train, drill, discipline, break in, cradle, inure, habituate, harden, case-harden, season, acclimatize, qualify, educate, teach.

Phrases: To take steps; prepare the ground; lay or fix the foundations, the basis, groundwork, etc.; to clear the ground or way or course; clear decks; clear for action; close one's ranks; plough the ground; dress the ground; till the soil; sow the seed; open the way; pave the way; lay a train; dig a mine; prepare a charge; erect the scaffolding; *reculer pour mieux sauter.*

Put in harness; sharpen one's tools; whet the knife; shoulder arms; put the horses to; oil up; crank up; warm up.

To prepare oneself; lay oneself out for; get into harvest; gird up one's loins; buckle on one's armour; serve one's time or apprenticeship; be at one's post; gather oneself together.

To set on foot; to lay the first stone; to break ground.

To erect the scaffold; to cut one's coat according to one's cloth; to keep one's powder dry; to beat up for recruits; to sound the note of preparation.

Adjectives: Preparing, etc., in preparation, in course of preparation, in hand, in train, brewing, hatching, forthcoming, in embryo, afoot, afloat, on the anvil, on the carpet, on the stocks, *sur le tapis.*

Preparative, preparatory, provisional, in the rough, rough and ready (111).

Prepared, trained, drilled, etc., forearmed, ready, in readiness, ripe, mature, mellow, fledged, ready to one's hand, on tap, cut and dried, annealed, concocted, laboured, elabrated, planned (626).

Phrases: Armed to the teeth; armed cap-à-pie; booted and spurred; in full feather; *in utrumque paratus*; in working order.

Adverbs: In preparation, in anticipation of, etc., against.

674 NON-PREPARATION
Substantives: want or absence of preparation, inculture, inconcoction, improvidence.

Immaturity, crudeness, crudity, greenness, rawness, disqualification.

Absence of art, state of nature, virgin soil.

An embryo, skeleton, rough copy, draft (626); germ, rudiment (153), raw material, rough diamond.

Tyro, beginner, novice, neophyte, greenhorn, new chum, pommy, recruit, sprog.

Verbs: To be unprepared, etc., to want or lack preparation.

To improvise, extemporize (612).

To render unprepared, etc., to dismantle, dismount, dismast, disqualify, disable (645), unrig, undress (226).

Phrases: To put *hors de combat*; to put out of gear; to spike the guns; to remove the sparking-plug.

Adjectives: Unprepared, rudimentary, immature, embryonic, unripe, raw, green, crude, rough, roughcast, rough-hewn, unhewn, unformed, unhatched, unfledged, unnurtured, uneducated, unlicked, unpolished, natural, in a state of nature, *au naturel,* unwrought, unconcocted, undigested, indigested, unrevised, unblown, unfashioned, unlaboured, unleavened, fallow, uncultivated, unsown, untilled, untrained, undrilled, unexercised, unseasoned, disqualified, unqualified, out of order, unseaworthy.

Unbegun, unready, unarranged, unorganized, unfurnished, unprovided, unequipped, undressed, in dishabille, dismantled, untrimmed.

Shiftless, improvident, unguarded, happy-go-lucky, feckless, thoughtless, unthrifty.

Unpremeditated, unseen, off-hand (612), from hand to mouth, extempore (111).

Phrases: Caught on the hop; with their trousers down.

675 ESSAY
Substantives: endeavour, try, trial, experiment (463), probation, attempt (676), venture, adventure, tentative, *ballon d'essai, coup d'essai,* go, crack, whack, slap, shot, speculation.

Verbs: To try, essay, make trial of, try on, experiment, make an experiment, endeavour, strive, attempt, grope, feel one's way; to venture, adventure, speculate, take upon oneself.

Phrases: To put out or throw out a feeler; to tempt fortune; to fly a kite; to send up a pilot balloon; to fish for information, compliments, etc.; to have a crack at; to try one's luck; to chance it; to risk it.

Adjectives: Essaying, etc., experimental, tentative, empirical, on trial, probative, probatory, probationary.

Adverbs: Experimentally, etc., at a venture.

676 UNDERTAKING
Substantives: enterprise, emprise, quest, mission, endeavour, attempt,

move, first move, the initiative, first step.

Verbs: To undertake, take in hand, set about, go about, set to, fall to, set to work, engage in, launch into, embark in, plunge into, take on, set one's hand to, tackle, grapple with, volunteer, take steps, launch out.

To endeavour, strive, use one's endeavours; to attempt, make an attempt, tempt.

To begin, set on foot, set agoing, take the first step.

Phrases: To break the neck of the business; take the initiative; to get cracking; to break ground; break the ice; break cover; to pass the Rubicon; to take upon oneself; to take on one's shoulders; to put one's shoulder to the wheel; *ce n'est que le premier pas qui coûte*; well begun is half done.

To take the bull by the horns; to rush *in medias res*; to have too many irons in the fire; to attempt impossibilities.

Adverbs: Undertaking, attempting, etc.

677 USE

Substantives: employment, employ, application, appliance, adhibition, disposal, exercise, exercitation.

Recourse, resort, avail, service, wear, usage, conversion to use, usufruct, utilization.

Agency (170); usefulness (644).

Verbs: To use, make use of, utilize, exploit, employ (134), apply, adhibit, dispose of, work, wield, manipulate, handle, put to use; turn or convert to use; avail oneself of, resort to, have recourse to, take up with, betake oneself to.

To render useful, serviceable, available, etc.; to utilize, draw, call forth, tax, task, try, exert, exercise, practise, ply, work up, consume, absorb, expend.

To be useful, to serve one's turn (644).

Phrases: To take advantage of; to turn to account; to make the most of; to make the best of; to bring to bear upon; to fall back upon; to press or enlist into the service; to make shift with; make a cat's-paw of.

To pull the strings or wires; put in action; set to work; set in motion; put in practice.

Adjectives: Used, employed, etc., applied, exercised, tried, etc.

678 DISUSE

Substantives: forbearance, abstinence, dispensation, desuetude (614), relinquishment, abandonment (624, 782).

Verbs: To disuse, not to use, to do without, to dispense with, neglect, to let alone, to spare, waive.

To lay by; set, put, or lay aside, to discard, dismiss (756); cast off, throw off, turn off, turn out, turn away, throw away, scrap, dismantle, shelve (133), shunt, side-track, get rid of, do away with; to keep back (636).

Phrases: To lay on the shelf; to lay up in a napkin; to consign to the scrap-heap; to cast, heave, or throw overboard; to cast to the winds; to turn out neck and crop; to send to the right-about; to send packing.

Adjectives: Disused, etc., not used, unused, unutilized, done with, unemployed, unapplied, unspent, unexercised, kept or held back.

Unessayed, untouched, uncalled-for, ungathered, unculled, untrodden.

679 MISUSE

Substantives: misusage, misemployment, misapplication, misappropriation, abuse, profanation, prostitution, desecration.

Waste (818), wasting, spilling, exhaustion (638).

Verbs: To misuse, misemploy, misapply, misappropriate, desecrate, abuse, profane, prostitute.

To waste, spill, fritter away,

exhaust, throw or fling away, squander (818).

Phrases: To waste powder and shot; cut blocks with a razor; cast pearls before swine.

Adjectives: Misused, etc.

Section 3 –
Voluntary Action

680 ACTION

Substantives: performance, work, operation, execution, perpetration, proceeding, procedure, *démarche,* process, handiwork, handicraft, workmanship, manœuvre, evolution, transaction, bout, turn, job, doings, dealings, business, affair.

Deed, act, overt act, touch, move, strike, blow, *coup,* feat, stunt, exploit, passage, measure, step, stroke of policy, *tour de force, coup de main, coup d'état.*

Verbs: To act, do, work, operate, do or transact business, practise, prosecute, perpetrate, perform, execute (729), officiate, exercise, commit, inflict, strike a blow, handle, take in hand, put in hand, run.

To labour, drudge, toil, ply, set to work, pull the oar, serve, officiate, go about, turn one's hand to, dabble; to have in hand.

Phrases: To have a finger in the pie; to take or play a part; to set to work; to put into execution (729); to lay one's hand to the plough; to ply one's task; to get on with the job; to discharge an office.

Adjectives: Acting, etc., in action, in operation, etc., operative, in harness, in play, on duty, on foot, at work, red-handed.

Interjection: Here goes!

681 INACTION

Substantives: abstinence from action, inactivity (683), non-intervention, non-interference, neutrality, strike, Fabian tactics.

Verbs: Not to do, to let be, abstain from doing; let or leave alone, refrain, desist, keep oneself from doing; let pass, lie by, let be, wait.

To undo, take down, take or pull to pieces, do away with.

Phrases: To bide one's time; to let well alone; to cool one's heels; to stay one's hand; to wash one's hands of; to strike work; nothing doing; *nihil fit; dolce far niente.*

Adjectives: Not doing, not done, let alone, undone, etc.; passive, neutral.

682 ACTIVITY

Substantives: briskness, quickness, promptness, promptitude, expedition, dispatch, readiness, alertness, smartness, sharpness, nimbleness, agility (274).

Spirit, ardour, animation, life, liveliness, vivacity, eagerness, *empressement, brio,* dash, *élan,* abandon, pep, go, alacrity, zeal, push, vim, energy (171), hustle, vigour, intentness.

Wakefulness, *pervigilium,* insomnia, sleeplessness.

Industry, assiduity, assiduousness, sedulity, sedulousness, diligence; perseverance, persistence, plodding, painstaking, drudgery, busyness, indefatigability, indefatigableness, patience, Business habits.

Movement, bustle, commotion, stir, fuss, fluster, bother, pother, ado, fidget, restlessness, fidgetiness.

Officiousness, meddling, interference, interposition, intermeddling, tampering with, intrigue, *tripotage,* supererogation.

A man of action, busy bee, busybody, go-getter, zealot, devotee, meddler, hustler, whizz-kid.

Phrases: The thick of the action; *in medias res;* too many cooks; new brooms sweep clean; too many irons in the fire.

Verbs: To be active, busy, stirring, etc., to busy oneself in, stir, bestir oneself, bustle, fuss, make a fuss, speed, hasten, push, make a push, go ahead, hustle; to industrialize.

To plod, drudge, keep on, hold on, persist, persevere, fag at, hammer at, peg away, stick to, buckle to, stick to work, take pains; to take or spend time in; to make progress.

To meddle, moil, intermeddle, interfere, interpose, kibitz, tamper with, fool with, get at, nobble, agitate, intrigue.

To overact, overdo, overlay, outdo, ride to death.

Phrases: To look sharp; to lay about one; to have one's hands full; to kick up a dust; to stir one's stumps; to exert one's energies; to put one's best foot foremost; to do one's best; to do all one can; to leave no stone unturned; to have all one's eyes about one; make the best of one's time; not to let the grass grow under one's feet; to make short work of; to seize the opportunity; to come up to the scratch.

To take time by the forelock; to improve the shining hour; to make hay while the sun shines; to keep the pot boiling; to strike while the iron is hot; to kill two birds with one stone; to move heaven and earth; to go through fire and water; to do wonders; to go all lengths; to stick at nothing; to go the whole hog; to keep the ball rolling; to put one's back into it; to make things hum.

To have a hand in; to poke one's nose in; to put in one's oar; to have a finger in the pie; to mix oneself up with; steal a march upon.

Adjectives: Active, brisk, quick, prompt, alert, on the alert, stirring, spry, sharp, smart, quick, nimble, agile, light-footed, tripping, ready, awake, broad awake, wide awake, alive, lively, live, animated, vivacious, frisky, forward, eager, strenuous, zealous, expeditious, enterprising, pushing, pushful, spirited, in earnest, up in arms, go-ahead.

Working, on duty, at work, hard at work, intent, industrious, up and coming, assiduous, diligent, sedulous, painstaking, business-like, practical, in harness, operose, plodding, toiling, hard-working, fagging, busy, bustling, restless, fussy, fidgety.

Persevering, indefatigable, untiring, unflagging, unremitting, unwearied, never-tiring, undrooping, unintermitting, unintermittent, unflinching, unsleeping, unslumbering, sleepless, persistent.

Meddling, meddlesome, pushing, intermeddling, tampering, etc., officious, over-officious, intriguing, managing.

Phrases: Up and doing; up and stirring; busy as a bee; on the *qui vive*; nimble as a quirrel; the fingers itching; no sooner said than done; *nulla dies sine linea*; a rolling stone gathers no moss; the used key is always bright.

Adverbs: Actively, etc. (684).

Interjections: Look alive! look sharp! get a move on! get cracking! get busy! hump yourself! get weaving!

683 INACTIVITY

Substantives: inaction (681), idleness, sloth, laziness, indolence, inertness, inertia (172), lumpishness, supineness, sluggishness, segnitude, languor, torpor, quiescence, stagnation, lentor, limpness, listlessness, remissnes, slackness.

Dilatoriness, cunctation, procrastination (133), relaxation, truancy, lagging, dawdling, rust, rustiness, want of occupation, resourcelessness.

Somnolence, drowsiness, doziness, nodding, oscitation, sleepiness, hypnosis.

Hypnology.

Sleep, nap, doze, slumber, shut-eye, bye-bye, snooze, dog-sleep, cat-nap, siesta, dream, faint, swoon, coma, trance, hypnotic state, snore, a wink of sleep, lethargy, hibernation, aestivation.

An idler, laggard, truant, do-nothing, lubber, sluggard, sleepy-head, slumberer, faineant, *flâneur,* loafer, drone, dormouse, slow-coach, stick-in-the-mud, lounger, slug, sundowner, bum, Weary Willie, lazy-bones, lotus-eater, slacker, trifler, dilettante.

Cause of inactivity (174), sedative, hypnotic, knock-out drops, hypnotism; lullaby.

Phrases: The Castle of Indolence; *dolce far niente;* the Land of Nod; the Fabian policy; *laissez aller; laissez faire;* masterly inactivity; the thief of time.

Sleeping partner; waiter on Providence.

Verbs: To be inactive, etc., to do nothing, let alone, lie by, lie idle, stagnate, lay to, keep quiet, hang fire, relax, slouch, loll, drawl, slug, dally, lag, dawdle, potter, lounge, loiter, laze, moon, moon about, loaf, hang about, stooge, mouch; to waste, lose, idle away, kill, trifle away, fritter away or fool away time; trifle, footle, dabble, fribble, peddle, fiddle-faddle.

To sleep, slumber, nod, close the eyes, close the eyelids, doze, drowse, fall asleep, take a nap, go off to sleep, hibernate, aestivate, vegetate.

To languish, expend itself, flag, hang fire.

To render idle, etc.; to sluggardize.

Phrases: To fold one's arms; to let well alone; play truant; while away the time; to rest upon one's oars; to burn daylight; to take it easy; slack off.

To get one's head down; to hit the hay; to have forty winks; to sleep like a top or like a log; to sleep like a dormouse; to swing the lead; to eat the bread of idleness; to twiddle one's thumbs.

Adjectives: Inactive, unoccupied, unemployed, unbusied, doing nothing (685), resourceless.

Indolent, easy-going, lazy, slothful, idle, thowless, fushionless, slack, inert, torpid, sluggish, languid, supine, heavy, dull, stagnant, lumpish, soulless, listless, moony, limp, languorous, exanimate.

Dilatory, laggard, lagging, tardigrade, drawling, creeping, dawdling, faddling, rusty, lackadaisical, fiddlefaddle, shilly-shally, unpractical, unbusiness-like.

Sleepy, dozy, dopy, dreamy, drowsy, somnolent, dormant, asleep, lethargic, comatose, napping, somniferous, soporific, soporous, soporose, somnific, hypnotic, narcotic, unawakened.

Phrases: With folded arms; *les bras croisés,* with the hands in the pockets; at a loose end.

In the arms or lap or Morpheus.

684 HASTE
Substantives: dispatch, precipitancy, precipitation, spurt, precipitousness, impetuosity, posthaste, acceleration, quickness (274).

Hurry, flurry, drive, bustle, fuss, splutter, scramble, brusquerie, fidget, fidgetiness (682).

Verbs: To haste, hasten, urge, press on, push on, bustle, hurry, hustle, buck up, precipitate, accelerate; to bustle, scramble, scuttle, scurry, scoot, plunge, rush, dash on, press on, scorch, speed.

Phrases: To make the most of one's time; to lose not a moment; *festina lente.*

Adjectives: Hasty, hurried, precipitate, scrambling, etc., headlong, boisterous, impetuous, brusque, abrupt, slapdash, cursory.

Adverbs: Hastily, etc., headlong, in haste, slapdash, slap-bang, amain,

263

hurry-scurry, helter-skelter, head and shoulders, head over heels, by fits and starts, by spurts.
Phrases: No sooner said than done; a word and a blow.

685 LEISURE
Substantives: leisureliness, spare time, breathing-space, off-time, slack time, holiday, bank holiday, Sunday, sabbath, vacation, recess, red-letter day, relaxation, rest, repose, halt, pause (142), respite.
Phrases: *Otium cum dignitate*; time to spare; time on one's hands.
Verbs: To have leisure, take one's ease, repose (687), pause.
Phrase: To shut up shop.
Adjectives: Leisurely, undisturbed, quiet, deliberate, calm, slow (683).
Adverbs: Leisurely, etc., at leisure.

686 EXERTION
Substantives: labour, work, toil, fag, exercise, travail, swink, sweat, exercitation, duty, trouble, pains, ado, drudgery, fagging, slavery, operoseness.

Effort, strain, grind, tug, stress, tension, throw, stretch, struggle, spell, heft.

Gymnastics, gym, physical jerks, PT.
Phrases: A stroke of work; the sweat of one's brow.
Verbs: To labour, work, exert oneself, toil, strive, use exertion, fag, strain, drudge, moil, take pains, take trouble, trouble oneself, slave, pull, tug, ply the oar, rough it, sweat, bestir oneself, get up steam, get a move on, fall to work, buckle to, stick to.
Phrases: To set one's shoulder to the wheel; to strain every nerve; to spare no pains; to do one's utmost or damnedest; to work day and night; to work one's fingers to the bone; to do double duty; to work double tides; to put forth one's strength; to work like a nigger or

a horse; to go through fire and water; to put one's best foot forward (682); to do one's level best, grub along; to lay oneself out, lean over backwards.
Adjectives: Labouring, etc., laborious, toilsome, troublesome, operose, herculean, gymnastic, palaestric.

Hard-working, painstaking, energetic, strenuous (682).
Adverbs: Laboriously, lustily, roundly.
Phrases: By the sweat of the brow; with all one's might; *totis viribus*; with might and main; *vi et armis*; tooth and nail; hammer and tongs; through thick and thin; heart and soul.

687 REPOSE
Substantives: rest, halt, pause, relaxation, breathing-space, respite (685).

Day of rest, *dies non*, sabbath, holiday.
Verbs: To repose, rest, relax, take rest, breathe, take breath, take one's ease, gather breath, recover one's breath, respire, pause, halt, stay one's hand, lay to, lie by, lie fallow, recline, lie down, go to rest, go to bed, go to sleep, etc., unbend, slacken.
Phrases: To rest upon one's oars, to take a holiday; to shut up shop.
Adjectives: Reposing, resting, etc., restful, unstrained; sabbatical.

688 FATIGUE
Substantives: lassitude, weariness (841), tiredness, exhaustion, sweat, collapse, prostration, swoon, faintness, faint, *deliquium,* syncope, yawning, anhelation; overstrain.
Verbs: To be fatigued, etc., to droop, sink, flag, wilt, lose breath, lose wind, gasp, pant, pech, puff, yawn, drop, swoon, faint, succumb.

To fatigue, tire, weary, fag, irk, jade, harass, exhaust, knock up, prostrate, wear out, strain, overtask, overwork, overburden, overtax, overstrain, drive, sweat.

Adjectives: Fatigued, tired, unrefreshed, weary, wearied, jaded; wayworn; overworked, hard-driven, toilworn, done up.

Breathless, out of breath, windless, out of wind, blown, winded, broken-winded.

Drooping, flagging, faint, fainting, doneup, knocked up, exhausted, sinking, prostrate, spent, overspent, deadbeat, dog-tired, fagged out.

Worn out, played out, battered, shattered, weather-beaten, footsore, *hors de combat,* done for.

Fatiguing, etc., tiresome, irksome, wearisome, trying.

Phrases: Ready to drop; tired to death; on one's last legs; run off one's legs; all in.

689 REFRESHMENT

Substantives: recovery of strength, recruiting, repair, refection, refocillation, relief, bracing, regalement, bait, restoration, revival; pick-up.

Phrase: A giant refreshed.

Verbs: To refresh, recruit, repair, refocillate, give tone, reinvigorate, reanimate, restore, recover.

To recover, regain, renew, etc., one's strength; perk up.

Adjectives: Refreshing, etc., recuperative, tonic; refreshed, etc., untired, unwearied, etc. (682).

690 AGENT

Substantives: doer, performer, actor, perpetrator, practitioner, operator, hand, employee, commissionaire, executor, executrix, maker, effector, consignee, steward, broker, factor, middleman, jobber.

Artist, workman, workwoman, charwoman, worker, artisan, artificer, architect, craftsman, handicraftsman, mechanic, roustabout, machinist, machineman, manufacturer, operative, journeyman, labourer, navvy, stevedore, docker, smith, wright, day-labourer, co-worker; *dramatis personae.*

Drudge, hack, fag, man or maid of all work, hired man, hired girl, factotum, handy-man.

Phrase: Hewers of wood and drawers of water.

691 WORKSHOP

Substantives: laboratory, manufactory, mill, shop, works, factory, mint, forge, smithy, loom, cabinet, office, bureau, studio, atelier, hive, hive of industry, workhouse, nursery, hothouse, hotbed, kitchen, dock, slip, yard, foundry.

Crucible, alembic, cauldron, matrix.

692 CONDUCT

Substantives: course of action, practice, drill, procedure, business (625), transaction, dealing, ways, tactics, policy, polity, generalship, statesmanship, economy, strategy, husbandry, seamanship, stewardship, housekeeping, housewifery, *ménage,* regime, *modus operandi,* economy.

Execution, manipulation, handling, treatment, process, working-out, course, campaign, career, walk.

Behaviour, deportment, comportment, carriage, mein, air, demeanour, bearing, manner, observance.

Verbs: To conduct, carry on, run, transact, execute, carry out, work out, get through, carry through, go through, dispatch, treat, deal with, proceed with, officiate, discharge, do duty, play a part or game, run a race.

To behave; to comport, acquit, demean, carry, hold oneself.

Phrases: To shape one's course; to paddle one's own canoe.

Adjectives: Conducting, etc., strategical, business-like, practical, executive.

693 DIRECTION

Substantives: management, government, bureaucracy, statesmanship, conduct (692), regulation, charge, agency, senatorship, ministry, ministration, managery, directorate, directorship, chairmanship, guidance, steerage, pilotage, superintendence, stewardship, supervision, surveillance, proctorship, chair, portfolio, statecraft, politics, *haute politique,* kingcraft, cybernetics; council (696).

Helm, rudder, compass, needle, radar.

Phrase: The reins of government.

Verbs: To direct, manage, govern, guide, conduct, regulate, order, prescribe, brief, steer, con, pilot, have or take the direction, take the helm, have the charge of, administer, superintend, overlook, supervise, look after, see to, control, boss, run, preside, hold office, hold the portfolio.

To head, lead, show the way, etc.

Phrase: To pull the wires.

Adjectives: Directing, etc., managerial, gubernatorial, executive; dirigible.

694 DIRECTOR

Substantives: manager, executive, master (745), prime minister, premier, governor, statesman, legislator, controller, comptroller, intendant, superintendent, rector, matron, supervisor, president, preses, chairman, headman, supercargo, inspector, moderator, monitor, overseer, overlooker, shopwalker, taskmaster, leader, ringleader, demagogue, conductor, precentor, fugleman; official, jack-in-office, bureaucrat, minister, office-bearer, red-tapist, officer (726).

Conductor, steersman, helmsman, pilot, coxswain, guide, cicerone, guard, driver, engine-driver, motorman, whip, charioteer, coachman, Jehu, muleteer, teamster, chauffeur, postilion, *vetturino.*

Steward, factor, factotum, bailiff, landreeve, foreman, forewoman, gaffer, charge-hand, whipper-in,

shepherd, proctor, procurator, housekeeper, major-domo, chef, master of ceremonies, MC.

695 ADVICE

Substantives: counsel, suggestion, recommendation, advocacy, hortation, exhortation, dehortation, instruction, charge, monition, admonition (668), admonishment, caution, warning, expostulation (616), obtestation, injunction, persuasion.

Guidance, guide, handbook, chart, compass, manual, itinerary, roadbook, reference.

An adviser, senator, counsellor, counsel, consultant, specialist, monitor, mentor, Nestor, guide, teacher (540), physician, leech, doctor.

Referee, arbiter, arbitrator, referendary, assessor.

Verbs: To advise, counsel, give advice, recommend, advocate, admonish, submonish, suggest, prompt, caution, warn, forewarn.

To persuade, dehort, exhort, enjoin, expostulate, charge, instruct.

To deliberate, consult together, hold a council, etc., confer, call in, refer to take advice, be closeted with.

Phrases: To lay their heads together; to compare notes; to go into a huddle; to take counsel of one's pillow; to take one's cue from.

Adjectives: Monitory, monitive, admonitory, recommendatory, hortatory, dehortatory, exhortatory, exhortative, warning, etc.

Phrases: A word to the wise; *verb sap.*

Interjection: Go to!

696 COUNCIL

Substantives: conclave, court, chamber, cabinet, cabinet council, house, committee, subcommittee, board, bench, brains trust, *comitia,* staff.

Senate, *senatus,* parliament, synod, soviet, convocation, convention, congress, consistory, conventicle, chapter, chapel, witenagemot, junta, states-general, diet, Cortes, Riksdag, Thing, Storthing, Reichsrat, Reichstag, Duma, Politburo, Presidium, Comintern, Sobranje, Skupshtina, Tynwald, divan, durbar, kgotla, indala, Areopagus, sanhedrin, directory.

A meeting, assembly, sitting, session, séance, sederunt.

Adjectives: Senatorial, curule.

697 PRECEPT
Substantives: direction, instruction, charge, prescript, prescription, recipe, receipt, order (741).

Rule, canon, code, formula, formulary, law, statute, act, rubric, maxim, apophthegm, etc. (496).

698 SKILL
Substantives: skilfulness, cleverness, ability, talent, genius, ingenuity, calibre, capacity, competence, shrewdness, sagacity, parts, endowment, faculty, gift, forte, strong point, turn, invention, headpiece.

Address, dexterity, adroitness, aptness, aptitude, facility, felicity, knack, expertness, quickness, sharpness, resourcefulness, smartness, readiness, excellence, habilitation, technique, virtuosity, artistry, ambidexterity, ambidextrousness, sleight of hand (545), know-how, knowingness.

Qualification, proficiency, panurgy, accomplishment, attainment, acquirement, craft, mastery, mastership.

Tact, knowledge of the world, *savoir faire,* discretion, finesse, worldly wisdom.

Prudence, discretion (864).

Art, science, management, tactics, manœuvring, sleight, trick, policy, strategy, jobbery, temporization, technology.

A masterstroke, *chef-d'œuvre,* a masterpiece, *tour de force,* a bold stroke, *coup be maître,* a good hit (650).

Verbs: To be skilful, skilled, etc., to excel in, to specialize in, have the trick of, be master of; to temporize, manœuvre.

Phrases: To play one's cards well; to stoop to conquer; to have all one's wits about one; to keep one's hand in; to know your stuff; to cut one's coat according to one's cloth; to know what one is about; to know what's what; to know the ropes.

Adjectives: Skilled, skilful, etc., clever, able, accomplished, talented, versatile, many-sided, resourceful, ingenious, inventive, shrewd, gifted, hard-headed, sagacious, sharp-witted.

Expert, crack, dexterous, scientific, adroit, apt, sharp, handy, deft, fluent, facile, ready, quick, smart, slick, spry, yare, nimble, ambidextrous, neat-handed, fine-fingered.

Conversant, versed, proficient, efficient, capable, competent, qualified, good at, up to, master of, cut out for, at home in, knowing.

Experienced, practised, hackneyed, trained, initiated, prepared, primed, finished, schooled, thoroughbred, masterly, consummate.

Technical, artistic, workmanlike, business-like, daedalian.

Discreet, politic, tactful, diplomatic, sure-footed, felicitous, strategic.

Phrases: Up to snuff; sharp as a needle; no flies on him.

Adverbs: Skilfully, etc., aright.

699 UNSKILFULNESS
Substantives: inability, incompetence, incompetency, inproficience, improficiency, infelicity, inexpertness, indexterity, unaptness, ineptitude, lefthandedness, awkwardness, maladroitness, clumsiness, gaucherie, rawness, slovenliness, greenness, inexperience, disability, disqualification.

Bungling, blundering, etc., blunder (495), *bêtise*; unteachableness, dumbness, dullness, stupidity (499).

Indescretion, imprudence (863), thoughtlessness, giddiness, wildness, mismanagement, misconduct, maladministration, misrule, misgovernment, misapplication, misdirection.

Phrases: Rule of thumb; a bad show.

Verbs: To be unskilled, unskilful, etc.

To mismanage, bungle, blunder, botch, boggle, fumble, flounder, stumble, muff, foozle, miscue, muddle, murder, mistake, misapply, misdirect, misconduct; stultify.

Phrases: To make a mess or hash of; to begin at the wrong end; to make sad work or a bad job of; to put one's foot in it; to lose or miss one's way; to lose one's balance; to stand in one's own light; to quarrel with one's bread and butter; to pay dear for one's whistle; to cut one's own throat; to kill the goose which lays the golden eggs; to reckon without one's host.

Adjectives: Unskilled, etc., unskilful, bungling, etc., awkward, clumsy, unhandy, unworkmanlike, unscientific, shiftless, lubberly, *gauche,* maladroit, left-handed, hobbling, slovenly, sloppy, slatternly, giddy, gawky, dumb, dull, unteachable, at fault.

Unapt, unqualified, inhabile, incompetent, disqualified, untalented, ill-qualified, inapt, inept, inexpert, inartistic, raw, green, rusty.

Unaccustomed, unused, unhackneyed, unexercised, untrained, unpractised, undisciplined, uneducated, undrilled, uninitiated, unschooled, unconversant, unversed, inexperienced, unstatesmanlike, non-professional.

Unadvised, misadvised, ill-judged, ill-advised, unguided, misguided, foolish, wild, ill-devised, misconducted.

Phrases: His fingers are all thumbs; penny wise and pound foolish.

700 PROFICIENT

Substantives: adept, expert, specialist, genius, dab, crack, whiz, master, *maître,* master-hand, virtuoso, champion, first string, first fiddle, protagonist, ace, artist, tactician, marksman, old stager, veteran, top-sawyer, picked man, cunning man, conjurer, wizard, etc. (994); connoisseur (850); prodigy (872), an Admirable Crichton.

Phrases: A man of the world; a practised hand; no slouch; a smart customer; an old file; an all-round man.

701 BUNGLER

Substantives: blunderer, marplot, greenhorn, lubber, landlubber, fumbler, muddler, duffer, butter-fingers, novice, no conjurer, flat, muff, babe.

Phrases: A poor hand at; no good at; a fish out of water; a freshwater sailor; the awkward squad; not likely to set the Thames on fire.

702 CUNNING

Substantives: craft, craftiness, wiliness, artfulness, subtlety, shrewdness, smartness, archness, insidiousness, slyness, opportunism, artificialness, artificiality.

Artifice, stratagem, wile, dodge, subterfuge, evasion, finesse, ruse, diplomacy, jobbery, backstairs influence.

Duplicity, guile, circumvention, chicane, chicanery, sharp practice, Machiavellism, legerdemain, trickery, etc. (545).

Net, toils, trap, etc. (667).

A slyboots, Ulysses, Machiavel, trickster, serpent, fox, intriguer, opportunist, time-server.

Verbs: To be cunning, etc., to contrive, design, manœuvre, gerrymander, finesse, shuffle, wriggle, wangle, intrigue, temporize, overreach (545), circumvent, get round, nobble, undermine.

Phrases: To play a deep game; to steal a march on; to know on which side one's bread is buttered.

Adjectives: Cunning, crafty, artful, knowing, wily, sly, fly, pawky, smooth, sharp, smart, slim, feline, subtle, arch, designing, intriguing, contriving, insidious, canny, downy, leery, tricky, deceitful (545), artificial, deep, profound, diplomatic, vulpine, Machiavellian, time-serving.

Phrases: Cunning as a fox; too clever by half; not born yesterday; not to be caught with chaff.

703 ARTLESSNESS

Substantives: nature, naturalness, simplicity, ingenuousness, *bonhomie*, frankness, naïveté, openness, *abandon*, candour, outspokenness, sincerity, straightforwardness, honesty (939), innocence (946).

Phrases: *Enfant terrible*; a rough diamond; a mere babe.

Verbs: To be artless, etc.

Phrases: To call a spade a spade; not to mince one's words; to speak one's mind; to wear one's heart upon one's sleeve.

Adjectives: Artless, natural, native, plain, simple-minded, ingenuous, candid, untutored, unsophisticated, simple, naïve, sincere, frank (543), open, frank-hearted, open-hearted, above-board, downright, unreserved, guileless, inartificial, undesigning, single-minded, honest, straightforward, outspoken, blunt, matter-of-fact.

Section 4 –
Antagonism.

704 DIFFICULTY

Substantives: hardness, toughness, hard work, uphill work, hard task, troublesomeness, laboriousness.

Impracticability, infeasibility, intractability, toughness, perverseness (471).

Embarrassment, awkwardness, perplexity, intricacy, intricateness, entanglement, knot, Gordian knot, labyrinth, net, meshes, maze, etc. (248).

Dilemma, nice point, delicate point, knotty point, stumbling-block, snag, vexed question, crux; *pons asinorum*, poser, puzzle, floorer, teaser, nonplus, quandary, strait, pass, critical situation, crisis, trial, pinch, emergency, exigency, scramble.

Scrape, hobble, fix, hole, lurch, contretemps, hitch, how-d'ye-do, slough, quagmire, hot water, pickle, stew, imbroglio, mess, ado, false position, stand, deadlock, encumbrance, cul-de-sac, impasse.

Phrases: A Herculean task; a labour of Sisyphus; a difficult role to play; a sea of troubles; horns of a dilemma; a peck of troubles; a kettle of fish; a pretty state of things; a handful; 'Ay, there's the rub.'

Verbs: To be difficult, etc.

To meet with, experience, labour under, get into, plunge into, be surrounded by, be encompassed with, be entangled by, struggle, contend against or grapple with difficulties.

To come to a stand, to stick fast, to be set fast, to boggle, flounder, get left.

To render difficult, etc., to embarrass, perplex, put one out, bother, pose, puzzle, floor, nonplus, ravel, entangle, gravel, faze, flummox, run hard.

Phrases: To come to a deadlock; to be at a loss; to get into hot water; to get into a mess; to be bunkered; to weave a tangled web; to fish in troubled waters; to buffet the waves; to be put to one's shifts; not to know which way to turn; to skate over thin ice.

To lead one a pretty dance; to put a spoke in one's wheel; to leave in the lurch.

Adjectives: Difficult, not easy, hard, stiff, troublesome, toilsome, formidable, laborious, onerous, operose,

269

awkward, unwieldy, beset with or full of difficulties, Herculean, Sisyphean.

Unmanageable, tough, stubborn, hard to deal with, *difficile,* trying, provoking, ill-conditioned, refractory, perverse, crabbed, intractable, against the grain.

Embarrassing, perplexing, delicate, ticklish, pernickety, complicated, intricate, thorny, spiny, knotty, tricky, critical, pathless, trackless, labyrinthine.

Impracticable, not possible, impossible (471), not practicable, not feasible, unachievable, un-come-at-able, inextricable, impassable, innavigable, desperate, insuperable, insurmountable, unplayable.

In difficulty, perplexed, etc., beset, water-logged, put to it, hard put to it, run hard, hard pressed, thrown out, adrift, at fault, abroad, pushed.

Stranded, aground, stuck fast, at bay.

Phrases: At a standstill; at a stand; up against it; up a gum-tree; out of one's depth; at the end of one's tether; in a cleft stick; on the wrong scent; driven from pillar to post; things being come to a pretty pass; at a pinch; between two stools; in the wrong box; in a fix; in a hole; in a tight place; in the cart; in the soup.

Adverbs: With difficulty, hardly, etc., against the stream, against the grain, uphill.

706 HINDRANCE
Substantives: prevention, preclusion, impedance, retardment, retardation.

Obstruction, stoppage, interruption, interclusion, oppilation, interception, restriction, restraint, inhibition, embargo, blockade, embarrassment.

Interference, interposition, obtrusion, discouragement, chill.

An impediment, hindrance, obstacle, obstruction, bunker, hazard, let, stumbling-block, snag, check,

impasse, countercheck, *contretemps,* set-back, hitch, bar, barrier, barrage, barricade, turnpike, wall, dead wall, bulkhead, portcullis, etc. (717), dam, weir, broom, turnstile, tourniquet.

Drawback, objection.

An encumbrance, impedimenta, onus, clog, skid, drag, weight, dead weight, lumber, top-hamper, pack, millstone, incubus, nightmare; trammel, etc. (752).

A hinderer, marplot; killjoy, interloper, passenger; opponent (710).

Phrases: A lion in the path; a millstone round one's neck; a wet blanket; the old man of the sea; *damnosa hereditas*; back to square one.

Verbs: To hinder, impede, prevent, preclude, retard, slacken, obviate, forefend, avert, turn aside, ward off, draw off, cut off, counteract, undermine.

To obstruct, stop, stay, let, make against, bar, debar, inhibit, scotch, squash, cramp, restrain, check, stonewall, set back, discourage, discountenance, foreclose.

To thwart, traverse, contravene, interrupt, intercept, interclude, frustrate, defeat, disconcert, embarrass, baffle, undo, intercept; to balk, unsight, cushion, stymie, spoil, mar.

To interpose, interfere, intermeddle, obtrude (682).

To hamper, clog, cumber, encumber, saddle with, load with, overload, overlay, lumber, block up, incommode, hustle; to curb, shackle, fetter; to embog.

Phrases: To lay under restraint; to tie the hands; to keep in swaddling bands.

To stand in the way of; to take the wind out of one's sails; to break in upon; to run or fall foul of; to put a spoke in the wheel; to throw cold water on; to nip in the bud; to apply the closure.

Adjectives: Hindering, etc., in the way of, impedimental, inimical, unfavourable, onerous, burdensome, cumbrous, intercipient, obstructive.

Hindered, etc., wind-bound, storm-stayed, water-logged, heavy-laden.

Unassisted, unaided, unhelped, unsupported, single-handed, un-befriended.

Phrase: Prevention is better than cure.

707 AID
Substantives: assistance, help, succour, support, advocacy, relief, advance, furtherance, promotion.

Coadjuvancy, patronage, interest, championship, countenance, favour, helpfulness.

Sustentation, subvention, subsidy, alimentation, nutrition, nourishment, ministration, ministry, accommodation.

Supplies, reinforcements, succours, contingents, recruits; physical support (215); relief, rescue.

Phrases: Corn in Egypt; a *deus ex machina*.

Verbs: To aid, assist, help, succour, support, sustain, uphold, subscribe to, finance, promote, further, abet, advance, foster, cherish, foment; to give, bring, furnish, afford or supply support, etc., to reinforce, recruit, nourish, nurture.

To favour, countenance, befriend, smile upon, encourage, patronize, make interest for.

To second, stand by, relieve, rescue, back, back up, take part with, side with, to come or pass over to, to join, to rally round, play up to.

To serve, do service, minister to, oblige, humour, cheer, accommodate, work for, administer to, pander to; to tend, attend, take care of, wait on, nurse, dry-nurse, entertain.

To speed, expedite, forward, quicken, hasten, set forward.

Phrases: To take the part of; consult the wishes of; to take up the cudgels for; to espouse the cause of; to enlist under the banners of; to lend or bear a hand; to hold out a helping hand; to give one a lift; to do one a good turn; to see one through; to take in tow; to pay the piper; to help a lame dog over the stile; to give a leg-up.

Adjectives: Aiding, helping, assisting, etc., auxiliary, adjuvant, ancillary, accessory, ministrant, subservient, subsidiary, helpful.

Friendly, amicable, favourable, propitious, well-disposed, neighbourly.

Adverbs: On or in behalf of; in the service of; under the auspices of; hand in hand.

Interjections: Help! save us! *à moi!*

708 OPPOSITION
Substantives: antagonism, oppugnancy, oppugnation, counteraction (179), contravention, impugnment, control, clashing, collision, competition, conflict, rivalry, emulation.

Absence of aid, etc., counterplot (718).

Phrase: A head wind.

Verbs: To oppose, antagonize, cross, counteract, control, contravene, countervail, counterwork, contradict, belie, controvert, oppugn, stultify, thwart, counter, countermine, run counter, go against, collide with, clash, rival, emulate, put against, militate against, beat against, stem, breast, encounter, compete with, withstand, to face, face down.

Phrases: To set one's face against; to make a dead set against; to match (or pit) oneself against; to stand out against; to fly in the face of; to fall foul of; to come into collision with; to be or to play at cross-purposes; to kick against the pricks; to buffet the waves; to cut one another's throats; to join issue.

Adjectives: Opposing, etc., adverse, antagonistic, opposed, conflicting, contrary, unfavourable, unfriendly, hostile, inimical; competitive, emulous.

Phrases: Up in arms; at daggers drawn.

Adverbs: Against, versus, counter to, against the grain; against the stream, tide, wind, etc., in the way of, in spite of, in despite of, in the teeth of, in the face of, *per contra*; single-handed.

Across, athwart, overthwart.

Though, although (179), even, *quand même,* all the same.

Phrases: In spite of one's teeth; with the wind in one's teeth.

709 CO-OPERATION

Substantives: coadjuvancy, collaboration, concert, collusion, participation, complicity, co-efficiency, concurrence (178).

Alliance, colleagueship, free-masonry, joint-stock, co-partnership, coalition, combine, syndicate (778), amalgamation, federation, confederation (712).

Phrases: A helping hand; a long pull.

Verbs: To co-operate, combine, concur, conspire, concert, collaborate, draw or pull together, to join with, collude, unite one's efforts, club together, fraternize, be in league, etc., with, be a party to, to side with.

Phrases: To make common cause; to be in the same boat; to stand shoulder to shoulder; to play into the hands of; to hunt in couples; to hit it off together; to lay their heads together; to play ball.

Adjectives: Co-operating, etc., co-operative, co-operant, in co-operation, etc., in concert, allied, clannish; favourable (707).

Unopposed, unobstructed, unimpeded.

Phrase: Wind and weather permitting.

Adverbs: As one man (488).

710 OPPONENT

Substantives: antagonist, adversary, adverse party, opposition, rival, competitor, pacemaker, enemy, foe (891), assailant; malcontent.

711 AUXILIARY

Substantives: assistant, adjuvant, adjunct, adjutant, help, helper, help-mate, helpmeet, colleague, partner, side-kick, *confrère,* coadjutor, co-operator, collaborator, co-belligerent, ally, aide-de-camp, accomplice, accessory, stand-in, stooge.

Friend (890), confidant, champion, partisan, right hand, stand-by; adherent, *particeps criminis,* confederate, bottleholder, second, candle-holder, servant (746); *fidus Achates.*

Phrase: *Deus ex machina.*

712 PARTY

Substantives: side, partnership, fraternity, sodality, company, society, firm, house, establishment, body, corporation, corporate body, union, association, syndicate, guild, tong, joint concern, combine, trust, cartel.

Fellowship, brotherhood, sisterhood, denomination, communion, community, clan, clanship, club, friendly society, clique, junto, coterie, faction, gang, ring, circle, *camarilla,* cabal, league, confederacy, confederation, federation; *esprit de corps;* alliance, partisanship.

Band, staff, crew, team, set, posse, phalanx, *dramatis personae.*

Verbs: To unite, join, club together, join forces, federate, co-operate, befriend, aid, etc. (707), cement, form a party, league, etc., to be in the same boat.

Adjectives: In partnership, alliance, etc., federal, federated, bounded, banded, linked, cemented, etc., together, embattled.

713 DISCORD

Substantives: disagreement (24), variance, difference, divergence, dissent, dissension, misunderstanding, jar, jarring, clashing, friction, odds, dissonance, disaccord.

Disunion, schism, breach, falling out, division, split, rupture, disruption, open rupture, *brouillerie*, feud, vendetta, contentiousness, litigiousness, strife, contention (720); enmity (889).

Dispute, controversy, polemics, quarrel, tiff, spat, *tracasserie*, altercation, imbroglio, bickering, snip-snap, chicanery, squabble, row, shemozzle, rumpus, racket, fracas, brawl, bear garden, Donnybrook, debate (476).

Litigation, words, war of words, battle of the books, logomachy, wrangling, wrangle, jangle, breach of the peace, declaration of war (722).

Subject of dispute, ground of quarrel, disputed point, vexed question, bone of contention, apple of discord, *casus belli.*

Verbs: To be discordant, etc., to differ, dissent, disagree, clash, jar, to misunderstand one another.

To fall out, dispute, controvert, litigate, to quarrel, argue, wrangle, squabble, bicker, spar, jangle, nag, brawl; to break with; to declare war.

To embroil, entangle, disunite, set against, pit against; to sow dissension, disunion, discord, etc. among.

Phrases: To be at odds with; to fall foul of: to have words with; to have a bone to pick with; to have a crow to pluck with; to have a chip on one's shoulder; to be at variance with; to be at cross purposes; to join issue; to pick a quarrel with; to part brass rags; to chew the fat or rag; to go to the mat with; to live like cat and dog.

To set by the ears; to put the cat among the pigeons; to sow or stir up contention.

Adjectives: Discordant, disagreeing, differing, disunited, clashing, jarring, discrepant, divergent, dissentient, sectarian, at variance, controversial.

Quarrelsome, disputatious, litigious, litigant, factious, pettifogging, polemic, schismatic; unpacified, unreconciled.

Phrases: At odds; on bad terms; in hot water; at daggers drawn; up in arms; out of tune; at sixes and sevens; at loggerheads; a house divided against itself; no love lost between them.

714 CONCORD
Substantives: accord, agreement (23), unison, unity, union, good understanding, quiet, peace, conciliation, unanimity (488), harmony, amity, sympathy (897), *entente cordiale, rapprochement,* alliance.

Phrases: The bonds of harmony; a happy family; kittens in a basket; a happy band of brothers.

Verbs: To agree, accord, be in unison, etc., to harmonize with, fraternize, stand in with.

Phrases: To understand one another; to see eye to eye with; to hit it off; to keep the peace; to pull together.

Adjectives: Concordant, congenial, agreeing, etc., united, in unison, etc., harmonious, allied, cemented, friendly (888), amicable, fraternal, at peace, peaceful, pacific, tranquil.

Phrases: At one with; with one voice.

715 DEFIANCE
Substantives: challenge, dare, cartel, daring, war-cry, slogan, college yell, war-whoop.

Verbs: To defy, challenge, dare, brave, beard, bluster, look big.

Phrases: To set at naught; snap the fingers at; to cock a snook at; to bid defiance to; to set at defiance; to hurl defiance at; to double the fist; to show a bold front; to brave it out; to show fight; to throw down the gauntlet or glove; to call out.

Adjectives: Defying, etc., defiant.

Adverbs: In defiance of; with arms akimbo.

Interjections: Come on! let 'em all come! do your worst!

Phrase: *Nemo me impune lacessit.*

716 ATTACK

Substantives: aggression, offence, assault, charge, onset, onslaught, battue, brunt, thrust, pass, passado, cut, sally, inroad, invasion, irruption, incursion, excursion, sortie, *camisade,* storm, storming, boarding, escalade, foray, raid, air raid, *razzia,* dragonnade (619); siege, investment.

Fire, volley, cannonade, barrage, blitz, broadside, bombardment, stonk, hate, raking fire, platoon-fire, fusillade.

Kick, punch (276), lunge, a run at, a dead set at, carte and tierce, a backhander.

An assailant, aggressor, invader.

Verbs: To attack, assault, assail, go for, fall upon, close with, charge, bear down upon, set on, have at, strike at, run at, make a run at, butt, tilt at, poke at, make a pass at, thrust at, stab, bayonet, cut and thrust, pitch into, kick, buffet, bonnet, beat (972), lay about one, lift a hand against, come on, have a fling at, slap on the face, pelt, throw stones, etc., to round on.

To shoot, shoot at, fire at, fire upon, let fly at, brown, pepper, bombard, shell, bomb, dive-bomb, blitz, strafe, prang.

To beset, besiege, lay siege to, invest, beleaguer, open the trenches, invade, raid, storm, board, scale the walls.

To press one hard, be hard upon, drive one hard.

Phrases: To draw the sword against; to launch an offensive; take the offensive; assume the aggressive; make a dead set at.

To give the cold steel to; to lay down a barrage; to pour in a broadside; to fire a volley.

Adjectives: Attacking, etc., aggressive, offensive, up in arms.

717 DEFENCE

Substantives: self-defence, self preservation, protection, ward, guard, guardianship, shielding, etc., resistance (719), safety (664).

Fence, wall, parapet, dike, ditch, fosse, moat (232), boom, mound, mole, outwork, trench, foxhole, dugout, shelter, Anderson shelter, Morrison shelter, entrenchment, fortification, embankment, bulwark, barbican, battlement, stockade, laager, zareba, abattis, turret, barbette, casemate, muniment, vallum, circumvallation, contravallation, barbed-wire entanglement, sunk fence, ha-ha, buttress, abutement, breastwork, portcullis, glacis, bastion, redoubt, rampart.

Hold, stronghold, keep, donjon, palladium, fort, fortress, blockhouse, pillbox, hedgehog, sconce, citadel, tower, castle, capitol, fastness, asylum (666).

Anchor, sheet-anchor.

Shield, armour, buckler, aegis, breastplate, coat of mail, cuirass, hauberk, habergeon, *chevaux de frise,* screen, etc. (666), helmet, tin hat, battle bowler, casque, shako, bearskin, gas-mask, panoply; fender, torpedonet, paravane, cow-catcher, buffer.

Defender, protector, guardian (664), champion, protagonist, knight errant; garrison, picket.

Verbs: To defend, shield, fend, fence, entrench, guard (664), keep off, keep at bay, ward off, beat off, parry, repel, bear the brunt of, put to flight.

Phrases: To act on the defensive; to maintain one's ground; to stand at bay; to give a warm reception to.

Adjectives: Defending, etc., defensive, defended, etc., armed, armoured, armour-plated, iron-clad, loopholed, sandbagged, castellated, panoplied, proof, bullet-proof, bomb-proof.

Phrases: Armed cap-à-pie; armed to the teeth.
Adverbs: Defensively, on the defence, on the defensive, at bay.

718 RETALIATION
Substantives: reprisal, retort, comeback, counter-stroke, reciprocation, *tu quoque,* recrimination, retribution, counterplot, counterproject, counterblast, *lex talionis,* revenge (919), compensation (30).
Phrases: Tit for tat; a *quid pro quo*; a Roland for an Oliver; diamond cut diamond; the biter bit; catching a Tartar; a game two can play at; hoist with his own petard.
Verbs: To retaliate, retort, cap, reciprocate, recriminate, counter, get even with one, pay off.
Phrases: To turn the tables; to return the compliment; to pay off old scores; to pay in one's own coin; to give as good as one got.
Adjectives: Retaliating, retaliatory, retaliative, recriminatory, recriminative.
Interjection: You're another!

719 RESISTANCE
Substantives: stand, oppugnation, reluctation, front, repulse, rebuff, opposition (708), disobedience (742), recalcitration.

Strike, industrial action, lockout, tumult, riot, pronunciamento, *émeute,* mutiny.

Revolt, rising, insurrection, rebellion, *coup d'état, putsch.*
Verbs: To resist, not to submit, etc., to withstand, stand against, stand firm, make a stand, repugn, reluct, reluctate, confront, grapple with, face down.

To kick, kick against, recalcitrate, lift the hand against (716), repel, repulse, rise, revolt, mutiny.
Phrases: To show a bold front; to make head against; to stand one's ground; to stand the brunt of; to hold

one's own; to keep at bay; to stem the torrent; to champ the bit; to sell one's life dearly.

To fly in the face of; to kick against the pricks; to take the bit between one's teeth.
Adjectives: Resisting, etc., resistive, resistant, refractory, mutinous, recalcitrant, rebellious, up in arms, out.

Unyielding, unconquered, indomitable.
Interjections: Hands off! keep off!

720 CONTENTION
Substantives: contest, struggle, contestation, debate (476), logomachy, paper war, litigation, high words, rivalry, corrivalry, corrivalship, competition, *concours,* gymkhana, race, heat, match, tie, bickering, strife (713).

Wrestling, jiu-jitsu, pugilism, boxing, fisticuffs, spar, prize-fighting, athletics, sports, gymnastics, set-to, round, fracas, row, shindy, scrap, dust, rumpus, shemozzle, stramash, outbreak, clash, collision, shock, breach of the peace, brawl, Donnybrook (713).

Conflict, skirmish, rencounter, scuffle, encounter, velitation, tussle, scrimmage, scrummage, broil, fray, affray, *mêlée,* affair, brush, bout, fight, battle, combat, action, engagement, battle royal, running fight, free fight, joust, tournament, tourney, pitched battle, death struggle, Armageddon.

Naval engagement, naumachy, seafight; air duel, dogfight.

Duel, satisfaction, monomachy, single combat, passage of arms, affair of honour, a triangular duel.
Verbs: To contend, struggle, vie with, emulate, rival, race, race with, outvie, battle with, cope with, compete, join issue, bandy words with, try conclusions with, close with, square, buckle with, spar, box, tussle, fence, wrestle, joust, enter the lists, take up arms, take the field, encounter, strug-

gle with, grapple with, tackle, engage with, pitch into, strive with, fall to, encounter, collide with.

Phrases: Join battle; fall foul of; have a brush with; break the peace; take up the cudgels; unsheath the sword; break a lance; to run a tilt at; give satisfaction; measure swords; exchange shots; lay about one; cut and thrust; fight without the gloves; go on the warpath.

Adjectives: Contending, etc., contentious, combative, bellicose (722); pugilistic, agnostic, competitive, rival, polemical (476), rough-and-tumble.

Phrases: A word and a blow; pull devil, pull baker.

721 PEACE

Substantives: amity, truce, armistice, harmony (714), tranquillity.

Phrases: Piping time of peace; a quiet life.

Verbs: To be at peace, etc., to keep the peace, etc. (714), pacify (723).

Adjectives: Pacific, peaceable, peaceful, tranquil, untroubled, bloodless, halcyon.

722 WARFARE

Substantives: war, hostilities, fighting, etc., arms, the sword, open war, *ultima ratio,* war to the knife.

Battle array, campaign, crusade, expedition, operation, mission, warpath.

Warlike spirit, military spirit, militarism, bellicosity.

The art of war, tactics, strategy, military evolutions, arms, service, campaigning, tented field; Mars, Bellona.

War-cry, slogan, fiery cross, trumpet, clarion, bugle, pibroch, war-whoop, beat of drum, tom-tom; mobilization.

Phrases: The mailed fist; wager of battle.

Verbs: To arm, fight, set to, spar, scrap, tussle, joust, tilt, box, skirmish,

fight hand to hand, fence, measure swords, engage, combat, give battle, go to battle, join battle, engage in battle, raise or mobilize troops, declare war, wage war, go to war, come to blows, break a lance with, appeal to arms, appeal to the sword, give satisfaction, take the field, keep the field, fight it out, fight to a finish, spill blood, carry on war, carry on hostilities, to fight one's way, to serve, to fight like devils, to sell one's life dearly.

Phrases: To see service; to smell powder; to go over the top.

Adjectives: Contending, etc., unpeaceful, unpacific, contentious, beligerent, bellicose, jingo, chauvinistic, martial, warlike, military, militant, soldierly, soldierlike, gladiatorial, chivalrous, in arms, embattled.

Phrases: Together by the ears; sword in hand.

Adverbs: *Pendente lite,* the battle raging, in the cannon's mouth; in the thick of the fray.

Interjections: To arms! the Philistines be upon thee!

723 PACIFICATION

Substantives: reconciliation, accommodation, arrangement, *modus vivendi,* adjustment, terms, amnesty.

Peace-offering, olive-branch, calcumet or pipe of peace, preliminaries of peace.

Pacifism, pacificism, appeasement.

Truce, armistice, suspension of arms, of hostilities, etc., convention, *détente.*

Flag of truce, white flag, cartel.

Phrases: Hollow truce; cold war; *pax in bello.*

Verbs: To make peace, pacify, make it up, reconcile, reconciliate, propitiate, appease, tranquillize, compose, allay, settle differences, restore harmony, heal the breach.

Phrases: To put up the sword; to

sheathe the sword; to beat swords into ploughshares; to bury the hatchet; to smoke the pipe of peace; to close the temple of Janus; to cry quits.
Adjectives: Pacified, etc., pacific, conciliatory.

724   MEDIATION
Substantives: intervention, interposition, interference, intermeddling, intercession, parley, negotiation, arbitration, conciliation, mediatorship, good offices, diplomacy, peace-offering, eirenicon.

A mediator, intermediary, go-between, intercessor, peacemaker, diplomat, diplomatist, negotiator, troubleshooter, ombudsman.
Verbs: To mediate, intermediate, intercede, interpose, interfere, intervene, negotiate, arbitrate, compromise, meet half-way.
Phrase: To split the difference.

725   SUBMISSION
Substantives: surrender, non-resistance, appeasement, deference, yielding, capitulation, cession.

Homage, obeisance, bow, curtsy, kneeling, genuflexion, prostration, kow-tow.
Verbs: To surrender, succumb, submit, yield, give in, bend, cringe, crawl, truckle to, knuckle down or under, knock under, capitulate, lay down or deliver up one's arms, retreat, give way, cave in.
Phrases: Beat a retreat; strike one's flag or colours; surrender at discretion; make a virtue of necessity; to come to terms.

To eat humble pie; to eat dirt; to swallow the pill; to kiss the rod; to turn the other cheek; to lick a person's boots.
Adjectives: Surrendering, etc., non-resisting, unresisting, submissive, down-trodden.

Undefended, untenable, indefensible.

726   COMBATANT
Substantives: belligerent, champion, disputant, controversialist, litigant, competitor, rival, corrival, assailant, bully, bruiser, fighter, duellist, fighting-man, pugilist, pug, boxer, the fancy, prize-fighter, fighting-cock, gladiator, swashbuckler, fire-eater, berserker; swordsman, wrestler, Amazon, Paladin, son of Mars; staff, *état-major,* brass hats; militarist.

Warrior, soldier, campaigner, veteran, man-at-arms, redcoat, man in khaki, Tommy Atkins, tommy, doughboy, GI, *poilu,* trooper, dragoon, hussar, grenadier, fusilier, guardsman, lifeguard, lancer, cuirassier, spearman, musketeer, carabineer, rifleman, sniper, sharpshooter, *bersagliere*; ensign, standard-bearer, halberdier; private, subaltern, conscript, recruit, cadet; effectives, line, rank and file, cannon fodder, PBI.

Engineer, artilleryman, gunner, cannoneer, bombadier, sapper, miner; archer, bowman.

Paratrooper, aircraftman, erk, pilot, observer, aircrew.

Marine, jolly, leatherneck; seaman, bluejacket, tar, AB.

Guerrilla, Maquis, partisan, cossack, sepoy, gurkha, spahi, janizary, zouave, bashi-bazouk.

Armed force, the army, the military, regulars, soldiery, infantry, mounted infantry, fencibles, volunteers, territorials, yeomanry, cavalry, artillery, guns, tanks, armour, commando.

Militia, irregulars, *francs-tireurs,* Home Guard, train-band.

Legion, phalanx, myrmidons, squadron, wing, group, troop, cohort, regiment, corps, platoon, battalion, unit, mob, company (72), column, detachment, brigade, division, garrison, battle array, order of battle.

726   NON-COMBATANT
Substantives: civilian; passive resister,

conscientious objector, conchy, Cuthbert, pacifist, pacificist; non-effective.

Quaker, Quirites.

Adjectives: Non-effective.

727 ARMS

Substantives: weapons, armament, armour, armoury, quiver, arsenal, magazine, armature.

Mail, chain-mail, lorication; ammunition, powder, gunpowder, gun-cotton, dynamite, gelignite, TNT, cordite, lyddite, cartridge, cartouche (635).

Artillery, park, ordnance piece, gun, cannon, swivel, howitzer, carronade, culverin, field-piece, machine-gun, Gatling, Maxim, submachine-gun, tommy-gun, mitrailleuse, pom-pom, mortar, grenade, petronel, petard, falconet.

Fire-arms, side-arms, stand of arms, musketry, musket, smooth-bore, muzzle-loader, firelock, match-lock, flint-lock, fowling-piece, rifle, revolver, six-shooter, carbine, blunderbuss, pistol, gat, rod, betsy, automatic pistol, derringer, Winchester, Lee-Metford, Mauser, Bren gun, Bofors, Sten gun, Lewis gun, bazooka.

Bow, arquebus (or harquebus), cross-bow, sling, catapult.

Missile, projectile, shot, round-shot, ball, shrapnel; grape, grape-shot, chain-shot, bullet, stone, shell, gas-shell, bomb, land-mine, block-buster, flying bomb, buzz-bomb, doodlebug, guided missile, V1, V2, atomic bomb, hydrogen bomb, torpedo, rocket, ballistics.

Pike, lance, spear, javelin, assagai, dart, arrow, reed, shaft, bolt, boomerang, harpoon.

Bayonet, sword, sabre, broadsword, cutlass, falchion, scimitar, rapier, skean, toledo, tuck, claymore, kris (or creese), dagger, dirk, hanger, poniard, stiletto, stylet, dudgeon, axe, bill, pole-axe, battle axe, halberd, tomahawk, bowie-knife, snickersnee, yataghan, kukri.

Club, mace, truncheon, staff, bludgeon, cudgel, knobkerrie, life-preserver, knuckle-duster, shillelagh, bat, cosh, sandbag, lathi.

Catapult, battering-ram; tank.

728 ARENA

Substantives: field, walk, battle-field, field of battle, lists, palaestra, campus, playing-field, recreation ground, playground, course, cinder-track, dirt-track, gridiron, diamond, pitch, links, rink, court, platform, stage, boards, racecourse, *corso,* circus, ring, cockpit, bear garden, scene of action, theatre of war, the enemy's camp, amphitheatre, hippodrome, coliseum (or colosseum), proscenium.

Section 5 –
Results of Voluntary
Action

729 COMPLETION

Substantives: accomplishment, performance, fulfilment, fruition, execution, achievement, dispatch, work done, superstructure, finish, termination, denouement, catastrophe, conclusion, culmination, climax, consummation, *fait accompli,* winding up, the last stroke, finishing stroke, *coup de grâce,* last finish, final touch, crowning touch, coping-stone, end (67), arrival (292), completeness (52).

Verbs: To complete, effect, perform, do, execute, go through, accomplish, fulfil, discharge, achieve, compass, effectuate, dispatch, knock off, close, terminate, conclude, finish, end (67), consummate, elaborate, bring about, bring to bear, bring to pass, get through, carry through, bring through, bring off, pull off, work out, make good, carry out, wind up, dispose of, bring to a close, termination, conclusion, etc.

To perfect, bring to perfection, stamp, put the seal to, polish off, crown.

To reach, arrive (292), touch, reach, attain the goal; to run one's race.

Phrases: To give the last finish or finishing touch; to be through with; to get it over; to deliver the goods; to shut up shop.

Adjectives: Completing, final, terminal, concluding, conclusive, exhaustive, crowning, etc., done, completed, wrought.

Phrases: It is all over; *finis coronat opus; actum est.*

Adverbs: Completely, etc. (52), out of hand, effectually, with a vengeance, with a witness.

730 NON-COMPLETION

Substantives: inexecution, shortcoming (304), non-fulfilment, nonperformance, neglect; incompleteness (53); a drawn battle or game, a draw, a stalemate.

Phrase: The web of Penelope; one swallow does not make a summer.

Verbs: Not to complete, perform, etc., to fall short of, leave unfinished, let slip, lose sight of, neglect, leave undone, etc., draw.

Phrases: To scotch the snake, not kill it; hang fire; do by halves.

Adjectives: Not completed, etc., uncompleted, incomplete, unfinished, left undone (53), short, unaccomplished, unperformed, unexecuted.

In progress, in hand, proceeding, going on, on the stocks.

Adverbs: *Re infecta; nihil fit.*

731 SUCCESS

Substantives: successfulness, speed, thrift, advance, luck, good fortune (734), godsend, prize, windfall, trump card, hit, stroke, lucky strike, break; lucky or fortunate hit; bold stroke, master-stroke, *coup de maître,* knockout blow (698), checkmate.

Continued success, run of luck, time well spent, tide, flood, high tide, heyday.

Advantage over, ascendancy, mastery, conquest, subdual, victory, subjugation, triumph, exultation (884).

A conqueror, victor, winner.

Phrase: A feather in one's cap.

Verbs: To succeed, to be successful, to come off successful, to be crowned with success, to come or go off well, catch on, to thrive, speed, prosper, bloom, blossom, flourish, go on well, be well off.

To gain, attain, carry, secure, or win a point or object; to triumph, be triumphant, etc.; to surmount, overcome, conquer, master, or get over a difficulty or obstacle; to score, make a hit.

To advance (282), come on, get on, gain ground, make one's way, make progress, progress, worry along, get by.

To bring to bear, to bring about, to effect, accomplish, complete (729), manage, contrive to, make sure; to reap, gather, etc., the benefit of.

To master, get the better of, conquer, subdue, subjugate, quell, reduce, overthrow, overpower, vanquish, get under; get or gain the ascendancy, obtain a victory; to worst, defeat, beat, lick, drub, trim, settle, floor, knock out, put down, trip up, beat hollow, checkmate, non-suit, trip up the heels of, capsize, shipwreck, ruin, kibosh, do for, victimize, put to flight, drown, etc.; to roll in the dust, to trample under foot, to wipe the floor with.

To baffle, disconcert, frustrate, confound, discomfit, dish, foil, out-general, outmanœuvre, outflank, outwit, overreach, balk, outvote, circumvent, score off, catch napping.

To answer, succeed, work well, turn out well.

Phrases: To sail before the wind; to swim with the tide; to stem the torrent; to turn a corner; to weather a point; to fall on one's legs or feet; *se tirer d'affaire*; to take a favourable turn; to turn up trumps; to have the ball at one's feet; to come off with flying colours; to win or gain the day; to win the palm; to win one's spurs; to breast the tape; to bear away the bell.

To get the upper hand; to gain an advantage; to get the whip-hand of; to have on the hip; to get the start of; to have a run of luck; to make a hit; to make a killing; to score a success; to reap or gather the harvest; to strike oil; to give a good account of oneself; to carry all before one; to put to rout; to cook one's goose; to settle one's hash.

Adjectives: Succeeding, etc., successful, home and dry, prosperous, felicitous, blooming, etc., set up, triumphant, victorious, cock-a-hoop.

Unfoiled, unbeaten, unsubdued, etc.

Effective, well-spent.

Phrases: Flushed with success; one's star being in the ascendant; the spoilt child of fortune.

Adverbs: Successfully, etc., triumphantly, with flying colours, in triumph, *à merveille,* to good purpose.

Phrase: *Veni, vidi, vici.*

732 FAILURE

Substantives: unsuccess, non-success, disappointment, blow, frustration, inefficacy, discomfiture, abortion, miscarriage, lost trouble; vain, ineffectual, or abortive attempt or effort.

A mistake, error, blunder, fault, miss, oversight, blot, slip, trip, stumble, claudication, breakdown, false step, wrong step, howler, floater, clanger, boner, *faux pas, bêtise,* titubation, scrape, botch, bungle, foozle, mess, washout, stalemate, botchery, fiasco, flop, frost, sad work, bad job, bad show, want of skill.

Mischance, mishap, misfortune, misadventure, disaster, bad or hard luck (735).

Repulse, rebuff, set-down, defeat, fall, downfall, rout, discomfiture, collapse, smash, crash, wreck, perdition, shipwreck, ruin, subjugation, overthrow, death-blow, quietus, knockout, destruction.

A victim, loser, bankrupt, insolvent (808).

Phrases: A losing game; a flash in the pan; a wild-goose chase; a mare's-nest; a fool's errand.

Verbs: To fail, to be unsuccessful, etc., to come off badly, go badly, go amiss, abort, go wrong, fall flat, flop, fall through, fizzle out, turn out ill, work ill, lose ground, recede (283), fall short of (304), prang (162, 176).

To miss, miss one's aim; to labour, toil, etc., in vain; to lose one's labour, flounder, limp, miss one's footing, miscarry, abort; to make vain, ineffectual, or abortive efforts; to make a slip; to make or commit a mistake, commit a fault, make a mess of; to botch, make a botch of, bungle, foozle.

To be defeated, overthrown, foiled, worsted, let down, etc.; to break down, sink, drown, founder, go to ruin, etc., fall, slip, tumble, stumble, falter, be capsized, run aground, pack up, crock up, collapse.

Phrases: To come to nothing; to end in smoke; to slip through one's fingers; to hang fire; to miss fire; to miss stays; to flash in the pan; to split upon a rock; to go to the wall; to have had it; to take a back seat; to get the worst of it; to go to the dogs; to go to pot; to be all up with; to be in the wrong box; to stand in one's own light; to catch a Tartar; to get hold of the wrong sow by the ear; to burn one's fingers; to shoot at a pigeon and kill a crow; to beat the air; to tilt against windmills; to roll the stone of Sisyphus; to fall between two stools; to pull a boner; to come a cropper or mucker.

Adjectives: Unsuccessful, failing, etc., unfortunate, in a bad way, unlucky, luckless, out of luck, ill-fated, ill-starred, disastrous.

Unavailing, abortive, addle, still-born, fruitless, bootless, ineffectual, stickit, unattained, lame, hobbling, impotent, futile.

Aground, grounded, swamped, stranded, cast away, wrecked, on the rocks, foundered, capsized, torpedoed, shipwrecked.

Defeated, overcome, overthrown, overpowered, mastered, worsted, vanquished, conquered, subjugated, routed, silenced, distanced, foiled, unhorsed, baffled, befooled, dished, tossed about, stultified, undone, done for, down and out, ruined, circumvented, planet-struck, nonplussed.

Phrases: At a loss; wide of the mark; not having a leg to stand upon; ruined root and branch; the sport of fortune; bitched, bothered, and bewildered; hoist by one's own petard; left in the lurch; out of the running.

Adverbs: Unsuccessfully, etc., in vain, to no purpose, all up with.

Phrases: The game is up; all is lost.

733 TROPHY
Substantives: laurel, palm, crown, bays, wreath, garland, chaplet, civic crown, medal, ribbon, cup, scalp, prize, award, oscar, triumphal arch, ovation, triumph (883), flourish of trumpets, flying colours.

Phrase: A feather in one's cap.

734 PROSPERITY
Substantives: affluence (803), success (731), thrift, good fortune, welfare, well-being, felicity, luck, good luck, a run of luck, fair weather, sunshine, fair wind, a bed of roses, palmy days, the smiles of fortune, halcyon days, *Saturnia regna,* golden age.

An upstart, parvenu, *nouveau riche,* profiteer, skipjack, mushroom, self-made man.

A made man, a lucky dog.

Phrase: A roaring trade.

Verbs: To prosper, thrive, flourish, be well off; to flower, blow, blossom, bloom, fructify.

Phrases: To feather one's nest; to line one's pockets; to make one's pile; to bask in the sunshine; to rise in the world; to make one's way; to better oneself; to light on one's feet.

Adjectives: Prosperous, fortunate, lucky, well-off, well-to-do, bein, affluent, solvent (803), thriving, set up, prospering, etc., blooming, palmy, halcyon.

Auspicious, propitous, in a fair way.

Phrases: Born with a silver spoon in one's mouth; the spoilt child of fortune; in clover; on velvet; in luck's way.

Adverbs: Prosperously, etc., swimmingly.

735 ADVERSITY
Substantives: bad, ill, evil, adverse, etc., fortune, hap, or luck, tough luck, hard lines, reverse, set-back, comedown, broken fortunes, falling or going down in the world, hard times, iron age, evil day, rainy day.

Fall, ruin, ruination, ruinousness, undoing, mishap, mischance, misadventure, misfortune, disaster, calamity, catastrophe (619), failure (732); a hard life; trouble, hardship, blight, curse, evil star, evil genius, evil dispensation.

Phrases: The frowns of fortune; the ups and downs of life; a black look-out; the time being out of joint.

Verbs: To be ill off; to decay, sink, go under, fall, decline, come down in the world, lose caste; to have had it.

Adjectives: Unfortunate, unlucky, luckless, untoward, ill-off, badly off, decayed, ill-fated, ill-starred, impecunious, necessitous (804), bankrupt (808), unprosperous, adverse, untoward.

Disastrous, calamitous, ruinous, dire, deplorable, etc.

Phrases: Down on one's luck; in a bad way; in poor shape; having seen better days; born with a wooden ladle in one's mouth; one's star on the wane; from bad to worse; down and out.

736 MEDIOCRITY

Substantives: the golden mean, *aurea mediocritas,* moderation (174), moderate circumstances; the middle classes, bourgeoisie.

Adjectives: Tolerable, fair, middling, passable, average, so-so, ordinary, mediocre; middle-class, bourgeois.

Verbs: To keep a middle course, jog on, get along, get by.

Phrase: *Medio tutissimus ibis.*

II

Section 1 –
General Intersocial
Volition

737 AUTHORITY

Substantives: influence, patronage, credit, power, prerogative, control, jurisdiction, censorship, autoritativeness, absoluteness, despotism, absolutism, tyranny.

Command, empire, sway, rule, dominion, domination, supremacy, sovereignty, suzerainty, lordship, headship, seigniory, seigniorship, mastery, mastership, office, government, administration, gubernation, empire, body politic, accession.

Hold, grasp, gripe, grip, reach, fang, clutches, talons, helm, reins.

Reign, dynasty, regime, directorship, proconsulship, prefecture, caliphate, seneschalship, magistrature, magistracy, presidency, presidentship, premiership.

Empire, autocracy, monarchy, kinghood, kingship, royalty, regality, kingcraft, aristocracy, oligarchy, feudalism, republic, republicanism, democracy, socialism, demagogy, ochlocracy, mobocracy, mob-rule, dictatorship of proletariat, ergatocracy, collectivism, communism, Bolshevism, bureaucracy, bumbledom, syndicalism, militarism, stratocracy, *imperium in imperio,* dictatorship, protectorate, protectorship, directorate, directory, executive, raj.

Limited monarchy, constitutional government, representative government, home rule, diarchy (or dyarchy), duumvirate, triumvirate.

Vicarious authority (755, 759).

Gynarchy, gynaecocracy, petticoat government, matriarchy; patriarchy, patriarchism.

Verbs: To have, hold, possess, or exercise authority, etc.

To be master, etc.; to have the control, etc.; to overrule, override, overawe, dominate.

To rule, govern, sway, command, control, direct, administer, lead, preside over, boss; to dictate, reign, hold the reins; to possess or be seated on the throne; to ascend or mount the throne; to sway or wield the sceptre.

Phrases: To have the upper hand; to have the whip-hand; to bend to one's will; to have one's own way; to rule the roost; to lay down the law; to be cock of the roost; to have under the thumb; to keep under; to lead by the nose; to wear the breeches; to have the ball at one's feet; to play first fiddle.

Adjectives: Ruling, etc., regnant, dominant, paramount, supreme, authoritative, executive, gubernatorial, administrative, official.

Imperial, regal, sovereign, royal, royalist, kingly, monarchical, imperatorial, princely, baronial, feudal, seigneurial, seigniorial, aristocratic, democratic, etc.; totalitarian, ultramontane, absolutist.

Imperative, peremptory, arbitrary, absolute, overruling.

Adverbs: In the name of, by the authority of, in virtue of, at one's command, under the auspices of, under the aegis of, *ex officio, ex cathedra.*

738 LAXITY

Substantives: laxness, licence, licentiousness, relaxation, looseness, loosening, slackness, toleration, *laissez-faire,* remission, liberty (748).

Misrule, anarchy, interregnum.

Deprivation of power, dethronement, deposition, usurpation.

Denial of authority: anarchism, nihilism; insubordination, mutiny (742).

Anarchist, nihilist, usurper, mutineer.

Phrases: A dead letter; *brutum fulmen.*

Verbs: To be lax, etc., to hold a loose rein, tolerate, to relax, to misrule.

To dethrone.

Phrases: To give a loose rein to; to give rope enough.

Adjectives: Lax, permissive, loose, slack, remiss, relaxed, licensed, reinless, unbridled, anarchic, anarchical, nihilistic.

Unauthorized (925).

739 SEVERITY

Substantives: strictness, rigour, rigidity, rigidness, sternness, stringency, austerity, inclemency, harshness, acerbity, stiffness, rigorousness, inexorability.

Arbitrary power, absolutism, despotism, dictatorship, autocracy, domineering, tyranny; Moloch.

Assumption, usurpation.

A tyrant, disciplinarian, martinet, stickler, despot, oppressor, hard master; King Stork.

Phrases: Iron rule; reign of terror; mailed fist; martial law; blood and iron; tender mercies; red tape.

Verbs: To be severe, etc.; to assume, usurp, arrogate, take liberties; to hold or keep a tight hand; to bear or lay a heavy hand on; to be down on; to dictate; to domineer, bully, oppress, override, tyrannize.

Phrases: To lord it over; to carry matters with a high hand; to ride roughshod over; to rule with a rod of iron; to put on the screw; to deal faithfully with; to keep a person's nose to the grindstone.

Adjectives: Severe, strict, rigid, stern, stiff, dour, strait-laced, rigorous, exacting, stringent, hard and fast, peremptory, absolute, positive, uncompromising, harsh, austere, arbitrary, haughty, overbearing, arrogant, autocratic, bossy, dictatorial, imperious, domineering, tyrannical, masterful, obdurate, unyielding, inflexible, inexorable, exigent, inclement, Spartan, Rhadamanthine, Draconian.

Adverbs: Severely, etc., with a heavy hand.

740 LENITY

Substantives: mildness, lenience, leniency, gentleness, indulgence, clemency, tolerance, forbearance.

Verbs: To be lenient, etc., to tolerate, indulge, spoil, bear with, to allow to have one's own way, to let down gently.

Adjectives: Lenient, mild, gentle, soft, indulgent, tolerant, easy-going, clement.

Phrase: Live and let live.

741 COMMAND

Substantives: order, fiat, bidding, dictum, hest, behest, call, beck, nod, message, direction, injunction, charge, instructions, appointment, demand, exaction, imposition, requisition, requirement, claim, reclamation, revendication.

Dictation, dictate, mandate, caveat, edict, decree, decretal, enactment, precept, prescript, writ, rescript, law, ordinance, ordination, bull, regulation, prescription, brevet, placet, ukase, firman, warrant, passport, mittimus, mandamus, summons, subpoena, interpellation, citation, word of command.

Verbs: To command, to issue a command, order, give order, bid, require, enjoin, charge, claim, call for, demand, exact, insist on, make a point of, impose, entail, set, tax, prescribe, direct, brief, appoint, dictate, ordain, decree, enact; to issue or promulgate a decree, etc.

To cite, summon, call for, call up, send for, requisition, subpoena; to set or prescribe a task, to set to work, to give the word of command, to call to order.

Phrase: The decree is gone forth.

Adjectives: Commanding, etc., authoritative, peremptory, decretive, decretory (737).

Adverbs: By order, with a dash of the pen.

Phrase: *Le roy le veult.*

742 DISOBEDIENCE

Substantives: non-compliance, insubordination, contumacy, defection, infringement, infraction, violation; defiance (715), resistance (719), non-observance (773).

Rising, insurrection, revolt, *coup d'état, putsch,* rebellion, turn-out, strike, riot, riotousness, mutinousness, mutiny, tumult, sedition, treason, lesemajesty.

An insurgent, mutineer, rebel, rioter, traitor, apostate, renegade, seceder, quisling, fifth columnist; *carbonaro,* sansculotte, *frondeur;* agitator, demagogue, Jack Cade, Wat Tyler; ringleader.

Verbs: To disobey, violate, infringe, resist (719), defy (715), turn restive, shirk, kick, strike, mutiny, rise, rebel, secede, lift the hand against, turn out, come out, go on strike.

Phrases: To champ the bit; to kick over the traces; to unfurl the red flag.

Adjectives: Disobedient, resisting, rebellious, unruly, unsubmissive, ungovernable, uncomplying, uncompliant, restive, insubordinate, contumacious, mutinous, riotous, seditious, disaffected, recusant, recalcitrant, refractory, naughty.

Unbidden, unobeyed, a dead letter.

Phrase: The grey mare being the better horse.

743 OBEDIENCE

Substantives: submission, non-resistance, passiveness, resignation, cession, compliance, surrender (725), subordination, deference, loyalty, devotion, allegiance, obeisance, homage, fealty, prostration, kneeling, genuflexion, curtsy, kowtow, salaam, submissiveness, obsequiousness (886), servitorship, subjection (749).

Verbs: To be obedient, etc.; to obey, submit, succumb, give in, knock under, cringe, yield (725), comply, surrender, follow, give up, give way, resign, bend to, bear obedience to.

To kneel, fall on one's knees, bend the knee, curtsy, kowtow, salaam, bow, pay homage to.

To attend upon, tend; to be under the orders of, to serve.

Phrases: To kiss the rod; to do one's bidding; to play second fiddle; to take it lying down; to dance attendance on.

Adjectives: Obedient, submissive, resigned, passive, complying, compliant, loyal, faithful, devoted, yielding, docile, tractable, amenable, biddable, unresisting, henpecked; restrainable, unresisted.

744 COMPULSION

Substantives: coercion, coaction, force, constraint, enforcement, press, *corvée,* conscription, levy, duress, brute force, main force, *force majeure,* the sword, club law, *ultima ratio, argumentum baculinum.*

Verbs: To compel, force, make, drive, coerce, constrain, steam-roller, enforce, put in force, oblige, force upon, press, conscribe, extort, put down, bind, pin down, bind over, impress, commandeer, requisition.

Phrases: To cram down the throat; to take no denial; to insist upon; to make a point of.

Adjectives: Compelling, etc., compulsory, compulsatory, obligatory, forcible, coercive, coactive, peremptory, rigorous, stringent, inexorable (739); being fain to do, having to do.

Adverbs: By force, perforce, under compulsion, *vi et armis,* in spite of one's teeth; *bon gré, mal gré*; willy-nilly, *nolens volens*; *de rigueur.*

745 MASTER

Substantives: lord, laird, chief, leader, captain, skipper, mate, protagonist, coryphaeus, head, chieftain, commander, commandant, director (694), captain of industry, ruler, potentate, dictator, liege, sovereign, monarch, autocrat, despot, tyrant, *führer, duce,* demagogue, ring-leader, boss, big shot, fugleman.

Crowned head, emperor, king, majesty, tetrarch, *imperator,* protector, president, stadtholder, governor.

Caesar, czar, sultan, soldan, caliph, sophy, khan, cacique, inca, lama, mogul, imam, shah, khedive, pasha (or bashaw), dey, cham, judge, aga, hospodar, mikado, shogun, tycoon, exarch.

Prince, seignior, highness, archduke, duke, marquis, earl, viscount, baron (875), margrave, landgrave, palatine, elector, doge, satrap, rajah, maharajah, emir, bey, effendi, nizam, nawab, mandarin, sirdar, ameer, sachem, sagamore.

Empress, queen, czarina, sultana, princess, duchess, marchioness, countess, viscountess, baroness, infanta, ranee, maharanee, margravine, etc.

Military authorities, marshal, field-marshal, *maréchal,* generalissimo, commander-in-chief, admiral, commodore, general, lieutenant-general, major-general, brigadier, colonel, lieutenant-colonel, officer, captain, major, lieutenant, adjutant, midshipman, quartermaster, aide-de-camp, ensign, cornet, cadet, subaltern, non-commissioned officer, drum-major, sergeant-major, sergeant, corporal, air-marshal, group-captain, wing-commander, squadron-leader, flight-lieutenant, centurion, *seraskier,* hetman, subahdar, *condottiere.*

Civil authorities, mayor, prefect, chancellor, provost, magistrate, syndic, alcade (or alcayde), burgomaster, *corregidor,* sheik, seneschal, burgrave, alderman, warden, constable (965), beadle, alguazil, kavass, tribune, consul, proconsul, quaestor, praetor, aedile, archon, pole-march.

Statesman, politician, statist, legislator, lawgiver.

President, chairman, speaker, moderator, vice-president, comptroller, director (694), monitor, monitress.

746 SERVANT

Substantives: servitor, employee, attaché, secretary, subordinate, clerk, retainer, vassal, protégé, dependant, hanger-on, pensioner, client, emissary, *âme damnée.*

Retinue, cortège, staff, court, train, entourage, clientele, suite.

An attendant, squire, henchman, led captain, chamberlain, follower, usher, page, train-bearer, domestic, help, butler, footman, lackey, flunkey, parlour-man, valet, waiter, *garçon,* equerry, groom, jockey, ostler (or hostler), stable-boy, tiger, buttons, boot-boy, boots, livery servant, hireling, mercenary, underling, menial, gillie, under-strapper, journeyman, whipper-in, bailiff, castellan, seneschal, major-domo, cup-bearer, bottle-washer, scout, gyp.

Serf, villein, slave, galley-slave, thrall, peon, helot, bondsman, *adscriptus glebae,* wage-slave.

A maid, handmaid, abigail, chamber-maid, lady's maid, house-keeper, lady help, soubrette, *fille de chambre,* parlour-maid, housemaid, between-maid, kitchen-maid, nurse, *bonne,* scullion, laundress, bed-maker, skivvy, slavey, daily.

Verbs: To serve, attend upon, dance attendance, wait upon, squire, valet.

Adverbs: In one's pay or employ, in the train of.

747 SCEPTRE

Substantives: regalia, insignia (550), crown, coronet, rod of empire, orb, mace, *fasces,* wand, baton, truncheon, staff, insignia (550), portfolio.

A throne, chair, divan, dais, wool-sack.

Diadem, tiara, ermine, purple, signet, seals, keys, talisman, cap of maintenance, toga, robes of state, decoration.

748 FREEDOM

Substantives: independence, liberty, licence (760), self-government, autonomy, scope, range, latitude, play, swing, free play, elbow-room, *lebensraum,* margin.

Franchise, immunity, exemption, emancipation (750), naturalization, denizenship.

Freeland, freehold, allodium (780).

A freeman, freedman, denizen.

Phrases: The four freedoms; *liberté, egalité, fraternité;* a place in the sun; Liberty Hall.

Verbs: To be free, to have scope, etc.

To render free, etc., to free, to emancipate, enfranchise (750), naturalize.

Phrases: To have the run of; to have one's own way; to have one's fling; to stand on one's own feet; to stand on one's rights; to have a will of one's own; to paddle one's own canoe; to play a lone hand.

To take a liberty; to make free with; to take the bit between one's teeth.

Adjectives: Free, independent, loose, at large, unconstrained, unrestrained, unchecked, unobstructed, unconfined, unsubdued, unsubjugated, self-governed, autonomous, self-supporting, untrammelled, unbound, uncontrolled, unchained, unshackled, unfettered, uncurbed, unbridled, unrestricted, unmuzzled, unbuttoned, unforced, uncompelled, unbiased, spontaneous, unhindered, unthwarted, heart-whole, uncaught, unenslaved, unclaimed, ungoverned, resting.

Free and easy, at ease, *dégagé,* wanton, rampant, irrepressible, unprevented, unvanquished, exempt, freehold, allodial, enfranchised, emancipated, released, disengaged (750), out of hand.

Phrases: Free as air; one's own master; *sui juris;* a law to oneself; on one's own; a cat may look at a king.

749 SUBJECTION

Substantives: dependence, thrall, thraldom, subjugation, subordination, bondage, serfdom, servitude, slavery, vassalage, villeinage, service, clientship, liability (177), enslavement, tutelage, constraint (751).

Yoke, harness, collar.

Verbs: To be subject, dependent, etc., to fall under, obey, serve (743).

To subject, subjugate, enthral, enslave, keep under, control, etc. (751), to reduce to slavery, mediatize, break in.

Phrases: To drag a chain; not dare to call one's soul one's own; to be led by the nose; to be or lie at the mercy of.

To keep in leading strings.

Adjectives: Subject, subordinate, dependent, subjected, in subjection to, in thrall to, feudatory, feudal, enslaved, a slave to, at the mercy of, downtrodden, overborne, henpecked, enthralled, controlled, constrained (751).

Phrases: Under the thumb of; at the feet of; tied to the apron-strings of; the puppet, sport, plaything of.

750 LIBERATION

Substantives: disengagement, release, enlargement, emancipation, affranchisement, enfranchisement, manumission, discharge, dismissal.

Escape (671), deliverance (672), redemption, extrication, absolution, acquittance, acquittal (970).

Licence, toleration; parole, ticket of leave.

Verbs: To gain, obtain, acquire, etc., one's liberty, freedom, etc., to get off, get clear, to deliver oneself from.

To break loose, escape, slip away, make one's escape, cut and run, slip the collar, bolt (671).

To liberate, free, set free, set at liberty, release, loose, let loose, loosen, relax, unloose, untie, unbind, unhand, unchain, unshackle, unfetter, unclog, disengage, unharness (44).

To enlarge, set clear, let go, let out, disenchain, disimprison, unbar, unbolt, uncage, unclose, uncork, discharge, disenthral, dismiss, deliver, extricate, let slip, enfranchise, affranchise, manumit, denizen, emancipate, assoil (748).

To clear, acquit, redeem, ransom, get off.

Phrases: To throw off the yoke; to burst one's bonds; to break prison.

To give one one's head.

Adjectives: Liberated, freed, etc.

751 RESTRAINT

Substantives: constraint, coercion, cohibition, repression, clamp down, control, discipline.

Confinement, durance, duress, detention, imprisonment, incarceration, prisonment, internment, blockade, quarantine, coarctation, mancipation, entombment, 'durance vile,' limbo, captivity, penal servitude.

Arrest, arrestation, custody, keep, care, charge, ward.

Prison, fetter (752); *lettre de cachet.*

Verbs: To be under restraint or arrest, to be coerced, etc.

To restrain, constrain, coerce, check, trammel, curb, cramp, keep under, enthral, put under restraint, restrict, repress, cohibit, detain, debar; to chain, enchain, fasten, tie up (43), picket, fetter, shackle, manacle, handcuff, bridle, muzzle, gag, suppress, pinion, pin down, tether, hobble.

To confine, shut up, shut in, clap up, lock up, cage, encage, impound, pen, coop, hem in, jam in, enclose, bottle up, cork up, seal up, mew, wall in, rail in, cloister, bolt in, close the door upon, imprison, incarcerate, immure, entomb, seclude, corral.

To take prisoner, lead captive, send or commit to prison, give in charge or in custody, arrest, commit, run in, lag; re-commit, remand.

Phrases: To put in irons; to clap under hatches; to put in a straitwaistcoat.

Adjectives: Restrained, coerced, etc., sewn up, pent up.

Held up, wind-bound, weather-bound, storm-stayed.

Coactive, stiff, restringent, strait-laced, hide-bound.

Phrases: In limbo; under lock and key; laid by the heels; 'cabined, cribbed, confined'; in quod; in durance vile; doing time; bound hand and foot.

752 PRISON

Substantives: jail (or gaol), prison-house, house of detention, lock-up, the cells, clink, glasshouse, brig, jug, quod, cooler, choky, stir, calaboose, cage, coop, den, cell, stronghold, fortress, keep, dungeon, bastille, oubliette, bridewell, tollbooth, panopticon, hulks, galleys, penitentiary, guard-room, hold, round-house, blackhole, station, enclosure, concentration camp, pen, fold, pound, paddock, stocks, bilboes, nick.

Newgate, King's Bench, Fleet, Marshalsea, Pentonville, Holloway, Dartmoor, Portland, Peterhead, Broadmoor, Sing Sing, the Bastille.

Fetter, shackle, trammel, bond, chain, irons, collar, cangue, pinion, gyve, fetterlock, manacle, handcuff, darbies, strait waistcoat; yoke, halter, harness, muzzle, gag, bridle, curb, bit, snaffle, rein, martingale, leading-strings, swaddling-bands, tether, hobble, picket, band, brake.

Bolt, bar, lock, padlock, rail, wall, paling, palisade (232), fence, corral, barrier, barricade.

753 KEEPER

Substantives: custodian, *custos,* warder, jailer (or gaoler), turnkey, castellan, guard, ranger, gamekeeper, watch, watchman, watch and ward, sentry, sentinel, coastguard, convoy, escort, *concierge,* caretaker, watch-dog.

Guardian, duenna, nurse, ayah, chaperon.

754 PRISONER

Substantives: prisoner-of-war, POW, kriegie, captive, *détenu,* convict, jailbird, lag; ticket-of-leave man.
Adjectives: In custody, in charge, imprisoned, locked up, incarcerated, pent.

755 COMMISSION

Substantives: delegation, consignment, assignment, devolution, procuration, deputation, legation, mission, agency, clerkship, agentship; power of attorney; errand, embassy, charge, brevet, diploma, exequatur, commit-

tal, commitment.

Appointment, nomination, ordination, installation, inauguration, return, accession, investiture, coronation.

Vicegerency, regency, regentship.

Deputy (759).

Verbs: To commission, delegate, depute, devolve, send out, assign, consign, charge, encharge, entrust with, commit to, enlist.

To appoint, name, nominate, accredit, engage, bespeak, ordain, install, induct, inaugurate, invest, crown, return, enrol.

Employ, empower, set over.

To be commissioned, to represent.

Adverbs: *Per procurationem per pro.,* p.p.

756 ABROGATION

Substantives: annulment, cancel, cancellation, revocation, repeal, rescission, rescinding, deposal, deposition, dethronement, defeasance, dismissal, sack, *congé,* demission, disestablishment, disendowment.

Abolition, abolishment, counter-order, countermand, repudiation, nullification, recantation, palinode, retractation (607).

Verbs: To abrogate, annul, cancel, revoke, repeal, rescind, reverse, override, overrule, abolish, disannul, dissolve, quash, repudiate, nullify, retract, recant, recall, countermand, counter-order, break off, disclaim, declare null and void, disestablish, disendow, deconsecrate, set aside, do away with.

To dismiss, send off, send away, discard, turn off, turn away, cashier, sack, fire, bounce, oust, unseat, unthrone, dethrone, depose, uncrown, unfrock, disbar, disbench.

Phrases: Send about one's business; put one's nose out of joint; give one the mitten, the chuck, the sack, the boot, the push.

To get one's books or cards; to get the key of the street.
Adjectives: Abrogated, etc.; *functus officio.*
Interjections: Get along with you! clear out! be off! beat it!

757 RESIGNATION
Substantives: retirement, abdication, renunciation, abjuration.
Verbs: To resign, give up, throw up, retire, abdicate, lay down, abjure, renounce, forgo, disclaim, retract (756); to tender one's resignation, send in one's papers.
Phrases: To swallow the anchor; to be given one's bowler.
Adjectives: Emeritus.
Phrase: 'Othello's occupation's gone.'

758 CONSIGNEE
Substantives: delegate, commissary, commissioner, vice-regent, legate, representative, secondary, nominee, surrogate, functionary, trustee, assignee.
Corps diplomatique, plenipotentiary, emissary, embassy, ambassador, diplomat(ist), consul, resident, nuncio, internuncio.
Agent, factor, attorney, broker, factotum, bailiff, man of business, go-between, intermediary, middleman, salesman, commission agent, commercial traveller, bagman, drummer, colporteur, commissionaire, employee, attaché, curator, clerk, placeman.

759 DEPUTY
Substantives: substitute, vice, proxy, locum tenens, baby-sitter, *chargé d'affaires,* delegate, representative, *alter ego,* surrogate, understudy, stooge, stand-in, stopgap, pinch-hitter.
Regent, viceroy, vicegerent, vicar, satrap, exarch, vizier, minister, premier, commissioner, chancellor, prefect, warden, lieutenant, proconsul, legate.

Verbs: To deputize; to be deputy, etc., for; to appear for; to understudy; to take duty for.
Phrase: To hold a watching brief for.
Adjectives: Acting, deputizing, etc.
Adverbs: In place of, vice.

Section 2 – Special Intersocial Volition

760 PERMISSION
Substantives: leave, allowance, sufferance, tolerance, toleration, liberty, law, licence, concession, grant, vouchsafement, authorization, sanction, accordance, admission, favour, dispensation, exemption, connivance.
A permit, warrant, brevet, precept, authority, firman, pass, passport, furlough, ticket, licence, charter, patent, *carte blanche,* exeat.
Verbs: To permit; to give leave or permission; to let, allow, admit, suffer, tolerate, concede, accord, vouchsafe, humour, indulge, to leave it to one; to leave alone; to grant, empower, charter, sanction, authorize, warrant, license; to give licence; to give a loose to.
To let off, absolve, exonerate, dispense with, favour, wink, connive at.
Phrases: To give *carte blanche;* to give rein to; to stretch a point; leave the door open; to let one have a chance; to give one a fair show.
To take a liberty; to use a freedom; to make so bold; to beg leave.
Adjectives: Permitting, etc., permissive, conceding, indulgent.
Allowable, permissible, lawful, legitimate, legal.
Unforbid, unforbidden, unconditional.

761 PROHIBITION
Substantives: inhibition, veto,

disallowance, interdiction, estoppage, hindrance (706), restriction, restraints (751), embargo, an interdict, ban, injunction, taboo, proscription; *index librorum prohibitorum*.

Verbs: To prohibit, forbid, inhibit, disallow, bar, debar, interdict, ban, estop, veto, keep in, hinder, restrain (751), restrict, withhold, limit, circumscribe, keep within bounds.

To exclude, shut out, proscribe.

Phrase: To clip the wings of; to forbid the banns.

Adjectives: Prohibitive, restrictive, exclusive, prohibitory, forbidding, etc.

Not permitted, prohibited, etc., unlicensed, contraband, unauthorized.

Phrases: Under the ban of; on the Index.

Interjections: Hands off! keep off! God forbid!

762 CONSENT

Substantives: compliance, acquiescence, assent (488), agreement, concession, yieldingness, acknowledgment, acceptance.

Settlement, ratification, confirmation.

Verbs: To consent, give consent, assent, comply with, acquiesce, agree to, subscribe to, accede, accept.

To concede, yield, satisfy, grant, settle, acknowledge, confirm, homologate, ratify, deign, vouchsafe.

Phrase: To take at one's word.

Adjectives: Consenting, etc., having no objection, unconditional.

Adverbs: Yes (488); if you please, as you please, by all means, by all manner of means, so be it, of course, certainly, sure, OK.

Phrases: Suits me; all right by me.

763 OFFER

Substantives: proffer, tender, present, overture, proposition, motion, proposal, invitation, candidature, presentation, offering, oblation, bid, bribe.

Sacrifice, immolation.

Verbs: To offer, proffer, tender, present, invite, volunteer, propose, move, make a motion, start, press, bid, hold out, hawk about.

To sacrifice, immolate.

Phrases: To be a candidate; to go abegging.

Adjectives: Offering, etc., in the market, for sale, on hire.

764 REFUSAL

Substantives: rejection, declining, non-compliance, declension, dissent (489), denial, repulse, rebuff, discountenance.

Disclaimer, recusancy, abnegation, protest.

Revocation, violation, abrogation (756), flat refusal, peremptory denial.

Verbs: To refuse, reject, deny, decline, disclaim, repudiate, protest, resist, repel, veto, refuse or withhold one's assent; to excuse oneself, to negative, turn down, rebuff, snub, spurn, resist, cross, grudge, begrudge.

To discard, set aside, rescind, revoke, discountenance, forswear.

Phrases: To turn a deaf ear to; to shake the head; not to hear of; to send to the right-about; to hang fire; to wash one's hands of; to declare off.

Adjectives: Refusing, etc., recusant, restive, uncomplying, unconsenting.

Refused, etc., out of the question, not to be thought of.

Adverbs: No, by no means, etc. (489).

Phrases: Excuse me; nix on that; not on your life; nothing doing.

765 REQUEST

Substantives: requisition, asking, petition, demand, suit, solicitation, craving, entreaty, begging, postulation, adjuration, canvass, candidature, prayer, supplication, impetration, imploration, instance, obsecration, obtestation, importunity, application, address, appeal, motion, invitation, overture, invocation, interpellation, apostrophe, orison, incantation, imprecation, conjuration.

Mendicancy, begging letter, round robin.

Claim, reclamation, revendication.

Verbs: To request, ask, sue, beg, cadge, crave, pray, petition, solicit, beg a boon, demand, prefer a request or petition, ply, apply to, make application, put to, make bold to ask, invite, beg leave, put up a prayer.

To beg hard, entreat, beseech, supplicate, implore, plead, conjure, adjure, invoke, evoke, kneel to, fall on one's knees, impetrate, imprecate, appeal to, apply to, put to, address, call for, press, urge, beset, importune, dun, tax, besiege, cry to, call on.

To bespeak, canvass, tout, make interest, court; to claim, reclaim.

Phrases: To send that hat round; to beg from door to door.

Adjectives: Requesting, asking, beseeching, etc., precatory, suppliant, supplicatory, postulant, importunate.

Phrases: Cap in hand; on one's knees.

Adverbs: Do, please, kindly, be good enough, pray, prithee, be so good as, have the goodness, vouchsafe.

For heaven's sake, for goodness' sake, for God's sake, for the love of Mike.

766 DEPRECATION

Substantives: expostulation, intercession, mediation.

Verbs: To deprecate, protest, expostulate; to enter a protest; to intercede for.

Adjectives: Deprecating, etc; deprecatory, expostulatory, intercessory; deprecated, protested.

Unsought, unbesought.

Interjections: God forbid! forbid it heaven! *Absit omen!*

767 PETITIONER

Substantives: solicitor, applicant,

suppliant, supplicant, mendicant, beggar, mumper, suitor, candidate, aspirant, claimant, postulant, canvasser, tout, cadger, sponger.

Section 3 –
Conditional Intersocial Volition

768 PROMISE

Substantives: word, troth, plight, profession, pledge, parole, word of honour, assurance, vow, oath.

Engagement, guarantee, undertaking, insurance, contract (769), obligation; affiance, betrothal, betrothment.

Verbs: To promise, give a promise, undertake, engage, assure; to give, pass, pledge or plight one's word, honour credit, faith, etc.; to covenant, warrant, guarantee (467); to swear, vow, be sworn; take oath, make oath, kiss the book; to attest, adjure; to betroth, plight troth, affiance.

To answer for, be answerable for, secure, give security (771).

Phrases: To enter on, make or form an engagement, take upon oneself; to bind, tie, commit, or pledge oneself; to be in for it; to contract an obligation; to be bound; to hold out an expectation.

To call heaven to witness; to swear by bell, book, and candle; to put on one's oath; to swear a witness.

Adjectives: Promising, etc., promised, pledged, sworn, etc.; votive, promissory.

Phrases: Under one's hand and seal; as one's head shall answer for.

Interjection: So help me God!

768a RELEASE FROM ENGAGEMENT

Substantives: disengagement, liberation (750).

Adjectives: Absolute, unconditional, uncovenanted, unsecured.

769 COMPACT
Substantives: contract, agreement, understanding, bargain, bond, deal, pact, paction, stipulation, covenant, settlement, convention, cartel, protocol, charter, treaty, indenture, concordat, *zollverein*.

Negotiation, transaction, bargaining, haggling, chaffering; diplomacy.

Ratification, settlement, signature, endorsement, seal, signet.

A negotiator, diplomatist, diplomat, agent, contractor, underwriter, attorney, broker (758).

Verbs: To contract, covenant, agree for, strike a bargain, engage (768); to underwrite.

To treat, negotiate, bargain, stipulate, haggle (or higgle), chaffer, stick out for, insist upon, make a point of, compound for.

To conclude, close, confirm, ratify, endorse, clench, come to an understanding, take one at one's word, come to terms.

To subscribe, sign, seal, indent, put the seal to, sign and seal.

Phrase: *Caveat emptor.*

770 CONDITIONS
Substantives: terms, articles, articles of agreement, clauses, proviso, provisions, salvo, covenant, stipulation, obligation, ultimatum, *sine qua non*.

Verbs: To make it a condition, make terms; to stipulate, insist upon; to tie up.

Adjectives: Conditional, provisional, guarded, fenced, hedged in.

Adverbs: Conditionally, on the understanding; provided (469).

Phrases: With a string tied to it; wind and weather permitting; God willing; DV; *Deo volente.*

771 SECURITY
Substantives: surety, guaranty, guarantee, mortgage, warranty, bond, debenture, pledge, tie, plight, pawn, lien, caution, sponsion, hostage, sponsor, bail, parole.

Deed, instrument, deed-poll, indenture, warrant, charter, cartel, protocol, recognizance; verification, acceptance, endorsement, signature, execution, seal, stamp, IOU.

Promissory note, bill of exchange, bill.

Stake, deposit, pool, kitty, jack-pot, earnest, handsel.

Docket, certificate, voucher, verification, authentication.

Verbs: To give security, go bail, pawn (787); guarantee, warrant, accept, endorse, underwrite, insure; execute, stamp.

To hold in pledge.

772 OBSERVANCE
Substantives: performance, fulfilment, satisfaction, discharge, compliance, acquittance, quittance, acquittal, adhesion, acknowledgment, fidelity (939).

Verbs: To observe, perform, keep, fulfil, discharge, comply with, make good, meet, satisfy, respect, abide by, adhere to, be faithful to, act up to, acquit oneself.

Phrase: To redeem one's pledge.

Adjectives: Observant, faithful, true, honourable (939), strict, rigid, punctilious.

Adverbs: Faithfully, etc., to the letter.

Phrase: As good as one's word.

773 NON-OBSERVANCE
Substantives: inobservance, evasion, omission, failure, neglect, laches, laxity, infringement, infraction, violation, forfeiture, transgression.

Retractation, repudiation, nullification, protest.

Informality, lawlessness, disobedience, bad faith (742).

Verbs: To break, violate, fail, neglect, omit, skip, cut, forfeit, infringe, transgress.

To retract, discard, protest, go back upon or from one's word, repudiate, nullify, ignore, set at naught, wipe off, cancel, etc. (552), to fob off, palter, elude, evade.

Phrases: To wash out; to shut one's eyes to; to drive a coach and six through.

Adjectives: Violating, etc., elusive, evasive, transgressive, unfulfilled; compensatory (30).

774 COMPROMISE
Substantives: composition, middle term, *mezzo termine, modus vivendi;* bribe, hush-money.

Verbs: To compromise, compound, commute, adjust, take the mean, split the difference, come to terms, come to an understanding, meet one half-way, give and take, submit to arbitration.

Section 4 –
Possessive Relations

775 ACQUISITION
Substantives: obtainment, gaining, earning, procuration, procuring, procurement, gathering, gleaning, picking, collecting, recovery, retrieval, totting, salvage, find.

Book-collecting, book-hunting, etc., philately, cartophily, phillumeny.

Gain, profit, benefit, emolument, the main chance, pelf, lucre, loaves and fishes, produce, product, proceeds, return, fruit, crop, harvest, scoop, takings, winnings.

Inheritance, bequest, legacy.

Fraudulent acquisition, subreption, stealing (791).

Profiteering, pot-hunting.

A collector, book-collector, etc., bird-fancier, etc., philatelist, cartophilist, phillumenist; a profiteer, money-grubber, pot-hunter.

Verbs: To acquire, get, gain, win, earn, realize, regain, receive (785), take (789), obtain, procure, derive, secure, collect, reap, gather, glean, come in for, step into, inherit, come by, rake in, scrape together, get hold of, scoop, pouch.

To profit, make profit, turn to profit, make money by, obtain a return, make a fortune, coin money, profiteer.

To be profitable, to pay, to answer.

To fall to, come to, accrue.

Phrases: To turn an honest penny; to earn an honest crust; to bring grist to the mill; to raise the wind; to line one's pockets; to feather one's nest; to reap or gain an advantage; to keep the wolf from the door; to keep the pot boiling.

Adjectives: Acquisitive, acquiring, acquired, etc., profitable, lucrative, remunerative, paying.

Phrase: On the make.

776 LOSS
Substantives: perdition, forfeiture, lapse.

Privation, bereavement, deprivation (789), dispossession, riddance.

Verbs: To lose; incur, experience, or meet with a loss; to miss, mislay, throw away, forfeit, drop, let slip, allow to slip through the fingers; to get rid of (782), to waste (638, 679).

To be lost, lapse.

Phrase: To throw good money after bad.

Adjectives: Losing, etc., lost, etc.

Devoid of, not having, unobtained, unpossessed, unblest with.

Shorn of, deprived of, bereaved of, bereft of, rid of, quit of, dispossessed, denuded, out of pocket, minus, cut off.

Irrecoverable, irretrievable, irremediable, irreparable.

Interjections: Farewell to! adieu to!

777 POSSESSION

Substantives: ownership, proprietorship, tenure, tenancy, seisin, occupancy, hold, holding, preoccupancy.

Exclusive possession, impropriation, monopoly, inalienability.

Future possession, heritage, heirship, inheritance, reversion.

Phrases: A bird in the hand; nine points of the law; the haves and the have-nots.

Verbs: To possess, have, hold, own, be master of, be in possession of, enjoy, occupy, be seized of, be worth, to have in hand or on hand; to inherit (775).

To engross, monopolize, corner, forestall, absorb, preoccupy.

To be the property of, belong to, appertain to, pertain to, be in the hands of, be in the possession of.

Adjectives: Possessing, etc., possessed of, seized of, worth, endowed with, instinct with, fraught, laden with, charged with.

Possessed, etc., proprietary, proprietorial; on hand, in hand, in store, in stock, unsold, unshared; inalienable.

778 PARTICIPATION

Substantives: joint stock, common stock, partnership, copartnership, possession in common, communion, community of possessions or goods, socialism, collectivism, communism, syndicalism.

Bottle party, share-out, picnic.

A syndicate, ring, corner, combine, cartel, trust, monopoly, pool.

A partner, co-partner, shareholder; co-tenant, co-heir; a communist, socialist.

Verbs: To participate, partake, share, communicate, go snacks, go halves, share and share alike; to have or possess, etc., in common; to come in for a share, to stand in with, to socialize, to pool.

Adjectives: Partaking, etc.; socialist, socialistic, communist.

Adverbs: Share and share alike, fifty-fifty, even Stephen.

779 POSSESSOR

Substantives: owner, holder, proprietor, proprietress, proprietary, master, mistress, heritor, occupier, occupant, landlord, landlady, landowner, lord of the manor, squire, laird, landed gentry; tenant, renter, lessee, lodger.

Future possessor, heir, heiress, inheritor.

780 PROPERTY

Substantives: possession, ownership, proprietorship, seisin, tenancy, tenure, lordship, title, claim, stake, legal estate, equitable estate, fee simple, fee tail, *meum et tuum*, occupancy.

Estate, effects, assets, resources, means, belongings, stock, goods, chattels, fixtures, plant, movables, furniture, things, traps, trappings, paraphernalia, luggage, baggage, bag and baggage, cargo, lading.

Lease, term, settlement, remainder, reversion, dower, jointure, apanage, heritage, inheritance, patrimony, heirloom.

Real property, land, landed estate, manor, demesne, domain, tenement, holding, hereditament, household, freehold, farm, ranch, *hacienda, estancia,* fief, feoff, seigniority, allodium.

Ground, acres, field, close.

State, realm, empire, kingdom, principality, territory, sphere of influence.

Adjectives: Predial, manorial, freehold, etc., copyhold, leasehold.

781 RETENTION

Substantives: keep, holding, keeping, retaining, detention, custody, grasp, gripe, grip, tenacity.

Fangs, teeth, clutches, hooks, tentacles, claws, talons, nails.

Forceps, pincers, pliers, tongs, vice.
Incommunicableness, incommunicability.
Phrase: A bird in the hand.
Verbs: To retain, keep, keep in hand, secure, detain, hold fast, grasp, clutch, clench, cinch, gripe, grip, hug, withhold, keep back.
Adjectives: Retaining, etc., retentive, tenacious.

Unforfeited, undeprived, undisposed, uncommunicated, incommunicable, inalienable, not transferable.

782 RELINQUISHMENT
Substantives: cession, abandonment (624), renunciation, surrender, dereliction, rendition, riddance (776), resignation (758).
Verbs: To relinquish, give up, let go, lay aside, resign, forgo, drop, discard, dismiss, waive, renounce, surrender, part with, get rid of, lay down, abandon, cede, yield, dispose of, divest oneself of, spare, give away, throw away, cast away, fling away, maroon, jettison, chuck up, let slip, make away with, make way for.
Phrases: To lay on the shelf; to throw overboard.
Adjectives: Relinquished, etc., derelict, left, residuary (40), unculled.

783 TRANSFER
Substantives: interchange, exchange, transmission, barter (794), conveyance, assignment, alienation, abalienation, demise, succession, reversion; matastasis.
Verbs: To transfer, convey, assign, consign, make over, pass, transmit, interchange, exchange (148).

To change hands, change from one to another, alienate, devolve.

To dispossess, abalienate, disinherit.
Adjectives: Alienable, negotiable, transferable.

784 GIVING
Substantives: bestowal, donation, accordance, presentation, oblation, presentment, delivery, award, investment, granting.

Cession, concession, consignment, dispensation, benefaction, charity, liberality, generosity, munificence, almsgiving.

Gift, donation, bonus, boon, present, testimonial, presentation, fairing, benefaction, grant, subsidy, subvention, offering, contribution, subscription, whip-round, donative, meed, tribute, gratuity, tip, Christmas box, handsel, trinkgeld, *douceur, pourboire*, baksheesh, cumshaw, dash, bribe, free gift, favour, bounty, largess, allowance, endowment, charity, alms, dole, peace-offering, payment (807).

Bequest, legacy, demise, dotation.

Giver, grantor, donor, benefactor.
Phrase: *Panem et circenses.*
Verbs: To give, bestow, accord, confer, grant, concede, present, give away, deliver, deliver over, make over, consign, entrust, hand, tip, render, impart, hand over, part with, fork out, yield, dispose of, put into the hands of, vest in, assign, put in possession, settle upon, endow, subsidize.

To bequeath, leave, demise, devise.

To give out, dispense, deal, deal out, dole out, mete out.

To contribute, subscribe, put up a purse, send round the hat, pay (807), spend (809).

To furnish, supply, administer, afford, spare, accommodate with, indulge with, shower upon, lavish.

To bribe, suborn, grease the palm, square.
Adjectives: Giving, etc., given, etc., charitable, eleemosynary, tributary.
Phrase: *Bis dat qui cito dat.*

785 RECEIVING
Substantives: acquisition (775), reception, acceptance, admission.

A recipient, donee, assignee, legatee, grantee, stipendiary, beneficiary, pensioner, almsman.

Verbs: To receive, take (789), accept, pocket, pouch, admit, catch, catch at, jump at, take in.

To be received, etc.; to accrue, come to hand.

Adjectives: Receiving, etc., recipient; pensionary, stipendiary.

786 APPORTIONMENT

Substantives: distribution, dispensation, allotment, assignment, consignment, partition, division, deal, share-out.

Dividend, portion, contingent, share, whack, meed, allotment, lot, measure, dole, pittance, quantum, ration, quota, modicum, allowance, appropriation.

Phrase: Cutting up the melon.

Verbs: To apportion, divide, distribute, administer, dispense, billet, allot, cast, share, mete, parcel out, serve out, deal, partition, appropriate, assign.

Adjectives: Apportioning, etc., respective.

Adverbs: Respectively, severally.

787 LENDING

Substantives: loan, advance, mortage, accommodation, lease-lend, subsistence money, sub, pawn, pignoration, hypothecation, investment; pawnshop, *mont de piété*.

Lender, pawnbroker, uncle.

Verbs: To lend, loan, advance, mortgage, invest, pawn, impawn, pop, hock, hypothecate, impignorate, place or put out to interest, entrust, accommodate with.

Adjectives: Lending, etc., lent, etc., unborrowed.

Adverb: In advance; up the spout.

788 BORROWING

Substantives: pledging, replevin, borrowed plumes, plagiarism, plagiary; a touch.

Verbs: To borrow, hire, rent, farm, raise money, raise the wind; to plagiarize.

Adjectives: Borrowing, etc., borrowed, second-hand.

Phrases: To borrow of Peter to pay Paul; to run into debt.

789 TAKING

Substantives: appropriation, prehension, capture, seizure, abduction, ablation, catching, seizing, apprehension, arrest, kidnapping, round-up.

Abstraction, subtraction, deduction, subduction.

Dispossession, deprivation, deprival, bereavement, divestment, sequestration, confiscation, disendowment.

Resumption, reprise, reprisal, recovery (775).

Clutch, swoop, wrench, catch, take, haul.

Verbs: To take, capture, lay one's hands on; lay, take, or get hold of; to help oneself to; to possess oneself of, take possession of, make sure of, make free with.

To appropriate, impropriate, pocket, put into one's pocket, pouch, bag; to ease one of.

To pick up, gather, collect, round up, net, absorb (296), reap, glean, crop, get in the harvest, cull, pluck; intercept, tap.

To take away, carry away, carry off, bear off, hurry off with, abduct, kidnap, crimp, shanghai.

To lay violent hands on, fasten upon, pounce upon, catch, seize, snatch, nip up, whip up, jump at, snap at, hook, claw, clinch, grasp, gripe, grip, grab, clutch, wring, wrest, wrench, pluck, tear away, catch, nab, capture, collar, throttle.

To take from, deduct, subduct (38), subtract, curtail, retrench, abridge of, dispossess, expropriate, take away from, abstract, deprive of, bereave, divest, disendow, despoil, strip, fleece, shear, impoverish, levy, distrain, confiscate, sequester, sequestrate, commandeer, requisition, oust, extort, usurp, suck, squeeze, drain, bleed, milk, gut, dry, exhaust.

Phrases: To suck like a leech; to be given an inch and take an ell; to sweep the board; to scoop the pool.

Adjectives: Taking, etc., privative, prehensile, predatory, rapacious, raptorial, predial, ravenous.

790 RESTITUTION

Substantives: return, reddition, rendition, restoration, rehabilitation, remission, reinvestment, reparation, atonement.

Redemption, recovery, recuperation, release, replevin.

Verbs: To return, restore, give back, bring back, derequisition, denationalize, render, refund, reimburse, recoup, remit, rehabilitate, repair, reinvest.

To let go, disgorge, regorge, regurgitate.

Adjectives: Restoring, etc., recuperative.

Phrase: *Suum cuique.*

791 STEALING

Substantives: theft, thieving, thievery, abstration, appropriation, plagiarism, depredation, pilfering, rape, larceny, robbery, shop-lifting, burglary, house-breaking, abaction (of cattle), cattle-lifting, kidnapping.

Spoilation, plunder, pillage, sack, rapine, brigandage, foray, raid, hold-up, dragonnade, marauding.

Peculation, embezzlement, swindling (545), blackmail, *chantage,* smuggling, black market; thievishness, rapacity, kleptomania; den of thieves, Alsatia.

Licence to plunder, letter of marque.

Verbs: To steal, thieve, rob, abstract, appropriate, filch, pilfer, purloin, nab, nim, prig, grab, bag, lift, pick, pinch, knock off.

To convey away, carry off, make off with, run or walk off with, abduct, spirit away, kidnap, crimp, seize, lay violent hands on, etc. (789), abact, rustle (of cattle), shanghai.

To scrounge, wangle, win, crib, sponge, rook, bilk, diddle, swindle (545), peculate, embezzle, fiddle, flog, poach, run, smuggle, hijack.

To plunder, pillage, rifle, sack, ransack, burgle, spoil, spoliate, despoil, hold up, stick up, bail up, strip, fleece, gut, loot, forage, levy blackmail, pirate, plagiarize.

Phrases: To live by one's wits; to rob Peter to pay Paul; to obtain under false pretences; to set a thief to catch a thief.

Adjectives: Stealing, etc., thievish, light-fingered, larcenous, stolen, furtive, piratical, predaceous.

792 THIEF

Substantives: robber, spoiler, pickpocket, curpurse, dip, depredator, yegg, yeggman, footpad, highwayman, burglar, house-breaker, larcener, larcenist, pilferer, filcher, sneak-thief, shop-lifter, poacher, rustler; swell mob; the light-fingered gentry; kleptomaniac.

Swindler, crook, spiv, welsher, smuggler, bootlegger, hijacker, gangster, cracksman, magsman, mobsman, sharper, blackleg, shark, trickster, harpy, *chevalier d'industrie,* peculator, plagiarist, blackmailer; receiver, fence.

Brigand, freebooter, bandit, pirate, viking, corsair, buccaneer, thug, dacoit, picaroon, moss-trooper, rapparee, marauder, filibuster, wrecker, bushranger; Autolycus, Turpin, Macheath, Bill Sikes, Jonathan Wild.

Phrases: A snapper-up of unconsidered trifles; *homo triarum literarum.*

793 BOOTY

Substantives: spoil, plunder, swag,

loot, boodle, prey, pickings, grab, forage, blackmail, graft, prize.

794 BARTER

Substantives: exchange, truck, swop (or swap), chop, interchange, commutation.

Traffic, trade, commerce, dealing, business, custom, negotiation, transaction, jobbing, agiotage, bargain, deal, package deal, commercial enterprise, speculation, brokery.

Phrases: A Roland for an Oliver, a *quid pro quo*; payment in kind.

Verbs: To barter, exchange, truck, interchange, commute, swap (or swop), traffice, trade, speculate, transact, or do business with, deal with, have dealings with; open or keep an account with; to carry on a trade; to rig the market.

To bargain; drive, make, or strike a bargain; negotiate, bid for, haggle (or higgle), chaffer, dicker, stickle, cheapen, compound for, beat down, outbid, underbid, outbargain, come to terms, do a deal, quote, underquote.

Phrase: To throw a sprat to catch a whale.

Adjectives: Commercial, mercantile, trading, interchangeable, marketable, negotiable; wholesale, retail.

795 PURCHASE

Substantives: emption, buying, purchasing, shopping, hire-purchase, never-never; pre-emption, bribery, co-emption.

A buyer, purchaser, customer, emptor, shopper, patron, client, clientele.

Verbs: To buy, purchase, procure, hire, rent, farm, pay, fee, repurchase, buy in, keep in one's pay; pre-empt; bribe, suborn, square, buy over; shop, market.

Adjectives: Purchased, etc.

Phrase: *Caveat emptor.*

796 SALE

Substantives: disposal, custom.

Auction, Dutch auction, roup.
Lease, mortgage.
Vendibility, salability.
A vendor, seller (797).

To sell, vend, dispose of, retail, dispense, auction, auctioneer, hawk, peddle, undersell.

To let, sublet, lease, mortgage.

Phrases: Put up to sale or auction; bring under the hammer.

Adjectives: Vendible, marketable, salable; unpurchased, unbought, on one's hands, unsalable.

797 MERCHANT

Substantives: trader, dealer, tradesman, buyer and seller, vendor, monger, chandler, shopkeeper, shopman, salesman, saleswoman, changer.

Retailer, chapman, hawker, huckster, regrater, higgler, pedlar, cadger, sutler, bumboatman, middleman, coster, costermonger; auctioneer, broker, money-broker, bill-broker, money-changer, jobber, factor, go-between, cambist, usurer, money-lender.

House, firm, concern, partnership, company, guild, syndicate.

798 MERCHANDISE

Substantives: ware, mercery, commodity, effects, goods, article, stock, stock-in-trade, cargo (190), produce, freight, lading, ship-load, staple commodity.

799 MART

Substantives: market, change (or 'change), exchange, bourse, market-place, fair, hall, staple, bazaar, guildhall, tollbooth (or tolbooth), custom-house.

Office, shop, counting-house, bureau, counter, stall, booth, chambers.

Warehouse, depot, store (636), *entrepôt*, emporium, godown.

800 MONEY

Substantives: funds, treasure, capital,

stock, proceeds, assets, cash, bullion, ingot, nugget; sum, amount, balance.

Currency, soft currency; hard currency, circulating medium, legal tender, specie, coin, hard cash, sterling, pounds shillings and pence, LSD.

Ready, rhino, blunt, oof, lolly, splosh, chink, dibs, plunks, bucks, bones, siller, dust, tin, dough, jack, spondulicks, simoleons, mazuma, ducats, the needful, the wherewithal.

Gold, silver, copper, nickel, rouleau, dollar, etc.

Finance, gold standard, monometallism, bimetallism.

Pocket-money, pin-money, chicken feed, petty cash, change, small coin; doit, farthing, bawbee, penny, shilling, stiver, mite, sou; plum, grand, monkey, pony, tenner, fiver, quid, wheel, bob, tanner, two bits.

Sum, amount, balance.

Paper money, note, bank-note, treasury note, greenback, note of hand, promissory note, IOU.

Cheque (or check), bill, draft (or draught), order, remittance, postal order, money order, warrant, coupon, debenture, bill of exchange, exchequer bill, treasury bill, assignat.

A drawer, a drawee.

False money, base coin, flash note, kite, stumer.

Science of coins, numismatics.
Phrases: The sinews of war; the almighty dollar.
Verbs: To draw, draw upon, endorse, issue, utter; to amount to, come to.
Adjectives: Monetary, pecuniary, fiscal, financial, sumptuary; mono-metallic, bimetallic; numismatical.
Phrases: To touch the pocket; *argumentum ad crumenam.*

801 TREASURER
Substantives: purse-bearer, purser, bursar, banker, moneyer, paymaster, cashier, teller, accountant, steward, trustee, almoner.

Chancellor of the Exchequer, minister of finance, Queen's Remembrancer.

802 TREASURY
Substantives: bank, savings-bank, exchequer, coffer, chest, money-box, money-bag, strong-box, strong-room, safe, bursary, till, note-case, wallet, purse, *porte-monnaie,* purse-strings, pocket, fisc.

Consolidated fund, sinking fund, the funds, consols, government securities, war loan, savings certificates.

803 WEALTH
Substantives: fortune, riches, opulence, affluence, independence, solvency, competence, easy circumstances, command of money; El Dorado, Golconda, plutocracy.

Means, provision, substance, resources, capital, revenue, income, alimony, livelihood, subsistence, loaves and fishes, pelf, mammon, lucre, dower (810), pension, superannuation, annuity, unearned increment, pin-money.

A rich man, capitalist, plutocrat, financier, money-bags, millionaire, a Nabob, Dives, Croesus, Midas; *rentier.*
Phrases: The golden calf; a well-lined purse; the purse of Fortunatus; a mint or pot of money.
Verbs: To be rich, etc., to afford.

To enrich, fill one's coffers, etc.; to capitalize.
Phrases: To roll in riches; to wallow in wealth; to make one's pile; to feather one's nest; to line one's pockets; to keep one's head above water.
Adjectives: Wealthy, rich, well-off, affluent, opulent, flush, oofy, solvent (734), moneyed, plutocratic.
Phrases: Made of money; in funds; rich as Croesus; rolling in riches; one's ship come home.

804 POVERTY
Substantives: indigence, penury,

pauperism, destitution, want, need, lack, necessity, privation, distress, an empty purse; bad, reduced, or straitened circumstances; narrow means, straits, insolvency, impecuniosity, beggary, mendicancy, mendicity.

A poor man, pauper, mendicant, beggar, tramp, bum, vagabond, gangrel, starveling; the proletariat; *un pauvre diable.*

Poorhouse, workhouse, the institution.

Phrases: *Res angusta domi*; the wolf at the door.

Verbs: To be poor, etc., to want, lack, starve.

To render poor, etc., to reduce, to impoverish, reduce to poverty, depauperate, ruin; to pauperize.

Phrases: To live from hand to mouth; come upon the parish; not to have a penny; to have seen better days; to beg one's bread.

Adjectives: Poor, indigent, penniless, moneyless, impecunious, short of money, out of money, out of cash, out of pocket, needy, destitute, necessitous, distressed, hard up, in need, in want, poverty-stricken, badly off, in distress, pinched, straitened, dowerless, fortuneless, reduced, insolvent (806), bereft, bereaved, fleeced, stripped, stony broke, stony, stumped.

Phrases: Unable to make both ends meet; out at elbows; in reduced circumstances; not worth a sou; poor as Job; poor as a church mouse; down at heels; on one's uppers; on the rocks.

805 CREDIT
Substantives: trust, tick, score, account.

Letter of credit, duplicate, traveller's cheque (or check); mortgage, lien, debenture.

A creditor, lender, lessor, mortgagee, debenture-holder; a dun, usurer, gombeen-man, Shylock.

Verbs: To keep an account with, to credit, accredit.

To place to one's credit or account, give credit.

Adjectives: Crediting.

Adverbs: On credit, on tick, on account, to pay, unpaid-for.

806 DEBT
Substantives: obligation, liability, debit, indebtment, arrears, deficit, default, insolvency.

Interest, usance, usury.

Floating debt, bad debt, floating capital, debentures; deferred payment, hire system, never-never system.

A debtor, debitor, borrower, lessee, mortgagor; a defaulter (808).

Verbs: To be in debt, to owe, to answer for, to incur a debt, borrow (788).

Phrases: To run up a hill; to go on tick; to outrun the constable.

Adjectives: In debt, indebted, owing, due, unpaid, outstanding, in arrear, being minus, out of pocket, liable, chargeable, answerable for, encumbered, involved, in difficulties, insolvent, in the red.

Unrequited, unrewarded.

807 PAYMENT
Substantives: defrayment, discharge, quittance, acquittance, settlement, clearance, liquidation, satisfaction, remittance, instalment, stake, reckoning, arrangement, composition, acknowledgment, release.

Repayment, reimbursement, retribution, reward (973).

Bill, cheque, cash, ready money (800).

Phrase: A *quid pro quo.*

Verbs: To pay, defray, discharge, settle, quit, acquit oneself of, reckon with, remit, clear, liquidate, release; repay, refund, reimburse.

Phrases: To honour a bill; to strike a

balance; to settle, balance, or square accounts with; to be even with; to wipe off old scores; to satisfy all demands; to pay one's way or shot; to pay in full.
Adjectives: Paying, etc., paid, owing nothing, out of debt.
Adverbs: On the nail, money down, COD.

808 NON-PAYMENT
Substantives: default, defalcation, repudiation, protest.

Insolvency, bankruptcy, failure, whitewashing, application of the sponge.

Waste paper, dishonoured bills.

A defaulter, bankrupt, welsher, levanter, insolvent debtor, man of straw, lame duck.
Verbs: Not to pay, to fail, break, become insolvent or bankrupt, default, defalcate.

To protest, dishonour, repudiate, nullify; hammer.
Phrases: To run up bills; to tighten the purse-strings.
Adjectives: Not paying, in debt, behindhand, in arrear, insolvent, bankrupt, gazetted.
Phrases: Being minus or worse than nothing; plunged or over head and ears in debt; in the gazette; in Queer Street.

809 EXPENDITURE
Substantives: money going out; outgoings, expenses, disbursement, outlay.

Pay, payment, fee, hire, wages, perquisites, vails, allowance, stipend, salary, screw, divided, tribute, subsidy, batta, bat-money, shot, scot.

Remuneration, recompense, reward (973), tips, *pourboire,* largess, honorarium, refresher, bribe, *douceur,* hush-money, extras, commission, rake-off.

Advance, subsistence money, sub, earnest, handsel, deposit, prepayment, entrance fee, entrance.

Contribution, donation, subscription, deposit, contingent, dole, quota.

Investment, purchase (795), alms (748).
Verbs: To expend, spend, pay, disburse, lay out, lay or pay down, to cash, to come down with, brass up, shell out, fork out, bleed, make up a sum, to invest, sink money, prepay, tip.
Phrases: To unloose the purse-strings; to pay the piper; to pay through the nose.
Adjectives: Expending, expended, etc., sumptuary.

810 RECEIPT
Substantives: money coming in, incomings.

Income, revenue, earnings (775), rent, rental, rent-roll, rentage, return, proceeds, premium, bonus, gate-money, royalty.

Pension, annuity, tontine, jointure, dower, dowry, dot, alimony, compensation.

Emoluments, perquisites, recompense (809), sinecure.
Verbs: To receive, pocket (789), to draw from, derive from.

To bring in, yield, return, afford, pay, accrue.
Phrases: To get what will make the pot boil; keep the wolf from the door; bring grist to the mill.
Adjectives: Receiving, etc., received, etc.

Gainful, profitable, remunerative, lucrative, advantageous (775).

811 ACCOUNTS
Substantives: money matters, finance, budget, bill, score, reckoning, balance-sheet, books, account-books, ledger, day-book, cash-book, cash account, current account, deposit account, pass-book.

Book-keeping, audit, double entry.

An accountant, CA, auditory, actuary, book-keeper.

Verbs: To keep accounts, to enter, post, credit, debit, tot up, carry over; balance, make up accounts, take stock, audit.

To falsify, garble, cook, or doctor accounts.

812 PRICE

Substantives: cost, expense, amount, figure, charge, demand, damage, fare, hire.

Dues, duty, toll, tax, supertax, pay-as-you-earn, PAYE, rate, impost, cess, levy, gabelle, octroi, assessment, benevolence, custom, tithe, exactment, ransom, salvage, excise, tariff, brokerage, demurrage.

Bill, account, score, reckoning.

Worth, rate, value, valuation, evaluation, appraisement, market price, quotation; money's worth, penny-worth; price-current, price list.

Verbs: To set or fix a price, appraise, assess, value, evaluate, price, charge, demand, ask, require, exact.

To fetch, sell for, cost, bring in, yield, make, change hands for, go for, realize, run into, stand one in; afford.

Phrases: To run up a bill; to amount to; to set one back.

Adjectives: Priced, charged, etc., to the tune of, *ad valorem*; mercenary, venal.

Phrases: No penny, no paternoster; *point d'argent, point de Suisse.*

813 DISCOUNT

Substantives: abatement, reduction, deduction, depreciation, allowance, drawback, poundage, *agio,* percentage, rebate, set-off, backwardation, contango, tare and tret, salvage.

Verbs: To discount, bate, abate, rebate, reduce, take off, allow, give, discount, tax.

Adjectives: Discounting, etc.

Adverb: At a discount.

814 DEARNESS

Substantives: costliness, high price, expensiveness, rise in price, overcharge, surcharge, extravagance, exorbitance, extortion.

Phrase: A pretty penny.

Verbs: To be dear, etc., to cost much, to come expensive; to overcharge, surcharge, bleed, fleece (791).

To pay too much, to pay through the nose.

Adjectives: Dear, high, high-priced, expensive, costly, dear-bought, precious, unreasonable, extortionate, extravagant, exorbitant, steep, stiff.

Adverbs: Dear, at great cost, at a premium.

815 CHEAPNESS

Substantives: low price, inexpensiveness, drop in price, undercharge, bargain; absence of charge, gratuity, free admission.

Phrases: A labour of love; the run of one's teeth; a drug in the market.

Verbs: To be cheap, etc., to cost little, to come down or fall in price, to cut prices.

Phrase: To have one's money's worth.

Adjectives: Cheap, low, moderate, reasonable, inexpensive, unexpensive, low-priced, dirt-cheap, worth the money, half-price; catchpenny.

Gratuitous, gratis, free, for nothing, given away, free of cost, without charge, not charged, untaxed, scot-free, shot-free, expenseless, free of expense, free of all demands, honorary, unpaid.

Phrases: Cheap as dirt; for a mere song; given away with a pound of tea; at cost price; at a reduction; at a sacrifice.

816 LIBERALITY

Substantives: generosity (942), bounty, munificence, bounteousness, boutifulness, charity (906), hospitality.

Verbs: To be liberal, etc., spend freely, lavish, shower upon.

Phrases: To loosen one's purse-strings; to give *carte blanche*; to spare no expense.
Adjectives: Liberal, free, generous, charitable, hospitable, bountiful, bounteous, handsome, lavish, ungrudging, free-handed, open-handed, open-hearted, free-hearted, munificent, princely.
Overpaid.

817 ECONOMY
Substantives: frugality, thrift, thriftiness, care, husbandry, good housewifery, austerity, retrenchment; parsimony (819).
Verbs: To be economical, etc., to save, economize, skimp, scrimp, scrape, meet one's expenses, retrench; to lay by, put by, save up, invest, bank, hoard, accumulate.
Phrases: To cut one's coat according to one's cloth; to make ends meet; to pay one's way; to look at both sides of a shilling; to provide for a rainy day.
Adjectives: Economical, frugal, thrifty, canny, careful, saving, chary, spare, sparing, cheese-paring.
Phrase: Take care of the pence and the pounds will take care of themselves.

818 PRODIGALITY
Substantives: unthriftiness, thriftlessness, unthrift, waste, profusion, profuseness, extravagance, dissipation, squandering, squandermania, malversation.
A prodigal, spendthrift, squanderer, waster, wastrel.
Verbs: To be prodigal, etc., to squander, lavish, waste, dissipate, exhaust, run through, spill, misspend, throw away money, drain.

Phrases: To burn the candle at both ends; to make ducks and drakes of one's money; to spend money like water; to outrun the constable; to fool away, potter, muddle away, fritter away, etc., one's money; to pour water into a sieve; to go the pace.
Adjectives: Prodigal, profuse, improvident, thriftless, unthrifty, wasteful, extravagant, lavish, dissipated.
Phrases: Penny wise and pound foolish; money burning a hole in one's pocket.

819 PARSIMONY
Substantives: parsimoniousness, stint, stinginess, niggardliness, cheese-paring, extortion, illiberality, closeness, penuriousness, avarice, tenacity, covetousness, greediness, avidity, rapacity, venality, mercenariness, cupidity.
A miser, niggard, churl, screw, skinflint, money-grubber, codger, muckworm, hunks, curmudgeon, harpy.
Phrase: *Auri sacra fames.*
Verbs: To be parsimonious, etc., to grudge, begrudge, stint, pinch, screw, dole out.
Phrases: To skin a flint; to drive a hard bargain; to tighten one's purse-strings.
Adjectives: Parsimonious, stingy, miserly, mean, mingy, penurious, shabby, near, niggardly, cheese-paring, close, close-fisted, close-handed, chary, illiberal, ungenerous, churlish, sordid, mercenary, venal, covetous, avaricious, greedy, grasping, griping, pinching, extortionate, rapacious.
Phrases: Having an itching palm; with a sparing hand.

Words relating to the sentient and moral powers

Section 1 –
Affections in General

820 AFFECTIONS
Substantives: character, qualities, disposition, nature, spirit, mood, tone, temper, temperament; cast or frame of mind or soul; turn, bent, idiosyncrasy, bias, turn of mind, predisposition, diathesis, predilection, propensity, proneness, proclivity, vein, humour, grain, mettle.

Soul, heart, breast, bosom, the inner man, inmost heart, heart's core, heart-strings, heart's-blood, heart of hearts, *penetralia mentis.*

Passion, pervading spirit, ruling passion, master-passion.

Phrases: Flow of soul; fullness of the heart; the cockles of one's heart; flesh and blood.

Verbs: To have or possess affections, etc.; be of a character, etc.; to breathe.

Adjectives: Affected, characterized, formed, moulded, cast, tempered, attempered, framed, disposed, predisposed, prone, inclined, having a bias, etc., imbued or penetrated with; inbred, inborn, engrained (or ingrained).

821 FEELING
Substantives: endurance, experience, suffering, tolerance, sufferance, experience, sensibility (822), passion (825).

Impression, sensation, affection, response, emotion, pathos, warmth, glow, fervour, fervency, heartiness, effusiveness, effusion, gush, cordiality, ardour, exuberance, zeal, eagerness, *empressement, élan,* enthusiasm, verve, inspiration.

Blush, suffusion, flush, tingling, thrill, kick, excitement (824), turn, shock, agitation (315), heaving, flutter, flurry, fluster, twitter, stew, tremor, throb, throbbing, panting, palpitation, trepidation, perturbation, hurry of spirits, the heart swelling, throbbing, thumping, pulsating, melting, bursting; transport, rapture, ecstasy, ravishment (827).

Verbs: To feel, receive an impression, etc.; to be impressed with, affected with, moved with, touched with, keen on.

To bear, bear with, suffer, endure, brook, tolerate, stomach, stand, thole, experience, taste, meet with, go through, put up with, prove; to harbour, cherish, support, abide, undergo.

To blush, change colour, mantle, tingle, twitter, throb, heave, pant, palpitate, go pit-a-pat, agitate, thrill, tremble, shake, quiver, wince, simmer, burble.

To swell, glow, warm, flush, redden, look blue, look black, catch the flame, catch the infection, respond, enthuse.

To possess, pervade, penetrate, imbue, absorb, etc., the soul.

Phrases: To bear the brunt of; to come home to one's feelings or bosom; to strike a chord.

Adjectives: Feeling, suffering, enduring; sentient, emotive, emotional.

Impressed, moved, touched, affected with, etc., penetrated, imbued.

Warm, quick, lively, smart, strong, sharp, keen, acute, cutting, incisive, piercing, pungent, racy, piquant, poignant, caustic.

Deep, profound, indelible, ineffaceable, impressive, effective, deep-felt, home-felt, heart-felt, warm-hearted, hearty, cordial, swelling, thrilling, rapturous, ecstatic, soul-stirring, emotive, deep-mouthed, heart-expanding, electric.

Earnest, hearty, eager, exuberant, gushing, effusive, breathless, glowing, fervent, fervid, ardent, soulful, burning, red-hot, fiery, flaming, boiling, boiling over, zealous, pervading, penetrating, absorbing, hectic, rabid, fanatical; the heart being big, full, swelling, overflowing, bursting.

Wrought up, excited, passionate, enthusiastic (825).

Phrase: Struck all of a heap.

Adverbs: Heartily, cordially, earnestly, etc.

Phrases: From the bottom of one's heart; *de profundis*; heart and soul; over head and ears.

822 SENSIBILITY

Substantives: impressibility, sensibleness, sensitiveness, hyperaesthesia (825), responsiveness, affectibility, susceptibleness, susceptibility, susceptivity, excitability, mobility, vivacity, vivaciousness, tenderness, softness, sentimentality, sentimentalism, schmalz.

Physical sensibility (375).

Verbs: To be sensible, etc., to shrink, have a tender heart.

Phrases: To be touched to the quick; to feel where the shoe pinches; to take it hard; to take to heart.

Adjectives: Sensible, sensitive, impressible, impressionable, suscep-

tive, susceptible, responsive, excitable, mobile, thin-skinned, touchy, alive, vivacious, lively, mettlesome, highstrung, intense, emotional, tender, soft, sentimental, maudlin, sloppy, romantic, enthusiastic, neurotic.

Adverbs: Sensibly, etc., to the quick.

823 INSENSIBILITY

Substantives: insensibleness, inertness, insensitivity, impassibility, impassibleness, impassivity, apathy, phlegm, dullness, hebetude, coolness, coldness, supineness, stoicism, insouciance, nonchalance, indifference, lukewarmness, frigidity, cold blood, sang-froid, dry eyes, cold heart, deadness, torpor, torpidity, ataraxia, pococurantism.

Lethargy, coma, trance, stupor, stupefaction, amnesia, paralysis, palsy, catalepsy, suspended animation, hebetation, anaesthesia (381), stock and stone, neutrality.

Physical insensibility (376).

Verbs: To disregard, be insensible, not to be affected by, not to mind, to vegetate, *laisser aller,* not to care; to take it easy.

To render insensible (376), numb, benumb, paralyse, deaden, render callous, sear, inure, harden, steel, caseharden, stun, daze, stupefy, brutalize, hebetate.

Phrases: To turn a deaf ear to; not care a straw (or a fig).

Adjectives: Insensible, unconscious, impassive, unsusceptible, insusceptible, impassible, unimpressionable, unresponsive, unfeeling, blind to, deaf to, dead to, passionless, spiritless, soulless, apathetic, listless, phlegmatic, callous, hard-boiled, thick-skinned, pachydermatous, obtuse, proof against, case-hardened, inured, steeled against, stoical, dull, frigid, cold, cold-blooded, cold-hearted, flat, inert, bovine, supine, sluggish, torpid, languid, tame, tepid, numb, numbed, sleepy, yawning, comatose, anaesthetic.

Indifferent, insouciant, lukewarm, careless, mindless, regardless, disregarding, nonchalant, unconcerned, uninterested, pococurante; taking no interest in.

Unfelt, unaffected, unruffled, unimpressed, unmoved, unperturbed, uninspired, untouched, etc.; platonic, imperturbable, vegetative, automatic.
Adverbs: Insensibly, etc., *aequo animo,* with dry eyes, with withers unwrung.
Phrases: No matter; never mind; *n'importe*; it matters not; it does not signify; it is of no consequence or importance (643); it cannot be helped; nothing coming amiss; it is all the same or all one to; what's the odds? *nichevo.*

824 EXCITATION
Substantives: of feeling, excitement, galvanism, stimulation, provocation, calling forth, infection, animation, inspiration, agitation, perturbation, subjugation, fascination, intoxication, enravishment, unction; a scene, sensation, tableau, shocker, thriller.
Verbs: To excite, affect, touch, move, stir, wake, awaken, raise, raise up, evoke, call up, summon up, rake up.

To impress, strike, hit, quicken, swell, work upon.

To warm, kindle, stimulate, pique, whet, animate, hearten, inspire, impassion, inspirit, spirit, provoke, irritate, infuriate, sting, rouse, work up, hurry on, ginger up, commove.

To agitate, ruffle, flutter, fluster, flush, shake, thrill, penetrate, pierce, cut; to work oneself up, to simmer, bubble, burble.

To soften, subdue, overcome, master, overpower, overwhelm, bring under.

To shock, stagger, jar, jolt, stun, astound, electrify, galvanize, give one a shock, petrify.

To madden, intoxicate, fascinate, transport, ravish, enrapture, enravish, entrance, send.
Phrases: To come home to one's feelings; to make a sensation; to prey on the mind; to give one a turn; to cut to the quick; to go through one; to strike one all of a heap; to make one's blood boil; to lash to a fury; to make one sit up.
Adjectives: Excited, affected (825), wrought up, worked up, strung up, lost, *éperdu,* wild, haggard, feverish, febrile.

Exciting, etc., impressive, pathetic, sensational, provocative, piquant, aphrodisiac, dramatic, warm, glowing, fervid, swelling.
Phrases: Being all of a twitter; all of a flutter; the head being turned.

825 EXCITABILITY
Substantives: intolerance, impatience, wincing, perturbation, trepidation, disquiet, disquietude, restlessness, fidgets, fidgetiness, fuss, hurry, agitation, flurry, fluster, flutter, irritability (901), hypersensitiveness, hyperaesthesia.

Passion, excitement, vehemence, impetuosity, flush, heat, fever, fire, flame, fume, wildness, turbulence, boisterousness, tumult, effervescence, ebullition, boiling, boiling over, whiff, gust, storm, tempest, outbreak, outburst, burst, explosion, fit, paroxysm, brain-storm, the blood boiling.

Fierceness, rage, fury, furore, tantrum, hysteria, hysterics, raving, delirium, frenzy, intoxication, fascination, infection, infatuation, fanaticism, Quixotism, *la tête montée.*
Verbs: To be intolerant, etc., not to bear, to bear ill, wince, chafe, fidget, fuss, not to be able to bear, stand, tolerate, etc.

To break out, fly out, burst out, explode, run riot, boil, boil over, fly off, flare up, fire, take fire, fume, rage, rampage, rave, run mad, run amuck, raise Cain.

Phrases: To fly off at a tangent; to be out of all patience; to go off the deep end; to get the wind up; to make a scene; to go up in a blue flame.

Adjectives: Exitable, etc., excited, etc.

Intolerant, impatient, unquiet, restless, restive, fidgety, irritable, mettlesome, chafing, wincing, etc.

Vehement, boisterous, impetuous, demonstrative, fierce, fiery, flaming, boiling, ebullient, over-zealous, passionate, impassioned, enthusiastic, rampant, mercurial, high-strung, skittish, overwrought, overstrung, hysterical, hot-headed, hurried, turbulent, furious, fuming, boiling, raging, raving, frantic, phrenetic, rampageous, wild, heady, delirious, intoxicated, demoniacal; hypersensitive.

Overpowering, overwhelming, uncontrolled, madcap, reckless, stanchless, irrepressible, ungovernable, uncontrollable, inextinguishable, volcanic.

Phrases: More than flesh and blood can stand; stung to the quick; all hot and bothered.

Interjections: Pish! pshaw! botheration!

826 INEXCITABILITY

Substantives: hebetude, tolerance, patience.

Coolness, composure, calmness, imperturbability, sang-froid, collectedness, tranquillity, quiet, quietude, quietness, sedateness, soberness, poise, staidness, gravity, placidity, sobriety, philosophy, stoicism, demureness, meekness, gentleness, mildness.

Submission, resignation, sufferance, endurance, longanimity, long-sufferance, forbearance, fortitude, equanimity.

Repression, restraint (174), hebetation, tranquillization.

Phrases: Patience of Job; even temper; cool head; Spartan endurance; a sobersides.

Verbs: To be composed, etc., to bear, to bear well, tolerate, put up with, bear with, stand, bide, abide, aby, take easily, rub on, rub along, make the best of, acquiesce, submit, yield, bow to, resign oneself, suffer, endure, support, go through, reconcile oneself to, bend under; subside, calm down, pipe down.

To brook, digest, eat, swallow, pocket, stomach, brave, make light of.

To be borne, endured, etc., to go down.

To allay, compose, calm, still, lull, pacify, placate, quiet, tranquillize, hush, smooth, appease, assuage, mitigate, soothe, soften, temper, chasten, alleviate, moderate, sober down, mollify, lenify, tame, blunt, obtund, dull, deaden (823), slacken, damp, repress, restrain, check, curb, bridle, rein in, smother (174).

Phrases: To take things as they come; to submit with a good grace; to shrug the shoulders.

To set one's heart at rest or at ease.

Adjectives: Inexcitable, unexcited, calm, cool, temperate, composed, collected, placid, quiet, tranquil, unstirred, undisturbed, unruffled, serene, demure, sedate, staid, sober, dispassionate, unimpassioned, passionless, good-natured, easy-going, platonic, philosophic, stoical, imperturbable, cold-blooded, insensible (823).

Meek, tolerant, patient, submissive, unoffended, unresenting, content, resigned, subdued, bearing with, long-suffering, gentle, mild, sober-minded, cool-headed.

Phrases: Gentle or meek as a lamb; mild as milk; patient as Job; armed with patience; cool as a cucumber.

307

Section 2 –
Personal Affections

827 PLEASURE
Substantives: gratification, delectation, enjoyment, fruition, relish, zest, gusto, kick.

Well-being, satisfaction, complacency, content (831), ease, comfort, bed of roses, bed of down, velvet.

Joy, gladness, delight, glee, cheer, sunshine.

Physical pleasure (377).

Treat, refreshment, feast, luxury, voluptuousness, clover.

Happiness, felicity, bliss, beatitude, beatification, enchantment, transport, rapture, ravishment, ecstasy, heaven, *summum bonum,* paradise, Eden, Arcadia, nirvana, elysium, empyrean (981).

Honeymoon, palmy days, halcyon days, golden age, *Saturnia regna.*

Verbs: To be pleased, etc., to feel, receive, or derive pleasure, etc.; to take pleasure or delight in; to delight in, joy in, rejoice in, relish, like, enjoy, take to, take in good part.

To indulge in, treat oneself, solace oneself, revel, riot, luxuriate in, gloat over; to be on velvet, in clover, in heaven, etc.; to enjoy oneself; to congratulate oneself, hug oneself.

Phrases: To slake the appetite; to bask in the sunshine; to tread on enchanted ground; to have a good time; to make whoopee.

Adjectives: Pleased, enjoying, relishing, liking, gratified, glad, gladdened, rejoiced, delighted, overjoyed, charmed.

Cheered, enlivened, flattered, tickled, indulged, regaled, treated.

Comfortable, at ease, easy, cosy, satisfied, content (831), luxurious, on velvet, in clover, on a bed of roses, *sans souci.*

Happy, blest, blessed, blissful, over-joyed, enchanted, captivated, fascinated, transported, raptured, rapt, enraptured, in raptures, in ecstasies, in a transport, beatified, in heaven, in the seventh heaven, in paradise.

Phrases: With a joyful face; with sparkling eyes; happy as a king; pleased as Punch; in the lap of luxury; happy as the day is long; *ter quaterque beatus.*

Adverbs: Happily, etc.

828 PAIN
Substantives: suffering; physical pain (378).

Displeasure, dissatisfaction, discontent, discomfort, discomposure, malaise.

Uneasiness, disquiet, inquietude, weariness (841), dejection (837).

Annoyance, irritation, plague, bore, bother, botheration, worry, infliction, stew.

Care, anxiety, concern, mortification, vexation, chagrin, trouble, trial, solicitude, cark, dole, dule, load, burden, fret.

Grief, sorrow, distress, affliction, woe, bitterness, heartache, a heavy heart, a bleeding heart, a broken heart, heavy affliction.

Unhappiness, infelicity, misery, wretchedness, desolation, tribulation.

Dolour, sufferance, ache, aching, hurt, smart, cut, twitch, twinge, stitch, cramp, spasm, nightmare, convulsion, throe, angina.

Pang, anguish, agony, torture, torment, rack, crucifixion, martyrdom, purgatory, hell (982).

A sufferer, victim, prey, martyr.

Phrases: Vexation of spirit; a peck of troubles; a sea of troubles; the ills that flesh is heir to; *mauvais quart d'heure*; the iron entering the soul.

Verbs: To feel, suffer, or experience pain, etc.; to suffer, ache, smart, ail, bleed, twinge, tingle, gripe, wince, writhe.

To grieve, fret, pine, mourn, bleed,

worry oneself, chafe, yearn, droop, sink, give way, despair (859).

Phrases: To sit on thorns; to be on pins and needles; to labour under afflictions; to have a bad or thin time; to drain the cup of misery to the dregs; to fall on evil days.

Adjectives: In pain; feeling, suffering, enduring, etc., pain; in a state of pain, of suffering, etc., sore, aching, suffering, ailing, etc., pained, hurt, stung (830).

Displeased, annoyed, dissatisfied, discontented, weary (832), uneasy, ungratified, uncomfortable, ill at ease.

Crushed, stricken, victimized, ill-used.

Concerned, afflicted, in affliction, sorry, sorrowful, in sorrow, cut up, bathed in tears (839).

Unhappy, unfortunate, hapless, unblest, luckless, unlucky, ill-fated, ill-starred, fretting, wretched, miserable, careworn, disconsolate, inconsolable, woebegone, poor, forlorn, comfortless, a prey to grief, etc., despairing, in despair (859), heart-broken, broken-hearted, the heart bleeding, doomed, devoted, accursed, undone.

829 PLEASURABLENESS

Substantives: pleasantness, gratefulness, welcomeness, acceptableness, acceptability, agreeableness, delectability, deliciousness, daintiness, sweetness, luxuriousness, lusciousness, voluptuousness, eroticism.

Charm, attraction, attractiveness, sex-appeal, SA, It, oomph, fascination, witchery, prestige, loveliness, takingness, winsomeness, likableness, invitingness, glamour.

A treat, dainty, titbit, bonbon, *bonne bouche,* sweet, sweetmeat, sugar-plum, nuts, *sauce piquante.*

Verbs: To cause, produce, create, give, afford, procure, offer, present, yield, etc., pleasure, gratification, etc.

To please, take, gratify, satisfy, indulge, flatter, tickle, humour, regale, refresh, interest.

To charm, rejoice, cheer, gladden, delight, enliven (836), to transport, captivate, fascinate, enchant, entrance, bewitch, ravish, enrapture, enravish, beatify, enthral, imparadise.

Phrases: To do one's heart good; to tickle one to death; to take one's fancy.

Adjectives: Causing or giving pleasure, etc., pleasing, agreeable, grateful, gratifying, pleasant, pleasurable, acceptable, welcome, glad, gladsome, comfortable.

Sweet, delectable, nice, jolly, palatable, dainty, delicate, delicious, dulcet, savoury, toothsome, tasty, luscious, luxurious, voluptuous, genial, cordial, refreshing, comfortable, scrumptious.

Fair, lovely, favourite, attractive, engaging, winsome, winning, taking, prepossessing, inviting, captivating, bewitching, fascinating, magnetic, seductive, killing, stunning, ripping, smashing, likable.

Charming, delightful, exquisite, enchanting, enthralling, ravishing, rapturous, heart-felt, thrilling, beatific, heavenly, celestial, elysian, empyrean, seraphic, ideal.

Palmy, halcyon, Saturnian, Arcadian.

Phrases: To one's heart's content; to one's taste.

830 PAINFULNESS

Substantives: disagreeableness, unpleasantness, irksomeness, displeasingness, unacceptableness, bitterness, vexatiousness, troublesomeness.

Trouble, care, cross, annoyance, burden, load, nuisance, pest, plague, bore, bother, botheration, vexation, sickener, pin-prick.

Scourge, bitter pill, worm, canker, cancer, ulcer, curse, gall and wormwood, sting, pricks, scorpion, thorn, brier, bramble, hornet, whip, lash, rack, wheel.

A mishap, misadventure, mischance, pressure, infestation, grievance, trial, crosses, hardship, blow, stroke, affliction, misfortune, reverse, infliction, dispensation, visitation, disaster, undoing, tragedy, calamity, catastrophe, adversity (735).

Provocation, infestation, affront, aggravation, indignity, outrage (900, 929).

Phrases: A thorn in one's side; a fly in the ointment; a sorry sight; a bitter pill; a crumpled rose-leaf.

Verbs: To cause, produce, give, etc., pain, uneasiness, suffering, etc.

To pain, hurt, wound, sting, pinch, grate upon, irk, gall, jar, chafe, gnaw, prick, lacerate, pierce, cut, cut up, stick, gravel, hurt one's feelings, mortify, horrify, shock, twinge, gripe.

To wring, harrow, torment, torture, rack, scarify, cruciate, crucify, convulse, agonize.

To displease, annoy, incommode, discompose, trouble, disquiet, grieve, cross, tease, rag, josh, bait, tire, vex, worry, try, plague, fash, faze, fret, haunt, obsess, bother, pester, bore, gravel, flummox, harass, importune, tantalize, aggravate.

To irritate, provoke, nettle, pique, rile, ruffle, aggrieve, enchafe, enrage.

To maltreat, bite, assail, badger, infest, harry, persecute, haze, roast.

To sicken, disgust, revolt, turn the stomach, nauseate, disenchant, repel, offend, shock.

To horrify, prostrate.

Phrases: To barb the dart; to set the teeth on edge; to stink in the nostrils; to stick in one's throat; to add a nail to one's coffin; to plant a dagger in the breast; to freeze the blood; to make one's flesh creep; to make one's hair stand on end; to break or wring the heart.

Adjectives: Causing, occasioning, giving, producing, creating, inflicting, etc., pain, etc., hurting, etc.

Painful, dolorific, dolorous, unpleasant, unpleasing, displeasing, unprepossessing, disagreeable, distasteful, uncomfortable, unwelcome, unsatisfactory, unpalatable, unacceptable, thankless, undesirable, untoward, unlucky, undesired, obnoxious.

Distressing, bitter, afflicting, afflictive, cheerless, joyless, comfortless, depressing, depressive, mournful, dreary, dismal, bleak, melancholy, grievous, pathetic, woeful, disastrous, calamitous, ruinous, sad, tragic, tragical, deplorable, dreadful, frightful, lamentable, ill-omened.

Irritating, provoking, provocative, stinging, biting, vexatious, annoying, unaccommodating, troublesome, fashious, wearisome, tiresome, irksome, plaguing, plaguy, teasing, pestering, bothering, bothersome, carking, mortifying, galling, harassing, worrying, tormenting, aggravating, racking, importunate, insistent.

Intolerable, insufferable, insupportable, unbearable, unendurable, shocking, frightful, terrific, grim, appalling, dire, heart-breaking, heart-rending, heart-wounding, heart-corroding, dreadful, horrid, harrowing, horrifying, horrific, execrable, accursed, damnable.

Odious, hateful, unpopular, repulsive, repellent, uninviting, offensive, nauseous, disgusting, sickening, nasty, execrable, revolting, shocking, vile, foul, abominable, loathsome, rotten.

Sharp, acute, sore, severe, grave, hard, harsh, bitter, cruel, biting, caustic, corroding, consuming, racking, excruciating, grinding, agonizing.

Phrase: More than flesh and blood can bear.

Adverbs: Painfully, etc.

831 CONTENT

Substantives: contentment, contentedness, satisfaction, peace of mind, complacency, serenity, sereneness, ease.

Comfort, snugness, well-being.

Moderation, patience (826), endurance, resignation, reconciliation.

Verbs: To be content, etc.; to rest satisfied, to put up with; to take up with; to be reconciled to.

To render content, etc., to set at ease, to conciliate, reconcile, disarm, propitiate, win over, satisfy, indulge, slake, gratify.

Phrases: To make the best of; to let well alone; to take in good part; to set one's heart at ease or at rest.

Adjectives: Content, contented, satisfied, at ease, easy, snug, comfortable, cosy.

Patient, resigned to, reconciled to, unrepining; disarming, conciliatory.

Unafflicted, unvexed, unmolested, unplagued, etc., serene, at rest, *sine cura, sans souci.*

Phrases: To one's heart's content; like patience on a monument.

Interjections: Very well, all right, suits me.

832 DISCONTENT

Substantives: discontentment, dissatisfaction, disappointment, mortification.

Repining, taking on, inquietude, heart-burning, regret (833).

Nostalgia, home-sickness, *maladie du pays.*

Grumbler, grouser, croaker.

Verbs: To be discontented, dissatisfied, etc.; to repine, regret (833), grumble (839).

To cause discontent, etc., to disappoint, dissatisfy, mortify.

Phrases: To take in bad part; to have the hump; to quarrel with one's bread and butter.

Adjectives: Discontented, dissatisfied, unsatisfied, malcontent, mortified, disappointed, cut up.

Repining, glum, grumbling, grous-

ing, grouchy, exigent, *exigeant,* exacting; nostalgic, home-sick; disgruntled.

Disappointing, unsatisfactory.

Phrases: Out of humour; in the dumps; in high dudgeon; down in the mouth.

833 REGRET

Substantives: bitterness, repining; lamentation (839); self-reproach, penitence (950).

Verbs: To regret, deplore, repine, lament, rue, repent (950).

Phrase: To rue the day.

Adjectives: Regretting, etc., regretful, regretted, regrettable, lamentable.

Phrase: What a pity!

834 RELIEF

Substantives: easement, alleviation, mitigation, palliation, solace, consolation, comfort, encouragement, refreshment (689), lullaby; deliverance, delivery.

Lenitive, balm, oil, restorative, cataplasm (662); cushion, pillow, bolster (215).

Phrases: A crumb of comfort; balm in Gilead.

Verbs: To relieve, ease, alleviate, mitigate, palliate, soften, soothe, assuage, allay, cheer, comfort, console, encourage, bear up, refresh, restore, remedy, cure.

Phrases: To dry the tears; to pour balm into; to lay the flattering unction to one's soul; to temper the wind to the shorn lamb; to breathe again; to breathe freely.

Adjectives: Relieving, etc., consolatory; balmy, balsamic, soothing, lenitive, anodyne (662), remedial, curative; easeful.

835 AGGRAVATION

Substantives: heightening, exacerbation, exasperation.

Verbs: To aggravate, render worse, heighten, intensify, embitter, sour, acerbate, envenom, exacerbate, exasperate.

Phrase: To add fuel to the flame.

Adjectives: Aggravating, etc., aggravated, etc., unrelieved; aggravable.

Phrases: Out of the frying-pan into the fire; from bad to worse.

836 CHEERFULNESS

Substantives: gaiety, cheer, spirits, high spirits, high glee, light-heartedness, joyfulness, joyousness, good humour, geniality, hilarity, exhilaration, livliness, sprightliness, briskness, vivacity, buoyancy, sunniness, jocundity, joviality, levity, sportiveness, playfulness, jocularity.

Mirth, merriment, merrymaking, laughter (838), amusement (840); nepenthe, Euphrosyne.

Gratulation, rejoicing, exultation, jubilation, jubilee, triumph, paean, Te Deum, heyday; joy-bells.

Verbs: To be cheerful, etc.; to be of good cheer, to cheer up, perk up, brighten up, light up; take heart, bear up.

To rejoice, make merry, exult, congratulate oneself, triumph, clap the hands, crow, sing, carol, lilt, frisk, prance, galumph, rollick, maffick, frivol.

To cheer, enliven, elate, exhilarate, entrance, inspirit, animate, gladden, buck up, liven up.

Phrases: To drive dull care away; to make whoopee; to keep up one's spirits; care killed the cat; *ride si sapis*; laugh and grow fat.

Adjectives: Cheerful, gay, blithe, cheery, jovial, genial, gleeful, of good cheer, in spirits, in good or high spirits, *allegro*, light, lightsome, buoyant, debonair, bright, glad, light-hearted, hearty, free and easy, airy, jaunty, canty, perky, spry, chipper, saucy, sprightly, lively, vivacious, sunny, breezy, chirpy, hopeful (858).

Merry, joyous, joyful, jocund, playful, waggish, frisky, frolicsome, sportive, gamesome, jokesome, joky, jocose, jocular, jolly, frivolous.

Rejoicing, elated, exulting, jubilant, hilarious, flushed, rollicking, cock-a-hoop.

Phrases: In high feather; walking on air; with one's head in the clouds; gay as a lark; happy as a king or as the day is long; playful as a kitten; jolly as a sandboy; merry as a grig; full of beans.

Adverbs: Cheerfully, cheerily, cheerly, etc.

Interjections: Cheer up! never say die! hurrah! huzza!

837 DEJECTION

Substantives: depression, low spirits, lowness or depression of spirits, dejectedness, sadness.

Heaviness, dullness, infestivity, joylessness, gloom, dolefulness, dolesomeness, weariness (841), heaviness of heart, heart-sickness.

Melancholy, melancholia, dismals, mumps, dumps, doldrums, blues, mulligrubs, blue devils, megrims, vapours, accidie, spleen, hypochondria; *taedium vitae; maladie du pays.*

Despondency, despair, pessimism, disconsolateness, prostration; the Slough of Despond (859).

Demureness, seriousness, gravity, solemnity, solemnness, sullenness.

A hypochondriac, self-tormentor, *malade imaginaire,* kill-joy, Job's comforter, wet blanket, pessimist, futilitarian.

Verbs: To be dejected, sad, etc.; to grieve, take on, take to heart, give way, droop, sink, lour, look downcast, mope, mump, pout, brood over, fret, pine, yearn, frown, despond (859).

To depress, discourage, dishearten, dispirit, dull, deject, lower, sink, dash, unman, prostrate, over-cloud.

Phrases: To look blue; to hang down the head; to wear the willow; to laugh on the wrong side of the mouth; to get the hump.

To prey on the mind or spirits; to dash one's hopes.

Adjectives: Cheerless, unmirthful, mirthless, joyless, dull, glum, flat, dispirited, out of spirits, out of sorts, out of heart, in low spirits, spiritless, lowering, frowning, sulky.

Discouraged, disheartened, downhearted, downcast, cast down, depressed, chap-fallen, crest-fallen, dashed, drooping, sunk, heart-sick, dumpish, mumpish, desponding, pessimistic.

Dismal, melancholy, sombre, tristful, *triste*, pensive, *penseroso*, mournful, doleful, moping, splenetic, gloomy, lugubrious, funereal, woebegone, comfortless, forlorn, overcome, prostrate, cut up, care-worn, care-laden.

Melancholic, hipped, hypochondriacal, bilious, jaundiced, atrabilious, atrabiliar, saturnine, adust.

Disconsolate, inconsolable, despairing, in despair (859).

Grave, serious, sedate, staid, sober, solemn, grim, grim-faced, grim-visaged (846), rueful, sullen.

Depressing, preying upon the mind (830).

Phrases: Down in the mouth; down on one's luck; sick at heart; with a long face; a prey to melancholy; dull as a beetle; dull as ditch-water; as melancholy as a gib-cat; grave as a judge.

838 REJOICING
Substantives: exultation, heyday, triumph, jubilation, jubilee (840), paean (990).

Smile, simper, smirk, grin, broad grin.

Laughter, giggle, titter, snigger, crow, cheer, chuckle, guffaw, shout, hearty laugh, horse-laugh, cachinnation; a shout, burst, or peal of laughter.

Derision, risibility (856).

Momus, Democritus the Abderite.
Verbs: To rejoice, exult, triumph (884), hug oneself, sing, carol, dance with joy.

To smile, simper, smirk, grin, mock; to laugh, giggle, titter, snigger, chuckle, chortle, burble, crow, cackle; to burst out, shout, guffaw.

To cause, create, occasion, raise, excite, or produce laughter, etc.; to tickle, titillate.

Phrases: To clap one's hands; to fling up one's cap; to laugh in one's sleeve; to shake one's sides; to hold both one's sides; to split one's sides; to die with laughter.

To tickle one's fancy; to set the table in a roar; to convulse with laughter; to be the death of one.

Adjectives: Laughing, rejoicing, etc.; jubilant (836), triumphant.

Laughable, risible, ludicrous (853), side-splitting.

Phrases: Ready to burst or split oneself; 'Laughter holding both his sides.'

Interjections: Hurrah! three cheers!

839 LAMENTATION
Substantives: complaint, murmur, mutter, plaint, lament, wail, sigh, suspiration, heaving.

Cry, whine, whimper, sob, tear, moan, snivel, grumble, groan.

Outcry, scream, screech, howl, whoop, yell, roar, (414).

Weeping, crying, etc.; lachrymation, complaining, frown, scowl, sardonic grin or laugh.

Dirge (363), elegy, requiem, monody, threnody, jeremiad; coronach, wake, keen, keening.

Plaintiveness, querimoniousness, languishment, querulousness.

Mourning, weeds, willow, cypress, crape, sackcloth and ashes.

A grumbler, grouser, croaker, drip; Heraclitus, Niobe.

Phrases: The melting mood; wringing

of hands; weeping and gnashing of teeth.

Verbs: To lament, mourne, grieve, keen, complain, murmur, mutter, grumble, grouse, belly-ache, beef, squawk, sigh; give, fetch, or heave a sigh.

To cry, weep, sob, greet, blubber, blub; snivel, whimper; to shed tears; pule, take on, pine.

To grumble, groan, grunt, croak, whine, moan, bemoan, wail, bewail, frown, scowl.

To cry out, growl, mew, mewl, squeak, squeal, sing out, scream, cry out lustily, screech, skirl, bawl, howl, holloa, bellow, yell, roar, yammer.

Phrases: To melt or burst into tears; to cry oneself blind; to cry one's eyes out; to beat one's breast; to wring one's hands; to gnash one's teeth; to tear one's hair; to cry before one is hurt; to laugh on the wrong side of one's mouth.

Adjectives: Lamenting, complaining, etc.; mournful, doleful, sad, tearful, lachrymose, plaintive, plaintful, querulous, querimonious, elegiac.

Phrases: With tears in one's eyes; bathed or dissolved in tears; the tears starting from the eyes.

Interjections: O dear! ah me! alas! alack! heigh-ho! ochone! well-a-day! well-a-way! alas the day! woe worth the day! *O tempora, O mores!*

840 AMUSEMENT

Substantives: diversion, entertainment, sport, divertissement, recreation, relaxation, distraction, avocation, pastime.

Fun, frolic, pleasantry, drollery, jollity, joviality, jovialness, jocoseness, laughter (838).

Play, game, gambol, romp, prank, quip, quirk, rig, lark, fling, bat, spree, burst, binge, razzle-dazzle, escapade, dido, monkey-shines, ploy, jamboree.

Dance (309), ball, ballet (599), hop,

shindig, jig, fling, reel, strathspey, cotillion, quadrille, lancers, rigadoon, saraband, lavolta, pavane, galliard, hornpipe, can-can, tarantella, cachucha, fandango, bolero, minuet, gavotte, polka, mazurka, schottische, waltz (or valse), fox-trot, tango, maxixe, rumba, samba, blues, two-step, one-step; folk-dance, morris-dance, square dance, round dance, country dance, step-dance, clog-dance, sword-dance, egg-dance, cake-walk, break-down.

Festivity, festival, jubilee, party (892), merrymaking, rejoicing, fête, gala, ridotto, revelry, revels, carnival, corroboree, saturnalia, high jinks, night out.

Feast, banquet, entertainment, carousal, bean-feast, beano, wayz-goose, jollification, junketing, junket, wake, field-day, regatta, fair, kermess, *fête champêtre*, symposium, wassail.

Buffoonery, mummery, tomfoolery, raree-show, puppet-show, masquerade.

Bonfire, fireworks, *feu de joie*.

A holiday, gala day, red-letter day.

A place of amusement, theatre, music-hall, concert-hall, cinema, circus, hippodrome, ballroom, dance hall, arena, auditorium, recreation ground, playground, playing field, park.

Toy, plaything, bauble, doll, puppet, teddy-bear.

A master of ceremonies or revels; a sportsman, sportswoman, gamester, reveller; devotee, votary, enthusiast, fan.

Phrases: A round of pleasure; a short life and a merry one; high days and holidays.

Verbs: To amuse, divert, entertain, rejoice, cheer, recreate, enliven, solace; to beguile or while away the time; to drown care.

To play, sport, disport, make merry, take one's pleasure, make holiday, keep holiday; to game, gambol, revel, frisk, frolic, romp, jollify, skylark, dally; to dance, hop, foot it, jump, caper, cut capers, skip.

To treat, feast, regale, carouse, banquet.

Phrases: To play the fool; to jump over the moon; to make a night of it; to make whoopee; to go on the bust; to have one's fling; *desipere in loco.*

Adjectives: Amusing, amusive, diverting, entertaining, etc., amused, etc.

Sportive, jovial, festive, jocose, tricksy, rompish.

Phrases: On with the dance! *vogue la galère! vive la bagatelle!*

841 WEARINESS

Substantives: tedium, ennui, boredom, lassitude, fatigue (688), dejection (837).

Disgust, nausea, loathing, sickness, disgust of life, *taedium vitae, Weltschmerz.*

Wearisomeness, irksomeness, tiresomeness, montony, sameness, treadmill, grind.

A bore, a buttonholer, proser, fossil, wet blanket.

Phrases: A twice-told tale; time hanging heavily on one's hands; a thin time.

Verbs: To tire, weary, fatigue, fag, jade, bore; set to sleep, send to sleep.

To sicken, disgust, nauseate.

Phrases: To harp on the same string; to bore to tears; never hear the last of.

Adjectives: Wearying, etc., wearisome, tiresome, irksome, uninteresting, devoid of interest, monotonous, humdrum, pedestrian, mortal, flat, tedious, prosy, prosing, slow, soporific, somniferous.

Disgusting, sickening, nauseating.

Weary, tired, etc.; aweary, uninterested, sick of, flagging, used up, blasé, bored, stale, fed up, browned off, brassed off, cheesed off, chokka, weary of life; drowsy, somnolent,

sleepy (683).

Adverbs: Wearily, etc.

Phrase: *Ad nauseam.*

842 WIT

Substantives: humour, comicality, imagination (515), fancy, fun, drollery, whim, jocularity, jocosity, facetiousness, waggery, waggishness, wittiness, salt, Atticism, Attic wit, Attic salt, *esprit,* smartness, banter, chaff, persiflage, badinage, farce, *espièglerie.*

Jest, joke, jape, conceit, quip, quirk, quiddity, crank, wheeze, side-splitter, *concetto,* witticism, gag, wisecrack, repartee, retort, comeback, *mot, bon mot,* pleasantry, funniment, flash of wit, happy thought, sally, point, dry joke, idle conceit, epigram, quibble, play upon words, pun (563), conundrum, anagram (533), quodlibet, *jeu d'esprit, facetiae;* a chestnut, a Joe Miller; an absurdity (497).

A practical joke, a rag.

Phrases: The cream of the jest; the joke of it; *le mot pour rire.*

Verbs: To joke, jest, jape, retort; to cut jokes, crack a joke, perpetrate a joke or pun.

To laugh at, banter, rally, chaff, josh, jolly, jeer (856), rag, guy, kid; to make fun of, make merry with.

Phrase: To set the table in a roar.

Adjectives: Witty, facetious, humorous, fanciful, quick-witted, ready-witted, nimble-witted, imaginative (515), sprightly, *spirituel,* smart, jocose, jocular, waggish, comic, comical, laughable, droll, ludicrous, side-splitting, killing, funny, risible, farcical, roguish, sportive, pleasant, playful, sparkling, entertaining, arch.

Adverbs: In joke, in jest, in sport, for fun.

843 DULLNESS

Substantives: heaviness, stolidness, stolidity, dumbness, stupidity (499), flatness, prosiness, gravity (837), solemnity; prose, matter of fact, platitude, commonplace, bromide.

Verbs: To be dull, prose, fall flat.

To render dull, etc., damp, depress.

Phrase: To throw cold water on.

Adjectives: Dull, prosaic, prosing, prosy, unentertaining, dismal (837), uninteresting, boring, flat, pointless, stolid, humdrum (841), pedestrian, literal, unimaginative, matter-of-fact, commonplace.

Slow, stupid, dumb, plodding, Boeotian.

Phrases: Dull as ditch-water; *Davus sum, non Oedipus; aliquando bonus dormitat Homerus.*

844 A HUMORIST

Substantives: wag, wit, funny man, caricaturist, cartoonist, epigrammatist, *bel esprit,* jester, joker, punster, wise-cracker.

A buffoon (599), comedian, *farceur,* merry-andrew, jack-pudding, tumbler, mountebank, harlequin, punch, punchinello, scaramouch, clown, pantaloon.

Phrase: The life and soul of the party.

845 BEAUTY

Substantives: handsomeness, beauteousness, beautifulness, pulchritude, aesthetics.

Form, elegance, grace, symmetry, *belle tournure;* good looks.

Comeliness, seemliness, shapeliness, fairness, prettiness, neatness, spruceness, atractiveness, loveliness, quaintness, speciousness, polish, gloss, nattiness; a good effect.

Bloom, brilliancy, radiance, splendour, magnificence, sublimity.

Concinnity, delicacy, refinement, charm, style.

A beautiful woman, belle, charmer, enchantress, goddess; Helen of Troy, Venus, Hebe, the Graces, Peri, Houri; Cupid, Apollo, Hyperion, Adonis, Antinous, Narcissus.

Peacock, butteryfly, flower, rose, lily; the flower of, the pink of, etc.; a garden, a picture.

Phrases: *Je ne sais quoi; le beau idéal;* a sight for sore eyes.

Verbs: To be beautiful; to shine, beam, bloom.

To render beautiful, etc., to beautify, embellish, adorn, deck, bedeck, decorate, set out, set off, ornament (847), dight, bedight, array, garnish, furbish, smarten, trick out, rig out, fig out, dandify, dress up, prank, prink, perk, preen, trim, embroider, emblazon, adonize.

To polish, burnish, gild, varnish, japan, enamel, lacquer.

To powder, rouge, make up, doll up, titivate.

Adjectives: Beautiful, handsome, good-looking, fine, pretty, lovely, graceful, elegant, delicate, refined, fair, personable, comely, seemly, bonny, braw, well-favoured, proper, shapely, well-made, well-formed, well-proportioned, symmetrical, sightly, becoming, goodly, neat, dapper, tight, trig, spruce, smart, stylish, chic, dashing, swagger, dandified, natty, sleek, quaint, jaunty, bright-eyed, attractive, seductive, stunning.

Blooming, rosy, brilliant, shining, beaming, splendid, resplendent, dazzling, gorgeous, superb, magnificent, sublime, grand.

Picturesque, statuesque, artistic, aesthetic, decorative, photogenic, well-composed, well-grouped.

Passable, presentable, not amiss, undefaced, spotless, unspotted.

Phrases: Easy to look at; dressed up to kill.

846 UGLINESS

Substantives: deformity, inelegance, plainness, homeliness, uncomeliness, ungainliness, uncouthness, clumsiness, stiffness, disfigurement, distortion, contortion, malformation, monstrosity, misproportion, inconcinnity, want of symmetry, roughness, repulsiveness, squalor, hideousness, unsightliness, odiousness.

An eyesore, object, figure, sight, fright, guy, spectre, scarecrow, hag, harridan, satyr, sibyl, toad, baboon, monster, gorgon, Caliban, Hecate.

Phrases: A forbidding countenance; a wry face; a blot on the landscape; no oil-painting; *'monstrum horrendum, informe, ingens, cui lumen ademptum.'*

Verbs: To be ugly, etc.

To render ugly, etc., to deform, deface, distort, disfigure (241), disfeature, misshape, blemish, spot, stain, distain, soil, tarnish, discolour, sully, blot, daub, bedaub, begrime, blur, smear, besmear (653), bespatter, maculate, denigrate, uglify.

Phrase: To make faces.

Adjectives: Ugly, plain, homely, unsightly, unornamental, unshapely, unlovely, ill-looking, ordinary, unseemly, ill-favoured, hard-favoured, evil-favoured, hard-featured, hard-visaged, ungainly, uncouth, gawky, hulking, lumbering, slouching, ungraceful, clumsy, graceless, rude, rough, rugged, homespun, gaunt, raw-boned, haggard, scraggy.

Misshapen, shapeless, misproportioned, ill-proportioned, deformed, ill-made, ill-shaped, inelegant, disfigured, distorted, unshapen, unshapely, humpbacked, crooked, bandy, stumpy, dumpy, squat, stubby, bald, rickety.

Squalid, grim, grisly, gruesome, grooly, macabre, grim-faced, grim-visaged, ghastly, ghost-like, death-like, cadaverous, repellent, repulsive, forbidding, grotesque.

Frightful, odious, hideous, horrid, shocking, monstrous, unprepossessing.

Foul, soiled, tarnished, stained, distained, sullied, blurred, blotted, spotted, maculated, spotty, splashed, smeared, begrimed, spattered, bedaubed, besmeared; ungarnished.

Phrases: Ugly as sin; not fit to be seen.

847 ORNAMENT

Substantives: ornamentation, adornment, decoration, embellishment, enrichment, illustration, illumination, ornature, ornateness, flamboyancy.

Garnish, polish, varnish, gilding, japanning, enamel, lacquer, ormolu.

Cosmetic, rouge, powder, lipstick, mascara, hair-oil, brilliantine.

Jewel, jewellery, bijouterie, spangle, trinket, locket, bracelet, bangle, anklet, necklace, earring, brooch, chain, chatelaine, carcanet, tiara, coronet, diadem.

Gem, precious stone, diamond, brilliant, emerald, sapphire, ruby, agate, garnet, beryl, onyx, topax, amethyst, opal; pearl, coral.

Embroidery, broidery, brocade, galloon, lace, fringe, trapping, trimming, edging, border, chiffon, hanging, tapestry, arras.

Wreath, festoon, garland, lei, chaplet, tassel, knot, epaulette, frog, star rosette, bow.

Feather, plume, *panache*, aigrette.

Nosegay, bouquet, posy, buttonhole.

Tracery, moulding, arabesque.

Frippery, finery, bravery, gewgaw, gaud, fal-lal, tinsel, spangle, clinquant, bric-à-brac, knick-knack.

Trope, flourish, flowers of rhetoric, purple patches (577).

Excess of ornament, tawdriness (851).

Verbs: To ornament, embellish, illustrate, illuminate, enrich, decorate, adorn, beautify, garnish, polish, gild, varnish, enamel, paint, white-wash, stain, japan, lacquer, fume, grain; bespangle, bedeck, bedizen (845), embroider, work, chase, emboss, fret, tool; emblazon, illuminate.

Adjectives: Ornamented, etc.,

beautified, rigged out, figged out, well-groomed, dolled up, ornate, showy, dressy, gaudy (851), garish, gorgeous, fine, gay, rich.

Phrases: Fine as fivepence; in full fig; in one's Sunday best; dressed up to the nines.

848 BLEMISH

Substantives: disfigurement, defacement, deformity, eyesore, defect, fault, deficiency, flaw, fleck.

Stain, blot, spot, speck, mote, blur, macula, blotch, speckle, spottiness; soil, tarnish, smudge, smut, dirt, soot (653); freckle, birthmark.

Excrescence, pimple, pustule (250).

Verbs: To blemish, disfigure, deface (846).

Adjectives: Blemished, disfigured, etc.; spotted, speckled, freckled, pitted.

849 SIMPLICITY

Substantives: plainness, undress, chastity, chasteness; freedom from ornament or affectation, homeliness.

Phrase: *Simplex munditiis.*

Verbs: To be simple, etc., to render simple, etc., to simplify.

Adjectives: Simple, plain, ordinary, household, homely, homespun, chaste, unaffected, severe, primitive.

Unadorned, unornamented, undecked, ungarnished, unarrayed, untrimmed, unsophisticated, in dishabille.

850 TASTE

Substantives: delicacy, refinement, gust, gusto, *goût,* virtuosity, virtuosoship, nicety, finesse, grace, culture, virtu, τὸ πρέπον, polish, elegance.

Science of taste, aesthetics.

A man of taste, connoisseur, judge, critic, *cognoscente,* virtuoso, dilettante, amateur, aesthete, purist, precision; an Aristarchus, Corinthian, *arbiter elegantiarum.*

Phrase: Caviare to the general.

Verbs: To appreciate, judge, discriminate, criticize (465).

Adjectives: In good taste, tasteful, unaffected, pure, chaste, classical, attic, refined, aesthetic, cultivated, cultured, artistic, elegant.

Adverb: Elegantly, etc.

Phrases: To one's taste or mind; after one's fancy; *comme il faut.*

851 VULGARITY

Substantives: vulgarism, barbarism, Vandalism, Gothicism, *mauvais goût,* sensationalism, flamboyance.

Coarseness, grossness, indecorum, lowness, low life, *mauvais ton,* bad form, ribaldry, clownishness, rusticity, boorishness, brutishness, brutality, rowdyism, ruffianism, awkwardness, *gaucherie,* want of tact, tactlessness.

Excess of ornament, false ornament, tawdriness, loudness, gaudiness, flashiness, ostentation.

A rough diamond, a hoyden, tomboy, slattern, sloven, dowdy, frump, cub, unlicked cub, clown, cad, guttersnipe, ragamuffin (876); a Goth, Vandal.

Verbs: To be vulgar, etc., to misbehave.

Adjectives: In bad taste, vulgar, coarse, unrefined, gross, ribald, heavy, rude, unpolished, indecorous, homespun, clownish, uncouth, awkward, *gauche,* ungraceful, slovenly, slatternly, dowdy, frumpish.

Ill-bred, ungenteel, impolite, ill-mannered, uncivil, tactless, underbred, caddish, ungentlemanly, unladylike, unfeminine, unmaidenly, unseemly, unpresentable, unkempt, uncombed.

Rustic, countrified, boorish, provincial, barbarous, barbaric, brutish, blackguardly, rowdy, raffish, Gothic, unclassical, heathenish, outlandish, untamed (876).

Obsolete, out of fashion, *démodé,* out

318

of date, unfashionable, antiquated, fossil, old-fashioned, old-world, gone by.

New-fangled, odd, fantastic, grotesque, ridiculous (853), affected, meretricious, extravagant, sensational, monstrous, shocking, horrid, revolting.

Gaudy, tawdry, tinsel, bedizened, flamboyant, baroque, tricked out, gingerbread, loud, flashy, showy.
Phrase: A back number.

852 FASHION
Substantives: style, tonishness, *ton, bon ton,* mode, vogue, craze, rage, fad.

Manners, breeding, politeness, gentlemanliness, courtesy (894), decorum, *bienséance, savoir faire, savoir vivre,* punctilio, convention, conventionality, propriety, the proprieties, Mrs Grundy, form, formality, etiquette, custom, demeanour, air, port, carriage, presence.

Show, equipage, turn-out (882).

The world, the fashionable world, the smart set, the *beau monde,* high life, society, town, court, gentility (875), civilization, civilized life, the *élite.*
Phrases: The height of fashion; *dernier cri;* the latest thing.
Verbs: To be fashionable, etc.
Phrases: To cut a dash; to be in the swim.
Adjectives: Fashionable, in fashion, in vogue, *à la mode,* modish, tony, tonish, stylish, smart, courtly, *recherché,* genteel, aristocratic, conventional, punctilious, *comme il faut,* well-bred, well-mannered, polished, gentlemanlike, ladylike, well-spoken, civil, presentable, *distingué,* refined, thorough-bred, county, *dégagé,* jaunty, swell, swagger, posh, dashing, unembarrassed; trendy.
Phrases: Having a run; all the go.
Adverbs: Fashionably, in fashion.

853 RIDICULOUSNESS
Substantives: ludicrousness, risibility.

Oddness, oddity, whimsicality, comicality, drollery, grotesqueness,

fancifulness, quaintness, frippery, gawkiness, preposterousness, extravagance, monstrosity, absurdity (497).

Bombast, bathos, fustian, doggerel, nonsense verse, amphigouri, extravaganza, clerihew, bull, Irish bull, spoonerism.
Adjectives: Ridiculous, absurd, extravagant, *outré,* monstrous, preposterous, irrational, nonsensical.

Odd, whimsical, quaint, queer, rum, droll, grotesque, fanciful, eccentric, bizarre, strange, out-of-the-way, outlandish, fantastic, baroque, rococo.

Laughable, risible, ludicrous, comic, serio-comic, mock-heroic, comical, funny, derisive, farcical, burlesque, *pour rire,* quizzical, bombastic, inflated, stilted.

Awkward, gawky, lumbering, lumpish, hulking, uncouth.

854 FOP
Substantives: dandy, exquisite, swell, toff, dude, nut, masher, lady-killer, coxcomb, beau, macaroni, blade, blood, buck, spark, dog, popinjay, puppy, *petit-maître,* jackanapes, jack-a-dandy, tailor's dummy, man-milliner, man about town.

855 AFFECTATION
Substantives: mannerism, pretension, airs, dandyism, coxcombry, frills, side, swank, dog, conceit, foppery, affectedness, preciosity, euphuism, charlatanism, quackery, foppishness, pedantry, acting a part, pose, gush.

Prudery, Grundyism, demureness, coquetry, *minauderie,* sentimentality, lackadaisicalness, stiffness, formality, buckram, mock modesty, *mauvaise honte.*

Pedant, precisian, prig, square, bluestocking, *bas bleu,* formalist, *poseur,* mannerist, *précieuse ridicule;* prude, Mrs Grundy.
Phrases: A lump of affectation; prunes and prisms.

Verbs: To affect, to give oneself airs, put on side or frills, to swank, simper, mince, to act a part, overact, attitudinize, gush, pose.

Adjectives: Affected, conceited, precious, pretentious, stilted, pedantic, pragmatical, priggish, smug, puritanical, prim, prudish, starchy, up-stage, high-hat, stiff, formal, demure, goody-goody.

Foppish, namby-pamby, slip-slop, coxcombical, slipshod, simpering, mincing, niminy-piminy, la-di-da, sentimental, lackadaisical.

Exaggerated (549), overacted, overdone, high-falutin, gushing, stagy, theatrical.

856 RIDICULE

Substantives: derision, mockery, quiz, banter, chaff, badinage, irony, persiflage, raillery, send-up.

Jeer, gibe, quip, taunt, satire, scurrility, scoffing.

A parody, burlesque, travesty, skit, farce, comedy, tragi-comedy, doggerel, blunder, bull, *lapsus linguae,* slip of the tongue, malapropism, spoonerism, anticlimax.

Buffoonery, vagary, antic, mummery, tomfoolery, grimace, monkey-trick, escapade, prank, gambade, extravaganza, practical joke, booby-trap.

Verbs: To ridicule, deride, laugh at (929), laugh down, scoff, mock, jeer, banter, quiz, rally, fleer, flout, rag, rot, chaff, josh, guy, rib, razz, roast, twit, taunt, point at, grin at.

To parody, caricature, burlesque, travesty, pillory, take off.

Phrases: To raise a smile; to set the table in a roar; to make fun of; to poke fun at; to make merry with; to make a fool of; to make an ass of; to make game of; to make faces at; to make mouths at; to lead one a dance; to run a rig upon; to make an April fool of; to laugh out of court; to laugh in one's

sleeve; to take the micky out of.

Adjectives: Derisory, derisive, sarcastic, ironical, quizzical, mock, scurrilous, burlesque, Hudibrastic.

857 LAUGHING-STOCK

Substantives: gazing-stock, butt, stooge, target, quiz; an original, guy, oddity, card, crank, eccentric, monkey, buffoon, jester (844), mime, mimer (599), scaramouch, punch, punchinello, mountebank, golliwog.

Phrases: A figure of fun; a queer fish; fair game.

858 HOPE

Substantives: trust, confidence, reliance, faith, assurance, credit, security, expectation, affiance, promise, assumption, presumption.

Hopefulness, buoyancy, reassurance, optimism, enthusiasm, aspiration.

A reverie, day-dream, pipe-dream, Utopia, millennium.

Anchor, mainstay, sheet-anchor, staff (215).

Phrases: Castles in the air; castles in Spain; a ray, gleam, or flash of hope; the silver lining of the cloud.

Verbs: To hope; to feel, entertain, harbour, cherish, feed, nourish, encourage, foster, etc., hope or confidence; to promise oneself.

To trust, confide, rely on, build upon, feel or rest assured, confident, secure, etc.; to flatter oneself, expect, aspire, presume, be reassured.

To give or inspire hope; to augur well, shape well, bid fair, be in a fair way; to encourage, assure, promise, flatter, buoy up, reassure, embolden, raise expectations.

Phrases: To see daylight; to live in hopes; to look on the bright side; to pin one's hope or faith upon; to catch at a straw; to hope against hope.

Adjectives: Hoping, etc., in hopes, hopeful, confident, secure, buoyant, buoyed up, in good heart, sanguine, optimistic, enthusiastic, utopian.

Fearless, unsuspecting, unsuspicious; free or exempt from fear, suspicion, distrust, etc., undespairing.

Auspicious, promising, propitious, bright, rose-coloured, rosy, of good omen, reassuring.

Phrases: *Nil desperandum*; while there's life there's hope; *dum spiro spero*; never say die; all for the best.

859 HOPELESSNESS
Substantives: despair, desperation, despondency, pessimism (837); forlornness, a forlorn hope, the Slough of Despond.

Phrases: A black look-out; a bad business.

Verbs: To despair, despond, give up, be hopeless; to lose, give up, abandon, relinquish, etc., all hope; to yield to despair.

To inspire or drive to despair; to dash, crush, or destroy one's hopes.

Phrases: To trust to a broken reed; *'lasciate ogni speranza voi ch' entrate.'*

Adjectives: Hopeless, having lost or given up hope, losing etc., hope, past hope, despondent, pessimistic, forlorn, desperate, despairing.

Incurable, irremediable, irreparable, irrevocable, incorrigible, beyond remedy.

Inauspicious, unpropitious, unpromising, threatening, ill-omened.

860 FEAR
Substantives: cowardice (862), timidity, diffidence, nervousness, restlessness, inquietude, disquietude, solicitude, anxiety, care, distrust, mistrust, hesitation, misgiving, suspicion, qualm, want of confidence, nerves.

Apprehension, flutter, trepidation, tremor, shaking, trembling, palpitation, jitters, the jumps, the creeps, the needle, ague-fit, fearfulness, despondency; stage fright, cold feet, wind up.

Fright, affright, alarm, dread, awe, terror, horror, dismay, obsession, panic, funk, flap, stampede, scare, consternation, despair (859).

Intimidation, terrorism, reign of terror; an alarmist, scaremonger.

Object of fear, bugbear, bugaboo, bogy, scarecrow, goblin (980), *bête noire*, nightmare, Gorgon, ogre.

Phrases: Raw head and bloody bones; fee-faw-fum; butterflies in the stomach.

Verbs: To fear, be afraid, etc., distrust, hesitate, have qualms, misgiving, suspicions.

To apprehend, take alarm, start, wince, boggle, skulk, cower, crouch, tremble, shake, quake, quaver, quiver, shudder, quail, cringe, turn pale, blench, flutter, flinch, funk.

To excite fear, raise apprehensions, to give, raise, or sound an alarm, to intimidate, put in fear, frighten, fright, affright, alarm, startle, scare, haunt, obsess, strike terror, daunt, terrify, unman, awe, horrify, dismay, petrify, appal.

To overawe, abash, cow, browbeat, bully, deter, discourage.

Phrases: To shake in one's shoes; to shake like an aspen leaf; to stand aghast; to eye askance.

To fright from one's propriety; to strike all of a heap; to make the flesh creep; to give one the creeps; to cause alarm and despondency.

Adjectives: Fearing, timid, timorous, faint-hearted, tremulous, fearful, nervous, nervy, jumpy, funky, diffident, apprehensive, restless, haunted with the fear, apprehension, dread, etc., of.

Frightened, afraid, cowed, pale, alarmed, scared, terrified, petrified, aghast, awestruck, dismayed, horror-struck, horrified, appalled, panic-stricken.

Inspiring fear, fearsome, alarming, formidable, redoubtable, portentous, perilous (665), ugly, fearful, dreadful, dire, shocking, terrible, tremendous, horrid, horrible, horrific, ghastly, awful, awesome, horripilant, hair-raising, creepy, crawly.

Phrases: White as a sheet; afraid of one's shadow; the hair standing on end; letting 'I dare not' wait upon 'I would'; more frightened than hurt; frightened out of one's senses or wits; in a blue funk.

861 COURAGE

Substantives: bravery, value, boldness, spirit, moral fibre, spiritedness, daring, gallantry, intrepidity, contempt of danger, self-reliance, confidence, fearlessness, audacity.

Manhood, manliness, nerve, pluck, grit, guts, sand, mettle, gameness, heart, spunk, smeddum, virtue, hardihood, fortitude, firmness, resolution, sportsmanship.

Prowess, derring-do, heroism, chivalry.

A hero, heroine, ace, paladin, *preux chevalier,* Hector, Hotspur, Amazon, Joan of Arc, *beau sabreur,* fire-eater (863).

A lion, tiger, bulldog, gamecock, fighting-cock, sportsman.

Verbs: To be courageous, etc., to face, front, affront, confront, despise, brave, defy, etc., danger; to take courage; to summon up, muster up, or pluck up courage; to rally.

To venture, make bold, face, dare, defy, brave (715), beard, hold out, bear up against, stand up to.

To give, infuse, or inspire courage; to encourage, embolden, inspirit, cheer, nerve.

Phrases: To take the bull by the horns; to come up to the scratch; to face the music; to 'screw one's courage to the sticking-place'; to die game.

To pat on the back; to make a man of.

Adjectives: Courageous, brave, valiant, valorous, gallant, intrepid.

Spirited, high-spirited, high-mettled, mettlesome, plucky, manly, manful, resolute, stout, stout-hearted, lion-hearted, heart of oak, firm, indomitable, game, sportsmanlike.

Bold, daring, audacious, fearless, unfearing, dauntless, undaunted, indomitable, unappalled, undismayed, unawed, unabashed, unalarmed, unflinching, unshrinking, unblenching, unblenched, unapprehensive, confident, self-reliant.

Enterprising, venturous, adventurous, venturesome, dashing, chivalrous, heroic, fierce, warlike (722).

Unfeared, undreaded, etc.

Phrases: One's blood is up; brave as a lion; bold as brass; full of beans.

862 COWARDICE

Substantives: fear (860), pusillanimity, cowardliness, timidity, fearfulness, spiritlessness, faint-heartedness, softness, effeminacy, funk.

Poltroonery, baseness, dastardliness, yellow streak, a faint heart.

A coward, poltroon, dastard, recreant, funk, mollycoddle, milksop, cry-baby, 'fraid-cat, chicken, cowardy custard.

A runaway, fugitive, deserter, quitter.

Verbs: To be cowardly, etc.; to quail (860), to flinch, fight shy, shy, turn tail, run away, cut and run, fly for one's life, stampede.

Phrases: To show the white feather; to be in a sweat.

Adjectives: Coward, cowardly, yellow, pusillanimous, shy, fearful, timid, skittish, timorous, poor-spirited, spiritless, weak-hearted, faint-hearted, chicken-hearted, white-livered.

Dastard, dastardly, base, craven, recreant, unwarlike, unheroic, unsoldierly, unmanly, womanish.

Phrase: 'In face a lion, but in heart a deer.'

Interjections: *Sauve qui peut!* the devil take the hindmost!

863 RASHNESS

Substantives: temerity, audacity, presumption, precipitancy, precipitation, impetuosity, recklessness, overboldness, foolhardiness, desperation, knight-errantry, Quixotism; carelessness (460), want of caution, over-confidence.

Imprudence, indiscretion.

A desperado, madcap, bravo, dare-devil, *enfant perdu,* gambler, adventurer, knight errant; Hotspur, Don Quixote, Icarus.

Phrases: A leap in the dark; a blind bargain; a wild-cat scheme.

Verbs: To be rash, incautious, etc.

Phrases: To buy a pig in a poke; to go on a forlorn hope; to go at it bald-headed; to play with fire; to tempt providence.

Adjectives: Rash, temerarious, head-strong, insane, foolhardy, slap-dash, dare-devil, devil-may-care, overbold, wild, reckless, desperate, hot-headed, hare-brained, headlong, hot-blooded, over-confident, precipitate, impetuous, venturesome, impulsive, Quix-otic.

Imprudent, indiscreet, uncalculating, incautious, improvident.

Phrases: Without ballast; neck or nothing.

Interjections: *Vogue la galère!* come what may!

864 CAUTION

Substantives: cautiousness, discretion, prudence, reserve, wariness, heed, circumspection, calculation, deliberation (459).

Coolness, self-possession, aplomb, presence of mind, sang-froid, self-command, steadiness, the Fabian policy.

Phrases: The better part of valour; masterly inactivity.

Verbs: To be cautious, etc., to beware, take care, have a care, take heed, ca' canny, be on one's guard, look about one, take no chances.

Phrases: To look before one leaps; to think twice; to let sleeping dogs lie; to see which way the wind blows; to see how the land lies; to feel one's way; to count the cost; to be on the safe side; steady as she goes.

Adjectives: Cautious, wary, careful, heedful, cautelous, chary, canny, cagey, circumspect, prudent, prudential, reserved, discreet, politic, non-committal.

Unenterprising, unadventurous, cool, steady, self-possessed.

Phrases: Safety first; better be sure than sorry.

865 DESIRE

Substantives: wish, mind, inclination, leaning, bent, fancy, partiality, penchant, predilection, liking, love, fondness, relish.

Want, need, exigency.

Longing, hankering, solicitude, anxiety, yearning, yen, coveting, eagerness, zeal, ardour, aspiration, ambition, over-anxiety.

Appetite, appetence, appetency, the edge of appetite, keenness, hunger, stomach, thirst, thirstiness, drouth, mouth-watering, dispomania, itch, itching, prurience, lickerishness, *cacoethes,* cupidity, lust, libido, concupiscence, greed.

Avidity, greediness, covetousness, craving, voracity, bulimia, rapacity.

Passion, rage, furore, mania, kleptomania, inextinguishable desire, vaulting ambition, impetuosity.

A gourmand, gourmet, glutton, cormorant (957).

An amateur, votary, devotee, fan, aspirant, solicitant, candidate.

Object of desire, desideratum,

attraction, lure, allurement, fancy, temptation, magnet, loadstone, whim, whimsy (608), maggot, hobby, hobby-horse, pursuit.

Phrases: The height of one's ambition; *hoc erat in votis*; the wish being father to the thought; the torments of Tantalus.

Verbs: To desire, wish, long for, fancy, affect, like, have a mind to, be glad of, want, miss, need, feel the want of, would fain have, to care for.

To hunger, thirst, crave, lust after; to hanker after, itch for.

To desiderate, covet; to sigh, cry, gasp, pine, pant, languish, yearn for; to aspire after, catch at, jump at.

To woo, court, solicit, ogle, fish for.

To cause, create, raise, excite, or provoke, desire; to allure, attract, solicit, tempt, hold out temptation or allurement, to tantalize, appetize.

To gratify desire, slake, satiate (827).

Phrases: To have at heart; to take a fancy to; to set one's heart upon; to make eyes at; to set one's cap at; to run mad after.

To whet the appetite; to make one's mouth water.

Adjectives: Desirous, inclinded, fain, keen, wishful, wishing, optative, desiring, wanting, needing, hankering after, dying for, partial to.

Craving, hungry, esurient, sharp-set, keen-set, peckish, thirsty, athirst, dry, drouthy.

Greedy, voracious, lickerish, open-mouthed, agog, covetous, ravenous, rapacious, extortionate; unsated, unslaked, insatiable, insatiate, omnivorous.

Eager, ardent, avid, fervent, bent on, intent on, aspiring, ambitious.

Desirable, desired, desiderated (829).

Phrases: Pinched or perished with hunger; hungry as a hunter; parched with thirst; having a sweet tooth; nothing loth.

Interjections: O for! would that!

866 INDIFFERENCE

Substantives: coldness, coolness, unconcern, nonchalance, insouciance, inappetency, listlessness, lukewarmness, neutrality, impartiality; apathy (823), supineness (683), disdain (930).

Verbs: To be indifferent, etc.; to have no desire, wish, taste, or relish for; to care nothing about, take no interest in, not mind, make light of; to disdain, spurn (930).

Phrase: Couldn't care less.

Adjectives: Indifferent, undesirous, cool, cold, frigid, unconcerned, insouciant, unsolicitous, unattracted, lukewarm, half-hearted, listless, lackadaisical, unambitious, unaspiring, phlegmatic.

Unattractive, unalluring, uninviting, undesired, undesirable, uncared-for, unwished, uncoveted, unvalued.

Vapid, tasteless, insipid (391), wersh, unappetizing, mawkish, namby-pamby, flat, stale, vain.

Phrases: Never mind; all one to Hippocleides.

867 DISLIKE

Substantives: distaste, disrelish, disinclination, reluctance, backwardness, demur (603).

Repugnance, disgust, queasiness, turn, nausea, loathing, averseness, aversion, abomination, antipathy, abhorrence, horror, hatred, detestation (898), resentment (900); claustrophobia, agoraphobia, Anglophobia, Gallophobia.

Verbs: To dislike, mislike, disrelish, mind, object to.

To shun, avoid, eschew, withdraw from, shrink from, shrug the shoulders at, recoil from, shudder at.

To loathe, nauseate, abominate, detest, abhor, hate (898).

To cause or excite dislike; to disincline, repel, sicken, render sick, nauseate, disgust, shock, pall.

Phrases: Not to be able to bear or

endure or stand; to have no taste for; to turn up one's nose at; to look askance at.

To go against the grain; to turn one's stomach; to stink in the nostrils; to stick in one's throat; to make one's blood run cold.

Adjectives: Disliking, disrelishing, etc., averse to, adverse, shy of, sick of, fed up with, queasy, disinclined.

Disliked, disagreeable, unpalatable, unpopular, offensive, loathsome, loathly, sickening, nauseous, nauseating, repulsive, disgusting, detestable, execrable, abhorrent, abhorred (830), disgustful.

Adverbs: Disajeeably, etc.

Phrase: *Usque ad nauseam.*

Interjections: Faugh! Ugh!

868 FASTIDIOUSNESS

Substantives: nicety, daintiness, squeamishness, niceness, particularity, finicality, meticulosity, difficulty in being pleased, epicurism.

Excess of delicacy, prudery.

Epicure, gourmet, gourmand, *bon vivant,* gastronomer.

Verbs: To be fastidious, etc, to discriminate, differentiate, disdain.

Phrases: To split hairs; to mince one's words; to see spots in the sun.

Adjectives: Fastidious, nice, difficult, dainty, delicate, finicky, lickerish, pernickety, squeamish, queasy, difficult to please, particular, choosy, punctilious, fussy, hypercritical; prudish, strait-laced.

869 SATIETY

Substantives: fullness, repletion, glut, saturation, surfeit.

A spoilt child; too much of a good thing.

Verbs: To sate, satiate, satisfy, saturate, quench, slake, pall, glut, overfeed, gorge, surfeit, cloy, tire, spoil, sicken.

Adjectives: Satiated, sated, blasé,

used up, fed up, browned off, brassed off, cheesed off, chokka, sick of.

Phrases: Enough is enough; *Toujours perdrix.*

Interjections: Enough! that'll do!

870 WONDER

Substantives: surprise, marvel, astonishment, amazement, amazedness, wonderment, admiration, awe, bewilderment, stupefaction, fascination, thaumaturgy (992).

Verbs: To wonder, marvel, be surprised, admire; to stare, gape, start.

To surprise, astonish, amaze, astound, dumbfound, dumbfounder, strike, dazzle, startle, take by surprise, take aback, strike with wonder, electrify, stun, petrify, flabbergast, confound, stagger, stupefy, bewilder, fascinate, boggle.

To be wonderful, etc.

Phrases: To open one's mouth or eyes; to look blank; to stand aghast; not to believe one's eyes; not to account for; not to know whether one stands on one's head or one's heels.

To make one sit up; to take one's breath away.

To beggar description; to stagger belief; imagination boggles at it.

Adjectives: Surprised, astonished, amazed, astounded, struck, startled, taken by surprise, taken aback, struck dumb, awestruck, aghast, agape, dumbfounded, flabbergasted, thunderstruck, planet-struck, stupefied, open-mouthed, petrified.

Wonderful, wondrous, surprising, astonishing, amazing, astounding, startling, stunning, unexpected, unforeseen, strange, uncommon, unheard-of, unaccountable, incredible, inexplicable, indescribable, inexpressible, ineffable, unutterable, unspeakable, monstrous, prodigious, stupendous, marvellous, miraculous, passing strange, uncanny, weird, phenomenal.

Phrases: Struck all of a heap; lost in

wonder; like a dying duck in a thunder-storm; you could have knocked me down with a feather.

Adverbs: Wonderingly, wonderfully, etc., with gaping mouth, all agog; *mirabile dictu.*

Interjections: What! indeed! really! hallo! humph! you don't say so! my stars! good heavens! my goodness! good gracious! bless my soul! bless my heart! my word! O gemini! great Scott! gee! *wunderbar!* dear me! well, I'm damned! well, I never! lo! heyday! who'd have thought it!

871 EXPECTANCE

Substantives: expectancy, expectation (507).

Verbs: To expect, not to be surprised, not to wonder, etc., *nil admirari.*

Phrase: To think nothing of.

Adjectives: Expecting, etc., blasé, unamazed, astonished at nothing, (841).

Common, ordinary (82); foreseen.

872 PRODIGY

Substantives: phenomenon, wonder, cynosure, marvel, miracle, monster (83), unicorn, phoenix, gazing-stock, curiosity, *rara avis,* lion, sight, spectacle, wonderment, sign, portent (512), eye-opener; wonderland, fairyland.

Thunderclap, thunderbolt, bursting of a shell or bomb, volcanic eruption.

Phrases: A nine days' wonder; *annus mirabilis.*

873 REPUTE

Substantives: distinction, note, notability, name, mark, reputation, figure, *réclame, éclat,* celebrity, vogue, fame, famousness, popularity, renown, memory, immortality.

Glory, honour, credit, prestige, kudos, account, regard, respect, reputableness, respectability, respectable-

ness, good name, illustriousness, gloriousness.

Dignity, stateliness, solemnity, grandeur, splendour, nobility, nobleness, lordliness, majesty, sublimity.

Greatness, highness, eminence, supereminence, pre-eminence, primacy, importance (642).

Elevation, ascent (305), exaltation, superexaltation, aggrandisement.

Rank, standing, condition, precedence, *pas,* station, place, status, order, degree, *locus standi.*

Dedication, consecration, enshrinement, glorification, beatification, canonization, deification, posthumous fame.

Chief, leader (745), hero, celebrity, notability, somebody, lion, cock of the roost, cock of the walk, man of mark, pillar of the state, prima donna.

A star, sun, constellation, galaxy, flower, pearl, paragon (650); honour, ornament, aureole.

Phrases: A halo of glory; a name to conjure with; blushing honours; a feather in one's cap; the top of the tree; a niche in the temple of fame.

Verbs: To glory in, to be proud of (878), to exult (884), to be vain of (880).

To be glorious, distinguished, etc., to shine, to figure, to make or cut a figure, dash, or splash; to rival, out-rival, surpass, emulate, outvie, eclipse, outshine, overshadow, throw into the shade.

To live, flourish, glitter, flaunt.

To honour, lionize, dignify, glorify, ennoble, nobilitate, exalt, enthrone, signalize, immortalize, deify.

To consecrate, dedicate to, devote to, to enshrine.

To confer or reflect honour, etc., on; to do, pay, or render honour to; to redound to one's honour.

Phrases: To acquire or gain honour, etc.; to bear the palm; to bear the bell; to take the cake; to win laurels; to make a noise in the world; to go far; to make a sensation; to be all the rage; to have a run; to catch on.

To exalt one's horn; to leave one's mark; to exalt to the skies.

Adjectives: Distinguished, *distingué*, noted, notable, respectable, reputable, celebrated, famous, famed, far-famed, honoured, renowned, popular, deathless, imperishable, immortal (112).

Illustrious, glorious, splendid, bright, brilliant, radiant, full-blown, heroic.

Eminent, prominent, conspicuous, kenspeckle, high, pre-eminent, peerless, signalized, exalted, dedicated, consecrated, enshrined.

Great, dignified, proud, noble, worshipful, lordly, grand, stately, august, imposing, transcendent, majestic, kingly, queenly, princely, sacred, sublime, commanding.

Phrases: Redounding to one's honour; one's name living for ever; *sic itur ad astra*.

Interjections: Hail! all hail! *vive! viva!* glory be to! honour be to!

874 DISREPUTE
Substantives: discredit, ingloriousness, derogation, abasement, degradation, odium, notoriety.

Dishonour, shame, disgrace, disfavour, disapprobation (932), slur, scandal, obloquy, opprobrium, ignominy, baseness, turpitude, vileness, infamy.

Tarnish, taint, defilement, pollution.

Stain, blot, spot, blur, stigma, brand, reproach, imputation, slur, black mark.

Phrases: A burning shame; *scandalum magnatum*; a badge of infamy; the bar sinister; a blot on the scutcheon; a byword of reproach; a bad reputation.

Verbs: To be conscious of shame, to feel shame, to blush, to be ashamed, humiliated, humbled (879, 881).

To cause shame, etc.; to shame, disgrace, put to shame, dishonour; to throw, cast, fling, or reflect shame, etc., upon; to be a reproach to, to derogate from.

To tarnish, stain, blot, sully, taint, discredit, degrade, debase, defile.

To impute shame to, to brand, stigmatize, vilify, defame, slur, run down, knock.

To abash, humiliate, humble, dishonour, discompose, disconcert, shame, show up, put out, put down, snub, confuse, mortify; to obscure, eclipse, outshine.

Phrases: To feel disgrace; to cut a poor figure; to hide one's face; to look foolish; to hang one's head; to laugh on the wrong side of the mouth; not to dare to show one's face; to hide one's diminished head; to lose caste; to be in one's black books.

To put to the blush; to put out of countenance; to put one's nose out of joint; to cast into the shade; to take one down a peg; to take the shine out of; to tread or trample under foot; to drag through the mud.

Adjectives: Feeling shame, disgrace, etc.; ashamed, abashed, disgraced, blown upon, branded, tarnished.

Inglorious, mean, base (940), shabby, nameless, unnoticed, unnoted, unhonoured.

Shameful, disgraceful, despicable, discreditable, unbecoming, degrading, humiliating, unworthy, disreputable, derogatory, vile, ribald, dishonourable, abject, scandalous, infamous, notorious.

Phrases: Unwept, unhonoured, and unsung; shorn of its beams; unknown to fame; in bad odour; under a cloud; down in the world.

Interjections: Fie! shame! for shame! *O tempora! O mores!*

875 NOBILITY
Substantives: noblesse, aristocracy, peerage, gentry, gentility, quality,

rank, blood, birth, donship, fashionable world (852), the *haute monde,* high life, the upper classes, the upper ten, the four hundred.

A personage, notability, celebrity, man of distinction, rank, etc.; a nobleman, noble, lord, peer, grandee, magnate, magnifico, hidalgo, don, gentleman, squire, patrician, lordling, nob, swell, dignitary, bigwig, big gun.

House of Lords, Lords Spiritual and Temporal.

Gentlefolk, landed proprietors, squirearchy, *optimates.*

Prince, duke, marquis, earl, viscount, baron, thane, banneret, baronet, knight, count, armiger, laird, esquire; nizam, maharajah, rajah, nawab, sultan, emir (or ameer), effendi, sheik, pasha.

Princess, duchess, marchioness, marquise, countess, viscountess, baroness, lady, dame, maharanee, ranee, sultana, begum.

Verbs: To be noble, etc.

Adjectives: Noble, exalted, titled, patrician, aristocratic, high-born, well-born, genteel, *comme il faut,* gentlemanlike, ladylike, princely, courtly, fashionable (852).

Phrases: *Noblesse oblige;* born in the purple.

876 COMMONALTY

Substantives: the lower classes or orders, the vulgar herd, the crowd, the people, the commons, the proletariat, the multitude, Demos, οι πολλοί, the populace, the million, the masses, the mobility, the peasantry.

The middle classes, bourgeoisie.

The mob, rabble, rabble-rout, ruck, *canaille,* the underworld, riff-raff, *profanum vulgus.*

A commoner, one of the people, a proletarian, *roturier,* plebeian; peasant, yeoman, crofter, boor, carle, churl, serf, kern, tyke, (or tike), chuff, ryot, fellah, cottar.

A swain, clown, hind, clodhopper, bog-trotter, chaw-bacon, hodge, joskin, yokel, bumpkin, hayseed, rube, hick, ploughman, plough-boy, gaffer, loon, looby, lout, *gamin,* street arab, guttersnipe, mudlark, slubberdegullion.

A beggar, tramp, vagrant, gangrel, gaberlunzie, bum, hobo, sundowner, panhandler, pariah, muckworm, sansculotte, raff, tatterdemalion, ragamuffin.

A Goth, Vandal, Hottentot, savage, barbarian, yahoo, rough diamond, unlicked cub.

An upstart, parvenu, skipjack, *novus homo, nouveau riche,* outsider, vulgarian, snob, mushroom.

Barbarousness, barbarism.

Phrases: The man in the street; the submerged tenth; ragtag and bobtail; the swinish multitude; hewers of wood and drawers of water; the great unwashed.

Verbs: To be ignoble, etc.

Adjectives: Ignoble, common, mean, low, plebeian, proletarian, vulgar, bourgeois, untitled, homespun, homely, Gorblimey.

Base, base-born, low-bred, beggarly, earth-born, rustic, agrestic, countrified, provincial, parochial; banausic, menial, sorry, scrubby, mushroom, dunghill, sordid, vile, uncivilized, loutish, boorish, churlish, rude, brutish, raffish, unlicked, barbarous, barbarian, barbaric.

877 TITLE

Substantives: honour, princedom, principality, dukedom, marquisate, earldom, viscounty, baronetcy, lordship, knighthood.

Highness, excellancy, grace, worship, reverence, esquire, sir, master, sahib, Mr, monsieur, signor, señor, Herr.

Decoration, laurel, palm, wreath, medal, gong, ribbon, cross, star, garter, feather, crest, epaulette, colours, cockade, livery; order, arms, shield, scutcheon.

Phrase: A handle to one's name.

878 PRIDE

Substantives: haughtiness, loftiness, hauteur, stateliness, pomposity, vainglory, superciliousness, assumption, lordliness, stiffness, primness, arrogance, *morgue,* starch, starchiness, side, swank, uppishness; self-respect, dignity.

A proud man, etc., a highflier.

Verbs: To be proud, etc., to presume, assume, swagger, strut, prance, peacock, bridle.

To pride oneself on, glory in, pique oneself, plume oneself, preen oneself.

Phrases: To look big; give oneself airs; to ride the high horse; to put on side; to put on dog; to hold up one's head; to get one's tail up.

To put a good face upon.

Adjectives: Proud, haughty, lofty, high, mighty, high-flown, high-minded, high-mettled, puffed up, flushed, supercilious, patronizing, condescending, disdainful, overweening, consequential, on stilts, swollen, arrogant, pompous.

Stately, dignified, stiff, starchy, prim, perked up, buckram, strait-laced, vainglorious, lordly, magisterial, purse-proud, stand-offish, upstage, toffee-nose.

Unabashed (880).

Phrases: High and mighty; proud as a peacock; proud as Lucifer.

Adverbs: Proudly, haughtily, arrogantly, etc.

879 HUMILITY

Substantives: humbleness, meekness, lowness, lowliness, abasement, self-abasement, self-contempt, humiliation, submission, resignation, verecundity, modesty (881).

Verbs: To be humble, etc.; to deign; vouchsafe, condescend; to humble or demean oneself; stoop, submit, knuckle under, look foolish, feel small.

To render humble; to humble, humiliate, set down, abash, abase, shame, mortify, crush, take down, snub.

Phrases: To sing small; to pipe down; to draw in one's horns; to hide one's diminished head; to eat humble-pie; to eat dirt; to kiss the rod; to pocket an affront; to stoop to conquer.

To throw into the shade; to put out of countenance; to put a person in his place; to put to the blush; to take down a peg, cut down to size; to send away with a flea in one's ear.

Adjectives: Humble, lowly, meek, sober-minded, submissive (725), resigned, self-contemptuous, under correction.

Humbled, humiliated, abashed, ashamed, chapfallen, crestfallen.

Phrases: Out of countenance; on one's bended knees; humbled in the dust; not having a word to say for oneself.

Adverbs: Humbly, meekly, etc.

880 VANITY

Substantives: conceit, conceitedness, self-conceit, self-confidence, self-sufficiency, self-esteem, self-approbation, self-importance, self-praise, self-laudation, self-admiration, complacency, self-complacency, swelled head, megalomania, *amour-propre.*

Pretensions, airs, mannerism, egotism, egoism, egomania, priggishness, coxcombry, gaudery, vainglory (943), elation, ostentation (882).

A coxcomb (854).

Verbs: To be vain, etc., to egotize.

To render vain, etc., to puff up, to inspire with vanity, turn one's head.

Phrases: To have a high or overweening opinion of oneself; to think no small beer of oneself; to thrust oneself forward; to give oneself airs; to show off; to fish for compliments.

Adjectives: Vain, conceited, overweening, forward, vainglorious, puffed up, high-flown, inflated, flushed, stuck-up.

Self-satisfied, self-confident, self-sufficient, self-flattering, self-admiring, self-applauding, self-opinionated, self-centred, egocentric, egoistic, egoistical, egotistic, egotistical, complacent, self-complacent, pretentious, priggish.

Unabashed, unblushing, unconstrained, unceremonious, free and easy.

Phrases: Vain as a peacock; wise in one's own conceit.

Adverbs: Vainly, etc., ostentatiously (882).

881 MODESTY
Substantives: humility (879), diffidence, timidity, bashfulness, shyness, coyness, sheepishness, *mauvaise honte,* shamefacedness, verecundity, self-consciousness.

Reserve, constraint, demureness.

Verbs: To be modest, humble, etc.; to retire, keep in the background, keep private, reserve oneself.

Phrases: To hide one's light under a bushel; to take a back seat.

Adjectives: Modest, diffident, humble (879), timid, bashful, timorous, shy, skittish, coy, sheepish, shamefaced, blushing, self-conscious.

Unpretending, unpretentious, unassuming, unostentatious, unboastful, unaspiring.

Abashed, ashamed, dashed, out of countenance, crestfallen (879).

Reserved, constrained, demure, undemonstrative.

Adverbs: Modestly, diffidently, quietly, privately, unostentatiously.

882 OSTENTATION
Substantives: display, show, flourish, parade, pomp, state, solemnity, pageantry, dash, splash, splurge, glitter, veneer, tinsel, magnificence, pomposity, showing off, swank, swagger, strut, *panache, coup de théâtre,* stage effect.

Flourish of trumpets, fanfare, salvo of artillery, salute, fireworks, *feu de joie.*

Pageant, spectacle, procession, march-past, review, promenade, turn-out, set-out, build-up, fête, gala, regatta, field-day.

Ceremony, ceremonial, mummery; formality, form, etiquette, ritual, protocol, punctilio, puncitiliousness.

Verbs: To be ostentatious, etc.; to display, exhibit, posture, attitudinize, show off, swank, come forward, put oneself forward, flaunt, emblazon, prink, glitter; make or cut a figure, dash, or splash.

To observe or stand on ceremony, etiquette, etc.

Adjectives: Ostentatious, showy, gaudy, garish, flashy, dashing, pretentious, flaunting, jaunty, glittering, sumptuous, spectacular, ceremonial, stagy, theatrical, histrionic.

Pompous, solemn, stately, high-sounding, formal, stiff, ritualistic, ceremonious, punctilious.

Phrases: With flourish of trumpets; with beat of drum; with flying colours; in one's Sunday best; in one's best bib and tucker.

883 CELEBRATION
Substantives: jubilee, jubilation, commemoration, festival, feast, solemnization, ovation, paean, triumph.

Triumphal arch, bonfire, illuminations, fireworks, salute, salvo, *feu de joie,* flourish of trumpets, fanfare.

Inauguration, installation, presentation, coronation, fête (882).

Anniversary, silver wedding, golden wedding, diamond wedding, diamond jubilee, centenary, bicentenary, tercentenary, quartercentenary, quingentenary (or quincentenary), sexcentenary, etc., millenary.

Verbs: To celebrate, keep, signalize, do honour to, pledge, drink to, toast, commemorate, solemnize.

To inaugurate, install.

Phrase: To paint the town red.

Adjectives: Celebrating, etc., in honour of, in commemoration of, in memoriam.

Interjections: Hail! all hail! 'See the conquering hero comes.' 'For he's a jolly good fellow.'

884 BOASTING

Substantives: boast, vaunt, vaunting, brag, bounce, *blague,* swank, bluff, puff, puffing, puffery, flourish, fanfaronade, gasconade, braggadocio, bravado, tall talk, heroics, vapouring, rodomontade, bombast, exaggeration (549), self-advertisement, *réclame*; jingoism, Chauvinism, spread-eagleism.

Exultation, triumph, flourish of trumpets (883).

A boaster, braggart, braggadocio, Gascon, peacock; a pretender, charlatan.

Verbs: To boast, make a boast of, brag, vaunt, puff, flourish, vapour, blow, strut, swagger, swank, skite, gas.

To exult, crow, chuckle, triumph, gloat, glory.

Phrases: To talk big; to shoot a line; to blow one's own trumpet.

Adjectives: Boasting, vaunting, etc., thrasonical, vainglorious, braggart, jingo, jingoistic, chauvinistic.

Elate, elated, flushed, jubilant.

Phrases: On stilts; cock-a-hoop; in high feather.

885 INSOLENCE

Substantives: haughtiness, arrogance, imperiousness, contumeliousness, superciliousness, bumptiousness, bounce, swagger, swank.

Impertinence, sauciness, pertness, flippancy, petulance, malapertness.

Assumption, presumption, presumptuousness, nerve, forwardness, impudence, assurance, front, face, neck, cheek, lip, side, brass, shamelessness, hardihood, a hardened front, effrontery, audacity, procacity, self-assertion, gall, crust.

Verbs: To be insolent, etc.; to bluster, vapour, swagger, swank, swell, roister, arrogate, assume, bluff.

To domineer, bully, beard, snub, huff, outface, outlook, outstare, outbrazen, bear down, beat down, trample on, tread under foot, outbrave, hector.

To presume, take liberties or freedoms.

Phrases: To give oneself airs; to lay down the law; to put on side; to ride the high horse; to lord it over; *traiter, ou regarder de haut en bas*; to ride roughshod over; to carry with a high hand; to throw one's weight about; to carry it off; to brave it out.

Adjectives: Insolent, etc.; haughty, arrogant, imperious, dictatorial, high-handed, contumelious, supercilious, snooty, uppish, self-assertive, bumptious, overbearing, intolerant, assumptive.

Flippant, pert, perky, cavalier, saucy, cheeky, fresh, forward, impertinent, malapert.

Blustering, swaggering, swanky, vapouring, bluff, roistering, rollicking, high-flown, assuming, presuming, presumptuous, self-assertive, impudent, free, brazen, brazen-faced, barefaced, shameless, unblushing, unabashed.

886 SERVILITY

Substantives: obsequiousness, suppleness, fawning, slavishness, abjectness, prostration, prosternation, genuflexion (900), abasement, subjection (749).

Fawning, mealy-mouthedness,

sycophancy, flattery (833), humility (879).

A sycophant, parasite, gate-crasher, toad-eater, toady, spaniel, bootlicker, lickspittle, flunkey, sponger, snob, hanger-on, tuft-hunter, time-server, reptile, cur (941); Uriah Heep.
Verbs: To cringe, bow, stoop, kneel, fall on one's knees, etc.

To sneak, crawl, crouch, cower, truckle to, grovel, fawn.
Phrases: To pay court to; to dance attendance on; to do the dirty work of; to lick the boots of.

To go with the stream; to worship the rising sun; to run with the hare and hunt with the hounds.
Adjectives: Servile, subservient, obsequious, sequacious, soapy, oily, unctuous, supple, mean, crouching, cringing, fawning, slavish, grovelling, snivelling, beggarly, sycophantic, parasitical, abject, prostrate.
Adverb: Cap in hand.

887 BLUSTERER
Substantives: bully, swaggerer, braggart (884), fire-eater, daredevil, roisterer, puppy, sauce-box, hussy, minx, malapert, jackanapes, jack-in-office, jingo, Drawcansir, Captain Bobadil, Sir Lucius O'Trigger, Bombastes Furioso, Hector, Thraso, Bumble.
Phrases: The Great Panjandrum himself; a cool hand.

Section 3 –
Sympathetic Affections

888 FRIENDSHIP
Substantives: amity, amicableness, amicability, friendliness, friendly regard, affection (897), goodwill, favour, brotherhood, fraternity, sodality, comradeship, *camaraderie,* confraternity, fraternization, cordiality, harmony, good understanding, concord (714), *entente cordiale.*

Acquaintance, introduction, intimacy, familiarity, fellowship, fellow-feeling, sympathy, welcomeness, partiality, favouritism.
Verbs: To be friends, to be friendly, etc., to fraternize, sympathize with (897), to be well with, to be thick with, to befriend (707), to be in with, to keep in with.

To become friendly, to make friends with, to chum up with.
Phrases: To take in good part; to hold out the right hand of fellowship; to break the ice; to scrape acquaintance with.
Adjectives: Friendly, amical, amicable, brotherly, fraternal, harmonious, cordial, social, chummy, pally, neighbourly, on good terms, on a friendly footing, on friendly terms, well-affected, well-disposed, favourable.

Acquainted, familiar, intimate, thick, hand and glove, welcome.

Firm, staunch, intimate, familiar, bosom, cordial, devoted.
Phrases: In one's good books; hail fellow well met.
Adverbs: Friendly, amicably, etc., *sans cérémonie.*

889 ENMITY
Substantives: hostility, unfriendliness, antagonism, animosity, hate (898), dislike (867), malevolence (907), ill will, ill feeling, spite, bad blood, aversion, antipathy, alienation, estrangement; umbrage, pique.
Verbs: To be inimical, etc.; to estrange, to fall out, alienate.
Phrases: To keep at arms's length; to bear malice; to set by the ears.
Adjectives: Inimical, unfriendly, hostile, antagonistic, adverse, at variance, at loggerheads, at daggers drawn, on bad terms.

Estranged, alienated, irreconcilable.

890 FRIEND
Substantives: well-wisher, *amicus*

curiae, alter ego, bosom friend, *fidus Achates,* partner (711); *persona grata.*

Partisan, sympathizer, ally, backer, patron, good genius, fairy godmother.

Neighbour, acquaintance, associate, compeer, comrade, companion, *confrère, camarade,* mate, messmate, shopmate, shipmate, crony, cummer, confidant, chum, pal, buddy, side-kick, boon companion, pot-companion, schoolfellow, playfellow, playmate, bedfellow, bed-mate, bunkie, room-mate.

Arcades ambo, Pylades and Orestes, Castor and Pollux, Nisus and Euryalus, Damon and Pythias, David and Jonathan, *par nobile fratrum.*

Host, guest, visitor, *habitué,* protégé.

891 ENEMY

Substantives: foe, opponent (710), antagonist.

Public enemy, enemy to society, anarchist, terrorist, Ishmael.

892 SOCIALITY

Substantives: sociability, sociableness, social intercourse, companionship, companionableness, consortship, intercommunication, intercommunion, consociation.

Conviviality, good fellowship, hospitality, heartiness, welcome, the glad hand, joviality, jollity, *savoir vivre,* festivity, merrymaking.

Society, association, union, co-partnership, fraternity, sodality, coterie, clan, club (72), circle, clique, knot.

Assembly-room, casino, clubhouse, common-room.

Esprit de corps, nepotism (11).

An entertainment, party, social gathering, reunion, gaudy, levee, soirée, conversazione, rout, *ridotto,* at-home, house-warming, bee, tea-party, bun-fight, picnic, garden-party, festival (840), interview, assignation, appointment, date, tryst, call, visit, visiting, reception (588).

A good fellow, good scout, boon companion, good mixer, *bon vivant.*

Verbs: To be sociable, etc., to associate with, keep company with, to club together, sort with, hobnob with, consort, make advances, fraternize, make the acquaintance of.

To visit, pay a visit, interchange visits or cards, call upon, leave a card.

To entertain, give a party, dance, etc.; to keep open house; to receive, to welcome.

Phrases: To make oneself at home; to crack a bottle with.

To be at home to; to do the honours; to receive with open arms; to give a warm reception to; to kill the fatted calf.

Adjectives: Sociable, social, companionable, neighbourly, gregarious, clannish, clubbable, conversable, affable, accessible, familiar, on visiting terms, welcome, hospitable, convivial, jovial, festive.

Phrases: Free and easy; hail fellow well met.

Adverbs: *En famille;* in the family circle; in the social whirl; *sans façon; sans cérémonie; sans gêne.*

893 SECLUSION

Substantives: privacy, retirement, withdrawal, reclusion, recess, retiredness, rustication.

Solitude, singleness, estrangement from the world, loneliness, lonesomeness, retiredness, isolation; hermitage, cloister, nunnery (1000); study, den; ivory tower, Shangri-la.

Wilderness, depopulation, desolation.

Agoraphobia, claustrophobia.

EXCLUSION

Substantives: excommunication, banishment, expatriation, exile, ostracism, cut, cut direct, dead cut, inhospitality, inhospitableness, unsociability.

A recluse, hermit, cenobite, anchoret (or anchorite), stylite, santon,

troglodyte, solitary, ruralist; displaced person, outcast, pariah; foundling, waif, wastrel, castaway; Timon of Athens, Simon Stylites.
Phrase: 'A lone lorn creetur.'
Verbs: To be secluded, etc., to retire, to live retired, secluded, etc.; to keep aloof, keep snug, shut oneself up, deny oneself.

To cut, refuse to associate with or acknowledge; repel, cold-shoulder, blackball, outlaw, proscribe, excommunicate, boycott, exclude, banish, exile, ostracize, rusticate, send down, abandon, maroon.

To depopulate, dispeople, unpeople.
Phrases: To retire from the world; to take the veil; to sport one's oak.

To send to Coventry; to turn one's back upon; to give one the cold shoulder.
Adjectives: Secluded, sequestered, retired, private, snug, domestic, claustral.

Unsociable, unsocial, aloof, eremitical, offish, stand-offish, unclubbable, inhospitable, cynical, inconversible, retiring, unneighbourly, exclusive, unforthcoming.

Solitary, lonely, lonesome, isolated, single, estranged, unfrequented, uninhabited, unoccupied, tenantless.

Unvisited, cut, blackballed, uninvited, unwelcome, friendless, deserted, abandoned, derelict, lorn, forlorn, homeless, out of it.
Phrase: Left to shift for oneself.

894 COURTESY

Substantives: good manners, good breeding, good form, mannerliness, manners, *bienséance,* urbanity, civilization, polish, politeness, gentility, comity, civility, amenity, suavity, discretion, diplomacy, good temper, easy temper, gentleness, mansuetude, gracious-ness, gallantry, affability, obligingness, *prévenance,* amiability, good humour.

Compliment, fair words, soft words, sweet words, honeyed phrases, attentions, *petits soins,* salutation, reception, presentation, introduction, *accueil,* greeting, regards, remembrances, welcome, *abord,* respect, devoir.

Obeisance, reverence, bow, curtsy, scrape, salaam, kowtow, capping, shaking hands, embrace, hug, squeeze, accolade, salute, kiss, buss, kissing hands, genuflexion, prostration, obsequiousness.

Mark of recognition, nod, wave, valediction (293).
Verbs: To be courteous, civil, etc., to show courtesy, civility, etc., to speak one fair; to make oneself agreeable; to unbend, thaw.

To visit, wait upon, present oneself, pay one's respects, kiss hands.

To receive, do the honours, greet, welcome, bid welcome, usher in, bid God speed; hold or stretch out the hand; shake, press, or squeeze the hand.

To salute, kiss, embrace, hug, drink to, pledge, hobnob; to wave to, nod to, smile upon, bow, curtsy, scrape, uncover, cap, present arms, take off the hat.

To pay homage or obeisance, kneel, bend the knee, prostrate oneself, etc.

To render polite, etc., to polish, civilize, humanize.
Phrases: To mind one's p's and q's; to do the polite; to greet with open arms; to speed the parting guest.
Adjectives: Courteous, courtly, civil, civilized, polite, Chesterfieldian, genteel, well-bred, well-mannered, mannerly, urbane, gentlemanly, ladylike, refined (850), polished, genial.

Gracious, affable, familiar, well-spoken, fair-spoken, soft-spoken, finespoken, suave, bland, mild, conciliatory, winning, obsequious, obliging, open-armed.

Phrases: With a good grace; *suaviter in modo; à bras ouverts.*

Interjections: Hail! welcome! good morning! good day! good afternoon! good evening! good night! well met! *pax vobiscum!*

895 DISCOURTESY
Substantives: ill-breeding; ill, bad, or ungainly manners; rusticity, inurbanity, impoliteness, ungraciousness, uncourtliness, insuavity, rudeness, incivility, tactlessness, disrespect, impertinence, impudence, cheek, barbarism, misbehaviour, *grossièreté,* brutality, blackguardism, roughness, ruggedness, brusqueness, brusquerie, bad form.

Bad or ill temper, churlishness, crabbedness, tartness, crossness, peevishness, moroseness, sullenness, sulkiness, grumpiness, grouchiness, acrimony, sternness, austerity, moodiness, asperity, captiousness, sharpness, snappishness, perversity, cussedness, irascibility (901).

Sulks, dudgeon, mumps, scowl, frown, hard words, black looks.

A bear, brute, boor, blackguard, beast, cross-patch, grouch, sorehead.

Verbs: To be rude, etc., frown, scowl, glower, lour, pout, snap, snarl, growl, nag; to cut, insult, etc.

To render rude, etc., to brutalize, decivilize, dehumanize.

Phrases: To turn one's back upon; to turn on one's heel; to look black upon; to give one the cold shoulder, or the frozen face, or the frozen mitt; to take liberties with.

Adjectives: Discourteous, uncourteous, uncourtly, ill-bred, ill-mannered, ill-behaved, unmannerly, mannerless, impolite, unpolished, ungenteel, ungentlemanly, unladylike, uncivilized.

Uncivil, rude, ungracious, cool, chilly, distant, stand-offish, offish, icy, repulsive, uncomplaisant, unaccommodating, ungainly, unceremonious, ungentle, rough, rugged, bluff, blunt, gruff, churlish, boorish, bearish, brutal, brusque, blackguardly, vulgar, stern, harsh, austere, cavalier.

Ill-tempered, out of temper or humour, cross, crusty, tart, sour, crabbed, sharp, short, snappish, testy, peevish, waspish, captious, grumpy, snarling, caustic, acrimonious, ungenial, petulant, pettish, pert.

Perverse, cross-grained, ill-conditioned, wayward, humoursome, naughty, cantankerous, intractable, curst, nagging, froward, sulky, glum, grim, morose, scowling, grouchy, glowering, surly, sullen, growling, splenetic, spleenful, spleeny, spleenish, moody, dogged, ugly.

Phrases: Cross as two sticks; sour as a crab; surly as a bear.

Adverbs: With a bad grace, grudgingly.

896 CONGRATULATION
Substantives: felicitation, wishing joy, the compliments of the season, good wishes.

Verbs: To congratulate, felicitate, give or wish joy, tender or offer one's congratulations.

Adjectives: Congratulatory, etc.

Phrases: Many happy returns of the day! merry Christmas! happy New Year!

897 LOVE
Substantives: fondness, liking, inclination (865), regard, good graces, partiality, benevolence (906), admiration, fancy, tenderness, leaning, penchant, predilection; amativeness, amorousness.

Affection, sympathy, fellow-feeling, heart, affectionateness.

Attachment, yearning, amour, romance, gallantry, love-affair, *affair de cœur,* passion, tender passion, *grande passion,* flame, pash, crush, rave, devotion, enthusiasm, fervour, enchantment, infatuation, adoration, idolatry, idolization.

Eros, Cupid, Aphrodite, Venus, Freya, the myrtle.

Maternal love, στοργή.

Attractiveness, etc., popularity.

Abode of love, love-nest, agapemone.

A lover, suitor, follower, admirer, adorer, wooer, beau, fiancé, gallant, young man, boy friend, sweetheart, flame, love, true-love, leman, paramour, amorist, *amoroso, cavaliere servente, cicisbeo*; turtle-doves.

Girl friend, lady-love, fiancée, sweetie, cutie, mistress, *inamorata,* idol, doxy, dona, Dulcinea, goddess.

Betrothed, affianced.

Verbs: To love, like, affect, fancy, care for, regard, revere, cherish, admire, dote on, adore, idolize, fall for, hold dear, prize.

To bear love to; to take to; to be in love with; to be taken, smitten, etc., with; to have, entertain, harbour, cherish, etc., a liking, love, etc., for; to be fond of, be gone on.

To excite love; to win, gain, secure, etc., the love, affections, heart, etc.; to take the fancy of, to attract, attach, seduce, charm, fascinate, captivate, enamour, enrapture.

To get into favour; to ingratiate oneself, insinuate oneself, curry favour with, pay one's court to, *faire l'aimable.*

Phrases: To take a fancy to; to make a fuss of; to look sweet upon; to cast sheep's eyes at; to fall in love with; to set one's affections on; to lose one's heart to.

To set one's cap at; to turn one's head.

Adjectives: Loving, liking, etc., attached to, fond of, taken with, struck with, gone on, sympathetic, sympathizing with, charmed, captivated, fascinated, smitten, bitten, *épris,* enamoured, lovesick, love-lorn.

Affectionate, tender, sweet upon, loving, lover-like, loverly, amorous, amatory, amative, spoony, erotic, uxorious, motherly, ardent, passionate, devoted, amatorial.

Loved, beloved, etc., dear, precious, darling, favourite (899), pet, popular.

Lovely, sweet, dear, charming, engaging, amiable, winning, winsome, lovesome, attractive, adorable, enchanting, captivating, fascinating, bewitching, taking, seductive (829).

Phrases: Head over ears in love; to one's mind, taste, or fancy; in one's good graces; nearest to one's heart.

898 HATE

Substantives: hatred, disaffection, disfavour, alienation, estrangement, odium, dislike (867), enmity (899), animus, animosity (900).

Umbrage, pique, grudge, dudgeon, spleen, bitterness, ill feeling, acrimony, acerbity, malice (907), implacability.

Disgust, repugnance, aversion, averseness, loathing, abomination, horror, detestation, antipathy, abhorrence.

Object of hatred, abomination, *bête noir.*

Verbs: To hate, dislike, disrelish (867), loathe, nauseate, execrate, detest, abominate, shudder at, recoil at, abhor, shrink from.

To excite hatred, estrange, incense, envenom, antagonize, rile, alienate, disaffect, set against; to be hateful, etc.

Phrases: To make one's blood run cold; to have a down on; to hate one's guts.

To sow dissension among; to set by the ears.

Adjectives: Hating, etc., averse to, set against.

Unloved, disliked, unwept, unlamented, undeplored, unmourned, unbeloved, uncared-for, unvalued.

Crossed in love, forsaken, jilted, rejected, love-lorn.

Obnoxious, hateful, abhorrent, odious, repulsive, offensive, shocking, loathsome, sickening, nauseous, disgusting, abominable, horrid (830).

Invidious, spiteful, malicious (907), spleenful, disgustful.

Insulting, irritating, provoking.

Phrases: Not on speaking terms; there being no love lost between them; at daggers drawn.

899 FAVOURITE

Substantives: pet, cosset, dear, darling, honey, duck, moppet, jewel, idol, minion, spoilt child, blue-eyed boy, *persona grata*.

Phrases: The apple of one's eye; a man after one's own heart; the idol of the people; the answer to the maiden's prayer.

900 RESENTMENT

Substantives: displeasure, animus, animosity, anger, wrath, indignation.

Pique, umbrage, huff, miff, soreness, dudgeon, moodiness, acerbity, bitterness, asperity, spleen, gall, heart-burning, heart-swelling, rankling; temper (901), bad blood, ill blood, ill humour.

Excitement, irritation, exasperation, warmth, bile, choler, ire, fume, dander, passion, fit, tantrum, burst, explosion, paroxysm, storm, rage, wax, fury, desperation.

Temper, petulance, procacity, angry mood, taking, snappishness.

Cause of umbrage, affront, provocation, offence, indignity, insult (929).

The Furies; the Eumenides.

Phrases: The blood being up or boiling; a towering passion; the vials of wrath; fire and fury.

A sore subject; a rap on the knuckles; *casus belli*.

Verbs: To resent, take amiss, take offence, take umbrage, take huff, bridle up, bristle up, frown, scowl, lour, snarl, growl, gnash, snap.

To chafe, mantle, redden, colour, fume, froth up, kindle; get, fall, or fly into a passion, rage, etc.; fly out, take fire, fire up, flare up, boil, boil over, rage, storm, foam.

To cause or raise anger; to affront, offend, give offence or umbrage; hurt the feelings; discompose, fret, ruffle, nettle, excite, irritate, provoke, rile, chafe, wound, sting, incense, inflame, enrage, aggravate, embitter, exasperate, rankle, infuriate, peeve.

Phrases: To take in bad part; to take it ill; to take exception to; to stick in one's gizzard; to take in dudgeon; to have a bone (or crow) to pick with one; to get up on one's hind legs; to show one's teeth; to lose one's temper; to stamp, quiver, swell, or foam with rage; to see red; to look as black as thunder; to breathe revenge; to cut up rough; to pour out the vials of one's wrath; to blaze up; to blow one's top; to go up in a blue flame; to go on the war-path; to raise Cain.

To put out of humour; to stir up one's bile; to raise one's dander or choler; to work up into a passion; to make one's blood boil; to lash into a fury; to drive one mad; to put one's monkey up; to get one's goat.

Adjectives: Angry, wroth, irate, ireful, warm, boiling, fuming, raging, etc., nettled, sore, bitter, riled, ruffled, chafed, exasperated, wrought up, worked up, snappish.

Fierce, wild, rageful, furious, infuriate, mad, fiery, savage, rabid, waxy, shirty, boiling over, rankling, bitter, virulent, set against.

Relentless, ruthless, implacable, unpitying, pitiless (919), inexorable, remorseless, stony-hearted, immitigable.

Phrases: One's back being up; up in arms; in a stew; the gorge rising; in the height of passion.

337

Interjections: Hell's bells! zounds! damme! For crying out loud!

901 IRASCIBILITY
Substantives: susceptibility, excitability, temper, bad temper, procacity, petulance, irritability, fretfulness, testiness, grouchiness, tetchiness, touchiness, frowardness, peevishness, snappishness, hastiness, tartness, huffiness, resentfulness, vindictiveness, acerbity, protervity, aggressiveness, pugnacity (895).

A shrew, vixen, termagant, virago, scold, spitfire, Xanthippe; a tartar, fire-eater, fury; *genus irritabile*.

Verbs: To be irascible, etc.; to take fire, fire up, flare up (900).

Adjectives: Irascible, susceptible, excitable, irritable, fretful, fretty, on the fret, fidgety, peevish, hasty, over-hasty, quick, warm, hot, huffish, huffy, touchy, testy, tetchy (or techy), grouchy, restive, pettish, waspish, snappish, petulant, peppery, fiery, passionate, choleric, short-tempered.

Ill-tempered, bad-tempered, cross, churlish, sour, crabbed, cross-grained, sullen, sulky, grumpy, fractious, splenetic, spleenful, froward, shrewish.

Quarrelsome, querulous, disputatious, contentious, cranky, cantankerous, sarcastic (932), resentful, vindictive, pugnacious, aggressive.

Phrases: Like touchwood or tinder; a word and a blow; as cross as two sticks.

902 ENDEARMENT
Substantives: caress, blandishment, fondling, billing and cooing, petting, necking, embrace, salute, kiss, buss, smack, osculation, deosculation.

Courtship, wooing, suit, addresses, attentions, *petits soins,* flirtation, coquetry, philandering, gallivanting, serenading, œillade, ogle, the glad eye, sheep's eyes, goo-goo eyes.

Love-tale, love-token, love-letter, *billet-doux,* valentine.

Flirt, coquette, gold digger, vamp; male flirt, masher, philanderer, lady killer, wolf, lounge lizard, cake eater, sheik.

Verbs: To caress, fondle, wheedle, dandle, dally, cuddle, cockle, cosset, nestle, nuzzle, snuggle, clasp, hug, embrace, kiss, salute, bill and coo.

To court, woo, flirt, coquette, philander, spoon, canoodle, mash, spark, serenade.

Phrases: To make much of; to smile upon; to make eyes et; to chuck under the chin; to pat on the cheek; to make love; to pay one's court or one's addresses to; to set one's cap at; to pop the question.

To win the heart, affections, love, etc., of.

Adjectives: Caressing, etc., caressed, etc., flirtatious, spoony.

903 MARRIAGE
Substantives: matrimony, wedlock, union, bridal, match, intermarriage, coverture, cohabitation, bed, the marriage bond, the nuptial tie.

Wedding, nuptials, Hymen, spousals, espousals; leading to the altar; the torch of Hymen; nuptial benediction, marriage song, epithalamium.

Bride, bridegroom, groom, bridesmaid, maid of honour, matron of honour, bridesman, groomsman, best man.

Honeymoon, honeymooner.

A married man, a husband, spouse benedick (or benedict), consort, goodman, lord and master, hubby.

A married woman, a wife, lady, matron, mate, helpmate, helpmeet, rib, better half, *femme couverte* (or *feme coverte*), squaw.

A married couple, wedded pair, Darby and Joan, man and wife.

A monogamist, bigamist, a Turk,

polygamist, a much-married man, a Bluebeard, a Mormon.

Monogamy, bigamy, digamy, deuterogamy, trigamy, polygamy, polygyny, polyandry, endogamy, exogamy.

A morgantic marriage, left-handed marriage, marriage of convenience, *mariage de convenance,* companionate marriage, trial marriage, misalliance, *mésalliance.*

Verbs: To marry, wed, espouse, wive.

To join, give away, handfast, splice.

Phrases: To lead to the altar; to take to oneself a wife; to take for better for worse; to give one's hand to; to get spliced.

To tie the nuptial knot; to give in marriage.

Adjectives: Matrimonial, conjugal, connubial, nuptial, wedded, hymeneal, spousal, bridal, marital, epithalamic.

Monogamous, bigamous, polygamous, etc.

904 CELIBACY

Substantives: singleness, misogamy; bachelorhood, bachelorship; virginity, maidenhood, maidenhead.

An unmarried man, bachelor, celibate, misogamist, misogynist.

An unmarried woman, spinster, maid, maiden, old maid, virgin, *feme sole,* bachelor girl.

Phrase: Single blessedness.

Verb: To live single.

Adjectives: Unwedded, unmarried, single, celibate, wifeless, spouseless, lone.

905 DIVORCE

Substantives: dissolution of marriage, separation, divorcement.

A divorcee, co-respondent, cuckold.

Verbs: To live separate, divorce, put away.

WIDOWHOOD, viduity, weeds.

Widow, relict, dowager, jointress, grass widow; widower, grass widower.

906 BENEVOLENCE

Substantives: goodwill, good nature, kindness, kindliness, benignity, brotherly love, beneficence, charity, humanity, fellow-feeling, sympathy, good feeling, kind-heartedness, amiability, complaisance, loving-kindness; toleration, consideration, generosity.

Charitableness, bounty, bounteousness, bountifulness almsgiving, philanthropy (910), unselfishness (942).

Acts of kindness, a good turn, good works, kind offices, attentions, good treatment.

Phrases: The milk of human kindness; the good Samaritan.

Verbs: To be benevolent, etc., to do good to, to benefit, confer a benefit, be of use, aid, assist (707), render a service, treat well, to sympathize with.

Phrases: To have one's heart in the right place; to enter into the feelings of others; to do a good turn to; to do as one would be done by.

Adjectives: Benevolent, well-meaning, kind, obliging, accommodating, kind-hearted, tender-hearted, charitable, generous, beneficent, bounteous, bountiful, humane, clement, benignant, benign, considerate.

Good-natured, *bon enfant, bon diable,* a good sort, sympathizing, sympathetic, responsive, complaisant, accommodating, amiable, gracious.

Kindly, well-meant, well-intentioned, brotherly, fraternal, friendly (888).

Adverbs: With a good intention, with the best intentions.

Interjections: Good luck! God speed!

907 MALEVOLENCE

Substantives: ill will, unkindness, ill nature, malignity, malice, maliciousness, spite, spitefulness, despite, despitefulness.

Uncharitableness, venom, gall, rancour, rankling, bitterness, acerbity, harshness, mordacity, acridity, virulence, *acharnement,* misanthropy (911).

Cruelty, hardness of heart, obduracy, cruelness, brutality, brutishness, hooliganism, savageness, savagery, ferocity, barbarity, blood-thirstiness, immanity, pitilessness, truculence, devilry (or deviltry), devilment.

An ill turn, a bad turn, outrage, atrocity, affront (929).
Phrases: A heart of stone; the evil eye; the cloven hoof.
Verbs: To be malevolent, etc.; to injure, hurt, harm, molest, disoblige, do harm to, ill treat, maltreat (649), do an ill office or turn to, (830), to wrong.

To worry, harass, bait, oppress, grind, haze, persecute, hunt down, dragoon, hound.
Phrases: To wreak one's malice on; to bear or harbour malice against; to do one's worst.
Adjectives: Malevolent, malicious, ill-disposed, evil-minded, ill-intentioned, maleficent, malign, malignant.

Ill-natured, disobliging, inofficious, unfriendly, unsympathetic, unkind, uncandid, unaccommodating, uncharitable, ungracious, unamiable.

Surley, churlish (895), grim, spiteful, despiteful, ill-conditioned, foulmouthed, acrid, rancorous, caustic, bitter, acrimonious, mordacious, vitriolic, venomous.

Cold, cold-blooded, cold-hearted, hard-hearted, iron-hearted, flinthearted, marble-hearted, stonyhearted.

Pitiless, unpitying, uncompassionate, without bowels, ruthless, merciless, unmerciful, inexorable, relentless, unrelenting, virulent, dispiteous.

Cruel, brutal, savage, ferocious, atrocious, untamed, ferine, inhuman, barbarous, fell, Hunnish, bloody, blood-stained, bloodthirsty, bloody-minded, sanguinary, truculent (919), butcherly.

Fiendish, fiendlike, infernal, demoniacal, diabolical, devilish, hellish.
Adverbs: Malevolently, etc., with bad intent or intention, despitefully.

908 MALEDICTION
Substantives: curse, malison, imprecation, denunciation, execration, anathema, ban, proscription, excommunication, commination, fulmination, *maranatha.*

Cursing, scolding, revilement, vilification, vituperation, invective, flyting, railing, Billingsgate, expletive, oath, bad language, unparliamentary language, ribaldry, scurrility.
Verbs: To censure, curse, imprecate, damn, scold, swear at, flyte on, rail at or against, execrate.

To denounce, proscribe, excommunicate, fulminate against, anathematize, blaspheme.
Phrases: To devote to destruction; to invoke or call down curses on one's head; to swear like a trooper; to rap out an oath; to curse with bell, book, and candle.
Adjectives: Cursing, etc., accursed, cursed, etc., blue-pencil, asterisk; maledictory, imprecatory, blasphemous.
Interjections: Curse! damn! blast! devil take it! dash! hang! blow! confound! plague on it! woe to! beshrew! *ruat coelum!* ill betide!

909 THREAT
Substantives: menace, defiance (715), abuse, minacity, intimidation, commination.
Verbs: To threaten, threat, menace, fulminate, thunder, bluster, defy, snarl; growl, gnarl, mutter; to intimidate (860).
Phrases: To hurl defiance; to throw down the gauntlet; to look daggers; to show one's teeth; to shake the fist at.

Adjectives: Threatening, menacing, minatory, comminatory, minacious, abusive, sinister, ominous, louring, defiant (715).
Interjections: Let them beware! You have been warned!

910 PHILANTHROPY
Substantives: humanity, humanitarianism, altruism, public spirit.

Patriotism, civicism, nationality, nationalism, love of country, *amor patriae,* sociology, socialism, utilitarianism.

A philanthropist, humanitarian, utilitarian, Benthamite, socialist, cosmopolitan, cosmopolite, citizen of the world, patriot, nationalist, lover of mankind.
Adjectives: Philanthropic, philanthropical, humanitarian, humane, utilitarian, patriotic, altruistic, public-spirited.
Phrases: '*Humani nihil a me alienum puto*'; *pro bono publico*; the greatest happiness of the greatest number.

911 MISANTHROPY
Substantives: egotism, egoism, incivism, want of patriotism, moroseness, selfishness (943); misogynism.

A misanthrope, egotist, cynic, man-hater, Timon, Diogenes.

Woman-hater, misogynist.
Adjectives: Misanthropic, misanthropical, antisocial, unpatriotic, fish, egotistical, morose, sullen, maladjusted.

912 BENEFACTOR
Substantives: saviour, good genius, tutelary saint, guardian angel, fairy godmother, good Samaritan.
Phrase: *Deus ex machina.*

913 EVILDOER
Substantives: wrong-doer, mischief-maker, marplot, anarchist, nihilist, terrorist, firebrand, incendiary, evil genius (980).

Frankenstein's monster.

Savage, brute, ruffian, blackguard, villain, scoundrel, cutthroat, barbarian, caitiff, desperado, jail-bird, hooligan, tough, rough, teddy boy, larrikin, hoodlum, gangster, crook, yegg, apache (949).

Fiend, tiger, hyena, bloodhound, butcher, blood-sucker, vampire, ogre, ghoul, serpent, snake, adder, viper, rattlesnake, scorpion, hell-hound, hag, hellbag, beldam, harpy, siren, fury, Jezebel.

Monster, demon, imp, devil (980), anthropophagi, Attila, vandal, Hun, Goth.
Phrases: A snake in the grass; a scourge of the human race; a fiend in human shape; worker of iniquity.

914 PITY
Substantives: compassion, commiseration, sympathy, fellow-feeling, tenderness, yearning.

Forbearance, mercy, humanity, clemency, leniency, ruth, long-suffering, quarter.
Phrases: The melting mood; *coup de grâce*; bowels of compassion; *argumentum ad misericordiam.*
Verbs: To pity, commiserate, compassionate, sympathize, feel for, yearn for, console, enter into the feelings of, have or take pity; show or have mercy; to forbear, relent, thaw, spare, relax, give quarter.

To excite pity, touch, soften, melt, propitiate, disarm.

To ask for pity, mercy, etc.; to supplicate, implore, deprecate, appeal to, cry for quarter, etc.; beg one's life, kneel, fall on one's knees, etc.
Phrase: To put one out of one's misery.
Adjectives: Pitying, commiserating, etc.

Pitiful, compassionate, tender, clement, merciful, lenient, relenting, etc.; soft-hearted, sympathetic, touched, weak, soft, melting, unhardened (740).

Piteous, pitiable, sorry, miserable.

Phrases: Tender as a woman; one's heart bleeding for.

Interjections: For pity's sake! mercy! God help you! poor thing! poor fellow!

915 CONDOLENCE

Substantives: lamentation, lament (839), sympathy, consolation.

Verbs: To condole with, console, solace, sympathize; express, testify, etc., pity; to afford or supply consolation, grieve for, lament with, weep with (839).

916 GRATITUDE

Substantives: gratefulness, thankfulness, feeling of obligation.

Acknowledgment, recognition, thanksgiving, giving thanks.

Thanks, praise, benediction, prace, paean, Te Deum (990).

Requital, thank-offering.

Verbs: To be grateful, etc.; to thank, to give, render, return, offer, tender thanks, acknowledgments, etc.; to acknowledge, appreciate, requite.

To lie under an obligation, to be obliged, beholden, etc.

Phrases: To overflow with gratitude; to thank one's stars; never to forget.

Adjectives: Grateful, thankful, obliged, beholden, indebted to, under obligation.

Interjections: Thanks! many thanks! ta! *merci!* gramercy! much obliged! thank heaven! heaven be praised!

917 INGRATITUDE

Substantives: ungratefulness, thanklessness, oblivion of benefits.

Phrases: 'Benefits forgot'; a thankless task.

Verbs: To be ungrateful, etc.; to forget benefits.

Phrases: To look a gift-horse in the mouth; to bite the hand that fed one.

Adjectives: Ungrateful, unmindful, unthankful, thankless, ingrate, inappreciative.

Forgotten, unacknowledged, unthanked, unrequited, unrewarded, ill-requited.

Phrase: Thank you for nothing.

918 FORGIVENESS

Substantives: pardon, condonation, grace, remission, absolution, amnesty, indemnity, oblivion, indulgence, reprieve.

Reconcilement, reconciliation, appeasement, mollification, shaking of hands, pacification (723).

Excuse, exoneration, quittance, acquittal, propitiation, exculpation.

Longanimity, forbearance, placability.

Verbs: To forgive, pardon, excuse, pass over, overlook, bear with, condone, absolve, pass, let off, remit, reprieve, exculpate, exonerate.

To allow for; to make allowance for.

To conciliate, propitiate, pacify, appease, placate, reconcile.

Phrases: To make it up; to forgive and forget; to shake hands; to heal the breach; to kiss and be friends; to bury the hatchet; to wipe the slate clean; to let bygones be bygones.

Adjectives: Forgiving, etc., unreproachful, placable, conciliatory.

Forgiven, etc., unresented.

919 REVENGE

Substantives: vengeance, revengement, avengement, vendetta, feud, retaliation.

Rancour, vindictiveness, implacability.

Revenger, avenger, vindicator, Nemesis, Furies.

Verbs: To revenge, take revenge, avenge.

Phrases: To wreak one's vengeance; to visit the sins on; to breathe vengeance; to have a bone to pick with; to have accounts to settle; to have a rod in pickle; to get one's knife into; to take one's change out of.

To harbour vindictive feelings; to rankle in the breast.

Adjectives: Revengeful, revanchist, vindictive, vengeful, rancorous, unforgiving, pitiless, ruthless, remorseless, unrelenting, relentless, implacable, rigorous.

920 JEALOUSY
Substantives: jealousness, heart-burning.
Phrases: A jaundiced eye; the green-eyed monster.
Verbs: To be jealous, etc.; to view with jealousy.
Adjectives: Jealous, jaundiced, yellow-eyed.
Phrase: Eaten up with jealousy.

921 ENVY
Substantives: rivalry, emulation, covetousness; a Thersites, Zoilus.
Verbs: To envy, rival, emulate, covet.
Adjectives: Envious, invidious, covetous.
Phrase: Bursting with envy.

Section 4 –
Moral Affections

922 RIGHT
Substantives: what ought to be, what should be; goodness, virtue (944), rectitude, probity (939).

Justice, equity, equitableness, fitness, fairness, fair play, impartiality, reasonableness, propriety.

Astraea, Themis.

Phrases: The scales of justice; even-handed justice; *suum cuique*; a fair field and no favour; *lex talionis*; 'Fiat justitia, ruat coelum.'

Morality, morals, ethics, duty (926).
Verbs: To stand to reason; to be right, just, etc.

To deserve, merit; to be worthy of, to be entitled to (924).
Phrases: To do justice to; to see justice done; to hold the scales even; to see fair play; to see one righted; to serve one right; to give the devil his due; to give and take; *audire alteram partem.*
Adjectives: Right, just, equitable, fair, equal, even-handed, impartial, judicial, legitimate, justifiable, rightful, reasonable, fit, proper, becoming, decorous, decent (926).

Deserved, merited, condign (924).
Adverbs: Rightly, in justice, in equity, fairly, etc., in reason, without distinction, without respect of persons.
Phrases: *En règle; de jure.*

923 WRONG
Substantives: what ought not to be, badness, evil (945), turpitude, improbity (940).

Injustice, unfairness, inequity, foul play, partiality, favour, favouritism, leaning, bias, party spirit, undueness (925), unreasonableness, tort, unlawfulness (964), encroachment, imposition.
Verbs: To be wrong, unjust, etc.; to favour, lean towards, show partiality, to encroach, impose upon.
Phrase: To rob Peter to pay Paul.
Adjectives: Wrong, wrongful, bad, unjust, unfair, undue, inequitable, unequal, partial, invidious, one-sided, improper, unreasonable, iniquitous, unfit, immoral (945).

Unjustified, unjustifiable, unwarranted, unauthorized, unallowable, unwarrantable.
Phrases: In the wrong; in the wrong box.
Adverbs: Wrongly, unjustly, etc., amiss.
Phrase: It won't do.

924 DUENESS
Substantives: due.

Right, privilege, prerogative, title,

claim, qualification, pretension, birth-right, prescription, immunity, exemption, licence, liberty, franchise, enfranchisement, vested interest.

Sanction, authority, warranty, tenure, bond, security, lien, constitution, charter, warrant (760), patent, letters patent, copyright, *imprimatur.*

A claimant, pretender, appellant, plaintiff (938).

Women's rights, feminism; feminist, suffragist, suffragette.

Verbs: To be due, etc., to.

To have a right to, to be entitled to, to be qualified for, to have a claim upon, a title to, etc.; to deserve, merit, be worthy of.

To demand, claim, call upon, exact, insist on, challenge, to come upon one for, to revendicate, make a point of, enforce, put in force, use a right.

To appertain to, belong to, etc. (777).

To lay claim to, assert, assume, arrogate, make good, substantiate; to vindicate a claim, etc., to make out a case.

To give or confer a right; to entitle, authorize, warrant, sanction, sanctify, privilege, enfranchise, license, legalize, ordain, prescribe, allot.

Adjectives: Having a right to, a claim to, etc.; due to, entitled to, deserving, meriting, worthy of, claiming, qualified.

Privileged, allowed, sanctioned, warranted, authorized, permitted, licit, ordained, prescribed, chartered, enfranchised, constitutional, official.

Prescriptive, presumptive, absolute, indefeasible, unalienable, inalienable, imprescriptible, inviolable, unimpeachable, unchallenged, sacred, sacrosanct.

Condign, merited, deserved.

Allowable, permissible, lawful, legitimate, legal, legalized (693), proper, square, equitable, unexceptionable, reasonable (922), right, correct, meet, fitting (926).

Adverbs: Duly, by right, by divine right, *ex officio, Dei gratia, de jure.*

925 UNDUENESS

Substantives: unlawfulness, impropriety, unfitness, illegality (964).

Falseness, spuriousness, emptiness of invalidity of title, illegitimacy.

Loss of right, forfeiture, disfranchisement.

Usurpation, violation, breach, encroachment, stretch, imposition, relaxation.

Verbs: Not to be due, etc., to; to be undue, etc.

To infringe, encroach, violate, do violence to; to stretch or strain a point; to trench on, usurp.

To disfranchise, disentitle, disfrock, unfrock; to disqualify, invalidate, relax.

To misbecome, misbehave (945).

Adjectives: Undue, unlawful, illicit, unconstitutional.

Unauthorized, unwarranted, unsanctioned, unofficial, unjustified, unprivileged, illegitimate, bastard, spurious, supposititious, false, usurped, unchartered, unfulfilled, unauthorized.

Unentitled, disentitled, unqualified underprivileged; difranchised, forfeit.

Undeserved, unmerited, unearned.

Improper, unmeet, unbecoming, unfit, misbecoming, unseemly, preposterous.

Phrases: Not the thing; out of the question; not to be thought of; out of court.

926 DUTY

Substantives: what ought to be done; moral obligation, accountableness, accountability, liability, onus, responsibility, bounden duty; dueness (924). Allegiance, fealty, tie, office, function, province, post, engagement (768).

Morality, morals, conscience,

accountableness, conscientiousness; the Decalogue, the Ten Commandments.

Dueness, propriety, fitness, decency, seemliness, decorum.

Observance, fulfilment, discharge, performance, acquittal, satisfaction, redemption, good behaviour.

Science of morals, ethics, deontology; moral or ethical philosophy, casuistry.

Phrases: The thing; the proper thing; a case of conscience; the still small voice.

Verbs: To be the duty of, to be due to, to be up to; ought to be; to be incumbent on, to behove, befit, become, beseem, belong to, pertain to, devolve on, to be on one's head; to be, or stand, or lie under and obligation; to have to answer for, to be accountable for, to owe it to oneself, to be in duty bound, to be committed to, to be on one's good behaviour.

To impose a duty or obligation; to enjoin, require, exact, bind, pin down, saddle with, prescribe, assign, call upon, look to, oblige.

To do one's duty, to enter upon a duty; to perform, observe, fulfil, discharge, adhere to; acquit oneself of an obligation.

Phrases: To be at one's post; to redeem one's pledge; to toe the mark or line.

Adjectives: Dutiful, duteous, docile, obedient, compliant, tractable.

Obligatory, binding, imperative peremptory, mandatory, behoving, incumbent on, chargeable on, meet, due to.

Being under obligation, under obedience, obliged by, beholden to, bound by, tied by, saddled with, indebted to.

Amenable, liable, accountable, responsible, answerable.

Right, proper, fit, due, correct, seemly, fitting, befitting, decent, meet.

Moral, ethical, casuistical, conscientious.

Adverbs: Conscientiously, with a safe conscience; as in duty bound; on one's own responsibility.

927 DERELICTION OF DUTY
Substantives: guilt (947), sin (945), neglect, negligence, non-observance, failure, evasion, dead letter.

Verbs: To violate, break, break through, infringe, set at naught, slight, neglect, trample on, evade, contravene, disregard, renounce, repudiate, quit, forswear, fail, transgress.

Phrase: To wash one's hands of.

927A EXEMPTION
Substantives: freedom, irresponsibility, immunity, liberty, licence, release, exoneration, excuse, dispensation, absolution, franchise, renunciation, discharge.

Verbs: To be exempt, free, at liberty, released, excused, exonerated, absolved, etc.

To exempt, release, excuse, exonerate, absolve, acquit, free, set at liberty, discharge, set aside, let off, remit, pass over, spare, excuse, license, dispense with; to give dispensation.

Phrase: To stretch a point.

Adjectives: Exempt, free, released, at liberty, absolved, exonerated, excused, let off, discharged, licensed, acquitted, unencumbered, dispensed, scot-free, immune.

Irresponsible, unaccountable, unanswerable, unbound.

928 RESPECT
Substantives: deference, reverence, regard, consideration, attention, honour, esteem, estimation, distance, decorum, veneration, admiration.

Homage, fealty, obeisance, genuflexion, kneeling, salaam, kowtow, presenting arms (896), prostration, obsequiousness, devotion, worship (990).

Verbs: To respect, honour, reverence,

regard, defer to, pay respect or deference to, render honour to, look up to, esteem, revere, think much of, think highly of, venerate, hallow.

To pay homage to, bow to, take off one's hat to, kneel to, bend the knee to, present arms, fall down before, prostrate oneself.

To command or inspire respect; to awe, overawe, dazzle.

Phrases: To keep one's distance; to make way for; to observe due decorum.

Adjectives: Respecting, etc., respectful, considerate, polite, attentive, reverential, obsequious, ceremonious, bare-headed, cap in hand, on one's knees, prostrate.

Respected, esteemed, honoured, hallowed, venerable, emeritus.

Phrases: Saving your presence; begging your honour's pardon.

929 DISRESPECT

Substantives: irreverence, dishonour, disparagement, slight, neglect, disesteem, disestimation, superciliousness, contumely, indignity, insult, rudeness.

Ridicule (856), sarcasm, derision, scurrility, mockery, scoffing, sibilation.

A jeer, gibe, taunt, scoff, sneer (930), hiss, hoot, fling, flout.

Verbs: To treat with disrespect, etc., to disparage, dishonour, misprise, vilipend, slight, insult, affront, disregard, make light of, hold in, no esteem, esteem of no account, set at naught, speak slightingly of, set down, pass by, overlook, look down upon, despise (930).

To deride, scoff, sneer at, laugh at, ridicule (856), roast, guy, rag, mock, jeer, taunt, twit, flout, gibe, hiss, hoot, boo.

Phrases: To make game of; to point the finger at; to make a fool of; to turn into ridicule; to laugh to scorn; to turn

one's back upon.

Adjectives: Disrespectful, slighting, disparaging (934), dishonouring, scornful (940), irreverent, supercilious, contumelious, scurrilous, deriding, derisive, derisory.

Unrespected, unworshipped, unregarded, disregarded, ignored.

Adverbs: Disrespectfully, cavalierly, etc.

930 CONTEMPT

Substantives: disdain, scorn, contumely, despisal, slight, sneer, spurn, sniff; a byword.

Scornfulness, disdainfulness, haughtiness, contemptuousness, superciliousness, derision (929).

The state of being despised, despisedness.

Verbs: To despise, contemn, scorn, disdain, scout, spurn, look down upon, disregard, slight, make light of, not mind, hold cheap, hold in contempt, pooh-pooh, sneeze at, sniff at, whistle at, hoot, flout, trample upon.

Phrases: Not to care a straw, fig, button, etc., for (643); to turn up one's nose at; to shrug one's shoulders; to snap one's fingers at; to take no account of; to laugh to scorn; to make light of; to tread or trample under foot; to set at naught; to point the finger of scorn at.

Adjectives: Contemptuous, disdainful, scornful, contumelious, cavalier, derisive, supercilious, toplofty, upstage, sniffy, sardonic.

Contemptible, despicable, poor, paltry (643), downtrodden, unenvied.

Interjections: A fig for! hoots! bah! pshaw! pish! shucks! pooh-pooh! fiddlestick! fiddle-de-dee! tush! tut!

931 APPROBATION

Substantives: approval, approvement, endorsement, sanction, esteem, admiration, estimation, good opinion, appreciation, regard, account, popularity, kudos.

Commendation, praise, laud, laudation, advocacy, good word; meed or tribute of praise, encomium, eulogium, eulogy, *éloge,* panegyric, puff, blurb, homage.

Applause, plaudit, cheer, clap, clapping, clapping of hands, acclamation; paean, benediction, blessing, benison, hosanna; claque.

Phrases: A peal, shout, or chorus of applause; golden opinions; *succès d'estime.*

Verbs: To approve, think well or highly of, esteem, appreciate, value, prize, admire, countenance, endorse.

To commend, speak well of, recommend, advocate, praise, laud, belaud, compliment, bepraise, clap, clap hands, applaud, cheer, panegyrize, celebrate, eulogize, cry up, root for, crack up, write up, extol, glorify, magnify, puff, boom, boost, exalt, swell, bless, give a blessing to.

To deserve praise, etc., to be praised, etc.

Phrases: To set great store by; to sing the praises of; to extol to the skies; to applaud to the echo; to stick up for; to say a good word for; to pat on the back.

To redound to the honour or praise of; to do credit to.

To win golden opinions; to be in high favour; to bring down the house.

Adjectives: Approving, etc., commendatory, complimentary, benedictory, laudatory, panegyrical eulogistic, encomiastic.

Approved, praised, uncensured, unimpeached, admired, popular, deserving or worthy of praise, praiseworthy, commendable, estimable, plausible, meritorious.

Phrases: Lavish of praise; lost in admiration.

Interjections: Well done! good man! stout fellow! good show! atta-boy!

bravo! bravissimo! *euge!* that's the stuff! hear, hear!

932 DISAPPROBATION
Substantives: disapproval, dislike (867), blame, censure, reprobation, obloquy, dispraise, contumely, odium, disesteem, depreciation, detraction (934), condemnation, ostracism.

Reprobation, exprobration, insinuation, innuendo, animadversion, reflection, stricture, objection, exception, criticism, critique, correction, discommendation.

Satire, sneer, fling, gibe, skit, squib, quip, taunt, sarcasm, lampoon, cavil, pasquinade, recrimination, castigation.

Remonstrance, reprehension, reproof, admonition, expostulation, reproach, rebuke, reprimand, talking-to, telling-off.

Evil speaking, hard words, foul language, personalities, ribaldry, Billingsgate, unparliamentary language.

Upbraiding, abuse, invective, vituperation, scolding, wigging, dressing-down, objurgation, jaw, railing, jobation, nagging, reviling, contumely, execration (908).

A set-down, trimming, rating, slap, snub, frown, scowl, black look.

A lecture, curtain lecture, diatribe, jeremiad, tirade, philippic; clamour, outcry, hue and cry, hiss, hissing, sibilation cat-call.

Phrases: A rap on the knuckles; a slap in the face; a left-handed compliment.

Verbs: To disapprove, dislike (867), dispraise, find fault with, criticize, glance at, insinuate, cut up, carp at, cavil, point at, peck at, nibble at, object to, take exception to, animadvert upon, protest against, frown upon, bar.

To disparage, depreciate, deprecate, crab, knock, traduce, smear, speak ill of, decry, vilify, vilipend, defame, detract (934), revile, satirize, sneer, gibe, lampoon, inveigh against, write down, scalp.

To blame; to lay or cast blame upon, reflect upon, cast a slur upon, censure, pass censure on, impugn, show up, denounce, censure, brand, stigmatize, reprobate, improbate.

To reprehend, reprimand, admonish, remonstrate, expostulate, reprove, pull up, take up, set down, snub, twit, taunt, reproach, load with reproaches, rebuke, come down upon, sit on, pitch into, get on to, tell off, tick off.

To chide, scold, wig, rate, objurgate, upbraid, vituperate, recriminate, anathematize, abuse, call names, exclaim against, jaw, mob, trounce, trim, rail at, nag, nag at, bark at, blackguard, revile, ballyrag, rag, natter, blow up, roast, lecture; castigate, chastise, correct, lash, flay; to fulminate against, fall foul of.

To cry out against, cry down, run down, clamour, hiss, hoot; to accuse (938), to find guilty, ostracize, blacklist, blackball.

To scandalize, shock, revolt, incur blame, excite disapprobation.

Phrases: To set one's face against; to shake the head at; to take a poor or dim view of; to view with dark or jaundiced eyes; to pick holes in; to give a thing the bird; to damn with faint praise; to pluck a crow with; to have a fling at; to read a lecture; to put on the carpet (or mat); to take to task; to bring to book; to haul over the coals; to tear one off a strip; to shoot down in flames; to pull to pieces; to cut up; to cast in one's teeth; to abuse like a pickpocket; to speak or look daggers; to rail in good set terms; to give it one hot; to throw mud; to give a person the rough side of one's tongue.

To forfeit the good opinion of; to catch it; to be under a cloud; to carry the can; to stand corrected.

Adjectives: Disapproving, disparaging, etc., condemnatory, damnatory,

denunciatory, reproachful, abusive, objurgatory, clamorous, vituperative, dyslogistic.

Censorious, critical, carping, satirical, sarcastic, sardonic, cynical, dry, hypercritical, captious; sharp, cutting, mordant, biting, withering, trenchant, caustic, severe, scathing; squeamish, fastidious, strait-laced (868).

Disapproved, chid, unapproved, blown upon, unblest, unlamented, unbewailed.

Blameworthy, uncommendable, exceptionable (649, 945).

Phrases: Hard upon one; weighed in the balance and found wanting; not to be thought of.

Interjections: Bad show! shame!

933 FLATTERY

Substantives: adulation, sycophancy, blandishment, cajolery, fawning, wheedling, coaxing, flunkeyism, toadeating, toadyism, tuft-hunting, backscratching, blandiloquence, schmalz.

Incense, honeyed words, flummery, soft sawder, soft soap, butter, applesauce, blarney, malarkey; mouth-honour, lip-service.

Verbs: To flatter, wheedle, cajole, fawn upon, coax (615), humour, gloze, butter, toady, sugar, bespatter, beslaver, earwig, jolly, flannel, truckle to, pander to, court, pay court to.

Phrases: To curry favour with; to lay it on thick; to lay it on with a trowel; to ingratiate oneself with; to fool to the top of one's bent.

Adjectives: Flattering, adulatory, mealy-mouthed, smooth, honeyed, candied, soapy, oily, unctuous, fairspoken, plausible, servile, sycophantic, fulsome; courtier-like.

934 DETRACTION

Substantives: obloquy, scurrility, scandal, vilification, smear, defamation, aspersion, traducement, slander, calumny, back-biting, criticism, slating, personality, evil-speaking, disparagement, depreciation (932).

Libel, lampoon, skit, squib, sarcasm.

Verbs: To detract, criticize, asperse, depreciate, derogate, disparage, cheapen, blow upon, bespatter, blacken, denigrate, defame, brand, malign, decry, vilify, vilipend, backbite, libel, slate, lampoon, traduce, slander, calumniate, run down, write down.

Phrases: To speak ill of one behind one's back; to damn with faint praise; to sell oneself short.

Adjectives: Detracting, disparaging, libellous, scurrilous, abusive, cynical (932), foul-tongued, foul-mouthed, slanderous, defamatory, calumnious, calumniatory.

935 FLATTERER

Substantives: adulator, eulogist, encomiast, white-washer, toady, sycophant, toad-eater, *prôneur,* touter, booster, *claqueur,* spaniel, backscratcher, flunkey, lick-spittle, pickthank, earwig, tuft-hunter, hanger-on, courtier, parasite, doer of dirty work, *âme damnée, Graeculus esuriens.*

936 DETRACTOR

Substantives: disapprover, critics, censor, caviller, carper, knocker, *frondeur,* defamer, backbiter, slanderer, traducer, libeller, calumniator, lampooner, satirist, candid friend, Thersites.

937 VINDICATION

Substantives: justification, exoneration, exculpation, acquittal, whitewashing.

Extenuation, palliation, mitigation, softening; extenuating circumstances.

Plea, excuse, apology, defence, gloss, varnish, salvo (617).

Vindicator, apologist, justifier, defender.

Verbs: To vindicate, justify, warrant, exculpate, acquit, clear, set right, exonerate, disculpate, whitewash.

To extenuate, palliate, excuse, soften, apologize, varnish, slur, gloze, gloss over, bolster up.

To plead, advocate, defend, stand up for, stick up for, speak for, make good, bear out, say in defence, contend for.

Phrases: To put in a good word for; to plead the cause of; to put a good face upon; to keep in countenance; to make allowance for.

Adjectives: Vindicatory, vindicative, palliative, exculpatory; vindicating, etc.

Excusable, defensible, pardonable, venial, specious, plausible, justifiable, warrantable.

Phrases: *'Honi soit qui mal y pense'; qui s'excuse s'accuse.*

938 ACCUSATION

Substantives: charge, imputation, inculpation, exprobration, delation, crimination, recrimination, invective, jeremiad (932).

Denunciation, denouncement, challenge, indictment, libel, delation, citation, arraignment, impeachment, appeachment, bill of indictment, true bill, condemnation (971), scandal (934), *scandalum magnatum.*

Accuser, prosecutor, plaintiff, pursuer, informer, appellant, complainant.

Accused, defendant, prisoner, panel, respondent.

Phrases: The gravamen of a charge; *argumentum ad hominem.*

Verbs: To accuse, charge, tax, impute, twit, taunt with, slur, reproach, brand with, stigmatize, criminate, incriminate, inculpate (932), implicate, saddle with.

To inform against; to indict, denounce, arraign, impeach, challenge, show up, pull up, cite, prosecute, summon.

Phrases: To lay to one's door; to lay to one's charge; bring home to; to call to account; to bring to book; to take to task; to trump up a charge; to brand with reproach.

Adjectives: Accusing, etc., accusatory, accusative, imputative, denunciatory, criminative, criminatory, incriminatory, accusable, imputable.

Indefensible, inexcusable, unpardonable, unjustifiable (945).

939 PROBITY

Substantives: integrity, uprightness, honesty, virtue (944), rectitude, faith, good faith, bona fides, fairness, honour, fair play, justice, principle, constancy, fidelity, incorruptibility.

Trustworthiness, trustiness, reliability, dependableness, grace, uncorruptedness, impartiality, equity, candour, veracity (545), straightforwardness, truth, equitableness, singleness of heart.

Conscientiousness, punctiliousness, nicety, scrupulosity, delicacy, sense of decency, strictness, punctuality.

Dignity, respectability, reputableness (873).

A man of honour, a gentleman, a man of his word, a sportsman, white man, trump, brick, *preux chevalier*.

Phrases: The court of honour; a fair field and no favour; 'a verray parfit gentil knight.'

Verbs: To be honourable, etc.; to keep one's word, to give and take, to deal honourably, squarely, impartially, fairly.

Phrases: To hit straight from the shoulder; to play the game.

Adjectives: Upright, honest, virtuous (944), honourable, fair, right, just, equitable, impartial, even-handed, square, constant, faithful, loyal, staunch, straight.

Trustworthy, trusty, reliable, dependable, tried, incorruptible, straightforward, ingenuous (703),

frank, open-hearted, candid.

Conscientious, tender-conscienced, high-principled, high-minded, high-toned, scrupulous, strict, nice, punctilious, correct, punctual, inviolable, inviolate, unviolated, unbroken, unbetrayed.

Chivalrous, gentlemanlike, respectable, unbought, unbribed, unstained, stainless, untarnished, unsullied, untainted, unperjured, innocent (946).

Phrases: Jealous of honour; as good as one's word; true to one's colours; *sans peur et sans reproche; integer vitae scelerisque purus.*

Adverbs: Honourably, etc., bona fide; on the square; on the up and up.

940 IMPROBITY

Substantives: wickedness (945), bad faith, unfairness, infidelity, faithlessness, want of faith, dishonesty, disloyalty, falseness, falsity, one-sidedness, disingenuousness, shabbiness, littleness, meanness, caddishness, baseness, villainy, roguery, rascality, vileness, abjectness, turpitude, unreliability, untrustworthiness, insidiousness, knavery, knavishness, fraud (545), falsehood (544), shenanigans.

Disgrace, ignominy, infamy, tarnish, blot, stain, spot, slur, pollution, derogation, degradation (874).

Perfidy, perfidiousness, treason, high treason, perjury, apostasy (607), backsliding, breach of faith, defection, disloyalty, disaffection, foul play, sharp practice, graft, double-dealing, betrayal, treacherousness, treachery.

Phrases: The kiss of Judas; divided allegiance; Punic faith.

Verbs: To be of bad faith, dishonest, etc.; to play false, break one's word or faith, betray, forswear, shuffle (545).

To disgrace oneself, derogate, stoop, demean oneself, lose caste, dishonour oneself, sneak, crawl, grovel.

Phrases: To seal one's infamy; to sell oneself; to go over to the enemy.

Adjectives: Dishonest, unfair, one-sided, fraudulent (545), bent, knavish, wicked (945), false, faithless, unfaithful, foul, disingenuous, trothless, trustless, untrustworthy, unreliable, slippery, double-faced, double-tongued, crooked, tortuous, unscrupulous, insidious, treacherous, perfidious, false-hearted, perjured, rascally.

Base, vile, grovelling, dirty, scurvy, scabby, low, low-down, abject, shabby, caddish, mean, paltry, pitiful, inglorious, scrubby, beggarly, putrid, unworthy, disgraceful, dishonourable, derogatory, low-thoughted, disreputable, unhandsome, unbecoming (925), unbefitting, ungentlemanly, unmanly, unwomanly, undignified, base-minded, recreant, low-minded, blackguard, pettifogging, underhand, underhanded, unsportsmanlike.

Phrases: Lost to shame; dead to honour.

Adverbs: Dishonestly, etc., *mala fide,* on the crook.

941 KNAVE
Substantives: bad man (949), rogue, rascal, scoundrel, villain, spiv, sharper, shyster, blackleg, scab, trimmer, time-server, timist, turncoat, badmash, Vicar of Bray, Judas (607).

Apostate, renegade, pervert, black sheep, traitor, arch-traitor, quisling, fifth columnist, deviationist, betrayer, recreant, miscreant, cullion, outcast, mean wretch, slubberdegullion, snake in the grass, wolf in sheep's clothing.

942 UNSELFISHNESS
Substantives: selflessness, disinterestedness, generosity, high-mindedness, nobleness, elevation, liberality, greatness, loftiness, exaltation, magnanimity, chivalry, chivalrous spirit, heroism, sublimity, altruism, self-forgetfulness, unworldliness.

Self-denial, self-abnegation, self-sacrifice, self-restraint, self-control, devotion, stoicism.

Phrases: To put oneself in the background, in the place of others; to do as one would be done by.

Adjectives: Unselfish, selfless, self-forgetful, handsome, generous, liberal, noble, princely, great, high, high-minded, elevated, lofty, exalted, spirited, stoical, self-denying, self-sacrificing, self-devoted, magnanimous, chivalrous, heroic, sublime, unworldly.

Unbought, unbribed, pure, uncorrupted, incorruptible.

Adverb: *En prince.*

943 SELFISHNESS
Substantives: egotism, egoism, self-regard, self-love, self-indulgence, worldliness, worldly-mindedness, earthly-mindedness, self-interest, opportunism.

Illiberality, meanness, baseness.

A time-server, tuft-hunter, fortune-hunter, gold-digger, jobber, worldling, self-seeker, opportunist, hog, road-hog.

Phrase: A dog in the manger.

Verbs: To be selfish, etc., to indulge oneself, coddle oneself.

Phrases: To look after one's own interest; to take care of number one; to have an eye for the main chance.

Adjectives: Selfish, egotistical, egoistical, self-indulgent, apolaustic, self-regarding, self-centred, illiberal, self-seeking, mercenary, venal, mean, ungenerous, interested.

Worldly, earthly, mundane, time-serving, worldly-minded.

Phrases: To serve one's private ends; from interested motives; charity begins at home; I'm all right, Jack.

944 VIRTUE
Substantives: virtuousness, goodness, righteousness, morals, morality (926), rectitude, correctness, dutifulness, conscientiousness, integrity, probity

(939), uprightness, nobleness, nobility; innocence (946).

Merit, worth, worthiness, desert, excellence, credit, self-control, self-conquest, self-government, self-respect.

Well-doing, good actions, good behaviour, a well-spent life.

Verbs: To be virtuous, etc.; to act well; to do, fulfil, perform, or discharge one's duty, to acquit oneself well, to practise virtue; to command or master one's passions (926).

Phrases: To have one's heart in the right place; to keep in the right path; to fight the good fight; to set an example; to be on one's good behaviour.

Adjectives: Virtuous, good, innocent (946), meritorious, deserving, worthy, correct, dutiful, duteous (926), moral, ethical, righteous, right-minded, (939), laudable, well-intentioned, creditable, commendable, praiseworthy, excellent, admirable, sterling, pure, noble, well-conducted, well-behaved.

Exemplary, matchless, peerless, saintly, saint-like, heaven-born, angelic, seraphic, godlike.

Phrase: *Mens sibi conscia recti.*

Adverb: Virtuously, etc.

945 VICE

Substantives: evildoing, wrongdoing, wickedness, sin, iniquity, unrighteousness, demerit, unworthiness, worthlessness, badness.

Immorality, impropriety, indecorum, laxity, looseness of morals, want of principle, obliquity, backsliding, recidivism, gracelessness, infamy, demoralization, pravity, depravity, depravation, obduracy, hardness of heart, brutality (907), corruption, pollution, dissoluteness, debauchery, grossness, baseness, knavery, roguery, rascality, villainy (940), profligacy, abandonment, flagrancy, atrocity, devilry (or deviltry), criminality, guilt (947).

Infirmity, weakness, feebleness, frailty, imperfection, error, weak side or point, blind side, foible, failing, failure, defect, deficiency, indiscretion, peccability.

Phrases: The cloven hoof; the old Adam; the lowest dregs of vice; a sink of iniquity; the primrose path.

Verbs: To be vicious, etc.; to sin, commit sin, do amiss, misdo, err, transgress, go astray, misdemean or misconduct oneself, misbehave; to fall, lapse, slip, trip, offend, trespass.

To render vicious, etc., to demoralize, corrupt, seduce, debauch, debase, vitiate.

Phrases: To deviate from the line of duty or from the paths of virtue, rectitude, etc.; to blot one's copybook; to hug a sin or fault; to sow one's wild oats.

Adjectives: Vicious, bad, sinful, wicked, evil, evil-minded, immoral, iniquitous, unprincipled, demoralized, unconscionable, worthless, unworthy, good for nothing, graceless, heartless, virtueless, undutiful, unrighteous, unmoral, amoral, guilty (947).

Wrong, culpable, naughty, incorrect, indictable, criminal, dissolute, debauched, disorderly, raffish, corrupt, profligate, depraved, degenerate, abandoned, graceless, shameless, recreant, villainous, sunk, lost, obdurate, reprobate, incorrigible, irreclaimable, ill-conditioned.

Weak, frail, lax, infirm, spineless, invertebrate, imperfect, indiscreet, erring, transgressing, sinning, etc., peccable, peccant.

Blamable, reprehensible, blameworthy, uncommendable, discreditable, disreputable, shady, exceptionable.

Indecorous, unseemly, improper, sinister, base, ignoble, scurvy, foul, gross, vile, black, felonious, nefarious, scandalous, infamous, villainous, heinous, grave, flagrant, flagitious, atrocious, satanic, satanical, diabolic,. diabolical, hellish, infernal, stygian, fiendlike, fiendish, devilish, miscreated, misbegotten, hell-born, demoniacal.

Unpardonable, unforgivable, indefensible, inexcusable, irremissible, inexpiable.

Phrases: Past praying for; of the deepest dye; not having a word to say for oneself; weighed in the balance and found wanting; *in flagrante delicto.*

Adverbs: Wrongly, etc.; without excuse, too bad.

946 INNOCENCE
Substantives: guiltlessness, harmlessness, innocuousness, incorruption, impeccability, inerrability, blamelessness, sinlessness.

A newborn babe, lamb, dove.

Phrases: Clean hands; a clear conscience.

Verbs: To be innocent, etc.

Adjectives: Innocent, guiltless, not guilty, faultless, sinless, clear, spotless, stainless, immaculate, unspotted, innocuous, unblemished, untarnished, unsullied, undefiled.

Inculpable, unblamed, blameless, unblamable, clean-handed, irreproachable, unreproached, unimpeachable, unimpeached, unexceptionable, inerrable, unerring.

Harmless, inoffensive, unoffending, dovelike, lamblike, pure, uncorrupted, undefiled, undepraved, undebauched, chaste, unhardened, unsophisticated, unreproved.

Phrases: Innocent as an unborn babe; in the clear; above suspicion; more sinned against than sinning.

Adverbs: Innocently, etc.

947 GUILT
Substantives: sin, guiltiness, culpability, criminality, criminousness, sinfulness.

Misconduct, misbehaviour, misdoing, malpractice, malefaction, malfeasance, misprision, dereliction, *corpus delicti.*

Indiscretion, peccadillo, lapse, slip, trip, *faux pas,* fault, error, flaw, blot, omission, failure.

Misdeed, offence, trespass, transgression, misdemeanour, delinquency, felony, sin, crime, enormity, atrocity.

Science of crime, criminology.

Phrases: Besetting sin; deviation from rectitude; a deed without a name.

948 GOOD MAN
Substantives: trump, brick, worthy, example, pattern, mirror, model, paragon, phoenix (650), superman, hero, demigod, seraph, angel, saint (987).

A good fellow, good sort, sportsman, white man.

Phrases: One of the best; one in a million; the salt of the earth.

949 BAD MAN
Substantives: wrong-doer, evildoer, culprit, delinquent, criminal, recidivist, malefactor, outlaw, felon, convict, lag, outcast, sinner (988).

Knave, rogue, rascal, scoundrel, spiv, scamp, scapegrace, black sheep, scallywag, spalpeen, varlet, *vaurien,* blighter, rotter, good-for-nothing, twerp, heel, jerk, creep, goon, son of a gun, dastard, blackguard, sweep, loose fish, bad egg, bad lot, hard case, lost soul, vagabond, bum, *mauvais sujet,* cur, sad dog, rip, rascallion, rapscallion, slubberdegullion, cullion, roisterer.

Mohock, rowdy, hooligan, larrikin, teddy boy, apache, thug, reprobate, *roué,* recreant, jail-bird, crook, tough, rough, roughneck, gangster, gunman, hoodlum, yegg, villain, ruffian, miscreant, caitiff, wretch, *âme damnée,* castaway, monster, Jonathan Wilde, Jack Sheppard, Lazarillo de Tormes, Scapin (941).

Cur, dog, hound, skunk, swine, rat,

viper, serpent, cockatrice, basilisk, reptile, urchin, tiger, imp, demon, devil, devil incarnate, Mephistopheles (978), hellhound, son of Belial, cut-throat, *particeps criminis,* incendiary.

Bad woman, hellcat, hellhag, bitch, witch, hag, harridan, trollop, jade, drab, hussy, minx, Jezebel.

Riff-raff, rabble, ragtag and bobtail, *canaille.*

Phrases: A fiend in human shape; scum of the earth; poor white trash.

Interjection: Sirrah!

950 PENITENCE

Substantives: contrition, compunction, regret (833), repentance, remorse.

Self-reproach, self-reproof, self-accusation, self-condemnation.

Confession, acknowledgment, shrift, apology, recantation (607).

A penitent, prodigal, Magdalen.

Phrases: The stool of repentance; the cutty-stool; sackcloth and ashes; qualms or prickings of conscience; a sadder and a wiser man.

Verbs: To repent, regret, rue, repine, deplore, be sorry for.

To confess (529), acknowledge, apologize, shrive oneself, humble oneself, reclaim, turn from sin.

Phrases: To have a weight on one's mind; to plead guilty; to sing small; to cry *peccavi;* to eat humble pie; to turn over a new leaf; to stand in a white sheet.

Adjectives: Penitent, repentant, contrite, repenting, remorseful, regretful, sorry, compunctious, self-reproachful, self-accusing, self-convicted, conscience-stricken, conscience-smitten.

Not hardened, unhardened, reclaimed.

Adverb: *Meâ culpâ.*

951 IMPENITENCE

Substantives: obduracy, recusance, irrepentance, hardness of heart, a seared conscience, induration.

Verbs: To be impenitent, etc.; to steel or harden the heart.

Phrases: To make no sign; to die game.

Adjectives: Impenitent, uncontrite, obdurate, hard, callous, unfeeling, hardened, seared, recusant, relentless, unrepentant, graceless, shiftless, lost, uncorrigible, irreclaimable, irredeemable, unatoned, unreclaimed, unreformed, unrepented.

952 ATONEMENT

Substantives: reparation, compromise, composition, compensation (30), quittance, quits; propitiation, expiation, redemption, conciliation.

Amends, *amende honorable,* apology, satisfaction, peace-offering, olive branch, sin-offering, scapegoat, sacrifice, burnt-offering.

Penance, fasting, maceration, flagellation, sackcloth and ashes, white sheet, lustration, purgation, purgatory.

Verbs: To atone, expiate, propitiate, make amends, redeem, make good, repair, ransom, absolve, do penance, apologize, purge, shrive, give satisfaction.

Phrases: To purge one's offence; to pay the forfeit or penalty.

Adjectives: Propitiatory, piacular, expiatory, expiational.

953 TEMPERANCE

Substantives: moderation, forbearance, abnegation, self-denial, self-conquest, self-control, self-command, self-discipline, sobriety, frugality, vegetarianism.

Abstinence, abstemiousness, teetotalism, prohibition, asceticism (955), gymnosophy, system of Pythagoras.

An abstainer, ascetic, gymnosophist, vegetarian, teetotaller, Pythagorean.

Phrases: The simple life; the blue ribbon.

Verbs: To be temperate, etc.; to abstain, forbear, refrain, deny oneself, spare.

Phrases: To sign the pledge; to go on the water wagon.

Adjectives: Temperate, moderate, sober, frugal, sparing, abstemious, abstinent, Pythagorean, vegetarian, teetotal, dry.

954 INTEMPERANCE

Substantives: excess, immoderation, unrestraint; epicurism, epicureanism, hedonism, sensuality, luxury, luxuriousness, animalism, carnality, effeminacy; the lap of pleasure or luxury; indulgence, self-indulgence, voluptuousness; drunkenness (959).

Dissipation, licentiousness, debauchery, dissolutenesss, crapulence, brutishness.

Revels, revelry, carousal, orgy, spree, jag, toot, drinking bout, debauch, jollification, saturnalia.

A sensualist, epicure, epicurean, voluptuary, rake, rip, *roué*, sybarite, drug addict, dope fiend, hophead.

Phrases: The Circean cup; a fast life; wine, women, and song.

Verbs: To be intemperate, sensual, etc.

To indulge, exceed, revel, dissipate; give a loose to indulgence, live hard.

To debauch, pander to, sensualize, animalize, brutalize.

Phrases: To wallow in voluptuousness, luxury, etc.; to plunge into dissipation; to paint the town red; to live on the fat of the land; to sow one's wild oats.

Adjectives: Intemperate, sensual, pampered, self-indulgent, fleshly, inabstinent, licentious, wild, dissolute, dissipated, fast, rakish, debauched, brutish, crapulous, hedonistic, epicurean, sybaritical, Sardanapalian, voluptuous, apolaustic, orgiastic, swinish, piggish, hoggish; indulged, pampered.

955 ASCETICISM

Substantives: austerity, puritanism, mortification, maceration, sackcloth and ashes, flagellation, martyrdom, yoga.

An ascetic, anchoret, yogi, martyr; a recluse, hermit (893); puritan, Cynic.

Adjectives: Ascetic, ascetical, austere, puritanical.

956 FASTING

Substantives: fast, spare diet, meagre diet, Lent, Quadragesima, a lenten entertainment, famishment, starvation, banian day, Ramadan.

Phrases: A Barmecide feast; a hunger strike; short commons.

Verbs: To fast, starve, clem, famish.

Phrases: To dine with Duke Humphrey; to perish with hunger.

Adjectives: Fasting, etc., unfed, famished, starved; lenten, Quadragesimal.

957 GLUTTONY

Substantives: epicurism, greediness, good cheer, high living, edacity, voracity, gulosity, crapulence, hoggishness, piggishness.

Gastronomy; feast, banquet, good cheer, blow-out.

A glutton, epicure, *bon vivant*, cormorant, gourmand, gourmet, bellygod, pig, hog, Apicius, gastronome, gastronomer, gastronomist.

Verbs: To gormandize, gorge, cram, stuff, guzzle, bolt, devour, gobble up, pamper.

Phrases: To eat out of house and home; to have the stomach of an ostrich; to play a good knife and fork.

Adjectives: Gluttonous, greedy, gormandizing, edacious, voracious, crapulent, swinish, piggish, hoggish, pampered, overfed; gastronomical.

958 SOBRIETY

Substantives: teetotalism, total abstinence, temperance (953).

355

Compulsory sobriety, prohibition.

A water-drinker, teetotaller, abstainer, total abstainer, blue-ribbonite, Rechabite, Band of Hope; prohibitionist.

Verbs: To abstain, to take the pledge.

Adjectives: Sober, abstemious, teetotal.

Phrases: Sober as a judge; on the water wagon.

959 DRUNKENNESS

Substantives: insobriety, ebriety, inebriety, inebriation, intoxication, ebriosity, bibacity, drinking, toping, tippling, sottishness, tipsiness, bacchanals, compotation, intemperance (954); dipsomania, alcoholism, delirium tremens, DT

A drunkard, sot, toper, tippler, hard drinker, winebag, winebibber, dramdrinker, soak, soaker, sponge, tun, tosspot, pub-crawler, reveller, carouser, Bacchanal, Bacchanalian, Bacchant, a devotee to Bacchus; a dipsomaniac.

Drink, hard drinks, intoxicant, alcohol, liquor, spirits, booze, blue ruin, grog, cocktail, highball, dram, peg, stirrup-cup, doch-an-doris.

Phrases: The flowing bowl; one for the road.

Verbs: To drink, tipple, tope, booze; to guzzle, swill, soak, swig, get or be drunk, etc.; to take to drinking, drink hard, drink deep.

To inebriate, intoxiate, fuddle.

Phrases: To liquor up; to wet one's whistle; to crack a bottle; to have a bucket; to look on the wine when it is red; to take a drop too much; to drink like a fish; to splice the main-brace; to crook or lift the elbow.

Adjectives: Drunk, drunken, tipsy, intoxicated, in liquor, inebriated, fuddled, mellow, boozy, high, fou, boiled, tiddly, stinko, blotto, lit up, groggy, top-heavy, pot-valiant, glorious, overcome, overtaken, elevated, whiffled, sozzled, screwed, corned, raddled, sewed up, lushy, squiffy, muddled, oiled, canned, muzzy, maudlin, dead-drunk, disguised, tight, beery.

Bibacious, bibulous, sottish, Bacchanal, Bacchanalian.

Phrases: In one's cups; *inter pocula*; the worse for liquor; half-seas-over; three sheets in the wind; under the table; drunk as a piper, as a fiddle, as a lord, as an owl, as David's sow; stewed to the eyebrows; pickled to the gills; one over the eight.

Interjections: Cheers! here's to you! down the hatch! mud in your eye! skin off your nose! *prosit! slainte! skoal!*

960 PURITY

Substantives: modesty, decency, decorum, delicacy, continence, chastity, honesty, pudency, virtue, virginity.

A virgin, maiden, maid, vestal; Joseph, Hippolytus, Lucrece.

Phrase: The white flower of a blameless life.

Adjectives: Pure, immaculate, undefiled, modest, delicate, decent, decorous.

Chaste, continent, honest, virtuous; Platonic.

961 IMPURITY

Substantives: immodesty, grossness, coarseness, indelicacy, impropriety, impudicity, indecency, obscenity, obsceneness, ribaldry, smut, smuttiness, bawdiness, bawdry, *double entendre*, equivoque, pornography.

Concupiscence, lust, carnality, flesh, salacity, lewdness, prurience, lechery, lasciviousness, voluptuousness, lubricity.

Incontinence, intrigue, gallantry, debauchery, libertinism, libertinage, fornication, liaison, wenching, whoring, whoredom, concubinage, hetaerism.

Seduction, defloration, violation, rape, adultery, defilement, *crim. con.*, incest, harlotry, stupration, procuration, white-slave traffic.

A seraglio, harem, brothel, bagnio, stew, bawdy-house, disorderly house, house of ill fame, red lamp district, Yoshiwara.

Phrases: The morals of the farmyard; the oldest profession.

Verbs: To intrigue, debauch, defile, seduce, abuse, violate, force, rape, ravish, deflower, ruin, prostitute, procure.

Adjectives: Impure, immodest, indecorous, indelicate, unclean, unmentionable, unseemly, improper, suggestive, indecent, loose, coarse, gross, broad, equivocal, risky, *risqué,* high-seasoned, nasty, smutty, scabrous, ribald, obscene, bawdy, lewd, pornographic, Rabelaisian, Aristophanic.

Concupiscent, prurient, lickerish, rampant, carnal, fleshy, sensual, lustful, lascivious, lecherous, libidinous, goatish, erotic, ruttish, salacious.

Unchaste, light, wanton, debauched, dissolute, carnal-minded, licentious, frail, riggish, incontinent, meretricious, rakish, gallant, dissipated, adulterous, incestous, bestial.

Phrases: On the streets; of easy virtue; no better than she should be.

Near the knuckle; not for ears polite; four-letter words.

962 A LIBERTINE

Substantives: voluptuary, man of pleasure, sensualist (954), rip, rake, *roué,* debauchee, loose fish, intriguant, gallant, seducer, fornicator, lecher, satyr, whoremonger, *paillard,* adulterer, a gay deceiver, Lothario, Don Juan, Bluebeard.

A prostitute, courtesan, tart, call-girl, strumpet, harlot, whore, punk, *fille de joie, cocotte, lorette,* woman of the town, streetwalker, pick-up, piece, the frail sisterhood, the *demi-monde,* soiled dove, demirep, wench, trollop, trull, baggage, hussy, drab, jade, quean, slut, harridan, an unfortunate, Jezebel, Messalina, Delilah, Thais, Aspasia, Phryne, Lais.

Concubine, odalisque, mistress, doxy, kept woman, *petite amie,* hetaera.

Pimp, pander, ponce, *souteneur,* bawd, procuress.

963 LEGALITY

Substantives: legitimateness, legitimacy, justice (922).

Law, legislature, code, constitution, pandect, enactment, edict, statute, charter, rule, order, ordinance, injunction, institution, precept, regulation, by-law, decree, firman, bull, ukase, decretal.

Legal process, form, formula, formality, rite.

Science of law, jurisprudence, legislation, codification.

Equity, common law, *lex non scripta,* unwritten law, law of nations, international law, *jus gentium,* civil law, canon law, statute law, *lex mercatoria,* ecclesiastical law.

Phrase: The arm of the law.

Verbs: To legalize, enact, ordain, enjoin, prescribe, order, decree (741); to pass a law, issue an edict or decree; to legislate, codify.

Adjectives: Legal, lawful, according to law, legitimate, constitutional, chartered, vested.

Legislative, statutable, statutory.

Adverbs: Legally, etc.

Phrases: In the eye of the law; *de jure.*

964 ILLEGALITY

Substantives: lawlessness, arbitrariness, antinomy, violence, brute force, despotism, outlawry.

Mob law, lynch law, club law, martial law.

Camorra, Ku Klux Klan, Judge Lynch.

Informality, unlawfulness, illegitimacy, bastardy, the baton or bar sinister.

Smuggling, poaching, bootlegging; black market, grey market.

Verbs: To smuggle, run, poach.

To invalidate, annual, illegalize, abrogate, void, nullify, quash.

Phrases: To take the law into one's own hands; to set the law at defiance; to drive a coach and six through the law.

Adjectives: Illegal, unlawful, illicit, illegitimate, injudicial, unofficial, lawless, unauthorized, unchartered, unconstitutional, informal, contraband, hot.

Arbitrary, extrajudicial, despotic, autocratic, irresponsible, unanswerable, unaccountable.

Adverbs: Illegally, with a high hand.

965 JURISDICTION

Substantives: judicature, soc (or soke), administration of justice.

Inquisition, inquest, coroner's inquest.

The executive, municipality, corporation, magistracy, police, police force, constabulary, posse, *gendarmerie.*

Lord lieutenant, sheriff, sheriff-substitute, deputy, officer, constable, policeman, state trooper, traffic warden, bailiff, tipstaff, bum-bailiff, catchpoll, beadle; *gendarme,* lictor, macebearer.

Adjectives: Juridical, judicial, forensic, municipal, executive, administrative, inquisitorial, causidical.

Phrases: *Coram judice; ex cathedra.*

966 TRIBUNAL

Substantives: court, guild, board, bench, judicatory, senate-house, court of law, court of justice, criminal court, police-court, Court of Chancery, of King's Bench; Probate, Divorce, Admiralty Court, Judicial Committee of the Privy Council, US Supreme

Court, durbar.

City hall, town hall, theatre, bar, dock, forum, hustings, drum-head, wool-sack, jury-box, witness-box.

Assize, sessions, quarter sessions, petty sessions, eyre, court-martial, ward-mote.

967 JUDGE

Substantives: justice, justiciar, justiciary, chancellor, magistrate, beak, recorder, common serjeant, stipendiary, coroner, arbiter, arbitrator, umpire, referee, jury, Justice of the Peace, JP, Lord Chancellor, Lord Chief Justice, Master of the Rolls.

Mullah, ulema, mufti, cadi (or kadi), kavass.

Prosecutor, plaintiff, accuser, appellant, pursuer.

Defendant, panel, prisoner, the accused.

Verbs: Judge, try, pass judgment, give verdict.

968 LAWYER

Substantives: the bar, advocate, counsellor, counsel, queen's or king's counsel, QC, KC, pleader, special pleader, conveyancer, bencher, proctor, civilian, barrister, barrister-at-law, jurist, jurisconsult, publicist, draughtsman, notary, notary public, scrivener, attorney, solicitor, legal adviser, writer to the signet, writer, marshal, pundit; pettifogger.

Phrases: The gentlemen of the long robe; the learned in the law; a limb of the law.

Verbs: To practise law, plead.

Phrases: To be called to the bar; to take silk.

969 LAWSUIT

Substantives: suit, action, case, cause, trial, litigation.

Denunciation, citation, arraignment, prosecution, indictment, impeachment, apprehension, arrest, committal, imprisonment (751).

Pleadings, writ, summons, sub-poena, plea, bill, affidavit, libel; answer, counterclaim, demurrer, rebutter, rejoinder, surrebutter, surrejoinder.

Verdict, sentence, judgment, finding, decree, arbitrament, adjudication, award, decision, precedent.
Verbs: To denounce, cite, apprehend, sue, writ, arraign, summons, prosecute, indict, contest, impeach, attach, distrain; to commit.

To try, hear a cause, sit in judgment.

To pronounce, find, judge, adjudge, sentence, give judgment; bring in a verdict; to doom, arbitrate, adjudicate, award, report.
Phrases: To go to law; to appeal to the law; to file a claim; to inform against; to lodge an information; to serve with a writ; to bring an action against; to bring to trial or the bar; to give in charge or custody; to throw into prison; to clap in jail.
Adjectives: Litigious, litigant, litigatory.
Adverbial phrases: *Sub judice; pendente lite.*

970 ACQUITTAL
Substantives: acquitment, absolution, exculpation, quietus, clearance, discharge, release, reprieve (918), respite, compurgation.

Exemption from punishment, impunity.
Verbs: To acquit, absolve, whitewash, extenuate, exculpate, exonerate, clear, assoil, discharge, release, reprieve, respite.
Adjectives: Acquitted, etc.

Uncondemned, unpunished, unchastised.

971 CONDEMNATION
Substantives: conviction, proscription, damnation, death-warrant.

Attainder, attainture, attaintment.

Verbs: To condemn, convict, cast, find guilty, proscribe, ban, outlaw, attaint, damn, doom, sentence, confiscate, sequestrate, non-suit.
Adjectives: Condemnatory, damnatory, condemned; self-convicted.

972 PUNISHMENT
Substantives: punition, chastisement, castigation, correction, chastening, discipline, infliction.

Retribution, requital (973), penalty (974), reckoning, Nemesis.

Imprisonment (751), transportation, exile (297), cucking-stool, ducking-stool, treadmill, crank, hulks, galleys, penal servitude, preventive detention.

A blow, slap, spank, skelp, swish, hit, knock, rap, thump, bang, buffet, stripe, stroke, cuff, clout, kick, whack, thwack, box, punch, pummel.

Beating, lash, flagellation, flogging, etc., dressing, lacing, tanning, knock-out, spiflication, bastinado, strappado, pillory (975), running the gauntlet, *coup de grâce, peine forte et dure.*

Execution, capital punishment, hanging, beheading, decollation, decapitation, electrocution, guillotine, garrotte, *auto da fé, noyade,* crucifixion, impalement, *hara-kiri,* martyrdom.
Verbs: To punish, chastise, castigate, chasten, correct, inflict punishment, pay, do for, sever out, pay out, visit upon, give it to, strafe, spiflicate.

To strike, hit, smite, knock, slap, flap, rap, bang, thwack, whack, thump, kick, punch, pelt, beat, buffet, thrash, swinge, pummel, clapper-claw, drub, trounce, baste, belabour, lace, strap, comb, lash, lick, whip, flog, scourge, knout, swish, spank, skelp, birch, tan, larrup, lay into, knock out, wallop, leather, flagellate, horsewhip, bastinado, lapidate, stone.

To execute, hang, behead, decapitate, decollate, electrocute, guillotine, garrotte, shoot, gibbet; to hang, draw, and quarter; break on the wheel;

crucify, impale, torture, flay, keelhaul; lynch.

To banish, exile, transport, deport, expel, drum out, disbar, disbench, unfrock.

To be hanged, etc., to be spread-eagled.

Phrases: To make an example of; to serve one out; to give it one; to dust one's jacket; to tweak or pull the nose; to box the ears; to beat to a jelly; to tar and feather; to give a black eye; to lay it on.

To come to the gallows; to swing for it; to go to the chair; to die in one's shoes.

Adjectives: Punishing, etc., punitory, punitive, inflictive, penal, disciplinary, castigatory, borstal.

Interjection: *A la lanterne!*

973 REWARD

Substantives: recompense, remuneration, meed, guerdon, premium, indemnity, indemnification, compensation, reparation, requital, retribution, quittance, hush-money, acknowledgment, amends, solatium, sop, atonement, redress, consideration, return, tribute, honorarium, perquisite, tip, vail; salvage.

Prize, purse, crown, laurel, bays, cross, medal, ribbon, decoration (877).

Verbs: To reward, recompense, repay, requite, recoup, remunerate, compensate, make amends, indemnify, atone, satisfy, acknowledge, acquit oneself.

Phrase: To get for one's pains.

Adjectives: Remunerative, munerary, compensatory, retributive, reparatory.

974 PENALTY

Substantives: punishment (972), pain, penance.

Fine, mulct, amercement, forfeit, forfeiture, escheat, damages, deodand, sequestration, confiscation.

Phrases: Pains and penalties; the devil to pay.

Verbs: To fine, mulct, amerce, sconce, confiscate, sequester, sequestrate, escheat, estreat.

975 SCOURGE

Substantives: rod, cane, stick, rattan, switch, ferule, birch, cudgel.

Whip, lash, strap, thong, knout, cowhide, cat, cat-o'-nine-tails, sjambok, rope's end.

Pillory, stocks, cangue, whipping-post, ducking-stool, triangle, wooden horse, boot, thumbscrew, rack, wheel, treadmill.

Stake, tree, block, scaffold, gallows, halter, bowstring, gibbet, axe, maiden, guillotine, garrotte, electric chair, hot squat, lethal chamber.

Executioner, hangman, electrocutioner, firing squad, headsman, Jack Ketch.

Section 5 – Religious Affections

976 DEITY

Substantives: Divinity, Godhead, Omnipotence, Omniscience, Providence.

Quality of being divine, divineness, divinity.

GOD, Lord, Jehovah, The Almighty; The Supreme Being; The First Cause, *Ens Entium*; The Author of all things, The Infinite, The Eternal, The All-powerful, The All-wise, The All-merciful, The All-holy.

Attributes and perfections, infinite power, wisdom, goodness, justice, mercy, omnipotence, omniscience, omnipresence, unity, immutability, holiness, glory, majesty, sovereignty, infinity, eternity.

The Trinity, The Holy Trinity, The Trinity in Unity, The Triune God.

GOD THE FATHER, The Maker, The Creator.

Functions: creation, preservation, divine government, theocracy, thearchy, providence; the ways, dispensations, visitations of Providence.

GOD THE SON, Christ, Jesus, The Messiah, The Anointed, The Saviour, The Redeemer, The Mediator, The Intercessor, The Advocate, The Judge, The Son of Man, The Lamb of God, The Word, The Logos, Emmanuel, The King of Kings and Lord of Lords, The King of Glory, The Prince of Peace, The Good Shepherd, The Way of Truth and Life, The Bread of Life, The Light of the World, The Sun of Righteousness, The Incarnation, the Word made Flesh.

Functions: salvation, redemption, atonement, propitiation, mediation, intercession, judgment.

GOD THE HOLY GHOST, The Holy Spirit, Paraclete, The Comforter, The Spirit of Truth, The Dove.

Functions: inspiration, unction, regeneration, sanctification, consolation.

Verbs: To create, uphold, preserve, govern.

To atone, redeem, save, propitiate, mediate.

To predestinate, elect, call, ordain, bless, justify, sanctify, glorify.

Adjectives: Almighty, all-powerful, omnipotent, omnipresent, omniscient, all-wise, holy, hallowed, sacred, divine, heavenly, celestial.

Superhuman, ghostly, spiritual, supernatural, theocratic.

977 ANGEL

Substantives: archangel.

The heavenly host; ministering spirits; the choir invisible.

Madonna, saint.

Seraphim, cherubim, thrones, principalities, powers, dominions.

Adjectives: Angelic, angelical, seraphic, cherubic, celestial, heavenly, saintly.

978 SATAN

Substantives: the Devil, Lucifer, Beelzebub, Belial, Mephistopheles, Mephisto, Abaddon, Apollyon, the Prince of the Devils.

His Satanic Majesty, the tempter, the evil one, the wicked one, the old Serpent, the Prince of darkness, the father of lies, the foul fiend, the archfiend, the common enemy, Old Harry, Old Nick, the Old Scratch, the Old Gentleman, Old Horny.

Diabolism, devilism, devilship; Satanism, the cloven hoof, the black mass.

Fallen angels, unclean spirits, devils, the powers of darkness, inhabitants of Pandemonium.

Adjectives: Satanic, diabolic, devilish.

979 GREAT SPIRIT

Substantives: deity, numen, god, goddess; Allah, Brahma, Vishnu, Siva, Krishna, Buddha, Mithra, Ormuzd, Isis, Osiris, Moloch, Baal, Asteroth.

Jupiter, Jove, Juno, Minerva, Apollo, Diana, Venus, Vulcan, Mars, Mercury, Neptune, Pluto; Zeus, Hera, Athena, Artemis, Aphrodite, Hephaestus, Ares, Hermes, Poseidon.

Odin or Woden, Frigga, Thor.

Good genius, demiurge, familiar; fairy, fay, sylph, peri, kelpie, nymph, nereid, dryad, hamadryad, naiad, merman, mermaid (341), undine; Oberon, Mab, Titania, Puck, Robin Goodfellow; the good folk, the little people.

Adjectives: Fairy, faery, fairy-like, sylph-like, sylphine.

Mythical, mythological, fabulous, legendary.

980 DEMON

Substantives: evil genius, fiend, unclean spirit, caco-demon, incubus, succubus, succuba, flibbertigibbet; fury, harpy, siren, faun, satyr, Eblis, Demogorgon.

Vampire, werewolf, ghoul, afreet (or afrite), ogre, ogress, gnome, djinn, imp, genie (or jinnee), lamia, bogy, bogle, nix, nixie, kobold, brownie, leprechaun, elf, pixy, troll, sprite, gremlin, spandule.

Supernatural appearance, ghost, spectre, apparition, shade, vision, goblin, hobgoblin, banshee, spook, wraith, *revenant, doppelgänger,* poltergeist.

Phrase: The powers of darkness.

Adjectives: Supernatural, ghostly, apparitional, elfin, elfish, unearthly, uncanny, eerie, weird, spectral, spookish, spooky, ghostlike, fiendish, fiendlike, impish, demoniacal, haunted.

981 HEAVEN

Substantives: the kingdom of heaven; the kingdom of God, the heavenly kingdom; the throne of God, the presence of God.

Paradise, Eden, Zion, the Celestial City, the New Jerusalem, the abode of the blessed; celestial bliss or glory.

Mythological heaven, Olympus; mythological paradise, Elysium, the Elysian Fields, the garden of the Hesperides; Valhalla, Nirvana, happy hunting grounds.

Translation, apotheosis, deification, resurrection.

Adjectives: Heavenly, celestial, supernal, unearthly, from on high, paradisaical, paradisical, paradisial, Elysian, beatific.

982 HELL

Substantives: bottomless pit, place of torment; the habitation of fallen angels, Pandemonium, Domdaniel.

Hell-fire, everlasting fire, the lake of fire and brimstone.

Purgatory, limbo, abyss.

Mythological hell, Tartarus, Hades, Pluto, Avernus, Styx, the Stygian creek, Acheron, Cocytus, Phlegethon, Lethe, Erebus, Tophet, Gehenna.

Phrases: The fire that is never quenched; the worm that never dies.

The infernal or nether regions; the shades below; the realms of Pluto.

Adjectives: Hellish, infernal, stygian, Tartarean, Plutonian.

983 THEOLOGY (natural and revealed)

Substantives: divinity, religion, monotheism, hagiology, hagiography, hierography, theosophy; comparative religion, comparative mythology.

Creed, belief, faith, persuasion, tenet, dogma, articles of faith, declaration, profession or confession of faith.

Theologian, divine, schoolman, the Fathers.

Adjectives: Theological, religious, patristic, ecumenical, denominational, sectarian.

983a CHRISTIAN RELIGION

Substantives: true faith, Christianity, Christianism, Christendom, Catholicism, orthodoxy.

A Christian, a true believer.

The Church, the Catholic or Universal Church, the Church of Christ, the body of Christ, the Church Militant.

The members of Christ, the disciples or followers of Christ, the Christian community.

Protestant, Church of England, Anglican, Church of Scotland; Church of Rome, Roman Catholic; Greek Church, Orthodox Church.

Adjectives: Christian, Catholic, orthodox, sound, faithful, true, scriptural, canonical, schismless.

984 OTHER RELIGIONS

Substantives: paganism, heathenism, ethnicism, polytheism, ditheism, tritheism, pantheism, hylotheism.

Judaism, Gentilism, Mohammedanism (or Mahometanism), Islam, Buddhism, Hinduism, Taoism, Confucianism, Shintoism, Sufism.

A pagan, heathen, paynim, infidel, unbeliever, pantheist, etc.

A Jew, Mohammedan (or Mahometan), Mussulman, Moslem, Brahmin (or Brahman), Parsee, Sufi, Magus, Gymnosophist, Fire-worshipper, Buddhist, Rosicrucian.

Adjectives: Pagan, heaten, ethnic, gentile, pantheistic, etc.

Judaical, Mohammedan, Brahminical, Buddhistic.

984a HERESY

Substantives: heterodoxy, false doctrine, schism, schismaticalness, latitudinarianism, recusancy, apostasy, backsliding, quietism, adiaphorism.

Bigotry, fanaticism, iconoclasm, bibliolatry, fundamentalism, puritanism, sabbatarianism.

Dissent, sectarianism, nonconformity, secularism, syncretism.

A heretic, deist, unitarian.

Adjectives: Heretical, heterodox, unorthodox, unscriptural, uncanonical, schismatic, sectarian, nonconformist, recusant, latitudinarian.

Credulous, bigoted, fanatical, idolatrous, superstitious, visionary.

985 CHRISTIAN REVELATION

Substantives: Word, Word of God, Scripture, the Scriptures, Holy Writ, the Bible, the Holy Book.

Old Testament: Septuagint, Vulgate, Pentateuch, Hagiographa, the Law, the Prophets, the Apocrypha.

New Testament: the Gospel, the Evangelists, the Epistles, the Apocalypse, Revelations.

Talmud, Mishna, Masorah, Torah.

A prophet, seer, evangelist, apostle, disciple, saint, the Fathers.

Adjectives: Scriptural, biblical, sacred, prophetic, evangelical, apostolic, apostolical, inspired, theopneustic, apocalyptic.

986 OTHER SACRED BOOKS

Substantives: the Koran (or Alcoran), Vedas, Upanishads, Puranas, Zend-Avesta.

Religious founders: Buddha (or Gautama), Zoroaster (or Zarathustra), Confucius, Lao-Tsze, Mohammed (or Mahomet).

Idols: Golden Calf, Baal, Moloch, Dagon.

Adjectives: Anti-scriptural, anti-christian, profane, idolatrous, pagan, heathen, heathenish.

987 PIETY

Substantives: religion, theism, faith, religiousness, godliness, reverence, humility, veneration, devoutness, devotion, spirituality, grace, unction, edification, unworldliness, other-worldliness; holiness, sanctity, sanctitude, sacredness, consecration; virtue (944).

Theopathy, beatification, adoption, regeneration, conversion, justification, salvation, inspiration.

A believer, convert, theist, Christian, saint, one of the elect, a devotee.

The good, righteous, faithful, godly, elect, just.

Phrases: The odour of sanctity; the beauty of holiness; spiritual existence.

The children of God, of light.

Verbs: To be pious, etc., to believe, have faith; to convert, edify, sanctify, hallow, beatify, regenerate, inspire; to consecrate, enshrine.

Phrases: To work out one's salvation; to stand up for Jesus; to fight the good fight.

Adjectives: Pious, religious, devout, reverent, reverential, godly, humble, heavenly-minded, pure, holy, spiritual, saintly, saint-like, unworldly, other-worldly.

Believing, faithful, Christian.

Sanctified, regenerated, born again,

justified, adopted, elected, inspired, consecrated, converted, unearthly, sacred, solemn, not of the earth.

988 IMPIETY

Substantives: irreverence, profaneness, profanity, blasphemy, desecration, sacrilege, sacrilegiousness, sin (945); scoffing, ribaldry, reviling.

Assumed piety, hypocrisy, cant, pietism, lip-devotion, lip-service, lip-reverence, formalism, sanctimony, sanctimoniousness, pharisaism, precisianism, sabbatism, sabbatarianism, sacerdotalism, religiosity, religionism, *odium theologicum.*

Hardening, backsliding, declension, reprobation, perversion.

Sinner, outcast, castaway, lost sheep, reprobate.

A scoffer, hypocrite, pietist, pervert, religionist, precisian, formalist; son of darkness, son of Belial, blasphemer, Pharisee; bigot, devotee, fanatic, sabbatarian.

The wicked, unjust, ungodly, unrighteous.

Phrase: The unco guid.

Verbs: To be impious, etc., to profane, desecrate, blaspheme, revile, scoff, commit sacrilege.

To play the hypocrite, cant.

Adjectives: Impious, profane, irreverent, sacrilegious, desecrating, blasphemous; unhallowed, unsanctified, hardened, perverted, reprobate.

Bigoted, priest-ridden, fanatical, churchy.

Hypocritical, canting, pietistical, sanctimonious, unctuous, pharisaical, over-righteous, righteous overmuch.

Phrases: Under the mask, cloak, or pretence of religion.

989 IRRELIGION

Substantives: ungodliness, unholiness, gracelessness, impiety (988).

Scepticism, doubt, unbelief, disbelief, incredulity, incredulousness, faith-lessness, want of faith or belief (485, 487).

Atheism, hylotheism, materialism, positivism.

Deism, infidelity, freethinking, rationalism, agnosticism, unchristianness, antichristianity, antichristianism.

An atheist, sceptic, unbeliever, deist, freethinker, rationalist, agnostic, nullifidian, infidel, alien, giaour, heathen.

Verbs: To be irreligious, disbelieve, lack faith, doubt.

To dechristianize, rationalize.

Adjectives: Irreligious, undevout, godless, atheistic, atheistical, ungodly, unholy, unhallowed, unsanctified, graceless, without God, carnal-minded.

Sceptical, unbelieving, freethinking, agnostic, rationalistic, incredulous, unconverted, faithless, lacking faith.

Deistical, antichristian, unchristian, worldly-minded, mundane, carnal, earthly-minded.

Adverbs: Irreligiously, etc.

990 WORSHIP

Substantives: adoration, devotion, cult, homage, service, humiliation, kneeling, genuflexion, prostration.

Prayer, invocation, supplication, rogation, petition, orison, litany, the Lord's prayer, paternoster, collect.

Thanksgiving, giving or returning thanks, praise, glorification, benediction, doxology, hosanna, hallelujah, paean, Te Deum, Magnificat, Ave Maria, De Profundis, Nunc dimittis, Non nobis, Domine.

Psalmody, psalm, hymn, plainsong, chant, antiphon, response, anthem, motet.

Oblation, sacrifice, incense, libation, burnt-offering, votive offering; offertory, collection.

Discipline, self-discipline, self-examination, self-denial, fasting.

Divine service, religious service, office, duty, prime, terce, sext, matins, mass (998), angelus, nones, evensong, vespers, vigils, lauds, compline; prayer meeting, revival.

Worshipper, congregation, communicant, celebrant.

Verbs: To worship, adore, reverence, venerate, do service, pay homage, humble oneself, bow down, kneel, bend the knee, prostrate oneself.

To pray, invoke, supplicate, petition, put up prayers or petitions; to ask, implore (765).

To return or give thanks; to say grace; to bless, praise, laud, glorify, magnify, sing praises, lead the choir, pronounce benediction.

To propitiate, offer sacrifice, fast, deny oneself; vow, offer vows, give alms.

Phrases: To lift up the heart; to say one's prayers; to tell one's beads; to go to church; to attend divine service.

Adjectives: Worshipping, etc., devout, solemn, devotional, reverent, pure, fervent, prayerful.

Interjections: Hallelujah! alleluia! hosanna! glory be to God! *sursum corda!*

991 IDOLATRY

Substantives: idol-worship, idolism, demonism, demonolatry, fire-worship, devil-worship, fetishism.

Sacrifices, hecatomb, holocaust; human sacrifices, immolation, mactation, infanticide, self-immolation, suttee.

Idol, image, fetish, ju-ju, Mumbo-Jumbo, Juggernaut, joss.

Verbs: To worship idols, pictures, relics, etc.; to idolize, idolatrize.

Adjectives: Idolatrous, fetishistic.

992 OCCULT ARTS

Substantives: occultism, sorcery, magic, the black art, black magic, necromancy, theurgy, thaumaturgy, psychomancy, *diablerie,* bedevilment, withcraft, witchery, bewitchment,

wizardry, glamour, fetishism, vampirism, shamanism, voodooism, obeah (or obi), sortilege, conjuration, exorcism, fascination, mesmerism, hypnotism, animal magnetism, clairvoyance, telegnosis, telekinesis, psychokinesis, mediumship, spiritualism, extra-sensory perception, telepathy, parapsychology, second sight, spirit-rapping, table-turning, psychometry, crystal-gazing, divination, enchantment, hocus-pocus (545).

Verbs: To practise sorcery, etc.; to conjure, exorcize, charm, enchant, bewitch, bedevil, hoodoo, entrance, mesmerize, hypnotize, fascinate; to taboo, wave a wand, cast a spell, call up spirits.

Adjectives: Magic, magical, cabbalistic, talismanic, phylacteric, necromantic, incantatory, occult, mediumistic, charmed, exorcized, etc.

993 SPELL

Substantives: charm, fascination, incantation, exorcism, weird, cabbala, exsufflation, jinx, cantrip, runes, abracadabra, open sesame, mumbo-jumbo, taboo, counter-charm, evil eye, hoodoo, Indian sign.

Talisman, amulet, mascot, periapt, phylactery, philtre, fetish, wishbone, merrythought.

Wand, caduceus, rod, divining-rod, the lamp of Aladdin, magic ring, wishing-cap, seven-league boots.

994 SORCERER

Substantives: sorceress, magician, conjurer, necromancer, enchanter, enchantress, thaumaturgist, occultist, adept, Mahatma, seer, wizard, witch, warlock, charmer, exorcist, mage, archimage, soothsayer (513), shaman, medicine-man, witch-doctor, mesmerist, hypnotist, medium, spiritualist, clairvoyant; control.

Phrase: *Deus ex machina.*

995 CHURCHDOM

Substantives: ministry, apostleship, priesthood, prelacy, hierarchy, church government, Christendom, church; clericalism, sacerdotalism, priestcraft, theocracy, popery, papistry.

Monachism, monasticism, monkdom, monkhood, monkery.

Ecclesiastical offices and dignities: Pontificate, papacy, primacy, archbishopric, archiepiscopacy, bishopric, bishopdom, episcopate, episcopacy, see, diocese, prelacy, deanery, stall, canonry, canonicate, prebend, prebendaryship; benefice, incumbency, advowson, living, cure, rectorship, vicarship, vicariate, deaconry, deaconship, curacy, chaplaincy, chaplainship; cardinalate, abbacy.

Holy orders, ordination, institution, consecration, induction, preferment, translation.

Council, conclave, sanhedrim, synod, presbytery, consistory, chapter, vestry (696).

Verbs: To call, ordain, induct, install, prefer, translate, consecrate, canonize, beatify; to take the veil, to take vows.

Adjectives: Ecclesiastical, clerical, sacerdotal, priestly, prelatical, hierarchical, pastoral, ministerial, capitular, theocratic.

Pontifical, papal, episcopal, archidiaconal, diaconal, canonical; monastic, monachal, monkish; levitical, rabbinical.

996 CLERGY

Substantives: ministry, priesthood, presbytery.

A clergyman, cleric, parson, divine, ecclesiastic, churchman, priest, presbyter, hierophant, pastor, father, shepherd, minister, father in Christ, patriarch, padre, abbé, curé; sky-pilot, holy Joe, devil-dodger.

Dignitaries of the church: Primate, archbishop, bishop, prelate, diocesan, suffragan; dean, subdean, archdeacon, prebendary, canon, capitular, residentiary, beneficiary; rector, vicar, incumbent, chaplain, curate, deacon, subdeacon, preacher, reader, evangelist, revivalist, missionary, missioner.

Churchwarden, sidesman; clerk, precentor, choir, chorister, almoner, verger, beadle, sexton, sacrist, sacristan, acolyte.

Roman Catholic priesthood: Pope, pontiff, cardinal, confessor, spiritual director.

Cenobite, conventual, abbot, prior, father superior, monk, oblate, friar, lay brother, mendicant, Franciscan (or Grey Friars, Friars minor, Minorites), Observant, Capuchin, Dominican (or Black Friars), Carmelite (or White Friars), Augustin (or Austin Friars), Crossed or Crutched Friars, Benedictine, Jesuit (or Society of Jesus).

Abbess, prioress, canoness, mother, mother superior, *religieuse,* nun, novice, postulant.

Greek Church: Patriarch, metropolitan, archimandrite, pope.

Under the Jewish dispensation: Prophet, priest, high-priest, Levite, rabbi (or rabbin), scribe.

Moslem: Imam, mullah, mufti, dervish, fakir, santon, hadji; muezzin.

Hindu: Brahmin, pundit, guru, yogi.

Buddhist: Lama, bonze.

Phrase: The cloth.

Adjectives: Reverend, ordained, in orders.

997 LAITY

Substantives: flock, fold, congregation, assembly, brethren, people.

Temporality, secularization.

A layman, parishioner.

Verb: To secularize.

Adjectives: Secular, lay, laical, civil, temporal, profane.

998 RITE

Substantives: ceremony, ordinance, observance, cult, duty, form, formulary, ceremonial, solemnity, sacrament.

Baptism, immersion, christening, chrism, baptismal regeneration.

Confirmation, imposition or laying on of hands, ordination (995), consecration.

The Eucharist, the Lord's Supper, the communion, the sacrament, consubstantiation, celebration, consecrated elements, bread and wine.

Matrimony (903), burial (363), visitation of the sick, offertory.

Roman Catholic rites and ceremonies: Mass, high mass, low mass, dry mass; the seven sacraments, transubstantiation, impanation, extreme unction, viaticum, invocation of saints, canonization, transfiguration, auricular confession, maceration, flagellation, penance (952), telling of beads.

Relics, rosary, beads, reliquary, pyx (or pix), host, crucifix, *Agnus Dei*, thurible, censer, patera.

Liturgy, ritual, euchology, book of common prayer, litany, etc.; rubric, breviary, missal, ordinal; psalter, psalm book, hymn book, hymnal.

Service, worship (990), ministration, psalmody; preaching, predication; sermon, homily, lecture, discourse, exhortation, address.

Ritualism, ceremonialism, liturgics, liturgiology.

Verbs: To perform service, do duty, minister, officiate; to baptize, dip, sprinkle; to confirm, lay hands on; to give or administer the sacrament; to take or receive the sacrament, communicate.

To preach, sermonize, predicate, lecture, harangue, hold forth, address the congregation.

Adjectives: Ritual, ceremonial, baptismal, eucharistical, pastoral, liturgical.

999 VESTMENTS

Substantives: canonicals, robe, gown, pallium, surplice, cassock, alb, scapular (or scapulary), dalmatic, cope, soutane, chasuble, tonsure, cowl, hood, amice, calotte, bands, apron, biretta.

Mitre, tiara, triple crown, crosier.

1000 TEMPLE

Substantives: cathedral, pro-cathedral, minster, church, kirk, chapel, meeting-house, tabernacle, conventicle, bethesda, little Bethel, basilica, fane, holy place, chantry, oratory.

Synagogue, mosque, pantheon, pagoda, joss-house, dagobah, tope.

Parsonage, rectory, vicarage, manse, presbytery, deanery, bishop's palace, the Vatican.

Altar, shrine, sanctuary, *sanctum sanctorum*, the Holy of Holies, sacristy, communion table, holy table, table of the Lord; piscina, baptistery, font, aumbry.

Chancel, choir, nave, aisle, transept, vestry, crypt, apse, belfry, stall, pew, pulpit, ambo, lectern, reading-desk, confessional, prothesis, credence.

Monastery, priory, abbey, convent, nunnery, cloister.

Adjectives: Claustral, monastic, monasterial, conventual.

INDEX

Index

The numbers refer to the headings under which the words occur.

Abeyance
expectation, 507
extinction, 2
suspense, 142
Abhor
hate, 898
dislike, 867
Abide
continue, 141, 143
exist, 1
diuturnity, 110
endure, 821
dwell, 186
expect, 507
Abide by
resolution, 604
assent, 488
observance, 772
Abigail
servant, 746
Ability
power, 157
intellect, 450
skill, 698
Abject
servile, 886
vile, 874, 940
Abjure
renounce, 607
resign, 757
deny, 536
Ablation
subduntion, 38
taking, 789
Ablaze
heat, 382
light, 420
Able
skilful, 157, 698
Able-bodied
strength, 159
Ablepsy
blindness, 442
Ablution
cleanness, 652
Abnegation
denial, 536, 764
self-denial, 942
forbearance, 953
Abnormality
unconformity, 83
Aboard
ship, 273
present, 186

Abode
abode, 189, 182
Abodement
prediction, 511
Abolish
destroy, 162
abrogate, 756
Abominable
hateful, 898
bad, 649
foul, 653
painful, 830
Abominate
hate, 898
dislike, 867
Abomination
foulness, 653
Abord
courtesy, 894
Aboriginal
beginning, 66
native, 188
Aborigines
inhabitants, 188
Abortion
failure, 732
Abound
sufficiency, 639
About
relative to, 9
near, 32, 197
around, 227
Above
height, 206
priority, 116
Above all
greatness, 31
Above-board
visible, 446
plain, 518
artless, 703
true, 543
Above ground
alive, 359
Above par
greatness, 31
Abracadabra
spell, 993
Abrade
subduct, 38
Abrasion
pulverulence, 330
friction, 331

Abreast
lateral, 236
parallel, 216
Abridge
shorten, 201
conciseness, 572
lessen, 36
deprive, 789
in writing, 596
Abroach
dispersion, 73
Abroad
extraneous, 57
exterior, 220
distant, 196
ignorant, 491
perplexed, 704
Abrogation
abrogation, 756, 764
illegality, 964
Abrupt
sudden, 132
hasty, 684
violent, 173
transient, 111
steep, 217
unexpected, 508
style, 579
Abruption
separation, 44
Abscess
disease, 655
Abscission
retrenchment, 38
division, 44
Abscond
escape, 671
fly from, 287
Absence
non-existence, 2
non-presence, 187
inattention, 458
thoughtlessness, 452
Absent-minded
inattentive, 458
Absentee
absence, 187
Absit omen
deprecation, 766
Absolute
not relative, 1
certain, 474, 31
positive, 535
true, 494
unconditional, 768a

simple, 42
authoritative, 737
severe, 739
due, 924
complete, 52
Absolutely
assent, 488
Absolve
forgive, 918
exempt, 927a
liberate, 750
permit, 760
acquir, 970
Absonant
unreasonable, 495
discordant, 414
Absorb
combination, 48
take in, 296
think, 451
attend to, 457
feel, 821
possess, 777
consume, 677
Absquatulate
go away, 287
Abstain
refrain, 603
temperance, 953
forbear, 623
Abstemious
temperance, 953, 958
Absterge
cleanness, 652
Abstersive
remedy, 662
Abstinence
disuse, 678
forbearance, 623, 953
Abstinent
temperance, 953
sobriety, 958
Abstract
separate, 44
deduct, 38
idea, 451
to abridge, 596, 572
to take, 789
to steal, 791
Abstraction
inattention, 458
deduction, 38
disjunction, 44
unity, 87

Abstruse
recondite, 519
hidden, 528
Absurd
nonsensical, 497, 499
impossible, 471
ridiculous, 853
Abundant
copious, 639
great, 31
Abuse
misuse, 679
ill treat, 649
threat, 909
upbraid, 932
defame, 934
debauch, 961
deceive, 545
of language, 523
Abut
rest on, 215
touch, 199
Abyss
depth, 208
space, 180
hell, 982
Academic
teaching, 537
Academician
artist, 559
Academy
school, 542
Accede
consent, 762
Accelerate
velocity, 173, 274
earliness, 132
haste, 684
Accension
calefaction, 384
Accent
tone of voice, 580
sound, 402
Accept
receive, 785
consent, 762
assent, 488
Acceptable
agreeable, 829
expedient, 646
Acceptance
security, 771
Acceptation
meaning, 516

Accepted
conformity, 82
habitual, 613
Access
method, 627
approach, 286
Accessible
facility, 705
possible, 470
sociability, 892
Accession
increase, 35
addition, 37
commission, 755
to power, 737
Accessory
addition, 37
adjunct, 39
means, 632
auxiliary, 711
aiding, 707
accompanying, 88
Accidence
grammar, 567
Accident
chance, 156, 621
event, 151
Accidental,
external, 6
music, 413
Accidie
dejection, 837
Acclamation
approbation, 931
assent, 488
Acclimatize
inure, 613
train, 673
Acclivity
obliquity, 217
Accolade
courtesy, 894
Accommodate
suit, 23
equalize, 27
reconcile, 723
lend, 787
prepare, 673
aid, 707
give, 784
Accommodating
kind, 906
Accommodation
lodging, 189

Accompaniment
musical, 415
adjunct, 37, 39

Accompanist
musician, 416

Accompany
coexist, 88
add, 37

Accomplice
auxiliary, 711

Accomplish
execute, 161
finish, 729

Accomplishment
talent, 698
learning, 490

Accord
agree, 23, 646
assent, 488
concord, 714
melody, 413
give, 784
grant, 760
spontaneous, 600

According to
relation, 9
conformably, 15
evidence, 467

Accordingly
reasoning, 476

Accordion
musical instrument, 417

Accost
allocation, 586

Accoucheur
instrument, 631

Account
money, 811
bill, 812
computation, 85
list, 86
record, 551
description, 594
value, 644
estimation, 484
judgment, 480
approbation, 931
fame, 873
sake, 615

Account for
attribution, 155

Accountable
duty, 926
liability, 177

Accountant
accounts, 811
treasurer, 801

Accouplement
junction, 43

Accoutre
dress, 225
equip, 673

Accoutrement
equipment, 633

Accredit
money, 805
honour, 873
commission, 755

Accretion
coherence, 46
increase, 35

Accrue
result, 154
add, 37
acquire, 775
receive, 785, 810
benefit, 644

Accueil
courtesy, 894

Accumulate
collect, 72
store, 636

Accurate
exact, 494
likeness, 17

Accursed
undone, 828
painful, 830
disastrous 649
cursed 908

Accuse
charge, 938
disapprove 932

Accuser
judge, 967

Accustom
habituate, 613
usual, 82

Ace
unit, 87
small in quantity, 32
small in size, 193
courage, 861

Acerbate
embitter, 659
aggravate, 835

Acerbity
sourness, 397
harshness, 739

spleen, 898, 900, 901
malevolence, 907

Acervate
assemblage, 72

Acetic
sour, 397

Acetous
sour, 397

Acharnement
malevolence, 907

Ache
physical pain, 378
moral pain, 838

Acheron
hell, 982

Achievable
possible, 470
easy, 705

Achieve
accomplish, 729
end, 67

Achievement
escutcheon, 551

Achromatism
achromatic, 429

Achtung
attention, 457

Acicular
sharpness, 253

Acid
sourness, 397

Acknowledge
avow, 535
disclose, 529
assent, 488
consent, 762
reward, 973
repent, 950
answer, 462
observe, 772
receive, 82

Acknowledged
habitual, 613

Acme
summit, 210
highest degree, 33
perfection, 650

Acolyte
clergy, 996

Aconite
bane, 663

Acoustics
sound, 402

Acquaint
information, 527

374

Acquaintance
knowledge, 490
friendship, 888
friend, 890

Acquiesce
assent, 488
consent, 762

Acquire
acquisition, 775

Acquirement
knowledge, 490
learning, 539
talent, 698

Acquisition
gain, 775
knowledge, 970

Acquit
absolve, 490
exempt, 927A
vindicate, 937
liberate, 750

Acquit oneself
of a duty, 926
of an agreement, 772

Acquittance
payment, 807

Acres
property, 780

Acrid
unsavouriness, 395

Acrimony,
taste, 395
hatred, 898
malevolence, 907
discourtesy, 895

Acrobat
athlete, 159

Across
transverse, 219
opposition, 708

Acrostic
neology, 563
puzzle, 533

Act
physical, 170
voluntary, 680
law, 697
to feign, 544
to personate, 599
deputize, 759
business, 625
to imitate, 19

Actinotherapy
remedy, 662

Action
physical, 170
voluntary, 680
battle, 720
at law, 969

Activity
physical, 171
voluntary, 682

Actor
impostor, 548
player, 599
doer, 690

Actual
existing, 1
real, 494
present, 118

Actualize
describe, 594
materialize, 3

Actuality
truly, 31

Actuary
accounts, 811

Actuate
motive, 615

Actum est
completion, 729

Acuity
sharpness, 253

Aculeated
sharpness, 253

Acumen
wisdom, 484

Acuminated
sharpness, 233

Acupuncture
opening, 260

Acute
pointed, 253
violent (physically), 173
sensible (physically), 375
painful (morally), 830
strong feeling, 820
musical tone, 410
perspicacious, 498

Acutely
much, 31

Ad arbitrium
will, 600

Ad captandum
plea, 617
deception, 545

Ad captandum vulgas
ostentation, 852

Ad eundem
equality, 27

Ad infinitum
infinity, 105

Ad interim
duration, 106

Ad-lib
improvise, 612

Ad libitum
will, 600
choice, 609
sufficiency, 639

Ad rem
reasoning, 473

Ad unguem
perfection, 650

Ad valorem
price, 812

Adage
maxim, 496

Adagio
slowness, 275
music, 415

Adamant
hard, 323
strong, 159

Adapt
fit, 646
adjust, 673
agree, 23

Add
addition, 37
increase, 35
numerically, 85

Addendum
adjunct, 39

Adder
viper, 663
maleficent being, 913

Addict
habit, 613

Addition
adjunction, 37
thing added, 39
arithmetical, 85

Addle
barren, 169
abortive, 732
to spoil, 659

Addle-headed
imbecile, 499

Address
speak to, 586
skill, 698
request, 765
residence, 189
direction, 550
lecture, 582
preach, 998
Addresses
courtship, 902
Adduce
bring to, 288
evidence, 467
Adept
proficient, 700
sorcerer, 994
Adequate
sufficient, 639
power, 157
strength, 159
for a purpose, 644
Adhere
stick, 46
fidelity, 772
resoluteness, 604
Adherent
follower, 711
Adhesive
coherence, 46
connective, 45
Adhibit
use, 677
Adiaphorism
heresy, 984A
Adieu
departure, 293
Andipose
unctuous, 355
Adiposity
corpulence, 192
Adit
conduit, 350
orifice, 260
way, 627
Adjacent
nearness, 197
Adjection
addition, 37
Adjective
adjunct, 39
Adjoin
nearness, 197
contiguity, 199
Adjourn
lateness, 133

Adjudge
lawsuit, 969
Adjudication
choice, 609
judgement, 480
lawsuit, 969
Adjunct
thing added, 39
accompaniment, 88
aid, 707
Adjuration
affirmation, 535
Adjure
request, 765
promise, 768
Adjust
fit, 27
preface, 673
settle, 723
compromise, 774
Adjutage (or ajutage),
pipe, 350
opening, 260
Adjutant
auxiliary, 711
military, 745
Adjuvant
helper, 707, 711
Admeasurement
measurement, 466
Administer
give, 784
apportion, 786
manage, 693
govern, 737
Administration
of justice, 965
Admirable
excellent, 648
virtuous, 944
Admiral
master, 745
Admire
approve, 931
love, 897
wonder, 870
Admissable
tolerable, 651
Admission
ingress, 294, 296
inclusion, 76
Admit
let in, 296
accept, 785
include, 76

composition, 54
concede in argument, 467
disclose, 529
allow, 760
assent, 488
Admit of
possibility, 470
Admixture
mixture, 41
Admonish
advise, 695
warn, 668
reprove, 932
predict, 511
Ado
exertion, 686
activity, 682
difficulty, 704
Adolescence
youth, 131
Adonis
beauty, 845
Adopt
choice, 609
Adore
love, 897
worship, 990
Adorn
beauty, 845
Adown
lowness, 207
Adrift
unrelated, 10
dispersed, 73
at fault, 704
Adroit
skill, 698
Adscititious
extrinsic, 6
added, 37
supplementary, 52
Adscriptus glebæ
servant, 746
Adulation
flattery, 933
Adulator
flatterer, 935
Adult
adolescence, 131
Adulterate
mix, 41
deteriorate, 659
falsify, 495

Adulterer
libertine, 962

Adultery
impurity, 961

Adumbrate
sketch, 594
representation, 554
painting, 556
faint likeness, 21
imitate, 19
personify, 521

Adust
burnt, 384
gloomy, 837

Advance
progress, 282, 731
to promote, 658
forward, 707
increase, 35
lend, 787
expenditure, 809
assert, 535

Advanced
progressive, 658
modern, 123

Advantage
good, 618
utility, 644
goodness, 648
superiority, 33
inequality, 28
success, 705, 731

Advene
addition, 37

Advent
arrival, 292
event, 151
futurity, 121

Adventitious
extrinsic, 6
casual, 156, 621

Adventure
event, 151
chance, 156, 621
pursuit, 622
trial, 675

Adventurer
deceiver, 548
rashness, 863

Adventurous
courageous, 861
dangerous, 665

Adversaria
register, 551
chronicle, 594

Adversary
opponent, 710

Adverse
opposed, 708
enmity, 889
disliking, 867
unprosperous, 735

Adversity
adversity, 735

Advert
attention, 457

Advertise
publication, 531

Advertisement
preface, 64
information, 527

Advice
counsel, 695
notice, 527
news, 532

Advisable
expediency, 646

Advise
inform, 527
counsel, 695
predict, 511

Advised
voluntary, 600
intentional, 620

Adviser
counsellor, 695
teacher, 540

Advocacy
aid, 707

Advocate
counsellor, 968
advise, 695
to prompt, 615
commend, 931
to vindicate, 937
Saviour, 967

Advocatus diaboli
sophistry, 477

Advowson
churchdom, 995

Adytum
secret place, 530
room, 191
prediction, 511

Aedile
authority, 745

Aegis
defence, 717
patronage, 175

Aeolus

wind, 349

Aeon
duration, 106, 110

Aequiparate
equate, 27

Aequo animo
insensible, 823

Aerate
air, 338

Aerial
aeriform, 334, 338
elevated, 206

Aerie
abode, 189
height, 206

Aeriform
gaseity, 334, 338

Aerodrome
destination, 292

Aeronautics
navigation, 267

Aeroplane
aircraft, 273A

Aerostat
balloon, 273A

Aerostatics
gaseity, 334
navigation, 267

Aesthetic
taste, 850
beauty, 845
sensibility, 375

Aestival
morning, 125

Aestivate
sleep, 68

Aetiology
knowledge, 490
attribution, 155
disease, 655

Afar
distance, 196

Affable
courteous, 894
sociable, 892

Affair
business, 625, 680
event, 151
topic, 454
battle, 720

Affaire de cœur
love, 897

Affect
desire, 865
love, 897
lend to, 176

touch, 824

Affectability
sensibility, 822

Affectation
pretension, 855
in style, 577

Affection
disposition, 820
love, 897
friendship, 888

Affiance
trust, 858
promise, 768

Affiche
publication, 531

Affidavit
evidence, 467
affirmation, 535
record, 551

Affiliation
relation, 9
kindred, 11
attribution, 155

Affinity
relation, 9
similarity, 17

Affirm
assert, 535
confirm, 488

Affirmatively
assent, 488

Affix
to join, 43
add, 37
sequel, 39
addition, 37

Afflatus
inspiration, 515

Afflict
painfulness, 830

Affliction
calamity, 619
pain, 828

Afflictive
painfulness, 830

Affluent
flowing, 348
sufficient, 639
prosperous, 734
wealthy, 803

Afflux
approach, 286

Afford
supply, 134, 784
wealth, 803

accrue, 810

Affranchise
liberation, 750

Affray
contention, 720

Affright
fear, 880

Affront
insult, 900, 929
courage, 861
molest, 830

Affuse
water, 337

Afire
heat, 382

Afloat,
at sea, 341
on shipboard, 273
unstable, 149
public, 531

Afoot
walking, 266
existing, 1
business, 625
in preparation, 673

Afore
priority, 116

Aforementioned
precedence, 62

Aforesaid
repetition, 104
precedence, 62
priority, 116

Aforethought
intention, 620
premeditation, 611

Afraid
fear, 860

Afreet
demon, 980

Afresh
new, 123
repeated, 104
frequent, 136

Aft
rear, 235

After
in order, 63
in time, 117

After all
qualification, 469

After-clap
disappointment, 509

After-course
plan, 626

After-game
plan, 626

After-life
futurity, 121

After-part
sequel, 65

After-piece
drama, 599

After-time
futurity, 121

Afterglow
light, 420

Aftermath
sequel, 65
effect, 154

Afternoon
evening, 126

Aftertaste
taste, 390

Afterthought
sequel, 65
thought, 451
memory, 505
plan, 626

Afterwards
posteriority, 117

Aga
master, 745

Agacerie
motive, 615

Again
repeated, 104
frequent, 136

Against
physical opposition, 179
voluntary opposition, 708
anteposition, 237
provision, 673

Agape
wonder, 870
curiosity, 455

Agate
ornament, 847

Age
period, 108
oldness, 124
duration, 106
present time, 118
advanced life, 128

Aged
veteran, 130

Ageless perpetual, 112

Agency
physical, 170
instrumentality, 157,

631, 755
direction, 693

Agenda
business, 625
plan, 626

Agent
physical, 153
voluntary, 690
consignee, 758, 769

Agentship
commission, 755

Agglomerate
assemblage, 72
coherence, 46

Agglutinate
coherence, 46

Aggrandize
in degree, 35
in bulk, 194
honour, 873

Aggravate
increase, 35
vehemence, 173
distress, 835
render worse, 659
exasperate, 900
exaggerate, 549
provoke, 830

Aggregate
whole, 50
collection, 72

Aggregation
coherence, 46

Aggression
attack, 716

Aggressive
pugnacious, 901

Aggrieve
distress, 830
injure, 649

Aghast
with wonder, 870
with fear, 860
disappointed, 509

Agile
swift, 274
active, 682

Agio
discount, 813

Agiotage
barter, 794

Agitate
motion, 315
activity, 682
to affect the mind, 821

to excite, 824

Aglow
hot, 382

Agnation
consanguinity, 11

Agnomen
nomenclature, 564

Agnosticism
unbelief, 485, 989

Agnus Dei
rite, 998

Ago
preterition, 122

Agog
curiosity, 455
expectation, 507
desire, 865

Agonstic
contention, 720

Agonize
painfulness, 830

Agony
physical, 378
mental, 828

Agoraphobia
seclusion, 893
dislike, 866

Agrarian
agriculture, 371

Agree
accord, 23
concur, 178
assent, 488
consent, 762
concord, 714

Agreeable
pleasant, 377, 829

Agreeably
conformably, 82

Agreement
bargain, 769

Agrestic
rural, 371
uncouth, 876

Agriculture
agriculture, 371

Agronomy
agriculture, 371

Aground
stranded, 265, 704
fixed, 150
failure, 732

Ague-fit
fear, 860

Anguish

cold, 383

Ahead
in front, 62, 234, 280

Ahead (go)
progression, 282
to improve, 658

Aid
to help, 707, 712
charity, 606

Aide-de-camp
auxiliary, 711
officer, 745

Aide-memoire
memory, 505

Aigrette
ornament, 847

Aiguille
sharp, 253

Ail
sick, 655
in pain, 828

Ailment
disease, 655

Aim
direction, 278
purpose, 620

Aimless
chance, 621
motiveless, 616

Air
gas, 334
atmospheric, 338
wind, 349
tune, 415
appearance, 448
conduct, 692
unsubstantial, 4
fashion, 852
affectation, 855
vanity, 880

Air-balloon
aircraft, 273A

Air-built
imagination, 515

Air-condition
air, 338

Airdrop
transference, 270

Airlift
transference, 270

Air-liner
aircraft, 273A

Air Marshal
master, 745

Air-pipe
air-pipe, 351

Air-pocket
  pitfall, 667
Air-raid
  attack, 716
Air-tight
  closed, 261
Airborne
  locomotion, 267
  aircraft, 273A
  lightness, 320
Aircraft
  aeroplane, 273A
Aircraft-carrier
  ship, 273
Aircraftman
  fighter, 726
Aircrew
  fighter, 726
Airfield
  arrival, 292
Airgraph
  news, 532
  letter, 592
Airiness
  levity, 320
Airing
  journey, 266
Airman
  navigation, 269
Airport
  arrival, 292
Airship
  aircraft, 273A
Airstop
  arrival, 292
Airstrip
  arrival, 292
'Airworthy
  safe, 664
Airy
  atmosphere, 338
  gay, 836
Aisle
  passage, 260, 627
  church, 1000
Ajutage
  see, Adjutage
Akimbo
  angular, 244
Akin
  consanguinity, 11
Alabaster
  whiteness, 430
Alack!

lamentation, 839
Alacrity activity, 682
  cheerfulness, 836
Alarm
  fear, 860
  notice of danger, 669
  signal, 550
  threatening, 665
Alarmist
  newsmonger, 532
Alarum
  warning, 669
  signal, 550;
  loudness, 404
Alas!
  lamentation, 839
Alb
  dress, 225
  vestments, 999
Albeit
  counteraction, 179
  counter-evidence, 468
  compensation, 30
Albescent
  white, 430
Albification
  white, 430
Albinism
  achromatism, 429
Albino
  dim-sightedness, 443
Album
  book, 553
  compendium, 596
  repertoire, 636
Albuminous
  semiliquidity, 352
Alcade
  master, 745
Alchemy
  conversion, 144
Alcohol
  drunkenness, 986
Alcoran
  sacred books, 986
Alcove
  cave, 252
  dwelling, 189
Alderman
  master, 745
Alembic
  vessel, 191
  laboratory, 691
Alentours
  nearness, 197

Alert
  active, 682
  watchful, 459
  alarm, 669
  signal, 550
Alexandrine
  verse, 597
Alexipharmic
  remedy, 662
Alfresco
  exterior, 220
  air, 338
Algebra
  numeration, 85
Algid
  cold, 383
Algorism
  numeration, 85
Alias
  misnomer, 565
Alibi
  absence, 187
Alien
  irrelevant, 10
  foreign, 57
Alienate
  transfer, 783
  estrange, 889
  set against, 898
Alienation (mental)
  insanity, 503
Alieni appetens
  desire, 865
  jealousy, 920
Alienist
  doctor, 662
Alight
  descend, 306
  stop, 265
  arrive, 292
  light, 420
  hot, 382
Align
  arrange, 60
  trend, 278
Alike
  similarity, 17
Aliment
  food, 298, 707
Alimentation
  aid, 707
Alimony
  dowry, 810
  provision, 803

Aline
see Align
Aliquot
part, 51
Alive
living, 359
attentive, 457
sensitive, 822
active, 682
Alkahest
solution, 335
All
whole, 50
complete, 52
general, 78
All-clear
signal, 550
All-embracing
inclusive, 76
All hands
generality, 76
All in
exhausted, 160
All-inclusive
generality, 78
All-pervading
generality, 78
Allah
great spirit, 979
Allay
moderate, 174
pacify, 723
repress excitement, 826
relieve, 834
Allege
evidence, 467
assert, 535
plea, 617
Allegiance
duty, 743, 926
Allegory
comparison, 464, 521
Allegresse
cheerfulness, 836
Allegretto
music, 415
Allegro
cheerfulness, 836
music, 415
Alleluia
worship, 990
Allemande
dance, 840
Allergy
sensitiveness, 375

Alleviate
moderate, 174
allay, 826
relieve, 834
Alley
passage, 260
way, 627
court, 189
Allez-vous-en
repulse, 297
Alliance
relation, 9
kindred, 11
physical co-operation,
178
voluntary co-operation,
709
union, 714
Alligation
junction, 43
Alliteration
similarity, 17
poetry, 597
Allocation
arrangement, 60
Allocution
allocution, 586
Allodial
free, 748
Allodium
property, 780
Alloquialism
address, 586
Allot
arrange, 60
distribute, 786
dueness, 924
Allotment
agriculture, 371
Allotropy
variation, 16
multiformity, 81
Allow
permit, 760
assent, 488
concede, 467
disclose, 529
give, 784
discount, 813
allot, 786
pay, 809
Allowable
dueness, 924
Allowance
qualification, 469

forgiveness, 918
Alloy
mixture, 41
debase, 65
Allude
mean, 516
suggest, 514
refer to, 521
hint, 527
Allure
motive, 615
Allurement
desire, 865
Allusion
meaning, 516
reference, 521
Allusive
relation, 9
meaning, 516
Alluvium
deposit, 40
land, 342
soil, 653
Ally
auxiliary, 711
friend, 890
Alma Mater
school, 542
Almanac
chronometry, 114
record, 551
Almighty
deity, 976
Almoner
clergy, 996
treasurer, 801
Almost
nearly, 32
Alms
giving, 784
Aloft
height, 206
Alone
unity, 87
Along
length, 200
Along with
together, 88
by means of, 631
Alongside
near, 197
parallel, 216
side by side, 236
Aloof
unsociable, 893
indifferent, 456

Aloud
  loudness, 404
Alp
  height, 206
Alpha
  beginning, 66
Alphabet
  letter, 561
  beginning, 66
Alphabetize
  arrange, 60
Alpinist
  ascent, 305
Already
  antecedently, 116
  even now, 118
  past time, 122
Also
  addition, 37
  accompaniment, 88
Altar
  marriage, 903
  church, 1000
Alter
  vary, 20
  change, 140
Alter ego
  identity, 13
  similarity, 17
  deputy, 759
  friend, 890
Alterable
  mutability, 149
Alterative
  salubrity, 656
Altercation
  discord, 713
Alternate
  reciprocal, 12
  periodic, 63, 138
  oscillating, 314
  discontinuous, 70
Alternative
  plan, 626
  choice, 609
Although
  counteraction, 179
  compensation, 30
  opposition, 708
  counterevidence, 468
Altiloquence
  floridity, 577
Altitude
  height, 206

Alto
  high note, 410
Alto rilievo
  convexity, 250
  sculpture, 557
Altogether
  collectively, 50
  entirely, 31
Altruism
  disinterestedness, 942
  philanthropy, 910
Alumnus
  learner, 541
Alveolus
  concavity, 252
Always
  perpetuity, 112
  uniformity, 16
  conformity, 82
Amalgam
  mixture, 41
  compound, 48
Amanuensis
  writing, 590
  secretary, 553
Amaranthine
  perpetual, 112
Amass
  whole, 50
  store, 636
  to collect, 72
Amateur
  desire, 865
  taste, 850
  ignoramus, 493
Amatory
  love, 897
Amaurosis
  blindness, 442
Amaze
  wonder, 870
Amazingly
  greatness, 31
Amazon
  warrior, 726
  courage, 861
Ambages
  deviation, 279
Ambassador
  messenger, 534
  diplomat, 758
Amber
  yellowness, 436
  semiliquid, 352
Ambergris

  oil, 356
  fragrance, 400
Ambidexter
  right, 238
  clever, 678
  fickle, 607
Ambient
  circumscription, 227
Ambiguous
  uncertain, 475, 520
  obscure, 571
  unintelligible, 519
Ambiloquy
  double meaning, 520
Ambit
  outline, 229
Ambition
  desire, 865
  intention, 620
Amble
  pace, 266
  slowness, 275
Amblyopia
  dim-sighted, 443
Ambo
  pulpit, 542, 1000
Ambrosial
  savouriness, 394
  fragrance, 400
Ambulance
  remedy, 662
Ambulation
  journey, 266
Ambuscade
  ambush, 530
Ambush
  ambush, 530
Âme damnée
  servant, 746
  flatterer, 935
  bad man, 949
Ameer
  master, 745
  noble, 875
Ameliorate
  improvement, 658
Amen
  assent, 488
Amenable
  duty, 926
  obedient, 743
Amend
  improvement, 658
Amende honorable
  atonement, 952

Amends
 compensation, 30
 reward, 3973
 atonement, 952
Amenity
 courtesy, 894
Amerce
 penalty, 974
Americanism
 language, 560
Amethyst
 ornament, 847
 purple, 437
Amiable
 lovable, 897
 benevolent, 906
Amicable
 friendly, 888
 assisting, 707
Amice
 vestments, 999
Amicus curiae
 friend, 890
Amidst
 interjacent, 228
 middle, 68
 mixture, 41
Amiss
 wrong, 619, 923
 inexpedient, 647
Amity
 friendship, 888
 concord, 714
 peace, 721
Ammunition
 materials, 635
 warlike, 727
Amnesia
 oblivion, 506
 insensibility, 823
Amnesty
 forgiveness, 918
 pacification, 723
Amoebean
 sequence, 63
Among
 interjacence, 228
 mixture, 41
Amorist
 love, 897
Amoroso
 love, 897
Amorous
 love, 897
Amorphous

 formless, 241
 irregular, 83
Amount
 quantity, 25
 whole, 50
 numeration, 85
 sum of money, 800
 price, 812
Amour
 love, 897
Amour-propre
 vanity, 880
Amphibian
 aircraft, 273A
Amphibious
 unconformity, 83
Amphibology
 equivocality, 520
Amphibrach
 verse, 597
Amphigouri
 ridiculous, 853
 absurdity, 497
Amphimacer
 verse, 597
Amphitheatre
 arena, 728
 theatre, 599
 prospect, 441
 school, 542
Ample
 much, 31
 copious, 639
 large, 192
 broad, 202
 spacious, 180
Amplify
 enlarge, 35
 loudness, 404
 dilate, 194
 expatiate, 573
 exaggerate, 549
Amplitude
 degree, 26
 space, 180
 size, 192
 breadth, 202
Amputate
 subduction, 38
Amtrac
 vehicle, 272
Amuck, run
 violence, 173
 insanity, 503
 excitability, 825

Amulet
 spell, 993
Amuse
 amusement, 840
Amylaceous
 semiliquidity, 352
An
 if, 514
Ana
 description, 594
Anachronism
 anachronism, 115
Anacoluthon
 discontinuity, 70
Anacreontic
 poetry, 597
Anaemia
 pallor, 429
 weakness, 160
 feebleness, 575
Anaesthesia
 insensibility, 376, 381, 823
Anaesthetist
 doctor, 662
'Ανάγκη,
 necessity, 601
Anaglyph
 sculpture, 557
Anagogic
 concealment, 528
Anagram
 letter, 561
 double meaning, 520
 puzzle, 533, 842
Analecta
 description, 594
Analeptic
 remedy, 662
Analgesia
 insensibility, 376
Analogy
 relation, 9
Analogy
 similarity, 17
 comparison, 464
Analysis
 decomposition, 49
 arrangement, 60
 compendium, 596
 grammar, 567
 algebra, 85
 inquiry, 461
 reasoning, 476

assert, 535

Announcement
programme, 510

Announcer
radio, 599B

Annoyance
pain, 828
painfulness, 830
evil, 619
badness, 649

Annual
year, 108
periodic, 138
book, 593

Annuity
wealth, 803, 810

Annul
abrogation, 756, 964

Annular
circularity, 247

Annulet
circularity, 247

Annunciate
inform, 527
publish, 531

Annus mirabilis
period, 108
prodigy, 872

Anodyne
remedy, 174, 662, 834

Anoint
coat, 222
lubricate, 332
oil, 355

Anointed
deity, 976

Anomalistic
unconformity, 83

Anomaly
irregularity, 83
disorder, 59

Anon
ere long, 132
shortly, 111

Anonymous
misnomer, 565

Another
difference, 15

Answer
to an inquiry, 462
reply, 468, 587
confutation, 479
lawsuit, 969
to succeed, 731
serve, 644

Answer for
promise, 768

Answer to
correspond, 9

Answerable
duty, 926
liable, 177

Antaean
huge, 192

Antagonism
difference, 14
enmity, 889
hate, 898
voluntary, 708
physical, 179

Antagonist
opponent, 710
enemy, 891

Antecedence
in order, 62
in time, 116

Antecedent
in order, 64
in time, 116

Antechamber
room, 191

Antedate
anachronism, 115

Antediluvian
oldness, 124
priority, 116

Antelope
velocity, 274

Antemundane
oldness, 124

Antenna
touch, 379

Antepenultimate
end, 67

Anteposition
precedence, 62

Anterior
in order, 62
in time, 116
in place, 234

Ante-room
room, 191

Anthem
worship, 990

Anthology
poem, 597
collection, 72, 596

Anthropology
mankind, 372

Anthropomorphic
mankind, 372

Anthropophagi
evil-doer, 913

Anthropophagous
eat, 296

Antibiotic
remedy, 662

Antic
ridicule, 856

Antichristian
irreligion, 989

Anticipate
early, 132
future, 121
anachronism, 115
expect, 507
foresee, 510
prepare, 673
priority, 116

Anticlimax
depth, 208
bathos, 856
decrease, 36

Anticyclone
rotation, 312

Antidote
remedy, 662
counteraction, 179

Antilogarithm
number, 84

Antinomy
illegality, 964

Antinous
beauty, 845

Antiparallel
obliquity, 217

Antipathy
enmity, 889

Antiphon
music, 415
answer, 462
worship, 990

Antiphrasis
misnomer, 565

Antipodes
distance, 196
antiposition, 237
difference, 14
depth, 208

Antiposition
antiposition, 237

Antiquary
past, 122

Antiquated
vulgarity, 851
Antique
oldness, 124
Anti-scriptural
pagan, 986
Antiseptic
remedy, 662
cleanness, 652
Antisocial
misanthropy, 911
Antistrophe
poetry, 597
Antithesis
contrast, 14
comparison, 464
style, 574
Antitoxin
remedy, 662
Antitype
prototype, 22
Antler
sharpness, 253
Antonomasia
substitution, 147
nomenclature, 564
Antonym
opposite, 14
Anvil
support, 215
preparing, 673
(on the)
plan, 626
Anxiety
pain, 828
fear, 860
desire, 865
Anyhow
careless, 460
Aorist
indefinite time, 119
Apace
swift, 274
short time, 111
early, 132
Apache
ruffian, 913, 949
Apanage
adjunct, 39
property, 780
Apart
distance, 196
singleness, 87
difference, 15

Apartment
room, 191
abode, 189
Apathy
physical, 376
moral, 823
indifference, 456, 866
Ape
imitation, 19
Apelles
artist, 559
Aperçu
compendium, 596
Aperitif
food, 298
Aperture
opening, 260
Apex
summit, 210
Aphasia
aphony, 581
Aphelion
distance, 196
Aphony
aphony, 581
Aphorism
maxim, 496
Aphrodisiac
excitation, 824
Aphrodite
goddess, 979
love, 897
Apiary
domestication, 370
Apicius
gluttony, 957
Apiece
disjunction, 44
particularity, 79
Aplomb
vertical, 212
intelligence, 498
self-possession, 864
Apocalypse
revelation, 985
Apocryphal
uncertain, 475
false, 495, 544
Apodictic
demonstration, 478
Apogee
distance, 196
summit, 210
Apolaustic
self-indulgent, 943

Apollo
god, 979
music, 415
beauty, 845
Apologue
description, 521, 594
Apology
penitence, 950
vindication, 937
reasoning, 476
atonement, 952
substitute, 147
Apophthegm
maxim, 496
Apoplexy
weakness, 160
Aposiopesis
taciturnity, 585
Apostasy
palinode, 607
dishonour, 940
heterodoxy, 984A
Apostate
knave, 941
renegade, 144, 742
Apostatize
tergiversation, 607
Apostle
teacher, 540
Apostolic
revelation, 985
Apostrophe
appeal, 765
address, 586, 589
Apothecary
doctor, 662
Apotheosis
deification, 981, 991
Apozem
solution, 335
Appal
fear, 860
Appalling
painfulness, 830
Appanage
see Apanage
Apparatus
instrument, 633
Apparel
vestment, 225
Apparent
visible, 446
manifest, 525
Apparition
ghost, 980

386

appearance, 448
Appeal
  request, 765
  address, 586
Appear
  come into being, 1, 448
  come to light, 525
  come into view, 446
Appear for
  deputy, 759
Appearance
  sight, 448
  probability, 472
Appease
  physically, 174
  morally, 826
  conciliate, 918
Appeasement
  pacifism, 723
  submission, 725
Appellant
  plaintiff, 924, 938, 967
Appellation
  nomenclature, 564
Append
  addition, 37
  sequence, 63
  hang, 214
Appendage
  adjunct, 39
Appendix
  sequel, 65
Apperception
  knowledge, 490
  conception, 453
Appertain
  belong, 777
  related to, 9
  right, 922
  inclusion, 76
Appetence
  desire, 865
Appetiser
  whet, 298, 615
Appetite
  desire, 865
Applaud
  approbation, 931
Apple-green
  greenness, 435
Apple of discord
  discord, 713
Apple-sauce
  flattery, 933

Appleton layer
  air, 338
Appliance
  means, 632
  instrument, 633
Applicable
  to use, 644
  expedient, 646
  relative, 23
Applicant
  petitioner, 767
Application
  use, 677
  request, 765
  metaphor, 521
  study, 457
Appoggiatura
  music, 415
Appoint
  commission, 755
  command, 741
Appointment
  salary, 809
  equipment, 633
  interview, 892
Apportion
  allot, 786
  arrange, 60
  portion, 51
Apportionment
  dispersion, 73
Apposite
  agreeing, 23
  relative, 9
Apposition
  agreement, 23
  closeness, 199
Appraise
  value, 812
  estimate, 466
Appreciate
  measure, 466
  taste, 850
  realize, 450
  gratitude, 916
  judge, 480
  approve, 931
Apprehend
  know, 490
  believe, 484
  fear, 860
  seize, 789, 969
Apprehension
  conception, 453

Apprentice
  learner, 541
Apprenticeship
  learning, 539
  training, 673
Apprise
  information, 527
Approach move, 286
  nearness, 197
  path, 627
  of time, 121
Approbation
  approbation, 931
Appropinquation
  approach, 197, 286
Appropriate
  fit, 23, 646
  special, 79
  to assign, 786
  to take, 789
  to steal, 791
Appropriation
  stealing, 791
Approve
  commend, 931
  corroborate, 467
  assent, 488
Approximate
  approach, 286
  nearness, 197
  in mathematics, 85
  resemble, 17
  related to, 9
Appulse
  convergence, 286, 290
  collision, 276
Appurtenance
  part, 51
  component, 56
Apricot
  colour, 439
April fool
  fool, 501
Apron
  dress, 225
  vestments, 999
Apropos
  relation, 9
  expedience, 646
  occasion, 134
Apse
  church, 1000
Apt
  consonant, 23
  clever, 698

docile, 539
willing, 602
expedient, 646
tendency, 176
Aptitude
intelligence, 498
skill, 698
Aquarium
domestication, 370
collection, 636
Aquatic
water, 337
Aquatint
engraving, 558
Aqueduct
conduit, 350
Aqueous
water, 337
Aquiline
angularity, 244
Arabesque
ornament, 847
Arable
agriculture, 371
Araeometer
density, 321
measure, 466
Arbiter
judge, 480, 967
adviser, 695
Arbiter elegantiarum
taste, 850
Arbitrament
sentence, 969
judgment, 480
choice, 609
Arbitrary
without law, 964
authority, 737
obstinate, 606
severity, 739
irregular, 83
without relation, 10
Arbitrate
mediate, 724, 969
judge, 480
Arbor
support, 215
Arborescence
branching, 205, 242, 256
Arboretum
agriculture, 371
Arboriculture
agriculture, 371

Arbour
abode, 189
Arc
curvature, 245
Arc-lamp
light, 423
Arcade
arch, 245
passage, 189
Arcades ambo
similarity, 17
friend, 890
Arcadian
delightful, 829
Arcanum
secret, 533
Arch
curve, 245
great, 31
cunning, 702
roguish, 842
greatness, 31
Archaeology
preterition, 122
Archaic
oldness, 124
Archaism
inelegance, 579
Archangel
angel, 977
Archbishop
clergy, 996
Archdeacon
clergy, 996
Archduke
master, 745
Archetype
prototype, 22
model, 80
Arch-fiend
Satan, 978
Archiepiscopacy
churchdom, 995
Archimandrite
sorcerer, 994
Archimage
clergy, 996
Archipelago
island, 346
Architect
constructor, 164
agent, 690
Architecture
construction, 161
fabric, 329

Architrave
summit, 210
Archive
record, 551
Archness
cunning, 702
cleverness, 498
intelligence, 450
Archon
master, 745
Arch-traitor
knave, 941
Arctic
polar, 237
cold, 383
Arcuation
curvature, 245
Ardent
fiery, 382
feeling, 821
desire, 865
expectant, 507
Ardour
activity, 682
Arduous
difficulty, 704
Area
region, 181
quantity, 25
Arefaction
dryness, 340
Arena
field, 181, 728
amusement, 840
workshop, 691
Arenaceous
pulverulence, 330
Areolar
crossing, 219
Areopagus
council, 696
Area
god, 979
Arête
height, 206
sharpness, 253
Argent
whiteness, 430
Argillaceous
softness, 324
Argosy
ship, 273
Argot
language, 560

Arrondissement
region, 181
Arrow
swift, 274
missile, 284
arms, 727
Arrow-headed
angular, 244
Arrowy
sharp, 253
Arsenal
store, 636
military, 727
Arson
calefaction, 384
Art
skill, 698
cunning, 702
deception, 545
representation, 554
business, 625
Artemis
goddess, 979
Arterialize
to aerate, 338
Artery
conduit, 350
Artesian well
conduit, 348
Artful
cunning, 702
deceitful, 544
Article
thing, 3, 316
goods, 798
part, 51
conditions, 770
dissertation, 595
Articles
belief, 484, 983
Articulation
speech, 580
junction, 43
Artifice
cunning, 702
plan, 626
deception, 545
Artificer
agent, 690
Artificial
cunning, 702
fictitious, 544
style, 579
Artillery
arms, 727

corps of, 726
explosion, 404
Artisan
agent, 690
Artist
contriver, 626
producer, 164
painter, 559
agent, 690
Artiste
the drama, 599
Artistic
skilful, 698
beautiful, 845
tasteful, 850
Artless
natural, 703
veracious, 543
plain, 576
As
motive, 615
Ascend
ascent, 305
Ascendancy
Power, 157, 175
success, 731
Ascent
rise, 305
acclivity, 217
glory, 873
Ascertain
find out, 480A
Asceticism
asceticism, 955
temperance, 953
Ascribable
effect, 154
Ascribe
attribution, 155
Asepsis
cleanness, 652
Ash colour
grey, 432
Ashamed
shame, 874
humility, 879
modest, 881
Ashes
residue, 40
corpse, 362
Ashore
land, 342
Ashy
colourless, 429
Aside

laterally, 236
privately, 528
soliloquy, 589
Aside (to put)
relinquish, 624
disuse, 678
Asinine
imbecile, 499
Ask
inquire, 461
request, 765
as price, 812
supplicate, 990
Askance
obliquity, 217
doubt, 485
Askew
oblique, 217
distorted, 243
Aslant
obliquity, 217
Asleep
inactivity, 683
Aslope
obliquity, 217
Aspect
appearance, 448
state, 7
feature, 5
situation, 183
relation, 9
of thought, 453
Asperge
sprinkle, 337
Aspergillum
spray, 348
Asperity
roughness, 256
tartness, 895
anger, 900
Asperse
detraction, 934
Aspersorium
spray, 348
Asphalt
semiliquid, 352
Asphyxiate
killing, 361
Aspirant
petitioner, 767
Aspirate
voice, 580
Aspire
rise, 305
desire, 865

hope, 858
project, 620
Ass
beast of burden, 271
fool, 501
Assagai
arms, 727
Assail
attack, 716
plain, 830
Assailant
opponent, 710
attacker 716, 726
Assassinate
killing, 361
Assault
attack, 716
Assay
experiment, 463
Assemble
assemblage, 72
Assembly-room
sociality, 892
Assent
agree, 488
consent, 762
Assert
affirm, 535
claim as a right, 924
Assess
measure, 466
judge, 480
price, 812
Assessor
adviser, 695
Assets
property, 780
money, 800
Asseverate
affirm, 535
Assiduous
activity, 682
Assign
attribute, 155
transfer, 783
give, 784
commission, 755
allot, 786
duty, 926
Assignat
money, 800
Assignation
sociality, 892
Assignee
receive, 785

Assignment
allotment, 786
business, 625
commission, 755
Assimilate
resemble, 17, 144
imitate, 19
agree, 23
Assist
aid, 707
benefit, 906
Assistant
auxiliary, 711
Assize
measure, 466
tribunal, 966
Associate
accompany, 88
concur, 178
unite, 43
mixture, 41
assemble, 72
friend, 890
society, 892
Association
relation, 9
intuition, 477
Assoil
free, 750
acquit, 970
Assonance
similarity, 17
poetry, 597
Assort
arrange, 60
Assortment
class, 75
collection, 72
Assuage
physically, 174
morally, 826
relieve, 834
Assume
suppose, 514
evidence, 467
hope, 858
right, 924
insolence, 739, 885
pride, 878
falsehood, 544
Assumption
qualification, 469
severity, 739
Assurance
assertion, 535

promise, 768
certainty, 474
belief, 484
hope, 858
insolence, 885
Assuredly
positively, 31
assert, 488
safety, 664
Asterisk
indication, 550
expletive, 908
Astern
rear, 235
Asteroid
world, 318
Asteroth
deity, 979
Asthenia
weakness, 160
Astigmatism
dim-sightedness, 443
Astonish
wonder, 870
Astonishing
great, 31
Astound
surprise, 870
excite, 824
Astraea
right, 922
Astral
world, 318
immaterial, 317
Astray
deviation, 279
Astriction
junction, 43
Astride
support, 215
Astringent
contraction, 195
Astrology
prediction, 511
Astronaut
navigator, 269
Astronautics
navigation, 267
Astronomy
world, 318
Astrophysics
world, 318
Astute
wisdom, 498

Asunder
separate, 44
distant, 196
disjunction, 44

Asylum
retreat, 666
hospital, 662
defence, 717

Asymmetry
disorder, 59, 243

Asymptote
converge, 290

At-home
sociality, 892

At once
transientness, 111

At the end of the day
finally, 67

Ataraxia
insensibility, 823

Atavism
reversion, 145

Atelier
workshop, 691

Atheism
irreligion, 989
unbelief, 485

Athena
goddess, 979

Athirst
desire, 865

Athletic
strength, 159

Athletics
training, 673
contention, 720

Athwart
oblique, 217
crossing, 219
opposing, 708

Atlantis
visionary, 515

Atlas
support, 215
strength, 159;
maps, 554

Atmosphere
air, 338
circumstances, 227

Atoll
island, 346

Atom
small in degree, 32
in size, 193
particle, 330

Atomic bomb
arms, 727

Atomizer
spray, 348

Atonality
melody, 413

Atonement
atonement, 952
religious, 976
reward, 973

Atony
weakness, 160

Atrabilious
dejection, 837

Atrocious
vice, 945
guilt, 947
malevolence, 907

Atrophy
shrinking, 195
disease, 655
decay, 659

Attaboy
approval, 931

Attach
join, 43
love, 897
legal, 969

Attaché
servant, 746
consignee, 758

Attaché-case
receptacle, 191

Attachment
see Attach

Attack
attack, 716
disease, 655

Attain
arrive, 292
succeed, 731

Attainable
possible, 470
easy, 705

Attainder
condemnation, 971

Attainment
learning, 539
knowledge, 490
skill, 698

Attar
fragrance, 400

Attemper
mix, 41
moderate, 174

Attempt
undertaking, 676
try, 675

Attend
accompany, 88
follow, 281
treat, 662
apply the mind, 457
frequent, 136
be present, 186

Attendant
servant, 746

Attention
attention, 451, 457
respect, 928

Attentions
courtesy, 894
courtship, 902
kindness, 906

Attenuate
lessen, 36
rarefy, 322
contract, 195
narrow, 203

Attest
bear testimony, 467
indicate, 550
adjure, 768

Attestation
record, 551

Attic
garret, 191
high, 206
elegant, 578
wit, 842
taste, 850

Atticism
wit, 842

Attila
evildoer, 913

Attire
vestment, 225

Attitude
posture, 183, 240
circumstance, 8

Attitudinize
affectation, 855
ostentation, 882

Attorney
consignee, 758, 769
in law, 968

Attract
bring towards, 288
please, 829
allure, 865

Attractability
motive, 615
Attractive
beautiful, 845
pleasing, 829
lovely, 897
alluring, 615
Attrahent
attraction, 288
Attributable
effect, 154
Attribute
power, 157
Attribution
attribution, 155
Attribution
friction, 331
Attroupement
assemblage, 72
Attune
music, 415
prepare, 673
Au courant
knowledge, 490
Au fait
knowledge, 490
Au fond
truth, 494
inbeing, 5
Au pied de la lettre
truth, 494
meaning, 516
Au revoir
departure, 293
Aubade
music, 415
Auburn
brown, 433
Auction
sale, 796
Auctorial
book, 593
Audacity
courage, 861
insolence, 863, 885
Audi alteram partem
evidence, 468
right, 922
Audible
sound, 402
Audience
hearing, 418
conversation, 588
Audiometer
hearing, 418

Audiphone
hearing, 418
Audit
accounts, 811
numeration, 85
Audition
hearing, 418
Auditor
hearer, 418
accounts, 811
Auditorium
amusement, 840
Auditory
hearing, 418
Auf wiedersehen
departure, 293
Auger
perforation, 262
Augment
to increase, 35
thing added, 39
Augmentation
expansion, 194
Augur
predict, 507, 511
soothsayer, 513
Augury
prediction, 511, 512
August
repute, 873
Augustine
clergy, 996
Aura
touch, 380
emanation, 295
Aureate
yellowness, 436
Aureole
light, 420
Aureolin
orange, 439
Auricular
hearing, 418
Aurist
doctor, 662
Aurora
light, 423
dawn, 125
Auroral
rosy, 434
Auscultation
hearing, 418
Auspices
patronage, 175
prediction, 511

Auspicious
hopeful, 858
prosperous, 734
expedient, 646
opportune, 134
Auster
wind, 349
Austere
harsh taste, 395
severe, 739
discourteous, 895
ascetic, 955
Austerity
economy, 817
Authentic
truth, 494
certain, 474
existence, 1
Authenticate
record, 551
evidence, 467
security, 771
Author
producer, 164
cause, 153
writer, 590
Authoritative
certain, 474
peremptory, 741
Authority
power, 157, 737
command, 741
right, 924
permission, 760
testimony, 467
sign, 500
Auto da fé
burning, 384
execution, 972
Autobahn
way, 627
Autobiography
description, 594
Autobus
vehicle, 272
Autocar
vehicle, 272
Autochrome
photograph, 556
Autochthonous
inhabitant, 188
Autocracy
severity, 739
authority, 737

Autocrat
   master, 745
Autocratic
   arbitrary, 739, 964
   will, 600
Autocycle
   vehicle, 272
Autogiro
   aircraft, 273A
Autograph
   warranty, 467
   signature, 550
   writing, 590
Autolycus
   thief, 792
Automatic
   mechanical, 601
   insensible, 823
Automation
   means, 632
Automobile
   vehicle, 272
Autonomy
   freedom, 748
Autopsy
   vision, 441
   disinter, 363
Autotype
   copy, 21
Aux abois
   death, 360
Aux aguets
   care, 459
Auxiliary
   aid, 707
   helper, 711
   intermediary, 631
Avail
   use, 677
   utility, 644
Avalanche
   fall, 306
   debacle, 348
Avant-courier
   pioneer, 673
   precursor, 64
Avant-garde
   go-ahead, 282
Avarice
   parsimony, 819
Avast
   quiescence, 265
   cessation, 142
Avaunt
   disappear, 449
   depart, 293

   repulse, 289
Ave
   arrival, 292
Avenge
   revenge, 919
Avenue
   street, 189
   method, 627
Aver
   affirmation, 535
Average
   mean, 29
   ordinary, 82, 736
Avernus
   hell, 982
Averse
   unwilling, 603
   repugnant, 616
Aversion
   dislike, 867
   enmity, 889;
   hate, 898
Avert
   hindrance, 706
Aviary
   collection, 636
   taming, 370
Aviation
   locomotion, 267
Avidity
   desire, 865
   avarice, 819
Avifauna
   animals, 366
Avocation
   business, 625
   diversion, 840
Avoid
   shun, 623, 867
Avoirdupois
   weight, 319
Avouch
   affirmation, 535
Avow
   assert, 535
   assent, 488
   disclose, 529
Avulsion
   separation, 44
   extraction, 301
Await
   future, 121
   impend, 152
Awake
   excite, 824

   incite, 615
   active, 682
   attentive, 457
   careful, 459
Award
   lawsuit, 969
   judgment, 480
   decision, 609
   giving, 784
   trophy, 733
Aware
   knowledge, 490
Away
   absence, 187
Awe
   wonder, 870
   fear, 860
Aweary
   weariness, 841
Awestruck
   fear, 860
Awful
   great, 31
   fearful, 860
Awhile
   transientness, 111
Awkward
   unskilful, 699
   vulgar, 851
   ridiculous, 853
   difficult, 704
Awl
   perforator, 262
Awn
   bristle, 253
Awning
   tent, 222
   shade, 424
   top, 210
Awry
   oblique, 217
   distorted, 243
Axe
   edge tool, 253
   weapon, 727
   for beheading, 975
Axiom
   maxim, 496
Axiomatic
   truth, 494
   certain, 474
   demonstrable, 469, 478
Axis
   rotation, 312
   length, 200

support, 215
centre, 223
Axle
rotation, 312
Ay
yes, 488
affirmation, 535
Ayah
keeper, 753
Aye
ever, 112
Azimuth
direction, 278
obliquity, 217
Azoic
inanimate, 358
Azure
blueness, 438
Azygous
unity, 87

Baa
animal sound, 412
Baal
divinity, 979
idol, 986
Babel
talk, 584
nonsense, 517
faint sound, 405
flow, 348
Babe
infant, 129
innocent, 946
novice, 701
Bable
confusion, 59
discord, 414
Baboon
ugliness, 846
Baby
fool, 501
Baby-sitter
deputy, 759
Babyhood
youth, 127
Babyish
folly, 499
Bacca
tobacco, 298A
Bacchanals
drunk, 959
Bacchus
drunkenness, 959
Bachelor

celibacy, 904
Bacillus
bane, 663
Back
rear, 235
convexity, 250
to recede, 283
to aid, 707
Back-blocks
interior, 221
Back down
revoke, 607
Back out
revoke, 607
relinquish, 624
Back to square one
hindrance, 706
Back-scratcher
flatterer, 935
Backbite
traduce, 932
detract, 934
Backbiter
detractor, 936
Backbone
frame, 215
interior, 221
strength, 159
decision, 604
intrinsic, 5
Backer
friend, 891
Backhanded
oblique, 717
unexpected, 508
Backhander
attack, 716
Backlash
recoil, 145
Backlog
leeway, 304
Backsheesh
see Baksheesh
Backsliding
dishonour, 940
delinquency, 945
relapse, 661
tergiversation, 607
heresy, 984A
Backward
regression, 283
traction, 285
unwilling, 603
Backwardation
discount, 813

Backwardness
unwillingness, 603
indocility, 538
dislike, 867
Backwoodsman
inhabitant, 188
forester, 371
Bacon, to save one's
escape, 671
Bad
badness, 649, 945
evil, 619
wrong, 923
putrid, 653
Bad blood
enmity, 889
Bad show
disapproval, 932
failure, 732
Badge
indication, 550
Badger
to maltreat, 830
question, 461
stink, 401
Badinage
wit, 842
ridicule, 856
Badmash
knave, 941
Baedeker
guide, 266
Baffle
thwart, 706
defeat, 731
Baffling
bewildering, 528
Baff
club, 276
Bag
receptacle, 191
to take, 789, 791
to receive, 810
to pocket, 184
Bagatelle
trifle, 643
Baggage
property, 780
materials, 634
hussy, 962
Baggy
loose, 47
bulging, 250
Bagman
agent, 758

Bagnio
impurity, 961
Bagpipe
musical instrument, 417
Bagpiper
musician, 416
Bags
greatness, 31
plenty, 639
Bah
contempt, 930
Baikie
receptacle, 191
Bail
security, 771
Bail up
rob, 791
Bailiff
director, 694
servant, 746
officer, 965
factor, 758
Bailiwick
region, 181
tribunal, 966
Bairn
infant, 129
Bait
allurement, 615
food, 298, 689
harass, 907, 830
Bake
heat, 384
Bakehouse
furnace, 386
Baker's dozen
thirteen, 98
Baksheesh
gratuity, 784
Balance
equality, 27
symmetry, 242
remainder, 40
numeration, 85
measure, 466
weight, 319
money, 800
accounts, 811
mean, 29
steadiness, 265
Balcony
convexity, 250
theatre, 599
Bald
bare, 226

ugly, 846
in style, 575
Baldachin
canopy, 222
Balderdash
absurdity, 497
nonsense, 517
Baldric
girdle, 247
Bale bundle, 72
evil, 619
Bale out
ejection, 297
Baleful
badness, 649
Balk
hinder, 706
fail, 731
disappoint, 509
deceive, 545
Ball
globe, 249
missile, 284, 727
dance, 840
Ball-point
pen, 590
Ballad
song, 415
poem, 597
Ballad opera
drama, 599
Ballade
poem, 597
music, 415
Ballast
weight, 319
compensation, 30
steadiness, 150
wisdom, 498
Ballet
amusement, 840
Ballistics
propulsion, 284
Ballon d'essai
feeler, 461, 463
Balloon
aircraft, 273A
Ballot
choice, 609
Ballyhoo
publicity, 531
Ballyrag
abuse, 932
Balm
fragrance, 400

relief, 834
lenitive, 174
remedy, 662
Balmoral
cap, 225
Balmy
foolish, 499
Balsam
see Balm
Balsamic
salubrious, 656
Baluster
support, 215
Balustrade
enclosure, 232
Bamboo curtain
secret, 533
Bamboozle
deception, 545
Ban
prohibition, 761
denunciation, 908
condemnation, 971
Banal
commonplace, 82, 643
feeble, 575
Banausic
menial, 876
Band
ligature, 45
assemblage, 72
party, 712
of music, 416
shackle, 752
Bandage
ligature, 45
to lie, 43
Bandbox
receptacle, 191
Banderole
flag, 550
Bandersnatch
swiftness, 274
Bandit
thief, 792
Bandog
warning, 668
Bandolier
roundness, 247
Bands
canonicals, 999
Bandy
agitate, 315
contest, 476, 720
exchange, 148

crooked, 245
deformed, 876
Bandy-legged
distorted, 243
curved, 245
Bane
badness, 649, 663
Bang
sound, 406
to impel, 276
to beat, 972
Bangle
ornament, 847
Banian day
fast, 956
scanty, 640
Banish
exclude, 55, 297
displace, 185
seclude, 893
punish, 972
Banister
support, 215
Banjo
musical instrument, 417
Bank
side of river, 342
acclivity, 217
store, 636
money, 802
deviate, 279
Banker
treasurer, 801
Bankruptcy
failure, 732
non-payment, 808
Banlieue
nearness, 197
Banner
indication, 550
Banneret
nobility, 875
Banquet
meal, 298
feast, 840
gluttony, 957
Banshee
demon, 980
Bantam
small, 193
low, 207
Banter
wit, 842
ridicule, 856
Bantling

child, 129
offspring, 167
Baptism
rite, 998
Baptistery
temple, 1000
Baptize
name, 564
Bar
hindrance, 706
line, 200
to exclude, 55
close, 261
enclosure, 232
prison, 752
prohibition, 761
tribunal, 966
legal profession, 968
drink, 298
Baragouin
absurdity, 497
Barb
spike, 253
horse, 271
Barbarian
evildoer, 913
Barbarism
discourtesy, 895
solecism, 568
Barbarous
maleficent, 907
vulgar, 851
rude, 876
style, 579
Barbette
defence, 717
Barbican
defence, 717
Bard
poetry, 597
Bare
mere, 32
nude, 226
scanty, 640
exposed to view, 446
Barefaced
visible, 446
shameless, 885
insolent, 886
Barefoot
divest, 226
Bareheaded
divest, 226
respect, 928
Barely

smallness, 32
Bargain
compact, 769
barter, 794
promise, 768
cheap, 813, 815
Bargain, into the
addition, 37
Barge
ship, 273
Bargee
mariner, 269
Baritone
deep-toned, 408
Bark
rind, 223
ship, 273
to yelp, 412
to censure, 932
Barker
interpreter, 524
publicity, 531
Barm
yeast, 353
Barmy
foolish, 499
Barn
abode, 189
Barnacles
spectacles, 445
Barometer
measurement, 466
air, 338
Baron
nobility, 875
master, 745
Baronet
nobility, 875
Baronetage
list, 86
Baronetcy
title, 877
Baroque
ridiculous, 853
Barque
ship, 273
Barquentine
ship, 273
Barrack
abode, 189
Barrage
obstacle, 706
Barred
crossed, 219
striped, 440

Barrel
vessel, 191
cylinder, 249
Barren
sterile, 169
useless, 645
Barricade
fence, 232
prison, 752
obstacle, 706
Barrier
fence, 232
obstacle, 706
Barring
except, 83
save, 38
Barrister
lawyer, 968
Barrow
vehicle, 272
grave, 363
Barter
exchange, 794
Bas bleu
affectation, 855
Bascule
instrument, 633
Base
lowest part, 211P
support, 215
bad, 649
dishonourable, 940
shameful, 874
vicious, 945
cowardly, 862
plebeian, 876
Base-minded
improbity, 940
Baseless
unreal, 2
erroneous, 495
Basement
base, 211
Bashaw
ruler, 745
Bashful
modesty, 881
Basic
support, 215
Basic English
language, 560
Basilica
temple, 1000
Basilisk
serpent, 949
monster, 83

evil eye, 441
Basin
hollow, 252
vessel, 191
plain, 344
dock, 189
Basis
preparation, 673
foundation, 215
Bask
warmth, 382
physical enjoyment, 377
moral enjoyment, 827
prosperity, 734
Basket
receptacle, 191
Basket-work
plaiting, 219
Basketry
plaiting, 219
Bas-relief
convexity, 250
Bass
deep-sounding, 408, 413
Bass/viol
musical instrument, 417
Bassinette
vehicle, 272
Basso rilievo
convexity, 250P
sculpture, 557
Bassoon
musical instrument, 417
Bastard
spurious, 544, 925
erroneous, 495
Bastardy
illegitimacy, 964
Baste
beat, 276
punish, 972
Bastille
prison, 752
Bastinado
punishment, 972
Bastion
defence, 717
Bat
club, 633, 727
spree, 840
Batch
assemblage, 72
quantity, 25
Bate
diminish, 36, 38

reduce price, 813
Bath
immersion, 300
water, 337
Bath-chair
vehicle, 272
Bath-room
room, 191
Bathe
immersion, 300
plunge, 310
Bathing-suit
dress, 225
Bathos
depth, 208
anticlimax, 497
ridiculous, 853
Bathymetry
depth, 208
Bathysphere
depth, 208
Baton
sceptre, 747
impact, 276
Bats
insane, 503
Battalion
troop, 726
assemblage, 72
Batten
feed, 296
Batter
beat, 276
destroy, 162
Battered
imperfect, 651
Battering-ram
weapon, 276, 727
Battery
instrument, 633
Battle
contention, 720
Battle array
warfare, 722
arrangement, 60
Battle-axe
arms, 727
Battle-bowler
defence, 717
Battle-cruiser
ship, 273
Battle-dress
dress, 225
Battle-field
arena, 728

Battlement
bulwark, 666
defence, 717
enclosure, 232
embrasure, 257
Battleship
ship, 273
Battue
pursuit, 622
killing, 361
Batty
insane, 503
Bauble
trifle, 643
toy, 840
Baulk
see Balk
Bavardage
absurdity, 497
Bawbee
money, 800
Bawd
libertine, 962
Bawdy
impurity, 961
Bawl
cry, 411, 839
Bay
gulf, 343
brown, 433
to howl, 412
Bay, at
defence, 717
Bayadère
dancer, 599
Bayard
carrier, 271
perfection, 650
Bayonet
arms, 727
attack, 716
kill, 361
Bays
trophy, 733
reward, 973
Bazaar
mart, 799
Bazooka
gun, 727
Be
existence, 1
Be of
inclusion, 76
Be off
departure, 293

ejection, 297
Beach
land, 342
Beacon
sign, 423, 550
warning, 668
Bead-roll
list, 86
Beadle
janitor, 263
officer, 745
law officer, 965
church, 996
Beads
rite, 998
Beak
front, 234
nose, 250
judge, 967
Beaker
receptacle, 191
Beam
support, 215
of a balance, 466
of light, 420
beauty, 845
Beamless
darkness, 421
Bean-feast
pleasure, 827, 840
meal, 298
Bear
sustain, 215
produce, 161
carry, 270
suffer, 821
admit, 470
brute, 895
Bear down upon
attack, 716
Bear-garden
arena, 728
brawl, 713
Bear-leader
teacher, 540
Bear off
taking, 789
Bear out
confirm, 467
vindicate, 937
Bear up
cheerfulness, 836
Bear upon
influence, 175
evidence, 467

to relate to, 9
Bear with
indulge, 740
Bearable
tolerable, 651
Beard
spike, 253
rough, 256
to defy, 715
courage, 861
insolence, 885
Beardless
youth, 127
Bearer
carrier, 271
Bearing
support, 215
direction, 278
meaning, 516
appearance, 448
demeanour, 692
circumstance, 8
situation, 183
Bearish
discourtesy, 895
Beast
animal, 366
blackguard, 895
Beastly
uncleanness, 653
Beat
strike, 716, 972
surpass, 33, 303
periodic, 138
oscillation, 314
agitation, 315
crush, 330
sound, 407
succeed, 731
line of pursuit, 625
news, 532
Beat down
chaffer, 794
insolent, 885
Beat hollow
superiority, 33
Beat it
go away, 293, 287
escape, 671
Beat off
defence, 717
Beat time
chronometry, 114
Beat up for
seek, 461

Beautify
enrapture, 829
honour, 873
sanctify, 987, 995
Beating
impulse, 276
Beatnik
hippy, 183
Beatitude
pleasure, 827
Beau
fop, 854
man, 373
admirer, 897
Beau idéal
beauty, 845
perfection, 650
Beau monde
fashion, 852
nobility, 875
Beau sabreur
hero, 861
Beauty
beauty, 845
ornament, 847
symmetry, 242
Beaver
hat, 225
Bebop
melody, 413
Becalm
quiescence, 265
Because
attribution, 155
reasoning, 476
motive, 615
Bechance
eventuality, 151
Beck
rill, 348
signal, 550
mandate, 741
Beckon
signal, 550
Becloud
darkness, 421
Become
change to, 144
behove, 926
Become of
event, 151
Becoming
proper, 646
beautiful, 845
just, 922

apt, 23
Bed
layer, 204
support, 215
lodgment, 191
Bed-maker
servant, 746
Bedabble
splash, 337
Bedarken
darkness, 421
Bedaub
cover, 222
dirt, 653
deface, 846
Bedazzle
light, 420
Bedeck
beauty, 845
ornament, 847
Bedevil
derange, 61
bewitch, 992
Bedew
moisture, 339
Bedfellow
friend, 890
Bedight
beauty, 845
Bedim
darkness, 421
Bedizen
beautify, 845
ornament, 851
Bedlam
insanity, 503
Bedlamite
madman, 504
Bedraggle
soil, 653
Bedridden
disease, 655
Bedstead
support, 215
Bedtime
evening, 126
Bee
active, 682
party, 892
Bee-line
direction, 278
Bee-witted
folly, 499
Beef
complain, 839

Beefy
corpulent, 192
Beelzebub
Satan, 978
Beery
drunken, 959
Beeswax
oil, 356
Beetle
high, 206
projecting, 250
impact, 276
Befall
eventuality, 151
Befit
agree, 23
Befitting
right, 926
expedient, 646
Befool
deceive, 503, 545
baffle, 732
Before
precedence, 62
Before Christ
period, 108
Beforehand
prior, 116, 132
Befoul
uncleanness, 653
Beg
request, 765
Beg the question
evidence, 467
Beget
produce, 161
Begetter
father, 166
Beggar
petitioner, 767
poor, 804
Beggarly
mean, 643
vulgar, 876
servile, 886
vile, 940
Begilt
ornament, 847
Begin
beginning, 66
Begin again
repetition, 104
Beginner
learner, 541
novice, 674

400

Beginning to end, from,
 whole, 50
 completeness, 52
 duration, 106
Begird
 encircle, 227, 231
Begone
 depart, 293
 repel, 289
Begrime
 soil, 653
 deface, 846
Begrudge
 refusal, 764
 parsimony, 819
Beguile
 deceive, 545
 amuse, 840
Beguine
 nun, 996
Begum
 nobility, 875
Behalf
 advantage, 618
 aid, 707
Behave
 conduct, 692
Behead
 punish, 972
 divide, 44
Behest
 command, 741
Behind
 in order, 63
 in space, 235
Behindhand
 late, 133
 adversity, 735
 insolvent, 808
 shortcoming, 304
Behold
 vision, 441
Beholden
 grateful, 916
 obligatory, 926
Behoof
 good, 618
Behove
 duty, 926
Bein
 prosperous, 734
Being
 abstract, 1
 conduct, 3
Bejan

 learner, 541
Bel canto
 music, 415
Bel esprit
 humorist, 844
Belabour
 thump, 972
 buffet, 276
Belated
 late, 133
 confused, 491
Belaud
 approbation, 931
Belay
 junction, 43
 stop, 265
Belch
 ejection, 297
Beldam
 old woman, 130
 hag, 913
Beleaguer
 attack, 716
Belfry
 height, 206
 church, 1000
 head, 450
Belie
 falsify, 544
 misinterpret, 523
 deny, 536
 disagreement, 24
 oppose, 708
Belief
 credence, 484
 supposition, 514
 religious creed, 983
Believer
 piety, 987
Belike
 probability, 472
Belittle
 disparage, 483
Bell
 sound, 417
 cry, 412
 funeral, 363
 alarm, 669
Bell-boy
 messenger, 534
Bell-shaped
 globose, 249
 concave, 252
Bell-washer
 precursor, 64

Belle
 woman, 374
 beauty, 845
Belles-lettres
 language, 560
 knowledge, 490
Bellicose
 warlike, 722
Belligerent
 warfare, 722
Bellow
 cry, 411, 412
 complain, 839
Bellows
 wind, 349
Belly
 receptacle, 191
 interior, 221
 to bulge, 250
Belly-ache
 complain, 839
Belly-god
 glutton, 957
Belly-timber
 food, 298
Bellyful
 sufficiency, 639
 fullness, 52
Belong
 related, 9
 property, 717
 attribute, 157
 duty, 926
 inclusion, 76
Belongings
 property, 780
Beloved
 lover, 897, 899
Below
 lowness, 207
 posterior, 117
Belt
 girdle, 247
 gulf, 343
 outline, 229
 blow, 276
Belvedere
 vision, 441
Bemire
 soil, 653
Bemoan
 lament, 839
Bemuddle
 bewilder, 458
Bemuse
 bewilder, 458

Ben
height, 206
interior, 221
Ben trovato
probable, 472
falsehood, 544
deception, 545
Bench
support, 215
council, 696
tribunal, 966
Bencher
lawyer, 968
Bend
curve, 245
angularity, 244
circle, 247
yield, 324, 725
circuit, 311
obliquity, 217
descent, 806
deviation, 279
bow, 308
humble, 879
Bend to
tend, 176
habit, 613
Bending
pliant, 324
Beneath
under, 207
unbecoming, 940
Benedick
marriage, 903
Benedictine
clergy, 996
Benediction
approval, 931
gratitude, 916
worship, 990
Benefaction
giving, 784
Benefactor
benevolence, 912
giver, 784
Benefice
churchdom, 995
Beneficent
benevolence, 906
Beneficial
useful, 644
good, 648
Beneficiary
clergy, 996

Benefit
advantage, 618
acquisition, 775
benevolence, 906
Benevolence
kindness, 906
love, 897;
tax, 812
Benighted
ignorance, 491
darkness, 421
Benignant
benevolence, 906
Benison
approbation, 931
Bent
direction, 278
inclination, 602
desire, 865
tendency, 176
intentions, 629
affections, 820
dishonest, 940
Bent on
willing, 602
resolved, 604, 620
desirous, 865
Benthamite
philanthropy, 910
Benumb
cold, 383
general insensibility,
376
tactual insensibility, 381
apathy, 823
Beplaster
cover, 222
Bepraise
approbation, 931
Bequeath
giving, 784
Bequest
gift, 784
acquisition, 775
Berceuse
music, 415
Bereave
take away, 789
Bereavement
loss, 789
Bereft
poor, 804
loss, 776
Bergschrund
interval, 198

Berlin
vehicle, 272
Berry
brown, 433
Bersagliere
combatant, 726
Berserker
combatant, 726
violence, 173
Berth
lodging, 189
bed, 191
repose, 215
Beryl
ornament, 847
Beseech
request, 765
Beseem
duty, 926
Beset
surround, 227
difficulty, 704
entreaty, 765
beshrew, 908
by the side of, 216
Besetting
habitual, 613
Beshrew
curse, 908
Beside
except, 83
accompaniment, 216
Beside, oneself
insanity, 503
Beside the mark
irrelation, 10
Besides
addition, 37, 88
Besiege
attack, 716
solicit, 765
Beslaver
flattery, 933
Beslime
uncleanness, 653
Beslobber
uncleanness, 653
Besmear
soil, 653
deface, 846
cover, 222
Besmirch
soil, 653
deface, 846

Besmudge
dirt, 653
Besom
cleanness, 652
Besotted
prejudiced, 481
foolish, 499
Bespangle
ornament, 847
Bespatter
soil, 653
spoil, 659
deface, 846
revile, 932
flatter, 933
Bespeak
indicate, 516
evidence, 467
commission, 755
earliness, 132
request, 765
Bespeckle
variegation, 440
Bespotted
variegation, 440
Besprinkle
mix, 41
wet, 337
Best
perfection, 650
to outwit, 545
Bestial
impurity, 961
Bestir
activity, 682, 686
Bestow
giving, 784
Bestraddle
sit, 215
Bestrew
disperse, 73
Bestride
mount, 206
sit, 215
Bestud
emboss, 250
Bet
chance, 621
Betake
business, 625
Bête noire
fear, 860
hate, 898
Bethink
memory, 505

Bethump
beat, 276
Betide
eventuality, 151
Betimes
earliness, 132
Bêtise
blunder, 699, 732
Betoken
indicate, 550
predict, 511
Betray
disclose, 529
deceive, 545
dishonour, 940
appear, 446
Betroth
promise, 768
Betrothed
affianced, 897
Betsy
gun, 727
Better (to)
improvement, 658
Between
interjacence, 228
Between-maid
servant, 746
Betwixt
interjacence, 228
Bevel
obliquity, 217
Bever
food, 298
Bevy
assemblage, 72, 102
Bewail
lamentation, 839
Beware
warn, 668
care, 459
afraid, 862
cautious, 864
Bewilder
confuse, 458
mislead, 538
perplex, 519, 528
astonish, 870
Bewildered
ignorant, 491
Bewitch
please, 829
exorcise, 992
influence, 615
Bewray

disclose, 529
Bey
master, 745
Beyond
distance, 196
Biannual
periodic, 138
Bias
slope, 217
prepossession, 481
unfairness, 923
inclination, 602
tendency, 176
motive, 615
disposition, 820
Biblacious
drunkenness, 959
Bibelot
trifle, 643
Bible
revelation, 985
Bibliography
list, 86
book, 593
Bibliolatry
heterodoxy, 984A
knowledge, 490
Bibliology
book, 593
Bibliomania
erudition, 490
book, 593
Bibliophile
book, 593
scholar, 492
Bibulous
spongy, 322
drunken, 959
Bicentenary
period, 138
celebration, 883
Bicentric
duality, 89
Bicker
flutter, 315
discord, 713
quarrel, 720
Bicuspid
bisection, 91
Bicycle
travel, 266
Bid
order, 741
offer, 763
Bid for
bargain, 794

Biddable
  obedient, 743
Bide
  tarry, 133
  remain, 141
Bide one's time
  future, 121
Biennial
  periodic, 138
Bienséance
  polish, 852
  manners, 894
Bier
  interment, 363
Bifacial
  duplication, 90
Bifarious
  duality, 89
Biff
  impact, 276
Bifocal
  duality, 89
Bifold
  duplication, 90
Biform
  duplication, 90
  bisection, 91
Biformity
  duality, 89
Bifurcation
  bisection, 91
  fork, 244
Big
  in degree, 31
  in size, 192
Big pot
  importance, 642
Bigamy
  marriage, 903
Bight
  gulf, 343
  bend, 245
Bigot
  impiety, 989
Bigoted
  imbecile, 499
  prejudiced, 481
  obstinate, 606
Bigotry
  prejudice, 481
  credulity, 486
  certainty, 474
  obstinacy, 606
  heterodoxy, 984A

Bigwig
  sage, 500
  pedant, 492
  notability, 642, 875
Bijou
  gem, 650
  little, 193
Bijouterie
  ornament, 847
Bike
  bicycle, 266
Bikini
  dress, 225
Bilateral
  duplication, 90
  side, 236
Bilbo
  arms, 727
Bilboes
  prison, 752
Bile
  resentment, 900
Bilge
  trash, 645
Bilge-water
  dirt, 653
Bilious
  dejection, 837
Bilk
  deception, 545
  swindle, 791
  disappointment, 509
Bill
  money, account, 811
  charge, 812
  money-order, 800
  security, 771
  in law, 969
  placard, 531
  ticket, 550
  instrument, 633
  weapon, 727
  sharpness, 253
Bill of fare
  food, 298
  list, 86
  plan, 626
Billabong
  river, 348
Billet
  epistle, 592
  ticket, 550
  to apportion, 786
  to locate, 184
Billet-doux

epistle, 592
endearment, 902
Billiard-table
  level, 213
Billingsgate
  scolding, 932
  imprecatory, 908
Billion
  numbers, 98
Billow
  wave, 348
Billycock
  hat, 225
Bimetallism
  money, 800
Bimonthly
  periodical, 138
Bin
  receptacle, 191
Binary
  duality, 89
Bind
  connect, 43
  compel, 744
  obligation, 926
  condition, 770
Binge
  amusement, 840
Bingle
  clip, 201
Binoculars
  lens, 445
Binomial
  duplication, 90
Bint
  girl, 374
Biograph
  spectacle, 448
Biographer
  recorder, 553
Biography
  description, 594
Biology
  organization, 357
  life, 359
Bioscope
  spectacle, 448
Bipartition
  duplication, 91
Biplane
  aircraft, 273A
Birch
  scourge, 975
  to punish, 972

Bird
  animal, 366
Bird of passage
  traveller, 268
Bird-fancier
  collector, 775
Bird-lime
  vinculum, 45
Bird's-eye
  tobacco, 298A
  general, 78
Bird's-eye view
  sight, 448
Birds of a feather
  inclusion, 76
  conformity, 82
Bireme
  ship, 273
Biretta
  cap, 225
  vestments, 999
Biro
  pen, 590
Birth
  beginning, 66
  production, 161
  nobility, 875
Birthday
  anniversary, 138
Birthmark
  blemish, 848
Birthplace
  origin, 153
Birthright
  dueness, 924
Bis
  duplication, 89
  repetition, 104
Bise
  wind, 349
Bisection
  duality, 91
Bishop
  clergy, 996
Bishopric
  churchdom, 995
Bissextile
  period, 108
Bistoury
  sharpness, 253
Bistre
  brown, 433
Bisulcate
  fold, 258, 259
Bit

part, 51
mixture, 41
small quantity, 32
money, 800
curb, 752
Bit by bit
  part, 51
  degree, 26
Bitch
  bad woman, 949
Bite
  pain, 378
  painful, 830
  cheat, 545
Biting
  cold, 383
  pungent, 392
  painful, 830
Bitter
  taste, 395
  cold, 383
  animosity, 898
  wrath, 900
  malevolence, 907
  regret, 833
  painful, 830
Bitumen
  semiliquid, 352
Bivouac
  repose, 265
  to encamp, 186
  camp, 189;
  watch, 664
Bizarre
  ridiculous, 853
  unconformity, 83
Blab
  disclosure, 529
Black
  colour, 431
  crime, 945
  copy, 590
Black-and-white
  colourless, 429
Black art
  sorcery, 992
Black hole
  prison, 752
Black-letter
  printing, 591
Black looks
  discourtesy, 598
Black market
  illegality, 964
  theft, 791

Black-out
  darkness, 421
Black out
  obliterate, 552
Black sheep
  bad man, 949
Blackamoor
  blackness, 431
Blackball
  exclude, 55
  reject, 610
  seclude, 893
  disapprove, 932
Blacken
  disapprobation, 932
Blackguard
  rude, 895
  vulgar, 851
  vagabond, 949
  evildoer, 913
  to revile, 932
Blackleg
  sharper, 548
  thief, 792
  traitor, 941
Blacklist
  disapprove, 932
Blackmail
  theft, 791
  booty, 793
Bladder
  receptacle, 191
Blade
  instrument, 633
  sharpness, 253
  man, 372
  fop, 854
Blague
  humbug, 545
  boast, 884
Blah
  nonsense, 497
Blain
  swelling, 250
Blamable
  vice, 945
Blame
  disapprobation, 932
Blameless
  innocence, 946
Blameworthy
  vice, 945
  disapproval, 932
Blanch
  whiteness, 430

Bland
courteous, 894
mild, 174
Blandiloquence
flattery, 933
Blandishment
flattery, 902, 933
motive, 615
Blank
insubstantiality, 2, 4
simple, 42
vacant, 187
verse, 597
Blare
loudness, 404
Blarney
flattery, 933
plea, 617
Blasé
weariness, 841
satiety, 869
Blasphemy
impiety, 988
malediction, 908
Blast
wind, 349
sound, 404
evil, 619
curse, 908
explosion, 173
destroy, 162
Blast-furnace
furnace, 386
Blatant
cry, 412
loud, 404
silly, 499
Blatherskite
chatter, 584
Blaze
light, 420
heat, 382
Blaze abroad
publish, 531
Blazon
publication, 531
Blazonry
colour, 428
Bleach
discolour, 429
whiten, 430
Bleak
cold, 383
dreary, 830

Blear-eyed
dim-sighted, 443
Bleat
animal cry, 412
Bleb
swelling, 250
bubble, 353
Bleed
physical pain, 378
moral pain, 828
overcharge, 814
despoil, 789
Bleeding
excretion, 299
Blemish
ugly, 846
defect, 651, 848
Blench
avoid, 623
fear, 860
Blend
mix, 41
combine, 48
Bless
approbation, 931
Blessed
happy, 827
Blessing
good, 618
Blether
nonsense, 497, 499
loquacity, 584
Blight
evil, 619
adversity, 735
decay, 659
Blighter
knave, 949
Blighty
home, 189
Blimp
balloon, 273A
die-hard, 606
Blimpish
prejudiced, 481
foolish, 499
Blind
blindness, 442
ignorant, 491
screen, 424
falsehood, 546
deception, 545
concealment, 528
necessity, 601
heedless, 458
pretext, 617

imperforate, 261
Blind alley
closure, 261
Blind side
obstinacy, 606
prejudice, 481
Blindfold
sightless, 442
ignorant, 491
Blink
wink, 442
neglect, 460
overlook, 458
shirk, 623
Blinkard
dim-sighted, 443
Blinkers
mask, 530
Bliss
pleasure, 827
Blister
swelling, 250
Blithe
cheerfulness, 836
Blitz
attack, 716
Blizzard
wind, 349
Bloated
swollen, 194
Block
mass, 192
dense, 321
fool, 501
execution, 975
Block-buster
bomb, 727
Block in
sketch, 556
Block out
form, 240
Block up
plug, 261
impede, 706
Blockade
closure, 261
hindrance, 706
restraint, 751
Blockhead
fool, 501
Blockhouse
defence, 716
Blockish
folly, 499

Bloke
man, 373
Blonde
whiteness, 430
Blood
relation, 11
killing, 361
fluid, 333
affections, 820
nobility, 875
fop, 854
Blood-guilty
killing, 361
Blood-letting
ejection, 297
Blood-red
redness, 434
Blood-stained
murderous, 361P
maleficent, 907
Bloodhound
evil-doer, 913
detective, 461
Bloodless
weak, 160
peaceful, 721
Bloodshed
killing, 361
Bloodsucker
evildoer, 913
Bloodthirsty
malevolence, 907
Bloody
malevolence, 907
killing, 361
Bloom
youth, 127
prosperity, 734
success, 731
blueness, 438
Bloomer
error, 495
dress, 225
Blooming
beauty, 845
health, 654
Blossom
plant, 367
success, 731
prosperity, 734
Blot
obliterate, 552
dry up, 340
darken, 431
disappear, 449

discoloration, 429
forget, 506
ugly, 846
blemish, 848
disgrace, 874
dishonour, 940
guilt, 947
Blotch
blackness, 431
blemish, 848
Blotto
drunk, 959
Blouse
dress, 225
Blow
wind, 349
boast, 884
knock, 276
action, 680
evil, 619
expletive, 908
pain, 828
disappointment, 732
inexpectation, 508
mishap, 830
to prosper, 734
Blowdown
destruction, 162
Blow-hole
air-pipe, 351
Blow out
extinguish, 385, 421
gluttony, 957
Blow over
preterition, 122
cessation, 142
Blow up
fan, 615
wind, 349
inflame, 194
eruption, 173
objurgation, 932
Blow upon
censure, 934
Blower
signal, 550
Blown
fatigued, 688
Blowpipe
wind, 349
Blowzy
red, 434
sluttish, 653
Blubber
cry, 839

fat, 356
Bludgeon
club, 276
weapon, 727
Blue
colour, 438
learned, 490
Blue-book
record, 551
Blue devils
dejection, 837
Blue lights
firework, 423
Blue-pencil
expletive, 908
Blue-print
model, 22
plan, 626
Blue ruin
drunkenness, 959
Blue water
ocean, 341
Blues
dance, 840
Bluestocking
scholar, 492
affectation, 855
Bluff
high, 206
blunt, 254
insolent, 885
discourteous, 895
boasting, 884
deception, 545
Blunder
error, 495
folly, 499
awkwardness, 699
mistake, 732
ridiculous, 856
Blunderbuss
arms, 727
Blunderer
bungler, 701
Blunderheaded
folly, 499
Blunge
water, 337
Blunt
inert, 172
obtuse, 254
insensible, 376
inexcitable, 826
stupid, 499
cash, 800

discourteous, 895
inelegant, 579
plain, 576
frank, 543
to moderate, 174
to damp, 616
Blunt-witted
folly, 499
Blur
deformity, 846
blemish, 848
disrepute, 874
Blurb
commendation, 931
publicity, 531
Blurred
invisibility, 447
Blurt out
disclosure, 529
Blush
redden, 434
feel, 821
be ashamed, 874
Bluster
violence, 173
insolence, 885
defiance, 715
threat, 909
Blusterer
swagger, 887
Blustering
windy, 349
Boa
dress, 225
Board
layer, 204
food, 298
to attach, 716
council, 696
tribunal, 966
theatre, 599
Boast
brag, 884
Boat
ship, 273
navigation, 267
Bop
leap, 309
bow, 308
oscillate, 314
agitate, 315
Bob
money, 800
Bobadil
bluster, 887

Bobbery
disturbance, 315
row, 404
disorder, 59
Bobbish
healthy, 654
Bobby
police, 664
Bobbysoxer
youngster, 129
Bod
man, 373
Bode
prediction, 511
Bodega
drink, 298
Bodice
dress, 225
Bodily
substantiality, 3
Bodkin
perforator, 262
sharpness, 253
go-between, 228
Body
substance, 3
matter, 316
whole, 50
person, 373
assemblage, 72
party, 712
political, 737
Boeotian
dull, 843
foolish, 499
Bofors
gun, 727
Bog
swamp, 343
dunghill, 653
Boggle
demur, 603
hesitate, 605
difficulty, 704
awkward, 699
wonder, 870
Bogle
demon, 980
Bogus
false, 495, 544
deceitful, 545
Bogy
demon, 980
alarm, 669
Bohemian

oddity, 83, 614
Boil
heat, 382, 384
disease, 655
swelling, 250
bubble, 353
effervesce, 315
be excited , 825
be irate, 900
Boil down
shorten, 201, 596
Boiled
drunk, 959
Boiler
furnace, 386
Boiler suit
dress, 225
Boisterous
violent, 173
hasty, 684
excitable, 825
Bold
brave, 861
prominent, 250
Bolero
dance, 840
Boloney
nonsense, 497
trash, 643
Bolshevism
authority, 737
Bolster
support, 215
aid, 707
repair, 658
relief, 834
Bolt
fastening, 45
to fasten, 43
shackle, 752
sort, 42
to propel, 284
decamp, 287
swallow, 296
gluttony, 957
move rapidly, 274
escape, 671, 750
upright, 212
Bolus
mouthful, 298
Bomb
arms, 727
Bomb-proof
defence, 717

Bombard
attack, 716
Bombardier
combatant, 726
Bombast
absurd, 497
ridiculous, 853
boasting, 884
style, 549, 573, 577, 853
Bomber
aircraft, 273A
Bon enfant
benevolence, 906
Bon gré
willing, 602
Bon gré, mal gré
unwilling, 603
Bon mot
wit, 842
Bon ton
fashion, 852
Bon vivant
glutton, 957
epicure, 868
sociality, 892
Bon voyage
departure, 293
Bona fide
veracity, 543
probity, 939
Bonanza
good luck, 618
Bonbon
sweet, 396
pleasurable, 829
Bond
relation, 95
tie, 45
compact, 769
security, 771
right, 924
fetters, 752
Bondage
subjection, 749
Bondsman
servant, 746
Bone
hardness, 323
money, 800
Bone of contention
discord, 713
Bone-shaker
bicycle, 266
Bonehead
fool, 499, 501

Boner
error, 495, 732
Bones
corpse, 362
Bonfire
rejoicing, 838
Bonhomie
veracity, 543
candour, 703
Bonne
servant, 746
Bonne bouche
dainty, 829
savoury, 394
Bonnet
hat, 225
to assault, 716
Bonny
pretty, 845
cheerful, 836
Bonus
advantage, 618
gift, 784
money, 810
addition, 39
Bony
hard, 323
Bonze
clergy, 996
Boo
cry, 412
deride, 927
Boob
fool, 501
Booby
fool, 501
ignoramus, 493
Boodle
booty, 793
Boogie-woogie
rhythm, 413
Book
volume, 593
enter account, 811
to record, 551
to register, 86
to bespeak, 132
Book-keeper
recorder, 553
Book-keeping
accounts, 811
Booked
dying, 360
Bookish
erudite, 490

scholarly, 492
Bookless
ignorant, 493
Bookworm
scholar, 492
Boom
bar, 633
defence, 717
obstacle, 706
support, 215
to sail, 267
rush, 274
cry, 402
sound, 404
impact, 276
praise, 931
Boomerang
arms, 727
recoil, 277
Boon
giving, 784
good, 618
Boor
clown, 876
discourteous, 895
ridiculous, 851
Boost
throw, 284
commend, 931
publicity, 531
Boot
addition, 37
dress, 225
advantage, 618
important, 642
punishment, 975
Boot-boy
servant, 746
Booth
abode, 189
shop, 799
Bootlegging
illegality, 964
Bootless
useless, 645
failing, 732
Bootlicker
toady, 886
Boots
servant, 746
Booty
plunder, 793
Booze
drunkenness, 959

409

Bo-peep
vision, 441
Border
edge, 230
limit, 233
ornament, 847
to be near, 197
Bore
hole, 260
diameter, 202
to trouble, 828
to plague, 830
to weary, 841
dull, 843
tide, 348
Boreal
polar, 237
cold, 383
Boreas
wind, 349
Borer
perforator, 262
Borné
folly, 499
Borough
abode, 189
Borrow
borrowing, 788
debt, 806
Borstal
school, 542
punishment, 972
Boscage
vegetation, 367
Bosh
nonsense, 517
Bosom
breast, 221
mind, 450
will, 600
affection, 820
Bosom friend
friend, 890
Boss
convexity, 250
to direct, 693, 737
master, 745
Bossy
will, 600
severity, 739
Botanic
plant, 367
Botany
botany, 369
Botch
to mend, 658

to fail, 732
unskilful, 699
inperfect, 651
Both
duality, 89
Bother
trouble, 828, 830
fuss, 682
Bottle
receptacle, 191
Bottle-neck
thinness, 203
Bottle-party
food, 298
sharing, 778
Bottle up
preserve, 670
enclose, 231
restrain, 751
remember, 505
Bottle-washer
servant, 746
Bottom
lowest part, 211
base, 215
valley, 252
ship, 273
pluck, 604
courage, 861
Bottom, at
intrinsicality, 5
Bottomless
depth, 208
Boudoir
room, 191
Bough
part, 51
plant, 367
curve, 245
Boulder
mass, 192
Boulevard
circumjacence, 227
way, 627
Bouleversement
change, 140
destruction, 162
Bounce
violence, 173
motion, 274
recoil, 277
eject, 297
dismiss, 756
boast, 884
insolence, 885

exaggeration, 549
Bounce upon
arrival, 292
surprise, 508
Bouncer
untruth, 546
Bouncing
large, 192
Bound
limit, 233
circumscribe, 231
speed, 274
leap, 309
Boundary
limit, 233
Bounder
upstart, 876
Boundless
great, 31
infinite, 105
space, 180
Bounteous
benevolent, 906
Bountiful
liberal, 816
Bounty
gift, 784
liberality, 816
benevolence, 906
Bouquet
fragrance, 400
ornament, 847
Bourgeois
middle class, 736, 876
Bourne
limit, 233
Bourse
mart, 799
Bout
turn, 138
job, 680
fight, 720
Boutade
absurdity, 497
caprice, 608
Bovine
inert, 172, 823
Bow
curve, 245
ornament, 847
fore-part, 234
shot, 284
arms, 727
to stoop, 308
reverence, 894

410

submission, 725
obeisance, 743
servility, 886
respect, 928
prominence, 250
Bow-legged
curvature, 245
distortion, 243
Bowdlerize
expurgate, 652
Bowels
interior, 221
of compassion, 914
Bower
alcove, 189
chamber, 191
Bowie-knife
arms, 727
sharpness, 253
Bowl
vessel, 191
hollow, 252
to propel, 284
Bowler
hat, 225
Bowling-green
horizontality, 213
Bowshot
nearness, 197
Bowstring
scourge, 975
Box
chest, 191
house, 189
theatre, 599
to strike, 972
to fight, 720
Boxer
combatant, 726
Boxing
contention, 720
Boy
infant, 129
Boy friend
love, 897
Boycott
exclude, 893
eject, 297
Boyhood
youth, 127
Bra
dress, 225
Brace
to tie, 43
fastening, 45

two, 89
to refresh, 689
to strengthen, 159
Brace and bit
perforator, 262
Bracelet
ornament, 847
circularity, 247
Bracer
remedy, 662
Brachygraphy
writing, 590
Bracing
strengthening, 159
refreshing, 689
Bracket
tie, 43
support, 215
vinculum, 45
couple, 89
Brackish
pungent, 392
Brad
vinculum, 45
Bradawl
perforator, 262
Brae
height, 206
Brag
boasting, 884
Braggadocio
boasting, 884
Braggart
boasting, 884
bully, 887
Brahma
god, 979
Brahmin
clergy, 996
religious, 984
Braid
to tie, 43
ligature, 45
intersection, 219
Braille
printing, 591
Brain
intellect, 450
skill, 498
Brain-sick
giddy, 460
Brain-storm
excitability, 825
Brainless
imbecile, 499

Brains trust
council, 696
Brainwash
teach, 537
Brake
copse, 367
curb, 752
vehicle, 272
Bramble
thorn, 253
painful, 830
Bran
pulverulence, 330
Bran-new
see Brand-new
Branch
member, 51
plant, 367
duality, 91
posterity, 167
ramification, 256
Branch off
divergence, 291
Branch out
style, 573
divide, 91
Brand
to burn, 384
fuel, 388
to stigmatize, 932
mark, 550
to accuse, 938
reproach, 874
Brand-new
new, 123
Brander
roast, 384
Brandish
oscillate, 314
flourish, 315
Bras croisés
inactive, 683
Brasier
furnace, 386
Brass
insolence, 885
colour, 439
Brass up
pay, 809
Brassed off
bored, 641
sated, 869
Brasserie
food, 298
Brassière
dress, 225

Brassy
club, 276
Brat
infant, 129
Bravado
boasting, 884
Brave
courage, 861
to defy, 715
Bravery
courage, 861
ornament, 847
Bravo
assassin, 361
applause, 931
Bravura
music, 415
Braw
handsome, 845
Brawl
cry, 411
discord, 713
contention, 720
Brawny
strong, 159
stout, 192
Bray
cry, 412
to grind, 330
Brazen-faced
insolent, 885
Breach
crack, 44
quarrel, 713
violation, 925
exception, 83
Bread
food, 298
Breadstuffs
food, 298
Breadth
thickness, 202
of mind, 498
Break
fracture, 44
shatter, 162
incompleteness, 53
interval, 70, 106, 198
opportunity, 134
luck, 621, 731
crumble, 328
violation, 773
bankruptcy, 808
to infringe, 927

to disclose, 529
to tame, 749
to decline, 659
to swerve, 311
Break down
fail, 158, 732
Break ground
undertaking, 676
Break in
teach, 537
train, 370, 673
Break loose
escape, 671
liberate, 750
Break off
a habit, 614
leave off, 142
abrogate, 756
Break out
fly out, 825
Break the ranks
derangement, 61
Break the record
superiority, 33
Break up
destroy, 162
deteriorate, 659
decompose, 49
Break with
discord, 713
Breaker
wave, 348
danger, 667
Breakfast
food, 298
Breakneck
perilous, 665
precipitous, 217
Breakwater
refuge, 666
enclosure, 232
Breast
interior, 221
convexity, 250
mind, 450
will, 600
soul, 820
to oppose, 708
Breastplate
defence, 717
Breastwork
defence, 717
Breath
air, 349
sound, 405

life, 359, 364
Breathe
exist, 1
live, 359
blow, 349
mean, 516
utter, 580, 582
repose, 687
Breather
preparation, 673
Breathing
lifelike, 17
Breathing-space
time, 106
pause, 141, 265
leisure, 685
Breathless
calm, 265
out of breath, 688
feeling, 821
Breech
rear, 235
Breeches
dress, 225
Breed
kind, 75
to multiply, 161
domesticate, 370
progeny, 167
Breeding
fashion, 852
Breeze
wind, 349
Breezy
lively, 836
Bren
gun, 727
Brevet
warrant, 741
commission, 755
permission, 760
Breviary
liturgy, 998
Brevity
space, 201
Brew
mix, 41
prepare, 673
impend, 121
Briar
tobacco, 298A
Bribe
buy, 795
offer, 763
gift, 784

fee, 809
tempt, 615
Bric-à-brac
trifle, 643
ornament, 847
Brick
materials, 635
hardness, 323
good man, 939, 946
Brickbat
missile, 284
Bride
marriage, 903
Bridegroom
marriage, 903
Bridewell
prison, 752
Bridge
intermedium, 45
way, 627
escape, 671
Bridge over
junction, 43
Bridle
curb, 752
to restrain, 751
to moderate, 174
to swagger, 878
Bridle up
resentment, 900
Brief
time, 111
space, 201
style, 572
compendium, 596
direct, 693, 741
Brief-case
receptacle, 191
Briefly
transientness, 111
Briefs
dress, 225
Brier
sharp, 253
painful, 830
Brig
ship, 273
prison, 752
Brigade
combatant, 726
Brigadier
master, 745
Brigand
thief, 792
Brigantine

ship, 273
Bright
shining, 420
colour, 428
cheerful, 836
auspicious, 858
glorious, 873
Brilliant
shining, 420
beautiful, 845
glorious, 873
perfect, 650
gem, 847
Brilliantine
ornament, 847
Brim
edge, 230
Brimful
sufficient, 639
fullness, 52
Brimmer
fullness, 52
Brindled
variegated, 440
Brine
salt, 392
sea, 341
Bring
transfer, 270
induce, 615
Bring about
cause, 153
achieve, 729
succeed, 731
Bring forth
produce, 161
Bring forward
manifest, 525
Bring home to
convince, 537
adduce, 467
Bring in
price, 812
Bring into
existence, 1
Bring off
deliver, 672
accomplish, 161, 729
Bring out
manifest, 525
publish, 531
Bring over
persuade, 484, 615
Bring to
restore, 658

Bring under
subdue, 824
Bring up
educate, 537
Brink
edge, 230
Brio
vivacity, 682
Briquette
fuel, 388
Brisk
quick, 274
energetic, 171
active, 682
prompt, 111
Bristle
sharpness, 253
Bristle up
resentment, 900
Bristle with
abound, 639
British warm
dress, 225
Brittle
brittleness, 328
Broach
begin, 66
tap, 297
put forth, 535
Broad
space, 292
indelicate, 961
meaning, 535
Broad-minded
wisdom, 498
Broadcast
scattered, 73
shed, 291
radio, 418, 599B
publication, 531
Broadmoor
prison, 752
Broadside
side, 236
cannonade, 716
Broadsword
arms, 727
Brobdingnagian
size, 192, 193
Brocade
ornament, 847
Brochure
book, 593
Brog
perforator, 262

Brogue
language, 560
shoe, 225
Broidery
ornament, 847
Broil
heat, 382
to fry, 384
fray, 720
Broken
weakness, 160
Broken-hearted
unhappy, 828
Broken-winded
fatigue, 688
Broker
agent, 690, 758, 769
merchant, 797
Brokerage
pay, 812
Bromide
photograph, 556
dull, 843
Bronze
brown, 433
sculpture, 557
Brooch
fastening, 45
ornament, 847
Brood
posterity, 167
Brood over
think, 451
mope, 837
Brook
stream, 348
to bear, 821, 826
Broom
cleanness, 652
Broth
food, 298
semiliquid, 352
Brothel
impurity, 961
Brother
kin, 11
similar, 17
equal, 27
friend, 888
Brother-in-law
kin, 11
Brougham
vehicle, 272
Brouillerie
discord, 713

Brow
summit, 210
edge, 230
Browbeat
intimidate, 860
swagger, 885
attack, 716
Brown
colour, 433
Brown-out
dim, 422
Brown study
reverie, 458
thought, 451
Browned off
bored, 841
sated, 869
Brownie
imp, 980
Browse
feed, 296
Bruise
hurt, 619
to injure, 649
pound, 330
Bruiser
fighter, 726
Bruit
publication, 531
news, 532
Brumal
cold, 383
evening, 126
Brummagem
spurious, 544
Brumous
foggy, 422
Brunette
brown, 433
Brunt
impulse, 276
attack, 716
Brush
rapid motion, 274
to clean, 652
painting, 559
fight, 720
rough, 256
Brush up
memo, 505
Brushwood
plant, 367
Brusque
discourteous, 895
inelegant, 579

rough, 173
Brutal
vicious, 945
ill-bred, 895
savage, 907
Brutalize
harden, 823, 895
Brute
animal, 366
rude, 895
maleficent, 913
Brute force
illegality, 964
Brute matter
materiality, 316
inanimate matter, 358
Brutish
vulgar, 851, 876
intemperate, 954
Brutum fulmen
impotence, 158
laxity, 738
Bubble
air, 353
light, 320
trifle, 643
error, 495
vision, 515
deceit, 545
excitement, 824
flow, 348
Buccaneer
thief, 792
Buck
leap, 309
to wash, 652
fop, 854
money, 800
Buck up
hasten, 274
stimulate, 615
cheer, 836
Bucket
receptacle, 191
Bucketful
quantity, 25
Buckle
to tie, 43
vinculum, 45
distort, 243
Buckle to
apply oneself, 682
Buckle with
grapple, 720

Buckler
defence, 666, 717
Buckram
hardness, 323
affectation, 855
Buckshee
superfluous, 641
Bucolic
domestication, 370
poem, 597
Bud
beginning, 66
to expand, 194
effect, 154
graft, 300
Buddha
deity, 979
religious founder, 986
Buddhism
religions, 984
Buddy
friend, 891
associate, 88
Budge
move, 264
Budget
heap, 72
store, 636
news, 532
accounts, 811
Buff
yellow, 436
grindstone, 331
Buffer
defence, 717
fellow, 373
Buffet
cupboard, 191
beat, 276, 972
Buffet car
vehicle, 272
Buffo
the drama, 599
Buffoon
humorist, 844
butt, 857
actor, 599
Buffoonery
amusement, 840
ridiculous, 856
Bugaboo
fear, 860
Bugbear
fear, 860

alarm, 669
imaginary, 515
Buggy
vehicle, 272
Bughouse
insane, 503
Bugle
instrument, 417
war-cry, 722
Bugs
insane, 503
Buhl
variegation, 440
Build
construct, 161
compose, 54
Build-up
display, 882
Build upon
expect, 507, 858
count upon, 484
Builder
producer, 164
Building
abode, 189
Bulb
knob, 249, 250
Bulbous
swollen, 194
rotund, 249
Bulge
convexity, 250
Bulimia
desire, 865
Bulk
whole, 50
size, 192
Bulkhead
hindrance, 706
Bulky
size, 192
Bull
absurdity, 497, 853
error, 495
solecism, 568
nonsense, 497, 517
law, 963
ordinance, 741
police, 664
Bull-calf
fool, 501
Bulldog
courage, 861
resolution, 604
Bullet

ball, 249
missile, 284
arms, 727
swiftness, 274
Bullet-proof
defence, 717
Bulletin
message, 532
Bullion
money, 800
Bull's-eye
middle, 68
Bully
bluster, 885
blusterer, 887
fight, 726
domineer, 739
frighten, 860
good, 648
Bulrush
unimportance, 643
Bulwark
defence, 717
refuge, 666
Bum
tramp, 268, 876
loafer, 683
pauper, 804
rascal, 949
Bumbledom
authority, 737
Bumboat
ship, 273
provision, 637
Bumboatman
trader, 797
Bump
projection, 250
thump, 276
Bump off
kill, 361
Bumper
sufficiency, 639
fullness, 52
Bumpkin
commonalty, 876
Bumptious
insolent, 885
Bun-fight
party, 892
Bunce
profit, 618
Bunch
protuberance, 250
collection, 72

Bundle
packet, 72
to move, 275
Bung
stopper, 263
throw, 284
Bung-ho
departure, 293
Bungalow
abode, 189
Bungle
unskilfulness, 699
failure, 732
Bungler
unskilful, 701
Bunion
swelling, 250
Bunk
bed, 191, 215
escape, 671
Bunker
receptacle, 191
obstruction, 706
Bunkie
friend, 891
Bunkum
humbug, 545
nonsense, 497
Bunt
inversion, 218
deviate, 279
Bunting
flag, 550
Buoy
float, 320
to raise, 307
to hope, 858
Buoyant
floating, 305
levity, 320
elastic, 325
hopeful, 858
cheerful, 836
Bur
rough, 256
clinging, 46
Burberry
dress, 225
Burden
weight, 319
clog, 706
chorus, 104, 415
frequency, 136
lading, 190
care, 830

oppresion, 828
Bureau
cabinet, 691
office, 799
Bureaucracy
direction, 693
authority, 737
Burgee
Flag, 550
Burgeon
expansion, 194
increase, 35
Burgess
citizen, 188, 373
Burgher
man, 373
Burglar
thief, 792
Burglary
stealing, 791
Burgomaster
master, 745
Burgrave
master, 745
Burial
corpse, 362
Buried
depth, 208
Burin
engraving, 559
Burke
kill, 361
destroy, 162
suppress, 528
Burlesque
imitation, 19
travesty, 21
drama, 599
ridicule, 856
ridiculous, 853
Burletta
the drama, 599
Burly
size, 192
Burn
heat, 382
consume, 384
detection, 480A
passions, 821
rivulet, 348
Burnish
polish, 255
beautify, 845
shine, 420
Burnous

dress, 225
Burp
belch, 297
Burrow
excavate, 252
lodge, 186
Bursar
treasurer, 801
Bursary
treasury, 802
Burst
explosion, 173
sound, 406
of anger, 900
paroxysm, 825
spree, 840
separate, 44
Burst forth
appear, 446
sprout, 194
Burst out
ejaculate, 580
Burst upon
inexpectation, 508
Bury
inter, 363
conceal, 528
Bus
vehicle, 272
Busby
hat, 225
Bush
branch, 51
shrub, 367
Bushel
receptacle, 191
Bushy
roughness, 256
Business
occupation, 625
event, 151
topic, 454
action, 680
barter, 794
Business-like
activity, 682
skilful, 698
order, 58
Buskin
dress, 225
drama, 599
Buss
ship, 272
kiss, 902

Bustle
  activity, 682
  agitation, 315
  haste, 684
  energy, 171
  earliness, 132
Busy
  activity, 682
Busybody
  activity, 682
  curiosity, 455
But
  exception, 83, 179
  counter-evidence, 468
Butcher
  evildoer, 913
Butchery
  killing, 361
Butler
  servant, 746
Butt
  aim, 620
  laughing-stock, 857
  remnant, 40
  part, 51;
  to push, 276
  to attack, 716
Butt-end
  end, 67
Butt in
  intervene, 228
Butte
  height, 206
Butter
  softness, 324
  oiliness, 356
  to flatter, 933
Butter-fingers
  bungler, 701
Butterfly
  beauty, 845
  fickleness, 605
  fear, 860
Butterscotch
  sweet, 396
Button
  knob, 250
  to fasten, 43
  fasten, 43
  fastening, 45
  hanging, 214
  trifle, 643
Buttoned up
  reserved, 528
  taciturn, 585

Buttonhole
  ornament, 847
  accost, 586
Buttonholer
  weariness, 841
Buttons
  servant, 746
Buttress
  support, 215
  defence, 717
  strengthen, 159
Buxom
  plump, 192
  cheerful, 836
Buy
  purchase, 795
Buzz
  sound, 409, 412
  to publish, 531
  news, 532
Buzz-bomb
  arms, 727
Buzz off
  depart, 293
Buzzard
  fool, 501
By and by
  transientness, 111
By fits and starts
  disorder, 59
  irregularity, 139
By jingo
  affirmation, 535
By-law
  legality, 963
Byname
  misnomer, 565
By the by
  opportunity, 134
Bye-bye
  departure, 293
  sleep, 683
Bygone
  former, 122
  forgotten, 506
Bypath
  road, 627
Byplay
  gesture, 550
Byssus
  roughness, 256
Bystander
  spectator, 444
  near, 197
Byway

  road, 627
Byword
  maxim, 496
  cant term, 563
  contempt, 930

C.A.
  accounts, 811
C.O.D.
  payment, 807
Ca' canny
  caution, 864
Cab
  vehicle, 272
  translation, 522
Cabal
  confederacy, 712
  plan, 626
Cabbage
  purloin, 791
Cabbala
  spell, 993
Cabbalistic
  mysterious, 528
Caber
  missile, 284
Cabin
  room, 189
  receptacle, 191
Cabin cruiser
  ship, 273
Cabinet
  receptacle, 191
  workshop, 691
  council, 696
Cable
  vinculum, 45
Cabriolet
  vehicle, 272
Cache
  hiding-place, 530
  conceal, 528
  store, 636
Cachexy
  disease, 655
  weakness, 160
Cachinnation
  rejoicing, 838
Cachucha
  dance, 840
Cacique
  master, 745
Cackle
  of geese, 412

talk, 588
laughter, 838
Cacodemon
demon, 980
Cacodyl
fetor, 401
Cacoethes
habit, 613
itch, 865
writing, 590
Cacoethes loquendi
loquacity, 584
Cacoethes scribendi
writing, 590
Cacography
writing, 590
Cacophony
stridor, 410
discord, 414
style, 579
Cad
vulgarity, 851
Cadastre
list, 86
Cadaverous
corpse, 362
pale, 429
thin, 203
hideous, 846
Caddish
mean, 940
Caddy
receptacle, 191
Cadence
accent, 580
music, 415
descent, 306
Cadenza
music, 415
Cadet
junior, 129
combatant, 726
officer, 745
Cadge
request, 765
Cadger
merchant, 797
Cadi
judge, 967
Cadmium
orange, 439
Cadre
framework, 215
Caduceus
spell, 993

Caducity
transientness, 111
Caecum
closure, 261
Caesar
master, 745
Caesura
break, 70
disjunction, 44
Caetera desunt
incomplete, 53
Caeteris paribus
circumstance, 8
equality, 27
Café
food, 298
Cafeteria
food, 298
Caftan
dress, 225
Cage
prison, 231, 752
to immure, 751
abode, 189
Cagey
cautious, 864
Caique
ship, 273
Cairn
grave, 363
sign, 550
Caisson
receptacle, 191
depth, 208
Caitiff
ruffian, 913
villain, 949
Cajole
persuade, 615
flatter, 933
Cake
cohesion, 46
density, 321
food, 298
Cake eater
philander, 902
Cakewalk
dance, 840
easy, 705
Calabash
receptacle, 191
tobacco-pipe, 298A
Calaboose
prison, 752
Calamity

evil, 619
adversity, 735
suffering, 830
Calash
vehicle, 272
cap, 225
Calcine
calefaction, 384
Calculate
reckon, 85
expect, 507
believe, 484
investigate, 461
Calculated,
tending to, 176
premeditated, 600, 611
Calculating
prudent, 498
Calculation
motive, 615
caution, 864
Calculus
numeration, 85
Caldron
see Cauldron
Calefaction
heating, 384
Calembour
pun, 563
Calendar
of time, 114
list, 86;
record, 551
Calender
to glaze, 255
Calf
fool, 501
Caliban
ugliness, 846
Calibre
size, 192
breadth, 202
degree, 26
opening, 260
intellectual capacity, 698
Calidity
heat, 382
Caliph
master, 745
Caliphate
authority, 737
Call
to name, 564
motive, 615
visit, 892

inspiration, 985
Call-boy
theatre, 599
Call down
malediction, 908
Call for
order, 741
ask, 765
require, 630
Call forth
resort to, 677
Call-girl
prostitute, 962
Call on
ask, 765
Call over
numeration, 85
Call up
memory, 505
summon, 741
Call upon
behove, 926
visit, 892
claim, 924
Callant
youth, 129
Caller
arrival, 292
Calligraphy
writing, 590
Calling
business, 625
Callipers
measurement, 466
Callisthenics
training, 537, 673
Callosity
hardness, 323
Callous
obtuse, 376
insensible, 823
impenitent, 951
Callow
infant, 129
young, 127
Calm
physical, 174
moral, 826
quiet, 265
dissuade, 616
Calorific
heat, 382
Calorimeter
thermometer, 389
Calotte

vestment, 225, 999
Caltrop
sharpness, 253
Calumet
pacification, 723
tobacco, 298A
Calumniator
detractor, 936
Calumny
detraction, 934
Calyx
integument, 222
Camarade
friend, 890
Camaraderie
friendship, 888
Camarilla
party, 712
Camber
curvature, 250
Cambist
merchant, 797
Camel
carrier, 271
Cameo
sculpture, 557
Camera
optical instrument, 445
Camerated
curved, 245
Camisade
attack, 716
Camisole
dress, 225
Camorra
illegality, 964
Camouflage
conceal, 528
deception, 545
Camp
to locate, 184
abode, 186
Campagna
space, 180
Campaign
warfare, 722
plan, 626
conduct, 692
Campaigner
combatant, 726
Campanile
tower, 206
Campaniliform
bell-shaped, 249
cupped, 252

Campanologist
musician, 416
Campus
field, 344
arena, 728
Can
power, 157
mug, 191
to preserve, 670
Canaille
commonalty, 876
rabble, 949
Canal
opening, 260
way, 627
Canard
deception, 545
news, 532
Can-can
dance, 840
Cancel
obliterate, 552, 773
abrogate, 756
Cancellated
crossing, 219
Cancelli
lattice, 219
Cancer
disease, 655
swelling, 250
foulness, 653
painful, 830
Candelabra
luminary, 423
Candescence
heat, 382
Candid
sincere, 543
ingenuous, 703
honourable, 939
Candidate
petitioner, 767, 865
Candidature
offer, 763
solicitation, 765
Candied
flattering, 933
Candle
luminary, 423
Candle-ends
remainder, 40
Candle-holder
auxiliary, 711
Candle-light
dimness, 422

Candlestick
luminary, 423

Candour
veracity, 543
artlessness, 703
honour, 939

Candy
sweetness, 396

Cane
scourge, 975
to beat, 276
punish, 972

Cangue
shackle, 752
stocks, 975

Canicular
heat, 382

Canister
receptacle, 191

Canker
disease, 655
bane, 663
deterioration, 659
pain, 830

Cankering
badness, 649

Canned
drunk, 959

Cannibal
sinner, 949

Cannibalize
repair, 658

Cannon
arms, 727
collision, 276

Cannonade
attack, 716

Cannoneer
combatant, 726

Canny
cautious, 459, 864
cunning, 702
intelligent, 498
thrifty, 817

Canoe
ship, 273

Canon
rule, 80
music, 415
precept, 697
priest, 996

Canonical
orthodox, 983A

Canonicals
holy orders, 999

Canonize
rites, 995, 998
honour, 873

Canoodle
endearment, 902

Canopy
height, 206
roof, 210
covering, 222

Canorous
resonant, 402
melodious, 415

Cant
neology, 563
language, 560
oblique, 217
hypocrisy, 544, 988

Cantankerous
discourtesy, 895

Cantata
music, 415

Cantatrice
musician, 416

Canted
obliquity, 217

Canteen
receptacle, 191
feeding, 298

Canter
move, 266
gallop, 274

Canticle
music, 415

Cantilever
support, 215

Cantle
part, 51

Canto
poetry, 597

Canton
region, 181

Cantonment
location, 184
abode, 189

Canty
cheerfulness, 836

Canvas
sail, 267

Canvass
investigate, 461
treat of, 595
solicit, 765

Canyon
ravine, 198

Canzonet

song, 415
poem, 597

Caoutchouc
elasticity, 325

Cap
hat, 225
height, 206
to be superior, 33, 194
counter, 718
to salute, 894

Cap-à-pie
preparation, 673
length, 200

Capability
power, 157
strength, 159
skill, 698
facility, 705
endowment, 5

Capacity
space, 180
size, 192
endowment, 5
power, 157
intellect, 450
aptitude, 539
talent, 698
wisdom, 498
utility, 644
office, 625

Caparison
vestment, 225

Cape
land, 342
projection, 250
height, 206
cloak, 225

Caper
leap, 309
dance, 840

Capillary
thinness, 203, 205

Capital
excellent, 648
important, 642
summit, 210
money, 800
wealth, 803

Capitalist
wealth, 803

Capitation
numeration, 85

Capitol
defence, 717

Capitular
clergy, 996
Capitulate
submission, 725
Capote
vestment, 224
Capriccio
caprice, 608
Caprice
chance, 608
irresolution, 605
music, 415
Capricious
irregular, 139
changeable, 149
whimsical, 608
Capriole
leap, 309
Capsize
inversion, 218
wreck, 731
Capsized
failure, 732
Capstan
instrument, 633
Capsule
vessel, 191
tunicle, 222
Captain
master, 745
of industry, 745
Caption
indication, 550
Captious
capricious, 608
censorious, 932
discourteous, 795
Captivated
fascinated, 827, 897
induced, 615
Captivating
pleasing, 829
lovely, 897
Captive
prisoner, 754
Captivity
restraint, 751
Capture
taking, 789
Capuchin
clergy, 996
Caput mortuum
remainder, 40
unclean, 653
Car

vehicle, 272
Carabineer
combatant, 726
Caracole
leap, 309
journey, 266
Carafe
receptacle, 191
Carambole
impulse, 276
Caramel
sweet, 396
Carapace
covering, 222
Caravan
vehicle, 272
Caravansary
abode, 189
Caravel
ship, 273
Carbine
arms, 727
Carbon
copy, 590
Carbon print
photograph, 556
Carbonize
calefaction, 384
Carborundum
sharpener, 253
Carboy
receptacle, 191
Carcass
corpse, 362
Card
ticket, 550
plan, 626
oddity, 857
to unravel, 60
Cardiac
remedy, 662
Cardigan
dress, 225
Cardinal
important, 642
excellent, 648
red, 434
dress, 225
priest, 995, 996
Care
attention, 459
fear, 860
pain, 828, 830
custody, 751
Care for

desire, 865
love, 642, 897
Care-worn
pain, 828
Careen
slant, 217, 306
repair, 658
Career
business, 625
conduct, 692
Careful
caution, 864
Careless
inattentive, 458
neglectful, 460
insensible, 823
Caress
endearment, 902
Caret
incomplete, 53
to want, 640
Caretaker
keeper, 753
Cargo
goods, 798
contents, 190
property, 780
materials, 635
large quantity, 31
Caricature
likeness, 19
misrepresentation, 555
ridicule, 856
Caricaturist
humorist, 844
Caries
disease, 655
Carillon
musical instrument, 417
Carking
painful, 830
Carle
boor, 876
Carmelite
clergy, 996
Carminative
remedy, 662
Carmine
redness, 434
Carnage
killing, 361
Carnal
impure, 961
animality, 364
intemperate, 954

irreligious, 989
material 316
Carnation
redness, 434
Carnival
amusement, 840
Carny
to coax, 615
Carol
music, 415
cheerful, 836
rejoice, 838
Carom
impulse, 276
Carouse
feast, 296
festivity, 840
drink, 959
intemperance, 954
Carp
disapprobation, 932
Carpe diem
occasion, 134
Carper
detractor, 936
Carpet
covering, 222
Carrack
ship, 273
Carrefour
road, 627
Carriage
transference, 270
vehicle, 272
gait, 264
aspect, 448
conduct, 692
fashion, 852
Carrier
porter, 271
Carriole
vehicle, 272
Carrion
carcass, 362
foulness, 653
Carronade
arms, 727
Carroty
redness, 434
Carry
support, 215
transfer, 270
assent, 488
tend, 176
induce, 615

Carry off
take, 789
steal, 791
Carry on
conduct, 692
continue, 143
pursue, 622
Carry out
complete, 729
conduct, 692
Carry through
complete, 729
conduct, 692
Cart
vehicle, 272
to transfer, 270
Cart-load
quantity, 31
abundance, 639
Cartage
transference, 270
Carte blanche
permission, 760
liberality, 816
Carte de visite
indication, 550
Carte du pays
plan, 626
Cartel
defiance, 715
truce, 723
compact, 769
security, 771
combine, 712, 778
Cartilage
toughness, 327
Cartography
representation, 554
Cartoon
painting, 556
Cartoonist
humorist, 844
Cartophilist
collector, 775
Cartouche
scroll, 248
Cartridge
arms, 727
Cartulary
record, 551
list, 86
Caruncle
convexity, 250
Carve
sculpture, 557, 857

to form, 240
to produce, 161
disjunction, 44
Carver
artist, 559
Caryatides
support, 215
Cascade
river, 348
Case
state, 7
affair, 454
disease, 655
sheath, 222
receptacle 191, 232
lawsuit, 969
grammar, 567
Case-harden
harden, 823
strengthen, 159
train, 673
Casemate
defence, 717
Casement
opening, 260
Cash
money, 800
Cash register
numeration, 85
Cashier
to dismiss, 756
treasurer, 801
Casing
covering, 222
Casino
sociality, 892
Cask
receptacle, 191
Casket
receptacle, 191
coffin, 363
Cassandra
warning, 668
Casserole
receptacle, 191
Cassock
dress, 225
canonicals, 999
Cast
to throw, 284
to throw down, 308
state, 7
bias, 820
mould, 21
form, 240

small quantity, 32
tinge, 428
squint, 443
aspect, 448
to peel, 226
reject, 610

Cast
to condemn, 971
to allot, 786
drama, 599

Cast about
inquiry, 461

Cast anchor
stop, 265
arrive, 293

Cast away
relinquish, 782

Cast down
dejection, 837

Cast forth
dispersion, 73

Cast off
remainder, 40
stop, 142
discard, 678

Cast out
ejection, 297

Cast up
add, 85
happen, 151
eject, 297

Castalian
poetry, 597

Castanet
musical instrument, 417

Castaway
lost, 732
outcast, 893
reprobate, 949
sinner, 949

Caste
class, 75

Castellan
keeper, 753
servant, 746

Castellated
defence, 717

Caster
receptacle, 191

Castigate
punish, 972
reprove, 932

Castle
defence, 717
edifice, 189

Castle building
imagination, 515

Castor
hat, 225
fragrance, 400

Castor oil
oil, 356

Castrate
mutilate, 38, 44, 53
sterilize , 169

Castrated
weakened, 160
purified, 652

Casual
by chance, 156, 621
irregular, 139
mutable, 149
liable, 177
uncertain, 475
unmethodical, 59

Casualty
event, 151
chance, 156, 621
killing, 361

Casuistry
sophistry, 477
scruple, 485
ethics, 926

Casus belli
discord, 713
resentment, 900

Cat
eye, 441
scourge, 975
to vomit, 297

Cat-call
abuse, 932

Cat-o'-nine-tails
scourge, 975

Catachresis
metaphor, 521
misinterpretation, 523

Cataclysm
deluge, 348
convulsion, 146
redundance, 641

Catacomb
interment, 363

Catafalque
interment, 363

Catalectic
poetry, 597

Catalepsy
quiescence, 265
insensibility, 376, 823

Catalogue
list, 86, 551
record, 551
arrangement, 60
classify, 75

Catalysis
decomposition, 49

Catamaran
vessel, 273

Cataplasm
remedy, 662

Catapult
projection, 276, 284
arms, 727

Cataract
river, 348
blindness, 442

Catastrophe
end, 67, 729
rear, 235
disaster, 619
adversity, 735
calamity, 830
convulsion, 146

Catch
take, 134, 789
receive, 785
learn, 539
gather meaning, 518
cheat, 545
vinculum, 45

Catch at
receiving, 785

Catch on
success, 731

Catch up
overtake, 292

Catching
infectious, 657

Catchpenny
trumpery, 643
cheap, 815
false, 544

Catchpoll
jurisprudence, 965

Catchword
formula, 80
maxim, 496

Catechetical
inquiry, 461

Catechize
inquiry, 461

Catechumen
learner, 541

Categorical
true, 494
positive, 474
demonstrative, 478
affirmative, 535
Category
class, 75
arrangement, 60
state, 7
Catenary
curve, 245
Catenation
continuity, 69
Cater
provision, 637
Caterwauling
cry, 412
discord, 414
Cates
food, 298
Cathedral
temple, 1000
Catholic
universal, 78
Christian, 983A
broad-minded, 448
Catholicity
generality, 78
broad-mindedness, 498
Catholicon
remedy, 662
Cat's-cradle
crossing, 219
Cat's-paw
instrument, 631
dupe, 547
Cattle-lifting
stealing, 791
Cattle-truck
vehicle, 272
Caucus
assemblage, 72
Caudal
end, 67
Caudate
pendency, 214
Cauldron
mixture, 41
vessel, 191
heating, 386
laboratory, 691
Caulk
repair, 658
Causality
cause, 153
power, 157

Causation
cause, 153
agency, 170
Cause
source, 153
final, 620
lawsuit, 969
Causless
casual, 156
aimless, 621
Causerie
chat, 588
Causeur
talker, 588
Causeway
road, 627
Causidical
juridical, 965
Caustic
feeling, 821
painful, 830
gruff, 895
disapproving, 932
malevolent, 907
Cautelous
caution, 864
Cauterize
calefaction, 384
Caution
care, 459
warning, 668
prudence, 864
advice, 695
security, 771
Cavalcade
continuity, 69
Cavalier
horseman, 268
insolent, 885
discourteous, 895
contemptuous, 930
Cavaliere servente
lover, 897
Cavalierly
inattention, 458
Cavalry
combatant, 726
Cavatina
music, 415
Cave
cavity, 252
cell, 91
dwelling, 189
warning, 668
care, 459

Cave in
submit, 729
Caveat
warning, 668
Cavendish
tobacco, 298A
Cavern
hollow, 252
cell, 191
dwelling, 189
Cavernous
hollow, 252
porous, 322
Caviare
pungent, 171, 392
Cavil
censure, 932
dissent, 489
split hairs, 477
Caviller
detractor, 936
Cavity
concavity, 252
Cavort
prance, 315
Caw
animal cry, 412
Cayenne
condiment, 393
pungent, 171
Cease
cessation, 142
Ceaseless
perpetuity, 112
Cecity
blindness, 442
Cede
relinquish, 782
Ceiling
height, 206
summit, 210
covering, 222
Cela va sans dire
conformity, 82
effect, 154
Celebrant
worship, 990
Celebrate
solemnize, 883
publish, 531
praise, 931
Celebration
fête, 883
rite, 998

Chain
series, 69
to fasten, 43
vinculum, 45
ornament, 847
to imprison, 752
Chain-mail
arms, 727
Chain-shot
arms, 727
Chair
support, 215
vehicle, 272
direction, 693
professorship, 542
throne, 747
Chairman
director, 694, 745
Chairmanship
direction, 693
Chaise
vehicle, 272
Chaise longue
support, 215
Chalcography
engraving, 558
Chalet
abode, 189
Chalice
cup, 191
hollow, 252
Chalk
mark, 550
drawing, 556, 559
soil, 342
Chalk out
plan, 626
Chalky
white, 430
Challenge
defy, 715
accuse, 938
claim, 924
Cham
master, 745
Chamber
room, 191
council, 696
mart, 799
Chamber music
music, 415
Chamberlain
servant, 746
Chambermaid
servant, 746
Chameleon

variegation, 440
inconstancy, 149, 605
Chamfer
furrow, 259
Champ
eat, 296
Champaign
plain, 344
Champion
auxiliary, 711
proficient, 700
good, 648
defence, 717
combatant, 726
Championship
aid, 707
superiority, 33
Chance
absence of cause, 156
absence of aim, 621
opportunity, 134
Chance-medley
chance, 156
Chancel
temple, 1000
Chancellor
president, 745
judge, 967
Chancy
risky, 665
uncertain, 475
Chandelier
luminary, 423
Chandler
merchant, 797
Change
alteration, 140
mart, 799
small coin, 800
Changeable
mutable, 149, 607
irresolute, 605
Changeful
mutable, 149
volition, 607
Changeling
changed, 147
fool, 501
Channel
opening, 260
conduit, 350
instrumentality, 631
way, 627
passage, 302
furrow, 259

Chant
sing, 415
worship, 990
rites, 998
Chantage
blackmail, 791
Chanty
music, 415
Chaos
disorder, 59
secret, 533
Chap
man, 373
fissure, 198
Chap-book
book, 593
Chap-fallen
dejected, 837
humiliated, 879
Chapel
temple, 1000
council, 696
Chaperon
safety, 664, 753
accompaniment, 88
Chaplain
clergy, 996
Chaplet
circle, 247
dress, 225
ornament, 847
trophy, 733
Chapman
merchant, 797
Chaps
orifice, 66
Chapter
part, 51
topic, 454
book, 593
church, 995
council, 696
Char
calefaction, 384
Charabanc
vehicle, 272
Character
nature, 5
disposition, 820
state, 7
letter, 561
type, 591
drama, 599
class, 75
unconformity, 83

Characteristic
special, 79
feature, 550
intrinsic, 5
Characterize
name, 564
description, 594
Charade
secret, 533
drama, 599
Charcoal
fuel, 388
black, 431
artist, 559
Charge
business, 625
direction, 693
advice, 695
precept, 697
commission, 755
load, 52, 639
order, 741
accusation, 938
attack, 716
impact, 276
price, 812
custody, 751
Charge-hand
director, 694
Chargé d'affaires
deputy, 759
Chargeable
debt, 806
Charger
carrier, 271
Chariot
vehicle, 272
Charioteer
director, 694
Charity
giving, 784
benevolence, 906
bounty, 816
Charivari
loudness, 404
discordance, 413
Charlatan
imposter, 548
ignoramus, 493
boaster, 884
Charlatanism
quackery, 545, 855
ignorance, 491
Charm
to please, 829

love, 897
beauty, 845
motive, 615
to conjure, 992
spell, 993
flock, 72
Charnel-house
interment, 363
Chart
representation, 554
Charter
privilege, 924
legality, 963
permit, 760
compact, 769
security, 771
commission, 755
Charwoman
clean, 652
Chary
economical, 817
cautious, 864
Chase
pursue, 622
follow, 281
shape, 240
adorn, 847
convexity, 250
wood, 367
Chasm
discontinuity, 4, 70
interval, 198
Chassis
framework, 215
Chaste
simple, 576, 849
good taste, 850
symmetry, 242
pure, 960
innocent, 946
style, 576
Chasten
punish, 972
refine, 658
moderate, 826
Chastise
punish, 932, 972
Chasuble
vestments, 999
Chat
interlocution, 588
Château
abode, 189
Chatelaine
ornament, 847

Chatoyant
variegation, 440
Chattels
goods, 635
property, 780
Chatter
talk, 584
cold, 383
Chatterbox
loquacity, 584
Chauffeur
driver, 694
Chauvinistic
bellicose, 722
boasting, 884
Chaw
food, 298
Chaw-bacon
boor, 876
Cheap
low price, 815
worthless, 643
Cheapen
barter, 794
depreciate, 483
Cheat
deceiver, 548
to deceive, 545
Check
restrain, 174, 751
pacify, 826
slacken, 275
counteract, 179
hinder, 706
impediment, 135
dissuade, 616
test, 463
evidence, 467
ticket, 550
money order, 800
numerical, 85
variegate, 440
Checkmate
success, 731
Cheek
side, 236
insolence, 885
discourtesy, 895
Cheer
mirth, 836
rejoicing, 838
Cheer
amusement, 840
pleasure, 827
to give pleasure, 829

relief, 834
cry, 411
repast, 298
applaud, 931
aid, 707
inspirit, 861
Cheered
pleasure, 827
Cheerful
pleasurable, 836
Cheerio
departure, 293
Cheerless
dejection, 830, 837
Cheers
drink, 959
Cheese-parings
remainder, 40
parsimony, 819
Cheesed off
bored, 841
sated, 869
Chef
director, 694
Chef-d'œuvre
masterpiece, 650
capability, 648
master-stroke, 698
Cheka
detective, 461
Chela
novice, 541
Chemise
dress, 225
Chemistry
conversion, 144
Cheque
money, 800
Chequer
variegation, 440
Cherish
love, 897
aid, 707
entertain, 820
Cheroot
tobacco, 298A
Cherry
red, 434
Cherub
angel, 977
Chessboard
variegated, 440
Chest
box, 191
money-box, 802

Chest-note
resonance, 408
Chesterfield
seat, 215
Chesterfieldian
courtesy, 894
Chestnut
brown, 433
joke, 842
Cheval-glass
mirror, 445
Chevalier d'industrie
thief, 792
Chevaux-de-frise
defence, 717
spikes, 253
Chevelure
hair, 256
Chevron
indication, 550
Chew eat, 296
tobacco, 298A
Chew the cud
thought, 451
Chez soi
at home, 221
Chiaroscuro
shade, 424
Chibouque
tobacco-pipe, 298A
Chic
beauty, 845
Chicane
cunning, 702
deception, 545
Chicanery
sophistry, 477
deception, 545
wrangling, 713
Chicken
youth, 127
weakness, 160
cowardice, 862
Chicken feed
money, 800
Chicken-hearted
cowardice, 862
Chide
disapprobation, 932
Chief
principal, 642
master, 745
Chieftain
master, 745
Chiffon

ornament, 847
Chignon
head-dress, 225
Chilblain
swelling, 250
Child
youth, 129
fool, 501
offspring, 167
Childish
foolish, 499
banal, 575
trifling, 643
Child's play
unimportance, 643
easy, 705
Chiliad
numbers, 98
duration, 106
Chill
cold, 383
discouragement, 616, 706
Chilly
ungracious, 895
Chime
resonance, 408
roll, 407
repetition, 104
to harmonize, 413
Chime in with
agree, 23
conformity, 82
assent, 488
Chimera
monster, 83
error, 495
imaginary, 515
Chimerical
impossible, 471
Chimney
air-pipe, 351
fissure, 198
opening, 260
egress, 295
Chin-chin
departure, 293
Chink
gap, 198
opening, 260
sound, 408
money, 800
Chip
bit, 51
small part, 193

to detach, 44
to reduce, 195
Chip in
interpose, 228
conversation, 588
Chip of the old block
similarity, 17
Chipper
gay, 836
healthy, 654
Chirography
writing, 590
Chiromancy
prediction, 511
Chirp
bird cry, 412
sing, 415
Chirpy
cheerful, 836
Chirrup
see Chirp
Chisel
sculpture, 557
sharpness, 253
form, 240
fabricate, 161
Chit
infant, 129
small, 193
letter, 592
Chit-chat
colloquy, 588
Chivalrous
martial, 722
honourable, 939
bold, 861
generous, 942
Chivy
chase, 622
Chloral
anaesthetic, 376
Chlorosis
achromatism, 429
Chlorotic
achromatism, 429
Chock-full
sufficiency, 639
fullness, 52
Chocolate
brown, 433
sweet, 396
Choice
election, 609
excellent, 648
Choir

music, 415
orchestra, 416
church, 1000
Choke
close, 261
hinder, 706
surfeit, 641
suffocate, 361
Choke off
dissuade, 616
Chokka
bored, 841
sated, 869
Choky
prison, 752
Choler
resentment, 900
Choleric
irascible, 901
Choose
choice, 609
will, 600
Choosy
particular, 868
Chop
disjoin, 44
change, 140
barter, 794
wave, 348
sign, 550
Chop logic
reasoning, 476
Chopping
large, 192
Chops
orifice, 66
Choral
music, 415
Chord
harmony, 413
Chore
business, 625
Choreography
dance, 840
Chorister
musician, 416
clergy, 996
Chorography
situation, 183, 554
Chortle
to laugh, 838
Chorus
sound, 404
voices, 411
musicians, 416

unanimity, 488
Chose jugée
judgment, 480
Chota hazri
food, 298
Chouse
deception, 545
Chrism
rite, 998
Christ
Deity, 976
Christen
nomenclature, 564
Christendom
Christianity, 983A
Christian
piety, 987
Christianity, 983A
Christianity
Christian religion, 983A
Christmas box
gift, 784
Chromatic
colour, 428
musical scale, 413
Chromatrope
optical instrument, 445
Chromolithograph
engraving, 558
Chronic
diuturnity, 110
Chronicle
annals, 551
measure of time, 114
account, 594
Chronicler
recorder, 553
Chronique scandaleuse
gossip, 532, 588
Chronology
time measurement, 114
Chronometry
time measurement, 114
Chrysalis
youth, 127, 129
Chubby
size, 192
Chuck
throw, 284
desist, 142
cry, 412
food, 298
Chuck out
expel, 297

Chuck up
abandon, 624
Chucker-out
doorkeeper, 263
Chuckle
laugh, 838
exult, 884
Chuckle-head
fool, 501
Chum
friend, 890
Chummy
friendly, 888
Chunk
size, 192
part, 51
Chunky
short, 201
broad, 202
Church
Christian religion,
983A
temple, 1000
Churchdom
churchdom, 995
Churchman
clergy, 996
Churchwarden
clergy, 996
tobacco-pipe, 298A
Churchy
bigoted, 988
Churchyard
interment, 363
Churl
boor, 876
rude, 895
irascible, 901
niggard, 819
Churn
agitation, 315, 352
Chute
obliquity, 217
Chutney
condiment, 393
Chyle
fluid, 333
Chyme
semiliquid, 352
Cicatrize
improvement, 658
Cicerone
teacher, 540
director, 694
Cicisbeo
love, 897

Ci-devant
preterition, 122
Cigar
tobacco, 298A
Cigar-case
receptacle, 191
Cigar-shaped
rotund, 249
Cigarette
tobacco, 298A
Cigarette-case
receptacle, 191
Ciliated
roughness, 256
Cimmerian
darkness, 421
Cinch
grip, 781
connection, 45
easy, 705
Cincture
circularity, 247
Cinders
remainder, 40
Cine-camera
lens, 445
Cinema
theatre, 599A
amusement, 840
Cinemaddict
cinema, 599A
Cinematograph
show, 448
Cinerary
burial, 363
Cineration
calefaction, 384
Cinerator
furnace, 386
Cinereous
grey, 432
Cingulum
belt, 229
Cinnabar
red, 434
Cinque
numbers, 98
Cipher
zero, 101
number, 84
to compute, 85
secret, 533
mark, 550
writing, 590
unimportant, 643

Circe
seductor, 615
sensuality, 954
Circle
form, 247
curvature, 245
space, 181
theatre, 599
party, 712
social, 892
Circuit
deviation, 279
indirect path, 629
winding, 248
turn, 311
tour, 266
space, 181
Circuitous
devious, 279
turning, 311
indirect, 629
Circular
round, 247
curved, 245
advertisement, 531
letter, 592
Circulate
rotate, 312
publish, 531
Circumambient
circumjacence, 227
Circumambulate
move, 266
wind, 311
Circumbendibus
winding, 248
circuit, 629
circuition, 311
Circumference
outline, 229
Circumfluent
circuition, 311
Circumfuse
dispersion, 73
Circumgyration
rotation, 312
Circumjacence
surrounding, 227
Circumlocution
phrase, 566, 573
Circumnavigation
navigation, 267
circuition, 311
Circumrotation
rotation, 312

Circumscribe
surround, 231
limit, 761
Circumspect
attentive, 457
careful, 459
cautious, 864
Circumstance
phrase, 8
event, 151
Circumstantial
diffuse, 573
evidence, 472
Circumvallation
enclosure, 232
defence, 717
Circumvent
cheat, 545
defeat, 731
cunning, 702
Circumvolution
rotation, 312
Circus
arena, 728
amusement, 840
edifice, 189
Cistern
receptacle, 191
store, 636
Citadel
fort, 666
defence, 717
Cite
quote as example, 82, 564
as evidence, 467
summon, 741
accuse, 938
arraign, 969
Cithern
musical instrument, 417
Citizen
inhabitant, 188
Citizen
man, 373
Citrine
yellow, 436
City
abode, 189
Civet
fragrance, 400
Civic
urban, 189
public, 372
Civicism

patriotism, 910
Civil
courteous, 894
laity, 997
Civilian
lawyer, 968
non-combatant, 726A
Civilization
courtesy, 894
mankind, 372
Civvies
dress, 225
Clachan
village, 189
Clack
talk, 588
snap, 406
animal cry, 412
Clad
dressed, 225
Claim
demand, 741, 765
property, 780
right, 924
Claimant
dueness, 924
petitioner, 767
Clairvoyance
occult arts, 992
insight, 490
foresight, 510
Clam
taciturn, 585
Clamant
cry, 411
Clamber
ascent, 305
Clammy
semiliquid, 352
Clamour
loudness, 404, 411
Clamp
to fasten, 43
fastening, 45
Clamp down
restrict, 751
Clan
class, 75
kindred, 11
clique, 892
Clandestine
concealment, 528
secret, 534
Clang
loudness, 404

resonance, 408
Clanger
error, 495, 732
solecism, 568
Clank
harsh sound, 410
Clannishness
prejudice, 481
co-operation, 709
Clap
explosion, 406
to applaud, 931
Clap on
addition, 37
Clap up
restraint, 751
Clapperclaw
beat, 972
Claptrap
plea, 617
pretence, 546
sophistry, 477
nonsense, 492
Claqueur
flatterer, 935
Clarence
vehicle, 272
Clarify
cleanness, 652
Clarinet
musical instrument, 417
Clarion
musical instrument, 417
Clarity
transparency, 425
perspicuity, 570
Clart
mud, 352
dirt, 653
Clash
oppose, 708
disagree, 24
discord, 713
contest, 720
concussion, 276
sound, 406
chatter, 584
Clasp
to unite, 43
fastening, 45
entrance, 903
come close, 197
Clasp-knife
sharpness, 253

Class
category, 75
to arrange, 60
learner, 541

Classic
masterpiece, 650
symmetry, 242
ancient, 124

Classical
taste, 578, 580

Classify
arrangement, 60
class, 75

Clatter
roll, 407
din, 404

Clause
part, 51
passage, 593
condition, 770

Claustral
secluded, 893

Claustrophobia
dislike, 867
seclusion, 893

Clavichord
musical, 417

Claw
hook, 633
to grasp, 789

Clay
earth, 342
corpse, 362
tobacco-pipe, 298A

Clay-cold
cold, 383

Claymore
arms, 727

Clean
unstained, 652
entirely, 31

Clean-handed
innocence, 946

Cleanse
purge, 652

Clear
transparent, 425
light, 420
visible, 446
intelligible, 518
perspicuous style, 570
to prepare, 673
to free, 750
to vindicate, 937
to acquit, 970
innocent, 946

simple, 42
easy, 705
to pay, 807
to pass, 302

Clear decks
prepare, 673

Clear of
distant, 196

Clear out
eject, 297
depart, 203

Clear-sighted
vision, 441
shrewd, 498

Clear up
interpret, 518, 522

Clearance
payment, 807

Clearway
way, 627

Cleave
adhere, 46
sunder, 44, 91

Cleek
club, 276

Clef
music, 413

Cleft
chink, 198

Clem
starve, 956

Clement
lenient, 740
kind, 906
pitiful, 914

Clench
see Clinch

Clepsydra
chronometry, 114

Clergy
clergy, 996

Clerical
churchdom, 995

Clerihew
drollery, 853
absurdity, 497

Clerk
scholar, 492
recorder, 553
writer, 590
servant, 746
agent, 758
church, 996

Clerkship
commission, 755

Clever
skill, 698

Cliché
platitude, 497

Click
snap, 406

Client
dependant, 746
buyer, 795
frequenter, 136

Clientship
subjection, 749

Cliff
height, 206
verticality, 212, 217

Cliff-hanging
suspense, 485

Climacteric
age, 128

Climate
region, 181
weather, 338

Climax
summit, 210
completion, 729
increase, 35
in degree, 33

Climb
ascent, 305

Clime
region, 181

Clinch
snatch, 789
fasten, 43
close, 261
an argument, 474, 478

Cling
cohere, 46

Clinic
medicine, 662

Clink
resonance, 408
prison, 752

Clinker
concretion, 321
dirt, 653

Clinometer
angularity, 244

Clinquant
ornament, 847

Clip
prune, 38
contract, 195
shorten, 201
stammer, 583

blow, 276
fastening, 45
hanging, 214
Clipper
ship, 273
swift, 274
Clipping
part, 51
extract, 596, 609
first-rate, 648
Clique
party, 712
sociality, 892
Cloaca
conduit, 350
foulness, 653
Cloak
dress, 225
conceal, 528
disguise, 546
Clock
chronometry, 114
Clockwise
rotation, 312
Clockwork
instrument, 633
Clod
earth, 342
fool, 591
Clod-pated
folly, 499
Clodhopper
boor, 876
Clodpoll
fool, 501
Clog
hindrance, 706
boot, 225
Clog-dance
dance, 840
Cloister
temple, 1000
seclusion, 893
Close
near, 197
short, 201
narrow, 203
dense, 321
tight, 43
similar, 17
warm, 382
to shut, 261
end, 67
to complete, 729
taciturn, 585

stingy, 819
piece of land, 780
house, 189
Close-fisted
parsimony, 819
Close in upon
converge, 290
Close quarters
nearness, 197
Close-up
cinema, 599A
Close with
arrive, 292
combat, 720
assent, 488
compact, 769
Closeness
junction, 43
Closet
room, 191
hide, 530
Closure
closing, 261
cessation, 142
Clot
concretion, 46
density, 321
earth, 342
Cloth
cover, 222
Clothes
dress, 225
Cloud
dimness, 422
shade, 424
opacity, 426
concealment, 528
crowd, 72
smoke, 334
Cloud-capt
height, 206
Clouded
variegated, 440
Cloudless
light, 420
Cloudy
opaque, 426
dark, 421
Clout
blow, 276
punishment, 972
to repair, 658
Cloven
bisection, 91
Cloven-footed

malevolent, 907
Clover
luxury, 377
comfort, 827
Clown
rustic, 876
buffoon, 844
pantomimic, 599
Clownish
vulgar, 851
Cloy
satiety, 641, 869
Club
bludgeon, 276
instrument, 633
weapon, 727
party, 712
to co-operate, 709
social meeting, 892
assemblage, 72
focus, 74
Club-footed
distorted, 243
Club-law
illegality, 964
compulsion, 744
Cluck
animal cry, 412
Clue
ball, 249
key, 462
Clueless
ignorant, 491
Clump
projecting mass, 250
assemblage, 72
trees, 367
to tread, 266
Clumsy
unskilful, 647, 699
graceless, 846
style, 579
Cluster
assemblage, 72
Clutch
seize, 134, 789
retain, 781
Clutches
authority, 737
Clutter
roll, 407
disorder, 59
Coacervation
crowd, 72

Coach
carriage, 272
to teach, 537
tutor, 540
Coachman
director, 694
Coaction
compulsion, 744
Coadjutor
auxiliary, 711
Coagency
co-operation, 709
Coagment
collect, 72
Coagulate
density, 321
Coagulum
density, 321
Coal
fuel, 388
Coal-black
blackness, 431
Coalesce
identity, 13
combine, 48
Coalition
co-operation, 709
Coaptation
agreement, 23
Coarctation
narrow, 203
decrease, 36
Coarse
texture, 329
vulgar, 851
dirty, 653
impure, 961
Coast
land, 342
to navigate, 267
to skirt, 230
to slide down, 306
Coaster
ship, 273
Coastguard
keeper, 753
Coat
layer, 204
exterior, 220
habit, 225
to paint, 222
lining, 224
Coating
lining, 224
Coax
flatter, 933

persuade, 615
Cob
horse, 271
Cobalt
blue, 438
Cobble
to mend, 658
Cobbler
dress, 225
Co-belligerent
helper, 711
Coble
ship, 273
Cobra
bane, 663
Cobweb
light, 320
flimsy, 643
dirty, 653
untruth, 546
Cochineal
red, 434
Cock-a-hoop
exulting, 731, 884
gay, 836
Cock-and-bull
absurdity, 497
Cock-crow
morning, 125
Cock-sure
belief, 484
Cock up
stick up, 212
project, 250
Cockade
badge, 550
title, 877
Cockatrice
bane, 663
monster, 83
evil eye, 441
miscreant, 949
Cockboat
ship, 273
Cocker
caress, 902
Cockle up
fold, 258
Cockney
townsman, 188
Cockpit
arena, 728
of a ship, 191
Cockshut time
twilight, 422

Cocktail
stimulus, 615
drunkenness, 959
Cocotte
prostitute, 962
Coction
calefaction, 384
Cocytus
hell, 982
Coda
end, 67
Code
law, 963
precept, 697
secret, 533
signal, 550
Codex
book, 593
Codger
parsimony, 819
Codicil
adjunct, 39
sequel, 65
Codify
legality, 963
Codswallop
nonsense, 643
Coefficient
co-operating, 709
accompanying, 88
factor, 84
Coemption
purchase, 795
Coenobite
seclusion, 893
Coequal
equality, 27
Coerce
restrain, 751
compel, 744
dissuade, 616
Coessential
identity, 13
Coetaneous
synchronism, 120
Coeternal
perpetuity, 112
Coeval
synchronism, 120
Coexist
synchronism, 120
accompany, 88
contiguity, 199
Coextension
equality, 27

parallelism, 216
Coffee-house
food, 298
Coffer
chest, 191
money-chest, 802
store, 636
Coffin
interment, 363
Coffin-nail
tobacco, 298A
Cog
tooth, 253
ship, 273
deceive, 545
flatter, 933
Cogent
powerful, 157
argument, 467, 476
Cogitate
thought, 451
Cognate
rule, 80
relation, 9
Cognation
relation, 9
Cognition
knowledge, 490
Cognizance
knowledge, 490
Cognomen
nomenclature, 564
Cognoscence
knowledge, 490
Cognoscente
taste, 850
Cognoscible
knowledge, 490
Cohabitation
marriage, 903
Co-heir
partner, 778
Cohere
unite, 46
dense, 321
Cohesive
uniting, 46
dense, 321
tenacious, 327
Cohibition
restraint, 751
Cohort
combatant, 726
Coif
dress, 225

Coiffure
dress, 225
Coil
convolution, 248
circuition, 311
disorder, 59
Coin
money, 800
to fabricate, 161
to imagine, 515
Coincidence
identity, 13
in time, 120
in place, 199
in opinion, 488
Coinstantaneity
synchronism, 120
Coke
fuel, 388
Colander
opening, 260
Cold
frigidity, 383
style, 575
insensible, 823
indifferent, 866
Cold-blooded
malevolent, 907
dispassionate, 823, 826
Cold-hearted
enmity, 889
Cold-shoulder
exclusion, 893
repulsion, 289
Cold war
truce, 723
Coliseum
arena, 728
Collaborate
accompany, 88
co-operate, 178, 709
Collapse
contraction, 195
prostration, 160
fatigue, 688
incapacity, 158
failure, 732
Collar
dress, 225
shackle, 749, 752
seize, 789
Collate
compare, 464
Collateral
relation, 11

lateral, 236
consequential, 467
Collation
food, 299
comparison, 464
Colleague
auxiliary, 711
co-operating, 709
Collect
assemble, 72
take, 789
acquire, 775
learn, 539
opine, 480
understand, 518
prayer, 990
Collectanea
assemblage, 72
compendium, 596
Collected
calm, 826
Collection
store, 636
offering, 990
assemblage, 72
Collectiveness
whole, 50
Collectivism
participation, 780
authority, 737
Collector
assemblage, 72
Colleen
woman, 374
girl, 129
College
school, 542
Collide
see Collision
Collier
ship, 273
man, 373
Colligate
assemblage, 72
Colligation
junction , 43
Collimation
direction, 278
Collimator
optical instrument, 445
Collision
approach, 286
percussion, 276
clashing, 179
opposition, 708

encounter, 720
Collocate
arrange, 60
assemble, 72
Collocution
interlocution, 588
Collogue
confer, 588
Colloid
semiliquid, 352
Collop
part, 51
Colloquialism
language, 560
Coloquy
interlocution, 588
Collotype
engraving, 558
Collusion
deceit, 545
concurrence, 178
conspiring, 709
Colon
stop, 142
Colonel
master, 745
Colonize
location, 184, 188
Colonnade
continuity, 69
Colony
region, 181
settlement, 184, 188
Colophon
end, 67
sequel, 65
Coloration
colour, 428
Coloratura
music, 415
Colossal
size, 192
height, 206
Colour
hue, 428
plea, 617
disguise, 545
qualify, 469
to blush, 434
Colourable
deceptive, 545
ostensible, 472
Colouring
meaning, 516
exaggeration, 549

Colourless
achromatism, 429
Colours
standard, 550
decoration, 877
Colporteur
agent, 758
Colt
fool, 501
horse, 271
Column
series, 69
height, 206
monument, 551
cylinder, 249
procession, 266
troop, 726
Colure
universe, 318
Coma
insensibility, 376, 823
inactivity, 683
Comb
sharpness, 253
Combat
contention, 720, 722
Combatant
contention, 726
Comber
wave, 348
Combination
union, 48
Combinations
arithmetical, 84
dress, 225
Combine
join, 48
co-operate, 709
union, 712
syndicate, 778
Combustible
heating, 384
fuel, 388
Come
arrive, 292
approach, 286
happen, 151
Come about
eventuality, 151
Come after
sequence, 63
Come-at-able
accessible, 705
Come away
recession, 287

Come-back
retort, 462, 479, 842
retaliation, 718
Come before
precedence, 62
Come by
acquisition, 775
Come down
descend, 306
cheapness, 815
pay, 809
Come-down
adversity, 735
Come forth
existence, 1
Come from
effect, 154
Come in for
obtain, 775
Come near
approach, 286
Come off
disjunction, 44
take place, 151
Come on
follow, 63
defy, 715
prosper, 731
Come out
egress, 294
Come over
induce, 615
Come to
whole, 50
Come up to
equal, 27
Come up with
arrival, 292
Come upon
arrival, 292
Comedian
the drama, 599
humorist, 844
Comedy
drama, 599
ridicule, 856
Comely
beauty, 845
Comestible
food, 298
Comet
wanderer, 268
universe, 318
Comfit
sweetness, 396

Comfort
pleasure, 377, 827
content, 831
relief, 834
Comfort station
toilet, 191, 653
Comfortable
pleased, 827
pleasing, 829
Comforter
deity, 976
dress, 225
Comfortless
unhappy, 828
painful, 830
dejected, 837
Comic
witty, 842
ridiculous, 853
Comintern
council, 696
Comitium
assemblage, 72
council, 696
Comity
courtesy, 894
Comma
stop, 141
Command
order, 741
authority, 737
Commandeer
impress, 744
take, 789
Commander
master, 745
Commanding
dignified, 873
Commando
combatant, 726
Comme il faut
taste, 850
fashion, 852
Commemorate
celebration, 883
record, 551
memory, 505
Commence
beginning, 66
Commend
approbation, 931
Commendable
virtuous, 944
Commensurate
accord, 23

adequate, 639
Comment
reason, 476
interpret, 522
dissertation, 595
Commerce
intercourse, 588
business, 625
barter, 794
Commercialese
verbiage, 573
Commination
threat, 909
Commingle
mixture, 41
Comminute
pulverulence, 330
disjunction, 44
incoherence, 47
Commiserate
pity, 914
Commissariat
provision, 298, 637
Commissary
consignee, 758
deputy, 759
Commission
business, 625
consignee, 755
fee, 809
Commissionaire
agent, 690
door-keeper, 263
Commissioner
consignee, 758
Commissure
junction, 43
Commit
act, 680
delegate, 755
imprison, 751
arrest, 969
Committee
council, 696
assemblage, 72
Commix
mixture, 41
Commodious
spacious, 180
expedience, 646
Commodity
merchandise, 798
Commodore
master, 745
Common

ordinary, 82
low, 876
unimportant, 643
general, 78
reciprocal, 12
frequent, 136
plain, 344
Common-room
sociality, 892
Common sense
intellect, 450
wisdom, 498
Commonalty
common, 876
people, 372
Commoner
commonalty, 876
Commonplace
unimportant, 643
habitual, 613
dull, 843
Commons
commonalty, 876
food, 298
Commonwealth
man, 373
Commotion
agitation, 315
Commune
muse, 451
converse, 588
territorial division, 181
Communicant
worship, 990
Communicate
tell, 527
participate, 778
join, 43
Communication
information , 527, 532
connection, 43
Communion
society, 712
participation, 778
sacrament, 998
Communism
participation, 778
authority, 737
Community
man, 373
fellowship, 712
participation, 778
Commute
barter, 794
substitution, 147

style, 569
compromise, 774
atonement, 952
materials, 635
Compositor
printer, 591
Compost
manure, 653
Composure
inexcitability, 826
moderation, 174
Compotation
drunkenness, 959
Compound
mix, 41
combination, 48
compromise, 774
Compound for
compact, 769
barter, 794
Comprehend
include, 76
compose, 54
understand, 518
know, 490
Comprehension
intelligence, 498
Comprehensive
general, 78
wide, 192
Compress
condense, 321, 572
narrow, 203
curtail, 201
contract, 195
remedy, 662
Comprise
inclusion, 76
Compromise
compound, 774
atone, 952
endanger, 665
mean, 29, 628
compensation, 30
Compte rendu
compendium, 596
Comptroller
director, 694
master, 745
Compulsion
force, 744
Compunction
penitence, 950
Compurgation

acquittal, 970
evidence, 467
Compute
numeration, 85
Comrade
friend, 890
Con
memory, 505
thought, 451
to steer, 693
Con amore
willing, 602
Con man
cheat, 548
Con moto
music, 415
Conation
will, 600
Concatenation
junction, 43
continuity, 69
Concave
concavity, 252
Conceal
hide, 528
invisible, 447
Concede
consent, 762
admit, 467, 529
give, 784
assent, 488
permit, 760
Conceit
idea, 453
belief, 484
supposition, 514
imagination, 515
affectation, 855
vanity, 880
wit, 842
Conceited
folly, 499
Conceivable
possible, 470
Conceive
believe, 484
imagine, 515
produce, 161, 168
Concent
melody, 413
Concentrate
assemble, 72
compress, 321
converge, 290
Concentric

centrality, 223
Concept
idea, 453
Conception
intellect, 450
idea, 453
belief, 484
knowledge, 490
imagination, 515
beginning, 66
Conceptual
thought, 451
Concern
relation, 9
grief, 828
importance, 642
business, 625
firm, 797
Concerning
relation, 9
Concert
music, 415
plan, 626
co-operation, 709
agreement, 23
Concert-hall
amusement, 840
Concertina
musical, 417
Concerto
music, 415
Concession
grant, 762, 784
assent, 488
permit, 760
Concetto
wit, 842
Conchoid
curvature, 245
Conchy
non-combatant, 726A
Concierge
keeper, 263, 753
Conciliate
talk over, 615
satisfy, 831
atone, 952
courtesy, 894
Conciliation
concord, 714
pacification, 723
mediation, 724
Concinnity
style, 578
beauty, 845

Concise
conciseness, 572
Conclave
assembly, 72
council, 696
church, 995
Conclude
end, 67
infer, 476
opine, 480, 484
complete, 729
determine, 604
Conclusion (to try)
contention, 720
Conclusive
demonstration, 478
Concoct
prepare, 673
falsify, 544
plan, 626
Concomitant
synchronous, 120
concurring, 178
accompanying, 88
Concord
agreement, 23
in music, 413
assent, 488
harmony, 714
amity, 888
Concordance
dictionary, 562
Concordat
compact, 769
Concours
contention, 720
Concourse
assemblage, 72
convergence, 290
Concrete
mass, 46
material, 3, 316
density, 321
Concubine
libertine, 962
Concupiscence
desire, 865
impurity, 961
Concur
co-operate, 178
in concert, 709
converge, 290
assent, 488
Concurrence
agreement, 23

coexistence, 120
Concussion
impulse, 276
Condemn
censure, 932
convict, 971
Condense
contraction, 195
density, 321
style, 572
Condescend
humility, 879
Condescending
patronizing, 878
Condign
dueness, 922, 924
Condiment
condiment, 393
Condition
state, 7
rank, 873
term, 770
modification, 469
sensitiveness, 375
teach, 537
habit, 613
Conditional
circumstance, 8
Condole
condolence, 915
Condonation
forgiveness, 918
Condottiere
master, 745
Conduce
tend, 176
concur, 178
avail, 644
contribute, 153
Conduct
lead, 693
transfer, 270
procedure, 692
music, 415
Conductor
guard, 666
director, 694
interpreter, 524
musician, 416
conveyor, 271
Conduit
conduit, 350
Condyle
convexity, 250
Cone

round, 249
pointed, 253
Confabulation
interlocution, 588
Confection
sweetness, 396
Confederacy
party, 712
co-operation, 709
Confederate
auxiliary, 711
Confer
give, 784
converse, 588
advise, 695
Confess
avow, 529, 535
assert, 488
penitence, 950
rite, 998
Confessedly
affirmation, 535
admission, 467
Confessional
temple, 1000
Confidant
auxiliary, 711
friend, 890
Confide
trust, 484
credulity, 486
hope, 858
Confidence
courage, 861
Confidence man
cheat, 548
Confidential
concealment, 528
Configuration
form, 240
Confine
limit, 233
imprison, 751
circumscribe, 231
frontier, 199
Confined
ailing, 655
Confirm
corroborate, 467
consent, 762
rites, 998
Confirmed
fixed, 150
Confiscate
condemn, 971

440

take, 789
Conflagration
calefaction, 384
Conflation
combination, 48
Conflict
contention, 720
disagreement, 24
Conflicting
opposing, 14, 179, 708
Confluence
convergence, 290
Conflux
assemblage, 72
Conform
assent, 488
accustom, 613
concur, 178
agree, 646
Conformation
form, 240
frame, 7
Conformity
to rule, 16, 82
Confound
disorder, 61
injure, 649
perplex, 475
baffle, 731
confuse, 519
astonish, 870
indiscriminate, 465A
expletive, 908
Confoundedly
greatness, 31
Confraternity
friendship, 888
Confrère
friend, 890
Confront
face, 234
compare, 467
resist, 719
Confucianism
religion, 984
Confucius
religious founder, 986
Confuse
derange, 61
indiscriminate, 465A
obscure, 519
perplex, 458, 475
abash, 874
style, 571
Confusion

disorder, 59
shame, 874
Confutation
disproof, 479
Confute
deny, 536
Congé
dismissal, 756
Congeal
cold, 385
Congealed
dense, 321
Congener
consanguinity, 11
similar, 17
included, 76
Congenial
agreeing, 23, 714
expedient, 646
Congenital
intrinsic, 5
habitual, 613
Congeries
assemblage, 72
Congestion
collection, 72
redundance, 641
disease, 655
Conglobation
assemblage, 72
Conglomerate
assemblage, 72
density, 321
Conglutinate
coherence, 46
Congratulate
congratulation, 896
Congregate
assemblage, 72
Congregation
laity, 997
worship, 990
Congress
assemblage, 72, 290
council, 696
Congruous
agreeing, 23
expedient, 646
Conical
round, 249
pointed, 253
Conjecture
supposition, 514
Conjoin
junction, 43

concur, 178
Conjointly
together, 37, 43
Conjugal
marriage, 903
Conjugate
word, 562
Conjugation
junction, 43
pair, 89
phase, 144
grammar, 567
Conjunct
junction, 43
Conjunction
vinculum, 45
Conjuncture
contingency, 8
occasion, 134
Conjuration
deception, 545
sorcery, 992
Conjure
entreat, 765
exorcise, 992
Conjure up
imagine, 515
Conjurer
sorcerer, 994
adept, 700
Connate
cause, 153
intrinsic, 5
Connatural
uniform, 16
similar, 17
Connect
relate, 9
link, 43
Connection
kindred, 11
link, 45
Connective
link, 45
Connive
overlook, 460
concur, 178
allow, 760
Connoisseur
taste, 850
judge, 480
proficient, 700
Connotation
indication, 550

Connubial
marriage, 903
Conquer
success, 731
Conquered
failure, 732
Conquest
success, 731
Consanguinity
kindred, 11
Conscience
moral sense, 926
knowledge, 490
Conscience-smitten
penitence, 950
Conscientious
virtuous, 944
scrupulous, 726A, 939
true, 494
Consciousness
intuition, 450
knowledge, 490
Conscript
soldier, 726
Conscription
compulsion, 744
Consecrate
dedicate, 873
sanctify, 987, 995, 998
Consectary
corollary, 480
Consecution
sequence, 63
Consecutive
following, 63
continuous, 69
Consecutively
gradually, 144
Consensus
agreement, 23
assent, 488
Consent
grant, 762
concur, 178
assent, 488
agreement, 23
Consentaneous
agreeing, 23
expedient, 646
Consequence
effect, 154
event, 151
importance, 642
Consequent
sequence, 63
Consequential

arrogant, 878
deducible, 467, 478
Consequently
reasoning, 154, 476
Conservation
preservation, 670
Conservative
permanence, 141
Conservatoire
school, 542
Conservatory
store, 636
hothouse, 386
Conserve
sweet, 396
Consider
think, 451
attend to, 457
inquire, 461
Considerable
in degree, 31
in size, 192
important, 642
Considerate
judicious, 498
benevolent, 906
respectful, 928
Consideration
motive, 615
qualification, 469
importance, 642
requital, 973
respect, 928
Considering
reasoning, 476
Consign
transfer, 783
commission, 755
give, 784
allot, 786
Consignee
delegate, 758
Consignment
commission, 755
Consist in
existence, 1
Consist of
composition, 54
Consistence
density, 321
Consistency
uniformity, 16
Consistent
agreement, 23
Consistory

council, 696
church, 995
Consociation
sociality, 892
Console
relieve, 834
pity, 914
table, 215
keyboard, 417
Consolidate
unite, 46, 48
condense, 321
Consols
treasury, 802
Consonance
agreement, 23
expedience, 646
music, 413
Consonant
letter, 561
Consort
accompany, 88
associate, 892
spouse, 903
Consort with
fit, 646
Consortship
sociality, 892
Conspectus
compendium, 596
Conspicuous
visible, 446
eminent, 873
Conspiracy
plot, 626
Conspire
concur, 178
Constable
governor, 745
police, 664
officer, 965
Constant
uniformity, 16
immutable, 150
regular, 80, 82
continuous, 69
resolute, 604
True, 494
faithful, 939
Constantly
frequently, 136
Constellation
stars, 318, 423
glory, 873

442

Consternation
fear, 860
Constipate
density, 321
Constituent
component, 54, 56
voter, 609
Constitute
compose, 54, 56
produce, 161
Constitution
nature, 5
state, 7
texture, 329
charter, 924
law, 963
Constrain
power, 157
restrain, 751
compel, 744
abash, 881
Constrict
narrow, 203
contract, 195
Constringe
narrow, 203
Construct
production, 161
Construction
form, 240
structure, 329
meaning, 522
Construe
meaning, 522
Consubstantiation
rite, 998
Consul
diplomat, 758
Consult
advice, 695
Consume
destroy, 162
waste, 638
use, 677
ravage, 649
Consuming
painful, 830
Consummate
great, 31
complete, 52, 729
skill, 698
Consummation
end, 67
Consumption
shrinking, 195

waste, 638
disease, 655
use, 677
Contact
contiguity, 199
meet, 292
Contadino
peasant, 876
Contagious
insalubrious, 657
Contain
include, 76
be composed of, 54
Contaminate
spoil, 659
soil, 653
Contango
discount, 813
Contemn
contempt, 930
Contemper
moderation, 174
Contemplate
view, 441
think, 451
purpose, 620
expect, 507
Contemporaneous
synchronism, 120
Contemporary
synchronism, 120
Contempt
despise, 930
Contemptible
unimportant, 643
Contend
fight, 720
assert, 535
Content
satisfied, 827, 831
calm, 826
assentient, 488
patience, 821
will, 600
willing, 602
Contention
discord, 713
struggle, 720
Contentious
bad-tempered, 901
Contents
ingredients, 56
components, 190
list, 86
compendium, 596

end, 67
Conterminal
end, 67
limit, 233
Conterminous
adjoining, 199
Contest
contention, 720
lawsuit, 969
Context
printing, 591
accompaniment, 88
Contexture
state, 7
texture, 329
Contiguous
touching, 199
Continence
purity, 960
Continent
land, 342
Contingent
conditional, 8
qualifying, 469
eventual, 151
chance, 156
liable, 177
possible, 470
uncertain, 475
casual, 621
allotment, 786
part, 51
duration, 108A
Continually
frequency, 136
Continuation
sequence, 63
sequel, 65
adjunct, 39
Continue
persist, 141, 143
endure, 106, 110
Continued, to be
sequel, 65
Continuity
persistence, 69
Continuum
substantiality, 3
Contortion
distortion, 243
convolution, 246
deformity, 846
Contour
outline, 229, 448

444

Conversion
change, 144
religious, 987
Convert
opinion, 484
learner, 541
piety, 987
to change to, 144
to use, 677
Convertible
identical, 13
equal, 27
Convex
convexity, 250
Convey
transfer, 270, 783
Conveyance
vehicle, 272
Conveyancer
lawyer, 968
Convict
condemn, 971
to convince, 537
prisoner, 754
condemned, 949
Conviction
belief, 484
Convince
teaching, 537
Convincement
belief, 484
Convivial
social, 892
Convocation
council, 696, 995
Convoke
assemblage, 72
Convolution
coil, 248
rotation, 312
crossing, 219
Convoy
transfer, 270
guard, 664, 753
Convulse
violent, 173
agitate, 315
pain, 378
torture, 830
Coo
animal cry, 412

Cook
heat, 384
prepare, 673

falsify, 544
accounts, 811
Cool
cold, 383
to refrigerate, 385
judicious, 498
to moderate, 174
to dissuade, 616
to allay, 826
indifferent, 866
torpid, 826
Cool-headed
torpid, 826
judicious, 498
Cooler
refrigerator, 387
prison, 752
Coolie
carrier, 271
Coombe
valley, 252
Coon
black, 431
Coop
confine, 752
restrain, 751
abode, 189
Co-operate
physically, 178
voluntarily, 709
Co-operation
agreement, 23
Co-operator
auxiliary, 711
Co-ordinate
equality, 27
arrange, 60
Cop
police, 664
Copal
semiliquid, 352
Copartner
participator, 778
associate, 892
accompanying, 88
Cope
contend, 720
equal, 27
canonicals, 999
Copia verborum
diffuseness, 573
speech, 582
Coping-stone
completion, 729

Copious
abundant, 639
style, 573
Copper
money, 800
colour, 439
police, 664
Copperplate
engraving, 558
Coppice
plant, 367
Coprology
impurity, 653
Copse
see Coppice
Copula
junction, 45
Copy
imitation, 19, 21
prototype, 22
to write, 590
represent, 554
Copyholder
printing, 591
Copying
imitating, 19
Copyist
writing, 590
Copyright
privilege, 924
Coquetry
affectation, 855
Coquette
flirt, 902
vacillate, 605
Cor anglais
musical, 417
Coracle
boat, 273
Coral
ornament, 847
Coram judice
jurisdiction, 965
Corbeille
receptacle, 191
Cord
tie, 45
filament, 205
furrow, 259
Cordage
junction, 45
Cordial
grateful, 829
warm, 821

willing, 602
friendly, 888
remedy, 662
Cordite
arms, 727
Cordon
outline, 229, 232
circular, 247
badge, 550
Corduroy
furrow, 259
Core
centrality, 223
importance, 642
Co-respondent
divorce, 905
Corgi
vehicle, 272
Coriaceous
tenacity, 327
Corinthian
taste, 850
Co-rival
see Corrival
Cork
lightness, 320
plug, 263
Cork up
closure, 261
restrain, 751
Corkscrew
extractor, 301
perforator, 262
spiral, 248
Cormorant
gluttony, 865, 957
Corn
projection, 250
Corncob
tobacco-pipe, 298A
Cornea
eye, 441
Corned
drunk, 959
Corneous
hard, 323
Corner
place, 182
receptacle, 191
angularity, 244
Corner-stone
support, 215
to engross, 777
syndicate, 778

Cornet
music, 417
officer, 745
Cornice
summit, 210
Cornucopia
sufficiency, 639
Cornute
sharp, 253
Corollary
deduction, 480
addition, 37, 39
Corona
circularity, 247
light, 420
Coronach
lamentation, 839
funeral, 363
Coronary
height, 206
summit, 210
Coronation
celebration, 883
Coronet
sceptre, 747
ornament, 847
Corporal
officer, 745
animality, 364
Corporality
materiality, 316
Corporate
junction, 43
Corporation
association, 712
convexity, 350
bulk, 192
Corporeal
materiality, 316
Corporeity
substantiality, 3
Corps
assemblage, 72
troops, 726
Corps de reserve
store, 636
Corps diplomatique
consignee, 758
Corpse
body, 362
Corpulent
size, 192
broad, 202

Corpus delicti
guilt, 947
Corpuscle
atom, 193
jot, 32
Corradiation
focus, 74
Corral
enclosure, 232, 752
Correct
true, 494
reason, 476
order, 58
virtuous, 939, 944
due, 924, 926
style, 570
elegant, 578
undeceive, 529
to improve, 658
to censure, 932
to punish, 972
Corrective
remedy, 662
counteraction, 179
Corregidor
master, 745
Correlation
relation, 9
reciprocity, 12
Correspond
agree, 23
concur, 178
write, 592
Correspondent
report, 527
Corridor
place, 191
passage, 627
Corrie
hollow, 252
Corrigible
improvement, 658
Corrival
combatant, 726
Corrivalry
contention, 720
Corrivation
river, 348
Corroborant
remedy, 662
assent, 488
Corroborate
evidence, 467

Corroboree
festivity, 840
Corrode
erode, 659
consume, 649
afflict, 830
Corrosion
evil, 619
Corrosive
destructive, 649
Corrugate
constrict, 195
narrow, 203
rumple, 258
derange, 61
Corrupt
foul, 653
noxious, 649
evil, 619
to spoil, 659
vicious, 945
Corruption
decomposition, 49
Corsage
dress, 225
Corsair
thief, 792
Corse
corpse, 362
Corset
dress, 225
Corse
arena, 728
Cortège
suite, 746
procession, 266
continuity, 39, 69
Cortes
council, 696
Cortex
covering, 222
Corundum
hardness, 323
Coruscate
light, 420
Corvée
compulsion, 744
Corvette
ship, 273
Corybantic
insanity, 503
Coryphaeus
leader, 745
Cosh

impact, 276
arms, 727
Cosmetic
ornament, 847
Cosmic
world, 318
Cosmogony
world, 318
Cosmography
world, 318
Cosmonaut
navigator, 269
Cosmopolitan
world-wide, 78
Cosmopolite
philanthropy, 910
Cosmorama
view, 448
Cossack
combatant, 726
Cosset
favourite, 899
Cost
price, 812
Costermonger
merchant, 797
Costly
dearness, 814
Costume
dress, 225
Cosy
comfortable, 377, 827,
829
Cot
abode, 189
Cote
hut, 189
Co-tenant
partner, 778
Coterie
party, 712
sociality, 892
Cotillion
amusement, 840
Cottage
abode, 189
Cottar
inhabitant, 188
peasant, 876
Cotton-wool
softness, 324
Couch
bed, 215
to lie, 213

recline, 308
lie in wait, 530
express, 566
Couchant
horizontal, 213
Couci-couci
imperfection, 651
Cough
puff, 349
Couloir
gully, 198
Coulter
sharpness, 253
Council
senate, 696
ecclesiastical, 995
Counsel
advice, 695
Counsellor
adviser, 695
lawyer, 968
Count
compute, 85
expect, 507
believe, 484
estimate, 480
signify, 642
lord, 875
Countenance
face, 234
favour, 707
appearance, 448
to approve, 931
Counter
contrary, 14
against, 179, 708
retort, 479
number, 84
token, 550
table, 215
shopboard, 799
to retaliate, 718
Counter-attraction
dissuasion, 616
avoidance, 623
Counter-claim
lawsuit, 969
Counter-evidence
contrary, 468
Counter-intelligence
secret, 533
Counter-irritant
counteraction, 179
Counter-movement
regression, 283

Counter-order
abrogation, 756
Counter-project
retaliation, 718
plan, 626
Counter-revolution
revolution, 146
Counter-stroke
retaliation, 718
Counter-subject
music, 415
Counter-tenor
melody, 413
high note, 410
Counteract
physically, 179
voluntarily, 708
hinder, 706
compensate, 30
Counterbalance
compensation, 30
Counterblast
counteraction, 179
retaliation, 718
Counterchange
reciprocality, 12, 148
Countercharm
spell, 993
Countercheck
hindrance, 706
Counterfeit
simulate, 544, 545
imitate, 19
copy, 21
Counterfoil
check, 550
Countermand
abrogation, 756
Countermarch
regression, 283
journey, 266
Countermark
indication, 550
Countermine
opposition, 708
Counterpane
covering, 222
Counterpart
copy, 21
match, 17
Counterplot
retaliation, 718
plan, 626
Counterpoint
harmony, 413

Counterpoise
compensation, 30
weight, 319
Counterpoison
remedy, 662
Countersign
indication, 550
assent, 488
Countervail
compensate, 28, 30
oppose, 179, 708
evidence, 468
Counterweight
weight, 319
Counterwork
opposition, 708
Countess
noble, 875
chief, 745
Counting-house
mart, 799
Countless
infinity, 105
Countrified
rural, 185
low, 876
Country
definite region, 181, 189
agriculture, 371
Countryman
inhabitant, 185
Counts
particulars, 79
County
region, 181
fashionable, 852
Coup
action, 680
Coup de grâce
death-blow, 361
destruction, 162
completion, 729
end, 67
pity, 914
punishment, 972
Coup de main
violence, 173
action, 680
Coup de maître
skill, 698
success, 731
Coup d'essai
essay, 675
Coup d'état
action, 680

plan, 626
revolt, 719, 742
Coup de théâtre
appearance, 448
ostentation, 882
Coup d'œil
vision, 441
appearance, 448
Coupé
vehicle, 272
Couple
two, 89
to unite, 43
Couplet
poetry, 597
Coupon
money, 800
ticket, 550
Courage
bravery, 861
Courier
messenger, 534
interpreter, 524
Course
order, 58
continuity, 69
of time, 109
layer, 204
direction, 278
motion, 264
locomotion, 266
effect, 154
rapidity, 274
pursuit, 622
teaching, 537
plan, 626
way, 627
conduct, 692
arena, 728
dinner, 298
Courser
carrier, 271
swift, 274
Court
house, 189
hall, 191
council, 696
arena, 728
to invite, 615
to pursue, 622
to solicit, 765
to wish, 865
to woo, 902
to flatter, 933
gentility, 852

tribunal, 966
retinue, 746
Court hand
writing, 590
Court-martial
tribunal, 966
Courtesan
libertine, 962
Courtesy
politeness, 894
manners, 852
Courtier
flatterer, 935
Courtier-like
flattery, 933
Courtly
fashion, 852
noble, 975
polite, 894
Courtship
endearment, 902
Cousin
consanguinity, 11
Coûte que coûte
resolution, 604
Cove
cell, 191
haunt, 189
hollow, 252
bay, 343
man, 373
Covenant
compact, 769, 770
promise, 768
Cover
dress, 225
superpose, 222
conceal, 528
retreat, 530
safety, 664, 666
to compensate, 30
stopper, 263
Coverlet
covering, 222
Covert
invisibility, 447
Coverture
marriage, 903
Covetous
miserly, 819
envious, 921
desirous, 865
Covey
assemblage, 72, 102
Cow

intimidate, 860
Cow-catcher
defence, 717
Coward
fearful, 860, 862
Cower
fear, 860
stoop, 308
grovel, 886
Cowl
dress, 225
sacerdotal, 999
Cowling
covering, 222
Co-worker
worker, 690
Coxcomb
fop, 854
Coxcombical
vain, 880
affected, 855
Coxswain
steersman, 694
Coy
modesty, 881
Cozen
deception, 545
Crab
sourness, 397
to depreciate, 932
Crab-like
deviation, 279
Crabbed
sour, 397
difficult, 704
inelegant, 579
uncivil, 895
testy, 901
Crack
split, 44
snap, 328
break up, 162
fissure, 198
furrow, 259
blow, 276
try, 675
sound, 406
chat, 588
excellent, 648
proficient, 698, 700
Crack, in a
instantaneity, 113
Crack-brained
imbecility, 499
Cracked

mad, 503
faulty, 651
Cracker
snap, 406
untruth, 546
Crackers
mad, 503
Crackle
snap, 406
Crackpot
madman, 504
Cradle
bed, 215
beginning, 66
origin, 153
infancy, 127
to place, 184
to train, 673
Craft
cunning, 702
skill, 698
plan, 626
apparatus, 633
business, 623
shipping, 273
Craftsman
doer, 690
Crag
height, 206
Cragged
rough, 256
Cram
stuff, 194
fill, 52, 639
collect, 72
gorge, 296, 957
teach, 537
choke, 261
Crambe repetita
repetition, 104
Crammer
teacher, 540
untruth, 546
Cramp
hinder, 706
restrain, 751
contract, 195
narrow, 203
fasten, 45
paralyse, 158
weaken, 160
spasm, 378, 828
Cramped
style, 572, 579

Crane
   instrument, 633
   raise, 307
Crane-neck
   curvature, 245
Cranium
   intellect, 450
Crank
   instrument, 633
   wit, 842
   eccentric, 83, 499
   punishment, 972
Crank up
   prepare, 673
Crankle
   to bend, 244
Cranky
   eccentric, 499
   opinionated, 606
   bad-tempered, 901
   insane, 503
Cranny
   interval, 198
Crape
   mourning, 839
Crapulence
   intemperance, 954
Crash
   sound, 406
   descent, 306
   destruction, 162, 732
   impulse, 276
Crasis
   coherence, 46
Crass
   great, 31
   ignorance, 491
   stupid, 499
Crassitude
   breadth, 202
   thickness, 352
Crate
   receptacle, 191
Crater
   hollow, 252
   depth, 208
   receptacle, 191
Cravat
   dress, 225
Crave
   ask, 765
   desire, 865
Craven
   cowardice, 862
Craw

   receptacle, 191
Crawl
   move, 275
   submission, 725
   servility, 886
   improbity, 940
Crayon
   painting, 556
   pencil, 559
Craze
   caprice, 608
   fashion, 852
Crazy
   weak, 160
   mad, 503
Creak
   stridor, 410
Cream
   emulsion, 354
   oil, 355
   perfection, 648, 650
   choice, 609
Cream-coloured
   white, 430
Creamy
   semiliquid, 352
Crease
   fold, 258
Create
   produce, 161
   cause, 153
   imagine, 515
Creation
   universe, 318
Creationism
   causation, 153
Creative
   productive, 168
Creator
   deity, 976
   producer, 164
Creature
   animal, 366
   thing, 3
   effect, 154
Creature comforts
   food, 298
Crèche
   nursery, 542
Credence
   belief, 484
Credential
   evidence, 467
Credible
   probable, 472, 484

   possible, 470
Credit
   belief, 484
   authority, 737
   pecuniary, 805
   account, 811
   influence, 737
   hope, 858
   repute, 873
   desert, 944
Creditor
   credit, 805
Credo
   belief, 484
Credulity
   belief, 486
   superstition, 984A
Creed
   belief, 484, 496
   tenet, 983
Creek
   gulf, 343
Creep
   crawl, 275
   bad man, 949
Creeper
   plant, 367
Creeping
   sensation, 380
Creepy
   fearsome, 860
Cremation
   burning, 384
   of corpses, 363
Crème de la crème
   goodness, 648
Cremona
   musical instrument, 417
Crenated
   notch, 257
Crenelated
   notched, 257
Crepitate
   snap, 406
Crepuscule
   dawn, 125
   dimness, 422
Crescendo
   increase, 35
   music, 415
Crescent
   curve, 245
   street, 189
Cressset
   torch, 423

Crest
  summit, 210
  tuft, 256
  armorial, 550, 877
Crestfallen
  dejected, 837
  humiliated, 879, 881
Cretin
  fool, 501
Crevasse
  interval, 198
Crevice
  interval, 198
  opening, 260
Crew
  assemblage, 72
  party, 712
  inhabitants, 188
Crib
  bed, 215
  to steal, 791
  interpretation, 522
Crick
  pain, 378
Crier
  messenger, 534
Crime
  guilt, 947
Criminal
  culprit, 949
  vicious, 945
Criminality
  guilty, 947
Criminate
  accusation, 938
Criminology
  crime, 947
Crimp
  curl, 248
  fold, 258
  to steal, 791
Crimson
  red, 434
Cringe
  submit, 725, 743
  servility, 886
  fear, 860
Crinkle
  fold, 258
  angle, 244
Crinoline
  dress, 225
Cripple
  weaken, 160
  disable, 158

injure, 649, 659
  disease, 655
Crisis
  conjuncture, 8
  event, 151
  difficulty, 704
  opportunity, 134
Crisp
  brittle, 328
  rough, 256
  rumpled, 248
  concise, 572
Criss-cross-row
  letter, 561
Criterion
  trial, 463
  evidence, 467
Critic
  taste, 850
  judge, 480
  reviewer, 590
  dissertation, 595
  detractor, 936
Critical
  opportune, 134
  important, 642
  difficult, 704
  dangerous, 665
Criticism
  disapprobation, 932
  dissertation, 595
Criticize
  taste, 850
Critique
  discrimination, 465
  dissertation, 595
  disapprobation, 932
Croak
  cry, 412
  stammer, 583
  complain, 839
  discontent, 832
  predict, 511
Croceate
  yellow, 436
Crochet
  knit, 43
Crock
  weakness, 160
Crock up
  failure, 732
Crocodile tears
  falsehood, 544
Croesus
  wealth, 803

Croft
  hut, 189
Crofter
  peasant, 876
Cromlech
  interment, 363
Crone
  veteran, 130
Crony
  friend, 890
Crook
  curvature, 245
  evildoer, 913
  swindler, 792
  ill, 655
Crooked
  angular, 244
  distorted, 243, 846
  sloping, 217
  dishonourable, 940
Croon
  to hum, 405, 415
Crop
  stomach, 191
  to shorten, 201
  to gather, 775
  to take, 789
  to eat, 297
  harvest, 154
Crop up
  inexpectation, 508
  event, 151
  appear, 446
Cropper
  fall, 306
Crosier
  canonicals, 999
Cross
  intersection, 219
  passage, 302
  swindle, 545
  opposition, 179, 708
  refusal, 572
  vexation, 828
  vexatiousness, 830
  ill-tempered, 895
  fretful, 901
  failure, 732
  mixture, 41
  decoration, 877
  reward, 973
  rites, 998
Cross-breed
  unconformity, 83

Cross-cut
method, 627
Cross-examine
inquiry, 461
Cross-grained
obstinate, 606
ill-tempered, 895, 901
Cross-purposes
error, 495
misinterpretation, 523
Cross-question
inquiry, 461
Cross-reading
misinterpretation, 523
Cross-road
way, 627
Crossbow
arms, 727
Crossing
crossing, 219
Crosspatch
ill-tempered, 895
Crossword
puzzle, 461, 533
Crotch
angularity, 244
Crotchet
music, 413
prejudice, 481
caprice, 608
Crotchety
folly, 499
Crouch
stoop, 308
lower, 207
servility, 886
fear, 860
Croup
rear, 235
Crow
cry, 412
laugh, 838
boast, 884
exult, 836
lever, 633
black, 431
Crowbar
instrument, 633
Crowd
assemblage, 72
multitude, 102
closeness, 197
the vulgar, 876
Crown
top, 210
end, 67

circle, 247
trophy, 733
sceptre, 747
reward, 973
to complete, 729
Crowning
superior, 33
Crow's nest
view, 441
Crucial
crossing, 219
experimental, 463
demonstrative, 478
Crucible
receptacle, 191
laboratory, 144, 691
Crucifix
rite, 998
canonicals, 999
Cruciform
crossing, 219
Crucify
torture (physical), 378
agony (mental), 828
painfulness, 830
execution, 972
Crude
unprepared, 674
inelegant, 579
Cruel
painful, 830
inhuman, 907
Cruet
receptacle, 191
Cruise
navigation, 267
Cruiser
ship, 273
Crumb
small part, 51
grain, 193
powder, 330
bit, 32
Crumble
pulverize, 330
destroy, 162
diminish, 36
spoil, 659
brittleness, 328
Crumple
ruffle, 256
crease, 258
contract, 195
Crunch
bruise, 44

masticate, 297
pulverize, 330
Crupper
rear, 235
Crusade
warfare, 722
Cruse
vessel, 191
Crush
pulverize, 330
destroy, 162
injure, 649
humiliate, 879
pain, 828
contract, 195
love, 897
Crust
covering, 222
insolence 885
Crusty
discourtesy, 895
Crutch
support, 215
angle, 244
instrument, 633
Crux
question, 461
mystery, 533
Cry
animal, 412
human, 411
loudness, 404
voice, 580
publish, 531
weep, 839
Cry down
disapprove, 932
Cry for
desire, 865
Cry to
beseech, 765
Cry up
praise, 931
Crypt
cell, 191
hide, 530
grave, 363
altar, 1000
Cryptic
latent, 526, 528
Cryptogram
cipher, 533
Cryptography
writing, 590

Crystal-gazing
  prediction, 511
Crystalline
  dense, 321
  transparent, 425
Cub
  young, 129
  clown, 876
Cube
  triality, 92
  angularity, 244
Cubist
  artist, 559
Cuckold
  divorce, 905
Cuckoo
  repetition, 104
  imitation, 19
  cry, 412
  fool, 501
  insane, 503
Cuddle
  caress, 902
Cuddy
  carrier, 271
Cudgel
  beat, 975
  bludgeon, 276, 727
Cue
  hint, 527
  watchword, 550
  plea, 617
Cuff
  beat, 276, 972
  dress, 225
Cui bono
  utility, 644
Cuirass
  defence, 717
Cuirassier
  combatant, 726
Cuisine
  food, 298
Cul-de-lampe
  tail-piece, 67
Cul-de-sac
  concavity, 252
  closure, 261
  difficulty, 704
Culbute
  inversion, 218
  descent, 306
Culinary
  food, 298
Cull

choice, 609
  take, 789
Cullender
  sieve, 260
Cullion
  wretch, 941, 949
Cully
  dupe, 547
Culminate
  maximum, 33
  height, 206, 210
Culmination
  completion, 729
Culpability
  guilt, 947
Culpable
  vice, 945
Culprit
  sinner, 949
Cult
  worship, 990
  rite, 998
Cultivate
  improve, 658
  sensitiveness, 375
  taste, 850
  till, 371
Culture
  tillage, 371
  taste, 850
  teaching, 537
  knowledge, 490
Culverin
  arms, 727
Culvert
  conduit, 350
Cum grano salis
  qualify, 469
  unbelief, 485
Cumber
  load, 319
  to incommode, 647
  to obstruct, 706
Cummer
  friend, 891
Cummerbund
  girdle, 247
Cumshaw
  gift, 784
Cumulation
  assemblage, 72
Cumulative
  increase, 35
  addition, 37
Cumulus

cloud, 353
Cunctation
  delay, 133
  inactivity, 683
Cuneiform
  angular, 244
  writing, 590
Cunning
  art, 702
  sagacity, 698
  well-planned, 626
Cup
  hollow, 252
  vessel, 191
Cupboard
  receptacle, 191
Cupid
  beauty, 845
  love, 897
Cupidity
  avarice, 819
  desire, 865
Cupola
  dome, 250
  height, 206
Cur
  knave, 949
Curable
  improvement, 658
Curacy
  churchdom, 995
Curate
  clergy, 996
Curative
  remedial, 834
Curator
  consignee, 758
Curb
  restrain, 751
  hinder, 706
  shackle, 752
  moderate, 174
  check, 826
  dissuade, 616
  counteract, 179
  slacken, 275
Curd
  mass, 46
  density, 321
  pulp, 354
Curdle
  condense, 321
  coagulate, 46, 352
Cure
  remedy, 662, 834

reinstate, 660
religious, 995
preserve, 670
improve, 656
Curé
priest, 996
Curfew
evening, 126
Curio
toy, 643
Curiosa felicitas
elegance, 578
Curiosity
curiosity, 455
phenomenon, 872
Curious
true, 494
exceptional, 83
Curl
bend, 245, 248
cockle up, 258
Curlicue
convolution, 248
Curliewurlie
convolution, 248
Curmudgeon
parsimony, 819
Currency
publicity, 531
money, 800
Current
existing, 1
present, 118
happening, 151
stream, 347
river, 348
wind, 349
course, 109
danger, 667
opinion, 484
public, 531
prevailing, 82
Currente calamo
diffuseness, 573
Curricle
vehicle, 272
Curriculum
teaching, 537
Curry
condiment, 393
rub, 331
Curry flavour
flattery, 933
Curse
malediction, 908

bane, 663
evil, 619
adversity, 735
badness, 649
painfulness, 830
Cursive
writing, 590
Cursory
transient, 111
inattentive, 458
neglecting, 460
hasty, 684
Curst
perverse, 895
Curt
short, 201
taciturn, 585
concise, 572
Curtail
shorten, 201, 572
retrench, 38
decrease, 36
deprive, 789
Curtain
shade, 424
ambush, 530
Curtain lecture
speech, 582
Curtain-raiser
play, 599
Curtsy
obeisance, 743, 894
submission, 725
stoop, 308
Curule
council, 696
Curve
curvature, 245
Curvet
leap, 309
oscillate, 314
agitate, 315
Cushion
pillow, 215
softness, 324
to frustrate, 706
relief, 834
Cushy
easy, 705
Cusp
point, 253
angle, 244
Cussedness
obstinacy, 606
Custodian

keeper, 753
Custody
captivity, 664, 751, 781
captive, 754
Custom
rule, 80
habit, 613
fashion, 852
sale, 796
barter, 794
tax, 812
Custom-house
mart, 799
Customer
purchaser, 795
Cut
divide, 44
bit, 51
interval, 70, 198
sculpture, 557
curtail, 201
cultivate, 371
layer, 204
notch, 257
form, 240
road, 627
print, 558
attach, 716
pain, 828
to give pain, 830
affect, 824
ignore, 460, 893, 895
neglect, 773
state, 7
cold, 385
Cut across
passage, 302
Cut along
velocity, 274
Cut and dried
ready, 673
trite, 82
Cut and run
escape, 671
Cut capers
leap, 309
dance, 840
Cut down
diminish, 36
destroy, 162
shorten, 201
lower, 308
kill, 361
Cut down to size
humiliate, 879

Cut off
kill, 361
subduct, 38
impede, 706
disjunction, 44
Cut out
surpass, 33
retrench, 38
plan, 626
supplant, 147
Cut short
shorten, 201, 572
stop, 142
decrease, 36
contract, 195
Cut-throat
killing, 361
sinner, 913, 949
Cut up
divide, 44
destroy, 162
censure, 932
unhappy, 828, 837
Cutaneous
covering, 222
Cuthbert
pacifist, 726A
Cuticle
covering, 222
Cutie
sweetheart, 897
Cutlass
arms, 727
Cutlery
sharpness, 253
Cutpurse
thief, 792
Cutter
ship, 273
Cutting
cold, 383
affecting, 821
censorious, 932
extract, 596, 609
Cutty
tobacco, 298A
Cybernetics
statecraft, 693
Cycle
period, 138
duration, 106
circle, 247
travel, 266
Cycloid
circularity, 247

Cyclone
violence, 173
rotation, 312
agitation, 315
wind, 349
Cyclopaedia
knowledge, 490
Cyclopean
huge, 192
Cyclops
monster, 83
Cylinder
rotundity, 249
Cymbal
musical instrument, 417
Cynical
censorious, 932
detracting, 483
unsociable, 893
cross, 895
Cynosure
indication, 550
prodigy, 872
Cypher
see Cipher
Cypress
lamentation, 839
Cyst
receptacle, 191
Czar
master, 745

D.T.
drunkenness, 959
D.V.
conditions, 770
Da capo
repetition, 104
duplication, 90
frequency, 136
Dab
clever, 700
to paint, 222
to slap, 276
Dabble
action, 680
trifle, 683
moisten, 337
Dacoit
thief, 792
Dactyl
verse, 597
Dactylonomy
numeration, 85

Dad
paternity, 166
Dadaist
artist, 559
Dado
lining, 224
base, 211
Daedal
variegated, 440
Daedalian
skill, 698
convoluted, 248
Daft
insane, 503
silly, 499
Dagger
arms, 727
sharpness, 253
Daggers drawn
discord, 713
enmity, 889
Daggle
pendency, 214
Dago
alien, 57
Dagon
idol, 986
Daguerreotype
painting, 556
copy, 21
Dahabeeyah
ship, 273
Daily
routine, 138
publication, 531
servant, 746
Dainty
savoury, 394
pleasing, 829
fastidious, 868
Dais
support, 215
Dak-bungalow
inn, 189
Dale
concavity, 252
Dally
irresolute, 605
delay, 133
inactive, 683
amuse, 840
fondle, 902
Dalmatic
vestments, 999

Dam
  parent, 166
  lock, 350
  close, 261
  confine, 231
  obstruct, 348, 706
  trifle, 643
Damage
  evil, 619
  to injure, 649
  to spoil, 659
  payment, 812
Damages
  penalty, 974
Damascene
  variegate, 440
Damask
  redness, 434
Dame
  woman, 374
  teacher, 540
Damn
  condemn, 971
  expletive, 908
Damn-all
  nothing, 4
Damnable
  execrable, 830
  spoil, 659
Damnify
  damage, 649
Damnosa hereditas
  burden, 706
Damp
  moist, 339
  cold, 386
  to moderate, 174
  to dissuade, 616
  depress, 837
  calm, 826
Damper
  silencer, 417
Damsel
  youth, 129
  lady, 374
Dance
  oscillate, 314
  agitate, 315
  jump, 309
  sport, 840
Dander
  resentment, 900
  journey, 266
Dandify
  adorn, 845
  dress, 225

Dandle
  endearment, 902
Dandruff
  uncleanness, 653
Dandy
  fop, 854
Dandyism
  affectation, 855
Danger
  danger, 665
Dangle
  hang, 214
  swing, 314
Dank
  moist, 339
Dapper
  thin, 203
  elegant, 845
Dapple
  brown, 433
Dappled
  variegation, 440
Darbies
  fetter, 752
Dare
  defy, 715
  face danger, 861
Dare-devil
  rashness, 863
  blusterer, 887
Darg
  work, 625
Daring
  courage, 861
Dark
  obscure, 421
  dim, 422
  invisible, 447
  unintelligible, 519
  mysterious, 528
  ignorant, 491
  blind, 442
  latent, 526
Darkie
  black, 431
Darling
  favourite, 899
  beloved, 897
Darn
  improve, 658
Dart
  missile, 727
  to propel, 284
  swift, 274
Darwinism

  causation, 153
Dash
  sprinkling, 32, 193
  to mix, 41
  throw down, 308
  display, 882
  depress, 837
  shine, 873
  mark, 550
  expletive, 908
  velocity, 274
  energy, 171
  vivacity, 682
  gift, 784
Dash off
  sketch, 556
Dash out
  rush, 274
  haste, 684
Dashing
  brave, 861
  smart, 845
  fashionable, 852
Dastard
  coward, 862
Data
  evidence, 467
  reasoning, 476
Date
  chronometry, 114
  party, 892
Daub
  cover, 222
  dirt, 653
  bad painting, 555
  to deform, 846
Daughter
  posterity, 167
Daunt
  frighten, 860
Dauntless
  courage, 861
Davenport
  receptacle, 191
  support, 215
Dawdle
  slow, 275
  tardy, 133
  inactive, 683
Dawn
  morning, 125
  precursor, 116
  to begin, 66
  dim, 422
  glimpse, 490

456

Day
period, 108
light, 420
Day-book
list, 86
record, 551
accounts, 811
Day-dream
imagination, 515
hope, 858
inattention, 458
Day-labourer
workman, 690
Day of Judgment
end, 67
Daybreak
morning, 125
dim, 422
beginning, 66
Daylight
light, 420
publicity, 531
Dayspring
morning, 125
Daze
light, 420
confuse, 442
stupefy, 823
Dazzle
light, 420
confuse, 442
De bon cœur
willingly, 602
De facto
existence, 1
truth, 494
De haut en bas
contempt, 930
De jure
right, 922
legal, 963
dueness, 924
De novo
repetition, 104
frequency, 136
De omnibus rebus
multiformity, 81
De Profundis
worship, 990
De règle
rule, 80
De rigueur
rule, 80
De trop
redundance, 641

Deacon
clergy, 996
Dead
lifeless, 360
inert, 172
insensible, 376, 823
colourless, 429
Dead-beat
fatigue, 688
weak, 160
Dead-drunk
drunkenness, 959
Dead-heat
equality, 27
Dead weight
hindrance, 706
Deaden
weaken, 158, 160
moderate, 174, 826
benumb, 823
Deadfall
trap, 667
Deadlock
stoppage, 265
hindrance, 706
Deadly
mortal, 361, 657
destructive, 162
pernicious, 649
Deadness
numbness, 381
inertness, 172, 823
Deaf
deafness, 419
Deafening
loud, 404
Deal
quantity, 31
mingle, 41
give, 784
allot, 786
barter, 794
Deal out
distribute, 73, 784
Dealer
merchant, 797
Dealings
action, 680
Dean
clergy, 996
Deanery
office, 995
house, 1000
Dear
loved, 897, 899

high-priced, 814
Dear-bought
worthless, 645
Dearth
insufficiency, 640
Death
death, 360
Death-blow
end, 67
killing, 361
failure, 732
Deathless
perpetuity, 112
celebrated, 873
Deathlike
hideous, 846
silence, 403
Debacle
river, 348
descent, 306
destruction, 162
Debag
divest, 226
Debar
prohibit, 761
hinder, 751
exclude, 77
Debark
arrive, 292
Debase
depress, 308
deteriorate, 659
foul, 653
vicious, 945
Debatable
uncertain, 475
Debate
reason, 476
dispute, 713, 720
hesitate, 605
talk, 588
Debauch
spoil, 659
vice, 945
intemperance, 954
impurity, 961
Debenture
certificate, 551
security, 771
credit, 805
Debility
weakness, 160
Debit
debt, 806
accounts, 811

Debonair
cheerfulness, 836
Debouch
march out, 292
flow out, 295, 348
Debrett
list, 86
Debris
part, 51
pulverulence, 330
unimportance, 643
Debt
debt, 806
Debtor
debt, 806
Debus
arrival, 292
Début
beginning, 66
Decade
number, 98
period, 108
duration, 106
Decadence
deterioration, 659
Decadent
feeble, 575
Decagon
number, 98
angularity, 244
Decahedron
ten, 98
Decalogue
duty, 926
Decamp
move off, 287, 293
escape, 671
Decant
transfer, 270
Decanter
receptacle, 191
Decapitate
kill, 361, 972
Decay
spoil, 659
disease, 655
shrivel, 195
decrease, 36
Decayed
imperfect, 651
old, 124
adversity, 735
Decease
death, 360
Deceit

deception, 544, 545
Deceiver
deceiver, 548
Decent
modest, 960
tolerable, 651
seemly, 926
right, 922
Decentralize
disperse, 73
Deception
deception, 545
sophistry, 477
Decide
judge, 480
choose, 609
make certain, 474
cause, 153
Decided
resolved, 604
positive, 535
certain, 475
great, 31
Deciduous
transitory, 111
falling, 306
spoiled, 659
Decimal
number, 84, 98
Decimate
subduct, 38, 103
kill, 361
Decipher
interpret, 522
solve, 462
Decision
intention, 620
conclusion, 480
resolution, 604
verdict, 969
Decisive
final, 67
evidence, 467
resolution, 604
demonstration, 478
Decivilize
brutalize, 895
Deck
floor, 211
to beautify, 845
Declaim
speech, 582
Declamatory
florid, 577
Declare

assert, 535
inform, 516, 527
Declension
descent, 306
deterioration, 659
grammar, 567
intrinsicality, 5
Decline
decrease, 36
descent, 306
weaken, 160
decay, 735
disease, 655
become worse, 659
reject, 610
refuse, 764
be unwilling, 603
grammar, 567
Declivity
obliquity, 217
Decoction
calefaction, 384
Decode
interpret, 522
Decollate
punishment, 972
Decoloration
achromatism, 429
Decompose
decomposition, 49, 653
Decomposite
combination, 48
Decompound
combination, 48
Deconsecrate
cancel, 756
Decontamination
cleanness, 652
Decorate
embellish, 845, 847
Decoration
repute, 873
title, 877
insignia, 747
Decorous
decent, 960
befitting, 922
Decorticate
divest, 226
Decorum
politeness, 852
respect, 928
purity, 960
Decoy
entice, 615

Definite
exact, 494
special, 79
visible, 446
limited, 233
intelligible, 518
Definitely
assent, 488
Definitive
decided, 535
final, 67
Deflagration
calefaction, 384
Deflate
contract, 195
Deflection
curvature, 245
deviation, 279
Defloration
impurity, 961
soil, 653
Defluxion
river, 348
Deform
deface, 241, 846
Deformity
blemish, 848
Defraud
cheat, 545
non-payment, 808
Defray
pay, 807
Defrost
melt, 384
Deft
clever, 698
suitable, 23
Defunct
dead, 360
Defy
dare, 715
disobey, 742
threaten, 909
Dégagé
freedom, 748
fashion, 825
Degenerate
deterioration, 659
vice, 945
Deglutition
swallowing, 296
Degradation
shame, 874
dishonour, 940
deterioration, 659

Degree
quantity, 26
term, 71
honour, 873
Degustation
taste, 390
Dehortation
dissuasion, 616
advice, 695
warning, 668
Dehumanize
brutalize, 895
Dehydrate
dry, 340
preserve, 670
De-ice
melt, 384
Dei gratiâ
dueness, 924
Deification
heaven, 981
idolatry, 991
honour, 873
Deign
condescend, 879
consent, 762
Deiseal
rotation, 312
Deism
irreligion, 989
heresy, 984A
Deity
deity, 976
great spirit, 979
Dejection
sadness, 828, 837, 841
Déjeuner
food, 298
Dekko
look, 441
Délâbrement
deterioration, 659
Delation
accusation, 938
Delay
lateness, 133
protraction, 110
slowness, 275
Dele
obliteration, 552
Delectable
savoury, 394
agreeable, 829
Delectation
pleasure, 827

Delegate
consignee, 758, 759
to commission, 755
Deleterious
pernicious, 649
unwholesome, 657
Deletion
obliteration, 552
Deliberate
think, 451
cautious, 864
slow, 275
leisurely, 685
advised, 620, 695
Deliberately
slowly, 133
designedly, 600, 611
Delicacy
of texture, 329
slenderness, 203
weak, 160
sickly, 655
savoury, 394
dainty, 298
of taste, 850
fastidiousness, 868
exactness, 494
pleasing, 829
beauty, 845
honour, 939
purity, 960
difficulty, 704
scruple, 603, 616
Delicatessen
food, 298
Delicious
taste, 394
pleasing, 829
Delight
pleasure, 827
Delightful
pleasurableness, 829
Delilah
temptress, 615
Delimit
circumscribe, 231
Delineate
describe, 594
represent, 554
Delineavit
painting, 556
Delinquency
guilt, 947
Delinquent
sinner, 949

Delinquescent
  liquid, 333
Delinquium
  weakness, 160
  fatigue, 688
Delirium
  raving, 503
  passion, 825
Delirium tremens
  drunkenness, 959
Delitescence
  latency, 526
Deliver
  transfer, 270
  give, 784
  liberate, 750
  relieve, 834
  utter, 582
  rescue, 672
  escape, 671
Dell
  concavity, 252
Delouse
  disinfect, 652
Delta
  land, 342
Delude
  deceive, 495, 545
Deluge
  flow, 337, 348
  redundance, 641
  multitude, 72
Delusion
  error, 495
  deceit, 545
Delve
  dig, 252
  cultivate, 371
  depth, 208
Demagogue
  leader, 745
  director, 694
  agitator, 742
Demagogy
  authority, 737
Demand
  claim, 924
  ask, 765
  require, 630
  inquire, 461
  order, 741
  price, 812
Demarcation
  limit, 199, 233
Démarche

procedure, 680
Dematerialize
  immateriality, 317
Demean
  humble, 879
  dishonour, 940
Demeanour
  conduct, 692
  air, 448
  fashion, 852
Dementation
  insanity, 503
Démenti
  contradiction, 536
Demerit
  vice, 945
  inutility, 645
Demesne
  property, 780
Demi
  bisection, 91
Demigod
  hero, 948
Demijohn
  receptacle, 191
Demi-rep
  libertine, 962
Demise
  death, 360
  to transfer, 783
  to give, 784
Demiurge
  deity, 979
Demivolt
  leap, 309
Demobilize
  disperse, 73
Democracy
  authority, 737
Démodé
  obsolete, 851
Demogorgon
  demon, 980
Demoiselle
  woman, 374
Demolish
  destroy, 162
  confute, 479
  damage, 649
Demolisher
  destroyer, 165
Demon
  devil, 980
  wretch, 913
  violent, 173

Demoniacal
  wicked, 945
  furious, 825
  diabolic, 649, 980
Demonism
  idolatry, 991
Demonolatry
  idolatry, 991
Demonstrate
  prove, 85, 478
  manifest, 525
Demonstrative
  evidential, 467, 478
  excitable, 825
Demonstrator
  scholar, 492
  teacher, 540
Demoralize
  vice, 945
  degrade, 659
Demos
  commonalty, 876
Demote
  abase, 308
  degrade, 659
Demotic
  writing, 590
Demulcent
  mild, 174
  soothing, 662
Demur
  unwillingness, 603
  hesitation, 605
  to disbelieve, 485
  dissent, 489
  dislike, 867
Demure
  grave, 826
  modest, 881
  affected, 855
Demurrage
  charge, 812
Demurrer
  lawsuit, 969
Den
  lair, 189
  room, 191, 893
  prison, 752
  sty, 653
Denary
  number, 98
Denationalize
  restore, 790
Denaturalized
  unconformity, 83

Dendriform
rough, 256
Denegation
negation, 536
Denial
negation, 536
Denigrate
blacken, 431
decry, 483, 934
Denization
liberation, 750
Denizen
inhabitant, 188
man, 373
Denominate
nomenclature, 564
Denomination
class, 75
party, 712
Denominational
theology, 983
Denominator
number, 84
Denote
indication, 550
Denouement
result, 154
end, 67
elucidation, 522
completion, 729
Denounce
accuse, 297
blame, 932
cite, 965
Dense
close, 321
crowded, 72
stupid, 499
Density
closeness, 46, 321
Dent
notch, 257
hollow, 252
Dental
letter, 561
Denticle
sharpness, 253
Denticulated
sharp, 253
Dentist
doctor, 662
Denude
divest, 226
deprive, 776
Denunciation

see Denounce
Deny
negative, 536
dissent, 489
refuse, 764
Deo volente
conditions, 770
Deodand
penalty, 974
Deodorize
disinfect, 652
Deontology
duty, 926
Depart
set out, 296
die, 360
Departed
gone, 2
Department
class, 75
part, 51
region, 181
business, 625
Depauperate
impoverish, 804
Depend
hang, 214
be contingent, 475
Depend upon
trust, 484
be the effect of, 154
affirm, 535
Dependable
belief, 484
probity, 939
Dependant
servant, 746
Dependence
subjection, 749
Dependent
liable, 177
Depict
paint, 556
represent, 554
describe, 594
Depletion
insufficiency, 640
Deplorable
bad, 649
disastrous, 735
painful, 830
Deplore
regret, 833
complain, 839
remorse, 950

Deploy
expansion, 194
Depone
affirm, 535
Deponent
evidence, 467
Depopulate
displace, 185
desert, 893
Deportation
displace, 185
exclusion, 55
transfer, 270
emigration, 297
punishment, 972
Deportment
conduct, 692
appearance, 448
Depose
evidence, 467
tell, 527
record, 551
dethrone, 738, 756
declare, 535
Deposit
place, 184
secure, 771
store, 636
expenditure, 809
solidify, 321
Depository
store, 636
Depot
store, 636
focus, 74
mart, 799
Deprave
spoil, 659
Depraved
bad, 649
vicious, 945
Deprecate
deprecation, 766
dissuade, 616
disapproval, 932
pity, 914
Depreciate
detract, 483
censure, 932
decrease, 36
Depreciation
discount, 813
stealing, 791
Depredation
stealing, 791

Depredator
thief, 792
Depression
lowering, 308
lowness, 207
depth, 208
concavity, 252
dejection, 837
Deprive
take, 789
subduct, 38
lose, 776
Depth
physical, 208
mental, 450, 490
Depurate
clean, 652
improve, 658
Depuratory
remedy, 662
Depute
commission, 755
Deputy
substitute, 147, 634, 759
jurisdiction, 965
Derangement
mental, 503
physical, 61
disorder, 59
Derelict
solitary, 893
Dereliction
relinquishment, 624, 782
guilt, 947
Derequisition
restore, 790
Deride
ridicule, 856
disrespect, 929
contempt, 930
trifle with, 643
scoff, 483
Derisive
ridiculous, 853
Derivation
origin, 153
verbal, 562
Derivative
effect, 154
Derive
attribute, 155
receive, 785
acquire, 755

income, 810
Dermal
covering, 222
Dernier cri
fashion, 852
newness, 123
Dernier ressort
plan, 626
Derogate
detract, 483, 934
demean, 940
shame, 874
Derrick
raise, 307
Derring-do
courage, 861
Derringer
arms, 727
Dervish
clergy, 996
Descale
clean, 652
Descant
dissert, 595
dwell upon, 584
diffuseness, 573
Descendant
posterity, 167
Descent
slope, 217
motion downwards, 306
order, 58
Describe
set forth, 594
Description
kind, 75
narration, 594
Descry
vision, 441
Desecrate
misuse, 679
profane, 988
Desert
solitude, 101, 893
waste, 645
merit, 944
to relinquish, 624
to escape, 671
Deserter
apostate, 607
coward, 862
Desertless
vice, 945
Deserve
merit, 944

right, 922, 924
Déshabillé
see Dishabille
Desiccate
dryness, 340
Desiderate
desire, 865
require, 630
Desideratum
desire, 865
inquiry, 461
requirement, 630
Design
intention, 620
cunning, 702
plan, 626
delineation, 554
prototype, 22
Designate
specify, 79, 564
Designation
kind, 75
Designed
intended, 600
Designer
artist, 559, 626
Designing
false, 544
artful, 702
Desirable
expedient, 646
Desire
longing, 865
Desist
discontinue, 142
relinquish, 624
inaction, 681
Desk
support, 215
receptacle, 191
Desolate
alone, 87
secluded, 893
afflicted, 828
to ravage, 162
Desolation
evil, 619
Désorienté
ignorance, 491
Despair
hopelessness, 859
dejection, 837
Despatch
see Dispatch
Desperado
rashness, 863

463

Desperate
great, 31
violent, 173
rash, 863
difficult, 704
impossible, 471

Desperation
hopelessness, 859

Despicable
shameful, 874
contemptible, 930
trifling, 643

Despise
contemn, 930
deride, 483, 929

Despite
notwithstanding, 179,
708

Despite
malevolence, 907

Despoil
take, 789
rob, 791
hurt, 649

Despondency
sadness, 837
fear, 860
despair, 859

Despot
master, 745

Despotism
arbitrariness, 964
authority, 737
severity, 739

Desquamation
divestment, 226

Dessert
food, 298

Destination
fate, 152, 601
arrival, 292
intention, 620

Destiny
fate, 601
chance, 152

Destitute
insufficient, 640
poor, 804

Destrier
carrier, 271

Destroy
demolish, 162
injure, 649
deface, 241

Destroyed
inexistence, 2

Destroyer
ship, 273

Destruction
demolition, 162, 732
evil, 619

Destructive
hurtful, 649

Desuetude
disuse, 614, 678

Desultory
discontinuous, 70
irregular in time, 139
disordered, 59
multiform, 81
deviating, 149, 279
agitated, 315

Detach
separate, 10, 44, 47

Detached
irrelated, 10, 47
indifferent, 456
unity, 87

Detachment
part, 51
army, 726

Detail
to describe, 594
special portion, 79

Detain
retention, 781

Detection
discovery, 480A

Detective
inquiry, 461

Detention
retention, 781
imprisonment, 751

Détenu
prisoner, 754

Deter
dissuasion, 616
fear, 860

Detergent
remedy, 662
remedial, 656
cleanness, 652

Deteriorate
deterioration, 659

Determinate
special, 79
exact, 474
resolute, 604

Determination

resolution, 604
will, 600
judgment, 480

Determine
find out, 480A
intend, 620
direction, 278
make certain, 474
cause, 153
resolve, 604
designate, 79

Determinism
necessity, 601

Deterrent
restraint, 616

Detersive
cleanness, 652

Detest
hate, 867, 898

Detestable
bad, 649, 867

Dethrone
abrogation, 756

Dethronement
anarchy, 738

Detonate
sound, 406
explode, 173

Detonator
signal, 550

Detour
circuit, 629
curvature, 245
deviation, 279

Detract
subduct, 38
depreciate, 483
censure, 932
slander, 934

Detractor
slanderer, 936

Detrain
arrival, 292

Detriment
evil, 619

Detrimental
hurtful, 649

Detritus
part, 51
pulverulence, 330

Detrude
cast out, 297
cast down, 308

Detruncation
subduction, 38

disjunction, 44
Deuce
  duality, 89
  demon, 980
Deuced
  great, 31
Deux ex machina
  helper, 707, 711
  wonder-worker, 994
Deuterogamy
  marriage, 903
Devastate
  destroy, 162
  injure, 649
Devastation
  havoc, 659
Develop
  cause, 153
  produce, 161
  increase, 35
  expand, 194
  evolve, 313
Development
  effect, 154
Deviate
  differ, 15
  vary, 20
  change, 140
  turn, 279
  diverge, 291
  circuit, 629
  bend, 245
Deviationist
  revolutionary, 146
  dissent, 489
Device
  expedient, 626
  instrument, 633
  motto, 550
Devices
  inclination, 602
Devil
  Satan, 978
  maleficent being, 913
  mediate, 631
  culprit, 949
  seasoned food, 392
Devil-may-care
  rash, 863
Devilish
  great, 31
  bad, 649
  hell, 982
Devilry (or Deviltry)
  evil, 619

cruelty, 907
  wickedness, 945
  sorcery, 992
Devious
  deviating, 245, 279
  different, 15
Devise
  plan, 620, 626
  imagine, 515
  bequeath, 784
Devitalize
  weaken, 160
Devoid
  empty, 640
  absent, 187
  not having, 776
Devoir
  courtesy, 894
Devolution
  delegation, 755
Devolve
  transfer, 783
Devolve on
  duty, 926
Devote
  attention, 457
  curse, 908
  employ, 677
  consecrate, 873
Devoted
  loving, 897
  friendly, 888
  doomed, 152, 735, 828
Devotee
  pious, 987
  resolute, 604
  enthusiast, 682, 840
Devotion
  piety, 987
  worship, 990
  respect, 928
  love, 897
  obedience, 743
  disinterestedness, 942
Devour
  eat, 296
  gluttony, 957
  destroy, 162
Devout
  pious, 897
Dew
  moisture, 339
Dew-pond
  lake, 343
Dexter

right, 238
Dexterous
  skill, 698
Dey
  master, 745
Dhow
  ship, 273
Diablerie
  sorcery, 992
Diabolic
  malevolent, 907
  wicked, 945
  bad, 649
  satanic, 978
Diacoustics
  sound, 402
Diacritical
  distinctive, 550
Diadem
  regalia, 747
  ornament, 847
Diagnostic
  intrinsicality, 5
  speciality, 79
  discrimination, 465
Diagonal
  oblique, 217
Diagram
  representation, 554
Diagraph
  imitation, 19
Dial
  clock, 114
  face, 234, 448
Dialect
  neology, 563
Dialectic
  argumentation, 476
  language, 560
Dialogue
  interlocution, 588
Diameter
  breadth, 202
Diamond
  lozenge, 244
  arena, 728
  gem, 650
  ornament, 847
  hardness, 323
Diana
  goddess, 979
Diapason
  melody, 413
Diaper
  reticulation, 219

Diaphanous
transparent, 425
Diaphoresis
excretion, 298
Diaphoretic
remedy, 662
Diaphragm
partition, 228
middle, 68
Diarchy
authority, 737
Diary
record, 551
journal, 114
Diastole
expansion, 194
pulse, 314
Diathermancy
calefaction, 384
Diathesis
state, 7
habit, 613
affections, 820
Diatonic
harmony, 413
Diatribe
disapprobation, 932
Dibble
perforator, 262
cultivate, 371
Dibs
money, 800
Dice
chance, 156
Dichotomy
bisection, 91
angularity, 244
Dichroism
variegation, 440
Dick
detective, 461
police, 664
Dicker
barter, 794
interchange, 148
Dicky
seat, 215
Dictaphone
hearing, 418
Dictate
command, 741
authority, 737
enjoin, 615
write, 590
Dictator

master, 745
Dictatorial
severe, 739
insolent, 885
Dictatorship
authority, 737
Diction
style, 569
Dictionary
word, 562
Dictum
maxim, 496
affirmation, 535
command, 741
Didactic
teaching, 537
Diddle
deception, 545
swindle, 791
Dido
leap, 309
prank, 840
foolery, 497
caprice, 608
Die
chance, 156
mould, 22
to expire, 2, 360
cease, 142
Die for
desire, 865
Die-hard
obstinacy, 606
Dies non
never, 107
repose, 687
Diet
food, 298
remedy, 662
council, 696
Dietetics
remedy, 662
Differ
dissent, 489
Difference
difference, 15
inequality, 28
dissimilarity, 18
discord, 713
numerical, 84
Differential
number, 84
Differentiation
numeration, 85
difference, 15

discrimination, 465
fastidiousness, 868
Difficile
troublesome, 704
Difficult
fastidious, 868
Difficulty
hardness, 704
question, 461
Diffident
modest, 881
fearful, 860
Diffluent
liquefaction, 335
flow, 348
Diffraction
curvature, 245
Diffuse
style, 573
disperse, 73, 291
publish, 531
permeate, 186
Dig
excavate, 252
Dig
cultivate, 371
deepen, 208
poke, 276
understand, 518
Dig up
past, 122
Digamy
marriage, 903
Digest
arrange, 60, 826
think, 451
plan, 626
book, 593
compendium, 596
Diggings
abode, 189
Dight
dressed, 225
Digit
number, 84
Digitated
pointed, 253
Dignify
honour, 873
Dignitary
cleric, 996
personage, 875
Dignity
glory, 873
pride, 878

honour, 939

Digress
deviate, 279
style, 573

Digs
abode, 189

Dike
ditch, 198, 232
defence, 666, 717

Dilaceration
disjunction, 44

Dilapidation
wreck, 162
deterioration, 659

Dilate
increase, 35
swell, 194
lengthen, 202
rarefy, 322
style, 573
discourse, 584

Dilatory
slow, 275
inactive, 683

Dilemma
difficulty, 704
logic, 476
doubt, 475, 485

Dilettante
ignoramus, 493
taste, 850
idler, 683

Diligence
coach, 272
activity, 682

Dilly-dally
irresolution, 605
lateness, 133

Dilution
weakness, 160
tenuity, 322
water, 337

Diluvian
old, 124

Dim
dark, 421
obscure, 422
invisible, 447

Dim-out
dim, 422

Dim-sighted
imperfect vision, 443
foolish, 499

Dime
trifle, 643

Dimension
size, 192

Dimidiation
bisection, 91

Diminish
lessen, 32, 36
contract, 195

Diminuendo
music, 415

Diminutive
in degree, 32
in size, 193

Dimness
dimness, 422

Dimple
concavity, 252
notch, 257

Din
noise, 404
repetition, 104
loquacity, 584

Dine
to feed, 297

Diner
vehicle, 272

Ding-dong
noise, 407

Dinghy
boat, 273

Dingle
hollow, 252

Dingus
euphemism, 565

Dingy
dark, 421, 431
dim, 422
colourless, 429
grey, 432

Dining-car
vehicle, 272

Dinner
food, 298

Dinner-jacket
dress, 225

Dint
power, 157
instrumentality, 631
dent, 257

Diocesan
clergy, 996

Diocese
churchdom, 995

Diorama
view, 448
painting, 556

Dip
plunge, 310
direction, 278
slope, 217
depth, 208
insert, 300
immerse, 337
thief, 792

Dip into
examine, 457
investigate, 461

Diphthong
letter, 561

Diploma
commission, 755
document, 551

Diplomacy
mediation, 724
artfulness, 702
courtesy, 894
negotiation, 769

Diplomatic
artful, 544, 702
tactful, 498, 698

Diplomat(ist)
messenger, 534
emissary, 758

Dippy
insane, 503

Dipsomania
drunkenness, 959
insanity, 503, 504
craving, 865

Dire
fearful, 860
grievous, 830
hateful, 649

Direct
straight, 246, 278, 628
to order, 737
to command, 741
to teach, 537
artless, 703

Direction
tendency, 278
course, 622
place, 183
management, 693
precept, 697

Directly
soon, 111
towards, 278

Director
manager, 694
master, 745

teacher, 540
Directorship
  authority, 737
Directory
  council, 696
  list, 86
Dirge
  song, 415
  lament, 839
  funeral, 363
Dirigible
  airship, 273A
Dirk
  arms, 727
Dirt
  uncleanness, 653
  trifle, 643
  ugly, 846
  blemish, 848
Dirt-cheap
  cheap, 815
Dirt-track
  arena, 728
Dirty
  dishonourable, 940
Disability
  impotence, 158
  fault, 651
  unskilfulness, 698
Disable
  weaken, 158, 160, 674
Disabuse
  disclosure, 529
Disadvantage
  evil, 649
  inexpedience, 647
  badness, 649
Disaffection
  hate, 898
  disobedience, 742
  disloyalty, 940
Disagreeable
  unpleasant, 830
  disliked, 867
Disagreement
  incongruity, 24
  difference, 15
  discord, 713
  dissent, 489
Disallow
  prohibit, 761
Disannul
  abrogate, 756
Disapparel
  divest, 226

Disappear
  vanish, 2, 449
Disappoint
  discontent, 832
  fail, 732
  baulk, 509
Disapprobation
  blame, 932
  disrepute, 874
Disarm
  incapacitate, 158
  weaken, 160
  conciliate, 831
  propitiate, 914
Disarrange
  derange, 61
Disarray
  disorder, 59
  undress, 226
Disaster
  evil, 619
  failure, 732
  adversity, 735
  calamity, 830
Disavow
  negation, 536
  retract, 607
Disband
  disperse, 73
  separate, 44
Disbar
  punish, 972
  dismiss, 756
Disbelief
  doubt, 485
  religious, 988
Disbench
  punish, 972
  dismiss, 756
Disbranch
  disjunction, 44
Disburden
  facilitate, 705
  disclose, 529
Disburse
  expend, 809
Disc
  see Disk
Discard
  dismiss, 624, 756
  disuse, 678
  refuse, 764
  thought, 452
  repudiate, 773
  relinquish, 782

Discern
  behold, 441
Discernible
  visibility, 446
Discerning
  wisdom, 498
Discernment
  wisdom, 498
  discrimination, 465
Discerption
  disjunction, 44
Discharge
  emit, 297
  sound, 406
  violence, 173
  propel, 284
  excrete, 299
  flow, 348
  duty, 926
  acquit oneself, 692
  observe, 772
  pay, 807
  exempt, 927A
  accomplish, 729
  liberate, 750
  forget, 506
  acquit, 970
Disciple
  learner, 541
Disciplinarian
  master, 540
  martinet, 739
Discipline
  order, 58
  teaching, 537
  training, 673
  restraint, 751
  punishment, 972
  religious, 990
Disclaim
  deny, 536
  refuse, 764
  repudiate, 756
  abjure, 757
Disclose
  disclosure, 529
Discoid
  horizontally, 213
Discolour
  achromatism, 429
  to stain, 846
Discomfit
  success, 731
Discomfiture
  failure, 732

Discomfort
pain, 378, 828
Discommendation
blame, 932
Discommodious
inutility, 645
hindrance, 706
Discommodity
inexpedience, 647
Discompose
derange, 61
hinder, 706
put out, 458
to vex, 830
disconcert, 874
provoke, 900
Discomposure
pain, 828
Disconcert
hinder, 706
frustrate, 731
disappoint, 509
distract, 458
confuse, 874
Disconcerted
inattention, 458
Disconformity
disagreement, 24
Discongruity
disagreement, 24
Disconnect
disjunction, 44
irrelation, 10
Disconnected
confused, 519
Disconsolate
sad, 837
grief, 828
Discontent
dissatisfaction, 832
Discontented
pain, 828
Discontinuance
cessation, 142
Discontinue
interrupt, 70
relinquish, 624
Discord
disagreement, 24
dissension, 713
musical, 414
Discordance
incongruity, 24
sound, 410
dissent, 489

Discount
abatement, 813
deduction, 38
to anticipate, 673
disregard, 460, 483
qualify, 469
Discountenance
refuse, 764
disfavour, 706
radeness, 895
Discourage
dissuade, 616
sadden, 837
disfavour, 706
fear, 860
Discourse
talk, 588
speech, 582
dissert, 595
Discourtesy
rudeness, 895
Discover
perceive, 441
find, 480a
solve, 462
Discredit
disbelief, 485
dishonour, 874
Discreditable
vice, 945
Discreet
careful, 459
cautious, 864
prudent, 498
clever, 698
Discrepancy
disagreement, 24
discord, 713
Discrete
separate, 44
single, 87
Discretion
wisdom, 498
foresight, 510
caution, 864
skill, 698
courtesy, 894
will, 600
care, 459
choice, 609
Discrimination
distinction, 465
difference, 15
taste, 850
fastidiousness, 868

wisdom, 498
Disculpate
vindicate, 937
Discursive
moving, 264
migratory, 266
wandering, 279
style, 573
chatty, 588
dissertation, 595
Discus
missile, 284
Discuss
reason, 476
inquire, 461
reflect, 451
treat of, 595
eat, 296
Disdain
contempt, 930
indifference, 866
fastidiousness, 868
Disdainful
proud, 878
Disease
illness, 655
Disembark
arrive, 292
Disembarrass
facilitate, 705
Disembodied
immaterial, 317
Disembody
decompose, 49
disperse, 73
Disembogue
flow out, 348
emit, 295
Disembowel
extraction, 300
disjunction, 44
Disenable
impotence, 158
Disenchant
dissuade, 616
Disencumber
facility, 705
Disendow
taking, 789
cancel, 756
Disengage
detach, 44
facilitate, 705
liberate, 750, 768a

469

Disentangle
separate, 44
arrange, 60
facilitate, 705
unfold, 313
decipher, 522
Disenthral
liberate, 750
Disentitled
undueness, 925
Disestablish
displace, 185
cancel, 756
Disesteem
disrespect, 929
censure, 932
Disfavour
hate, 898
disrepute, 874
to oppose, 708
Disfeature
deface, 241
deform, 846
Disfigure
deface, 241, 659
deform, 846
blemish, 848
Disfranchise
disentitle, 925
Disgorge
emit, 297
restore, 790
flow out, 348
Disgrace
shame, 874
dishonour, 940
Disguise
conceal, 528
falsify, 544
deceive, 545
mask, 530
untruth, 546
Disguised
in liquor, 959
Disgust
dislike, 867
hatred, 898
offensive, 830
weary, 841
taste, 395
Dish
plate, 191
food, 299
upset, 162
to foil, 731
Dishabille

undress, 225
unprepared, 674
simplicity, 849
Dishearten
dissuade, 616
deject, 837
Dished
failure, 732
Dishevelled
loose, 47
disordered, 61
intermixed, 219
twisted, 248
Dishonest
false, 544
faithless, 940
Dishonour
baseness, 940
to repudiate a bill, 808
disrespect, 929
disrepute, 874
Disillusion
dissuasion, 616
Disimprove
deteriorate, 659
Disincentive
check, 616
Disincline
dissuade, 616
Disinclined
unwilling, 603
disliking, 867
Disinfect
purify, 652
improve, 658
Disinfectant
remedy, 662
Disingenuous
false, 544
dishonourable, 940
Disinherit
transfer, 783
Disintegrate
separate, 44
decompose, 49
pulverize, 330
Disinter
exhume, 363
discover, 480a, 525
Disinterested
unselfish, 942
Disjoin
loosen, 44
Disjointed
loosened, 44

in disorder, 59
Disjunction
incoherence, 47
decomposition, 49
Disk
face, 234
exterior, 220
Dislike
distaste, 867
disapproval, 932
hate, 898
enmity, 889
reluctance, 603
Dislocate
loosen, 44
derange, 61
Dislodge
displace, 185
Disloyal
improbity, 940
Dismal
dejection, 837
dullness, 843
Dismantle
destroy, 162
disuse, 678
despoil, 649
injure, 659
divest, 226
Dismast
disuse, 678
dismantle, 659, 674
Dismay
fear, 860
Dismember
loosen, 44
Dismiss
discard, 678, 756, 782
eject, 297
liberate, 750
Dismount
descend, 306
arrive, 292
disable, 674
Disobey
disobedience, 742
Disobliging
malevolent, 907
Disorder
confusion, 59
to derange, 61
disease, 655
Disorderly
violent, 173
Disorganize

470

Dissemble
falsehood, 544
Dissembler
liar, 548
Disseminate
scatter, 73
diverge, 291
publish, 531
pervade, 186
Dissension
discord, 713
Dissent
disagree, 489
refuse, 764
heterodoxy, 984a
discord, 713
Dissertation
disquisition, 595
Disservice
disadvantage, 619
inexpedience, 647
Dissever
disjoin, 44
Dissidence
disagreement, 24
dissent, 489
Dissilience
violent, 173
Dissimilar
unlike, 18
Dissimulate
falsehood, 544
Dissipate
scatter, 73
waste, 638
prodigality, 818
dissolute, 961
licentiousness, 954
Dissociation
irrelation, 10
separation, 44
Dissolute
intemperate, 954
profligate, 945
debauched, 961
Dissolution
decomposition, 49
liquefaction, 335
death, 360
Dissolve
vanish, 2, 4
disappear, 449
abrogate, 756
liquefy, 335
Dissonance

disagreement, 24
discord, 414
Dissuade
dissuasion, 616
Distain
ugliness, 846
Distance
longinquity, 196
swiftness, 274
to overtake, 282
to leave behind, 303,
732
respect, 928
of time, 110
Distant
far, 196
discourteous, 895
Distaste
dislike, 867
Distasteful
disagreeable, 830
Distemper
disease, 655
painting, 556
Distend
expansion, 194
Distended
swollen, 194
Distich
poetry, 597
Distil
evaporate, 336
flow, 348
drop, 295
Distinct
visible, 446
audible, 402
intelligible, 518, 535
disjoined, 44
Distinction
difference, 15
discrimination, 465
fame, 873
style, 574
Distinctive
special, 75
Distingué
repute, 873
fashionable, 852
Distinguish
perceive, 441
Distortion
obliquity, 217
twist, 243, 555
falsehood, 544

of vision, 443
perversion, 523
ugliness, 846
Distracted
insane, 503
unthinking, 452
confused, 491
Distraction
inattention, 458
amusement, 840
Distrain
seize, 789, 969
Distrait
incogitancy, 452
inattention, 458
Distraught
see Distracted
Distress
affliction, 828
cause of pain, 830
poor, 804
Distribute
disperse, 73
arrange, 60
allot, 786
diverge, 291
District
region, 181
Distrust
disbelief, 485
fear, 860
Disturb
derange, 61
alter, 140
agitate, 315
Disunion
separation, 44
discord, 713
Disuse
unemployment, 678
desuetude, 614
Ditch
conduit, 350
hollow, 252
trench, 259, 343
defence, 717
upset, 162
sea, 341
Ditheism
heathen, 984
Dither
shiver, 315, 383
Dithyrambic
poetry, 597

Ditto
repetition, 104, 136
Ditty
music, 415
Diuretic
remedy, 662
Diurnal
period, 108, 138
Diuturnal
diuturnity, 110
Divan
sofa, 215
council, 696
Divarication
divergence, 291
deviation, 279
difference, 15
Dive
plunge, 310
descent, 306
depth, 208
Divellicate
disjoin, 44
Divergence
variation, 20
dissimilarity, 18
difference, 15
discord, 713
dispersion, 73
separation, 291
disagreement, 24
deviation, 279
Divers
many, 102
different, 15
multiform, 81
Diversified
varied, 15, 16A, 18, 20, 81
Diversion
amusement, 840
change, 140
Diversity
difference, 15
dissimilarity, 18
multiform, 16A, 81
Divert
turn, 279
amuse, 840
abstract, 452
Divertissement
drama, 599
amusement, 840
Dives
wealth, 803

Divest
denude, 226
take, 789
Divest oneself of
leave, 782
Divide
separate, 44
part, 51, 91
apportion, 786
Dividend
part, 51
number, 84
portion, 786
Dividers
measure, 466
Divination
prediction, 511
occult arts, 992
Divine
Diety, 976
clergyman, 996
theologian, 983
to guess, 514
predict, 510, 511
perfect, 650
Diving-bell
depth, 208
Divining-rod
spell, 993
Divinity
Deity, 976
theology, 983
Division
separation, 44
part, 51
class, 75
troop, 72, 726
arithmetical, 85
discord, 713
distribution, 786
Divisor
number, 84
Divorce
matrimonial, 905
separation, 44
Divulge
disclose, 529
Divulsion
disjoin, 44
Dizzard
fool, 501
Dizzy
confused, 458
vertigo, 503
foolish, 499

Djinn
demon, 980
Do
act, 680
fare, 7
produce, 161
suffice, 639
complete, 729
cheat, 545
Do away with
remove, 185, 678
destroy, 162, 681
Do for
injure, 659
defeat, 731
kill, 361
suit, 646
punish, 972
Do in
kill, 361
Do into
interpret, 522
Do-nothing
inactivity, 683
Do over
cover, 222
Do up
repair, 658
pack, 72
Doch-an-doris
departure, 293
intoxicant, 959
Docile
teachable, 539
tractable, 705
willing, 602
obedient, 743
dutiful, 926
Dock
cut off, 38
diminish, 36
incompleteness, 53
shorten, 201
port, 189
yard, 636, 691
tribunal, 966
Docker
workman, 690
Docket
indication, 467, 550
record, 551
security, 771
Doctor
sage, 492
physician, 695

to restore, 660
amend, 658
remedy, 662
falsify, 544
Doctrinaire
ignoramus, 493
Doctrinal
teaching, 537
Doctrine
tenet, 484
knowledge, 490
Document
record, 551
Documentary
film, 599A
Dodecahedron
angle, 244
Dodge
oscillate, 314
pursue, 461
deceive, 545
avoid, 623
shift, 264
contrivance, 626
cunning, 702
Doe
swiftness, 274
Doer
agent, 690
originator, 164
Doff
put off, 226
Dog
to pursue, 622
follow, 281
affectation, 855
Dog-cart
vehicle, 272
Dog-days
heat, 382
Dog-ear
fold, 258
Dog Latin
solecism, 568
Dog-tired
fatigue, 688
Dog-trot
slowness, 275
Doge
master, 745
Dogfight
contest, 720
Dogged
obstinate, 606
discourteous, 895

Dogger
ship, 273
Doggerel
verse, 597
ridiculous, 853
Dogma
tenet, 484
theological, 983
Dogmatic
obstinate, 606
certainty, 474
assertion, 535
intolerant, 481
Dog's-eared
fold, 258
Doings
actions, 680
events, 151
Doit
trifle, 643
coin, 800
Doited
insane, 503
Dolce far niente
inactivity, 638
Doldrums
dejection, 837
Dole
small quantity, 32
to give, 784
to allot, 786
expenditure, 809
grief, 828
Dole out
parsimony, 819
Doleful
dejected, 837
lament, 839
Doll
plaything, 840
image, 554
small, 193
Doll up
beautify, 845
adorn, 847
Dollar
money, 800
Dollop
part, 51
Dolman
dress, 225
Dolmen
grave, 363
Dolorous
pain, 830

Dolour
physical, 378
moral, 828
Dolphin
ocean, 341
Dolt
fool, 501
Doltish
folly, 499
Domain
region, 181
class, 75
property, 780
Domdaniel
hell, 982
Dome
convexity, 250
Domesday Book
list, 86
Domestic
interior, 188, 221
servant, 746
secluded, 893
Domesticate
tame, 537
Domicile
abode, 189
Dominance
influence, 175
Dominant
prevailing, 737
note in music, 413
Domination
authority, 737
Domineer
tyrannize, 739
insolence, 885
Dominican
clergy, 996
Dominie
teacher, 540
Dominion
region, 181
spirit, 977
Domino
dress, 225
mask, 530
Don
to put on, 225
noble, 875
scholar, 492
Dona
woman, 374
sweetheart, 897

Donation
gift, 784, 804
Done
finished, 729
cheated, 547
Donee
receive, 785
Donjon
defence, 717
Donkey
ass, 271
fool, 501
Donkey's breakfast
bed, 215
Donna
woman, 374
Donnybrook
disorder, 59
discord, 713
contention, 720
Donor
giver, 784
Doodlebug
bomb, 727
Doom
fate, 152
necessity, 601
destruction, 162, 360
to sentence, 969
condemn, 971
end, 67
Doomed
undone, 828
fated, 152, 601
Doomsday
futurity, 121
end, 67
Door
opening, 260
passage, 627
brink, 230
entrance, 66, 294
barrier, 232
Door-keeper
janitor, 263
Doorway
opening, 260
Dope
semiliquid, 352
stupefy, 376
Dope fiend
intemperance, 954
Doppelgänger
ghost, 980
Dopy

sleepy, 683
Dormant
latent, 526
inert, 172, 683
Dormitory
room, 191
Dormouse
inactivity, 683
Dorsal
rear, 235
Dorsum
rear, 235
convexity, 250
Dose
part, 51
mixture, 41
remedy, 662
Doss-house
inn, 189
Dossier
record, 551
evidence, 461
Dossil
stopper, 263
Dot
speck, 32, 193
mark, 550
dowry, 810
Dotage
age, 128
folly, 499
Dotard
fool, 501
Dote
drivel, 499, 503
love, 897
Dotted
variegated, 440
Double
duplex, 90
turn, 283
fold, 258
false, 544
similarity, 17
Double-dealing
falsehood, 544
dishonour, 940
Double Dutch
jargon, 497
Double-edged
energy, 171
equivocal, 520
Double entendre
equivocalness, 520
indecency, 961

Double-faced
deceitful, 544
trimming, 607
Double-quick
speed, 274
Double-tongued
false, 544
equivocal, 520
Doublet
dress, 225
Doubt
disbelief, 485
scepticism, 989
Doubtful
uncertain, 475
incredulous, 485
Doubtless
certainty, 474
assent, 488
Douceur
expenditure, 809
giving, 784
Douche
water, 337
Dough
pulp, 354
inelastic, 324
money, 800
Doughboy
fighter, 726
Doughty
courageous, 861
strong, 159
Dour
severe, 739
Douse
immerse, 310
splash, 337
Dove
deity, 976
Dovelike
innocent, 946
Dovetail
intervene, 228
intersect, 219
insert, 300
angular, 244
join, 43
agree, 23
Dowager
widow, 905
lady, 374
veteran, 130
Dowdy
vulgar, 851

475

dirty, 653
ugly, 846
Dower
wealth, 803, 810
property, 780
Dowerless
poverty, 804
Down
levity, 320
smoothness, 255
plumose, 256
bed of, 377
below, 207
Down-hearted
dejection, 837
Downcast
dejection, 837
Downfall
dejection, 837
calamity, 619
Downgrade
debase, 659
Downhill
obliquity, 217
Downright
absolute, 31
plain, 576
sincere, 703
Downs
plains, 344
uplands, 206
Downstairs
lowness, 207
Downtrodden
contemptible, 930
submission, 725
subject, 749
Downwards
lowness, 207
Downy
hairy, 256
soft, 324
cunning, 702
Dowry
wealth, 803, 810
Doxology
worship, 990
Doxy
belief, 484
Doyen
oldness, 124
Doze
inactivity, 683
Dozen
assemblage, 72

number, 98
Drab
colour, 432
hussy, 962, 949
Draconian
severe, 739
Draff
uncleanness, 653
Draft
copy, 21
transfer, 270
sketch, 554
write, 590
abstract, 596
plan, 626
cheque, 800
Drag
traction, 285
attract, 288
crawl, 275
brake, 752
Drag-net
generality, 78
assemblage, 72
Drag up
elevation, 307
Draggle
hang, 214
Dragoman
interpreter, 524
Dragon
fury, 173
monster, 83
Dragonnade
evil, 619, 791
Dragoon
combatant, 726
to persecute, 907
Drain
conduit, 350
to dry, 340
wash, 652
exhaust, 789
waste, 638
sewer, 653
dissipate, 818
flow out, 295
empty itself, 297, 348
drink up, 296
Dram
stimulus, 615
drink, 298
drunkenness, 959
Drama
the drama, 599

Dramatic
impressive, 824
Dramatis personae
the drama, 599
interlocution, 588
agent, 690
party, 712
Drapery
clothes, 225
Drastic
energy, 171
Draught
drink, 296
traction, 285
stream of air, 349
depth, 208
abundance, 639
remedy, 662
Draughtsman
artist, 559
Draw
pull, 285
attract, 288
extract, 301
tobacco, 298A
induce, 615
delineate, 556
equal, 27
unfinished, 730
money order, 800
Draw back
regress, 283, 287
avoid, 623
Draw in
contract, 195
Draw near
approach, 286
time, 121
Draw on
event, 151
entice, 615
Draw out
extract, 301
prolong, 200
protract, 110
exhibit, 525
Draw together
assemble, 72
Draw up
writing, 590
Drawback
hindrance, 706
imperfection, 651
discount, 813
evil, 619

Drawbridge
escape, 671
Drawcansir
blusterer, 887
Drawee
money, 800
Drawer
receptacle, 191
money, 800
Drawers
dress, 225
Drawing
sketch, 556
representation, 554
Drawing-room
room, 191
Drawl
creep, 275
prolong, 200
in speech, 583
sluggish, 683
Drawn
distorted, 217
Dray
vehicle, 272
Dread
fear, 860
Dreadful
great, 31
fearful, 860
calamitous, 830
Dreadnought
ship, 273
Dream
vision, 515
unsubstantial, 4
error, 495
inactivity, 683
Dream of
think, 451
intend, 620
Dreamy
inattentive, 458
sleepy, 683
Dreary
solitary, 87
melancholy, 830
Dredge
raise, 307
extract, 301
collect, 72
Dregs
refuse, 643
dirt, 653
remainder, 40

Drench
drink, 296
water, 337
redundance, 641
Dress
clothe, 225
prepare, 673
fit, 23
clip, 38
trim, 27
Dress-circle
theatre, 599
Dress up
adorn, 845
Dresser
support, 215
Dressing
punishment, 972
condiment, 393
Dressing-case
receptacle, 191
Dressing-down
reprimand, 932
Dressy
smart, 847
Dribble
flow out, 295
drop, 348
Driblet
part, 51
scanty, 193
small, 32
Drift
direction, 278
meaning, 516
intention, 620
tendency, 176
to float, 267
to accumulate, 72
Driftless
chance, 621
Drill
auger, 262
to train, 673
teach, 537
pierce, 260
procedure, 692
Drink
to swallow, 296
liquor, 298
to tipple, 959
sea, 341
Drink in
learn, 539
imbibe, 296

Drip
ooze, 295
flow out, 348
whirer, 839
Dripping
fat, 356
moist, 339
Drive
impel, 276
propel, 284
repel, 289
urge, 615
haste, 684
pursue, 622
fatigue, 688
compel, 744
airing, 266
Drive at
intend, 620
mean, 516
Drive in
insert, 300
ingress, 294
Drive out
ejection, 297
Drivel
folly, 499
fatuity, 503
Driveller
fool, 501
loquacious, 584
Driver
director, 694
Drizzle
distil, 295
rain, 348
Droll
witty, 842
odd, 853
Drollery
amusement, 840
ridiculousness, 853
Dromedary
carrier, 271
Drone
inactive, 683
slow, 275
sound, 412
Droop
sink, 306
flag, 688
weakness, 160
disease, 655
sorrow, 828
dejection, 837

decline, 659
Drop
fall, 306
discontinue, 142
expire, 360
relinquish, 624, 782
lose, 776
faint, 160
fatigue, 688
flow out, 348
spherule, 249
small quantity, 32, 193
Drop astern
regression, 283
Drop in
immerse, 300
arrive, 292
Drop off
die, 360
Droplet
smallness, 32
Dropsical
swollen, 194
redundant, 641
Droshky
vehicle, 272
Dross
dirt, 653
trash, 643
remainder, 40
Drought
insufficiency, 640
Drouth
thirst, 865
Drove
assemblage, 72, 102
Drown
kill, 361
immerse, 300
water, 337
surfeit, 641
ruin, 731, 732
Drowsy
slow, 275
inactive, 683
weary, 841
Drub
beat, 276
master, 731
punish, 972
Drudge
agent, 690
to work, 680
to plod, 682
Drug

remedy, 662
superfluity, 641
trash, 643
Drugget
covering, 222
Drum
cylinder, 249
music, 417
sound, 407
to repeat, 104
Drum-major
master, 745
Drum out
punish, 972
Drumhead
tribunal, 966
Drummer
agent, 758
Drunk
intoxication, 959
intemperance, 954
Dry
arid, 340
jejune, 575
thirsty, 865
teetotal, 953
scanty, 640
wit, 844
cynical, 932
Dry-nurse
tend, 707
teach, 537
teacher, 540
Dry point
engraving, 558
Dry rot
deterioration, 653, 659
Dry up
waste, 638
silent, 585
Dryasdust
past, 122
Duad
duality, 89
Duality
duality, 89
Dub
name, 465
cinema, 599A
Dubious
uncertain, 475
Dubitation
doubt, 485
Duce
master, 745

Duchess
noble, 875
Duchy
region, 181
Duck
immerse, 300
plunge, 310
wet, 337
stoop, 308
darling, 899
nothing, 4
vehicle, 272
Duck-pond
taming, 370
Ducking-stool
punishment, 975
Ducks and drakes
recoil, 277
Duct
conduit, 350
Ductile
flexible, 324
easy, 705
useless, 645
Dud
defective, 651
Dude
fop, 854
Dudeen
tobacco-pipe, 298A
Dudgeon
anger, 900
discourteous, 895
club, 727
Duds
clothes, 225
Due
proper, 924, 926
owing, 806
effect, 154
expedient, 646
Duel
contention, 720
Duellist
combatant, 726
Dueness
right, 924
Duenna
teacher, 540
accompaniment, 88
keeper, 753
Dues
price, 812
Duet
music, 815

Duff
false, 495
Duffer
fool, 501
bungler, 700
Duffle coat
dress, 225
Dug
convexity, 250
Dug-out
refuge, 666, 717
canoe, 273
Duke
noble, 875
ruler, 745
Dukedom
title, 877
Dulcet
sound, 405
melodious, 413
agreeable, 829
Dulcify
sweeten, 396
Dulcimer
musical instrument, 417
Dulcinea
favourite, 899
Dull
inert, 172
insensible, 376
tame, 575
callous, 823
blunt, 254
weak, 160
moderate, 174
colourless, 429
dejected, 837
inexcitable, 826
stolid, 699
prosing, 843
unapt, 499
Dull-brained
folly, 499
Dull-witted
folly, 499
Dullard
fool, 501
Duma
council, 696
Dumb
aphony, 581
stupid, 499, 843
unskilful, 699
Dumb-bell
fool, 501

Dumb show
the drama, 599
Dumbfound
astonish, 870
disappoint, 509
Dummy
aphony, 581
effigy, 554
Dump
deposit, 184
Dumps
sadness, 837
mortification, 832
Dumpy
broad, 202
short, 200
ugly, 846
Dun
colour, 432
to importune, 765
a creditor, 805
Dunce
ignoramus, 493
fool, 501
Dunderhead
fool, 501
Dundreary
whisker, 256
Dune
hillock, 206
Dung
uncleanness, 653
Dungarees
dress, 225
Dungeon
prison, 752
hide, 530
Dunghill
vulgar, 876
Dunt
blow, 619
Duodecimal
twelve, 98
Duodecimo
littleness, 193
book, 593
Duodenary
numbers, 98
Duologue
interlocution, 588
drama, 599
Dupe
to deceive, 545
deceived, 547
credulous, 486

Duplex
double, 89, 90
Duplicate
double, 89, 90
superfluous, 641
copy, 21, 590
pledge, 550, 805
Duplication
imitation, 19
Duplicity
false, 544, 702
Durable
lasting, 110
stable, 150
Durance
restraint, 751
Duration
period, 106
Durbar
tribunal, 966
assembly, 696
Duress
restraint, 751
compulsion, 744
During
lasting, 106
During pleasure
contingent, duration,
108a
Durity
hardness, 323
Dusk
evening, 126
obscurity, 422
Dusky
darkness, 421
Dust
powder, 330
corpse, 362
levity, 320
dirt, 653
trash, 643
to clean, 652
contest, 720
money, 800
Dustman
cleaner, 652
Duteous
virtue, 944
Dutiful
virtue, 944
filial, 167
Duty
obligation, 926
business, 625

peculiar, 79
exterior, 220
wrong-headed, 499
oddity, 857
Ecclesiastic
clergy, 996
Écervelé
insanity, 503
Echelon
series, 69
Echo
repeat, 104
assent, 488
imitate, 19
loudness, 404
resonance, 408
answer, 462
Éclaircissement
interpretation, 522
Éclat
repute, 873
Eclectic
choice, 609
Eclipse
hide, 528
invisible, 447
darkness, 421, 422
outshine, 33, 874
Ecliptic
universe, 318
Eclogue
poetry, 597
Ecology
organization, 357
Economy
order, 58
plan, 626
conduct, 692
frugality, 817
Ecstasy
fancy, 515
rapture, 821, 827
Ecumenical
theology, 983
Edacity
gluttony, 957
Eddy
current, 348
whirlpool, 312
Eden
heaven, 981
Edge
brink, 230
energy, 171
to move forward, 282

to move sideways, 236
to instigate, 615
Edge-tool
sharpness, 253
Edging
ornament, 847
Edible
food, 298
Edict
legality, 963
command, 741
Edifice
abode, 189
Edify
build, 161
teach, 537
piety, 987
Edit
publish, 531
alter, 140
Editorial
dissertation, 595
Educate
teach, 537
train, 673
Education
learning, 490
Educe
elicit, 525
Educt
remainder, 40
Edulcorate
sweeten, 396
clean, 652
Eel
convolution, 248
Eerie
unconformity, 83
supernatural, 980
Efface
obliterate, 552
oblivion, 506
disappear, 449
Effect
consequence, 154
to produce, 161
to complete, 729
Effective
capable, 157
impressive, 821
successful, 731
real, 1
Efects
property, 780
goods, 798

materials, 635
Effectual
useful, 644
Efeminate
weak, 160
womanish, 374
sensual, 954
timorous, 862
Effend
master, 745
noble, 875
Effervesce
bubble up, 353
agitate, 315
energy, 171
violence, 173
excited, 825
Effete
old, 124
weak, 160
useless, 645
spoiled, 659
Efficacy
power, 157
Efficiency
utility, 644
skill, 698
Effigy
representation, 554
copy, 21
Effleurer
skim, 267
slur over, 458
Efflorescence
pulverulence, 330
Effluence
egress, 295
river, 348
Effluvium
odour, 398
vapour, 334
Efflux
flow, 348
Effort
exertion, 686
Effrontery
insolence, 885
Effulgence
light, 420
Effusion
outpouring, 295
ejection, 297, 299
speech, 582
Effusiveness
feeling, 821

Eftsoons
soon, 111
early, 132
Egg
beginning, 66
Egg on
urge, 615
Egg-shaped
round, 247, 249
Egghead
sage, 500
Ego
self, 13
Egocentric
vanity, 880
Egoism
vanity, 880
selfishness, 911
Egomania
vanity, 880
Egotism
vanity, 880
selfishness, 911, 943
Egregious
exceptional, 83
important, 642
extravagant, 499
Egregiously
greatness, 31
Egress
emergence, 295
Eiderdown
covering, 222
Eidolon
idea, 453
Eirenicon
mediation, 724
Eisteddfod
assemblage, 72
Either
choice, 609
Ejaculate
propel, 284
utter, 580
Eject
displace, 185
emit, 297
Eke
addition, 37
to complete, 52
spin out, 110
Elaborate
preparation, 673
complete, 729
detail, 594

Élan
ardour, 821
vigour, 574
activity, 682
Elapse
pass, 122
flow, 109
Elastic
resilient, 325
strong, 159
Elate
to cheer, 836
boast, 884
Elbow
angle, 244, 258
projection, 250
to push, 276
Elbow-grease
rubbing, 331
Elbow-room
space, 180
freedom, 748
Eld
oldness, 124
Elder
oldness, 124
age, 128
veteran, 130
Elect
choice, 609
Election
necessity, 601
choice, 609
Elector
master, 745
voter, 609
Electric
feeling, 821
Electric bulb
light, 423
Electricity
velocity, 274
Electrify
excite, 824
astonish, 870
energize, 171
Electrocute
punish, 972, 975
Electrolier
light, 423
Electrolysis
decomposition, 49
Electron
atom, 193
Electroplate

to cover, 222
Electrotype
engraving, 558
imitation, 19
Eleemosynary
giving, 784
Elegance
beauty, 845
in style, 578
taste, 850
Elegy
dirge, 415
funeral, 363
plaint, 839
Element
component, 56
matter, 316
cause, 153
beginning, 66
rudimental knowledge,
490
Elemental
simple, 42
Elementary
simple, 42
Elenchus
sophistry, 477
Elephant
large, 192
carrier, 271
Elevation
height, 206
raising, 307
plan, 554
improvement, 658
of mind, 942
style, 574
glory, 873
Elevator
lift, 627
Elevenses
food, 298
Eleventh hour
occasion, 134
Elf
infant, 129
little, 193
demon, 980
Elicit
manifest, 525
discover, 480a
cause, 153
draw out, 301
Elide
strike out, 552

Eligible
expedience, 646
Eliminate
exclude, 55
extract, 301
weed, 103
Elimination
subduction, 38
Elision
separation, 44
shortening, 201
Élite
perfection, 650
Elixir
remedy, 662
Elixir vitae
remedy, 662
Ellipse
circularity, 247
curvature, 245
conciseness, 572
Ellipsis
curtailment, 201
style, 572
Ellipsoid
circularity, 247
rotundity, 249
Elocution
speech, 582
Éloge
approval, 931
Elongation
lengthening, 200
distance, 196
Elope
escape, 671
Eloquence
of style, 574
speech, 582
Else
addition, 37
Elsewhere
absence, 187
Elucidate
interpret, 522
Elude
avoid, 623
escape, 671
palter, 773
sophistry, 477
succeed, 731
Elusory
falsehood, 544
Elysium
paradise, 981

bliss, 827
Emaciation
contraction, 193
smallness, 195
slenderness, 203
decay, 659
Emanate
go out of, 295
excrete, 299
proceed from, 154
Emanation
odour, 398
Emancipate
free, 750
facilitate, 705
Emasculate
weakness, 160
style, 575
Embalm
preserve, 670
bury, 363
memory, 505
to perfume, 400
Embankment
defence, 717
Embargo
prohibition, 706, 761
stoppage, 265
Embark
depart, 293
undertake, 676
Embarrass
render difficult, 704
hinder, 706
perplex, 475, 528
hesitation, 485
Embase
deterioration, 659
Embassy
errand, 532, 755
diplomat, 758
Embattled
arranged, 60
warfare, 722
Embed
locate, 184
insert, 300
Embellish
beautify, 845
ornament, 847
Embers
fuel, 388
Embezzle
steal, 791
Embitter

aggravate, 835
deteriorate, 659
acerbate, 900
Emblazon
colour, 428
beautify, 845, 847
display, 882
Emblem
indication, 550
Embody
combine, 48
compose, 54
join, 43
form a whole, 50
materialize, 3, 316
Embolden
encourage, 861
hope, 858
Embolism
insertion, 300
Embonpoint
size, 192
Embosomed
middle, 68
lodged, 184
circumjacence, 227
Emboss
form, 240
adorn, 847
Embossed
convex, 250
Embouchure
opening, 260
lipping, 415
Embrace
include, 76
compose, 54
enclose, 227
courtesy, 894
endearment, 902
Embrangle
derange, 61
Embrasure
notch, 257
opening, 260
Embrocation
remedy, 662
Embroider
beauty, 845
ornament, 847
variegate, 440
falsify, 544
exaggerate, 549
Embroil
discord, 713

derange, 61
Embrown
  brown, 433
Embryo
  cause, 153
  preparation, 673
  beginning, 66
Embryonic
  latent, 526
Embus
  depart, 293
Emendation
  improvement, 658
Emerald
  green, 435
  gem, 847
Emerge
  egress, 295
Emergency
  difficulty, 704
  conjuncture, 8
  event, 151
Emeritus
  retired, 757
  respected, 928
Emersion
  egress, 295
Emery
  sharpener, 253
Emery paper
  smooth, 255
Emetic
  remedy, 662
Émeute
  resistance, 716
Emigrant
  traveller, 268
Emigrate
  remove, 266
  egress, 295
Eminence
  height, 206
  fame, 873
Eminently
  superiority, 33
  greatly, 31
Emir
  master, 745
  noble, 875
Emissary
  messenger, 534
  consignee, 758
Emission
  ejection, 297
Emmet

little, 193
Emollient
  remedy, 662
  softness, 324
Emolument
  acquisition, 775
  receipt, 810
Emotion
  feeling, 821
Emotive
  feeling, 821
Emotional
  sensibility, 822
Empale
  see Impale
Emperor
  master, 745
Emphasis
  accent, 580
Emphatic
  positive assertion, 535
  style, 574
  energetic, 171
  important, 642
Empire
  region, 181
  dominion, 737
  domain, 780
Empirical
  tentative, 675
Empiricism
  experiment, 463
  quackery, 545
Employ
  use, 677
  commission, 755
  business, 625
Employee
  servant, 746
  agent, 690, 758
Emporium
  mart, 799
Empower
  power, 157
  commission, 755
  permit, 760
Empress
  chief, 745
Empressement
  activity, 682
  feeling, 821
Emprise
  undertaking, 676
Emption
  purchase, 795

Empty
  vacant, 187
  transfer, 270
  insufficient, 640
  unimportant, 643
  useless, 645
  drain, 297
Empty-handed
  insufficient, 640
Empty-headed
  ignorant, 491
Empurple
  purple, 437
Empyrean
  sky, 318
  blissful, 827, 829
Emulate
  rival, 708, 720
  envy, 921
  imitate, 19
  glory, 873
Emulsion
  semiliquidity, 352
Emunctory
  conduit, 350
En bloc
  assent, 488
  whole, 50
En famille
  sociality, 892
En garçon
  celibacy, 904
En passant
  method, 627
  transitoriness, 111
  irrelation, 10
  journey, 266
En prince
  generosity, 942
En rapport
  agreement, 23
  relation, 9
En règle
  conformity, 82
En revanche
  compensation, 30
En route
  journey, 266
Enable
  power, 157
Enact
  order, 741
  a law, 963
  drama, 599

Enamel
painting, 556
covering, 222
smooth, 255
adorn, 845, 847
Enamour
love, 897
Encage
circumscribe, 231
restrain, 751
Encamp
locate, 184, 265
inhabit, 186
Encase
circumscribe, 231
Encaustic
painting, 556
Enceinte
region, 181
enclosure, 232
pregnant, 168
Enchain
bind, 43, 751
Enchant
please, 829
love, 897
conjure, 992, 994
Enchantress
beauty, 845
sorceress, 994
Encharge
consign, 755
Enchiridion
book, 593
Encircle
begird, 227
Enclave
enclosure, 232
region, 181
Enclose
circumscribe, 231
Enclosure
fence, 752
space, 181
Encomiast
flatterer, 935
Encomium
approval, 931
Encompass
begird, 227
Encore
repetition, 104
Encounter
meet, 292
clash, 276

contest, 720
withstand, 708
Encourage
animate, 615
aid, 707
embolden, 861
hope, 858
comfort, 834
Encroach
transgress, 303
infringe, 925
Encrust
line, 224
coat, 222
Encumbered
in debt, 806
Encumbrance
hindrance, 704, 706
Encyclical
publication, 531
Encyclopaedia
knowledge, 490
assembly, 72
generality, 78
End
termination, 67, 154
death, 360
object, 620
Endamage
injure, 659
harm, 649
Endanger
danger, 665
Endeavour
attempt, 675, 676
pursue, 622
intend, 620
Endemic
special, 79
disease, 655, 657
Endless
infinite, 105
multitudinous, 102
long, 200
Endogamy
marriage, 903
Endorsement
evidence, 467
sign, 550, 590
voucher, 771
ratification, 769
approval, 931
Endosmosis
passage, 302
Endow

confer power, 157
Endowment
gift, 784
capacity, 5
power, 157
talent, 698
Endue
empower, 157
Endure
time, 106
to continue, 141
to last, 110
event, 151
to bear, 821
to submit, 826
Endways
length, 200
vertical, 212
Enemy
enemy, 891
Energumen
madman, 503
fanatic, 515
Energy
physical, 171
strength, 159
style, 574
activity, 682
exertion, 686
resolution, 604
Enervate
weakness, 160
Enfant perdu
rashness, 863
Enfant terrible
artlessness, 703
Enfeeble
weaken, 160
Enfilade
pierce, 260
pass through, 302
Enfold
circumscribe, 231
Enforce
urge, 615
compel, 744
require, 924
Enfranchise
liberate, 748, 750, 924
Engage
induce, 615
the attention, 457
in a pursuit, 622
promise, 768, 769
commission, 755

undertake, 676
book, 132
Engagement
business, 625
contest, 720
promise, 768
duty, 926
Engaging
pleasing, 829
amiable, 897
Engender
produce, 161
Engine
instrument, 633
Engine-driver
director, 694
Engineering
means, 632
Engirdle
circumjacence, 227
English
translate, 522
Engorge
reception, 296
Engorgement
redundance, 641
Engraft
insert, 301
join, 43
add, 37
teach, 537
implant, 6
Engrained
imbued, 5
combined, 48
Engrave
mark, 550
on the memory, 505
Engraving
engraving, 558
Engross
possess, 777
write, 590
the thoughts, 451
the attention, 457
Engulf
destroy, 162
plunge, 310
swallow up, 296
Enhance
increase, 35
improve, 658
Enharmonic
harmony, 413
Enigma

secret, 533
question, 461
Enigmatic
concealed, 528
obscure, 519
uncertain, 475
Enjambement
transcursion, 303
Enjoin
command, 741
induce, 615
enact, 963
Enjoy
physically, 377
morally, 827
possess, 777
Enkindle
induce, 615
Enlace
surround, 227
entwine, 219, 248
join, 43
Enlarge
increase, 35
swell, 194
liberate, 750
in writing, 573
Enlighten
illuminate, 420
inform, 527
instruct, 537
Enlightened
wise, 498
Enlightenment
knowledge, 490
Enlist
commission, 755
engage, 615
Enliven
amuse, 840
cheer, 836
delight, 829
Enmesh
entwine, 219
Enmity
hostility, 889
hate, 898
discord, 713
Ennead
nine, 98
Enneagon
nine, 98
Ennoble
glorify, 873
Ennui

weariness, 841
Enormity
crime, 947
Enormous
in degree, 31
in size, 192
Enough
much, 31
sufficient, 639
satiety, 869
Enquiry
see Inquiry
Enrage
incense, 900
provoke, 830
Enrapture
excite, 824
beatify, 829
love, 897
Enravish
beatify, 829
Enrich
wealth, 803
ornament, 847
Enrobe
invest, 225
Enrol
record, 551
appoint, 755
Enrolment
list, 86
Ens
essence, 1
Ensanguined
red, 434
murderous, 361
Ensconce
settle, 184
render safe, 664
conceal, 528
Ensemble
whole, 50
Enshrine
memory, 505, 873
sanctify, 987
Enshroud
conceal, 528
Ensiform
sharpness, 253
Ensign
standard, 550
officer, 726
master, 745
Enslave
subjection, 749

Ensnare
cheat, 545
Ensue
follow, 63, 117
happen, 151
Ensure
certainty, 474
Entablature
summit, 210
Entail
cause, 153
involve, 467
impose, 741
Entangle
derange, 61
entwine, 219
disorder, 59
embroil, 713
perplex, 528
mixture, 41
Entente cordiale
friendship, 888
concord, 714
Enter
go in, 294
note, 551
accounts, 811
Enter in
converge, 290
Enter into
component, 56
Enter upon
begin, 66
Enterprise
pursuit, 622
attempt, 676
Enterprising
active, 682
energetic, 171
courageous, 861
Entertain
amuse, 840
support, 707
sociality, 892
an idea, 451, 484
Entertainment
repast, 298
Entêté
obstinate, 606
prejudiced, 481
Enthral
subdue, 749
delight, 829
Enthrone
repute, 873

Enthusiasm
feeling, 821
imagination, 515
love, 897
hope, 850, 858
Enthusiast
game, 840
zealot, 606
Enthusiastic
sensibility, 822
excitability, 825
Enthymeme
reasoning, 476
Entice
motive, 615
Enticing
pleasure, 829
Entire
whole, 50
complete, 52
Entirely
greatness, 31
Entitle
name, 564
give a right, 924
Entity
existence, 1
Entomb
inter, 231, 363
imprison, 751
Entourage
environment, 227
retinue, 746
Entr'acte
interval, 106
Entrails
interior, 221
Entrain
depart, 293
Entrance
beginning, 66
ingress, 294
fee, 809
to enrapture, 824, 829
to conjure, 992
Entrap
deceive, 545
Entre nous
concealment, 528
Entreat
request, 765
Entrechat
leap, 309
Entrée
ingress, 294

Entremet
food, 298
Entrench
defence, 717
Entrepôt
store, 636
mart, 799
Entrepreneur
organizer, 626
Entresol
interjacence, 228
Entrust
consign, 784
lend, 787
charge with, 755
Entry
ingress, 294
beginning, 66
record, 551
evidence, 467
Entwine
join, 43
intersect, 219
convolve, 248
Enumerate
number, 85
Enunciate
publish, 531
inform, 527
affirm, 535
voice, 580
Envelop
invest, 225
conceal, 528
Envelope
covering, 222
enclosure, 232
Envenom
poison, 649
deprave, 659
exasperate, 835, 898
Environs
nearness, 197
circumjacence, 227
Envisage
view, 441
confront, 234
intuition, 477
Envoy
messenger, 534
postscript, 39
Envy
jealousy, 921
Enwrap
invest, 225

Eolith
oldness, 124
Epaulet
badge, 550
decoration, 877
ornament, 847
Éperdu
excited, 824
Ephemeral
transient, 111
changeable, 149
Ephemeris
calendar, 114
record, 551
book, 593
Epic
poem, 597
Epicedium
interment, 363
Epicene
exceptional, 83
multiform, 81
Epicentre
focus, 223
Epicure
sensual, 954
glutton, 957
fastidious, 868
Epicycle
circularity, 247
Epicycloid
circularity, 247
Epidemic
disease, 655
dispersed, 73
general, 78
Epidermis
covering, 222
Epidiascope
spectacle, 448
Epigram
wit, 842
Epigrammatic
pithy, 516
concise, 572
Epigrammatist
humorist, 844
Epigraph
indication, 550
Epilepsy
convulsion, 315
Epilogue
sequel, 65
drama, 599
Episcopal

clergy, 995
Episode
event, 151
interjacence, 228
interruption, 70
Episodic
unrelated, 10
style, 573
Epistle
letter, 592
Epitaph
interment, 363
Epithalamium
marriage, 903
Epithem
remedy, 662
Epithet
nomenclature, 564
Epitome
compendium, 596
conciseness, 572
miniature, 193
Epizootic
insalubrity, 657
Epoch
time, 113
duration, 106
period, 114
Epode
poetry, 597
Epopee
poetry, 597
Épris
love, 897
Equable
right, 922
Equal
equality, 27
equitable, 922
Equanimity
inexcitability, 826
Equate
equality, 27
Equations
numeration, 85
Equator
middle, 68
Equerry
servant, 746
Equestrian
traveller, 268
Equidistant
Middle, 68
Equilibrium
equality, 27

steadiness, 265
Equip
dress, 225
prepare, 673
Equipage
vehicle, 272
instrument, 633
materials, 635
Equipoise
equal, 27
Equipollent
equal, 27
identical, 13
Equiponderant
equal, 27
Equitable
just, 922
fair, 480, 939
due, 924
Equitation
journey, 266
Equity
justice, 922
law, 963
honour, 939
Equivalence
equal, 27
Equivalent
identity, 13
compensation, 30
synonymous, 516
Equivocal
dubious, 475
double meaning, 520, 961
Equivocate
pervert, 477
prevaricate, 520
Equivoque
equivocal, 520
uncertainty, 475
impurity, 961
error, 495
Era
duration, 106
chronology, 114
Eradicate
destroy, 162
extract, 301
Erase
efface, 162, 499, 552
Ere
priority, 116
Ere long
earliness, 132

488

Erebus
 dark, 421
 hell, 982
Erect
 raise, 307
 build, 161
 vertical, 212
Erection
 house, 189
Eremitical
 seclusion, 893
Erewhile
 preterition, 122
 priority, 116
Ergatocracy
 rule, 737
Ergo
 reasoning, 476
Ergotism
 reasoning, 476
Eriometer
 optical, 445
Erk
 fighter, 726
Ermine
 badge of authority, 747
Erode
 destroy, 162
 injure, 659
Erotic
 amorous, 897
 impure, 961
Eroticism
 pleasantness, 829
Err
 in opinion, 495
 morally, 945
Errand
 commission, 755
 business, 625
 message, 532
Erratic
 capricious, 149, 608
 wandering, 264, 279
Erratum
 error, 495
 misprint, 555
Error
 false opinion, 495
 failure, 732
 vice, 945
 guilt, 947
Erst
 preterition, 122
Erubescence

 redness, 434
Eructate
 eject, 297
Erudite
 scholar, 492
Erudition
 knowledge, 490
Eruption
 egress, 295
 violence, 173
 disease, 655
Escalade
 mount, 305
 attack, 716
Escalate
 increase, 35
Escalator
 way, 627
 lift, 307
Escallop
 convolution, 248
Escapade
 freak, 608
 prank, 840
 vagary, 856
Escape
 flight, 671
 liberate, 750
 evade, 927
 forget, 506
Escarpment
 slope, 217
Eschatology
 intention, 620
 end, 67
Escheat
 penalty, 974
Eschew
 avoid, 623
 dislike, 867
Escort
 to accompany, 88
 safeguard, 664
 keeper, 753
Escritoire
 desk, 191
Esculent
 food, 298
Escutcheon
 indication, 550
Esoteric
 private, 79
 concealed, 528
Espalier
 agriculture, 371

Especial
 private, 79
Esperanto
 language, 560
Espial
 vision, 441
Espièglerie
 wit, 842
Espionage
 inquiry, 461
Esplanade
 flat, 213
 plain, 344
Espousal
 marriage, 903
Esprit
 shrewdness, 498
 wit, 842
Esprit de corps
 party, 712
 misjudgment, 781
 belief, 484
 sociality, 892
Esprit fort
 sage, 500
Espy
 vision, 441
Esquire
 title, 877
Essay
 try, 463
 endeavour, 675
 dissertation, 595
Essayist
 writing, 590
Essence
 nature, 5
 existence, 1
 odour, 398
 pith, 642
Essential
 great, 31
 requisite, 630
Establish
 fix, 184
 demonstrate, 478
 evidence, 467
 create, 161
 substantiate, 494
 settle, 150
Established
 received, 82
 habitual, 613
Establishment
 fixture, 141

party, 712
location, 184
Estancia
property, 780
Estate
condition, 7
property, 780
Esteem
judge, 480
believe, 484
approve, 931
Estimable
good, 648
commendable, 931
Estimate
measure, 466
judge, 480
count, 85
Estimation
opinion, 484
respect, 928
good, 648
Estoppage
prohibition, 761
Estrade
horizontal, 213
Estrange
alienate, 449
hate, 898
seclude, 893
Estreat
penalty, 974
Estuary
gulf, 343
Esurient
hungry, 865
État-major
combatant, 726
Etcetera
addition, 37
inclusion, 76
plurality, 100
Etch
engraving, 558
Eternal
perpetuity, 112
Ether
sky, 313, 338
void, 4
vapour, 334
Ethical
virtue, 944
Ethics
duty, 926
Ethiopic

blackness, 431
Ethnic
heathen, 984
racial, 372
Ethnology
mankind, 372
Ethos
nature, 5
Etiolate
bleach, 429, 430
Etiquette
fashion, 852
custom, 613
ceremony, 882
Étude
music, 415
Etymology
word, 562
language, 560
Etymon
origin, 153
verbal, 562
Eucharist
rite, 998
Euchology
rite, 998
Eugenics
production, 161
Eulogy
approval, 931
Euphemism
misnomer, 565
Euphonious
musical, 413
style, 578
Euphony
harmony, 413
Euphoria
health, 654
Euphuism
ornament, 577
affectation, 855
Eurasian
mixture, 41
Eureka
judgment, 480
answer, 462
Eurhythmics
training, 673
Eurhythmy
symmetry, 242
Euroclydon
wind, 349
Euterpe
music, 415

Euthanasia
death, 360
killing, 361
Evacuate
emit, 297
excrete, 299
Evacuee
escape, 671
Evade
avoid, 623
escape, 671
sophistry, 477
dereliction, 927
Evaluate
appraise, 466, 812
Evanescent
transient, 111
minute, 32, 193
disappearing, 449
Evangelist
revelation, 985
Evangelize
convert, 484
Evaporate
vapour, 336
gas, 334
unsubstantiality, 4
Evasion
escape, 623, 671
sophistry, 477
plea, 617
falsehood, 544
untruth, 546
cunning, 702
dereliction, 927
Eve
evening, 126
priority, 116
Even
equal, 27
uniform, 16
level, 213
flat, 251
smooth, 265
straight, 246
although, 179, 469
Even-handed
equitable, 922
honourable, 939
Even so
assent, 488
Evening
evening, 126
Evening
worship, 990

evening, 126
Event
  eventuality, 151
Eventful
  stirring, 151
  remarkable, 642
Eventide
  evening, 126
Eventual
  futurity, 121
Eventuate
  occur, 1
Ever
  always, 112
  seldom, 137
Ever and anon
  repetition, 104
Ever-changing
  mutability, 149
Ever-recurring
  repetition, 104
Evergreen
  newness, 123
  diuturnity, 110
  continuous, 69
  perpetuity, 112
Everlasting
  perpetual, 112, 136
Evermore
  perpetual, 112
Every
  generality, 78
Everyday
  conformity, 82
  perpetuity, 112
Everyman
  mankind, 372
Everywhere
  space, 180, 186
Eviction
  displacement, 185
Evidence
  evidence, 467
Evident
  visible, 446
  certain, 474
  demonstrable, 478
  manifest, 525
Evil
  harm, 619
  wrong, 923
  vice, 945
  producing evil, 649
Evil day
  adversity, 735

Evil eye
  malevolence, 907
  glance, 441
Evil-minded
  malevolent, 907
  vicious, 945
Evil-speaking
  detraction, 934
Evildoer
  maleficent, 913
  badness, 649
  culprit, 949
Evince
  show, 467
  prove, 478
Eviscerate
  extract, 301
  divide, 44
  mutilate, 38
Evoke
  call upon, 765
  excite, 824
Evolution
  numerical, 85
  effect, 154
  development, 161
  turning out, 313
  circuition, 311
Evulsion
  extraction, 301
Ewer
  receptacle, 191
Ex cathedra
  affirmation, 535
  insolence, 885
Ex concesso
  reasoning, 476
  assent, 488
Ex-libris
  label, 550
Ex mero motu
  will, 600
Ex necessitate rei
  destiny, 152
Ex officio
  truth, 494
  authority, 737
  dueness, 924
Ex parte
  evidence, 467
Ex post facto
  preterition, 122
Exacerbate
  increase, 35
  aggravate, 835

exasperate, 173
Exact
  true, 494
  similar, 17
  require, 741
  claim, 924
  tax, 812
Exacting
  severe, 739
Exactly
  just so, 488
Exaggerate
  increase, 35
  overestimate, 482
  misrepresent, 549
  boast, 884
Exalt
  increase, 35
  elevate, 307
  extol, 931
  boast, 884
Exalted
  heroic, 942
Examine
  inquiry, 457, 461
Example
  instance, 82
  pattern, 22
  model, 948
Exanimate
  listless, 683
  lifeless, 360
Exarch
  ruler, 745
  deputy, 759
Exasperate
  increase, 35
  exacerbate, 173
  aggravate, 835
  inflame, 900
Excavate
  dig, 252
Exceed
  surpass, 33
  expand, 194
  transgress, 303
Exceeding
  remaining, 40
Exceedingly
  greatness, 31
Excel
  superiority, 33
  goodness, 648, 650
Excellency
  skill, 698

title, 877
Excellent
  good, 648
  virtuous, 944
Excelsior
  ascent, 305
  height, 206
Except
  subduct, 38
  exclude, 55
Exception
  to a rule, 83
  qualification, 469
  censure, 932
Exceptionable
  vicious, 945
  blameworthy, 932
Exceptional
  special, 79
  irregular, 83
Excerpt
  extract, 596
  choice, 609
Excess
  superiority, 33
  remainder, 40
  redundance, 641
  intemperance, 954
Excessive
  greatness, 31
Exchange
  mutual change, 148
  reciprocalness, 12
  transfer, 783
  barter, 794
  mart, 799
Exchequer
  treasury, 802
Excise
  price, 812
Excision
  subduction, 38
Excitability
  excitement, 825
  irascibility, 901
Excitation
  excitation, 824
Excite
  violent, 173
  morally, 824
  anger, 900
Exclaim
  voice, 580
Exclosure
  region, 181

enclosure, 232
Exclude
  leave out, 55
  prohibit, 761
  ostracize, 893
  subduction, 38
Exclusive
  omitting, 55
  special, 79
  irregular, 83
  unsociable, 893
Excogitation
  thought, 451
  imagination, 515
Excommunicate
  exclude, 55, 893
  hate, 898
  curse, 908
Excoriate
  flay, 226
Excrement
  uncleanness, 653
Excrescence
  projection, 250
  blemish, 848
Excretion
  excretion, 299
Excruciating
  pain, 378, 830
Exculpate
  forgive, 918
  vindicate, 937
  acquit, 970
Excursion
  tour, 266
  circuit, 311
  attack, 716
Excursionist
  traveller, 268
Excursive
  style, 573
Excursus
  appendix, 65
Excuse
  plea, 617
  exempt, 927
  forgive, 918
  vindicate, 937
Exeat
  leave, 760
Exercrable
  bad, 649
  offensive, 830
  nauseous, 867
Execrate

malediction, 908
  hate, 898
Execute
  conduct, 692
  perform, 680, 739
  in law, 771
  music, 415
Executioner
  killing, 361
Executive
  jurisprudence, 965
  directing, 693
  director, 694
Executor
  agent, 690
Exegesis
  interpretation, 522
Exemplar
  prototype, 22
Exemplary
  virtue, 944
Exemplify
  quote, 82
  illustrate, 522
Exempt
  absolve, 927
  free, 748
  permit, 760
Exemption
  exception, 83
  dueness, 924
Exenterate
  extract, 301
  mutilate, 38
Exequatur
  commission, 755
Exequies
  interment, 363
Exercise
  employ, 677
  act, 680
  exert, 686
  teach, 537
  train, 673
  task, 625
Exercitation
  dissertation, 595
  use, 677
Exert
  exertion, 686
Exertion
  physical, 171
Exfoliation
  divestment, 226

Exhalation
vapour, 336
odour, 398
excretion, 299
Exhaust
drain, 638, 789
fatigue, 688
weaken, 160
misemploy, 679
squander, 818
complete, 52, 729
tube, 351
Exhaustless
infinite, 105
plentiful, 639
Exhibit
show, 525
display, 882
Exhilarate
cheer, 836
Exhort
advise, 695
induce, 615
preach, 998
Exhume
interment, 363
past, 122
Exigency
crisis, 8
chance, 621
difficulty, 704
requirement, 630
need, 865
dearth, 640
Exigent
severe, 640
exacting, 832
Exiguous
little, 193
Exile
displace, 185
send out, 297
seclude, 893
punish, 972
Exility
thinness, 203
Existence
being, 1
life, 359
thing, 3
in time, 118
in space, 186
Exit
departure, 293
egress, 295

escape, 671
Exodus
departure, 293
egress, 295
Exogamy
marriage, 903
Exonerate
exempt, 927
vindicate, 937
forgive, 918
acquit, 970
disburden, 705
absolve, 760
release, 756
Exorbitant
enormous, 31
redundant, 641
dear, 814
Exorcise
conjure, 992
Exorcism
theology, 993
Exorcist
heterodoxy, 994
Exordium
beginning, 66
Exosmosis
passage, 302
Exoteric
disclosed, 531
public, 529
Exotic
alien, 10
exceptional, 83
Expand
swell, 194
increase, 35
in breadth, 202
rarefy, 322
in writing, 573
Expanse
space, 180, 202
size, 192
Expansion
space, 180
Expatiate
in writing, 573
in discourse, 582, 584
Expatriate
deport, 295
displace, 185
exclude, 55, 893
Expect
look for, 121, 507
not wonder, 871

hope, 858
Expectorant
remedy, 662
Expectorate
eject, 296
Expedience
utility, 646
Expedient
means, 632
substitute, 634
plan, 626
Expedite
accelerate, 274
earliness, 132
aid, 707
Expedition
speed, 274
activity, 682
warfare, 722
march, 266
Expel
displace, 185
eject, 297
drive from, 289
punish, 972
Expend
use, 677
waste, 638
pay, 809
Expense
price, 812
Expensive
dear, 814
Experience
knowledge, 490
undergo, 821
event, 151
Experienced
skilled, 698
Experiment
trial, 463
endeavour, 675
Experimentum crucis
demonstration, 478
Expert
skill, 698
adept, 700
Experto crede
knowledge, 490
Expiate
atonement, 952
Expire
death, 360
end, 67
breathe out, 349

493

extract, 301
compel, 744
Extortionate
greedy, 865
dear, 814
parsimonious, 819
Extra
additional, 37, 39
supernumerary, 641
store, 636
Extra muros
exteriority, 220
Extra-sensory
occult, 992
thought, 451
immaterial, 317
Extract
take out, 301
part, 51
choice, 609
quotation, 596
Extradite
deport, 55, 270
displace, 185
eject, 297
Extrajudicial
illegal, 964
Extramundane
immateriality, 317
Extramural
exterior, 220
Extraneous
extrinsic, 6
not related, 10
foreign, 57
Extraordinary
unconformity, 83
greatness, 31
Extravagant
exaggerated, 549
irrational, 477
absurd, 497
ridiculous, 853
foolish, 499
redundant, 641
high-priced, 814
prodigal, 818
vulgar, 851
inordinate, 31
Extravaganza
fanciful, 515
burlesque, 853
the drama, 599
Extravasate
excretion, 299

Extreme
greatness, 31
revolutionary, 146
Extremist
zealot, 604
Extremity
end, 67
exterior, 220
Extricate
take out, 301
liberate, 750
deliver, 672
facilitate, 705
Extrinsic
extrinsicality, 6
Extrude
eject, 297
Exuberant
redundant, 641
style, 573
feeling, 821
Exude
excretion, 299
egress, 295
Exult
crow, 836
rejoice, 838
boast, 873, 884
Exuviae
remainder, 40
Eye
organ of sight, 441
opening, 260
circle, 247
Eye-opener
enlightenment, 527
portent, 870
Eye-shade
mask, 530
Eye-witness
evidence, 467
spectator, 414
Eyeglass
optical instrument, 445
Eyeless
blind, 442
Eyelet
opening, 260
Eyesight
vision, 441
Eyesore
ugliness, 846
Eyewash
deception, 545
Eyot

island, 346
Eyre
jurisprudence, 965
Eyrie
abode, 189

Fabian policy
inactivity, 681, 683
delay, 133
Fable
fiction, 546
error, 495
description, 594
Fabric
texture, 329
house, 189
effect, 154
state, 7
Fabricate
make, 161
invent, 515
forge, 544
falsify, 546
Fabulous
imagination, 515
mythical, 979
exaggerated, 549
greatness, 31
non-existent, 2
Façade
front, 234
Face
exterior, 220
front, 234
lining, 224
impudence, 885
confront, 861
aspect, 448
Face about
deviation, 279
Face-cloth
wash, 652
Face down
withstand, 719
Face to face
manifestation, 525
Facet
exterior, 220
Facetious
wit, 842
Facia
indication, 550
Facile
irresolute, 605

persuasible, 602, 615
easy, 705
skilful, 698
Facile princeps
superiority, 33
goodness, 648
Facility
ease, 705
aid, 707
skill, 698
Facing
lining, 224
covering, 222
Façon de parler
meaning, 516
metaphor, 521
exaggeration, 549
phrase, 566
Facsimile
copy, 21
identity, 13
representation, 554
Fact
event, 151
truth, 494
existence, 1, 2
Faction
party, 712
Factious
discord, 713
Factitious
artificial, 544
Factor
numerical, 84
agent, 690
director, 694
consignee, 758
merchant, 797
Factory
workshop, 691
Factotum
manager, 694
employee, 758
Faculty
power, 157
intellect, 450
skill, 698
profession, 625
Fad
caprice, 608
prejudice, 481
fashion, 852
Fade
vanish, 2, 4, 111, 449
dim, 422

expel, 297
lose colour, 429
spoil, 659
droop, 160
change, 149
become old, 124
Fade
insipid, 391
Fade-out
cinema, 599A
Fadge
agreement, 23
Faeces
excretion, 298
foulness, 653
Faery
fabulous being, 979
imagination, 515
Fag
labour, 686
activity, 682
fatigue, 688, 841
drudge, 690
Fag-end
remainder, 40
end, 67
Faggot
bundle, 72
fuel, 388
Fahrenheit
thermometer, 389
Fail
incomplete, 53, 651
shortcoming, 304
non-observance, 732
non-payment, 808
dereliction, 927
droop, 160
break down, 158
reject, 610
vice, 945
Fain
wish, 865
willing, 602
compulsive, 744
Fainéant
idler, 683
Faint
weak, 160
sound, 405
colour, 429
small in degree, 32
swoon, 683, 688
Faint-hearted
coward, 862

fear, 860
Fair
in degree, 31
white, 430
just, 922
impartial, 498
honourable, 939
true, 543
tolerable, 651
pleasing, 829
beautiful, 845
mart, 799
festivity, 840
Fair play
justice, 922
honour, 939
Fair sex
woman, 374
Fair-spoken
courteous, 894
flattering, 933
Fairing
gift, 784
Fairly
great, 31
Fairy
fabulous being, 979
Fairy-cycle
bicycle, 266
Fairy godmother
friend, 891
benefactor, 912
Fairy-tale
lie, 546
Fait accompli
completion, 729
Faith
belief, 484
hope, 858
honour, 939
creed, 983
piety, 987
Faithful
likeness, 17
true, 494
obedient, 743
observant, 772
Christian, 983A
godly, 987
Faithless
false, 544
dishonourable, 940
sceptical, 989
Fake
imitation, 19

496

deception, 545
to forge, 544
Fakir
clergy, 996
Falcated
curved, 245
sharp, 244
Falchion
arms, 727
Falciform
angularity, 244
curvature, 245
Fall
descend, 306
destruction, 162
slope, 217
fail, 732
die, 360
adversity, 735
decline, 659
happen, 151
vice, 945
autumn, 126
Fall away
decrease, 36
shrink, 195
Fall back
recede, 283, 287
relapse, 661
Fall behind
sequence, 281
Fall down
descend, 306.
worship, 990
Fall for
love, 897
Fall foul of
oppose, 708
encounter, 720
reprimand, 932
Fall in
marshal, 58, 60
happen, 151
Fall in with
find, 480A
uniformity, 16
agree, 23
Fall off
deterioration, 659
decrease, 36
disjunction, 44
Fall out
happen, 151
drop, 297
Fall short

shortcoming, 304, 730
fail, 53
insufficiency, 640
Fall through
failure, 732
Fall to
work, 686
devour, 296
fight, 722
Fall to pieces
disjunction, 44
Fall under
inclusion, 76
Fall upon
attack, 716
discover, 480A
devise, 626
Fallacy
error, 495
uncertainty, 475
sophistry, 477
Fal-lal
ornament, 847
trifle, 643
Fallible
uncertain, 475, 477
Fallow
yellow, 436
unproductive, 169
unready, 674
False
untrue, 544
error, 495
sophistry, 477
spurious, 925
dishonourable, 940
False-hearted
improbity, 940
Falsehood
lie, 546
Falsetto
music, 413
affected, 577
Falsify
misinterpret, 523
accounts, 811
deceive, 495
lie, 544
Falstaffian
fat, 192
Falter
stammer, 583
hesitate, 605
demur, 603
slowness, 275

Fame
renown, 873
rumour, 531
news, 532
Familiar
common, 82
habit, 613
known, 490
friendly, 888
affable, 892, 894
spirit, 979
Family
class, 75
consanguinity, 11
paternity, 166
posterity, 167
Famine
insufficiency, 640
Famished
fasting, 956
Famous
repute, 873
greatness, 31
Fan
blow, 349
excite, 615
enthusiast, 840, 865
frequenter, 136
Fanatic
extravagant, 515
Fanatical
feeling, 821
Fanaticism
folly, 499
obstinacy, 606
religious, 984A
Fanciful
capricious, 608
imaginative, 515
mistaken, 495
unreal, 2
Fancy
think, 451
believe, 484
wit, 842
idea, 453
suppose, 514
imagine, 515
caprice, 608
choice, 609
desire, 865
like, 394
love, 897
pugilism, 726

Fandango
dance, 840
Fane
temple, 1000
Fanfare
loudness, 404
ostentation, 882
Fanfaronade
boasting, 884
Fang
bane, 663
Fanlight
opening, 260
Fantasia
music, 415
imagination, 515
Fantastic
odd, 83
imaginary, 515
capricious, 608
ridiculous, 853
Fantasy
caprice, 608
imagination, 515
idea, 453
Fantoccini
marionettes, 554, 599
Far
distant, 196
Far-fetched
irrelation, 10
irrelevant, 24
irrational, 477
obscure, 519
Far from it
dissimilarity, 18
Far-seeing
foresight, 510
Farce
drama, 599
ridiculous, 856
Farceur
humorist, 844
Farcical
ridiculous, 856
witty, 842
trifling, 643
Fardel
assemblage, 72
Fare
circumstance, 8
event, 151
to eat, 296
food, 298
price, 812
Farewell

departure, 293
Farm
house, 189
property, 780
to rent, 788, 795
Farrago
mixture, 41
confusion, 59
Farthing
coin, 800
worthless, 643
Farthingale
dress, 225
Fasces
sceptre, 747
Fascia
band, 205
circle, 247
Fascicle
assemblage, 72
Fascinate
please, 829
excite, 824, 825
astonish, 870
love, 897
conjure, 992
Fascination
spell, 993
motive, 615
occult arts, 992
Fash
worry, 830
Fashion
form, 144, 240
custom, 613
mould, 140
mode, 627, 852
nobility, 875
Fast
rapid, 274
steadfast, 150
stuck, 265
joined, 43
dissolute, 954
not to eat, 640, 956
Fast and loose
false, 544
changeful, 607
Fasten
join, 45, 214
fix, 150
restrain, 751
Fastener
hanging, 214
Fastening

vinculum, 45
Fastidious
dainty, 868
squeamish, 932
Fasting
abstinence, 956
atonement, 952
insufficient, 640
Fastness
asylum, 666
defence, 717
Fat
oleaginous, 356
unctuous, 355
broad, 202
big, 192
Fat-head
fool, 501
Fat-witted
folly, 499
Fata morgana
phantasm, 4
dim sight, 443
imagination, 515
Fatal
lethal, 361
pernicious, 649
Fatalism
destiny, 152
necessity, 601
Fatality
killing, 361
Fate
necessity, 601
chance, 152, 621
end, 67, 360
Father
paternity, 166
priest, 996
theologian, 983
Father upon
attribute, 155
Fatherland
home, 189
Fatherless
unsustained, 160
Fathom
measure, 466
investigate, 461
answer, 462
Fathomless
depth, 208
Fatidical
prediction, 511
Fatigue

lassitude, 688
weariness, 841

Fatras
unimportance, 643

Fatten on
feeding, 296

Fatuity
folly, 499

Faubourg
suburb, 227

Fauces
beginning, 66

Faucet
opening, 260
channel, 350
outlet, 295

Faugh!
dislike, 867

Fault
imperfection, 651
blemish, 848
break, 70
vice, 945
guilt, 947
error, 495
failure, 732
ignorance, 491

Faultless
perfect, 650
innocent, 946

Fauna
animal, 366

Faute de mieux
shift, 147, 626

Fauteuil
support, 215

Faux pas
failure, 732
error, 495
vice, 945

Favour
aid, 707
permit, 760
friendship, 888
partiality, 923
gift, 784
letter, 592
to resemble, 17

Favourable
good, 648
willing, 602
friendly, 707, 888
co-operating, 709

Favourite
pleasing, 829

beloved, 897, 899

Favouritism
wrong, 923

Fawn
colour, 433
cringe, 886
flatter, 933

Fay
fairy, 979

Faze
worry, 830
discompose, 458
perplex, 704

Fealty
duty, 926
respect, 928
obedience, 743

Fear
fear, 860
cowardice, 862

Fearful
great, 31

Fearless
hopeful, 858
courageous, 861

Feasible
possible, 470
easy, 705

Feast
repast, 298
to devour, 296
gluttony, 957
revel, 840
enjoyment, 827
celebration, 883
anniversary, 138

Feast on
enjoy, 377

Feat
action, 680

Feather
tuft, 256
lightness, 320
trifle, 643
class, 75
ornament, 847
decoration, 877

Feather-bed
softness, 324

Feathery
roughness, 256

Feature
character, 5
form, 240
appearance, 448

lineament, 550
component, 56
to resemble, 17
cinema, 599A

Febrifuge
remedy, 662

Fecit
painting, 556

Feckless
feeble, 160
improvident, 674
useless, 645

Feculence
uncleanness, 653

Fecund
productive, 168

Fecundation
production, 161

Fed up
weariness, 841
dislike, 867
satiety, 869

Federation
co-operation, 709
party, 712

Fee
expenditure, 795, 809

Fee simple
property, 780

Feeble
weak, 160
imperfect, 651
scanty, 32
silly, 477
style, 575

Feeble-minded
foolish, 499
irresolute, 605

Feed
eat, 296
supply, 637
meal, 298

Feel
touch, 379
sensibility, 375
moral, 821

Feel for
seek, 461
sympathize, 914

Feeler
inquiry, 461

Feet
journey, 266

Feign
falsehood, 544

Feint
deception, 545
Felicitate
congratulate, 896
Felictious
expedient, 646
favourable, 648
skilful, 698
successful, 731
happy, 827
elegant, 578
apt, 23
Felicity
happiness, 827
prosperity, 734
skill, 698
Feline
stealthy, 528
sly, 702
Fell
mountain, 206
cut down, 308
knock down, 213
dire, 162
wicked, 907
Fellah
commonalty, 876
Fellow
similar, 17
equal, 27
companion, 88
man, 373
dual, 89
Fellow creature
man, 372, 373
Fellow-feeling
love, 897
friendship, 888
sympathy, 906, 914
Fellowship
sociality, 892
partnership, 712
friendship, 888
Felo-de-se
killing, 361
Felon
sinner, 949
Felonious
vice, 945
Felony
guilt, 947
Felt
matted, 219
Felucca
ship, 273

Female
woman, 374
Feminality
feebleness, 160
Feminine
woman, 374
Feminism
rights, 924
Femme couverte
marriage 903
Femme de chambre
servant, 746
Fen
marsh, 345
Fence
circumscribe, 231
enclose, 232
defence, 717
fight, 720, 722P
safety, 664
refuge, 666
prison, 752
to evade, 544
Fencible
combatant, 726
Fend
defence, 717
provision, 637
Fenestrated
windowed, 260
Feoff
property, 780
Ferine
malevolence, 907
Ferment
disorder, 59
energy, 171
violence, 173
agitation, 315
effervesce, 353
Fern
plant, 367
Ferocity
brutality, 907
violence, 173
Ferret
tape, 45
Ferret out
inquiry, 461
discover, 480A
Ferry
transference, 270
way, 627
Fertile
productive, 168

abundant, 639
Ferule
scourge, 975
Fervent
devout, 990
Fervour
heat, 382
animation, 821
desire, 865
love, 897
Fester
disease, 655
corruption, 653
Festina lente
haste, 684
Festival
celebration, 883
anniversary, 138
Festive
amusement, 840
sociality, 892
Festoon
ornament, 847
curvature, 245
Fetch
bring, 270
arrive, 292
stratagem, 626
evasion, 545
price, 812
Fête
amusement, 840
ostentation, 882
celebration, 883
convivial, 892
Fête champêtre
amusement, 840
Fetid
fetor, 401
Fetish
spell, 993
Fetishism
idolatry, 991P
sorcery, 992
Fetter
hinder, 706
restrain, 751
shackle, 752
join, 43
Fettle
preparation, 673
Fetus
see Foetus
Feud
discord, 713

revenge, 919
Feudal
authority, 737
Feudatory
subjection, 749
Feu de joie
firework, 840
salute, 882
Feuilleton
essay, 595
Fever
heat, 382
disease, 655
excitement, 825
Few
fewness, 103
plurality, 100
Fez
cap, 225
Fiancée
love, 897
Fiasco
failure, 732
Fiat
command, 741
Fib
falsehood, 544, 546
Fibre
link, 45
filament, 205
Fibrous
thin, 203
Fichu
dress, 225
Fickle
irresolute, 605
Fictile
form, 240
Fiction
untruth, 546
fancy, 515
story, 594
Fictitious
false, 544
Fiddle
to play, 415
violin, 417
deceive, 545
swindle, 791
falsify, 544
Fiddle-de-dee
trifling, 643
contemptible, 930
Fiddle-faddle
trifle, 643

dawdle, 683
Fiddler
musician, 416
Fiddlestick
contemptible, 930
absurd, 497
trifling, 643
Fiddling
trifling, 643
Fidelity
honour, 939
observance, 772
Fidget
excitability, 825
irascibility, 901
agitation, 315
activity, 682
Fidgety
changeable, 149
Fido
mist, 353
Fiducial
belief, 484
Fidus Achates
auxiliary, 711
Fie!
disrepute, 874
Fief
property, 780
Field
plain, 344
arena, 728
scope, 180
business, 625
property, 780
Field-day
pageant, 882
festivity, 840
Field-marshal
master, 745
Field of view
vista, 441
idea, 453
Field-piece
arms, 727
Fiend
demon, 980
ruffian, 913
Fiendish
malevolent, 907
wicked, 945
Fierce
violent, 173
passion, 825
daring, 861

angry, 900
Fiery
violent, 173
excitable, 825
hot, 382
fervent, 821
Fiery cross
warfare, 722
Fife
musical instrument, 417
Fifth columnist
traitor, 742
Fig
unimportant, 643
dress, 225
adorn, 845, 847
Fight
contention, 720, 722
Fighter
combatant, 726
aircraft, 273A
Fighter-bomber
aircraft, 273A
Figment
imagination, 515
Figurante
the drama, 599
Figuration
form, 240
Figurative
metaphorical, 521
style, 577
comparison, 464
Figure
state, 7
number, 84
price, 812
form, 240
metaphor, 521, 566
imagine, 515
represent, 550, 554
reputation, 873
ugliness, 846
parade, 882
Figurehead
effigy, 554
inaction, 683
Figurine
sculpture, 557
Fike
whim, 481
Filament
slender, 205
ligature, 45
light, 423

501

Filamentous
thin, 203
Filch
steal, 791, 792
File
to smooth, 255
to pulverize, 330
to string together, 60
row, 69
duality, 89
collection, 72
list, 86
store, 636
register, 551
File off
march, 266
diverge, 291
Filial
posterity, 167
Filiation
consanguinity, 11
posterity, 167
derivation, 155
Filibeg
dress, 225
Filibuster
thief, 792
delay, 133
Filigree
crossing, 219
Filings
pulverulence, 330
Fill
occupy, 186
fullness, 52
Fill out
expand, 194
Fill up
complete, 52
close, 261
satisfy, 639
composition, 54
compensate, 30
Fille de joie
libertine, 962
Fillet
band, 45
circle, 247
gut, 297
Filling
contents, 190
Fillip
stimulus, 615
impulse, 276
propulsion, 284

Filly
horse, 271
young, 129
Film
layer, 204
dimness, 421, 426
semitransparency, 427
cinema, 599A
Filmy
texture, 329
Filter
clean, 652
percolate, 295
amend, 658
Filth
uncleanness, 653
Filtration
passage, 302
Fimbriated
rough, 256
Fin
instrument, 267, 633
Final
end, 67
conclusive, 478
resolved, 604
Finale
music, 415
Finance
money, 800
accounts, 811
Find
discover, 480A
term, 71
provide, 637
sentence, 969
acquisition, 775
Fine
rare, 322
textural, 329
good, 648
beautiful, 845
adorned, 847
thin, 203
mulct, 974
to clarify, 652
Fine-draw
improve, 658
Fine-spoken
courtesy, 894
Fine-spun
thinness, 203
Finery
ornament, 847
Finesse

cunning, 702
manœuvre, 545
tact, 698
taste, 850
Finger
touch, 379
instrument, 633
Finger-post
indication, 550
Finger-print
evidence, 467
sign, 550
Finical
unimportant, 643
Finicky
fastidious, 868
Finikin
unimportant, 643
Finis
end, 67
Finish
complete, 52
achieve, 729
end, 67
symmetry, 242
Finished
perfect, 242, 650
accomplished, 698
greatness, 31
Finite
smallness, 32
Fiord
gulf, 343
Fire
heat, 382, 384
furnace, 386
vigour, 574
energy, 171
to excite, 825
to urge, 615
dismiss, 756
Fire at
attack, 716
Fire away
begin, 66
Fire-brigade
cooling, 385
Fire-bug
incendiary, 384
Fire-drake
light, 423
Fire-eater
blusterer, 887
Fire-eater
fury, 173, 901

cooling, 385
Fire-escape
escape, 671
Fireoff
propulsion, 284
Fire-place
furnace, 386
Fire-ship
ship, 273
burning, 384
Fireup
resentment, 900
Fire-worshipper
heathen, 984
Firebrand
brand, 388
incendiary, 913
Firefly
luminary, 423
Firelock
arms, 727
Fireman
cooling, 385
Fireproof
incombustible, 385
safe, 664
Fireside
abode, 189
Firework
fire, 382
light, 423
display, 882
celebration, 883
Firing
fuel, 388
explosion, 406
Firkin
receptacle, 191
Firm
hard, 323
junction, 43
stable, 150
resolute, 604
brave, 861
party, 712
partnership, 797
friendship, 888
Firmament
world, 318
Firman
order, 741
permit, 760
decree, 963
First
beginning, 66

First-born
age, 124, 128
First-rate
ship, 273
excellent, 648
superiority, 33
First string
proficient, 700
First to last, from
whole, 50
completeness, 52
duration, 106
Firth
gulf, 343
Fisc
treasury, 802
Fiscal
money, 800
Fish
animal, 366
Fish for
desire, 865
Fish out
discover, 480A
Fish out of water
disagreement, 24
Fish up
elevation, 307
Fishery
domestication, 370
Fishy
dubious, 475, 478
Fissile
brittle, 328
Fission
disjunction, 44
Fissure
chink, 198
Fist
writing, 590
Fistula
opening, 260
Fit
state, 7
paroxysm, 173
disease, 655
caprice, 608
to prepare, 673
equalize, 27
excitement, 825
anger, 900
duty, 926
agreement, 23
expedient, 646
right, 922

Fit out
preparation, 673
Fitful
capricious, 608
irresolute, 605
discontinuous, 70
irregular, 139
Fitness
agreement, 23
Fitting
expedient, 646
right, 922, 926
due, 924
instrument, 633
Five
number, 98
Fiver
money, 800
Fix
place, 150, 184
rectify, 658, 660
solidify, 321
arrangement, 60
situation, 8
difficulty, 704
Fix together
junction, 43
Fix upon
choose, 609
Fixed
determined, 604
permanent, 141, 150
quiescent, 265
Fixture
property, 780
stability, 150
Fizgig
firework, 423
Fizz
sibilation, 409
bubble, 353
Fizzle
hiss, 409
Fizzle out
failure, 158, 732
Fjord
see Fiord
Flabbergast
astound, 870
Flabby
soft, 324
Flaccid
shrivelled, 172, 193
soft, 324
empty, 640

Flag
streamer, 550
flat stone, 204
weakness, 160
floor, 211
droop, 688
inactive, 683
infirm, 160, 655
slowness, 275
Flagellation
flogging, 972
atonement, 952
asceticism, 955
Flageolet
musical, 417
Flagitious
vice, 945
Flagrant
notorious, 531
manifest, 525
great, 31
atrocious, 945
Flagstaff
sign, 550
high, 206
Flail
impulse, 276
Flair
intelligence, 498
Flake
layer, 204
Flam
untruth, 546
Flambeau
luminary, 423
Flamboyant
vulgar, 851
ornamented, 577, 847
Flame
light, 420
fire, 382
luminary, 423
passion, 825
love, 897
favourable, 899
Flame-coloured
orange, 439
Flaming
excited, 821, 825
Flâneur
idler, 683
Flange
support, 215
Flank
side, 236

safety, 664
Flannel
flattery, 933
Flannels
dress, 225
Flap
adjunct, 39
hanging, 214
move about, 315
beat, 972
fear, 860
Flapdoodle
deception, 546
nonsense, 497
Flapjack
receptacle, 191
Flapper
girl, 129, 374
Flapping
loose, 47
Flare
glare, 420
violence, 173
Flare up
kindle, 825
anger, 900
Flaring
colour, 428
Flash
instant, 113
fire, 382
light, 420
thought, 451
sudden act, 612
violence, 173
Flash-lamp
light, 423
Flash note
money, 800
Flashback
memory, 505
cinema, 599A
Flashy
gaudy colour, 428
bad taste, 851
ostentatious, 882
Flask
receptacle, 191
Flat
level, 251
uniform, 16
horizontal, 213
novice, 701
dupe, 547
low, 207

vapid, 391
inert, 172, 823
dull, 841, 843
insipid, 575
dejected, 837
sound, 408
indifferent, 866
positive, 535
abode, 189
apartment, 191
Flatlet
abode, 189
Flatter
pleasure, 829
encourage, 858
adulation, 933
servility, 886
Flatterer
eulogist, 935
Flattie
detective, 461
cinema, 599A
Flatulent
windy, 338
gaseous, 334
style, 573
Flaunt
display, 873, 882
gaudy, 428
ornament, 847
Flautist
musician, 416
Flavour
taste, 390
Flavous
yellow, 436
Flaw
crack, 198
error, 495
imperfection, 651
blemish, 848
fault, 947
Flay
divest, 226
punish, 972
Flea-bag
bed, 215
Flea-bite
trifle, 643
Flea-bitten
variegated, 440
Fleckered
variegation, 440
Fledged
preparation, 673

Flee
  escape, 671
  avoid, 623
Fleece
  tegument, 222
  to rob, 791
  to strip, 789
  impoverish, 804
Fleer
  ridicule, 956
Fleet
  swift, 274
  ships, 273
Fleeting
  transient, 111
  changeful, 607
Flesh
  mankind, 372
  carnality, 961
Flesh colour
  redness, 434
Flesh-pots
  food, 298
Fleshly
  sensual, 954, 961
Fleshy
  corpulent, 192
Flexible
  pliant, 324
  tractable, 705
Flexion
  bending, 245
  deviation, 279
  fold, 258
Flexuous
  convolution, 248
Flexure
  bending, 245
  fold, 258
Flibbertigibbet
  trifler, 460
Flick
  propel, 284
  cinema, 599A
Flicker
  flutter, 315
  oscillate, 314
  waver, 149, 605
  shine, 420
Flickering
  irregular, 139
Flight
  departure, 287, 293
  escape, 671
  volitation, 267

  swiftness, 174
  multitude, 102
Flight-lieutenant
  master, 745
Flight of Fancy
  imagination, 515
  idea, 453
Flighty
  insane, 503
  fickle, 605
Flim-flam
  lie, 546
  caprice, 608
Flimsy
  texture, 329
  soft, 324
  irrational, 477
  trifling, 643
  frail, 160, 651
  manuscript, 590
Flinch
  fear, 850, 862
  avoid, 623
  swerve, 607
Fling
  propel, 284
  censure, 932
  attack, 716
  jeer, 929
  amusement, 840
Fling away
  relinquish, 782
Flint
  hardness, 323
Flint-hearted
  malevolence, 907
Flip
  propel, 284
  aviation, 267
Flippant
  pert, 885
  fluent, 584
Flipper
  fin, 267
Flirt
  propel, 284
  coquette, 902
Flit
  move, 264, 266
  fluctuate, 149
  depart, 293
  escape, 671
  swift, 274
  thought, 451
Flitter

  flutter, 315
Flitting
  evanescent, 111, 149
  roving, 266
Float
  navigate, 267
  buoy up, 305
  lightness, 320
Float
  sound, 405
  vehicle, 272
Floater
  error, 495, 732
  solecism, 568
Flocculent
  soft, 324
  pulverulent, 330
Flock
  herd, 366
  assemblage, 72, 102
  laity, 997
Flog
  punishment, 972
  steal, 791
Flong
  engraving, 558
Flood
  water, 348
  abundance, 639
  multitude, 72
  superfluity, 641
  increase, 35
  of light, 420
Floodgate
  conduit, 350
Floor
  base, 221
  level, 23
  horizontal, 213
  support, 215
  to puzzle, 485, 704
  to overthrow, 731
Floosy
  girl, 374
Flop
  flutter, 315
  failure, 732
Flora
  plant, 367, 379
Florid
  colour, 428
  red, 434
  health, 654
  style, 577

Flotilla
  ship, 273
Flotsam
  fragments, 51
  little, 643
Flounce
  quick motion, 274
  agitation, 315
  trimming, 230
  fold, 258
Flounder
  toss, 315
  waver, 314
  mistake, 495
  to blunder, 499, 699,
    732
  struggle, 704
Flourish
  brandish, 314
  succeed, 731, 734
  display, 873, 882
  boast, 884
  exaggerate, 549
  of speech, 577, 582
Flout
  mock, 856, 929
  sneer, 929
Flow
  stream, 347
  motion, 264
  course, 109
  result from, 154
Flow out
  egress, 295
Flow over
  run over, 348
  abound, 641
Flower
  plant, 367
  beauty, 845
  perfection, 648, 650
  prosper, 734
  produce, 161
  of life, 127
  of speech, 577P
  honour, 873
Flowing
  style, 573
  sound, 405
  abundant, 639
Fluctuate
  oscillate, 314
  wavering, 605
Flue
  air-pipe, 351
  egress, 295

opening, 260
down, 320
dross, 643, 653
Fluent
  speech, 584
  style, 573
  flowing, 348
  skilful, 698
Fluff
  lightness, 320
Fluid
  liquidity, 333
Fluke
  angularity, 244
  chance, 621
Flummery
  vain, 643
  flattery, 933
  absurd, 497
Flummox
  bewilder, 458
Flunk
  break down, 158
Flunkey
  lackey, 746
  toady, 886
  flatterer, 935
Fluorescence
  light, 420
Flurry
  hurry, 684
  discompose, 458
  agitation, 821, 825
Flush
  flat, 251
  flood, 348
  heat, 382
  light, 420
  redness, 434
  abundance, 639
  feeling, 821
  passion, 825
  series, 69
  flock, 72
  rich, 803
  in liquor, 959
Flushed
  elated, 836, 884
  vain, 880
  proud, 878
Fluster
  excitement, 824
  fuss, 682
  discompose, 458
Flustered

tipsy, 959
Flute
  musical, 417
Fluted
  furrow, 259
Flutter
  move, 315
  fear, 860
  feeling, 821, 824, 825
Fluviatile
  river, 348
Flux
  flow, 109, 348
  excretion, 299
  motion, 264
  oscillation, 314
  changes, 140
Fly
  depart, 293
  take wing, 287
  speed, 274
  escape, 671
  recede, 287
  shun, 623
  run away, 862
  lose colour, 429
  minute, 193
  time, 109, 111
  burst, 173, 328
  vehicle, 272
  clever, 498
  cunning, 702
Fly at
  attack, 716
Fly back
  recoil, 277
  elastic, 325
Fly-down
  unclean, 653
Fly-leaf
  insertion, 228
  book, 593
Fly out
  burst, 173
  passion, 825
  anger, 900
Fly-boat
  ship, 273
Flying boat
  aircraft, 273A
Flying bomb
  arms, 727
Flying fortress
  aircraft, 273A

506

Flying wing
aircraft, 273A
Flyover
way, 627
Flyte
curse, 908
Flywheel
instrument, 633
rotation, 312
Foal
young, 129
carrier, 271
Foam
spray, 353
passion, 173, 900
Fob
pocket, 191
to cheat, 545
evade, 773
Focus
reunion, 74
centre, 223
Fodder
food, 298
Foe
antagonist, 710
enemy, 891
Foetid
see Fetid
Foetus
infant, 129
Fog
cloud, 353
dimness, 422
Foggy
obscure, 447
shaded, 426
Fogy
veteran, 130
Föhn
wind, 349
Foible
vice, 945
Foil
contrast, 14
success, 731
Foiled
failure, 732
Foist in
insert, 228, 300
Foist upon
deception, 545
Fold
plait, 258
enclosure, 232

pen, 752
congregation, 996
bisect, 91
Foliaceous
layer, 204
Foliage
plant, 367
Foliated
layer, 204
Folio
book, 593
Folk
man, 373
Folk-dance
dance, 840
Folk-tale
legend, 594
Follicle
hollow, 252
opening, 260
cyst, 191
Follow
in order, 63
in time, 117
in motion, 281
to imitate, 19
pursue, 622
result from, 154
understand, 518
demonstration, 478
obey, 743
Follow on
continue, 143
Follow suit
conformity, 82
Follow up
inquiry, 461
Follower
sequence, 281
partisan, 746
Folly
irrationality, 499
nonsense, 497
building, 189
Foment
promote, 707
excite, 173
Fond
love, 897
Fondle
endearment, 902
Fondling
favourite, 899
Fondness
love, 897

desire, 865
Font
altar, 1000
Food
eatable, 298
materials, 635, 637
Fool
silly, 501
to deceive, 548
Foolhardy
rashness, 863
Foolish
unwise, 499
trifling, 643
irrational, 477, 497
misguided, 699
Foot
stand, 211
metre, 597
Foot it
walk, 266
dance, 840
Foot-pace
slowness, 275
Footfall
motion, 264
trace, 551
Foothold
influence, 175
support, 215
Footing
situation, 8, 183
state, 7
foundation, 211
place, 58
rank, 71
influence, 175
Footle
trifle, 683
Footlights
drama, 599
Footling
silly, 499
Footman
servant, 746
Footmark
record, 551
Footpad
thief, 792
Footpath
way, 627
Footprint
record, 551
Footslog
journey, 266

Footstep
record, 551
Footstool
support, 215
Foozle
bungle, 699, 732
Fop
fop, 854
Foppery
affectation, 855
For
reason, 476
motive, 615
For good
diuturnity, 110
Forage
provision, 637
booty, 793
to steal, 791
food, 298
Forage-cap
dress, 225
Foraminous
opening, 260
Forasmuch as
reasoning, 476
Foray
attack, 716
robbery, 791
havoc, 619
Forbear
avoid, 623
spare, 678
pity, 914
abstain, 953
lenity, 740
forgiveness, 918
sufferance, 826
Forbears
ancestors, 130, 166
Forbid
prohibit, 761
Forbidding
repulsive, 289, 846
Forby
addition, 37
Force
power, 157
validity, 476
strength, 159
agency, 170
energy, 171
to compel, 744
rape, 961
to induce, 615

of style, 574
waterfall, 348
Forced
out of place, 10, 24
Forceps
extraction, 301
retention, 781
Ford
way, 627
Fore
front, 234
care, 459
Fore and aft
whole, 50
Forearmed
preparation, 673
Forebode
prediction, 511
Forecast
foresee, 510
predict, 511
plan, 626
prepare, 673
Foreclose
hindrance, 706
Foredoom
necessity, 601
Forefather
old, 130
ancestor, 166
Foregoing
past, 122
preceding, 62
Foreground
front, 234
Forehead
front, 234
Foreign
alien, 10
extraneous, 57
Forejudge
misjudgment, 481
Foreknow
foresight, 510
Foreland
high, 206
projection, 250
Foreman
director, 694
Foremost
front, 234
beginning, 66
superior, 33
Forename
name, 564

Forenoon
morning, 125
Forensic
jurisprudence, 965
Foreordain
predestine, 152, 601
Forerun
priority, 116
precession, 280
Forerunner
in order, 64
in time, 116
omen, 512
Foresee
foreknow, 510
expect, 507, 871
Foreshadow
prediction, 511
Foreshorten
shortness, 201
Foresight
foresight, 510
Forest
plant, 367
Forestall
early, 132
priority, 116
futurity, 121
expect, 507
possess, 777
Forestry
agriculture, 371
Foretaste
foresight, 510
Foretell
prediction, 511
priority, 116
Forethought
care, 459
Foretoken
prediction, 511
Forewarn
warn, 668
advise, 695
predict, 511
Foreword
preamble, 64
front, 234
Forfeit
lose, 776
fail, 773
undueness, 925
penalty, 974
Forfend
guard, 717

hinder, 706
Forge
produce, 161
furnace, 386
workshop, 691
trump up, 544
Forge ahead
advance, 282
Forgery
untruth, 546
imitation, 19
Forget
oblivion, 506
Forgive
foregiveness, 918
Forgo
relinquish, 624, 782
renounce, 757
Forgotten
unremembered, 506
ingratitude, 917
Fork
angularity, 244
bisection, 91
Fork out
give, 784
expend, 809
Forlorn
abandoned, 893
dejected, 837
woebegone, 828
Forlorn hope
hopeless, 859
danger, 665
Form
shape, 240
state, 7
arrange, 60
rule, 80
to make up, 54
produce, 161
educate, 537
habituate, 613
bench, 215
part, 569
fashion, 852
etiquette, 882
law, 963
rite, 998
fours, 58
manner, 627
beauty, 845
likeness, 21
pupils, 541
Formal

regular, 82
affected, 855
positive, 535
Formalism
hypocrisy, 988
Formality
ceremony, 852
parade, 882
law, 963
Format
style, 7
Formation
production, 161
shape, 240
Formed of
composition, 54
Former
in order, 62
in time, 122
Formication
itching, 380
Formidable
fear, 860
difficult, 704
great, 31
Formless
amorphism, 241
Formula
rule, 80
precept, 697
law, 963
number, 84
Fornication
impurity, 961
Fornicator
libertine, 962
Forsake
relinquish, 624
Forsooth
truth, 494
Forswear
renounce, 624
retract, 607
refuse, 764
perjure, 544, 940
violate, 927
Fort
defence, 717
refuge, 666
Forte
excellence, 698
Forte
loudness, 404
Forth
progression, 282

Forthcoming
futurity, 121, 673
Forthwith
transient, 111
Fortification
defence, 717
refuge, 666
Fortify
strength, 159
Fortitude
courage, 861
endurance, 826
Fortnight
period, 108, 138
Fortress
defence, 716
prison, 752
Fortuitous
chance, 156, 621
Fortunate
opportune, 134
prosperous, 734
Fortune
chance, 156
accident, 621
wealth, 803
Fortune-teller
oracle, 513
Fortune-telling
prediction, 511
Forum
tribunal, 966
school, 542
Forward
early, 132
to advance, 282
to help, 707
active, 682
willing, 602
vain, 880
impertinent, 885
Fosse
furrow, 259
gap, 198
defence, 717
enclosure, 232
Fossick
inquiry, 461
Fossil
antiquated, 851
old, 124
bore, 841
Foster
aid, 707

Fou
drunken, 959
Foul
bad, 649
corrupt, 653
odour, 401
offensive, 830
ugly, 846
vicious, 945
Foul-mouthed
malevolent, 907
Foul-tongued
scurrilous, 934
Found
cause, 153
prepare, 673
Foundation
base, 211
support, 215
Founder
originator, 164
sink, 310, 732
Foundling
outcast, 893
Fount
origin, 153
spring, 348
type, 591
Fountain
cause, 153
river, 348
store, 636
Fountain-pen
writing, 590
Four
number, 95
Four-square
number, 95
Fourfold
number, 96
Fourscore
number, 98
Fourth
number, 97
Fowl
animal, 366
Fowling-piece
arms, 727
Fox
cunning, 702
Fox-trot
dance, 840
Foxhole
refuge, 666
defence, 717
Foxhound

chase, 622
Foyer
room, 191
Fracas
contention, 720
brawl, 713
Fraction
part, 51
numerical, 84
Fractious
irascibility, 901
Fracture
disjunction, 44
discontinuity, 70, 198
to break, 328
Fragile
brittle, 328
frail, 149, 160
Fragment
part, 51
Fragrant
fragrant, 400
'Fraid-cat
coward, 862
Frail
brittle, 328
mutable, 149
weak, 160
irresolute, 605
imperfect, 651
unchaste, 961
failing, 945
Frame
condition, 7
support, 215
texture, 329
form, 240
substance, 316
to construct, 161
border, 230
Franc-tireur
fighter, 726
Franchise
right, 924
freedom, 748
exemption, 927
Franciscan
clergy, 996
Frangible
brittle, 328
Frank
artless, 703
open, 525
sincere, 543
honourable, 939

Frankincense
fragrant, 400
Frantic
delirious, 503
violent, 173
excited, 825
Fraternal
brotherly, 11
friendly, 888, 906
Fraternity
assemblage, 72
company, 712, 892
Fraternize
co-operate, 709
harmonize, 714
Fratricide
killing, 361
Fraud
deception, 544, 545
dishonour, 940
Fraught
having, 777
full of, 639
Fray
contention, 720
to abrade, 331
Freak
caprice, 608
unconformity, 83
Freakish
irresolution, 605
Freckle
blemish, 848
Freckled
variegation, 440
Free
detached, 44
at liberty, 748
spontaneous, 600, 602
exempt, 927
unobstructed, 705
liberal, 816
gratuitous, 815
insolent, 885
Free-born
freedom, 748
Free gift
giving, 784
Free play
freedom, 748
Free-spoken
veracity, 543
Free-thinking
religion, 989

Free will
will, 600
Freebooter
thief, 792
Freedom
liberty, 748
looseness, 47
full play, 705
exemption, 927
space, 180
Freehold
property, 780
freedom, 748
Freelance
writer, 590
Freemasonry
secrecy, 528
sign, 550
fraternity, 712
co-operation, 709
Freeze
frigefaction, 385
stop dead, 265
Freight
contents, 190
cargo, 798
transfer, 270
Freight train
vehicle, 272
Frenzy
insanity, 503
Frequency
repetition, 104
Frequent
in time, 136
in number, 102
in space, 186
Fresco
painting, 556
Fresh
new, 123
cold, 383
colour, 428
unforgotten, 505
healthy, 654
good, 648
cheeky, 885
tipsy, 959
Freshet
flood, 348
Freshman
learner, 541
Fret
suffer, 378
grieve, 828

to gall, 830
sadness, 837
to irritate, 900
adorn, 847
Fretful
irascibility, 901
Fretwork
crossing, 219
Freya
love, 897
Friable
pulverulence, 330
Friar
clergy, 996
Friar's lantern
light, 423
Fribble
trifle, 460, 643
dawdle, 683
Friction
rubbing, 331
obstacle, 179
discord, 713
Friend
well-wisher, 890
relation, 11
auxiliary, 711
Friendless
seclusion, 893
Friendly
amical, 714, 888
helping, 707
Friendship
amical, 714, 888
Frieze
summit, 210
Frig
refrigerator, 387
Frigate
ship, 273
Frigga
goddess, 979
Fright
alarm, 860
ugliness, 846
Frightful
great, 31
hideous, 846
dreadful, 830
Frigid
cold, 383
callous, 823
reluctant, 603
indifferent, 866
Frigorific

refrigeration, 385
Frill
border, 230
Frills
affectation, 855
Fringe
lace, 256
ornament, 847
Frippery
dress, 225
trifle, 643
ornament, 847
ridiculous, 853
Frisk
brisk, 682
gay, 836
amuse, 840
Frisky
nimble, 274
leap, 309
in spirits, 836
Frith
strait, 343
chasm, 198
Fritter
small part, 51
waste, 135, 638, 683
misuse, 679
diminish, 36
Frivol
trifle, 460
Frivolous
unimportant, 643
silly, 499
frisky, 836
Frizzle
curl, 248
fold, 258
Frock
dress, 225
Frog
ornament, 847
Frogman
depth, 208
dive, 310
Frolic
amusement, 840
Frolicsome
cheerful, 836
Front
fore-part, 234
precession, 280
beginning, 66
exterior, 220
resistance, 719

Fundamentalism
heterodoxy, 984A
Fundamentally
greatness, 31
Funds
money, 800
wealth, 803
treasury, 802
Funeral
interment, 363
Fungus
convexity, 250
Funicle
filament, 205
Funk
fear, 860
cowardice, 862
Funk-hole
refuge, 666
Funnel
opening, 260
channel, 350
air-pipe, 351
Funnel-shaped
concave, 252
Funny
witty, 842
ridiculous, 853
peculiar, 83
ship, 273
Fur
hair, 256
dirt, 653
Furbish
improve, 658
prepare, 673
beautify, 845
ornament, 847
Furfur
unclean, 653
Furfuraceous
pulverulent, 330
Furious
great, 31
violent, 173
passion, 825
enraged, 900
velocity, 274
Furl
roll up, 312
Furlough
permission, 760
Furnace
furnace, 386
Furnish

provide, 637
prepare, 673
give, 215, 784
Furniture
materials, 635
equipment, 633
goods, 780
Furor
excitement, 825
Furore
rage, 865
excitement, 825
Furrow
furrow, 198, 259
Further
aid, 707
Furthermore
addition, 37
Furtive
clandestine, 528
false, 544
stealing, 791
Fury
violence, 173
excitation, 825
anger, 900
temper, 901
demon, 980
revenge, 919
evildoer, 913
Fuscous
brown, 433
Fuse
melt, 335
heat, 382, 384
combine, 48
Fusee
fuel, 388
Fushionless
lazy, 683
Fusiform
pointed, 253
angular, 244
Fusilier
combatant, 726
Fusillade
killing, 361
Fusion
liquefaction, 335
heat, 384
union, 48
Fuss
haste, 684
activity, 682
agitation, 315

hurry, 825
Fussy
fastidious, 868
faddy, 481
Fustian
nonsense, 497
ridiculous, 853
style, 477
Fusty
fetor, 401
dirt, 653
Futile
useless, 645
unavailing, 732
Futilitarian
pessimist, 837
Future
futurity, 121
Futurist
artist, 559
Fylfot
cross, 219

G.I.
fighter, 726
G-man
detective, 461
G.P.
doctor, 662
Gab
speech, 582
Gabble
loquacity, 584
Gabby
loquacious, 584
Gabelle
tax, 812
Gaberdine
dress, 225
Gaberlunzie
tramp, 876
Gaby
fool, 501
Gad about
journey, 266
Gadget
contrivance, 626
tool, 633
Gaffer
man, 373
veteran, 130
clown, 876
foreman, 694

513

Gag
speechless, 581, 585
muzzle, 403, 751
interpolation, 228
wit, 842

Gaga
insane, 503

Gage
security, 771

Gaggle
flock, 72

Gaiety
see Gay

Gain
acquisition, 775
advantage, 618
to learn, 539

Gain ground
improve, 658

Gain upon
approach, 286
become a habit, 613

Gainful
utility, 644, 810

Gainless
inutility, 645

Gainsay
negation, 536

Gait
walk, 264
speed, 274
way, 627

Gaiter
dress, 225

Gala
festival, 840
display, 882

Galahad
perfection, 650

Galaxy
stars, 318
assembly, 72
luminary, 423
multitude, 102
glory, 873

Gale
wind, 349

Gall
bitterness, 395
pain, 378
to pain, 830
insolence, 885
malevolence, 907
anger, 900

Gallant
brave, 861

courteous, 894
lover, 897
licentious, 961, 962

Gallantry
love, 897

Galleon
ship, 273

Galley
room, 191
theatre, 599
passage, 260

Gallery
ship, 273
prison, 752

Galliard
dance, 840

Gallicism
neology, 563

Galligaskins
dress, 225

Gallimaufry
mixture, 41

Galliot
ship, 273

Gallipot
receptacle, 191

Gallivant
travel, 266

Gallop
ride, 266
scamper, 274

Gallophobia
dislike, 867

Galloway
carrier, 271

Gallows
scourge, 975

Gallup poll
inquiry, 461

Galore
multitude, 102
sufficiency, 639

Galosh
dress, 225

Galumph
exult, 836

Galvanic
violent, 173

Galvanism
excitation, 824

Galvanize
energize, 171

Gambade
leap, 309
prank, 856

Gamble
chance, 156, 621

Gambler
rashness, 863

Gambol
amusement, 840

Game
chance, 156
pursuit, 622
plan, 626
intent, 620
amusement, 840
resolute, 604
brave, 861

Game-cock
courage, 861

Game reserve
menagerie, 370

Gamekeeper
keeper, 753

Gamesome
cheerful, 836

Gamin
commonalty, 876

Gammon
untruth, 544, 546,
to hoax, 545

Gamut
harmony, 413

Gamy
pungent, 392

Gander
look, 441

Gang
party, 712
knot, 72

Gangling
lank, 203

Gangrel
tramp, 876
pauper, 804

Gangrene
disease, 655

Gangster
evildoer, 913, 949
swindler, 792

Gangway
way, 627
opening, 260

Gaol
see Jail

Gap
discontinuity, 70
chasm, 4, 198

Gape
open, 260
wonder, 870
curiosity, 455
desire, 865
Garage
house, 189
Garb
dress, 225
Garbage
unclean, 653
Garble
retrench, 38
misinterpret, 523
falsify, 544
Garbled
incomplete, 53
Garçon
servant, 746
Garden
beauty, 845
Gardening
agriculture, 371
Gargantuan
size, 192
Gargle
water, 337
Gargoyle
spout, 350
Garish
colour, 428
light, 420
ornament, 847
display, 882
Garland
ornament, 847
trophy, 733
Garlic
condiment, 393
Garment
dress, 225
Garner
collect, 72
store, 636
Garnet
ornament, 847
Garnish
adorn, 845
ornament, 847
addition, 39
Garret
room, 191
high, 206
Garrison
combatant, 726

defend, 664, 717
Garrotte
killing, 361
punishment, 972
gallows, 975
Garrulity
loquacity, 584
Gas
rarity, 322
gaseity, 334
to chatter, 584
to boast, 884
Gas-bag
loquacity, 584
Gas-mantle
light, 423
Gasconade
boasting, 884
Gaselier
light, 423
Gash
disjunction, 44, 198
Gaslight print
photograph, 556
Gasolene
oil, 356
Gasometer
gas, 334
store, 636
Gasp
pant, 349, 688
desire, 865
droop, 655
Gastronomy
gluttony, 957
epicurism, 868
Gat
gun, 727
Gate
beginning, 66
way, 627
mouth, 260
barrier, 232
Gate-crasher
parasite, 886
Gather
collect, 72, 789
acquire, 775
enlarge, 194
learn, 539
conclude, 480
fold, 258
unite in a focus, 74
Gathering
disease, 655

Gatling
gun, 727
Gauche
unskilful, 699
ill-mannered, 851
Gaud
ornament, 847
Gaudery
vanity, 880
Gaudy
colouring, 428
ornamental, 847
Gaudy
vulgar, 851
flaunting, 882
party, 72, 892
Gauge
measure, 466
Gaunt
spare, 203
ugliness, 846
Gauntlet
defiance, 715
punishment, 972
glove, 225
anger, 909
Gautama
religious founder, 986
Gauze
shade, 424
Gauzy
filmy, 329
Gavotte
dance, 840
music, 415
Gawky
awkward, 699
ridiculous, 853
ugly, 846
Gay
cheerful, 836
adorned, 847
colour, 428
Gaze
vision, 441
Gazebo
look-out, 441
building, 189
Gazelle
velocity, 274
Gazette
publication, 531
record, 551
Gazetted
bankrupt, 808

515

Get
  acquire, 775
  understand, 518
  become, 144
Get about
  publication, 531
Get among
  mixture, 41
Get at
  tamper with, 682
  find out, 480A
Get-at-able
  attainable, 705
Get back
  arrival, 292
Get before
  precedency, 62
Get by
  succeed, 731
Get down
  descend, 306
Get home
  arrive, 292
Get off
  depart, 293
  liberate, 750
  escape, 927
Get on
  advance, 282
  succeed, 731
  improve, 658
Get on to
  blame, 932
Get out
  repulsion, 289
  ejection, 297
Get-out
  plea, 617
Get round
  circumvent, 702
Get the start
  precede, 62
Get to
  arrive, 292
Get together
  assemble, 72
Get up
  rise, 305
  prepare, 673
  style, 7
Get wind
  come to light, 525
Getaway
  escape, 671
Gewgaw

trifle, 643
  ornament, 847
Geyser
  heat, 382
  furnace, 386
Ghastly
  tedious, 846
  frightful, 860
Ghost
  soul, 450
  apparition, 980
  shade, 362
  emaciated, 193
  Deity, 976
  instrumentality, 631
Ghoul
  demon, 980
  evildoer, 913
Giant
  tall, 206
  large, 192
Gibber
  stammer, 583
  unmeaning, 517
Gibberish
  jargon, 519
  nonsense, 517
  absurdity, 497
Gibbet
  gallows, 975
  to execute, 972
Gibbous
  globose, 249
  convex, 250
  distorted, 244
Gibe
  jeer, 856, 932
  taunt, 929
Giddiness
  caprice, 608
  inattention, 458
  bungling, 699
Giddy
  careless, 460
  irresolute, 605
  bungling, 699
  light-headed, 503
Gift
  given, 784
  power, 157
  talent, 698
Gig
  vehicle, 272
  ship, 273
Gigantic

large, 192
  tall, 206
Giggle
  laugh, 838
Gild
  adorn, 845
  ornament, 847
  coat, 222
Gill
  river, 348
Gillie
  servant, 746
Gimbals
  rotation, 312
Gimble
  rotate, 312
Gimcrack
  brittle, 328
  weak, 160
  valueless, 645
  imperfect, 651
  ornament, 847
  whim, 865
Gimlet
  perforator, 262
Gimmick
  speciality, 79
Gin
  trap, 667
Ginger
  pungency, 392
  condiment, 393
  vigour, 574
Ginger up
  excite, 824
Gingerbread
  flimsy, 651
  ornament, 847
Gingerly
  carefully, 459
  slowly, 275
Gipsy
  deceiver, 548
  fortune-teller, 513
Girandole
  luminary, 423
Gird
  bind, 43
  surround, 227
  enclose, 231
  strengthen, 159
Girder
  bond, 45
  beam, 215

Girdle
circular, 247
outline, 229
connection, 45
Girl
young, 129
female, 374
Girl friend
sweetheart, 897
Girth
band, 45
outline, 229
Gist
essence, 5
important, 642
meaning, 516
Gittern
musical instrument, 417
Give
giving, 784
regress, 283
bend, 324
Give and take
probity, 939
Give back
restitute, 790
Give ear
listen, 418
Give entrance to
reception, 296
Give forth
publish, 531
Give in
submit, 725
obey, 743
Give notice
inform, 527
warn, 668
Give out
emit, 297
bestow, 784
publish, 531
teach, 537
end, 67
Give over
relinquish, 624
cease, 142
lose hope, 859
Give up
relinquish, 624
resign, 757
yield, 743
cease, 142
reject, 610
property, 782
despair, 859

Give way
yield, 725
obey, 743
despond, 837
Gizzard
receptacle, 191
Glabrous
smooth, 255
Glacial
cold, 383
Glaciate
frigefaction, 385
Glacier
cold, 383
Glacis
defence, 717
Glad
pressure, 827, 829
cheerful, 836
Glad eye
ogle, 441, 902
Glad hand
conviviality, 892
Glade
opening, 260
hollow, 252
thicket, 367
Gladiator
combatant, 726
Gladiatorial
warfare, 722
Gladsome
pleasurable, 829
Glairy
semiliquid, 352
Glamour
sorcery, 992
Glance
look, 441
rapid motion, 274
attend to, 457
hint, 527, 550
Glare
light, 420
visible, 446
colour, 428
Glaring
greatness, 31
manifest, 518, 525
Glass
vessel, 191
brittle, 328
smooth, 255
spectacles, 445
Glasshouse

prison, 752
Glassy
dim, 422
transparent, 425
colourless, 429
Glaucous
green, 435
Glaur
mud, 352
dirt, 653
Glazed
smooth, 255
Gleam
ray, 429
smallness, 32
Glean
choose, 609
take, 789
acquire, 775
learn, 539
Glebe
land, 342
Glee
satisfaction, 827
merriment, 836
music, 415
Gleeman
musician, 416
Glen
concavity, 252
Glengarry
cap, 225
Glib
valuble, 584
facile, 705
Glide
move, 266
aviation, 267
slowly, 275
course, 109
Glider
aircraft, 273A
Glimmer
light, 420
dimness, 422
Glimmering
slight knowledge, 490,
491
Glimpse
sight, 441
acknowledge, 490
Glint
shine, 420
Glissade
descent, 306

Go over
    change sides, 607
Go round
    circuition, 311
Go through
    pass, 302
    complete, 729
    endure, 821
Go to
    direction, 278
    remonstrance, 695
Go under
    name, 564
    sink, 310
    ruin, 735
Go up
    ascent, 305
Go with
    assent, 488
    suit, 646
Goad
    motive, 615
Goal
    object, 620
    reach, 292
Goat
    fool, 501
Goatish
    impure, 961
Gobbet
    piece, 51
Gobble
    devour, 296
    gluttony, 957
    cry, 412
Gobbledygook
    verbiage, 573
Gobemouche
    credulous, 486
    fool, 501
    dupe, 547
Goblin
    ghost, 980
    bugbear, 860
God
    Deity, 976
Goddess
    great spirit, 979
    favourite, 899
    beauty, 845
Godless
    irreligion, 989
Godlike
    virtue, 944
Godliness

    piety, 987
Godown
    store, 636, 799
Godsend
    luck, 621
    advantage, 618
    success, 731
Goer
    horse, 271
Goggle
    optical instrument, 445
    to stare, 441
Goggle-eyed
    dimsighted, 443
Golconda
    wealth, 803
Gold
    money, 800
Gold-digger
    flirt, 902
    selfishness, 943
Golden
    yellow, 436
Golden age
    pleasure, 827
    prosperity, 734
    imagination, 515
Golden calf
    idols, 986
Golden-mouthed
    ornament, 577
Golden wedding
    celebration, 883
    anniversary, 138
Goldsmith
    artist, 559
Goliath
    strength, 159
    giant, 192
Gombeen-man
    usurer, 805
Gomeril
    fool, 501
Gondola
    ship, 273
Gondolier
    mariner, 269
Gone
    non-extant, 2
    absent, 187
    dead, 360
Gone by
    past, 123
Gone on
    loving, 897

Gonfalon
    flag, 550
Gong
    resonance, 417
    decoration, 877
Goniometer
    angle, 244
    measure, 466
Goo
    adhesive, 45
    viscid, 352
Good
    advantage, 618
    advantageous, 648
    virtuous, 944
    right, 922
    tasty, 394
Good-bye
    departure, 293
Good day
    arrival, 292
    salute, 894
Good-fellowship
    892
Good-for-nothing
    rascal, 949
Good humour
    cheerfulness, 836
Good-looking
    beauty, 845
Good manners
    courtesy, 894
Good morning
    salute, 894
Good nature
    benevolence, 906
    inexcitability, 826
Good show
    approval, 931
Goodly
    large, 192
    beautiful, 845
Goods
    effects, 780
Goods train
    vehicle, 272
Goodwill
    benevolence, 906
    friendship, 888
    merchandise, 798
    materials, 635
Goody
    woman, 374
Gooey
    sticky, 46

Goo-goo eyes
  ogle, 902
Goon
  rascal, 949
Goose
  fool, 501
Goose-skin
  cold, 383
Gorblimey
  vulgar, 876
Gordian knot
  problem, 461
  difficulty, 704
Gore
  opening, 260
  angularity, 244
Gorge
  ravine, 198
  narrowness, 203
  to devour, 296
  full, 641
  satiety, 869
  gluttony, 957
Gorgeous
  colour, 428
  splendid, 845
  ornamented, 847
Gorgon
  fear, 860
  ugliness, 846
Gormandize
  gluttony, 957
  reception, 296
Gory
  killing, 361
Gospel
  scripture, 985
  truth, 494
  certainty, 474
Gossamer
  texture, 329
  slender, 205
  light, 320
Gossip
  conversation, 588
  chatterer, 584
  news, 532
Gossoon
  boy, 129, 373
Goth
  barbarian, 876
  evildoer, 913
Gothic
  vulgarity, 851
  defacement, 241

Gouache
  painting, 556
Gouge
  concavity, 252
Gourmand
  gluttony, 957
  epicure, 868
Gourmet
  desire, 865
  epicure, 868
  gluttony, 957
Goût
  taste, 850
Govern
  direct, 693
  authority, 737
Governess
  teacher, 540
Governess-cart
  vehicle, 272
Governor
  director, 694
  master, 745
  tutor, 540
Gowk
  fool, 501
Gown
  dress, 225
Grab
  snatch, 789
  steal, 791
  booty, 793
Grabble
  fumble, 379
Grace
  elegance, 845
  polish, 850
  forgiveness, 918
  honour, 939
  title, 877
  piety, 987
  worship, 990
  thanks, 916
  style, 578
Grace-note
  music, 415
Grace-stroke
  killing, 361
Graceless
  ungraceful, 846
  vicious, 945
  impenitent, 951
Gracile
  slender, 203
Gracious

  courteous, 894
  good-natured, 906
Gradatim
  degree, 26
  order, 58
  conversion, 144
Gradation
  degree, 26
  order, 58
  arrangement, 60
  continuity, 69
Grade
  degree, 26
  term, 71
Gradely
  good, 648
Gradient
  obliquity, 217
Gradual
  degree, 26
  continuity, 69
Graduate
  to arrange, 60
  to adapt, 23
  to measure, 466
  scholar, 492
Gradus
  dictionary, 562
Graffito
  drawing, 556
Graft
  join, 300
  insert, 43
  cultivate, 371
  locate, 184
  teach, 537
  bribe, 615
  improbity, 940
Grain
  essence, 5'
  minute, 32
  particle, 193
  texture, 329
  roughness, 256
  disposition, 820
  adorn, 847
Graminivorous
  eat, 296
Grammar
  grammar, 567
Grammar school
  school, 542
Grammarian
  scholar, 492
Grammercy
  gratitude, 916

Gramophone
reproduction, 19
music, 417
hearing, 418
Granary
store, 636
Grand
important, 642
beautiful, 845
glorious, 873
money, 800
Grandam
veteran, 130
Grandchild
posterity, 167
Grandee
master, 875
Grandeur
repute, 873
Grandiloquence
eloquence, 582
style, 577
Grandiose
style, 577
Grandsire
old, 130
ancestor, 166
Grandson
posterity, 167
Grange
abode, 189
Grangerize
addition, 36
Granite
hardness, 323
Granivorous
eat, 296
Grant
give, 784
allow, 760
consent, 762
disclose, 529
assent, 488
Grantee
receive, 785
Grantor
give, 784
Granulate
pulverulence, 330
Granule
littleness, 193
Grape-shot
arms, 727
Grapevine

news, 532
Graphic
painting, 556
description, 594
intelligible, 518
Grapnel
anchor, 666
Grapple
contend, 720
undertake, 676
join, 43
Grappling-iron
fastening, 45
safety, 666
Grasp
seize, 789
retain, 781
comprehend, 518
power, 737
Grasping
parsimony, 819
Grass
plant, 367
green, 435
Grass widow
divorce, 905
Grate
rub, 330
friction, 331
harsh, 410, 414
furnace, 386
pain, physical, 378
pain, moral, 830
Grateful
thanks, 916
agreeable, 377, 829
Gratification
animal, 377
moral, 827
Gratify
pleasure, 829
Grating
noise, 410
lattice, 219
Gratis
cheap, 815
Gratitude
thanks, 916
Gratuitous
spontaneous, 600, 602
cheap, 815
Gratuity
giving, 784
Gratulation
rejoicing, 836

Gravamen
importance, 642
grievance, 619
Grave
sad, 836
serious, 642
distressing, 830
heinous, 945
great, 31
engrave, 559
impress, 505
shape, 240
tomb, 363
sound, 408
Gravel
offend, 830
puzzle, 704
soil, 342
Graveolent
odour, 398
Graver
artist, 559
Gravestone
interment, 363
Graveyard
interment, 363
Gravid
pregnant, 168
Gravitate
descent, 306
Gravitation
attraction, 288
Gravity
weight, 319
attraction, 288
dullness, 843
seriousness, 837
importance, 642
composure, 826
Gravy
liquid, 333
Graze
browse, 296
touch, 199
Grease
oil, 332, 356
unctuous, 355
Great
much, 31
big, 192
importance, 642
glorious, 873
magnanimous, 942
pregnant, 168

Great circle
direction, 278
Greatcoat
garment, 225
Greaten
enlarge, 35
Greaves
garment, 225
Greedy
voracious, 957
desirous, 865
avaricious, 819
Greek Church
Christian religion, 983A
Green
colour, 435
meadow, 344
new, 123
unskilled, 699
unprepared, 674
unaccustomed, 614
credulous, 484
ignorant, 491
Green belt
environs, 227
Green-eyed
jealousy, 920
Green light
signal, 550
Greenback
money, 800
Greenhorn
fool, 501
dupe, 547
novice, 493, 674
stranger, 57
bungler, 701
Greenroom
the drama, 599
Greet
hail, 894
weep, 839
Gregarious
social, 892
Gremlin
demon, 980
Grenade
arms, 727
Grenadier
soldier, 726
tall, 206
Grey
colour, 432
age, 128
Grey-headed

age, 128
veteran, 130
Grey market
illegality, 964
Grey matter
brain, 450
Greybeard
veteran, 130
Greyhound
swift, 274
Grid
lattice, 219
Gridelin
purple, 437
Gridiron
lattice, 219
arena, 728
Grief
dejection, 837
Grievance
injury, 619
pain, 830
Grieve
complain, 828, 839
afflict, 830
injure, 649
Griffin
unconformity, 83
keeper, 753
Grig
cheerful, 836
Grill
calefaction, 384
question, 461
Grille
lattice, 219
Grim
ugly, 846
frightful, 828
discourteous, 895
ferocious, 907
Grim-visaged
grave, 837
Grimace
ridicule, 856
Grime
unclean, 653
Grin
laugh, 838
ridicule, 856
scorn, 929
Grind
pulverize, 330
an organ, 415
oppress, 907

learn, 539
sharpen, 253
scholar, 492
Grinder
teacher, 540
Grinding
painful, 831
Grip
power, 737
bag, 191
Grip-sack
bag, 191
Gripe
seize, 789
retain, 781
pain, 378, 828
to give pain, 830
power, 737
Griping
avaricious, 819
Grisette
woman, 374
Grisly
ugliness, 846
Grist
provision, 637
materials, 635
Gristle
toughness, 327
Grit
pulverulence, 330
determination, 604
courage, 861
Gritty
hard, 323
Grizzled
variegation, 440
Grizzly
grey, 432
Groan
cry, 411
lament, 839
Groggy
drunk, 959
ill, 655
Groin
angular, 244
Grooly
ugly, 845
Groom
servant, 746
marriage, 903
Groomsman
marriage, 903

523

Groove
    furrow, 259
    habit, 613
Grope
    feel, 379
    experience, 463
    inquire, 461
    try, 675
Gross
    whole, 51
    greatness, 31
    vulgar, 851
    vicious, 945
    impure, 961
Grossièreté
    rudeness, 895
Grot
    see Grotto
Grotesque
    deformed, 846
    ridiculous, 851, 853
    outlandish, 83
Grotto
    alcove, 189
    hollow, 252
Grouchy
    discourteous, 895
    bad-tempered, 901
Ground
    land, 342
    support, 215
    base, 211
    region, 181
    cause, 153
    motive, 615
    plea, 617
    property, 780
    arena, 728
    teach, 537
Ground swell
    surge, 348
    agitation, 315
Grounded
    knowing, 490
    wrecked, 732
Groundless
    erroneous, 495
    sophistical, 477
Groundling
    commonalty, 876
Grounds
    lees, 653
Groundwork
    basis, 211
    support, 215
    cause, 153

    precursor, 64
    preparation, 673
Group
    cluster, 72
    troop, 726
    to marshal, 58
Group-captain
    master, 745
Grouse
    grumble, 832, 839
Grout
    vinculum, 45
Grove
    wood, 367
    house, 189
Grovel
    move slowly, 275
    be low, 207
    cringe, 886
    base, 940
Grow
    increase, 35
    expand, 194
Grow from
    effect, 154
Growl
    cry, 412
    complain, 839
    threaten, 909
    be rude, 895
    anger, 900
Growler
    vehicle, 272
Growth
    in degree, 35
    in size, 194
Groyne
    refuge, 666
Grub
    little, 193
    food, 298
Grub up
    extract, 301
    destroy, 162
    discover, 480A
Grudge
    hate, 898
    stingy, 640, 819
    unwilling, 603
Gruelling
    punishment, 972
Gruesome
    ugly, 846
Gruff
    morose, 895

    sound, 410
Grumble
    sound, 411
    complain, 832, 839
Grumous
    dense, 321
    pulpy, 354
Grumpy
    discourteous, 895
    bad-tempered, 901
Grundyism
    prudery, 855
Grunt
    cry, 412
    complain, 839
Guano
    manure, 653
Guarantee
    security, 771
    evidence, 467
    promise, 768
Guard
    defend, 717
    safety, 664
Guard-room
    prison, 752
Guarded
    circumspect, 459
    conditional, 770
Guardian
    safety, 664, 717
    keeper, 753
Guardless
    danger, 665
Guardsman
    combatant, 726
Gubernatorial
    directing, 693
    authority, 737
Gudgeon
    dupe, 547
Guerdon
    reward, 973
Guerrilla
    combatant, 726
Guess
    suppose, 514
Guest
    friend, 890
    arrival, 292
Guet-apens
    untruth, 546
    ambush, 530
Guffaw
    laughter, 834

Guggle
see Gurgle
Guide
direct, 693
director, 694
advice, 695
teach, 537
teacher, 540
road-book, 266
Guide-post
indicator, 550
warning, 668
Guideless
danger, 665
Guild
corporation, 712
tribunal, 966
partnership, 797
Guildhall
mart, 799
Guile
cunning, 702
deceit, 545
Guileless
artless, 703
sincere, 543
Guillotine
engine, 975
to decapitate, 972
Guilt
crime, 947
vice, 945
Guiltless
innocence, 946
Guindé
conciseness, 572
Guise
state, 7
appearance, 448
manner, 627
plea, 617
Guiser
the drama, 599
Guitar
music, 417
Gulch
gap, 198
Gules
redness, 434
Gulf
sea, 343
depth, 208
Gull
dupe, 547
credulous, 486

Gullet
throat, 260
rivulet, 348
Gullible
credulity, 486
Gully
conduit, 350
opening, 260
hollow, 252
ravine, 198
Gulosity
gluttony, 957
Gulp
swallow, 297
believe, 484
Gum
fastening, 45
coherence, 46
semiliquid, 352
Gum-boot
dress, 225
Gumption
capacity, 498
Gumshoe
prowl, 528
Gun
arms, 727
fighter, 726
Gun-cotton
arms, 727
Gunboat
ship, 273
Gunman
bad man, 949
Gunner
combatant, 726
Gurgitation
rotation, 312
Gurgle
sound, 405, 408
bubble, 353
Gurkha
soldier, 726
Guru
priest, 996
Gush
flow, 295
flood, 348
feeling, 821
affectation, 855
Gusset
angularity, 244
Gust
wind, 349
physical taste, 390

enjoyment, 826
moral taste, 850
Gustatory
taste, 390
Gusto
relish, 827
taste, 850
Gut
opening, 260
to sack, 789
vitals, 221
Guts
courage, 861
resolution, 604
Gutter
conduit, 350
groove, 259
Guttersnipe
commonalty, 876
vulgarity, 851
Guttle
devour, 296
Guttural
stammer, 583
letter, 561
Guy
rope, 45
ugliness, 846
man, 373
to ridicule, 842, 856
deride, 929
Guzzle
drink, 296
tipple, 959
gluttony, 957
Gymkhana
contention, 720
Gymnasium
school, 542
training, 673
Gymnast
strength, 159
Gymnastic
exertion, 686
contention, 720
teaching, 537
Gymnosophist
heathen, 984
temperance, 953
Gynaecocracy
rule, 737
Gynaecology
remedy, 662
Gyp
servant, 746

Gypsy
see Gipsy
Gyration
rotation, 312
Gyre
rotation, 312
Gyroscope
rotation, 312
Gyve
chain, 45
shackle, 752

Haberdashery
dress, 225
Habergeon
defence, 717
Habiliment
dress, 225
Habilitation
skill, 698
Habit
intrinsic, 5
custom, 613
coat, 225
Habitat
abode, 189
Habitation
abode, 189
location, 184
Habitual
regular, 82, 613
Habituate
accustom, 613
train, 673
Habitude
state, 7
relation, 9
habit, 613
Habitué
guest, 891
frequenter, 136
Hacienda
property, 780
Hack
cut, 44
shorten, 201
horse, 271
drudge, 690
writer, 590
Hackle
cut, 44
Hackneyed
regular, 82
trite, 496

habitual, 613
experienced, 698
Hades
hell, 982
Hadji
clergy, 996
pilgrim, 268
Haecceity
speciality, 79
Haemorrhage
excretion, 299
Haft
instrument, 633
Hag
ugly, 846
veteran, 130
wretch, 913
bad woman, 949
Haggard
ugly, 846
wild, 824
insane, 503
Haggle
bargain, 769, 794
Hagiography
theology, 983
Ha-ha
ditch, 198
defence, 717
Haik
dress, 225
Hail
call, 586
ice, 383
Hair
thread, 45
filement, 205
roughness, 256
Hair-oil
ornament, 847
Hair-raising
fear, 860
Hair's breadth
thin, 203
Halberd
arms, 727
Halberdier
combatant, 726
Halcyon
prosperous, 734, 829
joyful, 827
calm, 174
Hale
health, 654
Half

bisection, 91
Half a dozen
six, 98
Half and half
mixture, 41
Half-baked
incomplete, 53
witless, 499
Half-blood
unconformity, 83
Half-breed
unconformity, 83
Half-caste
mixture, 41
unconformity, 83
Half-hearted
indifferent, 866
irresolute, 605
timorous, 862
Half-moon
curvature, 245
Half-pint
little, 193
Half-seas-over
drunk, 959
Half-track
vehicle, 272
Half-way
middle, 68
Half-wit
fool, 501
Half-witted
folly, 499
Hall
chamber, 189
receptacle, 191
mart, 799
Hall-marked
genuine, 494
Hallelujah
worship, 990
Hallo!
call, 586
wonder, 870
arrival, 292
Halloo
cry, 411
Hallow
sanctify, 987
Hallowed
venerated, 928
Deity, 976
Hallucination
error, 495
delusion, 503

Halo
light, 420
glory, 873
Halt
stop, 142, 265
flag, 655
rest, 685, 687
limp, 275
Halter
rope, 45
fetter, 752
punishment, 975
Halting
lame, 160
Halve
bisect, 91
Halyard
rope, 45
Hamadryad
nymph, 979
Hamlet
abode, 189
Hammal
carrier, 271
Hammam
furnace, 386
Hammer
to knock, 276
instrument, 633
auction, 796
repetition, 104
bankrupt, 808
Hammer at
thought, 583
action, 682
Hammock
support, 215
Hamper
basket, 191
obstruct, 706
Hamstring
injure, 649
weaken, 160
incapacitate, 158
Hand
instrument, 633
indicator, 550
agent, 690
side, 236
writing, 590
to give, 784
agency, 170
Hand-barrow
vehicle, 272
Hand-gallop

velocity, 274
Hand-in-hand
accompaniment, 88
Hand over
transfer, 270
Handbook
advice, 695
Handcuff
tie together, 43
manacle, 751, 752
Handfast
marriage, 903
Handful
quantity, 25, 103
smallness, 32
Handicap
inequality, 28
disadvantage, 651
Handicraft
action, 680
Handicraftsman
agent, 690
Handiwork
action, 680
effect, 154
Handkerchief
dress, 225
clean, 652
Handle
instrument, 633
plea, 617
touch, 379
use, 677
describe, 594
dissert, 595
work, 680
Handling
treatment, 692
Handmaid
servant, 746
instrumentality, 631
Hands off!
resist, 719
prohibit, 761
Handsel
security, 771
give, 784
pay, 809
begin, 66
Handsome
beautiful, 845
liberal, 816
disinterested, 942
Handspike
instrument, 633

Handwriting
omen, 512
signature, 550
autograph, 590
Handy
near, 197
skilful, 698
useful, 644
attainable, 705
Hang
pendency, 214
kill, 361
execute, 972
expletive, 908
Hang about
loiter, 275
Hang back
hesitate, 603
Hang fire
reluctance, 603
vacillation, 605
stop, 142
refuse, 764
lateness, 133
slowness, 275
inactivity, 683
Hang out
reside, 188
Hang over
futurity, 121
destiny, 152
height, 206
Hang together
junction, 43
Hang up
defer, 133
Hangar
building, 189
Hanger
arms, 727
Hanger-on
servant, 746
accompany, 88
follow, 281
parasite, 886
flatterer, 935
Hangings
ornaments, 847
Hangman
executioner, 975
Hank
skein, 219
Hanker
desire, 865

Hanky-panky
fraud, 545
Hansard
record, 551
Hansel
see Handsel
Hansom
vehicle, 272
Hap
chance, 156, 621
Haphazard
chance, 156, 621
Hapless
hopeless, 859
miserable, 828
Haply
chance, 156
possibly, 470
Happen
event, 151
Happy
glad, 827
expedient, 646
agreement, 23
Happy-go-lucky
careless, 460
aimless, 621
improvident, 674
Happy medium
middle, 68
Happy thought
wit, 842
Hari-kiri
suicide, 361
execution, 972
Harangue
speech, 582
preach, 998
Harass
worry, 907
fatigue, 688
vex, 830
Harbinger
omen, 512
precursor, 64, 116
Harbour
anchorage, 189
refuge, 666
haven, 292
to cherish, 821
Harbourless
exposed, 665
Hard
dense, 323
difficult, 704
grievous, 830

strong, 159
obdurate, 951
sour, 397
Hard-and-fast
exact, 494
strict, 739
Hard-boiled
callous, 823
Hard case
bad man, 949
Hard currency
money, 800
Hard-favoured
ugly, 846
Hard-headed
skill, 698
wise, 498
Hard-hearted
cruel, 907
Hard lines
adversity, 735
Hard-mouthed
obstinacy, 606
Hard up
poverty, 804
Hard-working
exertion, 682, 686
Harden
accustom, 613
train, 673
render callous, 376, 823
impious, 988
impenitent, 951
Hardihood
courage, 861
insolence, 885
Hardly
scarcely, 32
infrequency, 137
Hardness of heart
vice, 945
Hardship
pain, 830
adversity, 735
Hardy
strong, 159
healthy, 654
Hare
velocity, 274
Hare-brained
rash, 460, 863
Harem
apartment, 191
impurity, 961
Hark

hearing, 418
Hark back
regression, 283
Harlequin
motley, 440
pantomimic, 599
humorist, 844
Harlot
libertine, 962
Harlotry
impurity, 961
Harm
evil, 619
badness, 649
malevolence, 907
Harmattan
wind, 349
Harmless
innocent, 946
innocuous, 648
impotent, 158
Harmonic
music, 413
Harmonica
musical, 417
Harmonium
musical instrument, 417
Harmonize
uniformity, 16
Harmony
agreement, 23
melody, 413
concord, 714
peace, 721
conformity, 82
friendship, 888
Harness
fasten, 43
fastening, 45
bond, 752
accoutrement, 225
instrument, 633
subjection, 749
Harp
musical instrument, 417
to repeat, 104
to weary, 841
Harper
musician, 416
Harpoon
arms, 727
Harpsichord
musical, 417
Harpy
demon, 980

evildoer, 913
thief, 792
miser, 819
Harquebus
arms, 727
Harridan
hag, 846
trollop, 962
bad woman, 949
Harrow
pain, 830
cultivate, 371
Harry
pain, 830
Harsh
severe, 739
morose, 895
disagreeable, 830
malevolent, 907
sound, 410
Harum-scarum
disorder, 59
Haruspex
oracle, 513
Harvest
acquisition, 775
effect, 154
Hash
mixture, 41
disorder, 59
to cut, 44
Hasp
lock, 45
to lock, 43
Hassock
support, 215
Hast la vista
departure, 293
Haste
in time, 132
in motion, 274
Haste
in action, 684
activity, 682
Hasten
to promote, 707
Hasty
transient, 111
irritable, 901
Hat
dress, 225
Hatch
produce, 161
plan, 626
prepare, 673

door, 66
opening, 260
Hatchet
instrument, 633
sharpness, 253
Hatchet-faced
thin, 203
Hatchment
record, 551
Hatchway
way, 627
opening, 260
Hate
hate, 898
enmity, 889
bombardment, 716
Hateful
noxious, 649
painful, 830
Hatter
dress, 225
Hauberk
arms, 717
Haughty
proud, 878
severe, 739
insolent, 885
Haul
traction, 285
catch, 789
Haunch
side, 236
Haunt
presence, 186
alarm, 860
abode, 189
resort, 74
frequent, 136
trouble, 830
Haut-goût
pungency, 392
Hautboy
musical instrument, 417
Haute monde
noble, 875
Haute politique
government, 693
Hauteur
pride, 878
Have
possession, 777
deceive, 545
Have it
belief, 484
Have oneself a ball

enjoy, 377
Haven
anchorage, 189
refuge, 292, 666
Havers
nonsense, 497
folly, 499
Haversack
receptacle, 191
Havoc
evil, 162, 619
Haw
stammering, 583
Hawk
sell, 796
publish, 531
Hawk-eyed
vision, 441
Hawker
merchant, 797
Hawser
rope, 45
Hay-cock
bundle, 72
Hayseed
peasant, 876
Haywire
insane, 503
Hazard
chance, 156, 621
danger, 665
obstacle, 706
Haze
mist, 353
dimness, 422
opacity, 426
to harass, 830, 907
Hazel
brown, 433
Hazy
indistinct, 447
Head
beginning, 66
class, 75
summit, 210
front, 234
to lead, 280
froth, 353
intellect, 450
wisdom, 498
master, 745
direction, 693
director, 694
topic, 454

Head and shoulders
whole, 50
Head-foremost
rash, 863
Head-rhyme
similarity, 17
poetry, 597
Head-work
thought, 451
Headache
pain, 378
Header
plunge, 310
Headgear
dress, 225
Heading
title, 550
precursor, 64
beginning, 66
Headlong
projection, 250
cape, 342
height, 206
Headlong
rashly, 460, 863
hastily, 684
swiftly, 274
Headpiece
intellect, 450, 498
skill, 698
Headquarters
focus, 74
abode, 189
Heads
compendium, 596
warning, 668
care, 459
toilet, 191, 653
Headship
authority, 737
Headstrong
rash, 863
obstinate, 606
violent, 173
Headway
space, 180
progress, 282
navigation, 267
Heal
repair, 658
forgive, 918
Health
health, 654
Healthy
salubrity, 656
Heap

collection, 72
store, 636
plenty, 639
much, 31, 50
Hear
audition, 418
learn, 539
Hearken
audition, 418
Hearsay
news, 532
Hearse
interment, 363
Heart
interior, 221
centre, 223
mind, 450
will, 600
affections, 820
courage, 861
love, 897
Heart-breaking
painful, 830
Heart-broken
pain, 828
Heart-felt
feeling, 821
Heart-rending
painful, 830
Heart-sick
dejected, 837
Heart-strings
affections, 820
Heart-swelling
resentment, 900
Heart-whole
free, 748
Heartache
pain, 828
Heartburning
resentment, 900
jealousy, 920
Hearten
inspirit, 824, 861
Hearth
abode, 189
fire, 386
Heartiness
feeling, 821
sociality, 892
Heartless
malevolent, 945
Hearty
healthy, 654
willing, 602

feeling, 821
cheerful, 831, 836
Heat
warmth, 382
calefaction, 384
contest, 720
violence, 173
excitement, 825
Heath
plain, 344
Heathen
pagan, 984, 986
irreligious, 988
Heathenish
vulgar, 851
Heave
raise, 307
pant, 821
throw, 284
Heave in sight
visibility, 446
Heave to
stop, 265
Heaven
paradise, 981
bliss, 827
Heaven-born
virtue, 944
Heaven-directed
wisdom, 498
Heavenly
divine, 976
rapturous, 829
celestial, 318
angelic, 977
Heavens
world, 318
Heaviness
inertia, 172
dejection, 837
dullness, 843
Heaviside layer
air, 338
Heavy
weighty, 319
inert, 172, 682
slow, 275
stupid, 499
rude, 851
large, 31
Hebdomadal
period, 108, 138
Hebe
beauty, 845

Hebetate
  insensible, 823
Hecate
  hag, 846
Hecatomb
  killing, 361
Heckle
  question, 461
Hectic
  fever, 382
  feeling, 821
Hector
  courage, 861
  bully, 885
Hedge
  enclosure, 232
  to shuffle, 544
  to compensate, 30
Hedge-hop
  fly, 267
Hedge in
  enclose, 231
  safe, 664
Hedgehog
  sharpness, 253
  defence, 717
Hedonism
  intemperance, 954
Heed
  attend, 457
  care, 459
  caution, 864
Heedless
  inattentive, 458
  neglectful, 460
Heel
  slope, 217
  rascal, 949
Heel-tap
  remainder, 40
Heels
  rear, 235
Heels over head
  reckless, 460
Heft
  handle, 633
  exertion, 686
Hefty
  heavy, 319
Hegemony
  authority, 737
Hegira
  departure, 293
Heigh-ho!
  lamentation, 839

Height
  altitude, 206
  degree, 26
  superiority, 33
Heighten
  increase, 35
  exalt, 206
  exaggerate, 549
  aggravate, 835
Heinous
  vice, 945
Heir
  possessor, 779
  posterity, 167
  futurity, 121
Heirloom
  property, 780
Heirship
  possess, 777
Helen
  beauty, 845
Helicon
  poetry, 597
Helicopter
  aircraft, 273A
Helidrome
  arrival, 292
Heliograph
  signal, 550
Heliotherapy
  remedy, 662
Helix
  convolution, 248
Hell
  gehenna, 982
  abyss, 208
Hell-born
  vice, 945
Hellcat
  bad woman, 949
  fury, 173
Hellebore
  bane, 663
Hellhag
  bad woman, 949
Hellhound
  miscreant, 949
  ruffian, 173, 913
Hellish
  bad, 649
  malevolent, 907
  vicious, 945
Hello
  see Hallo
Helm

  handle, 633
  direction, 693
  authority, 737
Helmet
  dress, 225
  defence, 717
Helot
  servant, 746
Help
  aid, 707
  auxiliary, 711
  utility, 644
  remedy, 662
  servant, 746
Helpless
  weak, 160
  incapable, 158
  exposed, 665
Helpmate
  auxiliary, 711
  wife, 903
Helter-skelter
  disorder, 59
  haste, 684
  slope, 217
Hem
  edge, 230
  fold, 258
  to stammer, 583
Hem in
  enclose, 231
  surround, 227
  restrain, 751
Hemlock
  bane, 663
Henbane
  bane, 663
Hence
  arising from, 155
  deduction, 476
  motive, 615
Henceforth
  futurity, 121
Henchman
  servant, 746
Henpecked
  obedience, 743
  subjection, 749
Hep
  knowing, 490
  informed, 527
Hephaestus
  god, 979
Heptad
  seven, 98

Heptagon
angularity, 244
seven, 98
Hera
goddess, 979
Herald
messenger, 534
precursor, 64
omen, 512
lead, 280
to predict, 511
to proclaim, 531
Herb
plant, 367
Herbarium
botany, 369
Herbivorous
eat, 296
Herculean
strength, 159
huge, 192
difficulty, 704
Herd
animal, 366
flock, 72, 102
Here
present, 186
Hereabouts
nearness, 197
Hereafter
futurity, 121
Hereditament
property, 780
Hereditary
derivative, 154
posterity, 167
habit, 613
intrinsic, 5
Heredity
paternity, 166
Heresy
error, 495
unbelief, 485
religious, 984A
Heretic
dissent, 489
heresy, 984A
Heretofore
preterition, 122
priority, 116
Herewith
accompaniment, 88
Heritage
futurity, 121
possession, 777

property, 780
Heritor
possessor, 779
Hermaphrodite
incongruity, 83
Hermeneutic
interpretation, 522
Hermes
god, 979
messenger, 534
Hermetically
closure, 261
Hermit
seclusion, 893
Hermitage
abode, 189
Hero
brave, 861
saint, 948
Heroic
brave, 861
glorious, 873
magnanimous, 942
verse, 597
Heroics
exaggeration, 549
boast, 884
Herr
title, 877
Herring-gutted
thin, 203
Hesitate
reluctant, 603
irresolute, 605
uncertainty, 475
fearful, 860
sceptical, 485
to stammer, 583
Hetaera
courtesan, 962
Heteroclite
incongruity, 83
Heterodox
heresy, 984A
Heterogeneous
mixed, 10, 15, 41
multiform, 81
exceptional, 83
Heteromorphic
difference, 15
Heuristic
inquiry, 461
Hew
cut, 44
shorten, 201

fashion, 240
Hexachord
melody, 413
Hexad
six, 98
Hexagon
numbers, 98
angularity, 244
Hexahedron
angularity, 244
six, 98
Hey
attention, 547
accost, 586
Heyday
wonder, 870
success, 731
exultation, 836, 838
youth, 127
Hiatus
interval, 198
opening, 260
unsubstantiality, 4
discontinuity, 70
Hibernal
cold, 383
Hibernate
sleep, 683
Hibernicism
absurdity, 497
Hic jacet
burial, 363
Hiccup
cough, 349
Hick
peasant, 876
Hid
invisible, 447
concealed, 528
Hidalgo
master, 875
Hide
conceal, 528
ambush, 530
skin, 222
Hide-bound
intolerant, 481
obstinate, 606
strait-laced, 751
Hideous
ugly, 846
Hiding-place
refuge, 666
ambush, 530

Hie
go, 264, 266, 274
Hiemal
cold, 383
evening, 126
Hierarchy
churchdom, 995
order, 58
Hieroglyphic
letter, 561
writing, 590
representation, 554
unintelligible, 519
Hierogram
revelation, 985
Hierography
theology, 983
Hierophant
churchman, 996
Higgle
chaffer, 794
bargain, 769
Higgledy-piggledy
disorder, 59
Higgler
merchant, 797
High
lofty, 206
pungent, 392
stinking, 401
proud, 878
magnanimous, 942
drunk, 959
High-born
master, 875
High-brow
scholar, 492
sage, 500
High-falutin
bombast, 549
affected, 855
florid, 577
High-flier
imagination, 515
pride, 878
High-flown
proud, 878, 880
insolent, 885
exaggerated, 549
High-handed
insolent, 885
High-hat
affected, 855
High jinks
festivity, 840

High life
fashion, 852
nobility, 875
High-mettled
spirited, 861
proud, 878
High-minded
proud, 878
generous, 942
honourable, 940
High-powered
power, 157
High-priced
dear, 814
High-seasoned
pungent, 932
obscene, 961
High-spirited
brave, 861
High-strung
excitable, 825
High-wrought
perfect, 650
finished, 729
excited, 825
Highball
intoxicant, 959
Higher
superiority, 33
Highland
land, 342
Highly
great, 31
Highness
title, 877
prince, 745
Hight
nomenclature, 564
Highway
road, 627
Highwayman
thief, 792
Hijack
rob, 791, 792
Hike
journey, 266
Hiker
traveller, 268
Hilarity
cheerfulness, 836
Hill
height, 206
Hillock
height, 206
Hilt

instrument, 633
Hind
back, 235
clown, 876
Hinder
back, 235; end, 67
to impede, 179
obstruct, 706
prohibit, 761
Hindrance
obstruction, 706
Hindsight
thought, 451
memory, 505
Hinduism
religions, 984
Hinge
depend upon, 154
cause, 153
rotate, 312
fastening, 43, 45
Hinny
beast of burden, 271
Hint
suggest, 505
inform, 527
suppose, 514
Hinterland
interior, 221
Hip
side, 236
Hipped
dejection, 837
Hippocentaur
oddity, 83
Hippodrome
arena, 728
amusement, 840
Hippogriff
incongruity, 83
Hippophagous
eat, 296
Hippy
unconformity, 83
Hire
commission, 755
fare, 812
purchase, 795
borrow, 788
Hire purchase
buy, 795
Hireling
servant, 746
Hirsute
rough, 256

Hispid
rough, 256
Hiss
sound, 409
disrespect, 929, 932
Histology
texture, 329
Historian
recorder, 553, 594
Historic
indication, 550
History
record, 551
narrative, 594
Histrionic
the drama, 599
ostentatious, 882
Hit
strike, 276
impress, 824
punish, 972
succeed, 731
chance, 156, 621
reach, 292
agree, 23
Hit off
imitate, 19, 554
Hit-or-miss
chance, 621
Hit upon
find, 480A
Hitch
difficulty, 704
impediment, 135
jerk, 315
hang, 43, 214
Hitch-hike
travel, 266
Hither
arrival, 292
Hitherto
preterition, 122
Hive
workshop, 691
multitude, 102
dwelling, 186
Hive-off
distribute, 73
Hoar
white, 430
aged, 128
Hoar-frost
cold, 383
Hoard
store, 636

assemblage, 72
Hoarding
screen, 530
Hoarse
sound, 405, 410
voice, 581
Hoary
white, 430
aged, 128
Hoax
deception, 545
Hob
support, 215
fire, 386
Hobble
limp, 275
difficulty, 704
lame, 732
tether, 751
bond, 752
awkward, 699
Hobbledehoy
youth, 129
Hobby
pursuit, 622
desire, 865
Hobgoblin
demon, 980
Hobnob
courtesy, 894
Hobo
traveller, 268
tramp, 876
Hobson's choice
necessity, 601
absence of choice, 610
Hock
pawn, 787
Hocus
deceive, 545
stupefy, 376
Hocus-pocus
cheat, 545
conjuration, 992
Hod
receptacle, 191
vehicle, 272
Hodge
clown, 876
Hodge-podge
mixture, 41
confusion, 59
Hog
sensuality, 954
gluttony, 957

selfishness, 943
Hog-wash
uncleanness, 653
Hoist
elevate, 307
lift, 627
Hoity-toity!
wonder, 870
Hokum
humbug, 497
deception, 545
Hold
possess, 777
believe, 484
retain, 781
cohere, 46
fix, 150
stop, 265
discontinue, 142
continue, 141, 143
refrain, 623
contain, 54
influence, 175
prison, 752
in a ship, 207
term, 71
Hold forth
declaim, 582
teach, 537
Hold good
truth, 494
Hold in
moderation, 174
Hold on
move, 264
continue, 141, 143
determination, 604
Hold out
resist, 718
offer, 763
Hold the tongue
silence, 403, 585
Hold together
junction, 43
Hold up
sustain, 707
continue, 143
delay, 133
plunder, 791
Holder
possessor, 779
Holdfast
vinculum, 45
Holding
property, 780

Hole
opening, 260
place, 182; den, 189
receptacle, 191
ambush, 530
difficulty, 704
Hole-and-corner
concealment, 528
Holiday
amusement, 840
repose, 687
leisure, 685; time, 134
Holiness
Deity, 976
Hollow
concavity, 252
depth, 208
imcomplete, 53
false, 544
sound, 408
specious, 477
unsubstantial, 4
Holm
island, 346
Holocaust
idolatry, 991
killing, 361
Holograph
writing, 590
Holt
plant, 367
Holy
Deity, 976
piety, 987
Holy Ghost
Deity, 976
Holy Writ
revelation, 985
truth, 494
Homage
reverence, 928
submission, 725
approbation, 931
fealty, 743
worship, 990
Home
habitation, 189
interior, 221
focus, 74; near, 197
arrival, 292
Home and dry
successful, 731
Home-felt
feeling, 821
Home Guard

combatant, 726
Homeless
outcast, 893
displaced, 185
Homeliness
ugliness, 846
simplicity, 849
style, 576
Homeric
poetry, 597
Homespun
simple, 849
ugly, 846
vulgar, 851
low, 876
coarse, 329
style, 576
Homestead
abode, 189
Homicide
killing, 361
Homily
advice, 595
speech, 582
sermon, 998
Homoeopathic
littleness, 32, 193
Homogeneity
relation, 9
uniformity, 16
simplicity, 42
Homologate
concede, 467, 762
Homology
relation, 9
uniformity, 16
Homonym
word, 562
equivocal, 520
Homunculus
littleness, 193
Hone
sharpener, 253
grind, 331
Honest
pure, 960
true, 543
candid, 703
honour, 939
Honey
sweetness, 396
darling, 899
Honeycomb
concavity, 252
opening, 260

Honeydew
tobacco, 298A
Honeyed
flattering, 933
Honeymoon
wedding, 903
happiness, 827
Honorarium
expenditure, 809
Honorary
gratuitous, 815
Honour
probity, 939
glory, 873
title, 877
respect, 928
to pay, 807
Hood
cowl, 999
cap, 225
Hoodlum
evildoer, 913, 949
Hoodoo
sorcery, 992
spell, 993
Hoodwink
blind, 442
conceal, 528
ignore, 491
Hooey
nonsense, 497
trash, 643
Hoof
to kick, 276
Hoof it
walking, 266
Hoof out
eject, 297
Hook
to fasten, 43
fastening, 45
Hook
grip, 781
hang, 214
curvature, 245
deviation, 279
take, 789
Hook-up
junction, 43
Hookah
tobacco-pipe, 298A
Hooker
ship, 273
Hooligan
ruffian, 913, 949

Hooliganism
brutality, 907
Hoop
circle, 247
Hoot
cry, 411
deride, 929, 930, 932
drink, 298
Hooter
indication, 550
Hoots
contempt, 930
Hop
leap, 309
dance, 840
Hop it
go away, 293, 287
escape, 671
Hop the twig
die, 360
Hope
hope, 858
probability, 472
Hopeful
probable, 472
Hopeless
desperate, 859
impossible, 471
Hophead
intemperance, 954
Horde
assemblage, 72
Horizon
distance, 196
view, 441
prospect, 507
futurity, 121
Horizontal
horizontality, 213
Horn
sharpness, 253
musical, 417
alarm, 669
Horn-mad
jealousy, 920
Horn of plenty
sufficient, 639
Hornbook
school, 542
Hornet
bane, 663, 830
Hornpipe
dance, 840
Hornswoggle
deceive, 545

Horny
hard, 323
Horology
chronometry, 114
Horoscope
prediction, 511
Horrible
great, 31
fearful, 860
Horrid
noxious, 649
ugly, 846
dire, 830
vulgar, 851
fearful, 860
hateful, 898
Horripilation
cold, 383
terror, 860
Horrisonous
strident, 410
Horror
dislike, 867
hate, 898
fear, 860
Hors de combat
impotence, 158
disease, 655
Hors-d'œuvre
food, 298
Horse
animal, 271
cavalry, 726
stand, 215
Horse-box
vehicle, 272
Horse-laugh
laugh, 838
Horse-power
measure, 466
Horse-sense
wisdom, 498
Horse-shoe
curvature, 245
Horseman
traveller, 268
Horseplay
violence, 173
Horsewhip
punishment, 972
Hortation
advice, 615, 695
Horticulture
agriculture, 371
Hortus siccus

botany, 369
Hosanna
worship, 990
Hose
dress, 225
conduit, 350
Hospice
abode, 189
Hospitable
social, 892
liberal, 816
Hospital
remedy, 662
Hospodar
master, 745
Host
multitude, 100
collection, 72
friend, 890
religious, 999
Hostage
security, 771
Hostel
inn, 189
Hostile
adverse, 708
Hostilities
warfare, 722
Hostility
enmity, 889
Hot
warm, 382
pungent, 392
irascible, 901
rhythm, 413
contraband, 964
Hot air
sophistry, 477
Hot-bed
workshop, 691
cause, 153
Hot-blooded
rash, 863
Hot-brained
rash, 863
excited, 825
Hot-headed
rash, 863
excited, 825
Hot-plate
heater, 386
Hot water
difficulty, 704
Hot-water bottle
heater, 386

Hotchpotch
  mixture, 41
  confusion, 59
Hotel
  inn, 189
Hothouse
  conservatory, 386
  workshop, 691
Hotspur
  rashness, 863
  courage, 861
Hottentot
  boor, 876
Hough
  maltreat, 649
Hound
  pursue, 281, 622
  oppress, 907
  wretch, 949
Hour
  period, 108
Hour-glass
  time, 114
  form, 203
Houri
  beauty, 845
Hourly
  routine, 138
House
  abode, 189
  to locate, 184
  safety, 664
  party, 712
  senate, 696
  partnership, 797
House-warming
  sociality, 892
Houseboat
  abode, 189
Housebreaker
  thief, 792
Household
  abode, 189
  conformity, 82
  plain, 849
  property, 780
Housekeeper
  director, 694
  servant, 746
Housekeeping
  conduct, 692
Houseless
  displaced, 185
Housemaid
  servant, 746

Housewifery
  conduct, 692
  economy, 817
Housing
  lodging, 189
Hovel
  abode, 189
Hover
  soar, 267
  rise, 305
  high, 206
Hoverplane
  aircraft, 273A
How
  in what way, 627
  by what means, 632
How-d'ye-do
  difficulty, 704
Howbeit
  counteraction, 179
Howdah
  seat, 215
However
  except, 83
  notwithstanding, 179
  degree, 23
  compensation, 30
Howff
  resort, 74
Howitzer
  arms, 727
Howl
  ululation, 411, 412,
    839
Howler
  error, 495
  solecism, 568
Howsoever
  degree, 26
Hoy
  ship, 273
  salutation, 586
Hoyden
  vulgarity, 851
Hub
  centre, 223
  middle, 68
Hubble-bubble
  tobacco-pipe, 298A
Hubbub
  din, 404
  discord, 713
  agitation, 315
Huckster
  merchant, 797

Huddle
  mix, 41
  disorder, 59
  derange, 61
  collect, 72
  don, 225
  nearness, 197
Hue
  colour, 428
Hue and cry
  noise, 404
  outcry, 931
  alarm, 669
  proclamation, 531
Hueless
  achromatism, 429
Huff
  anger, 900
  insolence, 885
Huffiness
  irascibility, 901
Hug
  cohere, 46
  retain, 781
  endearment, 894, 902
Hug oneself
  rejoice, 838
Hug the shore
  approach, 286
Huge
  in degree, 31
  in size, 192
Hugger-mugger
  confusion, 59
Hulk
  whole, 50
  ship, 273
Hulking
  big, 192
  awkward, 853
  ugly, 846
Hull
  whole, 50
Hullabaloo
  noise, 404
  cry, 411
Hullo
  see Hallo
Hum
  faint sound, 405
  continued sound, 407,
    412
  to sing, 415
  deceive, 545
  stink, 401

Hum and ha
hesitate, 583
demur, 605
Hum-note
melody, 413
Human
mankind, 372
Humane
benevolent, 906
philanthropic, 910
Humanism
knowledge, 490
Humanist
scholar, 492
Humanitarian
philanthropist, 906
Humanities
letters, 560
Humanity
human nature, 372
benevolence, 906
Humanize
courtesy, 894
Humble
meek, 879
modest, 881
to abash, 874
pious, 987
Humbug
deception, 545
falsehood, 544
Humdrum
dull, 843
Humectate
moisten, 339
Humid
moist, 339
Humiliate
humble, 879
shame, 874
worship, 990
Humility
piety, 987
Humming-top
musical, 417
Hummock
height, 206, 250
Humoresque
music, 415
Humorist
humorist, 844
Humour
essence, 5
liquid, 333
disposition, 602

tendency, 176
caprice, 608
indulge, 760
affections, 820
to please, 829
wit, 842
Humoursome
capricious, 608
discourteous, 895
Hump
convexity, 250
Hump bluey
journey, 266
Hump yourself
activity, 682
Humpbacked
distortion, 243
ugliness, 846
Humph!
wonder, 870
Humus
soil, 342
Hun
evildoer, 913
Hunch
convexity, 250
Hundred
number, 99
region, 181
Hunger
desire, 865
Hunks
parsimony, 819
Hunnish
malevolent, 907
Hunt
follow, 281
pursue, 622
inquire, 461
Hunter
carrier, 271
Hunting grounds
heaven, 981
Hurdle
fence, 232
Hurdy-gurdy
musical, 417
Hurl
propel, 284
Hurly-burly
confusion, 59
turmoil, 315
Hurrah!
cheerfulness, 836
rejoicing, 838

Hurricane
tempest, 349
violence, 173
Hurried
excitability, 825
Hurry
haste, 684
swiftness, 274
earliness, 132
to urge, 615
to excite, 824
Hurst
plant, 367
Hurt
evil, 619
physical pain, 378
moral pain, 828
to injure, 649, 907
to molest, 830
Hurtful
badness, 649
Hurtle
impulse, 276
Husband
spouse, 903
to store, 636
Husbandman
agriculture, 371
Husbandry
agriculture, 371
conduct, 692
economy, 817
Hush
silence, 403
latent, 526
moderate, 174
assuage, 826
pacify, 723
Hush-hush
secret, 534
Hush-money
bribe, 809
compensation, 30
Hush up
conceal, 526, 528
Husk
covering, 222
to strip, 226
Husky
dry, 340
big, 192
strong, 159
faint sound, 405, 501
Hussar
combatant, 726

Hussy
libertine, 962
bad woman, 949
impertinent, 887
Hustings
tribunal, 966
platform, 542
Hustle
push, 276
disarrange, 61
agitate, 315
bustle, 171, 682
haste, 684
Hut
abode, 189
Hutch
abode, 189
Huzza!
cheerfulness, 836
Hyaline
transparency, 425
Hybrid
mixture, 41
nondescript, 83
Hydra
unconformity, 83
Hydra-headed
reproduction, 163
Hydrant
spray, 348
Hydraulics
fluids, 348
Hydrogen bomb
arms, 727
Hydrographic
sea, 341
Hydrology
water, 333
Hydromel
sweetness, 396
Hydrometer
density, 321
Hydropathic
salubrity, 656
remedy, 662
Hydropathy
remedy, 662
Hydrophobia
dislike, 867
Hydroplane
aircraft, 273A
Hydroponics
agriculture, 371
Hydrostatics
water, 333

Hydrotherapy
remedy, 662
Hyena
evildoer, 913
Hygiene
salubrity, 656
Hygrology
moisture, 339
Hygrometer
moisture, 339
Hylotheism
heathen, 984
Hymen
marriage, 903
Hymn
worship, 990
Hymnal rite, 998
Hyperaesthesia
excitability, 825
sensibility, 376, 822
Hyperbole
exaggeration, 549
Hyperborean
cold, 383
Hypercritical
disapprobation, 932
fastidious, 868
Hyperion
beauty, 845
Hypermetropia
vision, 443
Hyperpyrexia
heat, 382
Hypersensitive
sensitive, 375, 825
Hypertrophy
expansion, 194
Hyphen
vinculum, 45
Hypnology
inactivity, 683
Hypnosis
inactivity, 683
Hypnotic
remedy, 662
sedative, 683
Hypnotize
occult, 992, 994
Hypocaust
furnace, 386
Hypochondriac
dejection, 837
insanity, 503, 504
Hypocrisy
deception, 545

religious, 988
Hypocrite
deceiver, 548
Hypocritical
falsehood, 544
Hypostasis
substantiality, 3
Hypostatic
Deity, 976
Hypothecation
lending, 787
Hypothesis
supposition, 514
Hysterical
violence, 173
excitement, 825
Hysteron proteron
inversion, 218
i.e. meaning, 516

IOU
security, 771
money, 800
Iambic
verse, 597
Ibidem
identity, 13
Icarus
ascent, 305
Ice
cold, 383
cool, 385
smooth, 255
Ice-house
refrigeratory, 387
Ice-pail
cooler, 387
Ichnography
representation, 554
Ichor
liquidity, 333
Ichthyophagous
eat, 296
Icicle
cold, 383
Icon
representation, 554
Iconoclasm
heresy, 984A
Iconoclast
destroyer, 165
Icosahedron
angularity, 244
twenty, 98

Ictus
rhythm, 138
Icy
discourteous, 895
Id
mind, 450
Id est
interpretation, 522
Idea
notion, 453
belief, 484
knowledge, 490
small degree, 32
small quantity, 192
inexistence, 2
Ideal
erroneous, 495
unreal, 2, 515
immaterial, 317
pleasurable, 829
Ideality
intellect, 450
imagination, 515
Ideate
imagine, 515
apprehend, 490
Idée fixe
misjudgment, 481
Identify
comparison, 464
Identity
identity, 13
Identity-card
sign, 550
Ideologist
doctrinaire, 493
Ideology
intellect, 450
knowledge, 490
belief, 484
Idiocy
folly, 499
Idiom
phrase, 566
style, 569
Idiosyncrasy
essence, 5
speciality, 79
characteristic, 550
abnormality, 83
tendency, 176
temperament, 820
sensitiveness, 375
Idiot
imbecile, 501

foolish, 499
Idle
slothful, 683
trivial, 643
Ido
language, 560
Idol
favourite, 899
Idolatry
superstition, 984A
heathen, 986
impious worship, 991
love, 897
Idolize
love, 897
Idyll
poetry, 597
If
supposition, 514
qualification, 469
Igloo
abode, 189
Igneous
heat, 382
Ignis fatuus
light, 423
phantom, 515
unsubstantial, 4
dim sight, 443
error, 495
Ignite
calefaction, 384
Ignition
heat, 382
Ignoble
base, 876, 945
Ignominy
dishonour, 940
shame, 874
Ignoramus
ignoramus, 493
Ignorant
ignorance, 491
Ignore
repudiate, 773
slight, 460, 929
dissent, 489
Ilk
identity, 13
Ill
sick, 655
evil, 619
Ill-advised
foolish, 499, 699
inexpedient, 647

Ill-assorted
disagreement, 24
Ill-bred
discourtesy, 895
vulgar, 851
Ill-conditioned
discourteous, 895
malevolent, 907
vicious, 945
Ill-favoured
ugliness, 846
Ill feeling
enmity, 889
hate, 898
Ill-flavoured
unsavouriness, 395
Ill humour
resentment, 900
Ill-judged
foolish, 499
ill-advised, 699
Ill-looking
ugliness, 846
Ill-made
distortion, 243
Ill-natured
malevolence, 907
Ill-off
adversity, 735
Ill-omened
evil, 649
disagreeable, 858
hopeless, 859
Ill-proportioned
distortion, 243
Ill-sorted
disagreement, 24
Ill-starred
adversity, 735
Ill-tempered
discourtesy, 895
irascibility, 901
Ill-timed
inappropriate, 24
untimely, 135
Ill-treat
injure, 649, 907
Ill turn
evil, 619
Ill-used
hurt, 828
Ill will
enmity, 889
malevolence, 907

Illapse
entry, 294
Illation
judgment, 480
Illegal
illegality, 964
Illegible
unintelligible, 519
Illegitimate
undue, 925
illegal, 964
erroneous, 495
Illiberal
selfish, 943
stingy, 819
intolerant, 481
Illicit
illegality, 964, 925
Illimitable
infinite, 105
great, 31
Illiterate
ignorance, 491
Illness
disease, 655
Illogical
sophistical, 477
erroneous, 495
Illuminate
enlighten, 420
colour, 428
adorn, 847
Illuminati
scholar, 492
Illumination
drawing, 556
ornament, 847
celebration, 883
Illusion
error, 495
deceit, 545
Illusionist
conjurer, 548
Illusive
erroneous, 495
sophistical, 477
deceitful, 544
Illusory
see Illusive
Illustration
interpretation, 522
drawing, 556
representation, 554
ornament, 847
example, 82

Illustrious
repute, 873
Image
representation, 554
idea, 453
statue, 557
idol, 991
likeness, 17
Imagery
metaphor, 521
fancy, 515
Imaginary
non-existing, 2
erroneous, 495
quantity, 84
Imagination
fancy, 515
wit, 842
Imam
clergy, 996
master, 745
Imbalance
inequality, 28
Imbecile
foolish, 477, 499
absence of intellect, 450A
weak, 160
incapable, 158
Imbed
see Embed
Imbibe
receive, 296
learn, 539
Imbrangle
derange, 61
Imbricated
covering, 222
Imbroglio
unintelligibility, 519
discord, 713
Imbrue
moisten, 339
impregnate, 300
Imbue
mix, 41
tinge, 428
impregnate, 300
moisten, 339
teach, 537
feel, 821
Imitate
to copy, 19
repetition, 104
to represent, 554
Imitation

copy, 21
Immaculate
excellent, 648
spotless, 652
faultless, 650
innocent, 946
pure, 960
Immanent
inherent, 5
Immanity
malevolence, 907
Immaterial
unsubstantial, 4
spiritual, 317
mental, 450
trifling, 643
Immature
new, 123
unprepared, 674
Immeasurable
infinite, 105
great, 31
Immediate
transient, 111
Immedicable
incurable, 655, 659
Immemorial
old, 124
Immense
in degree, 31
in size, 192
Immerse
introduce, 300
dip, 337
baptism, 998
Immethodical
disorder, 59
Immigrant
stranger, 57
Immigration
migration, 266
entrance, 294
Imminent
futurity, 121
destiny, 152
Immiscibility
incoherence, 47
Immission
reception, 296
Immitigable
ire, 900
violence, 173
Immobility
immutability, 150
quiescence, 265

541

resolution, 604
Immoderately
greatness, 31
Immoderation
intemperance, 954
Immodest
impurity, 961
Immolate
destroy, 162
kill, 361
offer, 763
Immolation
sacrifice, 991
Immoral
vicious, 945
wrong, 923
Immortal
perpetual, 112
glorious, 873
celebrated, 883
Immovable
unchangeable, 150
resolved, 604
obstinate, 606
Immunity
exemption, 927A
right, 924
freedom, 748
Immure
enclose, 231
imprison, 751
Immutable
immutability, 150
Imp
demon, 980
ruffian, 913
wretch, 943
Impact
contact, 43
impulse, 276
insertion, 300
Impair
deterioration, 659
Impale
transfix, 260
pierce, 302
execute, 972
Impalpable
small, 193
powder, 330
immaterial, 317
intangible, 381
Impanation
rite, 998
Imparity

inequality, 28
Impart
give, 784
inform, 527
Impartial
just, 922
wise, 498
indifferent, 866
honourable, 939
Impassable
closed, 261, 704
Impasse
hindrance, 706
situation, 8
difficulty, 704
Impassible
insensible, 376, 823
Impassion
excite, 824
Impassive
insensible, 823
Impasto
painting, 556
Impatient
excitable, 825
Impawn
lending, 787
Impeach
accuse, 938
Impeccability
perfection, 650
Impecunious
adversity, 735
poverty, 804
Impede
hindrance, 706
Impedimenta
hindrance, 706
baggage, 635
Impel
push, 276, 284
move, 264
induce, 615
Impend
future, 121
expectation, 507
height, 206
destiny, 152
Impenetrable
latent, 526
hidden, 528
Impenitence
impenitence, 951
Imperative
authority, 737

duty, 926
requirement, 630
Imperator
master, 745
Imperceptible
invisible, 447
minute, 193
Impercipient
insensibility, 376
Imperfect
incomplete, 53
failing, 651
shortcoming, 304
vicious, 945
small, 32
Imperforate
closure, 261
Imperial
authority, 737
beard, 256
Imperil
endanger, 665
Imperious
stern, 739
insolent, 885
Imperishable
external, 112, 150
glorious, 873
Impermanent
transitory, 111
Impermeable
closed, 261
dense, 321
Impersonal
generality, 78
material, 316
Impersonate
represent, 554
imitate, 19
Impertinence
inexpedience, 647
Impertinent
irrelevant, 10
disagreeing, 24
insolent, 885
discourteous, 895
Imperturbable
unruffled, 823, 826
Impervious
closure, 261
Impetrate
beseech, 765
Impetuous
boisterous, 173
hot, 825

hasty, 684
rash, 863
eager, 865
Impetus
impulse, 276
Impiety
impiety, 988
irreligion, 989
Impignorate
lending, 787
Impinge
impulse, 276
Impish
supernatural, 980
Implacable
hatred, 898
wrath, 900
unforgiving, 919
Implant
insert, 300
teach, 537
Implanted
adventitious, 6
inborn, 5
Implement
instrument, 633
Impletion
sufficiency, 639
fullness, 52
Implicate
accuse, 938
involve, 54
Implication
inference, 521
Implicit
understood, 516
metaphorical, 521
untold, 526
Implore
beseech, 765
pray, 990
pity, 914
Imply
mean, 516
latent, 526
evidence, 467
metaphor, 521
Impolite
rude, 895
vulgar, 851
Impolitic
folly, 499
inexpedient, 647
Imponderable
light, 320

immaterial, 317
Import
ingress, 294
transfer, 270
insert, 300
mean, 516
be of consequence, 642
receive, 296
Importance
greatness, 31
Important
importance, 642
repute, 873
Importunate
painfulness, 830
Importune
ask, 765
pester, 830
Impose
order, 741
cheat, 545
be unjust, 923, 925
palm off upon, 486
Imposing
grand, 873
Impossible
incredible, 471
impracticable, 704
Impost
price, 812
Impostor
deceiver, 548
Imposture
deception, 545
Impotence
impotence, 158
weakness, 160
failure, 732
Impound
enclose, 231
imprison, 751
Impoverish
drain, 638
fleece, 789
render poor, 804
Impracticable
difficult, 704
impossible, 471
obstinate, 606
Imprecation
request, 765
malediction, 908
Impregnable
safety, 664
Impregnate

insert, 300
produce, 161, 168
mix, 41
teach, 537
Impresario
drama, 599
Imprescriptible
dueness, 924
Impress
mark, 550
memory, 505
excite, 375, 824
compel, 744
Impressible
sensibility, 822
motive, 615
Impression
belief, 375, 484
idea, 453
feeling, 821
engraving, 558
Impressionist
artist, 559
Impressive
exciting, 824
notable, 642
Imprimatur
sanction, 924
Imprimis
beginning, 66
Imprint
indication, 550
Imprison
shut up, 751
circumscribe, 231
Improbable
improbability, 473
Improbity
improbity, 940
wrong, 923
Improficiency
unskilfulness, 699
Impromptu
impulse, 612
music, 415
Improper
wrong, 923, 925
inexpedient, 499, 647
incongruous, 24
unseemly, 961
Impropriate
take, 789
possess, 777
Improve
improvement, 658

Improvident
careless, 460
not preparing, 674, 863
prodigal, 818P
Improvise
impulse, 612
imagine, 515
Imprudent
rash, 863
unwise, 699
neglectful, 460
Impudent
insolence, 885
discourtesy, 895
Impudicity
impurity, 961
Impugn
blame, 932
deny, 536
oppose, 708
Impuissance
impotence, 158
Impulse
push, 276
unpremeditation, 612
necessity, 601
Impulsive
instinctive, 477
motive, 615
motiveless, 616
rash, 863
Impunity
acquittal, 970
Impure
foul, 653
licentious, 961
Imputation
disrepute, 874
Impute
ascribe, 155
accuse, 938
In esse
existence, 1
In extenso
whole, 50
diffuse, 573
In extremis
death, 360
In fine
end, 67
In hand
possession, 777
business, 625
In limine
beginning, 66

In loco
agreement, 23
In mediis rebus
middle, 68
In nubibus
inexistence, 2
incogitancy, 452
imagination, 515
unintelligibility, 519
In propria persona
speciality, 79
In puris naturalibus
divestment, 226
In re
relation, 9
In saecula saeculorum
perpetuity, 112
In statu pupillari
youth, 127
learner, 541
In statu quo
permanence, 141
restoration, 660
In terrorem
threat, 909
In toto
whole, 50
greatness, 31
In transitu
transient, 111
conversion, 144
motion, 264
transference, 270
method, 627
Inability
want of power, 158
want of skill, 699
Inaccessible
distance, 196
impossible, 471
Inaccurate
error, 495, 568
Inaction
inaction, 681
Inactivity
inactivity, 172, 683
Inadaptability
disagreement, 24
Inadequate
insufficient, 640, 645
imperfect, 651
weak, 158, 160
Inadmissible
inexpedient, 647
incongruous, 24

excluded, 55
Inadvertence
inattention, 458
unintentional, 621
Inalienable
right, 924
possession, 777
retention, 781
Inamorata
love, 897
Inane
trivial, 643
useless, 645
void, 4
Inanimate
dead, 360
inorganic, 358
Inanition
insufficiency, 640
Inanity
inutility, 645
absence of thought, 452
absence of meaning, 517
insignificance, 643
Inappetence
indifference, 866
Inapplicable
irrelation, 10
disagree, 24
Inapposite
disagree, 24
irrelevant, 10
Inappreciable
in size, 193
in degree, 32
unimportant, 643
Inappreciative
ungrateful, 917
Inapprehensible
unknowable, 519
Inappropriate
discordant, 24
inexpedient, 647
Inapt
inexpedient, 647
incongruous, 24
Inaptitude
impotence, 158
Inarticulate
stammering, 583
Inartificial
artlessness, 703
Inartistic
unskilled, 699
imperfect, 651

Incomparable
goodness, 648
Incompatible
disagree, 24
Incompetence
inability, 158
incapacity, 499
insufficiency, 640
unskilfulness, 699
Incomplete
defective, 53
not completed, 730
Incomprehensible
unintelligible, 519
Incomprehension
ignorance, 491
Incompressible
density, 321
Inconceivable
unintelligible, 519
incredible, 485
Inconcinnity
ugliness, 846
Inconclusive
sophistry, 477
Incondite
inelegant, 579
Incongruous
disagreement, 24
Inconsecutive
discontinuous, 70
Inconsequential
unreasonable, 477
Inconsiderable
in size, 193
in degree, 32
unimportant, 643
Inconsiderate
thoughtless, 452
heedless, 460
foolish, 699
Inconsistent
contrary, 14
unreasonable, 477
disagreeing, 24
multiform, 16A
absurd, 497
capricious, 608
Inconsolable
pain, 828
dejection, 837
Inconsonance
disagreement, 24
Inconspicuous
invisible, 447

latent, 526
Inconstant
irresolution, 605
Incontestable
certainty, 474
Incontinent
impurity, 961
Incontinently
transient, 111
Incontrovertible
certainty, 474
unchangeable, 150
Inconvenient
inexpedient, 647
Inconvincible
incredulity, 487
Incorporate
combination, 48
Incorporeal
immaterial, 317
Incorrect
erroneous, 495, 568
sophistical, 477
Incorrigible
vicious, 945
impenitent, 951
irremediable, 649
hopeless, 859
Incorruptible
honourable, 939
pure, 942
Incorruption
health, 654
innocence, 946
Incrassate
thickness, 202
density, 321
Increase
in degree, 35
in size, 194
Incredible
impossible, 471
improbable, 473, 485
much, 31
wonderful, 870
Incredulity
unbelief, 485, 487
religious, 989
Increment
increase,
in degree, 35
in size, 194
addition, 37, 39
Incrustation
covering, 222

Incubation
preparation, 673
Incubus
hindrance, 706
Inculcate
teach, 537
Inculpate
accuse, 938
Incumbent
height, 206
weight, 319
duty, 926
clergyman, 996
Incunabula
beginning, 66
book, 591
Incur
liable, 177
Incurable
disease, 655
Incuriosity
incurious, 456
Incursion
ingress, 294
attack, 716
Incurvation
curvature, 245
Indaba
council, 696
Indebted
owing, 806
duty, 926
gratitude, 916
Indecent
impure, 961
Indecision
irresolute, 605
absence of choice, 610
Indecisive
uncertain, 475
inconclusive, 477
Indeclinable
immutable, 150
Indecorum
vice, 945
impurity, 961
vulgarity, 851
Indeed
very, 31
wonder, 870
truth, 494
assertion, 535
Indefatigable
activity, 682
resolute, 604

Indefeasible
dueness, 150, 924
Indefectible
perfection, 650
Indefensible
wrong, 945
inexcusable, 938
weak, 160, 725
Indefinite
vague, 447, 519
uncertain, 475
inexact, 495
infinite, 105
in degree, 31
Indelible
mark, 550
condition, 150
memory, 505
feeling, 821
Indelicate
impurity, 961
Indemnify
reward, 973
compensate, 30
Indemnity
forgiveness, 918
Indentation
notch, 252, 257
Indenture
record, 551
security, 771
evidence, 467
compact, 769
Independence
irrelation, 10
wealth, 803
freedom, 748
Indescribable
wonder, 870
great, 31
Indestructible
perpetual, 112
Indeterminate
uncertain, 475
obscure, 519
chance, 156
Indetermination
irresolution, 605
Index
sign, 550
list, 86, 562
arrangement, 60
record, 551
numerical exponent, 84
Indian sign

spell, 993
Indian summer
autumn, 126
Indiarubber
elasticity, 325
Indicate
point out, 550
manifest, 525
mean, 516
evidence, 467
Indict
arraign, 969
accuse, 938
Indictable
criminal, 945
Indifference
unconcern, 866
absence of choice, 610
coldness, 823
unwillingness, 603
unimportance, 643
imperfect, 651
Indigene
inhabitant, 188
Indigenous
intrinsic, 5
Indigent
poor, 804
insufficient, 640
Indignation
resentment, 900
Indignity
insult, 929
affront, 900
outrage, 830
Indigo
blueness, 438
Indirect
obliquity, 217
Indiscernible
invisible, 447
Indiscerptible
unity, 50
whole, 87
dense, 321
Indiscreet
unskilful, 699
blamable, 945
neglectful, 460
foolish, 499
Indiscretion
guilt, 947
Indiscriminate
multiform, 81
unarranged, 59

casual, 621
Indiscrimination
neglect, 460
indistinction, 465A
Indispensable
requirement, 630
Indisposed
disincline, 603
to dissuade, 616
sick, 655
Indisputable
certainty, 474
Indissoluble
whole, 50
dense, 321
united, 43
unchangeable, 150
Indistinct
vague, 519
dim, 447
Indistinguishable
minute, 447
identical, 13
Indite
write, 590
Individual
special, 79
exceptional, 83
unity, 87
whole, 50
style, 574
Indivisible
whole, 50
dense, 321
Indocility
obstinacy, 606
incapacity, 538
Indoctrinate
teach, 484, 537
Indolence
inactivity, 683
Indomitable
resolution, 604
courage, 861
unyielding, 719
Indraught
current, 348
Indubitable
certainty, 474
Induce
motive, 615
cause, 153
produce, 161
Induction
investigation, 461

reasoning, 476
of a priest, 995
appointment, 755
Indulge
allow, 760
give, 784
lenity, 740
pleasure, 827
pleasing, 829
intemperance, 954
satisfy, 831
Induration
hardening, 323
impenitence, 951
Industrial action
strike, 719
Industry
activity, 682
learning, 539
business, 625
Indweller
inhabitant, 188
Inebriety
drunkenness, 959
Inedible
unsavoury, 395
Ineffable
wonder, 870
Ineffably
greatness, 31
Ineffaceable
memory, 505
feeling, 821
Ineffectual
incapable, 158
weak, 160
useless, 645
failing, 732
Inefficacious
see Ineffectual
Inefficient
see Ineffectual
Inelastic
not elastic, 326
soft, 324
Inelegant
ugly, 846
in style, 579
Ineligible
inexpedience, 647
Ineluctable
destiny, 152
Inept
incapable, 158, 699
useless, 645

unsuitable, 24
Inequality
inequality, 28
Inequitable
wrong, 923
Ineradicable
fixed, 150
Inerrable
innocence, 946
Inert
physically, 172, 683
morally, 823
Inertia
inertness, 172
inactivity, 683
Inestimable
goodness, 648
Inevitable
destiny, 152, 601
certain, 474
Inexact
error, 495
Inexactitude lie, 546
Inexcitability
inexcitability, 826
Inexcusable
vice, 938, 945
Inexecution
non-completion, 730
Inexhaustible
sufficiency, 639
Inexistence
inexistence, 2
Inexorable
resolved, 604
stern, 739
compelling, 744
wrathful, 900
relentless, 907
Inexpectation
inexpectation, 508
Inexpedient
inexpedience, 647
Inexpensive
cheapness, 815
Inexperience
ignorance, 491
disqualification, 699
Inexpert
unskilfulness, 699
Inexpiable
vice, 945
Inexplicable
unintelligible, 519
wonderful, 870

Inexpressible
unmeaning, 517
wonder, 870
great degree, 31
Inexpressive
unmeaning, 517, 519
Inexpugnable
safety, 664
Inextinguishable
immutable, 150
uncontrollable, 825
energetic, 157
Inextricable
difficult, 704
impossible, 471
disorder, 59
coherence, 46
Infallible
certainty, 474
perfect, 650
Infamy
dishonour, 940
shame, 874
vice, 945
Infancy
beginning, 66
youth, 127
Infant
infant, 129
Infanta
master, 745
Infanticide
killing, 361
Infantile
puerile, 643
foolish, 499
Infantry
combatant, 726
Infatuation
folly, 499
misjudgment, 481
obstinacy, 606
credulity, 486
passion, 825
love, 897
Infeasible
impossible, 471
difficult, 704
Infect
mix, 41
Infection
disease, 655
contamination, 659
excitation, 824

Infectious
insalubrity, 657
Infecund
unproductiveness, 169
Infelicity
unhappiness, 828
inexpertness, 699
Infer
judgment, 480
Inference
judgment, 480
interpretation, 522
Inferential
deducible, 478
Inferior
less, 34
imperfect, 651
Infernal
bad, 649
wicked, 945
malevolent, 907
Infertility
unproductiveness, 169
Infest
annoy, 649, 830
frequent, 136
Infibulation
junction, 43
Infidel
heathen, 984
Infidelity
dishonour, 940
irreligion, 989
Infiltrate
intervene, 228
influence, 175
imbue, 339
teach, 537
mixture, 41
Infiltration
ingress, 294
passage, 302
presence, 186
Infinite
in quantity, 105
in degree, 31
in size, 192
Infinitesimal
in degree, 32
in quantity, 193
Infinity
infinitude, 105
space, 180
Infirm
weak, 160

irresolute, 605
vicious, 945
Infirmary
remedy, 662
Infirmity
weakness, 160
disease, 655
failing, 945
Infix
teaching, 537
Inflame
burn, 384
stir up, 173
incense, 900
incite, 615
Inflammation
disease, 655
Inflate
expend, 194
rarefy, 322
blow, 349
style, 573, 577
ridiculous, 853
vanity, 880
Inflect
curvature, 245
grammar, 567
Inflexible
hard, 323
resolved, 604
obstinate, 606
stern, 739
Inflexion
curvature, 245
change, 140
appendage, 39
grammar, 567
Inflict
condemn, 971
act upon, 680
give pain, 830
Infliction
pain, 828
Influence
physical, 175
authority, 737
inducement, 615
importance, 642
Influential
important, 642
Influx
ingress, 294
Inform
information, 527
Inform against

accusation, 938
Informal
irregular, 83
lawless, 964
Information
knowledge, 490
communication, 527
Informer
witness, 467
Infra
posterior, 117
Infra dignitatem
disrepute, 874
Infra-microscopic
little, 193
Infraction
non-observance, 773
unconformity, 83
exemption, 927
disobedience, 742
violation, 614
Infrangible
coherence, 46, 321
Infrastructure
base, 211
Infrequency
infrequency, 137
fewness, 103
Infringe
transgress, 303
violate, 742, 773, 925,
927
break through, 614
Infundibular
concavity, 252
Infuriate
wrathful, 900
excite, 824
violent, 173
Infuse
mix, 41
insert, 300
teach, 537
Infusible
solid, 321
Ingeminate
duplication, 90
Ingenious
skill, 698
Ingénue
actress, 599
Ingenuous
artless, 703
sincere, 543
guileless, 939

Ingest
absorb, 296
Ingle
fuel, 388
Inglorious
disrepute, 874
base, 940
Ingoing
ingress, 294
Ingot
money, 800
Ingraft
see Engraft
Ingrate
ingratitude, 917
Ingratiate
love, 897
Ingratitude
ingratitude, 917
Ingredient
component, 56
Ingress
ingress, 294
Ingrowing
insertion, 300
Ingurgitate
reception, 296
Inhabile
unskilfulness, 699
Inhabit
presence, 186
Inhabitant
inhabitant, 188
Inhale
reception, 296
sniff, 398
Inharmonious
discordant, 414
incongruity, 24
Inherence
intrinsicality, 5
Inherit
acquire, 775
possess, 777
Inheritance
property, 780
Inhesion
intrinsicality, 5
Inhibit
prohibit, 761
not think of, 452
dissuade, 616
hinder, 706
Inhospitable
seclusion, 893

Inhuman
malevolence, 907
Inhume
interment, 363
Inimical
hostile, 708, 889
unfavourable, 706
Inimitable
perfect, 650
good, 648
Iniquitous
bad, 649
Iniquity
wrong, 923
vice, 945
Initiate
begin, 66
teach, 537
Initiated
skilful, 698
Initiative
enterprise, 676
beginning, 66
Inject
insertion, 300
Injudicious
folly, 499
inexpedient, 647
Injunction
command, 741
prohibition, 761
advice, 695
decree, 963
Injure
to damage, 659
malevolence, 907
Injury
harm, 649
Injustice
wrong, 923
Ink
blackness, 431
Ink-slinger
writer, 590
Inkle
connection, 45
Inkling
information, 527
supposition, 514
knowledge, 490
Inlaid
variegation, 440
Inland
interiority, 221
Inlay

variegation, 440
Inlet
opening, 260
way, 627
beginning, 66
of the sea, 343
Inly
interiority, 221
Inmate
inhabitant, 188
Inmost
interiority, 221
Inn
abode, 189
Innate
intrinsicality, 5
Innavigable
difficulty, 704
Inner
interiority, 221
Innocence
innocence, 946
probity, 939
virtue, 944
Innocuous
harmless, 648
wholesome, 656
Innominate
misnomer, 565
Innovation
newness, 123
change, 140
Innoxious
innocent, 946
salubrious, 656
harmless, 648
Innuendo
information, 527
insinuation, 932
Innumerable
infinity, 105
Inobservance
non-observance, 773
Inoculate
insert, 300
teach, 537
Inodorous
inodorousness, 399
Inoffensive
harmless, 648, 946
Inofficious
malevolence, 907
Inoperative
unproductive, 169
useless, 645

Inopportune
untimely, 135
inexpedient, 647
Inordinate
size, 192
superfluous, 641
excessive, 31
Inorganic
inorganization, 358
Inosculate
intersect, 219
convoluted, 248
joined, 43
Inquest
inquiry, 461
jurisdiction, 965
Inquietude
uneasiness, 828
apprehension, 860
discontent, 832
restlessness, 264
disorder, 59
Inquiry
search, 461
curiosity, 455
Inquisition
inquiry, 461
jurisdiction, 965
Inroad
ingress, 294
invasion, 716
devastation, 619
Insalubrity
insalubrity, 657
Insane
mad, 503
rash, 863
Insanitary
insalubrious, 657
Insatiable
desire, 865
Inscribe
write, 590
label, 551
represent, 554
Inscrutable
unintelligibility, 519
Insculpture
sculpture, 557
Insect
animal, 366
minute, 193
Insecure
danger, 665
Insensate

foolish, 499
mad, 503
Insensibility
physical, 376
moral, 823
Inseparable
cohering, 46
attached, 43
Insert
put in, 300
locate, 184
interpose, 228
enter, 294
Inseverable
junction, 43
unity, 87
Inside
interiority, 221
Insidious
false, 544
cunning, 702
dishonourable, 940
Insight
knowledge, 490
intuition, 477
Insignia
indication, 550
Insignificance
smallness, 32
Insignificant
unimportance, 643
Insincere
falsehood, 544
Insinuate
intervene, 228
ingress, 294
mean, 516
suppose, 514
hint, 527
blame, 932
insert, 300
Insipid
tasteless, 391
dull, 575
indifferent, 866
Insist
command, 741
Insistent
importunate, 830
Insobriety
drunkenness, 959
Insolence
insolence, 885
Insoluble
dense, 321

unintelligible, 519
Insolvent
non-payment, 808
Insomnia
wakefulness, 680
Insomuch
greatness, 31
Insouciance
thoughtlessness, 458
supineness, 823
indifference, 866
Inspan
harness, 43
depart, 293
Inspect
look, 441
attend to, 457
Inspector
spectator, 444
director, 694
inquirer, 461
Inspiration
breathing, 349
impulse, 612
excitation, 824
prompting, 615
imagination, 515
wisdom, 498
piety, 987
Inspire
prompt, 615
animate, 824
Inspirit
urge, 615
animate, 824
cheer, 836
courage, 861
Inspissation
semiliquidity, 352
Instability
mutability, 149
Install
locate, 184
commission, 755
celebrate, 883
ordain, 995
Instalment
portion, 51
payment, 807
Instance
example, 82
solicitation, 765
motive, 615
Instancy
urgency, 642

Instant
moment, 113
present, 118
future, 121
Instanter
earlier, 132
instantaneity, 113
Instauration
restoration, 600
Instead
substitution, 147
Instigate
motive, 615
Instil
insert, 300
teach, 537
mix, 41
Instinct
intellect, 450
intuition, 477
impulse, 601
innate, 5
Instinctive
habitual, 613
impulsive, 612
Institute
school, 542
beginning, 66
cause, 153
organize, 161
Institution
legality, 963
poorhouse, 804
Institutor
teacher, 540
Instruct
teach, 537
advise, 695
precept, 697
command, 741
Instructor
teacher, 540
Instrument
implement, 633
record, 551
security, 771
Instrumental
means, 632
music, 415
subservient, 631
Instrumentality
medium, 631
Insubordinate
disobedience, 742
anarchy, 738

Insubstantiality
nothingness, 4
Insufferable
painfulness, 830
Insufficient
insuffiency, 640
shortcoming, 304
Insufflation
wind, 349
Insular
island, 346
detach, 44
single, 87
Insulate
separate, 44
Insult
rudeness, 895
disrespect, 929
offence, 900
Insuperable
difficulty, 704
impossible, 471
Insupportable
painfulness, 830
Insuppressible
violence, 173
Insurance
promise, 768
security, 771
precaution, 664
Insurgent
disobedience, 742
Insurmountable
difficulty, 704
impossible, 471
Insurrection
disobedience, 742
resistance, 719
Insusceptible
insensibility, 823
Intact permanence, 141
preserve, 669
Intaglio
concavity, 252
sculpture, 557
Intake
inlet, 260
Intangible
numbness, 381
immaterial, 317
Integer
whole, 50
Integral calculus
number, 84
Integral part

component, 56
Integrate
consolidate, 50
complete, 52
Integration
number, 84
Integrity
whole, 50
virtue, 944
probity, 939
Integument
overing, 222
Intellect
intellect, 450
Intelligence
mind, 450
news, 532
wisdom, 498
Intelligible
intelligibility, 518, 570
Intemperate
intemperance, 954
drunkenness, 957
Intempestivity
unseasonableness, 135
Intend
design, 620
Intendant
director, 694
Intended
will, 600
Intensify
energize, 171
aggravate, 835
Intensity
degree, 26
greatness, 31
energy, 171
Intent
active, 682
thoughtful, 451, 457
Intention
design, 620
Intentional
will, 600
Intentness
attention, 457
thought, 451
Inter
bury, 363
insert, 300
Inter alia
conformity, 82
Interaction
reciprocal, 12

Interblend
  mix, 41
Interbreed
  mix, 41
Intercalate
  insert, 300
  intervene, 228
Intercede
  mediate, 724
  deprecate, 766
Intercept
  hinder, 706
  take, 789
Intercession
  deprecation, 766
Interchange
  interchange, 148
  reciprocate, 12
  barter, 794
  transfer, 783
Intercipient
  hinder, 706
Interclude
  hindrance, 706
Intercom
  hearing, 418
Intercommunicate
  interlocution, 588
  information, 527
Intercommunion
  society, 892
Intercostal
  interiority, 221
Intercourse
  converse, 588
Intercross
  mix, 41
Intercurrence
  passage, 302
Interdict
  prohibition, 761
Interdigitate
  intervene, 228
  intersect, 219
Interest
  advantage, 618
  concern, 9
  importance, 642
  curiosity, 455
  attention, 457
  aid, 707
  to please, 829
  debt, 806
Interested
  selfish, 943

Interesting
  style, 574
Interfere
  intervene, 228
  meddle, 682
  disagree, 24
  counteract, 179
  thwart, 706
  mediate, 724
  activity, 682
Interglossa
  language, 560
Interim
  duration, 106
  synchronism, 120
Interior
  interiority, 221
Interjacence
  coming between, 228
  middle, 68
Interject
  insert, 300
  interpose, 228
Interlace
  twine, 219
  join, 43
Interlard
  interpose, 228
  mix, 41
  insert, 300
Interleave
  interjacence, 228
  addition, 37
Interline
  insert, 228
  write, 590
Interlink
  junction, 43
Interlocation
  interjacence, 228
Interlock
  cross, 219
  join, 43
Interlocution
  interlocution, 588
Interloper
  intervene, 228
  obstruct, 706
  extraneous, 57
Interlude
  dramatic, 599
  time, 106
  interjacence, 228
  interruption, 70
Intermarriage

  marriage, 903
Intermeddle
  hinder, 706
  interfere, 682
Intermeddling
  mediation, 724
Intermediary
  messenger, 534
Intermediate
  mean, 29
  middle, 68
  intervening, 228
Intermedium
  link, 45
  instrument, 631
  intervention, 228
Interment
  interment, 300, 363
Intermezzo
  interlude, 106
  music, 415
Interminable
  infinite, 105
  eternal, 112
  long, 200
Intermingle
  mixture, 41
Intermission
  discontinuance, 142
Intermit
  interrupt, 70
  discontinue, 142
  recur, 138
  suspend, 265
  in time, 106
Intermix
  mixture, 41
Intermutation
  interchange, 148
Intern
  restrain, 751
Internal
  interior, 221
  intrinsic, 5
International
  reciprocal, 12
  law, 963
Internecine
  slaughter, 361
  war, 722
Internuncio
  messenger, 534
  consignee, 758
Interpellation
  inquiry, 461

address, 586
appeal, 765
summons, 741
Interpenetration
passage, 302
interjacence, 228
presence, 186
ingress, 294
Interpolate
intervene, 228
mix, 41
analytical, 85
Interpose
intervene, 228
mediate, 724
mix, 41
act, 682
hinder, 706
Interpret
explain, 522
answer, 462
Interpreter
interpretation, 524
Interregnum
laxity, 738
intermission, 106
transient, 111
cessation, 142
discontinuity, 70
Interrogate
inquiry, 461
Interrupt
discontinuity, 70
hindrance, 706
cessation, 142
pause, 265
Intersect
crossing, 219
Interspace
interval, 198
interior, 221
Intersperse
diffuse, 73
mix, 41
intervene, 228
Interstice
interval, 198
Interstitial
interjacent, 228
internal, 221
Intertexture
tissue, 329
intersection, 219
Intertwine
cross, 219

intervene, 228
Intertwist
unite, 43, 219P
Interval
of space, 198
of order, 70
of time, 106
Intervene
in space, 228, 300
in time, 106
in order, 68
Intervention
mediation, 724
instrumentality, 170,
631
Interview
conference, 588
society, 892
Intervolved
junction, 43
Interweave
crossing, 219
Intestate
obliteration, 552
Intestine
interiority, 221
Intimate
to tell, 527
friendly, 888
close, 197
Intimidate
frighten, 860
insolence, 885
threat, 909
Intolerable
painfulness, 830
Intolerant
impatient, 825
insolent, 885
prejudice, 481
Intonation
sound, 402
voice, 580
Intone
recite, 582
Intoxicate
excite, 824, 825
inebriate, 959
Intractable
difficult, 704
obstinate, 606
discourteous, 895
Intramural
interiority, 221
Intransient

diuturnity, 110
Intransigent
discordant, 24
revolutionary, 146
Intransitive
diuturnity, 110
Intransmutable
diuturnity, 110
Intraregarding
interiority, 221
Intrepid
courage, 861
Intricate
difficult, 704
confused, 59
perplexed, 519
Intriguant
activity, 682
libertine, 962
Intrigue
plot, 626
cunning, 702
activity, 682
licentiousness, 961
Intrinsic
intrinsicality, 5
interior, 221
Introduction
addition, 37
ingress, 294
admission, 296
insertion, 300
precursor, 64
precession, 280
aquaintance, 888
presentation, 894
musical, 415
Introductory
preceding, 62
precursory, 116
beginning, 66
Introgression
ingress, 294
Introit
music, 415
Intromit
receive, 294, 296
insert, 300
discontinue, 142
Introspection
look into, 441
thought, 451
attend to, 457
Introvert
invert, 140, 218

evolve, 313
Intrude
  intervene, 228
  enter, 294
  inopportune, 135
  interfere, 24
Intruder
  extraneous, 57, 228
Intrusion
  mixture, 41
Intuition
  mind, 450
  instinct, 477
  knowledge, 490
Intuitive
  instinctive, 477
Intumescence
  expansion, 194
  convexity, 250
Inunction
  covering, 222
Inundate
  effusion, 337
  flow, 348
  redundance, 641
Inurbanity
  discourteous, 895
Inure
  habituate, 613
  train, 673
  harden, 823
Inutility
  inutility, 645
Invade ingress, 294
  attack, 716
Invalid
  disease, 655
Invalidate
  disable, 158
  disentitle, 925
  illegalize, 964
  confute, 479
  rebut, 468
Invalidity
  confutation, 479
Invaluable
  goodness, 648
Invariable
  intrinsic, 5
  immutability, 150
Invasion
  ingress, 294
  attack, 716
Invective
  accusation, 938

malediction, 908
  abuse, 932
Inveigh
  blame, 932
Inveigle
  deceive, 546
  seduce, 615
Invent
  imagine, 515
  devise, 626
  falsehood, 544
Inventive
skilful, 698
  productive, 168
  original, 20
Inventory
  list, 86
  record, 551
Inversion
  reversion, 145
  of position, 218, 237
  of relation, 14
  of order, 59, 61
Invertebrate
  feeble, 160, 575
  vicious, 945
  irresolute, 605
Invest
  give, 784
  lend, 787
  empower, 157, 755
  ascribe, 155
  clothe, 225
  besiege, 716
Investigate
  inquiry, 461
Investiture
  see Invest
Investment
  see Invest
Inveterate
  habit, 613
  old, 124
Invidious
  envy, 921
  hatred, 898
  unfair, 923
Invigorate
  stimulate, 171
Invigoration
  strength, 159
Invincible
  strength, 159
Inviolable
  right, 924

honour, 939
  concealment, 528
Inviolate
  unchanged, 141
  concealed, 528
Invisible
  not to be seen, 447
  small, 193
  latent, 526
Invite
  ask, 765
  offer, 763
  induce, 615
Inviting
  pleasing, 899
  alluring, 615
Invoice
  list, 86
  record, 551
Invoke
  implore, 767
  pray, 990
  address, 586
  curse, 908
Involuntary
  compulsory, 601
  unintentional, 621
Involution
  disorder, 59
  convolution, 248
  numerical, 85
  style, 571
Involve
  derange, 61
  include, 54
  wrap, 225
  evidence, 467
  meaning, 516
Involved
  disorder, 59
  in debt, 806
Invulnerable
  safety, 664
Inward
  interiority, 221
Inweave
  crossing, 219
Ionosphere
  air, 338
Iota
  particle, 32
  minute, 193
Ipse dixit
  certainty, 474

Ipsissimis verbis
  word, 562
Ipso facto
  being, 1
  truth, 494
Irascible
  anger, 901
Irate
  resentment, 900
Ire
  resentment, 900
Iridiscent
  variegation, 440
  changeable, 149
Iris
  variegation, 440
  eye, 441
Irish bull
  ridiculousness, 853
  error, 495
Irishism
  absurdity, 497
  error, 495
Irk
  oppress, 830
  tire, 688
Irksome
  tiresome, 688
  tedious, 841
  oppressive, 830
Iron
  strength, 159
  hardness, 323
  club, 276
  to smooth, 255
Iron age
  adversity, 735
Iron curtain
  secret, 533
Iron-hearted
  malevolence, 907
Ironclad ship, 273
  covering, 222
  defence, 717
Irons
  fetters, 752
Irony
  ridicule, 856
  untruth, 544, 546
Irradiate
  light, 420
Irrational
  number, 84
  silly, 477, 499
  ridiculous, 853
Irreclaimable

vile, 945
  impenitent, 951
Irreconcilable
  discordant, 24
  unrelated, 10
  hostile, 889
Irrecoverable
  lost, 776
  past, 122
Irredeemable
  impenitent, 951
Irreducible
  out of order, 59
  discordant, 24
  fixed, 150
Irrefragable
  certain, 475
  proved, 478
Irrefutable
  certain, 475
  proved, 467, 478
Irregular
  out of order, 59
  against rule, 83
  in time, 139
  distorted, 243
  multiform, 16A, 81
  fighter, 726
Irrelation
  unrelated, 10
  disagreement, 24
Irrelevant
  unrelated, 10
  unaccordant, 24
  sophistical, 477
Irreligion
  atheism, 989
Irremediable
  lost, 776
  hopeless, 859
  bad, 649
Irremissible
  vice, 945
Irremovable
  immutable, 150
  quiescence, 265
Irreparable
  loss, 776
  bad, 649
  hopeless, 859
Irrepentance
  impenitence, 951
Irreplaceable
  indispensable, 630
Irrepressible

violent, 173
  excitement, 825
  free, 778
Irreproachable
  innocence, 946
Irresistible
  strength, 159
  compulsory, 601
  evidence, 467
Irresolute
  irresolution, 149, 605
Irresolvable
  unity, 87
Irrespective
  irrelation, 10
Irresponsible
  exempt, 279A
  arbitrary, 964
  silly, 499
Irretrievable
  lost, 776
Irreverence
  disrespect, 929
  impiety, 988
Irreversible
  past, 122
  immutable, 150
Irrevocable
  immutable, 150, 601,
    604
  hopeless, 859
Irrigate
  water, 337
Irritable
  excitable, 825
  irascible, 901
Irritate
  provoke, 898
  incense, 900
  fret, 828
  pain, 830
Irruption
  ingress, 294
  invasion, 716
Ishmael
  enemy, 891
Isis
  deity, 979
Islam
  religions, 984
Island
  island, 346
Isobar
  air, 338

Isocheimal
cold, 383
Isochimenal
cold, 383
Isochronous
synchronism, 120
Isolation
singleness, 87
seclusion, 893
safety, 644
detachment, 44
irrelation, 10
Isomeric
part, 51
Isomorphism
form, 240
Isothermal
heat, 382
Issue
effect, 154
event, 151
end, 67
posterity, 121, 167
disease, 655
kindred, 11
depart, 293
egress, 295
stream, 347
distribute, 73
money, 800
Issueless
unproductive, 169
Isthmus
narrowness, 203
land, 342
connection, 45
It
charm, 829
Italicize
emphasize, 642
Italics indication, 550
type, 591
Itch
desire, 865
titillation, 380
Item
addition, 37
speciality, 79
adjunct, 39
part, 51
Iteration
repetition, 90, 104
Itinerant
moving, 266
traveller, 268

Itinerary
description, 594
guide, 695
Ivory
whiteness, 430
Ivory-skulled
stupid, 499
Ivory tower
retirement, 893

Jab
stab, 260
poke, 276
Jabber
chatter, 584
nonsense, 517
stammer, 583
Jabot
frill, 230
Jacent
horizontal, 213
Jack
instrument, 633
raise, 307
ensign, 550
money, 800
Jack-a-dandy
fop, 854
Jack-in-office
blusterer, 887
Jack-o'-lantern
vision, 515
light, 423
Jack-pot
stake, 771
Jack-pudding
buffoon, 844
Jackal
provision, 637
mediate, 631
Jackanapes
fop, 854
bluster, 887
Jackass
carrier, 271
Jacket
dress, 225
Jacquerie
tumult, 719
Jactitation
tossing, 315
Jade
to fatigue, 688, 841
woman, 374

bad woman, 949
courtesan, 962
horse, 271
Jag
spree, 954
Jagged
angular, 244
notched, 257
pointed, 253
Jail
prison, 752
Jail-bird
prisoner, 754
Jailer
keeper, 753
Jake
good, 648
Jakes
privy, 653
Jalopy
vehicle, 272
Jam
to squeeze, 43
confession, 396
Jamb
support, 215
Jangle
sound, 410
discord, 713
Janitor
stopper, 263
Janizary
combatant, 726
Janus
deceiver, 548
Janus-headed
duality, 89
Japan
varnish, 222
beautify, 845
ornament, 847P
Jape
jest, 842
Jar
vessel, 191
stridor, 410
discord, 414, 713
agitation, 315
shock, 824
pain, 830
clash, 24
Jargon
unmeaning, 519
absurdity, 497

557

Jasper-coloured
green, 435
Jaundiced
prejudiced, 481
jealous, 920
dejected, 837
yellow, 436
Jaunt
journey, 266
Jaunting-car
vehicle, 272
Jaunty
fashionable, 852
pretty, 845
showy, 882
Javelin
arms, 727
Jaw
mouth, 230
loquacity, 584
to scold, 932
Jaw-breaker
neology, 563
Jay
loquacity, 584
Jazz
melody, 413
Je ne sais quoi
euphemism, 565
Jealousy
envy, 920
Jeans
dress, 225
Jeep
vehicle, 272
Jeer
gibe, 856, 929
joke, 842
Jehovah
Deity, 976
Jehu
director, 694
Jejune
scanty, 640
style, 575
Jell
set, 321
Jelly
pulpiness, 354
sweet, 396
Jellyfish
weakness, 160
Jennet
carrier, 271
Jeopardy
danger, 665

Jeremiad
invective, 932, 938
lamentations, 839
Jerk
throw, 146, 284
draw, 285
agitate, 315
bad man, 949
Jerry
flimsy, 643
Jerry-built
fragile, 328
Jersey
dress, 225
Jest
wit, 842
trifle, 643
Jester
humorist, 844
buffoon, 857
Jesuit
clergy, 996
Jesuitry
deception, 544
sophistry, 477
Jesus
Deity, 976
Jet
water, 347
stream, 348
aircraft, 273A
blackness, 431
Jetsam
fragments, 51
little, 643
Jettison
abandon, 782
Jetty
convexity, 250
Jeu d'esprit
wit, 842
Jeu de mots
neology, 563
Jeu de théâtre
appearance, 448
Jeune fille
girl, 129
Jew
religions, 984
Jewel
gem, 650
ornament, 847
goodness, 648
favourite, 899
Jew's harp

musical, 417
Jezebel
wretch, 949
courtesan, 962
Jib
deviation, 279
demur, 603
Jibe
accord, 23
Jiffy
instant, 113
Jig
dance, 840
Jilt
deception, 545
lovelorn, 898
Jimjams
insanity, 503
Jingle
resonance, 408
vehicle, 272
Jingo
warlike, 722
boasting, 884
blusterer, 887
Jinnee
demon, 980
Jinx
spell, 993
Jitters
fear, 860
Jiu-jitsu
contention, 720
Jive
rhythm, 413
Job
business, 625
action, 680
unfairness, 940
Jobation
upbraiding, 932
Jobber
merchant, 797
agent, 690
trickster, 943
Jobbernowl
fool, 501
Jobbery
cunning, 702
Jobbing
skill, 698
barter, 794
Jockey
horseman, 268
servant, 746

to deceive, 545
deceiver, 548

Jocose
witty, 836, 840, 842

Jocular
gay, 836
amusing, 840

Jocund
cheerful, 836

Joe Soap
fool, 501
dupe, 547

Jog
push, 276
shake, 315

Jog on
advance, 282
slowness, 275
trudge, 266

Jog-trot
routine, 613

Joggle
agitation, 315

Johnsonian
style, 577

Join
junction, 43
contiguity, 199

Joint
part, 44, 51
junction, 43
flexure, 258
accompanying, 88

Joint stock
share, 778

Jointly
addition, 37

Jointress
widow, 905

Jointure
receipt, 810
property, 780

Joist
support, 215

Joke
wit, 842
trifle, 643

Jollification
spree, 954

Jollity
amusement, 480

Jolly
gay, 836
conviviality, 892
pleasing, 829

plump, 192
joke, 842
flatter, 933

Jolly-boat
ship, 273

Jolt
impulse, 276
agitation, 315
shock, 824

Jonathan Wild
thief, 792

Jorum
receptacle, 191

Josh
tease, 830
joke, 842
ridicule, 856

Joskin
clown, 876

Joss
idolatry, 991

Joss-house
temple, 1000

Jostle
clash, 24
push, 276
agitate, 315

Jot
small quantity, 32
particle, 193
to record, 551

Jotting
writing, 590

Jounce
agitation, 315

Journal
annals, 114
record, 551
description, 594
book, 593

Journalism
publication, 531

Journalist
recorder, 553
writer, 590

Journey
journey, 266
progression, 282

Journeyman
agent, 690
servant, 746

Joust
contention, 720

Jove
god, 979

Jovial
gay, 836
convivial, 892
amusement, 840

Jowl
laterality, 236

Joy
pleasure, 827

Joy-ride
journey, 266

Joyful
cheerful, 836

Joyless
dejection, 830, 837

Joyous
cheerful, 836

Jubilant
joyous, 836
boastful, 884

Jubilation
celebration, 882

Jubilee
rejoicing, 836, 838
festival, 840
anniversary, 138
celebration, 883

Judaism
religions, 984

Judge
arbitrator, 967
master, 745
taste, 850

Judgmatic
wisdom, 498

Judgment
decision, 480
intellect, 450
belief, 484
wisdom, 498
sentence, 969

Judgment-seat
tribunal, 966

Judicature
law, 965

Judicial
discriminative, 465
impartial, 922

Judicious
wisdom, 498
expedient, 646

Jug
receptacle, 191
prison, 752

Juggernaut
idol, 991

Keep on
continue, 143
Keep pace with
equality, 27
Keep under
restrain, 751
Keep up
continue, 143
Keeper
keep, 753
Keeping
congruity, 23
Keepsake
memory, 505
Keg
receptacle, 191
Kelpie
fabulous being, 979
Ken
knowledge, 490
Kennel
ditch, 259
conduit, 350
hovel, 189
Kenspeckle
eminent, 873
Kerb
edge, 230
Kerchief
dress, 225
Kermess
amusement, 840
Kern
commonalty, 876
Kernel
central, 223
importance, 642
Ketch
ship, 273
Kettle
vessel, 191
cauldron, 386
Kettle-drum
musical, 417
Key
interpretation, 522
answer, 462
music, 413
cause, 153
opener, 260
instrument, 631
insignia, 747
Key up
stimulate, 615
Keyhole

opening, 260
Keynote
music, 413
model, 22
rule, 80
Keystone
support, 215
Kgotla
council, 696
Khaki
brown, 433
Khan
master, 745
Khedive
master, 745
Khidmutgar
servant, 746
Kibitka
vehicle, 272
Kibitz
meddle, 682
Kibosh
defeat, 731
Kick
strike, 276
attack, 716
recoil, 277
disobey, 742
resist, 719
punish, 972
feeling, 821
pleasure, 827
Kickshaw
trifle, 643
food, 298
Kid
child, 129
to hoax, 545
chaff, 842
Kidnap
stealing, 789, 791
Kidney
class, 75
Kilderkin
receptacle, 191
Kill
kill, 361
Kill-joy
dejection, 837
Killing
charming, 829
funny, 842
Kiln
furnace, 386
Kilt

dress, 225
Kimono
dress, 225
Kin
class, 75
Kind
class, 75
benevolent, 906
Kindle
set fire to, 384
cause, 153
quicken, 171
incite, 615
excite, 824
incense, 900
Kindly
request, 765
Kindred
consanguinity, 11
Kinematics
motion, 264
Kinematograph
see Cinematograph
King
master, 745
Kingcraft
authority, 737
Kingdom
property, 780
region, 181
Kingly
majestic, 873
authority, 737
King's Remembrancer
treasurer, 801
Kingship
authority, 737
King-sized,
192
Kink
distortion, 243
angle, 244
caprice, 608
Kinsfolk
consanguinity, 11
Kinsman
consanguinity, 11
Kipper
preservation, 670
Kirk
temple, 1000
Kirtle
dress, 225
Kismet
destiny, 152, 601

Kiss
endearment, 902
courtesy, 894
of death, 361
Kit
bag, 191
accoutrements, 225
fiddle, 417
Kitcat
painting, 556
Kitchen
workshop, 691
room, 191
Kitchen garden
agriculture, 371
Kitchen-maid
servant, 746
Kite
flying, 273A
bill, 800
Kith and kin
consanguinity, 11
Kittle
sensation, 380
Kitty
stake, 771
Kleptomania
desire, 865
insanity, 503, 504
Knack
skill, 698
toy, 840
Knap
ridge, 206
to break, 44
Knapsack
receptacle, 191
Knave
deceiver, 548
rouge, 941
dishonour, 949
Knavish
improbity, 940
Knead
mix, 41
soften, 324
Knee
angularity, 244
Kneel
beg, 765
respect, 928
submission, 725
stoop, 308
pray, 990
servility, 886

Knell
interment, 363
Knick-knack
unimportant, 643
ornament, 847
Knife
sharpness, 253
kill, 361
Knight
noble, 875
Knight errant
defence, 717
rash, 863
Knighthood
title, 877
Knit
junction, 43
Knob
protuberance, 250
ball, 249
Knobkerrie
arms, 727
club, 276
Knock
blow, 276, 619
sound, 406
beat, 972
disparage, 483, 932
vilify, 874
Knock about
maltreat, 649
wander, 266
boisterous, 173
Knock down
destroy, 162
overthrow, 308
Knock-kneed
curved, 245
distorted, 243
Knock off
finish, 729
cease, 142
steal, 791
Knock out
beating, 972
end, 67
combine, 778
Knock under
yield, 725
obey, 743
Knock up
fatigue, 688
distorted, 243
Knoll
height, 206

Knot
ligature, 45
to fasten, 43
entanglement, 59
group, 72, 892
intersection, 219
difficulty, 704
ornament, 847
Knotted
crossing, 219
Knotty
difficult, 704
dense, 321
Knout
scourge, 972, 975
Know-all
sage, 500
Know-how
skill, 698
Know no bounds
greatness, 31
Knowing
skill, 698
cunning, 702
Knowingly
intentionally, 620
Knowledge
know, 490
Knuckle
angularity, 244
Knuckle-duster
arms, 727
Knuckle under
submit, 725
humble, 879
Kobold
gnome, 980
Kodachrome
photograph, 556
Kopje
height, 206
Koran
sacred books, 986
Kowtow
bow, 308, 894
respect, 928
submission, 725
obedience, 743
Kraal
abode, 189
Kraken
monster, 83
Kriegie
prisoner, 753

Kris
knife, 727
Ku Klux Klan
illegality, 964
Kudos
repute, 873, 931
Kukri
arms, 727
Kyanize
preserve, 670
Kyle
gap, 198
gulf, 343
Kyte
belly, 191
convexity, 250

L.S.D.
money, 800
Laager
defence, 717
Labarum
flag, 550
Label
indication, 550
Labial
letter, 561
Laboratory
workshop, 691
Labour
exertion, 686
work, 680
difficulty, 704
Labourer
agent, 690
Labyrinth
secret, 533
difficulty, 704
disorder, 59
convolution, 248
Lace
tie, 43
net, 219
to beat, 972
Lacerable
fragile, 328
Lacerate
disjunction, 44
pain, 830
Laches
neglect, 460
omission, 773
Lachrymation
lamentation, 839

Lack
insufficiency, 640
destitution, 804
requisition, 630
number, 98
Lack-brain
fool, 501
Lack-lustre
dim, 423
discoloured, 429
Lackadaisical
affected, 855
indifferent, 866
Lacker
see Lacquer
Lackey
servant, 746
Laconic
conciseness, 572
shortness, 201
Lacquer
varnish, 22
adorn, 845, 847
Lacteal
semiliquid, 352
Lacuna
orifice, 260
pit, 252
deficiency, 53
interval, 198
break, 70
Lacuscular
lake, 343
Lacustrine
lake, 343
Lad
infant, 129
Ladder
method, 627
Lade
transfer, 270
Laden
charged, 639
La-di-da
foppish, 855P
Lading
cargo, 190, 635
baggage, 780
Ladle
spoon, 272
vessel, 191
Lady
woman, 374
wife, 903
noble, 875

Lady help
servant, 746
Lady-killer
fop, 854
philanderer, 902
Lady-love
sweetheart, 897
Ladylike
fashion, 852
courteous, 894
noble, 875
Lag
linger, 275
follow, 281
dawdle, 683
lateness, 133
imprison, 751
prisoner, 754
Laggard
slack, 603, 683
Lagoon
lake, 343
Laical
laity, 997
Lair
den, 189
sty, 653
Laird
nobility, 875
possessor, 779
Laissez aller
inactivity, 683
Laissez faire
laxity, 738
inactivity, 683
permanence, 141
Laity
laity, 997
Lake
lake, 343
Lama
priest, 996
master, 745
Lamarckism
causation, 153
Lamb
innocent, 946
nursling, 129
Saviour, 976
saint, 948
Lambent flame
light, 420
Lamblike
innocent, 946

Lame
  weak, 160
  bad, 649
  imperfect, 65
  failing, 732
  laxity, 738
Lamella
  layer, 204
Lament
  complain, 839
  regret, 833
  funeral, 363
  pity, 914
Lamentable
  greatness, 31
  painful, 830
  regret, 833
Lamia
  demon, 980
Lamina
  layer, 204
  part, 51
Lamp
  luminary, 423
Lampoon
  disparage, 932
  libel, 934
Lance
  perforate, 260
  javelin, 727
Lancer
  combatant, 726
Lancet
  perforator, 262
  sharpness, 253
Lancinate
  pain, 378
Land
  ground, 342
  to arrive, 292
  to stop, 265
  estate, 780
Land girl
  agriculture, 371
Land-mine
  arms, 727
Landau
  vehicle, 272
Landaulette
  vehicle, 272
Landgrave
  master, 745
Landing-ground
  arrival, 292
Landing-place
  support, 215

destination, 292
Landing-stage
  arrival, 292
Landlocked
  circumscribed, 231
Landlord
  possessor, 779
Landlubber
  bungler, 701
Landmark
  indicate, 550
Landowner
  possessor, 779
Landscape
  view, 448
  delineation, 556
Landslide
  fall, 306
Landslip
  fall, 306
Lane
  street, 189
  way, 627
Language
  words, 560
Languid
  weak, 160
  slow, 275
  torpid, 683, 823
  style, 575
Languish
  desire, 865
  illness, 655
  decline, 36
Languor
  weakness, 160
  inactivity, 683
Lank
  little, 193
Lanolin
  oil, 356
Lantern
  light, 423
Lantern-jawed
  lean, 193
Lao-Tsze
  religious founder, 986
Lap
  support, 215
  interior, 221
  to wrap, 222
  encompass, 227
  speed, 274
  surpass, 303
  drink, 296

Lapel
  fold, 258
Lapidary
  concise, 572
Lapidate
  kill, 361
Lapis lazuli
  blue, 438
Lappet
  adjunct, 39
Lapse
  of time, 109, 135
  past time, 122
  fall, 306
  be lost, 776
  degeneracy, 659
  guilt, 947
  error, 495
Lapsus linguae
  solecism, 568
  ridicule, 856
  error, 495
  equivocal, 520
Larboard
  left, 239
Larcener
  thief, 792
Larceny
  theft, 791
Lard
  unctuousness, 353, 256
Larder
  store, 636
  food, 298
Lares and Penates
  abode, 189
Large
  in quantity, 31
  in size, 192
Largess
  giving, 784, 809
Largo
  slowness, 275, 415
Lariat
  vinculum, 45
Lark
  mount, 305
  frolic, 840
Larrikin
  rowdy, 949
  evildoer, 913
Larrup
  strike, 972
Larva
  youth, 127

Larynx
air-pipe, 351
Lascivious
impure, 961
Lash
tie together, 43
punish, 972
scourge, 830, 975
censure, 932
violence, 173
Lashings
plenty, 639
Lass
girl, 129, 374
Lassitude
fatigue, 688
weariness, 841
Lasso
vinculum, 45
Last
in order, 67
endure, 106
continue, 141
durable, 110
model, 22
Last post
signal, 550
Latakia
tobacco, 298A
Latch
vinculum, 45
Latchet
vinculum, 45
Late
tardy, 133
past, 122
new, 123
Latent
concealed, 526
Latent
implied, 516
inert, 172
Later
posterior, 117
Lateral
side, 236
Lath
strip, 205
Lathe
instrument, 633
Lather
foam, 353
to flog, 972
Lathi
impact, 276

arms, 727
Latitude
scope, 180
situation, 183
breadth, 202
freedom, 748
Latitudinarian
heterodoxy, 984A
Latrine
room, 191
Latter
sequent, 63
past, 122
Lattice
crossing, 219
opening, 260
Laud
praise, 931
worship, 990
Laudable
virtue, 944
Laudanum
anaesthetic, 376
Laudation
approval, 931
Laudator temporis acti
oldness, 124
permanence, 141
discontent, 832
lamentation, 839
Lauds
worship, 990
Laugh
rejoice, 838
Laugh at
ridicule, 856
sneer, 929
underestimate, 483
joke, 842
Laughable
ridiculous, 853
Laughing gas
anaesthetic, 376
Laughing-stock
ridicule, 857
Laughter
rejoice, 836, 838, 840
Launch
propel, 284
begin, 66
adventure, 876
Launch out
expatiate, 584
style, 573
Laundress

servant, 746
Laundry
cleanness, 652
Laureate
poetry, 597
Laurel
trophy, 733
reward, 973
glory, 873
decoration, 877
Lava
semiliquid, 352
Lavatory
room, 191
privy, 653
Lave
cleanness, 652
water, 337
Lavender
colour, 437
fragrance, 400
Lavish
prodigal, 818
giving, 784
profuse, 639, 641
liberal, 816
Lavolta
dance, 840
Law
rule, 80, 697
ordination, 963
command, 741
permission, 760
Lawful
dueness, 924
allowable, 760
Lawless
arbitrary, 964
irregular, 83
Lawn
plain, 344
Lawsuit
law, 969
Lawyer
lawyer, 968
Lax
incoherent, 47
soft, 324
diffuse, 573
disuse, 614
remiss, 738
licentious, 945
Laxative
remedy, 662

Lay
place, 184
assuage, physically, 174
assuage, morally, 826
bet, 151
poetry, 597
music, 415
level, 213
secular, 997
Lay aside
relinquish, 624
give up, 782
cease, 142
reject, 610
Lay bare
manifest, 525
Lay brother
clergy, 996
Lay by
store, 636
economize, 817
Lay down
assert, 535
renounce, 757
Lay figure
prototype, 22
effigy, 554
nonentity, 643
Lay in
store, 636
Lay into
punish, 972
buffet, 276
Lay open
disclose, 529
show, 525
divest, 226
Lay out
level, 213
Lay to
stop, 265
be inactive, 683
repose, 687
Lay up
illness, 655
store, 636
Lay waste
ravage, 649
disorganize, 659
Layer
layer, 204
Layman
laity, 997
Laystall
unclean, 653

Lazaretto
remedy, 662
Lazy
inactive, 683
slow, 275
Lea
plain, 342, 344
Lead
to precede in order, 62
precede in motion, 280
to tend, 176
to direct, 693
to induce, 615
authority, 737
heaviness, 319
depth, 208
Lead-line
measurement, 466
Lead off
begin, 66
precursor, 64
Leader
master, 745
director, 694
dissertation, 595
Leading
important, 642
Leading strings
subjection, 749
Leaf
part, 51
plant, 367
layer, 204
of a book, 593
Leaflet
part, 51
League
party, 712
Leak
dribble, 295
waste, 638
Lean
thin, 193
narrow, 203
oblique, 217
recline, 215
Lean-to
building, 189
Leaning
direction, 278
tendency, 176
willingness, 602
Leap
jump, 309
Leap to

change, 140
Learned
knowledge, 490, 492
Learner
learner, 541
Learning
acquiring, 539
erudition, 490
Lease
sale, 796
property, 780
Lease-lend
lend, 787
Leash
tie, 43
three, 92
Least
inferiority, 34
Leat
conduit, 350
Leather
to beat, 972
toughness, 327
Leatherneck
fighter, 726
Leave
quit, 293
vacate, 185
relinquish, 624
permission, 760
bequeath, 784
Leave off
cessation, 142, 614, 624
Leave out
exclusion, 55
Leave over
postpone, 133
Leaven
cause, 153
Leavings
remainder, 40
Lebensraum
freedom, 748
Lecher
libertine, 962
Lechery
impurity, 961
Lectern
church, 1000
Lecture
teach, 537
censure, 932
discourse, 582, 595
Lecturer
learner, 541

Ledge
support, 215
Ledger
accounts, 811
record, 551
list, 86
Lee
laterality, 236
refuge, 666
Lee shore
pitfall, 667
Leech
suck, 789
physician, 695
Leer
vision, 441
signal, 550
Leery
cunning, 702
Lees
uncleanness, 653
Leeway
navigation, 267
shortcoming, 304
Left
remaining, 40
sinistral, 239
Left-handed
unskilful, 699
equivocal, 520
sinister, 649
Leg
swindler, 548
Leg-break
deviation, 279
Legacy
gift, 784
acquisition, 775
Legal
legitimate, 924
relating to law, 963
allowable, 760
Legate
consignee, 750
messenger, 534
deputy, 759
Legatee
receive, 785
Legation
commission, 755
Legend
narrative, 594
record, 551
Legendary
mythical, 979

imaginary, 515
Legerdemain
trick, 545, 702
cunning, 702
Legèreté
irresolution, 605
Legging
dress, 225
Legible
intelligible, 518
Legion
army, 726
multitude, 102
assemblage, 72
Legislate
legality, 963
Legislator
director, 694
Legislature
legality, 963
Legitimate
true, 494
allowable, 760
just, 922
due, 924
legal, 963
Legs
journey, 266
Lei
garland, 847
Leisure
unoccupied, 685
opportunity, 134
Leisurely
slowly, 133, 275
Leit-motiv
music, 415
Leman
favourite, 899
Lemma
evidence, 467
maxim, 496
Lemon
yellow, 430
Lend
lending, 787
credit, 805
Length
length, 200
Lengthy
diffuse, 573
Lenient
compassionate, 914
moderate, 174
mild, 740

Lenify
moderate, 174
Lenitive
remedy, 662
relief, 834
Lenity
lenity, 740
Lens
optical instrument, 445
Lent
fasting, 956
Lenticular
curvature, 245
Lentor
inertness, 172
inactivity, 683
Lentous
viscid, 352
Leopard
variegation, 440
Leprechaun
sprite, 980
Lese-majesty
disobedience, 742
Less
inferior, 34
subduction, 38
Lessee
debt, 806
possessor, 779
Lessen
in quantity or degree, 36
in size, 195
Lesson
teaching, 537
warning, 668
Lessor
credit, 805
Lest
avoidance, 623
Let
hindrance, 706
sell, 796
permit, 760
Let down
depress, 308
disappoint, 509
Let fall
depression, 308
speak, 582
Let fly
propulsion, 284
Let go
liberate, 750
relinquish, 782

servile, 886
Lictor
  law, 965
Lid
  cover, 263
  integument, 22
Lie
  place, 186
  position, 183
  exist, 1
  recline, 213, 215
  descend, 306
  to deceive, 545
  untruth, 546
  contradict, 489
Lie by
  inaction, 681
Lie doggo
  conceal, 528
Lie in wait
  ambush, 530
Lie low
  lowness, 207
  concealment, 528
Lie over
  postpone, 133
  future, 121
Lie to
  quiescence, 265
Lied
  music, 415
Lief
  willingness, 602
Liege
  master, 745
Lien
  dueness, 924
  security, 771
  credit, 805
Lieutenant
  officer, 745
  deputy, 759
Life
  vitality, 359
  activity, 682
  existence, 1
  events, 151
Life and death
  important, 642
Life-preserver
  impact, 276
Lifeblood
  life, 359
  inbeing, 5
Lifeboat

boat, 273
  safety, 666
Lifeless
  dead, 360
  inert, 172
Lifelike
  similarity, 17
Lift
  raise, 307
  way, 627
  aid, 707
  steal, 791
Ligament
  vinculum, 45
Ligation
  junction, 43
Ligature
  vinculum, 45
Light
  luminosity, 420
  opening, 260
  levity, 320
  colour, 428
  to kindle, 384
  luminary, 423
  small, 32
  trifling, 643
  gay, 836
  idea, 453
  knowledge, 490
  descent, 306
  to arrive, 292
  loose, 961
Light-fingered
  stealing, 791
Light-footed
  swift, 274
  active, 682
Light-headed
  delirious, 503
  foolish, 499
Light-hearted
  cheerful, 836
Light-legged
  velocity, 274
Light-minded
  irresolution, 605
Light up
  illuminate, 420
  cheer, 836
  awaken, 615
Light upon
  find, 480A
  arrive, 292
Lighten

render easy, 705
Lighter
  ship, 273
  fuel, 388
Lighterman
  mariner, 269
Lighthouse
  beacon, 668
  luminary, 423
Lightness
  see Light
Lightning
  velocity, 274
  luminousness, 420
Lightship
  light, 423
  warning, 668
Lightsome
  cheerful, 836
  fickle, 605
Likable
  attractive, 829
Like
  similar, 17
  to relish, 394
  will, 600
  enjoy, 827
Likely
  probable, 472
Likeness
  similitude, 17
  copy, 21
  representation, 554
  portrait, 556
Likewise
  addition, 37
Liking
  love, 897
  desire, 865
Lilac
  purple, 437
Lilliputian
  little, 193
  low, 207
Lilt
  music, 415
  rhythm, 138
  cheerful, 836
Lily
  whiteness, 430
  beauty, 845
Limature
  pulverulence, 330, 331
Limb
  member, 51

component, 56
instrument, 633
Limber
flexible, 324
Limbo
incarceration, 751
purgatory, 982
Lime
deception, 545
Limelight
publicity, 531
Limerick
absurdity, 497
Limit
boundary, 233
end, 67
to circumscribe, 231
qualify, 469
prohibit, 761
Limitless
infinity, 105
space, 180
Limn
painting, 556
Limner
artist, 559
Limousine
vehicle, 272
Limp
halt, 275
fail, 732
weak, 160
inert, 172, 683
soft, 324
Limpid
transparent, 425
Lincture
remedy, 662
Line
length, 200
filament, 205
to coat, 224
band, 45
order, 58
contour, 229
continuity, 69
direction, 278
business, 625
soldier, 726
feature, 550
appearance, 448
posterity, 167
epistle, 592
Lineage
posterity, 167

series, 69
kindred, 11
Lineament
appearance, 448
mark, 550
Linear
length, 200
Linger
loiter, 275
delay, 133
protract, 110
Lingo
language, 560
Lingua franca
neology, 563
Linguist
scholar, 492
language, 560
Liniment
unctuous, 355
remedy, 662
Lining
lining, 224
Link
relation, 9
connecting, 45
to connect, 43
part, 51
term, 71
flambeau, 423
Links
arena, 728
Linn
lake, 343
Linocut
engraving, 558
Linoleum
covering, 222
Linotype
printing, 591
Linsey-woolsey
mixed, 41
Lion
courage, 861
prodigy, 872
celebrity, 873
Lip
edge, 230
beginning, 66
prominence, 250
impudence, 885
Lip-devotion
impiety, 988
Lip-service
insincerity, 544

flattery, 933
impiety, 988
Lip-wisdom
folly, 499
Lipogram
misnomer, 565
Lippitude
dim sight, 443
Lipstick
ornament, 847
Liquation
calefaction, 384
Liquefaction
soluble, 335
calefaction, 384
Liquescence
calefaction, 384
Liquescent
soluble, 335
Liquid
fluid, 333
letter, 561
sound, 405
Liquidate
pay, 808
destroy, 162
Liquor
liquid, 333
intoxicant, 959
potable, 299
Liquorice
sweet, 396
Lisp
stammering, 583
Lissom
soft, 324
List
catalogue, 86
record, 551
strip, 205
fringe, 230
obliquity, 217
hear, 418
will, 600
choose, 609
Listed
variegation, 440
Listen
hearing, 418
Listen in
radio, 599B
Listless
inattentive, 458
inactive, 683
impassive, 823

indifferent, 866
Lists
   arena, 728
Lit up
   drunk, 959
Litany
   rite, 998
Literae humaniores
   language, 560
Literal
   exact, 19, 494
   meaning, 516
   unimaginative, 843
Literate
   knowledge, 491
Literati
   scholar, 492
Literatim
   imitation, 19
   word, 562
Literature
   learning, 490
   language, 560
Lithe
   softness, 324
Lithograph
   engraving, 558
Litigant
   combatant, 726
   lawsuit, 969
Litigate
   discord, 713
   contention, 720
Litigious
   discord, 713
   lawsuit, 969
Litter
   disorder, 59
   to derange, 61
   trash, 643
   useless, 645
   vehicle, 272
   offspring, 167
Little
   in degree, 32
   in size, 193
Littoral
   land, 342
Liturgy
   rite, 998
Live
   exist, 1
   continue, 141
   dwell, 186
   fame, 873

Livelihood
   wealth, 803
Livelong
   perpetuity, 110
Lively
   sprightly, 836
   acute, 821
   sensitive, 375, 822
   active, 682
   style, 574
Liver-coloured
   brown, 433
Livery
   badge, 550, 877
   colour, 428
   suit, 225
Livid
   dark, 431
   purple, 437
Living
   life, 359
   benefice, 995
Lixiviate
   cleanness, 652
   liquefaction, 335
Lixivium
   liquidity, 333
Llama
   carrier, 271
Llano
   plain, 344
Lo!
   see, 441
   wonder, 870
Load
   weight, 319
   cargo, 190
   quantity, 31
   redundance, 641
   hindrance, 706
   anxiety, 828
   fill up, 52
   to oppress, 830
Loadstone
   attraction, 289, 865
   motive, 615
Loaf
   head, 450
Loafer
   idler, 683
Loam
   soil, 342
Loan
   lending, 787
Loathe

dislike, 867
   hate, 898
Loathing
   nausea, 841
Loathsome
   hateful, 649, 898
   abhorrent, 867
   nauseous, 395
Lob
   toss, 284
Lobby
   room, 191
   passage, 627
Lobe
   part, 51
Lobster
   red, 434
Local
   situation, 183
   regional, 180
Locality
   situation, 183
Localize
   location, 184
   limit, 231
Locate
   location, 184
Loch
   lake, 343
Lock
   fasten, 43
   confine, 229
   rest, 265
   enclose, 232
   barrier, 706
   canal, 350
   tuft, 256
Lock up
   concealment, 528
   restraint, 751
Lock-up
   jail, 752
Locker
   receptacle, 191
Locket
   ornament, 847
Lockout
   resistance, 719
Loco
   insane, 503
Locomotion
   motion, 264
Locomotive
   traction, 285

Locum tenens
  deputy, 759
  substitute, 634
Locus standi
  influence, 175
  support, 215
  repute, 873
Lode
  conduit, 350
  mine, 636
Lodestar
  beacon, 289, 550
Lodestone
  see Loadstone
Lodge
  presence, 186
  dwelling, 189
  receptacle, 191
  place, 184
Lodger
  inhabitant, 188
Loft
  garret, 191
  toss, 184
Lofty
  high, 206
  proud, 878
  sublime, 574
  magnanimous, 942
Log
  fuel, 388
  measure, 466
  velocity, 274
  record, 551
Log-book
  dissertation, 595
Log-line
  velocity, 274
Logarithm
  number, 84
Loggerhead
  fool, 501
Loggerheads
  quarrel, 713, 889
Loggia
  place, 191
Logic
  reasoning, 476
Logogriph
  secret, 533
Logomachy
  words, 588
  dispute, 720
  reasoning, 476
Logometer
  numeration, 85

Loin
  laterality, 236
Loiter
  slow, 275
  inactive, 683
  tardy, 133
  linger, 110
Loll
  recline, 215
  lounge, 683
  sprawl, 213
Lollipop
  sweetness, 396
Lolly
  money, 800
Lone
  unity, 87
  unwedded, 904
Lonesome
  seclusion, 893
Long
  in space, 200
  in time, 110
Long dozen
  thirteen, 78
Long-headed
  wisdom, 498
Long-lived
  diuturnity, 110
Long-sighted
  wise, 498
  presbyopic, 443
Long-suffering
  inexcitable, 826
Long-tongued
  loquacious, 584
Long-winded
  diffuse, 573
  protracted, 110
  loquacious, 584
Longanimity
  patience, 826
Longboat
  ship, 273
Longeval
  diuturnity, 110
Longevity
  age, 128
Longhand
  writing, 590
Longing
  desire, 865
Longitude
  length, 200
Longo intervallo

  discontinuity, 7
Longsome
  long, 200
Longueur
  diffuseness, 573
Looby
  clown, 876
  fool, 501
Look
  see, 441
  appearance, 448
Look after
  attention, 457
  manage, 693
Look for
  seek, 461
  expect, 507
Look forward
  expect, 507
  foresee, 510
Look in
  radio, 599B
Look into
  examine, 461
Look-out
  prospect, 448
  futurity, 121
Look out
  warning, 668
Look out for
  expect, 507
Look over
  examine, 461
Look upon
  belief, 484
Looker-on
  spectator, 444
Looking-glass
  optical, 445
Loom
  dim, 422
  come in sight, 446
  impend, 152
  weaver's, 691
  future, 121
Loon
  clown, 876
  fool, 501
Loop
  curve, 245
  circle, 247
Loop the loop
  inversion, 218
Loophole
  opening, 260

vista, 441
plea, 617
refuge, 666, 717
escape, 671
feint, 545
Loopy
insane, 503
Loose
detach, 44
free, 748
liberate, 750
incoherent, 47
vague, 519
style, 573
lax, 738
dissolute, 961
Loosen
disjoin, 47, 750
Loot
stealing, 791
booty, 793
Lop
retrench, 38
shorten, 53, 201
Lope
velocity, 274
Loquacity
talk, 584
prolixity, 573
Lord
nobleman, 875
ruler, 745
GOD, 976
Lord it over
insolence, 885
Lordling
bluster, 875
Lordly
proud, 878
grand, 873
Lordship
title, 877
Lore
knowledge, 490
Lorn
seclusion, 893
Lorry
vehicle, 272
Lorry-hop
travel, 266
Lose
opportunity, 135
property, 776
time, 683
Loser

victim, 732
Loss
privation, 776
waste, 638
evil, 619
Lost
invisible, 449
non-existing, 2
bewildered, 491
inattentive, 458
demoralized, 945
Lot
destiny, 152
chance, 156, 621
group, 72
state, 7
allotment, 786
quantity, 25, 639
multitude, 102
Lotion
remedy, 662
Lottery
chance, 156, 621
Lotus-eater
inactivity, 683
Loud
loudness, 404
showy, 428
vulgar, 851
Lough
lake, 343
Lounge
inactive, 683
to loiter, 275
room, 191
seat, 215
Lounge lizard
flirt, 902
Lour
darken, 421, 422
mope, 837
frown, 895
threaten, 511, 908
resent, 900
Lousy
bad, 649
Lout
clown, 876
fool, 501
to stoop, 308
Love
attachment, 897
favourite, 899
nothing, 4
Love-nest

love, 897
Lovelorn
love-sick, 897
rejected, 898
Lovely
dear, 897
pleasing, 829
beautiful, 845
Lover
love, 897
Low
depressed, 207
debased, 940
vulgar, 876
cry, 412
price, 815
bad, 649
sound, 403
smallness, 32
Low-bred
commonalty, 876
Low-brow
ignoramus, 493
fool, 501
Low-down
information, 527
Low-lying
low, 207
Low-thoughted
improbity, 940
Lowboy
receptacle, 191
Lower
depress, 308
decrease, 36
inferior, 34
Lowering
unhealthy, 657
Lowlands
lowness, 207
Lowly
humility, 879
Lowness
see Low
Loyal
probity, 939
obedient, 743
Lozenge
angularity, 244
sweet, 396
Lubber
slow, 683
awkward, 699
fool, 501
big, 192

Lubricate
smooth, 255, 332
facilitate, 705
Lubricity
slippery, 255
impurity, 961
Lucid
luminous, 420
intelligible, 518
style, 570
sane, 502
Lucifer
Satan, 978
match, 388
Luck
chance, 156, 621
good, 618
success, 731
prosperity, 734
Luckless
failure, 732
adversity, 735
distressed, 828
Lucky
prosper, 134, 734
Lucrative
receipt, 810
useful, 644
profitable, 775
Lucre
gain, 775
wealth, 803
Lucubration
thought, 451
Luculent
light, 420
Ludicrous
laughable, 838
ridiculous, 853
witty, 842
Lug
traction, 285
Luggage
baggage, 635, 780
Lugger
ship, 273
Lugubrious
dejection, 837
Lukewarm
temperate, 382
unwilling, 603
indifferent, 866
torpid, 823
Lull
assuage, 174

mitigate, 826
silence, 403
quiescence, 142, 265
Lullaby
soothing, 174
sleep, 683
song, 415
relief, 834
Lum
funnel, chimney, 351
Lumber
useless, 645
slow, 275
trash, 643
disorder, 59
hindrance, 647, 706
Lumber-room
receptacle, 191, 636
Lumbering
ugly, 846
Lumberjacket
dress, 225
Luminary
light, 423
sage, 500
Luminous
light, 420
Lump
mass, 192
density, 321
concrete, 46
totality, 50
to amass, 72
Lumpish
heavy, 319
massive, 192
sluggish, 683
awkward, 853
Lunacy
insanity, 503
Lunar
world, 318
Lunatic
madman, 504
Lunation
period, 108
Luncheon
food, 298
Lunette
curvature, 245
Lunge
impulse, 276
attack, 716
Lunik
space ship, 273A

Lurch
sink, 306
difficulty, 704
deception, 545
oscillation, 314
slope, 217
Lure
entice, 615
allurement, 865
deception, 545
Lurid
dim, 422
dark, 421
yellow, 436
sensational, 549
Lurk
latent, 526
concealed, 528
hide, 530
unseen, 447
Luscious
savoury, 394, 396
grateful, 829
style, 577
Lush
succulent, 333
vegetation, 365
luxuriant, 639
Lushy
drunkenness, 959
Lust
desire, 865
concupiscence, 961
Lustily
exertion, 686
Lustration
purification, 652
atonement, 952
Lustre
brightness, 420
chandelier, 423
Lustrum
period, 108
Lusty
size, 192
strong, 159
Lusus naturae
unconformity, 83
Lute
cement, 45
to cement, 46
guitar, 417
Luxation
disjunction, 44

Luxuriant
  sufficiency, 639
  vegetation, 365
Luxuriate
  pleasure, 827
Luxurious
  pleasurableness, 829
Luxury
  physical, 377
  enjoyment, 827
  sensuality, 954
Lyceum
  school, 542
Lych-gate
  opening, 260
Lyddite
  arms, 727
Lying
  decumbent, 213
  deceptive, 546
Lyke-wake
  interment, 363
Lymph
  water, 337
Lymphatic
  inert, 172
  soft, 324
Lynch
  punish, 972
  kill, 361
Lynch law
  illegality, 964
Lynx-eyed
  vision, 441
Lyre
  musical instrument, 417
Lyrics
  poetry, 597

M.C.
  director, 694
Ma
  mother, 166
Mab
  fairy, 979
Macabre
  gruesome, 846
Macadam
  smoothness, 255
Macaroni
  fop, 854
Macaronic
  poetry, 597
Mace

club, 633
  weapon, 727
  sceptre, 747
Mace-bearer
  jurisprudence, 965
Macerate
  water, 337
Maceration
  asceticism, 955
  atonement, 952
Machiavellian
  falsehood, 544
Machiavellism
  cunning, 702
Machicolation
  embrasure, 257
Machination
  plan, 626
Machine
  instrument, 633
Machinist
  agent, 690
Mackerel sky
  cloud, 353
Mackintosh
  dress, 225
Macrobiotic
  lasting, 110
Macrocosm
  world, 318
  greatness, 31
Macrology
  diffuseness, 573
Mactation
  idolatry, 991
Macula
  blemish, 848
Maculated
  variegation, 440
Maculation
  ugliness, 846
Mad
  insane, 503
  violent, 173
Madcap
  caprice, 608
  rash, 863
  excitable, 825
Madden
  excite, 824
Madder
  red, 434
Made of
  composition, 54
Madefaction

moisture, 339
Madhouse
  hospital, 662
Madman
  madman, 504
Madness
  insanity, 503
Madrigal
  poetry, 597
Maelstrom
  whirlpool, 312, 348
  turmoil, turmoil, 59
Maenad
  violence, 173
Maffick
  make merry, 836
Magazine
  store, 636
  record, 551
  book, 593
Magdalen
  penitent, 950
Mage
  sorcerer, 994
Magenta
  purple, 437
Maggot
  whim, 608
  desire, 865
Maggoty
  uncleanness, 653
Magi
  sage, 500
  saint, 948
Magic
  sorcery, 992
Magic lantern
  optical, 445
  spectacle, 448
Magician
  sorcerer, 994
Magisterial
  pride, 878
Magistracy
  authority, 737
  jurisdiction, 965
Magistrate
  justiciary, 967
  ruler, 745
Magistrature
  authority, 737
Magma
  mixture, 41
Magnanimity
  disinterestedness, 942

575

Magnate
nobility, 875
Magnet
attraction, 288, 829
desire, 865
motive, 615
Magnificat
worship, 990
Magnificent
grand, 882
fine, 845
magnanimous, 942
Mangifico
nobility, 875
Magnifier
optical instrument, 445
Magnify
increase, 35
enlarge, 194
exaggerate, 549
praise, 990
approve, 931
Magniloquent
ornament, 577
extravagant, 549
speech, 582
Magnitude
quantity, 25
size, 192
Magpie
loquacity, 584
Magsman
thief, 792
Magus
heathen, 984
Maharajah
master, 745
noble, 875
Maharanee
noble, 875
chief, 745
Mahatma
sorcerer, 994
Mahogany colour
brown, 433
Mahomet
religious founder, 986
Mahometanism
religions, 984
Maid of honour
marriage, 903
Maiden
girl, 129, 374
servant, 746
spinster, 904

purity, 960
guillotine, 975
first, 66
Mail
letters, 592
news, 532
defence, 717
armoury, 727
Mail-cart
vehicle, 272
Maim
injure, 649, 659
weaken, 160
Main
whole, 50
tunnel, 260
conduit, 350
ocean, 341
principal, 642
Mainland
land, 342
Mainly
greatness, 31
Mainspring
cause, 153
motive, 615
Mainstay
instrument, 631
refuge, 666
hope, 858
Maintain
continue, 141, 143
preserve, 670
sustain, 170
assert, 535
Maison de santé
remedy, 662
Maître
expert, 700
Majestic
repute, 873
Majesty
king, 745
rank, 873
Deity, 976
Major
greater, 33
officer, 745
Majordomo
director, 694
commissary, 746
Majority
age, 131
greater number, 102
dead, 362

Majuscules
printing, 591
Make
produce, 161
constitute, 54
form, 240
arrive at, 292
price, 812
Make-believe
untruth, 546
Make fast
vinculum, 43
Make for
tend, 176
Make good
compensation, 30
substantiate, 467
Make it up
forgive, 918
Make known
information, 527
Make loose
incoherence, 47
Make out
decipher, 522
understand, 518
discover, 480A
Make over
transfer, 783
Make up
complete, 52
compose, 54
imagine, 515
invent, 544
improvise, 612
Make up for
compensate, 30
Make up to
accost, 586
approach, 286
Make way
progress, 282
improve, 658
Maker
artificer, 690
Deity, 976
Makeshift
substitute, 147
temporary, 111
plan, 626
plea, 617
Makeweight
compensate, 30
equality, 27
completeness, 52

Mala fide
  improbity, 940
Malachite
  green, 435
Malade imaginaire
  madman, 504
  dejection, 837
Maladie du pays
  discontent, 832
  dejection, 837
Maladjusted
  antisocial, 911
Maladministration
  unskilful, 699
Maladroit
  unskilful, 699
Malady
  disease, 655
Malaise
  pain, 378, 828
Malapert
  jackanapes, 887
  insolent, 885
Malaprop
  misnomer, 565
Malapropism
  ridicule, 856
  error, 495
Malapropos
  irrelevant, 10
  discordant, 24
  inopportune, 135
Malaria
  disease, 657
Malarkey
  flattery, 933
Malcontent
  discontent, 832
Male
  strength, 159
Malediction
  curse, 908
Malefactor
  evildoer, 949
Maleficent
  malevolence, 907
Malevolent
  malevolence, 907
  badness, 649
  enmity, 889
Malfeasance
  guilt, 947
Malformation
  ugliness, 846
Malice

spite, 907
  hate, 898
Malign
  detraction, 934
Malignant
  malevolent, 907
  pernicious, 649
Malignity
  violence, 173
  badness, 649
Malinger
  falsehood, 544
  disease, 655
Mall
  club, 633
  impact, 276
  street, 189
Malleable
  soft, 324
  facile, 705
Mallet
  hammer, 276, 633
Malodorous
  fetor, 401
Malpractice
  guilt, 947
Maltreat
  injure, 649
  aggrieve, 830
  molest, 907
Malversation
  waste, 818
Mamilla
  convexity, 250
Mamma
  mother, 166
Mammal
  animal, 366
Mammet
  representation, 554
Mammon
  wealth, 803
Mammoth
  size, 192
Man
  mankind, 372P
  person, 373
  to arm, 673
Man-handle
  maltreat, 649
Man of straw
  defaulter, 808
Man-of-war
  ship, 273
Manacle

shackle, 751, 752
  to fetter, 43
Manage
  direction, 693
  succeed, 731
Manageable
  facility, 705
Management
  skill, 698
Manager
  director, 694
Managing
  active, 682
Mancipation
  restraint, 751
Mandamus
  command, 741
Mandarin
  master, 745
Mandate
  command, 741
  region, 181
Mandatory
  obligatory, 926
Mandolin
  musical instrument, 417
Mandrel
  rotation, 312
Manducation
  feeding, 296
Mane
  rought, 256
Manège
  training, 370
Manes
  corpse, 362
Manful
  strong, 159
  brave, 861
Mangle
  disjunction 44
  smooth, 255
Mangy
  disease, 655
Manhood
  virility, 131, 373
  bravery, 861
Mania
  insanity, 503
  desire, 865
Maniac
  mad, 504
Manifest
  visible, 446
  obvious, 518

to show, 525
to appear, 448
Manifesto
publication, 531
Manifold
multitude, 102
Manikin
image, 554
dwarf, 193
Manila
tobacco, 298A
Manipulate
handle, 379
use, 677
conduct, 692
Mankind
man, 372
Manlike
strength, 159
Manly
adolescent, 131
resolute, 604
brave, 861
Manna
sweetness, 396
Mannequin
image, 554
Manner
intrinsic, 5
way, 627
appearance, 448
conduct, 692
kind, 75
Mannerism
singularity, 79, 83
phrase, 566
ornament, 577
affectation, 855
vanity, 880
Mannerly
courtesy, 894
Manners
breeding, 852
politeness, 894
Manœuvre
scheme, 626
operation, 680
skill, 698
stratagem, 545, 702
Manor
property, 780
Manse
temple, 1000
Mansion
abode, 189

Mansuetude
courtesy, 894
Mantel
support, 215
Mantilla
dress, 225
Mantle
cloak, 225
kindle, 900
flush, 821
spread, 194
Mantlet
dress, 225
Mantology
prediction, 511
Manual
book, 542, 593
reference, 695
Manufactory
workshop, 691
Manufacture
production, 161
Manufacturer
agent, 690
producer, 164
Manumit
liberate, 750
Manure
unclean, 653
Manuscript
writing, 590
Many
multitude, 102
Many-coloured
variegation, 440
Many-sided
accomplished, 698
Map
representation, 554
journey, 266
Maquis
fighter, 726
Mar
spoil, 649
obstruct, 706
Maranatha
malediction, 908
Marasmus
atrophy, 655
shrinking, 195
Marauder
thief, 792
Marauding
stealing, 791
Marble

ball, 249
hard, 323
sculpture, 557
Marble-hearted
malevolence, 907
Marbled
variegated, 440
March
journey, 266
progression, 282
March-past
display, 882
March with
contiguity, 199
Marches
limit, 233
Marchioness
noble, 875
chief, 745
Marchpane
sweet, 396
Marconigram
message, 532
Mare
carrier, 271
Maréchal
master, 745
Mare's nest
absurdity, 497
failure, 732
Mare's tail
cloud, 353
Margin
edge, 230
space, 180
latitude, 748
Marginalia
commentary, 522
Margrave
master, 745
Marinade
pickle, 670
Marine
oceanic, 341
fleet, 273
soldier, 726
Marish
marsh, 345
Marital
marriage, 903
Maritime
oceanic, 341
Mark
indication, 550
record, 551

repute, 873
object, 620
degree, 26, 71
observe, 441, 450
attend to, 457
Marked
great, 31
Market
mart, 799
buy, 795
Market garden
agriculture, 371
Marketable
trade, 794, 796
Marksman
proficient, 700
Marl
land, 342
Marmalade
sweet, 396
Maroon
seclusion, 893
abandon, 782
signal, 550, 669
Marplot
bungler, 701
obstacle, 706
malicious, 913
Marquee
tent, 189
Marquetry
mixture, 41
variegation, 440
Marquis
noble, 875
master, 745
Marquisate
title, 877
Marriage
marry, 903
union, 41
Marriageable
adolescence, 131
Marrow
essence, 5
interior, 221
central, 223
gist, 516
essential, 642
Mars
god, 979
Marsh
marsh, 345
moisture, 339
Marshal

arrange, 60
officer, 745
in law, 968
messenger, 534
Mart
mart, 799
Martellato
music, 415
Martial
contention, 720
Martinet
tyrant, 739
teacher, 540
Martingale
bridle, 752
Martyr
pain, 828
Martyrdom
torture, 378
agony, 828
killing, 361
asceticism, 955
Marvel
wonder, 870
prodigy, 872
Marvellous
great, 31
impossible, 471
Marzipan
sweet, 396
Mascara
ornament, 847
Mascot
talisman, 993
Masculine
strength, 159
man, 373
Mash
mix, 41
knead, 324
Masher
fop, 854
Mashie
club, 276
Mask
concealment, 528
ambush, 530
untruth, 546
shade, 424
dress, 225
Masked
invisible, 447
Masorah
revelation, 985
Masque

drama, 599
Masquerade
frolic, 840
concealment, 528
ambush, 530
deception, 546
Mass
quantity, 25
degree, 31
whole, 50
heap, 72
size, 192
weight, 319
density, 321
rites, 990, 998
Massacre
killing, 361
Massage
friction, 331
Masses
lower classes, 876
Massive
huge, 192
heavy, 319
dense, 321
Mast-head
summit, 210
Master
ruler, 745
director, 694
proficient, 700
of arts, 492
teacher, 540
to succeed, 731
possessor, 779
to learn, 539
to understand, 518
to overpower, 824
Master-hand
skilled, 698
Master-key
explanation, 462
opener, 260
instrumentality, 631
Master-mind
sage, 500
Mastered
failure, 732
Masterful
domineering, 736
Masterly
skill, 698
Masterpiece
perfection, 650, 698

Mastership
authority, 737
Masterstroke
plan, 626
skill, 698
Mastery
authority, 737
skill, 698
success, 731
Mastic
semiliquid, 352
Masticate
eat, 296
Mat
network, 219
Match
equal, 27
duality, 89
similar, 17
to copy, 19
agreement, 23
contention, 720
fuel, 388
marriage, 903
Matchless
good, 648
perfect, 650
virtuous, 944
greatness, 31
superior, 33
Matchlock
arms, 727
Mate
similar, 17
equal, 27
duality, 89
friend, 890
wife, 903
master, 745
Materfamilias
paternity, 166
Materia medica
remedy, 662
Material
substance, 3, 316
important, 642
embody, 316
Materialism
absence of intellect, 450A
irreligion, 989
Materiality
corporality, 316
Materialize
appear, 448
Materials
materials, 635

Maternity
paternity, 166
Mathematical
exact, 494
Mathematics
quantity, 25
Matinée
drama, 599
Matins
rite, 990, 998
morning, 125
Matriarchy
authority, 737
Matricide
killing, 361
Matriculation
learner, 541
Matrimony
wedlock, 903
mixture, 41
Matrix
mould, 22
engraving, 558
workshop, 691
Matron
woman, 374
wife, 903
old, 130
adolescent, 131
superintendent, 694
Matt
rough, 256
Matted
crossing, 219
Matter
substance, 3
material world, 316
topic, 454
business, 625
meaning, 516
importance, 642
pus, 653
Matter of course
conformity, 82
Matter of fact
being, 1
Matter-of-fact
prosaic, 843
Matting
plaiting, 219
Mattock
instrument, 633
sharpness, 253
Mattress
support, 215

Mature
ripe, 144, 673
scheme, 626
old, 124
adolescent, 131
Matutinal
early, 125, 132
Maudlin
drunk, 959
sensitive, 822
Maugre
counteraction, 179
Maul
maltreat, 649
impact, 276
Maunder
digress, 573
Mausoleum
interment, 363
Mauvais sujet
bad man, 949
Mauvaise honte
modesty, 881
affectation, 855
Mauvaise plaisanterie
vulgarity, 852
Mauve
purple, 437
Maw
receptacle, 191
Mawkish
insipid, 391
indifferent, 866
Maxim
maxim, 496, 697
gun, 727
Maximum
greatness, 33
Maxixe
dance, 840
May
possible, 470
chance, 156
supposition, 514
Maya
illusion, 495
Maybe
possible, 470
chance, 156
supposition, 514
Mayhap
possible, 470
chance, 156
supposition, 514

Mayhem
 evil, 619
Mayor
 master, 745
Maypole
 height, 206
Mazarine
 blue, 438
Maze
 convolution, 248
 bewilderment, 491
 enigma, 533
Mazuma
 money, 800
Mazurka
 dance, 840
 music, 415
Me
 personality, 317
Me judice
 belief, 484
Mea culpa
 penitence, 950
Mead
 plain, 344
 sweet, 396
Meadow
 plain, 344
Meagre
 thin, 193
 narrow, 203
 scanty, 640
 style, 575
Meal
 powder, 330
 repast, 298
Mealy-mouthed
 false, 544
 servile, 886
Mean
 average, 29
 middle, 68, 628
 small, 32
 contemptible, 643
 shabby, 874
 base, 940
 humble, 879
 sneaking, 886
 selfish, 943
 stingy, 819
 intend, 620
 to signify, 516
Meander
 circuition, 311
 convolution, 248

 river, 348
 wander, 279, 629
Meaningless
 nonsense, 517
Means
 appliances, 632
 fortune, 803
 property, 780
Meantime
 period, 106, 120
Meanwhile
 duration, 106, 120
Measure
 extent, 25
 degree, 26
 moderation, 174, 639
 to compute, 466
 proceeding, 626, 680
 to apportion, 786
 in music, 413
 in poetry, 597
Measure, in a great
 greatness, 31
Measure for measure
 compensation, 30
Meat
 food, 298
Meaty
 savoury, 394
Mechanic
 agent, 690
Mechanical
 automatic, 601
 style, 575
 imitative, 19
Mechanics
 force, 159
 machinery, 632
Mechanism
 means, 632
Medal
 reward, 973
 record, 551
 palm, 733
 decoration, 877
Medallion
 sculpture, 557
Meddle
 interpose, 682
 act, 680
Meddlesome
 interpose, 682
Medial
 middle, 68
Median

 mean, 29
Mediation
 mediation, 724
 deprecation, 766
Mediator
 Saviour, 976
Medicament
 remedy, 662
Medicaster
 deceiver, 548
Medicate
 heal, 660
 compound, 41
Medicine
 remedy, 662
Medieval
 oldness, 124
 past, 122
Mediocrity
 moderate, 32
 mean, 29
 of fortune, 736
 imperfect, 648, 651
Meditate
 think, 451
 purpose, 620
Mediterranean
 middle, 68
 interjacent, 228
Medium
 mean, 29
 pigment, 428
 instrument, 631
 spiritualist, 994
Medley
 mixture, 41
Meed
 reward, 973
 gift, 784
 share, 786
 praise, 931
Meek
 humble, 879
 gentle, 826
Meerschaum
 tobacco-pipe, 298A
Meet
 contact, 199, 292
 agreement, 23
 converge, 290
 assemble, 72
 expedient, 646
 proper, 924, 926
 fulfil, 772

Meet with
find, 480A
happen, 151
Meeting-place
focus, 74
Megalomania
insanity, 503
vanity, 880
Megalomaniac
madman, 504
Megaphone
loudness, 404
Megascope
optical instrument, 445
Megrims
dejection, 837
Melancholia
insanity, 503
Melancholy
distressing, 830
dejection, 837
Mélange
mixture, 41
Mêlée
contention, 720
disorder, 59
Meliorate
improve, 658
Mellifluous
sound, 405
melody, 413
style, 578
Mellow
sound, 413, 580
mature, 144, 673
old, 124
soft, 324
tipsy, 959
Melodeon
wind instrument, 417
Melodrama
the drama, 599
Melody
music, 413
Melpomene
the drama, 599
Melt
liquefy, 335
fuse, 384
change, 144
disappear, 449
pity, 914
Melt away
disappear, 2, 449
Member
part, 51

component, 56
Membrane
layer, 204
Memento
memory, 505
Memento mori
interment, 363
Memoir
description, 594
dissertation, 595
Memorabilia
memory, 505
Memorable
importance, 642
Memorandum
memory, 505
record, 551
Memorial
record, 551
epistle, 592
Memoriter
memory, 505
Memory
reminiscence, 505
fame, 873
Menace
threat, 908
Ménage
conduct, 692
Menagerie
taming, 370
collection, 72
store, 636
Mend
improve, 658
Mendacity
falsehood, 544
Mendelism
production, 161
Mendicant
beggar, 767
monk, 996
Mendicity
beggar, 804
Menial
servant, 746
servile, 876
Menstrual
period, 108
Mensuration
measure, 466
Mental
intellect, 450
Mention
information, 527

Mentor
adviser, 695
teacher, 540
Menu
list, 86
food, 298
plan, 626
Mephistopheles
Satan, 978
miscreant, 949
Mephitic
fetid, 401
pernicious, 649
deleterious, 657
poison, 663
Mercantile
merchant, 794
Mercenary
parsimonious, 819
price, 812
servant, 746
self-seeking, 943
Merchandise
goods, 798
Merchant
merchant, 797
Merchantman
ship, 273
Merci
thanks, 917
Merciful
pity, 914
Merciless
malevolence, 907
Mercurial
excitable, 825
mobile, 264
quick, 274
Mercury
god, 979
messenger, 534
Mercy
mercy, 914
Mercy-seat
tribunal, 966
Mere
simple, 32
unimportant, 643
lake, 343
Meretricious
false, 495, 544
vulgar, 851
licentious, 961
colour, 428

Merge
plunge, 337
insert, 300
include, 76
combine, 48
midst, 68
Meridian
summit, 210
noon, 125
desert, 944
to deserve, 922, 924
usefulness, 644
Merit
goodness, 648
Mermaid
ocean, 341
monster, 83
Merry
cheerful, 836
Merry-andrew
humorist, 844
Merry-go-round
rotation, 312
Merrymaking
amuse, 836, 840
sociality, 892
Merrythought
spell, 993
Merum sal
wit, 842
Mésalliance
ill-assorted, 24
marriage, 903
Meseems
belief, 484
Mesh
crossing, 219
interval, 198
Mesial
middle, 68
Mesmerism
occult arts, 992, 994
Mess
mixture, 41
disorder, 59
dirt, 653
failure, 732
meal, 298
Message
command, 741
intelligence, 532
Messenger
message, 534
Messiah
Deity, 976

Messmate
friend, 890
Messuage
abode, 189
Metabolism
change, 140
life, 369
Metachronism
anachronism, 115
Metal
material, 635
Metallurgy
mineral, 358
Metamorphosis
change, 140
Metaphor
metaphor, 521
comparison, 464
analogy, 17
Metaphorical
style, 557
Metaphrase
interpret, 522, 524
Metaphysics
intellect, 450
Metastasis
change, 140
Metathesis
transference, 270
inversion, 218
Mete
measure, 466
give, 784
distribute, 786
Metempsychosis
change, 140
Meteor
luminary, 423
light, 420
universe, 318
Meteoric
violent, 173
refulgent, 420
transient, 111
Meteorology
air, 338
Methinks
belief, 484
Method
order, 58
way, 627
Methodize
arrange, 60
Meticulous
careful, 459

Metonymy
metaphor, 521
substitution, 147
Metre
poetry, 597
Metrical
measurement, 466
Metropolis
abode, 189
Mettle
spirit, 820
courage, 861
Mettlesome
excitable, 822, 825
brave, 861
Mew
enclose, 231
restrain, 751
divest, 226
complain, 839
Mewl
ululation, 412
Mezzo-rilievo
sculpture, 557
Mezzo-soprano
melody, 413
Mezzo termine
middle, 68
mid-course, 628
Mezzotint
engraving, 558
Miasma
bane, 663
Miasmal
morbific, 649
Micawber
careless, 460
Microbe
bane, 663
insalubrity, 657
Microcosm
little, 32, 193
Microfilm
copy, 21
Microphone
loudness, 404
hearing, 418
Microscope
optical, 445
Microscopic
little, 193
Mid
middle, 68
Mid-course
middle, 628

Midas
wealth, 803
Midday
course, 125
Midden
uncleanness, 653
Middle
in order, 68
in degree, 29
in space, 223
Middleman
agent, 690
go-between, 631
salesman, 797
Middling
imperfect, 651
mean, 29
Midge
littleness, 193
Midget
dwarf, 193
Midland
land, 342
Midnight
evening, 126
darkness, 421
Midriff
interjacence, 228
Midshipman
master, 745
Midst
central, 223
Midsummer
morning, 125
Midway
middle, 68
Midwife
doctor, 662
Mien
appearance, 448
conduct, 692
Miff
resentment, 900
Might
power, 157
degree, 26
violence, 173
Mighty
much, 31
large, 192
powerful, 159
haughty, 878
Migrate
journey, 266
Mikado

master, 745
Mike
loudness, 404
hearing, 418
Milch cow
store 636'
Mild
moderate, 174
insipid, 391
lenient, 740
calm, 826
courteous, 894
warm, 382
Mildew
unclean, 653
Mileage
measurement, 466
Militant
contention, 720
Militarism
warfare, 722
authority, 737
Military
combatant, 726
Militate
opposition, 179, 608
Militia
combatant, 726
Milk
to despoil, 789
Milk-and-water
inperfect, 651
Milk-white
whiteness, 430
Milksop
coward, 862
Milky
semitransparent, 427
emulsive, 252
Milky Way
world, 318
Mill
machine, 330, 633
workshop, 691
Mill-pond
store, 636
Millenary
celebration, 883
Millennium
period, 108
thousand, 98
futurity, 121
Utopia, 515
hope, 858
Millesimal

thousand, 98
Millet-seed
littleness, 193
Milliner
dress, 225
Million
number, 98
Millionaire
wealth, 803
Millstone
incubus, 706
weight, 319
Miltonic
sublime, 574
poetry, 597
Mime
player, 599
buffoon, 856
Mimeograph
imitation, 19
Mimesis
imitation, 19
Mimic
imitation, 19
repeat, 104
Minacity
threat, 909
Minaret
height, 206
Minatory
threatening, 909
dangerous, 665
Minauderie
affected, 855
Mince
disjoin, 44
stammer, 583
Mincing
slow, 275
affected, 855
Mind
intellect, 450
will, 600
desire, 865
dislike, 867
purpose, 620
to attend to, 457
believe, 484
remember, 505
Minded
willing, 602
Mindful
attentive, 457
remembering, 505

584

Mindless
inattentive, 458
forgetful, 506
Mine
store, 636
abundance, 639
to hollow, 252
open, 260
snare, 545
sap, 162
damage, 659
Mine-layer
ship, 273
Mine-sweeper
ship, 273
Mineral
inorganic, 358
Mineralogy
inorganic, 358
Minerva
goddess, 979
Mingle
mix, 41
Mingy
parsimony, 819
Mini
small, 193
Miniature
portrait, 556
small, 193
Minikin
small, 193
Minim
small, 32, 193
Minimize
moderate, 174
underestimate, 483
Minumum
small, 32, 193
Mining
opening, 260
Minion
favourite, 899
Minister
deputy, 759
instrumentality, 631
director, 694
to aid, 707
rites, 998
Ministry
direction, 693
church, 995
Minnow
littleness, 193
Minor

inferior, 34
infant, 129
Minority
fewness, 103
Minotaur
unconformity, 83
Minster
temple, 1000
Minstrel
music, 416
Minstrelsy
musician, 415
Mint
workshop, 691
mould, 22
wealth, 803
Minuend
deduction, 38
Minuet
dance, 840
music, 415
Minus
less, 38
in debt, 806
deficient, 304
Minuscules
printing, 591
Minute
in quantity, 32
in size, 193
of time, 108
instant, 113
compendium, 596
record, 551
in style, 573
Minutest
inferior, 34
Minutiae
small, 32
little, 193
unimportant, 643
Minx
impertinent, 887
bad woman, 949
Mirabile dictu
wonder, 870
Miracle
prodigy, 872
Miraculous
wonder, 870
Mirage
dim sight, 443
appearance, 448
shadow, 4
Mire

uncleanness, 653
Mirk
darkness, 421
Mirror
reflector, 445
perfection, 650
saint, 948
imitate, 19
Mirth
cheerful, 836
Mirthless
dejected, 837
Misadventure
failure, 732
adversity, 735
misfortune, 830
Misalliance
marriage, 903
Misanthrope
recluse, 893, 911
Misapply
misuse, 679
misinterpret, 523
mismanage, 699
Misapprehend
mistake, 495
misinterpret, 523
Misappropriate
misuse, 679
Misarrange
derange, 61
Misbecome
vice, 945
Misbegotten
vice, 945
Misbehaviour
discourtesy, 895
vulgarity, 852
guilt, 947
Misbelief
doubt, 495
Miscalculate
sophistry, 477
disappoint, 509
Miscall
misnomer, 565
Miscarriage
failure, 732
Miscegenation
mixture, 41
Miscellany
mixture, 41
collection, 72
generality, 78

Mischance
misfortune, 830
adversity, 735
failure, 732
Mischief
evil, 619
Mischievous
badness, 649
Miscible
mix, 41
Miscompute
mistake, 495
Misconceive
mistake, 495
misinterpret, 481, 523
Misconduct
guilt, 947
bungling, 699
Misconstrue
misinterpret, 523
Miscount
error, 495
Miscreant
wretch, 949
apostate, 941
Miscreated
vice, 945
Miscue
unskilfulness, 699
Misdate
anachronism, 115
Misdeed
guilt, 947
Misdeem
misinterpret, 523
Misdemean
vice, 945
Misdevotion
impiety, 988
Misdirect
misteaching, 538
bungle, 699
Misdoing
guilt, 947
Mise en scène
appearance, 448
Misemploy
misuse, 679
Miser
parsimony, 819
Miserable
contemptible, 643
unhappy, 828
pitiable, 914
small, 32
Miserly

parsimony, 819
Misery
pain, 828
Misestimate
error, 495
Misfit
disparity, 24
Misfortune
evil, 619
failure, 732
adversity, 735
unhappiness, 830
Misgiving
fear, 860
doubt, 485
Misgovern
unskilful, 699
Misguide
misteaching, 538
Misguided
foolish, 699
Mishandle
maltreat, 649
Mishap
evil, 619
failure, 732
adversity, 735
disaster, 830
Mishmash
mixture, 41
Misinform
misteach, 538
ignorance, 491
error, 495
Misintelligence
misteach, 538
Misinterpret
misinterpret, 523
Misjoined
disagreement, 24
Misjudge
err, 495
sophistry, 477
Mislay
lose, 776
derange, 61
Mislead
deceive, 477, 545
misteach, 538
error, 495
Mislike
dislike, 867
Mismanage
unskilful, 699
Mismatch

difference, 15
Mismatched
disagreement, 24
Misname
misnomer, 565
Misnomer
misnomer, 565
Misogamy
celibacy, 904
Misogynist
celibacy, 904
Misplace
disorder, 59
unconformity, 83
Misplaced
unsuitable, 24
Misprint
error, 495
Mispronounce
speech, 583
Misproportioned
ugliness, 846
Misquote
misinterpret, 523
false, 544
Misreckon
error, 495
Misrelate
error, 495
Misremember
error, 495
Misreport
err, 495
falsify, 544
Misrepresent
untruth, 546
Misrepresentation
perversion, 523
falsehood, 544
caricature, 555
Misrule
misconduct, 699
laxity, 738
Miss
lose, 776
fail, 732
inattention, 458, 460
want, 865
girl, 374
Missal
rite, 998
Missay
stammer, 583
misnomer, 565

Misshapen
ugliness, 846
distortion, 243
Missile
thing thrown, 284
arms, 727
Missing
absence, 187
Mission
commission, 755
undertaking, 676
business, 625
warfare, 722
Missionary
clergy, 996
Missive
correspond, 592
Misspell
misinterpret, 523
Misspend
prodigal, 818
Misstate
misinterpret, 523
falsify, 544
Misstatement
error, 495
falsehood, 544
untruth, 546
perversion, 523
Mist
dimness, 422
Mistake
error, 495
failure, 732
mismanagement, 699
misconstrue, 523
Misteach
misteach, 538
Misterm
misnomer, 565
Misthink
error, 495
Mistime
intempestivity, 135
Mistral
wind, 349
Mistranslate
misinterpret, 523
Mistress
lady, 374
sweetheart, 897
concubine, 962
Mistrust
doubt, 485
Misty

opaque, 426
dim, 422
invisible, 447
Misunderstanding
error, 495
misinterpretation, 523
discord, 713
Misuse
misuse, 679
waste, 638
Mite
small, 193
bit, 32
money, 800
Mitigate
abate, 36, 174
relieve, 834
calm, 826
improve, 658
extenuate, 937
Mitrailleuse
gun, 727
Mitre
canonicals, 999
joint, 43
Mitten
dress, 225
Mittimus
command, 741
Mix
mix, 41
Mixed
disorder, 59
Mixture
mix, 41
Mizzle
rain, 348
Mnemonics
memory, 505
Mnemosyne
memory, 505
Moan
lamentation, 411, 839
Moat
enclosure, 232
ditch, 350
defence, 717
Mob
crowd, 31, 72
multitude, 102
troop, 726
plenty, 639
vulgar, 876
to scold, 932
Mob law

illegal, 964
Mobile
movable, 264
sensible, 822
inconstant, 607
Mobility
commonalty, 876
move, 264
Mobilization
warfare, 722
Mobocracy
authority, 737
Mobsman
thief, 792
Moccasin
dress, 225
Mock
imitate, 17
repeat, 104
erroneous, 495
false, 544
to ridicule, 483, 856
laugh at, 838
Mock-heroic
ridiculous, 853
Modal
extrinsic, 6
state, 7
circumstance, 8
Mode
fashion, 852
method, 627
Model
prototype, 22
to change, 140, 144
rule, 80
example, 82
to copy, 19
sculpture, 557
perfection, 650
saint, 948
Modeller
artist, 559
Moderate
small, 32
to allay, 174
to assuage, 826
temperate, 953
cheap, 815
Moderation
temperateness, 174
mediocrity, 736
Moderato
music, 415

Moderator
master, 745
director, 694
Modern
newness, 123
Modernize
change, 140
Modesty
humility, 881
purity, 960
Modicum
little, 33
allotment, 786
Modification
difference, 15
variation, 20
change, 140
qualification, 469
Modify
convert, 144
Modish
fashion, 852
Modulation
change, 140
harmony, 413
Modus operandi
method, 627
conduct, 692
Modus vivendi
arrangement, 723
compromise, 774
Mogul
master, 745
Mohammed
religious founder, 986
Mohammedanism
religions, 984
Mohock
roisterer, 949
Moider
bewilder, 475
inattention, 458
Moiety
bisection, 91
Moil
action, 680
work, 686
Moist
wet, 337
humid, 339
Moke
carrier, 271
Molasses
sweetness, 396
Mole
mound, 206

defence, 717
refuge, 666
Molecule
small, 32, 193
Molehill
lowness, 207
trifling, 643
Molestation
evil, 619
damage, 649
malevolence, 907
Mollify
allay, 174
soften, 324
conciliate, 918
assuage, 826
Mollusc
animal, 366
Mollycoddle
cowardice, 862
Moloch
tyranny, 739
divinity, 979
idol, 986
Molten
liquid, 335
Moment
of time, 113
importance, 642
Momentary
transient, 111
Momentum
impulse, 276
Momus
rejoicing, 838
Monachism
church, 995
Monad
littleness, 193
unity, 87
Monarch
master, 745
Monarchy
authority, 737
Monastery
temple, 1000
Monastic
churchdom, 995
Monetary
money, 800
Money
money, 800
Money-bag
treasury, 802
Money-changer

merchant, 797
Money-grubber
miser, 819
acquisition, 775
Moneyed
wealth, 803
Moneyer
treasurer, 801
Moneyless
poverty, 804
Monger
merchant, 797
Mongrel
mixture, 41
anomalous, 83
Moniker
name, 564
Moniliform
circular, 247
Monism
unity, 87
Monition
advice, 695
warning, 668
information, 527
omen, 512
Monitor
teacher, 540
director, 694
master, 745
ship, 723
Monitory
prediction, 511
warning, 668
Monk
clergy, 996
Monkery
churchdom, 995
Monkey
imitative, 19
engine, 276
ridiculous, 856
laughing-stock, 857
to play the fool, 499
money, 800
Monkey-shines
prank, 840
foolery, 497
caprice, 608
Monkish
clergy, 995
Monochord
musical, 417
Monochrome
colourless, 429

Monocular
lens, 445
Monody
lamentation, 839
Monogamy
marriage, 903
Monogram
sign, 550
cipher, 533
diagram, 554
Monograph
dissertation, 595
Monolith
record, 551
Monologue
soliloquy, 589
Monomania
insanity, 503
error, 495
obstinacy, 606
Monomaniac
madman, 504
Monometallism
money, 800
Monoplane
aircraft, 273a
Monopolize
possess, 777
engross, 457
Monopoly
syndicate, 778
Monosyllable
letter, 561
Monotheism
theology, 983
Monotonous
unchanging, 141
Monotony
identity, 13
uniformity, 16
repetition, 104, 141
in style, 575
weariness, 841
Monotype
printing, 591
Monsieur
title, 877
Monsoon
wind, 349
Monster
exception, 83
prodigy, 872
size, 192
ugly, 846
evildoer, 913

ruffian, 949
Monstrous
greatness, 31
huge, 192
wonderful, 870
ugly, 846
ridiculous, 853
Mont de piété
lending, 787
Montgolfier
balloon, 273a
Month
period, 108
Monthly
periodical, 138
Monticule
height, 206
Monument
record, 551
interment, 363
tallness, 206
Monumental
great, 31
Mood
nature, 5
state, 7
temper, 820
will, 600
tendency, 176
disposition, 602
affections, 820
variations, 20
change, 140
Moody
sullen, 895
fretful, 900
furious, 825
Moon
inaction, 681
changeable, 149
Moon-eyed
dim sight, 443
Moonbeam
light, 420
dimness, 422
Mooncalf
fool, 501
Moonless
dark, 421
Moonlight
light, 420
Moonshine
nonsense, 497, 517
excuse, 617
trumpery, 643

dimness, 422
Moonstruck
insanity, 503
Moony
dreamy, 458
foolish, 499
listless, 683
Moor
open space, 180
plain, 344
locate, 184
join, 43
rest, 265
Moorland
space, 180
plain, 344
Moot
inquire, 461
argue, 476
conjecture, 514
Moot point
topic, 454, 461
Mop
clean, 652
Mope
dejection, 837
Mope-eyed
dim sight, 443
Moped
vehicle, 272
Moppet
darling, 899
Moraine
debris, 330
Moral
right, 922
duty, 926
virtuous, 944
maxim, 496
Moral fibre
courage, 861
Morale
state, 7
Moralize
reason, 476
teach, 537
Morality
drama, 599
Morass
marsh, 345
Moratorium
delay, 133
Morbid
bad, 649
diseased, 655

noxious, 657
Morbific
  bad, 649
  diseased, 655
  noxious, 657
Mordacity
  malevolence, 907
Mordant
  pungent, 392
  vigorous, 574
  sarcastic, 932
Mordent
  grace-note, 415
More
  addition, 37
  superiority, 33
More or less
  smallness, 32
  equality, 27
More suo
  conformity, 82
Moreover
  addition, 37
  accompaniment, 88
Morganatic
  marriage, 903
Morgue
  pride, 878
  dead-house, 363
Moribund
  dying, 360
  sick, 655
Mormon
  polygamist, 903
Morning
  morning, 125
Moron
  fool, 501
Morose
  discourtesy, 895
Morphia
  anaesthetic, 376
Morphology
  form, 240
Morris-dance
  dance, 840
Morrison
  shelter, 717
Morrow
  futurity, 121
  morning, 125
Morsel
  small quantity, 32
  portion, 51
Mortal

man, 373
  fatal, 361
  bad, 649
  weariness, 841
Mortality
  death, 360
  evanescence, 111
  mankind, 372
Mortar
  cement, 45
  artillery, 727
  pulverization, 330
Mortgage
  sale, 796
  lend, 787
  security, 771
  credit, 805
Mortgagee
  credit, 805
Mortgagor
  debt, 806
Mortice
  see Mortise
Mortician
  interment, 363
Mortify
  pain, 828
  to vex, 830
  to discontent, 832
  to humiliate, 874, 879
  disease, 655
  asceticism, 955
Mortise
  unite, 43
  insert, 300
  intersect, 219
Mortuary
  interment, 363
Mosaic
  mixture, 41
  variegation, 440
  painting, 556
Moslem
  religions, 984
Mosque
  temple, 1000
Moss
  marsh, 345
  tuft, 256
Moss-grown
  deterioration, 659
Moss-trooper
  thief, 792
Most
  greatness, 31

Most part, for the
  general, 78
  conformity, 82
Mot
  maxim, 496
Mote
  particle, 193
  smallness, 32
  blemish, 848
  light, 320
Motel
  inn, 189
Motet
  music, 415
  worship, 990
Moth
  decay, 659
Moth-eaten
  imperfect, 651
Mother
  parent, 166
  mould, 653
  nun, 997
Mother-of-pearl
  variegation, 440
Mother tongue
  language, 560
Mother wit
  wisdom, 498
Motherland
  abode, 189
Motherly
  love, 897
Motif
  music, 415
  theme, 454
Motion
  change of place, 264
  proposition, 514
  topic, 454
  request, 765
  offer, 763
Motion picture
  drama, 599
Motionless
  quiescence, 265
Motive
  reason, 615
  music, 415
Motiveless
  absence of motive, 616
Motley
  multiform, 81
  mixed, 41
  variegated, 440

Motor
machine, 633
vehicle, 272
Motor-boat
ship, 273
Motor-bus
vehicle, 272
Motor-car
vehicle, 272
Motor-coach
vehicle, 272
Motor-cycle
vehicle, 272
Motor-van
vehicle, 272
Motorize
move, 264
Motorman
director, 694
Mottled
variegated, 440
Motto
device, 550
maxim, 496
phrase, 566
Mouch
inactivity, 688
Mould
form, 240, 329
condition, 7
earth, 342
mildew, 653
to model, 554
carve, 557
matrix, 22
Moulder
deterioration, 659
Moulding
ornament, 847
Mouldy
decayed, 653
fetid, 401
Moult
divestment, 226
Mound
defence, 717
hillock, 206
Mount
to rise, 305
hill, 206, 250
support, 215
to prepare, 673
Mountain
hill, 206
size, 192

weight, 319
Mountaineer
climber, 305
Mountebank
quack, 548
ignoramus, 493
buffoon, 844, 857
Mourn
grieve, 828
lament, 839
Mournful
sad, 837
aflicting, 830
Mouse
little, 193
to search, 461
Mouse-coloured
grey, 432
Mouse-hole
opening, 260
Mousseux
bubble, 353
Moustache
hair, 256
Mouth
entrance, 66
opening, 260
brink, 230
voice, 580
stammer, 583
Mouth-honour
flattery, 933
Mouth-watering
desire, 865
Mouthful
portion, 51, 193
Mouthpiece
speaker, 524, 540
speech, 582
Mouthy
style, 577
Movable
transference, 270
Movables
property, 780
Move
be in motion, 264
induce, 615
excite, 824
act, 680
undertaking, 676
propose, 514
Move off
recede, 287
depart, 293

Move on
progression, 282
Moved
impressed, 827
Moveless
quiescence, 265
Movement
motion, 264
stir, 682
Movie
cinema, 599a
Mow
cultivate, 371
destruction, 162
Mr.
title, 877
Much
greatness, 31
Mucilage
semiliquid, 352
adhesive, 45
Muck
uncleanness, 653
Muckle
greatness, 31
Muckworm
miser, 819
baseborn, 876
Mucronate
sharpness, 253
Mucus
semiliquid, 352
Mud
unclean, 653
Muddle
disorder, 59
derange, 61
bungle, 699
Muddled
confused, 458
tipsy, 959
foolish, 499
Muddy
opaque, 426
Mudlark
commonalty, 876
Muezzin
clergy, 996
Muff
bungler, 701
to bungle, 699
Muffle
silent, 403, 581
conceal, 528
taciturn, 585

wrap, 225
Muffler
dress, 225
Mufti
clergy, 996
judge, 966
dress, 225
Mug
receptacle, 191
fool, 501
face, 448
to study, 539
Muggy
dim, 422
moist, 339
Mulatto
unconformity, 83
mixture, 41
Mulct
penalty, 974
Mule
beast, 271
mongrel, 83
obstinate, 606
fool, 499
slipper, 225
Muleteer
director, 694
Muliebrity
woman, 374
Mull
cape, 250
sweeten, 396
Mull over
think, 451
Mullah
judge, 967
priest, 996
Mulligrubs
depression, 837
Mullion
support, 215
Multifarious
multiform, 81
various, 15
Multifid
divided, 51
Multifold
multiform, 16A, 81
Multiform
diversified, 16A, 81
Multigenerous
multiform, 81
Multilateral
side, 236

Multipartide
disjunction, 44
Multiple
numerous, 102
product, 84
Multiplicand
number, 84
Multiplication
arithmetical, 85
reproduction, 163
Multiplicator
number, 84
Multiplicity
multitude, 102
Multiplier
number, 84
Multisonous
loud, 404
Multitude
number, 102
greatness, 31
mob, 876
assemblage, 72
Multitudinous
multitude, 102
Multum in parvo
contraction, 195
conciseness, 572
Mum
silence, 403
aphony, 581
mother, 166
Mumble
eat, 296
mutter, 405, 583
Mumbo Jumbo
idol, 991
spell, 993
Mumchance
silent, 403
mute, 581
Mummer
the drama, 599
Mummery
absurdity, 497
ridicule, 856
parade, 882
imposture, 545
masquerade, 840
Mummify
preserve, 670
bury, 363
Mummy
corpse, 362
dryness, 340

mother, 166
Mump
dejection, 837
Mumper
beggar, 767
Mumps
sullenness, 895
Munch
eat, 296
Munchausen
exaggerate, 549
Mundane
world, 318
selfishness, 943
irreligion, 989
Munerary
reward, 973
Municipal
law, 965
distinct, 189
Munificent
liberality, 816
giving, 784
Muniment
record, 551
defence, 717
refuge, 666
Munition
material, 635
Murder
killing, 361
to bungle, 699
Murex
purple, 437
Muricate
sharpness, 253
Murky
darkness, 421
Murmur
sound, 405
complaint, 839
flow, 348
Murrain
disease, 655
Murrey
redness, 434
Muscle
strength, 159
Muse
to reflect, 451
poetry, 597
language, 560
Musette
musical instrument, 415

Museum
  store, 636
  collection, 72
  focus, 74
Mushroom
  small, 193
  newness, 123
  low-born, 876
  upstart, 734
  increase, 35
Music
  music, 415
Music-hall
  theatre, 599
  amusement, 840
Musical
  melodious, 413
Musician
  usician, 416
Musk
  fragrance, 400
Musket
  arms, 727
Musketeer
  combatant, 726
Muslin
  semitransparent, 427
Muss
  dishevel, 61
Mussulman
  religions, 984
Must
  mucor, 653
  necessity, 152
  obligation, 926
  compulsion, 744
  essential, 630
Mustard
  condiment, 393
  yellow, 436
Mustard-seed
  little, 193
Muster
  collect, 72
  numeration, 85
Muster-roll
  record, 551
  list, 86
Musty
  foul, 653
  rank, 401
Mutable
  changeable, 149
  irresolute, 605
Mutation

  change, 140
Mutatis mutandis
  reciprocalness, 12
  substitution, 147
Mutato nomine
  substitution, 147
Mute
  silent, 403
  letter, 561
  silencer, 417
  speechless, 581
  taciturn, 585
  interment, 363
Mutilate
  retrench, 38
  deform, 241
  garble, 651
  incomplete, 53
  injure, 649, 659
  spoliation, 619
Mutineer
  disobey, 742
Mutiny
  disobey, 742
  misrule, 738
  revolt, 719
Mutt
  fool, 501
Mutter
  speak, 583
  murmur, 405
  threaten, 909
Mutual
  reciprocal, 12, 148
Muzzle
  opening, 260
  edge, 230
  to silence, 403, 581
  taciturn, 585
  to incapacitate, 158
  restrain, 751
  imprison, 752
Muzzle-loader
  gun, 727
Muzzy
  confused, 458
  in liquor, 959
Myopic
  dim sight, 443
Myriad
  number, 98
  multitude, 102
Myrmidon
  troop, 726
Myrrh

  fragrance, 400
Myrtle
  love, 897
Mysterious
  concealed, 528
  obscure, 519
Mystery
  secret, 533
  latency, 526
  concealment, 528
  craft, 625
  drama, 599
Mystery-ship
  deception, 545
Mystic
  concealed, 528
  obscure, 519
Mystify
  to deceive, 545
  hide, 528
  falsify, 477
  misteach, 538
Myth
  imagination, 515
Mythological
  god, 979
  imaginary, 515

N.B.
  attention, 457
N or M
  generality, 78
Na
  dissent, 489
Nab
  seize, 789
Nabob
  wealth, 803
Nacreous
  variegation, 440
Nadir
  base, 211
Naffy
  food, 298
Nag
  carrier, 271
  be rude, 895
  discord, 713
  to scold, 932
Naiad
  mythological, 979
Nail
  to fasten, 43
  fastening, 45

Nail-brush
  clean, 652
Nailing
  good, 648
Naïveté
  artless, 703
Naked
  denuded, 226
  visible, 446
Namby-pamby
  affected, 855
  insipid, 866
  trifling, 643
  style, 575
Name
  appellation, 564
  fame, 873
  to appoint, 755
Nameless
  anonymous, 565
  obscure, 874
Namely
  conformity, 82
  specifically, 79
Namesake
  name, 564
Nap
  sleep, 683
  down, 256
  texture, 329
Napkin
  clean, 652
Napping
  inattentive, 458
Nappy
  frothy, 353
Narcissus
  beauty, 845
Narcotic
  noxious, 649
  somniferous, 683
Narghile
  tobacco-pipe, 298A
Nark
  informer, 527, 529
Narrate
  description, 594
Narrow
  thinness, 203
Narrow-minded
  bigoted, 499
  prejudiced, 481
Nasal
  accent, 583
Nascent

begin, 66
  new, 123
Nasty
  foul, 653
  unsavoury, 395
  offensive, 830
  ugly, 846
Natal
  beginning, 66
Natation
  navigation, 267
Nathless
  counteraction, 179
Nation
  mankind, 372
National
  inhabitant, 188
Nationality
  philanthropy, 910
Native
  inhabitant, 188
  artless, 703
Nativity
  prediction, 511
Natter
  nag, 932
Natty
  spruce, 845
Natural
  intrinsic, 5
  regular, 82
  true, 543
  artlessness, 703
  a fool, 501
  style, 578
Natural history
  organize, 357
Natural philosophy
  materiality, 316
Naturalistic
  description, 594
Naturalization
  conversion, 144
Naturalized
  habitual, 613
  established, 82
Nature
  essence, 5
  world, 318
  organization, 357
  affections, 820
  reality, 494
  rule, 82
  artless, 703
  unfashioned, 674

spontaneous, 612
  class, 75
  style, 578
Naught
  nothing, 4
  zero, 101
Naughty
  vicious, 945
  disobedient, 742
  perverse, 895
Naumachy
  conflict, 720
Nausea
  disgust, 867
  weariness, 841
  hatred, 898
  unsavoury, 395
Nautch-girl
  dancer, 599
Nautical
  navigation, 267
Nave
  middle, 68
  centre, 223
  church, 1000
Navel
  middle, 68
  centre, 223
Navigation
  ship, 267
Navigator
  mariner, 269
Navvy
  workman, 690
Navy
  ship, 273
Nawaub
  master, 745
Nay
  negation, 536
Ne plus ultra
  greatness, 31
  end, 67
  distance, 196
  superiority, 33
  goodness, 648
  perfection, 650
Neap
  lowness, 207
Near
  in space, 197
  in time, 121
  approach, 286
  stingy, 817
  likeness, 17

Near side
sinistrality, 239
Near-sighted
dim sight, 443
Nearly
small, 32
Neat
spruce, 845
clean, 652
in writing, 576
Neat-handed
skilful, 698
Neb
convexity, 250
Nebula
stars, 318
dimness, 422
misty, 353
invisible, 447
obscure, 519
Nebulosity
see Nebula
Necessitate
evidence, 467
Necessitous
adversity, 735
Necessity
fate, 601
indigence, 804
requirement, 630
Neck
contraction, 195
narrow, 203
insolence, 885
caress, 902
Neck and crop
whole, 50
Neck-cloth
dress, 225
Necklace
ornament, 847
circularity, 247
Necrology
description, 594
death, 360
Necromancer
sorcerer, 994
Necromancy
sorcery, 992
Necropsy
disinter, 363
Nectar
sweet, 394, 396
Need
requirement, 630

insufficiency, 640
indigence, 804
desire, 865
Needle
sharpness, 253
perforator, 262
fear, 860
compass, 693
Needless
redundance, 641
Needs
necessity, 601
Nefarious
vice, 945
Negation
negation, 536
Negative
inexisting, 2
contrariety, 14
quantity, 84
denial, 536
confute, 479
refusal, 764
prototype, 22
Neglect
disregard, 460
disuse, 678
non-observance, 773
to leave undone, 730
to slight, 929
to evade, 927
Negotiable
transferable, 783
Negotiate
bargain, 769
traffic, 794
mediate, 724
Negro
black, 431
Neigh
cry, 412
Neighbour
friend, 890
Neighbourhood
nearness, 197
Neighbourly
social, 892
friendly, 707, 888
Neither
rejection, 610
Nem. con.
assent, 488
Nemesis
revenge, 919
Nemine contradicente

assent, 488
Nemo
zero, 101
Nenia
dirge, 415
Neolithic
oldness, 124
Neology
language, 563
Neon lighting
light, 423
Neophyte
learner, 541
novice, 674
Neoteric
newness, 123
Nepenthe
remedy, 662
Nephelology
clouds, 353
Nepotism
relation, 11
sociality, 892
Neptune
god, 979
ocean, 341
Nereid
ocean, 341
goddess, 979
Nerve
strength, 159
courage, 861
Nerveless
weakness, 160
Nervous
weak, 160
timid, 860
powerful, 157
concise style, 572
vigorous style, 574
Nescience
ignorance, 491
Ness
cape, 250
Nest
lodging, 189
cradle, 153
Nest-egg
store, 636
Nested
layer, 204
Nestle
lodge, 186
safety, 664
endearment, 902

Nestling
infant, 129
Nestor
veteran, 130
Net
intersection, 219
snare, 667, 702
to capture, 789
difficulty, 704
remainder, 40
Nether
lowness, 207
Nettle
to sting, 830
incense, 900
Network
crossing, 219
disorder, 59
Neurasthenia
weakness, 160
Neurosis
insanity, 503
Neurotic
sensitive physically, 375
morally, 822
Neutral
mean, 29, 628
indifferent, 610, 866
non-interference, 681
Neutral tint
grey, 432
Neutralize
counteract, 179
compensate, 30
Never
neverness, 107
Never-ending
long, 200
Never-never
purchase, 795
debt, 806
Nevertheless
counter, 179
compensation, 30
New
newness, 123
New-born
newness, 123
New-fashioned
new, 123
Newcomer
extraneous, 57
Newfangled
new, 123
strange, 83

barbarous, 851
News
news, 532
Newscast
radio, 599B
Newspaper
record, 551
Next
after, 63, 117
Nib
point, 253
summit, 210
disjunction, 44
end, 67
Nibble
carp at, 932
eat, 296
Niblick
club, 276
Nice
savoury, 394
good, 648
exact, 494
pleasing, 829
honourable, 939
fastidious, 868
Nicely
greatness, 31
Nicety
taste, 850, 868
discrimination, 465
exactness, 494
Niche
recess, 182
receptacle, 191
Nichevo
indifference, 460, 823
Nick
notch, 257
mark, 550
deceive, 545
of time, 134
prison, 752
Nickelodeon
juke box, 417
Nicker
animal sound, 412
Nickname
misnomer, 565
Nicotian
tobacco, 298A
Nictitate
blind, 442
dim sight, 443
Nidification

abode, 189
Nidus
nest, 189
cradle, 153
Niff
stink, 401
Niggard
parsimony, 819
Nigger
blackness, 431
Niggle
trifle, 643
depreciate, 483
Nigh
nearness, 197
Night
darkness, 421
Night-glass
lens, 445
Nightfall
evening, 126
Nightgown
dress, 225
Nightingale
music, 416
Nightmare
pain, 378, 828
imagination, 515
hindrance, 706
Nightshade
bane, 663
Nightshirt
dress, 225
Nigrification
black, 431
Nihilism
non-existence, 1
scepticism, 487
anarchism, 738
Nihilist
evildoer, 913
Nihility
unsubstantiality, 4
Nil admirari
expectance, 871
Nil desperandum
hope, 858
Nil ultra
superiority, 33
Nimble
swift, 274
active, 682
skilful, 698
Nimbus
cloud, 353

light, 420
Nimiety
redundance, 641
Niminy-piminy
affectation, 855
N'importe
unimportance, 643
Nimrod
chase, 622
Nincompoop
fool, 501
Nine
number, 98
Nine days' wonder
transientness, 111
Ninny
fool, 501
Ninnyhammer
fool, 501
Niobe
lament, 839
Nip
cut, 44
destroy, 162
smallness, 32
Nip up
taking, 789
Nipper
youngster, 129
Nipping
cold, 383
Nipple
convexity, 250
Nirvana
extinction, 2
happiness, 827
heaven, 979
Nit
dissent, 489
Nitrous oxide
anaesthetic, 379
Niveous
white, 430
Nix
nothing, 4
Nixie
fairy, 980
Nizam
master, 745
No
dissent, 489
negation, 536
No go
impossible, 471
Nob

summit, 210
nobility, 875
Nobble
deceive, 545
tamper with, 682
circumvent, 702
Nobility
nobleness, 875
Noble
rank, 873
greatness, 31
generous, 942
virtue, 944
Nobleman
nobleness, 875
Noblesse
nobility, 875
Nobody
absence, 187
zero, 101
unimportant, 643
ignoble, 876
Noctivagant
darkness, 421
Nocturnal
dark, 421
black, 431
Nocturne
music, 415
picture, 556
Nod
sleep, 683
signal, 550
assent, 488
order, 741
information, 527
bow, 894;
to wag, 314
Noddle
head, 450
summit, 210
Noddy
fool, 501
Node
convexity, 250
Nodosity
roughness, 256
convexity, 250
Nodule
convexity, 250
Noetic
intellect, 450
Noggin
receptacle, 191
Nohow

negation, 536
Noise
sound, 402
Noiseless
silence, 403
Noisome
fetor, 401
Noisy
loud, 404
showy, 428
Nolens volens
compulsion, 744
necessity, 601
Nom de guerre
misnomer, 565
Nom de plume
misnomer, 565
Nomad
vagrant, 264
traveller, 268
locomotive, 266
No-man's-land
interjacence, 228
Nomenclature
name, 564
Nominate
commission, 755
name, 564
Nominee
consignee, 758
Non constat
sophistry, 477
Non est
non-existence, 2
Non nobis Domine
worship, 990
Non possumus
impossible, 471
obstinacy, 606
Non sequitur
sophistry, 477
Non-adhesion
incoherence, 47
Non-admission
exclusion, 55
Nonage
youth, 127
Nonagon
angularity, 244
nine, 98
Non-appearance
invisible, 447
Non-attendance
absence, 187
Nonce
present time, 118

Nonce word
neologism, 563
Nonchalance
neglect, 460
indifference, 456, 823, 866
unwillingness, 603
Non-coincidence
contrariety, 14
Non-combatant
non-combatant, 726A
Non-committal
cautious, 864
Non-completion
non-complete, 730
Non-compliance
disobey, 742
Nonconformity
dissent, 489
unconformity, 81
sectarianism, 984A
Non-content
dissent, 489
Nondescript
unconformity, 83
None
zero, 101
Non-effective
non-combatant, 726A
Nonentity
inexistence, 2
unimportance 643
Nones
worship, 990
Non-essential
unimportance, 643
Nonesuch
see Nonsuch
Non-existence
inexistence, 2
Non-expectance
inexpectation, 508
Non-fulfilment
incomplete, 730
Non-inflammable
fireproof, 385
Non-intervention
inaction, 681
Nonjuror
dissent, 489
Non-observance
non-observance, 773
Nonpareil
perfection, 650

Nonpayment
non-payment, 808
Non-performance
non-completion, 730
Nonplus
difficulty, 704
failure, 732
Non-preparation
non-preparation, 674
Non-residence
absence, 187
Non-resistance
submission, 725
obedience, 743
Nonsense
unmeaningness, 517
absurdity, 497
ridiculousness, 853
folly, 499
trash, 643
Nonsuch
perfection, 650
unconformity, 83
Nonsuit
to cast, 731
to fail, 732
condemn, 971
Non-uniformity
variety, 16A
Noodle
fool, 501
Nook
place, 182
receptacle, 191
Noon
midday, 125
light, 420
Noose
ligature, 45
loop, 247
snare, 667
Nope
dissent, 489
Norm
type, 80
mean, 29
Normal
regular, 82
vertical, 212
North
opposite, 237
Northern lights
light, 423
Nose
smell, 398

informer, 527, 529
prominence, 250
Nose out
detect, 480A
Nosegay
fragrance, 400
ornament, 847
Nosology
disease, 655
Nostalgia
discontent, 832
Nostril
air-pipe, 351
Nostrum
remedy, 662
Nosy
curiosity, 455
Not
dissent, 489
Not on your nelly
dissent, 489
Not-being
inexistence, 2
Nota bene
care, 457
Notability
personage, 642, 875
repute, 873
Notable
visible, 446
manifest, 525
important, 642
famous, 873
Notably
greatness, 31
Notary
recorder, 553
lawyer, 968
Notch
nick, 257
mark, 550
Note
sign, 550
record, 551
letter, 592
precursor, 64
music, 413
fame, 873
notice, 450, 457
minute, 596
money, 800
Note-book
compendium, 596
Note-case
purse, 802

Nuncupatory
naming, 564
informing, 527
Nunnery
temple, 1000
seclusion, 893
Nuptials
marriage, 903
Nurse
servant, 746
treat, 662
to help, 707
preserve, 670
Nursery
room, 191
school, 542
workshop, 691
for plants, 367
Nurseryman
horticulture, 371
Nursling
infant, 129
Nurture
food, 298
to support, 707
prepare, 673
Nut
head, 450
fop, 854
madman, 504
Nut-brown
brown, 433
Nutation
oscillation, 314
Nutmeg-grater
rough, 256
Nutriment
food, 298
Nutrition
aid, 707
Nuts
insane, 503
rubbish, 643
Nutshell
littleness, 193
compendium, 596
Nuzzle
endearment, 902
Nyctalopia
dim-sighted, 443
Nylons
dress, 225
Nymph
woman, 374
goddess, 979

Nystagmus
dim-sighted, 443

O.K.
assent, 488
consènt, 762
Oaf
fool, 501
Oak
strength, 159
Oar
instrument, 633
paddle, 267
Oasis
land, 342
Oath
promise, 768
assertion, 535
expletive, 908
Obbligato
music, 415
Obduracy
sin, 945
impenitence, 931
obstinacy, 606
severity, 739
malevolence, 907
Obeah
occult arts, 992
Obedience
obedience, 743
duty, 926
Obeisance
bow, 894
reverence, 928
submission, 725
worship, 990
fealty , 743
Obelisk
monument, 551
tall, 206
Obelize
indicate, 550
Oberon
sprite, 980
Obesity
size, 192
Obey
obedience, 743, 749
Obfuscate
darken, 421, 426
bewilder, 458
Obit
death, 360

Obiter dictum
irrelation, 10
Obituary
description, 594
death, 360
Object
thing, 3, 316
intention, 620
ugly, 846
to disapprove, 932
Object lesson
explanation, 522
Object to
dislike, 867
Objectify
existence, 1
Objective
extrinsic, 6
material, 316, 450A
Objurgate
disapprobation, 932
Oblate
shortness, 201
monk, 996
Oblation
gift, 789
proffer, 763
worship, 990
Obligation
duty, 926
promise, 768
conditions, 770
debt, 806
gratitude, 916
Oblige
compel, 744
benefit, 707
Obliging
kind, 906
courteous, 894
Oblique
obliquity, 217
Obliquity
vice, 945
Obliterate
efface, 552
Oblivion
oblivion, 506
Oblong
length, 200
Obloquy
censure, 932
disgrace, 874
Obmutescence
aphony, 581

Obnoxious
hateful, 898
unpleasing, 830
pernicious, 649
Oboe
musical instrument, 417
Obscene
impurity, 961
Obscurantist
ignoramus, 493
Obscure
dark, 421
unseen, 447
unintelligible, 519
style, 571
to eclipse, 874
Obscurum per obscurius
unintelligibility, 519
misteaching, 538
Obsecration
request, 765
Obsequies
interment, 363
Obsequious
respectful, 928
courteous, 894
servile, 886
Observance
fulfilment, 772
rule, 82
habit, 613
practice, 692
rites, 998
Observatory
universe, 318
Observe
note, 457
conform, 926
remark, 535
Observer
spectator, 444
fighter, 726
Obsess
preoccupy, 457
worry, 830
haunt, 860
Obsession
misjudgment, 481
fixed idea, 606
Obsolete
old, 124
effete, 645
vulgar, 851
Obstacle
physical, 179

moral, 706
Obstetrician
instrumentality, 631
Obstinate
stubborn, 606
resolute, 604
prejudiced, 481
Obstreperous
violent, 173
loud, 404
Obstruct
hinder, 706
close, 261
Obtain
exist, 1
acquire, 775
Obtainable
possibility, 470
Obtestation
entreaty, 765
injunction, 695
Obtrude
intervene, 228
insert, 300
obstruct, 706
Obtund
blunt, 254
deaden, 376
paralyse, 826
Obtuse
blunt, 254
stupid, 499
dull, 823
Obverse
front, 234
Obviate
hindrance, 706
Obvious
visible, 446
clear, 518
Ocarina
musical instrument, 417
Occasion
juncture, 8
opportunity, 134
cause, 153
Occasionally
frequency, 136
Occidental
lateral, 236
Occlusion
closure, 261
Occult
latent, 526
hidden, 528

supernatural, 992
Occupancy
presence, 18
property, 780
possession, 777
Occupant
dweller, 188
proprietor, 779
Occupation
business, 625
presence, 186
Occupier
dweller, 188
possessor, 779
Occupy
station, 71
place, 186
attention, 457
Occur
exist, 1
happen, 151
be present, 186
to the mind, 451
Ocean
ocean, 341
plenty, 639
Ochlocracy
authority, 737
Ochone
lamentation, 839
Ochre
brown, 433
orange, 439
O'clock
time, 114
Octad
number, 98
Octagon
angularity, 244
eight, 98
Octahedron
angularity, 244
eight, 98
Octavo
book, 593
Octodecimo
book, 593
Octonary
eight, 98
Octoroon
mixture, 41
Octroi
tax, 812
Octuple
number, 98

Ocular
vision, 441
Oculist
doctor, 662
Odalisque
concubine, 962
Odd
exception, 83
single, 87
remaining, 40
eccentric, 499
ludicrous, 853
vulgar, 851
Oddity
folly, 499
laughing-stock, 857
Oddments
part, 51
Odds
inequality, 28
chance, 156
discord, 713
Odds and ends
portions, 51
dispersion, 73
mixture, 41
Ode
poetry, 597
Odin
god, 979
Odious
ugly, 846
hateful, 898
offensive, 830
Odium
blame, 932
disgrace, 874
hatred, 898
Odontoid
sharpness, 253
Odour
odour, 398
Odourless
inodorous, 399
Odyssey
journey, 266
navigation, 267
Oecology
organization, 357
Oecumenical
generality, 78
Oedematous
soft, 324
swollen, 194
Oedipus

expounder, 524
answer, 462
Œillade
ogle, 441, 902
Off
distance, 196
Off-break
deviation, 279
Off-chance
chance, 621
Off-white
white, 430
Offal
uncleanness, 653
Offence
attack, 716
guilt, 947
Offend
affront, 900
Offensive
unsavoury, 395
fetid, 401
foul, 653
displeasing, 830
distasteful, 867
obnoxious, 898
Offer
proposal, 763
gift, 784
Offering
worship, 990
Offertory
worship, 990
Offhand
spontaneous, 612, 674
careless, 460
Office
function, 644
duty, 926
business, 625
mart, 799
room, 191
bureau, 691
authority, 737
worship, 990
Office-bearer
director, 694
Officer
director, 694
constable, 965
master, 745
Official
authority, 474. 737
business, 625
authorized, 924

Officialese
verbiage, 573
Officiate
conduct, 692
act, 625, 680
religious, 998
Officious
activity, 682
Offing
distance, 196
sea, 341
Offish
unsocial, 893
discourteous, 895
Offscourings
remains, 40
dirt, 653
trash, 643
Offset
compensation, 30
ridge, 250
Offshoot
part, 51
posterity, 167
Offspring
posterity, 167
produce, 154
Often
frequency, 136
Ogee
curve, 145
Ogham
writing, 590
Ogle
vision, 442
desire, 865
courtship, 902
Ogpu
detective, 461
Ogre
demon, 980
bugbear, 860
evildoer, 913
Oil
unctuosity, 355, 356
lubricate, 332
smooth, 255
flattery, 933
servility, 886
bland, 894
relief, 834
to assuage, 174
Oilcloth
covering, 222

Open
begin, 66
expand, 194
unclose, 260
manifest, 518, 525
reveal, 529
frank, 543
artless, 703
Open-air
air, 338
Open-eyed
attention, 457
Open-handed
liberal, 816
Open-hearted
sincere, 543
frank, 703
honourable, 939
Open-minded
intelligence, 498
Open-mouthed
loud, 404
loquacious, 584
gaping, 865
Open sesame
interpretation, 522
Opening
aperture, 198, 260
occasion, 134
beginning, 66
Opera
drama, 599
music, 415
Opéra bouffe
drama, 599
Operate
incite, 615
work, 170, 680
Operation
warfare, 722
Operative
agent, 690
Operator
agent, 690
Operculum
covering, 222
stopper, 263
Operose
difficult, 704
active, 683
exertive, 686
Ophicleide
musical, 417
Ophthalmic

vision, 441
Opiate
remedy, 174
sedative, 174
Opine
belief, 484
Opiniâtre
obstinacy, 606
Opinion
belief, 484
Opinionative
obstinacy, 606
Opium
moderation, 174
Oppilation
hindrance, 706
Opponent
antagonist, 710
enemy, 891
Opportune
well-timed, 134
expedient, 646
Opportunism
cunning, 702
Opportunist
time server, 607, 646,
943
Opportunity
occasion, 134
Oppose
antagonize, 179
clash, 708
resist, 719
evidence, 468
Opposite
contrary, 14
antiposition, 237
Oppress
molest, 649
domineer, 739
Oppression
injury, 619, 649
dejection, 837
Opprobrium
disrepute, 874
Oppugn
oppose, 708
Optative
desire, 865
Optics
light, 420
sight, 441
Optimates
nobility, 875
Optimism

hope, 858
Option
choice, 609
Opulence
wealth, 803
Opus
music, 415
Opuscule
book, 593
Oracle
prophet, 513
sage, 500
Oracular
wise, 498
prophetic, 511
Oral
voice, 580
Orange
orange, 439
Oration
speech, 582
Orator
speaker, 582
teacher, 540
Oratorio
music, 415
Oratory
speech, 582
temple, 1000
Orb
circle, 247
region, 181
luminary, 423
sphere of action, 625
insignia, 747
Orbicular
circularity, 247
Orbit
path, 627
world, 318
Orbital
space ship, 273A
Orchestra
musician, 416
Orchestration
music, 415
Orchestrion
musical, 417
Ordain
command, 741
churchdom, 976
Ordained
prescribed, 924
clergy, 996

Ordeal
experiment, 463
sorcery, 992
Order
regularity, 58
subordinate class, 75
rule, 80
law, 963
command, 741
direct, 693, 697
rank, 873, 875
of the day, 82
Orderless
disorder, 59
Orderly
conformity, 82
Orders, holy
churchdom, 995
Ordinal
rite, 998
Ordinance
command, 741
law, 963
rite, 998
Ordinary
usual, 82, 613
plain, 849
mean, 29, 736
ugly, 846
Ordination
command, 741
arrangement, 60
rite, 998
Ordure
uncleanness, 653
Ore
materials, 635
Ore rotundo
ornament, 577
speech, 582
Organ
instrument, 633
music, 417
Organic
state, 7
living beings, 357
Organism
state, 7
structure, 329
Organist
musician, 416
Organization
structure, 329
Organize
arrange, 60

plan, 626
prepare, 673
produce, 161
Organized
organization, 357
Orgasm
violence, 173
Orgy
intemperance, 954
Orient
light, 420
direction, 278
Orientate
direction, 278
Orientation
situation, 183
Orifice
opening, 66, 260
Oriflamme
indication, 550
Origin
cause, 153
beginning, 66
Original
model, 22
oddity, 83, 857
invented, 515
vigorous, 574
Originate
cause, 153
begin, 66
invent, 515
Originator
producer, 164
Orison
request, 765
prayer, 990
Ormolu
ornament, 847
Ormuzd
deity, 979
Ornament
ornament, 847
glory, 873
style, 577
Ornate
ornament, 847
style, 577
Orography
height, 206
Orotund
style, 577
Orphan
weakness, 160
Orpiment

yellow, 436
Orris root
fragrance, 400
Orthodox
true, 494
conformity, 82
in religion, 983A
Orthoepy
voice, 580
Orthogenesis
causation, 153
Orthography
writing, 590
Orthometry
measurement, 466
poetry, 597
Orts
remnants, 40
refuse, 643
useless, 645
Oscar
trophy, 733
Oscillation
oscillation, 314
Osculate
contiguity, 199
kiss, 902
Osmosis
percolation, 302
Osseous
hard, 323
Ossification
hardness, 323
Ossuary
interment, 363
Ostensible
visible, 446
apparent, 448
probable, 472
plea, 617
explicit, 576
Ostentation
ostentation, 882
vanity, 880
vulgarity, 851
Osteopathy
remedy, 662
Ostiary
door-keeper, 263
Ostler
servant, 746
Ostracize
exclude, 55
displace, 185
seclude, 893

605

censure, 932
Other
difference, 15
Other-guess
difference, 15
Other-worldliness
piety, 987
Otherwise
difference, 15
dissimilarity, 18
O'Trigger
blusterer, 887
Otto
see Attar
Ottoman
support, 215
Oubliette
prison, 752
hide, 530
Ought
duty, 926
Oui-dire
news, 532
Oust
displace, 185
deprive, 789
dismiss, 756
Out
exteriority, 220
up in arms, 719
Out and out
greatness, 31
Out-herod
bluster, 173
exaggerate, 549
Out of bounds
transcursion, 303
Out of date
old, 124
past, 122
obsolete, 851
Out of place
disorder, 59
unconformity, 83
Out-talk
loquacity, 584
Outbalance
superiority, 28, 33
Outbid
barter, 794
Outbrave
insolence, 885
Outbrazen
insolence, 885
Outbreak

egress, 295
violence, 173
contest, 720
passion, 825
Outburst
egress, 295
violence, 173
passion, 825
Outcast
secluded, 893
sinner, 949
apostate, 941
Outclass
superiority, 33
Outcome
result, 154
Outcry
noise, 411
complaint, 839
censure, 932
Outdistance
speed, 274
surpass, 303
Outdo
activity, 682
surpass, 303
superiority, 33
Outdoor
exteriority, 220
Outer
exteriority, 220
Outface
insolence, 885
Outfit
preparation, 673
equipment, 633
Outfitter
dress, 225
Outflank
baffle, 731
Outgeneral
success, 731
Outgo
transgress, 303
distance, 196
Outgoings
expenditure, 809
Outgrow
expansion, 194
Outhouse
abode, 189
Outing
journey, 266
Outlandish
irregular, 83

foreign, 10
barbarous, 851
ridiculous, 853
Outlast
diuturnity, 110
Outlaw
reprobate, 949
exclude, 893
condemn, 971
Outlawry
illegality, 964
Outlay
expenditure, 809
Outleap
transcursion, 303
Outlet
egress, 295
opening, 260
Outline
contour, 229
sketch, 554
features, 448
plan, 626
Outlive
survive, 110
continue, 141
Outlook
insolence, 885
futurity, 121
prospect, 507
view, 448
Outlying
exteriority, 220
remainder, 40
Outmanœuvre
success, 731
Outmarch
speed, 274
Outmatch
inequality, 28
superiority, 33
Outnumber
multitude, 102
Outpace
velocity, 274
transcursion, 303
Outpost
distance, 196
circumjacent, 227
front, 234
Outpouring
information, 527
Outrage
evil, 619, 649
malevolence, 907

grievance, 830
Outrageous
excessive, 31
violence, 173
Outré
ridiculous, 853
unconformity, 83
exaggerated, 549
Outreach
deception, 545
Outreckon
overestimation, 482
Outrider
precursor, 64
Outrigger
support, 215
boat, 273
Outright
greatness, 31
completeness, 52
Outrun
velocity, 274, 303
Outset
beginning, 66
departure, 293
Outshine
glory, 873
eclipse, 874
Outside
exteriority, 220
Outsider
extraneous, 57
upstart, 876
Outskirt
environs, 227
distance, 196
Outspan
arrival, 292
Outspoken
speech, 582
candour, 703
Outspread
thickness, 202
Outstanding
remainder, 40
salient, 642
unpaid, 806
Outstep
go beyond, 303
distance, 196
Outstretched
length, 200
breadth, 202
Outstrip
velocity, 274

surpass, 303
Outvie
contend, 720
shine, 873
Outvote
success, 731
Outward
exteriority, 220
extrinsic, 6
Outweigh
exceed, 33
preponderate, 28
predominate, 175
Outwit
deceive, 545
succeed, 731
Outwork
refuge, 666
defence, 717
Oval
circularity, 247
curvature, 245
Ovary
receptacle, 191
Ovate
circularity, 247
Ovation
triumph, 733
celebration, 883
Oven
furnace, 386
Over
more, 33
past time, 122
above, 206
Over against
antiposition, 237
Over-anxiety
desire, 865
Over and above
remainder, 40
Over and over
repetition, 104
Over head and ears
greatness, 31
Over-officious
activity, 682
Over-righteous
impiety, 989
Over-zealous
excitability, 825
Overabound
redundance, 641
Overact
bustle, 682

affect, 855
Overalls
dress, 225
Overawe
intimidate, 860
authority, 737
respect, 928
Overbalance
inequality, 28, 33
compensation, 30
Overbearing
severe, 739
Overblown
deterioration, 659
Overbold
rashness, 863
Overborne
subjection, 749
Overburden
fatigue, 688
redundant, 641
Overcast
dark, 421
dim, 422
Overcharge
exaggerate, 549
redundance, 641
dearness, 814
style, 577
Overcolour
exaggeration, 549
Overcome
conquer, 731
subdued, 732
shock, 824
dejected, 837
tipsy, 959
Overdo
activity, 682
exaggerate, 549
Overdose
redundance, 641
Overdue
anachronism, 115
late, 133
Overestimate
overestimation, 482
Overfed
gluttony, 957
satiety, 869
Overflow
stream, 348
redundance, 641
Overgo
transcursion, 303

Overgrown
size, 31
swollen, 194
Overhang
height, 206
jut out, 250
impend, 121
Overhaul
inquire, 461
attend to, 457
number, 85
overtake, 292
Overhead
height, 206
Overhear
hear, 418
learn, 539
Overjoyed
pleasure, 827
Overjump
transcursion, 303
Overland
journey, 266
Overlap
cover, 222
go beyond, 303
Overlay
excess, 641
oppress, 649
hinder, 706
style, 577
Overleap
transcursion, 303
Overload
excess, 641
obstruct, 706
Overlook
disregard, 458
neglect, 460
superintend, 693
forgive, 918
slight, 929
Overlooker
director, 694
Overmatch
inequality, 28, 149
Overmuch
redundance, 641
Overnight
preterition, 122
Overpass
exceed, 33
transgress, 303
Overplus
excess, 641

remainder, 40
Overpower
subdue, 731
emotion, 824
Overpowered
failure, 732
Overpowering
excitability, 825
Overprize
overestimation, 482
Overrate
overestimation, 482
Overreach
pass, 303
deceive, 545
cunning, 702
baffle, 731
Override
pass, 303
cancel, 756
overrule, 737
domineer, 739
be superior, 33
Overrule
control, 737
cancel, 736
Overrun
ravage, 649
pass, 303
excess, 641
Overseas
extraneous, 57
Overseer
director, 694
Overset
level, 308
invert, 218
subvert, 731
Overshadow
darkness, 421
superiority, 33
repute, 873
Overshoe
dress, 225
Overshoot
transcursion, 303
Oversight
error, 495
inattention, 458
failure, 732
Overspread
cover, 222
pervade, 73, 186
Overstate
exaggeration, 549

Overstep
transcursion, 303
Overstrain
overrate, 482
fatigue, 688
Overstrung
excitability, 825
Overt
visible, 446
manifest, 525
Overtake
arrive, 292
Overtaken
tipsy, 959
Overtask
fatigue, 688
Overtax
fatigue, 688
Overthrow
destroy, 162
level, 308
confute, 479
vanquish, 731, 732
Overtone
melody, 413
Overtop
surpass, 33
height, 206
perfection, 650
Overture
beginning, 66
precursor, 64
offer, 763
music, 415
request, 765
Overturn
destroy, 162
level, 308
confute, 571
invert, 218
Overvalue
overestimation, 482
Overweening
conceit, 880
pride, 878
Overweight
overrate, 482
exceed, 33
influence, 175
Overwhelm
destroy, 162
affect, 824
Overwhelming
excitability, 825

Overwork
fatigue, 688
Overwrought
excited, 825
Ovoid
rotundity, 249
Ovule
circularity, 247
Owe
debt, 806
Owing to
attribution, 155
Owl-light
dimness, 422
Own
assent, 488, 535
divulge, 529
possess, 777
Owner
possessor, 779
Ownership
property, 780
Oxygenate
air, 338
Oy
attention, 457
Oyez
hearing, 418
Oyster
taciturnity, 585

P.A.Y.E.
tax, 812
P.B.I.
soldier, 725
p.m.
evening, 126
P.O.P.
photograph, 556
P.O.W.
prisoner, 754
p.p.
commission, 755
P.T.
Teaching, 537
Exertion, 686
Pa
father, 166
Pabulum
food, 298
Pace
speed, 274
step, 266
measure, 466

Pachydermatous
insensible, 376, 823
Pacific
concord, 714, 721
Pacifism
pacification, 723
Pacifist
non-combatant, 726A
Pacify
allay, 174
compose, 826
give peace, 723
forgive, 918
Pack
to join, 43
arrange, 60
bring close, 197
locate, 184
assemblage, 72
Pack-horse
carrier, 271
Pack off
depart, 293
recede, 287
decamp, 671
Pack up
circumscribe, 231
fail, 732
Package
parcel, 72
Packet
parcel, 72
ship, 273
Packing-case
receptacle, 191
Packthread
vinculum, 45
Pact
agreement, 769
Pactolus
wealth, 803
Pad
carrier, 271
line, 224
expand, 194
diffuse, 573
Padding
softness, 324
Paddle
oar, 267, 633
to bathe, 337
Paddle-steamer
ship, 273
Paddle-wheel
navigation, 267

Paddock
arena, 181
enclosure, 232, 752
Padlock
fastening, 45
fetter, 752
Padre
clergy, 996
Paean
thanks, 916
rejoicing, 836
worship, 990
Paediatrics
remedy, 662
Paeon
verse, 597
Paganism
heathen, 984, 996
Page
attendant, 746
of a book, 593
Pageant
spectacle, 448
the drama, 599
show, 882
Pagoda
temple, 1000
Pail
receptacle, 191
Pailful
quantity, 25
Paillard
libertine, 962
Pain
physical, 378
moral, 828
penalty, 974
Painful
painfulness, 830
Pains
exertion, 686
Painstaking
active, 682
laborious, 686
Paint
coat, 222
colour, 428
adorn, 847
delineate, 556
describe, 594
Painter
artist, 559
rope, 45
Painting
painting, 556

Pair
couple, 89
similar, 17
Pair off
average, 29
Pal
friend, 890
Palace
abode, 189
Paladin
courage, 861
Palaeography
interpretation, 522
Palaeolithic
oldness, 142
Palaeology
preterition, 122
Palaeontology
zoology, 368
past, 122
Palaestra
school, 542
arena, 728
training, 673
Palaestric
exertion, 686
Palanquin
vehicle, 272
Palatable
savoury, 394
pleasant, 829
Palatal
letter, 561
Palate
taste, 390
Palatine
master, 745
Palaver
speech, 582
colloquy, 588
council, 696
nonsense, 497, 517
loquacity, 584
Pale
dim, 422
colourless, 429
enclosure, 232
Palfrey
carrier, 271
Palimpsest
substitution, 147
writing, 590
Palindrome
neology, 563
inversion, 218

Paling
prison, 752
enclosure, 232
Palingenesis
restore, 660
Palinode
denial, 536
recantation, 607
Palisade
prison, 752
enclosure, 232
Pall
funeral, 363
disgust, 395, 867
satiate, 869
Palladium
defence, 664, 717
Pallet
support, 215
Palliasse
support, 215
Palliate
mend, 658
relieve, 834
moderate, 174
extenuate, 937
Palliative
remedy, 662
Pallid
achromatism, 429
Palling
unsavouriness, 395
Pallium
dress, 225
canonicals, 999
Pally
friendship, 888
Palm
trophy, 733
glory, 873
laurel, 877
deceive, 545
impose upon, 486
Palmer
traveller, 268
Palmist
fortune-teller, 513
Palmistry
prediction, 511
Palmy
prosperous, 734
halcyon, 827, 829
Palpable
tactile, 379
tangible, 316

obvious, 446, 525
intelligible, 518
Palpitate
tremble, 315
emotion, 821
fear, 860
Palsy
disease, 655
weakness, 160
incapacity, 158
insensibility, 376, 823
Palter
falsehood, 544
shift, 605
elude, 773
Paltry
mean, 940
despicable, 643, 930
little, 32
Paludal
marsh, 345
Pampas
plain, 344
Pamper
indulge, 954
gorge, 957
Pampero
wind, 349
Pamphlet
book, 593
Pamphleteer
writing, 590
dissertation, 595
Pan
receptacle, 191
face, 234, 448
Panacea
remedy, 662
Panache
plume, 256
ornament, 847
Pandect
code, 963
compendium, 596
erudition, 490
Pandemic
insalubrity, 657
Pandemonium
hell, 982
disorder, 59
Pander
flatter, 933
indulge, 954
mediate, 631
help, 707

Pandora
evil, 619
Paned
variegation, 440
Panegyric
approbation, 931
Panel
list, 86
partition, 228
accused, 938
legal, 967
Panem et circenses
giving, 784
Pang
physical, 378
moral, 828
Panhandler
tramp, 876
Panic
fear, 860
Pannier
receptacle, 191
Panoply
defence, 717
Panopticon
prison, 752
Panorama
view, 448
painting, 556
Panoramic
general, 78
Pansophy
knowledge, 490
Pansy
effeminate, 374
Pant
breathless, 688
desire, 865
agitation, 821
Pantaloon
buffoon, 844
dress, 225
Pantechnicon
vehicle, 272
Pantheism
heathen, 984
Pantheon
temple, 1000
Pantograph
imitation, 19
Pantomime
sign, 550
language, 560
drama, 599
Pantry

receptacle, 191
Pap
pulp, 354
teat, 250
Papa
father, 166
Papacy
churchdom, 995
Paper
writing, 590
book, 593
record, 551
white, 430
Paperback
book, 593
Papilla
convexity, 250
Papoose
infant, 129
Pappy
semiliquidity, 352
Par
equality, 27
Parable
metaphor, 521
analogy, 464
story, 594
Parabolic
metaphor, 521
curve, 245
Parachronism
anachronism, 115
Parachute
refuge, 666
Paraclete
Deity, 976
Parade
walk, 189
ostentation, 882
Paradigm
prototype, 22
example, 80
Paradise
heaven, 981
bliss, 827
Paradox
obscurity, 519
absurdity, 497
mystery, 528
enigma, 533
Paragon
perfection, 650
saint, 948
glory, 873
Paragraph

phrase, 566
part, 51
article, 593
Paralipsis
neglect, 460
Parallax
distance, 196
Parallel
position, 216
similarity, 17
to imitate, 19
agreement, 23
comparison, 464
Parallelepiped
angularity, 244
Parallelogram
angularity, 244
Paralogism
sophistry, 477
Paralyse
weaken, 160
benumb, 381
deaden, 823
insensibility, 376
impassivity, 823
stillness, 265
disqualify, 158
disease, 655
Paramount
essential, 642
in degree, 33
authority, 737
Paramour
love, 897
Paranoia
insanity, 503, 504
Parapet
defence, 717
Paraph
writing, 590
Paraphernalia
machinery, 633
materials, 635
property, 780
Paraphrase
interpretation, 522, 524
phrase, 566
imitation, 19, 21
Paraplectic
disease, 655
Parapsychology
occult, 992
Parasite
flatterer, 935
servile, 886

follow, 88
Parasol
shade, 424
Paratrooper
fighter, 726
Paravane
defence, 717
Parboil
calefaction, 384
Parcel
group, 72
portion, 51
Parcel out
arrange, 60
allot, 786
Parch
dry, 340
heat, 382
bake, 384
Parchment
manuscript, 590
record, 551
Pardon
forgiveness, 918
Pardonable
vindication, 937
Pare
scrape, 38, 226, 331
shorten, 201
decrease, 36
Paregoric
salubrity, 656
Parenchyma
texture, 329
Parent
paternity, 166
Parentage
kindred, 11
Parenthesis
interjacence, 228
discontinue, 70
Parenthetical
irrelation, 10
occasion, 134
Par excellence
greatness, 31
superiority, 33
Pari passu
equality, 27
Pariah
commonalty, 876
outcast, 892
Paring
part, 51
smallness, 32

Parish
region, 181
Parishioner
laity, 997
Parity
equality, 27
Park
plain, 344
vegetation, 367
amusement, 840
artillery, 727
locate, 184
Parlance
speech, 582
Parlementaire
messenger, 534
Parley
talk, 588
mediation, 724
Parliament
council, 696
Parlour
room, 191
Parlour-car
vehicle, 272
Parlourmaid
servant, 746
Parnassus
poetry, 597
Parochial
regional, 181
ignoble, 876
Parody
imitation, 19
copy, 21
travesty, 856
misinterpret, 523
Parole
promise, 768
Paronomasia
pun, 563
Paronymous
word, 562
Paroxysm
violence, 173
emotion, 825
anger, 900
Parquetry
variegation, 440
Parricide
killing, 361
Parrot
imitation, 19
loquacity, 584
repetition, 104

Parry
avert, 623
confute, 479
defend, 717
Parse
grammar, 567
Parsee
religions, 984
Parsimony
parsimony, 819
Parson
clergy, 996
Parsonage
temple, 1000
Part
portion, 51
component, 56
to diverge, 291
to divide, 44
business, 625
function, 644
Part with
relinquish, 782
give, 784
Partake
participation, 778
Parterre
agriculture, 371
Parti
adolescence, 131
Parti pris
prejudgment, 481
predetermination, 611
Partial
unequal, 28
special, 79
one-sided, 481
unjust, 923
love, 897
friendship, 888
desire, 865
erroneous, 495
smallness, 32
harmonic, 413
Particeps criminis
auxiliary, 711
bad man, 949
Participation
participation, 778
co-operation, 709
Particle
quantity, 32
size, 193
Particoloured
variegation, 440

Particular
special, 79
event, 151
careful, 459
capricious, 608
fastidious, 868
item, 51
detail, 79
description, 594
Particularly
greatness, 31
Parting
disjunction, 44
Partisan
auxiliary, 711
friend, 891
fighter, 726
Partition
allot, 51, 786
wall, 228
Partner
auxiliary, 711
Partnership
participation, 778
company, 797
companionship, 88
Parts
intellect, 450
wisdom, 498
talents, 698
Party
assemblage, 72
association, 712
society, 892
merry-making, 840
special, 79
Party-wall
interjacence, 228
Parvenu
upstart, 876
intruder, 57
successful, 734
Pas
rank, 873
precedence, 62
term, 71
Pash
love, 897
Pasha
master, 745
noble, 875
Pasquinade
satire, 932
Pass
move, 264

move out, 295
move through, 302
exceed, 303
be superior, 33
happen, 151
lapse, 122
vanish, 449
passage, 260
gap, 198
defile, 203
way, 627
difficulty, 704
conjuncture, 8
forgive, 918
thrust, 716
passport, 760
time, 106
Pass away
cease, 2, 142
Pass-book
accounts, 811
Pass by
disregard, 929
Pass for
falsehood, 544
Pass in the mind
thought, 451
Pass over
disregard, 458
neglect, 460
forgive, 918
exclude, 55
exempt, 927A
traverse, 302
Pass the time
duration, 106
Pass through
experience, 151
Passable
imperfection, 651
tolerable, 736
Passage
passage, 302
motion, 264
opening, 260
eventuality, 151
method, 627
transfer, 270
text, 593
part, 50
act, 680
assault, 720
Passage d'armes
contention, 720
Passé

age, 128
deterioration, 659
Passe-partout, 462
instrumentality, 631
Passenger
traveller, 268
hindrance, 706
Passim
dispersion, 73
situation, 183
Passing
exceeding, 33
transient, 111
greatness, 31
Passion
emotion, 820, 821
desire, 865
love, 879
anger, 900
Passionate
warm, 825
irascible, 901
Passionless
insensibility, 823
Passive
inert, 172
inactive, 681
submissive, 743
Passive resister
non-combatant, 726A
Passport
permit, 760
sign, 550
instrument, 631
order, 741
Password
sign, 550
Past
preterition, 122
Paste
cement, 45
to cement, 46
pulp, 354
Pastel
colour, 428
artist, 559
Pasteurize
inject, 300
sterilize, 169
Pasticcio
mixture, 41
Pastille
sweet, 396
remedy, 662

Pastime
amusement, 840
Pastor
clergy, 996
Pastoral
domestication, 370
poem, 597
religious, 995, 998
Pastry
food, 298
Pasturage
plain, 344
Pasture
food, 298
Pasty
semiliquid, 352
colourless, 429
Pat
expedient, 646
pertinent, 9
to strike, 276
Patagonian
height, 206
Patch
region, 181
smallness, 193
repair, 658
Patchwork
mixture, 41
variegation, 440
Patchy
imperfect, 53
Pate
head, 450
Patent
open, 260
visible, 446
manifest, 525
permit, 760
privilege, 924
Patera
plate, 191
church, 1000
Paternity
parent, 155, 166
Path
way, 627
passage, 302
direction, 278
Pathetic
painful, 830
affecting, 824
Pathless
closure, 261
difficult, 704
spacious, 180

Pathogenic
unhealthy, 657
Pathognomonic
indication, 550
Pathology
disease, 655
Pathos
feeling, 821
Pathway
way, 627
Patience
endurance, 826
content, 831
perseverance, 682
Patient
invalid, 655
Patois
language, 560
Patriarch
veteran, 130
Patriarchal
paternity, 166
Patriarchy
authority, 737
Patrician
nobility, 875
Patrimony
property, 780
Patriot
philanthropy, 910
Patristic
theological, 983
Patrol
safeguard, 664
warning, 668
Patron
friend, 891
buyer, 795
Patronage
aid, 707
protection, 175
authority, 737
Patronize
aid, 707
Patronizing
condescending, 878
Patronymic
nomenclature, 564
Patter
to strike, 276
step, 266
sound, 407
chatter, 584
patois, 560
Pattern

model, 22
order, 58
type, 80
example, 82
perfection, 650
saint, 948
Patulous
opening, 260
Paucity
fewness, 103
scantiness, 640
smallness, 32
Paul Pry
curiosity, 455
Paunch
receptacle, 191
convexity, 250
Pauperism
poverty, 804
Pause
stop, 265
discontinuance, 142
rest, 685, 687
disbelief, 485
Pavane
dance, 840
Pave
prepare, 673
cover, 222
Pavement
base, 311
footway, 627
Pavilion
abode, 189
Paving
base, 211
Paw
touch, 379
finger, 633
Pawky
cunning, 702
Pawn
security, 771
lending, 787
Pax vobiscum
courtesy, 894
Pay
expend, 809
defray, 807
condemn, 971
punish, 972
Pay-as you earn
tax, 812
Paymaster
treasury, 801

Paynim
heathen, 984
Pea
rotundity, 249
Pea-green
greenness, 435
Pea-shooter
propulsion, 284
Peace
silence, 403
amity, 721
concord, 714
Peace-offering
pacify, 723
atonement, 952
Peaceable
gentle, 174
Peach
disclosure, 529
Peach colour
redness, 434
Peacock
variegation, 440
beauty, 845
pride, 878
boaster, 884
Peak
summit, 210
height, 206
Peaked
sharpness, 253
Peal
loudness, 404
laughter, 838
Pear-shaped
rotundity, 249
curved, 245
Pearl
gem, 650
ornament, 847
glory, 873
Pearly
nacreous, 440
semitransparent, 427
white, 439
Peasant
commonalty, 876
Peat
fuel, 388
Pebble
hardness, 323
trifle, 643
Peccability
vice, 945
Peccadillo

guilt, 947
Peccancy
disease, 655
imperfection, 651
badness, 649
Peccant
wrong, 945
Pech
pant, 688
Peck
quantity, 31
eat, 296
Pecking-order
precedence, 58
Peckish
desire, 865
Pecksniff
hypocrite, 548
Pectinated
sharpness, 253
Peculate
stealing, 791
Peculator
thief, 792
Peculiar
special, 5, 79
exceptional, 83
Peculiarly
greatness, 31, 33
Pecuniary
money, 800
Pedagogue
scholar, 492
teacher, 540
Pedant
scholar, 492
affected, 855
teacher, 540
Pedantic
affected, 855
Pedantic
half-learned, 491
style, 577
Peddle
trifle, 683
sell, 796
Pedestal
support, 215
Pedestrian
traveller, 268
dull, 842, 843
style, 573
Pedicel
pendency, 214
Pedigree

ancestry, 155, 166
continuity, 69
Pediment
capital, 210
base, 215
Pedlar
merchant, 797
Peduncle
pendency, 214
Peek
look, 441
Peel
skin, 222
to uncover, 226
Peeler
police, 664
Peep
vision, 441
Peep-hole
opening, 260
view, 441
Peep out
visibility, 446
Peep-show
spectacle, 448
Peeping Tom
curiosity, 455
Peer
equal, 27
nobleman, 875
pry, 441
inquire, 461
appear, 446
Peerage
list, 86
Peerless
perfect, 650
excellent, 648, 873
superior, 33
virtuous, 944
Peeve
irritate, 900
Peevish
cross, 895
irascible, 901
Peg
degree, 26, 71
project, 250
hang, 214
jog on, 266
drink, 298
intoxicant, 959
Peg away
persist, 143
activity, 682

Peg out
die, 360
Pegasus
imagination, 515
Peine forte et dure
punishment, 972
Pejoration
deterioration, 659
Pelagic
ocean, 341
Pelerine
dress, 225
Pelf
money, 803
materials, 635
gain, 775
Pellet
rotundity, 249
remedy, 662
Pellicle
film, 205
skin, 222
Pell-mell
disorder, 59
Pellucid
transparency, 425
Pelt
skin, 222
throw, 276
attack, 716
beat, 972
Pen
surround, 231
enclose, 232
restrain, 751
imprison, 752
draw, 559
write, 590
Pen-and-ink
drawing, 556
Pen-name
misnomer, 565
Penal
punishment, 972
Penalty
penalty, 974
Penance
atonement, 952
rite, 998
penalty, 974
Penchant
inclination, 865
love, 897
Pencil
bundle, 72

of light, 420
artist, 556, 559, 590
Pencraft
writing, 590
Pendant
adjunct, 39
flag, 550
pendency, 214
match, 17
Pendent
during, 106
hanging, 214
uncertain, 485
Pendente lite
warfare, 722
lawsuit, 969
Pending
duration, 106
lateness, 133
uncertain, 475
Pendulous
pendency, 214
Pendulum
clock, 114
oscillation, 314
Penetralia
interiority, 221
secret, 533
Penetrate
fill, 186
influence, 175
Penetrating
affecting, 821
Penetration
ingress, 294
passage, 302
discernment, 441
sagacity, 498
Penfold
enclosure, 232
Peninsula
land, 342
Penitent
penitence, 950
Penitentiary
prison, 752
Penmanship
writing, 590
Penniless
poverty, 804
Pennon
indication, 550
Penny-a-liner
writer, 590
Penny-farthing

bicycle, 266
Pennyworth
price, 812
Penseroso
dejection, 837
Pensile
pendency, 214
Pension
wealth, 803, 810
Pensioner
servant, 746
recipient, 785
Pensive
thoughtful, 451
sad, 837
Pent
imprisoned, 754
Pentad
five, 98
Pentagon
angularity, 244
five, 98
Pentahedron
angularity, 244
five, 98
Pentatonic
melody, 413
Penthouse
building, 189
Penultimate
end, 67
Penumbra
darkness, 421, 424
Penurious
parsimony, 819
Penury
poverty, 804
scantiness, 640
People
man, 373
inhabitant, 188
commonalty, 876
to colonize, 184
Pep
energy, 171, 682
vigour, 574
Pep-talk
speech, 582
Pepper
hot, 171
pungent, 392
condiment, 393
attack, 716
Peppercorn
unimportance, 643

Peppery
irascibility, 901
Peptic
remedy, 662
Per contra
contrariety, 14
opposition, 708
Per procurationem
commission, 755
Per saltum
discontinuity, 70
transientness, 111
instantaneity, 113
Per se
unity, 87
Peradventure
chance, 156
possibly, 470
uncertainty, 475
Perambulate
journey, 266
Perceivable
visible, 446
Percentage
proportion, 84
discount, 813
Perceptible
visibility, 446
Perception
idea, 453
of touch, 380
Perceptivity
sensibility, 375
Perch
support, 215
to alight, 186
tall, 206
habitation, 189
Perchance
chance, 156
possibly, 470
Percipience
intellect, 450
Percolate
distil, 295
Percolation
passage, 302
Percussion
impulse, 276
Perdition
ruin, 732
loss, 776
Perdu
concealment, 528
Perdurable

permanence, 141
Peregrination
journey, 266
Peremptory
assertion, 535
denial, 536
firm, 604
rigorous, 739
authoritative, 737
compulsory, 744
obligatory, 926
order, 740, 741
Perennial
diuturnity, 110, 150
Perfect
entire, 52
complete, 729
excellent, 650
Perfectly
greatness, 31
Perfidy
improbity, 940
Perforate
opening, 260
Perforator
perforator, 263
Perforce
compulsion, 744
Perform
do, 170, 680
achieve, 729
produce, 161
act, 599
fulfil, 772
duty, 926
Performable
facility, 705
possible, 470
Performance
effect, 154
Performer
musician, 416
actor, 599
workman, 164
agent, 690
Perfume
fragrance, 400
Perfunctory
neglect, 460
incomplete, 53
Perhaps
possibly, 470
chance, 156
supposition, 514
Peri

fairy, 979
Periapt
spell, 993
Perigee
nearness, 197
Perihelion,
nearness, 197
Peril
danger, 665
Perimeter
outline, 229
Period
end, 67
of time, 106, 108
stop, 142
point, 71
recurrence, 138
Periodical
book, 593
publication, 531
Peripatetic
traveller, 268
ambulatory, 266
Periphery
outline, 229
Periphrasis
phrase, 566
diffuseness, 573
Perique
tobacco, 298A
Periscope
vision, 441
optical instrument, 445
Perish
vanish, 2
be destroyed, 162
die, 360
decay, 659
Peristaltic
convolution, 248
Periwig
dress, 225
Perjured
false, 940
Perjury
falsehood, 544
untruth, 546
Perk
lift, 307
smarten, 845
Perk up
recover 689
Perky
saucy, 885
gay, 836

617

Perlustration
vision, 441
Perm
convolution, 248
Permanent
unchanged, 141
unchangeable, 150
lasting, 106, 110
Permeable
opening, 260
Permeate
pervade, 186
influence, 175
insinuate, 228
pass through, 302
Permissible
dueness, 924
Permissive
lax, 738
Permit
permission, 760
Permutation
change, 140
numerical, 84
Pernicious
badness, 649
destructive, 162
Pernickety
fastidious, 868
faddy, 481
difficult, 704
Peroration
end, 67
sequel, 65
speech, 582
Perpend
thought, 451
attend, 457
Perpendicular
verticality, 212
Perpetrate
action, 680
Perpetrator
doer, 690
Perpetual
perpetuity, 112
duration, 106, 110
frequent, 136
continual, 143
Perpetuate
immutable, 150
Perplex
to derange, 61
bewilder, 458, 519

bother, 830
embarrass, 475
puzzle, 528
Perplexity
disorder, 59
difficulty, 704
ignorance, 491
doubt, 475
unintelligibility, 519
maze, 533
Perquisite
receipt, 810
reward, 973
Perquisition
inquiry, 461
Persecute
worry, 830, 907
oppress, 619, 649
Perseverance
firmness, 604
activity, 682
continuance, 143
Persiflage
ridicule, 856
wit, 842
Persist
endure, 106, 143, 606
Persistence
continuance, 110, 141
resolution, 604
activity, 682
Person
man, 373
grammar, 567
Personable
beauty, 845
Personage
nobility, 875
important, 642
Persona grata
favourite, 899
friend, 890
Personal
special, 79, 317, 372
bodily, 3
Personalities
abuse, 932
Personate
imitate, 17
act, 554
Personify
metaphor, 521
Personnel
component, 56
Perspective

view, 448
painting, 556
futurity, 121
sagacity, 498
sight, 441
Perspicacious
foreseeing, 510
Perspicacity
intelligence, 498
Perspicuity
Perspicuity, 518, 570
Perspiration
excretion, 299
Perstringe
attention, 457
Persuade
induce, 609, 615
teach, 537
advise, 695
Persuasible
learning, 539
willing, 602
Persuasion
opinion, 484
creed, 983
Pert
vain, 880
saucy, 885
discourteous, 895
Pertain
belong, 76, 777
relate to, 9
behove, 926
Pertinacious
obstinacy, 606
determination, 604
Pertinent
relative, 9
congruous, 23
Pertinent
relevant, 476
applicable, 646
Perturb
derange, 61
agitate, 315
emotion, 821
excitability, 825
ferment, 171
Peruke
dress, 225
Peruse
learning, 539
examine, 461
Pervade
extend, 186

affect, 821
Perverse
  crotchety, 608
  difficult, 704
  wayward, 895
Perversion
  injury, 659
  sophistry, 477
  falsehood, 544
  misinterpretation, 523
  misteaching, 538
  impiety, 988
Pervert
  apostate, 144, 941
  turncoat, 607
  blasphemer, 988
Pervicacious
  obstinacy, 606
Pervigilium
  activity, 682
Pervious
  opening, 260
Pessimism
  dejection, 837
  hopelessness, 859
Pest
  bane, 663
  badness, 649
  bother, 830
Pest-house
  remedy, 662
Pester
  painfulness, 830
Pestiferous
  insalubrity, 657
Pestilent
  badness, 649
  poison, 663
Pestle
  pulverulence, 330
Pet
  plaything, 840
  favourite, 899
  passion, 900
  to love, 897
  to fondle, 902
Petard
  arms, 727
Peter out
  end, 67
Peterhead
  prison, 752
Petit-maître
  fop, 854
Petite

little, 193
Petite amie
  mistress, 962
Petitio principii
  sophistry, 477
Petition
  ask, 765
  pray, 990
Petitioner
  petitioner, 767
Petits soins
  courtesy, 894
  courtship, 903
Pétri
  feeling, 821
Petrify
  dense, 321
  hard, 323
  affright, 860
  astonish, 870
  thrill, 824
Petroleum
  oil, 356
Pétroleur
  incendiary, 384
Petronel
  arms, 727
Petticoat
  dress, 225
Pettifogger
  lawyer, 968
Pettifogging
  discord, 713
  hair-splitting, 477
Pettish
  irascibility, 895, 901
Petty
  in degree, 32
  in size, 193
Petulant
  insolent, 885
  snappish, 895
  angry, 900
  irascible, 901
Pew
  temple, 1000
Phaeton
  carriage, 272
Phalanx
  army, 726
  party, 712
  assemblage, 72
Phantasm
  unreal, 4
  appearance, 448

delusion, 443
Phantasmagoria
  optical, 445
Phantom
  vision, 448
  unreal, 4
  imaginary, 515
Pharisaical
  falsehood, 544
Pharmacology
  remedy, 662
Pharmacy
  remedy, 662
Pharos
  warning, 668
  indication, 550
Phase
  aspect, 8
  appearance, 448
  change, 144
  form, 240
Phenomenal
  great, 31
  apparent, 448
  wonderful, 870
Phenomenon
  appearance, 448
  event, 151
  prodigy, 872
Phial
  receptacle, 191
Phidias
  artist, 559
Philanderer
  flirt, 902
Philanthropy
  philanthropy, 910
Philatelist
  collector, 775
Philibeg
  dress, 225
Philippic
  disapproval, 932
Philistine
  uncultured, 491, 493
Phillumenist
  collector, 775
Philology
  grammar, 567
Philomath
  scholar, 492
  sage, 500
Philomel
  musician, 416

619

Philosopher
scholar, 492
Philosophy
calmness, 826
thought, 451
knowledge, 490
Philtre
charm, 993
Phiz
appearance, 448
Phlebotomy
ejection, 297
Phlegethon
hell, 982
Phlegm
insensibility, 823
semiliquid, 352
Phoenix
prodigy, 872
exception, 83
paragon, 650
saint, 948
renovation, 163, 660
Phonetics
sound, 402
speech, 580
Phoney
fasle, 495, 544
Phonic
sound, 402
Phonograph
musical instrument, 417
hearing, 418
Phonography
shorthand, 590
Phosphorescent
light, 420, 423
Photo-lithograph
engraving, 558
Photogenic
beauty, 845
Photograph
copy, 21
representation, 554
Photography
painting, 556
Photogravure
engraving, 558
Photology
light, 420
Photometer
optical instrument, 445
Photostat
copy, 21
Phrase
phrase, 566

Phrase-monger
floridity, 577
Phraseology
style, 569
Phratry
class, 75
Phrenetic
see Frantic
Phrenitis
insanity, 503
Phrenology
intellect, 450
Phrontistery
room, 191
Phylactery
spell, 993
Phylum
class, 75
Physic
remedy, 662
to cure, 660
Physical
materiality, 316
Physician
advice, 695
Physics
materiality, 316
Physiognomy
appearance, 448
face, 234
Physiology
life, 359
Physique
substance, 3
animality, 364
Phytography
botany, 369
Phytology
botany, 369
Piacular
atonement, 952
Pianissimo
faint, 405
Pianist
musician, 416
Piano
instrument, 417
slowly, 275
faint sound, 405
Pianola
instrument, 417
Piazza
street, 189
veranda, 191
Pibroch

music, 415
Picaroon
thief, 792
Piccaninny
child, 129
Piccolo
musical instrument, 417
Pick
select, 609
goodness, 648
extract, 301
eat, 296
clean, 652
sharpness, 253
Pick-me-up
stimulant, 615
remedy, 662
Pick-thank
flatterer, 935
Pick up
learn, 539
improve, 658
acquire, 775
Pickaxe
sharpness, 253
Picket
join, 43
tether, 265
fence, 231
defence, 717
guard, 664
imprison, 752
Pickings
part, 51
booty, 793
Pickle
difficulty, 704
preserve, 670
pungent, 392
condiment, 393
macerate, 337
Pickpocket
thief, 792
Picnic
food, 298
party, 892
Picture
painting, 556
representation, 554
fancy, 515
Picturesque
beautiful, 845
graphic, 556
Piddling
paltry, 643

Pidgin English
language, 560
Pie
type, 591
disorder, 59
Piebald
variegation, 440
Piece
bit, 51
cannon, 727
drama, 599
Piece out
completeness, 42
Piecemeal
part, 51
Pied
variegation, 440
Pied à terre
abode, 189
Pier
refuge, 666
Pier-glass
optical instrument, 445
Pierce
perforate, 260, 302
pain, 378, 830
affect, 824
Piercing
cold, 383
sound, 404
sagacious, 498
feeling, 821
sight, 441
Pierian spring
poetry, 597
Pierrot
actor, 599
Pietism
impiety, 988
Piety
piety, 987
Piffle
absurdity, 497
Pig
gluttony, 957
Pig-headed
prejudiced, 481
obstinate, 606
stupid, 499
Pigeon-chested
distorted, 243
Pigeon-hole
receptacle, 191
aperture, 260
arrange, 60

discard, 624
reject, 610
Piggish
intemperance, 954
gluttony, 957
Pigment
colour, 428
Pigmy
see Pygmy
Pigsty
uncleanness, 653
Pigtail
pendant, 214
Pi-jaw
speech, 582
Pike
arms, 727
sharpness, 253
hill, 206
Pikestaff
height, 206
Pilaster
height, 206
Pile
heap, 72
nap, 256
building, 189
store, 636
wealth, 803
Pile-driver
hammer, 276
Pilfer
stealing, 791, 792
Pilgrim
traveller, 268
Pilgrimage
journey, 266
Pill
rotundity, 249
remedy, 662
Pill-box
defence, 717
Pillage
rob, 971
rapine, 619
devastation, 649
Pillar
support, 150, 215
monument, 551
lofty, 206
Pillar-box,
red, 434
Pillion
support, 215
Pillory

scourge, 975
to ridicule, 856
Pillow
support, 215, 265
soft, 324
ease, 831
Pilot
director, 694
mariner, 269
to guide, 693
balloon, 273
fighter, 726
trial, 463
Pilous
roughness, 256
Pimp
libertine, 962
Pimple
tumour, 250
blemish, 848
Pin
fastening, 45
to fasten, 43
axis, 312
sharp, 253
trifle, 643
Pin down
restrain, 751
compel, 744
Pin-prick
annoyance, 830
Pinafore
dress, 225
Pincers
extraction, 301
grip, 781
Pinch
emergency, 8
difficulty, 704
to contract, 195
narrow, 203
chill, 385
pain, 378
stint, 640, 819
to hurt, 830
to steal, 791
Pinch-hitter
substitute, 147, 634
deputy, 759
Pinchbeck
spurious, 544
Pinched
chilled, 383
thin, 203
indigent, 804

Pinching
  miserly, 819
Pine
  desire, 865
  grieve, 828
  droop, 837
Ping
  sound, 406
Pinguid
  unctuousness, 355
Pinhole
  opening, 260
Pinion
  instrument, 633
  wing, 267
  fetter, 752
  to fasten, 43
  to restrain, 751
Pink
  colour, 434
  perfection, 650
  beauty, 845
  glory, 873
  to pierce, 260
Pinnace
  ship, 273
Pinnacle
  summit, 210
Pinxit
  painting, 556
Pioneer
  precursor, 64
  preparer, 673
  teacher, 540
Pious
  piety, 987
Pip-pip
  departure, 293
Pipe
  conduit, 350
  passage, 302
  vent, 351
Pipe
  tobacco, 298A
  tube, 160
  sound, 510
  cry, 411
  music, 415
  instrument, 417
  observe, 457
Pipe down
  subside, 826
Pipe-dream
  hope, 858
  imagination, 515

Piper
  musician, 416
Piping
  sound, 410
  hot, 382
Pipkin
  receptacle, 191
Piquant
  pungent, 392
  style, 574
  motive, 615
  feeling, 821
  exciting, 824
Pique
  enmity, 889
  hate, 898
  anger, 900
  irritate, 830
  stimulate, 615, 824
Pique oneself
  pride, 878
Pirate
  thief, 792
  to steal, 791
Pirouette
  rotation, 312
Pis aller
  substitute, 634
  necessity, 601
  plan, 626
Piscatory
  animal, 366
Pisciculture
  taming, 370
Piscina
  church, 1000
Pistol
  arms, 727
Pistol-shot
  nearness, 197
Piston
  stopper, 264
Pit
  hole, 252
  opening, 260
  deep, 208
  grave, 363
  hell, 982
  theatre, 599
Pit against
  opposition, 708
Pit-a-pat
  feeling, 821
Pitch
  degree, 26

  term, 51
  station, 182
  arena, 728
  height, 206
  descent, 306
  summit, 210
  musical note, 413
  dark, 421
  black, 431
  semiliquid, 352
  to throw, 294
  to reel, 314
  to place, 184
Pitch-and-toss
  gambling, 621
Pitch into
  contention, 720
Pitch-pipe
  musical, 417
Pitch tent
  settle, 265
Pitch upon
  choose, 609
  reach, 292
Pitcher
  receptacle, 191
Pitchfork
  propel, 284
Piteous
  painfulness, 830
  greatness, 31
Pitfall
  pitfall, 667
Pith
  gist, 5, 516
  strength, 159
  interior, 221
  central, 223
  important, 642
Pithy
  significant, 516
  concise, 572
Pitiable
  unimportance, 643
Pitiful
  unimportant, 643
  compassionate, 914
  paltry, 940
Pitiless
  malevolent, 907
  revengeful, 900, 919
Pittance
  allotment, 786
Pitted
  blemished, 848

Pity
    compassion, 914
    regret, 833
Pivot
    cause, 153
    axis, 312
Pix
    cinema, 599A
Pixillated
    mad, 503
Pixy
    sprite, 980
Pizzicato
    music, 415
Placable
    forgiveness, 918
Placard
    notice, 550
    to publish, 531
Placate
    pacify, 826
Place
    situation, 182, 183
    circumstances, 8
    rank, 873
    term, 71
    in order, 58
    abode, 189
    to locate, 184
    substitution, 147
    office, 625
Placebo
    remedy, 662
Placeman
    consignee, 758
Placet
    command, 741
Placid
    calm, 826
Placket
    dress, 225
Plagiarism
    stealing, 791
    borrowing, 788
    imitation, 19
Plagiarist
    thief, 792
Plagioclastic
    oblique, 217
Plague
    disease, 655
    pain, 828
    to worry, 830
    evil, 619
    badness, 649

Plaid
    dress, 225
    variegated, 440
Plain
    horizontal, 213
    country, 344
    obvious, 446, 518
    simple, 849
    artless, 703
    ugly, 846
    style, 576
Plain dealing
    veracity, 543
Plain-song
    worship, 990
    music, 415
Plain speaking
    veracity, 543
    perspicuity, 570
Plain-spoken
    veracity, 543
Plaint
    cry, 411
    lamentation, 839
Plaintiff
    accuser, 938, 967
Plaintive
    lamentation, 839
Plait
    fold, 258
    pendant, 214
    interlace, 219
Plan
    project, 626
    intention, 620
    order, 58
    model, 22
    diagram, 554
Planchette
    writing, 590
Plane
    flat, 251
    smooth, 255
    horizontal, 213
    to soar, 305
    aircraft, 273A
Planet-struck
    failure, 732
Planetarium
    universe, 318
Plangent
    loud, 404
Planicopter
    aircraft, 273A
Plank

    board, 204
    safely, 666
    plan, 626
Plant
    vegetable, 367
    cultivate, 371
    to insert, 300
    place, 184
    stop, 265
    swindle, 545
    equipment, 633
    effects, 780
Plantation
    plant, 367
Plash
    lake, 343
    plait, 219
Plashy
    marshy, 345
Plasm
    prototype, 22
Plasmic
    form, 240
Plaster
    cement, 45
    remedy, 662
    mend, 658
    cover, 223
Plastic
    soft, 324
    form, 240
    mutable, 149
    materials, 635
Plat
    crossing, 219
    plain, 344
Plate
    layer, 204
    engraving, 558
    to cover, 222
Plateau
    horizontality, 213
    height, 206
Platform
    support, 215
    stage, 542
    arena, 728
    horizontal, 213
    plan, 626
Platinotype
    photograph, 556
Platitude
    absurdity, 497
    dull, 843
Platitudinous
    feeble, 575

Platonic
cold, 823
chaste, 960
Platoon
army, 726
assemblage, 72
Platter
receptacle, 191
layer, 204
Plaudit
approbation, 931
Plausible
probable, 472
sophistical, 477
false, 544
specious, 937
Play
operation, 170
scope, 180, 748
chance, 186
drama, 599
amusement, 840
music, 415
oscillation, 314
appear to be, 448
to act, 680
Play a part
falsehood, 544
Play of colours
variegation, 440
Play-pen
enclosure, 232
Play upon
deception, 545
Play with
deride, 483
Played out
fatigue, 688
old, 124
imperfect, 651
Player
actor, 599
deceiver, 548
musician, 416
Playfellow
friend, 890
Playful
cheerfulness, 836
Playground
amusement, 840
arena, 728
Playhouse
the drama, 599
Playmate

friend, 890
Plaything
toy, 840
trifle, 643
dependence, 749
Plea
excuse, 617
vindication, 937
falsehood, 546
in law, 969
Pleach
plait, 219
Plead
argue, 467
lawyer, 968
encourage, 615
request, 765
vindicate, 937
Pleader
lawyer, 968
Pleasant
agreeable, 377, 829
witty, 842
amusing, 840
Please
pleasurableness, 829
Pleasure
will, 600
physical, 377
moral, 827
Pleat
fold, 258
Plebeian
commonalty, 876
Plebiscite
judgment, 480
choice, 609
Pledge
security, 771
promise, 768
to borrow, 788
drink to, 894
Pledget
remedy, 662
Plein-air
air, 338
Plenary
full, 31
complete, 52
abundant, 639
Plenipotentiary
consignee, 758
Plenitude
sufficiency, 639
Plenty

sufficiency, 639
Plenum
substantiality, 3
Pleonasm
diffuseness, 573
Pleonastic
diffuseness, 573
Plethora
redundance, 641
Plexus
crossing, 219
Pliable
softness, 324
Pliant
soft, 324
facile, 705
irresolute, 605
Plication
fold, 258
Pliers
extraction, 301
grip, 781
Plight
predicament, 8
to promise, 768
security, 771
Plimsoll
shoe, 225
Plimsoll line
measure, 466
Plinth
base, 211
rest, 215
Plod
trudge, 275
journey, 266
work, 682
Plodding
dull, 843
Plop
plunge, 310
sound, 406
Plot
plan, 626
of ground, 181, 344
agriculture, 371
Plough
preparation, 673
to furrow, 259
reject, 610
Plough in
insertion, 300
Ploughman
commonalty, 876
Ploughshare

sharpness, 253
Ploy
  prank, 840
  escapade, 497
  caprice, 608
Pluck
  take, 789
  cheat, 545
  extract, 301
  reject, 610
  courage, 861
  resolution, 604
Plug
  stopper, 263
  to close, 261
  repeat, 104
  publicity, 531
  tobacco, 298A
Plum
  sweetness, 396
  money, 800
Plum-coloured
  purple, 437
Plumb
  close, 261
  measure, 466
Plumb-line
  verticality, 212
Plume
  roughness, 256
Plume oneself
  pride, 878
Plummet
  measurement, 466
  depth, 208
  verticality, 212
Plumose
  roughness, 256
Plump
  size, 192
  instantaneous, 113
Plump down
  descent, 306
Plump upon
  arrival, 292
Plumper
  choice, 609
Plunder
  booty, 793
  to steal, 791
  ravage, 649
  evil, 619
Plunge
  dive, 310
  leap, 146, 309

insert, 300
immerse, 208, 337
precipitate, 308
gamble, 621
adventure, 676
hurry, 684
Plunk
  money, 800
Plurality
  plurality, 100
Plus
  addition, 37
Plus-fours
  dress, 225
Plush
  smooth, 255
  rough, 256
Pluto
  god, 979
  hell, 982
Plutocrat
  wealth, 803
Plutonic
  heat, 382
Pluvial
  river, 348
Ply
  use, 677
  work, 680
  fold, 258
Pneumatics
  gaseity, 334
Pneumatology
  intellect, 450
Poach
  steal, 791, 964
Poacher
  thief, 792
Poachy
  marsh, 345
Pocket
  pouch, 191
  to place, 184
  take, 789
  receive, 785
  endure, 826
  receipts, 810
  treasury, 802
  diminutive, 193
Pococurante
  indifferent, 603
Pod
  receptacle, 191
Podgy
  broad, 202

short, 200
Poem
  poetry, 597
Poet
  poetry, 597
  writer, 593
Poetic
  metrical, 597
Poignant
  physical, 171
  moral, 821
  vigorous, 574
Point
  condition, 8
  degree, 26
  term, 71
  place, 182
  question, 461
  topic, 454
  prominence, 250
  mark, 550
  intention, 620
  wit, 842
  style, 574
  punctilio, 939
  speck, 193
  poignancy, 171
  sharp, 253
Point-blank
  direction, 278
Point d'appui
  influence, 175
Point of view
  aspect, 441
  idea, 453
  relation, 9
Point to
  indicate, 550
  show, 525
  mean, 516
  predict, 511
Point-to-point
  direction, 278
  chase, 622
Pointed
  explicit, 535
  great, 31
Pointer
  index, 550
  hint, 527
Pointillism
  variegation, 440
Pointillist
  artist, 559

625

Pointless
dullness, 843
motiveless, 616
Poise
balance, 27
measure, 466
composure, 826
Poison
bane, 663
to injure, 659
Poisonous
deleterious, 657
injurious, 649
Poke
push, 276
project, 250
pocket, 191
Poker
stiff, 323
Polacca
ship, 273
Polar
summit, 210
Polariscope
optical, 445
Polarity
duality, 89
antagonism, 179, 237
Polder
land, 342
Pole
lever, 633
axis, 223
summit, 210
tallness, 206
Pole-axe
arms, 727
Pole-star
indication, 550
sharpness, 253
Polecat
fetor, 401
Polemarch
master, 745
Polemics
discussion, 476
discord, 713
Polemoscope
optical, 445
Police
jurisdiction, 965
safety, 664
Policy
plan, 626
conduct, 692
skill, 698

Polish
smooth, 255
to rub, 331
urbanity, 894
furbish, 658
beauty, 845
ornament, 847
taste, 850
Politburo
council, 696
Politeness
manners, 852
urbanity, 894
respect, 928
Politic
wise, 498
expedient, 646
skilful, 698
cautious, 864
cunning, 702
Politician
statesman, 745
Politics
government, 693
Polity
plan, 626
conduct, 692
community, 372
Polka
dance, 840
Poll
count, 85
choice, 609
crop, 201
parrot, 584
Pollard
clip, 201
Pollute
corrupt, 659
soil, 653
disgrace, 874
dishonour, 940
Pollution
vice, 945
disease, 655
Poltergeist
demon, 980
Poltroon
cowardice, 862
Polychord
musical, 417
Polychromatic
variegation, 440
Polygamy
marriage, 903

Polyglot
word, 562
interpretation, 522
Polygon
figure, 244
building, 189
Polygraphy
writing, 590
Polygyny
marriage, 903
Polymorphic
multiform, 81
Polyp
convexity, 250
Polyphonism
voice, 580
Polyphony
melody, 413
Polysyllable
letter, 561
Polytechnic
school, 542
Polytheism
heathen, 984
Pomade
oil, 356
Pomatum
oil, 356
Pommel
rotundity, 249
Pommy
stranger, 57
greenhorn, 674
Pomp
ostentation, 882
Pom-pom
gun, 727
Pomposity
pride, 878
style, 577
Ponce
libertine, 962
Poncho
dress, 225
Pond
lake, 343
Ponder
thought, 451
Ponderation
judgment, 480
Ponderous
gravity, 319
style, 577
Pong
stink, 501

Poniard
  arms, 727
Pons asinorum
  difficulty, 704
Pontiff
  clergy, 996
Pontifical
  churchdom, 995
Pontificals
  dress, 225
Pony
  carrier, 271
  money, 800
Pooh-pooh
  trifle, 643
  contempt, 930
  to make light of, 483
Pool
  lake, 343
  participation, 778
Poop
  rear, 235
  fool, 501
Poor
  indigent, 804
  afflicted, 828
  weak, 160
  insufficient, 640
  trifling, 643
  contemptible, 930
  style, 575
Poor-spirited
  cowardice, 862
Poorly
  disease, 655
Pop
  noise, 406
  unexpected, 508
  pawn, 787
Pop upon
  arrive, 292
  find, 480
Pope
  clergy, 996
Popgun
  snap, 406
Popinjay
  fop, 854
Popsy
  girl, 374
Populace
  commonalty, 876
Popular
  current, 484
  favourite, 897

celebrated, 873
Popularize
  facilitate, 705
Populate
  to stock, 184
Population
  mankind, 373
  inhabitants, 188
Populous
  crowded, 72
Porch
  entrance, 66
  opening, 260
  mouth, 230
  way, 627
  receptacle, 191
Porcupine
  sharpness, 253
Pore
  opening, 260
  conduit, 350
  look, 441
  learn, 539
  apply the mind, 457
Porism
  corollary, 480
Pornography
  impurity, 961
Porous
  foraminous, 260
  concavity, 252
  light, 322
Porpoise
  size, 192
Porringer
  receptacle, 191
Port
  harbour, 666
  gait, 264
  resting-place, 265
  arrival, 292
  carriage, 448
  demeanour, 852
Port-hole
  opening, 260
Portable
  movable, 268, 270
  light, 320
  little, 193
Portage
  transference, 270
Portal
  entrance, 66
  mouth, 230
  opening, 260

way, 627
Portative
  transference, 270
  small, 193
Portcullis
  defence, 706, 717
Porte-monnaie
  purse, 802
Portend
  prediction, 511
Portent
  omen, 512
  prodigy, 872
Portentous
  prophetic, 511
  fearful, 860
Porter
  carrier, 271
  janitor, 263
Porterage
  transference, 270
Portfolio
  record, 551
  miscellany, 72
  receptacle, 191
  badge, 747
  direction, 693
Portico
  entrance, 66
  room, 191
Portion
  piece, 51, 41
  allotment, 786
Portland
  prison, 752
Portly
  size, 192
Portmanteau
  receptacle, 191
Portmanteau word
  conciseness, 572
Portrait
  painting, 556
  copy, 21
Portray
  describe, 594
  represent, 554
  paint, 556
Pose
  puzzle, 485
  hide, 528
  difficulty, 704
  affirm, 535
  embarrassment, 491
  attitude, 240

affectation, 855
Poseidon
  god, 979
Poser
  secret, 533
Poseur
  affectation, 855
Posh
  fashion, 852
Posit
  locate, 184
  assume, 467, 514
  affirm, 535
Position
  circumstance, 7
  situation, 183
  assertion, 535
  degree, 26
Positive
  certain, 474
  real, 1
  true, 494
  unequivocal, 518
  absolute, 739
  obstinate, 481, 606
  assertion, 535
  quantity, 84
Positively
  great, 31
Positivism
  materiality, 316
  irreligion, 989
Posse
  party, 712
  jurisdiction, 965
Possess
  have, 777
  feel, 821
Possessed
  insane, 503
Possession
  property, 780
Possessor
  possessor, 779
Possible
  feasible, 470, 705
  casual, 156, 177, 621
Post
  support, 215
  place, 184
  beacon, 550
  swift, 274
  employment, 625
  office, 926
  to record, 551

accounts, 811
  mail, 592
  news, 532
  inform, 527
Post-chaise
  vehicle, 272
Post-classical
  posterior, 117
Post-date
  anachronism, 115
Post-diluvian
  posterity, 117
Post-existence
  futurity, 121
Post-haste
  fast, 274
Post hoc
  sophistry, 477
Post-impressionist
  artist, 559
Post-mortem
  death, 360
  disinter, 363
Post-obit
  death, 360
Postcard
  news, 532
  epistle, 592
Poster
  notice, 531
Posterior
  in time, 117
  in order, 63
  in space, 235
Posterity
  in time, 117, 121
  descendants, 167
Postern
  back, 235
  portal, 66
  opening, 260
Postfix
  appendage, 39
Posthumous
  late, 133
  subsequent, 117
Postiche
  artificial, 544
Postilion
  director, 694
Postlude
  music, 415
  posterior, 117
Postman
  messenger, 534

Postpone
  lateness, 133
Postscript
  sequel, 65
  appendix, 39
Postulant
  petitioner, 767
  request, 765
  nun, 997
Postulate
  supposition, 514
  evidence, 467
  reasoning, 476
Postulation
  request, 765
Posture
  circumstance, 8
  attitude, 240
  display, 882
Posy
  motto, 550
  poem, 597
  flowers, 847
Pot
  mug, 191
  stove, 386
  greatness, 31
  ruin, 732
Pot-companion
  friend, 890
Pot-hooks
  writing, 590
Pot-hunting
  acquisition, 775
Pot-luck
  food, 298
Pot-pourri
  mixture, 41
  fragrance, 400
  music, 415
Pot-valiant
  drunk, 959
Potable
  drinkable, 298
Potation
  drink, 296
Potency
  power, 157
Potentate
  master, 745
Potential
  virtual, 2
  possible, 470
  power, 157

preparation, 673

Precede
in order, 62
in time, 116
lead, 280

Precedence
rank, 873

Precedent
rule, 80
verdict, 969

Precentor
clergy, 996
director, 694

Precept
maxim, 697
order, 741
rule, 80
permit, 760
decree, 963

Preceptor
teacher, 540

Precession
in order, 62
in motion, 280

Précieuse ridicule
affectation, 855
style, 577

Precincts
environs, 227
boundary, 233
region, 181
place, 182

Preciosity
affectation, 855

Precious
excellent, 648
valuable, 814
beloved, 897

Precipice
slope, 217
vertical, 212
danger, 667

Precipitancy
haste, 274, 684

Precipitate
rash, 863
impulse, 612
early, 132
transient, 111
to sink, 308
refuse, 653
consolidate, 321
swift, 274

Precipitous
obliquity, 217

Précis
compendium, 596

Precise
exact, 494
definite, 518

Precisely
assent, 488

Precisian
formalist, 855
taste, 850

Preclude
hindrance, 706

Precocious
early, 132
immature, 674

Precognition
foresight, 510
knowledge, 490

Preconception
misjudgment, 481

Preconcert
preparation, 673
predetermine, 611

Preconcerted
will, 600

Precursor
forerunner, 64
precession, 280
harbinger, 512

Precursory
in order, 62
in time, 116

Predacious
stealing, 791

Predatory
stealing, 791

Predecessor
in order, 64
in time, 116

Predeliberation
care, 459

Predestination
fate, 152
necessity, 601

Predetermination
predetermination, 611

Predetermined
will, 600
predetermination, 611

Predial
property, 780

Predicament
situation, 8
class, 75

Predicate

affirmation, 535

Predication
rite, 998

Prediction
prediction, 511

Predilection
love, 897
desire, 865
choice, 609
prejudice, 481
inclination, 602
affections, 820

Predisposition
proneness, 602
tendency, 176
motive, 615
affection, 820
preparation, 673

Predominance
influence, 175
inequality, 28
superiority, 33

Pre-eminent
famed, 873
superior, 31, 33

Pre-emption
purchase, 795

Pre-emptive
early, 132

Preen
adorn, 845

Pre-establish
preparation, 673

Pre-examine
inquiry, 461

Pre-exist
priority, 116
past, 122

Prefab
abode, 189

Preface
precedence, 62
precursor, 64
front, 234

Prefatory
in order, 62, 64
in time, 106

Prefect
ruler, 745
deputy, 759

Prefecture
authority, 737

Prefer
choose, 609
a petition, 765

Presentation
offer, 763
manifestation, 525
gift, 784
celebration, 883
Presentiment
prejudgment, 481
instinct, 477
foresight, 510
Presently
soon, 111, 132
Preservation
continuance, 141
conservation, 670
Preserve
sweet, 396
Preses
director, 694
Preside
command, 737
direct, 693
Presidency
authority, 737
President
master, 694, 745
Presidium
council, 696
Press
hasten, 132, 684
beg, 765
compel, 744
offer, 763
weigh, 319
solicit, 615
crowd, 72
closet, 191
velocity, 274
Press in
insertion, 300
Pressing
urgent, 642
Pressman
writer, 590
printer, 591
Pressure
weight, 319
influence, 175
urgency, 642
affliction, 830
Prestidigitation
deception, 545
Prestige
attractiveness, 829
repute, 873
Prestigious
delusive, 545

Prestissimo
music, 415
Presto
transientness, 111
velocity, 274
music, 415
Presume
suppose, 514
hope, 858
believe, 484
prejudge, 481
take liberties, 885
Presumption
probable, 472
right, 924
rashness, 863
insolence, 885
Presumptive
conjectural, 514
rightful, 924
probable, 472
indicative, 467
Presumptuous
rash, 863
insolent, 885
Presuppose
prejudge, 481
conjecture, 514
Presurmise
prejudge, 481
conjecture, 514
Pretence
untruth, 544, 546
excuse, 617
Pretend
simulate, 544
assert, 535
Pretender
boaster, 884
claimant, 924
deceiver, 548
Pretension
claim, 924
affectation, 855
vanity, 880, 884
ostentation, 882
Preterition
preterition, 122
Preterlapsed
preterition, 122
Pretermit
omit, 460
Preternatural
irregular, 83
Pretext

excuse, 617
falsehood, 546
Pretty
beauty, 845
Pretty well
much, 31
imperfect, 651
Prevail
influence, 175
be general, 78
be superior, 33
exist, 1
Prevail upon
motive, 615
Prevailing
preponderating, 28
usual, 82
Prevalence
influence, 175
usage, 613
superiority, 33
Prevaricate
falsehood, 544
equivocate, 520
Prévenance
courtesy, 894
Prevenient
precedence, 62
Prevention
hindrance, 706
counteraction, 179
prejudice, 481
Previous
in order, 62
in time, 116
Prevision
foresight, 510
Prey
food, 298
booty, 793
object, 620
victim, 828
Price
money, 812
value, 648
Priceless
goodness, 648
Prick
sharpness, 253
to incite, 615
sensation, 380
pain, 378, 830
Prick off
weed, 103

Prick up
  raise, 212
Prickle
  sharpness, 253
  sensation, 380
Pride
  loftiness, 878
Priest
  clergy, 996
Priest-ridden
  impiety, 988
Priestcraft
  churchdom, 995
Priesthood
  clergy, 996
Prig
  affectation, 855
  to steal, 791
Priggish
  affectation, 855
  vanity, 880
Prim
  affectation, 855, 878
Prima donna
  the drama, 599
  repute, 873
Prima facie
  appearance, 448
Primacy
  churchdom, 995
  pre-eminence, 33
  repute, 873
Primary
  importance, 642
Primate
  clergy, 996
Prime
  early, 132
  primeval, 124
  excellent, 648, 650
  important, 642
  to prepare, 673
  teach, 537
  number, 84
  worship, 990
Primed
  prepared, 698
Primer
  school, 542
Primeval
  oldness, 124
Primigenial
  beginning, 66
Primitive
  old, 124

  simple, 849
Primogeniture
  posterity, 167
Primordial
  oldness, 124
Primrose-coloured
  yellowness, 436
Primum mobile
  cause, 153
Prince
  master, 745
  noble, 875
Princedom
  title, 877
Princely
  authoritative, 737
  liberal, 816
  generous, 942
  noble, 873, 875
Princess
  noble, 875
Principal
  importance, 642
  money, 800
Principality
  property, 780
  spirit, 977
  title, 877
Principle
  element, 316
  cause, 153
  truth, 494
  reasoning, 476
  law, 80
  tenet, 484
  motive, 615
Prink
  adorn, 845
  show off, 882
Print
  mark, 550
  record, 551
  engraving, 558
  letterpess, 591
Printless
  obliteration, 552
Prior
  in order, 62
  in time, 116
  religious, 996
Prioress
  clergy, 996
Priory
  temple, 1000
Prise

  extract, 301
Prism
  optical instrument, 445
  angularity, 244
Prismatic
  colour, 428, 440
  changeable, 149
Prison
  prison, 752
  restraint, 751
Prisoner
  captive, 754
  defendant, 967
Pristine
  preterition, 122
Prithee
  request, 765
Prittle-prattle
  interlocution, 588
Privacy
  secrecy, 526
  concealment, 528
  seclusion, 893
Private
  special, 79
Private eye
  inquiry agent, 461
Privateer
  combatant, 726
Privation
  loss, 776
  poverty, 804
Privative
  taking, 789
Privilege
  dueness, 924
Privity
  knowledge, 490
Privy
  concealed, 528
Prize
  booty, 793
  reward, 973
  success, 731
  palm, 733
  good, 618
  love, 897
  approve, 931
Prize-fighter
  combatant, 726
Pro and con
  reasoning, 476
Pro bono publico
  utility, 644
  philanthropy, 910

Pro forma
habit, 613
Pro hac vice
present, 118
Pro more
conformity, 62
habit, 613
Pro rata
relation, 9
Pro re nata
circumstance, 8
occasion, 134
Pro tanto
greatness, 31
smallness, 32
Proa
ship, 273
Probable
probability, 472
chance, 156
Probate
evidence, 467
Probation
trial, 463
essay, 675
demonstration, 478
Probationer
learner, 541
Probe
stiletto, 262
measure, 466
depth, 208
investigate, 461
Probity
virtue, 944
right, 922
integrity, 939
Problem
enigma, 533
Problem
inquiry, 461
Problematical
uncertain, 475
hidden, 528
Proboscis
convexity, 250
Procedure
conduct, 692
action, 680
plan, 626
Proceed
advance, 282
from, 154
elapse, 109
happen, 151

Proceeding
action, 680
event, 151
plan, 626
incomplete, 53
Proceeds
money, 800
receipts, 810
gain, 775
Procerity
height, 206
Procès-verbal
compendium, 596
Process
projection, 250
plan, 626
action, 680
conduct, 692
engraving, 558
time, 109
Procession
train, 69
ceremony, 882
Prochronism
anachronism, 115
Proclaim
publication, 531
Proclivity
disposition, 602
proneness, 176, 820
Proconsul
deputy, 759
master, 745
Proconsulship
authority, 737
Procrastination
delay, 133, 683
Procreant
productiveness, 168
Procreate
production, 161
Procreator
paternity, 166
Proctor
officer, 694
law, 968
Proctorship
direction, 693
Procumbent
horizontality, 213
Procuration
commission, 755
pimping, 961
Procurator
director, 694

Procure
get, 775
cause, 153
buy, 795
pimp, 962
Prod
poke, 276
Prodigal
extravagant, 818
lavish, 641
penitent, 950
Prodigious
wonderful, 870
much, 31
Prodigy
prodigy, 872
Prodromal
precedence, 62
Prodrome
precursor, 64
Produce
cause, 153
create, 161
prolong, 200
show, 525, 599
evidence, 467
result, 154
fruit, 775
ware, 798
Product
effect, 154
acquisition, 775
multiple, 84
Productive
productiveness, 168
Proem
precursor, 64
Proemial
preceding, in order, 62
in time, 106
beginning, 66
Profane
impious, 988
pagan, 986
desecrate, 679
laical, 997
Profess
affirmation, 535
Profession
business, 625
promise, 768
Professor
teacher, 540
Proffer
offer, 763

Proficiency
skill, 698
Proficient
adept, 700
knowledge, 490
skilful, 698
Profile
lateral, 236
outline, 229
appearance, 448
Profit
acquisition, 775
advantage, 618
Profitable
useful, 644
gainful, 810
Profiteer
acquisition, 775
upstart, 734
Profitless
inutility, 645
Profligacy
vice, 945
Profluent
advancing, 282
flowing, 348
Profound
deep, 208
sagacity, 702
feeling, 821
thought, 451
Profoundly
great, 31
Profuse
prodigal, 818
lavish, 641
Prog
food, 298
Progenitor
paternity, 166
Progeny
posterity, 121, 167
Prognostic
omen, 512
Prognosticate
prediction, 511
Programme
catalogue, 86
announcement, 510
plan, 626
Progress
advance, 282
speed, 274
of time, 109
improvement, 658

success, 731
Progression
series, 69
gradation, 58
numerical, 84
motion, 282
Prohibit
forbid, 761
Prohibition
sobriety, 953, 958
Project
bulge, 250
propel, 284
eject, 297
move, 264
plan, 626
intend, 620
Projectile
missile, 284
weapon, 727
Projection
map, 554
Prolegomena
precursor, 64
Prolepsis
anachronism, 115
Prolétaire
commonalty, 876
Proletarian
commonalty, 876
Proliferate
reproduction, 161
Prolific
productive, 168
Prolix
diffuse, 573
Prolocuter
teacher, 540
speaker, 582
Prologue
precursor, 64
drama, 599
Prolong
lengthen, 200
protract, 110, 133
Prolusion
beginning, 64
lesson, 537
dissertation, 595
Promenade
journey, 266
causeway, 627
display, 882
Promethean
life, 359

Prominent
convex, 250, 252
conspicuous, 446, 525
important, 642
famous, 873
Prominently
great, 31
Promiscuous
irregular, 59
casual, 621
Promise
engage, 768
augur, 507
hope, 858
Promissory
pledged, 768
Promissory note
security, 771
money, 800
Promontory
cape, 206, 342
projection, 250
Promote
aid, 707
plan, 626
Promotion
improvement, 658
Prompt
in time, 111
early, 132
quick, 274
suggest, 514, 695
tell, 527
remind, 505
induce, 615
active, 682
Promptuary
store, 636
Promulgate
publication, 531
Pronation
inversion, 218
Prone
horizontal, 213
tending, 176
inclined, 602
disposed, 820
Prong
sharpness, 253
Pronounce
articulate, 580
speak, 582
assert, 535
judge, 480
sentence, 969

635

Pronounced
great, 31
obvious, 518
emphatic, 535
Pronunciamento
revolt, 719
Proof
demonstration, 478
test, 463
copy, 21
defence, 717
insensible, 376
Prop
support, 215
help, 707
refuge, 666
Propagable
productive, 168
Propaganda
publicity, 531
Propagandism
teaching, 537
proselytism, 484
Propagate
produce, 161
publish, 531
Propel
propulsion, 284
move, 264
Propensity
tendency, 176
disposition, 602
affections, 820
Proper
special, 79
right, 922, 926
expedient, 646
consonant, 23
handsome, 845
Property
possession, 780
power, 157
Prophecy
prediction, 511
scriptural, 985
Prophesy
predict, 511
Prophet
oracle, 513
Prophylactic
remedy, 662
preservative, 670
Prophylaxis
preservation, 670
salubrity, 656

Propinquity
nearness, 197
Propitiate
conciliate, 831, 918
pacify, 723
atone, 952
pity, 914
religious, 976
worship, 990
Propitious
favouring, 707
opportune, 134
prosperous, 734
auspicious, 858
Proplasm
prototype, 22
Proportion
relation, 9
mathematical, 84, 85
symmetry, 242
Proposal
plan, 626
Propose
offer, 763
intend, 620
suggest, 514
broach, 535
ask, 461
Proposition
reasoning, 476
problem, 461
supposition, 454
Propound
broach, 535
inquire, 461
suggest, 514
Propria persona
speciality, 79
Proprietary
possessor, 779
Proprietor
possessor, 779
Proprietorship
possession, 777
property, 780
Propriety
consonance, 23
expedience, 646
taste, 850
duty, 922, 926
Proprio motu
will, 600
Propter hoc
attribution, 155
Propulsion

propulsion, 284
impulse, 276
Prorogue
lateness, 133
Prosaic
dull, 843
style, 575, 598
Proscenium
front, 234
Proscribe
interdict, 761
curse, 908
condemn, 971
denounce, 938
exclude, 77, 893
Prose
not verse, 598
dullness, 843
to prate, 584
to weary, 841
Prosector
anatomist, 44
Prosecute
pursue, 622
accuse, 938
arraign, 969
action, 680
Prosecutor
judge, 967
Proselyte
learner, 541
convert, 484
Proselytism
teaching, 537
belief, 484
Prosit
drink, 959
Prosody
poetry, 597
Prosopopoeia
metaphor, 521
Prospect
view, 448
probability, 472
futurity, 121, 507
Prospectus
scheme, 626
compendium, 596
programme, 86
Prosperity
success, 731, 734
Prostitute
to corrupt, 659
misuse, 679
dishonour, 961, 962

Prostrate
low, 207
level, 213
to depress, 308
weak, 160
exhausted, 688
laid up, 655
dejected, 837
heart-broken, 830
Prostration
ruin, 619
disease, 655
servility, 886
obeisance, 725, 743,
928
worship, 990
Prosy
diffuse, 573
dull, 575, 843
Prosyllogism
reasoning, 476
Protagonist
leader, 745
champion, 711
proficient, 700
Protasis
precursor, 64
Protean
mutable, 149, 605
Protect
shield, 664
defend, 717
Protection
influence, 175
Protector
master, 745
Protectorate
region, 181
authority, 737
Protégé
servant, 746
friend, 890
Protein
living beings, 357
Protervity
petulance, 901
Protest
dissent, 489
denial, 536
affirmation, 535
refusal, 764
deprecate, 766
censure, 932
non-observance, 773
non-payment, 808

Protestant
Christian religion, 983A
Proteus
change, 149
Prothonotary
recorder, 553
Protocol
document, 551
compact, 769
warrant, 771
etiquette, 613
ceremony, 882
Protoplasm
substance, 3
living beings, 357
Protoplast
prototype, 22
Prototype
thing copied, 22
Protract
time, 110, 133
length, 200
Protractor
angularity, 244
Protrude
convexity, 250
Protuberance
convexity, 250
Proud
lofty, 878
dignified, 873
Prove
demonstrate, 85, 478
try, 463
turn out, 151
affect, 821
Provenance
cause, 153
Provender
food, 298
materials, 635
provision, 637
Proverb
maxim, 496
Proverbial
knowledge, 490
Provide
furnish, 637
prepare, 673
Provided
qualification, 469
condition, 770
conditionally, 8
Providence
foresight, 510

divine government, 976
Provident
careful, 459
foresight, 510
wise, 498
prepared, 673
Providential
opportune, 134
Province
region, 181
department, 75
office, 625
duty, 926
Provincialism
language, 560
vulgarity, 851, 876
Provision
supply, 637
materials, 635
preparation, 673
wealth, 803
food, 298
Provisional
preparing, 673
substituted, 147
temporary, 111
conditional, 8
Proviso
qualification, 469
condition, 770
Provoke
incite, 615
cause, 153
excite, 824
vex, 830
hatred, 898
anger, 900
Provoking
difficult, 704
Provost
master, 745
Prow
front, 234
Prowess
courage, 861
Prowl
journey, 266
conceal, 528
Proximity
nearness, 197
contiguity, 199
Proximo
futurity, 121
posterior, 117

Proxy
deputy, 759
substitute, 634
Prude
affectation, 855
Prudent
cautious, 864
foresight, 510
careful, 459
wise, 498
discreet, 698
Prudery
affectation, 855
Prune
shorten, 201
correct, 658
purple, 437
Prunella
unimportance, 643
Prurient
desire, 865
lust, 961
Pry
inquire, 461
curiosity, 455
look, 441
Psalm
worship, 990
Psalmody
music, 415
Psalter
rite, 998
Pseudo
spurious, 495
sham, 544
Pseudonym
misnomer, 565
Pseudoscope
optical, 445
Pshaw
contempt, 930
Psst
accost, 586
Psyche
soul, 450
Psychiatrist
mind, 450
remedy, 662
Psychical
immaterial, 317
intellectual, 450
Psycho-analysis
remedy, 662
Psychokinesis
occult, 992
Psychology

intellect, 450
Psychomancy
divination, 992
Psychopath
madman, 504
Psychosis
insanity, 503
Psycho-therapist
intellect, 450
remedy, 662
Ptisan
remedy, 662
Pub-crawler
drunkard, 959
Puberty
youth, 127
Public
people, 373
open, 529, 531
Public-house
drink, 298
Public-spirited
philanthropy, 910
Publication
promulgation, 531
showing, 525
printing, 591
book, 593
Publicist
writer, 593
lawyer, 968
Publicity
publication, 531
Publish
inform, 527
Puce
purple, 437
Puck
imp, 980
Pucker
fold, 258
Pudder
disorder, 59
Pudding
food, 298
Puddle
lakelet, 343
lining, 224
Pudency
purity, 960
Puerile
boyish, 127, 129
trifling, 643
foolish, 499
weak, 477, 575

Puff
wind, 349
vapour, 334
tobacco, 298A
inflate, 194
commendation, 931
advertisement, 531
boast, 884
pant, 688
Puffed up
vain, 770
proud, 878
Puffy
swollen, 194
wind, 349
Pug
shortness, 201
footprint, 551
boxer, 726
Pugilism
contention, 720
Pugilist
combatant, 726
Pugnacity
anger, 901
Puisne
posterior, 117
Puissant
strong, 157, 159
Puke
ejection, 297
Pukka
true, 494
goodness, 648
Pulchritude
beauty, 845
Pule
cry, 411, 412
weep, 839
Pull
draw, 285
attract, 288
row, 267
swerve, 279
advantage, 33
proof, 21, 591
Pull down
destroy, 162
lay low, 308
Pull off
accomplish, 729
Pull out
extract, 301
Pull through
recover, 658

Pull together
concord, 714
Pull up
stop, 142, 265
accuse, 938
Pullet
infant, 129
Pulley
instrument, 633
Pullman car
vehicle, 272
Pullover
dress, 225
Pullulate
grow, 194
multiply, 168
Pulp
pulpiness, 354
soften, 324
semiliquid, 352
Pulpit
rostrum, 542
church, 1000
Pulsate
see Pulse
Pulse
oscillate, 314
agitate, 315
periodically, 138
Pultaceous
pulpy, 354
Pulverize
maltreat, 649
Pulverulence
powder, 330
Pulvil
fragrance, 400
Pummel
handle, 633
beat, 276, 972
Pump
inquire, 461
spray, 348
reservoir, 636
Pun
verbal, 520, 563
wit, 842
similarity, 17
Punch
to perforate, 260
perforator, 262
to strike, 276
punish, 972
energy, 171
vigour, 574

buffoon, 857
humorist, 844
puppet, 599
horse, 271
Punctate
spotted, 440
Punctilio
ostentation, 882
Punctilious
correct, 494
fashionable, 852
observant, 772
fastidious, 868
scrupulous, 939
Punctual
early, 132
periodical, 138
scrupulous, 939
Punctuation
grammar, 567
Puncture
opening, 260
Pundit
scholar, 462
sage, 500
clergy, 996
Pungent
taste, 392
caustic, 171
feeling, 821
Punic faith
improbity, 940
Punish
punishment, 972
Punk
prostitute, 962
trash, 645
Punka
fan, 349
Punnet
receptacle, 191
Punster
humorist, 844
Punt
ship, 273
propel, 267, 284
gamble, 621
Puny
in degree, 32
in size, 193
weak, 160
Pup
infant, 129
Pupil
learner, 541

eye, 441
Puppet
subjection, 749
effigy, 554
plaything, 840
dupe, 547
little, 193
Puppet-show
the drama, 599
amusement, 840
Puppy
fop, 854
blusterer, 887
Puranas
sacred books, 986
Purblind
dim-sighted, 443
undiscerning, 499
Purchase
buy, 795
leverage, 175
Pure
simple, 42
true, 494
good taste, 850
clean, 652
innocent, 946
virtuous, 944
Purely
smallness, 32
greatness, 31
Purgation
cleansing, 652
atonement, 952
Purgative
remedy, 662
Purgatory
suffering, 828
atonement, 952
hell, 982
Purge
clean, 652
improve, 658
atone, 952
subduction, 38
Purify
cleanse, 652
improve, 658
Purist
style, 578
taste, 850
Puritanical
ascetic, 955
pedantic, 855

Puritanism
heterodoxy, 984A
Purity
purity, 960
of style, 578
Purl
gargle, 405
flow, 348
Purler
fall, 306
Purlieus
suburbs, 197, 227
Purloin
steal, 791
Purple
purple, 437
insignia, 747
Purport
meaning, 516
intent, 620
Purpose
intention, 620
Purposeless
chance, 621
motiveless, 616
Purposely
will, 600, 620
Purr
animal sound, 412
Purse
money-bag, 802
wealth, 803
to shrivel, 195
prize, 973
Purse-bearer
treasurer, 801
Purse-proud
pride, 878
Purse-strings
treasury, 802
Purser
treasurer, 801
Pursuant to
intention, 620
Pursue
follow, 281
continue, 143
aim, 622
inquire, 461
Pursuer
prosecutor, 938, 967
Pursuit
hobby, 865
business, 625
Pursuivant
messenger, 534

Pursy
size, 192
Purulent
unclean, 653
Purvey
provision, 637
Purview
extent, 180
intention, 620
Pus
dirt, 653
Push
exigency, 8
accelerate, 274
impel, 276
propel, 284
repel, 289
activity, 682
dismissal, 756
Push on
progress, 282, 684
Push-button
instant, 113
Pusher
girl, 374
Pushover
dupe, 547
Pusillanimity
cowardice, 862
Puss
face, 234, 448
Pustule
pimple, 250
blemish, 848
Put
place, 184
a question, 461
fool, 501
Put about
turn back, 283
circuition, 311
Put away
relinquish, 624
Put by
economy, 817
Put down
destroy, 162
confute, 479
coerce, 744;
baffle, 731
humiliate, 874
Put forth
assert, 535
suggest, 514
Put in

interject, 228
Put into
insert, 300
arrive, 292
Put off
delay, 133
deter, 616
Put on
clothe, 225
deceive, 544
Put out
quench, 385
darken, 421
perplex, 458
difficulty, 704
Put up to
teach, 537
Put up with
feeling, 821
Put upon
deception, 545
Putative
attribution, 155, 514
Putid
improbity, 940
Putrefy
unclean, 653
Putrid
unclean, 653
Putsch
revolt, 719, 742
Putt
impel, 276
Puttee
dress, 225
Putty
vinculum, 45
Puzzle
enigma, 533
obscurity, 519
mystify, 528
stagger, 485
bewilder, 491
Puzzle-headed
fool, 499
Puzzling
uncertain, 475
Pygmy
little, 193
low, 207
Pylades
friend, 890
Pyramid
point, 253
heap, 72

Pyre
  interment, 363
Pyretic
  hot, 382
Pyrexia
  heat, 382
Pyrometer
  thermometer, 389
Pyrotechny
  heat, 382
Pyrrhonism
  incredulity, 487
Pythagorean
  temperance, 953
Python
  oracle, 513
Pyx
  receptacle, 191
  assay, 463
  ritual, 998

Q-boat
  ship, 273
  deception, 545
Q.C.
  lawyer, 968
Q.E.D.
  answer, 462
Quack
  impostor, 548
  ignoramus, 493
  cry, 412
Quackery
  deception, 545
  ignorance, 491
  affectation, 855
Quacksalver
  deceiver, 548
Quadragesima
  fasting, 956
Quadragesimal
  forty, 98
Quadrangular
  angularity, 244
Quadrant
  measure, 466
  angularity, 244
Quadrate with
  agreement, 23
Quadratic
  number, 95
Quadrifid
  number, 97
Quadrilateral

  side, 236
Quadrille
  dance, 840
Quadripartition
  number, 97
Quadrireme
  ship, 273
Quadrisection
  number, 97
Quadruped
  animal, 366
Quadruple
  number, 96
Quaere
  inquiry, 461
Quaestor
  master, 745
Quaff
  reception, 296
Quag
  bog, 345
Quagmire
  bog, 345
  mire, 653
  difficulty, 704
Quaich
  bowl, 191
Quail
  fear, 800, 862
Quaint
  odd, 83
  ridiculous, 853
  pretty, 845
Quake
  shake, 315
  fear, 860
  cold, 383
Qualification
  modification, 469
  accomplishment, 698
  change, 140
  retraction, 536
  training, 673
  right, 924
Qualify
  train, 673
  modify, 469
  change, 140
  teach, 537
Quality
  power, 157
  nature, 5
  tendency, 176
  character, 820
  nobility, 875

Qualm
  fear, 860
  scruple, 603, 616
  disbelief, 485
  penitence, 950
Quandary
  difficulty, 704
Quand même
  opposition, 708
Quantitative
  amount, 25
  allotment, 786
Quantity
  amount, 25
Quantum
  amount, 25
  apportionment, 786
Quantum sufficit
  sufficiency, 639
Quaquaversum
  direction, 278
Quarantine
  safety, 664
  confinement, 751
Quarrel
  discord, 713
Quarrelsome
  enemy, 901
Quarry
  mine, 636
  object, 620
Quarter
  fourth, 97
  region, 181
  side, 236
  direction, 278
  to place, 184
  mercy, 914
Quartering
  number, 97
Quartermaster
  provision, 637
  master, 745
Quarters
  abode, 189
Quartet
  number, 95
Quarto
  book, 593
Quash
  destroy, 162
  annul, 756, 964
Quasi
  similarity, 17

Quatercentenary
celebration, 883
Quaternal
number, 95
Quaternity
number, 95
Quatrain
poetry, 597
Quaver
oscillate, 314
shake, 315
sound, 407
music, 413
hesitate, 605
fear, 860
shiver, 383
Quay
abode, 189
Quean
libertine, 962
Queasiness
dislike, 867
fastidious, 868
Queen
master, 745
Queenly
majestic, 873
Queer
unconformity, 83
sick, 655
whimsical, 853
Quell
destroy, 162
hush, 265
calm, 826
moderate, 174
subdue, 732
Quench
cool, 385
dissuade, 616
extinguish, 162
satiate, 869
Querimonious
lament, 839
Querist
inquiry, 461
Quern
mill, 330
Querulous
complaining, 839
quarrelsome, 901
Query
inquiry, 461
to doubt, 485
Quest
inquiry, 461

pursuit, 622
undertaking, 676
Question
inquiry, 461
topic, 454
to doubt, 485
to deny, 536
Questionable
uncertainty, 475, 485
Questionless
certainty, 474
Questor
treasurer, 801
Queue
appendix, 39, 214
sequel, 65
row, 69
Quibble
sophistry, 477
equivocate, 544
absurdity, 497
wit, 842
Quick
rapid, 274
transient, 111
active, 682
haste, 684
early, 132
skilful, 698
irascible, 901
feeling, 821, 822
Quick-sighted
quick-eyed, 441
sagacious, 498
Quick-witted
wit, 842
clever, 498
Quicken
hasten, 132
animate, 163
vivify, 359
operate, 170
urge, 615
excite, 824
promote, 907
violence, 173
Quicksand
pitfall, 667
Quicksilver
velocity, 274
Quid
tobacco, 298A
money, 800
Quid pro quo
compensation, 30

payment, 807
exchange, 794
interchange, 148
Quiddity
essence, 1, 5
quibble, 477
wit, 842
Quidnunc
curiosity, 455
Quiescence
cessation, 142
inertness, 172
inactivity, 683
rest, 265
Quiet
rest, 265
silent, 403
calm, 174, 826
dissuade, 616
peace, 714
Quietism
piety, 987
heresy, 984A
Quietus
death, 360
downfall, 732
Quill
writing, 590
Quill-driver
writing, 590
Quinary
number, 98
Quincentenary
see Quingentenary
Quinary
number, 98
Quincunx
number, 98
Quingentenary
celebration, 883
Quinquagesimal
fifty, 98
Quinquefid
number, 99
Quinquereme
ship, 273
Quinquesection
number, 99
Quint
number, 98
Quintessence
essence, 5
importance, 642
Quintet
five, 98

Quintuple
number, 98
Quip
wit, 842
amusement, 840
ridicule, 856
satire, 932
Quirites
non-combatant, 726A
Quirk
caprice, 608
evasion, 617
wit, 842
Quisling
traitor, 742
Quit
depart, 293
relinquish, 624
loss, 776
neglect, 927
pay, 807
Quite
greatness, 31
Quits
equality, 27
atonement, 952
Quittance
forgiveness, 918
atonement, 952
reward, 973
payment, 807
observance, 772
Quitter
coward, 862
shirker, 623
Quiver
agitate, 315
vibrate, 314
shiver, 383
fear, 860
affect, 821
store, 636
arm, 727
Quixotic
imaginary, 515
rash, 863
enthusiastic, 825
Quiz
to ridicule, 856
inquiry, 461
Quizzical
ridiculous, 853
Quocumque modo
means, 632
Quod

prison, 752
Quodlibet
sophism, 477
subtle point, 454
enigma, 461
wit, 842
Quondam
preterition, 122
Quorum
assembly, 72
Quota
apportionment, 786
Quotation
imitation, 19
citation, 82
price, 812
Quote
cite, 82, 467
bargain, 794
Quotidian
period, 108, 138
Quotient
number, 84

R.A.
artist, 559
R.I.P.
burial, 363
Rabbet
junction, 43
Rabbi
clergy, 996
Rabble
mob, 876
bad man, 949
assemblage, 72
Rabelaisian
coarse, 961
Rabid
insanity, 503
headstrong, 606
angry, 900
feeling, 821
Race
to run, 274
contest, 720
course, 622
career, 625
torrent, 348
lineage, 11, 69
kind, 75
people, 372
Racehorse
horse, 271

fleetness, 274
Racer
horse, 271
fleetness, 274
Racial
ethnic, 372
Rack
frame, 215
physical pain, 378
moral pain, 828
to torture, 830
punish, 975
purify, 652
refine, 658
cloud, 353
Racket
noise, 402, 404
brawl, 713
roll, 407
bat, 633
plan, 626
Raconteur
narrator, 594
Racy
strong, 171
pungent, 392
feeling, 821
style, 574
Radar
direction, 693
Raddle
weave, 219
red, 434
Radiant
diverging, 291
light, 420, 423
beauty, 845
glory, 873
Radiator
fire, 386
Radical
cause, 153
algebraic root, 84
complete, 52
intrinsic, 5
reformer, 658
revolution, 146
Radically
thorough, 31
Radio
hearing, 418
publication, 531
news, 532
wireless, 599B
Radioactivity
light, 420

Radiogram
hearing, 418
news, 532
Radioscopy
light, 420
Radiotherapy
light, 420
Radius
length, 200
degree, 26
Radix
cause, 153
Raff
refuse, 653
rabble, 876
Raffia
tape, 45
Raffish
vulgar, 851
Raffle
chance, 156, 621
Raft
ship, 273
Rafter
support, 215
Rag
shred, 51
clothes, 225
escapade, 497
to tease, 830
joke, 842
deride, 929
revile, 932
Ragamuffin
rabble, 876
Rage
violence, 173
fury, 825
wrath, 900
desire, 865
fashion, 852
Ragged
bare, 226
Ragout
food, 298
Ragtag
commonalty, 876
bad man, 949
Raid
attack, 716
robbery, 791
Rail
enclosure, 232
fence, 666

imprison, 752
Rail at
disapprove, 932
Rail-car
vehicle, 272
Rail in
circumscribe, 231
Raillery
ridicule, 856
Railroad
way, 627
Railway
road, 627
Raiment
dress, 225
Rain
river, 348
Rainbow
variegation, 440
Raise
elevate, 307
increase, 35
produce, 161
excite, 824
Raison d'être
cause, 253
motive, 615, 620
Raj
authority, 737
Rajah
master, 745
Rake
cultivate, 371
Rake-off
payment, 809
Rake up
collect, 72
extract, 301
recall, 504
excite, 824
Rakehell
intemperate, 954
Rakish
intemperate, 954
licentious, 961
Rally
ridicule, 856
joke, 842
recover, 658
stand by, 707
pluck up courage, 861
Ram
impel, 276
press in, 261
insert, 300

Ram down
condense, 321
fill up, 261
Ramadan
fasting, 956
Ramble
stroll, 266
wander, 279
diffuse, 572
delirium, 503
folly, 499
Rambler
traveller, 268
Ramification
branch, 51, 256
divergence, 291
posterity, 167
Rammer
plug, 263
impeller, 276
Ramp
rise up, 307
slope, 217
Rampage
violence, 173
excitement, 825
Rampant
violent, 173
vehement, 825
licentious, 961
free, 748
rearing, 307
Rampart
defence, 717
Ramrod
stopper, 263
Ramshackle
imperfect, 651
Ranch
farm, 780
Rancid
fetid, 401
rotten, 653
Rancour
malevolence, 907
revenge, 919
Randem
row, 69
Random
casual, 156, 621
Random
uncertain, 475
Ranee
noble, 875
chief, 745

Range
space, 180
extent, 26
draw up, 58
to collocate, 60
roam, 266
direction, 278
series, 69
term, 71
class, 75
freedom, 748
Range-finder
lens, 445
Ranger
keeper, 753
Rangy
lank, 203
Rank
degree, 26
thorough, 31
collocate, 60
row, 69
term, 71
luxuriant, 365
fetid, 401
bad, 649
to estimate, 480
nobility, 875
glory, 873
Rankle
animosity, 505, 900
Rannygazoo
fraud, 545
Ransack
seek, 461
plunder, 791
Ransom
price, 812
deliverance, 672
liberation, 750
Rant
nonsense, 497
speech, 582
acting, 599
style, 573, 577
Rantipole
fool, 499, 501
Rap
knock, 276
snap, 406
beat, 972
Rap out
voice, 580
Rapacious
avaricious, 819

greedy, 865
predatory, 789
Rape
violation, 961
seizure, 791
Rapid
velocity, 274
Rapids
river, 348
danger, 667
Rapier
arms, 727
Rapine
spoliation, 791
evil, 791
Rapparee
thief, 792
Rappee
tobacco, 298A
Rapscallion
sinner, 949
Rapt
thought, 451
pleasure, 827
Rapture
emotion, 821
bliss, 827
Rara avis
unconformity, 83
Rare
infrequent, 137
few, 103
exceptional, 83
excellent, 648
Raree-show
sight, 448
amusement, 840
Rarefy
expand, 194
render light, 322
Rascal
sinner, 949
knave, 941
Rascality
vice, 945
improbity, 940
Rase
see Raze
Rash
reckless, 863
careless, 460
disease, 655
Rasher
layer, 204
Rasp

grate, 330, 331
Rat
tergiversation, 607
Rataplan
roll, 407
Ratchet
sharpness, 253
Rate
degree, 26
speed, 274
measure, 466
estimation, 480
price, 812
to abuse, 932
Rathe
early, 132
Rather
somewhat, 32
choice, 609
Ratify
consent, 762
affirm, 488
compact, 769
Ratio
relation, 9
proportion, 84
degree, 26
Ratiocination
reasoning, 476
Ration
apportion, 786
Rational
sane, 502
intellectual, 450
reasoning, 476
judicious, 480, 498
Rationale
cause, 153
attribution, 155
answer, 462
interpretation, 522
Rationalist
sceptic, 989
Rations
food, 298
Rats
rubbish, 643
Rattan
scourge, 975
Ratting
tergiversation, 607
Rattle
noise, 407
prattle, 584
discompose, 458

645

Rattle off
speech, 582
Rattlesnake
bane, 663, 913
Rattletrap
imperfect, 651
Raucous
hoarse, 581
Ravage
destroy, 162
evil, 619
despoil, 649
Rave
madness, 503
excitement, 825
love, 897
Ravel
entangle, 219
convolution, 248
difficulty, 704
untwist, 44, 61
Raven
black, 431
gorge, 296
Ravenous
desire, 789, 865
Raver
madman, 504
Ravine
pass, 198, 203
dike, 259
Raving
mad, 503
violent, 825
Ravish
emotion, 824
ecstasy, 829
rape, 961
Raw
immature, 123
unprepared, 674
unskilful, 699
cold, 383
sensitive, 378
Raw-boned
gaunt, 193, 203
ugly, 846
Ray
light, 420
Rayless
darkness, 421
Raze
level, 308
obliterate, 552
demolish, 649

Razor
sharp, 253
Razz
ridicule, 856
Razzle-dazzle
frolic, 840
Re
concerning, 454
Reabsorb
reception, 296
Reach
length, 200
river, 348
degree, 26
distance, 196
fetch, 270
arrive at, 292
grasp, 737
React
recoil, 277
revert, 145
counteract, 179
sensibility, 375
relapse, 661
Reactionary
mulish, 499
reversion, 145
Read
interpret, 522
learn, 539
Readable
intelligible, 518
Reader
teacher, 492, 540
clergy, 996
Reading
meaning, 516
Reading-glass
lens, 445
Readjust
equality, 27
Readmit
reception, 296
Ready
prepared, 673
capable, 157
willing, 602
useful, 644
eager, 682
dexterous, 698
early, 132
cash, 800
Ready money
payment, 807
Reagent

criterion, 467
test, 463
Real
existing, 1
substantial, 3
true, 494
Realism
truth, 494
Realistic
description, 594
Reality
existence, 1
Realize
attribute, 155
produce, 161
substantiate, 494
be aware of, 450
imagine, 515
price, 812
Really
very, 31
indeed, 870
Realm
region, 181
property, 780
land, 372
Reanimate
revivify, 163
refresh, 689
reinstate, 660
Reap
cultivate, 371
acquire, 775
succeed, 731
take, 789
Reaping-hook
sharpness, 253
Reappear
repetition, 104, 163
frequency, 136
Rear
back, 67, 235
erect, 161, 307
sequel, 65
bring up, 537
room, 191
privy, 653
Rearrange
arrangement, 60
Reason
cause, 153
motive, 615
intellect, 450
evidence, 467
argue, 476

wisdom, 498
moderation, 174
Reasonable
judicious, 498
right, 922
equitable, 924
probable, 472
sane, 502
moderate, 174
cheap, 815
Reasoning
logic, 476
Reasonless
fool, 499
Reassemble
gather, 72
Reassure
hope, 858
Reasty
foul, 653
fetid, 401
Réaumur
thermometer, 389
Rebate
moderate, 174, 813
Rebeck
musical instrument, 417
Rebel
disobey, 742
Rebellion
resistance, 719
revolution, 146
Rebellow
ululation, 412
Rebound
recoil, 277, 283
revert, 144
react, 179
Rebours
regression, 283
Rebuff
refuse, 764
repulse, 732
resist, 719
recoil, 277, 325
Rebuild
reconstruct, 163
restore, 660
Rebuke
disapprove, 932
Rebus
secret, 533
Rebut
answer, 462
confute, 479

deny, 536
counter-evidence, 468
Rebutter
lawsuit, 969
Recalcitrant
disobedient, 742
Recalcitrate
'resist, 276, 719
counteract, 179
Recall
recollect, 505
cancel, 756
Recant
retract, 607
repent, 950
deny, 536
resign, 757
Recapitulate
summary, 596
describe, 594
repeat, 104
enumerate, 85
Recast
plan, 626, 660
refashion, 146
Recede
move back, 283
move from, 287
decline, 659
Receipt
money, 810
recipe, 697
Receive
admit, 296
take in, 785
include, 76
acquire, 775
learn, 539
believe, 484
welcome, 892, 894
money, 810
Received
ordinary, 82
habitual, 613
Recension
revision, 457
improvement, 658
Recent
past, 122
new, 123
Receptacle
recipient, 191
store, 636
Reception
arrival, 292

comprehension, 54
inclusion, 76
ingestion, 296
conference, 588
admission, 785
visit, 892, 894
Receptive
intelligent, 498
Recess
place, 182
regression, 283
ambush, 530
holiday, 685
interval, 106
retirement, 893
Recession
motion from, 287
motion backwards, 283
Réchauffé
copy, 21
improve, 658
Recherché
goodness, 648
Recidivism
relapse, 661
reversion, 145
vice, 945
Recidivist
criminal, 949
turncoat, 607
Recipe
remedy, 662
precept, 697
Recipient
receptacle, 191
receiving, 785
Reciprocal
mutual, 12
quantity, 84
interchange, 148
Reciprocation
retaliation, 718
Recital
music, 415
Recitative
music, 415
Recite
narrate, 594
speak, 582
enumerate, 85
Reck
care, 459
Reckless
rash, 863
excitable, 825

careless, 460
Reckon
count, 85
measure, 466
believe, 484
Reckon upon
expect, 507
Reckoning
accounts, 811
price, 812
Reclaim
restoration, 660
Réclame
advertisement, 531
self-advertisement, 884
Recline
lie flat, 213
rest upon, 215
repose, 687
lowering, 308
Recluse
seclusion, 893, 955
Recognizable
visible, 446
Recognizance
security, 771
Recognize
see, 441
know, 490
assent, 488
remember, 505
discover, 480A
acknowledge, 535
Recognized
received, 82
habitual, 613
Recoil
repercussion, 277, 325
revert, 145
shun, 623
reluctance, 603
dislike, 867
hate, 898
reaction, 179
Recollect
remember, 505
Recommence
repetition, 104
Recommend
advise, 695
approve, 931
induce, 615
Recompense
reward, 973
payment, 809

Reconcile
agree, 23
content, 831
pacify, 723
forgive, 918
Recondite
obscure, 519
hidden, 529
Reconnaissance
survey, 441
Reconnoitre
see, 441
remodel, 146
restore, 660
Reconvert
restore, 660
Record
note, 551
list, 86
Recorder
recorder, 553
judge, 967
Recording
copy, 21
Recount
description, 594
Recoup
restore, 660, 790
reward, 973
Recourse
use, 677
Recovery
reinstatement, 660P
improvement, 658
recruit, 689
Recreant
coward, 862
base, 940, 945
apostate, 941
wretch, 949
Recreation
amusement, 840
Recrement
unclean, 653
Recrimination
accusation, 938
reprobation, 932
retaliation, 718
Recrudescence
recurrence, 104, 136
Recruit
refresh, 689
reinstate, 660
health, 654
repair, 658

aid, 707
provide, 637
strengthen, 159
beginner, 674
fighter, 726
Rectangle
angularity, 244
Rectify
straighten, 246
improve, 658
re-establish, 660
Rectilinear
straightness, 246
Rectitude
virtue, 944
right, 922
probity, 939
Recto
dextrality, 228
Rector
clergy, 996
director, 694
Rectory
office, 995
house, 1000
Reculons
regression, 283
Recumbent
horizontal, 213
oblique, 217
Recuperation
restitution, 790
improvement, 658
restore, 660
refresh, 689
Recur
repeat, 104
frequent, 136
periodic, 138
Recurvation
curvature, 245
Recusant
denying, 536
dissenting, 489
disobedient, 742
unwilling, 603
refusing, 764
heterodox, 984A
impenitent, 951
Red
redness, 434
Red book
list, 86
Red cent
trifle, 643

648

Red-handed
  murderous, 361
  action, 681
Red-hot
  heat, 382
Red lamp
  brothel, 961
Red letter
  indication, 550
Red light
  signal, 550
Red tape
  custom, 613
Red-tapist
  director, 695
Redaction
  publication, 531
  improvement, 658
Redargue
  confute, 479
Redcoat
  combatant, 726
Redden
  flush, 821
Reddition
  restoration, 790
Redeem
  reinstate, 660
  deliver, 672
  liberate, 750
  fulfil, 772
  atone, 952
  compensate, 30
  restore, 790
Redemption
  salvation, 976
Redintegrate
  reinstate, 660
  renovate, 658
Redolence
  odour, 398
  fragrance, 400
Redouble
  duplication, 90
  repeat, 104
  increase, 35
Redoubt
  defence, 717
Redoubtable
  fear, 860
Redound
  conduce, 176
Redress
  remedy, 662
  rectify, 658

restore, 660
  reward, 873
Reduce
  lesson, 36
  contract, 195
  shorten, 201
  lower, 308
  weaken, 160
  convert, 144
  subdue, 731
  impoverish, 804
  in number, 103
Reductio ad absurdum
  confutation, 479
Reduction
  arithmetical, 85
Redundant
  ample, 641
  diffuse, 573
  remaining, 40
Reduplication
  imitation, 19
  doubling, 90
Re-echo
  imitate, 19
  repeat, 104
  reduplication, 90
  sound, 404, 408
Reechy
  uncleanness, 653
Reed
  musical instrument, 417
Re-educate
  teach, 537
Reef
  slacken, 275
  shoal, 346
  danger, 667
Reek
  hot, 382
  fume, 334
Reel
  rock, 314
  agitate, 315
  rotate, 312
  cinema, 599
  dance, 840
Re-embody
  combine, 43
  junction, 48
Re-entrant
  angle, 244
Re-establishment
  restoration, 145, 660
Refashion

remodel, 146
Refection
  refreshment, 689
  meal, 298
Refectory
  room, 191
Refer
  attribute, 155
  relate, 9
Referee
  judge, 480, 967
  adviser, 695
Referendum
  vote, 609
  inquiry, 461
Refinement
  elegance, 845
  fashion, 852
  taste, 850
  discrimination, 465
  improvement, 658
  wisdom, 498
  sophistry, 477
Refit
  repair, 658
  reinstate, 660
Reflect
  think, 451
  imitation, 19
Reflect upon
  blame, 932
Reflecting
  thoughtful, 498
Reflection
  maxim, 496
  likeness, 21
  imitation, 19
  blame, 932
Reflector
  optical instrument, 445
Reflet
  variegation, 440
Reflex
  regress, 283
  recoil, 277
Reflux
  regress, 283
  recoil, 277
Refocillate
  refresh, 689
  restore, 660
Reform
  improve, 658
  change, 140
Reformatory
  school, 542

Refraction
deviation, 279
angularity, 244
Refractor
optical instrument, 445
Refractory
resisting, 719
obstinate, 606
disobedient, 742
difficult, 704
Refrain
avoid, 623
reject, 610
unwilling, 603
abstain, 616, 681
temperance, 953
repetition, 104, 415
Refresh
cool, 385
relieve, 834
refit, 658
restore, 660
strengthen, 159
Refresher
fee, 809
Refreshing
pleasing, 377, 829
Refreshment
food, 298
pleasure, 827
recruiting, 689
Refrigeration
refrigerate, 385
Refrigeratory
cold, 387
Reft
disjoin, 44
Refuge
refuge, 666
Refugee
escape, 671
Refulgence
light, 420
Refund
restore, 790
pay, 807
Refurbish
improve, 658
Refuse
decline, 764
reject, 610
remains, 40
offscourings, 643
Refute

confute, 479
Regain
acquisition, 775
Regal
authority, 737
Regale
feast, 298
pleasing, 377, 829
Regalia
sceptre, 747
Regard
esteem, 931
respect, 928
love, 897
compliment, 894
view, 441
judge, 480
conceive, 484
credit, 873
Regarding
relation, 9
Regardless
inattention, 458
Regatta
amusement, 840
Regency
commission, 755
Regenerate
reproduce, 163
restore, 660
piety, 987
Regent
deputy, 759
governor, 745
Regicide
killing, 361
Regime
authority, 737
circumstance, 8
conduct, 692
Regimen
diet, 298
remedy, 662
Regiment
army, 726
assemblage, 72
Regimentals
dress, 225
Region
region, 181
Register
record, 551
list, 86
to arrange, 60
range, 26

to coincide, 199
ventilator, 351
fire-place, 386
Registrar
recorder, 553
Regorge
restitution, 790
Regrater
merchant, 797
Regress
regression, 283
Regressive
reversion, 145
Regret
sorrow, 833
penitence, 950
Regular
orderly, 58
complete, 52
rule, 80, 82
symmetric, 242
periodic, 138
soldier, 726
Regulation
arrangement, 60
direction, 693
usage, 80
order, 741
law, 963
Regurgitate
return, 283
flow, 348
restore, 790
Rehabilitate
reinstate, 660
restore, 790
Rehash
repetition, 104
improvement, 658
Rehearse
repeat, 104
trial, 463
describe, 594
prepare, 673
dramatic, 599
Reify
materialize, 3
Reign
authority, 175, 737
Reimburse
restore, 790
pay, 807
Rein
moderate, 174
check, 179

slacken, 275
restrain, 616
hold, 737
Reincarnation
reproduction, 163
Reindeer
carrier, 271
Reinforce
strengthen, 159
aid, 707
add, 37, 39
Reinforcement
supplies, 635, 637
Reinstate
restore, 660
Reinvigorate
restore, 660
refresh, 689
Reiterate
frequent, 136
repeat, 104, 535
multitude, 102
Reject
decline, 610
refuse, 764
exclude, 55
eject, 297
Rejoice
exult, 838
gratify, 829
cheer, 836
amuse, 840
Rejoinder
answer, 462
evidence, 468
lawsuit, 969
Rejuvenate
restore, 660
Rekindle
ignite, 384
motive, 615
Relapse
reversion, 145
retrogression, 661
Relate
narrate, 594
refer, 9
Relation
relation, 9
Relative
consanguinity, 11
Relax
weaken, 160
soften, 324
slacken, 275

unbend the mind, 452
repose, 687
leisure, 685
amuse, 840
lounge, 863
loose, 47
misrule, 738
relent, 914
Relaxing
unhealthy, 657
Relay
materials, 635
Release
liberate, 750
deliver, 672
discharge, 970
restore, 790
exempt, 927A
repay, 807
death, 360
Relegate
transfer, 270
remove, 185
banish, 55
Relent
moderate, 174
pity, 914
relax, 324
Relentless
malevolent, 907
wrathful, 900
revengeful, 919
flagitious, 945
impenitent, 951
Relevancy
pertinence, 9
congruity, 23
Reliable
believable, 484
trustworthy, 939
Reliance
confidence, 484
hope, 858
Relic
remainder, 40
reminiscence, 505
token, 551
sacred, 998
Relict
widow, 905
Relief
sculpture, 557
convexity, 250
aid, 707
Relieve

comfort, 834
refresh, 689
help, 707
improve, 658
Religion
theology, 983
belief, 484
piety, 987
Religiosity
sanctimony, 988
Religious
exact, 494
pious, 987
Relinquish
a purpose, 607, 624
property, 782
to discontinue, 142
Reliquary
rite, 998
Relish
like, 377, 827
taste, 390
savoury, 394
desire, 865
Relucent
luminous, 420
transparent, 425
Reluct
resist, 719
Reluctance
dislike, 867
unwillingness, 603
dissuasion, 616
Reluctation
resistance, 719
Relume
light, 384
Rely
confidence, 484
expectation, 507
hope, 858
Remain
endure, 106, 110
exist, 1
to be left, 40
rest, 265
continue, 141
Remainder
left, 40
property, 780
Remains
corpse, 362
vestige, 551
Remand
restraint, 751

651

delay, 133
Remark
observe, 457
assert, 535
Remarkable
important, 642
Remarkably
greatness, 31
Remedy
cure, 662
salubrious, 656
to restore, 660, 834
Remember
recollect, 505
Remembrance
compliment, 894
Remembrancer
recorder, 553
Remigration
egress, 295
Remind
recollect, 505
Reminiscence
remember, 505
Remiss
neglectful, 460
idle, 683
reluctant, 603
laxity, 738
Remission
see Remit
Remit
relax, 174
forgive, 918
restore, 790
discontinue, 142
pay, 807
Remnant
remainder, 40
Remodel
conversion, 140, 144
improve, 658
Remonstrate
dissuade, 616
expostulate, 932
Remorse
penitence, 950
Remorseless
resentment, 900
revenge, 919
Remote
distant, 196
not related, 10
Remotion
see Remove

Remove
displace, 185
retrench, 38
depart, 293
recede, 287
transfer, 270
extract, 301
term, 71
Removed
distant, 196
Remunerate
reward, 973
pay, 810
Renaissance
revival, 660
Renascent
reproduction, 163
Recontre
see Rencounter
Rencounter
fight, 720
meeting, 197, 292
Rend
disjoin, 44
Render
give, 784
restore, 790
interpret, 522
music, 415
Rendezvous
focus, 74
assemblage, 72
Rending
loud, 404
painful, 830
Rendition
surrender, 782
interpretation, 522
Renegade
apostate, 742, 941
turncoat, 144, 607
Renew
repeat, 104
reproduce, 163
frequent, 136
newness, 123
repair, 658
restore, 660
Reniform
curvature, 245
Renounce
relinquish, 624
property, 782
recant, 607
resign, 757

deny, 536
repudiate, 927
exempt, 927A
Renovate
reproduce, 163
newness, 123
restore, 660
Renown
repute, 873
Rent
fissure, 44, 198
hire, 788, 794
receipt, 810
Renter
possessor, 779
Rentier
wealth, 803
Renunciation
see Renounce
Reorganize
conversion, 144
restore, 660
Repair
mend, 658
refresh, 689
restore, 660, 790
atone, 952
Repair to
journey, 266
Reparation
compensation, 973
Repartee
wit, 842
answer, 462
Repast
food, 298
Repatriation
egress, 295
Repay
payment, 807
recompense, 973
Repeal
abrogation, 756
Repeat
iterate, 104, 143
imitate, 19
duplication, 90
frequent, 136
multiplied, 102
Repeater
watch, 114
Repel
repulse, 289
defend, 717
resist, 719

652

Rescind
cut off, 44
abrogate, 756
refuse, 764
Rescission
see Rescind
Rescript
order, 741
letter, 592
answer, 462
Rescue
deliver, 672
preserve, 670
aid, 707
Research
inquiry, 461
Reseat
restore, 660
Resection
disjunction, 44
Resemblance
similarity, 17
Resent
resentment, 900
Reservation
concealment, 528
silence, 585
shyness, 881
store, 636
Reserve
concealment, 528
silence, 585
shyness, 881
caution, 864
store, 636
Reservoir
store, 636
receptacle, 191
lake, 343
Reside
inhabit, 184, 186
Residence
abode, 189
location, 184
Resident
inhabitant, 188
emissary, 758
Residue
remainder, 40
Resign
give up, 757
relinquish, 624, 782
submit, 743
Resignation
endurance, 826
content, 831

Resignation
abdication, 757
humility, 743, 879
renunciation, 872
Resilient
elasticity, 325
rebound, 283
Resin
semiliquid, 352
Resist
withstand, 719
disobey, 742
refuse, 764
oppose, 179
tenacity, 327
Resistant
tough, 327
Resistless
strength, 159
Resolute
determined, 604
brave, 861
Resolution
decomposition, 49
investigation, 461
solution, 462
topic, 454
determination, 604
courage, 861
Resolve
purpose, 620
to liquefy, 335
decompose, 49
investigate, 461
discover, 480A
interpret, 522
Resonant
sonorous , 402
ringing, 408
Resorb
reception, 296
Resort
employ, 677
converge, 290
focus, 74
assemble, 72
frequent, 136
move, 266
dwell, 189
Resound
be loud, 402, 404
ring, 408
praises, 931
Resourceful
skill, 698

Resourceless
inactive, 683
Resources
means, 632, 780
wealth, 803
Respect
deference, 928
fame, 873
salutation, 894
observe, 772
reference, 9
Respectable
repute, 873
upright, 939
tolerable, 651
Respecting
relation, 9
Respective
speciality, 79
apportionment, 786
Respectless
inattention, 458
Respire
breathe, 359
repose, 687
Respite
pause, 265
intermission, 106
rest, 142, 685, 687
escape, 671, 672
reprieve, 970
Resplendent
luminous, 420
splendid, 845
Respond
agree, 23
sensibility, 375, 822
Respondent
accused, 938
Response
answer, 462
verbal, 587
rites, 998
Responsible
duty, 926
liable, 177
Responsive
see Respond
Rest
quiescence, 265
repose, 687
leisure, 685
remainder, 40
remain, 141
pause, 142

satisfaction, 831
recumbence, 215
Rest-house
inn, 189
Rest on
support, 215
Restaurant
food, 298
Restaurant-car
vehicle, 272
Restaurateur
provision, 637
Restful
soothing, 174
Resting-place
support, 215
quiescence, 165
arrival, 292
Restitution
restitution, 790
Restive
obstinate, 606
disobedient, 742
refusing, 764
impatient, 825
bad-tempered, 901
Restless
moving, 264
agitated, 315
active, 682
excited, 825
fearful, 860
Restorative
remedial, 662
salubrious, 656
relieving, 834
Restore
reinstate, 145, 660
newness, 123
improve, 658
refresh, 689
return, 790
meaning, 522
Restrain
moderate, 174
emotion, 826
check, 706
curb, 751
prohibit, 761
circumscribe, 231
dissuade, 616
Restrict
moderate, 174
emotion, 826
check, 706

curb, 751
prohibit, 761
circumscribe, 231
dissuade, 616
Result
effect, 154, 476
remainder, 40
Resultant
combination, 48
Resume
taking, 789
restore, 660
Résumé
compendium, 596
Resurgence
reproduction, 163
Resurrection
reproduction, 163
Resuscitate
reanimate, 163
reinstate, 660
Retail
sell, 796
particularize, 594
Retailer
merchant, 797
Retain
keep in place, 150
keep possession, 781
enlist, 615
Retainer
servant, 746
Retaliate
retort, 718
revenge, 919
Retard
hinder, 706
slacken, 275
Retch
rejection, 297
Retention
keeping, 781
in the memory, 505
Retentive
retention, 781
Reticence
latency, 526
taciturnity, 585
concealment, 528
Reticle
crossing, 219
Reticulate
crossing, 219
Reticule
receptacle, 191

Retiform
crossing, 219
Retinue
followers, 65
suite, 69
servants, 746
Retire
recede, 283, 287
depart, 293
avoid, 623
resign, 757
Retirement
seclusion, 893
privacy, 526
Retort
answer, 462
confutation, 479
retaliation, 718
wit, 842
vessel, 191
vaporizer, 336
Retouch
improve, 658
restore, 660
Retrace
memory, 505
Retrace steps
recede, 283
Retract
deny, 536
recant, 607
abjure, 757
annul, 756
violate, 773
Retreat
recede, 283, 287
surrender, 725
abode, 189
asylum, 666
escape, 671
hiding-place, 530
Retrench
subduct, 38
shorten, 201
lose, 789
economize, 817
Retribution
retaliation, 718
payment, 807
punishment, 972
Retrieval
acquisition, 775
Retrieve
restore, 660

Rheum
humour, 333
water, 337
Rhine
ditch, 350
Rhino
money, 800
Rhomb
angularity, 244
rhombohedron
angularity, 244
Rhomboid
angularity, 244
Rhombus
angularity, 244
Rhumb
direction, 278
Rhyme
poetry, 597
similarity, 17
Rhymeless
prose, 598
Rhythm
harmony, 413
regularity, 138
poetry, 597
Rib
ridge, 250
banter, 256
wife, 903
Ribald
vile, 874, 961
vulgar, 851
maledictory, 908
impious, 988
abuse, 932
Ribbed
furrow, 259
Ribbon
filament, 205
tie, 45
trophy, 733
decoration, 877
Rich
wealthy, 803
abundant, 639
savoury, 394
adorned, 847
style, 577
Richly
great, 31
Rick
store, 636
accumulation, 72
Rickety

weak, 160
imperfect, 651
ugly, 846
Rickshaw
vehicle, 272
Ricochet
recoil, 277
reversion, 145
Rid
loss, 776
relinquish, 782
abandon, 624
deliver, 672
Riddle
enigma, 533
obscurity, 519
question, 461
confute, 479
sieve, 260
arrange, 60
Ride
move, 266
get above, 206
road, 627
Rider
equestrian, 268
corollary, 480
appendix, 39
Ridge
narrowness, 203
projection, 250
Ridicule
deride, 856
depreciate, 483
disrespect, 929
Ridiculous
grotesque, 853
vulgar, 851
absurd, 497
silly, 499
trifling, 643
Riding
region, 181
Ridotto
gala, 840
rout, 892
Rifacimento
recast, 660
Rife
ordinary, 82
frequent, 136
prevailing, 175
Riff-raff
rabble, 876, 949
dirt, 653

Rifle
to plunder, 791
arms, 727
Rifleman
combatant, 726
Rift
separation, 44
fissure, 198
Rig
dress, 225
prepare, 673
frolic, 840
deception, 545
adorn, 845
Rigadoon
dance, 840
Rigescence
hardness, 323
Rigging
gear, 225
cordage, 45
Right
just, 922
privilege, 924
duty, 926
honour, 939
straight, 246
true, 494
suitable, 646
Righteous
virtuous, 944
just, 922
Rigid
hard, 323
exact, 494
strict, 772
severe, 739
stubborn, 606
regular, 82
Rigmarole
nonsense, 497, 517
unintelligible, 519
Rigour
severity, 739
compulsion, 744
exactness, 494
Rile
irritate, 830, 900
alienate, 898
Rill
river, 348
Rim
edge, 230
Rime
cold, 383

Rind
covering, 222
Ring
circle, 247
sound, 408
arena, 728
party, 712
syndicate, 778
Ring-fence
enclosure, 232
Ringleader
master, 745
director, 694
Ringlet
circle, 247
Rink
arena, 728
Rinse
cleanness, 652
Riot
violence, 173
revolt, 719, 742
confusion, 59
luxuriate, 377, 827
Rip
tear, 44
rush, 274
sensualist, 954
rascal, 949
Riparian
and, 342
Ripe
preparation, 673
Riposte
answer, 462
Ripping
excellent, 648
delightful, 827
Ripple
shake, 315
murmur, 405
wave, 348
Rise
ascend, 206, 305
slope, 217
resist, 719
revolt, 742
spring, 154
grow, 35
Risible
laughable, 828
ridiculous, 853
witty, 842
Risk
danger, 665

chance, 621
Risky
improper, 961
Rite
law, 963
religious, 998
Ritornello
frequency, 136
Ritual
rite, 998
ceremony, 882
Rival
emulate, 720
envy, 921
oppose, 708
competitor, 710, 726
Rive
disjoin, 44
Rivel
fold, 258
River
water, 348
Rivet
to fasten, 43, 150
fastening, 45
Rivulet
water, 348
Road
way, 189, 627
direction, 278
Road-hog
selfishness, 943
Roadhouse
inn, 189
Roadstead
anchorage, 189
gulf, 343
refuge, 666
Roadster
carrier, 271
Roadway
way, 627
Roam
journey, 266
Roan
variegation, 271
Roar
sound, 404
cry, 411
weep, 839
Roast
heat, 384
ridicule, 856
deride, 929
persecute, 830

censure, 932
Rob
plunder, 791
Robber
thief, 792
Robe
dress, 225
Robin Goodfellow
imp, 980
Robot
automaton, 601
Robust
strength, 159
Roc
monster, 83
Rock
hardness, 323
land, 342
to oscillate, 314
pitfall, 667
Rock-and-roll
melody, 413
Rock-bottom
base, 211
Rockery
garden, 371
Rocket
signal, 550
arms, 727
light, 423
space ship, 273A
rise, 305
rapid, 274
Rocky
unsteady, 149
Rococo
fantastic, 853
Rod
sceptre, 747
scourge, 975
bane, 663
measure, 466
divining, 992
gun, 727
Rodomontade
rant, 497
unintelligible, 519
boasting, 884
Rogation
worship, 990
Rogue
cheat, 548
knave, 941
scamp, 949

Roguery
vice, 945
dishonour, 940
Roguish
sportive, 842
Roily
opaque, 426
Roister
insolence, 885
Role
business, 625
drama, 599
Roll
rotate, 312
move, 264
push, 284
flow, 348
smooth, 255
sound, 407
cylinder, 249
convolution, 248
fillet, 205
record, 551
list, 86
Roll-call
number, 85
Roll in
abound, 639
Roller
rotundity, 249
Rollicking
frolicsome, 836
blustering, 885
Rolling-stock
vehicle, 292
Rolling stone
traveller, 268
Roly-poly
size, 192
Roman
type, 591
Roman Catholic
Christian religion, 983A
Romance
fiction, 515
falsehood, 544
absurdity, 497
fable, 594
love, 897
Romantic
sentimental, 822
Romp
leap, 309
Rompers
dress, 225

Rondeau
poem, 597
Rondo
music, 415
Roof
summit, 210
height, 206
cover, 222
house, 189
Roofless
divestment, 226
Rook
deceiver, 548
swindle, 791
Rookery
abode, 189
Room
space, 180
occasion, 124
chamber, 191
Roommate
friend, 891
Roomy
space, 180
Roost
abode, 186, 189
Root
cause, 153
base, 211
word, 562
algebraic, 84
to place, 184
Root for
commend, 931
Root out
destroy, 162
displace, 185
eject, 301
discover, 480A
Rooted
fixed, 265
permanent, 141
old, 124
habitual, 613
Rope
cord, 205
fastening, 45
Ropy
demiliquidity, 352
Roral
moisture, 339
Rosary
rite, 998
garden, 371
Roscid

moisture, 339
Roscius
actor, 599
Rose
redness, 434
beauty, 845
spout, 350
Rosette
cluster, 72
ornament, 847
Rosicrucian
heathen, 984
Rosin
semiliquid, 352
Roster
list, 86
record, 551
Rostrum
beak, 234
pulpit, 542
Rosy
red, 434
auspicious, 858
Rot
disease, 655
decay, 659
decompose, 48
putrefy, 653
nonsense, 497, 517
to banter, 856
Rota
periodicity, 138
list, 86
record, 551
Rotate
rotation, 312
Rote
memory, 505
Rotor
navigation, 267
ship, 273
Rotten
foul, 653
fetid, 401
Rotter
knave, 949
Rotund
fat, 192
round, 249
Rotunda
abode, 189
Rotundity
roundness, 249
Roturier
commonalty, 876

659

Roué
scoundrel, 949
sensualist, 954
libertine, 962
Rouge
red, 434
ornament, 847
Rouge-et-noir
chance, 156, 621
Rough
uneven, 256
shapeless, 241
pungent, 392
sour, 397
austere, 395
violent, 173
windy, 349
sound, 410
unprepared, 674
ugly, 846
churlish, 895
brute, 913
bad man, 949
to fag, 686
Rough and ready
transient, 111
provisional, 673
Rough-grained
texture, 329
Rough-hewn
rugged, 256
unprepared, 674
Rough-house
disorder, 59
Roughcast
unprepared, 674
Roughly
near, 197
Roughneck
ruffian, 949
Rouleau
cylinder, 249
money, 800
Roulette
engraving, 558
gambling, 621
Round
circular, 247
rotund, 249
assertion, 535
periodicity, 138
song, 415
fight, 720
rung, 71
work, 625

Round-house
prison, 752
Round on
attack, 716
peach, 529
Round robin
record, 551
request, 765
Round-shot
arms, 727
Round-shouldered
distorted, 243
Round up
assemblage, 72
capture, 789
Roundabout
circuitous, 31
way, 629
circumlocutory, 566,
573
Roundelay
poetry, 597
Roundlet
circular, 247
Roundly
exertion, 686
Roup
sale, 796
Rouse
stimulate, 615
passion, 824
Roustabout
labourer, 690
Rout
discomfort, 732
assembly, 892
rabble, 876
Rout out
destruction, 162
Route
method, 627
direction, 278
Route march
journey, 266
Routine
order, 58
uniformity, 16
cycle, 138
rule, 60
custom, 613
work, 625
Rove
wander, 266, 279
Rover
traveller, 268

Row
series, 69
navigate, 267
violence, 173
brawl, 713
riot, 720
din, 404
Rowdy
violent, 173
vulgar, 851
Rowel
sharpness, 253
stimulus, 615
Royalty
authority, 737
receipt, 810
Rozzer
police, 664
Rub
friction, 331
difficulty, 703
Rub-a-dub
roll, 407
Rub down
pulverulence, 330
Rub out
disappear, 449
efface, 552
Rub up
improve, 658
Rubber
elasticity, 325
shoe, 225
pry, 455
Rubberneck
spectator, 444
curiosity, 455
Rubbing
copy, 21
Rubbish
inutility, 645
nonsense, 497, 517
Rubble
unimportance, 643
Rube
peasant, 876
Rubefy
red, 434
Rubicon
limit, 233
passage, 303
undertaking, 676
Rubicund
red, 434

Rubric
precept, 697
liturgy, 998
Rubricate
red, 434
Ruby
red, 434
gem, 650
ornament, 847
Ruche
fold, 258
Ruck
fold, 258
commonalty, 876
Rucksack
receptacle, 191
Rudder
guidance, 693
Ruddle
red, 434
Ruddy
red, 434
Rude
violent, 173
vulgar, 851
uncivil, 895
disrespectful, 929
ugly, 846
shapeless, 241
uncivilized, 876
Rudiment
beginning, 66
cause, 153
smallness, 193
non-preparation, 674
Rudiments
elementary knowledge,
490
beginning, 66
school, 542
Rue
regret, 833
repent, 950
Rueful
doleful, 837
Ruffian
maleficent, 913
scoundrel, 949
vulgarity, 851
Ruffle
derange, 61
fold, 258
edge, 230
discompose, 830
excite, 824

anger, 900
Rufous
red, 434
Rug
covering, 222
Rugged
rough, 256
ugly, 846
churlish, 895
style, 579
Rugose
wrinkled, 256
Ruin
decay, 659
failure, 732
evil, 619
debauch, 961
impoverish, 804
adversity, 735
ruins, 40
Ruinous
painful, 830
Rule
regularity, 80
length, 200
measure, 466
government, 737
precept, 697
custom, 613
law, 963
to decide, 480
Rule out
exclude, 77
Ruler
master, 745
Rum
odd, 853
Rumba
dance, 840
Rumble
noise, 407
understand, 518
Rumbustious
violent, 173
Ruminate
thought, 451
chew, 296
Rummage
seek, 461
Rumour
publicity, 531
report, 532
Rump
rear, 235
remnant, 40

part, 51
Rumple
fold, 258
derange, 61
rough, 256
Rumpus
confusion, 59
din, 404
violence, 173
brawl, 713
contention, 720
Run
move quickly, 274
move out, 295
recurrence, 104, 136
flow, 109, 333
continue, 143
operate, 680
conduct, 692, 693
smuggle, 791
Run across
encounter, 292
Run after
pursue, 622
Run away
escape, 671
avoid, 623
from fear, 862
recede, 287
Run down
censure, 932
depreciate, 483
weakness, 160
Run high
violence, 173
Run in
insert, 300
arrest, 751
Run into
become, 144
Run low
decrease, 36
Run on
continue, 143
Run out
elapse, 122
waste, 638
Run over
redundant, 641
describe, 594
count, 85
examine, 457, 596
Run riot
violence, 173

Run through
peruse, 539
squander, 818
Run up
expend, 809
increase, 35
Runabout
vehicle, 272
Runaway
fugitive, 623, 671
Rundle
circle, 247
convolution, 248
rotundity, 249
Rune
writing, 590
Runlet
receptacle, 191
Runnel
river, 348
Runner
courier, 268
messenger, 534
Runner-up
sequel, 65
Running
continuously, 69
Runt
littleness, 193
Rupture
break, 44, 713
Rural
country, 189, 371
Ruralist
recluse, 893
Rurbania
suburbs, 227
Ruse
cunning, 702
deception, 545
Rush
rapidity, 274
haste, 684
violence, 173
to pursue, 622
trifle, 643
Rushlight
light, 423
Russet
red, 433
Rust
decay, 659
sluggishness, 683
canker, 663
red, 434
Rustic

rural, 189, 371
clown, 876
vulgar, 851
Rusticate
expel, 185
exclude, 55
Rustication
seclusion, 895
Rusticity
inurbanity, 895
Rustle
noise, 405, 409, 410
rob, 791
Rustler
robber, 792
Rusty
sluggish, 683
old, 128
unserviceable, 645
dirty, 653
deteriorated, 659
Rut
groove, 259
habit, 613
Ruth
pity, 914
Ruthless
pitiless, 907
revenge, 919
angry, 900
Rutilant
light, 420
Ruttish
impurity, 961
Ryot
commonalty, 876

S.A.
charm, 829
S O S
signal, 550
alarm, 669
Sabbatarian
bigot, 988
heterodoxy, 984A
Sabbath
rest, 685
Sable
black, 431
Sabot
dress, 225
Sabotage
damage, 649
Sabre

weapon, 727
to kill, 361
Sabretache
bag, 191
Sabulous
pulverulence, 330
Saccharine
sweet, 396
Sacerdotal
clergy, 995
pietism, 988
Sachem
master, 745
Sachet
fragrance, 400
Sack
bag, 191
to ravage, 649
havoc, 619
plunder, 791
dismiss, 297, 756
Sackcloth
asceticism, 955
atonement, 952
mourning, 839
Sacrament
rite, 998
Sacred
holy, 976
pious, 987
books, 986
inviolable, 924
Sacrifice
destroy, 162
offering, 763
self-denial, 942
atonement, 952
worship, 990
Sacrilege
irreligion, 989
impiety, 988
Sacristan
churchman, 996
Sacristy
temple, 1000
Sacrosanct
inviolable, 924
Sad
dejected, 837
mournful, 839
bad, 649
painful, 830
Saddle
clog, 706
add, 37

Safe
secure, 664
cupboard, 191
Safe-conduct
safety, 664
passport, 631
Safeguard
safety, 664
Safety-valve
means of safety, 666
Saffron
yellowness, 436
Sag
obliquity, 217
Saga
description, 594
Sagacious
intelligent, 498
foreseeing, 510
skilful, 698
Sagittate
angular, 244
Sahib
title, 877
Saic
ship, 273
Said
precedence, 62
priority, 116
repetition, 104
Sail
navigate, 267
set out, 293
Saint
holy, 948
pious, 987
spirit, 977
St. Luke's summer
autumn, 126
St. Martin's summer
autumn, 126
Saintly
virtuous, 944
pious, 987
angelic, 977
Sake
cause, 615
Salaam
respect, 743, 928
bow, 308
Salacity
impurity, 961
Salad
mixture, 41
Salamander

furnace, 386
Salary
pay, 809
Sale
merchandize, 796
Salesman
merchant, 797
representative, 758
Salient
projecting, 250
sharp, 253
manifest, 525
important, 643
Saline
pungent, 392
Saliva
excretion, 299
lubricant, 332
Sallow
yellow, 436
pale, 429
Sally
issue, 293
attack, 716
wit, 842
Salmagundi
mixture, 41
Salmon-coloured
red, 434
Salon
room, 191
Saloon
room, 191
vehicle, 272
Salt
pungent, 392
condiment, 393
wit, 842
preserve, 670
Saltation
dancing, 309
Saltatory
leap, 309
agitation, 351
Saltimbanco
quack, 548
Salubrity
health, 656
Salutary
salubrious, 656
remedial, 662
Salute
compliment, 894
kiss, 902
address, 586

firing, 882, 883
Salvage
tax, 812
discount, 813
reward, 973
acquisition, 775
to save, 672
Salvation
deliverance, 672
preservation, 670
religious, 976
Salve
to relieve, 834
remedy, 662
Salver
dish, 191
Salvo
exception, 83
condition, 770
excuse, 937
plea, 617
explosion, 406
salute, 882
Samaritan
benefactor, 912
Samba
dance, 840
Sambo
mixture, 41
Same
identity, 13
Sameness
monotony, 841
Samiel
wind, 349
Samovar
vessel, 191
Sampan
ship, 273
Sample
specimen, 82
San fairy ann
indifference, 456
neglect, 460
Sanatorium
salubrity, 656
Sanatory
improvement, 658
remedy, 662
Sanctify
authorize, 924
piety, 987
Sanctimony
hypocrisy, 988
falsehood, 544

Sanction
authority, 924
approbation, 931
permission, 760
Sanctity
piety, 987
Sanctuary
refuge, 666
altar, 1000
Sanctum
holy, 1000
room, 191
Sand
pulverulence, 330
manliness, 604
courage, 861
Sand-blind
dim-sighted, 443
Sand-shoe
dress, 225
Sandal
dress, 225
Sandalwood
fragrance, 400
Sandbag
defence, 717
arms, 727
Sandpaper
smooth, 255
Sands
pitfall, 667
Sandwich
interpose, 228
Sandy
pulverulence, 330
Sane
intelligent, 498
rational, 502
Sang-froid
insensibility, 823
inexcitability, 826
caution, 864
Sanguinary
brutal, 907
Sanguine
expectant, 507
hopeful, 858
Sanhedrim
tribunal, 696
Sanies
fluidity, 333
Sanitary
salubrity, 656
Sanity
rationality, 502

health, 654
Sans
absence, 187
Sans cérémonie
modesty, 881
sociality, 892
friendship, 888
Sans façon
modesty, 881
sociality, 892
Sans pareil
superiority, 33
Sans phrase
frankness, 543, 566
Sans souci
pleasure, 827
content, 831
Sansculotte
rebel, 742
commonalty, 876
Santon
hermit, 893
priest, 996
Sap
juice, 333
inbeing, 5
to destroy, 162
damage, 659
fool, 501
Sapid
tasty, 390
Sapient
wisdom, 498
Sapless
dry, 340
Sapling
youth, 129
Saponaceous
soapy, 355
Sapor
flavour, 390
Sapphire
ornament, 847
Sappy
juicy, 333
foolish, 499
Saraband
dance, 840
Sarcasm
satire, 932
disrespect, 929
Sarcastic
irascible, 901
derisory, 856
Sarcoma

disease, 655
Sarcophagus
interment, 363
Sardonic
contempt, 838
Sartorial
dress, 225
Sash
central, 247
Satan
devil, 978
Satanic
evil, 649
hellish, 982
vicious, 945
Satchel
bag, 191
Sate
see Satiate
Satellite
follower, 281
companion, 88
space ship, 273A
Satiate
sufficient, 639
redundant, 641
cloy, 869
Satiety
see Satiate
Satin
smooth, 255
Satire
ridicule, 856
censure, 932
Satirist
detractor, 936
Satisfaction
duel, 720
reward, 973
Satisfactorily
well, 618
Satisfy
content, 831
gratify, 827, 829
convince, 484
fulfil a duty, 926
an obligation, 772
reward, 973
pay, 807
suffice, 639
satiate, 869
grant, 762
Satrap
ruler, 745
deputy, 759

Satrapy
province, 181
Saturate
fill, 52, 639
soak, 337
moisten, 339
satiate, 869
Saturated
greatness, 31
Saturnalia
amusement, 840
intemperance, 954
disorder, 59
Saturnian
halcyon, 734, 829
Saturnine
grim, 837
Satyr
ugly, 846
demon, 980
rake, 961
Sauce
mixture, 41
adjunct, 39
abuse, 832
Sauce-box
impudence, 887
Saucepan
stove, 386
Saucer
receptacle, 191
Saucy
insolent, 885
flippant, 895
cheerful, 836
Saunter
ramble, 266
dawdle, 275
Sauve qui peut
speed, 274
recession, 287
avoidance, 623
escape, 671
cowardice, 862
Savage
violent, 173
brutal, 876;
angry, 900
malevolent, 907
a wretch, 913
Savanna
plain, 344
Savant
scholar, 492
wisdom, 500

Save
except, 38, 55, 83
to preserve, 670
deliver, 672
lay by, 636
economize, 817
Savings certificates
treasury, 802
Saviour
Deity, 976
benefactor, 912
Savoir faire
tact, 698
manners, 852
Savoir vivre
sociality, 892
breeding, 852
Savour
taste, 390
fragrance, 400
Savour of
similarity, 17
Savourless
insipid, 391
Savoury
palatable, 394
delectable, 829
Savvy
know, 490
Saw
jagged, 257
saying, 496
Sawder
flattery, 933
Sawdust
pulverulence, 330
Sawney
fool, 501
Saxophone
musical instrument, 417
Say
speak, 582
assert, 535
attention, 457
about, 32
Saying
assertion, 535
maxim, 496
Sayonara
departure, 293
Scab
traitor, 941
Scabbard
receptacle, 191, 222
Scabby

improbity, 940
Scabrous
rough, 256
indelicate, 961
Scaffold
frame, 215
preparation, 673
way, 627
execution, 975
Scald
burn, 384
poet, 597
Scalding
hot, 382
burning, 384
Scale
slice, 204
skin, 222
order, 58
measure, 58
measure, 466
weight, 319
series, 69
gamut, 413
to mount, 305
attack, 716
Scale, on a large
greatness, 31
Scale, on a small
small, 32
Scale, turn the
superiority, 33
Scallop
convolution, 248
notch, 257
Scalp
trophy, 733
to criticize, 932
Scalpel
sharpness, 253
Scamp
rascal, 949
to neglect, 460
Scamper
velocity, 274
Scan
vision, 441
inquire, 461
metre, 597
Scandal
disgrace, 874
vice, 945
news, 532
Scandalize
disgust, 932

Scandent
climb, 305
Scansion
metre, 597
Scant
narrowness, 203
smallness, 32
Scanties
dress, 225
Scantling
dimensions, 192
example, 82
small quantity, 32
scrap, 51
prototype, 22
Scanty
smallness, 32
narrow, 203
few, 103
insufficient, 640
Scapegoat
blame, 952
substitute, 147
Scapegrace
vice, 949
Scapular
vestments, 999
Scar
blemish, 848
Scaramouch
humorist, 844
buffoon, 857
Scarce
insufficiency, 640
infrequent, 137
Scarcely
little, 32
rare, 137
Scare
frighten, 860
Scarecrow
ugly, 846
bugbear, 860
Scaremonger
news, 532
Scarf
dress, 225
Scarf-skin
covering, 222
Scarify
torment, 830
Scarlet
red, 434
Scarp
slope, 217

Scarper
escape, 671
Scat
expel, 297
Scathe
evil, 619
bane, 663
injury, 659
badness, 649
Scatheless
secure, 664
saved, 672
Scathing
censorious, 932
Scatology
uncleanness, 653
Scatter
disperse, 73
diverge, 291
derange, 59
Scatter-brained
foolish, 499
Scattered
discontinuous, 70
Scatty
insane, 503
Scavenger
clean, 652
Scenario
plan, 626
cinema, 599A
Scene
appearance, 448
surroundings, 227
arena, 728
painting, 556
drama, 599
Scenery
vista, 448
Scent
smell, 398
knowledge, 490
suspect, 485
trail, 551
Scent-bag
smell, 400
Scentless
absence of smell, 399
Scepticism
doubt, 485, 497
religious, 989
Sceptre
sceptre, 747
Schedule
list, 86

récord, 551
draft, 554
Scheme
plan, 626
draft, 554
Schemer
plot, 626
Scherzando
music, 415
Scherzo
music, 415
Schesis
state, 7
Schism
discord, 713
dissent, 489
heresy, 984A
Schizophrenia
insanity, 503, 504
Schmalz
sentiment, 822
flattery, 933
Scholar
learner, 541
erudite, 492
Scholarship
school, 490
learning, 539
Scholastic
learning, 490, 539
Scholiast
interpreter, 524
Scholium
interpretation, 496, 522
School
teach, 537, 542
flock, 72
belief, 484
School-days
youth, 127
Schoolboy
pupil, 541
Schooled
trained, 698
Schoolfellow
friend, 890
Schooling
teaching, 538
Schoolman
scholar, 492
sage, 500
theologian, 983
Schoolmaster
teacher, 540

Schoolmistress
teacher, 540
Schooner
ship, 273
Schottische
dance, 840
Schwärmerei
imagination, 515
Sciamachy
absurdity, 497
Science
knowledge, 490
skill, 698
Scientific
exact, 494
Scientist
scholar, 492
Scimitar
arms, 727
Scintilla
small, 32
spark, 420
Sciolism
smattering, 491
Sciolist
smatterer, 493
Scion
child, 129
posterity, 167
Scire facias
inquiry, 641
Scission
cut, 44
Scissors
sharpness, 253
Sclerosis
hardness, 323
Scobs
pulverulence, 330
Scoff
ridicule, 856
deride, 929
impiety, 988
Scold
abuse, 932
vixen, 936, 901
Scollop
see Scallop
Sconce
summit, 210
mulct, 974
candlestick, 423
Scoop
depth, 208
depression, 252

perforator, 262
profit, 775
news, 532
Scoot
hurry, 274, 684
escape, 671
Scooter
locomotion, 266
Scope
degree, 26
extent, 180
intention, 620
freedom, 748
Scorch
burn, 384
hurry, 684
Score
mark, 550, 842
furrow, 259
motive, 615
price, 812
accounts, 805, 811
record, 551
twenty, 98
musical, 415
to count, 85
to succeed, 731
Scoriae
unimportance, 643
uncleanness, 653
Scorify
calefaction, 384
Scorn
contempt, 930
Scorpion
bane, 663, 913
painful, 830
Scot-free
gratuitous, 815
deliverance, 672
exemption, 927A
Scotch
maltreat, 649
stop, 706
notch, 257
Scotch mist
rain, 348
Scotomy
dim-sightedness, 443
Scotticism
language, 560
Scoundrel
vice, 949
evildoer, 913
Scour

rub, 331
run, 274
clean, 652
Scourge
whip, 972, 975
bane, 663
painful, 830
bad, 649
Scourings
refuse, 643
Scout
messenger, 534
servant, 746
watch, 664
to disdain, 930
deride, 643
Scowl
frown, 895
complain, 839
anger, 900
Scrabble
fumble, 379
nonsense, 517
Scraggy
narrow, 203
ugly, 846
Scram
go away, 287, 293
escape, 671
repel, 289
ejection, 297
Scramble
confusion, 59
haste, 684
difficulty, 704
mount, 305
Scrannel
stridulous, 410
meagre, 643
Scrap
piece, 51
small portion, 32, 193
disuse, 678
contention, 720
to fight, 722
Scrap-book
collection, 596
Scrape
difficulty, 704
mischance, 732
abrade, 330, 331
bow, 894
save, 817
Scrape together
collect, 72

get, 775
Scratch
groove, 259
mark, 550
write, 590
daub, 555
abrade, 331
hurt, 619
to wound, 649
Scratch out
obliteration, 552
Scrawl
write, 590
Scrawny
lean, 193, 203
Scream
cry, 410
complain, 839
Screech
cry, 410
complain, 839
Screech-owl
noise, 412
Screed
speech, 582
Screen
concealment, 528
asylum, 666, 717
ambush, 530
to shield, 664
sieve, 260
sift, 652
inquire, 461
discriminate, 465
sort, 42, 60
exclude, 55
shade, 424
cinema, 599A
Screened
safe, 664
invisible, 447
Screever
artist, 559
Screw
fasten, 43
joining, 45
instrument, 267, 633
rotation, 312
salary, 809
miser, 819
Screw-steamer
ship, 273
Screw up
strengthen, 159
Screwball

madman, 504
Screwed
drunk, 959
Scribble
write, 590
unmeaning, 517
Scribe
writer, 553, 590
priest, 996
Scrimp
shorten, 201
stint, 640
save, 817
Scrip
receptacle, 191
Script
writing, 590
radio, 599B
Scriptural
Christian, 983A
Scripture
revelation, 985
certain, 474
Scrivener
writing, 590
Scroll
record, 551
convolution, 248
Scrounge
steal, 791
Scrub
clean, 652
plant, 367
Scrubby
vulgar, 876
shabby, 940
bad, 649
trifling, 643
small, 193
rough, 256
Scrumptious
pleasing, 829
Scrunch
pulverulence, 330
Scruple
doubt, 485
dissuasion, 616
smallness, 32
Scrupulous
careful, 459
incredulous, 487
exact, 494
reluctant, 603
punctilious, 939
virtuous, 944

Scrutator
inquiry, 461
Scrutinize
examine, 457, 461
Scud
speed, 274
sail, 267
shower, 348
haze, 353
Scuffle
contention, 720
Scull
navigation, 267
Scullery
room, 191
Scullion
servant, 746
Sculp
produce, 161
Sculptor
artist, 559
Sculpture
carving, 557
form, 240
Scum
dregs, 643, 653
Scunner
disgust, 395
Scupper
conduit, 350
Scurf
uncleanness, 653
Scurrility
ridicule, 856
malediction, 908
detraction, 934
disrespect, 929
Scurry
hasten, 274, 684
Scurvy
bad, 649
base, 940, 945
Scut
tail, 235
Scutcheon
standard, 550
honour, 877
Scuttle
tray, 191
opening, 260
to destroy, 162
hasten, 274, 684
Scythe
angularity, 244
sharpness, 253

Sea
water, 341
blue, 438
Sea-nymph
sea, 341
Seaboard
edge, 342
Seal
to close, 67, 261
sigil, 550
mould, 22
evidence, 467
record, 551
compact, 769
security, 771
authority, 747
Seal up
shut up, 231, 751
Seam
junction, 43
Seaman
mariner, 269
Seamanship
conduct, 603
Seamstress
see Sempstress
Séance
council, 696
Seaplane
aircraft, 273A
Sear
burn, 384
deaden, 823
Search
seek, 461
pursuit, 622
Searching
thorough, 52
Searchless
unintelligible, 519
Seared
impenitent, 951
Seascape
spectacle, 448
Seaside
edge, 342
Season
time, 106
opportunity, 134
pungent, 392, 393
to preserve, 670
prepare, 673
accustom, 613
Seasonable
opportune, 134

expedient, 646
agreement, 23
Seasonal
period, 108
Seasoning
mixture, 41
pungency, 171, 393
Seat
abode, 189
position, 183
to place, 184
support, 215
Seaworthy
useful, 644
fit, 673
Sebaceous
unctuous, 355
Secateurs
sharpness, 253
Secede
dissent, 489
disobedience, 742
Seclude
restrain, 751
Seclusion
retirement, 526, 893
Second
of time, 108
instant, 113
abet, 707
auxiliary, 711
duplication, 90
Second-best
imperfection, 651
inferiority, 34
Second-hand
borrowed, 788
indifferent, 651
imitated, 19
Second-rate
imperfection, 651
inferiority, 34
Second sight
prediction, 510
intuition, 477
witchcraft, 992
Secondary
following, 63
consignee, 758
deputy, 759
inferior, 34, 643
imperfect, 651
Secondly
bisection, 91
Secret

latent, 526
hidden, 528
riddle, 533
Secretary
recorder, 553
writer, 590
Secrete
hide, 528
Secretive
reserved, 528
Sect
division, 75
Sectarian
dissenter, 984A
theology, 983
Section
part, 51
division, 44
class, 75
chapter, 593
Sector
part, 51
circularity, 247
Secular
number, 99
laity, 997
Secularism
heterodoxy, 984A
Secure
fasten, 43
safe, 664
engage, 768
gain, 775
retain, 781
confident, 858
Security
pledge, 771
warranty, 924
Sedan
vehicle, 272
Sedan chair
vehicle, 272
Sedate
thoughtful, 451
calm, 826
grave, 837
Sedative
calming, 174
sleep, 683
remedy, 662
Sedentary
quiescence, 265
Sederunt
council, 696

Self-reproof
blame, 950
Self-respect
virtue, 944
pride, 878
Self-restraint
self-control, 942
Self-sacrifice
unselfishness, 942
Self-satisfied
vanity, 880
Self-seeking
selfishness, 943
Self-styled
pretence, 544
Self-sufficient
vanity, 880
Self-supporting
freedom, 748
Self-taught
knowledge, 490
Self-tormentor
dejection, 837
Self-willed
obstinate, 606
Selfish
selfishness, 943
Selfless
unselfish, 942
Sell
sale, 796
deception, 545
Sell short
detract, 284
Selvedge
edge, 230
Semantics
interpretation, 522
Semaphore
sign, 550
Sematology
sign, 550
Semblance
likeness, 19
Semeiology
sign, 550
Semi-
half, 91
Semicircle
roundness, 247
Semicolon
stop, 142
Semi-diaphanous
semi-transparent, 427
Semifluid

semiliquidity, 352
Semiliquid
semiliquidity, 352
Semilunar
curvature, 245
Seminary
school, 542
Semi-opaque
semitransparent, 427
Semitransparent
semi-transparency, 427
Semmit
dress, 225
Semper idem
identity, 13
Sempiternal
duration, 112
Sempstress
dress, 225
Senary
number, 98
Senate
council, 696
Senator
adviser, 695
Send
propel, 284
transfer, 270
errand, 755
affect, 824
Send down
expel, 893
Send up
ridicule, 856
Seneschal
master, 745
Seneschalship
power, 737
Senile
age, 128
Seniority
age, 128
Señor
title, 877
Sendation
physical, 375
affective, 820
excitement, 824
Sensational
exaggerated, 549
Sensationalism
vulgarity, 851
Sense
intellect, 450
wisdom, 498

meaning, 516
Senseless
foolish, 499
absurd, 497
insensible, 376
unmeaning, 517
Senses
feeling, 375
Sensibility
physical, 375
moral, 822
Sensible
material, 316
wise, 498
Sensitive
physical, 375
morally, 822
Sensorium
intellect, 450
Sensual
intemperance, 954
libertine, 962
Sensuous
perception, 375
Sentence
phrase, 566
maxim, 496
judgment, 969
condemn, 971
decision, 480
Sententious
concise, 572
pompous, 577
energetic, 574
Sentient
feeling, 375, 821, 822
Sentiment
opinion, 484
maxim, 496
idea, 453
Sentimental
sensibility, 822
affectation, 855
Sentinel
guardian, 664
keeper, 753
watch, 668
Sentry
see Sentinel
Separate
simple, 42
to disjoin, 44, 91, 198
exclude, 55
diverge, 291
divorce, 905

Sepia
brown, 433
Sepoy
combatant, 726
Sept
class, 75
Septenary
seven, 98
Septentrional
opposite, 237
Septet
number, 98
Septic
insalubrity, 657
Septuagint
revelation, 985
Septum
partition, 228
Septuple
seven, 98
Sepulchral
sound, 408, 410
Sepulchre
interment, 363
Sepulture
interment, 363
Sequacious
following, 63
servile, 886
Sequel
following, 65
in time, 117
addition, 39
Sequence
in order, 63
in time, 117
motion, 281
Sequester
take, 789
hide, 526
seclude, 893
confiscate, 974
Sequestrate
take, 789
condemn, 971
confiscate, 974
Seraglio
harem, 961
room, 191
Seraph
angel, 977
saint, 948
Seraphic
blissful, 829
virtuous, 944

Seraskier
master, 745
Serenade
music, 415
compliment, 902
Serendipity
windfall, 618
Serene
calm, 826
content, 831
Serf
clown, 876
slave, 746
Serfdom
subjection, 749
Sergeant
master, 745
Seriatim
continuity, 69
order, 59
speciality, 79
continuance, 144
Series
sequence, 69
book, 593
Serio-comic
ridiculous, 853
Serious
great, 31
important, 642
dejected, 837
resolved, 604
Serjeant
judge, 967
Sermon
dissertation, 595
lesson, 537
speech, 582
pastoral, 998
Serosity
fluidity, 333
Serpent
tortuous, 248
Satan, 978
deceiver, 548
cunning, 702
evil, 663
Serpentine
convolution, 248
Serrated
angular, 244
notched, 257
Serried
crowded, 72
dense, 321

Serum
lymph, 333
water, 337
Servant
servant, 711, 746
Serve
aid, 707
obey, 743, 749
work, 625, 680
suffice, 639
Serve out
apportion, 786
punish, 972
Service
good, 618
use, 677
utility, 644
worship, 990
servitude, 749
warfare, 722
Serviceable
useful, 644
good, 648
Servile
obsequious, 886
flattery, 933
Servitor
servant, 746
Servitude
subjection, 749
Sesqui-
number, 87
Sesquipedalia verba
ornament, 577
Sesquipedalian
long, 200
Sessions
legal, 966
council, 696
Sestina
poetry, 597
Set
condition, 7
group, 72
class, 75
firm, 43
to place, 184
establish, 150
prepare, 673
sharpen, 253
solidify, 321
leaning, 278
gang, 712
lease, 796
habitual, 613

Set about
  begin, 676
Set apart
  disjoin, 55
Set aside
  disregard, 460
  annul, 756
  release, 927A
Set-back
  hindrance, 706
  adversity, 735
  relapse, 661
Set down
  humiliate, 879
  censure, 932
  slight, 929
  rebuff, 732
Set fire to
  burn, 384
Set foot in
  ingress, 294
Set forth
  publish, 531
  tell, 527
  show, 525
  assert, 535
  describe, 594
Set forward
  depart, 293
Set in
  begin, 66
  tide, 348
  approach, 286
Set off
  depart, 293
  compensate, 30
  adorn, 845
Set-off
  foil, 14
Set on
  attack, 615
Set out
  begin, 66
  depart, 293
  decorate, 845
Set right
  reinstate, 660
Set sail
  depart, 293
Set-square
  angularity, 244
Set-to
  combat, 720
Set to work
  begin, 676

Set up
  raise, 307
  prosperous, 734
Set-up
  state, 7
  structure, 329
  plan, 626
Set upon
  attack, 716
  desire, 865
  willing, 602
  determined, 604, 620
Setaceous
  rough, 256
Settee
  support, 215
Setting
  surroundings, 227
Settle
  decide, 480
  be fixed, 141
  be stationary, 265
  place, 184
  dwell, 186
  sink, 306
  arrange, 60
  pacify, 723
  defeat, 731
  consent, 762
  pay, 807
  give, 784
  bench, 215
Settlement
  location, 184
  colony, 188
  dregs, 653
  compact, 762, 769
  property, 780
Settler
  inhabitant, 188
Seven
  number, 98
Seventy-four
  ship, 273
Sever
  disjoin, 44
Several
  repetition, 102
  special, 79
Severally
  one by one, 44, 79
  sharing, 786
Severe
  harsh, 739
  energetic, 171

  painful, 830
  unadorned, 576, 849
  critical, 932
  greatness, 31
Sew
  join, 43
Sewer
  drain, 295, 350
  cloaca, 653
Sex
  kind, 75
  women, 374
Sex-appeal
  charm, 829
Sexagesimal
  sixty, 98
Sexcententary
  celebration, 883
Sext
  worship, 990
Sextant
  angularity, 244
  roundness, 247
Sextet
  number, 98
Sextodecimo
  book, 593
Sexton
  church, 996
  interment, 363
Sextuple
  number, 98
Sforzando
  music, 415
Sgraffito
  see Graffito
Shabby
  mean, 819, 874
  bad, 649
  disgraceful, 940
  trifling, 643
  smallness, 32
Shack
  abode, 189
Shackle
  to tie, 43
  hinder, 706
  restrain, 751
  fetter, 752
Shade
  darkness, 421
  shadow, 424
  colour, 428
  degree, 26
  difference, 15, 41

673

small quantity, 32
screen, 530
manes, 362
ghost, 980
decrease, 36
Shaded
invisible, 447
Shades
hell, 982
Shading off
degree, 26
Shadow
darkness, 421
shade, 424
error, 495
phantom, 4
little, 193, 203
small in degree, 32
part, 51
sequence, 281
Shadow forth
show, 525
Sindicate, 550
Sadumbrate, 521
describe, 594
Shadow of doubt
unbelief, 485
Shadow out
represent, 554
Shadowy
imaginary, 2
invisible, 447
erroneous, 495
Shady
umbrageous, 424
dishonest, 544
disreputable, 945
Shaft
pit, 260
air-pipe, 351
deep, 208
frame, 215
missile, 284
shank, 633
weapon, 727
Shag
roughness, 256
tobacco, 298A
Shaggy
hirsute, 256
Shah
master, 745
Shake
agitate, 315
fluctuate, 149

trill, 314, 407
musical, 415
dissuade, 616
injure, 659
impress, 821
flutter, 824
shiver, 383
Shake-down
bed, 215
Shake off
ejection, 297
Shake up
agitation, 315
Shaken
weak, 160
Shakespearian
poetry, 597
Shaky
in danger, 665
frail, 149
Shallop
ship, 273
Shallow
not deep, 209
ignorant, 491
foolish, 499
Shallow-brained
foolish, 499
Shallow-pated
foolish, 499
Shallows
dangers, 667
Sham
humbug, 544
deceive, 545
Shamble
shuffle, 275, 315
Shambles
butchery, 361
Shame
disgrace, 874
humiliation, 879
Shamefaced
abashed, 881
Shameful
disgraceful, 874
profligate, 945
Shameless
profligate, 945
impudent, 885
Shampoo
friction, 331
cleanness, 652
Shandrydan
vehicle, 272

Shanghai
kidnap, 789
Shangri-la
fancy, 515
retirement, 893
Shank
shaft, 633
Shape
form, 240
condition, 7
to fashion, 144
aspect, 448
Shape well
hopeful, 858
Shapeless
amorphous, 241
ugly, 846
Shapely
comely, 845
symmetrical, 242
Share
part, 51
participate, 778
allotted portion, 786
Shark
thief, 792
cheat, 548
Sharp
acute, 253, 376
musical tone, 410
pungent, 392, 821
energetic, 171
violent, 173
intelligent, 498
clever, 698
cunning, 702
active, 682
rude, 895
censorious, 932
Sharper
cheat, 548
thief, 792
knave, 941
Sharp-sighted
vision, 441
Sharpshooter
combatant, 726
Shatter
destroy, 162
weaken, 160
Shave
cut, 203
Shaving
layer, 204
filament, 205

675

Shock
  concussion, 276
  violence, 173
  sheaf, 72
  contest, 720
  affect, 821
  move, 824
  pain, 830
  inexpectation, 508
  dislike, 867
  hate, 898
  scandalize, 932
Shocking
  ugly, 846
  vulgar, 851
  fearful, 860
  painful, 830
  considerable, 31
Shoe
  dress, 225
Shogun
  master, 745
Shoogle
  oscillate, 314
Shoot
  propel, 284
  dart, 274
  kill, 361
  grow, 194
  attack, 716
  pain, 378
  offspring, 167
Shoot up
  increase, 35
  ascend, 305
  prominent, 250
Shop
  mart, 799
  buy, 795
  workshop, 691
Shopkeeper
  merchant, 797
Shoplifting
  stealing, 791
Shopman
  merchant, 797
Shopwalker
  director, 694
Shore
  support, 215
  land, 342
  edge, 230
  sewer, 653
Shoreless
  space, 180

Shorn
  deprived, 776
  reduced, 36
Short
  not long, 201
  concise, 572
  incomplete, 53
  unaccomplished, 730
  insufficient, 640
  brittle, 328
  uncivil, 895
Shortfall
  deficit, 204
Short-lived
  youth, 111
Short of
  inferiority, 34
Short-sighted
  myopic, 443
  foolish, 499
Short-tempered
  irascible, 901
Short-witted
  foolish, 499
Shortage
  insufficiency, 640
Shortcoming
  failing, 304
  fault, 651
Shorten
  diminish, 36
Shorthand
  write, 590
Shortly
  soon, 132
Shorts
  dress, 225
Shot
  missile, 284
  weapon, 727
  variegated, 440
  changeable, 149
  guess, 514
Shoulder
  projection, 250
  support, 215
  to shove, 276
Shout
  loudness, 404
  cry, 411
  voice, 580
Shove
  impulse, 276
Shovel
  vehicle, 272

  to transfer, 270
  receptacle, 191
Show
  manifest, 525
  appear, 446, 448
  evince, 467
  demonstrate, 478
  parade, 852, 882
  drama, 599
Show-down
  disclosure, 529
  opportunity, 134
Show of
  similarity, 17
Show up
  accuse, 874, 938
  appear, 446
Shower
  rain, 348
  abundance, 639
  liberality, 816
  assemblage, 72
Showman
  interpreter, 524
Showy
  coloured, 428
  gaudy, 847, 882
  vulgar, 851
Shrapnel
  arms, 727
Shred
  bit, 51
  filament, 205
Shrew
  vixen, 901
Shrewd
  intelligent, 498
  wise, 490
  clever, 698
  cunning, 702
Shriek
  cry, 410, 411
Shrill
  noise, 410
Shrimp
  little, 193
Shrine
  altar, 1000
  interment, 363
Shrink
  shrivel, 195
  narrow, 203
  decrease, 36
  small, 32
  recoil, 287, 898

677

Sight
vision, 441
spectacle, 448
prodigy, 872
large quantity, 31
Sightless
blind, 442
invisible, 447
Sightly
beauty, 845
Sightseer
spectator, 444
Sigil
seal, 550
evidence, 467
Sigmoidal
convolution, 248
Sign
indication, 550
omen, 512
record, 551
write, 590
prodigy, 872
evidence, 467
compact, 769
Sign manual
sign, 550
Signal
sign, 550
manifest, 525
important, 642
greatness, 31
Signalize
celebrate, 883
glory, 873
Signally
great, 31
Signature
mark, 550
writing, 590
Signboard
indication, 550
Signet
evidence, 467
signature, 550
sign of authority, 747
Significant
meaning, 516, 527
clear, 518
foreboding, 511
important, 642
Signify
mean, 516
inform, 527
forebode, 511

Signor
title, 877
Silence
no sound, 403
aphony, 581
confute, 479
taciturn, 585
to check, 731
Silhouette
portrait, 556
outline, 229
Silk
smooth, 255
Silk hat
dress, 225
Siller
money, 800
Silly
irrational, 477
credulous, 486
foolish, 499
Silt
dirt, 653
dregs, 50
Silver
money, 800
Silver-toned
harmony, 413
Silver wedding
celebration, 883
anniversary, 138
Silversmith
artist, 559
Silvery
colour, 430
voice, 580
Similar
relation, 9
resembling, 17
comparison, 464
Simile, Similitude
see Similar
Simmer
heat, 382, 384
excitement, 824
Simoleons
money, 800
Simon Stylites
hermit, 893
Simony
churchdom, 995
Simoon
blast, 349
heat, 382
Simp

fool, 501
Simper
smile, 838
affectation, 855
Simple
unmixed, 42
unadorned, 576, 849
small, 32
credulous, 486
silly, 499
true, 543
Simpleton
fool, 501
Simplify
meaning, 518
Simulate
resemble, 17
imitate, 19
cheat, 544
Simultaneous
contemporary, 120
Sin
guilt, 947
vice, 945
Sin-offering
atonement, 952
Since
in order, 8, 63
in time, 117
because, 155, 476, 615
Sincere
veracious, 543
ingenuous, 703
Sinecure
receipt, 810
Sine die
neverness, 107
long duration, 110
Sine qua non
condition, 770
importance, 642
requirement, 630
Sinewy
strong, 159
tough, 327
Sinfonietta
music, 415
Sinful
evil, 947
Sing
music, 415P
poetry, 597
cheerful, 836
rejoice, 838

Sing out
  cry, 411
Sing-song
  untuneful, 414
  concert, 415
  repetition, 104
Singe
  burn, 384
Singer
  musician, 416
Single
  unit, 87
  unmixed, 42
  secluded, 893
  unmarried, 904
Single-handed
  unaided, 708
Single-minded
  honest, 543
Single out
  select, 609
Singlet
  dress, 225
Sing Sing
  prison, 752
Singspiel
  drama, 599
Singular
  exceptional, 79, 83
  one, 87
  remarkable, 31
Sinister
  left, 239
  bad, 649
  discourtesy, 895
  menacing, 909
  vicious, 945
Sink
  descend, 306
  lower, 308
  submerge, 310
  deep, 208
  fail, 732
  destroy, 162
  decay, 659
  fatigue, 688
  cloaca, 653
  depressed, 837
  droop, 828
  conceal, 528
  neglect, 460
  in the memory, 505
Sinless
  good, 946
Sinner

sinner, 949
  impiety, 988
Sinuous
  curved, 245
  convoluted, 248
Sinus
  concavity, 252
Sip
  drink, 296
  smallness, 32
Siphon
  conduit, 350
Sir
  respect, 877
Sirdar
  master, 745
Sire
  elder, 166
Siren
  musician, 416
  indication, 550
  alarm, 669
  seducing, 615
  sea, 341
  demon, 980
  evildoer, 913
Sirocco
  wind, 349
  heat, 382
Sissy
  weakness, 160
Sister
  kindred, 11
  likeness, 17
Sisterhood
  assembly, 72
  party, 712
Sisyphean
  difficulty, 704
Sit
  repose, 215
  lie, 213
  lowering, 308
Site
  situation, 183
Sitting
  consultation, 696
Situate
  location, 184
Situation
  circumstances, 8
  place, 183
  business, 625
Siva
  deity, 979

Six
  number, 98
Six-shooter
  gun, 727
Sixth sense
  intuition, 477
Size
  magnitude, 31, 192
  grade, 60
  glue, 45, 352
  quantity, 25
Size up
  measure, 466
  estimate, 480
  scrutinize, 457
Sizy
  sticky, 350
Sjambok
  scourge, 975
Skate
  locomotion, 266
Skean
  arms, 727
Skedaddle
  escape, 671
  go away, 293, 287
Skein
  knot, 219
  disorder, 59
Skeleton
  corpse, 362
  frame, 626
  small, 193
  lean, 203
  imperfect, 651
  essential part, 50
Skelp
  impact, 276
  punishment, 972
Sketch
  painting, 556
  description, 594
  plan, 626
Sketcher
  artist, 559
Sketchy
  imperfect, 53, 651
Skew
  obliquity, 217
Skew-whiff
  oblique, 217
Skewbald
  variegation, 440
Skew
  vinculum, 45

Ski
  locomotion, 266
Skid
  deviation, 279
  hindrance, 706
Skiff
  boat, 273
Skiffle
  melody, 413
Skill
  ability, 450, 698
Skim
  move, 266
  rapid, 274
  attend lightly, 458, 460
Skimp
  shorten, 201
  stint, 640
  save, 817
Skin
  tegument, 222
  to peel, 226
Skin-deep
  shallow, 220
Skinflint
  miser, 819
Skinful
  fullness, 52
Skinny
  small, 193
  slender, 203
  tegumentary, 222
Skip
  jump, 309
  neglect, 460
  omit, 773
  escape, 671
  dance, 840
Skipjack
  upstart, 734, 876
Skipper
  master, 745
Skirl
  shriek, 410, 411
  lamentation, 839
Skirmish
  fight, 720, 722
Skirt
  edge, 230
  appendix, 39
  pendent, 214
  circumjacent, 227
  woman, 374
Skirting-board
  base, 211

Skit
  parody, 856
  satire, 932
Skite
  boast, 884
Skittish
  capricious, 608
  bashful, 881
  excitable, 825
  timid, 862
Skivvy
  servant, 746
Skoal
  drink, 959
Skulk
  hide, 447, 528
  coward, 860
  flock, 72
Skull
  head, 450
Skunk
  fetid, 401
  bad man, 949
Sky
  world, 318
  air, 338
  summit, 210
Sky-line
  outline, 229
Sky-rocket
  ascent, 350
Skylark
  frolic, 840
Skylight
  opening, 260
Skymaster
  aircraft, 273A
Skyscraper
  height, 206
Slab
  layer, 204
  flatness, 251
  record, 551
Slabber
  ejection, 297
Slack
  loose, 47
  weak, 160
  slow, 275
  inert, 172
  inactive, 683
  unwilling, 603
  laxity, 738
  to moderate, 174
  retard, 706

  calm, 826
Slacken
  relax, 687
Slacker
  evasion, 623
Slacks
  dress, 225
Slag
  refuse, 40
  dirt, 653
Slainté
  drink, 959
Slake
  quench, 174
  indulge, 954
  gratify, 831, 865
  satiate, 869
Slam
  shut, 406
  slap, 276
Slander
  detraction, 934
Slanderer
  detractor, 936
Slang
  neology, 563
  language, 560
Slant
  obliquity, 217
Slap
  to strike, 276
  hit, 972
  try, 675
  instantaneous, 113
  quick, 274
  haste, 684
Slapdash
  careless, 460
  hasty, 684
  reckless, 863
Slapstick
  drama, 599
Slash
  cut, 44
  notch, 257
Slashing
  vigour, 574
Slat
  strip, 205
Slate
  writing-tablet, 590
  covering, 222
  to criticize, 934
Slate-coloured
  grey, 432

Slating
  roof, 210
Slattern
  negligent, 460
  dirty, 653
  awkward, 701
Slatternly
  vulgar, 851
  unskilful, 699
Slaughter
  to kill, 361
Slave
  servant, 746
  to toil, 686
Slaver
  slobber, 297
  ship, 273
Slavery
  servitude, 749
Slavey
  servant, 746
Slavish
  imitative, 19
Slay
  kill, 361
Sledge
  vehicle, 272
Sledge-hammer
  impel, 276
  engine, 633
Sleek
  smooth, 255
  pretty, 845
Sleep
  inactivity, 141, 683
  insensibility, 376
Sleeper
  support, 215
  vehicle, 272
Sleeping-bag
  bed, 215
Sleeping-car
  vehicle, 272
Sleepless
  active, 682
Sleepy
  inactive, 683, 823
  slow, 275
  weary, 841
Sleet
  rain, 383
Sleeve
  dress, 225
Sleight
  cleverness, 698

Sleight of hand
  quickness, 146, 545
Slender
  narrow, 203
  small, 32
  trifling, 643
Sleuth-hound
  inquiry, 461
  pursuit, 623
Slice
  layer, 204
  part, 44, 51
  swerve, 279
Slick
  dexterous, 698
  smooth, 255
Slicker
  dress, 225
Slide
  pass, 264
  relapse, 661
  descend, 306
  elapse, 109
  become, 144
  skate, 266
Slide-rule
  numeration, 85
  measurement, 466
Slight
  small, 32
  slender, 203
  tenuous, 322
  trifle, 643
  to neglect, 460, 927
  to dishonour, 929
Slim
  thin, 203
  cunning, 702
Slimy
  viscous, 352
  dirt, 653
Sling
  hang, 214
  project, 284
  weapon, 727
Slink
  recede, 287
  prowl, 528
  escape, 671
Slip
  descend, 306
  strip, 205
  part, 51
  transfer, 270
  fail, 732

  liberate, 750
  workshop, 691
  guilt, 947
  smallness, 32
  dress, 225
  scion, 167
Slip away
  escape, 287, 671, 750
Slip cable
  departure, 293
Slip of tongue
  mistake, 495
  solecism, 568
Slip on
  dress, 225
Slip over
  cover, 460
Slipover
  dress, 225
Slipper
  dress, 225
Slippery
  smooth, 255
  uncertain, 475
  changeable, 149
  dangerous, 665
  not trustworthy, 940
Slipshod
  untidy, 653
  ungrammatical, 568
Slipslop
  affected, 855
  absurd, 497
  style, 573
Slit
  to divide, 44
  chink, 198
  groove, 259
Sliver
  part, 51
  strip, 205
Slobber
  slop, 337
  emit, 297
  soil, 653
Sloe
  colour, 431
Slog
  hit, 277
Slogan
  indication, 550
  defiance, 715
  war, 722
  maxim, 496
Sloop
  ship, 273

Slop
water, 337
insipid, 391
emit, 297
dirt, 653
police, 664
Slope
oblique, 217
flee, 623
Sloppy
wet, 337
disorder, 59
slovenly, 699
maudlin, 822
Slops
dress, 225
Slot
opening, 260
track, 551
degree, 26
Sloth
inactivity, 683
inertness, 172
Slouch
oblique, 217
low, 207
inactive, 683
ugly, 846
Slouch-hat
dress, 225
Slough
difficulty, 704
quagmire, 345
residuum, 40
Sloven
drab, 653
careless, 460
awkward, 699
bungler, 701
vulgar, 851
Slovenly
style, 573
disorder, 59
Slow
sluggish, 275
tardy, 133
dull, 843
wearisome, 841
inert, 172
inactive, 683
Slubberdegullion
knave, 941, 949
commonalty, 876
Sludge

mud, 653
Slug
slow, 275
Sluggard
slow, 275
sleepy, 683
Sluggish
slow, 275
inert, 172
sleepy, 683
callous, 823
Sluice
conduit, 350
outlet, 295
river, 348
to wash, 652
Slum
abode, 189
dirt, 653
Slump
fall, 306
Slur
stigma, 874
gloss, 937
reproach, 938
Slur over
neglect, 460
inattention, 458
conceal, 528
exclude, 55
Slush
pulp, 354
dirt, 653
Slut
hussy, 962
Sluttish
unclean, 653
neglect, 460
Sly
cunning, 702
false, 544
Smack
blow, 27
ship, 273
taste, 390
mixture, 41
small quantity, 32
kiss, 902
Small
in degree, 32
in size, 193
Smaller
inferiority, 34
Smart pain, 378
grief, 828

active, 682
clever, 498, 698
cunning, 702
to feel, 821
witty, 842
neat, 845
fashionable, 852
Smash
destroy, 162
failure, 732
Smashing
pleasing, 829
good, 648
Smatterer
ignoramus, 493
Smattering
ignorance, 491
Smear
daub, 222
ugly, 846
vilify, 483, 932, 934
Smeddum
courage, 861
Smell
odour, 398
Smelt
heat, 384
Smile
risible, 838
Smile upon
approve, 894
Smirch
soil, 653
blacken, 431
Smirk
grin, 838
Smirr
rain, 348
Smite
strike, 276
punish, 972
bad, 694
Smith
workman, 690
Smithereens
fragments, 51
Smithy
workshop, 691
Smitten
love, 897
Smock
dress, 225
Smog
mist, 353
dimness, 422

Smoke
  cloud, 334
  dimness, 422
  heat, 382
  trifle, 643
  dirt, 653
  preserve, 670
Smoke-stack
  funnel, 351
Smooth
  not rough, 16, 255
  to calm, 174
  lubricate, 332
  easy, 705
  to flatter, 933
  cunning, 702
Smooth-bore
  gun, 727
Smooth-faced
  falsehood, 544
Smooth-spoken
  falsehood, 544
Smooth-tongued
  falsehood, 544
Smother
  kill, 361
  repress, 174
  calm, 826
  silence, 581
  suppress, 528, 585
Smoulder
  burn, 382
  inert, 172
  latent, 528
Smout
  littleness, 193
Smudge
  dirt, 653
  blemish, 848
Smug
  affected, 855
Smuggle
  contraband, 791
  introduce, 294
Smuggler
  thief, 792
Smut
  dirt, 653
  black, 431
  blemish, 848
  impurity, 961
Smutch
  blacken, 431
Snack
  participate, 778

  food, 298
Snaffle
  restraint, 752
Snag
  danger, 667
  difficulty, 704
  hindrance, 706
  sharp, 253
  projection, 250
Snail
  slow, 275
Snake
  miscreant, 913
Snaky
  winding, 248
Snap
  noise, 406
  brittle, 328;
  break, 44
  be rude, 895, 900
  seize, 789
  vigour, 574
  easy, 705
Snappy
  concise, 572
Snare
  trap, 667
Snarl
  growl, 412
  angry, 900
  rude, 895
  threaten, 909
  disorder, 59
Snatch
  to seize, 789
  opportunity, 134
  part, 51
Sneak
  servility, 886
  basement, 940
  to hide, 528
  retire, 287
Sneakers
  shoes, 225
Sneer
  contempt, 930
  blame, 932
  disparage, 929
Sneeze
  snuffle, 409
  blow, 349
Snick
  part, 51
Snickersnee
  weapon, 727

Snide
  false, 544
Sniff
  odour, 398
Sniff at
  despise, 930
Sniffy
  contemptuous, 930
Snigger
  laugh, 838
Snip
  cut, 44
Snip-snap
  discord, 713
Sniper
  fighter, 726
Snippet
  smallness, 32
Snivel
  cry, 839
Snivelling
  servile, 886
Snob
  commonalty, 876
  sycophant, 886
Snood
  dress, 225
  fastening, 45
Snooper
  spectator, 444
  curiosity, 455
  inquire, 461
Snooty
  insolence, 885
Snooze
  sleep, 683
Snore
  noise, 411
  sleep, 683
Snort
  noise, 411
  sleep, 683
  drink, 298
Snout
  prominence, 250
Snow
  ice, 383
  white, 430
Snow-shoe
  locomotion, 266
Snowball
  collection, 72
Snowk
  sniff, 398
Snub
  bluster, 885

Snub
blame, 932
refuse, 764
abash, 874
short, 201
Snuff
odour, 398
tobacco, 298A
Snuff-box
receptacle, 191
Snuff out
die, 360
Snuff up
inhale, 296
Snuffle
hiss, 409
blow, 349
stammer, 583
Snug
comfortable, 377, 831
safe, 664
latent, 526
secluded, 893
Snuggery
room, 189
Snuggle
draw near, 286
cuddle, 902
So-and-so
euphemism, 565
So-called
miscall, 565
So long
departure, 293
So-so
unimportant, 643
imperfection, 651
smallness, 32
tolerable, 736
Soak
immerse, 300
water, 337
moisture, 339
Soaker
drunkenness, 959
Soap
oil, 356
cleanness, 652
Soapy
unctuous, 355
servile, 886
flattering, 933
Soar
rise, 305

height, 206
great, 31
fly, 267
Sob
weep, 839
Sober
moderate, 174
temperate, 953
abstinent, 958
sane, 502
wise, 498
calm, 826
grave, 837
Sober-minded
wise, 502
calm, 826
Sobranje
council, 696
Sobriquet
misnomer, 565
Sociable
friendly, 892
Social
friendly, 888, 892
Socialism
participation, 778
philanthropy, 910
authority, 737
Society
man, 372
friendly, 892
party, 712
fashion, 852
Sociology
mankind, 372
philanthropy, 910
Sock
stocking, 225
drama, 599
Socket
receptacle, 191, 252
Socrates
sage, 500
Socratic method
quiz, 461
Sod
turf, 344
Soda-water
bubble, 353
Sodality
fraternity, 712
association, 892
friendship, 888
Sodden
wet, 339

overcharged, 641
Sofa
support, 215
Soft
not hard, 324
marshy, 345
moderate, 174
sound, 405
smooth, 255
weak, 160
silly, 499
irresolute, 605
timid, 862
lenient, 740
compassionate, 914
tender, 822
Soft currency
money, 800
Soft mark
dupe, 547
Soften
soothe, 826
mitigate, 834
palliate, 937
subdue, 824
Softy
wool, 501
Soggy
wet, 337
Soi-disant
deceiver, 548
misnomer, 565
boaster, 884
Soil
land, 342
dirt, 653
spoil, 659
deface, 846
tarnish, 848
Soiled dove
courtesan, 962
Soirée
assemblage, 72
reception, 892
Sojourn
abode, 189
inhabit, 186
settle, 265
Sol-fa
melody, 413
Solace
relief, 834
comfort, 827
condolence, 915
recreation, 840

Solar
world, 318
Solatium
recompense, 973
Soldan
master, 745
Solder
cohere, 46
join, 43
cement, 45
Soldier
combatant, 726
warfare, 722
Sole
alone, 87
base, 211
Solecism
ungrammatical, 568
sophistry, 477
Solemn
awful, 873
sacred, 987
grave, 837
pompous, 882
positive, 535
important, 642
Solemnity
parade, 882
rite, 998
dullness, 843
Solemnize
celebrate, 883
Solfeggio
melody, 413
Solicit
induce, 615
request, 765
desire, 865
Solicitor
law, 968
Solicitude
anxiety, 860
care, 459
desire, 865
Solid
complete, 52
dense, 321
certain, 474
true, 494
firm, 604
wise, 498
Solidify
coherence, 46
density, 321
Soliloquy

speech, 589
Solitary
alone, 87
secluded, 893
Solitude
see Solitary
Solmization
melody, 413
Solo
music, 415
Soloist
musician, 416
Solomon
sage, 500
Solon
sage, 500
wise, 498
Soluble
dissolve, 335
Solution
dissolving, 335
explanation, 462
interpretation, 522
Solve
explain, 462
discover, 480A
Solvency
wealth, 803
Somatics
material, 316
Sombre
dark, 421
grey, 432
black, 431
melancholy, 837
Some
a few, 100
Somebody
one, 87
man, 373
celebrity, 873
Somehow
manner, 155
Somersault
inversion, 218
Somerset
inversion, 218
Something
thing, 3
small degree, 32
Sometimes
frequency, 136
Somewhat
small, 32
Somewhere

place, 182
Somnambulism
imagination, 515
Somniferous
sleepy, 683
weary, 841
Somnolence
sleepy, 683
weary, 841
Son
relation, 167
Sonance
sound, 402
Sonata
music, 415
Song
music, 415
Song, old
unimportant, 643
Songster
musician, 416
Soniferous
sound, 402
Sonnet
poetry, 597
Sonorous
sound, 402
loud, 404
Sonsy
fat, 102
Soon
early, 132
transient, 111
Soot
black, 431
dirt, 653
blemish, 846
Sooth
truth, 494
Soothe
allay, 174
calm, 826
relieve, 834
Soothsay
predict, 511
Soothsayer
omen, 513
magician, 994
Sop
bribe, 615
reward, 973
wet, 337
Sophism
bad logic, 477
absurdity, 497

Sophisticate
  mix, 41
  mislead, 477
  debase, 659
Sophistry
  false reasoning, 477
  misteaching, 538
Sophomore
  learner, 541
Sophy
  ruler, 745
Soporific
  sleepy, 683
  boring, 841
Sopping
  moist, 339
Soprano
  music, 413
  high note, 409, 410
Sorcerer
  sorcerer, 994
Sorcery
  occult arts, 992
Sordes
  uncleanness, 653
Sordid
  mean, 819
  base, 876
Sordine
  silencer, 417
  damper, 403
Sore
  pain, 378
  grievance, 828
  painful, 830
  angry, 900
Sorehead
  discourtesy, 895
Sorely
  greatness, 31
Sorites
  reasoning, 476
Sororicide
  killing, 361
Sorrel
  redness, 434
Sorrow
  pain, 828
Sorry
  grieved, 828
  penitent, 950
  pitiful, 914
  bad, 649
  mean, 876
  trifling, 643

  smallness, 32
Sort
  kind, 75
  degree, 26
  rectify, 658, 660
  to arrange, 60
  simplify, 42
Sortes
  chance, 156, 621
  prediction, 511
Sortie
  attack, 716
Sortilege
  sorcery, 992
  prediction, 511
  chance, 621
Sorting
  arrangement, 60
Sostenuto
  music, 415
Sot
  fool, 501
  drunkard, 959
Sotto voce
  faintness, 405
  aphony, 581
  stammering, 583
Sou
  money, 800
Soubrette
  actress, 599
  servant, 746
Sough
  conduit, 350
  cloaca, 653
  wind, 349
Soul
  intrinsic, 5
  intellect, 450
  affections, 820
  man, 373
  important part, 50, 642
Soulful
  feeling, 821
Soulless
  insensible, 823
Sound
  noise, 402
  healthy, 654
  perfect, 650
  good, 648
  great, 31
  to measure, 466
  to investigate, 461
  true, 494

  wise, 498
  orthodox, 983A
  bay, 343
  gap, 198
Sounder
  herd, 72
Sounding-rod
  depth, 208
Soundings
  deep, 208
Soundless
  deep, 208
  silent, 403
Soundly
  great, 31
Soup
  food, 298
  pulp, 354
Soup-and-fish
  dress, 225
Soupçon
  little, 32, 193
  mixture, 41
Sour
  acid, 397
  uncivil, 895
  misanthropic, 901
  to embitter, 835
Source
  origin, 66, 153
Sourdine
  silencer, 417
Souse
  immerse, 300
  water, 337
Soutane
  canonicals, 999
Souteneur
  libertine, 962
South
  opposite, 237
Souvenir
  memory, 505
Sou'wester
  dress, 225
Sovereign
  great, 31
  superiority, 33
  strong, 157
  ruler, 745
Sovereignty
  authority, 737
Soviet
  council, 696

Sow
  scatter, 73
  cultivate, 371
  prepare, 673
Sozzled
  drunk, 959
Spa
  salubrity, 656
  remedy, 662
Space
  room, 180
  separate, 44
Space ship
  aircraft, 273A
Space travel
  voyage, 267
Spacious
  roomy, 180
Spade
  sharpness, 253
Spaewife
  oracle, 513
Spahi
  combatant, 726
Spalpeen
  bad man, 949
Span
  distance, 196
  nearness, 197
  length, 200
  measure, 466
  time, 106
  duality, 89
Spandule
  demon, 980
Spangle
  spark, 420
  ornament, 847
Spaniel
  servile, 886
  flatterer, 935
Spank
  impact, 276
  beat, 972
Spanking
  size, 192
Spar
  discord, 713
  contention, 720, 722
Spare
  meagre, 203
  scanty, 640
  to give, 784
  relinquish, 782
  disuse, 678

  exempt, 927A
  refrain, 623
  pity, 914
  frugal, 953
  economic, 817
Spare
  superfluous, 641
  in reserve, 636
Spare time
  leisure, 685
Sparge
  sprinkle, 73
Sparing
  temperate, 953
  small, 32
  economic, 817
Spark
  light, 420
  fire, 382
  fop, 854
  court, 902
Sparkle
  glisten, 420
  bubble, 353
Sparkling
  vigorous, 574
Sparse
  scattered, 73
  tenuous, 322
  few, 103
Sparsim
  non-assemblage, 73
Spartan
  severe, 739
Spasm
  fit, 173
  throe, 146
  pain, 378, 828
Spasmodic
  fitful, 139
Spat
  quarrel, 713
Spatial
  space, 99
Spatter
  dirt, 653
  damage, 659
Spatterdash
  dress, 225
Spatula
  layer, 204
  trowel, 191
Spawn
  dirt, 653
  offspring, 167

Spray
  sterilize, 169
Speak
  speech, 582
Speak fair
  conciliate, 615
Speak of
  mean, 516
Speak to
  allocution, 586
Speak out
  disclose, 529
Speaker
  speech, 582
  teacher, 540
  interpreter, 524
  president, 745
Spear
  lance, 727
  to pierce, 260
  pass through, 302
Spearman
  combatant, 726
Special
  particular, 79
  peculiar, 5
Special pleading
  sophistry, 477
Specialist
  adviser, 695
  doctor, 662
  proficient, 700
Speciality
  intrinsic, 5
  particular, 79
Specie
  money, 800
Species
  kind, 75
  appearance, 448
Specific
  special, 79
Specification
  description, 594
Specify
  name, 564
  tell, 527
Specimen
  example, 82
Specious
  probable, 472
  sophistical, 477
  plausible, 937
Speck
  dot, 193

small quantity, 32
blemish, 848
Speckle
variegated, 400
blemish, 848
Spectacle
appearance, 448
show, 882
prodigy, 872
Spectacles
optical instrument, 445
Spectator
spectator, 444
Spectre
vision, 448
ugly, 846
ghost, 980
Spectroscope
optical, 445
colour, 428
Spectrum
colour, 428
appearance, 448
Speculate
think, 451
suppose, 514
chance, 621
venture, 675
traffic, 794
view, 441
Speculum
mirror, 445
Speech
speech, 582
Speechless
silence, 581
Speed
velocity, 274
activity, 682
haste, 684
to help, 707
succeed, 731
Speedometer
velocity, 274
measure, 466
Speedwalk
way, 627
Speer
ask, 461
Spell
interpret, 522
read, 539
period, 106
charm, 993
necessity, 601

motive, 615
exertion, 686
Spellbound
motive, 615
Spelling
letters, 561
Spencer
dress, 225
Spencerism
causation, 153
Spend
expend, 809
waste, 638
Spendthrift
prodigal, 818
Spent
exhausted, 688
Spermaceti
oil, 356
Spew
ejection, 297
Sphere
ball, 249
region, 181
world, 318
rank, 26
business, 625
Spheroid
round, 249
Spherule
round, 249
Sphinx
oracle, 513
monster, 83
Spice
small quantity, 32
mixture, 41
pungent, 392
condiment, 393
Spick and span
clean, 123
Spicule
sharp, 253
Spidery
narrowness, 203
Spiflicate
trounce, 972
Spike
to pierce, 260
plug, 263
pass through, 302
sharp, 253
Spile
stopper, 263
Spill

filament, 205
fuel, 388
to shed, 297
waste, 638
splash, 348
disclose, 529
lavish, 818
misuse, 679
fall, 306
Spin
rotation, 312
excursion, 266
velocity, 274
reject, 610
Spin out
prolong, 200
protract, 110, 133
style, 573
Spindle
rotation, 312
Spindle-shanked
thin, 193, 203
Spindrift
spray, 353
Spine
sharpness, 253
Spineless
vicious, 945
weak, 160
irresolute, 605
Spinet
musical instrument, 417
Spinney
plant, 367
Spinster
celibacy, 904
Spiracle
air-pipe, 351
Spiral
convolution, 248
Spire
peak, 253
height, 206
soar, 305
Spirit
essence, 5
immateriality, 317
intellect, 450
affections, 820
resolutions, 604
courage, 861
ghost, 980
style, 576
activity, 682
to stimulate, 824

Spirit-level
  horizontal, 213
Spirited
  brave, 861
  generous, 942
Spiritless
  torpid, 823
  dejected, 837
  timid, 862
Spirits
  cheerfulness, 836
  intoxicant, 959
Spiritual
  immaterial, 317
  mental, 450
  divine, 976
  piety, 987
Spiritualism
  occult arts, 992
Spirituel
  witty, 842
Spirituoso
  music, 415
Spirt
  see Spurt
Spissitude
  density, 321, 352
Spit
  eject, 297
  pierce, 302
  rain, 348
  bar, 253
Spite
  malevolence, 907
  enmity, 889
  notwithstanding, 179
Spitfire
  fury, 173, 901
Spittle
  excretion, 299
Spittoon
  receptacle, 191
Spiv
  knave, 941
  bad man, 949
  cheat, 548
  swindler, 792
Splanchnic
  interior, 221
Splash
  affuse, 337
  spill, 348
  spatter, 653
  sully, 846
  parade, 882

publicity, 531
Splatter
  wet, 337
Splay
  angularity, 244
Splay-footed
  distorted, 243
Spleen
  melancholy, 837
  hatred, 898
  anger, 900
  discourteous, 895
Spleenless
  good-natured, 906
Splendid
  beautiful, 845
  glorious, 873
  excellent, 648
Splendour
  light, 420
Splenetic
  sad, 837
  ill-tempered, 895
  irascible, 901
Splice
  join, 43
  entwine, 219
  marry, 903
Splinter
  divide, 44
  brittle, 328
  bit, 51, 205
Split
  divide, 44, 91
  quarrel, 713
  fail, 732
  laugh, 838
Split hairs
  argue, 465
  sophistry, 477
Split-new
  new, 123
Splosh
  money, 800
Splurge
  ostentation, 882
Splutter
  stammer, 583
  haste, 684
  energy, 171
  spitting, 297
Spoil
  vitiate, 659
  hinder, 706
  plunder, 791

booty, 793
  injure, 649
  indulge, 740
  satiate, 869
Spoke
  tooth, 253
  radius, 200
  obstruct, 706
Spokesman
  interpreter, 524
  speaker, 582
Spoliate
  plunder, 791
  evil, 619
Spondulicks
  money, 800
Sponge
  clean, 652
  despoil, 791
  porous, 322
  oblivion, 506
  petitioner, 767
  parasite, 886
Spongy
  soft, 324
Sponsion
  security, 771
Sponson
  support, 215
Sponsor
  security, 771
  evidence, 467
Spontaneous
  voluntary, 600, 602
  free, 748
  impulsive, 612
Spoof
  deception, 545
Spook
  ghost, 980
Spoon
  receptacle, 191
  ladle, 272
  club, 276
  to make love, 902
Spoonerism
  blunder, 495
  inversion, 218
  ridiculousness, 853, 856
Spoonful
  quantity, 25
Spoony
  fool, 499
  amorous, 897

689

Spoor
track, 551
Spore
particle, 330
Sporran
pouch, 191
Sport
amusement, 840
gaiety, 836
wit, 842
enjoyment, 827
contention, 720
subjection, 749
abnormality, 83
Sports car
vehicle, 272
Sportsman
courage, 861
game, 840
good man, 948
Spot
place, 182
decoloration, 429
blemish, 848
to sully, 846
blot, 874
disgrace, 940
to detect, 457, 480A
Spotless
innocent, 946
clean, 652
good, 648, 650
fair, 845
Spotty
spotted, 440
Spousals
marriage, 903
Spouse
married, 903
companion, 88
Spouseless
celibacy, 904
Spout
conduit, 350
egress, 295
flow out, 348
speak, 582
act, 599
Sprain
strain, 160
Sprawl
lie, 213
leap, 309
Spray
sprig, 51
plant, 367

cover, 222
sprinkle, 337
sprinkler, 348
Spread
enlarge, 35
expand, 194
disperse, 73
diverge, 291
expanse, 180
publish, 531
Spread-eagleism
boasting, 884
bombast, 577
Spree
frolic, 840
intemperance, 954
Sprig
part, 51
scion, 167
Sprightly
cheerful, 836
witty, 842
Spring
early, 125
cause, 153
arise from, 154
ensue, 151
strength, 159
velocity, 274
leap, 309
rivulet, 348
instrument, 633
store, 636
Spring back
elastic, 325
recoil, 277
Spring tide
flow, 348
abundance, 639
Spring up
grow, 194
Springe
snare, 667
deception, 545
Sprinkle
mix, 41
disperse, 73, 291
omit, 297
wet, 337
Sprinkler
spray, 348
Sprinkling
smallness, 32
little, 193
Sprint

velocity, 274
Sprite
ghost, 890
Sprocket
tooth, 257
Sprog
recruit, 674
Sprout
grow, 35
expand, 194
arise from, 154
offspring, 167
Spruce
neat, 652
beautiful, 845
Spry
active, 682
healthy, 654
clever, 698
cheerful, 836
Spume
foam, 353
Spunk
courage, 861
Spur
sharp, 253
incite, 615
ridge, 250
Spurious
false, 544
erroneous, 495
illegitimate, 925
Spurn
disdain, 866, 930
refuse, 764
Spurt
impulse, 612
haste, 684
swift, 274
gush, 348
Sputnik
space ship, 273A
Sputter
emit, 297
stammer, 583
Spy
see, 441
spectator, 444
emissary, 534
Spy-glass
optical instrument, 445
Squab
large, 192
short, 201
broad, 202

690

recumbent, 215
Squabble
 quarrel, 713
Squabby
 broad, 202
 short, 201
Squad
 assembly, 72
Squadron
 navy, 726
 army, 273
 assemblage, 72
Squadron-leader
 master, 745
Squalid
 dirty, 653
 unattractive, 846
Squall
 cry, 411
 win, 349
 violence, 173
Squalor
 see Squalid
Squamous
 scaly, 204
 covering, 222
Squander
 waste, 638, 818
Squandermania
 waste, 818
Square
 number, 95
 buildings, 189
 congruity, 23
 expedience, 646
 justice, 924
 honour, 939
 form, 244
 prig, 855
 to equalize, 27
 to bribe, 784, 795
Square-toes
 butt, 857
Squash
 destroy, 162
 check, 706
 throw, 276
 soft, 324
 water, 337
Squashy
 pulpy, 352
Squat
 to encamp, 186
 sit, 308
 short, 201

broad, 202
flat, 213
ugly, 846
Squatter
 inhabitant, 188
Squatting
 horizontal, 213
Squaw
 marriage, 903
Squawk
 cry, 411, 412
 complain, 839
Squeak
 cry, 411, 412
 complain, 839
Squeal
 cry, 410, 411, 412
 blab, 529
 complain, 839
Squeamish
 fastidious, 868
 censorious, 932
Squeeze
 contract, 195
 narrow, 203
 condense, 321
 extort, 789
 copy, 21
Squeeze out
 extraction, 301
Squelch
 squash, 162
Squib
 sound, 406
 lampoon, 932
Squiffy
 drunk, 959
Squiggle
 convolution, 248
Squint
 dim-sighted, 443
 look, 441
Squire
 gentry, 875
 possessor, 779
 attendant, 746
Squirm
 wriggle, 315
Squirrel
 velocity, 274
Squirt
 eject, 297
 spurt, 348
Stab
 pierce, 260

attack, 716
kill, 361
injure, 649, 659
Stable
 house, 189
 at rest, 265
 immutable, 150
 resolute, 604
Stable-boy
 servant, 746
Staccato
 music, 415
Stack
 assembly, 72
Stadtholder
 master, 745
Staff
 support, 215
 instrument, 633
 weapon, 727
 impact, 276
 sceptre, 747
 retinue, 746
 party, 712
 hope, 858
Stage
 degree, 26
 term, 71
 step, 58
 layer, 204
 forum, 542
 vehicle, 272
 arena, 728
 drama, 599
Stage effect
 drama, 599
 ostentation, 882
Stage-play
 the drama, 599
Stager, old
 proficient, 700
Stagger
 totter, 314
 slow, 275
 agitate, 315
 doubt, 485
 dissuade, 616
 affect, 824
 astonish, 508, 870
Stagnant
 quiescent, 265
 unchanging, 141
 insert, 172
 inactive, 683

Stagy
  affected, 855
  ostentatious, 882
Staid
  steady, 604
  calm, 826
  wise, 498
  grave, 837
Stain
  colour, 428
  adorn, 847
  deface, 846
  blemish, 848
  spoil, 659
  disgrace, 874
  dishonour, 940
Stainless
  clean, 652
  innocent, 946
Stair
  way, 627
Stake
  wager, 621
  payment, 807
  danger, 665
  security, 771
  property, 780
  execution, 975
Stalactite
  lining, 224
Stalagmite
  lining, 224
Stale
  old, 124
  vapid, 866
  weary, 841
Stalemate
  non-completion, 730
Stalk
  follow, 266
  pursue, 622
Stalking-horse
  plea, 617
  deception, 545
Stall
  lodge, 189
  mart, 799
  theatre, 599
  cathedral, 1000
  delay, 133
Stallion
  horse, 271
Stalwart
  strong, 159
  large, 192
Stamina

strength, 159
  resolution, 604
Stammel
  redness, 434
Stammer
  stutter, 583
Stamp
  character, 7
  form, 240
  mould, 22
  to impress, 505
  mark, 550
  record, 551
  complete, 729
  security, 771
Stampede
  flight, 287
  fear, 860, 862
Stance
  footing, 175
Stanch
  dam up, 348
  stop, 658
Stanchion
  support, 215
Stand
  to be, 1
  rest, 265
  be present, 186
  to continue, 141, 143
  endure, 110
  station, 58
  rank, 71
  support, 215
  resistance, 719
Stand against
  resist, 719
Stand by
  near, 197
  be firm, 604
  befriend, 707
  auxiliary, 711
Stand for
  represent, 550
  signify, 516
Stand-in
  substitute, 147, 634
  deputy, 759
  assistant, 711
Stand in with
  participation, 778
Stand off
  distance, 196, 287
Stand-offish
  unsociable, 893

Stand on
  support, 215
Stand out
  project, 250
  appear, 446
  opposition, 708
Stand still
  stop, 265
  remain, 141
Stand over
  lateness, 133
Stand up
  vertical, 212
  elevation, 307
  disappoint, 509
Stand up for
  vindicate, 937
Stand up to
  courage, 861
Standard
  rule, 80
  measure, 466
  degree, 26
  pupil, 541
  colours, 550
  good, 648
  prototype, 22
Standard-bearer
  combatant, 726
Standardize
  conformity, 82
Standing
  footing, 8
  term, 71
  situation, 183
  degree, 26
  repute, 873
  vertical, 212
Standpoint
  aspect, 453
Stanza
  poetry, 597
Staple
  whole, 50
  peg, 214
  mart, 799
Star
  luminary, 423
  decoration, 877
  ornament, 847
  glory, 873
  actor, 599, 599A
Star Chamber
  jurisprudence, 966
Star-gazer

astronomer, 318
Starbeam
light, 420
dimness, 422
Starbord
dextrality, 238
Starch
viscidity, 352
Starchy
stiff, 323
proud, 878
affected, 855
Stare
look, 441
curiosity, 455
wonder, 870
Staring
visible, 446
Stark
stiff, 323
stubborn, 606
Starless
dark, 421
Starlight
light, 420
dimness, 422
Stars
celestial, 318
necessity, 601
Stars and Stripes
flag, 550
Start
depart, 293
begin, 66
desultory, 139
jump, 139
arise, 151
suggest, 514
from surprise, 508
from fear, 860
from wonder, 870
Start up
project, 250
appear, 446
Starting-point
beginning, 66
departure, 293
Startle
unexpected, 508
wonder, 870
fear, 860
doubt, 485
Starve
fast, 956
with cold, 383, 385

want, 804
Starved
lean, 193
insufficient, 640
Starveling
pinched, 203
poor, 804
famished, 540
State
condition, 7
nation, 372
ostentation, 882
property, 780
to inform, 527
assert, 535
describe, 594
State trooper
police, 965
Stateless
displaced, 185
Stately
pompous, 882
proud, 878, 873
Statement
information, 527
assertion, 535
Stateroom
chamber, 191
Statesman
master, 745
Statesmanship
direction, 694
Statics
gravity, 319
Station
stage, 58
term, 71
place, 182, 183
to locate, 184
stopping-place, 292
rank, 26, 873
Stationary
quiecence, 265
Stationery
writing, 590
Statist
statesman, 745
Statistics
numeration, 85
list, 86
Statue
sculpture, 557
representation, 554
Stature
height, 206

Status
standing, 8, 71
situation, 183
order, 58
rank, 873
Status quo
reversion, 145
Statute
law, 697, 963
Staunch
spirited, 604
trusty, 939
healthy, 654
Stave
verse, 597
Stave in
open, 260
concavity, 252
Stave off
defer, 133
Stay
wait, 133
continue, 141
exist, 1
support, 215
refuge, 666
rest, 265;
prevent, 706
dissuade, 616
corset, 225
Stead
utility, 644
Steadfast
resolved, 604
stable, 150
quiescent, 265
thought, 451
Steading
farm, 189
Steady
resolved, 604
cautious, 864
still, 265
constant, 138, 150
normal, 82
Steady as she goes
caution, 864
Steal
rob, 791
creep, 275, 528
Steal away
evade, 671
Stealth
concealment, 528

Steam
vapour, 334, 353
to sail, 267
Steamboat
ship, 273
Steamer
ship, 273
Steam-roller
compel, 744
Stearic
unctuous, 355
Stearin
fat, 356
Steed
horse, 271
Steek
close, 261
Steel
strength, 159
sharpener, 253
inure, 823
Steel-cut
engraving, 558
Steeled
resolved, 604
Steelyard
scale, 466
weight, 319
Steep
slope, 217
height, 206
immerse, 300
soak, 337
clean, 652
Steeple
spire, 253
high, 206
Steeplechase
race, 274
pursuit, 282, 622
Steer
guide, 693
Steer for
direction, 278
Steersman
director, 694
Steganography
writing, 590
Stegophilist
climber, 305
Stele
record, 551
Stellar
heavens, 318
Stem
origin, 153

result, 154
front, 234
to oppose, 708
to resist, 718
Sten
gun, 727
Stench
fetor, 401
Stencil
copy, 556
Stenographer
secretary, 553
Stenography
writing, 590
Stentorian
loud, 404
Step
degree, 26
station, 58
term, 71
near, 197
support, 215
motion, 264, 266
measure, 466
expedient, 626
means, 632
action, 680
Steppe
plain, 344
Stepping-stone
link, 45
way, 627
preparation, 763
resource, 666
Stercoraceous
unclean, 653
Stereoscope
optical, 445
Stereoscopic
visible, 446
Stereotype
printing, 591
engraving, 558
Stereotyped
ordinary, 82
habitual, 613
fixed, 141, 150
Sterile
unproductive, 169
useless, 645
clean, 652
Sterling
true, 494
good, 648
virtuous, 944

money, 800
Stern
back, 235
severe, 739
forbidding, 895
Stern-wheeler
ship, 273
Sternutation
sneeze, 349
sound, 409
Sternway
navigation, 267
Stertorous
sound, 411
Stet
unchanged, 150
Stetson
hat, 225
Stevedore
doer, 271, 690
Stew
confusion, 59
fluster, 821
difficulty, 704
heat, 382
cook, 384
perplex, 828
bagnio, 961
Steward
director, 694
agent, 690
treasurer, 801
Stewardship
charge, 693
conduct, 692
Stick
adhere, 46
stop, 142
continue, 143
staff, 215
to stab, 260, 830
pierce, 302
difficulty, 704
fool, 501
scourge, 975
Stick at
demur, 603
Stick in
insert, 300
locate, 184
Stick-in-the-mud
inactivity, 683
Stick out
project, 250
erect, 212

Stick up
project, 250
erect, 212, 307
rob, 791
Stickit
failure, 732
Stickle
haggle, 769
barter, 794
reluctant, 603
Stickler
obstinacy, 606
severity, 739
Sticky
cohering, 46
semiliquid, 352
Stiff
rigid, 323
resolute, 604
difficult, 704
restrained, 751
severe, 739
dear, 814
affected, 855
haughty, 878
pompous, 882
ugly, 846
style, 572, 579
Stiff-necked
obstinate, 606
resolute, 604
Stifle
silence, 403
conceal, 528
destroy, 162
kill, 361
sound, 405
Stigma
disgrace, 874
blame, 932
Stigmatize
accuse, 938
Stile
way, 627
Stiletto
piercer, 262
dagger, 727
Still
ever, 112
silent, 403
quiet, 174
quiescence, 265
photograph, 556
calm, 826
notwithstanding, 179

compensation, 30
vaporizer, 336
Still-born
failure, 732
dead, 360
Stilted
bombastic, 577
affected, 855
Stilts
support, 215
height, 206
journey, 266
boasting, 884
Stimulate
incite, 615
violence, 173
energize, 171
passion, 824
Stimulus
zest, 615
Sting
pain, 378
sensation, 380
pungent, 392
suffering, 824, 830
provoke, 900
Stingy
mean, 817
Stink
stench, 401
Stinkard
stink, 401
Stinking
bad, 649
Stinko
drunk, 959
Stint
degree, 26
limit, 233
scanty, 640
parsimony, 819
Stipend
salary, 809
Stipendiary
receiving, 785
subjected, 749
magistrate, 967
Stipple
engraving, 558
variegation, 440
Stipulate
conditions, 770
bargain, 769
Stir
move, 264

agitation, 315
activity, 682
energy, 171
emotion, 824
discuss, 476
prison, 752
Stir up
mix, 41
excite, 615
violence, 173
Stirrup-cup
departure, 293
intoxicant, 959
Stitch
work, 680
to join, 43
pain, 828
Stiver
money, 800
Stock
cause, 153
store, 636
materials, 635
provision, 637
property, 780
money, 800
merchandise, 798
collar, 225
offspring, 166
relation, 11
quantity, 25
habitual, 613
Stock-still
immovable, 265
Stockade
defence, 717
Stocking
dress, 225
Stockpile
store, 636
provide, 637
Stocks
funds, 802
punishment, 975
restraint, 752
Stocky
short, 201
broad, 202
Stoic
insensible, 823
inexcitable, 826
disinterested, 942
Stole
dress, 225

Stolid
dull, 843
stupid, 499
Stomach
pouch, 191
taste, 390
liking, 865
Stomacher
dress, 225
Stone
dense, 321
hard, 323
materials, 635
missile, 284
weapon, 727
kill, 361
Stone-blind
blind, 442
Stone-coloured
grey, 432
Stone-wall
hinder, 706
Stonk
bombardment, 716
Stony broke
poor, 804
Stony-hearted
cruel, 900
Stooge
substitute, 147
assistant, 711
deputy, 759
loaf, 683
Stook
assemblage, 76
Stool
support, 215
Stool-pigeon
deceiver, 548
informer, 527, 529
Stoop
bow, 308
slope, 217
humble, 879
servile, 886
porch, 191
Stoor
see Stour
Stop
close, 67, 261
halt, 265
lodge, 186
prevent, 706
silence, 403
continue, 141
discontinue, 142

Stopcock
stopper, 263
Stopgap
shift, 626
substitute, 634
Stopgap
deputy, 759
plug, 263
Stopper
stopper, 263
Store
magazine, 636
provision, 637
shop, 799
the memory, 595
greatness, 31
Storehouse
store, 636
Storey
layer, 204
rooms, 191
Στοργή, love, 897
Storm
wind, 349
violence, 173
agitation, 315
passion, 825
convulsion, 146
anger, 900
to attack, 716
assemblage, 72
Storm-stayed
hindered, 706
restraint, 751
Story
narrative, 582, 594
news, 532
lie, 546
Stot
rebound, 277
Stound
wonder, 870
Stour
dust, 330
dirt, 653
Stout
strong, 159
lusty, 192
brave, 861
Stove
furnace, 386
Stow
locate, 184
desist, 142

Stow it
silent, 585
Stowage
space, 180
location, 184
Strabismus
dim sight, 443
Straddle
sit, 215
stride, 266
trim, 607
Stradivarius
violin, 417
Strafe
punish, 972
maltreat, 649
attack, 716
Straggle
stroll, 266
deviate, 279
disjunction, 44
disorder, 59
Straggler
rover, 268
Straight
rectilinear, 246
vertical, 212
direction, 278, 628
undiluted, 42
Straightforward
artless, 703
honest, 939
true, 543
style, 576
mid-course, 628
Straightway
time, 111
Strain
effort, 686
violence, 173
fatigue, 688
sound, 402
melody, 413
clean, 652
to clarify, 658
percolate, 295
transgress, 304
poetry, 597
voice, 580
misinterpret, 523
kindred, 11
style, 569
Strainer
sieve, 260

696

Strait
maritime, 343
gap, 198
difficulty, 704
want, 804
narrow, 203
Strait-laced
severe, 739
censorious, 932
haughty, 878
stiff, 751
fastidious, 868
Strait waistcoat
restraint, 752
Straitened
poor, 804
Stramash
agitation, 315
contention, 720
Strand
shore, 342
Stranded
difficulty, 704
fixed, 150
failure, 732
Strange
exceptional, 83
wonderful, 870
ridiculous, 853
Stranger
extraneous, 57
ignorant, 491
Strangle
choke, 361
Strap
to tie, 43
ligature, 45
scourge, 975
Strap-oil
punishment, 972
Strappado
punishment, 972
Strapping
large, 192
strong, 159
Stratagem
plan, 626
artifice, 702
deception, 545
Strategy
conduct, 692
skill, 698
warfare, 722
plan, 626
Strath

valley, 252
Strathspey
dance, 840
Stratification
layer, 204
Stratocracy
authority, 737
Stratocruiser
aircraft, 273A
Statoliner
aircraft, 273A
Stratosphere
air, 338
Stratum
layer, 204
Straw
light, 320
trifling, 643
Straw-coloured
yellow, 436
Straw vote
inquiry, 461
Stray
wander, 266
deviate, 279
exceptional, 83
Streak
colour, 420
stripe, 440
furrow, 259
narrow, 203
intersection, 219
Stream
flow, 347
river, 348
of light, 420
of time, 109
of events, 151
abundance, 639
Streamer
flag, 550
Streaming
incoherent, 47
Streamlet
river, 348
Street
buildings, 189
way, 627
Street arab
commonalty, 876
Street-car
vehicle, 272
Streetscape
spectacle, 448
Streetwalker

libertine, 962
Strength
vigour, 159
power, 157
greatness, 31
energy, 171
tenacity, 327
degree, 26
Strengthen
to increase, 35
Strenuous
active, 682, 686
resolved, 604
Strepitoso
music, 415
Stress
weight, 642
intonation, 580
strain, 686
Stretch
increase, 35
expand, 194
lengthen, 200
space, 180
distance, 196
exertion, 686
encroachment, 925
misinterpret, 523
exaggeration, 549
Stretcher
vehicle, 272
support, 215
Strew
spread, 73
Stria
spot, 440
furrow, 259
Striate
furrowed, 259
spotted, 440
Stricken
hurt, 828
Strict
severe, 739
exact, 494
Stricture
disapprobation, 932
Stride
walk, 266
motion, 264
Strident
harsh, 410
Stridulous
shrill, 410
Strife
quarrel, 713, 720

697

Strike
hit, 276
luck, 618
beat, 649, 972
revolt, 719, 742
inaction, 681
impress, 824
wonder, 870
operate, 170
music, 415
Strike off
exclude, 55
Strike out
invent, 515
plan, 626
efface, 552
Strike up
begin, 66
Striking
manifest, 525
String
continuity, 69
to tie, 43
fibre, 205
ligature, 45
to arrange, 60
String up
kill, 361
Stringendo
music, 415
Stringent
severe, 739
compulsory, 744
Stringy
narrow, 203
tough, 327
viscous, 352
Strip
to divest, 226
rob, 789, 791
narrowness, 203
filament, 205
Stripe
length, 200
blow, 972
mark, 550
type, 75
variegation, 440
Stripling
youth, 129
Stripped
poor, 804
Strive
exert, 686

endeavour, 675, 676
contend, 720
Stroke
impulse, 276
mark, 550
work, 680
expedient, 626
success, 731
disease, 655
Stroll
walk, 266
Strong
powerful, 159
energetic, 171
vigorous, 574
tenacious, 327
pungent, 390, 392
cogent, 467
feeling, 821
Strong-box
treasury, 802
Strong-room
treasury, 802
Strong-willed
resolute, 604
Stronghold
defence, 717
refuge, 666
prison, 752
Strongly
great, 31
Strop
sharpen, 253
rub, 331
Strophe
poetry, 597
Structure
state, 7
texture, 329
building, 189
Struggle
contend, 720
exert, 686
Strum
music, 415
Strumpet
libertine, 962
Strut
parade, 882
boast, 884
pride, 878
support, 215
Stub
part, 51
end, 67

check, 550
Stubble
remainder, 40
rough, 256
Stubborn
obstinate, 606
unmanageable, 704
Stubby
short, 201
broad, 202
ugly, 846
Stucco
cement, 45
covering, 222
Stuck fast
difficulty, 704
stopped, 265
Stuck-up
vanity, 880
Stud
knob, 250
hanging, 214
point, 253
horses, 271
Studded
spotted, 440
Student
learner, 541
scholar, 492
Studied
intentional, 620
Studio
workshop, 691
Studious
thoughtful, 451
docile, 539
Studiously
purposely, 600
Study
thought, 451
learning, 539
research, 461
privacy, 893
intention, 620
copy, 21
music, 415
Stuff
substance, 3, 329
matter, 316
materials, 632
absurdity, 497
trifle, 643
to feed, 296
to line, 224
cram, 104

hoax, 545
Stuffing
contents, 190
Stuffy
musty, 401
hot, 382
Stultified
failure, 732
Stultify
counteract, 708
muddle, 699
Stultiloquy
absurdity, 497
Stumble
fall, 306
fail, 732
unskilful, 699
flounder, 315
Stumble upon
ascertain, 480A
Stumbling-block
difficulty, 704
hindrance, 706
Stumer
money, 800
Stump
trunk, 51
remnant, 40
to step, 266
speech, 582
Stumped
penniless, 804
Stumpy
short, 201
ugly, 846
Stun
stupefy, 376, 823
affect, 824
deafen, 419
astonish, 508, 865
loud, 404
Stunning
beauty, 845
Stung
pain, 828
Stunt
feat, 680
task, 625
Stunted
small, 193
contracted, 195
Stupefy
stun, 376, 823
wonder, 870
Stupendous

great, 31
large, 192
wonderful, 870
Stupid
dull, 843
credulous, 486
foolish, 499
Stupor
lethargy, 823
insensibility, 376
Sturdy
strong, 157, 159
Stutter
stammer, 583
Sty
dirt, 653
pen, 189
Stygian
infernal, 982
dark, 421
diabolic, 945
Style
state, 7
time, 114
fashion, 852
taste, 850
beauty, 845
to name, 564
diction, 569
pencil, 559
Stylet
arms, 727
Stylish
fashionable, 852
Stylist
style, 569
Stylite
recluse, 893
Stylograph
writing, 590
Stymie
to hinder, 706
Styptic
remedy, 662
contracting, 195
Suasion
persuade, 615
Suavity
courtesy, 894
Sub
loan, 787
advance, 809
Sub judice
inquiry, 461
Subacid

acid, 397
Subahdar
master, 745
Subalpine
height, 206
Subaltern
plebeian, 876
inferior, 24
officer, 726, 745
Subaqueous
depth, 208
Subastral
terrestrial, 318
Subcommittee
committee, 696
Subconsciousness
intellect, 450
Subcontrary
antiposition, 237
Subcutaneous
interiority, 221
Subdeacon
church, 996
Subdean
church, 996
Subdititious
substitution, 147
Sublimation
see Sublimate
Sublime
high, 206
beauty, 845
glory, 873
lofty, 574
magnanimous, 942
Subliminal
subconscious, 450
Sublunary
world, 318
Submachine-gun
arms, 727
Submarine
depth, 208
ship, 273
Submerge
immerse, 300
steep, 337
sink, 162, 208
plunge, 310
Submission
surrender, 725, 879
Submissive
humble, 725, 879
enduring, 826

Submit
 surrender, 725
 obey, 743
Subordinate
 inferior, 34
 unimportant, 643
 servant, 746
 subjection, 749
Subordination
 order, 58
Suborn
 hire, 795
 bribe, 784
Subpoena
 mandate, 741
Subscribe
 assent, 488
 agree to, 762, 769
 give, 707, 784
Subscription
 donation, 809
Subsequent
 in time, 117
 in order, 63, 65
Subservient
 utility, 644
 intermediate, 631
 aiding, 707
 servility, 886
Subside
 sink, 306
 cave in, 252
 decrease, 36
 calm down, 826
Subsidiary
 tending, 176
 means, 632
 auxiliary, 707
Subsidy
 pay, 809
 gift, 784
 aid, 707
Subsist
 existence, 1
 life, 359
 continuance, 141
Subsistence
 food, 298
 livelihood, 803
Subsistence money
 loan, 787
 advance, 809
Subsoil
 earth, 342
 interior, 221
Substance

thing, 3
 matter, 316
 interior, 221
 quantity, 25
 texture, 329
 compendium, 596
 meaning, 516
 important, 642
 wealth, 803
Substantial
 dense, 321
 existence, 1
 true, 494
Substantially
 intrinsically, 5
Substantiate
 demonstrate, 478
 make good, 494, 924
Substantive
 substance, 3
Substitute
 means, 634
 deputy, 759
Substitution
 change, 147
Substratum
 substance, 3
 interior, 221
 layer, 204
 base, 211
 support, 215
 materiality, 316
Subsumption
 inclusion, 76
Subterfuge
 lie, 546
 sophistry, 477
 cunning, 702
Subterranean
 underground, 208
Subtilize
 sophistry, 477
Subtle
 cunning, 702
 wise, 498
 rare, 322
 light, 320
 texture, 329
Subtract
 retrench, 38
 diminish, 36
 arithmetical, 84
 to take, 789
Subtrahend
 deduction, 38

number, 84
Suburban
 environs, 227
 distance, 197
Subvention
 aid, 707
 gift, 784
Subvert
 invert, 218
 depress, 308
 change, 140
 destroy, 162
Subway
 road, 627
Succedaneum
 substitute, 147, 634
Succeed
 answer, 731
 follow, 63
Succès d'estime
 approbation, 931
Success
 success, 731
Succession
 sequence, 63
 transfer, 783
 continuity, 69
 of time, 109
 lateness, 117
Successor
 sequel, 65
 posterior, 117
Succinct
 concise, 572
Succour
 help, 707
Succubus
 demon, 980
Succulent
 juicy, 333
 edible, 298
 semiliquid, 352
Succumb
 yield, 725
 obey, 743
 fatigue, 688
Such
 similarity, 17
Suck
 imbibe, 296
 deprive, 789
Sucker
 dupe, 547
Suckling
 youth, 129

Suction
imbibition, 296
Sudatorium
furnace, 386
Sudden
early, 132
abrupt, 508
transient, 111
Suds
froth, 353
Sue
demand, 765
at law, 969
Suet
fat, 356
Suffer
physical pain, 378
moral pain, 828
to endure, 821
to allow, 760
disease, 655
experience, 151
Sufferance
permission, 760
Sufficient
enough, 639
Suffix
sequel, 65
adjunct, 39
Sufflation
wind, 349
Suffocate
choke, 361
Suffragan
church, 996
Suffrage
vote, 609
prayer, 990
Suffragist
dueness, 924
Suffuse
mix, 41
feel, 821
blush, 874
Sufism
religions, 984
Sugar
sweet, 396
to flatter, 933
Sugarloaf
convexity, 250
Suggest
suppose, 514
advise, 695
inform, 527

recall, 505
occur, 451
Suggestio falsi
equivocalness, 520
falsehood, 544
Suggestion
plan, 626
Suggestive
impure, 961
Sui generis
special, 79
unconformity, 83
Sui juris
freedom, 748
Suicide
kill, 361
Suit
accord, 23
class, 75
expedient, 646
series, 69
clothes, 225
courtship, 902
at law, 969
Suit-case
receptacle, 191
Suite
series, 69
adjunct, 39
sequel, 65
retinue, 746
Suiting
accord, 23
Suitor
love, 897
Sulcated
furrow, 259
Sulky
discourteous, 895
bad-tempered, 901
gloomy, 837
Sullen
discourteous, 895
bad-tempered, 901
gloomy, 837
misanthropical, 911
Sully
deface, 846
dirty, 653
dishonour, 874, 940
Sulphur
colour, 436
Sultan
master, 745
noble, 875

Sultry
heat, 382
Sum
total, 50
number, 84
to reckon, 85
money, 800
Sum up
description, 594
Sumless
infinity, 105
Summary
transient, 111
early, 132
concise, 572
compendium, 201, 596
Summation
numeration, 85
Summer
heat, 382
support, 215
Summer-house
abode, 189
Summit
top, 210
climax, 33
Summon
command, 741
accuse, 938
Summon up
evoke, 824
Sump
marsh, 345
sink, 653
Sumptuary
expenditure, 800, 809
Sumptuous
ostentation, 882
Sun
luminary, 423
Sun-bonnet
dress, 225
Sun-up
morning, 125
Sunbeam
light, 420
Sundae
food, 298
Sunday
rest, 685
Sunder
disjoin, 44
Sundown
evening, 126

Sundowner
tramp, 268, 876
loafer, 683
Sundries
oddments, 51
Sundry
multitude, 102
Sunk
low, 208
vice, 945
Sunless
dark, 421
Sunlight
light, 420
cheerful, 836
pleasing, 827
prosperous, 734
Sunny
see Sunlight
Sunshade
shade, 424
Sunshine
see Sunlight
Sup
eat, 296
drink, 298
Super
good, 648
Superable
facility, 705
Superabundant
sufficient, 641
Superadd
addition, 37
increase, 35
Superannuated
age, 128
Superannuation
pension, 803
Superb
proud, 845
Supercargo
overload, 694
Supercherie
deception, 545
Supercilious
haughty, 878
insolent, 885
contemptuous, 929
Superdreadnought
ship, 273
Supereminence
repute, 873
Supererogation
uselessness, 645
superfluity, 641

activity, 682
Superexalted
repute, 873
Superexcellent
goodness, 648
Superfetation
addition, 37
Superficial
shallow, 209, 220
ignorant, 491
Superficies
face, 220
Superfine
best, 648
Superfluity
excess, 641
remainder, 40
Superfortress
aircraft, 273A
Superhuman
divine, 976
perfect, 650
great, 31
Superimpose
cover, 220
Superincumbent
above, 206
weight, 319
resting, 215
Superinduce
production, 161
change, 140
addition, 37
Superintend
direction, 693
Superintendent
director, 694
Superior
greater, 33
important, 642
good, 648
Superlative
perfect, 650
great, 31
Superman
hero, 948
Supernal
lofty, 206
Supernatant
overlying, 206
Supernatural
deity, 976
spiritual, 317
Supernumerary
redundant, 641

remaining, 40
actor, 599
Superpose
addition, 37
cover, 222
Superscription
mark, 550
writing, 590
evidence, 467
Supersede
disuse, 678
substitute, 147
Superstition
credulity, 486
heresy, 984A
Superstratum
exteriority, 220
Superstructure
completion, 729
Supertax
tax, 812
Supervacaneous
useless, 645
redundant, 641
Supervene
happen, 151
succeed, 117
addition, 37
Supervise
direction, 693
Supervisor
director, 694
Supine
horizontal, 213
inverted, 218
inert, 172
sluggish, 683
torpid, 823
indifferent, 866
Supper
food, 298
Supplant
substitution, 147
Supple
soft, 324
servile, 886
Supplement
adjunct, 39
completion, 52
addition, 37
Suppletory
addition, 37
Suppliant
petitioner, 767
Supplicant

petitioner, 767
Supplicate
beg, 765
pity, 914
worship, 990
Supplies
materials, 635
aid, 707
Supply
give, 784
provide, 637
store, 636
Support
sustain, 215
operate, 170
evidence, 467
aid, 707
preserve, 670
endure, 821, 826
Supporter
prop, 215
Suppose
supposition, 514
Supposing
provided, 469
Supposition
supposition, 514
Supposititious
false, 544, 925
non-existing, 2
Suppository
remedy, 662
Suppress
conceal, 528
silence, 581
destroy, 162
Suppurate
fester, 653
Supra
priority, 116
Supranatural
spiritual, 317
Supremacy
superior, 33
authority, 737
summit, 210
Supremely
great, 31
Surcease
cessation, 142
Surcharge
redundance, 641
dearness, 814
Surcingle
fastening, 45

Surd
number, 84
Sure
certain, 474
assent, 488
consent, 762
safe, 664
Sure-footed
careful, 459
skilful, 698
Surely
wonder, 870
Surety
security, 771
evidence, 467
Surf
foam, 353
tide, 458
Surf-riding
navigation, 267
Surface
exterior, 220
Surfeit
satiety, 869
redundance, 641
Surge
ocean, 341
rotation, 312
swell, 305
wave, 348
Surgery
remedy, 662
Surly
gruff, 895
unkind, 907
Surmise
supposition, 514
Surmount
rise, 305
tower, 206
overcome, 731
Surmountable
facility, 705
possible, 470
Surname
nomenclature, 564
Surpass
superior, 33
grow, 194
go beyond, 303
repute, 873
Surpassing
greatness, 31
Surplice
gown, 225

canonical, 999
Surplus
remainder, 40
store, 326
redundance, 641
Surprise
wonder, 870
non-expectation, 508
disappoint, 509
Surprisingly
great, 31
Surrealist
artist, 559
Surrebutter
lawsuit, 969
reply, 462
Surrejoinder
lawsuit, 969
reply, 462
Surrender
submit, 725
obey, 743
relinquish, 782
Surreptitious
false, 544
furtive, 528
Surrogate
consignee, 758
deputy, 634, 759
Surround
circumjacence, 227, 231
Surtout
dress, 225
Surveillance
care, 459
direction, 693
Survey
view, 441
measure, 466
Survive
remain, 40
continue, 141
endure, 110
Susceptible
liable, 177
impressible, 822
excitable, 901
Suscitate
cause, 153
produce, 161
induce, 615
excite, 825
stir up, 173
Suspect
doubt, 485

suppose, 514
Suspend
  hang, 214
  continue, 141
  discontinue, 142
  defer, 133
  stop, 265
Suspense
  doubt, 485
  uncertainty, 475
  expectancy, 507
  hesitation, 603
  irresolution, 605
Suspicion
  doubt, 485
  incredulity, 487
  uncertainty, 475
  fear, 860
  particle, 32, 193
  mixture, 41
Suspiration
  lamentation, 839
Sustain
  support, 215
  strengthen, 159
  aid, 707
  operate, 170
  preserve, 670
  continue, 143
Sustenance
  food, 298
Sustentation
  provision, 637
Susurration
  whisper, 405
Sutler
  trader, 797
  provision, 637
Suttee
  religion, 991
  burning, 384
  killing, 361
Suture
  joint, 43
Suzerainty
  authority, 737
Svelte
  lissom, 324
Swab
  cleanness, 562
  dry, 340
Swaddle
  dress, 225
Swag
  hang, 214

lean, 217
oscillation, 314
drop, 306
booty, 793
Swag-bellied
  wollen, 194
Swagger
  boast, 884
  bluster, 885
  smart, 845
Swaggerer
  blusterer, 887
Swagman
  tramp, 268
Swain
  rustic, 876
Swallow
  gulp, 296
  believe, 484
  destroy, 162
Swamp
  marsh, 345
  destroy, 162
Swamped
  failure, 732
Swan-song
  end, 67
  death, 360
Swank
  ostentation, 882
  boasting, 884
  pride, 878
  affectation, 855
Swap
  interchange, 148
  barter, 794
Sward
  plain, 344
Swarm
  crowd, 72
  sufficiency, 639
  multitude, 102
  to climb, 305
Swarthy
  black, 431
Swash
  spurt, 348
  affuse, 337
Swashbuckler
  fighter, 726
Swastika
  cross, 219
Swat
  blow, 276
Swatch

part, 51
Swathe
  clothe, 225
  fasten, 43
Sway
  power, 157
  influence, 175
  authority, 737
  induce, 615
  oscillate, 314
  agitate, 315
Sweal
  calefaction, 384
Swear
  promise, 768
  affirm, 535
  malediction, 908
Sweat
  transude, 348
  heat, 382
  excretion, 299
  labour, 686
  to fatigue, 688
Sweater
  dress, 225
Sweep
  space, 180
  degree, 26
  curve, 245
  rapidity, 274
  clean, 652
  displace, 185
  destroy, 162
  devastation, 619, 649
  blackguard, 949
Sweeping
  wholesale, 50
  complete, 52
  indiscriminate, 465A
Sweepings
  refuse, 653
  trifle, 643
Sweet
  saccharine, 396
  agreeable, 829
  lovely, 897
  melodious, 413
Sweetheart
  love, 897
Sweetie
  sweetheart, 897
Sweetmeat
  sweet, 396
Swell
  increase, 35

expand, 194, 202
bulge, 250
tide, 348
fop, 854
personage, 875
emotion, 821, 824
extol, 931
swagger, 885
good, 648
Swell mob
thief, 792
Swelled head
vanity, 880
Swelling
bombastic, 577
Swelter
heat, 382
Swerve
deviate, 279
diverge, 291
irresolution, 605
tergiversation, 607
Swift
velocity, 274
Swig
drink, 296
tope, 959
Swill
drink, 296
tope, 959
Swim
float, 305
navigate, 267
vertigo, 503
Swim in
abound, 639
Swim-suit
dress, 225
Swimming
successful, 731
buoyant, 320
Swimmingly
easily, 705
prosperously, 734
Swindle
peculate, 791
cheat, 545
Swindler
defrauder, 792
sharper, 548
Swing
space, 180
hang, 214
play, 170
oscillate, 314

rhythm, 138, 413
freedom, 748
Swinge
punish, 972
Swingeing
great, 31
Swinish
intemperance, 954
gluttony, 957
Swink
work, 686
Swipe
blow, 276
Swish
hiss, 409
Switch
scourge, 975
shift, 279
whisk, 311, 315
Switchback
obliquity, 217
Swivel
hinge, 312
cannon, 727
Swivel-eye
squint, 443
Swollen
proud, 878
expanded, 194
Swoon
fainting, 160
inactivity, 683
fatigue, 688
Swoop
seizure, 789
descent, 306
Swop
see Swap
Sword
arms, 722, 727
sharpness, 253
Swordsman
combatant, 726
Swot
to study, 539
scholar, 492
Sybarite
intemperance, 954
Sybo
condiment, 393
Sycophant
servility, 886
assent, 488
adulation, 933
flatterer, 935

Syllable
word, 561
Syllabus
list, 86
compendium, 596
Syllogism
logic, 476
Sylph
sprite, 979
Sylvan
woody, 367
Symbol
sign, 550
metaphor, 521
mathematical, 84
Symmetry
form, 252
order, 58
beauty, 845
equality, 27
Sympathy
kindness, 906
love, 897
friendship, 888, 891
pity, 914
Symphonic
harmony, 413
Symphony
music, 415
Symposium
feast, 299
festivity, 840
discussion, 461
Symptom
sign, 550
Synagogue
temple, 1000
Synchronism
time, 120
Syncopate
shorten, 201
Syncopation
rhythm, 413
Syncope
cut, 160
conciseness, 572
Syncretism
heresy, 984A
Syndic
master, 745
Syndicalism
participation, 778
Syndicate
partnership, 712, 797
co-operation, 709

follow, 281, 461
Tailor
dress, 225
Tailpiece
rear, 235
sequel, 65
end, 67
adjunct, 39
Taint
disease, 655
decay, 659
dirt, 653
stink, 401
fault, 651
disgrace, 874
Taintless
pure, 652
Take
to appropriate, 789
receive, 785
eat, 296
believe, 484
understand, 518
please, 829
Take aback
surprise, 508, 870
Take after
similarity, 17
Take away
remove, 38, 789
Take back
retract, 607
Take care
caution, 864
Take down
swallow, 296
note, 551
lower, 308
humiliate, 879
Take effect
agency, 170
Take heed
attention, 457
Take hold
taking, 789
Take in
include, 64
admit, 296
realize, 450
understand, 518
cheat, 545
Take it
believe, 484
suppose, 514
Take off

remove, 185
divest, 226
imitate, 19
personate, 554
ridicule, 856
jump, 305
Take on
anger, 837
undertake, 676
Take out
extract, 301
obliterate, 552
Take part with
aid, 707
Take place
happen, 151
Take root
dwell, 186
Take tent
care, 459
Take the mickey out of
ridicule, 856
Take to
like, 827
Take up
inquire, 461
Take up with
sociality, 892
Take wing
departure, 293
Taking
vexation, 828
anger, 900
acquisition, 775
pleasing, 829, 897
Tale
narrative, 582, 594
counting, 85
Tale-teller
tell, 534
Talebearer
tell, 534
Talent
skill, 698
intellect, 450
intelligence, 498
Talisman
spell, 993
Talk
speak, 582
rumour, 532
conversation, 588
Talkative
talk, 584
prolix, 573

Talkie
cinema, 599A
Tall
height, 206
Tallboy
receptacle, 191
Tallow
fat, 356
Tally
agreement, 23
numeration, 85
record, 551
check, 550
Talmud
revelation, 985
Talons
claw, 633
authority, 737
Talus
slope, 217
Tam-o'-shanter
hat, 225
Tambourine
music, 417
Tame
inert, 172
moderate, 174
feeble, 575
calm, 826
domesticate, 370
teach, 537
Tamis
strainer, 260
Tammy
hat, 225
Tamper with
change, 140
meddle, 682
bribe, 615
Tan
yellow, 433
to thrash, 972
Tandem
journey, 266
sequence, 69
Tang
taste, 390
Tangent
contiguity, 199
Tangible
touch, 379
real, 1
material, 316
Tangle
derange, 61

707

Tangled
  disordered, 59
  matted, 219
Tango
  dance, 840
Tank
  recipient, 191
  reservoir, 636
  fighter, 726
  arms, 727
  vehicle, 272
Tankard
  receptacle, 191
Tanker
  ship, 273
Tanner
  money, 800
Tantalize
  entice, 615
  disappoint, 509
  tease, 830
  tempt, 865
Tantalus
  receptacle, 191
  desire, 865
Tantamount
  equal, 27
  identical, 13
  synonymous, 516
Tantara
  loudness, 404
  roll, 407
Tantrum
  passion, 900
  excitability, 825
Taoism
  religions, 984
Tap
  hit, 276
  opening, 260
  channel, 350
  plug, 263
  noise, 406
  to let out, 297
  to intercept, 789
Tape
  joint, 45
Tape recorder
  mechanical instruments, 417
Taper
  narrow, 203
  sharp, 253
  candle, 423
Tapestry

  art, 556
  ornament, 847
Taps
  signal, 550
Tar
  mariner, 269
  semiliquid, 352
Taradiddle
  untruth, 546
Tarantella
  dance, 840
Tardy
  dilatory, 133
  slow, 275
Tare and tret
  discount, 813
Target
  object, 620
  laughing-stock, 857
Tariff
  price, 812
Tarn
  lake, 343
Tarnish
  discoloration, 429
  deface, 846
  spoil, 659
  dirt, 653
  disgrace, 874, 940
Tarpaulin
  covering, 222
Tarry
  remain, 110
  continue, 141
  late, 133
  expect, 507
  rest, 265
Tart
  acid, 397
  rude, 895
  irascible, 901
  courtesan, 962
Tartan
  dress, 225
  variegated, 440
  ship, 273
Tartar
  irascible, 901
Tartarus
  hell, 982
Tartuffe
  hypocrite, 544, 548
  impiety, 989
Task
  business, 625

  to put to use, 677
  function, 644
Taskmaster
  director, 694
Tassel
  ornament, 847
  pendant, 214
Taste
  sapidity, 390
  to experience, 821
  discrimination, 850
  small quantity, 32
Tasteless
  vapid, 391
  unattractive, 866
Tasty
  savoury, 394
  delicious, 829
Tat
  knit, 43
Tâtonnement
  trial, 463
Tatter
  part, 51
Tatterdemalion
  commonalty, 876
Tattle
  talk, 588
Tattler
  newsmonger, 532
Tattoo
  roll, 407
  variegate, 440
Taunt
  reproach, 938
  ridicule, 856
  hoot, 929
Tautology
  repetition, 104
  identity, 13
  diffusiveness, 573
Tavern
  inn, 189
Tawdry
  vulgar, 851
  colour, 428
Tawny
  yellow, 436
  brown, 433
Tax
  impost, 812
  to accuse, 938
  require, 765
  impose, 741
  employ, 677

opportunity, 134
Tempt
  entice, 615
  desire, 865
  try, 676
Ten
  number, 98
Tenable
  probable, 472
Tenacious
  retentive, 781
  avaricious, 819
  resolved, 604
  obstinate, 606
  prejudiced, 481
Tenacity
  toughness, 327
Tenancy
  possession, 777
Tenant
  occupier, 188
  possessor, 779
  present, 186
Tenantless
  empty, 187
  solitary, 893
Tend
  aid, 107
  train, 370
  contribute, 153
  conduce, 176
  direct to, 278
Tendentious
  misjudgment, 481
Tender
  soft, 324
  susceptible, 822
  loving, 897
  compassionate, 914
  to offer, 763
  ship, 273
  vehicle, 272
Tenderfoot
  stranger, 57
  learner, 541
Tendon
  fastening, 45
Tendril
  infant, 129
  filament, 205
  fastening, 45
Tenebrific
  darkness, 421
Tenement
  house, 189

property, 780
Tenet
  belief, 484
  creed, 983
Tenner
  money, 800
Tennysonian
  poetry, 597
Tenon
  dovetail, 300
Tenor
  course, 7
  degree, 26
  direction, 278
  meaning, 516
  musical, 413
Tense
  hard, 323
Tensile
  elasticity, 325
Tension
  strength, 159
  length, 200
  hardness, 323
  strain, 686
Tent
  receptacle, 189
  covering, 222
Tentacle
  instrument, 633
  grip, 781
Tentative
  experimental, 463
  essaying, 675
Tenterhooks
  expectation, 507
Tenuity
  rarity, 322
  thinness, 203
  smallness, 32
Tenure
  dueness, 924
  possession, 777
Tepefaction
  heating, 384
Tepid
  warm, 382
  passionless, 823
Terce
  worship, 990
Tercentenary
  period, 138
  celebration, 883
Terebration
  opening, 260

piercing, 302
Tergiversation
  change, 140, 607
  equivocation, 520
Term
  place in series, 71
  end, 67
  limit, 233
  period of time, 106
  property, 780
  word, 562
  name, 564
Termagant
  irascibility, 901
  fury, 173
Terminal
  end, 67
Terminate
  completion, 729
Terminology
  word, 562
Terminus
  end, 67
Termless
  infinity, 105
Terms
  conditions, 770
  circumstances, 8
  reasoning, 476
Ternary
  number, 92, 93
Terpsichore
  music, 415
Terpsichorean
  leap, 309
Terrace
  plain, 344
  level, 213
  buildings, 189
Terra firma
  support, 215
Terra incognita
  ignorance, 491
Terraqueous
  land, 342
  world, 318
Terrene
  land, 342
  world, 318
Terrestrial
  land, 342
  world, 318
Terrible
  fearful, 860
  great, 31

canonicals, 999
Tick
sound, 407
oscillation, 314
indicate, 550
credit, 805
Tick off
reprimand, 932
Ticket
indication, 550
permission, 760
plan, 626
Tickle
touch, 380
please, 377, 829
laugh, 838
Tickled
amused, 827
Ticklish
difficult, 704
uncertain, 475
dangerous, 665
Tiddly
drunk, 959
Tide
ocean, 341
flood, 348
abundance, 639
Tidings
news, 532
Tidy
clean, 652
trim, 673
Tie
relation, 9
fasten, 43, 45
security, 771
equality, 27
obligation, 926
contention, 720
Tie-beam
support, 215
Tier
continuity, 69
layer, 204
Tiff
discord, 713
anger, 900
Tiffin
food, 298
Tiger
violence, 173
courage, 861
servant, 746
wretch, 913

miscreant, 949
Tight
fast, 43
closed, 261
smart, 845
drunk, 959
Tight-lipped
taciturn, 585
Tike
commonalty, 876
Tile
covering, 222
hat, 225
Till
to cultivate, 371
coffer, 191, 802
up to the time, 108
Tilt
slope, 217
tumble, 306
cover, 222
Tilt at
attack, 716
Tilt over
obliquity, 218
Timber
materials, 635
Timbre
music, 413
Timbrel
musical instrument, 417
Time
period, 106
Time-ball
indication, 550
Time-server
servility, 886
apostate, 941
cunning, 702
expedient, 646
irresolution, 605
versatile, 607
selfish, 943
Time-worn
old, 124
exhausted, 659
Timelessness
never, 107
Timely
early, 132
opportune, 134
Timepiece
chronometer, 114
Timid
fearful, 860

cowardly, 862
humble, 881
Timon of Athens
recluse, 893
Timorous
see Timid
Timpanist
musician, 416
Tin
money, 800
to preserve, 670
Tin hat
defence, 717
Tin-opener
open, 260
Tinct
colour, 428
Tincture
mixture, 41
to colour, 428
Tinder
burn, 388
Tine
sharpness, 253
Ting
ring, 408
Tinge
colour, 428
mix, 41
Tingle
pain, 378, 828
feeling, 821
Tingling
titillation, 380
Tink
resonance, 408
Tinker
improve, 658
Tinkety-tonk
departure, 293
Tinkle
resonance, 408
faint sound, 405
Tinsel
ornament, 847
glitter, 420
display, 882
tawdry, 851
false, 544
Tint
colour, 428
Tintinnabulation
resonance, 408
Tiny
little, 32

small, 193
Tip
summit, 210
end, 67
hint, 527
to give, 784, 809
reward, 973
of iceberg, 193
Tippet
dress, 225
Tipple
drink, 296, 298
drunkenness, 959
Tipstaff
police, 965
Tipsy
drunk, 959
Tiptoe
high, 206
curiosity, 455
Tiptop
summit, 210
first-rate, 648
Tirade
disapproval, 932
declamation, 582
Tire
weary, 841
worry, 830
fatigue, 688
Tiresome
wearisome, 841
Tiro
see Tyro
Tirrivee
agitation, 315
Tissue
texture, 329
Tit
small, 193
pony, 271
Tit for tat
retaliation, 718
compensation, 30
Titanic
greatness, 31, 192
Titbit
dainty, 829
Tithe
tenth, 99
dues, 812
Titillate
touch, 380
please, 377, 838
Titivate

dress, 225
beautify, 845
Title
distinction, 877
name, 564
mark, 550
property, 780
right, 924
Title-page
beginning, 66, 593
Titter
laugh, 838
Tittle
small quantity, 32
little, 192
Tittle-tattle
chat, 588
news, 532
Tittup
frisk, 266, 274
Titubation
fall, 306
failure, 732
Titular
title, 564
Toad
ugliness, 846
Toad-eater
servile, 886
flatterer, 935
Toady
to flatter, 933
Toast
roast, 384
celebrate, 883
Tobacco
tobacco, 298A
Toccata
music, 415
Tocsin
alarm, 669
indication, 550
Toddle
walk, 266
limp, 275
Toddler
child, 129
Toe
base, 211
Toehold
support, 215
Toff
notability, 642
fop, 854
Toffee

sweet, 396
Toffee-nose
proud, 878
Toga
dress, 225
Together
added, 37
simultaneous, 120
accompanying, 88
Tohu-bohu
tumult, 315
Toil
exertion, 682, 686
trap, 667
Toilet
dress, 225
room, 191
Toilsome
difficult, 704
Token
sign, 550
Toledo
arms, 727
Tolerable
endurable, 651
Tolerant
patient, 826
Tolerate
endure, 821
permit, 760
licence, 750
lenity, 740
laxity, 738
Toll
sound, 407
tax, 812
Tollbooth
mart, 799
prison, 752
Tolling
interment, 363
Tomahawk
arms, 727
Tomb
interment, 363
Tomboy
vulgar, 851
Tome
volume, 593
Tomfoolery
absurdity, 497
ridiculous, 856
amusement, 840
Tommy
soldier, 726

Tommy-gun
arms, 727
Tompion
stopper, 263
Tom-tom
drum, 416, 722
Ton
taste, 852
Tonality
melody, 413
Tone
state, 7
affections, 820
strength, 159
sound, 402
melody, 413
minstrelsy, 415
colour, 428
Tone down
modify, 174, 469
discoloration, 429
Tone-poem
music, 415
Tong
guild, 712
Tongs
grip, 781
Tongue
language, 560
Tongue-tied
dumb, 581
Tongueless
dumb, 581
Tonic
remedy, 662, 656
refresh, 689
music, 413
Tonnage
size, 192
Tonsure
canonicals, 999
Tontine
income, 810
Too
addition, 37
Too much
redundance, 641
Tool
instrument, 631, 633
adorn, 847
Toot
sound, 408
intemperance, 954
Tooth
projection, 250

notch, 257
sharp, 253
link, 45
taste, 390
Toothache
pain, 378
Toothbrush
clean, 652
Toothful
smallness, 32
Toothsome
savoury, 394
agreeable, 829
Tootle-oo!
departure, 293
Top
summit, 210
good, 648
to surpass, 33
Top-boot
dress, 225
Top-hamper
hindrance, 706
Top-heavy
inverted, 218
dangerous, 665
tipsy, 959
unbalanced, 28
Top-hole
excellent, 648
Top-sawyer
proficient, 700
Topaz
yellow, 436
ornament, 847
Toper
drunkard, 959
Tophet
hell, 982
Topi
hat, 225
Topic
topic, 454
Topical
situation, 183
apt, 23
Toplofty
contempt, 930
Topmast
height, 200
Topmost
great, 33
high, 210
Topography
situation, 183

Topping
excellent, 648
Topple
fall, 306
ruin, 659
Topple over
inversion, 218
Topsy-turvy
upside down, 218
nonsensical, 497
Toque
hat, 225
Torah
revelation, 985
Torch
light, 423
Torchlight
light, 420
Toreador
combatant, 726
Torment
physical, 378
moral, 828, 830
Tornado
violence, 173
wind, 349
Torpedo
weapon, 727
wreck, 732
car, 272
Torpedo-boat
ship, 273
Torpedo-boat
destroyer
ship, 273
Torpedo-net
defence, 717
Torpid
inert, 172
insensible, 823
inactive, 683
Torrefy
burn, 384
Torrent
flow, 348
violence, 173
Torrid
heat, 382
Torsion
twist, 311
Torso
part, 51
Tort
wrong, 923

Tortoise
slow, 275
Tortoise-shell
variegation, 440
Tortuous
twist, 248
dishonest, 939
style, 571
Torture
physical, 378
moral, 828, 830
Tosh
nonsense, 517
Toss
throw, 284
oscillate, 314
agitate, 315
derange, 61
Toss-up
chance, 156, 621
Tosspot
drunk, 959
Tot
dram, 298
Tot up
numeration, 85
accounts, 811
Total
whole, 50
Totalitarian
authority, 737
Totalizator
numeration, 85
Totem
indication, 550
Toto coelo
contrariety, 14
difference, 15
greatness, 31
completeness, 52
Totter
limp, 275
droop, 160
oscillate, 314
agitate, 315
decay, 659
Tottering
dangerous, 665
imperfect, 651
Totting
retrieve, 775
Touch
tact, 379
contiguity, 199
to relate to, 9

music, 415
mix, 41
small quantity, 32, 39
act, 680
treat of, 516, 595
excite, 824
pity, 914
test, 463
borrow, 788
Touch-and-go
uncertainty, 475
danger, 665
Touch up
improve, 658
Touched
feeling, 821
Touching
relation, 9
Touchstone
evidence, 467
Touchwood
fuel, 388
Touchy
irascibility, 901
sensitive, 822
Tough
strong, 327
violent, 173
difficult, 704
brute, 913
bad man, 949
Toupee
wig, 225
roughness, 256
Tour
journey, 266
Tourer
vehicle, 272
Touring-car
vehicle, 272
Tourist
traveller, 268
Tournament
combat, 720
Tourney
combat, 720
Tourniquet
stopper, 263
hindrance, 706
Tournure
outline, 229
appearance, 448
beauty, 845
Tousle
derange, 61

Tousled
disorder, 59
Tout
solicit, 765, 767
publicity, 531
Tout ensemble
whole, 50
Touter
eulogist, 935
solicitor, 767
Toutie
ill, 655
Tow
pull, 285
Towards
direction, 278
Towel
clean, 652
Tower
height, 206
building, 189
defence, 717
to soar, 305
Towering
great, 31
passion, 900
Town
city, 189
fashion, 852
Town crier
publicity, 531
Town talk
news, 532
Township
region, 181
Townsman
inhabitant, 188
Toxic
poisonous, 657
Toxicology
poison, 663
Toxin
poison, 663
Toy
amusement, 840
trifle, 643
Tracasserie
discord, 713
Trace
inquire, 461
discover, 480A
vestige, 551
Trace to
discover, 155

Tracery
  lattice, 219
  ornament, 847
Traces
  harness, 45
Trachea
  air-pipe, 351
Tracing
  copy, 21
  representation, 554
Track
  way, 627
  trail, 551
  to trace, 461
Trackless
  difficult, 704
  space, 180
Tract
  region, 181
  dissertation, 595
Tractable
  easy, 705
  willing, 602
  obedient, 743
  malleable, 324
  dutiful, 926
Tractile
  easy, 705
  malleable, 324
Traction
  drawing, 285
  transmission, 270
Trade
  business, 625
  traffic, 794
Trade mark
  indication, 550
Trader
  merchant, 797
Tradition
  record, 551
  description, 594
Traditional
  old, 124
Traduce
  detract, 932, 934
Traffic
  barter, 794
  business, 625
Traffic warden
  police, 965
Tragedy
  drama, 599
  disaster, 830
Tragelaph
  unconformity, 83

Tragic
  distressing, 830
Tragi-comedy
  ridicule, 856
Tragi-comic
  the drama, 599
Trail
  sequel, 65
  pendent, 214
  slow, 275
  drag, 285
  odour, 398
  indication, 551
  pursue, 622
  to track, 281, 461
Trailer
  cinema, 599asa
Train
  series, 69
  sequel, 65
  sequence, 281
  retinue, 746
  appendix, 39
  traction, 285
  vehicle, 272
  teach, 537, 540
  cultivate, 375
  tame, 370
  accustom, 613
  drill, 673
Train-bearer
  servant, 746
Train oil
  oil, 356
Trained
  skill, 698
Trait
  appearance, 448
  lineament, 550
Traitor
  knave, 941
  disobedient, 742
Trajectory
  path, 627
Tram
  vehicle, 272
Tram-car
  vehicle, 272
Trammel
  fetter, 752
  restrain, 751
  hinder, 706
Tramontana
  wind, 349
Tramontane

  distant, 196
  alien, 57
Tramp
  to stroll, 266
  stroller, 268
  commonalty, 876
  ship, 273
Trample
  violate, 927
  bully, 885
  spurn, 930
Tramway
  way, 627
Trance
  lethargy, 823
  insensibility, 376
  inactivity, 683
Tranquil
  calm, 174, 826
  peaceful, 721
  quiet, 165
  to pacify, 723
Tranquillizer
  drug, 662
Transact
  conduct, 692
  traffic, 794
Transaction
  event, 151
Transalpine
  distance, 196
Transatlantic
  distance, 196
Transcend
  go beyond, 303
Transcendent
  great, 31, 33
  spiritual, 317
  perfect, 650
  good, 648
  glorious, 873
Transcendental
  recondite, 519
  spiritual, 317, 450
Transcribe
  write, 590
  copy, 21
Transcript
  write, 590
  copy, 21
Transcursion
  trespass, 303
Transept
  of church, 1000
  crossing, 219

Transfer
things, 270
property, 783
remove, 185
Transfiguration
change, 140
divine, 998
Transfix
perforate, 260
Transform
change, 140
Transformation
wig, 225
Transfuse
transfer, 270
mix, 41
translate, 522
Transgress
go beyond, 303
infringe, 773
violate, 927
sin, 947
Tranship
transfer, 270
Transient
passing, 111
Transilient
transcursion, 303
Transistor
radio, 599
Transit
conversion, 144
motion, 264
transference, 270
Transition
motion, 264
conversion, 144
transference, 270
Transitive
passing, 111
Transitory
passing, 111
Translate
interpret, 522
transfer, 270
promote, 995
Translucent
transparent, 425
Transmigration
change, 140
conversion, 144
Transmission
moving, 270
of property, 783
passage, 302

Transmitter
hearing, 418
Transmogrify
change, 140, 144
Transmute
change, 140
conversion, 144
Transparent
pellucid, 425
obvious, 518
perspicuous, 570
Transpicuous
transparent, 425
Transpierce
pierce, 260
Transpire
appear, 525
disclose, 529
Transplant
displace, 185
transfer, 270
Transpontine
drama, 599
Transport
transfer, 185, 270
punish, 972
ship, 272
feeling, 821, 824
please, 827, 829
Transpose
displace, 185
invert, 218
transfer, 270
exchange, 148
Transubstantiation
rite, 998
Transude
ooze, 295
pass through, 302
exude, 348
Transverse
oblique, 217
Trap
snare, 667
vehicle, 272
Trap-door
escape, 671
pitfall, 667
Trapes
journey, 266
Trappings
clothes, 39, 225
gear, 633
ornament, 847
property, 780

Trash
absurdity, 497
nonsense, 517
trifle, 643
Travail
work, 686
Travel
journey, 266
motion, 264
Traveller
traveller, 268
Traverse
move, 266
pass, 302
investigate, 461
obstruct, 706
Travesty
copy, 21
to imitate, 19
misinterpret, 523
burlesque, 856
Travolator
way, 627
Tray
receptacle, 191
Treachery
deceit, 940
Treacle
sweet, 396
semiliquid, 352
Tread
journey, 266
motion, 264
Treadle
instrument, 633
Treadmill
punishment, 975
wearisome, 841
Treason
revolt, 742
treachery, 940
Treasure
money, 800
goodness, 648
perfection, 650
windfall, 618
Treasurer
treasurer, 801
Treasury
treasury, 802
store, 636
Treat
manage, 692
bargain, 769
amuse, 840

Trilateral
side, 236
Trilby
hat, 225
Trill
sound, 407
resonance, 408
music, 415
Trilogy
triality, 92
Trim
state, 7
form, 240
dress, 225
ornament, 845, 847
order, 58
to adjust, 27
prepare, 673
beat, 731
scold, 932
change sides, 607
Trimmer
fickle, 605, 607
apostate, 941
Trimming
edge, 230
ornament, 847
Trinal
number, 92
Trine
triplication, 93
Trinity
Deity, 976
Trinket
ornament, 847
Trinkgeld
gift, 784
Trinomial
triality, 92
triplication, 93
Trio
number, 92
Triolet
poetry, 597
Trip
jaunt, 266
to fall, 306
hasten, 274
mistake, 495
fail, 945
guilt, 947
Trip up
overthrow, 731
deceive, 545
Tripartition

trisection, 94
Triphthong
letter, 561
Triple
triplication, 93
Triplet
triality, 92
poetry, 597
Triplicate
triplication, 93
Tripod
support, 215
Tripper
traveller, 268
Tripping
nimble, 682
failing, 495
Triquetra
triality, 92
Trireme
ship, 273
Trisect
tripartition, 94
Triste
dejected, 837
Tristful
dejected, 837
Trisulcate
tripartition, 94
furrow, 259
Trisyllable
letter, 561
Trite
old, 82
hackneyed, 496
unimportant, 643
Tritheism
heathen, 984
Triturate
pulverulence, 330
Triumph
success, 731
trophy, 733
exult, 838
boast, 884
celebrate, 883
Triumphant
elated, 836
Trivet
support, 215
Trivial
trifling, 643
useless, 645
flimsy, 477
smallness, 32

Trochee
verse, 597
Troglodyte
seclusion, 893
Troll
roll, 312
sing, 415
fairy, 980
Trolley
vehicle, 272
Trolley-bus
vehicle, 272
Trollop
libertine, 962
Trombone
musical instrument, 417
Troop
army, 726
assemblage, 72
Troop-ship
ship, 273
Trooper
combatant, 726
ship, 273
Trope
metaphor, 521
Trophy
triumph, 733
record, 551
Tropical
heat, 382
metaphor, 520
Tropology
metaphor, 520
Tropopause
air, 338
Troposphere
air, 338
Trot
run, 266
velocity, 274
Trot out
manifestation, 525
Troth
truth, 494
promise, 768
belief, 484
Trothless
faithless, 940
false, 544
Troubadour
musician, 416
Trouble
derange, 61
evil, 619, 649

adversity, 735
pain, 828, 830
exertion, 686
Troubleshooter
mediator, 724
Troublesome
difficulty, 704
Troublous
disorder, 59
Trough
conduit, 250
trench, 259
hollow, 252
Trounce
censure, 932
punish, 972
Trousers
dress, 225
Trousseau
dress, 225
Trow
think, 451, 484
know, 490
Trowel
instrument, 191
Truant
absent, 187
fugitive, 623
idle, 683
Truce
pacification, 723
suspension, 141, 142
Truck
vehicle, 272
barter, 794
summit, 210
Truckle to
submission, 725
Truculent
malevolence, 907
Trudge
slowness, 275
True
real, 1, 3
veracious, 543
good, 648
faithful, 772
orthodox, 983A
True-love
love, 897
Truepenny
probity, 939
Truism
absurdity, 497
Trull

impurity, 962
Truly
really, 31
assent, 488
verily, 494, 543
Trump
good man, 939, 948
Trump card
device, 626
success, 731
Trump up
falsehood, 544
Trumpery
unimportance, 643
nonsense, 517
Trumpet
musical instrument, 417
to publish, 531
roar, 412
war-cry, 722
Trumpet-tongued
publication, 531
Trumpeter
messenger, 534
Truncate
shorten, 201
incomplete, 53
subduct, 38
Truncheon
club, 727
staff of office, 747
mace, 633
Trundle
roll, 312
propel, 284
Trunk
whole, 50
origin, 153
paternity, 166
box, 191
Truss
join, 43
support, 215
packet, 72
Trust
credit, 805
belief, 484
credulity, 486
hope, 858
Trustee
consignee, 758
treasurer, 801
Trustless
improbity, 940
Trustworthy

probity, 939
certainty, 474
Trusty
probity, 939
Truth
truth, 494
Truthful
veracity, 543
Truthless
falsehood, 544
Try
experiment, 463
endeavour, 675
use, 677
annoy, 830
judge, 967
Try-out
trial, 463
Trying
difficult, 704
Tryst
party, 892
Tsar
see Czar
Tu quoque
retaliation, 718
Tub
vessel, 191
to bathe, 337
Tub-thumper
ranter, 584
Tuba
wind instrument, 417
Tubby
corpulent, 192
Tube
opening, 260
way, 627
Tubercle
convexity, 250
Tuberosity
convexity, 250
Tubular
opening, 260
Tuck
fold, 258
dagger, 727
Tuck in
insert, 300
eat, 296
locate, 184
Tuft
rough, 256
collection, 72

Turnpike
hindrance, 706
Turnpike road
way, 627
Turnstile
hindrance, 706
Turpitude
dishonour, 940
wrong, 923
disgrace, 874
Turquoise
blue, 438
Turret
height, 206
defence, 717
Turtle-dove
love, 897
Tush
contempt, 930
Tusk
sharpness, 253
Tussle
contention, 720
Tutelage
safety, 664
subjection, 749
learner, 541
Tutelary
safety, 664
Tutor
teacher, 540
to teach, 537
cultivate, 375
Tuxedo
dress, 225
Twaddle
absurdity, 497
nonsense, 517
loquacity, 584
Twain
duplication, 90
Twang
taste, 390
sound, 402, 410
voice, 583
Tweak
squeeze, 195, 203
punish, 972
Tweeds
dress, 225
Twelve
number, 98
Twenty
number, 98
Twerp

bad man, 949
Twice
duplication, 90
Twiddle
rotation, 312
Twig
part, 51
plant, 367
to notice, 457
comprehend, 518
Twilight
morning, 125
evening, 126
grey, 432
Twill
fold, 258
Twilled
crossing, 219
Twin
duplicate, 90
accompaniment, 88
similar, 17
Twine
thread, 45
fibre, 205
intersect, 219
convolution, 248
cling, 46
Twinge
bodily pain, 378
mental, 828, 830
Twinkle
light, 420
Twinkling
moment, 113
Twirl
agitation, 315
convolution, 248
turn, 311, 312
Twist
cord, 45
distort, 243
falsehood, 544
obliquity, 217
convolution, 248
bend, 311
imperfection, 651
prejudice, 481
Twit
disapprove, 932
ridicule, 856
slight, 929
Twitch
pull, 285
convulsion, 315

pain, 378
mental, 828
Twitter
agitation, 315
cry, 412
music, 415
emotion, 821
Two
duality, 89
Two-by-four
trifling, 643
Two-seater
vehicle, 272
Two-step
dance, 840
Twofold
duplication, 89, 90
Twopenny
paltry, 643
Tycoon
master, 745
Tyke
commonalty, 876
Tympanum
hearing, 418
Tympany
expansion, 194
Tynewald
council, 696
Type
pattern, 22
class, 75
nature, 5
person, 372
man, 373
rule, 80
indication, 550
printing, 591
Typewriting
writing, 590
Typhoon
violence, 173
rotation, 312
wind, 349
Typical
ordinary, 82
special, 79
Typify
indication, 550
Typography
printing, 591
Tyrannicide
killing, 361
Tyranny
severity, 739

724

authority, 737
Tyrant
  master, 745
Tyro
  learner, 541
  novice, 674

Uberty
  sufficiency, 639
Ubiety
  presence, 186
Ubiquitous
  presence, 186
Udder
  teat, 250
Ugly
  ugliness, 846
  cantankerous, 895
  formidable, 860
Uh-huh
  assent, 488
Ukase
  order, 741
  law, 963
Ukelele
  stringed instrument, 417
Ulcer
  disease, 655
  care, 830
Ulema
  judge, 967
Ullage
  deficiency, 53
Ulster
  coat, 225
Ulterior
  in space, 196
  in time, 121
Ultimate
  end, 67
Ultimatum
  conditions, 770
Ultimo
  priority, 116
Ultimogeniture
  descent, 167
Ultra
  superiority, 33
  greatness, 31
  extremist, 604
Ultramarine
  blueness, 438
Ultramontane
  authority, 737

alien, 57
Ululation
  cry, 412
Ulysses
  cunning, 702
Umber
  brown, 433
Umbilical
  centrality, 223
Umbra
  darkness, 421
Umbrage
  shade, 424
  darkness, 421
  offence, 900
  enmity, 889
  grudge, 898
Umbrella
  shelter, 666
Umpire
  judge, 480, 967
Umpteen
  plurality, 100
Unabashed
  bold, 861
  haughty, 873, 878
  insolent, 885
  conceited, 880
Unabated
  great, 31
Unable
  impotence, 158
Unacceptable
  painfulness, 830
Unaccommodating
  disagreeing, 24
  uncivil, 895
  disobliging, 907
Unaccompanied
  alone, 87
Unaccomplished
  incomplete, 730
Unaccountable
  obscure, 519
  wonderful, 870
  arbitrary, 964
  irresponsible, 927A
Unaccustomed
  unused, 614
  unskilled, 699
  unusual, 83
Unachievable
  difficult, 704
  impossible, 471
Unacknowledged

ignored, 489
  unrequited, 917
Unacquainted
  ignorant, 491
Unactuated
  unmoved, 616
Unadmonished
  unwarned, 665
Unadorned
  simple, 849
  style, 575
Unadulterated
  simple, 42
  genuine, 494, 648
Unadventurous
  quiet, 864
Unadvisable
  inexpedient, 647
Unadvised
  unwarned, 665
  foolish, 699
Unaffected
  callous, 376
  genuine, 494
  sincere, 543
  simple, 576, 849
  elegant, 578
  in good taste, 850
Unafflicted
  serene, 831
Unaided
  meak, 160
Unalarmed
  courage, 861
Unalienable
  dueness, 924
Unallayed
  strength, 159
Unallied
  irrelative, 10
Unallowable
  wrong, 923
Unalluring
  indifference, 866
Unalterable
  identical, 13
  unchanged, 141
  unchangeable, 150
Unamazed
  expectance, 871
Unambiguous
  intelligibility, 518
Unambitious
  indifference, 866
Unamiable
  ill-natured, 907

spontaneous, 602
uninfluenced, 616
free, 748
Unbidden
spontaneous, 600
disobedient, 742
Unbind
detach, 44
release, 750
Unblameable
innocence, 946
Unblemished
innocence, 946
Unblenching
courage, 861
Unblended
unmixed, 42
Unblest
unhappy, 838
unapproved, 932
Unblown
non-preparation, 674
Unblushing
impudent, 885
proud, 878
vain, 880
Unboastful
modest, 881
Unbodied
immateriality, 317
Unbolt
liberate, 750
Unbonnet
divestment, 226
Unborn
future, 121
not existing, 2
Unborrowed
lending, 787
Unbosom
disclosure, 529
Unbound
free, 748
exempt, 927A
Unbounded
great, 31
large, 192
infinite, 105
space, 180
Unbrace
relax, 655
weaken, 160
Unbreathed
latent, 526
Unbribed

disinterested, 942
Unbridled
lax, 738
violent, 173
free, 748
Unbroken
entire, 50
continuous, 69
unviolated, 939
Unbruised
whole, 50
Unbuckle
disjunction, 44
Unbusiness-like
inactivity, 683
Unbutton
unfasten, 44
Unbuttoned
freedom, 748
Uncage
liberation, 750
Uncalled-for
useless, 645
superfluous, 641
not used, 678
Uncandid
morose, 907
insincere, 544
Uncanny
strange, 83
wonderful, 870
supernatural, 980
Uncanonical
heterodox, 984A
Uncared-for
indifferent, 866
hated, 898
Uncase
divestment, 226
Uncaught
freedom, 748
Uncaused
chance, 156
Unceasing
perpetuity, 112
Uncensured
approbation, 931
Unceremonious
rude, 895
Uncertain
uncertainty, 475
irresolute, 605
irregular, 139
Unchain
unfasten, 44

liberate, 750
free, 748
Unchallenged
dueness, 924
assent, 488
Unchangeable
immutable, 150
firm, 604
Unchanged
permanent, 141
Uncharitable
malevolent, 907
Uncharted
unknown, 491
Unchartered
unauthorized, 925
illegal, 964
Unchaste
impure, 961
Unchastized
acquittal, 970
Unchecked
freedom, 748
Unchristian
irreligion, 989
Uncial
writing, 590
Uncircumscribed
spacious, 180
Uncivil
rude, 895
vulgar, 851
Unclad
naked, 226
Unclaimed
freedom, 748
Unclasp
loosen, 44
Unclassed
disorder, 59
Unclassical
vulgarity, 851
Unclassified
disorder, 59
Uncle
relative, 11
pawnbroker, 787
Unclean
uncleanness, 653
impurity, 961
Unclinch
disjunction, 44
Unclipped
whole, 50
Unclog
liberate, 705, 750

Uncouth
  ugly, 846
  ridiculous, 853
  style, 579
  rude, 851
Uncovenanted
  unsecured, 768A
Uncover
  open, 260
  denude, 226
  disclose, 529
  bow, 894
Uncreated
  inexistence, 2
Uncropped
  whole, 50
Uncrown
  abrogation, 756
Unction
  emotion, 824
  piety, 987
  extreme,
  rite, 998
Unctuous
  oily, 355
  hypocritical, 988
  flattering, 933
  servile, 886
Unculled
  untouched, 678
  relinquished, 782
Uncultivated
  ignorant, 491
  unprepared, 674
Uncultured
  ignorant, 491
Uncurbed
  freedom, 748
Uncurl
  straightness, 246
Uncut
  whole, 50
Undamaged
  goodness, 648
Undamped
  dryness, 340
Undated
  waving, 248
  time, 115
Undaunted
  courage, 861
Undazzled
  wisdom, 498
Undebauched
  innocence, 946

Undecayed
  goodness, 648
Undeceive
  inform, 527, 529
Undeceived
  knowledge, 490
Undecided
  in question, 461
  uncertain, 475
  irresolute, 605
  indifferent, 610
Undecipherable
  unintelligible, 519
Undecked
  simplicity, 849
Undecomposed
  simpleness, 42
Undefaced
  beauty, 845
Undefended
  submission, 725
Undefiled
  innocence, 946
  purity, 960
Undefinable
  unmeaning, 517, 519
  uncertain, 475
Undefined
  see Undefinable
Undemolished
  tire, 50
  good, 648
Undemonstrative
  modesty, 881
Undeniable
  certainty, 474
Undeplored
  hate, 898
Undepraved
  innocence, 946
Undeprived
  retention, 781
Under
  below, 207
  less, 34
Under-bodice
  dress, 225
Under breath
  faintness, 405
Under-reckon
  depreciation, 483
Underbid
  bargain, 794
Underbred
  rude, 861.

Undercharge
  cheap, 815
Undercover
  secret, 534
Undercurrent
  stream, 347
  latency, 526
Underestimate
  depreciation, 483
Undergo
  feeling 821
Undergraduate
  learner, 541
Underground
  low, 207
  deep, 208
  way, 627
Undergrowth
  plant, 367
Underhand
  hidden, 528
  false, 544
  base, 940
Underlie
  latent, 526
Underline
  mark, 550
  emphatic, 642
Underling
  servant, 746
Underlying
  lowness, 207
Undermanned
  insufficiency, 640
Undermine
  burrow, 252
  counteract, 706
  damage, 659
Undermost
  base, 211
Underneath
  lowness, 207
Underpin
  support, 215
Underplot
  plan, 626
Underprivileged
  forfeit, 925
Underprize
  underrate, 483
Underprop
  support, 215
Underquote
  bargain, 794

Underrate
depreciation, 483
Undersell
sale, 796
Undersized
littleness, 193
Understaffed
insufficiency, 640
Understand
know, 490
meaning, 516
intelligible, 518
Understanding
intellect, 450, 498
agreement, 714
compact, 769
Understatement
falsehood, 544
Understood
implied, 516
metaphorical, 521
Understrapper
servant, 746
Understudy
deputy, 159, 634
substitute, 147
Undertake
promise, 768
pursue, 622
endeavour, 676
Undertaker
interment, 363
Undertaking
enterprise, 676
business, 625
Undertone
faintness, 405
Undertow
danger, 667
Undervalue
depreciation, 483
Underwear
dress, 225
Underworld
commonalty, 876
Underwood
plant, 367
Underwrite
insure, 769, 771
Undescribed
unconformity, 83
Undescried
invisible, 447
Undeserved
undueness, 925
Undesigned

necessity, 601
chance, 621
Undesigning
artlessness, 703
Undesirable
unpleasant, 830
unattractive, 866
inexpedient, 647
Undesirous
indifference, 866
Undespairing
hope, 858
Undestroyed
whole, 50
persisting, 141
existing, 1
Undetermined
irresolute, 605
untried, 461
uncertain, 475
obscure, 519
chance, 156
Undeterred
resolute, 604
Undeveloped
latent, 526
Undeviating
progressing, 282
straight, 246
direct, 278
mid-course, 628
unchanged, 150
Undevout
irreligion, 989
Undigested
unarranged, 59
crude, 674
Undiluted
strength, 159
purity, 42
Undiminished
whole, 50
great, 31
increase, 35
Undine
sprite, 980
Undirected
deviating, 279
casual, 621
Undiscerned
invisibility, 447
Undiscerning
blind, 442
stupid, 499
Undisciplined

unskilfulness, 699
Undisclosed
concealment, 528
Undiscoverable
concealment, 528
Undisguised
sincere, 543
true, 494
Undismayed
courage, 861
Undispersed
assemblage, 72
Undisposed of
disuse, 678
retention, 781
Undisputed
certainty, 474
Undissolved
entire, 50
dense, 321
Undistinguished
indiscrimination, 465A
Undistorted
straight, 246
true, 494
Undistracted
attention, 457
Undisturbed
quiet, 265, 685
calm, 826
orderly, 58
Undiverted
resolution, 604
Undivided
whole, 50
Undivulged
concealment, 528
Undo
untie, 44
do away with, 681
counteract, 179, 706
reverse, 145
Undoing
ruin, 735, 830
Undone
non-assemblage, 73
incomplete, 730
foiled, 732
hapless, 828
Undoubted
certainty, 474
Undraped
nudity, 226
Undreaded
courage, 861

Undreamed
  incogitancy, 452
Undress
  nudity, 226
  morning dress, 225
Undressed
  unprepared, 674
  unadorned, 849
Undrilled
  unprepared, 674
  unaccustomed, 699
Undriven
  willing, 602
Undrooping
  activity, 682
Undue
  wrong, 923, 925
Undulate
  oscillate, 314
  wave, 248
Undutiful
  vice, 945
Undyed
  achromatism, 429
Undying
  perpetual, 112
  immutable, 150
Unearth
  manifestation, 525
  discovery, 480A
  inquiry, 461
Unearthly
  immaterial, 317
  heavenly, 981
  pious, 987
Uneasy
  pain, 828
Uneatable
  unsavoury, 395
Unedifying
  misteaching, 538
Uneducated
  ignorant, 491
  unprepared, 674
  unskilful, 699
Unembarrassed
  manners, 852
Unemployed
  inactive, 683
  not used, 678
Unencumbered
  easy, 705
  exempt, 927A
Unending
  infinite, 105

long, 200
Unendowed
  impotence, 158
Unendurable
  painfulness, 830
Unenjoyed
  weary, 841
Unenlightened
  ignorant, 491
  foolish, 499
Unenslaved
  free, 748
Unenterprising
  caution, 864
Unentertaining
  dullness, 843
Unentitled
  undueness, 925
Unequal
  inequality, 28
  unable, 158
  unjust, 923
Unequalled
  superior, 33
Unequipped
  non-preparation, 674
Unequivocal
  sure, 474
  clear, 518
Unequivocally
  greatly, 31
Unerring
  certain, 474
  true, 494
  innocent, 946
Unespied
  invisible, 447
  hidden, 526
Unessayed
  disuse, 678
Unessential
  unimportance, 643
Uneven
  rough, 256
  unequal, 28
  irregular, 16A, 83
Unexaggerated
  truth, 494
Unexamined
  neglect, 460
Unexampled
  unconformity, 83
Unexceptionable
  good, 648
  legitimate, 924

innocent, 946
Unexcited
  inexcitability, 826
Unexciting
  moderate, 174
Unexecuted
  non-completion, 730
Unexempt
  liability, 177
Unexercised
  unused, 678
  unprepared, 674
  unskilled, 699
Unexerted
  inertness, 172
Unexhausted
  vigorous, 159
  abundant, 639
Unexpanded
  contraction, 195
Unexpected
  unlooked-for, 508
  sudden, 132
  wonderful, 870
Unexpensive
  cheapness, 815
Unexplained
  latent, 526
  unknown, 491
Unexplored
  latent, 526
  unknown, 491
Unexposed
  latent, 526
Unexpressed
  latent, 526
Unextended
  immateriality, 317
Unextinguished
  violent, 172
  burning, 382
Unfaded
  colour, 428
  fresh, 648
Unfading
  perpetuity, 112
Unfailing
  constant, 141
Unfair
  unjust, 923
  dishonourable, 940
  false, 544
Unfaithful
  faithless, 940

731

Unfaltering
resolution, 604
Unfamiliar
unconformity, 83
Unfashionable
vulgarity, 851
abnormal, 83
Unfashioned
formless, 241
unwrought, 674
Unfasten
disjunction, 44
Unfathomable
deep, 208
infinite, 105
unintelligible, 519
Unfavourable
obstructive, 708
out of season, 135
Unfearing
courage, 861
Unfeasible
impracticable, 471
Unfed
fasting, 956
deficient, 640
Unfeeling
insensibility, 823
impenitence, 951
Unfeigned
veracity, 543
Unfelt
insensibility, 823
Unfeminine
vulgarity, 851
manly, 373
Unfetter
unfasten, 44
release, 750
Unfettered
spontaneous, 600
Unfinished
non-completion, 53, 730
Unfit
inappropriate, 24
incapacitate, 158
inexpedient, 647
Unfix
disjoin, 44
Unfixed
irresolute, 605
mutable, 149
Unflagging
activity, 682
resolution, 604
Unflattering

sincere, 543
true, 494
Unfledged
unprepared, 674
young, 129
Unflinching
resolute, 604
bravery, 861
persevering, 682
Unfoiled
success, 731
Unfold
evolve, 313
straighten, 246
disclose, 529
interpret, 522
Unforbidden
permission, 760
Unforced
free, 748
willing, 602
Unforeseen
unexpected, 508
surprising, 870
Unforfeited
retention, 781
Unforgettable
importance, 642
Unforgivable
vice, 945
Unforgiving
revenge, 919
Unforgotten
memory, 505
Unformed
non-preparation, 674
Unforthcoming
unsociable, 893
Unfortified
weakness, 160
Unfortunate
failure, 732
adversity, 735
unhappy, 828
untimely, 135
Unfounded
falsehood, 544
Unfrequent
seldom, 137
Unfrequented
seclusion, 893
Unfriended
weak, 160
enmity, 889
Unfriendly

enmity, 889
opposed, 708
malevolent, 907
Unfrock
disqualify, 925
punish, 972
dismiss, 756
Unfruitful
unproductiveness, 169
Unfulfilled
non-observance, 773, 925
Unfurl
evolution, 213
Unfurnished
unprepared, 674
insufficient, 640
Ungainly
ugly, 846
rude, 895
Ungarnished
unadorned, 849
Ungathered
disuse, 678
Ungenerous
stingy, 819
selfish, 943
Ungenial
insalubrious, 657
uncivil, 895
Ungenteel
vulgar, 851
rude, 895
Ungentle
rude, 895
violent, 173
Ungentlemanly
vulgar, 851
rude, 895
dishonourable, 940
Un-get-at-able
distant, 196
Ungird
disjunction, 44
Unglue
disjunction, 44
incoherence, 47
Ungodly
irreligion, 989
Ungovernable
violent, 173
disobedient, 742
passion, 825
Ungoverned
freedom, 748

Ungraceful
ugly, 846
inelegant, 579
vulgar, 851
Ungracious
uncivil, 895
unfriendly, 907
Ungrammatical
solecism, 568
Ungrateful
ingratitude, 917
Ungratified
pain, 828
Ungrounded
error, 495
Ungrudging
liberality, 816
Unguarded
neglected, 460
improvident, 674
dangerous, 665
spontaneous, 612
Unguent
oil, 356
Unguided
ignorant, 491
unskilful, 699
Unhackneyed
desuetude, 614
Unhallowed
irreligion, 989
profane, 988
Unhand
liberation, 750
Unhandsome
ugly, 940
Unhandy
unskilfulness, 699
Unhappy
pain, 828
Unhardened
tender, 914
penitent, 950
innocent, 946
Unharmed
safety, 664
Unharness
disjoin, 44
liberate, 750
Unhatched
non-preparation, 674
Unhazarded
safety, 664
Unhealthy
ill, 655

unwholesome, 657
Unheard-of
ignorant, 491
exceptional, 83, 137
impossible, 471
improbable, 473
wonderful, 870
Unheeded
neglected, 460
Unheralded
inexpectation, 507
Unheroic
cowardly, 862
Unhesitating
resolution, 604
Unhewn
formless, 241
unprepared, 674
Unhindered
free, 748
Unhinge
weaken, 169
derange, 61
Unhinged
unsettled, 605
insane, 503
Unholy
evil, 989
Unhonoured
disrespect, 874
Unhook
disjoin, 44
Unhoped
unexpected, 508
Unhouse
displace, 185
Unhurt
uninjured, 670
Unicorn
monster, 83
prodigy, 872
Unidea'd
unthinking, 452
Unideal
true, 494
existing, 1
Uniform
homogeneous, 16
simple, 42
orderly, 58
regular, 82
symmetrical, 242
livery, 225
insignia, 550
uniformity, 23

Unify
combine, 48
make one, 87
Unilluminated
dark, 421
ignorant, 491
Unimaginable
inconceivable, 519
Unimaginative
dull, 843
Unimagined
truth, 494
Unimitated
original, 20
Unimpaired
preserved, 670
sound, 648
Unimpassioned
inexcitable, 826
Unimpeachable
innocent, 946
irrefutable, 474, 478
inalienable, 924
perfect, 650
Unimpeded
facility, 705
Unimpelled
uninduced, 616
Unimportant
insignificant, 643
Unimpressionable
insensible, 823
Unimproved
deterioration, 659
Uninfluenced
unbiased, 616
obstinate, 606
Uninfluential
inert, 172
Uninformed
ignorance, 491
Uninhabited
empty, 187
solitary, 893
Uninitiated
unschooled, 699
Uninjured
good, 648
preserved, 670
healthy, 644
Uninquisitive
indifferent, 456
Uninspired
unexcited, 823
unactuated, 616

Uninstructed
ignorant, 491
Unintellectual
ignorant, 452
imbecile, 499
Unintelligent
foolish, 499
Unintelligible
difficult, 519
style, 571
Unintentional
change, 621
Uninterested
incurious, 456
inattentive, 458
indifferent, 823
weary, 841
Uninteresting
wearisome, 841
dull, 843
Unintermitting
unbroken, 69
durable, 110
continuing, 143
active, 682
Uninterrupted
continuous, 69
unremitting, 143
Uninvestigated
unknown, 491
Uninvited
exclusion, 893
Uninviting
unattractive, 866
unpleasant, 830
Union
junction, 43
combination, 48
concord, 23, 714
concurrence, 178
marriage, 903
Union Jack
flag, 550
Unique
special, 79
alone, 87
exceptional, 83
dissimilarity, 18
non-imitation, 20
Unison
agreement, 23
concord, 714
uniformity, 16
melody, 413
Unisonant

harmony, 413
Unit
number, 87
troop, 726
Unitarian
heterodoxy, 984A
Unite
join, 43
agree, 23
concur, 178
assemble, 72
converge, 290
league, 712
Unity
singleness, 87
integrity, 50
concord, 714
Universal
general, 78
Universe
world, 318
University
school, 542
Unjust
wrong, 923
Unjustified
undue, 925
Unkempt
careless, 653
slovenly, 851
Unkennel
turn out, 185
disclose, 529
Unkind
malevolent, 907
Unknit
disjoin, 44
Unknowable
concealment, 528
Unknown
ignorant, 491
latent, 526
to fame, 874
Unlaboured
unprepared, 674
style, 578
Unlace
disjoin, 44
Unlade
ejection, 297
Unladylike
vulgar, 851
rude, 895
Unlamented
disliked, 898

unapproved, 932
Unlatch
disjoin, 44
Unlawful
undue, 925
illegal, 964
Unlearn
forget, 506
Unlearned
ignorant, 491
Unleavened
non-preparation, 674
Unless
circumstances, 8
qualification, 469
condition, 770
Unlettered
ignorant, 491
Unlicensed
unpermitted, 761
Unlicked
clownish, 876
vulgar, 851
unprepared, 674
Unlike
dissimilar, 18
Unlikely
improbable, 473
Unlimited
infinite, 105
space, 180
great, 31
Unlink
disjoin, 44
Unliquefied
solid, 321
Unlit
darkness, 421
Unload
unpack, 297
disencumber, 705
transfer, 270
Unlock
unfasten, 44
explain, 462
Unlooked-for
unexpected, 508
Unloose
unfasten, 44
liberate, 750
Unloved
hate, 898
Unlovely
ugly, 846

Unlucky
  inopportune, 135
  failing, 732
  unfortunate, 735
  luckless, 828
  painful, 830
  bad, 649
Unmade
  non-existent, 2
Unmaidenly
  ill-mannered, 851
Unmaimed
  uninjured, 654
Unmake
  reversion, 145
Unmanageable
  perverse, 704
  unwieldy, 647
Unmanly
  improbity, 940
  effeminate, 374
  cowardly, 862
Unmanned
  weak, 160
  sad, 837
Unmannerly
  rude, 895
Unmarked
  neglect, 460
Unmarred
  sound, 654
  preserved, 670
Unmarried
  celibacy, 904
Unmask
  show, 525
  disclose, 529
Unmatched
  different, 15
  unparalleled, 20
  dissimilar, 18
Unmeaning
  nonsense, 517
Unmeasured
  abundant, 639
  infinite, 105
  undistinguished, 465A
  casual, 621
Unmeet
  undue, 925
Unmelodious
  discord, 414
Unmelted
  density, 321
Unmentionable

  unseemly, 961
Unmentioned
  latency, 526
Unmerciful
  malevolence, 907
Unmerited
  undueness, 925
Unmethodical
  disorder, 59
Unmindful
  inattention, 458
  neglect, 460
  forgetful, 506
  ungrateful, 917
Unmingled
  simpleness, 42
Unmirthful
  dejection, 837
Unmissed
  neglect, 460
Unmistakable
  clear, 518
  visible, 446
Unmitigated
  greatness, 31
  complete, 52P
Unmixed
  simpleness, 42
Unmodified
  permanence, 141
Unmolested
  content, 831
  safe, 664
Unmoral
  vice, 945
Unmourned
  hate, 898
Unmoved
  quiescent, 265
  resolute, 604
  obstinate, 606
  torpid, 823
  uninduced, 616
Unmusical
  discord, 414
Unmuzzled
  freedom, 748
Unnamed
  misnomer, 565
Unnatural
  unconformity, 83
Unnecessary
  inutility, 645
  superfluous, 641
Unneeded

  inutility, 645
Unneighbourly
  unsociable, 893
Unnerved
  impotence, 158
  weakness, 160
Unnoted
  neglected, 460
  ignoble, 874
Unnoticed
  neglected, 460
  ignoble, 874
Unnumbered
  infinity, 105
Unobjectionable
  goodness, 648
Unobscured
  vision, 420
Unobservant
  inattention, 458
Unobserved
  unseen, 460
Unobstructed
  unopposed, 709
  free, 748
  clear, 705
Unobtainable
  impossibility, 471
Unobtained
  loss, 776
Unobtrusive
  modesty, 881
Unoccupied
  vacant, 187
  solitary, 893
  unthinking, 452
  inactive, 683
Unoffending
  innocuous, 648
  innocent, 946
Unofficial
  unauthorized, 925
Unopened
  closure, 261
Unopposed
  co-operation, 709
Unorganized
  mineral, 358
  unprepared, 674
Unornamental
  ugly, 846
Unornamented
  simple, 849
  style, 576

Unorthodox
heterodox, 984A
abnormal, 83
Unostentatious
modesty, 881
Unpacified
discord, 713
Unpack
ejection, 297
Unpaid
debt, 806
gratuitous, 815
Unpaid-for
credit, 805
Unpalatable
unsavoury, 395
disagreeable, 830, 867
Unparagoned
perfection, 650
Unparalleled
great, 31
superiority, 33
exceptional, 83
unmatched, 20
Unpardonable
vice, 945
Unpatriotic
selfish, 911
Unpeaceful
warfare, 722
Unpeople
displacement, 185
exclusion, 893
Unpeopled
empty, 187
Unperceived
latent, 526
neglected, 460
unknown, 491
Unperformed
non-completion, 730
Unperjured
probity, 939
Unperplexed
wisdom, 498
Unpersuadable
obstinacy, 606
dissuasion, 616
Unperturbed
impassive, 823
Unphilosophical
folly, 499
Unpick
disjunction, 44
Unpierced
closure, 261

Unpin
disjunction, 44
Unpitying
ruthless, 907
angry, 900
Unplagued
content, 831
Unplayable
difficult, 704
Unpleasant
pain, 830
Unplumbed
deep, 208
Unpoetical
prose, 598
Unpolished
rude, 895
vulgar, 851
unprepared, 674
Unpolluted
goodness, 648
Unpopular
disliked, 830
Unpossessed
loss, 776
Unpractical
inactivity, 683
Unpractised
unskilfulness, 699
disuse, 614
Unprecedented
unconformity, 83
dissimilarity, 18
infrequency, 137
Unprejudiced
judicious, 480
wise, 498
Unpremeditated
impulsive, 612
unprepared, 674
Unprepared
non-preparation, 674
Unprepossessed
wisdom, 498
Unprepossessing
unpleasing, 829
ugly, 846
Unpresentable
vulgarity, 851
Unpretending
modesty, 881
Unpretentious
modest, 881
Unprincipled
vice, 945

Unprivileged
undueness, 925
Unproclaimed
latency, 526
Unprocurable
impossibility, 471
Unproduced
non-existent, 2
Unproductive
barren, 169
useless, 645
Unprofessional
non-observance, 614
Unprofitable
useless, 645
inexpedient, 647
bad, 649
unproductive, 169
Unprogressive
unchanged, 141
Unprolific
barren, 169
Unpromising
hopeless, 859
Unprompted
impulse, 612
Unpromulgated
latent, 526
Unpronounced
latent, 526
Unpropitious
hopeless, 859
inauspicious, 135
Unproportioned
disagreement, 24
Unprosperous
adversity, 735
Unprotected
danger, 665
Unproved
sophistry, 477
Unprovided
scanty, 640
unprepared, 674
Unprovoked
uninduced, 616
Unpublished
latency, 526
Unpunctual
tardy, 133
untimely, 135
irregular, 139
Unpunished
exempt, 960

Unpurified
uncleanness, 653
Unpurposed
chance, 621
Unpursued
relinquishment, 624
Unqualified
inexpert, 699
unentitled, 925
unprepared, 674
complete, 52
Unquelled
violence, 173
Unquenched
violence, 173
burning, 382
Unquestionable
certainty, 474
Unquestioned
certainty, 474
assent, 488
Unquiet
excitement, 825
Unravaged
undamaged, 648
Unravel
untie, 44
straighten, 246
unfold, 313
decompose, 49
solve, 462, 480A
interpret, 522
disembarrass, 705
arrange, 60
Unravelled
arranged, 58
Unreachable
distance, 196
Unreached
shortcoming, 304
Unread
ignorance, 491
Unready
non-preparation, 674
incompleteness, 53
Unreal
non-existing, 2
erroneous, 495
imaginary, 515
Unreasonable
foolish, 499
exorbitant, 814
unjust, 923
impossible, 471
erroneous, 495

Unreasoning
material, 450A
instinctive, 477
Unreclaimed
impenitence, 951
Unreconciled
discord, 713
Unrecorded
obliteration, 552
Unrecounted
exclusion, 55
Unrecovered
deterioration, 659
Unrectified
imperfection, 651
Unredeemed
greatness, 31
Unreduced
greatness, 31
Unrefined
vulgarity, 851
Unreflecting
impulse, 612
Unreformed
impenitence, 951
Unrefreshed
fatigue, 688
Unrefuted
demonstrated, 478
true, 494
Unregarded
neglected, 460
unrespected, 929
Unregistered
unrecorded, 552
Unrehearsed
impulse, 612
Unrelated
irrelation, 10
Unrelaxed
unweakened, 159
Unrelenting
malevolent, 907
revengeful, 919
Unreliable
dubious, 475, 485
untrustworthy, 940
Unrelieved
aggravation, 835
Unremarked
neglected, 460
Unremembered
forgotten, 506
Unremitting
continuing, 69, 110

industrious, 682
Unremoved
location, 184
Unremunerative
inutility, 645
Unrenewed
unchanged, 141
Unrepealed
unchanged, 141
Unrepeated
fewness, 103
unity, 87
Unrepentant
impenitent, 951
Unrepining
patient, 831
Unreplenished
insufficient, 640
Unreported
untold, 526
Unrepressed
violent, 173
Unreproached
innocence, 946
Unreproachful
forgiveness, 918
Unreproved
innocence, 946
Unrequited
owing, 806
ingratitude, 917
Unresented
forgiven, 918
Unresenting
enduring, 826
Unreserved
frank, 543
Unresisting
obedience, 743
Unresolved
irresolute, 605
Unrespected
disrespect, 929
Unresponsive
insensibility, 823
Unrest
moving, 264
change, 140
changeable, 149
Unrestored
deterioration, 659
Unrestrained
free, 748
unencumbered, 705
Unrestraint
intemperance, 954

Unrestricted
undiminished, 31
free, 748
Unretracted
affirmation, 535
Unrevealed
concealed, 528
Unrevenged
jealousy, 920
Unreversed
permanence, 141
continuance, 143
Unrevoked
continuance, 143
Unrewarded
debt, 806
ingratitude, 917
Unrhymed
prose, 598
Unriddle
solve, 462
interpret, 522
disclose, 529
Unrighteous
evil, 945
Unrip
uncover, 260
Unripe
unprepared, 674
Unrivalled
goodness, 648
Unrivet
disjoin, 44
Unrobe
divest, 226
Unroll
straighten, 246
evolve, 313
display, 525
unravel, 47
Unromantic
true, 494
Unroof
divest, 226
Unroot
pull up, 162
Unruffled
calm, 174
placid, 826
unaffected, 823
quiet, 265
orderly, 58
Unruly
disobedient, 742

obstinate, 606
violent, 173
Unsafe
dangerous, 665
Unsaid
unspoken, 581
untold, 526
Unsanctified
unholy, 988, 989
Unsanctioned
undue, 925
Unsanitary
insalubrious, 657
Unsated
desire, 865
Unsatisfactory
discontent, 832
displeasing, 830
Unsatisfied
discontent, 832
Unsavoury
unsavouriness, 395
Unsay
retract, 607
Unscanned
neglected, 460
Unscathed
health, 654
Unschooled
illiterate, 491
uneducated, 699
Unscientific
ignorant, 495
unskilled, 699
Unscoured
unclean, 653
Unscreened
danger, 665
Unscrew
disjoin, 44
Unscriptural
heterodoxy, 984A
Unscrupulous
evil, 940
Unseal
disclosure, 529
Unseam
disjoin, 44
Unsearched
neglect, 460
Unseasonable
intempestivity, 135
inexpedient, 647
inappropriate, 24
Unseasoned

unprepared, 674
unaccustomed, 614
Unseat
dismiss, 756
Unsecured
uncovenanted, 768A
Unseemly
undue, 925
vicious, 945, 961
vulgar, 851
ugly, 846
inexpedient, 647
Unseen
invisible, 447
unprepared, 674
neglected, 460
Unselfish
generous, 942
Unserviceable
useless, 645
Unset
disjoin, 44
Unsettle
derange, 61
irresolute, 475, 605
mutable, 149
insane, 503
Unsevered
whole, 50
Unshackle
free, 748
liberate, 750
untie, 44
Unshaken
strong, 159
resolute, 604
Unshapely
ugly, 846
Unshapen
amorphous, 241
ugly, 846
Unshared
possession, 777
Unsheathe
uncover, 226
Unsheltered
danger, 665
Unshifting
continuance, 143
Unshocked
unmoved, 823
Unshod
divestment, 226
Unshorn
whole, 50

Unshrinking
resolution, 604
courage, 861
Unsifted
neglected, 460
Unsight
hinder, 706
Unsightly
ugly, 846
Unsinged
uninjured, 670
Unskilful
unskilled, 699
useless, 645
Unslaked
desire, 865
Unsleeping
activity, 682
Unsociable
exclusive, 893
Unsocial
exclusive, 893
Unsoiled
clean, 652
Unsold
possessed, 777
Unsolder
disjoin, 47
Unsoldierly
cowardly, 862
Unsolicited
willing, 602
Unsolicitous
indifferent, 866
Unsolved
secret, 526
Unsophisticated
genuine, 494
simple, 42, 849
good, 648
innocent, 946
Unsorted
unarranged, 59
Unsought
avoided, 623
unrequested, 766
Unsound
imperfect, 651
unhealthy, 655
sophistical, 477
Unsounded
deep, 208
Unsown
unprepared, 674
Unsparing

ample, 639
Unspeakable
great, 31
wonderful, 870
Unspecified
general, 78
Unspent
unused, 678
Unspoiled
goodness, 648
Unspoken
unsaid, 581
Unsportsmanlike
improbity, 940
Unspotted
clean, 652
innocent, 946
beautiful, 845
Unstable
mutable, 149
irresolute, 605
Unstained
untouched, 652
honourable, 939
Unstatesmanlike
unskilful, 699
Unsteadfast
irresolute, 605
Unsteady
mutable, 149
irresolute, 605, 607
dangerous, 665
Unstinted
plenteous, 639
Unstirred
unmoved, 826
calm, 265
Unstitch
disjoin, 44
Unstopped
open, 260
continuing, 143
Unstored
unprovided, 640
Unstrained
unexerted, 172
relaxed, 687
turbid, 653
Unstrengthened
weak, 160
Unstrung
weak, 160
Unsubdued
free, 748
Unsubjugated

free, 748
Unsubmissive
disobedient, 742
Unsubstantial
unsubstantiality, 4
rare, 322
texture, 329
imaginary, 515
erroneous, 495
Unsubstantiated
erroneous, 495
Unsuccessful
failure, 732
Unsuccessive
discontinuous, 70
Unsuitable
incongruous, 24
inexpedient, 647
time, 135
Unsuited
see Unsuitable
Unsullied
clean, 652
honourable, 939
guiltless, 946
Unsummed
infinity, 105
Unsummoned
voluntary, 600
Unsung
untold, 526
Unsunned
dark, 421
Unsupplied
insufficiency, 640
Unsupported
weak, 160
Unsuppressed
persisting, 141
Unsurpassed
great, 31
superior, 33
Unsusceptible
unfeeling, 823
Unsuspected
latent, 526
Unsuspicious
credulous, 484, 486
hopeful, 858
Unsustained
weak, 160
Unswayed
uninfluenced, 616
Unsweetened
unsavoury, 395

untouched, 678
Unusual
  unconformity, 83
  greatness, 31
Unutilized
  disuse, 678
Unutterable
  wonderful, 870
  great, 31
Unvalued
  depreciated, 483
  undesired, 866
  disliked, 898
Unvanquished
  free, 748
Unvaried
  permanent, 141
  continued, 143
  monotonous, 576
Unvarnished
  truth, 494
Unvarying
  uniform, 16
Unveil
  manifest, 525
  disclose, 529
Unventilated
  close, 261
Unveracious
  false, 544
Unverified
  indiscrimination, 465A
Unversed
  unconversant, 491
  unskilled, 699
Unvexed
  content, 831
Unviolated
  probity, 939
Unvisited
  exclusion, 893
Unvitiated
  unspoiled, 648
Unvouched-for
  unattested, 468
Unwakened
  dormant, 683
Unwanted
  unnecessary, 645
Unwarlike
  cowardly, 862
Unwarmed
  cold, 383
Unwarned
  danger, 665

Unwarped
  unprejudiced, 480
Unwarranted
  unjustifiable, 923, 925
  inconclusive, 477
Unwary
  heedless, 460
Unwashed
  unclean, 653
  vulgar, 851
Unwasted
  unexhausted, 639
Unwatched
  neglected, 460
Unwatchful
  inattentive, 458
Unwatered
  dry, 340
  undiluted, 159
Unwavering
  resolute, 604
Unweakened
  strong, 159
Unwearied
  indefatigable, 682
  refreshed, 689
Unwedded
  celibacy, 904
Unweeded
  neglected, 460
Unweighed
  neglected, 460
Unwelcome
  disagreeable, 830
Unwell
  ill, 655
Unwept
  hate, 898
Unwholesome
  insalubrious, 657
Unwieldy
  large, 192
  heavy, 319
  difficult, 704
  cumbersome, 647
Unwilling
  unwillingness, 603
  dissent, 489
Unwind
  evolve, 313
  straighten, 246
Unwinking
  vigilant, 457
Unwiped
  unclean, 653

Unwise
  fool, 499
Unwished
  undesirable, 866
Unwithered
  strong, 159
Unwitnessed
  unseen, 526
Unwitting
  ignorant, 491
  involuntary, 601
Unwomanly
  unbecoming, 940
Unwonted
  unaccustomed, 614
  unusual, 83
Unworkmanlike
  unskilful, 699
Unworldly
  disinterested, 943
  pious, 987
Unworn
  unused, 159
Unworthy
  vicious, 945
  base, 940
  shameful, 874
Unwrap
  straighten, 246
Unwreathe
  straighten, 246
Unwrinkled
  smooth, 255
Unwritten
  untold, 526
Unwrought
  unprepared, 674
Unyielding
  tough, 323
  resolute, 604
  severe, 739
  obstinate, 606
  resisting, 719
Unyoke
  disjoin, 44
Up
  fizzy, 353
Up in arms
  resist, 719
Up-country
  interiority, 221
Upanishads
  sacred books, 986
Upbear
  support, 215

Upbraid
disapprove, 932
Upbringing
teaching, 537
Upcast
elevation, 307
Upgrow
height, 206
Upgrowth
ascent, 305
Upheave
elevation, 307
Uphill
activity, 217
ascent, 305
difficult, 704
Uphold
support, 215
evidence, 467
aid, 707
continue, 143
Upholster
cover, 222
furnish, 637
Upkeep
preservation, 670
Uplands
height, 206
Uplift
elevation, 307
Upper
height, 206
Upper hand
authority, 737
success, 731
Upper storey
brain, 450
Uppermost
height, 206, 210
Uppish
self-assertive, 885
Upraise
elevation, 307
Uprear
elevation, 307
Upright
vertical, 212
honest, 939
virtuous, 944
Uprise
ascent, 305
Uproar
noise, 404
turmoil, 173
Uproar

disorder, 59
Uproot
destruction, 162
extraction, 301
Upset
throw down, 308
disorder, 59
derange, 61
change, 140
invert, 218
destroy, 162
Upshot
end, 66
total, 50
Upside-down
inversion, 218
Upstage
affected, 855
supercilious, 930
proud, 878
Upstairs
height, 207
Upstart
plebeian, 876
prosperous, 734
Upturn
inversion, 218
Upwards
height, 206
Uranology
world, 318
Urban
abode, 189
Urbane
courtesy, 894
Urchin
small, 193
child, 129
wretch, 949
Urge
impel, 276
incite, 615
solicit, 765
hasten, 684
accelerate, 274
violence, 173
Urgent
important, 642
required, 630
Uriah Heep
servility, 886
Urinal
room, 191
privy, 653
Urinate

excrete, 299
Urn
vase, 191
funereal, 363
kettle, 386
Usage
custom, 613
rule, 80
use, 677
Usance
debt, 806
Use
employment, 677
waste, 638
utility, 644
habit, 613
rule, 80
Used up
worn, 651
surfeited, 869
Useful
use, 644
Useless
misuse, 645
Usher
teacher, 540
servant, 746
announce, 511
receive, 296, 894
begin, 66
precede, 62, 280
prior, 116
Ustulation
heating, 384
Usual
ordinary, 82
customary, 613
Usufruct
use, 677
Usurer
merchant, 797
Usurp
assume, 739
dethrone, 738
seize, 789
illegality, 925
Usury
debt, 806
Utensil
instrument, 633
Utilitarian
philanthropy, 910
Utilize
use, 644, 677

742

Vanquished
failure, 732
Vantage-ground
influence, 175
Vapid
insipid, 391
unattractive, 866
style, 575
Vaporize
vaporization, 336
Vapour
gas, 334
bubble, 353
insolence, 885
boasting, 884
chimera, 515
rare, 322
Vapour bath
furnace, 386
Vapours
dejection, 837
Variable
changeable, 149
irresolute, 605
Variance
difference, 15
disagreement, 24
discord, 713
Variation
non-imitation, 20
irrelation, 10
music, 415
Varied
different, 15
Variegation
colour, 440
Variety
difference, 15
multiformity, 16A
exception, 83
class, 75
Variform
difference, 15
variety, 81
Various
different, 15
many, 102
variation, 20
Varlet
sinner, 949
Varnish
coat, 222
decorate, 845, 847
semiliquid, 352

sophistry, 477
falsehood, 544
excuse, 937
Vary
differ, 15
diversify, 18
modify, 20
change, 140
fluctuate, 149
Vasculum
botany, 369
Vase
receptacle, 191
Vassal
servant, 746
Vassalage
subjection, 749
Vast
in quantity, 31
in size, 192
Vat
receptacle, 191
Vatican
temple, 1000
Vaticide
killing, 361
Vaticination
prediction, 511
Vaudeville
the drama, 599
Vault
cellar, 191
sepulchre, 363
to leap, 305, 309
Vaulting
superiority, 33
Vaunt
boasting, 884
Vaurien
sinner, 949
Veda
sacred books, 986
Vedette
safety, 664
warning, 668
Veer
regression, 283
change, 140
deviate, 279
change intention, 607
Vegetable
vegetable, 365
plant, 367
Vegetarian
temperance, 953

Vegetate
grow, 194
exist, 1
inactivity, 683
insensibility, 823
quiescence, 265
Vehemence
violence, 173
emotion, 825
Vehicle
vehicle, 272
instrumentality, 631
Vehmgericht
illegality, 964
Veil
mask, 530
to conceal, 528
shade, 424
covering, 225
Veiled
invisible, 447
latent, 526
Vein
humour, 602
tendency, 176
cast of mind, 820
mine, 636
Veined
variegation, 440
Velleity
will, 600
Vellum
writing, 590
Velocipede
locomotion, 266
Velocity
swiftness, 274
Velour
smooth, 255
rough, 256
Velvet
smooth, 255
rough, 256
ease, 705
physical pleasure, 277
moral pleasure, 827
profit, 618
Velveteen
smooth, 255
rough, 256
Venal
parsimony, 819
mercenary, 812, 943
Vend
sell, 796

Vendetta
feud, 713
revenge, 919
Vendible
sale, 796
Vendor
merchant, 797
Veneer
covering, 222
ostentation, 882
Venerable
old, 128
Veneration
respect, 928
piety, 987
worship, 990
Venery
chase, 622
Venesection
ejection, 297
Vengeance
revenge, 919
(with a),
greatness, 31
Vengeful
revenge, 919
Venial
excusable, 937
Venom
bane, 663
malignity, 907
Venomous
evil, 649
malignant, 907
Vent
air-pipe, 351
opening, 260
emit, 295
disclose, 529
Vent-peg
stopper, 263
Ventilate
perflate, 349
air, 338
clean, 652
discuss, 595
examine, 461
publicity, 531
Ventilator
wind, 349
Ventricle
receptacle, 191
Ventriloquism
voice, 580
Venture

chance, 156
to try, 621, 675
danger, 665
courage, 861
Venturesome
brave, 861
rash, 863
Venue
place, 182
Venus
goddess, 979
beauty, 845
love, 897
Veracity
truth, 494, 543
Veranda
portico, 191
Verb. sap.
advice, 695
Verbal
word, 562
Verbatim
imitation, 19
interpretation, 522
word, 562
Verbiage
diffuse, 573
nonsense, 497
Verbose
diffuse, 573
loquacious, 584
Verdant
green, 435
vegetation, 367
credulous, 486
ignorant, 491
Verd-antique
green, 435
Verdict
opinion, 480
sentence, 969
Verdigris
green, 435
Verdure
green, 435
plant, 367
Verecundity
modesty, 881
humility, 879
Verge
brink, 230
to tend, 278
contribute, 176
Verger
churchman, 996

Veridical
truthful, 543
Verify
test, 463
demonstrate, 478
judge, 480
warrant, 771
Verily
positively, 32
truly, 494
Verisimilitude
probable, 472
Veritable
truth, 494
Verity
truth, 494
Verjuice
sourness, 397
Vermicular
convolution, 248
Vermiform
convolution, 248
Vermilion
redness, 434
Vermin
base, 876
unclean, 653
Vernacular
language, 560
familiar, 82
Vernal
early, 123
spring, 125
Vers de société
poetry, 597
Vers libre
poetry, 597
Versatile
changeable, 605
skilful, 698
Verse
poetry, 597
Versed
skill, 698
Versicolour
variegation, 440
Versifier
poetry, 597
Version
interpretation, 522
Verso
left hand, 239
Vert
change belief, 144, 484
green, 435

745

Vertex
summit, 210
Vertical
verticality, 212
Vertigo
insanity, 503
Verve
imagination, 515
feeling, 821
Very
great, 31
Very light
light, 423
Vesicle
cell, 191
globe, 249
Vespers
rite, 990, 998
Vespertine
evening, 126
Vessel
recipient, 191
ship, 273
tube, 260
Vest
dress, 225
give, 784
Vestal
purity, 960
Vested
legal, 963
Vestibule
entrance, 66
room, 191
Vestige
record, 551
Vestments
canonicals, 999
Vestry
conclave, 995
church, 1000
Vesture
dress, 225
Veteran
old, 130
adept, 700
fighter, 726
Veterinary
remedy, 662
taming, 370
Veto
prohibit, 761
refuse, 764
Vetturino
director, 694

Vex
painful, 830
Vexation
pain, 828
Vexatious
painful, 830
Via
way, 627
direction, 278
Via media
mean, 29
middle, 68
Viability
life, 359
Viable
practicable, 470
Viaduct
way, 627
Vial
bottle, 191
wrath, 900
Viands
food, 298
Viaticum
rite, 998
Vibrate
fluctuate, 149
oscillate, 314
Vicar
clergy, 996
deputy, 759
Vicarage
office, 995
house, 1000
Vicarious
substituted, 149, 755
Vice
guiltiness, 945
imperfection, 651
deputy, 759
grip, 781
vinculum, 45
Vice versa
correlation, 12
contrariety, 14
interchange, 148
Vicegerency
agency, 755
Vicegerent
consignee, 758
deputy, 759
Vice-president
master, 745
Viceroy
deputy, 759

Vicinity
nearness, 197
Vicious
fallacious, 477
faulty, 651
immoral, 945
Vicissitude
change, 140
mutable, 149
Victim
injured, 732
dupe, 547
sufferer, 828
Victimize
deceive, 545
baffle, 731
Victoria
vehicle, 272
Victory
success, 731
Victualling
provision, 637
Victuals
food, 298
Videlicet
namely, 522
specification, 79
Video
radio, 599B
Viduity
widowhood, 905
Vie
emulate, 648
contend, 720
View
sight, 441
appearance, 448
to attend to, 457
landscape, 556
opinion, 484
intention, 620
radio, 599B
View-finder
optical, 445
Viewless
invisible, 447
Viewy
caprice, 608
Vigesimal
twenty, 98
Vigil
watch, 459
eve, 116
Vigilance
attention, 457

care, 459
Vigils
worship, 990
Vignette
engraving, 558
Vigour
strong, 159
healthy, 654
activity, 683
energy, 171
style, 574
Viking
pirate, 792
Vile
bad, 649
odious, 830
valueless, 643
disgraceful, 874, 940
plebeian, 876
Vilify
censure, 932
defame, 934
scold, 908
shame, 874
Vilipend
censure, 932
defame, 934
shame, 874
disrespect, 929
Villa
abode, 189
Village
abode, 189
Villager
inhabitant, 188
Villain
vice, 945
knave, 941
Villainage
subjection, 749
Villainy
vice, 945
improbity, 940
Villanelle
poetry, 597
Villous
roughness, 256
Vim
energy, 171, 682
style, 574
Vincible
weakness, 160
Vinculum
junction, 45
Vindicate

justify, 924, 937
Vindictive
revengeful, 919
irascible, 901
Vinegar
sourness, 397
condiment, 393
Vineyard
agriculture, 371
Vintage
agriculture, 371
Viola
musical instrument, 417
Violate
disobey, 742
engagement, 773
right, 925
duty, 927
a usage, 614
Violence
physical, 173
arbitrariness, 964
Violently
great, 31
Violet
purple, 437
Violin
musical instrument, 417
Violinist
musician, 416
Violoncello
musical instrument, 417
Viper
bane, 663, 913
miscreant, 949
Virago
irascibility, 901
fury, 173
Virescent
green, 435
Virgin
girl, 129
celibacy, 904
purity, 960
Virginal
musical instrument, 417
Virginia
tobacco, 298AA
Viridescent
green, 435
Viridity
green, 435
Virile
manly, 373
adolescent, 131

strong, 159
style, 574
Virtu
taste, 850
Virtual
real, 1
potential, 2
Virtually
truth, 494
Virtue
goodness, 944
right, 922
probity, 939
purity, 960
power, 157
courage, 861
Virtueless
vice, 945
Virtuosity
taste, 850
skill, 698
Virtuoso
taste, 850
performer, 416
proficient, 700
Virulence
insalubrity, 657
poison, 663
malignity, 649
page, 900
malevolence, 907
Virus
poison, 663
disease, 655
insalubrity, 657
Visage
ront, 234
appearance, 448
Vis-à-vis
front, 234
opposite, 237
Viscera
interior, 221
Viscid
semiliquid, 352
Viscount
noble, 875
master, 745
Viscounty
title, 877
Viscous
semiliquid, 352
Visé
indication, 550
Vishnu
deity, 979

Visible
visibility, 446
Vision
sight, 441
imagination, 515
apparition, 980
Visionary
erroneous, 495
imaginary, 515
impossible, 471
heterodox, 984A
Visit
sociality, 892
frequent, 136
arrival, 292
Visitation
pain, 828
disease, 655
calamity, 830
Visiting-card
indication, 560
Visitor
arrival, 292
director, 694
Visor
concealment, 528
Vista
point of view, 441
prospect, 448, 507
Visual
vision, 441
Vital
importance, 642
Vitality
life, 359
strength, 159
Vitals
interior, 221
Vitiate
deteriorate, 659
debase, 945
Vitreous
density, 321
Vitrify
density, 321
harden, 323
Vitriolic
malevolent, 907
Vituperate
disapprove, 932
scold, 908
Viva
honour, 873
Viva voce

speech, 582
Vivacious
active, 682
sensitive, 822
cheerful, 836
Vivarium
taming, 370
Vive
honour, 873
Vivid
light, 420
colour, 428
lively, 375
energetic, 171
style, 574
Vivify
life, 359
Vivisect
anatomize, 44
Vixen
scold, 901
fury, 173
Viz.
meaning, 516
Vizier
deputy, 759
Vizor
see Visor
Vocable
word, 562
Vocabulary
word, 562
Vocal
voice, 580
loudness, 404
music, 415
Vocalist
musician, 416
Vocalize
speech, 580
Vocation
business, 625
Vociferate
cry, 411
loudness, 404
voice, 580
Vogue
fashion, 852
custom, 613
repute, 873
Vogue word
neology, 563
Voice
speech, 580
grammar, 567

sound, 402
cry, 411
choice, 609
affirmation, 535
opinion, 484
Void
vacuum, 2, 4
absence, 187
to emit, 297
invalidate, 964
Voivode
master, 745
Volant
flight, 267
Volapük
language, 560
Volatile
vaporizable, 336
changeable, 149
irresolute, 605
Volatility
caprice, 608
Volcanic
violence, 173
excitable, 825
Volitation
flight, 267
Volition
will, 600
Volley
impulse, 276
attack, 716
violence, 173
collection, 72
Volplane
descent, 306
Volte-face
recantation, 607
Voluble
loquacity, 584
Volume
bulk, 192
quantity, 25
greatness, 31
book, 593
Voluntary
willing, 600, 602
music, 415
Volunteer
endeavour, 676
offer, 600, 763
Voluptuary
libertine, 962
Voluptuous
sensual, 954

pleasure, 377
joy, 827
delight, 829
Volute
convolution, 248
Vomit
ejection, 297
Vomitory
opening, 260
Voodooism
occult arts, 992
Voracity
appetite, 865
gluttony, 957
Vortex
rotation, 312
whirlpool, 348
Votary
devotee, 840, 865
Vote
choice, 609
affirmation, 535
Vote for
assent, 488
Votive
promise, 768
Vouch
testify, 467
assert, 535
Voucher
evidence, 467
record, 551
security, 771
Vouchsafe
permit, 760
consent, 762
ask, 765
deign, 879
Vow
promise, 768
assert, 535
worship, 990
Voyage
journey, 267
motion, 264
Voyageur
boatman, 269
Voyeur
curiosity, 455
Vraisemblance
probability, 472
Vulcan
god, 979
Vulgar
unrefined, 851

discourteous, 895
commonalty, 876
Vulgarism
solecism, 568
language, 560
Vulgate
revelation, 985
Vulnerable
danger, 665
Vulpine
cunning, 702
Vulture
bane, 663

W.C.
lavatory, 653
Wabble
oscillation, 314
Wacky
mad, 503
Wadding
lining, 224
softness, 324
stopping, 263
Waddle
slowness, 275
oscillation, 314
Wade
swim, 267
Wafer
layer, 204
Waft
transfer, 270
blow, 267, 349
Wag
oscillate, 314
agitate, 315
wit, 844
Wage war
contention, 720
Wager
chance, 621
Wages
expenditure, 809
Waggery
wit, 842
Waggish
merry, 836
Waggle
oscillation, 314
agitation, 315
Wagon
vehicle, 272
Wagonette

vehicle, 272
Waif
outcast, 893
Wail
lamentation, 839
Wain
vehicle, 272
Wainscot
lining, 224
base, 211
Waist
narrow, 203
Waistcoat
dress, 225
Wait
tarry, 110, 133
expect, 121, 507
inaction, 681
Wait on
accompany, 88
help, 707
call on, 894
Waiter
servant, 746
Waits
musicians, 416
Waive
relinquish, 624, 782
dispense with, 678
Wake
sequel, 65
back, 235
trace, 551
to excite, 824
funeral, 363
lamentation, 839
Wale
ridge, 250
Walk
move, 266
slowness, 275
region, 181
business, 625
way, 627
conduct, 692
arena, 728
Walkie-talkie
hearing, 418
radio, 599B
Walkover
easy, 705
Wall
lining, 224
circumscription, 231
enclosure, 232

749

Washy
watery, 337
weak, 160
valueless, 645
style, 573
Wasp-waisted
thin, 203
Waspish
discourteous, 895
irascible, 901
Wassail
feast, 840
Waste
decrease, 36
contract, 195
expend, 638
destroy, 162
vacant space, 180
plain, 344
misuse, 679
useless, 645
prodigality, 818
refuse, 643
loss, 776
Waste-pipe
conduit, 350
Wasted
weakness, 160
Wasteful
useless, 645
prodigal, 818
Wastrel
outcast, 893
prodigal, 818
Watch
observe, 441
attend to, 457
expect, 507
sentinel, 753
clock, 114
Watch-fire
indication, 550
Watch-tower
warning, 668
Watcher
spectator, 444
Watchet
blue, 438
Watchful
care, 459
Watchman
safety, 664
Watchword
indication, 550
Water

fluid, 337
to weaken, 160
Water-cart
spray, 348
Water-clock
chronology, 114
Water-closet
room, 191
lavatory, 653
Water-gate
conduit, 350
Watercourse
conduit, 350
Watered
variegated, 440
Waterfall
river, 348
Watering-can
spray, 348
Waterlogged
difficulty, 704
Waterproof
dryness, 340
safe, 664
dress, 225
Watershed
summit, 210
Waterspout
river, 349
rotation, 312
Watertight
closed, 261
Wattle
plaiting, 219
Wave
of water, 348
the sea, 341
sinuous, 248
oscillate, 314
hint, 527
curl, 245
salute, 894
Waver
unwilling, 603
hesitate, 475, 605
fluctuate, 149
Wavy
convolution, 248
Wax
become, 144
increase, 35
soft, 324
semiliquid, 352
unctuous, 355
lubricate, 332

substance, 356
rage, 900
Waxcloth
covering, 222
Way
road, 627
space, 180
passage, 302
conduct, 692
habit, 613
Wayfarer
traveller, 268
Wayfaring
journey, 266
Waylay
deception, 545
Ways and means
means, 632
Wayward
obstinate, 606
capricious, 608
discourteous, 895
changeable, 149
Wayworn
fatigue, 688
Wayzgoose
picnic, 298
festivity, 840
Weak
feeble, 160
powerless, 158
insipid, 391, 575
small in degree, 32
foolish, 499
irrational, 477
irresolute, 605
compassionate, 914
vicious, 945
Weak-headed
fool, 499
Weak-hearted
coward, 862
Weak-kneed
irresolute, 605
Weak side
vice, 945
Weaken
enfeeble, 160
decrease, 36
invalidate, 468
impair, 659
Weal
good, 618
ridge, 250

Weald
plant, 367
plain, 344
Wealth
rich, 803
Wean
change habit, 614
change opinion, 484
infant, 129
Weapon
instrument, 633
arms, 727
Weaponless
impotent, 158
Wear
decrease, 36
decay, 659
use, 677
clothe, 225
alter course, 279
Wear and tear
waste, 638
injury, 619
Wear off
diminish, 36
cease, 142
habit, 614
Wear out
damage, 659
fatigue, 688
Wearisome
fatigue, 688
painful, 830
ennui, 841
Weary
fatigue, 688
ennui, 841
uneasy, 828
Weary Willie
loafer, 683
Weasand
air-pipe, 260, 351
Weather
air, 338
succeed, 731
disintegrate, 330
Weather-beaten
weak, 160
Weather-bound
restraint, 751
Weather-glass
measure, 466
air, 338
Weather-ship
air, 338
Weather-wise

prediction, 511
air, 338
Weathercock
irresolute, 605
mutable, 149
Weave
interlace, 219
wind, 248
produce, 161
Web
texture, 329
intersection, 219
Wed
marriage, 903
Wedded to
habit, 613
opinion, 484
obstinate, 606
Wedge
angular, 244
intervention, 228
instrument, 633
to insert, 300
locate, 184
join, 43
ingress, 294
flock, 72
Wedlock
marriage, 903
Wee
small, 32, 34
Weed
rubbish, 643, 645
plant, 367
cultivate, 371
reduce, 103
mourning, 225, 839
widow, 905
reject, 55
tobacco, 298A
Weedy
thin, 203
Weekly
period, 108, 138
publication, 531
Weeny
little, 193
Weep
lament, 839
Weigh
heavy, 319
ponder, 451
measure, 466
lift, 307
influence, 175

Weigh anchor
depart, 293
Weigh down
aggrieve, 649
Weigh with
motive, 615
Weighbridge
weight, 319
Weight
influence, 175
gravity, 319
importance, 642
Weightless
levity, 320
Weir
hindrance, 706
dam, 350
Weird
strange, 83
wonderful, 870
prediction, 511
supernatural, 980
destiny, 601
Welcome
grateful, 829
sociality, 892
reception, 894
friendly, 888
Weld
coherence, 46
join, 43
Welfare
prosperity, 734
Welkin
world, 318
Well
water, 343
to flow, 348
much, 31
healthy, 654
deep, 208
store, 636
origin, 153
Well-behaved
good, 944
Well-being
prosperity, 734
gratification, 827
Well-born
patrician, 875
Well-bred
courteous, 894
genteel, 852
Well-conducted
good, 944

Well-disposed
friendly, 707, 888
Well-doing
virtue, 944
Well done
approbation, 931
Well enough
imperfection, 651
Well-favoured
beauty, 845
Well-founded
probable, 472
Well-groomed
adornment, 847
Well-grounded
knowledge, 490
Well-informed
knowledge, 490
Well-intended
virtue, 944
Well-judged
intelligence, 498
Well-knit
strength, 159
Well-mannered
courtesy, 894
Well-meant
benevolent, 906
Well-off
prosperity, 734
wealth, 803
Well out
egress, 295
Well-proportioned
symmetry, 242
Well-set
strength, 159
Well-spent
success, 731
Well-tasted
savoury, 394
Well-timed
opportune, 134, 646
Well-to-do
prosperity, 734
Well-wisher
friend, 890
Welladay
lamentation, 839
Wellington
boot, 225
Wellnigh
almost, 32
Welsh
to cheat, 545

Welsher
deceiver, 548
swindler, 792
defaulter, 808
Welt
edge, 230
Welter
rotation, 312
agitation, 315
Weltschmerz
weariness, 841
Wen
convexity, 250
Wench
young girl, 129
woman, 374
Wend
journey, 266
Werewolf
demon, 980
Wersh
tasteless, 391, 866
insipid, 575
West
side, 236
Wet
water, 337
moisture, 339
Wet-nurse
to pamper, 954
Whack
blow, 276, 972
share, 786
try, 675
Whacked
exhausted, 160
Whacker
size, 31, 192
Whale
monster, 192
Whaler
ship, 273
Wham
impact, 276
Whang
impact, 276
Wharf
anchorage, 189
Whatnot
receptacle, 191
What's-his-name
euphemism, 565
Wheedle
flatter, 933
coax, 615

endearment, 902
Wheel
circle, 247
circuition, 311
deviation, 279
rotation, 212
instrument, 633
means, 632
money, 800
torture, 378, 975
pain, 830
execution, 972
Wheel-chair
vehicle, 272
Wheelbarrow
vehicle, 272
Wheen
plurality, 100
multitude, 102
Wheeze
blow, 349
hiss, 409
joke, 842
Whelm
redundance, 641
Whelp
young, 129
When
time, 119
Whence
attribution, 155
inquiry, 461
reasoning, 476
departure, 293
Whenever
time, 119
Whensoever
time, 119
Where
presence, 186
Whereabouts
situation, 183
nearness, 197
Whereas
reason, 476
Wherefore
reason, 476
attribution, 155
inquiry, 461
motive, 615
Whereupon
futurity, 121
Wherever
space, 180
Wherewith
instrument, 631

753

Wherewithal
means, 632
money, 800
Wherry
boat, 273
Whet
excite, 824
incite, 615
sharpen, 253
desire, 865
meal, 298
Whey
fluid, 337
Whiff
wind, 349
Whiffy
smelly, 401
Whigmaleerie
trifle, 643
While
duration, 106, 120
Whilom
preterition, 122
Whim
caprice, 608
prejudice, 481
desire, 865
imagination, 515
wit, 842
Whim-wham
trifle, 643
Whimper
lamentation, 839
Whimsical
fancy, 515, 608
ridiculous, 853
Whimsy
desire, 865
Whine
cry, 411
complain, 839
Whinny
animal cry, 412
Whip
to beat, 276, 972
scourge, 975
rapidity, 274
driver, 694
trouble, 830
Whip-hand
success, 731
Whip off
escape, 671
Whip-round

giving, 784
Whip up
snatch, 789
Whipper-in
director, 694
servant, 746
Whippersnapper
youth, 129
Whippet
chase, 622
Whipping-post
scourge, 975
Whirl
rotation, 312
Whirligig
rotation, 312
Whirlpool
vortex, 312
eddy, 348
danger, 667
confusion, 59
Whirlwind
wind, 349
vortex, 312
agitation, 315
Whirlybird
aircraft, 273A
Whirr
roll, 407
Whisk
rapidity, 274
circuition, 311
agitation, 315
Whisker
hair, 256
Whisky
vehicle, 272
Whisper
faint sound, 405
stammer, 583
tell, 527
prompt, 615
remind, 505
Whist!
silence, 403, 585
Whistle
hiss, 409
music, 415
instrument, 417
Whistle at
depreciate, 483
Whit
point, 32
part, 51
small, 193

White
whiteness, 430
eye, 441
White feather
coward, 862
White horses
wave, 348
White lie
equivocalness, 520
plea, 617
White-livered
cowardice, 862
Whitewash
whiten, 430
adorn, 847
vindicate, 937
acquit, 970
insolvency, 808
Whither
tendency, 176
direction, 278
Whittle
disjoin, 44
abbreviate, 201
Whiz
sibilation, 409
expert, 700
Whizz-kid
go-getter, 682
Whodunit
story, 594
Whole
entire, 50
complete, 52
healthy, 654
Whole-hearted
cordial, 602
Wholesale
greatness, 31
whole, 50
indiscriminate, 465A
plenty, 639
barter, 794
Wholesome
salubrity, 656
Wholly
great, 31
whole, 50
Whoop
cry, 411
loud, 404
weep, 839
Whoopee
merry, 836

Whopper
 untruth, 546
Whopping
 size, 192
Whore
 libertine, 962
 impurity, 961
Why
 reason, 615
 inquiry, 461
 cause, 155
Wicked
 vice, 945
 improbity, 940
Wicker
 crossing, 219
Wicket
 entrance, 66
 opening, 260
Wide
 broad, 202
Wide-awake
 hat, 225
Wide of
 distance, 196
Widen
 expand, 194
Widespread
 dispersed, 73
Widow
 widowhood, 905
Width
 breadth, 202
Wield
 use, 677
 brandish, 315
Wife
 marriage, 903
Wifeless
 celibacy, 904
Wig
 dress, 225
 to scold, 932
Wiggle
 oscillate, 314
Wight
 man, 373
Wigwam
 abode, 189
Wild
 violent, 173
 mad, 503
 excited, 825
 rash, 863
 licentious, 954

 foolish, 499, 699
 useless, 645
 desert, 344
Wilderness
 space, 180
 useless, 645
 seclusion, 893
Wildfire
 heat, 382
Wile
 cunning, 702
 stratagem, 545
Wilful
 obstinacy, 606
Will
 volition, 600
 resolution, 604
Will-o'-the-wisp
 light, 423
 phantom, 515
Willing
 acquiescent, 488
 voluntary, 600, 602
Willow
 lamentation, 839
Willowy
 pliant, 324
Willy-nilly
 compulsion, 744
 necessity, 601
Willy-willy
 vortex, 312
Wily
 sly, 702
Wimble
 perforator, 262
Wimple
 dress, 225
Win
 get, 775
 steal, 791
 succeed, 731
 engage, 897
Win over
 conciliate, 831
Wince
 flinch, 860
 feel, 821, 825
 pain, 378, 828
Winch
 instrument, 633
 raise, 307
Wind
 blast, 349
 circuition, 311

 convolution, 248
 rapidity, 274
Wind-bound
 hindrance, 706
 restraint, 751
Wind up
 screw up, 159
 end, 67
 complete, 729
 fear, 860
Windbreaker
 dress, 225
Windcheater
 dress, 225
Windfall
 good, 618
 luck, 621
 success, 731
Winding
 curved, 245
 undulating, 248
Winding-sheet
 shroud, 363
Windlass
 instrument, 633
 raise, 307
Windmill
 rotation, 312
Window
 opening, 260
Windpipe
 air-pipe, 351
Windy
 air, 338
 verbose, 573
Winebag
 drunken, 959
Winebibber
 drunken, 959
Wing
 side, 236
 limb, 633
 troop, 726
 asylum, 666
 move, 267
Wing-commander
 master, 745
Winged
 rapid, 274
Wink
 blind, 442
 nictitate, 443
 hint, 527
 indicate, 550

Wink at
permit, 760
overlook, 460
Winning
pleasing, 829
courteous, 894
lovely, 897
Winnow
sift, 42
exclude, 55
clean, 652
inquire, 461
pick, 609
Winsome
pleasing, 829
lovely, 897
Winter
cold, 383
Wintry
cold, 383
Wipe
clean, 652
dry, 340
strike, 276
Wipe off
non-observance, 773
Wipe out
obliterate, 552
demolish, 162
Wire
filament, 205
ligature, 45
message, 532
Wiredrawn
lengthy, 200
thin, 203
style, 571
Wireless
message, 532
publication, 531
hearing, 418
radio, 599B
Wireworm
bane, 663
Wiry
tough, 327
Wisdom
wisdom, 498
intellect, 450
Wise
wisdom, 498
way, 627
Wise to
knowing, 490
Wiseacre
sage, 500

Wisecrack
wit, 842
maxim, 496
phrase, 566
Wish
desire, 865
Wishbone
spell, 993
Wish joy
congratulation, 896
Wishing-cap
spell, 993
Wishy-washy
insipid, 391
absurd, 497
feeble, 575
trifling, 643
Wisp
assemblage, 72
Wistful
thoughtful, 451
Wit
intellect, 450
humour, 842
wisdom, 498
humorist, 844
Witch
oracle, 513
proficient, 700
sorceress, 994
bad woman, 949
Witchcraft
sorcery, 992
Witchery
attraction, 615
charm, 829
sorcery, 992
With
addition, 37
accompanying, 88
instrumental, 631
Withal
addition, 37
accompanying, 88
Withdraw
subduct, 38
recede, 283, 287
diverge, 291
deny, 536
depart, 293
retire, 893
Withe
fastening, 45
Wither
shrink, 195

decay, 659
Withering
disapproving, 932
Withershins
rotation, 312
Withhold
retain, 781
conceal, 528
stint, 640
prohibit, 761
dissuade, 616
Within
interior, 221
Without
unless, 8
absence, 187
exterior, 220
subduction, 38
exception, 83
circumjacent, 227
Withstand
resist, 719
oppose, 179, 708
Withy
fastening, 45
Witless
ignorant, 491
neglectful, 460
imbecile, 499
Witling
fool, 501
Witness
evidence, 467
voucher, 550
Wits
intellect, 450
Witticism
wit, 842
Wittingly
purposely, 620
Witty
wit, 842
Wive
marriage, 903
Wizard
sorcerer, 994
oracle, 513
good, 648
Wizardry
occult, 992
Wizened
withered, 193, 195
Wobble
oscillate, 314

Woden
god, 979
Woe
pain, 828
evil, 619
Woebegone
pain, 828
dejection, 837
Woeful
painfulness, 830
Wold
plain, 344
Wolf
to devour, 296
alarm, 669
philanderer, 902
Woman
woman, 131, 374
Womanish
cowardly, 862
Womanly
weakness, 160
Womb
interior, 221
cause, 153
Wonder
astonishment, 870
prodigy, 872
Wonderfully
great, 31
Wonderment
prodigy, 872
Wondrous
wonder, 870
Wonky
imperfect, 651
Wont
habitual, 613
usual, 82
Woo
desire, 865
courtship, 902
Wood
plant, 367
Wood-note
animal cry, 412
Woodcut
engraving, 558
Woodcutter
forester, 371
Wooer
love, 897
Woof
texture, 329
Wool

hair, 256
Wool-gathering
folly, 499
inattention, 458
madness, 503
Woolsack
pillow, 215
authority, 747
tribunal, 966
Wop
alien, 57
Word
vocable, 562
intelligence, 532
promise, 768
revelation, 985
Deity, 976
maxim, 496
Wording
expression, 566
style, 569
Wordless
aphony, 581
Words
quarrel, 713
Wordy
diffuseness, 573
Work
product, 154
agency, 170
to use, 677
shape, 240
adorn, 847
action, 680
book, 593
Work in
introduce, 37
Work off
get rid of, 545, 672
Work out
conduct, 692
achieve, 729
Work up
incite, 615
inflame, 824
Work upon
influence, 175
Workhouse
poverty, 804
Working
activity, 682
Workman
agent, 690
originator, 164
Workmanlike

skill, 698
Workmanship
produce, 161
handiwork, 680
Workshop
workshop, 691
World
universe, 318
mankind, 373
fashion, 852
events, 151
great, 31
Worldling
selfish, 943
Worldly
selfish, 943
irreligious, 989
Worldwide
world, 318
Worm
small, 193
animal, 366
spiral, 248
Worm in
insert, 300
interpose, 228
Worm out
ascertain, 480A
Wormeaten
imperfect, 651
decayed, 659
Wormwood
unsavoury, 395
Worn
imperfect, 651
decayed, 659
Worry
vexation, 828
to tease, 830
harass, 907
Worse
badness, 649
Worsen
deteriorate, 659
Worship
religious, 990
title, 877
servility, 886
Worshipful
repute, 873
Worst
defeat, 731
Worsted
defeated, 732

Worth
goodness, 648
value, 644
virtue, 994
price, 812
Worth while
utility, 644
Worthless
useless, 645
profligate, 945
Worthy
virtuous, 944
good, 648
saint, 948
Wot
knowledge, 490
Wound
evil, 619
badness, 649
injure, 659
hurt, 900
Wrack
evil, 619
Wraith
spirit, 980
Wrangle
dispute, 713
reason, 476
Wrangler
scholar, 492
Wrap
cover, 222
circumscribe, 231
Wrapped in
attention, 457
Wrapper
cover, 222
dress, 225
Wrapt
see Rapt
Wrath
anger, 900
Wreak
inflict, 918
Wreath
trophy, 733
ornament, 847
honour, 877
Wreck
remainder, 40
destruction, 162
failure, 732
Wrecker
thief, 792
Wrench
extract, 301

seize, 789
twist, 243
draw, 285
Wrest
seize, 789
twist, 243
distort, 523, 555
Wrestle
contention, 720
Wrestler
combatant, 726
Wretch
sinner, 949
apostate, 941
Wretched
unhappy, 828
bad, 649
contemptible, 643
petty, 32
Wriggle
agitation, 315
cunning, 702
Wright
workman, 690
Wring
pain, 378
to torment, 830
distort, 243
Wring from
taking, 789
Wrinkle
fold, 258
hint, 527
Writ
order, 741
in law, 969
Write
writing, 590
Write off
cancel, 552
Write up
praise, 931
detail, 594
Writer
lawyer, 968
Writhe
agitate, 315
pain, 378, 828
Writing
book, 593
Writing-case
receptacle, 191
Wrong
evil, 619
badness, 649

erroneous, 495
vice, 945
immoral, 923
to injure, 907
Wrong-headed
foolish, 499
obstinate, 606
Wrongdoer
sinner, 949
evildoer, 913
Wrought up
excitation, 824
Wry
oblique, 217
distorted, 243
Wunderbar
wonder, 870
Wynd
abode, 189
Wyvern
monster, 83

Xanthin
yellow, 436
Xanthippe
shrew, 901
Xebec
ship, 273
Xylography
engraving, 558
Xylophone
musical instrument, 417

Y
bifurcation, 91
Yacht
ship, 273
navigation, 267
Yahoo
commonalty, 876
Yak
carrier, 271
Yammer
cry, 411
complain, 839
Yank
jerk, 285
Yap
animal cry, 412
Yard
workshop, 691
abode, 189
support, 215

759

Zion
  heaven, 981
Zipper
  pendent, 214
Zither
  musical instrument, 417
Zodiac
  outline, 229
  universe, 318
Zoilus
  envy, 921
Zollverein
  compact, 769

Zombie
  fool, 501
Zone
  circle, 247
  belt, 229
  region, 181
  layer, 204
Zoography
  zoology, 368
Zoological garden
  taming, 370
Zoology
  zoology, 368

Zoom
  deviation, 279
  ascent, 305
Zoophyte
  animal, 366
Zootomy
  zoology, 368
Zoroaster
  religious founder, 986
Zouave
  combatant, 726
Zymotic
  insalubrity, 657